SHELL[illegible]MAN SERIES®

INCLUDES USER GUIDES FOR [illegible] COURSEMATE & WEBTUTOR!!

Discovering COMPUTERS

Student Success Guide

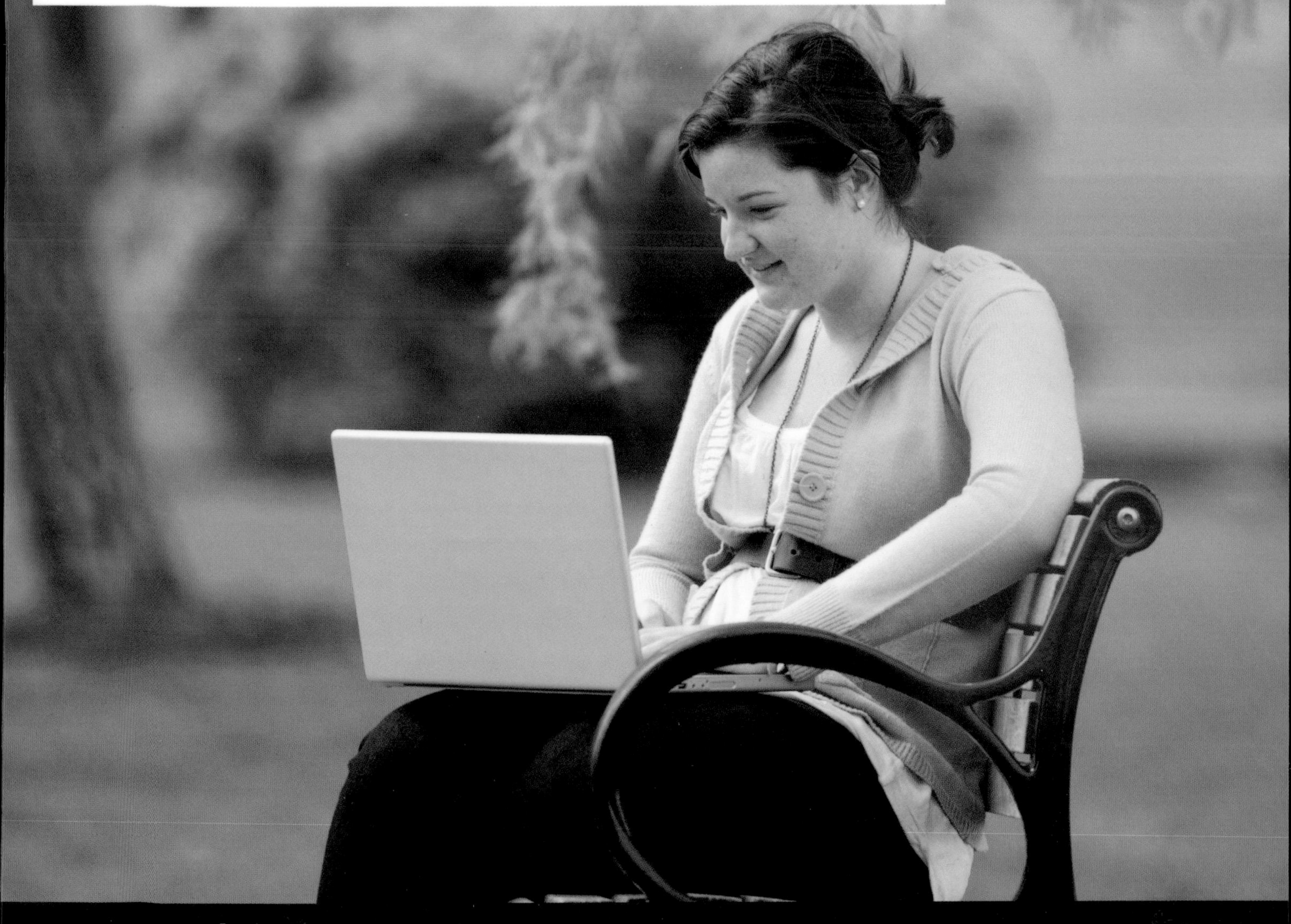

SHELLY | VERMAAT

COURSE TECHNOLOGY
CENGAGE Learning
24/7 Support
Tell us what you think!
HOME
EBOOK
GLOSSARY
Select Chapter
Home Page
Browse:
This Chapter
All Chapters
eBook
Key Terms
Quizzes
Student Edition Labs
Activities and Tutorials
Video Study Tools
Audio Study Tools
Beyond the Book
Features
Timeline
Enhanced: Discovering Computers Complete:
Your Interactive Guide to the Digital World
SHELLY CASHMAN SERIES
Discovering
COMPUTERS
COMPLETE
Your Interactive Guide to the Digital World

Discovering Computers
Student Success Guide

Discovering Computers
Student Success Guide

Gary B. Shelly
Misty E. Vermaat

Contributing Authors
Susan L. Sebok
Steven M. Freund

COURSE TECHNOLOGY
CENGAGE Learning™

SHELLY CASHMAN SERIES®

Australia • Canada • Denmark • Japan • Mexico • New Zealand • Philippines • Puerto Rico • Singapore • South Africa • Spain • United Kingdom • United States

COURSE TECHNOLOGY
CENGAGE Learning™

Discovering Computers: Student Success Guide
Gary B. Shelly, Misty E. Vermaat

Vice President, Career & Consulting: David Garza
Executive Editor: Kathleen McMahon
Associate Acquisitions Editor: Reed Curry
Associate Product Manager: Caitlin Womersley
Editorial Assistant: Sarah Ryan
Director of Marketing: Elisa Roberts
Senior Marketing Manager: Tristen Kendall
Marketing Coordinator: Michael Saver
Print Buyer: Julio Esperas
Content Project Manager: Matthew Hutchinson
Development Editor: Lyn Markowicz
Management Services: PreMediaGlobal
Interior Designer: Joel Sadagursky
Art Director: Jackie Bates
Text Design: Joel Sadagursky
Cover Design: Curio Press
Cover Photos: Tom Kates Photography
Illustrator: PreMediaGlobal
Compositor: PreMediaGlobal
Printer: RRD Jefferson City

For product information and technology assistance, contact us at
Cengage Learning Customer & Sales Support, 1-800-354-9706
For permission to use material from this text or product,
submit all requests online at **cengage.com/permissions**
Further permissions questions can be emailed to
permissionrequest@cengage.com

Library of Congress Control Number: 2012930421

ISBN-13: 978-1-133-59345-4

ISBN-10: 1-133-59345-3

Course Technology
20 Channel Center Street
Boston, MA 02210
USA

Cengage Learning is a leading provider of customized learning solutions with office locations around the globe, including Singapore, the United Kingdom, Australia, Mexico, Brazil, and Japan. Locate your local office at: **international.cengage.com/region**

Cengage Learning products are represented in Canada by Nelson Education, Ltd.

Visit our website www.cengage.com/ct/shellycashman to share and gain ideas on our textbooks!

To learn more about Course Technology, visit **www.cengage.com/coursetechnology**

Purchase any of our products at your local college store or at our preferred online store **www.CengageBrain.com**

Printed in the United States of America
2 3 4 5 6 18 17 16 15 14 13 12

Discovering Computers
Student Success Guide

Every student can be successful in classes utilizing *Discovering Computers*. Establishing goals for what students want to achieve in the course and knowing how to best use the tools available in the textbook and in the Computer Concepts CourseMate will help every student succeed in this course.

This Student Success Guide can help students succeed in this course in the following ways:

Perform better on tests and quizzes
This guide points to content and resources in the textbook and in the Computer Concepts CourseMate to assist with learning key terms, studying important concepts, and reviewing essential material. The Chapter Study Guide focuses on the most important material in each chapter and challenges students to complete questions in the Study Guide, helping reinforce the concepts learned.

Enable retention of material and promote transference of knowledge
Each chapter is organized into several different general goals students might have for the course, like being an informed digital consumer, and categorizes the content and resources available in the textbook and in the Computer Concepts CourseMate to help students achieve those goals. The Chapter Study Guide in each chapter helps solidify and confirm that students understand the material presented.

Understand the relevance of this material
Computing and technology is everywhere. Learn about why this material matters in everyday life with the scenarios and thought-provoking questions at the beginning of each chapter that relate chapter content and resources to students' day-to-day life.

Keep current with technology
This guide presents ways for students to learn about the latest advances, changes, trends, breakthroughs, and products associated with computers, devices, and related technologies. Search phrases enable students to explore independently for information online.

Learn how to most effectively use the Computer Concepts CourseMate and WebTutor content
A comprehensive user guide demystifies the wealth of learning tools available on the Computer Concepts CourseMate and enables students to take advantage of all the Computer Concepts CourseMate has to offer learners. The WebTutor user guide will help students to best utilize the additional study tools available on WebTutor to maximize the learning experience.

New Learning Opportunities

New to the Computer Concepts CourseMate for *Discovering Computers* are three Web applications that can help student comprehension of the material when students are away from a computer. The Web applications available only via the Computer Concepts CourseMate are developed for use on smart phones, as well as on tablets, laptops, and desktop computers.

Improve retention of the chapter terms with the Flashcard Web application. Study for an exam by reviewing the major points in each chapter with the Study Guide Web application or with the Practice Test Web application that provides multiple choice quizzing.

Computer Concepts CourseMate enriches the *Discovering Computers* learning experience. For more information about the Computer Concepts CourseMate see the Preface of the *Discovering Computers: Your Interactive Guide to the Digital World* textbook for a Computer Concepts CourseMate walkthrough to learn more about the resources available on the Computer Concepts CourseMate for *Discovering Computers*.

Like us on Facebook and follow us on Twitter
Facebook posts and Twitter tweets will enable students and instructors to keep up-to-date quickly and easily with relevant technology changes and events in the computing industry. Become part of the Shelly Cashman *Discovering Computers* community.

For Instructors A brand new testbank of questions for this edition of *Discovering Computers* promotes problem-solving and critical thinking, rather than requiring students merely to memorize and repeat the content in each chapter. Questions that challenge students to *think* about answers before responding ultimately creates a more solid, meaningful exam and assessment of student understanding of the material. All questions in the testbank relate to the Chapter Study Guide in the Student Success Guide.

Table of Contents

Discovering Computers
Student Success Guide Chapters

Chapter 1

Student Success Guide

Introduction to Computers

Why Should I Learn About Computers?

"I use computers to do homework, search the Internet, check e-mail, play games, post updates on Facebook, talk on Skype, upload photos from my digital camera, sync music with my phone, and so much more! So, why am I in this class? What could I possibly learn?"

True, you may be familiar with some of the material in this chapter, but do you know . . .

"Why am I in this class?"

- How to protect yourself from identity theft? (p. 13, Ethics & Issues)
- Which game system you might use in physical therapy? (p. 24, Innovative Computing)
- What types of embedded computers you use every day? (p. 26, Embedded Computers)
- What types of computerized equipment an airplane's pilot uses to transport you safely to a destination? (p. 39, Computer Usage @ Work)
- How a GPS knows where you are all the time? (p. 40, High-Tech Talk)
- Which computer company sold more than five million units of a single phone model during just one quarter? (p. 41, Companies on the Cutting Edge)
- How to create a blog? (pp. 50–51 and Computer Concepts CourseMate, Learn How To)
- What steps to perform on your computer to determine its speed, its processor, and the amount of RAM it contains? (Windows Exercises, Computer Concepts CourseMate)

For these answers and to discover much more information essential to this course, read Chapter 1 and visit the associated Computer Concepts CourseMate at www.cengagebrain.com.

Q & A

How can I meet one or more of these goals?

Make use of the goal's resources for each chapter in the book and you should meet that goal by the end of the course.

Customize Your Learning Experience

Adapt this book to meet your needs by determining your goal. Would you like to be an informed digital consumer? A productive technology user? A safe user, protected from the risks in a digital world? A competent digital citizen? A future entrepreneur or professional in a digital society?

Every chapter in this Student Success Guide identifies resources targeted toward each of these goals, along with criteria to verify you understand the resources' content. Resources may be located in the textbook, on the Computer Concepts CourseMate Web site, in the interactive eBook, and on the Web.

Informed Digital Consumer

Goal: I would like to understand the terminology used in Web or print advertisements that sell computers, mobile devices, and related technology, as well as the jargon used by sales associates in computer or electronics stores, so that I can make informed purchasing decisions.

Topic	Resource	Location	Now you should . . .
Computer Hardware Components	Text/Figures	pp. 6–8	Know the purpose of input devices, output devices, the system unit, storage devices, and communications devices
	Drag and Drop Figure 1-3	eBook p. 7 or CourseMate	Be able to identify images on the Web or in magazines that show common computer hardware components
Types of Software	Text/Figures	pp. 15–16	Know the difference between system and application software
Personal Computers	Text/Figures	pp. 19–20	Know the difference between desktop and notebook computers
Mobile Devices	Text/Figures	pp. 20–23	Know the functions of tablets, smart phones, e-book readers, portable media players, and digital cameras
Camera Phones	Web Link	eBook p. 22 or CourseMate	Be able to identify the top camera phones and their features

Continued on next page

Continued from previous page

Topic	Resource	Location	Now you should . . .
Digital Cameras	Web Link	eBook p. 23 or CourseMate	Be able to identify the top point-and-shoot and SLR digital cameras, their features, and their current prices
Game Consoles	Text/Figure	p. 24	Know the types of game consoles
Apple	Text	p. 41	Be familiar with Apple's recent products and developments
	Link	eBook p. 41 or CourseMate	
Amazon	Text	p. 41	Be familiar with products and services available through Amazon
	Link	eBook p. 41 or CourseMate	
Learning About Your Computer	Windows Exercise	CourseMate	Know how to determine the processor type, speed, and amount of memory (RAM) on a Windows computer

Productive Technology User

Goal: I would like to learn ways that technology can benefit me at home, work, and school. I also would like to learn helpful techniques for using technology so that I can perform tasks more efficiently and be more productive in daily activities.

Topic	Resource	Location	Now you should . . .
Using the Internet	Text/Figures	pp. 11–14	Know why people use the Internet and the Web sites they use to share and interact with others
Most Visited Web Sites	FAQ Link	eBook p. 14, or Top Web Sites link, CourseMate	Know how to find widely used Web sites and how to determine any Web site's current ranking
Windows	Web Link	eBook p. 15 or CourseMate	Know how to access Microsoft's online tips and help for using Windows
	Labs	CourseMate	Be familiar with how to use the Windows interface
	Learn How To	p. 50 and CourseMate	Know how to start and close a program in Windows
Installing and Running Programs	Text/Figures and FAQ	pp. 16–17	Understand the processes of installing a program and running an installed program
	Drag and Drop Figure 1-12	eBook p. 17 or CourseMate	
Embedded Computers	Text/Figure	p. 26	Be familiar with everyday products that contain or could contain embedded computers
	Looking Ahead	p. 34	
	Link and Video	eBook p. 34 or CourseMate	
Home User	Text/Figure and FAQ	pp. 28–29	Know how technology can help home users
Mobile User	Text/Figure	p. 31	Know how technology can help mobile users
Education	Text/Figure	p. 34	Be able to identify ways people in education use computers
Finance	Text/Figure	pp. 34–35	Know how people use computers to assist with finances
Government	Text/Figure	p. 35	Be familiar with services offered online through government agencies
Travel	Text/Figure	p. 38	Know how people use computers in travel or with travel arrangements
	Web Link	eBook p. 38 or CourseMate	Know about OnStar and how to find vehicles with which it works
Using Input Devices	Labs	CourseMate	Know how to use a mouse and keyboard
Google Maps	Web Apps	CourseMate	Know how to use Google Maps to locate places and obtain directions

Safe User, Protected from the Risks in a Digital World

Goal: I would like to take measures to (1) protect my computers, devices, and data from loss, damage, or misuse; (2) minimize or prevent risks associated with using technology; and (3) minimize the environmental impact of using computers and related devices.

Topic	Resource	Location	Now you should . . .
Disadvantages of Using Computers	Text	pp. 9–10	Know the risks associated with using computers
Technology Overload	Ethics & Issues	p. 9	Recognize behaviors associated with technology overload
Green Computing	Text	p. 10	Know strategies that support green computing
	Web Link	eBook p. 10 or CourseMate	Know where to find the latest news related to green computing
Identify Theft and Phishing	Ethics & Issues	p. 13	Know the steps you can take to deter identity theft
	Video	eBook p. 13 or CourseMate	Describe ways to be safe from phishing attempts
Safety of Social Networking Web Sites	Ethics & Issues	p. 29	Know the types of problems that can arise from use of social networking Web sites
Privacy of Personal Information	Ethics & Issues	p. 35	Recognize the trade-offs associated with surrendering personal information
E-Waste	Ethics & Issues	p. 39	Know the potential hazards of e-waste and issues with recycling efforts

Competent Digital Citizen

Goal: I would like to be knowledgeable and well-informed about computers, mobile devices, and related technology, so that I am digitally literate in my personal and professional use of digital devices.

Topic	Resource	Location	Now you should . . .
Digital Literacy	Text	p. 5	Know why computer, or digital, literacy is vital to success
How Computers Process Data into Information	Text/Figure	p. 6	Be able to define the term, computer, and distinguish between data and information
	Figure 1-2 Animation	eBook p. 6 or CourseMate	Be able to identify examples of data, processes, and information
Advantages of Using Computers	Text	p. 9	Know the benefits of using computers
Google History	FAQ Video	eBook p. 14 or CourseMate	Be familiar with technological developments from Google
Computer and Video Games	FAQ Link	eBook p. 16, or Game Demographics link, CourseMate	Be familiar with demographics and statistics related to computer and video games and their players
Convergence	Text	p. 18	Be able to give examples of technological convergence
Categories of Computers	Drag and Drop Figure 1-14	eBook p. 19 or CourseMate	Be able to identify images on the Web or in magazines that show each category of computer
Users' Technology Requirements	Figure 1-35	p. 33	Be able to identify the hardware and software requirements for various types of users
Science	Text/Figure	pp. 36–37	Recognize how scientists' breakthroughs in technology assist society
	Figure 1-35 Video	eBook p. 37 or CourseMate	Understand the benefits of using camera pills for 3-D imaging

Continued on next page

Continued from previous page

Topic	Resource	Location	Now you should . . .
Determining Locations	Text/Figure	p. 40	Be familiar with how the Wii game console, GPS, and cell phones use triangulation to determine your location
	Link and Video	eBook p. 40 or CourseMate	
Bill Gates	Text	p. 41	Be familiar with Bill Gates impact on the personal computer and gaming industries and on society
	Link and Video	eBook p. 41 or CourseMate	
History of Computers and Other Digital Devices	Text/Figures	pp. 54–71	Be familiar with milestones in the history of computers and other digital devices
	Video	eBook p. 54 or CourseMate	
	Video	At the Movies, CourseMate	

Future Entrepreneur or Professional in a Digital Society

Goal: As I ponder my future, I envision myself as an entrepreneur or skilled professional using technology to support my business endeavors or job responsibilities. Along the way, I may interact with a variety of computer professionals — or I may just become one myself!

Topic	Resource	Location	Now you should . . .
Sharing Resources	Text	p. 10	Know why a business shares network resources
Software Development	Text	p. 18	Be able to identify the role of a computer programmer in a business
Apple vs. PC	FAQ Link	eBook p. 20, or Personal Computer Sales link, CourseMate	Be familiar with the types of personal computers being used in industry today
Handheld Computers	Text/Figure	pp. 22–23	Know how businesses use handheld computers
Servers, Mainframes, and Supercomputers	Text/Figures	p. 25	Know the purpose of servers, mainframes, and supercomputers, and their role in organizations
Information Systems	Text/Figure	p. 27	Understand how hardware, software, data, people, and procedures interact in an organization
	Drag and Drop Figure 1-29	eBook p. 27 or CourseMate	
SOHO User	Text/Figure	p. 30	Know how technology can help small office/home office users
Power User	Text/Figure	p. 31	Know how technology can help power users
Enterprise User	Text/Figure	p. 32	Know how technology can help an enterprise and its users
Health Care	Innovative Computing	p. 24	Understand how game consoles are used in the medical field to assist professionals and patients
	Link and Video	eBook p. 24 or CourseMate	
	Text/Figure	p. 36	Understand how technology assists medical professionals
Publishing	Text/Figure	p. 37	Understand how publishers use technology
Manufacturing	Text/Figure	p. 38	Understand how the manufacturing industry uses computers
Transportation	Computer Usage @ Work	p. 39	Know how professionals in the transportation industry use computers to support their activities
	Link and Video	eBook p. 39 or CourseMate	
Personal Computer Salesperson	Exploring Computer Careers	CourseMate	Be familiar with the responsibilities of and education required for a personal computer salesperson
Create and Use Your Own Blog	Learn How To	pp. 50–51 and CourseMate	Understand the benefits of blogs to business owners; know how to create a blog and format it for display on a mobile device

Preparing for a Test

Visit the Computer Concepts CourseMate at www.cengagebrain.com and then navigate to the Chapter 1 Web Apps resource for this book to prepare for your test.

Does your class use the Computer Concepts CourseMate Web site? If so, prepare for your test by using the Flash Cards, Study Guide, and Practice Test Web apps — available for your smart phone or tablet.

If your class does not use the Computer Concepts CourseMate Web site or you prefer to use your book, you can prepare for the test by doing the Quiz Yourself activities on pages 10, 18, and 38; reading the Chapter Review on pages 42–43; ensuring you know the definitions for the terms on page 44; and completing the Checkpoint exercises on pages 45–46. You also should know the material identified in the Chapter 1 Study Guide that follows.

Chapter 1 Study Guide

This study guide identifies material you should know for the Chapter 1 exam. You may want to write the answers in a notebook, enter them on your digital device, record them into a phone, or highlight them in your book. Choose whichever method helps you remember the best.

1. Define computer literacy, or digital literacy, and describe how its requirements change.
2. Define the term, computer.
3. Differentiate between data and information. Give an example of each.
4. Identify the activities in the information processing cycle.
5. Define the term, hardware. Give examples.
6. Describe the purpose of each of the five components of a computer: input devices, output devices, system unit, storage devices, and communications devices.
7. Identify examples of commonly used input devices, output devices, and storage devices.
8. The two main components on the motherboard are the _____ and _____.
9. List and describe five different advantages of using computers.
10. List and describe five different disadvantages of using computers.
11. Define the term, green computing. Describe strategies that support green computing.
12. Define the terms, network and online.
13. List two benefits of sharing resources on a network. Identify four types of resources that can be shared on a network.
14. Define the term, Internet. Identify reasons people use the Internet.
15. Differentiate between a Web page and a Web site.
16. Understand how phishing can lead to identity theft. Identify three ways to deter identity theft.
17. Explain the purpose of a social networking Web site. _____ is a popular social networking Web site.
18. Define the term, blog. _____ is a popular microblog.
19. Define the term, podcast.
20. Define the term, Web application. Give some examples of software available as Web applications.
21. Name three characteristics that classify a Web site as Web 2.0.
22. FAQ stands for _____.
23. Define the term, software, and then give a synonym for this term. Identify where you can obtain software.
24. Describe the characteristics of a graphical user interface.
25. Differentiate between system software and application software.
26. Microsoft's personal computer operating system is called _____. Apple's is called _____.
27. Distinguish between installing a program and running a program. Describe how to determine if software will run on a computer.
28. Define the term, programmer. A computer programmer may be called a _____. Name some programming languages.
29. Know the categories of computers. Explain the concept of convergence, with respect to technology.
30. List the components of a personal computer. Identify two popular architectures.
31. Differentiate between a desktop computer and a notebook computer. Notebook computers are also known as _____ computers.
32. Describe a digital tablet, or tablet computer.
33. Describe the purpose of these mobile devices: smart phone, PDA, e-book reader, handheld computer, portable media player, and digital camera.
34. Differentiate among a text message, picture message, and video message.
35. Describe the purpose of earbuds.
36. Distinguish between a standard game console and a handheld game console. Identify popular models of game consoles. Explain how the medical field uses the Wii game console.
37. Differentiate among a server, mainframe, and supercomputer.
38. Define the term, embedded computer. Give examples of products that contain embedded computers.

Continued on next page

Continued from previous page

39. Identify the five elements of an information system.
40. Explain the role of an IT department.
41. Name the five categories of users and describe how each uses technology.
42. Describe how technology is used in education, finance, government, health care, science, publishing, travel, manufacturing, and transportation.
43. Identify reasons e-waste can be hazardous and issues with recycling efforts.
44. Explain uses of triangulation and how a GPS determines a location.
45. Identify Apple's tablet, portable media player, smart phone, and its online music store.
46. Amazon's e-reader is called the _____.
47. Bill Gates founded _____.
48. Technology milestones: Who was Dr. Grace Hopper? Who built the first Apple computer? When did the IBM PC enter the personal computer marketplace? Who invented the World Wide Web? Which online company started as a bookstore? Which online social network was originally available only to college students? When did federal law require all full-power television stations broadcast only in digital format? What was the benefit of HTML5?

Check This Out

As technology changes, you must keep up with updates, new products, breakthroughs, and recent advances to remain digitally literate. The list below identifies topics related to this chapter that you should explore to keep current. In parentheses beside each topic, you will find a search term to help begin your research using a search engine, such as Google.

1. **popular Web applications** (search for: Web apps)
2. **widely used Web sites** (search for: best Web sites, or popular Web sites)
3. **latest version of the Windows operating system** (search for: Microsoft Windows versions)
4. **latest version of the Mac OS operating system** (search for: Apple Mac OS versions)
5. **latest version of the iPad and iPhone operating system** (search for: iOS version)
6. **latest version of the Android operating system** (search for: Android version)
7. **widely used apps for tablets** (search for: best tablet apps)
8. **widely used apps for smart phones** (search for: best phone apps)
9. **latest models of e-book readers** (search for: e-reader reviews)
10. **features of popular portable media players** (search for: portable media player features)
11. **widely used digital cameras** (search for: popular digital cameras)
12. **popular Xbox 360 games** (search for: top Xbox games)
13. **popular Wii games** (search for: top Wii games)
14. **popular PlayStation games** (search for: top PlayStation games)
15. **widely used travel Web sites** (search for: popular travel Web sites)

For current news and information
Check us out on Facebook and Twitter. See your instructor or the Computer Concepts CourseMate for specific information.

Chapter 2

Student Success Guide

The Internet and the World Wide Web

Why Should I Learn About the Internet and the Web?

"I use the Internet and Web to shop for bargains, browse Google for all sorts of information, manage my fantasy sports teams, download music from iTunes, check e-mail on my phone, and so much more! Really, what more could I gain from the Internet or the Web?"

True, you may be familiar with some of the material in this chapter, but do you know . . .

"What more could I gain from the Internet or the Web?"

- Why you might support a do-not-track list? (p. 84, Ethics & Issues)
- Where you can obtain free plug-ins? (p. 97, Figure 2-24)
- How to create and publish your own Web page? (pp. 98 and 121 and Computer Concepts CourseMate, Learn How To)
- If you follow the code of acceptable behavior for online activities? (p. 108, Netiquette)
- How lighting technicians and audio engineers use computers to enhance your concert-going experiences? (p. 109, Computer Usage @ Work)
- How Mark Zuckerberg's college experiences led him to develop Facebook? (p. 111, Technology Trailblazers)
- How to search for a job online? (Student Edition Labs, Computer Concepts CourseMate)
- Which Web sites list job openings? (p. 138, Making Use of the Web Special Feature)

For these answers and to discover much more information essential to this course, read Chapter 2 and visit the associated Computer Concepts CourseMate at www.cengagebrain.com.

Q & A

How can I meet one or more of these goals?

Make use of the goal's resources for each chapter in the book and you should meet that goal by the end of the course.

Customize Your Learning Experience

Adapt this book to meet your needs by determining your goal. Would you like to be an informed digital consumer? A productive technology user? A safe user, protected from the risks in a digital world? A competent digital citizen? A future entrepreneur or professional in a digital society?

Every chapter in this Student Success Guide identifies resources targeted toward each of these goals, along with criteria to verify you understand the resources' content. Resources may be located in the textbook, on the Computer Concepts CourseMate Web site, in the interactive eBook, and on the Web.

Informed Digital Consumer

Goal: I would like to understand the terminology used in Web or print advertisements that sell computers, mobile devices, and related technology, as well as the jargon used by sales associates in computer or electronics stores, so that I can make informed purchasing decisions.

Topic	Resource	Location	Now you should . . .
Broadband Internet Service and Providers	Text and FAQ	pp. 76–78	Know various high-speed alternatives for connecting to and accessing the Internet
	Labs	CourseMate	
Wireless Modems	Web Link	p. 78	Be able to identify various wireless modem options
Mobile Devices	FAQ Link	eBook p. 78, or Mobile Internet link, CourseMate	Be able to identify top mobile devices and accessories
iPhone	Web Link	p. 82	Know the features of the latest iPhone model
E-Commerce	Text	pp. 98–100	Know how to shop online or how an online auction works

Continued on next page

Continued from previous page

Topic	Resource	Location	Now you should . . .
Cartoon Animation Software	Video	eBook p. 109 or CourseMate	Be familiar with software that animates artwork
eBay	Text	p. 111	Be familiar with services offered by eBay
	Link	eBook p. 111 or CourseMate	

Productive Technology User

Goal: I would like to learn ways that technology can benefit me at home, work, and school. I also would like to learn helpful techniques for using technology so that I can perform tasks more efficiently and be more productive in daily activities.

Topic	Resource	Location	Now you should . . .
Internet Addresses	Text	pp. 79–80	Know the components of IP addresses and their relationship to domain names
Internet Connections	Labs	CourseMate	Know how to connect to and disconnect from the Internet
Internet Properties and Internet Explorer	Windows Exercises	CourseMate	Know how to modify Internet properties, including browsing history, security settings, and privacy controls; and how to use Internet Explorer
Web Browsing	Text	pp. 81–82	Be able to use and customize a Web browser
	Labs	CourseMate	
Web Addresses	Text	pp. 82–83	Know how to enter a Web address in a browser
	Drag and Drop Figure 2-8	eBook p. 83 or CourseMate	Know the components of a Web address (URL)
Navigating Web Pages	Text	pp. 83–84	Know how to use links to navigate Web pages
Tabbed Browsing	Web Link	eBook p. 84 or CourseMate	Be able to use tabbed browsing in Firefox
Searching the Web	Text and FAQ	pp. 85–88	Know how to use search engines and subject directories
	Drag and Drop Figure 2-11	p. 86	
	Drag and Drop Figure 2-13	p. 87	
	Labs	CourseMate	
	Learn How To	pp. 120–121 and CourseMate	
Evaluating a Web Site	Text	p. 92	Know the seven criteria for evaluating a Web site
	Drag and Drop Figure 2-16	eBook p. 92 or CourseMate	
WorldWide Telescope	Innovative Computing	p. 93	Know how to use a computer as a telescope
	Link	eBook p. 93 or CourseMate	
Downloading Music	Text	pp. 94–95	Know how to purchase, download, and listen to music
Web Video	Text and FAQ	p. 96	Know how to view video on a computer or device
	Web Link	eBook p. 96 or CourseMate	
	Figure 2-22 Video	eBook p. 96 or CourseMate	
Plug-Ins	Text	p. 97	Know the purpose of widely used plug-ins and where to download them

Continued on next page

Continued from previous page

Topic	Resource	Location	Now you should . . .
E-Mail	Text	pp. 101–103	Know various e-mail programs, and how to compose and send e-mail messages
	Figure 2-27 Animation	eBook p. 102 or CourseMate	
	Web Link	eBook p. 103 or CourseMate	
	FAQ	p. 105	
	Labs	CourseMate	
	Web Apps	CourseMate	
	Learn How To	p. 120 and CourseMate	
Instant Messaging	Text	pp. 104–105	Know how use instant messaging
Chat Rooms	Text	p. 105	Know how to use a chat room
VoIP	Text	p. 106	Know how VoIP works
Newsgroups	Text	p. 107	Be familiar with newsgroups
FTP	Text	p. 107	Know how to use FTP
	Web Link	eBook p. 107 or CourseMate	
Using Web Sites	Text	pp. 124–139	Be familiar with a variety of useful Web sites

Safe User, Protected from the Risks in a Digital World

Goal: I would like to take measures to (1) protect my computers, devices, and data from loss, damage, or misuse; (2) minimize or prevent risks associated with using technology; and (3) minimize the environmental impact of using computers and related devices.

Topic	Resource	Location	Now you should . . .
Web Site Tracking	Ethics & Issues	p. 84	Know the issues with Web site tracking and online profiles
Google Bombing	Ethics & Issues	p. 87	Recognize the effects of skewed search results
Using Wikis for Research	Ethics & Issues	p. 90	Describe the controversy surrounding using a wiki as a valid source of research
Shopping Online	FAQ	p. 99	Know safeguards when using credit cards online
	FAQ Video	eBook pg. 99 or CourseMate	
Online Payment Services	Text	p. 100	Be familiar with various online payment services designed to provide fraud protection
	Web Link	eBook p. 100 or CourseMate	
Communications	Ethics & Issues	p. 100	Be aware of how technology affects written and spoken words
E-Mail Viruses	FAQ	p. 103	Recognize that viruses can spread through infected e-mail attachments
Cyberbullying	Ethics & Issues	p. 108	Know how to identify cyberbullying and recognize ways to protect yourself from it
	Video	eBook p. 108 or CourseMate	
	Web Link	eBook p. 108 or CourseMate	

Competent Digital Citizen

Goal: I would like to be knowledgeable and well-informed about computers, mobile devices, and related technology, so that I am digitally literate in my personal and professional use of digital devices.

Topic	Resource	Location	Now you should . . .
Evolution of the Internet	Text	pp. 75–76	Know how the Internet evolved to its present day form
W3C	Text	p. 76	Know the role of W3C with the Internet and Web
	Web Link	eBook p. 76 or CourseMate	
Internet2	Text	p. 76	Know the goal of Internet2 and its projects
Internet Backbone	Text	pp. 78–79	Understand the basics of how data and information travel the Internet
	Drag and Drop Figure 2-3	eBook p. 79 or CourseMate	
Web and Web 2.0	Text	pp. 80–81	Recognize static and dynamic Web pages, and Web 2.0 sites
Web 3.0	Looking Ahead	p. 81	Understand the significance of Web 3.0
Web Site Types	Text	pp. 88–92	Know the purpose of various types of Web sites
Netiquette	Text	p. 108	Know the code of acceptable online behavior
Computers in Entertainment	Computer Usage @ Work	p. 109	Recognize how computers are used in music, movies, games, and performances
IP Addresses	Text	p. 110	Know the difference between an iPv4 and iPv6 address
	Video	eBook p. 110 or CourseMate	Know how to trace an IP address location
Google	Text	p. 111	Be familiar with Google's products and services
	Link	eBook p. 111 or Coursemate	
Tim Berners-Lee	Text	p. 111	Be familiar with the Internet and Web accomplishments and current endeavors of Tim Berners-Lee
	Link	eBook p. 111 or CourseMate	
Mark Zuckerburg	Text	p. 111	Be familiar with Mark Zuckerburg's impact on online social networks
	Link and Video	eBook p. 111 or CourseMate	

Future Entrepreneur or Professional in a Digital Society

Goal: As I ponder my future, I envision myself as an entrepreneur or skilled professional using technology to support my business endeavors or job responsibilities. Along the way, I may interact with a variety of computer professionals — or I may just become one myself!

Topic	Resource	Location	Now you should . . .
Popular Browsers	FAQ Link	eBook p. 82, or Browser Market Share link, CourseMate	Know the market share of browsers for desktop and mobile devices
Business/Marketing Web Sites	Text	p. 89	Know the purpose of a business Web site
RSS	Text	p. 92	Recognize the purpose of RSS and other feeds
Web Graphics Formats	Text	pp. 93–94	Know the available graphics formats for creating Web pages
Web Animation	Text	p. 94	Know ways that developers incorporate animation in Web pages

Continued on next page

Continued from previous page

Topic	Resource	Location	Now you should . . .
Web Audio - Formats and Distribution	Text	pp. 94–95	Know the available audio formats compatible with Web pages, and various methods of distributing audio on a Web page
Virtual Reality	Text	pp. 96–97	Know the reasons a business would use virtual reality
Web Publishing	Text	pp. 97–98	Know the steps to follow when developing and publishing a Web page
	Drag and Drop	p. 98	
	Learn How To	p. 121 and CourseMate	
Web Page Authoring	Web Link	eBook p. 98 or CourseMate	Know the tools developers use to create Web pages
Mailing Lists	Text	p. 103	Recognize why businesses use mailing lists
Video Blogs	Video	At the Movies, CourseMate	Know how to create and publish a video blog
Web Developer	Exploring Computer Careers	CourseMate	Be familiar with the responsibilities of and education required for a Web developer

Preparing for a Test

Visit the Computer Concepts CourseMate at www.cengagebrain.com and then navigate to the Chapter 2 Web Apps resource for this book to prepare for your test.

Does your class use the Computer Concepts CourseMate Web site? If so, prepare for your test by using the Flash Cards, Study Guide, and Practice Test Web apps — available for your smart phone or tablet.

If your class does not use the Computer Concepts CourseMate Web site or you prefer to use your book, you can prepare for the test by doing the Quiz Yourself activities on pages 80, 98, and 109; reading the Chapter Review on pages 112–113; ensuring you know the definitions for the terms on page 114; and completing the Checkpoint exercises on pages 115–116. You also should know the material identified in the Chapter 2 Study Guide that follows.

Chapter 2 Study Guide

This study guide identifies material you should know for the Chapter 2 exam. You may want to write the answers in a notebook, enter them on your digital device, record them into a phone, or highlight them in your book. Choose whichever method helps you remember the best.

1. List the two goals of ARPANET. Name the year it became functional.
2. Describe the role of a host on a network.
3. Explain how ARPANET, hosts, and NSFnet contributed to the evolution of the Internet.
4. Communications activity on a network is called ______.
5. Identify the role of the W3C.
6. Describe the goal of Internet2. Give some examples of its projects.
7. Briefly describe seven types of broadband Internet service.
8. State the purpose of a hot spot. Name locations you might find one.
9. Define the term, access provider.
10. Differentiate among a regional ISP, a national ISP, an online service provider, and a wireless Internet service provider.
11. Major carriers of Internet traffic are known collectively as the Internet _____.
12. Describe the purpose and composition of an IP address.
13. Define the term, domain name. Cite an example of one.
14. Know the purpose of several generic TLDs. Identify ICANN's role with TLDs.
15. State the purpose of a DNS server.
16. Differentiate between an iPv4 and iPv6 address. Discuss why iPv6 eventually will replace iPv4.
17. Distinguish among the Web, a Web page, a Web site, and a Web server. Describe the role of each when a browser displays a home page.
18. Explain the purpose of a Web browser. Name five popular browsers for personal computers.
19. A _____ is a built-in connection to another related Web page or part of a Web page.

Continued on next page

Continued from previous page

20. Define the terms, downloading and uploading.
21. Define the term, Web address. Name a synonym.
22. Name and give examples of the four components of a Web address. Identify the two components that may be optional.
23. State the purpose of a bookmark.
24. Describe what happens when you click a link.
25. Describe the function and purpose of tabbed browsing.
26. Differentiate between a search engine and a subject directory.
27. Besides Web pages, identify other types of items a search engine can find.
28. Describe how to use a search engine to search for information. Give an example of search text.
29. Relevancy and _____ are two criteria search engines use to determine the priority of search results. Describe ways to improve search results.
30. Know how and when to use these search engine operators: +, OR, ( ), -, " ", and *.
31. Describe the purpose of these types of Web sites: portal, news, informational, business/marketing, blog, wiki, online social network, educational, entertainment, advocacy, Web app, content aggregator, and personal.
32. Explain the controversy surrounding using a wiki as a valid source of research. Name a widely used wiki.
33. Describe seven criteria for evaluating a Web site's content.
34. Define the term, multimedia.
35. Explain how Web pages use graphics, animation, audio, video, virtual reality, and plug-ins.
36. Name the types of graphics formats used on the Web.
37. Define the term, thumbnail.
38. Name some popular audio file players.
39. Define the term, streaming. Identify uses of streaming audio.
40. Identify the purpose of popular plug-ins.
41. Identify and briefly describe the steps in Web publishing.
42. Define the term, e-commerce. Describe and give examples of the types of e-commerce: B2C, C2C, and B2B.
43. Describe the purpose of these Internet services and explain how each works: e-mail, mailing lists, instant messaging, chat rooms, VoIP, and FTP.
44. _____ and _____ are two popular free e-mail Web apps.
45. Describe the components of an e-mail address.
46. Define the term, real time.
47. Define the term, netiquette. Identify the rules of netiquette.
48. Describe cyberbullying, how it occurs, and why it is difficult to catch the perpetrators.
49. Describe the purpose of these Web sites: Google, Webopedia, Blogger, Bloglines, Twitter, Facebook, LinkedIn, flickr, Shutterfly, YouTube, Expedia, Maps.com, E*TRADE, THOMAS, craigslist, eBay, Amazon, The Weather Channel, Yahoo! Sports, MSNBC, HowStuffWorks, NASA, WebMD, Monster, and Project Gutenberg.

Check This Out

As technology changes, you must keep up with updates, new products, breakthroughs, and recent advances to remain digitally literate. The list below identifies topics related to this chapter that you should explore to keep current. In parentheses beside each topic, you will find a search term to help begin your research using a search engine, such as Google.

1. **standards that alert users to unauthorized Web tracking** (search for: W3C Web tracking alerts)
2. **broadband Internet service in rural areas** (search for: extend broadband rural)
3. **broadband upload and download speed tests** (search for: broadband speed test)
4. **new ICANN top-level domains** (search for: ICANN domain)
5. **popular mobile Internet Web sites** (search for: top mobile device sites)
6. **today's most common search queries** (search for: top search terms)
7. **widely used online social networks** (search for: online social networks)
8. **errors found in Wikipedia** (search for: Wikipedia mistakes)
9. **computer games and game player statistics** (search for: computer game industry statistics)
10. **latest Web graphics formats** (search for: latest Web image file types)
11. **latest version of iTunes** (search for: iTunes version)
12. **recent uses of virtual reality** (search for: virtual reality news)
13. **latest news about cyberbullying** (search for: cyberbullying laws)
14. **latest music apps** (search for: music apps)
15. **popular weather Web sites** (search for: weather sites)

For current news and information
Check us out on Facebook and Twitter. See your instructor or the Computer Concepts CourseMate for specific information.

Chapter 3

Student Success Guide

Application Software

Why Should I Learn About Application Software?

"I use my computer mostly to type homework assignments, pay bills online, enhance digital photos, update my blog, and play games. Several years ago, a friend installed an antivirus program to protect my computer from viruses. What more software could I possibly need?"

True, you may be familiar with some of the material in this chapter, but do you know . . .

"What more software could I possibly need?"

- Which software can help you take notes? (p. 148, Figure 3-4, and p. 156)
- How teachers can detect Internet plagiarism in typed documents? (p. 149, Ethics & Issues)
- How fireworks shows use software to synchronize their displays with music? (p. 160, Innovative Computing)
- How CAD software helps architects and engineers design and construct buildings? (p. 160, Computer-Aided Design; p. 177, Computer Usage @ Work)
- How a computer virus unleashes its payload? (p. 178, High-Tech Talk)
- Which software company is the largest? (p. 179, Companies on the Cutting Edge)
- How to zip a file? (p. 189 and Computer Concepts CourseMate, Learn How To)
- How to use WordPad? (Windows Exercises, Computer Concepts CourseMate)
- Why texting can be harmful? (p. 196, Digital Communications Special Feature)

For these answers and to discover much more information essential to this course, read Chapter 3 and visit the associated Computer Concepts CourseMate at www.cengagebrain.com.

Q & A How can I meet one or more of these goals?
Make use of the goal's resources for each chapter in the book and you should meet that goal by the end of the course.

Customize Your Learning Experience

Adapt this book to meet your needs by determining your goal. Would you like to be an informed digital consumer? A productive technology user? A safe user, protected from the risks in a digital world? A competent digital citizen? A future entrepreneur or professional in a digital society?

Every chapter in this Student Success Guide identifies resources targeted toward each of these goals, along with criteria to verify you understand the resources' content. Resources may be located in the textbook, on the Computer Concepts CourseMate Web site, in the interactive eBook, and on the Web.

Informed Digital Consumer

Goal: I would like to understand the terminology used in Web or print advertisements that sell computers, mobile devices, and related technology, as well as the jargon used by sales associates in computer or electronics stores, so that I can make informed purchasing decisions.

Topic	Resource	Location	Now you should . . .
Software Availability	Text	pp. 142–143	Know the seven forms through which software is available
Registration	Text	p. 143	Be able to differentiate software registration from product activation
Business Software	Text/Figure	p. 146	Be able to identify widely used business programs
Business Software for Phones and PIM	Text/Figure	pp. 156–157	Know the types of business software available for phones and features of personal information manager software
Graphics and Multimedia	Text/Figure	pp. 159–160	Be able to identify widely used graphics and multimedia software
Graphics Software	Web Link	eBook p. 160 or CourseMate	Be able to identify the top graphics software and supporting devices

Continued on next page

Continued from previous page

Topic	Resource	Location	Now you should . . .
Home, Personal, Educational Software	Text/Figure	p. 165	Be able to identify widely used programs for home/personal/educational use
Tax Preparation	Link and Video	eBook p. 167 or CourseMate	Be able to identify the features of the top tax preparation programs
Adobe	Text	p. 179	Be familiar with Adobe's software
	Link	eBook p. 179 or CourseMate	
Microsoft	Text	p. 179	Be familiar with Microsoft's products and services
	Link and Video	eBook p. 179 or CourseMate	

Productive Technology User

Goal: I would like to learn ways that technology can benefit me at home, work, and school. I also would like to learn helpful techniques for using technology so that I can perform tasks more efficiently and be more productive in daily activities.

Topic	Resource	Location	Now you should . . .
Windows Programs	Text/Figure	pp. 144–145	Know Windows elements and how to start and use a program
	Drag and Drop Figure 3-3	p. 145	
Word Processing Software	Text/Figures	pp. 147–148	Know the features available in word processing software
	Web Link	eBook p. 148 or CourseMate	
	Ethics & Issues	p. 150	Know the issues surrounding word processing use
	Labs, Windows Exercises	CourseMate	Be able to use word processing software
Developing a Document	Text/Figure and FAQ	pp. 149–150	Understand the tasks involved with creating, editing, formatting, saving, and printing documents
	FAQ Link	eBook p. 150, or Saving Documents link, CourseMate	
	Windows Exercises	CourseMate	Know how to create a document in WordPad and use its Help feature
	Learn How To	eBook pp. 188–189 or CourseMate	Know how to save a file, install and uninstall a program, and zip a file
Spreadsheet Software	Text/Figures	pp. 150–153	Know the organization of and features in spreadsheet software
	Labs	CourseMate	Be able to use spreadsheet software
Database Software	Text/Figure and FAQ	pp. 153–154	Be able to describe a database, its organization, and how database software works
	Labs	CourseMate	Be able to use database software
Presentation Software	Text/Figures	pp. 154–155	Know the features available in presentation software
Note Taking Software	Text/Figure	p. 156	Know the function of note taking software
Business Software Suite	Text	p. 156	Know the programs in and advantages of a business software suite; give examples
	Web Link	eBook p. 156 or CourseMate	
Document Mgmt.	Text/Figure	p. 158	Know the purpose of document management software and PDF files

Continued on next page

Continued from previous page

Topic	Resource	Location	Now you should . . .
Personal Finance	Text/Figure and FAQ	p. 166	Know how to use personal finance software and online banking
Legal Software	Text/Figure	p. 167	Know the benefits of using legal software and types of documents provided
	FAQ Link	eBook p. 167, or Legal Software link, CourseMate	
Tax Preparation	Text/Figure	p. 167	Know the features of tax preparation software and benefits of e-filing
DTP Software	Text/Figure	pp. 167–168	Know the purpose of and how to use personal DTP software
	Web Link	eBook p. 168 or CourseMate	
Paint/Image/Photo Editing	Text/Figures	pp. 168–169	Know the purpose and capabilities of personal paint/image editing and photo editing software
	Figure Video	eBook p. 169 or CourseMate	
Clip Art/Image Gallery	Text/Figure	p. 169	Know the benefits of clip art/image gallery software
Video and Audio Editing	Text/Figure	p. 170	Know the basic features of video and audio editing software
	Video	At the Movies, CourseMate	Know how to convert media files to a format for mobile devices
Design/Landscaping	Text/Figure	p. 170	Know the basic features of home design/landscaping software
Travel and Mapping	Text/Figure	p. 170	Know the benefits of using travel and mapping software
Reference	Text/Figures	p. 171	Know various types of reference and educational software
Web Apps	Text/Figures	pp. 172–173	Know the purpose of several Web apps
	Web Link	eBook p. 173 or CourseMate	
	Web Apps	CourseMate	Know how to use Britannica.com
Communications	Text/Figure	p. 174	Know the purpose of a variety of programs used for home and business communications
	Drag and Drop Figure 3-44	eBook p. 174 or CourseMate	
Help	Text/Figure	p. 175	Understand how to use online and Web-based Help
iTunes U	Innovative Computing	p. 175	Know how to access lectures, demonstrations, and performances on iTunes U
	Link and Video		
Digital Communications – Personal Use	Text/Figures	pp. 194, 196, 198, 200, 202, and 204	Understand the advantages, disadvantages, and good practices in personal use of e-mail, text/picture/video messaging, blogs, wikis, online social networks, Web conferences, and content sharing

Safe User, Protected from the Risks in a Digital World

Goal: I would like to take measures to (1) protect my computers, devices, and data from loss, damage, or misuse; (2) minimize or prevent risks associated with using technology; and (3) minimize the environmental impact of using computers and related devices.

Topic	Resource	Location	Now you should . . .
Viruses and Antivirus Programs	Text & FAQ	p. 144	Know how computer viruses work, the role of an antivirus program, and how to protect a computer from viruses and other malware
	FAQ Link and Video	eBook p. 144, or Computer Viruses link, CourseMate	
	Web Link	eBook p. 144 or CourseMate	
	High-Tech Talk	p. 178	
	Link and Video		
Mapping Services	Ethics & Issues	p. 173	Be aware of issues surrounding mapping services

Competent Digital Citizen

Goal: I would like to be knowledgeable and well-informed about computers, mobile devices, and related technology, so that I am digitally literate in my personal and professional use of digital devices.

Topic	Resource	Location	Now you should . . .
Application Software	Text/Figure	p. 142	Be able to identify the primary use of various application software
System Software	Text/Figure	pp. 143–144	Know the role of system software with respect to application software
	Figure 3-2 Animation	eBook p. 143 or CourseMate	
Plagiarism	Ethics & Issues	p. 149	Know how teachers use software to detect plagiarism
Fireworks Software	Innovative Computing	p. 160	Understand how fireworks shows use software to coordinate music with the display
	Link	eBook p. 160 or CourseMate	
Digital Photo Alteration	Ethics & Issues	p. 162	Recognize how commercial or professional photos may be altered to a degree they are considered digital forgery
	Video	eBook p. 162 or CourseMate	
Driving Aids	Looking Ahead	p. 171	Be familiar with developments underway to assist drivers
	Link and Video	eBook p. 171 or CourseMate	
Entertainment	Text/Figure and FAQ	p. 172	Know examples of entertainment software
	Web Link	eBook p. 172 or CourseMate	
	FAQ Link	eBook p.172, or Entertainment Software link, CourseMate	
Distance Learning	Text/Figure	p. 176	Be familiar with the uses and benefits of DL training and education
Dan Bricklin	Text	p. 179	Be familiar with Dan Bricklin's contributions to the software industry
	Link	eBook p. 179 or CourseMate	

Future Entrepreneur or Professional in a Digital Society

Goal: As I ponder my future, I envision myself as an entrepreneur or skilled professional using technology to support my business endeavors or job responsibilities. Along the way, I may interact with a variety of computer professionals — or I may just become one myself!

Topic	Resource	Location	Now you should . . .
Database Options	Web Link	eBook p. 154 or CourseMate	Know the various database options for a business
Project Management	Text/Figure	p. 157	Know the purpose of project management software in business
Accounting Software	Text/Figure	p. 158	Know how companies use accounting software
Enterprise Computing	Text	p. 159	Know how functional business units use software
CAD	Text/Figure	p. 160	Know how engineers, architects, and scientists use CAD software
	Computer Usage @ Work	p. 177	
	Link and Video	eBook p. 177 or CourseMate	
DTP	Text/Figure	pp. 160–161	Know how professional designers use DTP software
Paint/Image Editing	Text/Figure	p. 161	Know how professionals use paint/image editing software
Photo Editing	Text/Figure	p. 162	Know how photo editing software assists professional photo users

Continued on next page

Continued from previous page

Topic	Resource	Location	Now you should . . .
Video and Audio Editing	Text/Figure	pp. 162–163	Know how professionals use video editing software and audio editing software
Multimedia Authoring	Text/Figure	pp. 162–163	Know how multimedia authoring software is used in business
Web Page Authoring	Text/Figure	p. 164	Know the purpose of Web page authoring software
	Web Link	eBook p. 164 or CourseMate	Be able to identify Web authoring tools and HTML editors
Help Desk Specialist	Exploring Computer Careers	CourseMate	Be familiar with the responsibilities of and education required for a help desk specialist
Digital Communications – Business Use	Text/Figures	pp. 195, 197, 199, 201, 203, and 205	Understand the advantages, disadvantages, and good practices in business use of e-mail, text/picture/video messaging, blogs, wikis, online social networks, Web conferences, and content sharing

Preparing for a Test

Visit the Computer Concepts CourseMate at www.cengagebrain.com and then navigate to the Chapter 3 Web Apps resource for this book to prepare for your test.

Does your class use the Computer Concepts CourseMate Web site? If so, prepare for your test by using the Flash Cards, Study Guide, and Practice Test Web apps — available for your smart phone or tablet.

If your class does not use the Computer Concepts CourseMate Web site or you prefer to use your book, you can prepare for the test by doing the Quiz Yourself activities on pages 146, 164, and 177; reading the Chapter Review on pages 180–181; ensuring you know the definitions for the terms on page 182; and completing the Checkpoint exercises on pages 183–184. You also should know the material identified in the Chapter 3 Study Guide that follows.

Chapter 3 Study Guide

This study guide identifies material you should know for the Chapter 3 exam. You may want to write the answers in a notebook, enter them on your digital device, record them into a phone, or highlight them in your book. Choose whichever method helps you remember the best.

1. Name four uses for application software.
2. Differentiate among packaged software, custom software, Web apps, open source software, shareware, freeware, and public-domain software.
3. Describe software registration and product activation.
4. Explain how the operating system and utility programs work with application software.
5. Name three popular personal computer operating systems.
6. Malicious software also is known as _____.
7. Identify ways a computer can be infected with a virus.
8. Describe common elements of the Windows user interface.
9. Explain the purpose of a file. Give an example of a file name.
10. Know how to start a Windows program.
11. Describe the features available in word processing software. Name popular word processing programs.
12. Explain the process of creating, editing, formatting, saving, and printing a document.
13. Differentiate between a serif font and a sans serif font.
14. Font size is gauged by a measurement system called _____.
15. Describe the features of spreadsheet software and the organization of a spreadsheet. Name popular spreadsheet programs.
16. Define the term, database. Describe how a database is organized and the purpose of database software. Name popular database programs.
17. Describe the features available in presentation software. Name popular presentation programs.
18. Identify the function and benefit of note taking software.
19. Identify programs typically in a business software suite and advantages of using a suite. Name popular business software suites.
20. Identify types of business software available for phones.
21. Describe the purpose and key features of project management software, accounting software, and document management software.

Continued on next page

Continued from previous page

22. Adobe Reader enables you to view any ____ file.
23. Briefly describe how functional business units in an enterprise use software.
24. Explain how engineers, architects, and scientists use CAD software.
25. Explain how professionals use DTP software, paint software, image editing software, photo editing software, video and editing software, and multimedia authoring software.
26. Identify the purpose and users of Web page authoring software.
27. Describe the benefits of personal finance software and online banking.
28. Identify the purpose of legal software.
29. Describe the purpose of tax preparation software. Define the term, e-filing.
30. Identify key features of these programs for personal use: desktop publishing, paint/image editing, photo editing, photo management, clip art/image gallery, video and audio editing, and home design/landscaping.
31. Describe features of travel and mapping software. Identify devices on which it usually is preinstalled.
32. Describe types of reference software and educational software.
33. Another word for computer-based training (CBT) is _____ (CAI). Identify some uses of CBT.
34. Describe types of entertainment software.
35. Define the term, cloud storage.
36. Describe the purpose of a Web app and various distribution methods. Name popular Web apps.
37. Identify issues surrounding online mapping services.
38. Describe the purpose of these application programs for communications: Web browser, e-mail, text/picture/video messaging, RSS aggregator, blogging, FTP, VoIP, and video conferencing.
39. Define the terms, online Help and Web-based Help.
40. Describe the purpose of iTunes U. Identify who posts its content.
41. Define the term, Web-based training.
42. Explain the advantages of distance learning.
43. Describe how instructors use e-learning providers to enhance their courses.
44. Briefly describe three actions a virus may perform during its infection phase.
45. Give examples of what might occur when a virus unleashes its payload.
46. Identify steps to protect a computer from virus infections.
47. Identify the names of Adobe's widely used programs.
48. Identify some of Microsoft's products and services.
49. Identify the advantages with personal and business use of e-mail, text/picture/video messaging, blogs, wikis, online social networks, Web conferences, and content sharing.

Check This Out

As technology changes, you must keep up with updates, new products, breakthroughs, and recent advances to remain digitally literate. The list below identifies topics related to this chapter that you should explore to keep current. In parentheses beside each topic, you will find a search term to help begin your research using a search engine, such as Google.

1. **widely used freeware** (search for: popular freeware)
2. **malware attacks on mobile devices** (search for: mobile malware)
3. **business letter writing tips** (search for: writing business letters)
4. **presentation software design principles** (search for: presentation software slide design)
5. **business software apps for smart phones** (search for: best business apps)
6. **latest version of Adobe Reader** (search for: Adobe Reader version)
7. **check deposit using a smart phone** (search for: remote deposit smart phone)
8. **popular photo editing software** (search for: best photo editing software)
9. **widely used computer games** (search for: top computer games)
10. **current productivity Web apps** (search for: productivity Web apps)
11. **new iTunes U course lectures** (search for: iTunes U lectures)
12. **recent computer viruses** (search for: latest computer viruses)
13. **latest Microsoft news** (search for: Microsoft news)
14. **latest news about online social networks** (search for: social network news)
15. **top blogs** (search for: best blogs)

For current news and information
Check us out on Facebook and Twitter. See your instructor or the Computer Concepts CourseMate for specific information.

Student Success Guide

Chapter 4

The Components of the System Unit

Why Should I Learn About System Unit Components?

"I bought my computer a few years ago, and it appears to be working well. Although at times it seems to run a little slow and it generates a lot of heat, I have not had problems with it. So, why do I need to learn about hardware in the system unit?"

True, you may be familiar with some of the material in this chapter, but do you know . . .

"Why do I need to learn about hardware in the system unit?"

- What types of processors can improve your computer's speed? (p. 213, Processor)
- How computer chips can help you locate a lost pet? (p. 213, Innovative Computing)
- How manufacturers name their processors? (p. 217, Comparison of Personal Computer Processors)
- Why the Department of Homeland Security may search your notebook computer at the airport? (p. 217, Ethics & Issues)
- How the sports industry uses computers? (p. 241, Computer Usage @ Work)
- Which company is the world's leading chip manufacturer? (p. 243, Companies on the Cutting Edge)
- How to purchase and install computer memory? (pp. 252–253 and Computer Concepts CourseMate, Learn How To)
- How to monitor your computer's electric consumption? (Windows Exercises, Computer Concepts CourseMate)

For these answers and to discover much more information essential to this course, read Chapter 4 and visit the associated Computer Concepts CourseMate at www.cengagebrain.com.

Q & A
How can I meet one or more of these goals?
Make use of the goal's resources for each chapter in the book and you should meet that goal by the end of the course.

Customize Your Learning Experience

Adapt this book to meet your needs by determining your goal. Would you like to be an informed digital consumer? A productive technology user? A safe user, protected from the risks in a digital world? A competent digital citizen? A future entrepreneur or professional in a digital society?

Every chapter in this Student Success Guide identifies resources targeted toward each of these goals, along with criteria to verify you understand the resources' content. Resources may be located in the textbook, on the Computer Concepts CourseMate Web site, in the interactive eBook, and on the Web.

Informed Digital Consumer

Goal: I would like to understand the terminology used in Web or print advertisements that sell computers, mobile devices, and related technology, as well as the jargon used by sales associates in computer or electronics stores, so that I can make informed purchasing decisions.

Topic	Resource	Location	Now you should . . .
ID Chips	Innovative Computing	p. 213	Know how ID chips help locate lost pets, along with other uses of the chips and approximate cost
	Link	eBook p. 213 or CourseMate	
Personal Computer Processors	Text/Figures	pp. 216–218	Know the popular chips by AMD and Intel, and their intended use
Chip Technology	Web Link	eBook p. 217 or CourseMate	Be familiar with current and future chip-making technologies
Cooling Kits	Web Link	eBook p. 220 or CourseMate	Know the features and approximate prices of computer cooling kits

Continued on next page

Continued from previous page

Topic	Resource	Location	Now you should . . .
Memory Sizes	Text/Figure	p. 223	Know the terms and acronyms used to define memory sizes
	Drag and Drop Figure 4-17	eBook p. 223 or CourseMate	
RAM Types and Requirements	Text/Figure	pp. 224–226	Know the types of RAM chips and guidelines for amount of RAM needed when purchasing or upgrading
	Drag and Drop Figure 4-19	eBook p. 225 or CourseMate	
	FAQ and Link	eBook p. 226 or CourseMate	
	Learn How To	pp. 252–253	
Cache	Text/Figure	p. 227	Know the types of cache and their capacities
Memory Access Times	Text/Figures	p. 229	Know the terms and acronyms used to define memory access times
	Drag and Drop Figure 4-24	eBook p. 229 or CourseMate	
Adapter Cards	Text/Figure	pp. 230–231	Know the purpose of widely used types of adapter cards
	Drag and Drop Figure 4-26	eBook p. 230 or CourseMate	
Video Cards, etc.	Web Link	eBook p. 230 or CourseMate	Be familiar with video cards and other components you can purchase
Removable Flash Memory	Text/Figure	p. 231	Be familiar with the purpose and use of memory cards, USB flash drives, and ExpressCard modules
Ports and Connectors	Text/Figures	pp. 232–236	Know the purpose of and be able to identify ports on desktop computers, notebook computers, and mobile devices
	Drag and Drop Figure 4-31	eBook p. 233 or CourseMate	
Processor and RAM	Figure 4-38	p. 239	Be familiar with processor and RAM recommendations for various users
NVIDIA	Text	p. 243	Be familiar with NVIDIA's products
	Link	eBook p. 243 or CourseMate	
Intel	Text	p. 243	Be familiar with Intel's products
	Link and Video	eBook p. 243 or CourseMate	

Productive Technology User

Goal: I would like to learn ways that technology can benefit me at home, work, and school. I also would like to learn helpful techniques for using technology so that I can perform tasks more efficiently and be more productive in daily activities.

Topic	Resource	Location	Now you should . . .
Windows ReadyBoost	Text	p. 227	Know how to use Windows ReadyBoost to increase a computer's memory
	Web Link	eBook p. 227 or CourseMate	
System Clock	Windows Exercises	CourseMate	Be able to set the system clock on a Windows computer
Flash Memory	Text/Figure	p. 228	Know examples of flash memory and how mobile devices use it

Continued on next page

Continued from previous page

Topic	Resource	Location	Now you should . . .
Portable Media Players	Figure and FAQ	pp. 228–229	Know how portable media players store music
	FAQ Link	eBook p. 229, or Portable Media Players link, CourseMate	
USB Ports	Text	p. 234	Know how to use a USB port
	Link and Video	eBook p. 234 or CourseMate	
FireWire	Text	p. 234	Know how FireWire works
	Web Link	eBook p. 238 or CourseMate	
Connecting Wireless Devices	FAQ	p. 235	Know how to connect wireless devices
	FAQ Link	eBook p. 235, or Wireless Devices link, CourseMate	
Installing Hardware	Windows Exercises	CourseMate	Be able to install a new device
Port Replicators and Docking Stations	Text/Figure	p. 236	Know the purpose of port replicators and docking stations, and their current prices
	Web Link	eBook p. 236 or CourseMate	
Bays	Text/Figure	p. 238	Know and be able to identify various types of bays
Power Supply and Fans	Text and FAQ	p. 239	Be familiar with the role of the power supply and types of computer fans and coolers
	FAQ Link	eBook p. 239, or Computer Fans link, CourseMate	
Apps for Sports Fans	Computer Usage @ Work	eBook p. 241 or CourseMate	Be familiar with phone and tablet apps for professional baseball and football
	Video		
Installing RAM	Video	eBook p. 242 or CourseMate	Know how to install RAM
	Learn How To	pp. 252–253	
Time Machine	Video	At the Movies, CourseMate	Know how to use Time Machine on an Apple computer to restore any previous files, data, or programs
Calculator	Labs and Windows Exercises	CourseMate	Know how to use Windows Calculator
Google Docs	Web Apps	CourseMate	Know how to use Google Docs to create documents, presentations, etc.

Safe User, Protected from the Risks in a Digital World

Goal: I would like to take measures to (1) protect my computers, devices, and data from loss, damage, or misuse; (2) minimize or prevent risks associated with using technology; and (3) minimize the environmental impact of using computers and related devices.

Topic	Resource	Location	Now you should . . .
Computer Search and Seizure	Ethics & Issues	p. 217	Be aware that the Dept. of Homeland Security can search and seize any mobile computer or device upon its arrival in the U.S.
Cleaning Computers and Mobile Devices	Text/Figure and FAQ	pp. 240–241	Know how to keep your computer and mobile device clean
Power Management	Windows Exercises	CourseMate	Be able to manage the power usage on your computer

Competent Digital Citizen

Goal: I would like to be knowledgeable and well-informed about computers, mobile devices, and related technology, so that I am digitally literate in my personal and professional use of digital devices.

Topic	Resource	Location	Now you should . . .
System Units	Text/Figures	pp. 210–212	Know the size and shape of system units on various computers and devices
Motherboard	Text/Figure	p. 212	Recognize the various slots, chips, and other items on a motherboard
	Labs	CourseMate	
System Unit Components	Drag and Drop Figure 4-3	p. 212	Be able to identify the items in and on a system unit
Processor	Text/Figures	pp. 213–215	Know the purpose of processors, relative speed of multi-core processors, and the role of the control unit and ALU
	Drag and Drop Figure 4-4	p. 213	
Robots	Innovative Computing	p. 214	Understand how robots assist with household and industrial tasks
	Link and Video	eBook p. 214 or CourseMate	
Turing Test	Ethics & Issues	p. 214	Be familiar with the Turing Test's relationship to computer intelligence
Machine Cycle	Text/Figures	pp. 215–216	Know the steps in a machine cycle and their relationship to processing speed
	Figure 4-5 Animation	p. 215	
Registers	Text	p. 216	Know the function of registers
System Clock	Text	p. 216	Know the purpose of the system clock and how clock speed is measured
Real-Time Clock	FAQ	p. 216	Know the difference between the system clock and the real-time clock
Processor Cooling	Text/Figures	pp. 219–220	Know the ways processor chips are cooled
Parallel Processing	Text/Figure	p. 220	Know the definition of parallel processing
Data Representation	Text/Figures	pp. 221–222	Understand how a computer represents data and uses coding schemes
	Labs	CourseMate	
Memory Storage	Text/Figure	p. 223	Know what items memory stores and how items are stored
Memory Types	Text	p. 223	Understand the difference between volatile and nonvolatile memory and types of RAM
	Link	eBook p. 242 or CourseMate	
RAM	Text/Figure	p. 224	Understand how program instructions transfer in and out of RAM
	Text/Figure	p. 242	Know the technical details about how RAM works
	Labs	CourseMate	
One Laptop per Child	Ethics & Issues	p. 226	Know the intent of the OLPC plan endorsed by the United Nations
	Video		See how the OLPCs work
ROM	Text	p. 228	Understand the purpose and types of ROM chips
	Labs	CourseMate	
CMOS	Text	p. 229	Be able to identify examples of CMOS use
Future Notebook Computers	Looking Ahead	p. 236	Know some of the current and future developments with respect to notebook computers
	Link and Video	eBook p. 236 or CourseMate	

Continued on next page

Continued from previous page

Topic	Resource	Location	Now you should . . .
Buses	Text/Figure	pp. 237–238	Know the parts of a bus, bus widths, and types of buses
Computers in Sports	Computer Usage @ Work	p. 241	Recognize how computers are used in professional baseball and NASCAR
	Link		
Jack Kilby	Text	p. 243	Be familiar with Jack Kilby's most significant patent
	Link	eBook p. 243 or CourseMate	
Gordon Moore	Text	p. 243	Be familiar with Moore's Law and other contributions from Gordon Moore
	Link	eBook p. 243 or CourseMate	

Future Entrepreneur or Professional in a Digital Society

Goal: As I ponder my future, I envision myself as an entrepreneur or skilled professional using technology to support my business endeavors or job responsibilities. Along the way, I may interact with a variety of computer professionals — or I may just become one myself!

Topic	Resource	Location	Now you should . . .
PC Market Share	FAQ	p. 219	Know the top PC vendors
Computer Factory	FAQ Video	eBook p. 219 or CourseMate	See how one PC vendor manufactures computers and fulfills orders
Computer Engineer	Exploring Computer Careers	CourseMate	Be familiar with the responsibilities of and education required for a computer engineer

Preparing for a Test

Visit the Computer Concepts CourseMate at www.cengagebrain.com and then navigate to the Chapter 4 Web Apps resource for this book to prepare for your test.

Does your class use the Computer Concepts CourseMate Web site? If so, prepare for your test by using the Flash Cards, Study Guide, and Practice Test Web apps — available for your smart phone or tablet.

If your class does not use the Computer Concepts CourseMate Web site or you prefer to use your book, you can prepare for the test by doing the Quiz Yourself activities on pages 220, 230, and 241; reading the Chapter Review on pages 244–245; ensuring you know the definitions for the terms on page 246; and completing the Checkpoint exercises on pages 247–248. You also should know the material identified in the Chapter 4 Study Guide that follows.

Chapter 4 Study Guide

This study guide identifies material you should know for the Chapter 4 exam. You may want to write the answers in a notebook, enter them on your digital device, record them into a phone, or highlight them in your book. Choose whichever method helps you remember the best.

1. Differentiate among the various styles of system units on desktop computers, notebook computers, and mobile devices.
2. Define the term, motherboard. Identify components that attach to the motherboard.
3. Define the term, computer chip.
4. Describe uses of chip implants.
5. A processor also is called a CPU, which stands for _____.
6. Describe the purpose of a processor. Describe multi-core processors.
7. Explain the role of the control unit and ALU in a computer.
8. Describe the purpose of the Turing Test.
9. Explain the four steps in a machine cycle.
10. Describe the benefit of pipelining.
11. Define the term, register. Identify functions of registers.
12. Identify the purpose of the system clock. Explain its relationship to the processor and devices.
13. One _____ (GHz) equals one billion ticks of the system clock per second.
14. Identify the clock that keeps track of the date and time in a computer and how it runs when the computer is off.
15. The leading manufacturers of personal computer processor chips are _____ and _____.

Continued on next page

Continued from previous page

16. Explain how processor manufacturers identify their chips.
17. Identify processor features unique to notebook computers and tablets.
18. Explain techniques used to dissipate processor heat.
19. Define the term, bit. The two digits used to represent bits are the _____ and _____.
20. Describe how a series of bits represents data.
21. Define the term, memory. Describe three types of items it stores.
22. Explain how memory uses addresses.
23. Differentiate among a kilobyte, megabyte, gigabyte, and terabyte. State their abbreviations.
24. Explain the difference between volatile and nonvolatile memory.
25. Explain how program instructions transfer in and out of memory.
26. Differentiate among DRAM, SRAM, and MRAM.
27. RAM chips usually reside on a _____ module.
28. Describe how to determine the amount of RAM necessary in a computer.
29. State the purpose of memory cache. Describe three types of memory cache.
30. Define the terms, ROM and firmware.
31. Define flash memory. Identify examples of its use.
32. Describe the advantage and uses of CMOS technology.
33. Define access time.
34. Differentiate among a millisecond, microsecond, nanosecond, and picosecond. State their abbreviations.
35. Describe the purpose of expansion slots and adapter cards.
36. Differentiate among a sound card, network card, and video card.
37. Define the term, Plug and Play.
38. Differentiate among a memory card, USB flash drive, PC Card, and ExpressCard module.
39. Explain the difference between a port and a connector.
40. Differentiate between a USB port and a FireWire port.
41. Explain the purpose of USB and FireWire hubs.
42. Briefly describe the purpose of a Bluetooth port, SCSI port, eSATA port, IrDA port, serial port, and MIDI port.
43. Explain the purpose of a port replicator and docking station.
44. Define the terms, bus and bus width.
45. Differentiate between the data bus and the address bus.
46. Describe the purpose of a front side bus, backside bus, and expansion buses.
47. Explain the purpose of a power supply.
48. Identify the various types of fans in a system unit.
49. Describe Moore's Law.

Check This Out

As technology changes, you must keep up with updates, new products, breakthroughs, and recent advances to remain digitally literate. The list below identifies topics related to this chapter that you should explore to keep current. In parentheses beside each topic, you will find a search term to help begin your research using a search engine, such as Google.

1. **latest tablet computers** (search for: tablets)
2. **recent uses of robotic technologies** (search for: new robot trends)
3. **fastest processor clock speeds** (search for: fastest processor)
4. **latest personal computer processors** (search for: processor comparison)
5. **top personal computer vendors** (search for: personal computer market share)
6. **new liquid cooling technology** (search for: liquid cooled computers)
7. **recent computer memory developments** (search for: new computer memory)
8. **One Laptop per Child notebook computers** (search for: OLPC stories)
9. **new removable flash memory devices** (search for: flash memory update)
10. **latest USB developments** (search for: USB news)
11. **latest Bluetooth technologies** (search for: Bluetooth improvements)
12. **docking stations for mobile devices** (search for: mobile device docking station)
13. **power supply heat problems** (search for: computer power supply heat)
14. **tablet computer use in professional sports** (search for: tablet professional sports)
15. **predictions based on Moore's Law** (search for: Moore's Law future)

For current news and information
Check us out on Facebook and Twitter. See your instructor or the Computer Concepts CourseMate for specific information.

Student Success Guide

Input

Why Should I Learn About Input Devices?

"After work or school, I video chat with my friends and discuss our gaming strategies. My computer has a wireless keyboard and mouse. I talk on a Bluetooth headset paired with my smart phone. I use my bank's ATM and the self-serve checkout at the grocery store. So, why do I need to learn about more input devices?"

True, you may be familiar with some of the material in this chapter, but do you know . . .

"Why do I need to learn about more input devices?"

- How your boss may monitor all the Web sites you visit while at work? (p. 261, Ethics & Issues)
- How to reduce the risk of injuring your wrists when you are typing? (p. 262, Keyboard Ergonomics)
- Which tabletop display Microsoft developed that has a touch screen and the ability to recognize fingers and objects? (p. 267, Touch Screens and Touch-Sensitive Pads)
- How a flatbed scanner converts a document into a digital image? (p. 278, Optical Scanners)
- How computers have increased accuracy and efficiency in the hospitality industry? (p. 287, Computer Usage @ Work)
- Who conceptualized the computer mouse more than 60 years ago? (p. 289, Technology Trailblazers)
- How to download music? (pp. 298–299 and Computer Concepts CourseMate, Learn How To)
- How to use the numeric keypad keys to move the mouse pointer, click, right-click, double-click, and drag? (Windows Exercises, Computer Concepts CourseMate)

For these answers and to discover much more information essential to this course, read Chapter 5 and visit the associated Computer Concepts CourseMate at www.cengagebrain.com.

Q & A How can I meet one or more of these goals?
Make use of the goal's resources for each chapter in the book and you should meet that goal by the end of the course.

Customize Your Learning Experience

Adapt this book to meet your needs by determining your goal. Would you like to be an informed digital consumer? A productive technology user? A safe user, protected from the risks in a digital world? A competent digital citizen? A future entrepreneur or professional in a digital society?

Every chapter in this Student Success Guide identifies resources targeted toward each of these goals, along with criteria to verify you understand the resources' content. Resources may be located in the textbook, on the Computer Concepts CourseMate Web site, in the interactive eBook, and on the Web.

Informed Digital Consumer

Goal: I would like to understand the terminology used in Web or print advertisements that sell computers, mobile devices, and related technology, as well as the jargon used by sales associates in computer or electronics stores, so that I can make informed purchasing decisions.

Topic	Resource	Location	Now you should . . .
Keyboard Types	Text/Figures	pp. 260–262	Know keyboard types including enhanced, gaming, and wireless
Mouse Types	Text/Figures	pp. 263–264	Know mouse types including optical, laser, air, and wireless
Portable Media Player	FAQ	p. 267	Know which companies sell the most portable media players
Smart Phone	Text/Figure	pp. 268–269	Be familiar with various types of input for smart phones

Continued on next page

Continued from previous page

Topic	Resource	Location	Now you should . . .
Game Controllers	Text/Figures	pp. 270–271	Be able to identify and know the purpose of various game controllers
	Drag and Drop Figure 5-19	eBook p. 270 or CourseMate	
	Web Link		Know about the Wii Remote
	Video		Know about the xBox Kinect
Digital Camera Types	Text	p. 272	Know the differences of studio, field, and point-and-shoot cameras
Resolution	Text/Figure	p. 273	Be able to explain resolution and its relationship to digital cameras
Web Cams	Text/Figure	pp. 275–276	Know the purpose and approximate costs of Web cams
Flatbed Scanner	Text	p. 278	Know flatbed scanner resolutions
Bar Code Reader	Video	eBook p. 280 or CourseMate	Be familiar with the benefits of a bar code reader
Fingerprint Reader	Text/Figure	p. 282	Be familiar with features and costs of fingerprint readers
Terminals	Text/Figures	pp. 284–285	Know the purpose and uses of POS terminals, ATMs, and DVD kiosks
Input Device Recommendations	Text/Figure	p. 285	Be familiar with input device recommendations for various users
Logitech	Text	p. 289	Be familiar with Logitech's recent products
	Link	eBook p. 289 or CourseMate	
Nokia	Text	p. 289	Be familiar with Nokia's recent products
	Link	eBook p. 289 or CourseMate	

Productive Technology User

Goal: I would like to learn ways that technology can benefit me at home, work, and school. I also would like to learn helpful techniques for using technology so that I can perform tasks more efficiently and be more productive in daily activities.

Topic	Resource	Location	Now you should . . .
Keyboard Keys	Text/Figure	pp. 260–261	Be able to identify and know the function of various keyboard keys
	Drag and Drop Figure 5-2	eBook p. 261 or CourseMate	
	Windows Exercises	CourseMate	Be able to use Windows to customize a keyboard, use mouse keys, and open the on-screen keyboard
Mobile Computer and Device Keyboards	Text/Figure	pp. 262–263	Know the types of keyboards on notebook computers and mobile devices and the advantage of predictive text input
	Drag and Drop Figure 5-5	eBook p. 263 or CourseMate	
Using a Mouse	Text/Figure	p. 264	Know how to use a mouse
	Drag and Drop Figure 5-8	eBook p. 264 or CourseMate	
Other Pointing Devices	Text/Figures	pp. 265–266	Know the look and purpose of a trackball, touchpad, and pointing stick
Touch Screens	Text/Figures	pp. 266–267	Know the function of touch screens and their various uses
	Web Link	eBook p. 266 or CourseMate	Be familiar with various multi-touch screen uses
Touch-Sensitive Pads	Text/Figure	p. 267	Know the functions of a touch-sensitive pad and its uses

Continued on next page

Continued from previous page

Topic	Resource	Location	Now you should . . .
Stylus and Digital Pen	Text/Figure	p. 268	Be familiar with uses of a stylus and digital pen
Digital Camera Use	Text/Figure and FAQ	pp. 272–273	Know ways users work with images from a digital camera and how a digital camera works
	Figure 5-20 Animation	eBook p. 272 or CourseMate	
Voice Input	Text/Figure	p. 274	Know the uses of voice input and how voice recognition works
Audio Input	Text/Figure	pp. 274–275	Know uses of audio input and ports used to connect music devices
	Innovative Computing	p. 275	Be familiar with music production software
	Link	eBook p. 275 or CourseMate	
	Labs	CourseMate	Know how to import and download audio files, and burn audio CDs
	Learn How To	pp. 298–299 and CourseMate	Know how to download songs to a portable media player
DV Cameras	Text/Figure	p. 275	Know how users work with digital video cameras
Web Cam	Learn How To	p. 298 and CourseMate	Know how to install and use a Web cam
Video Editing	Video	At the Movies, CourseMate	Know how to edit videos, import clips, and work with clips and transitions
	Labs	CourseMate	
Health Video Conference	Innovative Computing	p. 276	Be familiar with an example of how patients video conference with medical professionals
	Link	eBook p. 276 or CourseMate	
Flatbed Scanner	Text/Figure	p. 278	Know how flatbed scanners work and the benefit of OCR software
Scanning	FAQ	p. 278	Be familiar with how to use a scanner
	FAQ Link	eBook p. 278, or Scanning link, CourseMate	
Input Devices	Windows Exercises	CourseMate	Be able to use Windows to identify input devices on a computer
Photo Editing	Web Apps	CourseMate	Be able to upload photos to Flickr, crop them, and share them

Safe User, Protected from the Risks in a Digital World

Goal: I would like to take measures to (1) protect my computers, devices, and data from loss, damage, or misuse; (2) minimize or prevent risks associated with using technology; and (3) minimize the environmental impact of using computers and related devices.

Topic	Resource	Location	Now you should . . .
Keyboard Monitors	Ethics & Issues	p. 261	Recognize how your keystrokes can be logged and monitored
Keyboard Ergonomics	Text/Figure	p. 262	Know the purpose and design of an ergonomic keyboard
Ergonomics	Web Link	eBook p. 262 or CourseMate	Be familiar with the latest information regarding ergonomics
RSIs	FAQ	p. 263	Know ways to reduce your chance of experiencing RSIs and recognize the symptoms
	Link and Video	eBook p. 262 or CourseMate	
	Ethics & Issues	p. 265	Know the issues surrounding workplace RSIs

Continued on next page

Continued from previous page

Topic	Resource	Location	Now you should . . .
Mobile Device Threats	FAQ	p. 269	Be familiar with threats to mobile computers and devices
Medical Advice	Ethics & Issues	p. 271	Be familiar with issues of video game makers providing medical advice
RFID Tracking	Ethics & Issues	p. 280	Be aware of privacy issues surrounding RFID use
Biometric Monitoring	Ethics & Issues	p. 283	Be aware of privacy issues surrounding biometric facial recognition
	Video	eBook p. 283 or CourseMate	

Competent Digital Citizen

Goal: I would like to be knowledgeable and well-informed about computers, mobile devices, and related technology, so that I am digitally literate in my personal and professional use of digital devices.

Topic	Resource	Location	Now you should . . .
Input	Text/Figure	pp. 258–259	Know the difference among a program, command, and user response
Key Arrangement	FAQ	p. 261	Know the rationale for the arrangement of keyboard typing keys
	FAQ Link	eBook p. 261, or Keyboards link, CourseMate	
Pointing Device	Text	p. 261 Figure 5-3 and p. 263	Know the purpose of a pointing device and its relationship to a pointer
Scanners	Text/Figure	p. 277	Know the various types of scanners and their primary uses
	Drag and Drop Figure 5-27	eBook p. 277 or CourseMate	
Optical Readers	Text/Figures	p. 279	Know the difference between OCR and OMR
Bar Code Readers	Text/Figure	p. 280	Know the purpose of bar code readers and uses of bar codes
RFID Readers	Text/Figure	pp. 280–281	Know the purpose of RFID readers and uses of RFID tags
Magstripe Reader	Text/Figure	p. 281	Know the purpose of magstripe readers and what is stored in stripes
MICR	Text/Figure	p. 281	Know the purpose of MICR readers and what they read on a check
Biometric Input	Text/Figure	pp. 282–283	Know the purpose and uses of various biometric devices
	Video	eBook p. 288 or CourseMate	
	Text	p. 288	Be familiar with the process of authentication in finger-scan and other biometric technology
	Link	eBook p. 288 or CourseMate	
Input Devices for Physically Challenged Users	Text/Figures	p. 286	Be familiar with the ADA and input devices designed to assist users who are physically challenged
	Looking Ahead		
	Video and Link	eBook p. 286 or CourseMate	
Gesture Recognition	Text	p. 286	Be familiar with the purpose and uses of gesture recognition
	Web Link	eBook p. 286 or CourseMate	
Satoru Iwata	Text	p. 289	Be familiar with Satoru Iwata's accomplishments at Nintendo
	Link and Video	eBook p. 289 or CourseMate	
Douglas Engelbart	Text	p. 289	Be familiar with Douglas Engelbart's contribution to the computing industry
	Link	eBook p. 289 or CourseMate	

Future Entrepreneur or Professional in a Digital Society

Goal: As I ponder my future, I envision myself as an entrepreneur or skilled professional using technology to support my business endeavors or job responsibilities. Along the way, I may interact with a variety of computer professionals — or I may just become one myself!

Topic	Resource	Location	Now you should . . .
Signature Capture Pads	Web Link	eBook p. 268 or CourseMate	Be able to describe signature capture pads, along with their features and costs
Graphics Tablet	Text/Figure	p. 268	Know how professionals use a graphics tablet
Web Cams	Text	pp. 275–276	Know how businesses might use a Web cam
	Web Link	eBook p. 276 or CourseMate	
Video Conference	Text/Figure	pp. 276–277	Know what is required for a video conference and how it works, and give examples of its uses
	Innovative Computing Video	eBook p. 276 or CourseMate	
Bar Code Readers	Web Link	eBook p. 280 or CourseMate	Be familiar with features and prices of bar code readers
RFID Readers	Text	p. 280	Know why some retailers prefer RFID to bar code technology
Data Collection	Text/Figure	p. 282	Be familiar with uses of data collection devices
Computers in Hospitality Industry	Computer Usage @ Work	p. 287	Recognize how personnel and customers use computers in hotels and restaurants
	Link and Video	eBook p. 287 or CourseMate	
Data Entry Clerk	Exploring Computer Careers	CourseMate	Be familiar with the responsibilities of and education required for a data entry clerk

Preparing for a Test

Visit the Computer Concepts CourseMate at www.cengagebrain.com and then navigate to the Chapter 5 Web Apps resource for this book to prepare for your test.

Does your class use the Computer Concepts CourseMate Web site? If so, prepare for your test by using the Flash Cards, Study Guide, and Practice Test Web apps — available for your smart phone or tablet.

If your class does not use the Computer Concepts CourseMate Web site or you prefer to use your book, you can prepare for the test by doing the Quiz Yourself activities on pages 271, 277, and 287; reading the Chapter Review on pages 290–291; ensuring you know the definitions for the terms on page 292; and completing the Checkpoint exercises on pages 293–294. You also should know the material identified in the Chapter 5 Study Guide that follows.

Chapter 5 Study Guide

This study guide identifies material you should know for the Chapter 5 exam. You may want to write the answers in a notebook, enter them on your digital device, record them into a phone, or highlight them in your book. Choose whichever method helps you remember the best.

1. Define the terms, input and input device.
2. Differentiate among a program, command, and user response.
3. Describe the arrangement of keys on an enhanced keyboard, and identify the function of commonly used keys and buttons on desktop computer keyboards.
4. Explain the purpose of keyboard monitoring software.
5. Identify two types of wireless technologies that a wireless keyboard or wireless mouse might use.
6. The goal of _____ is to incorporate comfort, efficiency, and safety in the design of the workplace.
7. Identify ways to reduce chances of experiencing RSIs.
8. Describe how keyboards for mobile computers and devices differ from desktop computer keyboards.
9. Describe the function and purpose of predictive text input.
10. Identify the purpose of a pointing device and its relationship to a pointer.

Continued on next page

Continued from previous page

11. Describe the differences among mouse types: optical mouse, laser mouse, air mouse, and wireless mouse.
12. Explain how to use a mouse and common mouse operations.
13. Describe a trackball, touchpad, and pointing stick.
14. Identify uses of touch screens.
15. Touch screens that recognize multiple points of contact at the same time are known as _____.
16. Explain how to use a touch-sensitive pad.
17. Describe various types of pen input.
18. Identify various types of input for smart phones.
19. Identify security risks for mobile computers and devices.
20. Summarize the purpose of various game controllers: gamepads, joysticks and wheels, light guns, dance pads, and motion-sensing game controllers.
21. Differentiate among types of digital cameras: studio, field, and point-and-shoot.
22. Explain how resolution affects the quality of a picture captured on a digital camera.
23. MP stands for _____.
24. Differentiate between optical and enhanced resolution.
25. Describe the uses of voice input.
26. Explain the purpose of music production software.
27. Describe a DV camera.
28. Identify the purpose of a Web cam.
29. Describe how a video conference works.
30. Differentiate among flatbed, pen, sheet-fed, and drum scanners. State ways to improve scanned document quality.
31. Identify the purpose of OCR software.
32. Describe how optical readers work. Differentiate between OCR and OMR. Give examples of their uses.
33. Describe how bar code readers work. Identify uses of bar codes.
34. Describe how RFID readers work. State uses of RFID tags.
35. Identify privacy issues surrounding use of RFID.
36. Identify the purpose of magstripe readers. State types of information stored on a stripe.
37. The _____ industry almost exclusively uses MICR readers.
38. Give examples where data collection devices are used.
39. Define the term, biometrics. Give examples of biometric identifiers.
40. Describe the purpose and use of these biometric devices: fingerprint reader, face recognition system, hand geometry system, voice verification system, signature verification system, and iris recognition system.
41. Identify privacy issues surrounding biometric face recognition systems.
42. Identify the purpose of POS terminals, ATMs, and DVD kiosks.
43. PIN stands for _____.
44. Briefly describe the Americans with Disabilities Act.
45. Identify input devices for physically challenged users.
46. Describe how restaurants and hotels use computers.
47. Briefly explain the enrollment and matching steps in biometric technology.
48. Identify types of devices sold by Logitech.

Check This Out

As technology changes, you must keep up with updates, new products, breakthroughs, and recent advances to remain digitally literate. The list below identifies topics related to this chapter that you should explore to keep current. In parentheses beside each topic, you will find a search term to help begin your research using a search engine, such as Google.

1. **new virtual keyboards** (search for: virtual keyboard)
2. **recent keyboard monitoring software hacking** (search for: keylogging)
3. **health injuries resulting from using tablet computers** (search for: tablet ergonomics)
4. **new pointing devices** (search for: latest pointing devices)
5. **latest Microsoft Surface table** (search for: Microsoft Surface)
6. **input devices for smart phones** (search for: new smart phone input devices)
7. **popular game controllers** (search for: game controllers)
8. **input accessories for the Xbox** (search for: Xbox accessories)
9. **3-D motion control input device** (search for: 3D motion controller)
10. **digital camera features** (search for: digital camera specification review)
11. **smart phone voice recognition technology** (search for: smart phone input speech)
12. **features of new 3-D digital video cameras** (search for: 3D video camera)
13. **video conferencing on mobile devices** (search for: mobile device video conferencing)
14. **popular types of 2-D bar codes** (search for: 2D bar codes)
15. **mobile payments made using fingerprint scanning technology** (search for: mobile payment fingerprint)

For current news and information
Check us out on Facebook and Twitter. See your instructor or the Computer Concepts CourseMate for specific information.

Chapter 6

Student Success Guide

Output

Why Should I Learn About Output Devices?

"On Sunday afternoons, I relax by watching sports on my 60-inch HDTV. My wireless surround sound system makes me feel like I am sitting in the stadium's front-row seat. I even have produced flyers on my ink-jet printer inviting my friends to watch playoff games with me. What other output devices could I possibly use?"

True, you may be familiar with some of the material in this chapter, but do you know . . .

"What other output devices could I possibly use?"

- Which features to consider when purchasing an LCD screen or monitor? (pp. 308–309, LCD Quality)
- How ink-jet printers form characters and graphics on paper? (pp. 316–317, Ink-Jet Printers)
- Where you can discard depleted toner cartridges in an environmentally safe manner? (p. 320, FAQ)
- How 3-D graphics are generated for video games? (p. 330, High-Tech Talk)
- Who helped build the first desktop computer and was on the cover of *Time* magazine by age 26? (p. 331, Technology Trailblazers)
- How to make a video and upload it to YouTube? (pp. 340–341 and Computer Concepts CourseMate, Learn How To)
- How to use video editing software? (p. 348, Digital Video Technology Special Feature)
- Which Windows options assist those with hearing or visual impairments? (Windows Exercises, Computer Concepts CourseMate)

For these answers and to discover much more information essential to this course, read Chapter 6 and visit the associated Computer Concepts CourseMate at www.cengagebrain.com.

Q & A How can I meet one or more of these goals?

Make use of the goal's resources for each chapter in the book and you should meet that goal by the end of the course.

Customize Your Learning Experience

Adapt this book to meet your needs by determining your goal. Would you like to be an informed digital consumer? A productive technology user? A safe user, protected from the risks in a digital world? A competent digital citizen? A future entrepreneur or professional in a digital society?

Every chapter in this Student Success Guide identifies resources targeted toward each of these goals, along with criteria to verify you understand the resources' content. Resources may be located in the textbook, on the Computer Concepts CourseMate Web site, in the interactive eBook, and on the Web.

Informed Digital Consumer

Goal: I would like to understand the terminology used in Web or print advertisements that sell computers, mobile devices, and related technology, as well as the jargon used by sales associates in computer or electronics stores, so that I can make informed purchasing decisions.

Topic	Resource	Location	Now you should . . .
LCD Monitors and Screens	Text/Figures	pp. 307–309	Be familiar with features of LCD monitors and screens
	Web Link	eBook p. 307 or CourseMate	
	Video	At the Movies, CourseMate	
Digital Frames	Innovative Computing	p. 308	Be familiar with features and costs of digital frames
	Link and Video	eBook p. 308 or CourseMate	
LCD Quality	Text/Figure and FAQ	pp. 308–310	Know how resolution, response time, brightness, dot pitch, and contrast ratio affect quality of an LCD monitor or screen

Continued on next page

Continued from previous page

Topic	Resource	Location	Now you should . . .
Video Standards	Text/Figure	pp. 310–311	Know the video standards and typical resolutions for display devices
Plasma Monitors	Text/Figure	p. 311	Be familiar with features of plasma monitors
HDTV	Text/Figure	p. 312	Know the benefits of HDTV
Printer Purchase	Text/Figure	p. 314	Be familiar with questions to ask when purchasing a printer
Ink-Jet Printers	Text/Figures	pp. 316–317	Know the features, resolution, costs, and uses of ink-jet printers and ink
Photo Printers	Text/Figure	p. 318	Know the features, costs, and uses of photo printers
	Web Link	eBook p. 318 or CourseMate	
Photo Paper	FAQ	p. 318	Be familiar with paper to use for photo printing
	FAQ Link	eBook p. 318, or Photo Paper link, CourseMate	
Laser Printers	Text/Figure	pp. 319–320	Know the features, costs, and uses of laser printers and toner
Multifunction Peripherals	Text/Figure	pp. 320–321	Know the features, advantages, and disadvantages of multifunction peripherals
Digital Photo Printer	Text/Figure	p. 321	Know the features of digital photo printers for home use
Speakers	Text/Figure	pp. 323–324	Be familiar with features and types of speakers, configurations of surround sound systems, and audio resolution
Headphones and Earbuds	Text/Figures	pp. 324–325	Understand the difference between headphones, headsets, and earbuds
	Web Link	eBook p. 324 or CourseMate	
Game Controllers	Text/Figure	pp. 326–327	Know the purpose of force-feedback game controllers
Output Device Recommendations	Text/Figure	p. 327	Be familiar with output device recommendations for various users
HP	Text	p. 331	Be familiar with HP's products and services
	Link	eBook p. 331 or CourseMate	
Samsung	Text	p. 331	Be familiar with Samsung's products
	Link	eBook p. 331 or CourseMate	
Digital Video Technology	Text/Figures	pp. 344–349	Know how to select a video camera, record a video, transfer and manage videos, edit videos, and distribute videos
	Figure 6-3 Animation	p. 346	
	Drag and Drop Figure 6-6	p. 347	

Productive Technology User

Goal: I would like to learn ways that technology can benefit me at home, work, and school. I also would like to learn helpful techniques for using technology so that I can perform tasks more efficiently and be more productive in daily activities.

Topic	Resource	Location	Now you should . . .
Monitors	Text	p. 306	Know the adjustments available on computer monitors
Graphics Ports	Text/Figure	pp. 310–311	Be familiar with the purpose of DVI, HDMI, and other graphics ports
	Drag and Drop Figure 6-6		
	Web Link	eBook p. 310 or CourseMate	

Continued on next page

Continued from previous page

Topic	Resource	Location	Now you should . . .
Hard Copy Output	Text/Figures	pp. 313–314	Understand the difference between portrait and landscape orientation
Printing Methods	Text/Figure	pp. 314–315	Be familiar with the various printing methods
Wireless Printing	Text	pp. 314–315	Know the wireless technologies for printing
Accessibility Options	Windows Exercises	CourseMate	Know how to use Sound Sentry, Narrator, and Magnifier in Windows
Paint	Windows Exercises	CourseMate	Know how to use Paint
Sound	Windows Exercises	CourseMate	Know how to adjust sound in Windows
Make and Upload a Video	Learn How To	pp. 340–341 and CourseMate	Know how to transfer a video to a computer, upload the video to YouTube, and view the video
Control Printing	Learn How To	p. 341 and CourseMate	Know how to control printing on a Windows computer
Sending Files	Web Apps	CourseMate	Know how to use YouSendIt

Safe User, Protected from the Risks in a Digital World

Goal: I would like to take measures to (1) protect my computers, devices, and data from loss, damage, or misuse; (2) minimize or prevent risks associated with using technology; and (3) minimize the environmental impact of using computers and related devices.

Topic	Resource	Location	Now you should . . .
Computer Eye Strain	FAQ	p. 306	Know how to ease eyestrain while using a computer
	FAQ Link	eBook p. 306, or Eye Strain link, CourseMate	
Digital Billboards	Ethics & Issues	p. 306	Recognize the controversy surrounding digital billboards
Reusable Paper	Looking Ahead	p. 314	Know how reusable paper works
	Link and Video	eBook p. 314 or CourseMate	
Toner Disposal	FAQ	p. 320	Know how to dispose of toner cartridges properly
	FAQ Link and Video	eBook p. 320, or Recycling Toner Cartridges link, CourseMate	Be familiar with recycling guidelines
Green Graffiti	Ethics & Issues	p. 325	Be familiar with issues surrounding green graffiti
	Video	eBook p. 325 or CourseMate	

Competent Digital Citizen

Goal: I would like to be knowledgeable and well-informed about computers, mobile devices, and related technology, so that I am digitally literate in my personal and professional use of digital devices.

Topic	Resource	Location	Now you should . . .
Output	Text/Figure	pp. 304–305	Be able to identify various output devices and types of output
Display Devices	Text	p. 306	Be familiar with display devices on various computers and devices
	Labs	CourseMate	
LCD Technology	Text	p. 308	Know various types of LCD technology

Continued on next page

Continued from previous page

Topic	Resource	Location	Now you should . . .
Video Cards	Text	pp. 310–311	Know about bit depth and video memory on video cards
Video Content	FAQ	p. 311	Know the type of video content most often viewed
	FAQ Link	eBook p. 311, or Video Output Content link, CourseMate	Know about video apps
Largest HDTV	FAQ	p. 312	Be familiar with specs for the largest HDTV
	FAQ Link	eBook p. 312, or Largest High-Definition Display link, CourseMate	
CRT Monitors	Text/Figure	p. 313	Know how CRT monitors work and that their popularity has declined
Nonimpact Printers	Text	p. 315	Describe how nonimpact printers work and name examples
	Labs	CourseMate	
Ink-Jet Printers	Text/Figure	pp. 316–317	Know how ink-jet printers work
	Drag and Drop Figure 6-16	eBook p. 317 or CourseMate	
	Web Link		
Laser Printers	Text/Figure	p. 320	Know how laser printers work
	Drag and Drop Figure 6-19	eBook p. 320 or CourseMate	
	Web Link		
Output Devices for Physically Challenged	Text/Figures	pp. 328–329	Be familiar output devices designed to assist users who are physically challenged
	Ethics & Issues		
Computers in Space Exploration	Computer Usage @ Work	p. 329	Recognize how computers are used in space exploration
	Link and Video	eBook p. 329 or CourseMate	
Steve Jobs	Text	p. 331	Be familiar with Steve Jobs's impact on the computing industry and his accomplishments
	Video	eBook p. 331 or CourseMate	
Ursula Burns	Text	p. 331	Know the company of which Ursula Burns is chair and CEO
	Link	eBook p. 331 or CourseMate	

Future Entrepreneur or Professional in a Digital Society

Goal: As I ponder my future, I envision myself as an entrepreneur or skilled professional using technology to support my business endeavors or job responsibilities. Along the way, I may interact with a variety of computer professionals — or I may just become one myself!

Topic	Resource	Location	Now you should . . .
Thermal Printers	Text/Figure	p. 321	Know the uses of thermal printers in businesses
Mobile Printers	Text/Figure	p. 321	Know the features and technology used in mobile printers
Label and Postage Printers	Text/Figure	p. 322	Know the functions of label and postage printers

Continued on next page

Continued from previous page

Topic	Resource	Location	Now you should . . .
Plotters and Large-Format Printers	Text/Figure	p. 322	Know the features, technology, costs, and uses of plotters and large-format printers
	Web Link	eBook p. 322 or CourseMate	
	Figure 6-24 Video		
Impact Printers	Text/Figure	pp. 322–323	Know how impact printers work, and uses of dot-matrix and line printers
Data Projectors	Text/Figure	pp. 325–326	Know the function and types of data projectors
Interactive Whiteboards	Text/Figure	p. 326	Know the function, technologies, and uses of interactive whiteboards
	Web Link and Video	eBook p. 326 or CourseMate	
3-D Graphics	Text	p. 330	Know how professionals, such as game programmers, create 3-D graphics, and how 3-D graphics work
	Link and Video	eBook p. 330 or CourseMate	
	Labs	CourseMate	
Graphic Designer/ Illustrator	Exploring Computer Careers	CourseMate	Be familiar with the responsibilities of and education required for a graphic designer/illustrator

Preparing for a Test

Visit the Computer Concepts CourseMate at www.cengagebrain.com and then navigate to the Chapter 6 Web Apps resource for this book to prepare for your test.

Does your class use the Computer Concepts CourseMate Web site? If so, prepare for your test by using the Flash Cards, Study Guide, and Practice Test Web apps — available for your smart phone or tablet.

If your class does not use the Computer Concepts CourseMate Web site or you prefer to use your book, you can prepare for the test by doing the Quiz Yourself activities on pages 313, 323, and 329; reading the Chapter Review on pages 332–333; ensuring you know the definitions for the terms on page 334; and completing the Checkpoint exercises on pages 335–336. You also should know the material identified in the Chapter 6 Study Guide that follows.

Chapter 6 Study Guide

This study guide identifies material you should know for the Chapter 6 exam. You may want to write the answers in a notebook, enter them on your digital device, record them into a phone, or highlight them in your book. Choose whichever method helps you remember the best.

1. Define the terms, output and output device.
2. Describe the types of output: text, graphics, audio, and video.
3. Identify ways most monitors can be adjusted.
4. List ways to ease eyestrain while using a computer.
5. Describe a digital billboard.
6. LCD stands for _____.
7. Identify characteristics of LCD monitors and LCD screens.
8. Describe how LCD monitors and screens work.
9. Identify the advantages of active-matrix displays.
10. Describe the factors that affect the quality of an LCD monitor or LCD screen: resolution, response time, brightness, dot pitch, and contrast ratio.
11. Differentiate among these ports: DVI, HDMI, and S-video.
12. _____ defines a display's width relative to its height.
13. Explain the relationship of bit depth and video memory to video cards.
14. Explain the characteristics of plasma monitors.
15. Describe advantages of digital television signals over analog signals.
16. HDTV stands for _____.
17. Differentiate between portrait and landscape orientation.
18. Identify questions to ask when purchasing a printer.
19. Describe how reusable paper works.
20. Describe various ways to print.

Continued on next page

Continued from previous page

21. Differentiate between a nonimpact printer and an impact printer.
22. Describe characteristics and uses of ink-jet printers.
23. DPI stands for _____.
24. Describe characteristics of photo printers.
25. Describe characteristics and uses of laser printers. Identify proper ways to dispose of toner cartridges.
26. Identify the features, advantages, and disadvantage of multifunction peripherals.
27. Explain how thermal printers work. Give examples of their use.
28. Describe a mobile printer.
29. Describe how label and postage printers work.
30. Describe characteristics of plotters and large-format printers.
31. Describe the uses of speakers. Explain various surround sound system configurations.
32. Define the term, audio resolution.
33. Differentiate among headphones, earbuds, and headsets.
34. Identify the purpose of data projectors. Differentiate between LCD and DLP projectors.
35. Describe green graffiti.
36. Describe the purpose of interactive whiteboards and technologies for displaying computer images on them.
37. Describe how force-feed game controllers and tactile output work.
38. Identify output options for physically challenged users.
39. Explain a 3-D graphic. Identify the purpose of wireframes and considerations when adding surface to a wireframe.
40. Identify products manufactured by HP.
41. Identify products manufactured by Samsung.
42. ____ cofounded Apple with Steve Wozniak.
43. Describe how to transfer videos from a DV camera to a computer.
44. Name popular video file formats.
45. Explain ways to edit a video.

Check This Out

As technology changes, you must keep up with updates, new products, breakthroughs, and recent advances to remain digitally literate. The list below identifies topics related to this chapter that you should explore to keep current. In parentheses beside each topic, you will find a search term to help begin your research using a search engine, such as Google.

1. **top LCD monitors** (search for: LCD monitor reviews)
2. **latest plasma monitors** (search for: best plasma monitors)
3. **popular HDTV models** (search for: top high definition TVs)
4. **new wireless printers** (search for: wireless printers)
5. **best ink-jet printers** (search for: top ink jet printers)
6. **latest photo printer characteristics** (search for: photo printer features)
7. **new laser printers** (search for: latest laser printers)
8. **widely used multifunction products** (search for: multifunction peripherals)
9. **popular mobile printer features** (search for: top mobile printers)
10. **latest wireless speaker systems** (search for: wireless speakers)
11. **popular force-feedback game controllers** (search for: force feedback gaming accessories)
12. **new output devices for physically challenged users** (search for: output devices physically challenged)
13. **3-D graphics creation** (search for: new 3D technology)
14. **Steve Jobs's influence on consumer technology** (search for: Steve Jobs legacy)
15. **latest digital video technology** (search for: digital video equipment)

For current news and information
Check us out on Facebook and Twitter. See your instructor or the Computer Concepts CourseMate for specific information.

Student Success Guide

Storage

Why Should I Learn About Storage?

"My USB flash drive stores all the files I need for my classes. I transfer all of my digital photos from an SD card to my computer's hard disk, which also has plenty of space for my programs and music. Weekly, I back up files on my computer to an external hard disk. What other types of storage could I need?"

True, you may be familiar with some of the material in this chapter, but do you know . . .

"What other types of storage could I need?"

- How your hard disk reads and writes data? (p. 358, How a Hard Disk Works)
- How to safeguard data on your mobile media when traveling on commercial aircraft? (p. 367, FAQ)
- Where you can save and share your audio, video, graphics, and other important files on the Internet? (pp. 368–369, Cloud Storage)
- When law enforcement officials may read your e-mail messages? (p. 369, Ethics & Issues)
- How meteorologists use computers to forecast storms and hurricanes? (p. 381, Computer Usage @ Work)
- Which company developed the first hard disk for the personal computer? (p. 383, Companies on the Cutting Edge)
- How to increase space on your hard disk? (p. 392 and Computer Concepts CourseMate, Learn How To)
- How to recover a file you deleted accidentally? (Windows Exercises, Computer Concepts CourseMate)

For these answers and to discover much more information essential to this course, read Chapter 7 and visit the associated Computer Concepts CourseMate at www.cengagebrain.com.

Q & A
How can I meet one or more of these goals?
Make use of the goal's resources for each chapter in the book and you should meet that goal by the end of the course.

Customize Your Learning Experience

Adapt this book to meet your needs by determining your goal. Would you like to be an informed digital consumer? A productive technology user? A safe user, protected from the risks in a digital world? A competent digital citizen? A future entrepreneur or professional in a digital society?

Every chapter in this Student Success Guide identifies resources targeted toward each of these goals, along with criteria to verify you understand the resources' content. Resources may be located in the textbook, on the Computer Concepts CourseMate Web site, in the interactive eBook, and on the Web.

Informed Digital Consumer

Goal: I would like to understand the terminology used in Web or print advertisements that sell computers, mobile devices, and related technology, as well as the jargon used by sales associates in computer or electronics stores, so that I can make informed purchasing decisions.

Topic	Resource	Location	Now you should . . .
Storage Capacity	Text/Figure	p. 354	Know terms and abbreviations that define capacity of storage media
	Drag and Drop Figure 7-2	eBook p. 354 or CourseMate	
Transfer Rate	Text/Figure	p. 355 and p. 358	Be familiar with storage media transfer rates and relative speed compared to memory
	Drag and Drop Figure 7-4	eBook p. 355 or CourseMate	
Hard Disks	Text	pp. 355–356	Know the purpose of hard disks, their capacities, and uses

Continued on next page

Continued from previous page

Topic	Resource	Location	Now you should . . .
RAID	Text	p. 360	Know the purpose of RAID
External Hard Disks	Text/Figures	pp. 360–361	Know the capacities and advantages of external and removable hard disks
Hard Disk Controllers	Text	pp. 361–362	Know the differences of SATA, EIDE, SCSI, and SAS controllers
	Web Link	eBook p. 361 or CourseMate	
SSDs	Text/Figure and FAQ	p. 363	Know the purpose, form factors, capacities, speeds, advantages, and disadvantages of solid state drives
	FAQ Link	eBook p. 363, or Project Quicksilver link, CourseMate	
	Web Link	eBook p. 363 or CourseMate	
Memory Cards	Text/Figures	pp. 364–366	Know the types, capacities, and uses of various memory cards
	Web Link	eBook p. 365 or CourseMate	
USB Flash Drives	Text/Figure	p. 367	Know the uses and capacities of USB flash drives
ExpressCard Modules	Text/Figure	p. 367	Know the uses and sizes of ExpressCard modules
Optical Discs	Text/Figure	p. 370	Know the uses and sizes of optical discs
Optical Disc Types	Text/Figure	p. 372	Know the various optical disc formats and their capabilities
	Drag and Drop Figure 7-29	eBook p. 372 or CourseMate	
	Innovative Computing Link		
CDs	Text/Figure	pp. 372–373	Know the purpose and capacities of CD media and their drive speeds
Archive Disc	Text/Figure	p. 374	Know the use and cost of an archive disc or Picture CD
DVDs	Text/Figures and FAQ	pp. 375–376	Know the use and storage capacities of various DVD media
Blu-Ray	Text/Figure	p. 375	Know the use and storage capacities of Blu-ray media
	Web Link	eBook p. 375 or CourseMate	
Seagate	Text	p. 383	Be familiar with Seagate's products
	Link and Video	eBook p. 383 or CourseMate	
SanDisk	Text	p. 383	Be familiar with SanDisk's products
	Link	eBook p. 383 or CourseMate	

Productive Technology User

Goal: I would like to learn ways that technology can benefit me at home, work, and school. I also would like to learn helpful techniques for using technology so that I can perform tasks more efficiently and be more productive in daily activities.

Topic	Resource	Location	Now you should . . .
Miniature Hard Disks	Text/Figures	p. 361	Know the uses of miniature hard disks
Cloud Storage	Text/Figures	pp. 368–369	Know the purpose, advantages, services offered, and providers of cloud storage
	Innovative Computing	p. 368	
	Link and Video	eBook p. 368 or CourseMate	
	Web Link	eBook p. 369 or CourseMate	

Continued on next page

Continued from previous page

Topic	Resource	Location	Now you should . . .
Optical Discs	Text	p. 370	Know the use of LightScribe technology and drive designations
Archive Discs	Figure	p. 374	Know how an archive disc works
Converting to DVD	FAQ Link	eBook p. 376, or Transferring Movies link, CourseMate	Know about converting VHS to DVD
Managing Files and Folders; Hard Disks	Labs and Windows Exercises	CourseMate	Know how to use Windows to work with folders, to delete and restore files, and to learn statistics about the hard disk on a computer
TurboTax Online	Web Apps	CourseMate	Know how to use TurboTax Online to print and file a tax return

Safe User, Protected from the Risks in a Digital World

Goal: I would like to take measures to (1) protect my computers, devices, and data from loss, damage, or misuse; (2) minimize or prevent risks associated with using technology; and (3) minimize the environmental impact of using computers and related devices.

Topic	Resource	Location	Now you should . . .
Erasing Hard Disks	Ethics & Issues	p. 356	Be familiar with issues surrounding purchase of used hard disks
Crashes	Text/Figure	pp. 358–359	Know how to avoid a head crash
Disk Recovery	FAQ FAQ Link	p. 360 eBook p. 360, or Hard Disk Recovery link, CourseMate	Be familiar with how to recover a hard disk if it fails
	FAQ Video	eBook p. 360 or CourseMate	
Maintaining Hard Disk	Text and FAQ	p. 362	Know ways to maintain a hard disk: Check Disk, Cleanup Disk, and Defragment Disk
	Learn How To	pp. 392–393 and CourseMate	
	Labs and Windows Exercises	CourseMate	
Airport Screenings	FAQ	p. 367	Know how to safeguard data during air travel
	FAQ Link	eBook p. 367, or Airport Screening Equipment link, CourseMate	
Cloud Storage	Ethics & Issues	p. 369	Be familiar with privacy issues surrounding cloud storage
	Link and Video	eBook p. 369 or CourseMate	
Care for and Clean Discs	Text/Figure and FAQ	p. 371	Know how to care for, clean, and repair an optical disc
	FAQ Link	eBook p. 371, or Cleaning and Repairing Discs link, CourseMate	
Medical Records	Ethics & Issues	p. 380	Be aware of privacy issues surrounding medical records
Encrypting USB	Video	At the Movies, CourseMate	Know how to encrypt files on a USB flash drive
Recycle Bin	Windows Exercises	CourseMate	Know how to recover files from the Recycle Bin

Competent Digital Citizen

Goal: I would like to be knowledgeable and well-informed about computers, mobile devices, and related technology, so that I am digitally literate in my personal and professional use of digital devices.

Topic	Resource	Location	Now you should . . .
Program Storage	Text	p. 352	Know where application and system software are stored
Storage Media	Text/Figure	p. 353	Be able to state examples of storage media
Volatility	Text/Figure	p. 354	Understand the difference between volatile and nonvolatile storage
Access Time	Text	p. 355	Know what access time measures
Hard Disk Recording Methods	Text/Figures	p. 356	Know the difference between perpendicular and longitudinal recording
	Web Link	eBook p. 356 or CourseMate	
	Figure Video		
Hard Disk Characteristics and Trends	FAQ	p. 356	Be familiar with density, formatting, clusters, cylinders, platters, form factors, disk cache and other hard disk characteristics; how hard disks work; and trends related to hard disks
	FAQ Link	eBook p. 356, or Hard Disk Capacity link, CourseMate	
	Text	pp. 357–359	
	Figure 7-9 Animation	p. 358	
	Drag and Drop Figure 7-12	p. 359	
	FAQ Link	eBook p. 362, or Hard Disk Performance link, CourseMate	
Memory Cards	Text/Figure	p. 366	Know how a memory card works
Optical Discs	Text/Figure	pp. 370–371	Know how a laser reads data on an optical disc
Media Life	Figure	p. 378	Know the life expectancies of various media
	Drag and Drop Figure 7-38	eBook p. 378 or CourseMate	
Rosetta Project	Looking Ahead	p. 379	Know about the Rosetta Project's long-term storage
	Link and Video	eBook p. 379 or CourseMate	
Computers in Meteorology	Computer Usage @ Work	p. 381	Know how meteorologists use computers in weather forecasting and to predict storm patterns and paths
	Link and Video	eBook p. 381 or CourseMate	
DNS Servers	Text/Figure	p. 382	Know how devices on the Internet locate each other
	Drag and Drop Figure 7-41	eBook p. 382 or CourseMate	
	Link and Video		

Future Entrepreneur or Professional in a Digital Society

Goal: As I ponder my future, I envision myself as an entrepreneur or skilled professional using technology to support my business endeavors or job responsibilities. Along the way, I may interact with a variety of computer professionals — or I may just become one myself!

Topic	Resource	Location	Now you should . . .
NAS	Text/Figure	p. 360	Know the purpose, features, and costs of network attached storage
	Web Link	eBook p. 360 or CourseMate	
Tape	Text/Figure	p. 376	Know how businesses use tape storage and how it works

Continued on next page

Continued from previous page

Topic	Resource	Location	Now you should . . .
Magnetic Stripe Cards and Smart Cards	Text/Figure	p. 377	Know how businesses use magnetic stripe cards and smart cards and how they work
	Ethics & Issues		
	Web Link and Video	eBook p. 377 or CourseMate	
Microfilm, Microfiche	Text/Figure	p. 378	Know the purposes and uses of microfilm and microfiche
Enterprise Storage	Text/Figure	p. 379	Know how large businesses store data, information, and programs
	Web Link	eBook p. 379 or CourseMate	
Storage Recommendations	Text/Figure	p. 380	Be familiar with storage recommendations for various users
Computer Technician	Exploring Computer Careers	CourseMate	Be familiar with the responsibilities and education required for a computer technician

Preparing for a Test

Visit the Computer Concepts CourseMate at www.cengagebrain.com and then navigate to the Chapter 7 Web Apps resource for this book to prepare for your test.

Does your class use the Computer Concepts CourseMate Web site? If so, prepare for your test by using the Flash Cards, Study Guide, and Practice Test Web apps — available for your smart phone or tablet.

If your class does not use the Computer Concepts CourseMate Web site or you prefer to use your book, you can prepare for the test by doing the Quiz Yourself activities on pages 362, 369, and 381; reading the Chapter Review on pages 384–385; ensuring you know the definitions for the terms on page 386; and completing the Checkpoint exercises on pages 387–388. You also should know the material identified in the Chapter 7 Study Guide that follows.

Chapter 7 Study Guide

This study guide identifies material you should know for the Chapter 7 exam. You may want to write the answers in a notebook, enter them on your digital device, record them into a phone, or highlight them in your book. Choose whichever method helps you remember the best.

1. Differentiate between storage devices and storage media.
2. Define storage capacity. Know the terms and abbreviations used to define storage capacity.
3. Describe why most memory is considered volatile and most storage is considered nonvolatile.
4. Differentiate between writing and reading, with respect to storage media.
5. Describe what access time measures.
6. MBps stands for _____, and GBps stands for _____.
7. Define transfer rate. Know which storage media have faster transfer rates.
8. Describe a hard disk. Differentiate between a fixed disk and a portable disk.
9. Differentiate between longitudinal and perpendicular recording.
10. Describe the purpose of a wiping utility.
11. Describe the characteristics of an internal hard disk including capacity, platters, form factor, read/write heads, cylinders, sectors and tracks, revolutions per minute, transfer rate, access time, and density.
12. Explain how a hard disk works.
13. Describe what causes a head crash.
14. Define the term, backup.
15. Identify the purpose of disk cache.
16. A group of two or more integrated hard disks is called a(n) _____.
17. Discuss the purpose of network attached storage devices.
18. Differentiate between external hard disks and removable hard disks. Identify their advantages over fixed disks.
19. Identify devices that contain miniature hard disks.
20. Differentiate among hard disk controllers: SATA, EIDE, SCSI, and SAS.

Continued on next page

Continued from previous page

21. Identify Windows tools that can improve the performance on a hard disk.
22. Describe the purpose and advantages of solid state drives.
23. Differentiate among various types of memory cards.
24. Describe the function of a card reader/writer.
25. Identify advantages and capacities of USB flash drives.
26. Describe the purpose and shapes of ExpressCard modules.
27. Describe cloud storage, examples of services provided, and reasons to use cloud storage.
28. Describe the characteristics of optical discs.
29. Define LightScribe technology.
30. Explain how a laser reads data on an optical disc.
31. Identify guidelines for proper care of optical discs.
32. Explain how to clean an optical disc.
33. Describe a single-session disc.
34. State the typical storage capacity of a CD. Differentiate among a CD-ROM, a CD-R, and a CD-RW.
35. Explain why the speed of a CD-ROM drive is significant. Describe how manufacturers measure optical disc speed.
36. _____ is the process of writing on an optical disc.
37. Describe ripping, with respect to CDs.
38. Explain the purpose of an archive disc or Picture CD.
39. State the storage capacities of DVDs. Differentiate among DVD-ROMs, recordable DVDs, and rewritable DVDs.
40. Describe features of Blu-ray Discs and drives.
41. Describe tape storage and identify its primary use today.
42. Identify uses of magnetic stripe cards and smart cards.
43. Identify uses of microfilm and microfiche.
44. Order these media in terms of life expectancy, from shortest to longest: optical discs, solid state drives, magnetic disks, and microfilm.
45. Explain why an enterprise's storage needs may change.
46. Describe the types of standards set by HIPAA.
47. Explain how meteorologists use computers to predict the weather.
48. Name the company that has the rights to design, develop, manufacture, and market every type of flash memory card format.

Check This Out

As technology changes, you must keep up with updates, new products, breakthroughs, and recent advances to remain digitally literate. The list below identifies topics related to this chapter that you should explore to keep current. In parentheses beside each topic, you will find a search term to help begin your research using a search engine, such as Google.

1. **largest storage medium capacity** (search for: largest storage medium bytes)
2. **latest hard disk technologies** (search for: latest hard disks)
3. **popular failed hard disk data recovery methods** (search for: hard disk recovery software)
4. **widely used network attached storage devices** (search for: top network attached storage)
5. **new external hard disks** (search for: latest external hard disks)
6. **top removable hard disks** (search for: best removable hard disks)
7. **recent miniature hard disks** (search for: latest mini hard disks)
8. **widely used eSATA hard disk controllers** (search for: eSATA hard disk)
9. **popular solid state drives** (search for: top solid state drives)
10. **widely used memory cards** (search for: popular memory cards)
11. **innovative USB flash drives** (search for: latest USB flash drives)
12. **new ExpressCard modules** (search for: ExpressCard module growth)
13. **cloud storage developments** (search for: cloud storage news)
14. **latest Blu-ray Disc formats** (search for: new Blu-ray disc specifications)
15. **smart card technology advancements** (search for: smart card news)

For current news and information
Check us out on Facebook and Twitter. See your instructor or the Computer Concepts CourseMate for specific information.

Chapter 8

Student Success Guide

Operating Systems and Utility Programs

Why Should I Learn About Operating Systems and Utility Programs?

"My computer is running slower than when I bought it, but it seems to be working properly. I installed an antivirus program and update it and my Windows software occasionally. Aside from looking into ways to speed up my computer, why do I need to learn about operating systems and utility programs?"

True, you may be familiar with some of the material in this chapter, but do you know . . .

"Why do I need to learn about operating systems and utility programs?"

- Which combination of characters you should use to create a secure password? (p. 411, FAQ)
- Why a personal firewall may protect against unauthorized intrusions? (p. 425, Personal Firewall)
- What signs may indicate your computer is infected with a virus? (p. 425, Antivirus Programs)
- Who developed an operating system when he was a 21-year-old computer science student in Finland? (p. 431, Technology Trailblazers)
- How to update Windows regularly? (p. 440–441 and Computer Concepts CourseMate, Learn How To)
- How Windows can back up files? (Windows Exercises, Computer Concepts CourseMate)
- How to purchase a desktop or notebook computer, smart phone, portable media player, and digital camera? (p. 444–456, Buyer's Guide Special Feature)

For these answers and to discover much more information essential to this course, read Chapter 8 and visit the associated Computer Concepts CourseMate at www.cengagebrain.com.

Q & A How can I meet one or more of these goals?
Make use of the goal's resources for each chapter in the book and you should meet that goal by the end of the course.

Customize Your Learning Experience

Adapt this book to meet your needs by determining your goal. Would you like to be an informed digital consumer? A productive technology user? A safe user, protected from the risks in a digital world? A competent digital citizen? A future entrepreneur or professional in a digital society?

Every chapter in this Student Success Guide identifies resources targeted toward each of these goals, along with criteria to verify you understand the resources' content. Resources may be located in the textbook, on the Computer Concepts CourseMate Web site, in the interactive eBook, and on the Web.

Informed Digital Consumer

Goal: I would like to understand the terminology used in Web or print advertisements that sell computers, mobile devices, and related technology, as well as the jargon used by sales associates in computer or electronics stores, so that I can make informed purchasing decisions.

Topic	Resource	Location	Now you should . . .
Platform	Text	p. 399	Know the meaning of a required platform on a software package
Aero Interface	Text/Figure	pp. 402–403	Know RAM requirements for Windows Aero vs. Windows 7 Basic
RAM	Text	p. 406	Know how to determine RAM requirements
Embedded Operating Systems	Text/Figures	pp. 418–421	Know the features of Windows Embedded CE, Windows Phone, iPhone OS, Blackberry, and Google Android
	Web Links	eBook p. 420 or CourseMate	
File Compression	Text	p. 427	Be familiar with file compression utilities and popular programs
	Web Link	eBook p. 427 or CourseMate	Be familiar with WinZip
Media Players	Text/Figure	pp. 427–428	Know the purpose of media players and popular players

Continued on next page

Continued from previous page

Topic	Resource	Location	Now you should . . .
Disc Burning	Text/Figure	p. 428	Know the purpose of disc burning software
Personal Computers	Text/Figure	p. 428	Know the purpose of personal computer maintenance utilities
RIM	Text	p. 431	Be familiar with RIM's products and services
	Link	eBook p. 431 or CourseMate	
Buyer's Guide	Text/Figures	pp. 444–456	Know some considerations when purchasing a desktop computer, notebook computer, smart phone, portable media player, and digital camera
	Drag and Drop Figure 8-2	eBook pp. 446–447 or CourseMate	
	Videos and Links	eBook p. 444, 450, 452, 454, and 456 or CourseMate	

Productive Technology User

Goal: I would like to learn ways that technology can benefit me at home, work, and school. I also would like to learn helpful techniques for using technology so that I can perform tasks more efficiently and be more productive in daily activities.

Topic	Resource	Location	Now you should . . .
Starting and Shutting Down a Computer	Text/Figure	p. 400	Know how to perform a cold boot, warm boot, restart, and shut down the computer
Boot Disk	Text	p. 402	Know the reason to have a boot or recovery disk
Shut Down Options	Text and FAQ	p. 402	Know the purpose of various options for shutting down a computer
	Web Link and FAQ Video	eBook p. 402 or CourseMate	
Windows User Interface	Drag and Drop Figure 8-4	eBook p. 403 or CourseMate	Know the elements of the Windows user interface
Foreground Program	Text	pp. 404–405	Know how to make a program active (in the foreground)
Thrashing	FAQ	p. 407	Know how to stop a computer from thrashing
	FAQ Link	eBook p. 407 or CourseMate	
Plug and Play	Text	p. 408	Know how Plug and Play works
USB Flash Drives	FAQ	p. 408	Know how to safely remove a USB flash drive
Network Connections	Text/Figure	p. 408	Know how to connect to a network using Windows
Performance	Text/Figure	pp. 408–409	Know how to monitor performance using Windows
Automatic Update	Text/Figure	pp. 409–410	Know the benefits of using automatic update
Passwords	Text/Figure FAQ	pp. 410–411	Know how to select a good password
	FAQ Link	eBook p. 411 or CourseMate	
Windows	Text/Figures	pp. 413–415	Know some features and editions of Windows 7
	Web Link and Figure Video	eBook p. 414 or CourseMate	
	Windows Exercises	CourseMate	Know how to determine the Windows version on a computer
	Learn How To	pp. 440–441 and CourseMate	Know how to keep Windows up-to-date
Mac OS X	Text/Figure	p. 415	Know some features of Mac OS X
	Link and Video	eBook p. 415 or CourseMate	

Continued on next page

Continued from previous page

Topic	Resource	Location	Now you should . . .
UNIX	Text/Figure	p. 417	Know some features of UNIX
Linux	Text	pp. 416–417	Know some features of Linux
	Web Link	eBook p. 417 or CourseMate	
File Manager	Text/Figure	p. 422	Know the purpose of a file manager
Search Utility	Text/Figure	p. 422	Know the purpose of a search utility
Image Viewer	Text/Figure	p. 423	Know the purpose of an image viewer
Uninstaller	Text and FAQ	p. 423	Know the purpose of an uninstaller and how to delete a program properly
	FAQ Link	eBook p. 423 or CourseMate	
	Labs	CourseMate	
Disk Cleanup	Text/Figure	p. 423	Know the purpose of a disk cleanup utility
Disk Defragmenter	Text/Figure	pp. 423–424	Know the purpose of a disk defragmenter utility
	Figure 8-32 Animation	eBook p. 424 or CourseMate	
Backup and Restore	Text/Figure	p. 424	Know the purpose of a backup and a restore utility and how to use Windows Backup and Restore
	Windows Exercises	CourseMate	
Screen Saver	Text/Figure	p. 425	Know the purpose of a screen saver and how to use one
	Windows Exercises	CourseMate	
Burning Video Discs	Web Link	eBook p. 428 or CourseMate	Know how to use RealPlayer to burn a video disc
	Learn How To	p. 440 and CourseMate	Know how to use Windows Explorer to burn a disc
Verisign	Text	p. 431	Be familiar with Verisign's services
	Link	eBook p. 431 or CourseMate	
Install and Maintain	Learn How To	p. 440 and CourseMate	Be familiar with how to install and maintain a computer
Photo Editing	Web Apps	CourseMate	Know how to use Photoshop Express to edit and share photos

Safe User, Protected from the Risks in a Digital World

Goal: I would like to take measures to (1) protect my computers, devices, and data from loss, damage, or misuse; (2) minimize or prevent risks associated with using technology; and (3) minimize the environmental impact of using computers and related devices.

Topic	Resource	Location	Now you should . . .
Automatic Update	Ethics & Issues	p. 410	Be aware of controversial issues surrounding automatic updates
Recover Deleted Files	Innovative Computing	p. 421	Be familiar with utilities that enable you to recover deleted files
	Link and Video	eBook p. 421 or CourseMate	
Personal Firewall	Text/Figure	p. 425	Know how a personal firewall can protect your computer
Antivirus Programs	Text/Figures	pp. 425–426	Know how antivirus programs protect your computer

Continued on next page

Continued from previous page

Topic	Resource	Location	Now you should . . .
Computer Viruses	FAQ	p. 426	Recognize signs of virus infection and steps to prevent computer virus infection
	FAQ Link	eBook p. 426 or CourseMate	
	Video	At the Movies, CourseMate	
	Labs	CourseMate	
Spyware Removers	Text	p. 426	Know the purpose of spyware and adware removers
Internet Filters	Text and FAQ	pp. 426–427	Know the purpose of Web filters, anti-spam programs, phishing filters, and pop-up blockers
	FAQ Link	eBook p. 427 or CourseMate	

Competent Digital Citizen

Goal: I would like to be knowledgeable and well-informed about computers, mobile devices, and related technology, so that I am digitally literate in my personal and professional use of digital devices.

Topic	Resource	Location	Now you should . . .
System Software	Text	p. 398	Know the definition of system software
Start Up Process	Text/Figures	pp. 400–401	Be able to describe what occurs when you boot up a personal computer, and know the purpose of the registry
	Web Link	eBook p. 401 or CourseMate	
Command Language	Text	p. 403	Know the purpose of a command-line interface
Program Management	Text/Figures	pp. 404–405	Know various ways an operating system can handle programs
Virtual Memory	Text/Figure	p. 406	Know how a computer might use virtual memory
Spooling and Drivers	Text/Figure	pp. 407–408	Know how buffers and spooling work and the purpose of drivers
Eye Monitor	Looking Ahead	p. 409	Be familiar with a health-based performance monitor
	Link and Video	eBook p. 409 or CourseMate	
Operating Systems	Text/Figure	pp. 411–412	Know examples of operating systems in each category: stand-alone, server, and embedded
Windows History	Figure 8-15	p. 412	Be familiar with highlights of stand-alone Windows versions
Open vs. Closed Source	Ethics & Issues	p. 416	Be familiar with the issues around open and closed source programs
	Video	eBook p. 416 or CourseMate	
User Lockdown	Ethics & Issues	p. 418	Know how user lockdown relates to the smart phone industry
Computers in Education	Computer Usage @ Work	p. 429	Recognize how students and instructors use computers in school
	Link and Video	eBook p. 429 or CourseMate	
Touch Screens	Text	p. 430	Know how touch screens work
	Link and Video	eBook p. 430 or CourseMate	
Steve Wozniak	Text	p. 431	Be familiar with Steve Wozniak's impact on the computing industry
	Link and Video	eBook p. 431 or CourseMate	
Linus Torvalds	Text	p. 431	Be familiar with Linus Torvald's role with operating systems
	Link	eBook p. 431 or CourseMate	

Future Entrepreneur or Professional in a Digital Society

Goal: As I ponder my future, I envision myself as an entrepreneur or skilled professional using technology to support my business endeavors or job responsibilities. Along the way, I may interact with a variety of computer professionals — or I may just become one myself!

Topic	Resource	Location	Now you should . . .
Network Admin.	Text	p. 410	Know the role of a network administrator
Operating Systems	FAQ	p. 412	Know the market shares of various operating systems
	FAQ Link	eBook p. 412 or CourseMate	
Server Operating Systems	Text	pp. 417–418	Know the features of server operating systems: Windows Server, UNIX, Linus, Solaris, and NetWare
	Web Link	eBook p. 418 or CourseMate	
Systems Programmer	Exploring Computer Careers	CourseMate	Be familiar with the responsibilities and education required for a systems programmer

Preparing for a Test

Visit the Computer Concepts CourseMate at www.cengagebrain.com and then navigate to the Chapter 8 Web Apps resource for this book to prepare for your test.

Does your class use the Computer Concepts CourseMate Web site? If so, prepare for your test by using the Flash Cards, Study Guide, and Practice Test Web apps — available for your smart phone or tablet.

If your class does not use the Computer Concepts CourseMate Web site or you prefer to use your book, you can prepare for the test by doing the Quiz Yourself activities on pages 411, 421, and 429; reading the Chapter Review on pages 432–433; ensuring you know the definitions for the terms on page 434; and completing the Checkpoint exercises on pages 435–436. You also should know the material identified in the Chapter 8 Study Guide that follows.

Chapter 8 Study Guide

This study guide identifies material you should know for the Chapter 8 exam. You may want to write the answers in a notebook, enter them on your digital device, record them into a phone, or highlight them in your book. Choose whichever method helps you remember the best.

1. Define the term, system software. Identify the two types of system software.
2. Define operating system.
3. Define the terms, platform and cross-platform.
4. _____ is the process of starting or restarting a computer.
5. Differentiate a cold boot from a warm boot.
6. Define kernel.
7. Differentiate memory resident from nonresident.
8. Summarize the startup process on a personal computer.
9. Describe the purpose of the BIOS.
10. POST stands for _____.
11. Explain the purpose of the registry.
12. Differentiate between a boot drive and recovery disk.
13. Describe various shut down options: powering off, sleep mode, and hibernate.
14. Describe the purpose of a user interface. Differentiate between a GUI and command-line interface.
15. In relation to operating systems, explain the difference between single user/single tasking, single user/multitasking, preemptive multitasking, multiuser, and multiprocessing.
16. Differentiate between foreground and background.
17. Describe a fault-tolerant computer.
18. Describe how an operating system manages memory.
19. Describe virtual memory.
20. Define the term, thrashing. Identify ways to stop a computer from thrashing.
21. Explain how an operating system coordinates tasks or jobs.
22. Define the term, buffer. Explain how spooling uses buffers and a queue.
23. Define the term, driver. Explain how the operating system uses drivers and the role of Plug and Play.
24. Explain how properly to remove a USB flash drive.
25. Describe the purpose of a performance monitor.
26. _____ is a term that means computer error.

27. Briefly explain the types of updates that occur in an automatic update.
28. Describe a server operating system.
29. Describe the role of a network administrator. Differentiate administrator account from user account.
30. Define the terms, user name and password. Identify guidelines for selecting a good password.
31. Explain the reason for encryption.
32. Differentiate device-dependent from device-independent.
33. Differentiate among a stand-alone operating system, a server operating system, and an embedded operating system.
34. Summarize the features of these stand-alone operating systems: Windows, Mac OS, UNIX, and Linux.
35. State advantages of open source software.
36. Briefly describe various server operating systems: Windows Server, UNIX, Linux, Solaris, and NetWare.
37. Briefly describe and identify uses of Windows Embedded CE, Windows Phone, iPhone OS, BlackBerry, and Google Android.
38. Explain how it is possible to recover a deleted file.
39. Describe the purpose of a file manager, search utility, image viewer, uninstaller, and disk cleanup utility.
40. Describe the purpose of a disk defragmenter. Describe why a fragmented disk is slower than one that is defragmented.
41. Describe the purpose of a backup and restore utility, screen saver, and personal firewall.
42. Define computer virus and its relationship to malware. Identify signs of a virus infection. Describe the purpose of an antivirus program.
43. Describe the purpose of spyware and adware removers, Web filters, anti-spam programs, phishing filters, pop-up blockers, file compression utilities, media players, disc burning software, and personal computer maintenance utilities.
44. Explain the use of e-learning systems.
45. RIM's key product is its _____ smart phone.
46. _____ cofounded Apple with Steve Jobs.
47. Linus Torvalds created the open source operating system called _____.
48. Briefly describe some considerations when purchasing a desktop computer, notebook computer, smart phone, portable media player, and digital camera.

Check This Out

As technology changes, you must keep up with updates, new products, breakthroughs, and recent advances to remain digitally literate. The list below identifies topics related to this chapter that you should explore to keep current. In parentheses beside each topic, you will find a search term to help begin your research using a search engine, such as Google.

1. **largest operating system market share** (search for: top market share operating systems)
2. **features of latest Windows operating system** (search for: latest Microsoft Windows features)
3. **features of newest Apple OS operating system** (search for: latest Macintosh OS features)
4. **recent UNIX operating system elements** (search for: new UNIX features)
5. **new Linux GUI enhancements** (search for: Linux GUI)
6. **latest Windows Server edition** (search for: recent Windows Server)
7. **recent Windows Phone operating system** (search for: latest Windows mobile OS)
8. **new iPhone and iPad OS features** (search for: iOS news)
9. **popular utility software** (search for: best utility programs)
10. **best utilities to back up data** (search for: backup utilities review)
11. **top antivirus programs** (search for: popular antivirus software)
12. **widely used spyware removal programs** (search for: popular spyware programs)
13. **popular e-learning management systems** (search for: top e-learning software)
14. **updates about Steve Wozniak's projects** (search for: Steve Wozniak news)
15. **latest guidelines for purchasing computers** (search for: computer buying guide)

For current news and information
Check us out on Facebook and Twitter. See your instructor or the Computer Concepts CourseMate for specific information.

Student Success Guide

Communications and Networks

Why Should I Learn About Communications and Networks?

"I use my new smart phone to send text messages, send and receive voice mail, and navigate using a GPS app. At home, I have a broadband Internet connection, and I also access the Internet wirelessly at local hot spots or anywhere on campus. What more do I need to learn about communications and networks?"

True, you may be familiar with some of the material in this chapter, but do you know . . .

"What more do I need to learn about communications and networks?"

- How to determine hot spot locations throughout the country? (p. 480, FAQ)
- How tolls are collected automatically at tollbooths using a RFID reader? (p. 481, RFID)
- How you are able to access your school network wirelessly? (p. 487, Wireless Access Points)
- Why your Internet access provider may not be stating accurate connection speeds? (p. 492, Ethics & Issues)
- How the agriculture industry uses computers to help grow crops? (p. 497, Computer Usage @ Work)
- Which communications company's name is derived from the Roman goddess of truth? (p. 499, Companies on the Cutting Edge)
- How to set up and install a Wi-Fi home network? (p. 508–509 and Computer Concepts CourseMate, Learn How To)
- How to view Windows Firewall security settings? (Windows Exercises, Computer Concepts CourseMate)

For these answers and to discover much more information essential to this course, read Chapter 9 and visit the associated Computer Concepts CourseMate at www.cengagebrain.com.

Customize Your Learning Experience

Q & A How can I meet one or more of these goals?
Make use of the goal's resources for each chapter in the book and you should meet that goal by the end of the course.

Adapt this book to meet your needs by determining your goal. Would you like to be an informed digital consumer? A productive technology user? A safe user, protected from the risks in a digital world? A competent digital citizen? A future entrepreneur or professional in a digital society?

Every chapter in this Student Success Guide identifies resources targeted toward each of these goals, along with criteria to verify you understand the resources' content. Resources may be located in the textbook, on the Computer Concepts CourseMate Web site, in the interactive eBook, and on the Web.

Informed Digital Consumer

Goal: I would like to understand the terminology used in Web or print advertisements that sell computers, mobile devices, and related technology, as well as the jargon used by sales associates in computer or electronics stores, so that I can make informed purchasing decisions.

Topic	Resource	Location	Now you should . . .
Internet Connections	Text/Figure	pp. 483–484	Be aware of costs and transfer rates of various Internet connections
	Drag and Drop Figure 9-24	eBook p. 483 or CourseMate	
Modems	Text/Figures and FAQ	pp. 485–487	Know the purpose and uses of various modem types: dial-up modems, digital modems (ISDN, DSL, and cable), and wireless modems
	Web Links	eBook p. 486 or CourseMate	
	FAQ Link	eBook p. 486, or Cable Internet Service link, CourseMate	

Continued on next page

Continued from previous page

Topic	Resource	Location	Now you should . . .
Network Cards	Text/Figure	p. 487	Know the purpose and styles of network cards
Wireless Access Point	Text/Figure	p. 487	Know the purpose of a wireless access point
Routers	Text/Figure and FAQ	p. 488	Know the purpose of routers
	Web Link	eBook p. 488 or CourseMate	Be familiar with the features and costs of wireless routers
Mobile TV	Links and Video	eBook p. 495 or CourseMate	Be familiar with how to watch live programs on a computer or mobile device
	Innovative Computing	p. 495	
	Video	At the Movies, CourseMate	
Verizon	Text	p. 499	Be familiar with Verizon's products and services
	Link	eBook p. 499 or CourseMate	

Productive Technology User

Goal: I would like to learn ways that technology can benefit me at home, work, and school. I also would like to learn helpful techniques for using technology so that I can perform tasks more efficiently and be more productive in daily activities.

Topic	Resource	Location	Now you should . . .
Uses of Computer Communications	Text/Figure	pp. 461–462	Know the uses of computer communications previously discussed
	Drag and Drop Figure 9-2	eBook p. 462 or CourseMate	
	Web Link		
Wireless Messaging	Text/Figure and FAQ	pp. 462–464	Know the guidelines and uses of text, picture/video, and wireless instant messaging
	Figure Video	eBook p. 463 or CourseMate	
	FAQ and Web Link		
Wireless Internet Access Points	Text/Figure	pp. 464–465	Be familiar with hot spots and mobile wireless networks
Cybercafés	Text/Figure	p. 466	Know the services offered by cybercafés
GPS	Text/Figure	pp. 466–467	Know how GPS works, and name devices with GPS capability
	Web Link	eBook p. 466 or CourseMate	
Voice Mail	Text	p. 467	Know how voice mail and visual voice mail work
Internet Peer-to-Peer	Text/Figure	p. 475	Know the uses of a file sharing or P2P network
	Web Link	eBook p. 475 or CourseMate	
Wi-Fi	Text/Figure and FAQ	pp. 479–480	Know 802.11 series standards and transfer rates and uses of Wi-Fi and hot spots
	Drag and Drop Figure 9-20	eBook p. 479 or CourseMate	
	FAQ Link	eBook p. 480, or Hot Spots link, CourseMate	

Continued on next page

Continued from previous page

Topic	Resource	Location	Now you should . . .
Bluetooth, UWB, IrDA	Text	pp. 480–481	Know some uses of Bluetooth, UWB, and IrDA communications
Communications Software	Text	p. 482	Know the purpose of communications software
Internet Connections	Text/Figures	pp. 482–485	Know how these Internet connections work: dial-up, ISDN, DSL, FTTP, T-carrier, and ATM
	Web Link	eBook p. 484 or CourseMate	
Home Networks	Text/Figure	pp. 489–490	Know benefits of a home network, the types of wired and wireless home networks, and how to set up a home network
	Web Link	eBook p. 489 or CourseMate	
	Figure 9-33 Animation		
	Learn How To	pp. 508–509 and CourseMate	
Modems and Network Connections	Windows Exercises	CourseMate	Know how to use Windows to learn about the modem connected to a computer and view the computer's network connections
Gmail	Web Apps	CourseMate	Know how to use Gmail to send and receive e-mail messages

Safe User, Protected from the Risks in a Digital World

Goal: I would like to take measures to (1) protect my computers, devices, and data from loss, damage, or misuse; (2) minimize or prevent risks associated with using technology; and (3) minimize the environmental impact of using computers and related devices.

Topic	Resource	Location	Now you should . . .
IP Addresses	FAQ	p. 478	Know if an IP address can be used to determine a device's location and recover stolen computers
	FAQ Video	eBook p. 478 or CourseMate	
Unsecured Networks	Ethics & Issues	p. 480	Know some issues associated with unsecured wireless networks
Internet Connection Speeds	Ethics & Issues	p. 492	Know that advertised connection speeds may differ from actual speeds
Cellular and Wi-Fi Radiation	Ethics & Issues	p. 494	Know about potential health effects from cell phones, cellular antennas, and Wi-Fi devices
Wireless Security	Labs	CourseMate	Be familiar with ways to secure an access point
Windows Firewall	Windows Exercises	CourseMate	Be familiar with how to use Windows Firewall

Competent Digital Citizen

Goal: I would like to be knowledgeable and well-informed about computers, mobile devices, and related technology, so that I am digitally literate in my personal and professional use of digital devices.

Topic	Resource	Location	Now you should . . .
Communications	Text/Figure	pp. 460–461	Know the components required in a communications system
Print Media	Ethics & Issues	p. 465	Be aware of the impact of high-speed broadband on print media
	Video	eBook p. 465 or CourseMate	
Geocaching	Innovative Computing	p. 466	Be familiar with how geocaching uses GPS technology
	Link and Video	eBook p. 466 or CourseMate	

Continued on next page

Continued from previous page

Topic	Resource	Location	Now you should . . .
Body Area Network	Looking Ahead	p. 471	Be familiar with the uses of body area networks
	Link and Video	eBook p. 471 or CourseMate	
LANs, MANs, WANs	Text/Figures	pp. 471–473	Know the differences among LANs, MANs, and WANs
	Labs	CourseMate	
Internet Usage	Ethics & Issues	p. 474	Be familiar with issues surrounding Internet usage controls
IP Addresses	FAQ Link	eBook p. 478, or IP Addresses link, CourseMate	Know how IP addresses work
WAP	Text/Figure	p. 482	Know the uses of WAP
Communications Channel	Text/Figure	pp. 491–492	Know the meaning of bandwidth and latency, and the types of transmission media used on a communications channel
Physical Transmission Media	Text/Figures	pp. 492–493	Be familiar with transfer rates and composition of twisted-pair cable, coaxial cable, and fiber-optic cable
	Drag and Drop Figures 9-35, 9-37, and 9-38	eBook pp. 492–493 or CourseMate	
Wireless Transmission Media	Text/Figures	pp. 494–496	Be familiar with transfer rates of and technologies used in infrared, broadcast radio, cellular radio, microwaves, and communications satellite
	Drag and Drop Figure 9-39	eBook p. 494 or CourseMate	
Computers in Agriculture	Computer Usage @ Work	p. 497	Recognize how computers are used in the agriculture industry
	Link and Video	eBook p. 497 or CourseMate	
Network Communications	Text	p. 498	Recognize that data in a network flows through several layers
	Link and Video	eBook p. 498 or CourseMate	
Cisco	Text	p. 499	Be familiar with Cisco's products and services
	Link and Video	eBook p. 499 or CourseMate	
Robert Metcalf	Text	p. 499	Be familiar with Robert Metcalf's impact on network communications
	Link	eBook p. 499 or CourseMate	

Future Entrepreneur or Professional in a Digital Society

Goal: As I ponder my future, I envision myself as an entrepreneur or skilled professional using technology to support my business endeavors or job responsibilities. Along the way, I may interact with a variety of computer professionals — or I may just become one myself!

Topic	Resource	Location	Now you should . . .
Groupware	Text	p. 467	Be familiar with the benefits of groupware in business
Collaboration	Text/Figure	p. 468	Be familiar with collaboration tools: collaborative software, reviewing via e-mail, and document management systems
	Web Link	eBook p. 468 or CourseMate	
Web Services	Text/Figure	p. 469	Know the purpose of Web services in business
Network Advantages	Text/Figure	pp. 470–471	Know the reasons businesses use networks
Network Architectures	Text/Figures	pp. 473–474	Know the difference between client/server and peer-to-peer networks

Continued on next page

Continued from previous page

Topic	Resource	Location	Now you should . . .
Network Topologies	Text/Figures	pp. 475–477	Know the differences among star, bus, and ring networks
Intranets	Text	p. 477	Know how businesses use Intranets and extranets
Ethernet, Token Ring, TCP/IP	Text	pp. 477–478	Be able to differentiate among the Ethernet, token ring, and TCP/IP network communications standards
RFID	Text/Figure	p. 481	Know how RFID works and its uses
	Web Link	eBook p. 481 or CourseMate	
WiMAX	Text	p. 482	Know the purpose, types, and uses of WiMAX
Hubs and Switches	Text/Figure	pp. 488–489	Know the purpose of hubs and switches
Network Specialist	Exploring Computer Careers	CourseMate	Be familiar with the responsibilities and education required for a network specialist

Preparing for a Test

Visit the Computer Concepts CourseMate at www.cengagebrain.com and then navigate to the Chapter 9 Web Apps resource for this book to prepare for your test.

Does your class use the Computer Concepts CourseMate Web site? If so, prepare for your test by using the Flash Cards, Study Guide, and Practice Test Web apps — available for your smart phone or tablet.

If your class does not use the Computer Concepts CourseMate Web site or you prefer to use your book, you can prepare for the test by doing the Quiz Yourself activities on pages 469, 485, and 497; reading the Chapter Review on pages 500–501; ensuring you know the definitions for the terms on page 502; and completing the Checkpoint exercises on pages 503–504. You also should know the material identified in the Chapter 9 Study Guide that follows.

Chapter 9 Study Guide

This study guide identifies material you should know for the Chapter 9 exam. You may want to write the answers in a notebook, enter them on your digital device, record them into a phone, or highlight them in your book. Choose whichever method helps you remember the best.

1. Define computer communications.
2. Discuss the purpose of the components required for successful communications: sending device, communications device, communications channel, and receiving device.
3. Identify various sending and receiving devices.
4. Briefly describe these communications: blogs, chat rooms, e-mail, fax, FTP, instant messaging, Internet, RSS, video conferencing, VoIP, Web, Web 2.0, and wikis.
5. A synonym for text messaging is _____.
6. Describe text messaging. Identify a use of a CSC (common short code).
7. Describe picture messaging and video messaging.
8. A synonym for picture/video messaging is _____.
9. Define wireless Internet access point.
10. Define hot spot. Describe three hot spot technologies.
11. Describe a mobile wireless network.
12. Describe a cybercafé.
13. GPS stands for _____. Give examples of GPS receivers. Cite uses of GPS technology.
14. Explain geocaching.
15. Describe uses of these computer communications: groupware, collaboration, voice mail, and Web services.
16. Define the term, network. List advantages of using a network.
17. EFT stands for _____.
18. Differentiate among LANs, MANs, and WANs.
19. Describe how sensors might work in a body area network (BAN). Identify potential uses of BANs.
20. A server sometimes is called a(n) _____ computer. State examples of dedicated servers.
21. Differentiate between client/server and peer-to-peer networks.
22. Describe how a P2P network works.

Continued on next page

Continued from previous page

23. Differentiate among a star network, bus network, and ring network.
24. Describe how an intranet works. Identify the relationship of an extranet to an intranet.
25. Describe the purpose of network standards and protocols.
26. Differentiate among the Ethernet, token ring, and TCP/IP standards.
27. Describe the Wi-Fi standard. Identify its distance limitations. Name some uses of Wi-Fi.
28. Describe the Bluetooth standard. Identify its distance limitations. Give examples of some Bluetooth devices.
29. Describe UWB and IrDA standards.
30. RFID stands for _____. Explain how RFID works.
31. Describe the WiMAX standard.
32. Explain the purpose of communications software.
33. Describe various types of lines for communications over the telephone network: dial-up, ISDN, DSL, FTTP, T-carrier, and ATM.
34. Differentiate a dial-up modem from a digital modem. Explain differences between ISDN modems, DSL modems, and cable modems.
35. Describe the purpose of wireless modems and network cards. Identify types of each.
36. State the purpose of a wireless access point and a router. Explain security features built into some routers. Identify the best location for a router.
37. Define the purpose of a hub and/or switch.
38. Describe the advantages of a home network. Discuss different wired and wireless ways to set up a home network.
39. Define the terms, bandwidth and latency.
40. Describe the purpose of transmission media. Define the term, broadband media.
41. Explain why advertised Internet connections speeds may differ from actual speeds.
42. Define noise, as it relates to computer communications.
43. Describe characteristics of these physical transmission media: twisted-pair cable, coaxial cable, and fiber-optic cable.
44. Describe characteristics of these wireless transmission media: infrared, broadcast radio, cellular radio, microwaves, and communications satellite.
45. Describe the purpose of the OSI reference model.
46. Cisco manufactures _____ equipment.
47. Identify services by Verizon.
48. Robert Metcalfe coinvented the _____ standard for computer communications.

Check This Out

As technology changes, you must keep up with updates, new products, breakthroughs, and recent advances to remain digitally literate. The list below identifies topics related to this chapter that you should explore to keep current. In parentheses beside each topic, you will find a search term to help begin your research using a search engine, such as Google.

1. **news of using a cell phone as a primary telephone** (search for: cell phone primary phone)
2. **latest developments of working securely from a hot spot** (search for: wireless security hot spot)
3. **recent company use of GPS applications for tracking** (search for: GPS tracking system)
4. **recent geocaching developments** (search for: new geocaching adventures)
5. **popular online groupware applications** (search for: best groupware reviews)
6. **new document management systems for collaboration** (search for: electronic document management software)
7. **widely used mashups** (search for: best mashups)
8. **latest electronic funds transfers using cell phones** (search for: cell phone transfer funds news)
9. **popular wireless LAN devices** (search for: best wireless LAN hardware)
10. **recent software to monitor Internet use** (search for: Internet usage control)
11. **widely used network communications standards** (search for: network communications standards reviews)
12. **Wi-Fi Internet access developments** (search for: new Wi-Fi Internet technology)
13. **popular Bluetooth products** (search for: top Bluetooth devices)
14. **latest digital modems** (search for: digital modem news)
15. **useful advice for creating a wireless home network** (search for: wireless home network guide)

For current news and information
Check us out on Facebook and Twitter. See your instructor or the Computer Concepts CourseMate for specific information.

Chapter 10

Student Success Guide

Database Management

Why Should I Learn About Database Management?

"I realize my school maintains data about me on its computer system, including my contact information, schedule, and grades. At home, I use my computer to keep track of my income and expenses. I also have a list of repairs and modifications I have made to the car I am restoring. So, why do I need to learn about managing databases?"

True, you may be familiar with some of the material in this chapter, but do you know . . .

"Why do I need to learn about managing databases?"

- Why your privacy may be compromised when your personal data is stored in Internet databases? (p. 516, Ethics & Issues)
- How to verify the accuracy of your credit report? (p. 517, FAQ)
- What action you should take if you accidentally discover a file with private data on a publically accessible area of the Internet? (p. 531, Ethics & Issues)
- How a GIS works? (p. 534, Object-Oriented Databases)
- How databases automate processes in the health care industry? (p. 539, Computer Usage @ Work)
- Who developed the relational database design structure that is used for most databases used today? (p. 541, Technology Trailblazers)
- How to organize files using folders? (p. 550 and Computer Concepts CourseMate, Learn How To)
- How to manage folders on a storage device? (Windows Exercises, Computer Concepts CourseMate)

For these answers and to discover much more information essential to this course, read Chapter 10 and visit the associated Computer Concepts CourseMate at www.cengagebrain.com.

Q & A How can I meet one or more of these goals?

Make use of the goal's resources for each chapter in the book and you should meet that goal by the end of the course.

Customize Your Learning Experience

Adapt this book to meet your needs by determining your goal. Would you like to be an informed digital consumer? A productive technology user? A safe user, protected from the risks in a digital world? A competent digital citizen? A future entrepreneur or professional in a digital society?

Every chapter in this Student Success Guide identifies resources targeted toward each of these goals, along with criteria to verify you understand the resources' content. Resources may be located in the textbook, on the Computer Concepts CourseMate Web site, in the interactive eBook, and on the Web.

Informed Digital Consumer

Goal: I would like to understand the terminology used in Web or print advertisements that sell computers, mobile devices, and related technology, as well as the jargon used by sales associates in computer or electronics stores, so that I can make informed purchasing decisions.

Topic	Resource	Location	Now you should . . .
DBMSs	Figure	p. 527	Know the popular DBMSs
	Web Link	eBook p. 527 or CourseMate	
Database Vendors	FAQ	p. 527	Know the market share of database vendors
Data Models and Terminology	Text/Figures	p. 533	Know the various data models and data terminology used in file processing and relational database environments
	Drag and Drop Figure 10-19	eBook p. 533 or CourseMate	

Productive Technology User

Goal: I would like to learn ways that technology can benefit me at home, work, and school. I also would like to learn helpful techniques for using technology so that I can perform tasks more efficiently and be more productive in daily activities.

Topic	Resource	Location	Now you should . . .
Information	Text	pp. 516–517	Know the qualities of valuable information for decision making
Database vs. Spreadsheets	FAQ	p. 519	Know when to use a database versus a spreadsheet
	FAQ Link	eBook p. 519, or Databases and Spreadsheets link, CourseMate	
Adding Records	Text/Figure	p. 520	Be familiar with reasons for and process of adding records to a file
Modifying Records	Text/Figure	p. 521	Be familiar with reasons for and process of modifying records in a file
Deleting Records	Text/Figure	p. 522	Be familiar with reasons for and process of deleting records in a file
Data Dictionary	Text/Figure	pp. 527–528	Be familiar with the use of a data dictionary
	Drag and Drop Figure 10-12	eBook p. 528 or CourseMate	
File Retrieval and Maintenance	Text/Figures	pp. 528–531	Be familiar with the use of query languages, query by example, forms, and report generators
	Drag and Drop Figure 10-13	eBook p. 529 or CourseMate	
SQL	Text/Figure	p. 534	Be familiar with SQL
	Link and Video	eBook p. 534 or CourseMate	
Employee as a User	Text/Figure	p. 538	Know how employees uses databases
Photo Sharing Site	Video	At the Movies, CourseMate	Know how a photo sharing site keeps its data
Spreadsheets	Labs	CourseMate	Be familiar with advanced uses of spreadsheets
Databases	Labs	CourseMate	Be familiar with advanced uses of databases
Files and Folders	Learn How To	pp. 550–551 and CourseMate	Know how to use Windows to organize, manage, and search for files and folders
	Windows Exercises		
Calendar	Web Apps	CourseMate	Know how to use Windows Live Calendar

Safe User, Protected from the Risks in a Digital World

Goal: I would like to take measures to (1) protect my computers, devices, and data from loss, damage, or misuse; (2) minimize or prevent risks associated with using technology; and (3) minimize the environmental impact of using computers and related devices.

Topic	Resource	Location	Now you should . . .
Privacy	Ethics & Issues	p. 516	Realize privacy issues associated with Internet databases
Credit Report	FAQ	p. 517	Know how to check the accuracy of your credit report
	Link and Video	eBook p. 517 or CourseMate	
Government Data	Ethics & Issues	p. 519	Know the type of data the government stores about citizens and foreigners who travel to the United States
Criminal Databases	Ethics & Issues	p. 526	Know issues related to criminal databases
Data Security	Text	p. 531	Be familiar with levels of access privileges
Backup and Recovery	Text/Figure	pp. 531–532	Know the purpose of a backup, a log, a recovery utility, and continuous backup
Security Breaches	Ethics & Issues	p. 537	Know the privacy issues surrounding database security
	Video	eBook p. 537 or CourseMate	

Competent Digital Citizen

Goal: I would like to be knowledgeable and well-informed about computers, mobile devices, and related technology, so that I am digitally literate in my personal and professional use of digital devices.

Topic	Resource	Location	Now you should . . .
Databases	Text/Figure	pp. 514–516	Know the purpose of a database and database software, and how database software is used to process data into information
	Figure 10-1 Animation	eBook p. 514 or CourseMate	
Data Integrity	Text	p. 516	Understand the importance of data integrity
Hierarchy of Data	Text/Figures	pp. 517–519	Know the difference between characters, fields, records, and files; know data types of fields
	Drag and Drop Figure 10-2	p. 517	
Baseball Databases	Innovative Computing	p. 523	Know how databases are used in baseball memorabilia authentication and online baseball games
	Link and Video	eBook p. 523 or CourseMate	
Voter Databases	Innovative Computing	p. 530	Be familiar with how political campaigners use voter databases
Relational Databases	Text/Figure	pp. 533–534	Know the organization and uses of relational databases
Object-Oriented Databases	Text/Figure	pp. 534–535	Know the organization and uses of object-oriented databases
GIS Databases	FAQ	p. 535	Know about geographic information system databases
	FAQ Link	eBook p. 535, or GIS Databases link, CourseMate	
	Figure Video		
Multidimensional Databases	Text	p. 535	Know the organization and uses of multidimensional databases
Web Databases	Text/Figure	pp. 536–537	Be familiar with the uses and operation of Web databases
Portable Media Player	FAQ	p. 537	Know how portable media players use databases
	FAQ Link	eBook p. 537, or Media Player Databases link, CourseMate	
DNA Barcoding	Looking Ahead	p. 538	Be familiar with how databases are used to catalog species of plants, animals, and microbes
	Link and Video	eBook p. 538 or CourseMate	
Normalization	Text/Figure	p. 540	Know how databases are normalized
	Link and Video	eBook p. 540 or CourseMate	
E. F. Codd	Text	p. 541	Be familiar with E. F. Codd's impact on relational databases
	Link	eBook p. 541 or CourseMate	
Larry Ellison	Text	p. 541	Be familiar with Larry Ellison's impact on relational databases
	Link and Video	eBook p. 541 or CourseMate	

Future Entrepreneur or Professional in a Digital Society

Goal: As I ponder my future, I envision myself as an entrepreneur or skilled professional using technology to support my business endeavors or job responsibilities. Along the way, I may interact with a variety of computer professionals — or I may just become one myself!

Topic	Resource	Location	Now you should . . .
Data Validation	Text/Figure	pp. 522–524	Know the various checks programmers use to validate data
	Web Link	eBook p. 523 or CourseMate	
File Processing System	Text	p. 524	Be familiar with how organizations use file processing systems and potential disadvantages
Database Approach	Text and FAQ	p. 524-526	Be familiar with how organizations use a database approach and potential benefits over file processing systems
	Drag and Drop Figure 10-10	eBook p. 525 or CourseMate	
E-Forms	Web Link	eBook p. 530 or CourseMate	Know how to use e-forms for surveys and database connectivity
Data Warehouses	Text	p. 536	Know how organizations use data warehouses
Database Design Guidelines	Text	pp. 537–538	Be familiar with guidelines for database design
	Web Link	eBook p. 537 or CourseMate	
Database Analysts and Administrators	Text	p. 538	Know the role of database analysts and administrators, and be familiar with responsibilities and education required for database administrators
	Web Link	eBook p. 538 or CourseMate	
	Exploring Computer Careers	CourseMate	
Health Sciences	Computer Usage @ Work	p. 539	Know how professionals in the health sciences field use computers to support their activities
	Link and Video	eBook p. 539 or CourseMate	
Oracle	Text	p. 541	Be familiar with Oracle's enterprise products and services
	Link	eBook p. 541 or CourseMate	
Sybase	Text	p. 541	Be familiar with Sybase's enterprise products and services
	Link	eBook p. 541 or CourseMate	

Preparing for a Test

Visit the Computer Concepts CourseMate at www.cengagebrain.com and then navigate to the Chapter 10 Web Apps resource for this book to prepare for your test.

Does your class use the Computer Concepts CourseMate Web site? If so, prepare for your test by using the Flash Cards, Study Guide, and Practice Test Web apps — available for your smart phone or tablet.

If your class does not use the Computer Concepts CourseMate Web site or you prefer to use your book, you can prepare for the test by doing the Quiz Yourself activities on pages 524, 532, and 539; reading the Chapter Review on pages 542–543; ensuring you know the definitions for the terms on page 544; and completing the Checkpoint exercises on pages 545–546. You also should know the material identified in the Chapter 10 Study Guide that follows.

Chapter 10 Study Guide

This study guide identifies material you should know for the Chapter 10 exam. You may want to write the answers in a notebook, enter them on your digital device, record them into a phone, or highlight them in your book. Choose whichever method helps you remember the best.

1. Define database. Explain the purpose of a database management system (DBMS).
2. Explain the meaning of data integrity.
3. GIGO stands for _____. Describe the meaning of this term.
4. Describe seven qualities of valuable information.
5. Identify ways to verify the accuracy of your credit report.
6. Order these terms from smallest to largest: records, characters, files, fields. Define and give an example for each term.
7. Identify common data types.
8. Define file maintenance.
9. Identify reasons these activities are performed: adding records to a file, modifying records in a file, and deleting records from a file.
10. Describe ways DBMSs manage deleted records.
11. Explain the purpose of validation.
12. Describe and give an example of each of these types of validity checks: alphabetic, numeric, range, consistency, completeness, and check digit.
13. Explain how a file processing system works. Identify two weaknesses of a file processing system.
14. Explain how the database approach works. Identify five strengths of the database approach. Identify some disadvantages of the database approach.
15. Differentiate a front-end program from a back-end program.
16. Explain the significance of Megan's Law.
17. Explain why a database cannot completely eliminate redundant data.
18. Identify the database vendors with the largest market share.
19. Another term for data dictionary is _____.
20. Identify the types of details stored in a data dictionary.
21. Define the term, default value. Give an example.
22. Define the term, query.
23. Describe the purpose of these file retrieval and maintenance tools: query language, query by example (QBE), form, and report generator.
24. Identify the purpose of a wizard.
25. Describe how political campaigners can use databases.
26. Explain how e-forms can work with databases.
27. Define access privileges. Identify various levels of access privileges. Explain the intent of the principle of least privilege.
28. Describe how a DBMS uses backups.
29. Define the use and contents of a log.
30. Define how a DBMS uses recovery utilities. Differentiate between a rollforward and a rollback.
31. Describe advantages and disadvantages of continuous backup.
32. Define data model. Name examples.
33. A user of a relational database refers to a file as a(n) _____, a record as a(n) _____, and a field as a(n) _____.
34. A developer of a relational database refers to a file as a(n) _____, a record as a(n) _____, and a field as a(n) _____.
35. Describe the organization of relational databases. Define the terms, relationship and normalization.
36. SQL stands for _____.
37. Differentiate between SQL and OQL.

Continued on next page

Continued from previous page

38. Describe the organization of object-oriented databases. Give examples of applications that use object-oriented databases.
39. Describe the organization of multidimensional databases.
40. Explain the purpose of data warehouses and the reason they use data mining.
41. Give examples of databases on the Web.
42. Explain the purpose of a CGI script.
43. Identify guidelines for designing a database.
44. Differentiate between a database analyst and a database administrator.
45. Identify ways computers and databases are used in the health sciences field.
46. Briefly describe the normalization process.
47. Larry Ellison founded _____.

Check This Out

As technology changes, you must keep up with updates, new products, breakthroughs, and recent advances to remain digitally literate. The list below identifies topics related to this chapter that you should explore to keep current. In parentheses beside each topic, you will find a search term to help begin your research using a search engine, such as Google.

1. **widely used databases in education** (search for: popular databases education)
2. **recent government dragnets used to fight crime** (search for: latest government dragnets)
3. **popular data validation techniques** (search for: latest data validation checks)
4. **updates about database management systems** (search for: recent database management systems features)
5. **largest database management systems market share** (search for: top market share database management systems)
6. **recent data security breaches** (search for: security breaches news)
7. **popular database backup and recovery techniques** (search for: latest database backup recovery)
8. **new relational database software** (search for: relational database news)
9. **popular business object-oriented databases** (search for: objected-oriented database business)
10. **recent uses of multidimensional databases** (search for: multidimensional database examples)
11. **new GIS databases available from the U.S. Geological Survey** (search for: USGS Global GIS)
12. **widely used Web databases** (search for: popular Web databases)
13. **updates about database administrator jobs** (search for: database administrator duties)
14. **developments of identifying species using DNA barcoding** (search for: DNA barcoding news)
15. **updates about Oracle's social network applications** (search for: Oracle Public Cloud)

For current news and information
Check us out on Facebook and Twitter. See your instructor or the Computer Concepts CourseMate for specific information.

Student Success Guide

Computer Security and Safety, Ethics, and Privacy

Why Should I Learn About Computer Security and Safety, Ethics, and Privacy?

"I am careful when browsing the Internet and never open e-mail messages from unknown senders. No one would guess that I use my dog's name as my password on home and school networks. I use a surge protector and an ENERGY STAR monitor. What more do I need to know about security, ethics, and privacy while using a computer or mobile device?"

True, you may be familiar with some of the material in this chapter, but do you know . . .

"What more do I need to know about security, ethics, and privacy while using a computer or mobile device?"

- Which popular online services may protect your computer from Internet security breaches? (p. 558, Internet and Network Attacks)
- How to prevent tendonitis, eye strain, and other injuries? (p. 579, Computers and Health Risks)
- Which merchants analyze your conversations and shopping habits? (p. 585, Innovative Computing)
- How computers monitor and maintain national and local security? (p. 591, Computer Usage @ Work)
- Who is one of the world's leading computer security experts? (p. 593, Technology Trailblazers)
- How to back up files on an offsite Internet server? (p. 602 and Computer Concepts CourseMate, Learn How To)
- How to receive system updates automatically? (Windows Exercises, Computer Concepts CourseMate)
- How law enforcement officials investigate evidence found on computers and digital devices? (pp. 606–616, Digital Forensics Special Feature)

For these answers and to discover much more information essential to this course, read Chapter 11 and visit the associated Computer Concepts CourseMate at www.cengagebrain.com.

Q & A How can I meet one or more of these goals?
Make use of the goal's resources for each chapter in the book and you should meet that goal by the end of the course.

Customize Your Learning Experience

Adapt this book to meet your needs by determining your goal. Would you like to be an informed digital consumer? A productive technology user? A safe user, protected from the risks in a digital world? A competent digital citizen? A future entrepreneur or professional in a digital society?

Every chapter in this Student Success Guide identifies resources targeted toward each of these goals, along with criteria to verify you understand the resources' content. Resources may be located in the textbook, on the Computer Concepts CourseMate Web site, in the interactive eBook, and on the Web.

Informed Digital Consumer

Goal: I would like to understand the terminology used in Web or print advertisements that sell computers, mobile devices, and related technology, as well as the jargon used by sales associates in computer or electronics stores, so that I can make informed purchasing decisions.

Topic	Resource	Location	Now you should . . .
Antivirus Programs	Text/Figure	p. 560	Be familiar with names of popular antivirus programs
Firewall Software	Text/Figure	p. 564	Be familiar with names of personal firewall software
McAfee	Text	p. 593	Be familiar with McAfee's products and services
	Link	eBook p. 593 or CourseMate	
Symantec	Text	p. 593	Be familiar with Symantec's products and services
	Link	eBook p. 593 or CourseMate	

Productive Technology User

Goal: I would like to learn ways that technology can benefit me at home, work, and school. I also would like to learn helpful techniques for using technology so that I can perform tasks more efficiently and be more productive in daily activities.

Topic	Resource	Location	Now you should . . .
License Agreement	Text/Figure	pp. 571–572	Know what is allowed and not allowed with a software license
Wireless Network	FAQ Link	eBook p. 578 or CourseMate	Know how to set up a home wireless network
Computer Ethics	Text/Figure	p. 581	Be aware of ethical/unethical computer uses
	Labs	CourseMate	
Code of Conduct	Text/Figure	pp. 582–583	Be familiar with the IT code of conduct
Cookies	Text/Figure	pp. 585–587	Know the uses of cookies, how they work, how to view accepted cookies, and how to adjust cookie settings
	Web Link	eBook p. 586 or CourseMate	
	Labs	CourseMate	
Privacy Laws	Text/Figure	pp. 588–589	Be familiar with the intent of various privacy laws
Windows Media Player	Windows Exercises	CourseMate	Know how to use Windows Media Player to play a CD
Windows Updates	Windows Exercises	CourseMate	Know how to use Windows Update
Offsite Backup	Learn How To	p. 602 and CourseMate	Know how to back up files to an offsite Internet server
Windows Firewall	Learn How To	p. 603 and CourseMate	Know how to use Windows Firewall
Dictionary	Web Apps	CourseMate	Know how to use Dictionary.com

Safe User, Protected from the Risks in a Digital World

Goal: I would like to take measures to (1) protect my computers, devices, and data from loss, damage, or misuse; (2) minimize or prevent risks associated with using technology; and (3) minimize the environmental impact of using computers and related devices.

Topic	Resource	Location	Now you should . . .
Online Security	Text/Figure	p. 558	Be familiar with popular online security services
CERT/CC	Text	p. 558	Know the role of the Computer Emergency Response Team Coordination Center
	Web Link	eBook p. 558 or CourseMate	
Viruses and Other Malware	Text/Figures	pp. 560–561	Know ways to protect computers and devices from viruses and other malware
	Videos	eBook p. 561 or CourseMate, and At the Movies, CourseMate	
Botnets	FAQ Link and Video	eBook p. 562 or CourseMate	Know how to protect a computer from botnets
Firewalls	Text/Figures	pp. 563–564	Know how firewalls protect network resources
Unauthorized Access	Text/Figure	p. 565	Know how to protect your computer from unauthorized intrusions
Passwords	Text/Figure/FAQ	pp. 566–567	Know how to select a good password and protect it
PINs	Text	p. 568	Know the uses of PINs and why you should select them carefully
Biometrics and Privacy	Ethics & Issues	p. 568	Be aware of privacy issues surrounding use of biometric devices
	Video	eBook p. 568 or CourseMate	
Identity Theft	FAQ Link	eBook p. 569 or CourseMate	Know ways to protect yourself from identity theft

Continued on next page

Continued from previous page

Topic	Resource	Location	Now you should . . .
Hardware Theft	Text/Figure	p. 570	Be aware of ways to protect against hardware theft
Surge Protectors	Text/Figures/FAQ	pp. 576–677	Know the purpose of surge protectors and how they work
	Web Link	eBook p. 576 or CourseMate	
Wireless Security	Text and FAQ	pp. 578–579	Be familiar with ways to improve the security of wireless networks
Health Risks	Text/Figures	pp. 579–580	Know how to protect yourself from RSIs and CVS, how to design an ergonomic work area, and recognize computer addiction
Information Accuracy	Text/Figure	p. 582	Recognize that not all information is accurate
Green Computing	Text/Figure	pp. 583–584	Know strategies that support green computing
Information Privacy	Text/Figure	p. 584	Know ways to safeguard personal information
Consumer Privacy	Innovative Computing	p. 585	Be aware that your shopping behaviors may be recorded and tracked to create consumer profiles
	Link	eBook p. 585 or CourseMate	
Electronic Profiles	Text/Figure	p. 585	Be aware how direct marketers create electronic profiles
Spam	Text/Figure/FAQ	p. 587	Know how to reduce the amount of spam received
	FAQ Link	eBook p. 587 or CourseMate	
Phishing	Text/Figure/FAQ Ethics & Issues	pp. 587–588	Know how to protect yourself from phishing and pharming scams
	FAQ Link	eBook p. 588 or CourseMate	
Spyware and Adware	Text	p. 588	Know how to remove spyware and adware
Social Engineering	Text	p. 590	Be familiar with social engineering scams
Content Filtering	Text/Figure	pp. 590–591	Be familiar with issues of content filtering and Web filtering

Competent Digital Citizen

Goal: I would like to be knowledgeable and well-informed about computers, mobile devices, and related technology, so that I am digitally literate in my personal and professional use of digital devices.

Topic	Resource	Location	Now you should . . .
Security Risks	Text	p. 556	Know the definition of computer security risks
Cybercrime	Text	pp. 556–557	Be familiar with the categories of cybercriminals and punishments
	Ethics & Issues	p. 562	
Malware	Text/Figure/FAQ	pp. 558–559	Know the types of malware, how infections spread, and common symptoms of their infection
	FAQ Link	eBook p. 559 or CourseMate	
Botnets, DoS Attacks, Back Doors, Spoofing	Text and FAQ	pp. 562–563	Know the intent of botnets, DoS attacks, back doors, and spoofing
	Web Link	eBook p. 562 or CourseMate	
CAPTCHAs and RECAPTCHAs	Text/Figure Innovative Computing	p. 567	Know the purpose of CAPTCHAs and how RECAPTCHAs help digitize books and newspapers
	Link and Video	eBook p. 567 or CourseMate	
Brain Fingerprinting	Looking Ahead	p. 569	Know how brain fingerprints and behavior detection systems could be used in crime scene investigations
	Link and Video	eBook p. 569 or CourseMate	

Continued on next page

Continued from previous page

Topic	Resource	Location	Now you should . . .
Software Theft	Text	pp. 571 and 582	Be familiar with types of software theft
Encryption	Text/Figures	pp. 573–574	Know how encryption works
	Drag and Drop Figure 11-17	eBook p. 573 or CourseMate	
	Figure 11-18 Animation		
	Link and Video	eBook p. 592 or CourseMate	
Electrical Disturbances	Text	p. 575	Know the differences among noise, undervoltages, and overvoltages
War Driving	Text/Figure	p. 578	Be able to describe war driving
IP Rights	Text	p. 582	Be aware of intellectual property rights
Richard Stallman	Text	p. 593	Be familiar with Richard Stallman's copyleft concept
	Link and Video	eBook p. 593 or CourseMate	
Gene Spafford	Text	p. 593	Be familiar with Gene Spafford's role in computer security
	Link	eBook p. 593 or CourseMate	

Future Entrepreneur or Professional in a Digital Society

Goal: As I ponder my future, I envision myself as an entrepreneur or skilled professional using technology to support my business endeavors or job responsibilities. Along the way, I may interact with a variety of computer professionals — or I may just become one myself!

Topic	Resource	Location	Now you should . . .
Firewalls	Text	pp. 563–564	Be familiar with how enterprises use hardware firewalls
	Video	eBook p. 564 or CourseMate	
Intrusion Detection	Text	p. 564	Know why organizations use intrusion detection software
Honeypots	Text	p. 564	Know why an organization might use a honeypot
Authenticating Users	Text/Figures	pp. 565–568	Know how organizations identify and authenticate users through user names, passwords, possessed objects, and biometrics
	Web Link	eBook p. 568 or CourseMate	
Digital Forensics	Text	p. 569 and pp. 606–616	Know the purpose, uses, and steps in digital forensics
RTLS	Text	p. 570	Know the purpose and uses of real time location systems
	Web Link	eBook p. 570 or CourseMate	
BSA	Text	p. 572	Know the purpose of the Business Software Alliance
	Web Link	eBook p. 572 or CourseMate	
Digital Signatures and Certificates	Text/Figures	pp. 574–575	Know why organizations use digital signatures, digital certificates, and security protocols
UPS	Text/Figure	pp. 576–577	Know how organizations use UPS devices
Backing Up	Text	p. 577	Know the types of backups used by organizations
Employee Monitoring	Text Ethics & Issues	p. 590	Know issues surrounding employers monitoring employee communications

Continued on next page

Continued from previous page

Topic	Resource	Location	Now you should . . .
National and Local Security	Computer Usage @ Work	p. 591	Know how governments and businesses have implemented new security measures
	Link and Video	eBook p. 591 or CourseMate	
Digital Forensics Examiner	Exploring Computer Careers	CourseMate	Be familiar with responsibilities and education required for digital forensics examiners

Preparing for a Test

Visit the Computer Concepts CourseMate at www.cengagebrain.com and then navigate to the Chapter 11 Web Apps resource for this book to prepare for your test.

Does your class use the Computer Concepts CourseMate Web site? If so, prepare for your test by using the Flash Cards, Study Guide, and Practice Test Web apps — available for your smart phone or tablet.

If your class does not use the Computer Concepts CourseMate Web site or you prefer to use your book, you can prepare for the test by doing the Quiz Yourself activities on pages 569, 579, and 591; reading the Chapter Review on pages 594–595; ensuring you know the definitions for the terms on page 596; and completing the Checkpoint exercises on pages 597–598. You also should know the material identified in the Chapter 11 Study Guide that follows.

Chapter 11 Study Guide

This study guide identifies material you should know for the Chapter 11 exam. You may want to write the answers in a notebook, enter them on your digital device, record them into a phone, or highlight them in your book. Choose whichever method helps you remember the best.

1. Define the term, computer security risk.
2. Define the terms, computer crime and cybercrime.
3. Differentiate among a hacker, cracker, script kiddie, corporate spy, unethical employee, cyberextortionist, and cyberterrorist.
4. Describe the purpose of an online security service.
5. Differentiate among a computer virus, worm, Trojan horse, and rootkit.
6. Malware is short for _____.
7. Define payload. Identify various ways a payload is delivered.
8. Identify ways to safeguard against computer viruses and other malware.
9. Describe the purpose of an antivirus program. Explain techniques used by antivirus programs.
10. Define a botnet and a zombie. Describe ways to tell if a computer is a zombie or in a botnet.
11. DoS stands for _____. Explain how a DoS attack works. Identify reasons perpetrators claim to carry out a DoS attack.
12. Explain how a back door works.
13. Describe spoofing.
14. Define the term, firewall. Identify uses of firewalls.
15. Describe the purpose of intrusion detection software and honeypots.
16. AUP stands for _____.
17. Describe an access control.
18. Define the terms, user name and password. Identify ways to protect a password. Explain the purpose of a passphrase.
19. Explain the purpose and use of CAPTCHAs. Explain the benefits of RECAPTCHAs.
20. Give examples of possessed objects that might use a PIN.
21. Identify advantages and disadvantages of biometric devices.
22. Define digital forensics. Describe requirements of a digital forensics examiner.
23. Identify safeguards against hardware theft and vandalism.
24. Define software piracy. Explain the ways software manufacturers protect against software piracy.
25. Define a license agreement. Identify actions that are allowed and not allowed according to a license agreement.
26. Discuss the encryption process. Differentiate between private key and public key encryption.
27. Describe the purpose of digital signatures, digital certificates, transport layer security, secure HTTP, and VPN.
28. Identify causes of system failure.
29. Explain these electrical disturbances: noise, undervoltage, and overvoltage. Discuss surge protectors and UPSs.
30. Explain the options available for backing up computer resources.

Continued on next page

Continued from previous page

31. Describe the purpose of war driving. Identify ways to secure a wireless network.
32. RSI stands for _____. Identify two types of RSIs and precautions to prevent these injuries.
33. Describe symptoms of computer vision syndrome. Identify techniques to ease eyestrain.
34. Define ergonomics. Give examples of an ergonomically designed work area.
35. Identify symptoms of computer addiction.
36. Explain why users cannot assume information always is correct.
37. Describe intellectual property rights. Explain issues related to copyright law.
38. Define the purpose of an IT code of conduct.
39. Describe green computing strategies.
40. Identify ways to safeguard personal information.
41. Explain how electronic profiles are created.
42. Define cookie. Identify uses of cookies.
43. Describe spam, spyware, and adware. Explain ways to reduce spam, and remove spyware and adware.
44. Define phishing. Identify ways to protect yourself from phishing scams.
45. Identify common points in laws surrounding privacy.
46. Define social engineering.
47. Discuss issues of employee monitoring and content filtering.
48. Name two companies that sell products that protect computers and devices from malware, spam, and unauthorized access.
49. In digital forensics, identify the types of data and information that are examined and the software tasks that are performed.

Check This Out

As technology changes, you must keep up with updates, new products, breakthroughs, and recent advances to remain digitally literate. The list below identifies topics related to this chapter that you should explore to keep current. In parentheses beside each topic, you will find a search term to help begin your research using a search engine, such as Google.

1. **recent attempts to stop cybercrime activities** (search for: fighting cybercrime)
2. **latest CERT/CC security breach notices** (search for: CERT announcements)
3. **popular malware block and removal tools** (search for: top malware removal software)
4. **news of denial of service attacks** (search for: recent DoS DDoS attacks)
5. **popular antivirus programs** (search for: top antivirus programs)
6. **new biometric identification devices** (search for: biometric device systems)
7. **recent real time location system applications** (search for: latest RTLS)
8. **new products to curb hardware theft and vandalism** (search for: computer hardware theft deterrent)
9. **current Business Software Alliance efforts to fight software piracy** (search for: BSA piracy news)
10. **current encryption software** (search for: new encryption technology)
11. **new surge protectors and uninterruptible power supplies** (search for: popular surge protectors UPS)
12. **latest home wireless security network trends** (search for: home wireless network security software)
13. **current green computing initiatives** (search for: green computing concepts)
14. **recent phishing and smishing scams** (search for: phishing smishing attacks)
15. **updates about digital forensics procedures** (search for: digital forensics news)

For current news and information
Check us out on Facebook and Twitter. See your instructor or the Computer Concepts CourseMate for specific information.

Chapter 12

Student Success Guide

Information System Development

Why Should I Learn About Information System Development?

"My school is starting to implement a new computer system, and the conversion process is taking a long time. Although the system sometimes does not work correctly for a few hours, some of the new features make registering for classes and checking my grades easy to do. Why should I learn about how this new computer system is being developed?"

True, you may be familiar with some of the material in this chapter, but do you know . . .

"Why should I learn about how this new computer system is being developed?"

- Who is involved in developing a new information system? (p. 622, Who Participates in System Development?)
- Why people may lie when writing e-mail messages? (p. 627, Ethics & Issues)
- Which types of organizations are likely to use outside service providers? (p. 636, FAQ)
- How you can view billions of remote galaxy images on your computer? (p. 640, Looking Ahead)
- How computers are used to design and manufacture products in the textile industry? (p. 647, Computer Usage @ Work)
- Which nonprofit organization supports Wikipedia? (p. 649, Companies on the Cutting Edge)
- How to gather information in a personal interview? (p. 658 and Computer Concepts CourseMate, Learn How To)
- How to capture and print screen images? (Windows Exercises, Computer Concepts CourseMate)

For these answers and to discover much more information essential to this course, read Chapter 12 and visit the associated Computer Concepts CourseMate at www.cengagebrain.com.

Q & A

How can I meet one or more of these goals?

Make use of the goal's resources for each chapter in the book and you should meet that goal by the end of the course.

Customize Your Learning Experience

Adapt this book to meet your needs by determining your goal. Would you like to be an informed digital consumer? A productive technology user? A safe user, protected from the risks in a digital world? A competent digital citizen? A future entrepreneur or professional in a digital society?

Every chapter in this Student Success Guide identifies resources targeted toward each of these goals, along with criteria to verify you understand the resources' content. Resources may be located in the textbook, on the Computer Concepts CourseMate Web site, in the interactive eBook, and on the Web.

Informed Digital Consumer

Goal: I would like to understand the terminology used in Web or print advertisements that sell computers, mobile devices, and related technology, as well as the jargon used by sales associates in computer or electronics stores, so that I can make informed purchasing decisions.

Topic	Resource	Location	Now you should . . .
Project Management Software	Text	p. 623	Know the purpose of project management software

Productive Technology User

Goal: I would like to learn ways that technology can benefit me at home, work, and school. I also would like to learn helpful techniques for using technology so that I can perform tasks more efficiently and be more productive in daily activities.

Topic	Resource	Location	Now you should . . .
Interviews	FAQ Link	eBook p. 626 or CourseMate	Know how to conduct various types of interviews and questions to expect as an interviewee
	Learn How To	pp. 658–659	

Continued on next page

Continued from previous page

Topic	Resource	Location	Now you should . . .
Project Request	Text	pp. 626–627	Know how to initiate a system development project
E-Zine	Text	p. 638	Be familiar with an e-zine and name popular ones
	Web Link	eBook p. 638 or CourseMate	
Prototype	Text	pp. 641–642	Know the purpose of a prototype
Wikimedia	Text	p. 649	Be familiar with Wikimedia Foundation's role with Wikipedia
	Link and Video	eBook p. 649 or CourseMate	
Windows Error Reporting	Windows Exercises	CourseMate	Know how to use Windows Error Reporting
Paint	Windows Exercises	CourseMate	Know how to use Paint to create a drawing
Capture Screen Images	Windows Exercises	CourseMate	Know how to capture screen images
Picnik	Web Apps	CourseMate	Know how to use Picnik to upload, crop, and e-mail photos

Safe User, Protected from the Risks in a Digital World

Goal: I would like to take measures to (1) protect my computers, devices, and data from loss, damage, or misuse; (2) minimize or prevent risks associated with using technology; and (3) minimize the environmental impact of using computers and related devices.

Topic	Resource	Location	Now you should . . .
Outsourcing	Ethics & Issues	p. 637	Be familiar with security issues related to outsourcing
Financial Web Site Vulnerabilities	FAQ	p. 646	Be aware of vulnerabilities associated with financial Web sites
Computer Security Plan	Text	p. 646	Be familiar with the elements of a computer security plan

Competent Digital Citizen

Goal: I would like to be knowledgeable and well-informed about computers, mobile devices, and related technology, so that I am digitally literate in my personal and professional use of digital devices.

Topic	Resource	Location	Now you should . . .
SDLC	Text/Figure	pp. 620–621	Be able to identify the phases in an SDLC
Documentation	Text	p. 625	Know the types of documentation generated in system development
Data and Information Gathering	Text/Figure and FAQ	pp. 625–626	Know the purpose of reviewing documentation, observing, surveying, interviewing, conducting JAD sessions, and researching; be able to explain the Hawthorne Effect
	Ethics & Issues		
	Video	eBook p. 625 or CourseMate	
Process Modeling	Text/Figures	pp. 631–634	Know the purpose and elements of tools used in process modeling: entity-relationship diagrams, data flow diagrams, and the project dictionary
	Web Link	eBook p. 631 or CourseMate	
	Drag and Drop Figures 12-7, 12-8, 12-10	eBook pp. 632–633 or CourseMate	
	Video	eBook p. 633 or CourseMate	

Continued on next page

Continued from previous page

Topic	Resource	Location	Now you should . . .
Object Modeling	Text/Figures	pp. 634–635	Be able to define an object, its properties, and methods; know the purpose of the UML; and be familiar with use case and class diagrams
	Web Link	eBook p. 634 or CourseMate	
Packaged vs. Custom Software	Text	pp. 635–636	Know the difference between packaged and custom software, and the difference between horizontal and vertical market software
	Web Link	eBook p. 636 or CourseMate	
LSST	Looking Ahead	p. 640	Know how the Large Synoptic Survey Telescope will provide a graphical view of the universe's evolution
	Link and Video	eBook p. 640 or CourseMate	
CASE Tools	Text/Figure	p. 642	Know the purpose and use of CASE tools
Phoenix Lander	Innovative Computing	p. 643	Be familiar with the role software played in the *Phoenix Mars Lander* Mission
	Link and Video	eBook p. 643 or CourseMate	
Conversion Strategies	Text/Figure	pp. 644–645	Know the differences between direct, parallel, phased, and pilot conversions
	Figure 12-22 Animation	eBook p. 645 or CourseMate	
Web App Vulnerabilities	FAQ Link	eBook p. 646, or Web Site Vulnerabilities link, CourseMate	Know how to test a Web application's vulnerabilities
Computers in the Textile Industry	Computer Usage @ Work	p. 647	Know how computers assist with the design and manufacturing of fabrics and clothing
	Link and Video	eBook p. 647 or CourseMate	
Benchmarking	Text/Figure	p. 648	Know how benchmarks are used to measure the performance of hardware or software
	Link and Video	eBook p. 648 or CourseMate	
	Drag and Drop Figure 12-23		
Ed Yourdon	Text	p. 649	Be familiar with Ed Yourdon's contributions to computer technology
	Link	eBook p. 649 or CourseMate	
Tom DeMarco	Text	p. 649	Be familiar with Tom Demarco's role with software development
	Link	eBook p. 649 or CourseMate	

Future Entrepreneur or Professional in a Digital Society

Goal: As I ponder my future, I envision myself as an entrepreneur or skilled professional using technology to support my business endeavors or job responsibilities. Along the way, I may interact with a variety of computer professionals — or I may just become one myself!

Topic	Resource	Location	Now you should . . .
System Development	Text/Figure	p. 620	Be able to describe an information system and system development
System Development Guidelines	Text	pp. 621–622	Know how system development groups activities into phases, involves users, and defines standards
System Development Participants	Text/Figure	pp. 622–623	Know the role of analysts, users, the steering committee, and others during system development
	Drag and Drop Figure 12-2	eBook p. 622 or CourseMate	

Continued on next page

Continued from previous page

Topic	Resource	Location	Now you should . . .
Project Management	Text/Figures and FAQ	pp. 623–624	Know how organizations use project management and the difference between Gantt and PERT charts
	Link and Video	eBook p. 623 or CourseMate	
	Web Links	eBook p. 624–625 or CourseMate	
	FAQ Link	eBook p. 624, or Project Failures link, CourseMate	
	Labs	CourseMate	
Feasibility	Text and FAQ	pp. 624–625 and p. 643	Know the tests organizations use to assess project feasibility
Planning Phase	Text	pp. 628–629	Know the major activities performed in the planning phase
Analysis Phase	Text	p. 629	Know the major activities performed in the analysis phase
Preliminary Investigation	Text/Figure	pp. 629–631	Know the purpose of the preliminary investigation and contents of the feasibility report
	Web Link	eBook p. 629 or CourseMate	
Detailed Analysis	Text	p. 631	Know the major activities performed during detailed analysis
Systems Analyst	FAQ	p. 631	Know the role of, responsibilities of, and education required for a systems analyst
	FAQ Link	eBook p. 631, or Systems Analyst link, CourseMate	
	Exploring Computer Careers	CourseMate	
System Proposal	Text	p. 635	Know the purpose of the system proposal
Outsourcing	Text/Figure	pp. 636–637	Know reasons organizations outsource software development
	FAQ Video	eBook p. 636 or CourseMate	
Design Phase	Text/Figures	pp. 638–640	Know the major activities performed in the design phase
RFQ, RFP, RFI	Text	p. 638	Know the difference of an RFQ, an RFP, and an RFI
VAR	Text and FAQ	pp. 638–639	Know the purpose of a value-added reseller
IT Consultants	Text and FAQ	p. 639	Know the role of IT consultants
	FAQ Link	eBook p. 639 or CourseMate	
Detailed Design	Text	pp. 640–641	Know the major activities performed during detailed design
Quality Review	Text	p. 642	Be familiar with quality review techniques
Implementation Phase	Text/Figures	pp. 643–645	Know the major activities performed during the implementation phase
Operation, Support, and Security Phase	Text	pp. 645–646	Know the major activities performed during the operation, support, and security phase
Chief Security Officer	Text	p. 646	Know the role and responsibilities of a chief security officer
	Web Link	eBook p. 646 or CourseMate	
Web Design	Labs	CourseMate	Be familiar with Web design principles
CSC	Text	p. 649	Be familiar with services provided by Computer Sciences Corporation
	Link	eBook p. 649 or CourseMate	

Preparing for a Test

Visit the Computer Concepts CourseMate at www.cengagebrain.com and then navigate to the Chapter 12 Web Apps resource for this book to prepare for your test.

Does your class use the Computer Concepts CourseMate Web site? If so, prepare for your test by using the Flash Cards, Study Guide, and Practice Test Web apps — available for your smart phone or tablet.

If your class does not use the Computer Concepts CourseMate Web site or you prefer to use your book, you can prepare for the test by doing the Quiz Yourself activities on pages 629, 637, and 647; reading the Chapter Review on pages 650–651; ensuring you know the definitions for the terms on page 652; and completing the Checkpoint exercises on pages 653–654. You also should know the material identified in the Chapter 12 Study Guide that follows.

Chapter 12 Study Guide

This study guide identifies material you should know for the Chapter 12 exam. You may want to write the answers in a notebook, enter them on your digital device, record them into a phone, or highlight them in your book. Choose whichever method helps you remember the best.

1. Describe an information system. Define system development.
2. SDLC stands for _____. Name the five phases that often are part of an SDLC.
3. Describe the three guidelines that system development should follow.
4. Describe the role of a systems analyst.
5. Define the purpose of a steering committee. Identify the composition of a project team.
6. Explain project management. Differentiate between a Gantt chart and a PERT chart. Explain how scope creep occurs.
7. Describe the purpose of change management.
8. Give examples of deliverables.
9. Define feasibility. Differentiate among operational feasibility, schedule feasibility, technical feasibility, and economic feasibility.
10. Describe data and information gathering techniques: review documentation, observe, survey, interview, conduct JAD sessions, and research.
11. Explain the Hawthorne Effect.
12. Differentiate between open-ended and closed-ended questions.
13. Explain the purpose of a project request. Name a synonym for project request.
14. Name and briefly describe the four major activities performed in the planning phase.
15. Name and briefly describe the two major activities performed in the analysis phase.
16. State the purpose of a feasibility study.
17. Name and briefly describe the three major activities performed in the detailed analysis phase.
18. Detailed analysis sometimes is called _____ design.
19. Describe user buy-in.
20. Process modeling sometimes is called _____.
21. Define process modeling. Describe the tools used during process modeling: entity-relationship diagrams, data flow diagrams, and the project dictionary.
22. Object modeling sometimes is called _____.
23. Define object modeling and objects. Give an example of an object. Define UML. Describe use case diagrams and class diagrams.
24. Identify the purpose of the system proposal.
25. Differentiate between packaged software and custom software. Describe outsourcing.
26. Differentiate between horizontal and vertical market software.
27. Name and briefly describe the two major activities performed in the design phase.
28. Name and briefly describe the four major tasks performed when acquiring hardware and software.
29. RFQ stands for _____. RFP stands for _____. RFI stands for _____. Differentiate among these three documents.
30. Describe the function of a VAR (value-added reseller).
31. Describe an IT consultant.
32. Detailed design sometimes is called _____.
33. Name and briefly describe the activities performed during detailed design.
34. Define the term, mockup.
35. Describe the purpose of a prototype.
36. Explain the purpose of CASE tools.
37. Describe the purpose of an inspection.
38. Name and briefly describe the four major activities performed in the implementation phase.

Continued on next page

Continued from previous page

39. Differentiate among a unit test, systems test, integration test, and acceptance test.
40. Describe various training methods.
41. Differentiate among direct conversion, parallel conversion, phased conversion, and pilot conversion.
42. Name and briefly describe the three major activities performed in the operation, support, and security phase.
43. Differentiate among corrective maintenance, adaptive maintenance, and perfective maintenance.
44. Identify the role of a CSO (chief security officer).
45. Identify the purpose of a computer security plan.
46. Define benchmark. Explain how benchmarks are used in the computer field.
47. Describe the purpose of the Wikimedia Foundation.
48. Identify Ed Yourdon's contributions to computer technology.

Check This Out

As technology changes, you must keep up with updates, new products, breakthroughs, and recent advances to remain digitally literate. The list below identifies topics related to this chapter that you should explore to keep current. In parentheses beside each topic, you will find a search term to help begin your research using a search engine, such as Google.

1. **latest information system developments** (search for: information system news)
2. **popular project management software** (search for: top project management software)
3. **recent Hawthorne Effect research** (search for: latest Hawthorne Effect studies)
4. **updates on developing effective JAD session questions** (search for: JAD questions)
5. **news on SDLC trends** (search for: SDLC planning)
6. **recent data flow diagram examples** (search for: data flow diagram news)
7. **popular unified modeling language tools** (search for: latest unified modeling language uses)
8. **latest outsourcing statistics** (search for: outsourcing trends)
9. **popular e-zine articles and publications** (search for: top e-zines)
10. **popular value-added resellers** (search for: top value-added software hardware resellers)
11. **current required IT consultant skills** (search for: IT consulting jobs)
12. **widely used conversion strategies** (search for: conversion strategies)
13. **updates on post-implementation system reviews** (search for: post-implementation system review news)
14. **new CAD and CAM systems for the textile industry** (search for: textile CAD CAM)
15. **latest news and views posted on the Wikimedia Foundation blog** (search for: Wikimedia blog)

For current news and information
Check us out on Facebook and Twitter. See your instructor or the Computer Concepts CourseMate for specific information.

Chapter 13

Student Success Guide

Programming Languages and Program Development

Why Should I Learn About Programming Languages and Program Development?

"When my boss needs to update his payroll program, he hires a programmer to make changes. I would like to help, but the only software customizations I have made are adding some gadgets and widgets to my social networking home page. Other than assisting my boss, what else do I need to learn about programs and programming languages?"

True, you may be familiar with some of the material in this chapter, but do you know . . .

"What else do I need to learn about programs and programming languages?"

- Why some students learn to write computer viruses in their classes? (p. 681, Ethics & Issues)
- How Web page authoring software is used to create Web pages? (p. 685, Web Page Authoring Software)
- Why the term, bug, is used to refer to a computer error? (p. 696, Step 5 – Test Solution)
- How automakers use computers to streamline manufacturing? (p. 697, Computer Usage @ Work)
- Which software company develops the FIFA, Madden NFL, and Need for Speed video games? (p. 699, Companies on the Cutting Edge)
- How to evaluate a graphical user interface? (p. 708 and Computer Concepts CourseMate, Learn How To)
- How to adjust the speed of your keyboard? (Windows Exercises, Computer Concepts CourseMate)
- How developers create Web 2.0 applications for social networks and the cloud? (p. 712, Web 2.0 Program Development Special Feature)

For these answers and to discover much more information essential to this course, read Chapter 13 and visit the associated Computer Concepts CourseMate at www.cengagebrain.com.

Q&A How can I meet one or more of these goals?
Make use of the goal's resources for each chapter in the book and you should meet that goal by the end of the course.

Customize Your Learning Experience

Adapt this book to meet your needs by determining your goal. Would you like to be an informed digital consumer? A productive technology user? A safe user, protected from the risks in a digital world? A competent digital citizen? A future entrepreneur or professional in a digital society?

Every chapter in this Student Success Guide identifies resources targeted toward each of these goals, along with criteria to verify you understand the resources' content. Resources may be located in the textbook, on the Computer Concepts CourseMate Web site, in the interactive eBook, and on the Web.

Informed Digital Consumer

Goal: I would like to understand the terminology used in Web or print advertisements that sell computers, mobile devices, and related technology, as well as the jargon used by sales associates in computer or electronics stores, so that I can make informed purchasing decisions.

Topic	Resource	Location	Now you should . . .
Flowcharting Software	Text/Figure	p. 691–692	Be familiar with uses of flowcharting software
	Web Link	eBook p. 692 or CourseMate	
EA	Text	p. 699	Be familiar with entertainment products by Electronic Arts
	Link	eBook p. 699 or CourseMate	
	Video	At the Movies, CourseMate	

Productive Technology User

Goal: I would like to learn ways that technology can benefit me at home, work, and school. I also would like to learn helpful techniques for using technology so that I can perform tasks more efficiently and be more productive in daily activities.

Topic	Resource	Location	Now you should . . .
Online Calculators	Innovative Computing	p. 668	Know popular calculators on the Web
	Link	eBook p. 668 or CourseMate	
4GLs	Text/Figure and FAQ	pp. 674–675	Know the uses of 4GLs and SQL
	FAQ Link	eBook p. 675, or SQL link, CourseMate	
Application Generators	Text/Figure	p. 676	Be familiar with the use of application generators
Macros	Text/Figure	pp. 676–677	Know the purpose of macros and how to create them
	Web Link	eBook p. 677 or CourseMate	
Earth Album	Innovative Computing	p. 684	Know the purpose of the Earth Album mashup
Mashups	Videos	eBook p. 684 or CourseMate	Be able to state examples and uses of mashups
		eBook p. 715 or CourseMate	
Beta Testers	Web Link	eBook p. 696 or CourseMate	Know the role of beta testers
Creating Web Pages	Labs	CourseMate	Know how to create Web pages (formatting, graphics, backgrounds, links)
Program Files	Windows Exercises	CourseMate	Know how to search for executable files
Keyboard Speed	Windows Exercises	CourseMate	Know how to adjust keyboard speed
Loans	Windows Exercises	CourseMate	Know how to use the Loan Payment Calculator program
Google Earth	Web Apps	CourseMate	Know how to use Google Earth to view locations and satellite images

Safe User, Protected from the Risks in a Digital World

Goal: I would like to take measures to (1) protect my computers, devices, and data from loss, damage, or misuse; (2) minimize or prevent risks associated with using technology; and (3) minimize the environmental impact of using computers and related devices.

Topic	Resource	Location	Now you should . . .
Macro Security	Ethics & Issues	p. 677	Be aware of security threats surrounding macros
ActiveX Controls and Plug-Ins	FAQ	p. 680	Know when to install or disable a control or plug-in
	Video	eBook p. 680 or CourseMate	
Ethical Hacking	Ethics & Issues	p. 681	Be aware that some colleges teach hacking and know the meaning of ethical hacking
	Video	eBook p. 681 or CourseMate	
Digital Facelifts	Ethics & Issues	p. 688	Know the issues surrounding digital facelifts

Competent Digital Citizen

Goal: I would like to be knowledgeable and well-informed about computers, mobile devices, and related technology, so that I am digitally literate in my personal and professional use of digital devices.

Topic	Resource	Location	Now you should . . .
Programming Lang.	Text/Figure	p. 664	Be able to describe programming languages
Low- vs. High-Level	Text	pp. 664–665	Know the difference between low-level and high-level languages
Machine Language	Text/Figure	p. 665	Know the purpose of machine language
Assembly Language	Text/Figure	pp. 665–666	Know the purpose of an assembly language
Source Program	Text	p. 666	Be able to define source program
Procedural Languages	Text	p. 666	Describe procedural languages
Compilers vs. Interpreters	Text/Figures	pp. 666–667	Be able to differentiate between compilers and interpreters
	Drag and Drop Figures 13-4 and 13-5	eBook p. 667 or CourseMate	
C and COBOL	Text/Figures	pp. 668–669	Know the uses of C and COBOL
	Web Link	eBook p. 668 or CourseMate	
OOP Languages/Tools	Text/Figures	pp. 669–674	Describe object-oriented programming languages, RAD, and IDE
Java, .NET, C++, C#, and F#	Text/Figure	pp. 670–671	Know the characteristics and uses of Java, .NET, C++, C#, and F#
	Web Link	eBook p. 670 or CourseMate	
Visual Studio	Text/Figure	pp. 671–673	Know the purpose of and languages in the Visual Studio suite, visual programming, and user interface design
	Web Link	eBook p. 671 or CourseMate	
	Labs	CourseMate	
	Learn How To	pp. 708–709	
Delphi and PowerBuilder	Text/Figures	pp. 673–675	Know the uses of Delphi and PowerBuilder
Classic Programming Languages	Text/Figure	p. 675	Know the purpose of several classic programming languages
HTML, XHTML, XML, and WML	Text/Figures	pp. 678–679	Know the characteristics and uses of HTML, XHTML, XML, and WML
	Link and Video	eBook p. 679 or CourseMate	
Scripts, Applets, Servlets, and ActiveX	Text	p. 680	Know the differences among scripts, applets, servlets, and ActiveX controls
	FAQ Link	eBook p. 680, or Web Browser Prompts link, CourseMate	
CGI Scripts	Text/Figure	pp. 680–681	Know the purpose of CGI scripts
	Drag and Drop Figure 13-19	eBook p. 681 or CourseMate	
Scripting Languages	Text/Figure	pp. 682–683	Know the purpose of JavaScript, Perl, PHP, Rexx, Tcl, and VBScript
	Web Link	eBook p. 682 or CourseMate	
Sandbox	FAQ	p. 683	Know why developers use sandboxes
	FAQ Link	eBook p. 683, or Sandboxes link, CourseMate	

Continued on next page

Continued from previous page

Topic	Resource	Location	Now you should . . .
Dynamic HTML	Text	p. 683	Know the characteristics and uses of DHTML
	Web Link	eBook p. 683 or CourseMate	
Ruby on Rails	Text	p. 683	Be familiar with the purpose of Ruby on Rails
Web 2.0 Development	Text	p. 684	Be familiar with tools and languages used to develop Web 2.0 sites and the purpose of APIs
	Web Link	eBook p. 684 or CourseMate	
Web Page Authoring	Text	p. 685	Know about Dreamweaver, Expression Web, Flash, and SharePoint Designer
Multimedia Develop.	Text/Figure	p. 685	Be familiar with the purpose of ToolBook and Director
Program Development	Text/Figures	pp. 686–697	Know and be able to describe the steps in the program development life cycle and how it relates to the SDLC
	Drag and Drop Figure 13-23	eBook p. 686 or CourseMate	
Structured Design	Text/Figure	p. 688	Know the purpose of and charts used in structured design
Object-Oriented Design	Text/Figure	p. 689	Know the purpose of and charts used in object-oriented design
	Web Link	eBook p. 689 or CourseMate	
Control Structures	Text/Figures	pp. 689–690	Know the differences among sequence, selection, and repetition control structures
	Figure 13-31 Animation	eBook p. 690 or CourseMate	
Design Tools	Text/Figures	pp. 691–693	Know the purpose of program flowcharts, pseudocode, and the UML diagrams
	Figure Video	eBook p. 691 or CourseMate	
	Drag and Drop Figures 13-32 and 13-36	eBook p. 691 and 693 or CourseMate	
Test Data	Text and FAQ	pp. 693–694	Be familiar with types of test data and desk checking steps
	FAQ Link	eBook p. 694, or Test Data link, CourseMate	
Program Errors	Text	pp. 695–696	Know the difference between syntax and logic errors
Documentation	FAQ	p. 697	Know the types of documentation to include with programs
	FAQ Link	eBook p. 697 or CourseMate	
Acid3 Browser Test	Text/Figure	p. 698	Be familiar with the purpose of the Acid3 Browser Test
	Link and Video	eBook p. 698 or CourseMate	
Sun	Text	p. 699	Be familiar with Sun's products and services
	Link	eBook p. 699 or CourseMate	
Alan Kay	Text	p. 693	Be familiar with Alan Kay's computing research
	Link and Video	eBook p. 699 or CourseMate	
James Gosling	Text	p. 699	Be familiar with James Gosling's contributions to the computer field
	Link and Video	eBook p. 699 or CourseMate	
Web 2.0 Development	Text/Figures	pp. 712–717	Be familiar with tools used in Web 2.0 program development

Future Entrepreneur or Professional in a Digital Society

Goal: As I ponder my future, I envision myself as an entrepreneur or skilled professional using technology to support my business endeavors or job responsibilities. Along the way, I may interact with a variety of computer professionals — or I may just become one myself!

Topic	Resource	Location	Now you should . . .
Programmer	Text	p. 664	Know the role and responsibilities of and the education required for a computer programmer
	Exploring Computer Careers	CourseMate	
Programming Language Trends	Looking Ahead	p. 675	Be familiar with trends related to programming languages
	Link and Video	eBook p. 675 or CourseMate	
Popular Web Programming Languages	FAQ	p. 683	Be familiar with popular Web programming languages
	FAQ Link	eBook p. 683 or Web Programming Languages link, CourseMate	
Programming Team	Text	p. 687	Know the purpose of a programming team
Computers in Manufacturing	Computer Usage @ Work	p. 697	Know how computers are used in the manufacture of cars
	Link and Video	eBook p. 697 or CourseMate	

Preparing for a Test

Visit the Computer Concepts CourseMate at www.cengagebrain.com and then navigate to the Chapter 13 Web Apps resource for this book to prepare for your test.

Does your class use the Computer Concepts CourseMate Web site? If so, prepare for your test by using the Flash Cards, Study Guide, and Practice Test Web apps — available for your smart phone or tablet.

If your class does not use the Computer Concepts CourseMate Web site or you prefer to use your book, you can prepare for the test by doing the Quiz Yourself activities on pages 674, 686, and 697; reading the Chapter Review on pages 700–701; ensuring you know the definitions for the terms on page 702; and completing the Checkpoint exercises on pages 703–704. You also should know the material identified in the Chapter 13 Study Guide that follows.

Chapter 13 Study Guide

This study guide identifies material you should know for the Chapter 13 exam. You may want to write the answers in a notebook, enter them on your digital device, record them into a phone, or highlight them in your book. Choose whichever method helps you remember the best.

1. Define computer program and programming language.
2. Another term for programmer is _____.
3. Differentiate between low-level and high-level languages.
4. Define machine language.
5. Describe how a programmer writes assembly language instructions and the purpose of an assembler.
6. Define source program.
7. Describe how a programmer writes procedural language instructions.
8. Differentiate between a compiler and an interpreter.
9. Define the term, algorithm.
10. Identify uses of C and COBOL.
11. Define an object. Describe advantages of object-oriented programming languages.
12. RAD stands for _____. Describe RAD.
13. IDE stands for _____. Identify tools in an IDE.
14. Name the company that developed Java.
15. Describe the purpose of the .NET Framework.
16. Briefly discuss characteristics of C++, C#, and F#.
17. Describe Visual Studio. Differentiate among Visual Basic, Visual C++, and Visual C#.
18. Define visual programming language.

Continued on next page

Continued from previous page

19. Briefly describe the use of Delphi and PowerBuilder.
20. 4GL stands for _____.
21. Describe how a programmer writes nonprocedural language instructions.
22. Describe the purpose of SQL.
23. Describe the purpose of application generators.
24. Define macro. Describe two techniques for creating macros.
25. Describe the purpose of HTML and XHTML. Define a tag.
26. Describe the purpose of XML and WML. Explain the purpose of style sheets.
27. Identify the use of RSS 2.0 and ATOM.
28. Discuss and identify uses of scripts, applets, servlets, and ActiveX controls.
29. Identify the purpose of counters and image maps.
30. Describe the purpose of a CGI script.
31. Differentiate among JavaScript, Perl, PHP, Rexx, Tcl, and VBScript.
32. Describe the purpose of a sandbox.
33. Identify the purpose of DHTML. Describe how it uses the document object model, cascading style sheets, and scripting languages.
34. Identify the use of Ruby on Rails. Describe the purpose of Ajax.
35. API stands for _____. Define mashup. Explain the relationship between API and mashup.
36. Describe the purpose of Web page authoring software. Name some examples.
37. Describe the purpose of multimedia authoring software. Name some examples.
38. PDLC stands for _____. Name the six steps in the PDLC. Identify tasks performed during each step.
39. Define solution algorithm.
40. Differentiate between structured design and object-oriented design.
41. Differentiate between sequence, selection, and repetition control structures.
42. Describe the purpose of flowcharts, pseudocode, and the UML.
43. Identify steps performed by programmers during a desk check.
44. Describe extreme programming.
45. Differentiate a syntax error from a logic error.
46. Define the terms, bug and debugging.
47. Identify the type of software developed by Electronic Arts.
48. Identify an advantage of Web 2.0 program development. Describe the tiers in Web applications. Differentiate Web 2.0 program development from traditional Web page development.

Check This Out

As technology changes, you must keep up with updates, new products, breakthroughs, and recent advances to remain digitally literate. The list below identifies topics related to this chapter that you should explore to keep current. In parentheses beside each topic, you will find a search term to help begin your research using a search engine, such as Google.

1. **widely used programming languages** (search for: popular programming languages)
2. **high-level programming languages to know** (search for: best high-level programming learn)
3. **current uses of assembly languages** (search for: assembly code example)
4. **new object-oriented programming languages** (search for: recent OOP languages)
5. **popular rapid application development components** (search for: top RAD environment tools)
6. **new Microsoft Visual Studio tools** (search for: Visual Studio features)
7. **recent visual programming languages** (search for: latest visual programming languages)
8. **new fourth-generation languages** (search for: latest fourth-generation programming languages)
9. **widely used Visual Basic for Applications macros** (search for: popular VBA macro examples)
10. **popular RSS and ATOM XML applications** (search for: XML applications RSS ATOM)
11. **new common gateway interface scripts** (search for: CGI script examples)
12. **popular Web programming languages** (search for: top Web programming languages)
13. **widely used Web page authoring software** (search for: popular Web page authoring programs)
14. **popular flowcharting programs** (search for: best flowcharting software)
15. **latest Web 2.0 program development technologies** (search for: Web 2.0 program development toolkits)

For current news and information
Check us out on Facebook and Twitter. See your instructor or the Computer Concepts CourseMate for specific information.

Chapter 14

Student Success Guide

Enterprise Computing

Why Should I Learn About Enterprise Computing?

"My neighbor owns a small manufacturing business, and I often assist him on weekends by billing his customers and updating his budget. I back up the data on his computer to a USB flash drive and plan to expand his business interactions over the Internet. These computer functions seem adequate, so why should I learn about enterprise computing?"

True, you may be familiar with some of the material in this chapter, but do you know . . .

"Why should I learn about enterprise computing?"

- How various units function within a business? (p. 726, Information Systems in the Enterprise)
- Why practically everyone soon may be using cloud computing? (p. 746, Cloud and Grid Computing)
- What hardware you can use to back up data on your computer continuously? (p. 755, FAQ)
- How PS3s are used in astrophysics labs to study black holes? (p. 756, Innovative Computing)
- How municipalities use computers to enhance services? (p. 757, Computer Usage @ Work)
- Which YouTube cofounder created PayPal's original logo? (p. 759, Companies on the Cutting Edge)
- How to use Skype to make unlimited calls? (p. 768 and Computer Concepts CourseMate, Learn How To)
- How to create a desktop shortcut to print? (Windows Exercises, Computer Concepts CourseMate)

For these answers and to discover much more information essential to this course, read Chapter 14 and visit the associated Computer Concepts CourseMate at www.cengagebrain.com.

Q & A

How can I meet one or more of these goals?

Make use of the goal's resources for each chapter in the book and you should meet that goal by the end of the course.

Customize Your Learning Experience

Adapt this book to meet your needs by determining your goal. Would you like to be an informed digital consumer? A productive technology user? A safe user, protected from the risks in a digital world? A competent digital citizen? A future entrepreneur or professional in a digital society?

Every chapter in this Student Success Guide identifies resources targeted toward each of these goals, along with criteria to verify you understand the resources' content. Resources may be located in the textbook, on the Computer Concepts CourseMate Web site, in the interactive eBook, and on the Web.

Informed Digital Consumer

Goal: I would like to understand the terminology used in Web or print advertisements that sell computers, mobile devices, and related technology, as well as the jargon used by sales associates in computer or electronics stores, so that I can make informed purchasing decisions.

Topic	Resource	Location	Now you should . . .
Order Processing	Text/Figures	pp. 772–781	Be familiar with the steps involved with order processing from the customer creating a shopping cart to the customer receiving the order and requesting support

Productive Technology User

Goal: I would like to learn ways that technology can benefit me at home, work, and school. I also would like to learn helpful techniques for using technology so that I can perform tasks more efficiently and be more productive in daily activities.

Topic	Resource	Location	Now you should . . .
Telecommuting	Ethics & Issues	p. 745	Know the benefits of telecommuting
	Video	eBook p. 745 or CourseMate	
E-Commerce	Text	p. 747	Know the online services that users find beneficial: e-retail, finance, travel, entertainment and media, and health
	Drag and Drop Figure 14-25	eBook p. 747 or CourseMate	
Computers in Municipal Services	Computer Usage @ Work	p. 757	Know how you interact with or benefit from computers in various municipal services
	Link and Video	eBook p. 757 or CourseMate	
VoIP	Learn How To	pp. 768–769 and CourseMate	Know how to use VoIP (Voice over Internet Protocol)
Changing Windows Views	Windows Exercises	CourseMate	Know how to change views in Windows
Desktop Shortcuts	Windows Exercises	CourseMate	Know how to create a desktop shortcut in Windows
Sounds Cards and Audio Devices	Windows Exercises	CourseMate	Know how to determine the brand and model of sound cards and audio devices on your computer
Microsoft Office Web Apps	Web Apps	CourseMate	Know how to use Microsoft Office Web Apps to create, edit, and share documents, workbooks, presentations, and notes

Safe User, Protected from the Risks in a Digital World

Goal: I would like to take measures to (1) protect my computers, devices, and data from loss, damage, or misuse; (2) minimize or prevent risks associated with using technology; and (3) minimize the environmental impact of using computers and related devices.

Topic	Resource	Location	Now you should . . .
Personal Information	FAQ	p. 730	Know to be careful when supplying personal information to companies
	FAQ Link	eBook p. 730, or Sharing Personal Information link, CourseMate	
Online Purchases	Ethics & Issues	p. 747	Be familiar with ways to safeguard online purchases
Energy Consumption	FAQ	p. 748	Be familiar with power-saving practices in data centers
	FAQ Link	eBook p. 748, or Energy Reduction link, CourseMate	
Backup Procedures	Text/Figure and FAQ	pp. 754–755	Know the difference in various backup methods: full, differential, incremental, selective, and continuous
	Drag and Drop Figure 14-33	eBook p. 754 or CourseMate	
Disaster Recovery Plan	Text	pp. 755–756	Know the components of a disaster recovery plan
	Link and Video	eBook p. 756 or CourseMate	

Competent Digital Citizen

Goal: I would like to be knowledgeable and well-informed about computers, mobile devices, and related technology, so that I am digitally literate in my personal and professional use of digital devices.

Topic	Resource	Location	Now you should . . .
Portals	Text/Figure	pp. 740–741	Know the purpose and use of a portal
Data Warehouses	Text/Figure	pp. 741–742	Know the purpose and use of data warehouses
EDI	Text	p. 742	Know the purpose of electronic data interchange
Extranets	Text	p. 742	Know the benefits of an extranet
Web Services	Text/Figure	pp. 742–743	Know how Web services work
	Drag and Drop Figure 14-22	eBook p. 743 or CourseMate	
	Web Link		
SOA	Text	p. 743	Know the purpose of a service-oriented architecture
Document Management Systems	Text	p. 743	Know the benefits of document management systems
Workflow	Text/Figure	p. 744	Be familiar with workflow and workflow applications
VPN	Text/Figure	pp. 744–745	Know the purpose of a virtual private network
Virtualization	Text and FAQ	pp. 745–746	Be familiar with benefits of and various types of virtualization
	Links and Video	eBook p. 746 or CourseMate	
Cloud Computing	Text	p. 746	Be familiar with trends in cloud computing
	Looking Ahead		
	Video	eBook p. 746 or CourseMate	
Grid Computing	Text	p. 746	Know the purpose of grid computing
RAID	Text/Figure	pp. 748–749	Know how RAID works
	Figure 14-26 Animation	eBook p. 748 or CourseMate	
NAS and SAN	Text/Figure	pp. 749–750	Know the purpose of network attached storage and storage area networks
	Web Link	eBook p. 750 or CourseMate	
Blade Servers	Text/Figure and FAQ	p. 751	Know the purpose and advantages of blade servers
Thin Clients	Text/Figure	p. 752	Know the purpose of a thin client
High-Availability Systems	Text/Figure	pp. 752–753	Be familiar with uses of high-availability systems and the purpose of redundant components
Scalability	Text	p. 753	Know the definition of scalability
Interoperability	Text	pp. 753–754	Know the definition of interoperability
PS3 Gravity Grid	Innovative Computing	p. 756	Know how PS3s are simulating black hole activity
	Link	eBook p. 756 or CourseMate	

Continued on next page

Continued from previous page

Topic	Resource	Location	Now you should . . .
Neural Networks	Text/Figure	p. 758	Know how neural networks work and uses of neural networks
	Link and Video	eBook p. 758 or CourseMate	
EMC	Text	p. 759	Be familiar with EMC's products and services
	Link	eBook p. 759 or CourseMate	
IBM	Text	p. 759	Be familiar with IBM's products and services
	Link	eBook p. 759 or CourseMate	
Chad Hurley	Text	p. 759	Be familiar with Chad Hurley's contributions to technology
	Link and Video	eBook p. 759 or CourseMate	
Anita Borg	Text	p. 759	Be familiar with Anita Borg's role with women in technology
	Link	eBook p. 759 or CourseMate	

Future Entrepreneur or Professional in a Digital Society

Goal: As I ponder my future, I envision myself as an entrepreneur or skilled professional using technology to support my business endeavors or job responsibilities. Along the way, I may interact with a variety of computer professionals — or I may just become one myself!

Topic	Resource	Location	Now you should . . .
Enterprise Computing	Text/Figure	pp. 720–722	Know the meaning of enterprise computing
Enterprise Types	Text	p. 722	Be familiar with various types of enterprises
Organizational Structure	Text/Figure	p. 723	Know the difference between supporting and core activities, and the difference between a decentralized and centralized IT approach
Levels of Users	Text/Figure	p. 724	Know the difference between decision levels and job titles for executive management, middle management, operational management, and nonmanagement employees
	Drag and Drop Figure 14-3	eBook p. 724 or CourseMate	
Management	Text	pp. 725–726	Know how managers plan, organize, lead, and control; know how they use business intelligence, business process management, and business process automation
	Drag and Drop Figure 14-4	eBook p. 725 or CourseMate	
	Web Link		
Functional Units	Text/Figures	pp. 726–732	Know the role of functional units in most organizations: accounting and finance, human resources, engineering, manufacturing, quality control, marketing, sales, distribution, customer service, and information technology
	Drag and Drop Figure 14-6	eBook p. 727 or CourseMate	
	Figure Video	eBook p. 730 or CourseMate	
	Web Link	eBook p. 731 or CourseMate	
General Information Systems	Text/Figures	pp. 732–737	Be able to describe each type of general information system: office information system (OIS), transaction processing system (TPS), management information system (MIS), decision support system (DSS), and expert system
Integrated Information Systems	Text/Figures	pp. 737–739	Be able to describe each type of integrated information system: customer relationship management (CRM), enterprise resource planning (ERP), and content management system (CMS)
	Web Link	eBook p. 738 or CourseMate	

Continued on next page

Continued from previous page

Topic	Resource	Location	Now you should . . .
Data Centers	Text	p. 740	Be aware of the purpose of a data center and be familiar with some examples
	Innovative Computing		
	Link and Video	eBook p. 740 or CourseMate	
	Web Link		
	Video	At the Movies, CourseMate	
Wikis	FAQ	p. 742	Know why enterprises use wikis
Enterprise Storage	Text/Figure	pp. 750–751	Be familiar with storage strategies used by enterprises
Sarbanes-Oxley Act	Ethics & Issues	p. 751	Be familiar with financial reporting requirements defined by the Sarbanes-Oxley Act
CIO	Exploring Computer Careers	CourseMate	Be familiar with the responsibilities of and education required for a chief information officer (CIO)

Preparing for a Test

Visit the Computer Concepts CourseMate at www.cengagebrain.com and then navigate to the Chapter 14 Web Apps resource for this book to prepare for your test.

Does your class use the Computer Concepts CourseMate Web site? If so, prepare for your test by using the Flash Cards, Study Guide, and Practice Test Web apps — available for your smart phone or tablet.

If your class does not use the Computer Concepts CourseMate Web site or you prefer to use your book, you can prepare for the test by doing the Quiz Yourself activities on pages 740, 748, and 757; reading the Chapter Review on pages 760–761; ensuring you know the definitions for the terms on page 762; and completing the Checkpoint exercises on pages 763–764. You also should know the material identified in the Chapter 14 Study Guide that follows.

Chapter 14 Study Guide

This study guide identifies material you should know for the Chapter 14 exam. You may want to write the answers in a notebook, enter them on your digital device, record them into a phone, or highlight them in your book. Choose whichever method helps you remember the best.

1. Define enterprise computing.
2. Know the purpose of these types of enterprises: retail, manufacturing, service, wholesale, government, educational, and transportation.
3. Differentiate between supporting and core business activities.
4. Differentiate between a decentralized and centralized approach to information technology.
5. Identify the types of decisions and sample job titles of executive management, middle management, operational management, and nonmanagement employees.
6. Describe how managers plan, organize, lead, and control.
7. Define business intelligence, business process management, and business process automation.
8. Describe the purpose of and software used by these business functional units: accounting and finance, human resources, engineering or product development, manufacturing, quality control, marketing, sales, distribution, customer service, and information technology.
9. ERM stands for _____.
10. MRP stands for _____. Describe MRP.
11. Describe these general information systems: office information system (OIS), transaction processing system (TPS), management information system (MIS), decision support system (DSS), and expert system.
12. Differentiate online transaction processing (OLTP) from online analytical processing (OLAP).
13. Define the purpose of an executive information system (EIS).

Continued on next page

Continued from previous page

14. AI stands for _____.
15. Describe AI.
16. Describe these integrated information systems: customer relationship management (CRM), enterprise resource planning (ERP), and content management systems (CMS).
17. Define data center.
18. Describe the purpose and capabilities of a portal.
19. Describe how data warehouses work.
20. Define click stream.
21. Explain reasons enterprises use wikis.
22. Identify uses of extranets.
23. Describe the purpose of Web services.
24. Identify a benefit of using a service-oriented architecture.
25. Identify benefits of document management systems.
26. Describe a workflow and a workflow application.
27. Describe the purpose of a virtual private network (VPN).
28. Define virtualization. Give examples.
29. Identify benefits of cloud computing.
30. Define grid computing.
31. Explain the purpose of these e-commerce market segments: e-retail, finance, travel, entertainment and media, and health.
32. Identify ways to shop safely online.
33. Define legacy system.
34. Identify techniques data centers use to reduce energy consumption.
35. Describe the purpose of RAID. Differentiate between mirroring and striping.
36. Describe the purpose of network attached storage and storage area networks.
37. Identify the goal of an enterprise storage system. Describe storage techniques used by enterprise storage systems.
38. State the purpose of the Sarbanes-Oxley Act.
39. Describe a blade server.
40. Describe a thin client.
41. Define high-availability system and redundant components.
42. Explain scalability and interoperability.
43. Differentiate among these backup methods: full, differential, incremental, selective, and continuous.
44. Describe the components of a disaster recovery plan.
45. Define neural network. Briefly describe how neural networks work.
46. Identify services provided by EMC.
47. _____ cofounded YouTube.
48. Briefly describe the steps in order processing.

Check This Out

As technology changes, you must keep up with updates, new products, breakthroughs, and recent advances to remain digitally literate. The list below identifies topics related to this chapter that you should explore to keep current. In parentheses beside each topic, you will find a search term to help begin your research using a search engine, such as Google.

1. **new enterprise organizational structure developments** (search for: enterprise organization structure)
2. **recent iPad and tablet computer uses in corporations** (search for: iPad tablet corporations)
3. **recent business process management developments** (search for: business process management news)
4. **updates on information systems research** (search for: information system news)
5. **new software and information systems used in human resources** (search for: HRIS software)
6. **recent models created using 3-D visualization** (search for: 3D visualization)
7. **popular quality control programs** (search for: latest quality control software)
8. **latest online transaction processing applications** (search for: online transaction processing news)
9. **top content management systems** (search for: best content management systems)
10. **widely used Web service business applications** (search for: top business Web services)
11. **latest predictions on the future of cloud computing** (search for: trends cloud computing)
12. **widely used enterprise hardware** (search for: enterprise hardware storage)
13. **updates on backup and recovery methods** (search for: backup recovery procedures news)
14. **new real-life neural network uses** (search for: neural networks applications)
15. **latest news about IBM enterprise technology** (search for: IBM enterprise systems)

For current news and information
Check us out on Facebook and Twitter. See your instructor or the Computer Concepts CourseMate for specific information.

Chapter 15

Student Success Guide

Computer Careers and Certification

Why Should I Learn About Computer Careers and Certification?

"I have enjoyed discovering many facets of the computer field in this course. I would like to continue learning about technology, especially because I have heard that jobs for computer majors are available in a variety of fields throughout the world. How can I learn more about employment in the computer industry and required certifications?"

You may be familiar with some of the material in this chapter, but do you know . . .

"How can I learn more about employment in the computer industry and required certifications?"

- How younger and older workers can blend their skills in the office? (p. 786, Looking Ahead)
- How lucrative starting salaries are for computer science majors? (p. 787, FAQ)
- When you can copy software legally? (p. 791, Ethics & Issues)
- How publishers use computers to develop and print textbooks? (p. 809, Computer Usage @ Work)
- Which Microsoft executive was Bill Gates's college classmate? (p. 811, Technology Trailblazers)
- How to create a video resume? (p. 820 and Computer Concepts CourseMate, Learn How To)
- How to plan regular hard disk maintenance? (Windows Exercises, Computer Concepts CourseMate)
- Which digital products affect most facets of life? (p. 824, Living Digitally Special Feature)

For these answers and to discover much more information essential to this course, read Chapter 15 and visit the associated Computer Concepts CourseMate at www.cengagebrain.com.

Customize Your Learning Experience

Q & A

How can I meet one or more of these goals?

Make use of the goal's resources for each chapter in the book and you should meet that goal by the end of the course.

Adapt this book to meet your needs by determining your goal. Would you like to be an informed digital consumer? A productive technology user? A safe user, protected from the risks in a digital world? A competent digital citizen? A future entrepreneur or professional in a digital society?

Every chapter in this Student Success Guide identifies resources targeted toward each of these goals, along with criteria to verify you understand the resources' content. Resources may be located in the textbook, on the Computer Concepts CourseMate Web site, in the interactive eBook, and on the Web.

Informed Digital Consumer

Goal: I would like to understand the terminology used in Web or print advertisements that sell computers, mobile devices, and related technology, as well as the jargon used by sales associates in computer or electronics stores, so that I can make informed purchasing decisions.

Topic	Resource	Location	Now you should . . .
Online Classes	Innovative Computing	eBook p. 794 or CourseMate	Know about one school's online offering
	Link and Video		
Living Digitally	Text/Figures	pp. 824–830	Be familiar with audio, video, recording, gaming, and digital home products you may find useful

Productive Technology User

Goal: I would like to learn ways that technology can benefit me at home, work, and school. I also would like to learn helpful techniques for using technology so that I can perform tasks more efficiently and be more productive in daily activities.

Topic	Resource	Location	Now you should . . .
Trade School	Text	p. 794	Know the benefits of attending a trade school
	Web Link	eBook p. 794 or CourseMate	
Colleges and Universities	Text/Figure	pp. 794–795	Know the differences among computer disciplines at colleges or universities
	Drag and Drop Figure 15-8	eBook p. 795 or CourseMate	
	Web Link		
Searching for a Job	Text/Figure	pp. 796–797	Know how to search for a job online
	Figure 15-10 Animation	eBook p. 796 or CourseMate	
	Labs	CourseMate	
Dice	Text	p. 811	Be familiar with Dice's services
	Link	eBook p. 811 or CourseMate	
Dell	Text	p. 811	Be familiar with Dell's products and services
	Link	eBook p. 811 or CourseMate	
Video Resume	Learn How To	pp. 820–821 and CourseMate	Know how to create a video resume
Character Map Utility	Windows Exercises	CourseMate	Know how to use the Character Map Utility
Toggle Keys	Windows Exercises	CourseMate	Know how to use Ease of Access Options to set toggle key actions
Disk Maintenance	Windows Exercises	CourseMate	Know how to use Task Scheduler to schedule disk maintenance
TaxACT Online	Web Apps	CourseMate	Know how to use TaxACT Online to file federal and state taxes

Safe User, Protected from the Risks in a Digital World

Goal: I would like to take measures to (1) protect my computers, devices, and data from loss, damage, or misuse; (2) minimize or prevent risks associated with using technology; and (3) minimize the environmental impact of using computers and related devices.

Topic	Resource	Location	Now you should . . .
Outsourcing	Ethics & Issues	p. 785	Know issues surrounding outsourcing computer jobs
	Video	eBook p. 785 or CourseMate	
Computer Security	FAQ	p. 790	Be familiar with the importance of computer security and ways to secure data and computers
	Link and Video	eBook p. 790 or CourseMate	
Recycling Ink	FAQ	p. 790	Know how to recycle used printer ink cartridges
	FAQ Link	eBook p. 790, or Ink Cartridges link, CourseMate	
Copying Software	Ethics & Issues	p. 791	Know that copying software for purposes other than a backup is illegal

Continued on next page

Continued from previous page

Topic	Resource	Location	Now you should . . .
Personal Information	Ethics & Issues	p. 792	Be aware that IT professionals have access to your personal information
Green Organizations	FAQ	p. 797	Be familiar with strategies organizations use to preserve the environment
	FAQ Link	eBook p. 797, or Green Companies link, CourseMate	

Competent Digital Citizen

Goal: I would like to be knowledgeable and well-informed about computers, mobile devices, and related technology, so that I am digitally literate in my personal and professional use of digital devices.

Topic	Resource	Location	Now you should . . .
Trends	Text/Figure	pp. 784–785	Be familiar with trends related to computer professionals
Generation Gap	Looking Ahead	p. 786	Be familiar with how the generation gap affects IT departments
	Link and Video	eBook p. 786 or CourseMate	
DBA	FAQ	p. 807	Know the difference between database administrator and administration
Computers in Publishing	Computer Usage @ Work	p. 809	Know how authors, writers, and compositors use computers
	Link and Video	eBook p. 809 or CourseMate	
Bioinformatics	Text/Figure	p. 810	Be familiar with informatics and bioinformatics
	Link and Video	eBook p. 810 or CourseMate	
Steve Ballmer	Text	p. 811	Be familiar with Steve Ballmer's contributions to the computer industry
	Link and Video	eBook p. 811 or CourseMate	
Jerry Yang and David Filo	Text	p. 811	Be familiar with Jerry Yang and David Filo's creation
	Link	eBook p. 811 or CourseMate	
Google Tour	Video	At the Movies, CourseMate	Be familiar with Google's facility

Future Entrepreneur or Professional in a Digital Society

Goal: As I ponder my future, I envision myself as an entrepreneur or skilled professional using technology to support my business endeavors or job responsibilities. Along the way, I may interact with a variety of computer professionals — or I may just become one myself!

Topic	Resource	Location	Now you should . . .
IT Department Jobs and Salaries	Text/Figures and FAQ	pp. 786–789	Be familiar with jobs available in an IT department, along with responsibilities and salary ranges
	Drag and Drop Figure 15-3	eBook p. 788-789 or CourseMate	
	FAQ Link	eBook p. 787, or College Graduates' Starting Salaries link, CourseMate	
	Web Link	eBook p. 787 or CourseMate	

Continued on next page

Continued from previous page

Topic	Resource	Location	Now you should . . .
Equipment Field	Text/Figure	p. 790	Be familiar with types of companies and career options in the computer equipment field
Software Field	Text	pp. 790–791	Be familiar with types of companies and career options in the computer software field
Service and Repair Field	Text/Figure and FAQ	pp. 791–792	Be familiar with types of companies and career options in the computer service and repair field
	Figure Video	eBook p. 791 or CourseMate	
	FAQ Link	eBook p. 792, or Diagnostic Tools link, CourseMate	
Sales	Text/Figure	p. 792	Be familiar with types of companies and career options in the computer sales field
Education and Training Field	Text/Figure	pp. 792–793	Be familiar with types of companies and career options in the computer education and training field
IT Consulting	Text and Ethics & Issues	p. 793	Be familiar with career options in the IT consulting field and issues related to consulting mistakes
Career Development	Text/Figures	pp. 797–799	Know ways to keep up to date with industry trends and technologies and to develop new skills: professional organizations and personal networks, professional growth and continuing education, and computer publications and Web sites
	Web Link	eBook p. 797 or CourseMate	
Noncompete Agreements	Ethics & Issues	p. 798	Be aware that some employers require that employees sign a noncompete agreement
Computer Certification	Text/Figures	pp. 800–803	Know the benefits of certification, factors to consider when choosing a certification, how to prepare for certification, and what to expect on the exams
	Link and Video	eBook p. 800 or CourseMate	
	Web Link	eBook p. 801 or CourseMate	
Mainframe Careers	FAQ	p. 802	Know whether a career in mainframes is still a good choice
Application Software Certifications	Text/Figure	p. 804	Be familiar with popular application software certifications, along with careers suited for these certifications
	Web Link	eBook p. 804 or CourseMate	
Operating System Certifications	Text/Figure	p. 804	Be familiar with popular operating system certifications, along with careers suited for these certifications
Programmer/ Developer Certifications	Text/Figure	p. 805	Be familiar with popular programmer/developer certifications, along with careers suited for these certifications
Hardware Certifications	Text/Figure	p. 805	Be familiar with popular hardware certifications, along with careers suited for these certifications
Networking Certifications	Text/Figure	p. 806	Be familiar with popular networking certifications, along with careers suited for these certifications
	Web Link	eBook p. 806	
Digital Forensics Certifications	Text/Figure	p. 806	Be familiar with popular digital forensics certifications, along with careers suited for these certifications
Security Certifications	Text/Figure	p. 807	Be familiar with popular security certifications, along with careers suited for these certifications
Internet Certifications	Text/Figure	p. 807	Be familiar with popular Internet certifications, along with careers suited for these certifications

Continued on next page

Continued from previous page

Topic	Resource	Location	Now you should . . .
Database System Certifications	Text/Figure	pp. 807–808	Be familiar with popular operating system certifications, along with careers suited for these certifications
	FAQ Link	eBook p. 807, or DBA link, CourseMate	
Computer Science/IT Instructor	Exploring Computer Careers	CourseMate	Be familiar with the responsibilities of and education required for a computer science/IT instructor

Preparing for a Test

Visit the Computer Concepts CourseMate at www.cengagebrain.com and then navigate to the Chapter 15 Web Apps resource for this book to prepare for your test.

Does your class use the Computer Concepts CourseMate Web site? If so, prepare for your test by using the Flash Cards, Study Guide, and Practice Test Web apps — available for your smart phone or tablet.

If your class does not use the Computer Concepts CourseMate Web site or you prefer to use your book, you can prepare for the test by doing the Quiz Yourself activities on pages 793, 799, and 808; reading the Chapter Review on pages 812–813; ensuring you know the definitions for the terms on page 814; and completing the Checkpoint exercises on pages 815–816. You also should know the material identified in the Chapter 15 Study Guide that follows.

Chapter 15 Study Guide

This study guide identifies material you should know for the Chapter 15 exam. You may want to write the answers in a notebook, enter them on your digital device, record them into a phone, or highlight them in your book. Choose whichever method helps you remember the best.

1. Identify trends with occupations in computer-related fields.
2. Describe issues associated with outsourcing computer jobs.
3. Explain the effect of the generation gap on IT departments.
4. Describe the role of each of these areas in an IT department: management, system development and programming, technical services, operations, training, and security.
5. Identify the function of these IT department jobs: CIO, network administrator, project manager, computer games designer, computer scientist, software engineer, systems analyst, systems programmer, Web software developer, database administrator, digital forensics examiner, graphic designer, Web designer, computer operator, corporate trainer, help desk specialist, CSO, and security administrator.
6. Identify the types of companies involved and career opportunities available in these market segments: computer equipment field, computer software field, computer service and repair field, computer sales, computer education and training field, and IT consulting.
7. Identify recycling programs available for used printer ink cartridges.
8. Describe issues associated with illegal copying of software.
9. Explain how a technician knows how to diagnose a computer problem.
10. Distinguish between trade schools and colleges.
11. Differentiate among various computer-related majors for college students.
12. Identify ways to search for jobs.
13. ACM stands for _____.
14. AITP stands for _____.
15. Define user group.
16. Identify ways to stay current with changing technology after graduation.
17. Identify the purpose of the International Consumer Electronics Show.
18. Identify reasons an employer would want an IT employee to sign a noncompete agreement.
19. Define certification.
20. Explain the role of a sponsoring organization.
21. List the benefits of certification.
22. Identify factors to consider when selecting a certification.
23. Identify ways to prepare for certification.
24. Describe the types of certification exams.
25. List the general areas of IT certification.
26. Describe careers suited for application software certifications. Describe the purpose of these application software certifications: MOS – Core, MOS – Expert, ACE, and ACI.

Continued on next page

Continued from previous page

27. Describe careers suited for operating system certifications. Describe the purpose of these operating system certifications: MCITP, RHCE, and SCSA.
28. Describe careers suited for programmer/developer certifications. Describe the purpose of these programmer/developer certifications: CSDA, IBM Certified Solution Developer, MCPD, and SCMAD.
29. Describe careers suited for hardware certifications. Describe the purpose of this hardware certification: A+.
30. Describe careers suited for networking certifications. Describe the purpose of these networking certifications: NCA, CCNA, Network+, and SCNA.
31. Describe careers suited for digital forensics certifications. Describe the purpose of these digital forensics certifications: CCE and CIFI.
32. Describe careers suited for security certifications. Describe the purpose of these security certifications: CISSP and SCNS.
33. Describe careers suited for Internet certifications. Describe the purpose of this Internet certification: CIW.
34. Describe careers suited for database certifications. Describe the purpose of these database certifications: MCITP and OCP.
35. Define informatics and bioinformatics. Describe the purpose of the Human Genome Project.
36. Describe the purpose of Dice.
37. Identify Steve Ballmer's role with Microsoft.
38. _____ and _____ cofounded Yahoo!.

Check This Out

As technology changes, you must keep up with updates, new products, breakthroughs, and recent advances to remain digitally literate. The list below identifies topics related to this chapter that you should explore to keep current. In parentheses beside each topic, you will find a search term to help begin your research using a search engine, such as Google.

1. **new research of how outsourcing actually creates new corporate IT jobs** (search for: outsource IT job)
2. **recent starting salaries for computer science graduates** (search for: starting salary computer science)
3. **updates on IT department job functions and salaries** (search for: computer job description salary)
4. **updates on computer information security jobs** (search for: employment computer security)
5. **new jobs in the computer equipment field** (search for: computer manufacturing distribution jobs)
6. **recent computer software career opportunities** (search for: software developer manufacture support jobs)
7. **popular computer service and repair field jobs** (search for: computer service repair jobs)
8. **top employment opportunities for computer salespeople** (search for: computer sales jobs)
9. **current jobs in computer education and training** (search for: computer education training jobs)
10. **latest IT consulting employment prospects** (search for: IT consultant jobs)
11. **widely used computer job search techniques and career advice** (search for: computer career advice)
12. **new recommendations for computer certification training** (search for: computer certification)
13. **updates about the bioinformatics Human Genome Project** (search for: Human Genome Project informatics)
14. **latest news about Dell products and company strategies** (search for: Dell headlines)
15. **popular consumer electronics devices for the home** (search for: new consumer electronics home)

For current news and information
Check us out on Facebook and Twitter. See your instructor or the Computer Concepts CourseMate for specific information.

Quick Reference

Quick Reference

Every chapter in this Student Success Guide presents tables of resources targeted toward one of five student goals: informed digital consumer; productive technology user; safe user, protected from the risks in a digital world; competent digital citizen; and future entrepreneur or professional in a digital society. Resources may be located in the textbook, on the Computer Concepts CourseMate Web site, in the Interactive eBook, and on the Web.

Some of the tables throughout the Student Success Guide identify text and/or a figure(s) as the resource, which you will find self-explanatory. For those resources that are not identified as text or figures, the following table provides a quick reference to help you locate each type of resource. The first and second columns name and briefly describe the resource and its purpose. The third column identifies where you can find the resource and, in brackets, outlines how to navigate to resources on the Computer Concepts CourseMate Web site (www.cengagebrain.com). For more detailed instructions about the Computer Concepts CourseMate, refer to the pages specified in the fourth column.

Resource	Purpose	Location [Navigation]	Additional Information
Animations	Strengthen your understanding of chapter topics through animations that correspond directly to book content		• 1 per chapter
		Interactive eBook	For further instruction, see page 97 in CourseMate Student Guide
		CourseMate [eBook Interactive Activities link on navigation menu | Animations tab]	For further instruction, see page 97 in CourseMate Student Guide
Companies on the Cutting Edge	Expose you to companies you should know in the computer industry	Last page in chapter before Student Assignments	• 2 per chapter
		CourseMate [Beyond the Book link on navigation menu | Beyond the Book tab]	For further instruction, see page 104 in CourseMate Student Guide
Computer Usage @ Work	Familiarize you with ways various industries use computers and related technology	Follows Chapter Summary	• 1 per chapter
		External links with more information on **CourseMate** [Beyond the Book link on navigation menu | Beyond the Book tab]	For further instruction, see page 104 in CourseMate Student Guide
Drag and Drop Figures	Boost your understanding of chapter visuals through interactive figure activities	Interactive eBook	For further instruction, see page 97 in CourseMate Student Guide
		CourseMate [eBook Interactive Activities link on navigation menu | Drag and Drop Figures tab]	For further instruction, see page 97 in CourseMate Student Guide
Ethics & Issues	Heighten your awareness of ethical and controversial computer-related issues	Boxes throughout textbook	• 4 to 5 per chapter • For complete list of topics, see page xii in textbook
		CourseMate [Beyond the Book link on navigation menu | Ethics & Issues tab]	For further instruction, see page 104 in CourseMate Student Guide
Exploring Computer Careers	Familiarize you with various professions in the computer industry	**CourseMate** [Activities and Tutorials link on navigation menu | Exploring Computer Careers tab]	For further instruction, see page 97 in CourseMate Student Guide
FAQs	Ask and answer intriguing or current event questions related to technology	Boxes throughout textbook	• 6 to 8 per chapter • For complete list of topics, see pages xii-xiii in textbook
		External links with more information on **CourseMate** [Beyond the Book link on navigation menu | Beyond the Book tab]	For further instruction, see page 104 in CourseMate Student Guide

Continued on next page

Continued from previous page

High-Tech Talk	Deepen your knowledge of computer-related topics through technical discussions	Page following Chapter Summary	• 1 per chapter
		External links with more information on **CourseMate** [Beyond the Book link on navigation menu | Beyond the Book tab]	For further instruction, see page 104 in CourseMate Student Guide
Innovative Computing	Explore original or creative uses of technology to solve traditional problems	Boxes throughout textbook	• 1 to 2 per chapter • For complete list of topics, see page xiii in textbook
		External links with more information on **CourseMate** [Beyond the Book link on navigation menu | Beyond the Book tab]	For further instruction, see page 104 in CourseMate Student Guide
Labs (Student Edition Labs)	Reinforce and expand your knowledge about basic computer topics	**CourseMate** [Student Edition Labs link on navigation menu]	For further instruction, see page 100 in CourseMate Student Guide
Learn How To	Learn fundamental technology skills for practical everyday tasks through hands-on activities and exercises	Student Assignments in textbook	• 1 to 3 per chapter
		CourseMate [Video Study Tools link on navigation menu | Learn How To tab]	For further instruction, see page 103 in CourseMate Student Guide
Looking Ahead	Alert you to upcoming technological breakthroughs or recent advances in the industry	Boxes throughout textbook	• 1 per chapter • For complete list of topics, see page xiii in textbook
		External links with more information on **CourseMate** [Beyond the Book link on navigation menu | Beyond the Book tab]	For further instruction, see page 104 in CourseMate Student Guide
Technology Trailblazers	Expose you to leaders you should know in the computer industry	Last page in chapter before Student Assignments	• 2 per chapter
		CourseMate [Beyond the Book link on navigation menu | Beyond the Book tab]	For further instruction, see page 104 in CourseMate Student Guide
Videos	Show you current information or varying perspectives through third-party videos	Interactive eBook	For further instruction, see page 97 in CourseMate Student Guide
		CourseMate [eBook Interactive Activities link on navigation menu | Videos tab] **CourseMate** [Video Study Tools link on navigation menu | At the Movies tab]	For further instruction, see page 97 in CourseMate Student Guide For further instruction, see page 103 in CourseMate Student Guide
Web Apps	Learn how to use popular Web apps through practical exercises	**CourseMate** [Activities and Tutorials link on navigation menu | Web Apps tab]	For further instruction, see page 97 in CourseMate Student Guide
Web Links	Present you with current information or varying perspectives through external Web sites	**CourseMate** [Beyond the Book link on navigation menu | Beyond the Book tab]	For further instruction, see page 104 in CourseMate Student Guide
Windows Exercises	Sharpen your Windows skills by stepping through exercises on your computer	**CourseMate** [Activities and Tutorials link on navigation menu | Activities and Tutorials tab]	For further instruction, see page 100 in CourseMate Student Guide

Computer Concepts CourseMate Student Guide

Computer Concepts CourseMate Student Guide

Introduction

Welcome to this Computer Concepts CourseMate Student Guide. Computer Concepts CourseMate is an online collection of tools and resources you can use to enrich the learning process with the *Discovering Computers: Your Interactive Guide to the Digital World* textbook. This guide will help familiarize you with the navigation of the tools and resources contained in Computer Concepts CourseMate.

To use Computer Concepts CourseMate while following along in this guide, you will need access to:

- A computer
- An Internet connection
- A Web browser

Getting Started on Computer Concepts CourseMate

Computer Concepts CourseMate, which is a Web-based companion to the *Discovering Computers* textbook, is an easy-to-use and innovative product designed to enhance your learning experience. Access Computer Concepts CourseMate by navigating to http://login.cengagebrain.com in a Web browser. Set up a user name if you do not have one already, log in, and then use the printed access code to register your Computer Concepts CourseMate product.

After successful login to Computer Concepts CourseMate, the My Dashboard page will be displayed (Figure 1). On the My Dashboard page, follow these steps to add the *Discovering Computers* textbook to your bookshelf:

1. Type the title ISBN, author name, or title in the 'Add a title to your bookshelf' text box.
2. Click the Search button to display the Discovering Computers product on your bookshelf.

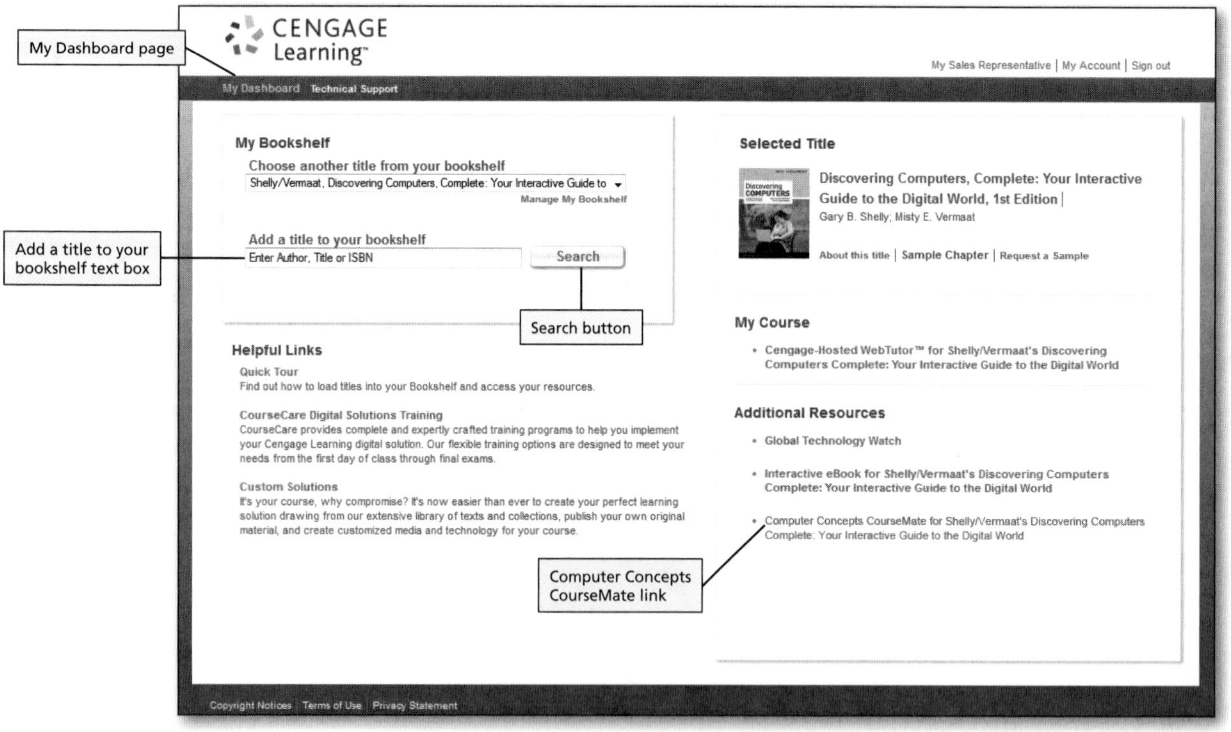

Figure 1

Once the book is added to your bookshelf, its associated Computer Concepts CourseMate link will be listed in the Additional Resources area of this page (shown in Figure 1). Click the Computer Concepts CourseMate link, which in this case, is called Computer Concepts CourseMate for Shelly/Vermaat's Discovering Computers Complete: Your Interactive Guide to the Digital World, to open the Computer Concepts CourseMate for *Discovering Computers* (Figure 2).

Figure 2

Using the Interactive eBook

You can access all of the textbook content through Computer Concepts CourseMate's Interactive eBook on your desktop or mobile computer, as long as you have an Internet connection. Open the Interactive eBook by clicking the Chapter eBook link on the navigation menu (shown in Figure 2), which is located on the left side of Computer Concepts CourseMate. The Interactive eBook not only displays all of the information in the text but also includes many interactive tools that are not available in the printed textbook. Figure 3 on the next page identifies specific tools in the Interactive eBook. For a brief description about how to use each of the tools, click the Help button in the upper-right corner of the Interactive eBook.

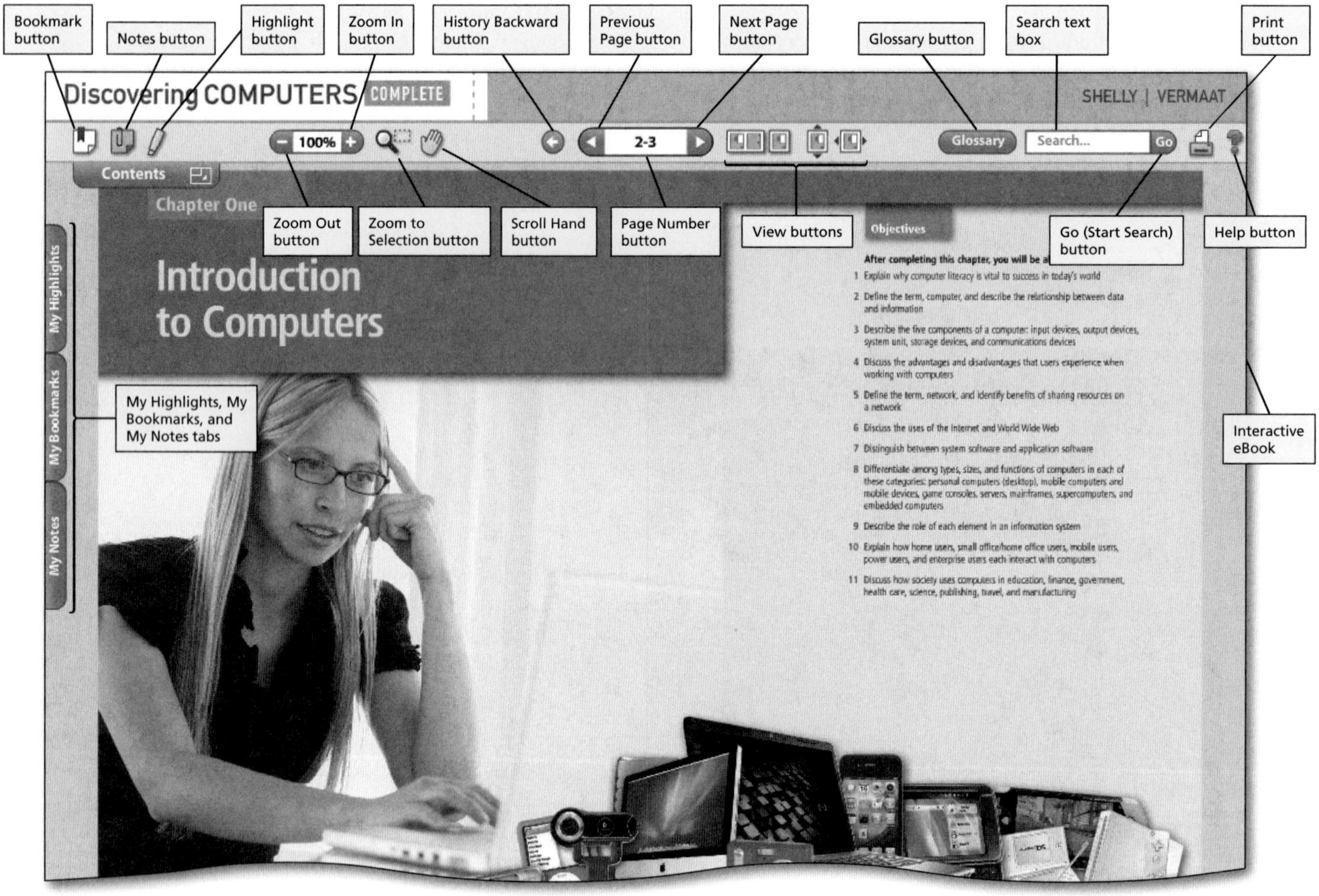

Figure 3

You can browse quickly through pages of text in the Interactive eBook, search for a term, zoom in to a section of a page, view multiple page layouts, take notes on a specific item, highlight text, bookmark a section, or search the glossary for a specific key term by using the buttons identified in Figure 3. To display all of your highlights, bookmarks, or notes, click the respective tabs on the left side of the Interactive eBook; or, you can print your highlights or notes using the Print button in the upper-right corner of the Interactive eBook. To display a different chapter or feature, click the Table of Contents button in the upper-left corner and then click the desired chapter on the menu.

Key terms, which are shaded gray throughout the Interactive eBook for easy identification, are links. Click any key term to display the Mini Glossary, where you can view the definition of the key term, listen to an audio recording of the term, and display external links associated with the term (Figure 4).

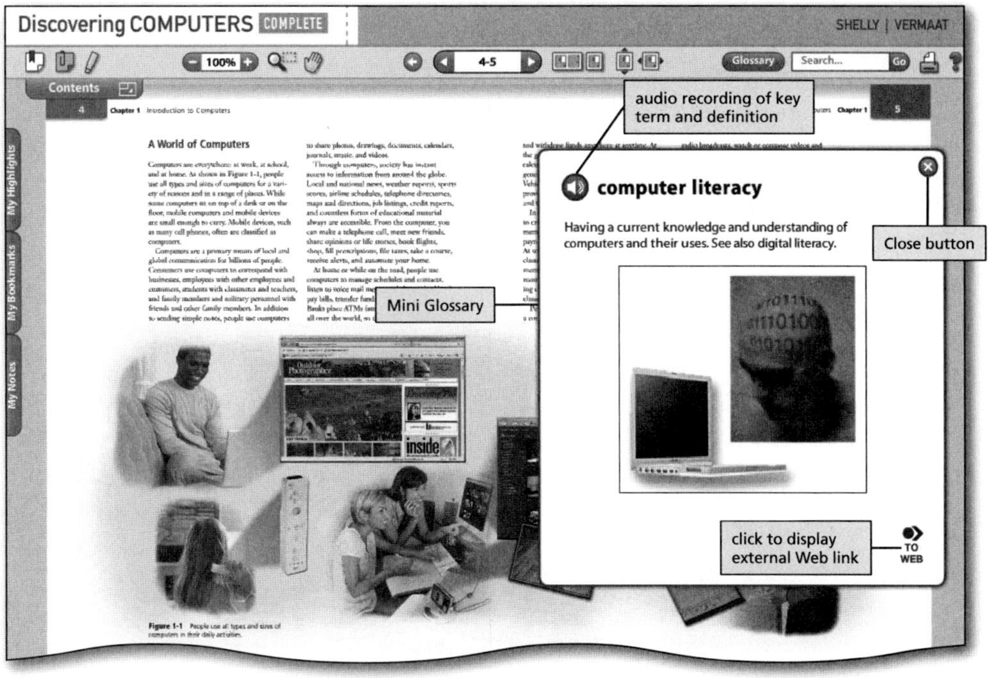

Figure 4

Learning Key Terms and Definitions

Computer Concepts CourseMate includes multiple resources to help you learn the terms and concepts in the *Discovering Computers* textbook. These resources include Interactive Flashcards, Key Terms, and games.

Instead of using index cards to create your own flashcards, you can use the Interactive Flashcards in Computer Concepts CourseMate to learn, review, and test your knowledge of key terms (Figure 5). These flashcards appear on the screen and look similar to those you would make yourself. While using the Interactive Flashcards, you can choose to display the definition or the term first, shuffle the deck, remove terms, or show all cards. If you simply want a list of the glossary items in one place for quick reference, click the Key Terms link, instead of the Interactive Flashcards link, on the navigation menu on the left side of Computer Concepts CourseMate.

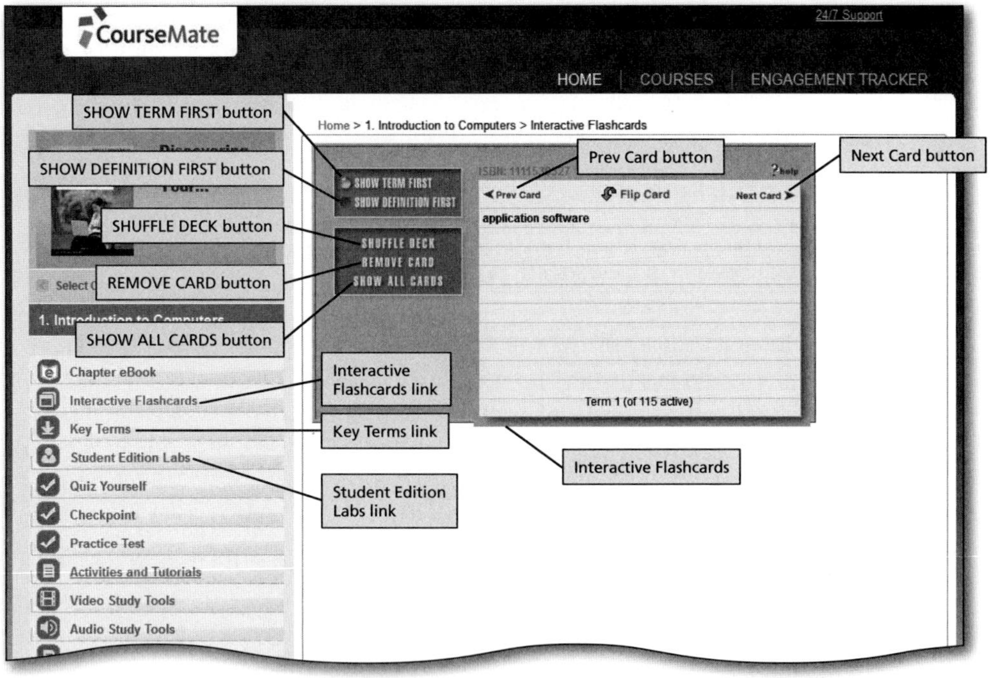

Figure 5

Do you want to challenge your knowledge of chapter content? The Crossword Puzzle resource covers the chapter's key terms and definitions. The Crossword Puzzle is a timed activity, which provides options to check your answers, undo incorrect answers, and submit your final solution. Complete the crossword puzzle to solidify your knowledge of the key terms and their definitions. To access the Crossword Puzzle resource, click the Activities and Tutorials link on the navigation menu on the left side of Computer Concepts CourseMate.

Wheel of Terms is another fun Computer Concepts CourseMate learning tool that tests your key term knowledge (Figure 6). Spin the wheel, pick a letter, buy a vowel, or submit your answer to the definition shown above the board. As you solve the puzzle and earn game money, you also build confidence for an upcoming exam. To access the Wheel of Terms resource, click the Activities and Tutorials link on the navigation menu on the left side of Computer Concepts CourseMate.

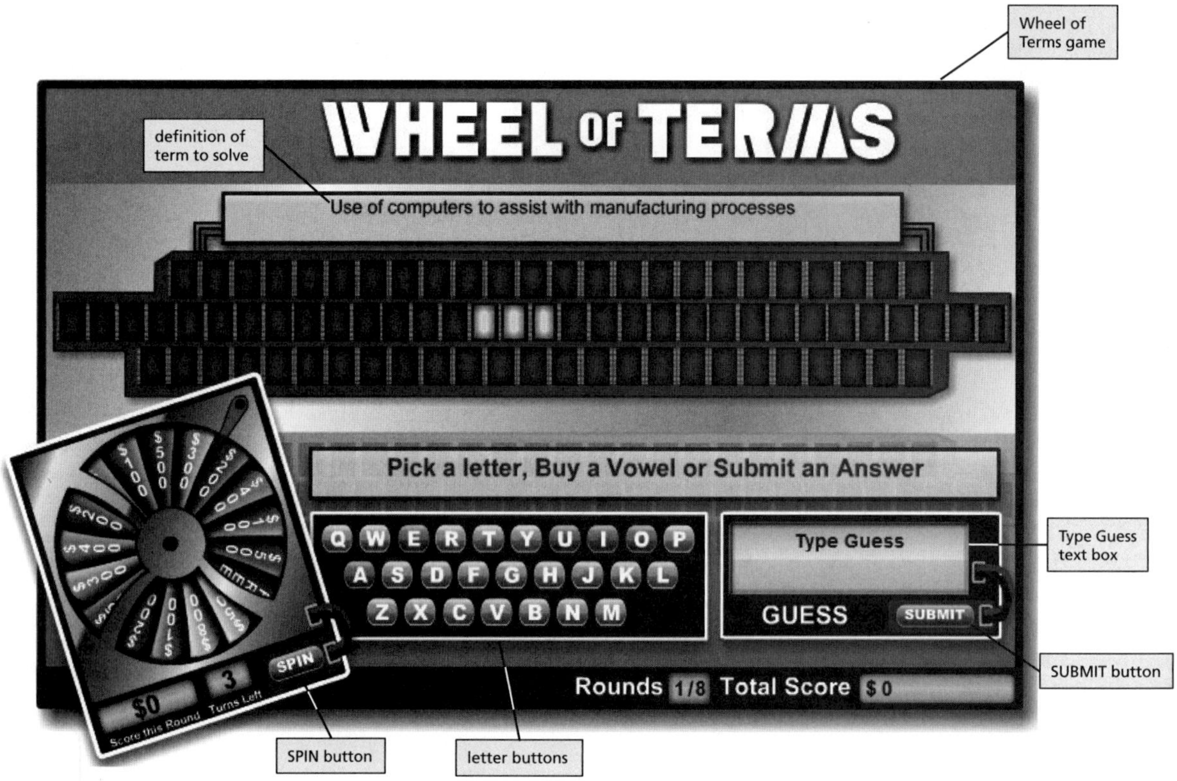

Figure 6

Hands-On Labs and Exercises

Computer Concepts CourseMate includes a variety of hands-on resources so that you can practice items covered in the textbook. Two of these resources are the Student Edition Labs and Windows Exercises.

To display the Student Edition Labs associated with a chapter, click the Student Edition Labs link on the navigation menu, which is located on the left side of Computer Concepts CourseMate (shown in Figure 5 on the previous page). You can start any individual lab in the list by clicking its link and then clicking the Start button for the lab. Figure 7 shows a sample lab and identifies elements of the interface.

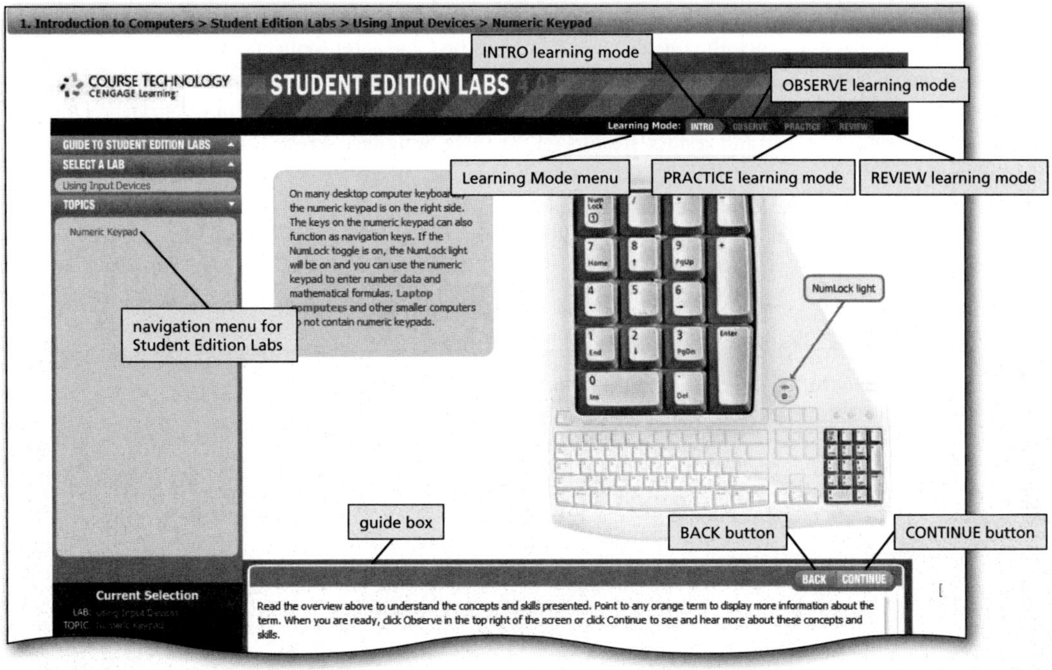

Figure 7

You interact with labs through four learning modes: Intro, Observe, Practice, and Review (shown in Figure 7). Each mode is designed to provide a cohesive path to learning the task. The Intro learning mode presents an overview of the topic; the Observe learning mode provides audio and visual guides; the Practice learning mode offers step-by-step instructions; and the Review learning mode supplies a series of multiple choice questions. At the bottom of each learning mode screen is a guide box that contains instructions for completing the lab and buttons for navigating through the lab.

Each Computer Concepts CourseMate chapter offers several Windows Exercises tailored to accompany the textbook and expand your knowledge of Windows. These step-by-step exercises vary by chapter and should be performed on a local computer. To access the Windows Exercises, click the Activities and Tutorials link on the navigation menu on the left side of the Computer Concepts CourseMate and then click the desired Windows Exercise.

Comprehensive Test Preparation

Computer Concepts CourseMate not only supplies resources to help you learn the chapter content, it also can help prepare you for quizzes and tests. Gauge your knowledge before a chapter exam using these resources: Computer Genius, Quiz Yourself, Checkpoint, You're Hired!, and Practice Test.

Who wants to be a Computer Genius? Are you ready to test your knowledge? Computer Genius tests your knowledge of the chapter content in a game-show environment. Start the Computer Genius game by clicking the Activities and Tutorials link on the Computer Concepts CourseMate navigation menu and then clicking the Computer Genius link. Computer Genius is a timed, multiple choice quiz that will test your knowledge of important concepts, terms, and ideas in the chapter text. If you are stumped on a question, use the Panic Buttons, such as the Book, 50/50, Survey, Double-Dip, and 3 Professors, before submitting your final answer.

Are you ready to look for a job? The You're Hired! game tests your understanding of chapter key terms in an interactive, timed simulation. In this simulation, you answer questions based on chapter content at a career fair, in an internship, and then in a job interview, to prove you are the right person for the job. If you answer questions incorrectly, the You're Hired! game allows you to repeat the level or to print a study guide to refine your answers for the time you play. To access You're Hired!, click the Activities and Tutorials link on the Computer Concepts CourseMate navigation menu and then click the You're Hired! link.

Prepare for your next quiz using the Quiz Yourself resource. The quizzes are grouped by chapter objectives. To begin a quiz, click the Quiz Yourself link on the Computer Concepts CourseMate navigation menu, click the desired objective groups on the Objectives tabs at the top of the screen, read the instructions, and then click the Start button. When you are finished taking the quiz, click the Done button and review your score and results. Results on the Quiz Summary screen are cross-referenced with the textbook and the Interactive eBook. If you have an incorrect answer, you can click the magnifying glass icon to the right of the answer to display the location of the correct answer in the textbook and the Interactive eBook (Figure 8).

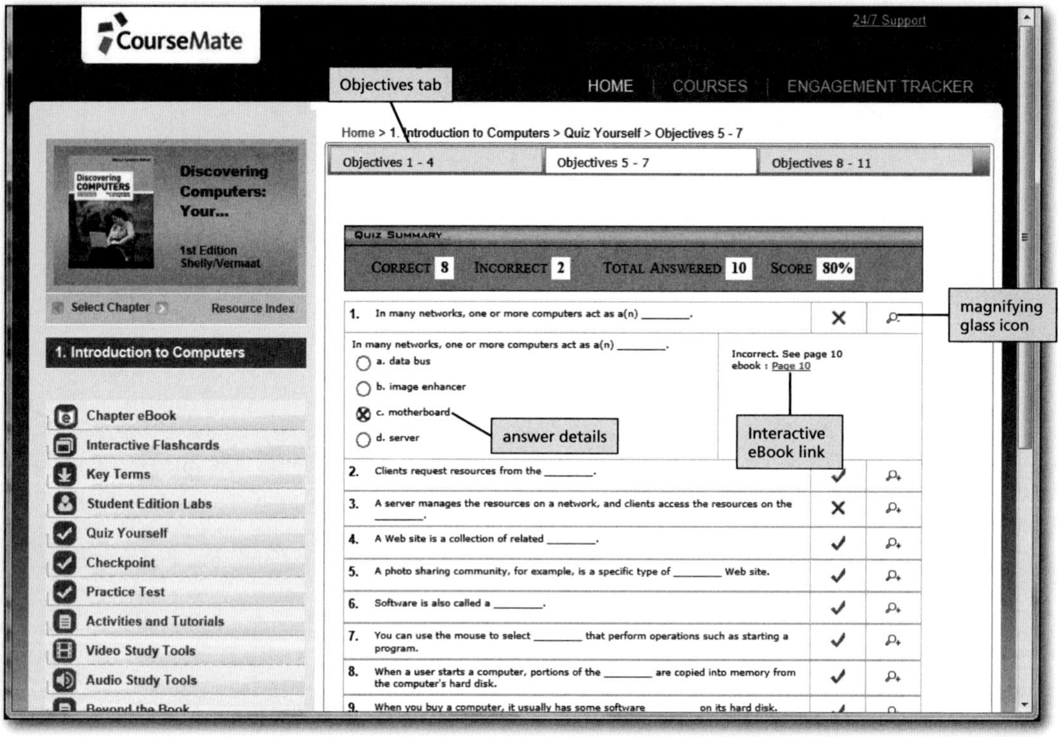

Figure 8

The Checkpoint resource checks your key term and chapter knowledge using matching, true/false, and multiple choice questions. When you click the Checkpoint link on the Computer Concepts CourseMate navigation menu, the first screen displays the Matching activity; to switch to True/False or Multiple Choice, click the desired name on the Checkpoint tabs at the top of the screen. Begin any of the activities by clicking the Start button. When you are finished with the activity, click the Done button, and review your results. Like the Quiz Yourself activity, you can cross-reference your responses using the magnifying glass icon.

The Practice Test is the most comprehensive tool to test your chapter knowledge (Figure 9). Because the Practice Test simulates a real test, it is an extremely important resource on Computer Concepts CourseMate. Click the Practice Test link on the Computer Concepts CourseMate navigation menu to begin the test. As with the other quizzes on Computer Concepts CourseMate, all answers are verified and your score appears after you click the Done button. All answers include a magnifying glass icon, which, when clicked, provides a cross-reference to the textbook and the Interactive eBook. In preparation for the best results on the real exam, try to achieve a 100 percent score on the Practice Test.

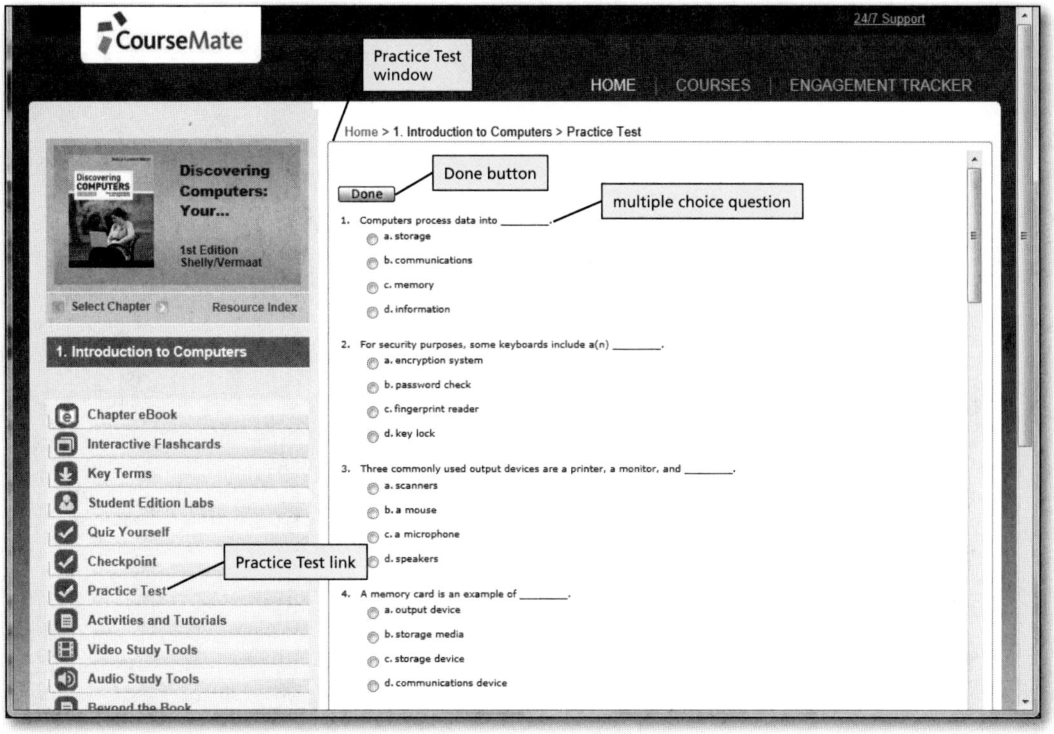

Figure 9

Enhanced Study Aids

Computer Concepts CourseMate includes both audio and video tools to further enhance your learning experience with the *Discovering Computers* textbook. The Video Study Tools, accessed from the Computer Concepts CourseMate navigation menu by clicking the Video Study Tools link, include these tools: You Review It, At the Movies, Learn How To, and Quiz: Learn How To. To use a particular tool, click its name on the Video Study Tools tabs at the top of the screen. The first three tools use videos, podcasts, or vodcasts of content related to the textbook; the Learn How To Quiz tests your knowledge of the material in the Learn How To video resource.

Sometimes, if you listen to text being read, you might absorb it into memory better than if you read it. For this reason, Computer Concepts CourseMate provides audio files of key terms and chapter content. To access these audio files, click the Audio Study Tools link on the Computer Concepts CourseMate navigation menu (Figure 10 on the next page). Audio tools are available for both the Chapter Review and the chapter key terms. Access each by clicking the respective resource name on the Audio Study Tools tabs at the top of the screen. Read the on-screen instructions, then download the audio files to a local computer or preferred portable media player, so that you can listen to the audio files offline.

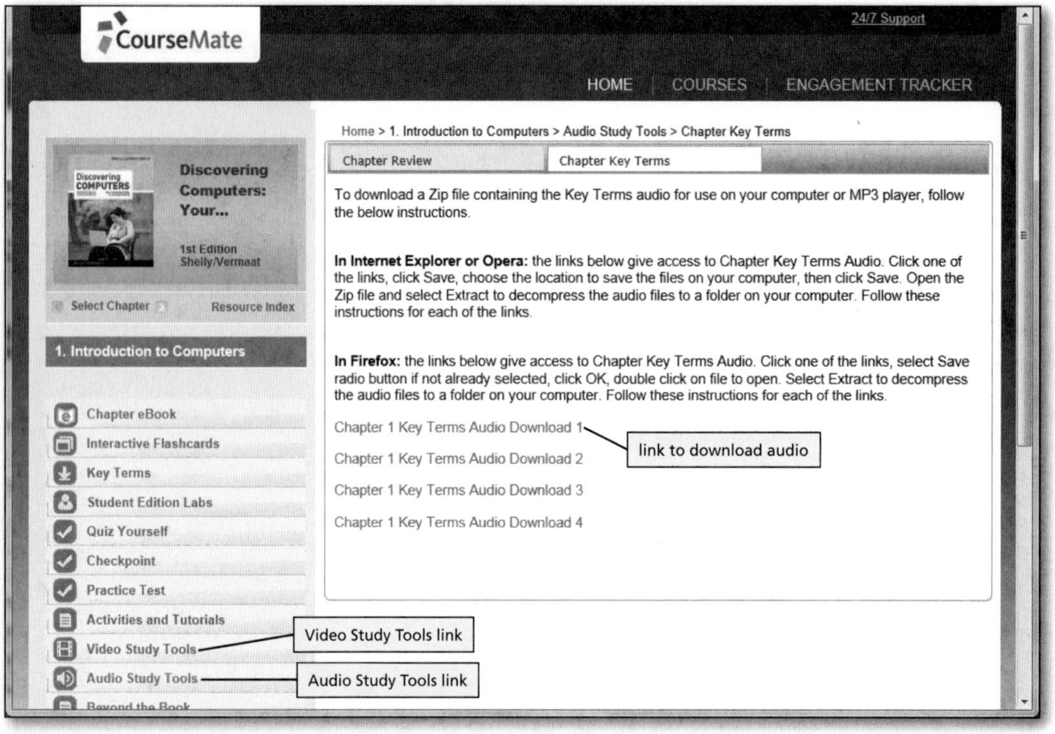

Figure 10

Explore Other Resources

Your *Discovering Computers* textbook presents a great wealth of information; Computer Concepts CourseMate expands on this information with the Beyond the Book and Ethics & Issues resources. Click the Beyond the Book link on the Computer Concepts CourseMate navigation menu to display a host of external links that are referenced throughout the chapter text. Click any link to explore resources outside of the Computer Concepts CourseMate interface. If you click Ethics & Issues on the Beyond the Book tabs at the top of the screen, text from all of the Ethics & Issues boxes in the chapter will be displayed in one convenient location. Learn, explore, and provide answers to various ethical questions pertaining to chapter topics.

Book-Level Resources at the bottom of the Computer Concepts CourseMate navigation menu include the following: Install Computer, Maintain Computer, Timeline, Buyer's Guide, Digital Forensics, Making Use of the Web, and Global Technology Watch (Figure 11). Each of these tools is designed to enhance your *Discovering Computers* experience by providing additional information or external, third-party links.

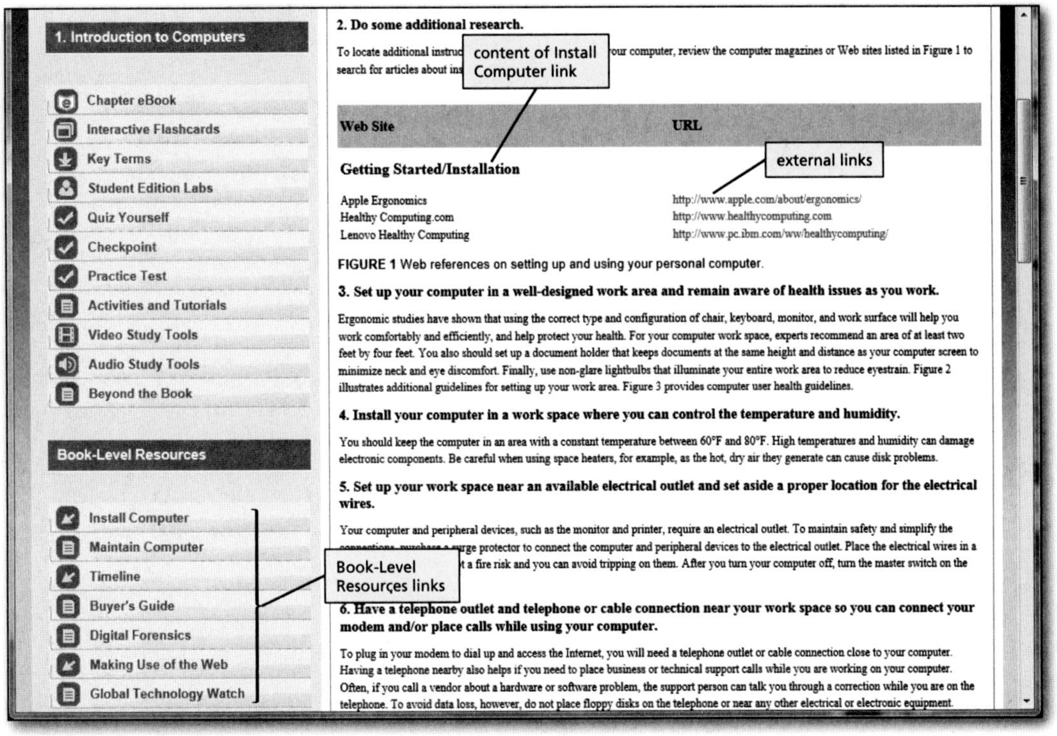

Figure 11

New Web Apps

New to Computer Concepts CourseMate for *Discovering Computers* are three Web applications (Web apps) that aid student comprehension of chapter material. These Web apps are available only via Computer Concepts CourseMate and are developed for use on smart phones, as well as on tablets, notebook computers, and desktop computers.

Improve retention of the chapter key terms with the Flashcard Web app. Study for an exam by reviewing major points in each chapter with the Study Guide Web app or with the Practice Test Web app that provides multiple choice questions.

Use the new Web apps as part of your overall *Discovering Computers* learning experience to help you succeed using *Discovering Computers*.

Summary

Computer Concepts CourseMate is designed for use as a companion to the *Discovering Computers: Your Interactive Guide to the Digital World* textbook. Conveniently organized in one location, all of the tools and resources in Computer Concepts CourseMate will help you learn. You can leave your book at home and use the Interactive eBook, study key terms, work on a simulated lab or explore other activities, download audio of key terms, watch a video related to the chapter text, take a practice quiz or exam, extend your learning experience outside of the book with external resources, and much more! Computer Concepts CourseMate is designed carefully to help you succeed using *Discovering Computers*.

WebTutor
Student Guide

WebTutor Student Guide

Objectives

You will have mastered the material in this guide when you can:

- Log in to Angel and Blackboard to access WebTutor content
- View Topic Reviews, PowerPoint Presentations, Practice Tests, and Topic Review Questions in Course Documents
- View Assignments
- Access and complete Assessments and Activities

Introduction

Welcome to the Discovering Computers 2012 Student Guide to WebTutor. The purpose of this guide is to orient you to the WebTutor online tools, which supplement the *Discovering Computers: Your Interactive Guide to the Digital World* textbooks. The WebTutor online materials will assist you with interactive ways of learning the material in your textbook.

Log in to Angel or Blackboard

You can access WebTutor via the Web applications Angel or Blackboard. In this section, you will log in to each of these applications.

Access WebTutor in Angel

Log in to Angel The following steps log in to Angel to access WebTutor.

- Start a Web browser, navigate to your school's Angel site, and then log in.
- Click the appropriate Discovering Computers ©2012 title in the Courses list to display information for the course in which you are enrolled (Figure 1).

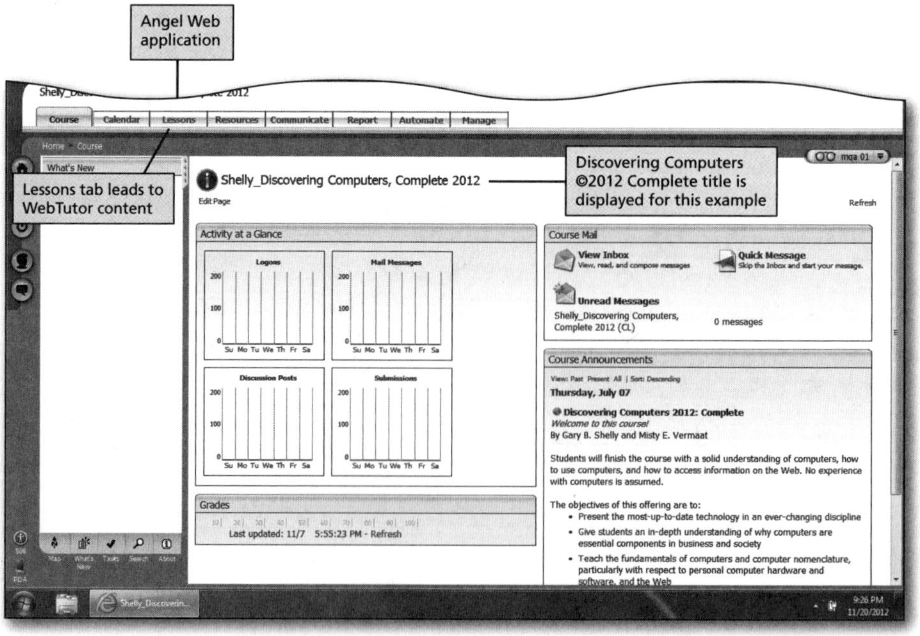

Figure 1

Access WebTutor in Blackboard

Log in to Blackboard The following steps log in to Blackboard to access WebTutor.

- Start a Web browser, navigate to your school's Blackboard site, and then log in.
- Click the Courses tab, if necessary, to view the course list.
- Click the appropriate Discovering Computers ©2012 title in the course list to display information for the course in which you are enrolled (Figure 2).

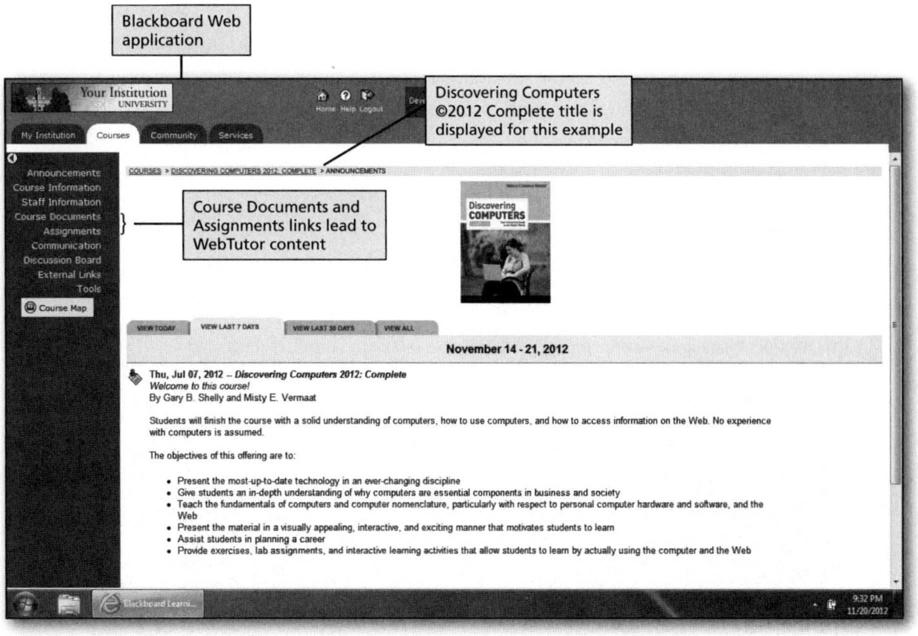

Figure 2

Course Documents

WebTutor contains course documents that reinforce the textbook content. The types of course documents are Topic Review, PowerPoint Presentations, Practice Test, and Topic Review Questions. In order to access course documents, log in to a WebTutor application (Angel or Blackboard) and then navigate to the course documents. Within the course documents are links to each chapter of the textbook. Click a chapter's link to display the list of WebTutor course documents for that chapter.

Topic Review

The WebTutor Topic Review is a course document that corresponds to the textbook's Chapter Review, which is located in the Student Assignments section of each chapter. Figure 3 shows a sample WebTutor Topic Review course document in Angel and Blackboard. Each link in the Topic Review corresponds to one of the statements or questions in bold in the textbook's Chapter Review. After thinking about the instruction and your response, click the corresponding link to view the answer, which also is located in the Chapter Review in the textbook. Table 1 shows the click path to the WebTutor Topic Review in each application.

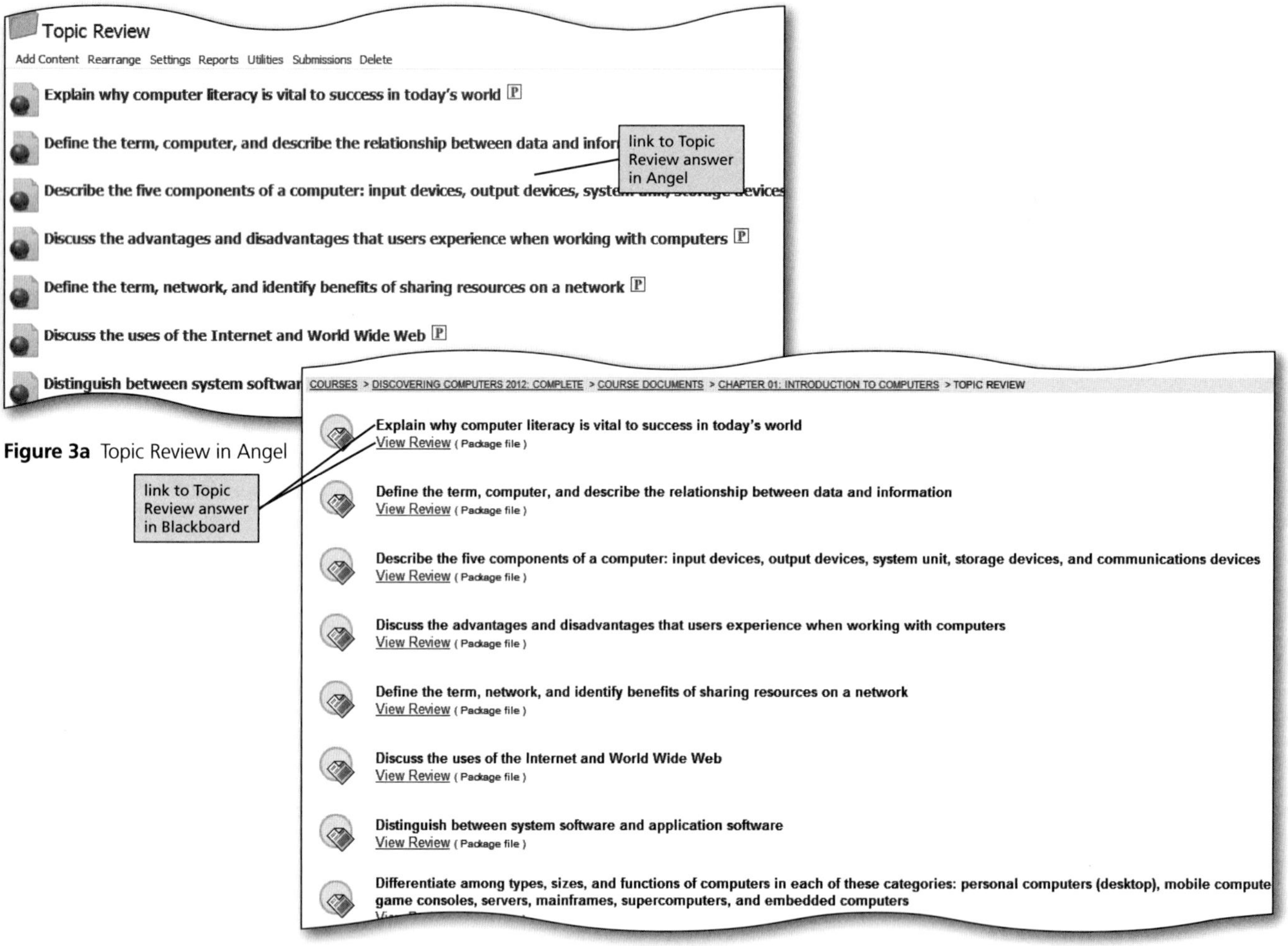

Figure 3a Topic Review in Angel

Figure 3b Topic Review in Blackboard

Figure 3

Table 1 Topic Review Click Path (substitute the chapter number in place of the * in the path)	
WEB APPLICATION	PATH
Angel	Lessons tab > Course Documents > Chapter * > Topic Review
Blackboard	Courses tab > Course Documents > Chapter * > Topic Review

PowerPoint Presentations

WebTutor contains PowerPoint presentations to reinforce the textbook content. Each PowerPoint presentation shows a high-level overview of the textbook chapter's contents. The presentations begin with the same image contained on the textbook chapter's first page, and the slides highlight key terms and figures in the chapter. The slides also contain graphical representations of lists of important information to remember. For example, Figure 4 shows slides from the presentation for Chapter 1 of the Discovering Computers 2012 Complete textbook. On the PowerPoint Presentations in each WebTutor application, you either can view a presentation online in a browser or download the presentation. Table 2 shows the click path to the WebTutor PowerPoint Presentations in each application.

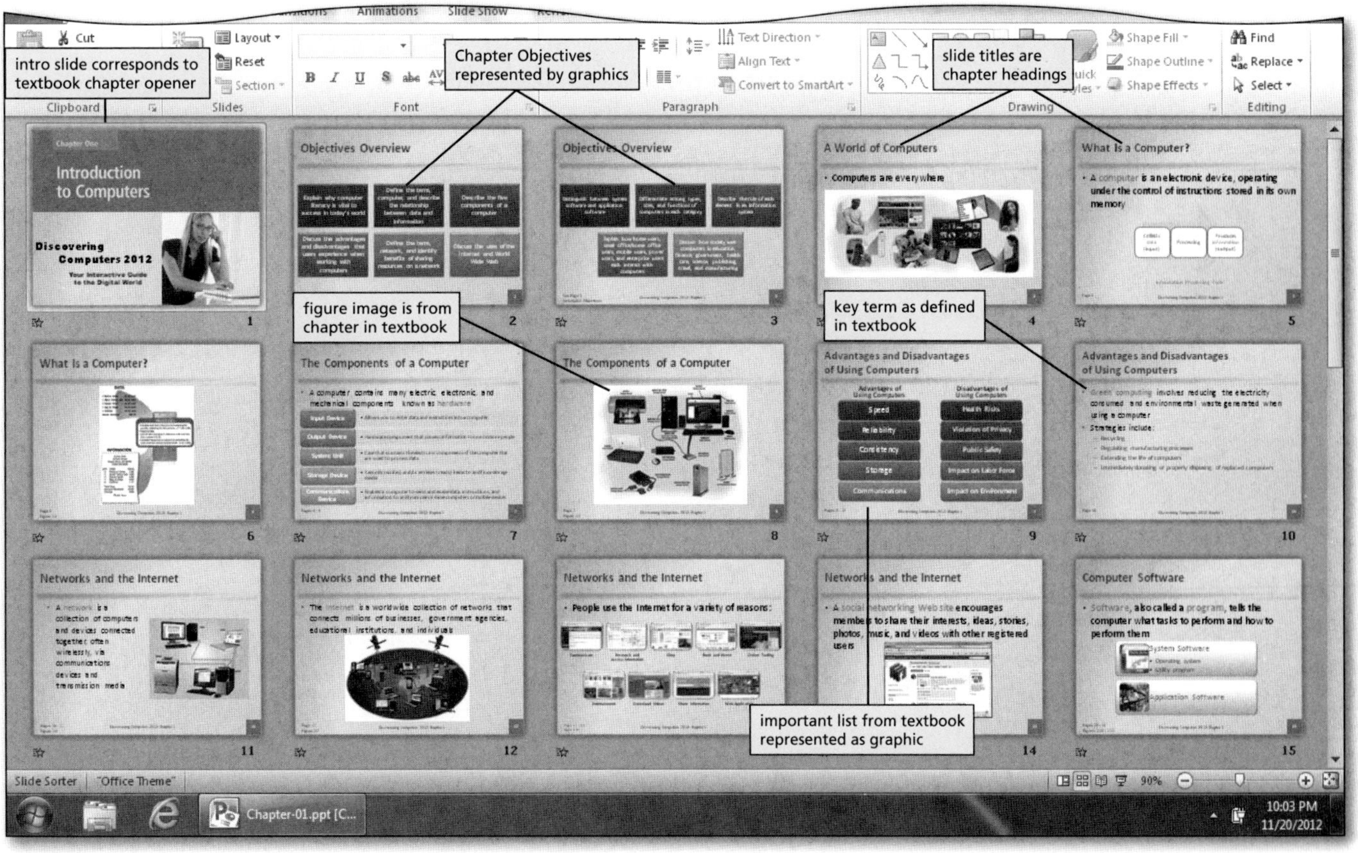

Figure 4

Table 2 PowerPoint Presentations Click Path (substitute the chapter number in place of the * in the path)	
WEB APPLICATION	PATH
Angel	Lessons tab > Course Documents > Chapter * > PowerPoint Presentations
Blackboard	Courses tab > Course Documents > Chapter * > PowerPoint Presentations

Practice Test

The WebTutor Practice Test is a course document that presents an extensive online test, which you can use to practice answering questions about the material covered in a chapter (Figure 5). Because the Practice Test is not printed in the textbook, you will find this tool useful in studying for your exams. The content for the questions is taken from the textbook and will reinforce the information. Also, practicing answering the questions will help prepare you for answering exam questions.

When you have completed a Practice Test, you can submit it for a grade. If desired, you can retake the test to improve your grade; only the latest grade is recorded in the online grade book. The test likely will include multiple choice, true/false, completion, matching, and/or essay questions. Table 3 shows the click path to the WebTutor Practice Test in each application.

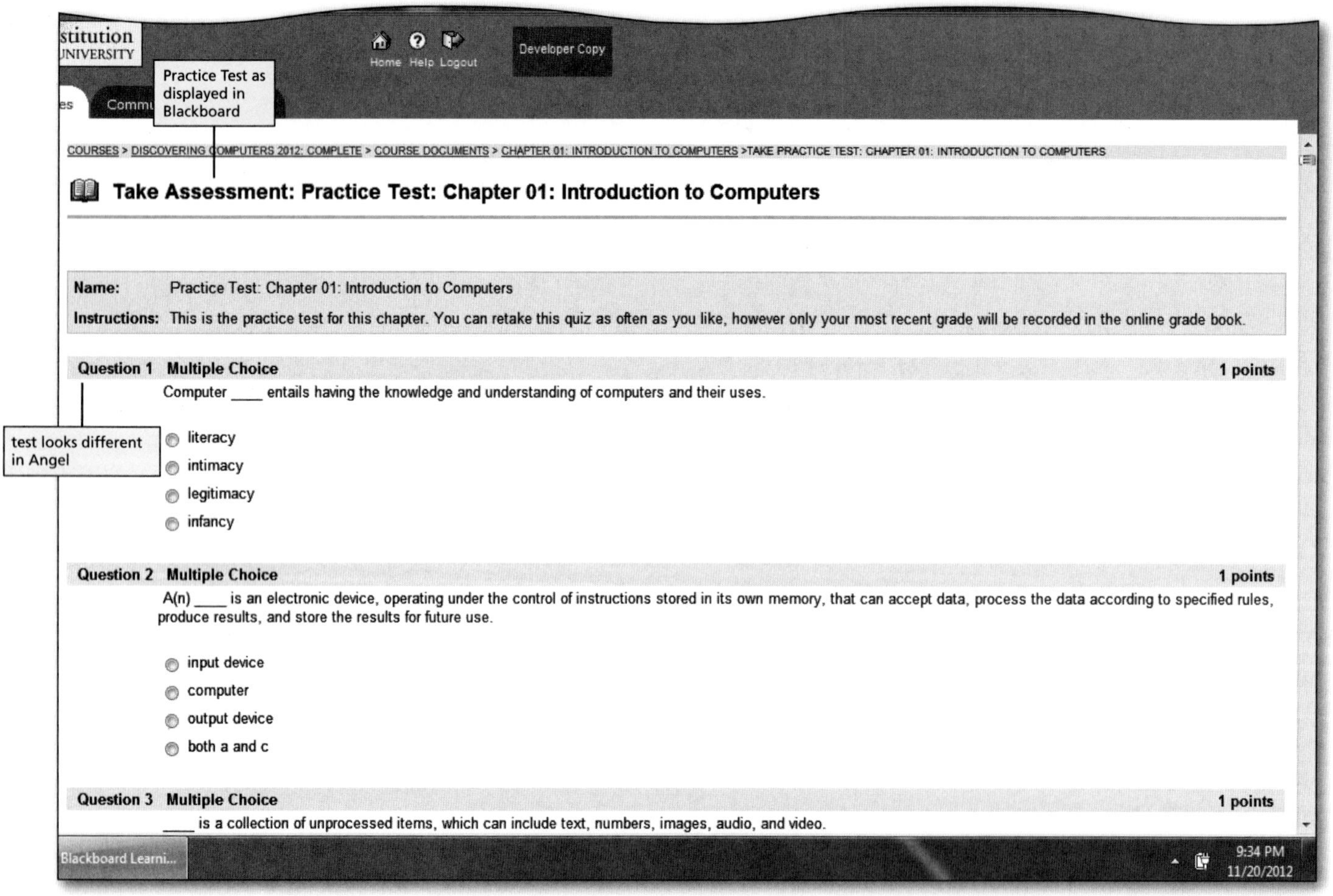

Figure 5

Table 3 Practice Test Click Path (substitute the chapter number in place of the * in the path)

WEB APPLICATION	PATH
Angel	Lessons tab > Quizzes > Practice Test: Chapter *
	Lessons tab > Question Banks > Practice Test: Chapter *
Blackboard	Courses tab > Course Documents > Chapter * > Practice Test

Topic Review Questions

The Topic Review Questions are an abbreviated version of the Practice Tests that you can use to practice answering possible test questions about the material covered in the chapter (Figure 6). Like the Practice Test, the Topic Review Questions are not located in the textbook. Topic Review Questions can be used as a quick self-assessment tool to gauge how well you know the textbook chapter's material. As with the Practice Test, practicing answering the questions will help prepare you for answering exam questions.

After completing the quiz, you can submit it for a grade. If desired, you can retake the quiz to improve your grade; only the latest grade is recorded in the online grade book. This short quiz could include true/false, multiple choice, and completion questions. Table 4 shows the click path to the WebTutor Topic Review Questions in each application.

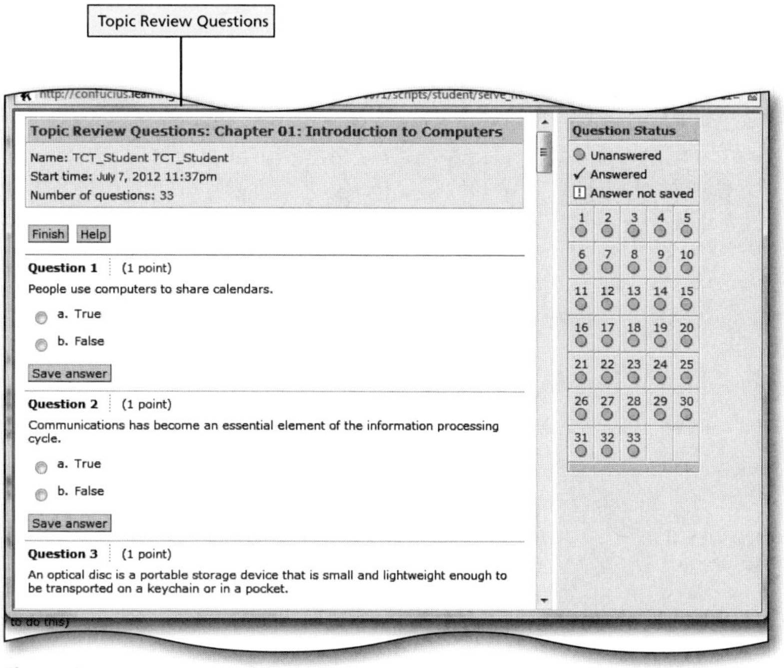

Figure 6

Table 4 Topic Review Questions Click Path (substitute the chapter number in place of the * in the path)

WEB APPLICATION	PATH
Angel	Lessons tab > Quizzes > Topic Review Questions: Chapter *
	Lessons tab > Question Banks > Topic Review Questions: Chapter *
Blackboard	Courses tab > Course Documents > Chapter * > Topic Review Questions

Assignments

Assignments in WebTutor are additional materials designed to enhance your understanding of the information in the textbook. The content of the assignments varies by title and chapter and includes an assignment topic that links to a suggested exercise (Figure 7a). When you click a link, the suggested exercise will appear (Figure 7b). Your instructor may assign the essay to you, or you may choose to complete an assignment to better understand topics in the textbook. Table 5 shows the click path to the WebTutor Assignments in each application.

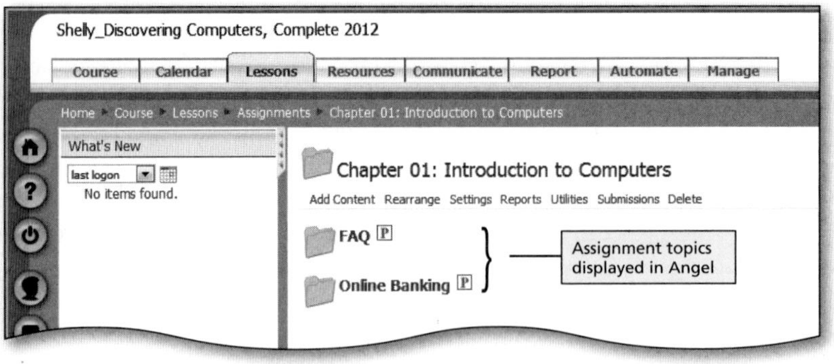

Figure 7a Assignment Topics

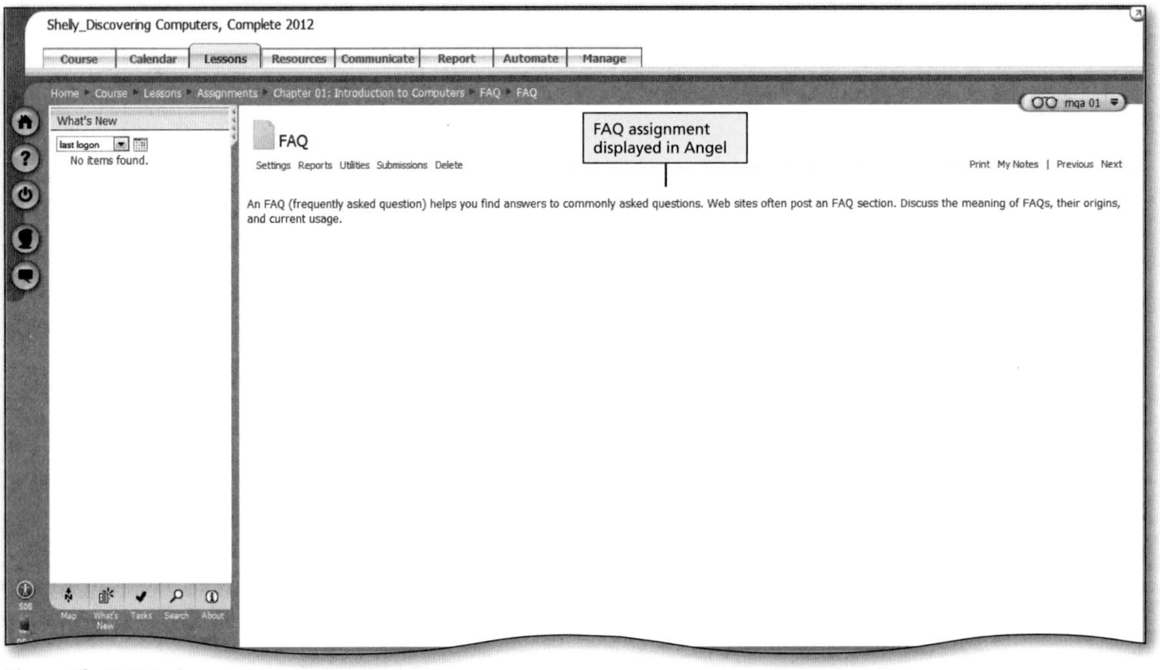

Figure 7b FAQ Assignment

Figure 7

Table 5 Assignments Click Path (substitute the chapter number in place of the * in the path)

WEB APPLICATION	PATH
Angel	Lessons tab > Assignments > Chapter *
Blackboard	Courses tab > Assignments > Chapter *

Summary

The WebTutor online course documents — Topic Reviews, PowerPoint Presentations, Practice Tests, and Topic Review Questions, and Assignments — reinforce the information in the Discovering Computers ©2012 textbooks. You can access the WebTutor online tools using the Angel or Blackboard Web applications.

Discovering COMPUTERS

Your Interactive Guide to the Digital World

BRIEF

Gary B. Shelly
Misty E. Vermaat

Contributing Authors
Jeffrey J. Quasney
Susan L. Sebok
Steven M. Freund

Shelly Cashman Series®
A part of Course Technology, Cengage Learning

COURSE TECHNOLOGY
CENGAGE Learning™

Australia • Brazil • Japan • Korea • Mexico • Singapore • Spain • United Kingdom • United States

COURSE TECHNOLOGY
CENGAGE Learning

Discovering Computers: Your Interactive Guide to the Digital World, Brief
Gary B. Shelly
Misty E. Vermaat

Vice President, Publisher: Nicole Pinard
Executive Editor: Kathleen McMahon
Associate Acquisitions Editor: Reed Curry
Associate Product Manager: Aimee Poirier
Editorial Assistant: Angela Giannopoulos
Director of Marketing: Elisa Roberts
Marketing Manager: Tristen Kendall
Marketing Coordinator: Adrienne Fung
Print Buyer: Julio Esperas
Content Project Manager: Matthew Hutchinson
Researcher: F. William Vermaat
Development Editor: Lyn Markowicz
Management Services: PreMediaGlobal
Interior Designer: Joel Sadagursky
Art Director: Marissa Falco
Text Design: Joel Sadagursky
Cover Design: Curio Press
Cover Photos: Tom Kates Photography
Illustrator: PreMediaGlobal
Compositor: PreMediaGlobal
Printer: RRD Menasha

Library of Congress Control Number: 2010943260

ISBN-13: 978-1-111-53047-1

ISBN-10: 1-111-53047-5

Course Technology
20 Channel Center Street
Boston, MA 02210
USA

Cengage Learning is a leading provider of customized learning solutions with office locations around the globe, including Singapore, the United Kingdom, Australia, Mexico, Brazil and Japan. Locate your local office at: **international.cengage.com/region**

Cengage Learning products are represented in Canada by Nelson Education, Ltd.

Visit our Web site **www.cengage.com/ct/shellycashman** to share and gain ideas on our textbooks!

To learn more about Course Technology, visit **www.cengage.com/coursetechnology**

Purchase any of our products at your local college bookstore or at our preferred online store at **www.cengagebrain.com**

Printed in the United States of America
3 4 5 6 17 16 15 14 13 12

Discovering Computers Brief

Your Interactive Guide to the Digital World

Table of Contents at a Glance

Table of Contents

CHAPTER 1

Introduction to Computers 2

Special Feature

CHAPTER 2

The Internet and World Wide Web 72

Table of Boxed Elements

ETHICS & ISSUES

FAQs

INNOVATIVE COMPUTING

LOOKING AHEAD

Preface

The Shelly Cashman Series® offers the finest textbooks in computer education. We are proud of the fact that the previous sixteen editions of this textbook have been the most widely used in computer education. With this edition of *Discovering Computers,* we have implemented significant improvements based on current computer trends and comments made by instructors and students, and are introducing an interactive, multi-media e-book and CourseMate Web site. *Discovering Computers: Your Interactive Guide to the Digital World* continues with the innovation, quality, and reliability you have come to expect from the Shelly Cashman Series.

In *Discovering Computers: Your Interactive Guide to the Digital World,* you will find an educationally sound, highly visual, interactive, and easy-to-follow pedagogy that, with the help of animated figures, relevant video, and interactive activities in the e-book, presents an in-depth treatment of introductory computer subjects. Students will finish the course with a solid understanding of computers, how to use computers, and how to access information on the Web.

Objectives of this Text, e-Book, and CourseMate Web Site

Discovering Computers: Your Interactive Guide to the Digital World, Brief is intended for use as a stand-alone solution or in combination with an applications, Internet, or programming textbook in a full-semester introductory computer course. No experience with computers is assumed. The objectives of this offering are to:

- Present the most-up-to-date technology in an ever-changing discipline
- Give students an in-depth understanding of why computers are essential components in business and society
- Teach the fundamentals of computers and computer nomenclature, particularly with respect to personal computer hardware and software, and the Web
- Present the material in a visually appealing, interactive, and exciting manner that motivates students to learn
- Assist students in planning a career
- Provide exercises, lab assignments, and interactive learning activities that allow students to learn by actually using the computer and the Web

Hallmarks of Discovering Computers

To date, more than six million students have learned about computers using *Discovering Computers*. With the Web integration and interactivity, streaming up-to-date audio and video, extraordinary step-by-step visual drawings and photographs, unparalleled currency, and the Shelly and Cashman touch, this book will make your computer concepts course exciting and dynamic. Hallmarks of Shelly Cashman Series *Discovering Computers* include:

A Proven Pedagogy

Careful explanations of complex concepts, educationally-sound elements, and reinforcement highlight this proven method of presentation.

A Visually Appealing Book that Maintains Student Interest

The latest technology, pictures, drawings, and text are combined artfully to produce a visually appealing and easy-to-understand book. Many of the figures include a step-by-step presentation (see page 145), which simplifies the more complex computer concepts. Pictures and drawings reflect the latest trends in computer technology. This combination of pictures, step-by-step drawings, and easy-to-read text layout sets the standard for computer textbook design.

- Present strategies for purchasing a desktop computer, a notebook computer, a Tablet PC, and personal mobile devices
- Provide alternative learning techniques and reinforcement via the Web
- Offer distance-education providers a textbook with a meaningful and exercise-rich digital learning experience

Distinguishing Features

Discovering Computers: Your Interactive Guide to the Digital World includes a variety of compelling features, certain to engage and challenge students, making learning with *Discovering Computers* an enriched experience. These compelling features include:

- Multi-media rich and interactive e-book and CourseMate Web site that engage students in learning about computer concepts.
- Animations, relevant and timely video, interactive in-chapter activities and Quiz Yourself reinforcement exercises embedded in the e-book, combined with the integration of interactive activities, videos, and end-of-chapter student assignments on the CourseMate Web site offer students an exceptional learning solution.
- Digital Communications and Buyer's Guide features introduce and familiarize students with new and developing technology, making the technology accessible for introductory students.
- Innovative Computing, FAQ and Ethics & Issues boxes, Companies on the Cutting Edge, Technology Trailblazers, and High-Tech Talk articles enable relevant classroom discussion.

Latest Technologies and Terms

The technologies and terms your students see in *Discovering Computers* are those they will encounter when they start using computers. Only the latest application software is shown throughout the book.

Web Integrated

This book uses the Web as a major learning tool. The purpose of integrating the Web into the book is to (1) offer students additional information and currency on important topics; (2) use its interactive capabilities to offer creative reinforcement and online quizzes; (3) make available alternative learning techniques with Web-based learning games, practice tests, and interactive labs; (4) underscore the relevance of the Web as a basic information tool that can be used in all facets of society; (5) introduce students to doing research on the Web; and (6) offer instructors the opportunity to organize and administer their traditional campus-based or distance-education-based courses on the Web using various learning management systems.

Extensive End-of-Chapter Student Assignments

A notable strength of *Discovering Computers* is the extensive student assignments and activities at the end of each chapter. Well-structured student assignments can make the difference between students merely participating in a class and students retaining the information they learn. The student assignments in *Discovering Computers: Your Interactive Guide to the Digital World* include: Chapter Review, Key Terms, Checkpoint, Problem Solving @ Home, Problem Solving @ Work, Learn It Online, Learn How To, Web Research, and Critical Thinking. The Problem Solving and Critical Thinking student assignments also include Collaboration exercises, encouraging team work amongst students.

Instructor Resources

The Instructor Resources include both teaching and testing aids.

Instructor's Manual Includes lecture notes summarizing the chapter sections, figures and boxed elements found in every chapter, teacher tips, classroom activities, lab activities, and quick quizzes in Microsoft Word files.

Syllabus Easily customizable sample syllabi that cover policies, assignments, exams, and other course information.

Figure Files Illustrations for every figure in the textbook in electronic form. Figures are provided both with and without callouts.

Solutions to Exercises Includes solutions for all end-of-chapter student assignments. Also includes Tip Sheets, which are suggested starting points for the Problem Solving exercises.

PowerPoint Presentations — Course Presenter A one-click-per-slide presentation system that provides PowerPoint slides for every subject in each chapter. Several brand new computer-related video clips are available for optional presentation. Course Presenter provides consistent coverage for multiple lecturers.

Test Bank & Test Engine Test Banks include 220 questions for every chapter, featuring objective-based and critical thinking question types, and including page number references and figure references, when appropriate. Also included is the test engine, ExamView, the ultimate tool for your objective-based testing needs.

Printed Test Bank A Rich Text Format (.rtf) version of the test bank that you can print.

Test Out/Final Exam Objective-based exam that can be used to test students out of your course, or as a final examination. Includes a master answer sheet.

Pretest/Posttest Carefully prepared tests that can be used at the beginning and the end of the semester to measure student progress. Includes master answer sheet.

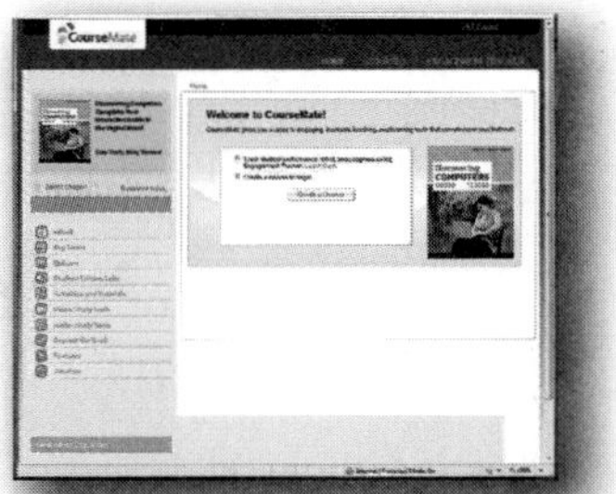

NEW! Computer Concepts CourseMate

The new Computer Concepts CourseMate for *Discovering Computers* is the most expansive digital site for any computer concepts text in the market today! The content in the CourseMate solution is integrated into each page of the text, giving students easy access to current information on important topics, reinforcements activities, and alternative learning techniques. Integrating the Computer Concepts CourseMate into the classroom keeps today's students engaged and involved in the learning experience.

The Computer Concepts CourseMate includes an integrated, multi-media rich and interactive digital book, and a variety of interactive Quizzes and Learning Games, Exercises, Web Links, Videos, and other features that specifically reinforce and build on the concepts presented in the chapter. These interactive activities are tracked within the CourseMate EngagementTracker, making it easy to assess students' retention of concepts. This digital solution encourages students to take learning into their own hands and explore related content on their own to learn even more about subjects in which they are especially interested.

All of these resources on the Computer Concepts CourseMate for *Discovering Computers* enable students to get more comfortable using technology and help prepare students to use the Internet as a tool to enrich their lives.

Contact Us

Colleges, Universities, Continuing Education Departments, Post-Secondary Vocational Schools, Career Colleges, Business, Industry, Government, Trade, Retailer, Wholesaler, Library, and Resellers
Call Cengage Learning at 800-354-9706

K-12 Schools, Secondary Vocational Schools, Adult Education, and School Districts
Call Cengage Learning at 800-354-9706

In Canada
Call Nelson Cengage Learning at 800-268-2222

Anywhere
www.cengage.com/coursetechnology

Visual Walkthrough of the Book

Current. Relevant. Innovative.
Teaching the Significance of Today's Digital World.

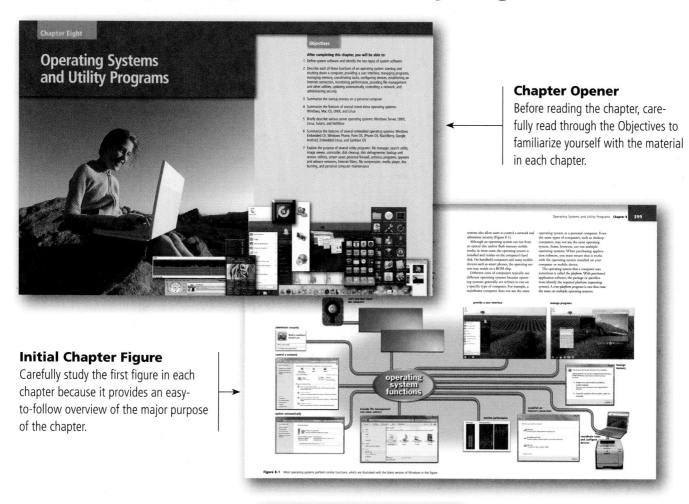

Chapter Opener
Before reading the chapter, carefully read through the Objectives to familiarize yourself with the material in each chapter.

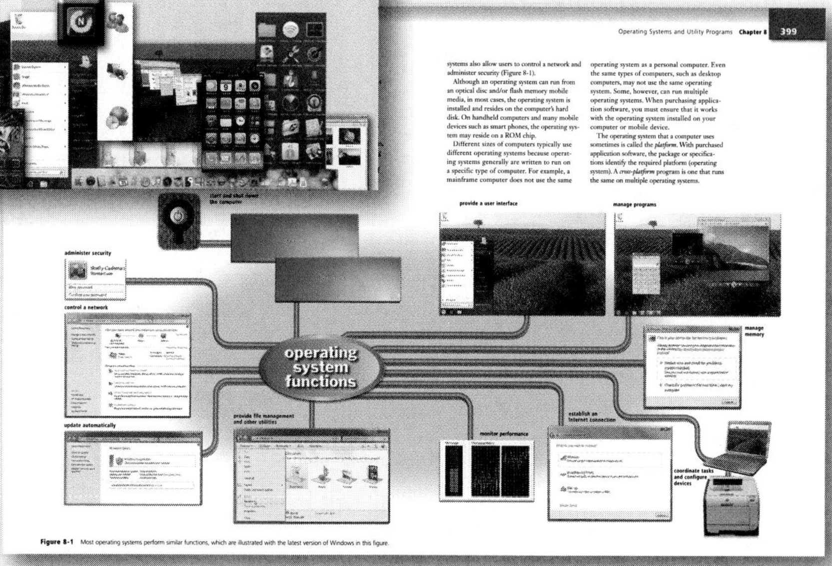

Initial Chapter Figure
Carefully study the first figure in each chapter because it provides an easy-to-follow overview of the major purpose of the chapter.

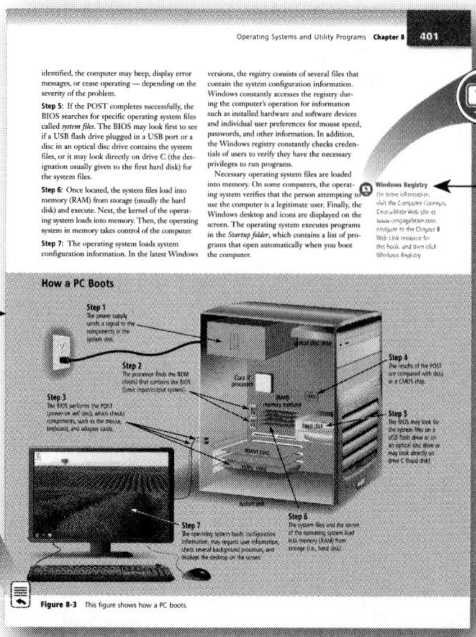

CourseMate Icon
Visit the Computer Concepts CourseMate Web site for access to many of the interactive chapter elements.

Step Figures
Each chapter includes numerous step figures that present the more complex computer concepts using a step-by-step pedagogy.

Web Links
Obtain current information and a different perspective about key terms and concepts by visiting the Web Links found in the margins throughout the book.

Interactive e-Book Activity Icon
Several elements in each chapter are interactive learning activities in the e-book and are identified by this icon.

FAQs

FAQ (frequently asked questions) boxes offer common questions and answers about subjects related to the topic at hand.

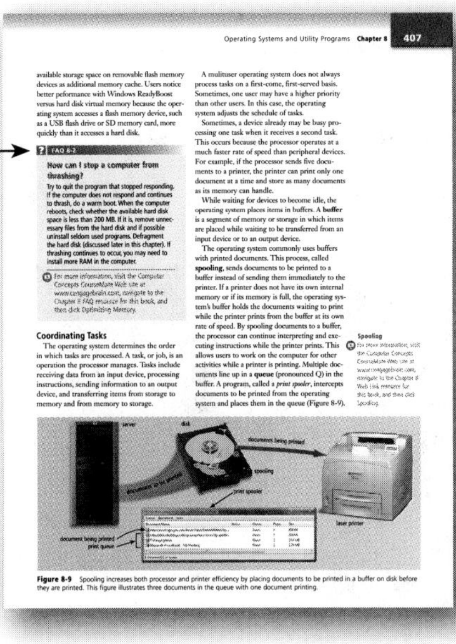

Quiz Yourself

Three Quiz Yourself boxes per chapter help ensure retention by reinforcing sections of the chapter material, rather than waiting for the end of chapter to test. Use Appendix A for a quick check of the answers, and access additional Quiz Yourself quizzes via the Computer Concepts CourseMate Web site for interactivity and easy use.

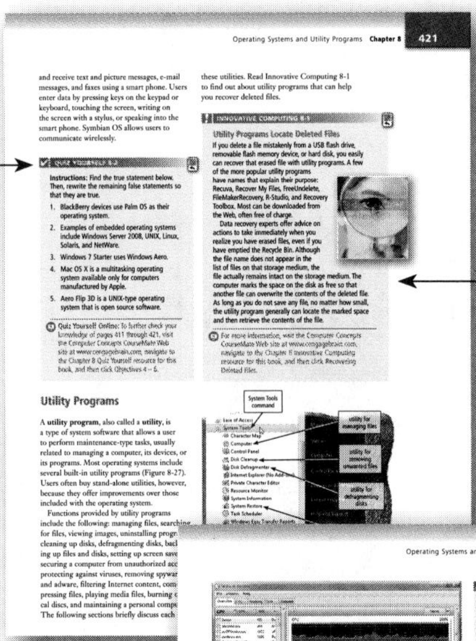

Innovative Computing

Discover different and innovative ways of using various technologies and learn how computing is applied creatively to solve problems.

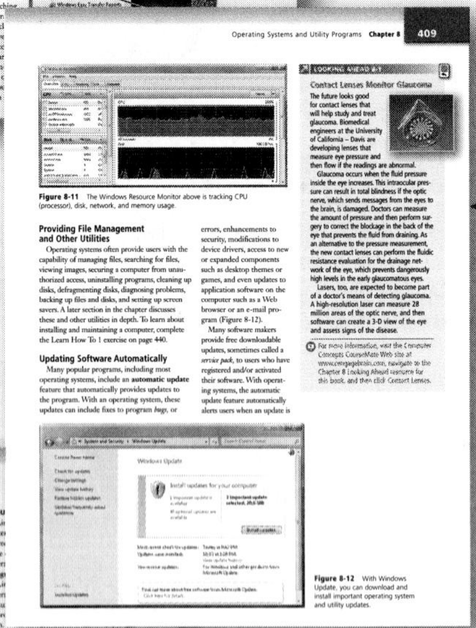

Looking Ahead

The Looking Ahead boxes offer a glimpse of the latest advances in computer technology that will be available, usually within five years.

Ethics & Issues

Ethics & Issues boxes raise controversial, computer-related topics of the day, challenging readers to consider closely general concerns of computers in society.

Computer Usage @ Work

Learn about how computers are used in fifteen different professional industries, including transportation, hospitality, education, sports, and construction.

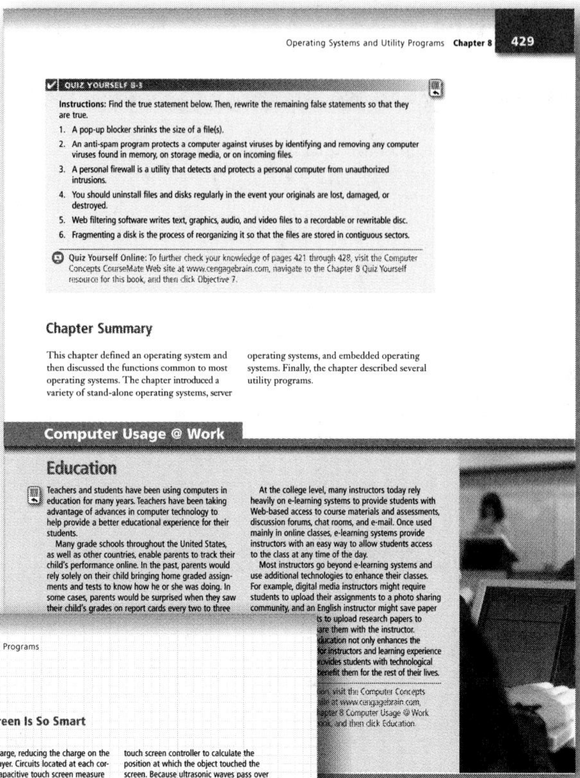

Operating Systems and Utility Programs **Chapter 8** 429

QUIZ YOURSELF 8-3

Instructions: Find the true statement below. Then, rewrite the remaining false statements so that they are true.

1. A pop-up blocker shrinks the size of a file(s).
2. An anti-spam program protects a computer against viruses by identifying and removing any computer viruses found in memory, on storage media, or on incoming files.
3. A personal firewall is a utility that detects and protects a personal computer from unauthorized intrusions.
4. You should uninstall files and disks regularly in the event your originals are lost, damaged, or destroyed.
5. Web filtering software writes text, graphics, audio, and video files to a recordable or rewritable disc.
6. Fragmenting a disk is the process of reorganizing it so that the files are stored in contiguous sectors.

Quiz Yourself Online: To further check your knowledge of pages 421 through 428, visit the Computer Concepts CourseMate Web site at www.cengagebrain.com, navigate to the Chapter 8 Quiz Yourself resource for this book, and then click Objective 7.

Chapter Summary

This chapter defined an operating system and then discussed the functions common to most operating systems. The chapter introduced a variety of stand-alone operating systems, server operating systems, and embedded operating systems. Finally, the chapter described several utility programs.

Computer Usage @ Work

Education

Teachers and students have been using computers in education for many years. Teachers have been taking advantage of advances in computer technology to help provide a better educational experience for their students.

Many grade schools throughout the United States, as well as other countries, enable parents to track their child's performance online. In the past, parents would rely solely on their child bringing home graded assignments and tests to know how he or she was doing. In some cases, parents would be surprised when they saw their child's grades on report cards every two to three

At the college level, many instructors today rely heavily on e-learning systems to provide students with Web-based access to course materials and assessments, discussion forums, chat rooms, and e-mail. Once used mainly in online classes, e-learning systems provide instructors with an easy way to allow students access to the class at any time of the day.

Most instructors go beyond e-learning systems and use additional technologies to enhance their classes. For example, digital media instructors might require students to upload their assignments to a photo sharing community, and an English instructor might save paper

High-Tech Talk

The High-Tech Talk article at the end of each chapter expands on a topic covered in the chapter and presents a more technical discussion.

430 **Chapter 8** Operating Systems and Utility Programs

High-Tech Talk

Touch Screen Technology: How the Screen Is So Smart

Touch screen technology is becoming a larger part of everyday life for many individuals. As presented in Chapter 5, a touch screen is a touch-sensitive display device that users can interact with by touching areas of the screen. People have been using touch screens for more than 30 years, and this technology now is being used in more places, such as in smart phones, point-of-sale terminals, automated teller machines, remote controls, GPS receivers, home security systems, and Tablet PCs.

Touch screen technology has evolved since its creation in the late 1960s. The first touch screens developed allowed users to press only one area at a time with the tip of their finger, and they were much less accurate than today's touch screens. As the technology is advancing, users are able to perform additional tasks, such as dragging their finger across the screen and touching more than one area of the screen at a time. For example, the iPhone and iPod touch allow you to zoom in pictures or other objects on the screen by placing two fingers close together on the screen, and then slowly moving them apart. Three types of touch screens most in use today are capacitive, resistive,

electrical charge, reducing the charge on the capacitive layer. Circuits located at each corner of the capacitive touch screen measure the change in electrical charge. The circuits then send this data to the touch screen controller, or software that is running on the computer. The controller then uses the data to calculate the location where the finger is touching the screen. Capacitive touch screens typically are high-quality and unaffected by items that do not conduct electrical charges. An example of the components of a capacitive touch screen is shown in Figure 8-41.

The second type of touch screen is a resistive touch screen. A metallic conductive and resistive layer held apart by spacers cover a *resistive touch screen*. When a user touches a resistive touch screen, the conductive and resistive layers connect in the location of the touch. An electronic current runs between the two layers, and the interruption in the current enables the touch screen controller to calculate the exact location of the touch. Although resistive touch screens usually are more affordable than capacitive touch screens, they are not as clear and can be damaged more easily.

The third type of touch screen uses surface wave technology. *Surface wave technology* passes ultrasonic waves over the touch screen. Touching the screen absorbs portions of the waves, which then allows the touch screen controller to calculate the position at which the object touched the screen. Because ultrasonic waves pass over the touch screen, it is easy for outside elements to damage the device. Touch screens using surface wave technology are the most advanced and often the most expensive of the three types.

Additional types of touch screen technologies exist, but they are not used as widely as the capacitive, resistive, and surface wave touch screens. *Optical touch screens* use cameras mounted at two corners of the screen to detect objects close to the surface. *Infrared touch screens* use light emitting diodes and light detectors at the edges of the touch screen to detect objects that break the beams of light traveling across the screen.

As touch screen prices continue to decrease, they most likely will be incorporated in an increasing number of computers and devices. Touch screens have increased productivity by allowing people to interact with devices more quickly than they can with a mouse or keyboard.

For more information, visit the Computer Concepts CourseMate Web site at www.cengagebrain.com, navigate to the Chapter 8 High-Tech Talk resource for this book, and then click Touch Screen Technology.

capacitive touch screen identifies where someone touches the screen by
nces in electrical charges.

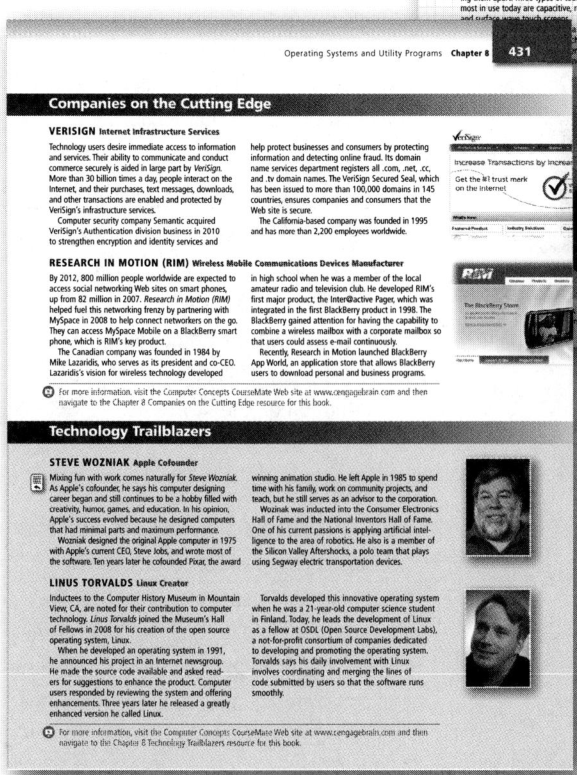

Operating Systems and Utility Programs **Chapter 8** 431

Companies on the Cutting Edge

VERISIGN Internet Infrastructure Services

Technology users desire immediate access to information and services. Their ability to communicate and conduct commerce securely is aided in large part by *VeriSign*. More than 30 billion times a day, people interact on the Internet, and their purchases, text messages, downloads, and other transactions are enabled and protected by VeriSign's infrastructure services.

Computer security company Semantic acquired VeriSign's Authentication division business in 2010 to strengthen encryption and identity services and help protect businesses and consumers by protecting information and detecting online fraud. Its domain name services department registers all .com, .net, .cc, and .tv domain names. The VeriSign Secured Seal, which has been issued to more than 100,000 domains in 145 countries, ensures companies and consumers that the Web site is secure.

The California-based company was founded in 1995 and has more than 2,200 employees worldwide.

RESEARCH IN MOTION (RIM) Wireless Mobile Communications Devices Manufacturer

By 2012, 800 million people worldwide are expected to access social networking Web sites on smart phones, up from 82 million in 2007. *Research in Motion (RIM)* helped fuel this networking frenzy by partnering with MySpace in 2008 to help connect networkers on the go. They can access MySpace Mobile on a BlackBerry smart phone, which is RIM's key product.

The Canadian company was founded in 1984 by Mike Lazaridis, who serves as its president and co-CEO. Lazaridis's vision for wireless technology developed in high school when he was a member of the local amateur radio and television club. He developed RIM's first major product, the Inter@active Pager, which was integrated in the first BlackBerry product in 1998. The BlackBerry gained attention for having the capability to combine a wireless mailbox with a corporate mailbox so that users could assess e-mail continuously.

Recently, Research in Motion launched BlackBerry App World, an application store that allows BlackBerry users to download personal and business programs.

For more information, visit the Computer Concepts CourseMate Web site at www.cengagebrain.com and then navigate to the Chapter 8 Companies on the Cutting Edge resource for this book.

Technology Trailblazers

STEVE WOZNIAK Apple Cofounder

Mixing fun with work comes naturally for *Steve Wozniak*. As Apple's cofounder, he says his computer designing career began and still continues to be a hobby filled with creativity, humor, games, and education. In his opinion, Apple's success evolved because he designed computers that had minimal parts and maximum performance.

Wozniak designed the original Apple computer in 1975 with Apple's current CEO, Steve Jobs, and wrote most of the software. Ten years later he cofounded Pixar, the award winning animation studio. He left Apple in 1985 to spend time with his family, work on community projects, and teach, but he still serves as an advisor to the corporation.

Wozinak was inducted into the Consumer Electronics Hall of Fame and the National Inventors Hall of Fame. One of his current passions is applying artificial intelligence to the area of robotics. He also is a member of the Silicon Valley Aftershocks, a polo team that plays using Segway electric transportation devices.

LINUS TORVALDS Linux Creator

Inductees to the Computer History Museum in Mountain View, CA, are noted for their contribution to computer technology. *Linus Torvalds* joined the Museum's Hall of Fellows in 2008 for his creation of the open source operating system, Linux.

When he developed an operating system in 1991, he announced his project in an Internet newsgroup. He made the source code available and asked readers for suggestions to enhance the product. Computer users responded by reviewing the system and offering enhancements. Three years later he released a greatly enhanced version he called Linux.

Torvalds developed this innovative operating system when he was a 21-year-old computer science student in Finland. Today, he leads the development of Linux as a fellow at OSDL (Open Source Development Labs), a not-for-profit consortium of companies dedicated to developing and promoting the operating system. Torvalds says his daily involvement with Linux involves coordinating and merging the lines of code submitted by users so that the software runs smoothly.

For more information, visit the Computer Concepts CourseMate Web site at www.cengagebrain.com and then navigate to the Chapter 8 Technology Trailblazers resource for this book.

Companies on the Cutting Edge and Technology Trailblazers

Everyone who interacts with computers should be aware of the key computer-related companies and of the more famous leaders of the computer industry.

STUDENT ASSIGNMENTS

End-of-Chapter Student Assignments

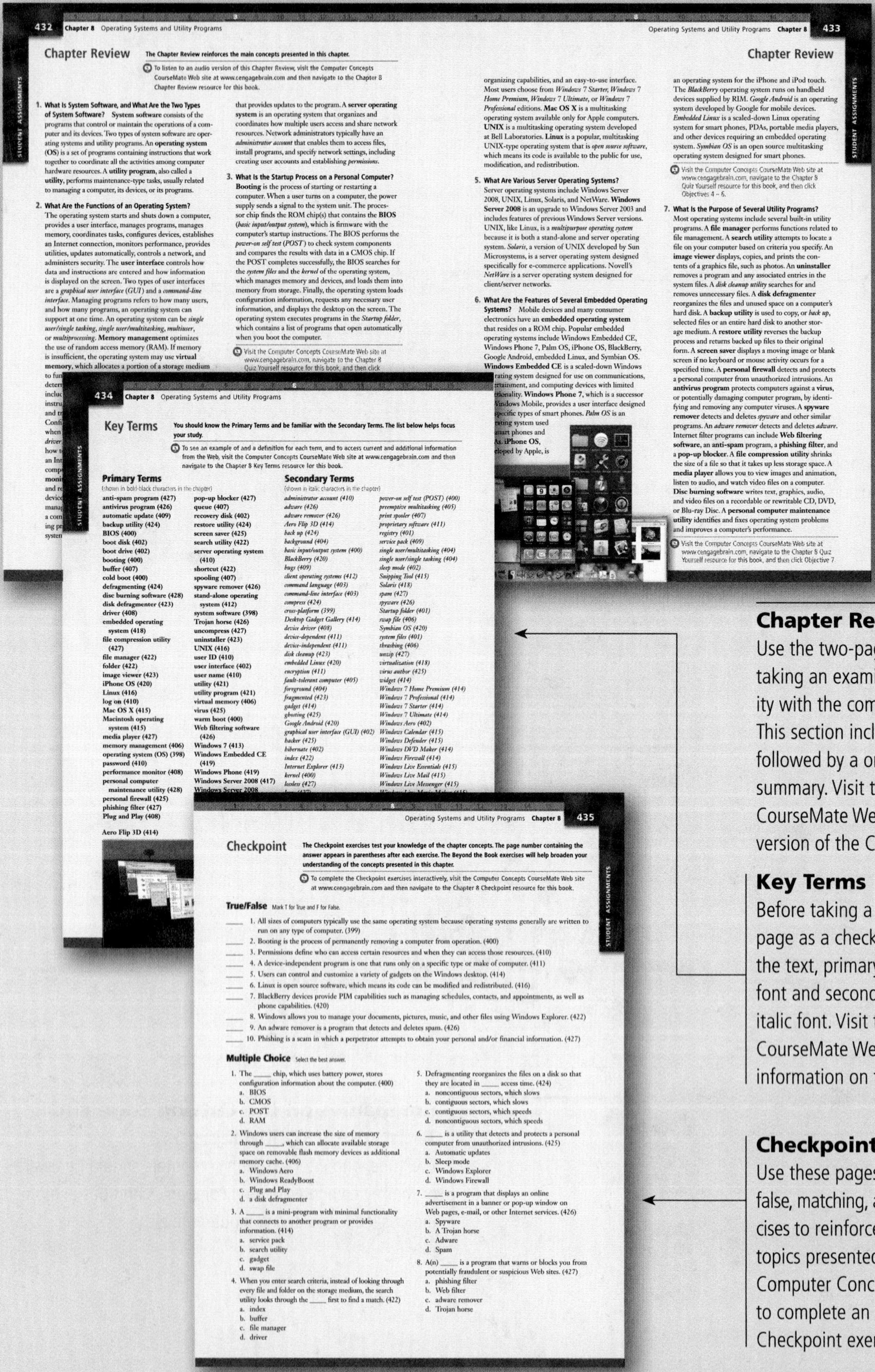

Chapter Review

Use the two-page Chapter Review before taking an examination to ensure familiarity with the computer concepts presented. This section includes each objective, followed by a one- or two-paragraph summary. Visit the Computer Concepts CourseMate Web site to hear an audio version of the Chapter Review.

Key Terms

Before taking a test, use the Key Terms page as a checklist of terms to know. In the text, primary key terms appear in bold font and secondary key terms appear in italic font. Visit the Computer Concepts CourseMate Web site for additional information on the Key Terms.

Checkpoint

Use these pages of multiple-choice, true/false, matching, and short answer exercises to reinforce understanding of the topics presented in the chapter. Visit the Computer Concepts CourseMate Web site to complete an interactive version of the Checkpoint exercises.

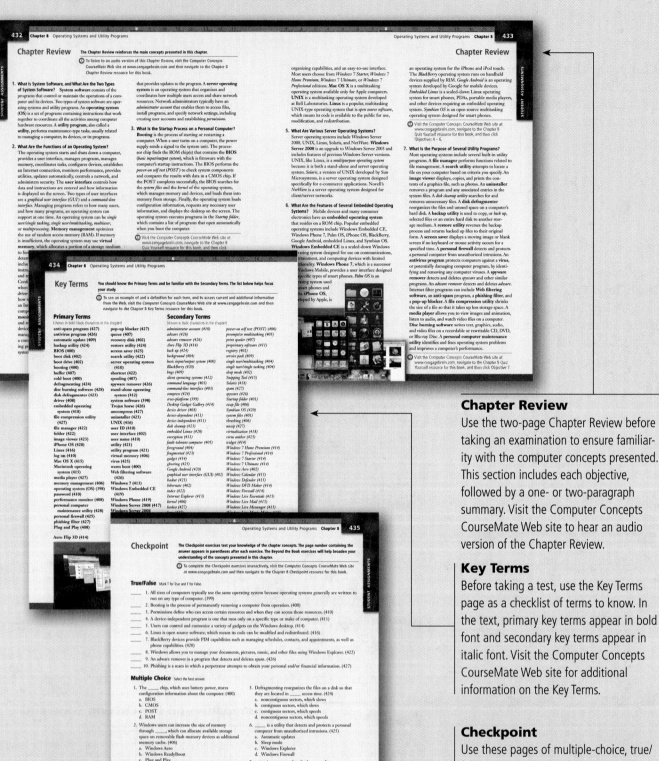

Learn It Online

The Learn It Online exercises, which include At the Movies online CNET videos, practice tests, interactive labs, learning games, and Web-based activities offer a wealth of online reinforcement.

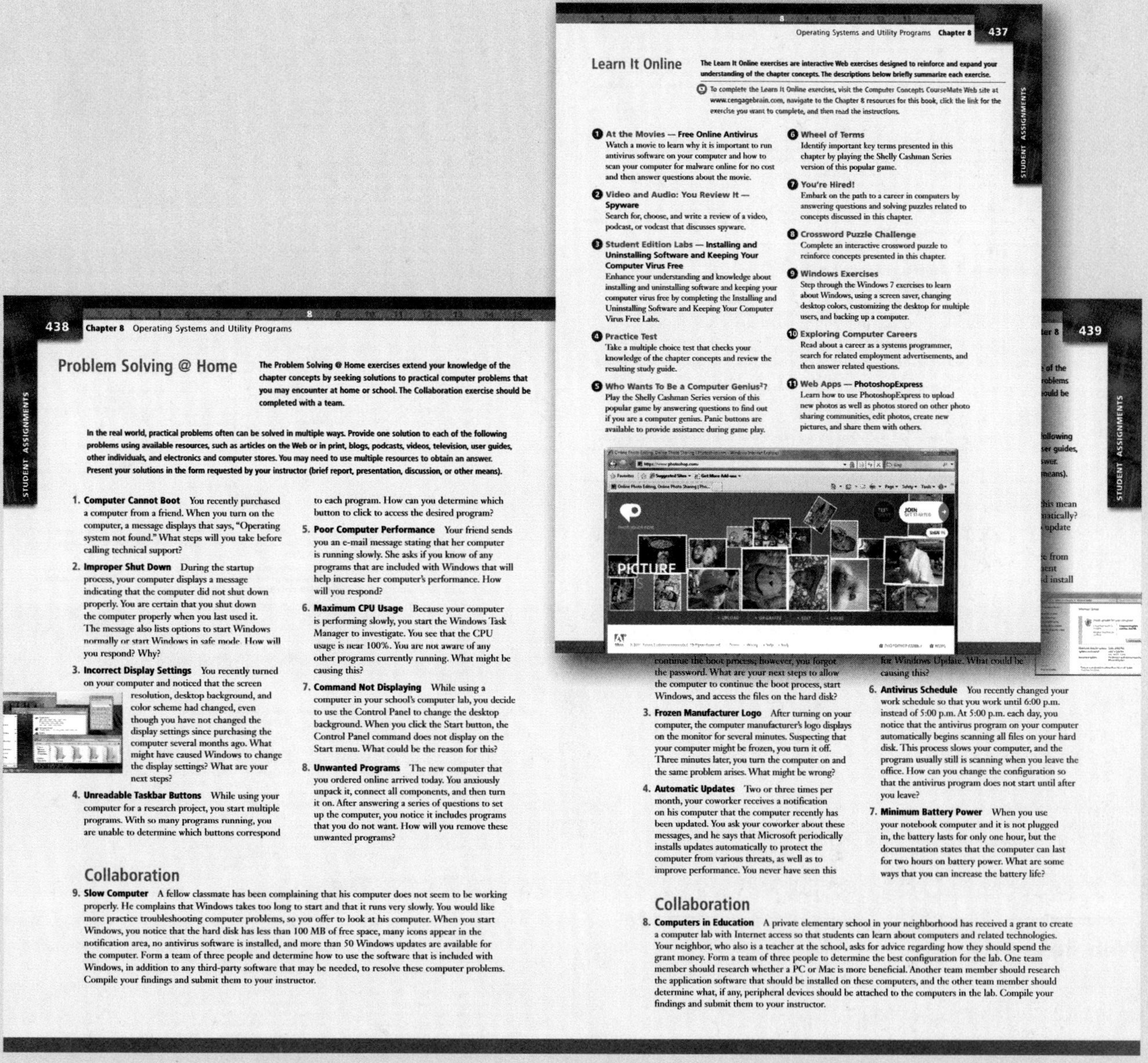

Operating Systems and Utility Programs **Chapter 8** 437

Learn It Online

The Learn It Online exercises are interactive Web exercises designed to reinforce and expand your understanding of the chapter concepts. The descriptions below briefly summarize each exercise.

To complete the Learn It Online exercises, visit the Computer Concepts CourseMate Web site at www.cengagebrain.com, navigate to the Chapter 8 resources for this book, click the link for the exercise you want to complete, and then read the instructions.

1. **At the Movies — Free Online Antivirus** Watch a movie to learn why it is important to run antivirus software on your computer and how to scan your computer for malware online for no cost and then answer questions about the movie.
2. **Video and Audio: You Review It — Spyware** Search for, choose, and write a review of a video, podcast, or vodcast that discusses spyware.
3. **Student Edition Labs — Installing and Uninstalling Software and Keeping Your Computer Virus Free** Enhance your understanding and knowledge about installing and uninstalling software and keeping your computer virus free by completing the Installing and Uninstalling Software and Keeping Your Computer Virus Free Labs.
4. **Practice Test** Take a multiple choice test that checks your knowledge of the chapter concepts and review the resulting study guide.
5. **Who Wants To Be a Computer Genius²?** Play the Shelly Cashman Series version of this popular game by answering questions to find out if you are a computer genius. Panic buttons are available to provide assistance during game play.
6. **Wheel of Terms** Identify important key terms presented in this chapter by playing the Shelly Cashman Series version of this popular game.
7. **You're Hired!** Embark on the path to a career in computers by answering questions and solving puzzles related to concepts discussed in this chapter.
8. **Crossword Puzzle Challenge** Complete an interactive crossword puzzle to reinforce concepts presented in this chapter.
9. **Windows Exercises** Step through the Windows 7 exercises to learn about Windows, using a screen saver, changing desktop colors, customizing the desktop for multiple users, and backing up a computer.
10. **Exploring Computer Careers** Read about a career as a systems programmer, search for related employment advertisements, and then answer related questions.
11. **Web Apps — PhotoshopExpress** Learn how to use PhotoshopExpress to upload new photos as well as photos stored on other photo sharing communities, edit photos, create new pictures, and share them with others.

438 **Chapter 8** Operating Systems and Utility Programs

Problem Solving @ Home

The Problem Solving @ Home exercises extend your knowledge of the chapter concepts by seeking solutions to practical computer problems that you may encounter at home or school. The Collaboration exercise should be completed with a team.

In the real world, practical problems often can be solved in multiple ways. Provide one solution to each of the following problems using available resources, such as articles on the Web or in print, blogs, podcasts, videos, television, user guides, other individuals, and electronics and computer stores. You may need to use multiple resources to obtain an answer. Present your solutions in the form requested by your instructor (brief report, presentation, discussion, or other means).

1. **Computer Cannot Boot** You recently purchased a computer from a friend. When you turn on the computer, a message displays that says, "Operating system not found." What steps will you take before calling technical support?
2. **Improper Shut Down** During the startup process, your computer displays a message indicating that the computer did not shut down properly. You are certain that you shut down the computer properly when you last used it. The message also lists options to start Windows normally or start Windows in safe mode. How will you respond? Why?
3. **Incorrect Display Settings** You recently turned on your computer and noticed that the screen resolution, desktop background, and color scheme had changed, even though you have not changed the display settings since purchasing the computer several months ago. What might have caused Windows to change the display settings? What are your next steps?
4. **Unreadable Taskbar Buttons** While using your computer for a research project, you start multiple programs. With so many programs running, you are unable to determine which buttons correspond to each program. How can you determine which button to click to access the desired program?
5. **Poor Computer Performance** Your friend sends you an e-mail message stating that her computer is running slowly. She asks if you know of any programs that are included with Windows that will help increase her computer's performance. How will you respond?
6. **Maximum CPU Usage** Because your computer is performing slowly, you start the Windows Task Manager to investigate. You see that the CPU usage is near 100%. You are not aware of any other programs currently running. What might be causing this?
7. **Command Not Displaying** While using a computer in your school's computer lab, you decide to use the Control Panel to change the desktop background. When you click the Start button, the Control Panel command does not display on the Start menu. What could be the reason for this?
8. **Unwanted Programs** The new computer that you ordered online arrived today. You anxiously unpack it, connect all components, and then turn it on. After answering a series of questions to set up the computer, you notice it includes programs that you do not want. How will you remove these unwanted programs?

Collaboration

9. **Slow Computer** A fellow classmate has been complaining that his computer does not seem to be working properly. He complains that Windows takes too long to start and that it runs very slowly. You would like more practice troubleshooting computer problems, so you offer to look at his computer. When you start Windows, you notice that the hard disk has less than 100 MB of free space, many icons appear in the notification area, no antivirus software is installed, and more than 50 Windows updates are available for the computer. Form a team of three people and determine how to use the software that is included with Windows, in addition to any third-party software that may be needed, to resolve these computer problems. Compile your findings and submit them to your instructor.

439

continue the boot process; however, you forgot the password. What are your next steps to allow the computer to continue the boot process, start Windows, and access the files on the hard disk?

3. **Frozen Manufacturer Logo** After turning on your computer, the computer manufacturer's logo displays on the monitor for several minutes. Suspecting that your computer might be frozen, you turn it off. Three minutes later, you turn the computer on and the same problem arises. What might be wrong?
4. **Automatic Updates** Two or three times per month, your coworker receives a notification on his computer that the computer recently has been updated. You ask your coworker about these messages, and he says that Microsoft periodically installs updates automatically to protect the computer from various threats, as well as to improve performance. You never have seen this

for Windows Update. What could be causing this?

6. **Antivirus Schedule** You recently changed your work schedule so that you work until 6:00 p.m. instead of 5:00 p.m. At 5:00 p.m. each day, you notice that the antivirus program on your computer automatically begins scanning all files on your hard disk. This process slows your computer, and the program usually still is scanning when you leave the office. How can you change the configuration so that the antivirus program does not start until after you leave?
7. **Minimum Battery Power** When you use your notebook computer and it is not plugged in, the battery lasts for only one hour, but the documentation states that the computer can last for two hours on battery power. What are some ways that you can increase the battery life?

Collaboration

8. **Computers in Education** A private elementary school in your neighborhood has received a grant to create a computer lab with Internet access so that students can learn about computers and related technologies. Your neighbor, who also is a teacher at the school, asks for advice regarding how they should spend the grant money. Form a team of three people to determine the best configuration for the lab. One team member should research whether a PC or Mac is more beneficial. Another team member should research the application software that should be installed on these computers, and the other team member should determine what, if any, peripheral devices should be attached to the computers in the lab. Compile your findings and submit them to your instructor.

Problem Solving @ Home, Problem Solving @ Work, and Collaboration

Tackle everyday computer problems and put the information presented in each chapter to practical use with the Problem Solving @ Home and Problem Solving @ Work exercises. Work as a team to solve the Collaboration exercises.

STUDENT ASSIGNMENTS

Learn How To

Apply the concepts in the chapter to everyday life with these hands-on activities. Learn how the Learn How To activities fit into your life with relevant scenarios, visual demonstrations, and practice questions via the Computer Concepts CourseMate Web site.

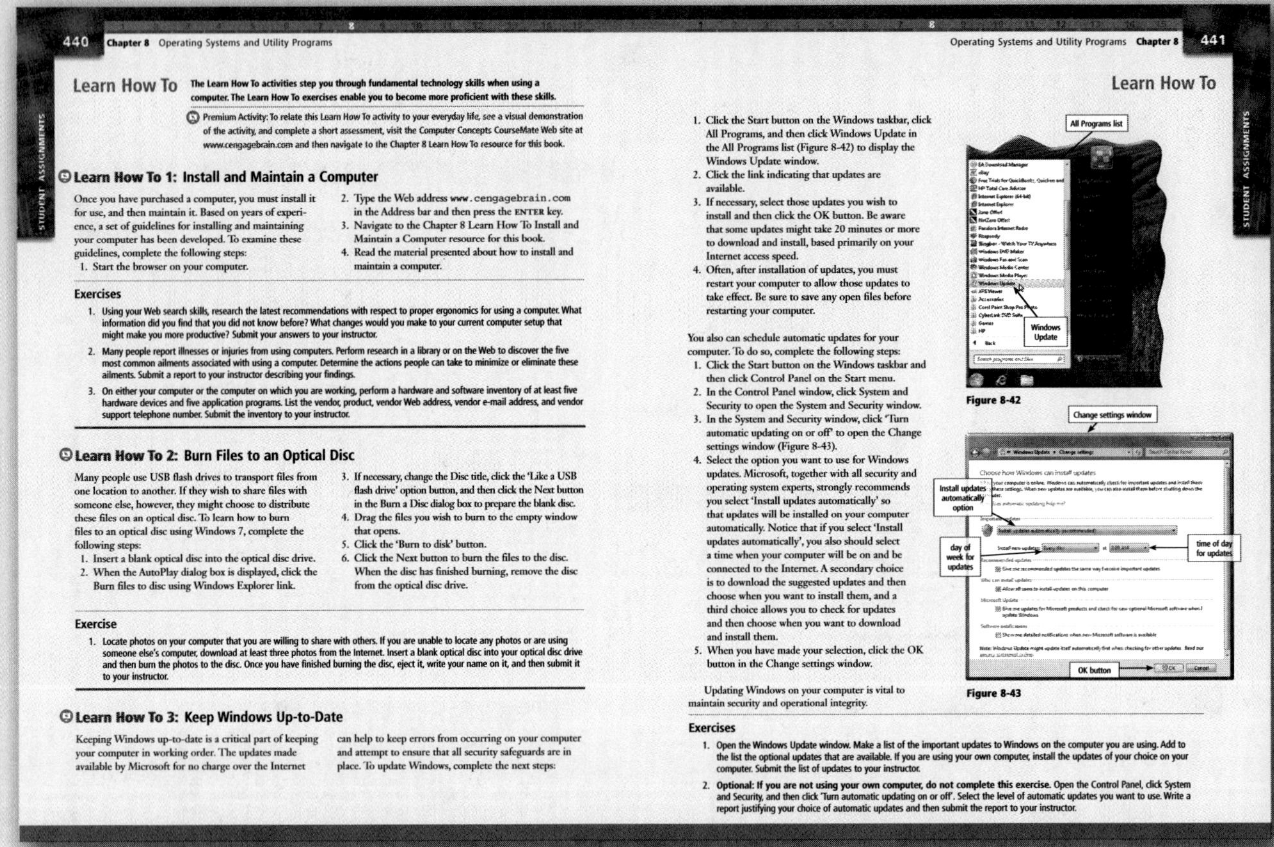

440 Chapter 8 Operating Systems and Utility Programs

STUDENT ASSIGNMENTS

Learn How To **The Learn How To activities step you through fundamental technology skills when using a computer. The Learn How To exercises enable you to become more proficient with these skills.**

Premium Activity: To relate this Learn How To activity to your everyday life, see a visual demonstration of the activity, and complete a short assessment, visit the Computer Concepts CourseMate Web site at www.cengagebrain.com and then navigate to the Chapter 8 Learn How To resource for this book.

Learn How To 1: Install and Maintain a Computer

Once you have purchased a computer, you must install it for use, and then maintain it. Based on years of experience, a set of guidelines for installing and maintaining your computer has been developed. To examine these guidelines, complete the following steps:

1. Start the browser on your computer.
2. Type the Web address www.cengagebrain.com in the Address bar and then press the ENTER key.
3. Navigate to the Chapter 8 Learn How To Install and Maintain a Computer resource for this book.
4. Read the material presented about how to install and maintain a computer.

Exercises

1. Using your Web search skills, research the latest recommendations with respect to proper ergonomics for using a computer. What information did you find that you did not know before? What changes would you make to your current computer setup that might make you more productive? Submit your answers to your instructor.
2. Many people report illnesses or injuries from using computers. Perform research in a library or on the Web to discover the five most common ailments associated with using a computer. Determine the actions people can take to minimize or eliminate these ailments. Submit a report to your instructor describing your findings.
3. On either your computer or the computer on which you are working, perform a hardware and software inventory of at least five hardware devices and five application programs. List the vendor, product, vendor Web address, vendor e-mail address, and vendor support telephone number. Submit the inventory to your instructor.

Learn How To 2: Burn Files to an Optical Disc

Many people use USB flash drives to transport files from one location to another. If they wish to share files with someone else, however, they might choose to distribute these files on an optical disc. To learn how to burn files to an optical disc using Windows 7, complete the following steps:

1. Insert a blank optical disc into the optical disc drive.
2. When the AutoPlay dialog box is displayed, click the Burn files to disc using Windows Explorer link.
3. If necessary, change the Disc title, click the 'Like a USB flash drive' option button, and then click the Next button in the Burn a Disc dialog box to prepare the blank disc.
4. Drag the files you wish to burn to the empty window that opens.
5. Click the 'Burn to disk' button.
6. Click the Next button to burn the files to the disc. When the disc has finished burning, remove the disc from the optical disc drive.

Exercise

1. Locate photos on your computer that you are willing to share with others. If you are unable to locate any photos or are using someone else's computer, download at least three photos from the Internet. Insert a blank optical disc into your optical disc drive and then burn the photos to the disc. Once you have finished burning the disc, eject it, write your name on it, and then submit it to your instructor.

Learn How To 3: Keep Windows Up-to-Date

Keeping Windows up-to-date is a critical part of keeping your computer in working order. The updates made available by Microsoft for no charge over the Internet can help to keep errors from occurring on your computer and attempt to ensure that all security safeguards are in place. To update Windows, complete the next steps:

Operating Systems and Utility Programs Chapter 8 441

Learn How To

1. Click the Start button on the Windows taskbar, click All Programs, and then click Windows Update in the All Programs list (Figure 8-42) to display the Windows Update window.
2. Click the link indicating that updates are available.
3. If necessary, select those updates you wish to install and then click the OK button. Be aware that some updates might take 20 minutes or more to download and install, based primarily on your Internet access speed.
4. Often, after installation of updates, you must restart your computer to allow those updates to take effect. Be sure to save any open files before restarting your computer.

You also can schedule automatic updates for your computer. To do so, complete the following steps:

1. Click the Start button on the Windows taskbar and then click Control Panel on the Start menu.
2. In the Control Panel window, click System and Security to open the System and Security window.
3. In the System and Security window, click 'Turn automatic updating on or off' to open the Change settings window (Figure 8-43).
4. Select the option you want to use for Windows updates. Microsoft, together with all security and operating system experts, strongly recommends you select 'Install updates automatically' so that updates will be installed on your computer automatically. Notice that if you select 'Install updates automatically', you also should select a time when your computer will be on and be connected to the Internet. A secondary choice is to download the suggested updates and then choose when you want to install them, and a third choice allows you to check for updates and then choose when you want to download and install them.
5. When you have made your selection, click the OK button in the Change settings window.

Updating Windows on your computer is vital to maintain security and operational integrity.

Figure 8-42

Figure 8-43

Exercises

1. Open the Windows Update window. Make a list of the important updates to Windows on the computer you are using. Add to the list the optional updates that are available. If you are using your own computer, install the updates of your choice on your computer. Submit the list of updates to your instructor.
2. **Optional: If you are not using your own computer, do not complete this exercise.** Open the Control Panel, click System and Security, and then click 'Turn automatic updating on or off'. Select the level of automatic updates you want to use. Write a report justifying your choice of automatic updates and then submit the report to your instructor.

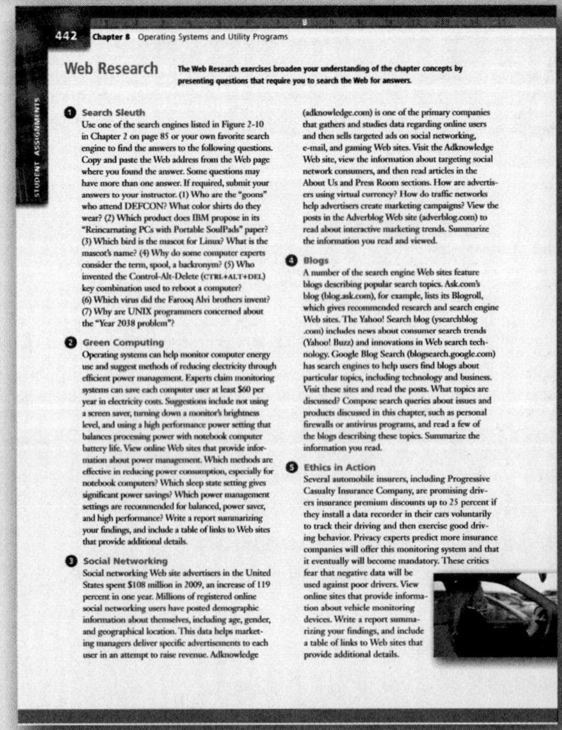

442 Chapter 8 Operating Systems and Utility Programs

STUDENT ASSIGNMENTS

Web Research **The Web Research exercises broaden your understanding of the chapter concepts by presenting questions that require you to search the Web for answers.**

1 **Search Sleuth**
Use one of the search engines listed in Figure 2-10 in Chapter 2 on page 85 or your own favorite search engine to find the answers to the following questions. Copy and paste the Web address from the Web page where you found the answer. Some questions may have more than one answer. If required, submit your answers to your instructor. (1) Who are the "goons" who attend DEFCON? What color shirts do they wear? (2) Which product does IBM propose in its "Reincarnating PCs with Portable SoulPads" paper? (3) Which bird is the mascot for Linux? What is the mascot's name? (4) Why do some computer experts consider the term, spool, a backronym? (5) Who invented the Control-Alt-Delete (CTRL+ALT+DEL) key combination used to reboot a computer? (6) Which virus did the Farooq Alvi brothers invent? (7) Why are UNIX programmers concerned about the "Year 2038 problem"?

2 **Green Computing**
Operating systems can help monitor computer energy use and suggest methods of reducing electricity through efficient power management. Experts claim monitoring systems can save each computer user at least $60 per year in electricity costs. Suggestions include not using a screen saver, turning down a monitor's brightness level, and using a high performance power setting that balances processing power with notebook computer battery life. View online Web sites that provide information about power management. Which methods are effective in reducing power consumption, especially for notebook computers? Which sleep state setting gives significant power savings? Which power management settings are recommended for balanced, power saver, and high performance? Write a report summarizing your findings, and include a table of links to Web sites that provide additional details.

3 **Social Networking**
Social networking Web site advertisers in the United States spent $108 million in 2009, an increase of 119 percent in one year. Millions of registered online social networking users have posted demographic information about themselves, including age, gender, and geographical location. This data helps marketing managers deliver specific advertisements to each user in an attempt to raise revenue. Adknowledge (adknowledge.com) is one of the primary companies that gathers and studies data regarding online users and then sells targeted ads on social networking, e-mail, and gaming Web sites. Visit the Adknowledge Web site, view the information about targeting social network consumers, and then read articles in the About Us and Press Room sections. How are advertisers using virtual currency? How do traffic networks help advertisers create marketing campaigns? View the posts in the Adverblog Web site (adverblog.com) to read about interactive marketing trends. Summarize the information you read and viewed.

4 **Blogs**
A number of the search engine Web sites feature blogs describing popular search topics. Ask.com's blog (blog.ask.com), for example, lists its Blogroll, which gives recommended research and search engine Web sites. The Yahoo! Search blog (ysearchblog.com) includes news about consumer search trends (Yahoo! Buzz) and innovations in Web search technology. Google Blog Search (blogsearch.google.com) has search engines to help users find blogs about particular topics, including technology and business. Visit these sites and read the posts. What topics are discussed? Compose search queries about issues and products discussed in this chapter, such as personal firewalls or antivirus programs, and read a few of the blogs describing these topics. Summarize the information you read.

5 **Ethics in Action**
Several automobile insurers, including Progressive Casualty Insurance Company, are promising drivers insurance premium discounts up to 25 percent if they install a data recorder in their cars voluntarily to track their driving and then exercise good driving behavior. Privacy experts predict more insurance companies will offer this monitoring system and that it eventually will become mandatory. These critics fear that negative data will be used against poor drivers. View online sites that provide information about vehicle monitoring devices. Write a report summarizing your findings, and include a table of links to Web sites that provide additional details.

Web Research

Each Web Research exercise requires follow-up research on the Web and suggests writing a short article or presenting the findings of the research to the class.

Critical Thinking

Exercise your mind and construct creative solutions to these thought-provoking exercises presented in each chapter. The Critical Thinking exercises are constructed for class discussion, presentation, and independent research. The Collaboration exercise is designed for a team environment.

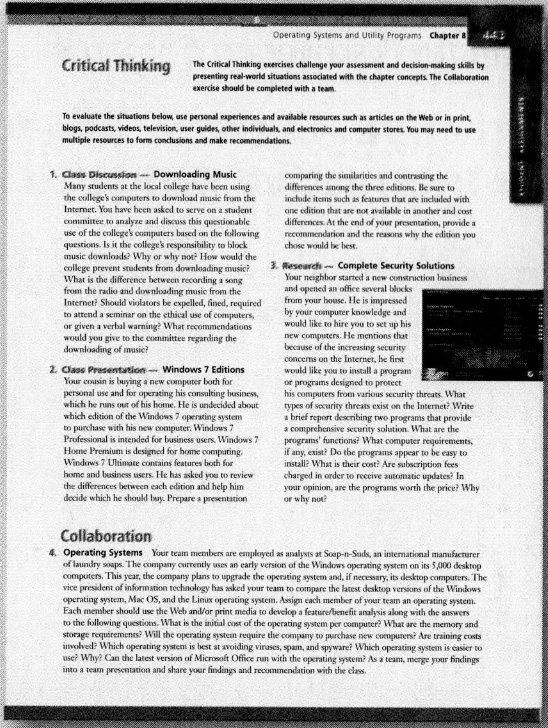
Operating Systems and Utility Programs **Chapter 8**

Critical Thinking The Critical Thinking exercises challenge your assessment and decision-making skills by presenting real-world situations associated with the chapter concepts. The Collaboration exercise should be completed with a team.

To evaluate the situations below, use personal experiences and available resources such as articles on the Web or in print, blogs, podcasts, videos, television, user guides, other individuals, and electronics and computer stores. You may need to use multiple resources to form conclusions and make recommendations.

1. **Class Discussion — Downloading Music** Many students at the local college have been using the college's computers to download music from the Internet. You have been asked to serve on a student committee to analyze and discuss this questionable use of the college's computers based on the following questions. Is it the college's responsibility to block music downloads? Why or why not? How would the college prevent students from downloading music? What is the difference between recording a song from the radio and downloading music from the Internet? Should violators be expelled, fined, required to attend a seminar on the ethical use of computers, or given a verbal warning? What recommendations would you give to the committee regarding the downloading of music?

2. **Class Presentation — Windows 7 Editions** Your cousin is buying a new computer both for personal use and for operating his consulting business, which he runs out of his home. He is undecided about which edition of the Windows 7 operating system to purchase with his new computer. Windows 7 Professional is intended for business users. Windows 7 Home Premium is designed for home computing. Windows 7 Ultimate contains features both for home and business users. He has asked you to review the differences between each edition and help him decide which he should buy. Prepare a presentation comparing the similarities and contrasting the differences among the three editions. Be sure to include items such as features that are included with one edition that are not available in another and cost differences. At the end of your presentation, provide a recommendation and the reasons why the edition you chose would be best.

3. **Research — Complete Security Solutions** Your neighbor started a new construction business and opened an office several blocks from your house. He is impressed by your computer knowledge and would like to hire you to set up his new computers. He mentions that because of the increasing security concerns on the Internet, he first would like you to install a program or programs designed to protect his computers from various security threats. What types of security threats exist on the Internet? Write a brief report describing two programs that provide a comprehensive security solution. What are the programs' functions? What computer requirements, if any, exist? Do the programs appear to be easy to install? What is their cost? Are subscription fees charged in order to receive automatic updates? In your opinion, are the programs worth the price? Why or why not?

Collaboration

4. **Operating Systems** Your team members are employed as analysts at Soap-n-Suds, an international manufacturer of laundry soaps. The company currently uses an early version of the Windows operating system on its 5,000 desktop computers. This year, the company plans to upgrade the operating system and, if necessary, its desktop computers. The vice president of information technology has asked your team to compare the latest desktop versions of the Windows operating system, Mac OS, and the Linux operating system. Assign each member of your team an operating system. Each member should use the Web and/or print media to develop a feature/benefit analysis along with the answers to the following questions. What is the initial cost of the operating system per computer? What are the memory and storage requirements? Will the operating system require the company to purchase new computers? Are training costs involved? Which operating system is best at avoiding viruses, spam, and spyware? Which operating system is easier to use? Why? Can the latest version of Microsoft Office run with the operating system? As a team, merge your findings into a team presentation and share your findings and recommendation with the class.

STUDENT ASSIGNMENTS

Special Features

Five special features following Chapters 1, 2, 3, 6, and 8 encompass topics from the history of computers, to hot topics on the Web, including Web 2.0, to a buyer's guide, to the latest in new technology and digital communications.

Visual Walkthrough of the Computer Concepts CourseMate for Discovering Computers

Interactive. Current. Engaging.
Your Interactive Guide to the Digital World!

Introduce the most current technology into the classroom with the Computer Concepts CourseMate for Discovering Computers. An integrated e-book and a wide range of online learning games, quizzes, practice tests, videos, and Web links expand on the topics covered in the text with hands-on reinforcement. The Pointer Icon integrated into each page of the text illustrates when to access the CourseMate Web site and quickly shows students the connection between the text and the digital solution.

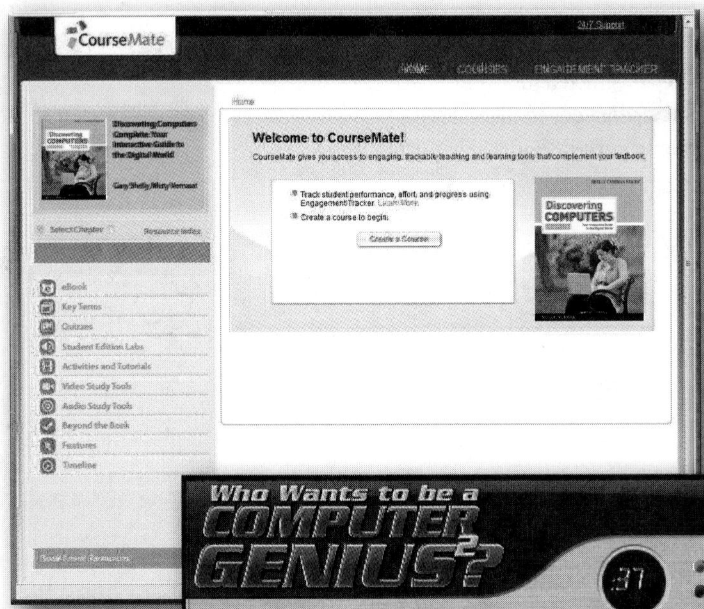

Who Wants to Be a Computer Genius?[2]

The Who Wants to Be a Computer Genius?[2] learning game allows students to quiz themselves on chapter content within a dynamic and entertaining game scenario. Question results are provided instantly so that students quickly see which concepts they understand and which concepts they need to study. Page remediation is included with question results so students know exactly where in the text to find the information they need.

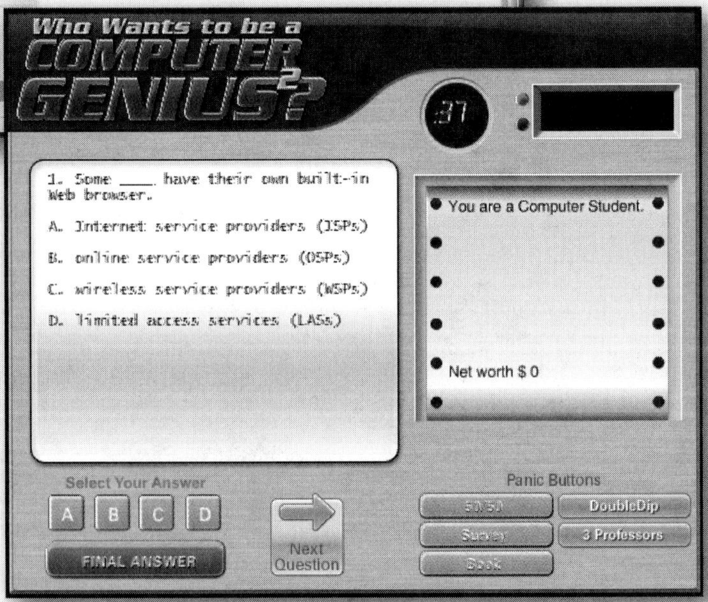

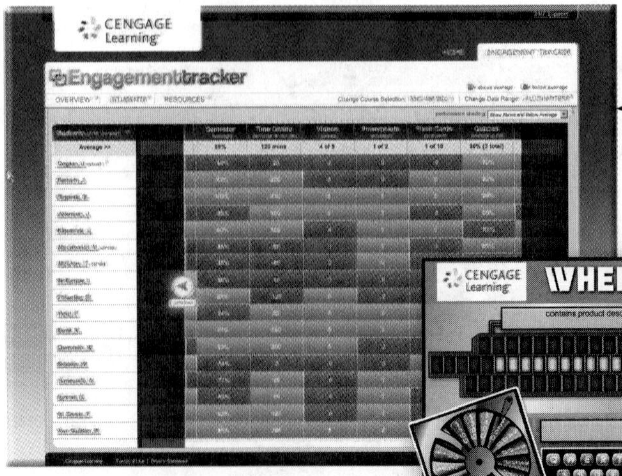

EngagementTracker

EngagementTracker makes assessing students easy by tracking student progress on the interactive activities. Clear and visual reports illustrate the class progress as a whole.

Wheel of Terms

Wheel of Terms is an interactive study tool for learning the Key Terms in each chapter. This learning game presents students with a short definition of one of the chapter's Key Terms and prompts them to type the correct term as the answer.

Online Content

Student Edition Labs

Our Web-based interactive labs help students master hundreds of computer concepts, including input and output devices, file management and desktop applications, computer ethics, virus protection, and much more. Featuring up-to-the-minute content, eye-popping graphics, and rich animation, the highly interactive Student Edition Labs offer students an alternative way to learn through dynamic observation, step-by-step practice, and challenging review questions. Access the Student Edition Labs from the Discovering Computers: Your Interactive Guide to the Digital World Computer Concepts CourseMate Web site at www.cengagebrain.com or see the Student Edition Lab exercises on the Learn It Online pages at the end of each chapter. Also available on CD at an additional cost.

SAM 2010: Assessment & Training and Project Grading Solutions

SAM (Skills Assessment Manager) is a robust assessment, training and project-based system that enables students to be active participants in learning valuable Microsoft Office 2010 skills. A set of testbank questions ties directly to each chapter in this book. Let SAM be an integral part of your students' learning experience!

Content for Online Learning

Course Technology has partnered with the leading distance learning solution providers and class-management platforms today. To access this material, instructors will visit our password-protected instructor resources available at http://www.cengage.com/coursecare/cartridge/. Instructor resources include the following: additional case projects, sample syllabi, PowerPoint presentations per chapter, and more. For additional information or for an instructor username and password, please contact your sales representative. For students to access this material, they must have purchased a Course Cartridge PIN-code specific to this title and your campus platform. The resources for students may include (based on instructor preferences), but not limited to: topic review, review questions and practice tests.

CourseCasts Learning on the Go

Always available. . . always relevant.

Our fast-paced world is driven by technology. You know because you are an active participant — always on the go, always keeping up with technological trends, and always learning new ways to embrace technology to power your life. Let CourseCasts, hosted by Ken Baldauf of Florida State University, be your guide to weekly updates in this ever-changing space. These timely, relevant podcasts are produced weekly and are available for download at http://coursecasts.course.com or directly from iTunes (search by CourseCasts). CourseCasts are a perfect solution to getting students (and even instructors) to learn on the go!

CourseNotes — Technology in a Flash!

Course Technology's CourseNotes are six-panel quick reference cards that reinforce the most important and widely used features of a software application in a visual and user-friendly format. CourseNotes serve as a great reference tool during and after the student completes the course. CourseNotes are available for software applications, such as Microsoft Office 2010, Word 2010, PowerPoint 2010, Excel 2010, Access 2010, and Windows 7. Topic-based CourseNotes are available for Best Practices in Social Networking, Hot Topics in Technology, and Web 2.0. Visit www.cengage.com/ct/coursenotes to learn more!

About Our Covers

The Shelly Cashman Series is continually updating our approach and content to reflect the way today's students learn and experience new technology. This focus on student success is reflected on our covers, which feature real students from Bryant University using the Shelly Cashman Series in their courses, and reflect the varied ages and backgrounds of the students learning with our books. When you use the Shelly Cashman Series, you can be assured that you are learning computer skills using the most effective courseware available.

Chapter One

Introduction to Computers

Objectives

After completing this chapter, you will be able to:

1 Explain why computer literacy is vital to success in today's world

2 Define the term, computer, and describe the relationship between data and information

3 Describe the five components of a computer: input devices, output devices, system unit, storage devices, and communications devices

4 Discuss the advantages and disadvantages that users experience when working with computers

5 Define the term, network, and identify benefits of sharing resources on a network

6 Discuss the uses of the Internet and World Wide Web

7 Distinguish between system software and application software

8 Differentiate among types, sizes, and functions of computers in each of these categories: personal computers (desktop), mobile computers and mobile devices, game consoles, servers, mainframes, supercomputers, and embedded computers

9 Describe the role of each element in an information system

10 Explain how home users, small office/home office users, mobile users, power users, and enterprise users each interact with computers

11 Discuss how society uses computers in education, finance, government, health care, science, publishing, travel, and manufacturing

A World of Computers

Computers are everywhere: at work, at school, and at home. As shown in Figure 1-1, people use all types and sizes of computers for a variety of reasons and in a range of places. While some computers sit on top of a desk or on the floor, mobile computers and mobile devices are small enough to carry. Mobile devices, such as many cell phones, often are classified as computers.

Computers are a primary means of local and global communication for billions of people. Consumers use computers to correspond with businesses, employees with other employees and customers, students with classmates and teachers, and family members and military personnel with friends and other family members. In addition to sending simple notes, people use computers to share photos, drawings, documents, calendars, journals, music, and videos.

Through computers, society has instant access to information from around the globe. Local and national news, weather reports, sports scores, airline schedules, telephone directories, maps and directions, job listings, credit reports, and countless forms of educational material always are accessible. From the computer, you can make a telephone call, meet new friends, share opinions or life stories, book flights, shop, fill prescriptions, file taxes, take a course, receive alerts, and automate your home.

At home or while on the road, people use computers to manage schedules and contacts, listen to voice mail messages, balance checkbooks, pay bills, transfer funds, and buy or sell stocks. Banks place ATMs (automated teller machines) all over the world, so that customers can deposit

Figure 1-1 People use all types and sizes of computers in their daily activities.

and withdraw funds anywhere at anytime. At the grocery store, a computer tracks purchases, calculates the amount of money due, and often generates coupons customized to buying patterns. Vehicles include onboard navigation systems that provide directions, call for emergency services, and track the vehicle if it is stolen.

In the workplace, employees use computers to create correspondence such as e-mail messages, memos, and letters; manage calendars; calculate payroll; track inventory; and generate invoices. At school, teachers use computers to assist with classroom instruction. Students complete assignments and conduct research on computers in lab rooms, at home, or elsewhere. Instead of attending class on campus, some students take entire classes directly from their computer.

People also spend hours of leisure time using a computer. They play games, listen to music or radio broadcasts, watch or compose videos and movies, read books and magazines, share stories, research genealogy, retouch photos, and plan vacations.

As technology continues to advance, computers have become a part of everyday life. Thus, many people believe that computer literacy is vital to success in today's world. **Computer literacy**, also known as *digital literacy*, involves having a current knowledge and understanding of computers and their uses. Because the requirements that determine computer literacy change as technology changes, you must keep up with these changes to remain computer literate.

This book presents the knowledge you need to be computer literate today. As you read this first chapter, keep in mind it is an overview. Many of the terms and concepts introduced in this chapter will be discussed in more depth later in the book.

What Is a Computer?

A **computer** is an electronic device, operating under the control of instructions stored in its own memory, that can accept data, process the data according to specified rules, produce results, and store the results for future use.

Data and Information

Computers process data into information. **Data** is a collection of unprocessed items, which can include text, numbers, images, audio, and video. **Information** conveys meaning and is useful to people.

Many daily activities either involve the use of or depend on information from a computer. As shown in Figure 1-2, for example, computers process several data items to print information in the form of a cash register receipt.

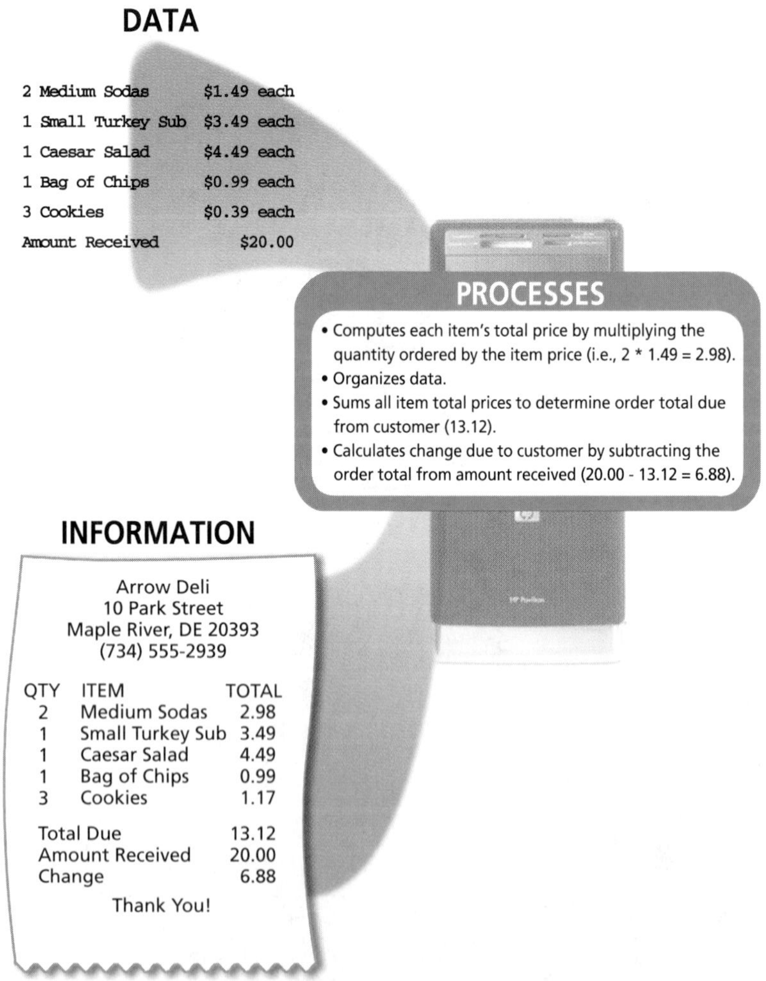
DATA
2 Medium Sodas $1.49 each
1 Small Turkey Sub $3.49 each
1 Caesar Salad $4.49 each
1 Bag of Chips $0.99 each
3 Cookies $0.39 each
Amount Received $20.00
PROCESSES
• Computes each item's total price by multiplying the quantity ordered by the item price (i.e., 2 * 1.49 = 2.98).
• Organizes data.
• Sums all item total prices to determine order total due from customer (13.12).
• Calculates change due to customer by subtracting the order total from amount received (20.00 - 13.12 = 6.88).
INFORMATION
Arrow Deli
10 Park Street
Maple River, DE 20393
(734) 555-2939
QTY ITEM TOTAL
2 Medium Sodas 2.98
1 Small Turkey Sub 3.49
1 Caesar Salad 4.49
1 Bag of Chips 0.99
3 Cookies 1.17
Total Due 13.12
Amount Received 20.00
Change 6.88
Thank You!

Figure 1-2 A computer processes data into information. In this simplified example, the item ordered, item price, quantity ordered, and amount received all represent data. The computer processes the data to produce the cash register receipt (information).

Information Processing Cycle

Computers process data (input) into information (output). Computers carry out processes using *instructions*, which are the steps that tell the computer how to perform a particular task. A collection of related instructions organized for a common purpose is referred to as software. A computer often holds data, information, and instructions in storage for future use. Some people refer to the series of input, process, output, and storage activities as the *information processing cycle*.

Most computers today communicate with other computers. As a result, communications also has become an essential element of the information processing cycle.

The Components of a Computer

A computer contains many electric, electronic, and mechanical components known as **hardware**. These components include input devices, output devices, a system unit, storage devices, and communications devices. Figure 1-3 shows some common computer hardware components.

Input Devices

An **input device** is any hardware component that allows you to enter data and instructions into a computer. Five widely used input devices are the keyboard, mouse, microphone, scanner, and Web cam (Figure 1-3).

A computer keyboard contains keys you press to enter data into the computer. For security purposes, some keyboards include a fingerprint reader, which allows you to work with the computer only if your fingerprint is recognized.

A mouse is a small handheld device. With the mouse, you control movement of a small symbol on the screen, called the pointer, and you make selections from the screen.

A microphone allows you to speak into the computer. A scanner converts printed material (such as text and pictures) into a form the computer can use.

A Web cam is a digital video camera that allows you to create movies or take pictures and store them on the computer instead of on tape or film.

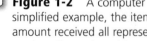

Output Devices

An **output device** is any hardware component that conveys information to one or more people. Three commonly used output devices are a printer, a monitor, and speakers (Figure 1-3).

A printer produces text and graphics on a physical medium such as paper. A monitor displays text, graphics, and videos on a screen. Speakers allow you to hear music, voice, and other audio (sounds).

System Unit

The **system unit** is a case that contains the electronic components of the computer that are used to process data (Figure 1-3). The circuitry of the system unit usually is part of or is connected to a circuit board called the motherboard.

Two main components on the motherboard are the processor and memory. The *processor*, also called a *CPU* (*central processing unit*), is the electronic component that interprets and carries out the basic instructions that operate the computer. *Memory* consists of electronic components that store instructions waiting to be executed and data needed by those instructions. Although some forms of memory are permanent, most memory keeps data and instructions temporarily, which means its contents are erased when the computer is shut off.

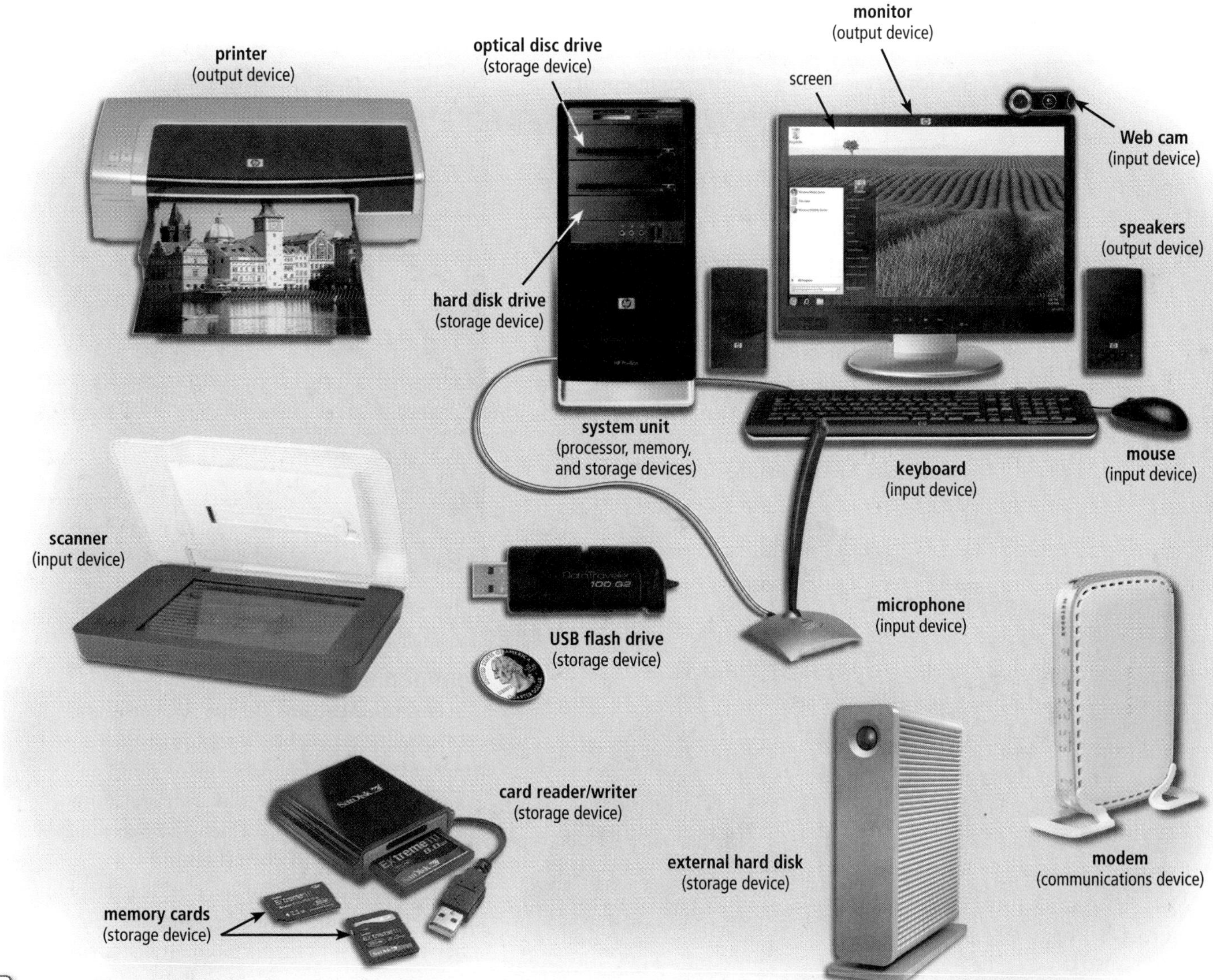

Figure 1-3 Common computer hardware components include a keyboard, mouse, microphone, scanner, Web cam, printer, monitor, speakers, system unit, hard disk drive, external hard disk, optical disc drive(s), USB flash drive, card reader/writer, memory cards, and modem.

Storage Devices

Storage holds data, instructions, and information for future use. For example, computers can store hundreds or millions of customer names and addresses. Storage holds these items permanently.

A computer keeps data, instructions, and information on **storage media**. Examples of storage media are USB flash drives, hard disks, optical discs, and memory cards. A **storage device** records (writes) and/or retrieves (reads) items to and from storage media. Drives and readers/writers, which are types of storage devices (Figure 1-3 on the previous page), accept a specific kind of storage media. For example, a DVD drive (storage device) accepts a DVD (storage media). Storage devices often function as a source of input because they transfer items from storage to memory.

A USB flash drive is a portable storage device that is small and lightweight enough to be transported on a keychain or in a pocket (Figure 1-3). The average USB flash drive can hold about 4 billion characters. You plug a USB flash drive in a special, easily accessible opening on the computer.

A hard disk provides much greater storage capacity than a USB flash drive. The average hard disk can hold more than 320 billion characters. Hard disks are enclosed in an airtight, sealed case. Although some are portable, most are housed inside the system unit (Figure 1-4). Portable hard disks are either external or removable. An external hard disk is a separate, freestanding unit, whereas you insert and remove a removable hard disk from the computer or a device connected to the computer.

Figure 1-4 Hard disks are self-contained devices. The hard disk shown here must be installed in the system unit before it can be used.

An optical disc is a flat, round, portable metal disc with a plastic coating. CDs, DVDs, and Blu-ray Discs are three types of optical discs. A CD can hold from 650 million to 1 billion characters. Some DVDs can store two full-length movies or 17 billion characters (Figure 1-5). Blu-ray Discs can store about 46 hours of standard video, or 100 billion characters.

Some mobile devices, such as digital cameras, use memory cards as the storage media. You can use a card reader/writer (Figure 1-3) to transfer the stored items, such as digital photos, from the memory card to a computer or printer.

Figure 1-5 A DVD in a DVD drive.

Communications Devices

A **communications device** is a hardware component that enables a computer to send (transmit) and receive data, instructions, and information to and from one or more computers or mobile devices. A widely used communications device is a modem (Figure 1-3).

Communications occur over cables, telephone lines, cellular radio networks, satellites, and other transmission media. Some transmission media, such as satellites and cellular radio networks, are wireless, which means they have no physical lines or wires.

Advantages and Disadvantages of Using Computers

Society has reaped many benefits from using computers. A **user** is anyone who communicates with a computer or utilizes the information it generates. Both business and home users can make well-informed decisions because they have instant access to information from anywhere in the world. Students, another type of user, have more tools to assist them in the learning process.

Advantages of Using Computers

Benefits from using computers are possible because computers have the advantages of speed, reliability, consistency, storage, and communications.

- **Speed:** When data, instructions, and information flow along electronic circuits in a computer, they travel at incredibly fast speeds. Many computers process billions or trillions of operations in a single second. Processing involves computing (e.g., adding, subtracting), sorting (e.g., alphabetizing), organizing, displaying images, recording audio, playing music, and showing a movie or video.
- **Reliability:** The electronic components in modern computers are dependable and reliable because they rarely break or fail.
- **Consistency:** Given the same input and processes, a computer will produce the same results — consistently. A computing phrase — known as *garbage in, garbage out* — points out that the accuracy of a computer's output depends on the accuracy of the input. For example, if you do not use the flash on a digital camera when indoors, the resulting pictures that are displayed on the computer screen may be unusable because they are too dark.
- **Storage:** A computer can transfer data quickly from storage to memory, process it, and then store it again for future use. Many computers store enormous amounts of data and make this data available for processing anytime it is needed.
- **Communications:** Most computers today can communicate with other computers, often wirelessly. Computers with this capability can share any of the four information processing cycle operations — input, process, output, and storage — with another computer or a user.

Disadvantages of Using Computers

Some disadvantages of computers relate to health risks, the violation of privacy, public safety, the impact on the labor force, and the impact on the environment.

- **Health Risks:** Prolonged or improper computer use can lead to injuries or disorders of the hands, wrists, elbows, eyes, neck, and back. Computer users can protect themselves from these health risks through proper workplace design, good posture while at the computer, and appropriately spaced work breaks. Two behavioral health risks are computer addiction and technology overload. Computer addiction occurs when someone becomes obsessed with using a computer. Individuals suffering from technology overload feel distressed when deprived of computers and mobile devices. Once recognized, both computer addiction and technology overload are treatable disorders. Read Ethics & Issues 1-1 for a related discussion.

ETHICS & ISSUES 1-1

How Can People Best Cope with Technology Overload?

Most people enjoy the benefits that technology brings to their lives, such as increased productivity. A growing problem, however, is observed among those suffering the effects of technology overload. People overloaded with technology often feel uncomfortable or nervous when they cannot use the Internet or a cell phone for even a short length of time. Some mental health experts believe that technology overload is a health problem that can be treated just as other compulsions are treated. While some disagreement exists over the specific definition, the general consensus is that a person has a problem with technology overload when the overuse of technology negatively impacts health, personal life, and professional life. For some, technology overload often leads to less time spent with family and has proven to be as potent a cause for divorce as gambling or substance abuse. Experts suggest balancing the use of technology in one's life and listening to others if they suggest that the overuse of technology is causing personal problems.

What steps can people or society take to cope with technology overload? How might one determine if he or she suffers from technology overload? How can technology companies help to alleviate the problem of technology overload? Should those identified as technology addicts be able to receive health insurance benefits for counseling services? Why or why not?

Ethics & Issues

For the complete text of the Ethics & Issues boxes found in this chapter, visit the Computer Concepts CourseMate Web site at www.cengagebrain.com and then navigate to the Chapter 1 Ethics & Issues resource for this book.

- **Violation of Privacy:** Nearly every life event is stored in a computer somewhere . . . in medical records, credit reports, tax records, etc. In many instances, where personal and confidential records were not protected properly, individuals have found their privacy violated and identities stolen.
- **Public Safety:** Adults, teens, and children around the world are using computers to share publicly their photos, videos, journals, music, and other personal information. Some of these unsuspecting, innocent computer users have fallen victim to crimes committed by dangerous strangers. Protect yourself and your dependents from these criminals by being cautious in e-mail messages and on Web sites. For example, do not share information that would allow others to identify or locate you and do not disclose identification numbers, passwords, or other personal security details.
- **Impact on Labor Force:** Although computers have improved productivity in many ways and created an entire industry with hundreds of thousands of new jobs, the skills of millions of employees have been replaced by computers. Thus, it is crucial that workers keep their education up-to-date. A separate impact on the labor force is that some companies are outsourcing jobs to foreign countries instead of keeping their homeland labor force employed.
- **Impact on Environment:** Computer manufacturing processes and computer waste are depleting natural resources and polluting the environment. When computers are discarded in landfills, they can release toxic materials and potentially dangerous levels of lead, mercury, and flame retardants.

Green computing involves reducing the electricity consumed and environmental waste generated when using a computer. Strategies that support green computing include recycling, regulating manufacturing processes, extending the life of computers, and immediately donating or properly disposing of replaced computers. When you purchase a new computer, some retailers offer to dispose of your old computer properly.

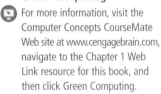

Green Computing

For more information, visit the Computer Concepts CourseMate Web site at www.cengagebrain.com, navigate to the Chapter 1 Web Link resource for this book, and then click Green Computing.

✔ QUIZ YOURSELF 1-1

Instructions: Find the true statement below. Then, rewrite the remaining false statements so that they are true.

1. A computer is a motorized device that processes output into input.
2. A storage device records (reads) and/or retrieves (writes) items to and from storage media.
3. An output device is any hardware component that allows you to enter data and instructions into a computer.
4. Computer literacy involves having a current knowledge and understanding of computers and their uses.
5. Computers have the disadvantages of fast speeds, high failure rates, producing consistent results, storing small amounts of data, and communicating with others.
6. Three commonly used input devices are a printer, a monitor, and speakers.

Quiz Yourself Online: To further check your knowledge of pages 4 through 10, visit the Computer Concepts CourseMate Web site at www.cengagebrain.com, navigate to the Chapter 1 Quiz Yourself resource for this book, and then click Objectives 1 – 4.

Networks and the Internet

A **network** is a collection of computers and devices connected together, often wirelessly, via communications devices and transmission media. When a computer connects to a network, it is **online**.

Networks allow computers to share *resources*, such as hardware, software, data, and information. Sharing resources saves time and money. In many networks, one or more computers act as a server. The *server* controls access to the resources on a network. The other computers on the network, each called a *client* or workstation, request resources from the server (Figure 1-6). The major differences between the server and client computers are that the server ordinarily has more power, more storage space, and expanded communications capabilities.

Many homes and most businesses and schools network their computers and devices. Most allow users to connect their computers wirelessly to the network. Home networks usually are small, existing within a single structure. Business and school networks can be small, such as in a room or building, or widespread, connecting computers and devices across a city, country, or the globe. The world's largest computer network is the Internet.

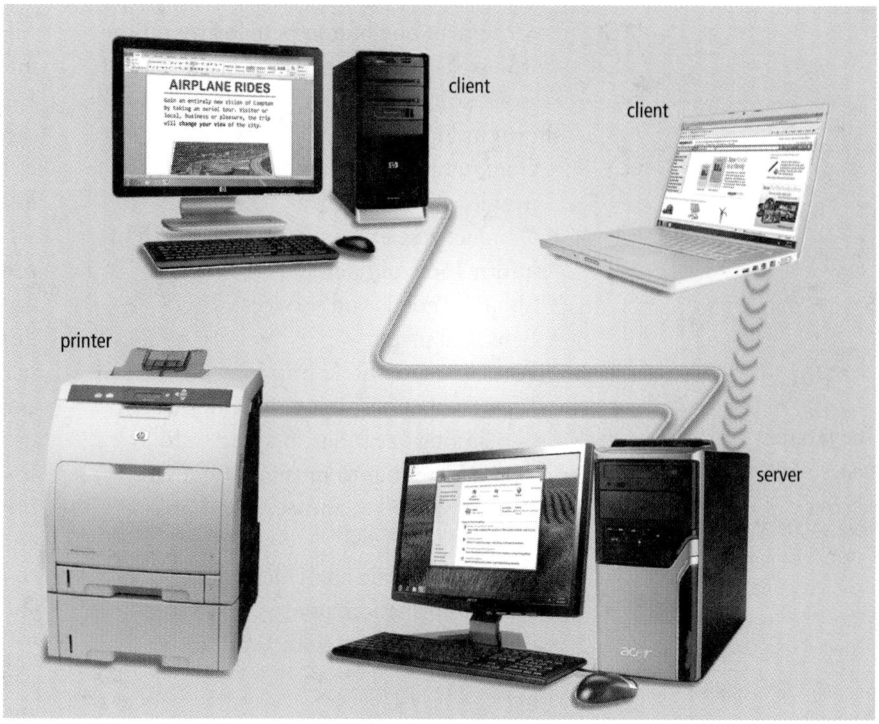

Figure 1-6 A server manages the resources on a network, and clients access the resources on the server. This network enables three separate computers to share the same printer, one wirelessly.

The Internet

The **Internet** is a worldwide collection of networks that connects millions of businesses, government agencies, educational institutions, and individuals (Figure 1-7).

Figure 1-7 The Internet is the largest computer network, connecting millions of computers and devices around the world.

More than one billion people around the world use the Internet daily for a variety of reasons, some of which are listed below and shown in Figure 1-8:

- Communicate with and meet other people
- Conduct research and access a wealth of information and news
- Shop for goods and services
- Bank and invest
- Participate in online training
- Engage in entertaining activities, such as planning vacations, playing online games, listening to music, watching or editing videos, and reading books and magazines
- Download music and videos
- Share information, photos, and videos
- Access and interact with Web applications

The Internet

For more information, visit the Computer Concepts CourseMate Web site at www.cengagebrain.com, navigate to the Chapter 1 Web Link resource for this book, and then click The Internet.

People connect to the Internet to share information with others around the world. E-mail allows you to send and receive messages to and from other users (read Ethics & Issues 1-2 for a related discussion). With instant messaging, you can have a live conversation with another connected user. In a chat room, you can communicate with multiple users at the same time — much like a group discussion. You also can use the Internet to make a telephone call.

Businesses, called access providers, offer users and organizations access to the Internet free or for a fee. By subscribing to an access provider, you can use your computer and a communications device, such as a modem, to connect to the many services of the Internet.

The Web, short for World Wide Web, is one of the more popular services on the Internet. Think of the Web as a global library of information available to anyone connected

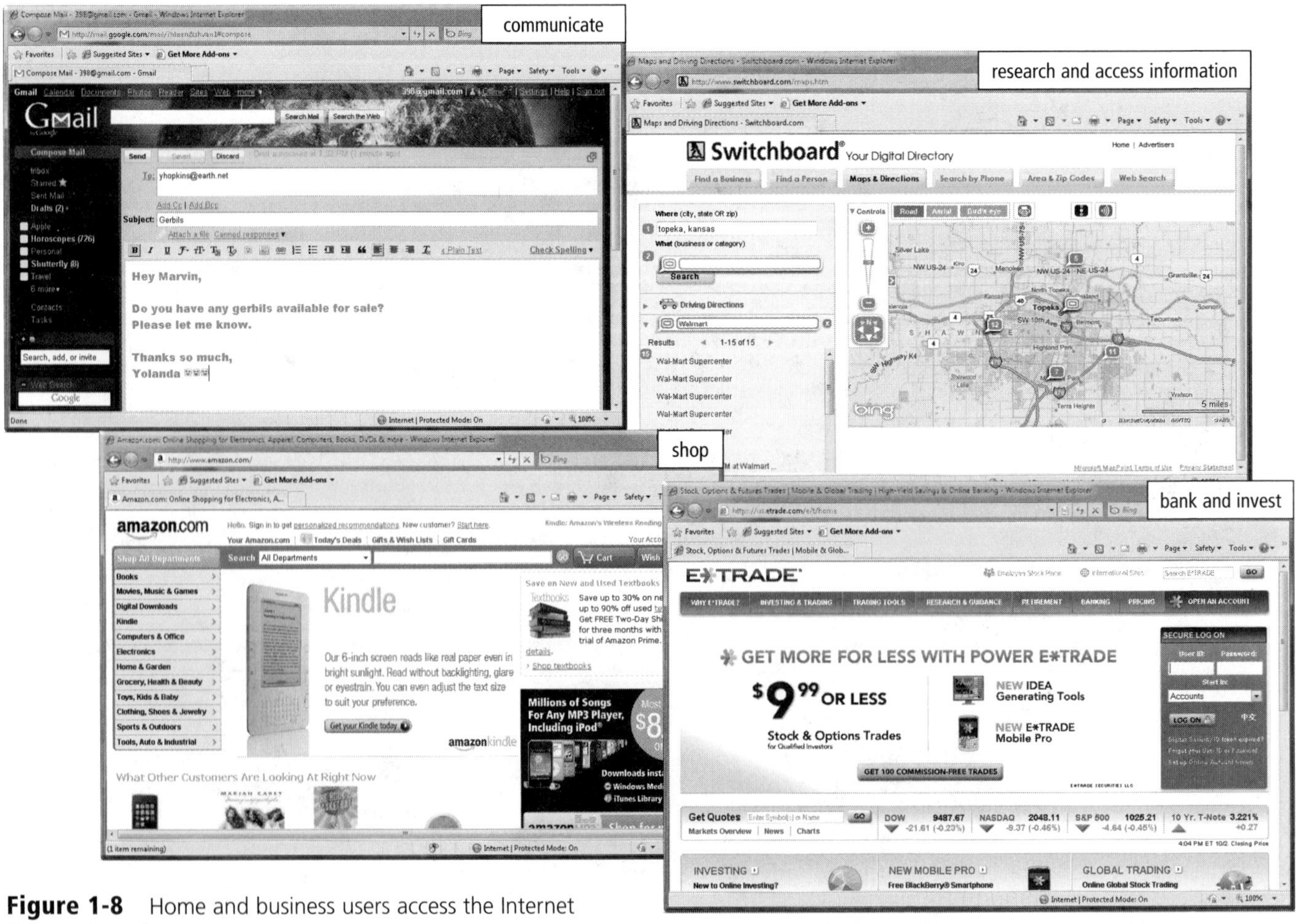

Figure 1-8 Home and business users access the Internet for a variety of reasons.

to the Internet. The **Web** contains billions of documents called Web pages. A **Web page** can contain text, graphics, animation, audio, and video. The nine screens shown in Figure 1-8 are examples of Web pages. Web pages often have built-in connections, or links, to other documents, graphics, other Web pages, or Web sites. A **Web site** is a collection of related Web pages. Some Web sites allow users to access music and videos that can be downloaded, or transferred to storage media in a computer or portable media player. Once downloaded, you can listen to the music through speakers, headphones, or earbuds, or view the videos on a display device.

Many people use the Web as a means to share personal information, photos, and videos with the world. For example, you can create a Web page and then make it available, or *publish* it, on the Internet for others to see.

ETHICS & ISSUES 1-2

What Should Be Done about Identity Theft?

Using e-mail and other techniques on the Internet, scam artists are employing a technique known as *phishing* to try to steal your personal information, such as credit card numbers, banking information, and passwords. For example, an e-mail message may appear to be a request from your bank to verify your Social Security number and online banking password. Instead, the information you submit ends up in the hands of the scammer, who then uses the information for a variety of unethical and illegal acts. Sadly, the result often is identity theft. You can help to deter identity theft in several ways: 1) shred your financial documents before discarding them, 2) do not click links in unsolicited e-mail messages, and 3) enroll in a credit monitoring service. Consumer advocates often blame credit card companies and credit bureaus for lax security standards. Meanwhile, the companies blame consumers for being too gullible and forthcoming with private information. Both sides blame the government for poor privacy laws and light punishments for identity thieves. But while the arguments go on, law enforcement agencies bear the brunt of the problem by spending hundreds of millions of dollars responding to complaints and finding and processing the criminals.

Who should be responsible for protecting the public from online identity theft? Why? Should laws be changed to stop it, or should consumers change behavior? What is an appropriate punishment for identity thieves? Given the international nature of the Internet, how should foreign identity thieves be handled? Why?

You also can join millions of people worldwide in an online community, called a **social networking Web site** or an *online social network*, that encourages members to share their interests, ideas, stories, photos, music, and videos with other registered users (Figure 1-9). Some social networking Web sites are college oriented, some business oriented, and others are more focused. A **photo sharing community**, for example, is a specific type of social networking Web site that allows users to create an online photo album and store and share their digital photos. Similarly, a **video sharing community** is a type of social networking Web site that allows users to store and share their personal videos.

Hundreds of thousands of people today also use blogs to publish their thoughts on the Web. A *blog* is an informal Web site consisting of time-stamped articles in a diary or journal format, usually listed in reverse chronological order. As others read the articles in a blog, they reply with their own thoughts. A blog that contains video clips is called a *video blog*. A *microblog*, such as Twitter, allows users to publish short messages, usually between 100 and 200 characters, for others to read. To learn more about creating and using blogs, complete the Learn How To 2 activity on pages 50 and 51.

Facebook

For more information, visit the Computer Concepts CourseMate Web site at www.cengagebrain.com, navigate to the Chapter 1 Web Link resource for this book, and then click Facebook.

Podcasts are a popular way people verbally share information on the Web. A *podcast* is recorded audio stored on a Web site that can be downloaded to a computer or a portable media player such as an iPod. A video podcast is a podcast that contains video and usually audio. At a convenient time and location, the user listens to or watches the downloaded podcast.

A **Web application** is a Web site that allows users to access and interact with software from any computer or device that is connected to the Internet. Examples of software available as Web applications include those that allow you to send and receive e-mail messages, prepare your taxes, organize digital photos, create documents, and play games.

Web sites such as social networking Web sites, blogs, and Web applications are categorized as Web 2.0 sites. The term **Web 2.0** refers to Web sites that provide a means for users to share personal information (such as social networking Web sites), allow users to modify the Web site contents (such as some blogs), and/or have software built into the site for users to access (such as Web applications).

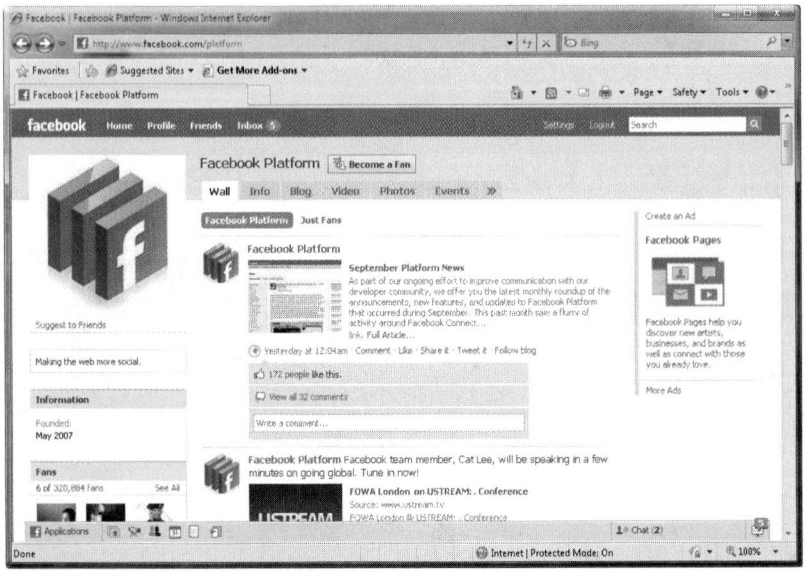

Figure 1-9 Facebook is a popular social networking Web site.

FAQ 1-1

What U.S. Web sites are visited most frequently?

A recent survey found that Google's Web site is visited most frequently, with Microsoft and Yahoo! not far behind. The chart below shows the five most frequently visited Web sites, as well as the approximate number of unique visitors per month.

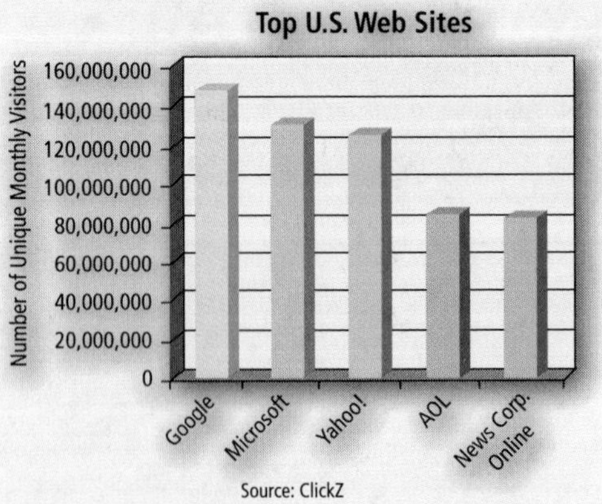

For more information, visit the Computer Concepts CourseMate Web site at www.cengagebrain.com, navigate to the Chapter 1 FAQ resource for this book, and then click Top Web Sites.

An *FAQ* (frequently asked question) helps you find answers to commonly asked questions. Web sites often post an FAQ section, and each chapter in this book includes FAQ boxes related to topics in the text.

Computer Software

Software, also called a **program**, consists of a series of related instructions, organized for a common purpose, that tells the computer what tasks to perform and how to perform them.

You interact with a program through its user interface. The user interface controls how you enter data and instructions and how information is displayed on the screen. Software today often has a graphical user interface. With a **graphical user interface** (**GUI** pronounced gooey), you interact with the software using text, graphics, and visual images such as icons. An *icon* is a miniature image that represents a program, an instruction, or some other object. You can use the mouse to select icons that perform operations such as starting a program.

The two categories of software are system software and application software. Figure 1-10 shows an example of each of these categories of software, which are explained in the following sections.

System Software

System software consists of the programs that control or maintain the operations of the computer and its devices. System software serves as the interface between the user, the application software, and the computer's hardware. Two types of system software are the operating system and utility programs.

Operating System An *operating system* is a set of programs that coordinates all the activities among computer hardware devices. It provides a means for users to communicate with the computer and other software. Many of today's computers use Microsoft's Windows, the latest version of which is shown in Figure 1-10, or Mac OS, Apple's operating system.

When a user starts a computer, portions of the operating system are copied into memory from the computer's hard disk. These parts of the operating system remain in memory while the computer is on.

Windows
For more information, visit the Computer Concepts CourseMate Web site at www.cengagebrain.com, navigate to the Chapter 1 Web Link resource for this book, and then click Windows.

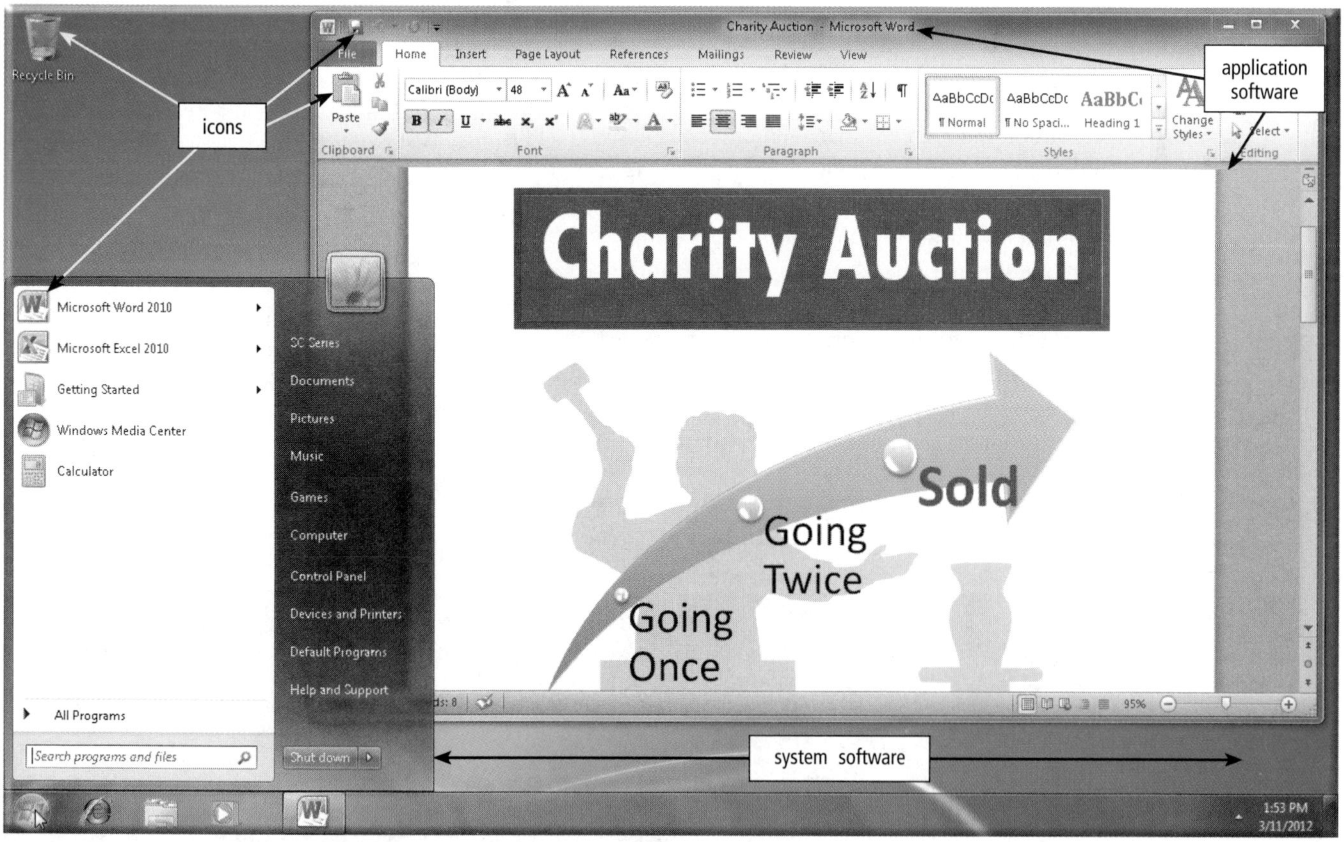

Figure 1-10 Today's system software and application software usually have a graphical user interface.

Utility Program A *utility program* allows a user to perform maintenance-type tasks usually related to managing a computer, its devices, or its programs. For example, you can use a utility program to transfer digital photos to an optical disc. Most operating systems include several utility programs for managing disk drives, printers, and other devices and media. You also can buy utility programs that allow you to perform additional computer management functions.

Application Software

Application software consists of programs designed to make users more productive and/or assist them with personal tasks. A widely used type of application software related to communications is a Web browser, which allows users with an Internet connection to access and view Web pages or access programs. Other popular application software includes word processing software, spreadsheet software, database software, and presentation software.

Many other types of application software exist that enable users to perform a variety of tasks. These include personal information management, note taking, project management, accounting, document management, computer-aided design, desktop publishing, paint/image editing, photo editing, audio and video editing, multimedia authoring, Web page authoring, personal finance, legal, tax preparation, home design/landscaping, travel and mapping, education, reference, and entertainment (e.g., games or simulations, etc.).

Software is available at stores that sell computer products (Figure 1-11) and also online at many Web sites.

FAQ 1-2

Who plays video games?

The introduction of computer and video games that cater to a broader audience has greatly increased the number of people who play them. According to the Entertainment Software Association, approximately 68 percent of the U.S. population plays video games. Of these, 40 percent are women. Further, 25 percent of Americans over 50 play video games, and the average game player is 35 years old.

For more information, visit the Computer Concepts CourseMate Web site at www.cengagebrain.com, navigate to the Chapter 1 FAQ resource for this book, and then click Game Demographics.

Installing and Running Programs

When purchasing software from a retailer, you typically receive a box that includes an optical disc(s) that contains the program. If you acquire software from a Web site on the Internet, you may be able to download the program; that is, the program transfers from the Web site to the hard disk in your computer.

The instructions in software are placed on storage media, either locally or online. To use software that is stored locally, such as on a hard disk or optical disc, you usually need to install the software. Web applications that are stored online, by contrast, usually do not need to be installed.

Installing is the process of setting up software to work with the computer, printer, and other hardware. When you buy a computer, it usually has some software preinstalled on its hard disk. This enables you to use the computer the first time you turn it on. To begin installing additional software from an optical disc, insert the program disc in an optical disc drive and follow the instructions to begin installation. To install downloaded software, the Web site typically provides instructions for how to install the program on your hard disk.

Figure 1-11
Stores that sell computer products have shelves stocked with software for sale.

Once installed, you can run the program. When you instruct the computer to **run** an installed program, the computer *loads* it, which means the program is copied from storage to memory. Once in memory, the computer can carry out, or *execute*, the instructions in the program so that you can use the program. Figure 1-12 illustrates the steps that occur when a user installs and runs a program. To learn more about starting and closing programs, complete the Learn How To 1 activity on page 50.

FAQ 1-3

How do I know if computer software will run on my computer?

When you buy a computer, the box, the manufacturer's Web site, or the order summary will list the computer's specifications. Similarly, when you buy software, the software box or the product's Web site lists specifications. Your computer's specifications should be the same as or greater than the software specifications.

For more information, visit the Computer Concepts CourseMate Web site at www.cengagebrain.com, navigate to the Chapter 1 FAQ resource for this book, and then click Computer Software.

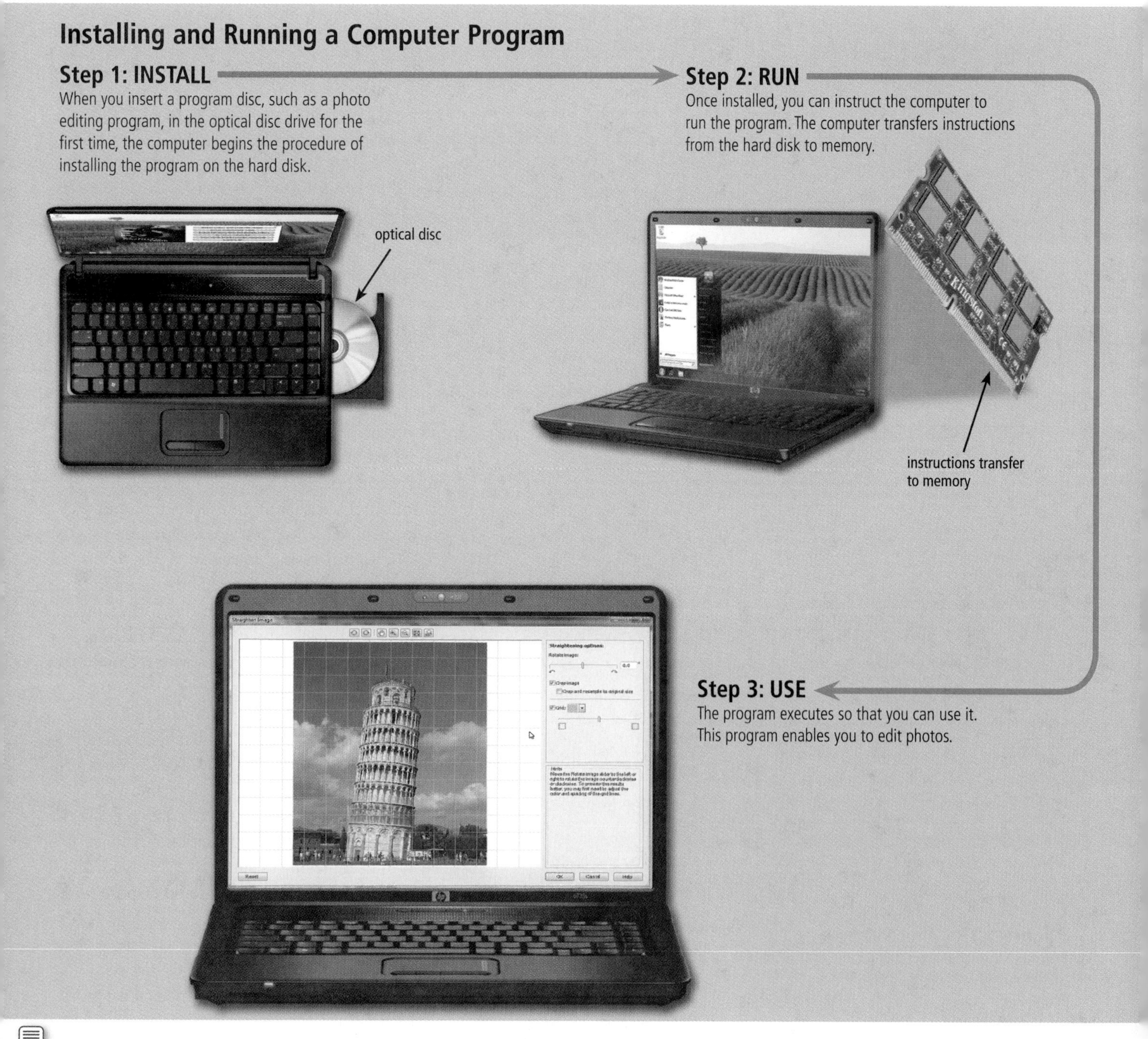

Installing and Running a Computer Program
Step 1: INSTALL
When you insert a program disc, such as a photo editing program, in the optical disc drive for the first time, the computer begins the procedure of installing the program on the hard disk.
optical disc
Step 2: RUN
Once installed, you can instruct the computer to run the program. The computer transfers instructions from the hard disk to memory.
instructions transfer to memory
Step 3: USE
The program executes so that you can use it. This program enables you to edit photos.

Figure 1-12 This figure shows how to install and run a computer program.

Software Development

A *programmer*, sometimes called a computer programmer or *developer*, is someone who develops software or writes the instructions that direct the computer to process data into information. When writing instructions, a programmer must be sure the program works properly so that the computer generates the desired results. Complex programs can require thousands to millions of instructions.

Programmers use a programming language or program development tool to create computer programs. Popular programming languages include C++, Java, JavaScript, Visual C#, and Visual Basic. Figure 1-13 shows some of the Visual Basic instructions a programmer may write to create a simple payroll program.

Figure 1-13a (Visual Basic program instructions)

```
Public Class frmPayrollInformation

    Private Sub btnCalculatePay_Click(ByVal sender As System.Object, ByVal e As System.
    EventArgs) Handles btnCalculatePay.Click
        'This procedure executes when the user clicks the
        'Calculate Pay button. It calculates regular
        'and overtime pay and displays it in the window.

        ' Declare variables
        Dim strHoursWorked As String
        Dim strHourlyRate As String
        Dim decHoursWorked As Decimal
        Dim decHourlyRate As Decimal
        Dim decRegularPay As Decimal
        Dim decOvertimeHours As Decimal
        Dim decOvertimePay As Decimal
        Dim decTotalPay As Decimal

        ' Calculate and display payroll information
        strHoursWorked = Me.txtHoursWorked.Text
        strHourlyRate = Me.txtHourlyRate.Text
        decHoursWorked = Convert.ToDecimal(strHoursWorked)
        decHourlyRate = Convert.ToDecimal(strHourlyRate)

        If decHoursWorked > 40 Then
            decRegularPay = 40 * decHourlyRate
            Me.txtRegularPay.Text = decRegularPay.ToString("C")
            decOvertimeHours = decHoursWorked - 40
            decOvertimePay = (1.5 * decOvertimeHours) * decHourlyRate
            Me.txtOvertimePay.Text = decOvertimePay.ToString("C")
            decTotalPay = decRegularPay + decOvertimePay
            Me.txtTotalPay.Text = decTotalPay.ToString("C")
        Else
            decRegularPay = decHoursWorked * decHourlyRate
            Me.txtRegularPay.Text = decRegularPay.ToString("C")
            Me.txtOvertimePay.Text = "$0.00"
            Me.txtTotalPay.Text = decRegularPay.ToString("C")
        End If
    End Sub
End Class
```

Figure 1-13b (window appears when user runs program)

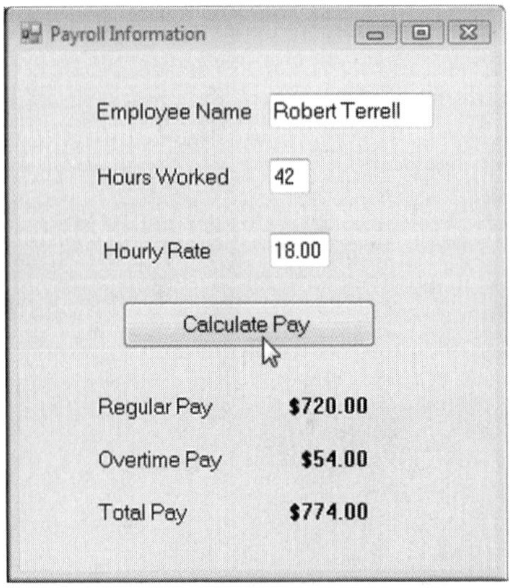

Figure 1-13 A programmer writes Visual Basic instructions to create the Payroll Information window.

QUIZ YOURSELF 1-2

Instructions: Find the true statement below. Then, rewrite the remaining false statements so that they are true.

1. A resource is a collection of computers and devices connected together via communications devices and transmission media.
2. Installing is the process of setting up software to work with the computer, printer, and other hardware.
3. Popular system software includes Web browsers, word processing software, spreadsheet software, database software, and presentation software.
4. The Internet is one of the more popular services on the Web.
5. Two types of application software are the operating system and utility programs.

Quiz Yourself Online: To further check your knowledge of pages 10 through 18, visit the Computer Concepts CourseMate Web site at www.cengagebrain.com, navigate to the Chapter 1 Quiz Yourself resource for this book, and then click Objectives 5 – 7.

Categories of Computers

Industry experts typically classify computers in seven categories: personal computers (desktop), mobile computers and mobile devices, game consoles, servers, mainframes, supercomputers, and embedded computers. A computer's size, speed, processing power, and price determine the category it best fits. Due to rapidly changing technology, however, the distinction among categories is not always clear-cut. This trend of computers and devices with technologies that overlap, called *convergence*, leads to computer manufacturers continually releasing newer models that include similar functionality and features. For example, newer cell phones often include media player, camera, and Web browsing capabilities. As devices converge, users need fewer devices for the functionality that they require. When consumers replace outdated computers and devices, they should dispose of them properly.

Figure 1-14 summarizes the seven categories of computers. The following pages discuss computers and devices that fall in each category.

Categories of Computers

Category	Physical Size	Number of Simultaneously Connected Users	General Price Range
Personal computers (desktop)	Fits on a desk	Usually one (can be more if networked)	Several hundred to several thousand dollars
Mobile computers and mobile devices	Fits on your lap or in your hand	Usually one	Less than a hundred dollars to several thousand dollars
Game consoles	Small box or handheld device	One to several	Several hundred dollars or less
Servers	Small cabinet	Two to thousands	Several hundred to a million dollars
Mainframes	Partial room to a full room of equipment	Hundreds to thousands	$300,000 to several million dollars
Supercomputers	Full room of equipment	Hundreds to thousands	$500,000 to several billion dollars
Embedded computers	Miniature	Usually one	Embedded in the price of the product

Figure 1-14 This table summarizes some of the differences among the categories of computers. These should be considered general guidelines only because of rapid changes in technology.

Personal Computers

A **personal computer** is a computer that can perform all of its input, processing, output, and storage activities by itself. A personal computer contains a processor, memory, and one or more input, output, and storage devices. Personal computers also often contain a communications device.

Two popular architectures of personal computers are the PC (Figure 1-15) and the Apple (Figure 1-16). The term, *PC-compatible*, refers to any personal computer based on the original IBM personal computer design. Companies such as Dell, HP, and Toshiba sell PC-compatible computers. PC and PC-compatible computers usually use a Windows operating system. Apple computers usually use a Macintosh operating system (Mac OS).

Two types of personal computers are desktop computers and notebook computers.

Figure 1-15 PC and PC-compatible computers usually use a Windows operating system.

Figure 1-16 Apple computers, such as the iMac, usually use a Macintosh operating system.

FAQ 1-4

Are PCs or Apple computers more popular?

While PCs still are more popular than Apple computers, Apple computer sales have been rising consistently during the past few years. In fact, Apple computer sales now account for more than 20 percent of all computer sales in the United States, with that number estimated to grow for the foreseeable future.

For more information, visit the Computer Concepts CourseMate Web site at www.cengagebrain.com, navigate to the Chapter 1 FAQ resource for this book, and then click Personal Computer Sales.

Desktop Computers

A **desktop computer** is designed so that the system unit, input devices, output devices, and any other devices fit entirely on or under a desk or table (Figures 1-15 and 1-16 on the previous page). In many models, the system unit is a tall and narrow *tower*, which can sit on the floor vertically — if desktop space is limited.

Some desktop computers function as a server on a network. Others, such as a gaming desktop computer and home theater PC, target a specific audience. The *gaming desktop computer* offers high-quality audio, video, and graphics with optimal performance for sophisticated single-user and networked or Internet multiplayer games. A *home theater PC (HTPC)* combines the features of a high-definition video/audio entertainment system with a desktop computer that is designed to be connected to a television and includes a Blu-ray Disc, digital video recorder, and digital cable television connectivity. These high-end computers cost more than the basic desktop computer.

Another expensive, powerful desktop computer is the workstation, which is geared for work that requires intense calculations and graphics capabilities. An architect uses a workstation to design buildings and homes. A graphic artist uses a workstation to create computer-animated special effects for full-length motion pictures and video games.

FAQ 1-5

Does the term, workstation, have multiple meanings?

Yes. In the computer industry, a *workstation* can be a high-powered computer or a client computer on a network. In an office environment, a workstation can refer to a work area assigned to an employee.

For more information, visit the Computer Concepts CourseMate Web site at www.cengagebrain.com, navigate to the Chapter 1 FAQ resource for this book, and then click Workstation.

Mobile Computers and Mobile Devices

A **mobile computer** is a personal computer you can carry from place to place. Similarly, a **mobile device** is a computing device small enough to hold in your hand.

The most popular type of mobile computer is the notebook computer. The following sections discuss the notebook computer and widely used mobile devices.

Notebook Computers

A **notebook computer**, also called a **laptop computer**, is a portable, personal computer often designed to fit on your lap. Notebook computers are thin and lightweight, yet they can be as powerful as the average desktop computer. A *netbook*, which is a type of notebook computer, is smaller, lighter, and often not as powerful as a traditional notebook computer. Most netbooks cost less than traditional notebook computers, usually only a few hundred dollars. An ultra-thin is another type of notebook computer that is lightweight and usually less than one-inch thick. Some notebook computers have touch screens, allowing you to interact with the device by touching the screen, usually with the tip of a finger.

On a typical notebook computer, the keyboard is on top of the system unit, and the monitor attaches to the system unit with hinges (Figure 1-17). These computers weigh on average from 2.5 to more than 10 pounds (depending on configuration), which allows users to transport the computers from place to place. Most notebook computers can operate on batteries or a power supply or both.

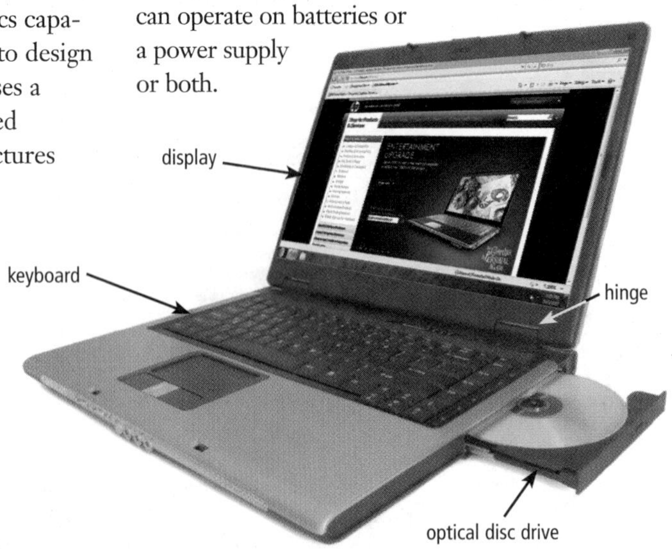

Figure 1-17 On a typical notebook computer, the keyboard is on top of the system unit, and the display attaches to the system unit with hinges.

Tablet PCs Resembling a letter-sized slate, the **Tablet PC**, or tablet computer, is a special type of notebook computer that you can interact with by touching the screen with your finger or a digital pen. A *digital pen* looks like a small ink pen but uses pressure instead of ink. Users write or draw on a Tablet PC by pressing a finger or digital pen on the screen, and issue instructions by tapping on the screen. One design of Tablet PC, called a *convertible tablet*, has an attached keyboard. Another design, which does not include a keyboard, is called a *slate tablet* (Figure 1-18) and provides other means for typing. Some Tablet PCs also support voice input so that users can speak into the computer.

Tablet PCs are useful especially for taking notes in lectures, at meetings, conferences, and other forums where the standard notebook computer is not practical.

Figure 1-18 The iPad is a widely used slate tablet.

Mobile Devices

Mobile devices, which are small enough to carry in a pocket, usually do not have disk drives. Instead, these devices store programs and data permanently on special memory inside the system unit or on small storage media such as memory cards. You often can connect a mobile device to a personal computer to exchange information between the computer and the mobile device.

Some mobile devices are **Internet-enabled**, meaning they can connect to the Internet wirelessly. With an Internet-enabled device, users can chat, send e-mail and instant messages, and access the Web. Because of their reduced size, the screens on mobile devices are small, but usually are in color.

Popular types of mobile devices are smart phones and PDAs, e-book readers, handheld computers, portable media players, and digital cameras.

Smart Phones and PDAs Offering the convenience of one-handed operation, a **smart phone** (Figure 1-19) is an Internet-enabled phone that usually also provides personal information management functions such as a calendar, an appointment book, an address book, a calculator, and a notepad. In addition to basic phone capabilities, a smart phone allows you to send and receive e-mail messages and access the Web — usually for an additional fee. Some smart phones communicate wirelessly with other devices or computers. Many also function as a portable media player and include built-in digital cameras so that you can share photos or videos with others as soon as you capture the image. Many smart phones also offer a variety of application software such as word processing, spreadsheet, and games, and the capability of conducting live video conferences.

Many smart phones have keypads that contain both numbers and letters so that you can use the same keypad to dial phone numbers

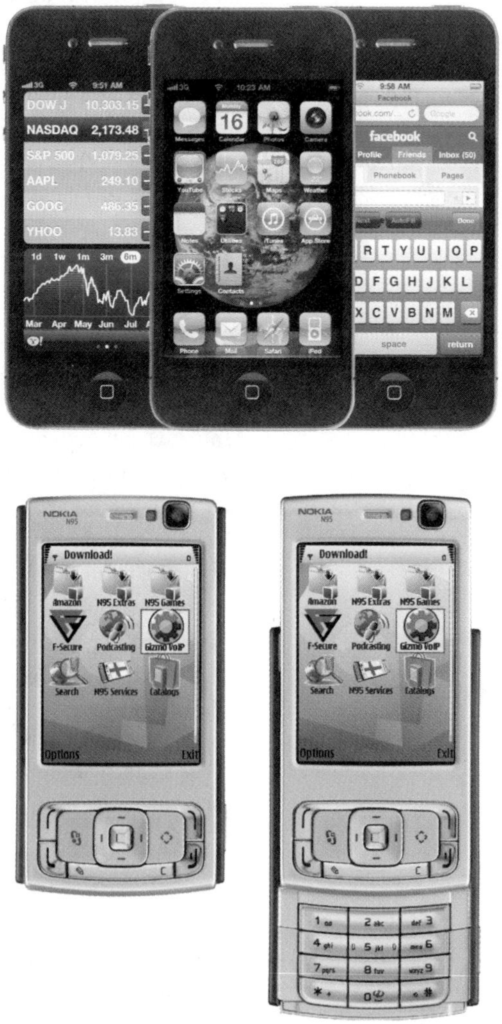

Figure 1-19 Some smart phones have touch screens; others have mini keyboards.

and enter messages. Others have a built-in mini keyboard on the front of the phone or a keyboard that slides in and out from behind the phone. Some have touch screens, where you press objects on the screen to make selections and enter text through an on-screen keyboard. Others include a stylus, which is similar to a digital pen but smaller and has less functionality.

Instead of calling someone's smart phone or cell phone, users often send messages to others by pressing buttons on their phone's keypad, keys on the mini keyboard, or images on an on-screen keyboard. Types of messages users send with smart phones include text messages, instant messages, picture messages, and video messages.

- A *text message* is a short note, typically fewer than 300 characters, sent to or from a smart phone or other mobile device.
- An *instant message* is a real-time Internet communication, where you exchange messages with other connected users.
- A *picture message* is a photo or other image, sometimes along with sound and text, sent to or from a smart phone or other mobile device. A phone that can send picture messages often is called a *camera phone*.
- A *video message* is a short video clip, usually about 30 seconds, sent to or from a smart phone or other mobile device. A phone that can send video messages often is called a *video phone*.

Camera Phone
For more information, visit the Computer Concepts CourseMate Web site at www.cengagebrain.com, navigate to the Chapter 1 Web Link resource for this book, and then click Camera Phone.

A **PDA** (*personal digital assistant*), which often looks like a smart phone, provides personal information management functions such as a calendar, an appointment book, an address book, a calculator, and a notepad. A PDA differs from a smart phone in that it usually does not provide phone capabilities and may not be Internet-enabled, support voice input, have a built-in camera, or function as a portable media player.

As smart phones and PDAs continue a trend of convergence, it is becoming increasingly difficult to differentiate between the two devices. This has led some manufacturers to refer to PDAs and smart phones simply as *handhelds*.

E-Book Readers An **e-book reader** (short for electronic book reader), or *e-reader*, is a handheld device that is used primarily for reading e-books (Figure 1-20). An *e-book*, or digital book, is an electronic version of a printed book, readable on computers and other digital devices. In addition to books, users typically can purchase and read other forms of digital media such as newspapers and magazines.

Most e-book readers have a touch screen and are Internet-enabled. These devices usually are smaller than tablet computers but larger than smart phones.

Figure 1-20 An e-book reader.

Handheld Computers A **handheld computer**, sometimes referred to as an *Ultra-Mobile PC* (*UMPC*), is a computer small enough to fit in one hand. Many handheld computers communicate wirelessly with other devices or computers and also include a digital pen or stylus for input.

Some handheld computers have miniature or specialized keyboards. Many handheld computers are industry-specific and serve the needs of mobile employees, such as meter readers and parcel delivery people (Figure 1-21), whose jobs require them to move from place to place.

? FAQ 1-6

How popular is text messaging?

A recent study indicates that people are using their smart phones and cell phones for voice communications and text messaging more frequently than in previous years. Because of the increase in smart phone sales and the ease with which individuals can send text messages, approximately two billion text messages are sent each day.

For more information, visit the Computer Concepts CourseMate Web site at www.cengagebrain.com, navigate to the Chapter 1 FAQ resource for this book, and then click Text Messaging.

Figure 1-21 This handheld computer is a lightweight computer that enables delivery people to obtain and record information about their deliveries.

Portable Media Players A **portable media player** is a mobile device on which you can store, organize, and play digital media (Figure 1-22). For example, you can listen to music; watch videos, movies, and television shows; and view photos on the device's screen. With most, you download the digital media from a computer to the portable media player or to media that you insert in the device.

Figure 1-22 The iPod, shown here, is a popular portable media player.

Some portable media players are Internet-enabled so that you can access Web sites and send e-mail messages directly from the device. Many offer personal information management functions such as a calendar and address book, and include a variety of games and other application software.

Portable media players usually include a set of earbuds, which are small speakers that rest inside each ear canal. Some portable media players have a touch screen, while others have a touch-sensitive pad that you operate with a thumb or finger, to navigate through digital media, adjust volume, and customize settings.

Digital Cameras A **digital camera** is a device that allows users to take pictures and store the photographed images digitally, instead of on traditional film (Figure 1-23). While many digital cameras look like a traditional camera, some are built into smart phones and other mobile devices.

Although digital cameras usually have some amount of internal storage to hold images, most users store images on small storage media such as memory cards. Digital cameras typically allow users to review, and sometimes modify, images while they are in the camera. Some digital cameras connect to or communicate wirelessly with a computer or printer, allowing users to print or view images directly from the printer. Some memory cards can connect to a network wirelessly, so that you can transfer photos directly from the memory card in the camera to the Internet without requiring a computer.

Often users prefer to download images from the digital camera to the computer. Or, you can remove the storage media such as a memory card from the digital camera and insert it in a card reader in or attached to the computer.

Digital Cameras

For more information, visit the Computer Concepts CourseMate Web site at www.cengagebrain.com, navigate to the Chapter 1 Web Link resource for this book, and then click Digital Cameras.

Figure 1-23 With a digital camera, users can view photographed images immediately through a small screen on the camera to see if the picture is worth keeping.

Game Consoles

A **game console** is a mobile computing device designed for single-player or multiplayer video games (Figure 1-24). Standard game consoles use a handheld controller(s) as an input device(s); a television screen as an output device; and hard disks, optical discs, and/or memory cards for storage. Weighing on average between two and nine pounds, the compact size of game consoles makes them easy to use at home, in the car, in a hotel, or any location that has an electrical outlet. Three popular models are Microsoft's Xbox 360, Nintendo's Wii (pronounced wee), and Sony's PlayStation 3. Read Innovative Computing 1-1 to find out how the medical field uses the Nintendo Wii.

A handheld game console is small enough to fit in one hand, making it more portable than the standard game console. With the handheld game console, the controls, screen, and speakers are built into the device. Because of their reduced size, the screens are small — three to four inches. Some models use cartridges to store games; others use a memory card or a miniature optical disc. Many handheld game consoles can communicate wirelessly with other similar consoles for multiplayer gaming. Two popular models are Nintendo DS Lite and Sony's PlayStation Portable (PSP).

In addition to gaming, many game console models allow users to listen to music, watch movies, keep fit, and connect to the Internet. Game consoles can cost from a couple hundred dollars to more than $500.

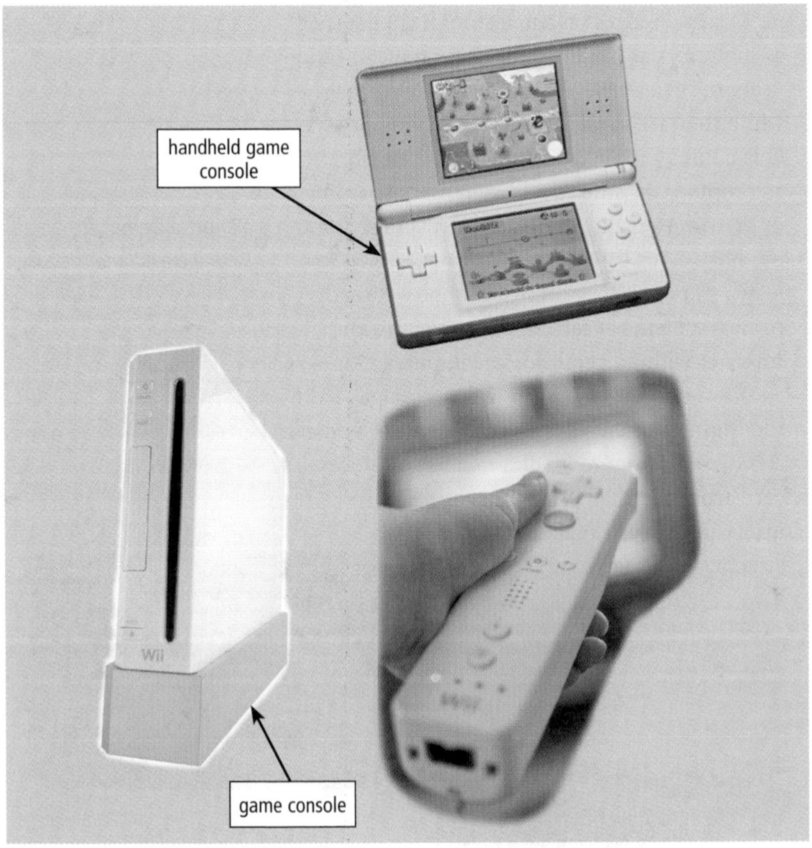

Figure 1-24 Game consoles provide hours of video game entertainment.

INNOVATIVE COMPUTING 1-1

Wii a Welcome Medical Skill Builder

A patient awaiting laparoscopic procedures may be less tense knowing that the surgeons have honed their dexterity and coordination using a Nintendo Wii. Preliminary studies have found that doctors can improve their fine motor control by playing video games that emphasize subtle hand movements used in minimally invasive surgeries. Researchers are developing Wii surgery simulators that will allow doctors to practice their skills at home or in break rooms at hospitals.

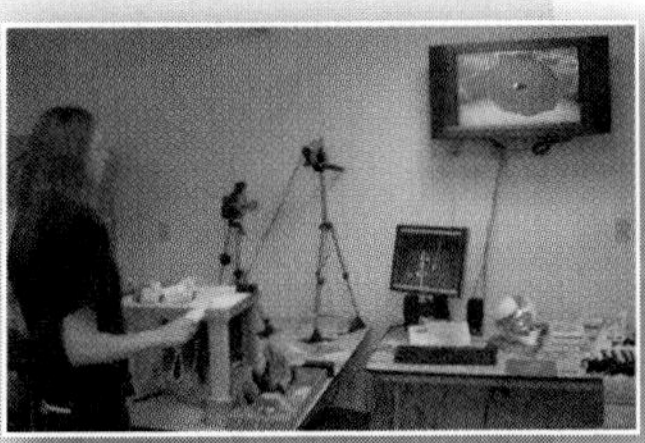

The Wii game system is finding a medical home in other nontraditional places. Physical therapists urge arthritic patients to use *Wiihabilitation* to build endurance and increase their range of motion. Therapeutic recreation with the Wii's sports games may help patients recovering from strokes, fractures, and combat injuries.

Researchers in a testing lab in California are experimenting with using the Wii's motion-activated controls in non-gaming applications, such as allowing doctors to explain X-ray images to patients.

For more information, visit the Computer Concepts CourseMate Web site at www.cengagebrain.com, navigate to the Chapter 1 Innovative Computing resource for this book, and then click Medical Wii.

Servers

Figure 1-25
A server controls access to resources on a network.

A **server** controls access to the hardware, software, and other resources on a network and provides a centralized storage area for programs, data, and information (Figure 1-25). Servers can support from two to several thousand connected computers at the same time.

In many cases, one server accesses data, information, and programs on another server. In other cases, people use personal computers or terminals to access data, information, and programs on a server. A terminal is a device with a monitor, keyboard, and memory.

Mainframes

Figure 1-26
Mainframe computers can handle thousands of connected computers and process millions of instructions per second.

A **mainframe** is a large, expensive, powerful computer that can handle hundreds or thousands of connected users simultaneously (Figure 1-26). Mainframes store tremendous amounts of data, instructions, and information. Most major corporations use mainframes for business activities. With mainframes, enterprises are able to bill millions of customers, prepare payroll for thousands of employees, and manage thousands of items in inventory. One study reported that mainframes process more than 83 percent of transactions around the world.

Mainframes also can act as servers in a network environment. Servers and other mainframes can access data and information from a mainframe. People also can access programs on the mainframe using terminals or personal computers.

Supercomputers

Figure 1-27 This supercomputer, IBM's Roadrunner, can process more than one quadrillion instructions in a single second.

A **supercomputer** is the fastest, most powerful computer — and the most expensive (Figure 1-27). The fastest supercomputers are capable of processing more than one quadrillion instructions in a single second. With weights that exceed 100 tons, these computers can store more than 20,000 times the data and information of an average desktop computer.

Applications requiring complex, sophisticated mathematical calculations use supercomputers. Large-scale simulations and applications in medicine, aerospace, automotive design, online banking, weather forecasting, nuclear energy research, and petroleum exploration use a supercomputer.

Embedded Computers

An **embedded computer** is a special-purpose computer that functions as a component in a larger product. Embedded computers are everywhere — at home, in your car, and at work. The following list identifies a variety of everyday products that contain embedded computers.

- Consumer Electronics: mobile and digital telephones, digital televisions, cameras, video recorders, DVD players and recorders, answering machines
- Home Automation Devices: thermostats, sprinkling systems, security monitoring systems, appliances, lights
- Automobiles: antilock brakes, engine control modules, airbag controller, cruise control
- Process Controllers and Robotics: remote monitoring systems, power monitors, machine controllers, medical devices
- Computer Devices and Office Machines: keyboards, printers, fax and copy machines

Because embedded computers are components in larger products, they usually are small and have limited hardware. These computers perform various functions, depending on the requirements of the product in which they reside. Embedded computers in printers, for example, monitor the amount of paper in the tray, check the ink or toner level, signal if a paper jam has occurred, and so on. Figure 1-28 shows some of the many embedded computers in cars.

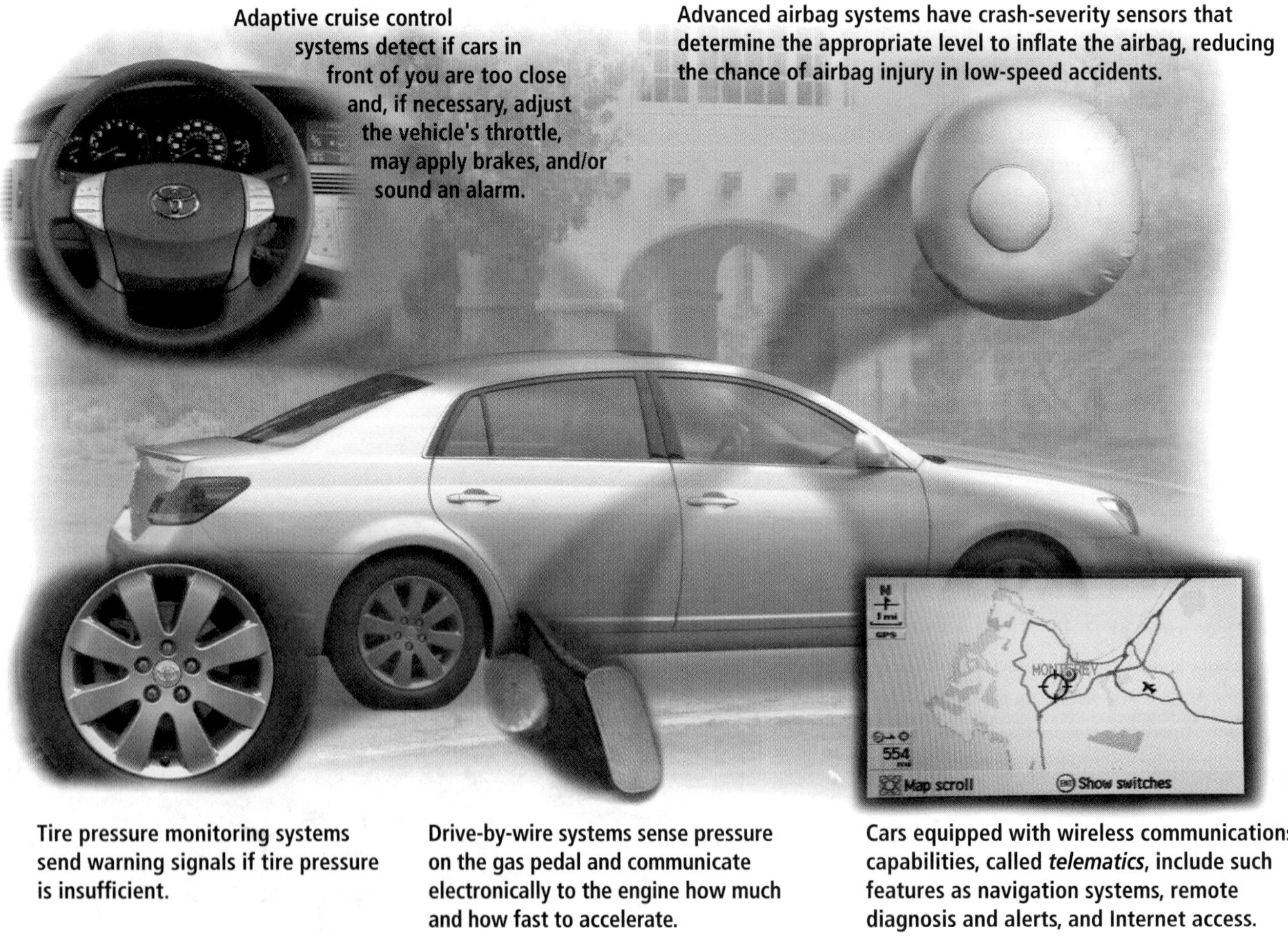
Adaptive cruise control systems detect if cars in front of you are too close and, if necessary, adjust the vehicle's throttle, may apply brakes, and/or sound an alarm.
Advanced airbag systems have crash-severity sensors that determine the appropriate level to inflate the airbag, reducing the chance of airbag injury in low-speed accidents.
MONTEREY
554
Map scroll
Show switches
Tire pressure monitoring systems send warning signals if tire pressure is insufficient.
Drive-by-wire systems sense pressure on the gas pedal and communicate electronically to the engine how much and how fast to accelerate.
Cars equipped with wireless communications capabilities, called *telematics*, include such features as navigation systems, remote diagnosis and alerts, and Internet access.

Figure 1-28 Some of the embedded computers designed to improve your safety, security, and performance in today's automobiles.

Elements of an Information System

To be valuable, information must be accurate, organized, timely, accessible, useful, and cost-effective to produce. Generating information from a computer requires the following five elements:

- Hardware
- Software
- Data
- People
- Procedures

Together, these elements (hardware, software, data, people, and procedures) comprise an *information system*. Figure 1-29 shows how each of the elements of an information system in an enterprise might interact.

The hardware must be reliable and capable of handling the expected workload. The software must be developed carefully and tested thoroughly. The data entered into the computer must be accurate.

Most companies with mid-sized and large computers have an IT (information technology) department. Staff in the IT department should be skilled and up-to-date on the latest technology. IT staff also should train users so that they understand how to use the computer properly. Today's users also work closely with IT staff in the development of computer applications that relate to their areas of work.

Finally, all the IT applications should have readily available documented procedures that address operating the computer and using its programs.

Women in Technology
For more information, visit the Computer Concepts CourseMate Web site at www.cengagebrain.com, navigate to the Chapter 1 Web Link resource for this book, and then click Women in Technology.

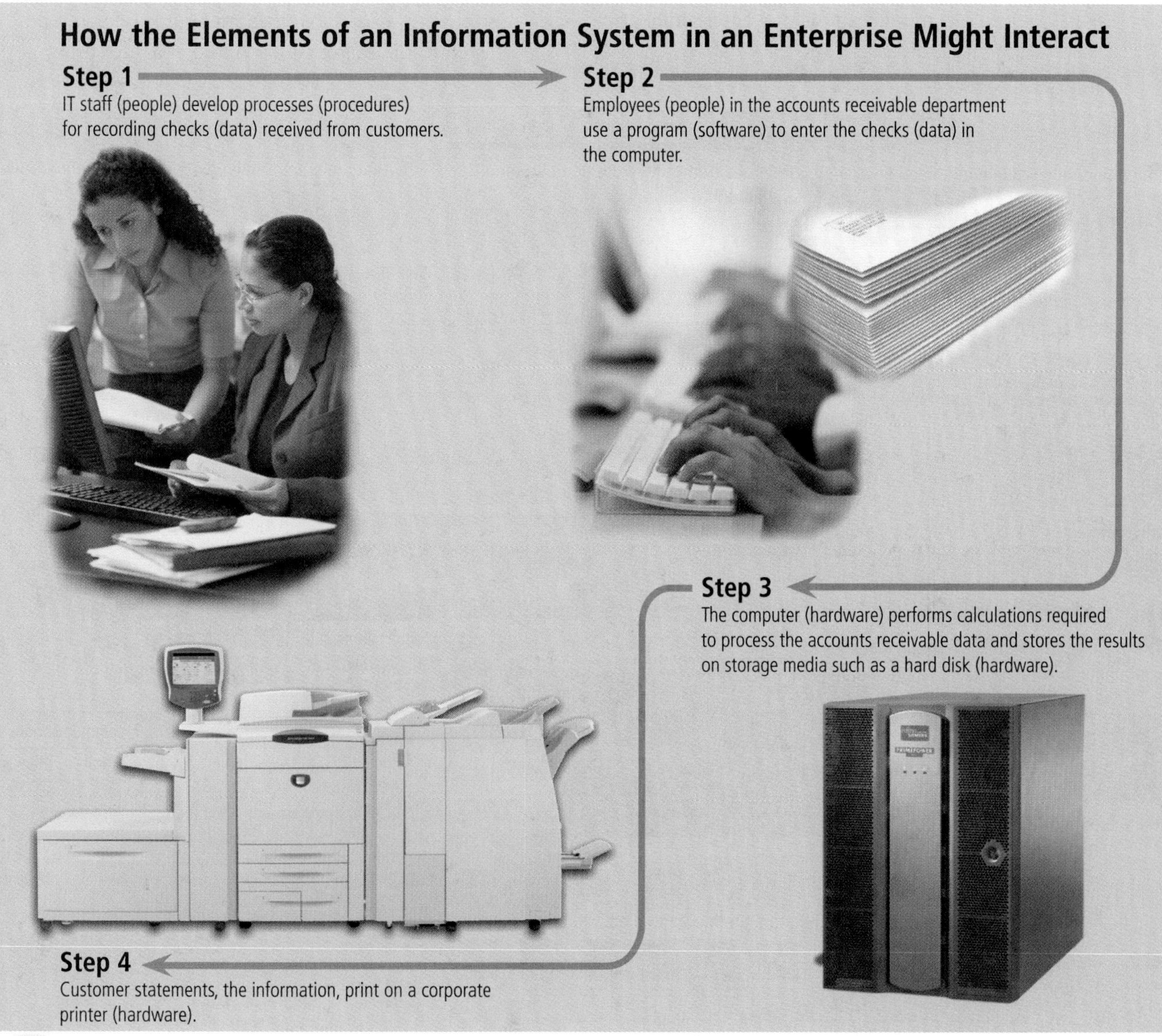
How the Elements of an Information System in an Enterprise Might Interact
Step 1
IT staff (people) develop processes (procedures) for recording checks (data) received from customers.
Step 2
Employees (people) in the accounts receivable department use a program (software) to enter the checks (data) in the computer.
Step 3
The computer (hardware) performs calculations required to process the accounts receivable data and stores the results on storage media such as a hard disk (hardware).
Step 4
Customer statements, the information, print on a corporate printer (hardware).

Figure 1-29 This figure shows how the elements of an information system in an enterprise might interact.

Examples of Computer Usage

Minorities in Technology

For more information, visit the Computer Concepts CourseMate Web site at www.cengagebrain.com, navigate to the Chapter 1 Web Link resource for this book, and then click Minorities in Technology.

Every day, people around the world rely on different types of computers for a variety of applications. To illustrate the range of uses for computers, this section takes you on a visual and narrative tour of five categories of users:

- Home user
- Small office/home office (SOHO) user
- Mobile user
- Power user
- Enterprise user

Home User

In an increasing number of homes, the computer no longer is a convenience. Instead, it is a basic necessity. Each family member, or **home user**, spends time on the computer for different reasons that include personal financial management, Web access, communications, and entertainment (Figure 1-30).

On the Internet, home users access a huge amount of information, conduct research, take college classes, pay bills, manage investments, shop, listen to the radio, watch movies, read books, file taxes, book airline reservations, make telephone calls, and play games (read Innovative Computing 1-2 to find out how some retailers use the Internet to help the environment). They also communicate with others around the world through e-mail, blogs, instant messages, and chat rooms using personal computers, smart phones, and other mobile devices. Home users share ideas, interests, photos, music, and videos on social networking Web sites (read Ethics & Issues 1-3 for a related discussion). With a digital camera, home users take photos and then send the electronic images to others. Using a Web cam, home users easily have live video calls with friends, family members, and others.

Many home users have a portable media player, so that they can download music or podcasts, and listen to the music and/or audio at a later time

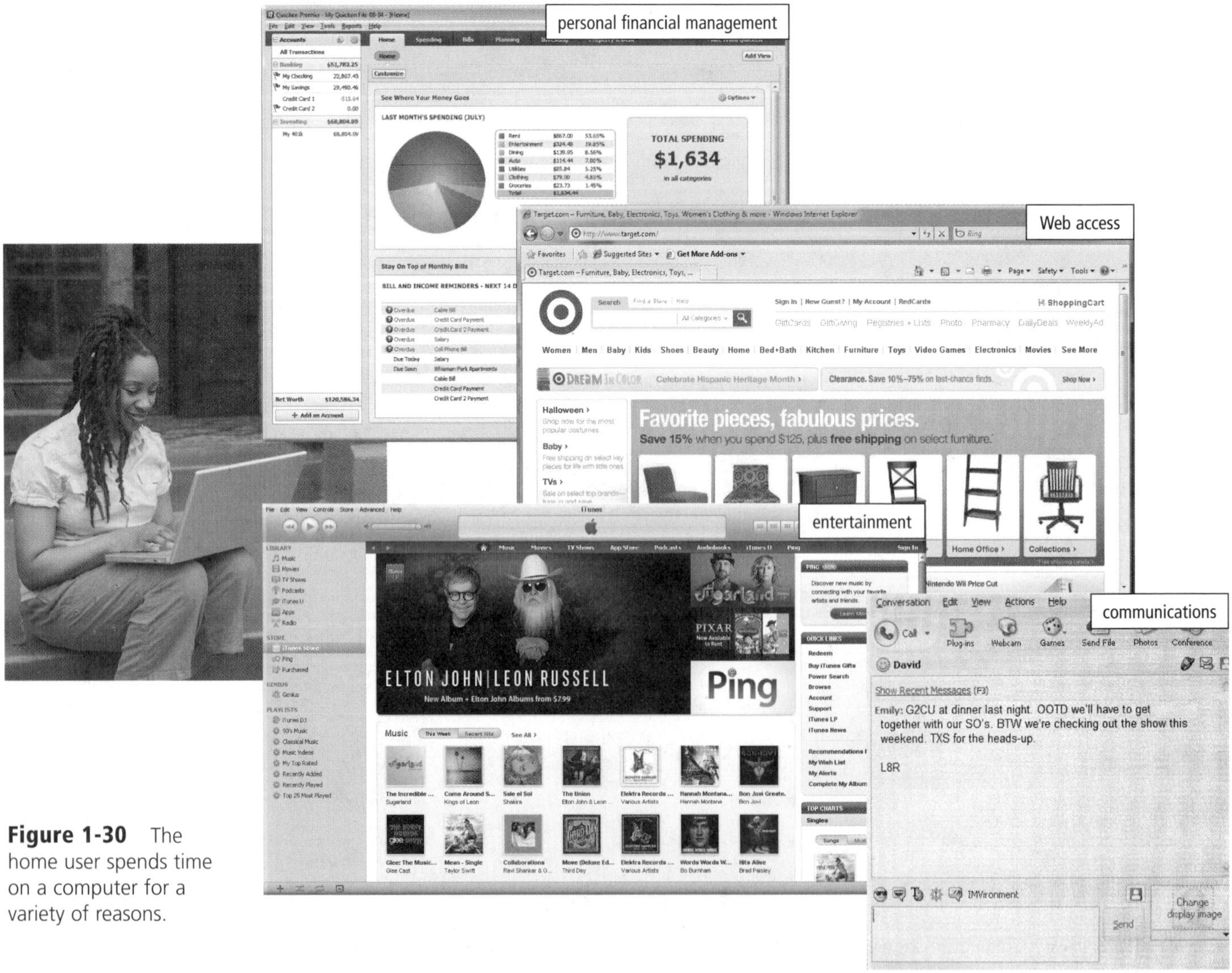

Figure 1-30 The home user spends time on a computer for a variety of reasons.

through earbuds attached to the player. They also usually have one or more game consoles to play video games individually or with friends and family members.

Today's homes also typically have one or more desktop computers. Many home users network multiple desktop computers throughout the house, often wirelessly. These small networks allow family members to share an Internet connection and a printer.

Home users have a variety of software. They type letters, homework assignments, and other documents with word processing software. Personal finance software helps the home user with personal finances, investments, and family budgets. Other software assists with preparing taxes, keeping a household inventory, setting up maintenance schedules, and protecting home computers against threats and unauthorized intrusions.

Reference software, such as encyclopedias, medical dictionaries, or a road atlas, provides valuable information for everyone in the family. With entertainment software, the home user can play games, compose music, research genealogy, or create greeting cards. Educational software helps adults learn to speak a foreign language and youngsters to read, write, count, and spell.

FAQ 1-7

How many households do not use the Internet or related technologies?

A recent survey estimates that 18 percent of U.S. households have no Internet access. Furthermore, about 20 percent of U.S. heads of households have never sent an e-mail message. The chart below illustrates the lack of experience with computer and Internet technology.

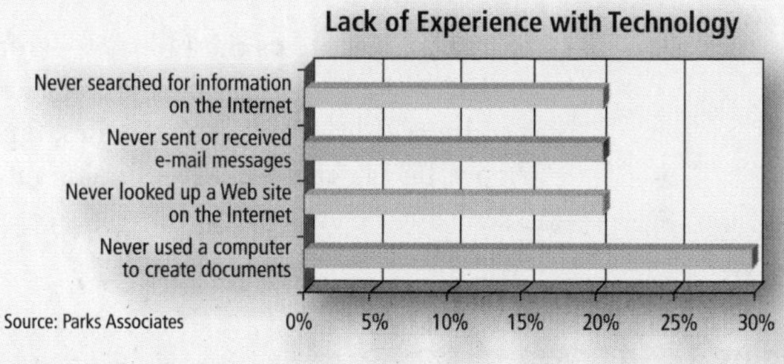

For more information, visit the Computer Concepts CourseMate Web site at www.cengagebrain.com, navigate to the Chapter 1 FAQ resource for this book, and then click Experience with Technology.

INNOVATIVE COMPUTING 1-2

E-Receipts Save Paper, Organize Life

You may need to find a new use for the old shoeboxes that are storing your receipts. Some environmentally conscious retailers are providing a service that issues receipts electronically so that consumers never will need to hunt for a little white slip of paper when returning an item or declaring an expense for income taxes.

Digital receipts, also called *e-receipts*, are sent automatically to an e-mail account or Web site where they can be sorted or deleted. One service links a consumer's credit cards to a receipt account on a specific Web site, so that every time the cards are swiped for a purchase, a receipt is sent to the consumer's account.

More than 70 percent of consumers say they would prefer having an e-receipt rather than a paper receipt. According to one estimate, nine million trees would be saved if no paper receipts were issued for one year.

For more information, visit the Computer Concepts CourseMate Web site at www.cengagebrain.com, navigate to the Chapter 1 Innovative Computing resource for this book, and then click Digital Receipts.

ETHICS & ISSUES 1-3

Who Should Look Out for the Safety of Social Networking Web Site Users?

In recent years, social networking Web site usage by children and adults exploded as a new means of communicating and socializing. Not surprisingly, the problems associated with this exciting way to interact with others mirror some problems in society in general. Problems include bullying, smear campaigns against individuals, and inappropriate contact between adults and minors. Recently, a high-school-aged girl secretly left the country with the intent of marrying an adult in a foreign country whom she met on a social networking Web site. Fortunately, authorities in the foreign country intercepted her at the airport and sent her home. Some parents claim that the government should intervene to ensure better monitoring of inappropriate behavior. While some social networking Web site companies have stepped up monitoring, they often claim that they are not responsible for the behavior of individuals, and parents and individuals should be responsible for inappropriate actions. Many individuals feel that the problems are simply a matter of personal responsibility and following some simple guidelines, such as the "golden rule."

Should social networking Web sites do a better job of telling their users what is safe or unsafe information to share? Why or why not? What role should parents play in overseeing their child's involvement in social networking Web sites? Why? Should police or other government authorities be responsible for maintaining order on social networking Web sites in the same way they are charged with maintaining order in society in general? Why or why not?

Small Office/Home Office User

Computers assist small business and home office users in managing their resources effectively. A **small office/home office** (*SOHO*) includes any company with fewer than 50 employees, as well as the self-employed who work from home. Small offices include local law practices, accounting firms, travel agencies, and florists. SOHO users typically have a desktop computer to perform some or all of their duties. Many also have smart phones or other mobile devices to manage appointments and contact information.

SOHO users access the Internet — often wirelessly — to look up information such as addresses, directions, postal codes, flights (Figure 1-31a), and package shipping rates or to send and receive e-mail messages or make telephone calls.

Many have entered the *e-commerce* arena and conduct business on the Web. Their Web sites advertise products and services and may provide a means for taking orders. Small business Web sites sometimes use a *Web cam* to show the world a live view of some aspect of their business.

To save money on hardware and software, small offices often network their computers. For example, the small office connects one printer to a network for all employees to share.

SOHO users often work with basic business software such as word processing and spreadsheet programs that assist with document preparation and finances (Figure 1-31b). They are likely to use other industry-specific types of software. An auto parts store, for example, will have software that allows for looking up parts, taking orders and payments, and updating inventory.

Figure 1-31a (Web access)

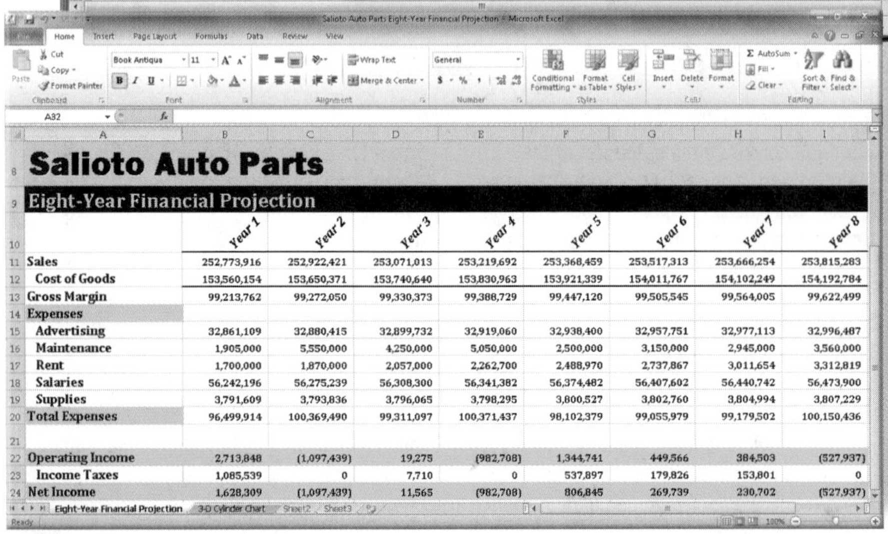

Figure 1-31b (spreadsheet program)

Figure 1-31 People with a home office and employees in small offices typically use a personal computer for some or all of their duties.

Mobile User

Today, businesses and schools are expanding to serve people across the country and around the world. Thus, increasingly more employees and students are **mobile users**, who work on a computer or mobile device while away from a main office, home office, or school (Figure 1-32). Examples of mobile users are sales representatives, real estate agents, insurance agents, meter readers, package delivery people, journalists, consultants, and students.

Mobile users often have mobile computers and/or mobile devices. With these computers and devices, the mobile user connects to other computers on a network or the Internet, often wirelessly accessing services such as e-mail and the Web. Mobile users can transfer information between their mobile device and another computer, such as one at the main office or school. For entertainment, the mobile user plays video games on a handheld game console and listens to music or watches movies on a portable media player.

The mobile user works with basic business software such as word processing. With presentation software, the mobile user can create and deliver presentations to a large audience by connecting a mobile computer or device to a video projector that displays the presentation on a full screen. Many scaled-down programs are available for mobile devices such as smart phones.

Figure 1-32 Mobile users have a variety of mobile computers and devices so that they can work, do homework, send messages, connect to the Internet, or play games while away from a wired connection.

Power User

Another category of user, called a **power user**, requires the capabilities of a workstation or other type of powerful computer. Examples of power users include engineers, scientists, architects, desktop publishers, and graphic artists (Figure 1-33). Power users often work with *multimedia*, combining text, graphics, audio, and video into one application. These users need computers with extremely fast processors because of the nature of their work.

The power user's workstation often contains industry-specific software. For example, engineers and architects use software to draft and design floor plans, mechanical assemblies, or vehicles. A desktop publisher uses software to prepare marketing literature. A graphic artist uses software to create sophisticated drawings. This software usually is expensive because of its specialized design.

Power users exist in all types of businesses. Some work at home. Their computers typically have network connections and Internet access.

Figure 1-33 This graphic artist uses a powerful computer to develop computer games.

Enterprise User

An enterprise has hundreds or thousands of employees or customers that work in or do business with offices across a region, the country, or the world. Each employee or customer who uses a computer in the enterprise is an **enterprise user** (Figure 1-34).

Many large companies use the words, *enterprise computing*, to refer to the huge network of computers that meets their diverse computing needs. The network facilitates communications among employees at all locations. Users access the network of servers or mainframes through desktop computers, mobile computers, and mobile devices.

Enterprises use computers and the computer network to process high volumes of transactions in a single day. Although they may differ in size and in the products or services offered, all generally use computers for basic business activities. For example, they bill millions of customers, prepare payroll for thousands of employees, and manage thousands of items in inventory. Some enterprises use blogs to open communications among employees, customers, and/or vendors.

Enterprise Computing
For more information, visit the Computer Concepts CourseMate Web site at www.cengagebrain.com, navigate to the Chapter 1 Web Link resource for this book, and then click Enterprise Computing.

Enterprises typically have e-commerce Web sites, allowing customers and vendors to conduct business online. The Web site also showcases products, services, and other company information.

The marketing department in an enterprise uses desktop publishing software to prepare marketing literature. The accounting department uses software for accounts receivable, accounts payable, billing, general ledger, and payroll activities.

The employees in the *information technology (IT) department* keep the computers and the network running. They determine when the company requires new hardware or software.

Enterprise users work with word processing, spreadsheet, database, and presentation software. They also may use calendar programs to post their schedules on the network. And, they might use smart phones or mobile devices to maintain contact information. E-mail programs and Web browsers enable communications among employees, vendors, and customers.

Many employees of enterprises telecommute. **Telecommuting** is a work arrangement in which employees work away from a company's standard workplace and often communicate with the office through the computer. Employees who telecommute have flexible work schedules so that they can combine work and personal responsibilities, such as child care.

Putting It All Together

The previous pages discussed the hardware and software requirements for the home user, small office/home office user, mobile user, power user, and enterprise user. The table in Figure 1-35 summarizes these requirements.

Figure 1-34 An enterprise can have hundreds or thousands of users in offices across a region, the country, or the world.

Categories of Users

User	Hardware	Software
Home 	• Desktop or notebook computer • Smart phone or other mobile device • Game consoles	• Business (e.g., word processing) • Personal information manager • Personal finance, online banking, tax preparation • Web browser • E-mail, blogging, instant messaging, chat rooms, and online social networking • Internet telephone calls • Photo and video editing • Reference (e.g., encyclopedias, medical dictionaries, road atlas) • Entertainment (e.g., games, music composition, greeting cards) • Education (e.g., tutorials, children's math and reading software)
Small Office/Home Office 	• Desktop or notebook computer • Smart phone or other mobile device • Shared network printer	• Business (e.g., word processing, spreadsheet, database) • Personal information manager • Company specific (e.g., accounting, legal reference) • Network management • Web browser • E-mail • Internet telephone calls
Mobile 	• Notebook computer equipped with a wireless modem, or a netbook or Tablet PC • Video projector • Smart phone or other mobile device • Handheld game consoles	• Business (e.g., word processing, note taking, presentation) • Personal information manager • Web browser • E-mail
Power 	• Workstation or other powerful computer with multimedia capabilities • Smart phone or other mobile device	• Desktop publishing • Multimedia authoring • Computer-aided design • Photo, audio, and video editing • Personal information manager • Web browser • E-mail
Enterprise 	• Server or mainframe • Desktop or notebook computer • Industry-specific handheld computer • Smart phone or other mobile device	• Business (e.g., word processing, spreadsheet, database) • Personal information manager • Accounting • Network management • Web browser • E-mail • Blogging

Figure 1-35 Today, computers are used by millions of people for work tasks, school assignments, and leisure activities. Different computer users require different kinds of hardware and software to meet their needs effectively.

Computer Applications in Society

The computer has changed society today as much as the industrial revolution changed society in the eighteenth and nineteenth centuries.

People interact directly with computers in fields such as education, finance, government, health care, science, publishing, travel, and manufacturing. In addition, they can reap the benefits from breakthroughs and advances in these fields. The following pages describe how computers have made a difference in people's interactions with these disciplines. Read Looking Ahead 1-1 for a look at how embedded computers may improve the quality of life.

LOOKING AHEAD 1-1

Embedded Computers May Improve Quality of Life

The weather forecast may be as close as your fingertips if plans to integrate embedded computers in everyday objects become a reality. Researchers are envisioning an umbrella with an embedded cell phone in the handle that will dial and then download the local forecast. The handle will glow green for good weather and flash red for imminent storms.

Dancers can pin a small flower with an embedded motion-detecting computer to their clothes. When they move, the embedded computer senses action and then synchronizes the tempo of music to this movement. Other embedded computers woven into clothing can monitor heart and breathing rates.

Wearing hidden embedded computers can help the elderly and people recovering from accidents and surgeries monitor their walking stride and pace. When their steps are uneven, the embedded computer can sound a warning and perhaps prevent a fall. Other embedded computers can give subtle feedback on the quality of physical activity.

For more information, visit the Computer Concepts CourseMate Web site at www.cengagebrain.com, navigate to the Chapter 1 Looking Ahead resource for this book, and then click Embedded Computers.

Education

Education is the process of acquiring knowledge. In the traditional model, people learn from other people such as parents, teachers, and employers. Many forms of printed material such as books and manuals are used as learning tools. Today, educators also are turning to computers to assist with education (Figure 1-36).

Many schools and companies equip labs and classrooms with computers. Some schools require students to have a mobile computer or mobile device to access the school's network or Internet wirelessly. To promote education by computer, many vendors offer substantial student discounts on software.

Sometimes, the delivery of education occurs at one place while the learning occurs at other locations. For example, students can take a class on the Web. Some classes are blended; that is, part of the learning occurs in a classroom and the other part occurs on the Web. More than 70 percent of colleges offer distance learning classes. A few even offer entire degrees online.

Figure 1-36 In some schools, students have mobile computers on their desks during classroom lectures.

Finance

Many people and companies use computers to help manage their finances. Some use finance software to balance checkbooks, pay bills, track personal income and expenses, manage investments, and evaluate financial plans. This software usually includes a variety of online services. For example, computer users can track investments and do online banking. With **online banking**, users access account balances, pay bills, and copy monthly transactions from the bank's computer right into their personal computers.

Many financial institutions' Web sites also offer online banking. When using a Web site instead of finance software on your computer, all your account information is stored on the bank's computer. The advantage is you can access your financial records from anywhere in the world (Figure 1-37).

Investors often use **online investing** to buy and sell stocks and bonds — without using a broker. With online investing, the transaction fee for each trade usually is much less than when trading through a broker.

Government

A government provides society with direction by making and administering policies. To provide citizens with up-to-date information, most government offices have Web sites. People in the United States access government Web sites to file taxes, apply for permits and licenses, pay parking tickets, buy stamps, report crimes, apply for financial aid, and renew vehicle registrations and driver's licenses. To provide these services, some Web sites require users provide personal information (read Ethics & Issues 1-4 for a related discussion).

Employees of government agencies use computers as part of their daily routine. North American 911 call centers use computers to dispatch calls for fire, police, and medical assistance. Military and other agency officials use the U.S. Department of Homeland Security's network of information about domestic security threats to help protect against terrorist attacks. Law enforcement officers have online access to the FBI's National Crime Information Center (NCIC) through in-vehicle notebook computers, fingerprint readers, and mobile devices (Figure 1-38). The NCIC contains more than 52 million missing persons and criminal records, including names, fingerprints, parole/probation records, mug shots, and other information.

Figure 1-37 An online banking Web site.

Figure 1-38 Law enforcement officials have in-vehicle computers and mobile devices to access emergency, missing person, and criminal records in computer networks in local, state, and federal agencies.

ETHICS & ISSUES 1-4

Should You Surrender Privacy for Convenience, Security, Money, or Social Connections?

The chief executive officer of a large computer software company once declared, "Privacy is dead, deal with it." While a vast majority of people demand increased privacy, many of those same people do not hesitate to surrender personal information in exchange for some short-term benefit. In a recent study, one-third of Internet users admitted to making detailed personal information available on the Internet. Personal information has become similar to a currency that people give up in order to obtain a benefit. Benefits might be in the form of increased convenience, increased security, money savings, or social connections online. For example, increased convenience may be in the form of an automated toll collection device that also can track the user's location and speed, and allow the government to maintain a record of the user's whereabouts. Insistence on safety or security may mean tolerating video cameras in many public and private places. The use of a grocery store affinity card saves a few dollars but also allows the store to track an individual buyer's every purchase. Signing up for an online social network often requires the divulgence of personal information so that the service better can locate other members with similar interests. In each of these examples, some measure of privacy is sacrificed.

Should people limit the amount of personal information they exchange? Why or why not? What are the dangers and disadvantages of giving up some amount of privacy in exchange for a short-term benefit? What are some possible alternatives to exchanging privacy for a perceived benefit? Should companies or government organizations be required to purge your personal information if you request so? Why or why not?

Health Care

Nearly every area of health care today uses computers. Whether you are visiting a family doctor for a regular checkup, having lab work or an outpatient test, or being rushed in for emergency surgery, the medical staff around you will be using computers for various purposes:

- Hospitals and doctors use computers and mobile devices to maintain and access patient records.
- Computers monitor patients' vital signs in hospital rooms and at home.
- Robots deliver medication to nurse stations in hospitals.
- Computers and computerized devices assist doctors, nurses, and technicians with medical tests (Figure 1-39).
- Doctors use the Web and medical software to assist with researching and diagnosing health conditions.
- Doctors use e-mail to correspond with patients.
- Pharmacists use computers to file insurance claims.
- Surgeons implant computerized devices, such as pacemakers, that allow patients to live longer.
- Surgeons use computer-controlled devices to provide them with greater precision during operations, such as for laser eye surgery and robot-assisted heart surgery.

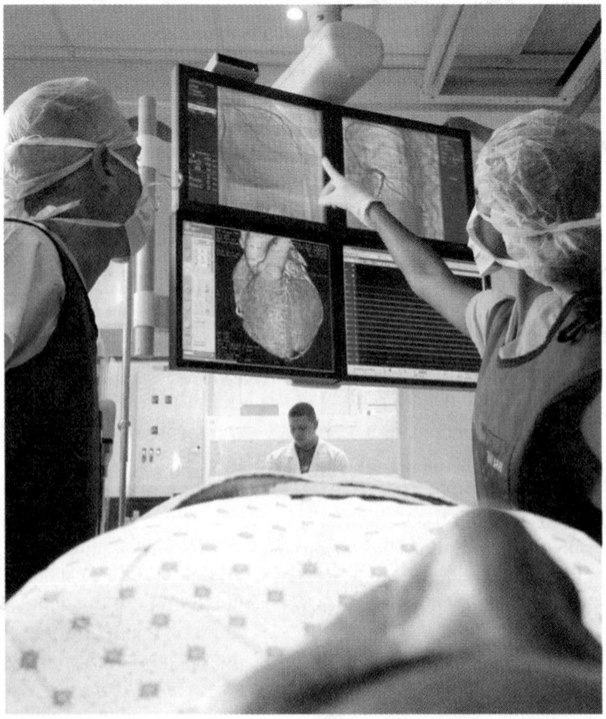

Figure 1-39 Doctors, nurses, technicians, and other medical staff use computers and computerized devices to assist with medical tests.

Many Web sites provide up-to-date medical, fitness, nutrition, or exercise information. These Web sites also maintain lists of doctors and dentists to help you find the one that suits your needs. They have chat rooms, so that you can talk to others diagnosed with similar conditions. Some Web sites even allow you to order prescriptions online.

Two forms of long-distance health care are telemedicine and telesurgery. Through *telemedicine*, health-care professionals in separate locations conduct live conferences on the computer. For example, a doctor at one location can have a conference with a doctor at another location to discuss a bone X-ray. Live images of each doctor, along with the X-ray, are displayed on each doctor's computer.

With *telesurgery*, also called *remote surgery*, a surgeon performs an operation on a patient who is not located in the same physical room as the surgeon. Telesurgery enables surgeons to direct robots to perform an operation via computers connected to a high-speed network.

Science

All branches of science, from biology to astronomy to meteorology, use computers to assist them with collecting, analyzing, and modeling data. Scientists also use the Internet to communicate with colleagues around the world.

Breakthroughs in surgery, medicine, and treatments often result from scientists' use of computers. Tiny computers now imitate functions of the central nervous system, retina of the eye, and cochlea of the ear. A cochlear implant allows a deaf person to listen. Electrodes implanted in the brain stop tremors associated with Parkinson's disease. Cameras small enough to swallow — sometimes called a camera pill — take pictures inside your body to detect polyps, cancer, and other abnormalities (Figure 1-40).

A *neural network* is a system that attempts to imitate the behavior of the human brain. Scientists create neural networks by connecting thousands of processors together much like the neurons in the brain are connected. The capability of a personal computer to recognize spoken words is a direct result of scientific experimentation with neural networks.

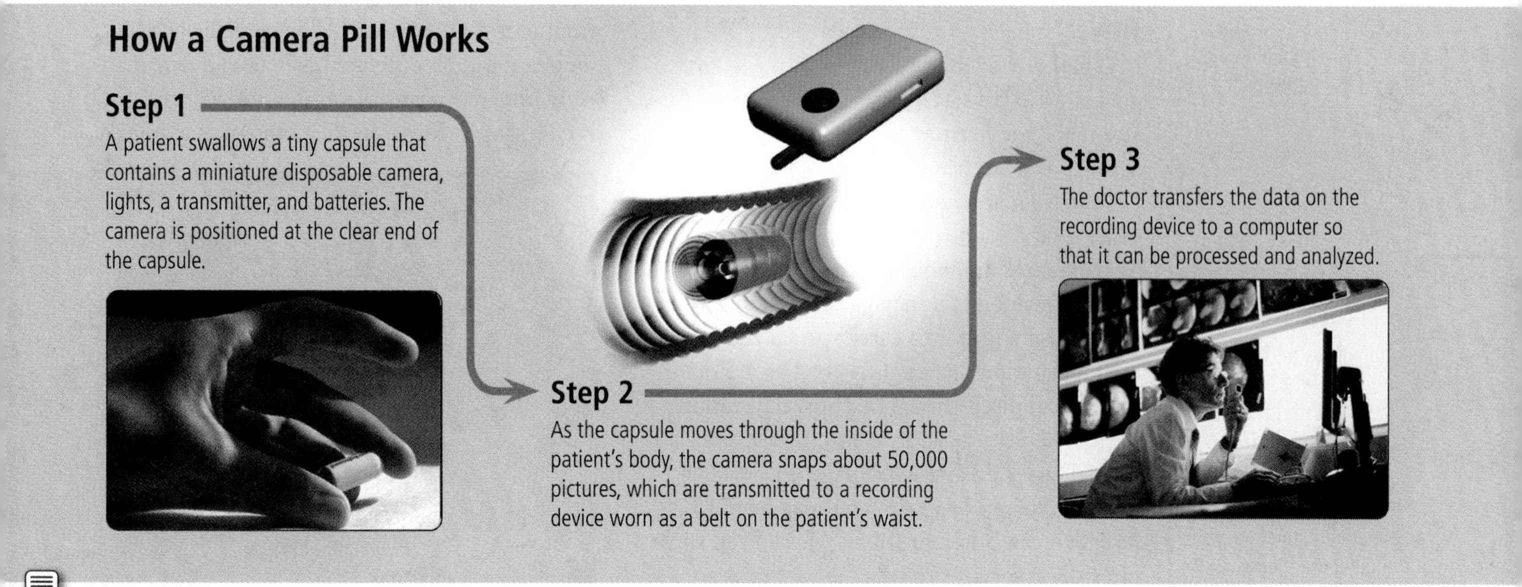
How a Camera Pill Works
Step 1
A patient swallows a tiny capsule that contains a miniature disposable camera, lights, a transmitter, and batteries. The camera is positioned at the clear end of the capsule.
Step 2
As the capsule moves through the inside of the patient's body, the camera snaps about 50,000 pictures, which are transmitted to a recording device worn as a belt on the patient's waist.
Step 3
The doctor transfers the data on the recording device to a computer so that it can be processed and analyzed.

Figure 1-40 This figure shows how a camera pill works.

Publishing

Publishing is the process of making works available to the public. These works include books, magazines, newspapers, music, film, and video. Special software assists graphic designers in developing pages that include text, graphics, and photos; artists in composing and enhancing songs; filmmakers in creating and editing film; and journalists and mobile users in capturing and modifying video clips.

Many publishers make their works available online (Figure 1-41). Some Web sites allow you to copy the work, such as a book or music, to your desktop computer, mobile computer, smart phone, or other mobile device.

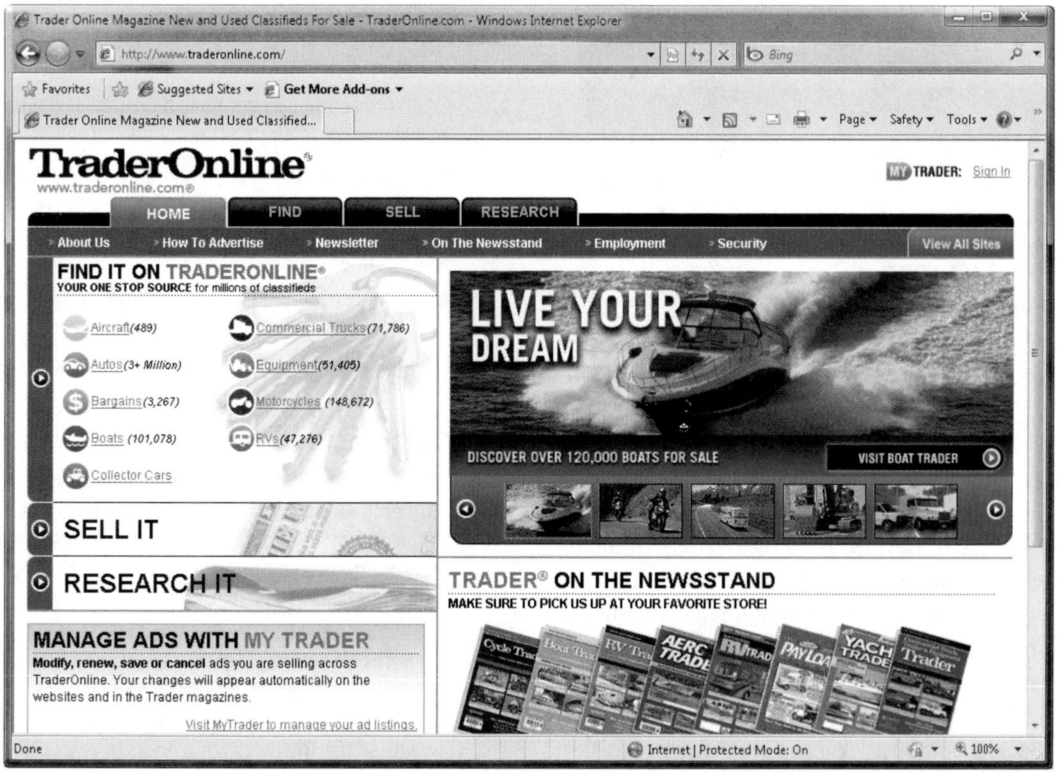

Figure 1-41 Many magazine and newspaper publishers make the content of their publications available online.

Travel

Whether traveling by car or airplane, your goal is to arrive safely at your destination. As you make the journey, you may interact with some of the latest technology.

Vehicles manufactured today often include some type of onboard navigation system, such as OnStar. Many mobile devices such as smart phones have built-in navigation systems. Some mobile users prefer to carry specialized handheld navigation devices (Figure 1-42). For a technical discussion about how navigation devices determine your location, read the High-Tech Talk article on page 40.

In preparing for a trip, you may need to reserve a car, hotel, or flight. Many Web sites offer these services to the public. For example, you can order airline tickets on the Web. If you plan to drive somewhere and are unsure of the road to take to your destination, you can print directions and a map from the Web.

OnStar

For more information, visit the Computer Concepts CourseMate Web site at www.cengagebrain.com, navigate to the Chapter 1 Web Link resource for this book, and then click OnStar.

Figure 1-42 This handheld navigation device gives users turn-by-turn voice-prompted directions to a destination.

Manufacturing

Computer-aided manufacturing (*CAM*) refers to the use of computers to assist with manufacturing processes such as fabrication and assembly. Industries use CAM to reduce product development costs, shorten a product's time to market, and stay ahead of the competition.

Often, robots carry out processes in a CAM environment. CAM is used by a variety of industries, including oil drilling, power generation, food production, and automobile manufacturing. Automobile plants, for example, have an entire line of industrial robots that assemble a car (Figure 1-43).

Special computers on the shop floor record actual labor, material, machine, and computer time used to manufacture a particular product. The computers process this data and automatically update inventory, production, payroll, and accounting records on the company's network.

Figure 1-43 Automotive factories use industrial robots to weld car bodies.

✔ QUIZ YOURSELF 1-3

Instructions: Find the true statement below. Then, rewrite the remaining false statements so that they are true.

1. A desktop computer is a portable, personal computer designed to fit on your lap.
2. A personal computer contains a processor, memory, and one or more input, output, and storage devices.
3. Each enterprise user spends time on the computer for different reasons that include personal financial management, Web access, communications, and entertainment.
4. A home user requires the capabilities of a workstation or other powerful computer.
5. Mainframes are the fastest, most powerful computers — and the most expensive.
6. The elements of an information system are hardware, e-mail, data, people, and the Internet.
7. With embedded computers, users access account balances, pay bills, and copy monthly transactions from the bank's computer right into their personal computers.

Quiz Yourself Online: To further check your knowledge of pages 18 through 38, visit the Computer Concepts CourseMate Web site at www.cengagebrain.com, navigate to the Chapter 1 Quiz Yourself resource for this book, and then click Objectives 8 – 11.

Chapter Summary

Chapter 1 introduced you to basic computer concepts such as what a computer is, how it works, and its advantages and disadvantages (read Ethics & Issues 1-5 for a related discussion). You learned about the components of a computer. Next, the chapter discussed networks, the Internet, and computer software. The many different categories of computers, computer users, and computer applications in society also were presented.

This chapter is an overview. Many of the terms and concepts introduced will be discussed further in later chapters. For a history of hardware and software developments, read the Timeline feature that follows this chapter.

ETHICS & ISSUES 1-5

Should Recycling of Electronics Be Made Easier?

Experts estimate that more than one billion computers have been discarded to date. The discarded items often are known as *e-waste*. As technology advances and prices fall, many people think of computers, cell phones, and portable media players as disposable items. These items often contain several toxic elements, including lead, mercury, and barium. Computers and mobile devices thrown into landfills or burned in incinerators can pollute the ground and the air. A vast amount of e-waste ends up polluting third world countries. One solution is to recycle old electronic equipment, but the recycling effort has made little progress especially when compared to recycling programs for paper, glass, and plastic.

Some lawmakers prefer an aggressive approach, such as setting up a recycling program that would be paid for by adding a small fee to the purchase price of computers and computer equipment, or forcing computer manufacturers to be responsible for collecting and recycling their products. California already requires a recycling fee for any products sold that include certain electronic equipment. Manufacturers have taken steps, such as offering to recycle old computers and using energy efficient and environmentally friendly manufacturing techniques, but some claim that consumers should bear the responsibility of disposing of their old computer parts. While some companies have set up recycling programs, many claim that forcing them to bear the cost of recycling programs puts the company at a competitive disadvantage when compared to foreign companies that may not be forced to maintain a recycling program.

Why is electronics recycling not as popular as other types of recycling? How can companies make it easier to recycle electronics while being compensated fairly for the cost of recycling? Should the government, manufacturers, or users be responsible for recycling of obsolete equipment? Why? Should the government mandate a recycling program for electronics? Why or why not?

Computer Usage @ Work

Transportation

What is transportation like without computers? Delivery drivers use clipboards to hold their records. Human navigators use paper maps to track routes for pilots. Ship captains rely solely on experience to navigate through shallow waters. Today, the transportation industry relies heavily on computer usage.

As presented in this chapter, many vehicles include onboard navigation systems to help you navigate from one location to another. These systems also usually provide other services such as dispatching roadside assistance, unlocking the driver's side door if you lock the keys in your vehicle, and tracking the vehicle if it is stolen.

The shipping and travel industries identify items during transport using bar codes, which are identification codes that consist of lines and spaces of different lengths. When you ship a package, the shipping company, such as UPS or FedEx, places a bar code on the package to indicate its destination to a computer. Because a package might travel to its destination by way of several trucks, trains, and airplanes, computers automatically route the package as efficiently as possible.

When you travel by airplane, baggage handling systems ensure that your luggage reaches its destination on time. When you check in your baggage at the airport, a bar code identifies the airplane on which the bags should be placed. If you change planes, automated baggage handling systems route your bags to connecting flights with very little, if any, human intervention. When the bags reach their destination, they are routed automatically to the baggage carousel in the airport's terminal building.

Pilots of high-technology commercial, military, and space aircraft today work in a glass cockpit, which features computerized instrumentation, navigation, communication, weather reports, and an autopilot. The electronic flight information shown on high-resolution displays is designed to reduce pilot workload, decrease fatigue, and enable pilots to concentrate on flying safely.

Boats and ships also are equipped with computers that include detailed electronic maps, help the captain navigate, as well as calculate the water depth and provide a layout of the underwater surface so that the captain can avoid obstructions.

As you travel the roadways, airways, and waterways, bear in mind that computers often are responsible for helping you to reach your destination as quickly and safely as possible.

For more information, visit the Computer Concepts CourseMate Web site at www.cengagebrain.com, navigate to the Chapter 1 Computer Usage @ Work resource for this book, and then click Transportation.

High-Tech Talk

Triangulation: Can You Find Me Now?

Have you wondered how a Nintendo Wii game console is able to determine the precise location of a Wii Remote while a player interacts with a game? How does the Wii console know where the player is pointing the Wii Remote, swinging it like a golf club, or motioning as if you are throwing a bowling ball? The answer is triangulation.

Triangulation is the process by which you can use trigonometry to determine the location of an object by measuring the angles from two or more fixed points. Surveyors often use triangulation to measure distance. Starting at a known location and elevation, surveyors measure a predetermined length to create a base line and then use an instrument called a theodolite to measure the angle to the unknown point from each side of the base line. The length of the base line along with the two known angles allows a computer or individual to determine the exact location of the third point (Figure 1-44). Electronic theodolites calculate angles automatically and then send the calculated angles to a computer for analysis.

In Figure 1-44, the distance between points A and B is known. The theodolite calculates angle CAB (α) and also calculates angle ABC (β). A human or computer can calculate the location of point C by determining the distance between points A and C and between points B and C. The formula used to determine the location of an object will vary depending upon the number of fixed points used in the measurement. With two fixed points, a relatively simple formula calculates the location of the third point. As the number of fixed points increases, the calculation becomes more complex.

Similarly, the Nintendo Wii game console uses triangulation to determine the location of a Wii Remote. When you set up a Wii game system, you place a sensor bar, which contains two infrared transmitters, near or on top of a television set. While you are using a Wii Remote, the Wii console determines the remote's location by calculating the distance and angles between the Wii Remote and the two transmitters on the sensor bar. Determining the location of a Wii Remote is relatively simple because the sensor bar only contains two fixed points: the transmitters.

A more complex application of triangulation occurs in global positioning systems. A *global positioning system* (*GPS*) is a navigation system that consists of one or more earth-based receivers that accept and analyze signals sent by satellites in order to determine the receiver's geographic location. GPS receivers are found in handheld navigation devices and many vehicles. GPS receivers use triangulation to determine their location relative to at least three geostationary satellites. Geostationary satellites, the fixed points in the triangulation formula, remain in the same location above the earth. Because 24 geostationary GPS satellites orbit the earth, a GPS receiver can increase its accuracy by using more than three satellites to determine its location by measuring the distance from each of the satellites, which always are a fixed distance apart, that are in range. In addition to determining position, GPS receivers also are able to calculate the speed of a moving object by recording its change in location from each satellite during a period of time. For instance, if a GPS receiver determines that you travel two-hundredths of a mile in one second, it automatically would be able to calculate that you are traveling at a rate of 72 miles per hour.

Another form of triangulation also can be used to determine the exact location of certain cell phones, usually after a caller dials for emergency assistance. Although some cell phones are not equipped with a GPS receiver, computers still can determine the phone's distance from other known locations, which might include cell towers. Because the location of two or more cell towers within range are known, computers easily can calculate the location of the cell phone. If you are unsure of whether the position of your cell phone can be determined automatically, always be prepared to give your location to an emergency dispatcher.

The next time you are passing a surveyor, playing a Nintendo Wii, following a prescribed route on a vehicle's navigation system, or observing emergency personnel respond to an accident, keep in mind that none of it might have been possible without the concept of triangulation.

For more information, visit the Computer Concepts CourseMate Web site at www.cengagebrain.com, navigate to the Chapter 1 High-Tech Talk resource for this book, and then click Triangulation.

Figure 1-44 Triangulation example.

Companies on the Cutting Edge

APPLE Innovative Industry Products

Apple recently sold a record 5.2 million of its latest iPhone models in one quarter, establishing the company's appeal to both consumer and corporate cell phone users. Apple is noted for introducing innovative products, starting with the Apple II, which was the first mass-marketed personal computer, in 1977 and the Macintosh, which featured a graphical user interface, in 1984.

Steve Jobs and Steve Wozniak founded Apple in 1976 when they marketed the Apple I, a circuit board they had developed in Jobs's garage. Under Jobs's direction as CEO, Apple developed the OS X operating system; iLife for working with photos, music, videos, and Web sites; and iWork, a collection of business programs. Apple also is leading the digital media revolution with its iPod portable media players, iPad tablet computer, and iTunes online store, which is the most popular Web site selling music. More than 10 million downloads occur each day from Apple's App Store, for a total download count exceeding 7 billion.

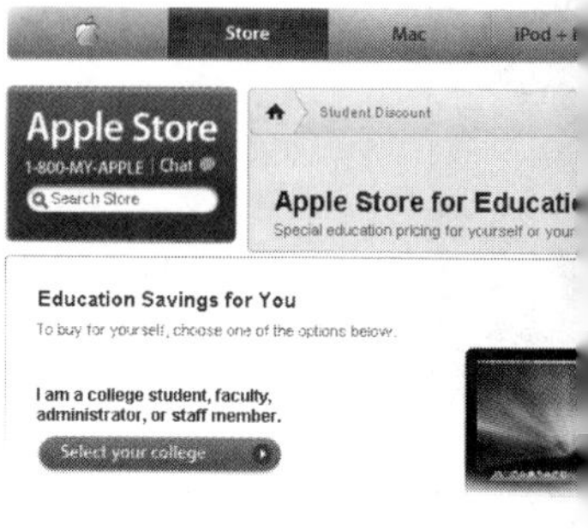

AMAZON Retailer Focused on Consumers

Online shoppers can find practically any product they desire on *Amazon*.com. Billing itself as the "Earth's most customer-centric company," it offers books, movies, electronics, clothing, toys, and many other items.

Jeff Bezos founded Amazon in 1995 knowing that book lovers would gravitate toward a Web site offering the convenience of browsing through millions of book titles in one sitting. He fulfilled orders for customers in every U.S. state and 45 additional countries during the first 30 days of business, all shipped from his Seattle-area garage.

The company has grown to permit third parties to sell products on its Web site. Its Kindle portable reader wirelessly downloads more than 450,000 books along with blogs, magazines, and newspapers to a high-resolution electronic paper display. Recently, it launched Kindle Singles, which are Kindle books with up to 30,000 words, the equivalent of two chapters of a typical book.

For more information, visit the Computer Concepts CourseMate Web site at www.cengagebrain.com and then navigate to the Chapter 1 Companies on the Cutting Edge resource for this book.

Technology Trailblazers

BILL GATES Microsoft Founder

When *Bill Gates* stepped down from his day-to-day activities at Microsoft in 2008, his action marked the end of an era that shaped the computer world. He remains the company's chairman and advisor, but he now devotes much of his time directing the Bill & Melinda Gates Foundation, a philanthropic organization working to help people worldwide lead healthy, productive lives. His foundation currently is awarding $3 billion in grants to improve education and graduation rates via technology, with an emphasis on online learning.

Gates learned to program computers when he was 13 years old. Early in his career, he developed the BASIC programming language for the MITS Altair, one of the first microcomputers. He founded Microsoft in 1975 with Paul Allen, and five years later they licensed the first operating system, called PC-DOS, to IBM for $80,000. This decision to license, rather than sell, the software is considered one of the wisest business decisions Gates ever made. Today, Microsoft's Windows and Office products dominate the software market.

TOM ANDERSON MySpace Cofounder and President

Having more than 11 million friends is all in a day's work for *Tom Anderson*, the current president and one of the founders of MySpace, one of the world's largest online social networks. Every MySpace account includes Anderson as a default first friend who is invited to view each personal network.

When Anderson's own rock group failed, he needed a place to post his songs. He started MySpace in 2003 with his friend, Chris DeWolfe, as a free tool to help musicians promote their songs and allow music lovers to create their own Web pages devoted to sharing their favorite music with like-minded admirers. Two years later they sold the business to Rupert Murdoch's News Corporation for $580 million. Anderson graduated from the University of California – Los Angeles in 2001 with a master's degree in film and from the University of California – Berkeley in 1998 with a bachelor's degree in English and rhetoric.

For more information, visit the Computer Concepts CourseMate Web site at www.cengagebrain.com and then navigate to the Chapter 1 Technology Trailblazers resource for this book.

Chapter Review

The Chapter Review reinforces the main concepts presented in this chapter.

To listen to an audio version of this Chapter Review, visit the Computer Concepts CourseMate Web site at www.cengagebrain.com and then navigate to the Chapter 1 Chapter Review resource for this book.

1. Why Is Computer Literacy Vital in Today's World? **Computer literacy**, or *digital literacy*, involves having current knowledge and understanding of computers and their uses. The requirements that determine computer literacy change as technology changes. As computers become more a part of everyday life, many people believe that computer literacy is vital to success.

2. What Is a Computer, and What Is the Relationship between Data and Information? A **computer** is an electronic device, operating under the control of instructions stored in its own memory, that can accept data, process the data according to specified rules, produce results, and store the results for future use. **Data** is a collection of unprocessed items, which can include text, numbers, images, audio, and video. **Information** conveys meaning and is useful to people.

3. List and Describe the Five Components of a Computer. The electric, electronic, and mechanical components of a computer, or **hardware**, include input devices, output devices, a system unit, storage devices, and communications devices. An **input device** allows you to enter data or instructions into a computer. An **output device** conveys information to one or more people. The **system unit** is a case that contains the electronic components of a computer that are used to process data. A **storage device** records and/or retrieves items to and from **storage media.** A **communications device** enables a computer to send and receive data, instructions, and information to and from one or more computers.

4. What Are the Advantages and Disadvantages That Users Experience When Working with Computers? A **user** is anyone who communicates with a computer or utilizes the information it generates. Computers have the advantages of speed, reliability, consistency, storage, and communications. They perform operations at incredibly fast speeds, are dependable and reliable, consistently generate error-free results, can store enormous amounts of data, and can share processing with other computers. Disadvantages of computers relate to health risks, the violation of privacy, public safety, the impact on the labor force, and the impact on the environment.

Visit the Computer Concepts CourseMate Web site at www.cengagebrain.com, navigate to the Chapter 1 Quiz Yourself resource for this book, and then click Objectives 1 – 4.

5. What Is a Network, and What Are Its Benefits? A **network** is a collection of computers and devices connected together, often wirelessly, via communications devices and transmission media. Networks allow computers to share *resources*, such as hardware, software, data, and information. Sharing resources saves time and money. The world's largest computer network is the Internet.

6. How Are the Internet and World Wide Web Used? The Internet is a worldwide collection of networks that connects millions of businesses, government agencies, educational institutions, and individuals. People use the Internet to communicate with and meet other people; conduct research and access information and news; shop for goods and services; bank and invest; participate in online training; engage in entertaining activities; download music and videos; share information, photos, and videos; and access and interact with Web applications. The **Web**, short for World Wide Web, is a global library of documents containing information that is available to anyone connected to the Internet.

7. How Is System Software Different from Application Software? **Software**, also called a **program**, is a series of related instructions, organized for a common purpose, that tells the computer what actions to perform and how to perform them. **System software** consists of the programs that control or maintain the operations of a computer and its devices. Two types of system software are the *operating system*, which coordinates activities among computer hardware devices, and *utility programs*, which perform maintenance-type tasks usually related to managing a computer, its devices, or its programs. **Application software** consists of programs designed to make users more productive and/or assists them with personal tasks. Popular application software includes Web browsers, word processing software, spreadsheet software, database software, and presentation software.

Visit the Computer Concepts CourseMate Web site at www.cengagebrain.com, navigate to the Chapter 1 Quiz Yourself resource for this book, and then click Objectives 5 – 7.

Chapter Review

8. What Are the Differences among the Types, Sizes, and Functions in the Following Categories: Personal Computers (Desktop), Mobile Computers and Mobile Devices, Game Consoles, Servers, Mainframes, Supercomputers, and Embedded Computers? Industry experts typically classify computers in seven categories: personal computers (desktop), mobile computers and mobile devices, game consoles, servers, mainframes, supercomputers, and embedded computers. A **personal computer** is a computer that can perform all of its input, processing, output, and storage activities by itself. A **mobile computer** is a personal computer you can carry from place to place, and a **mobile device** is a computing device small enough to hold in your hand. A **game console** is a mobile computing device designed for single-player or multiplayer video games. A **server** controls access to the hardware, software, and other resources on a network and provides a centralized storage area for programs, data, and information. A **mainframe** is a large, expensive, powerful computer that can handle hundreds or thousands of connected users simultaneously and can store tremendous amounts of data, instructions, and information. A **supercomputer** is the fastest, most powerful, and most expensive computer and is used for applications requiring complex, sophisticated mathematical calculations. An **embedded computer** is a special-purpose computer that functions as a component in a larger product.

9. What Is the Role of Each Element in an Information System? An *information system* combines hardware, software, data, people, and procedures to produce timely and useful information. People in an information technology (IT) department develop procedures for processing data. Following these procedures, people use hardware and software to enter the data into a computer. Software processes the data and directs the computer hardware to store changes on storage media and produce information in a desired form.

10. How Do the Various Types of Computer Users Interact with Computers? Computer users can be separated into five categories: home user, small office/home office user, mobile user, power user, and enterprise user. A **home user** is a family member who uses a computer for a variety of reasons, such as budgeting and personal financial management, Web access, communications, and entertainment. A **small office/home office** (*SOHO*) includes any company with fewer than 50 employees, as well as the self-employed individual who works from home. SOHO users access the Internet to look up information and use basic business software and sometimes industry-specific software. **Mobile users** are employees and students who work on a computer while away from a main office, home office, or school. A **power user** uses a workstation or other powerful computer to work with industry-specific software. Power users exist in all types of businesses. An **enterprise user** works in or interacts with a company with many employees and uses a computer and computer network that processes high volumes of transactions in a single day.

11. How Does Society Use Computers in Education, Finance, Government, Health Care, Science, Publishing, Travel, and Manufacturing? In education, students use computers and software to assist with learning or take distance learning classes. In finance, people use computers for **online banking** and **online investing**. Government offices have Web sites to provide citizens with up-to-date information, and government employees use computers as part of their daily routines. In health care, computers are used to maintain patient records, monitor patients, deliver medication to nurse stations via robots, assist with medical tests and research, correspond with patients, file insurance claims, provide greater precision during operations, and as implants. All branches of science use computers to assist with collecting, analyzing, and modeling data and to communicate with colleagues around the world. Publishers use computers to assist in designing pages and make the content of their works available online. Many vehicles use some type of online navigation system to help people travel more quickly and safely. Manufacturers use **computer-aided manufacturing** (*CAM*) to assist with manufacturing processes.

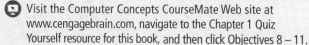

Visit the Computer Concepts CourseMate Web site at www.cengagebrain.com, navigate to the Chapter 1 Quiz Yourself resource for this book, and then click Objectives 8 – 11.

STUDENT ASSIGNMENTS

Key Terms

You should know the Primary Terms and be familiar with the Secondary Terms. The list below helps focus your study.

To see an example of and a definition for each term, and to access current and additional information from the Web, visit the Computer Concepts CourseMate Web site at www.cengagebrain.com and then navigate to the Chapter 1 Key Terms resource for this book.

Primary Terms

(shown in bold-black characters in the chapter)

application software (16)
communications device (8)
computer (6)
computer literacy (5)
computer-aided manufacturing (38)
data (6)
desktop computer (20)
digital camera (23)
e-book reader (22)
embedded computer (26)
enterprise user (32)
game console (24)
graphical user interface (GUI) (15)
green computing (10)
handheld computer (22)
hardware (6)
home user (28)
information (6)
input device (6)
installing (16)
Internet (11)
Internet-enabled (21)
laptop computer (20)
mainframe (25)
mobile computer (20)
mobile device (20)
mobile users (31)
network (10)
notebook computer (20)
online (10)
online banking (34)
online investing (35)
output device (7)
PDA (22)
personal computer (19)
photo sharing community (14)
portable media player (23)
power user (31)
program (15)
run (17)
server (25)
small office/home office (30)
smart phone (21)
social networking Web site (14)
software (15)
storage device (8)
storage media (8)
supercomputer (25)
system software (15)
system unit (7)
Tablet PC (21)
telecommuting (32)
user (9)
video sharing community (14)
Web (13)
Web 2.0 (14)
Web application (14)
Web page (13)
Web site (13)

handheld computer (22)

Secondary Terms

(shown in italic characters in the chapter)

blog (14)
CAM (38)
camera phone (22)
client (10)
convergence (18)
convertible tablet (21)
CPU (central processing unit) (7)
developer (18)
digital literacy (5)
digital pen (21)
e-book (22)
e-commerce (30)
e-reader (22)
enterprise computing (32)
execute (17)
FAQ (14)
gaming desktop computer (20)
garbage in, garbage out (9)
handhelds (22)
home theater PC (HTPC) (20)
icon (15)
information processing cycle (6)
information system (27)
information technology (IT) department (32)
instant message (22)
instructions (6)
loads (17)
memory (7)
microblog (14)
multimedia (31)
netbook (20)
neural network (36)
online social network (14)
operating system (15)
PC-compatible (19)
personal digital assistant (22)
picture message (22)
podcast (14)
processor (7)
programmer (18)
publish (13)
remote surgery (36)
resources (10)
server (10)
slate tablet (21)
SOHO (30)
telematics (26)
telemedicine (36)
telesurgery (36)
text message (22)
tower (20)
Ultra-Mobile PC (UMPC) (22)
utility program (16)
video blog (14)
video message (22)
video phone (22)
Web cam (30)

Checkpoint

The Checkpoint exercises test your knowledge of the chapter concepts. The page number containing the answer appears in parentheses after each exercise. The Beyond the Book exercises will help broaden your understanding of the concepts presented in this chapter.

To complete the Checkpoint exercises interactively, visit the Computer Concepts CourseMate Web site at www.cengagebrain.com and then navigate to the Chapter 1 Checkpoint resource for this book.

True/False Mark T for True and F for False.

_____ 1. Many people believe that computer literacy is vital to success in today's world. (5)

_____ 2. Hardware consists of a series of instructions that tells the computer what actions to perform and how to perform them. (6)

_____ 3. The circuitry of the system unit usually is part of or is connected to a circuit board called the server. (7)

_____ 4. Green computing involves reducing the electricity consumed and environmental waste generated when using a computer. (10)

_____ 5. The client controls access to the resources on a network. (10)

_____ 6. Web pages rarely have built-in connections, or links, to other documents, graphics, other Web pages, or Web sites. (13)

_____ 7. A video sharing community is a type of social networking Web site that allows users to store and share their personal videos. (14)

_____ 8. A text message is a short note, typically fewer than 300 characters, sent to or from a smart phone or other mobile device. (22)

_____ 9. Because embedded computers are components in larger products, they usually are small and have limited hardware. (26)

_____ 10. Telecommuting is a work arrangement in which employees work away from a company's standard workplace and often communicate with the office through the computer. (32)

_____ 11. With online investing, the transaction fee for each trade usually is much more than when trading through a broker. (35)

Multiple Choice Select the best answer.

1. Computer literacy, also known as digital literacy, involves having a current knowledge and understanding of _____. (5)
   a. computer programming
   b. computers and their uses
   c. computer repair
   d. all of the above

2. _____ is/are a collection of unprocessed items, which can include text, numbers, images, audio, and video. (6)
   a. Data
   b. Instructions
   c. Programs
   d. Information

3. A _____ is a specific type of social networking Web site that allows users to create an online photo album and store and share their digital photos. (14)
   a. vodcast
   b. blog
   c. photo sharing community
   d. chat room

4. A _____ is recorded audio stored on a Web site that can be downloaded to a computer or portable media player. (14)
   a. podcast
   b. social networking Web site
   c. blog
   d. speaker

5. _____ consists of the programs that control or maintain the operations of the computer and its devices. (15)
   a. System software
   b. A communications device
   c. A graphical user interface (GUI)
   d. Application software

6. A(n) _____ message is a real-time Internet communication, where you exchange messages with other connected users. (22)
   a. text
   b. instant
   c. picture
   d. video

7. Many large companies use the word(s), _____, to refer to the huge network of computers that meets their diverse computing needs. (32)
   a. information technology
   b. enterprise computing
   c. telecommuting
   d. multimedia

8. _____ is a system that attempts to imitate the behavior of the human brain. (36)
   a. Telemedicine
   b. A kiosk
   c. E-commerce
   d. A neural network

STUDENT ASSIGNMENTS

Checkpoint

Matching Match the terms with their definitions.

____ 1. processor (7)
____ 2. storage device (8)
____ 3. online social network (14)
____ 4. application software (16)
____ 5. install (16)
____ 6. execute (17)
____ 7. portable media player (23)
____ 8. digital camera (23)
____ 9. multimedia (31)
____ 10. neural network (36)

a. interprets and carries out basic instructions that operate a computer
b. carry out the instructions in a computer program
c. combines text, graphics, audio, and video into one application
d. programs designed to make users more productive and/or assist them with personal tasks
e. a system that attempts to imitate the behavior of the human brain
f. mobile device on which you can store, organize, and play digital media
g. online community that encourages members to share their interests, ideas, stories, photos, music, and videos with other registered users
h. set up software to work with a computer and other hardware components
i. device that allows users to take pictures and store the photographed images digitally, instead of on traditional film
j. records (writes) and/or retrieves (reads) items to and from storage media

Short Answer Write a brief answer to each of the following questions.

1. What is a computer? ____________ What is the information processing cycle? ____________
2. Describe two health risks posed by computers. ____________ How might computers have a negative effect on the environment? ____________
3. What is a Web application? ____________ What are some features of a Web 2.0 site? ____________
4. What are seven categories of computers? ____________ What determines how a computer is categorized? ____________
5. How do Web sites benefit individuals' health care? ____________ How does telesurgery differ from telemedicine? ____________

Beyond the Book Follow the book element instructions below; present your findings (brief report, presentation, discussion, or other means).

1. Ethics & Issues — Select an Ethics & Issues in this chapter (9, 13, 29, 35, 39), find a recent newspaper/magazine article that supports one point of view presented, and then evaluate the article.
2. Computer Usage @ Work — Use the Web or a recent newspaper/magazine to locate three additional unique usages of computer technology in the transportation industry (39). What makes the use of these technologies unique to the transportation industry?
3. Companies on the Cutting Edge and Technology Trailblazers — Use the Web or a recent business newspaper/magazine to locate an interesting fact about Apple, Amazon, Bill Gates, or Tom Anderson that was not presented in the chapter (41).
4. High-Tech Talk — Locate a recent newspaper/magazine article that discusses topics related to Triangulation (40). Would you recommend the article you found? Why or why not?
5. FAQs and Web Links — Use the Web or a recent newspaper/magazine to locate three additional facts about an FAQ (14, 16, 17, 20, 22, 29) and Web Link (10, 12, 14, 15, 22, 23, 27, 28, 32, 38) that were not presented in the chapter.
6. Looking Ahead — Use the Web or a recent newspaper/magazine to discover additional uses of the technology presented in Embedded Computers May Improve Quality of Life (34).
7. Innovative Computing — Use the Web or a recent newspaper/magazine to locate two additional interesting facts about Wii a Welcome Medical Skill Builder (24) and E-Receipts Save Paper, Organize Life (29).
8. Making Use of the Web — Visit three of the Fun and Entertainment Web Sites (125) and outline the information on each Web site and the possible uses for each Web site.
9. Timeline — Select an event from the Timeline (54) and then research the history surrounding the event using the Web or a magazine article.

Learn It Online

The Learn It Online exercises are interactive Web exercises designed to reinforce and expand your understanding of the chapter concepts. The descriptions below briefly summarize each exercise.

To complete the Learn It Online exercises, visit the Computer Concepts CourseMate Web site at www.cengagebrain.com, navigate to the Chapter 1 resources for this book, click the link for the exercise you want to complete, and then read the instructions.

1 At the Movies — Computer History in a Barn

Watch a movie to tour the Digibarn Computer Museum and then answer questions about the movie.

2 Video and Audio: You Review It — Social Networking

Search for, choose, and write a review of a video, podcast, or vodcast that discusses social networking.

3 Student Edition Labs — Using Input Devices and Using Windows

Enhance your understanding and knowledge about input devices and the Windows operating system by completing the Using Input Devices and Using Windows Labs.

4 Practice Test

Take a multiple choice test that checks your knowledge of the chapter concepts and review the resulting study guide.

5 Who Wants To Be a Computer Genius^2?

Play the Shelly Cashman Series version of this popular game by answering questions to find out if you are a computer genius. Panic buttons are available to provide assistance during game play.

6 Wheel of Terms

Identify important key terms presented in this chapter by playing the Shelly Cashman Series version of this popular game.

7 You're Hired!

Embark on the path to a career in computers by answering questions and solving puzzles related to concepts discussed in this chapter.

8 Crossword Puzzle Challenge

Complete an interactive crossword puzzle to reinforce concepts presented in this chapter.

9 Windows Exercises

Step through the Windows 7 exercises to learn how to use help, improve mouse skills, and identify computer information.

10 Exploring Computer Careers

Read about a career as a computer salesperson, search for relevant employment advertisements, and then answer related questions.

11 Web Apps — Google Maps

Learn how to locate businesses in your area, view a location's surroundings via satellite, and find directions from one location to another using Google Maps.

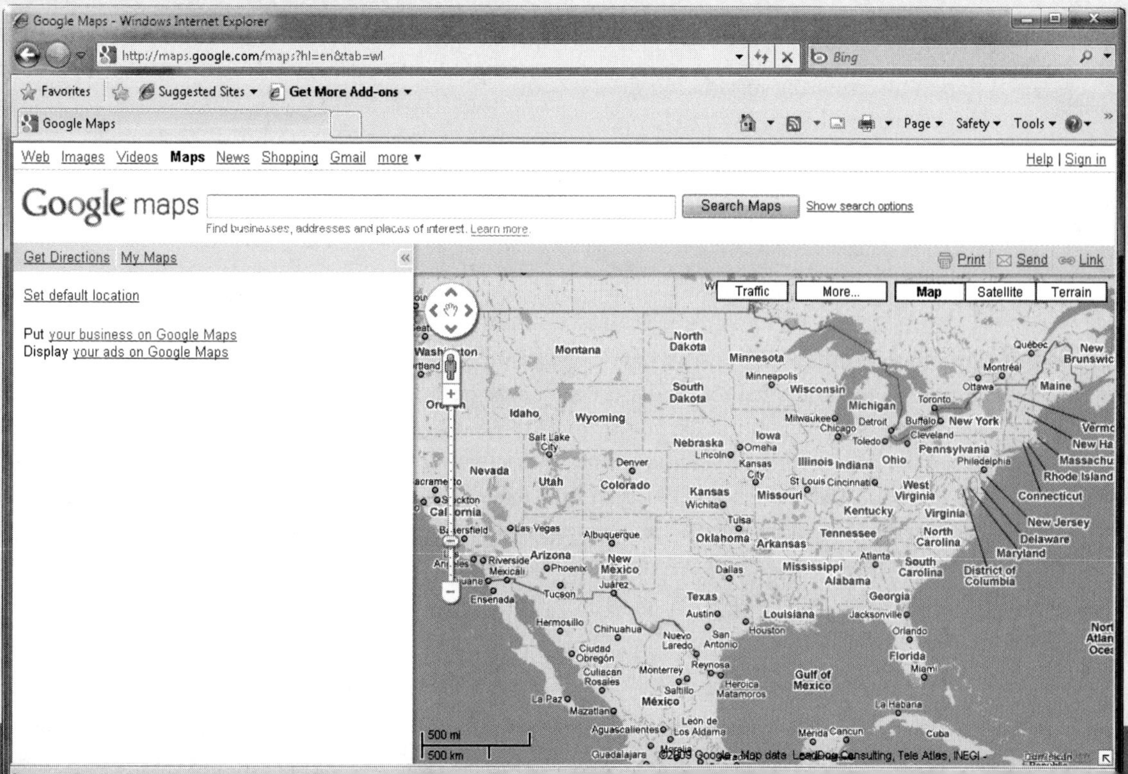

Problem Solving @ Home

The Problem Solving @ Home exercises extend your knowledge of the chapter concepts by seeking solutions to practical computer problems that you may encounter at home or school. The Collaboration exercise should be completed with a team.

In the real world, practical problems often can be solved in multiple ways. Provide one solution to each of the following problems using available resources, such as articles on the Web or in print, blogs, podcasts, videos, television, user guides, other individuals, and electronics and computer stores. You may need to use multiple resources to obtain an answer. Present your solutions in the form requested by your instructor (brief report, presentation, discussion, or other means).

1. **Incorrect Grade Report** Your grade report came in the mail today. On the grade report, your grade point average (GPA) is not what you expect. After computing it manually, you discover that the GPA on your grade report is incorrect. What might be causing the error?
2. **Suspicious Charges** Your credit card company called to inform you that your account has a suspicious charge. Upon further investigation, you realize that the charge does not belong to you. What will you do?
3. **Shared Printer Error** At the beginning of the semester, your roommate configured your computer so that it could print on the printer in his bedroom. He left for vacation three days ago, and you recently have noticed that you are unable to print to his printer from your computer. Each time you attempt to print, you receive an error message stating that the printer is unavailable. What might be wrong?

4. **Software Installation Trouble** You have purchased a new video game for your home computer and attempt to install it. Upon inserting the installation disc, however, nothing appears to happen on your computer. What is your next step?
5. **Problematic Player** After charging your portable media player overnight, you turn it on only to find that it is reporting a low battery. Seconds later, it shuts off automatically. What might be wrong?
6. **Inaccessible Media** You insert an optical disc with digital photos from your most recent family vacation, and discover that your computer will not read the optical disc. What might be wrong?
7. **Bank Account Postings** While reviewing your checking account balance online, you notice that debit card purchases have not posted to your account for the past several days. Because you use online banking to balance your account, you become concerned about your unknown account balance. What steps will you take to correct this situation?
8. **GPS Error** You are driving to your friend's house and are using your GPS receiver for directions. While approaching your destination, you realize that the GPS receiver instructed you to turn the wrong way on your friend's street. How could this have happened?
9. **Shopping for Software** You are shopping for software that will assist with your home landscape design. The package for the program you would like to purchase states that it was designed for the most recent version of Windows, but an older version is installed on your computer. How can you determine whether the program will run on your computer?

Collaboration

10. **Unsolicited Communications** Lately, you have been receiving many unsolicited e-mail messages, text messages, instant messages, and telephone calls. These messages not only are annoying, but they also are consuming large amounts of your time. Form a team of three people and decide what steps are necessary to minimize these unsolicited communications. One team member should research how to stop unsolicited e-mail messages, one team member should research how to stop unsolicited text messages and instant messages, and another team member should research how to stop unsolicited telephone calls. Finally, all team members should research where these unsolicited calls and messages might be originating and how to prevent being added to distribution lists in the future.

STUDENT ASSIGNMENTS

Problem Solving @ Work

The Problem Solving @ Work exercises extend your knowledge of the chapter concepts by seeking solutions to practical computer problems that you may encounter at work. The Collaboration exercise should be completed with a team.

In the real world, practical problems often can be solved in multiple ways. Provide one solution to each of the following problems using available resources, such as articles on the Web or in print, blogs, podcasts, videos, television, user guides, other individuals, and electronics and computer stores. You may need to use multiple resources to obtain an answer. Present your solutions in the form requested by your instructor (brief report, presentation, discussion, or other means).

1. **Insufficient Disk Space** Recently, you purchased a USB flash drive that you plan to use to store work-related files. When you attempt to store a file on the USB flash drive, the computer displays an error message indicating that the file will not fit. How could a brand new USB flash drive not have enough room to store the first file you attempted to store on it?
2. **Computer Replacement** The technical support department at your company has informed you that you will be receiving a new computer within the next week. Before they will replace your computer, they told you to back up anything that is important. What types of files do you feel are important to back up?
3. **Power Outage** The power in your office has been out for the last two hours and has just come back on. When you attempt to start your computer by pressing the power button, nothing happens. What is your next step before calling technical support?
4. **Incorrect Login Credentials** Upon returning to the office from a well-deserved two-week vacation, you turn on your computer. Upon entering your user name and password, an error message appears stating that your password is incorrect. What are your next steps?
5. **Software Installation** You are attempting to install a program on your office computer. After inserting the installation disc and specifying that you would like to begin the installation, your computer appears to begin installing the software. Halfway through the installation process, an error message appears stating that you must have administrative privileges to perform the installation. Why were you not informed immediately upon beginning the installation? What are your next steps?

6. **Dead Battery** While traveling for business, you realize that you forgot to bring the battery charger for your notebook computer. Knowing that you need to use the notebook computer to give a presentation tomorrow, what will you do to make sure that you have enough battery power?
7. **Discarding Old Computer Equipment** Your company has just given you a new computer to replace your current, outdated computer. Because of the negative environmental impact of throwing the computer away, your supervisor has asked you to suggest options for its disposal. How will you respond?

Collaboration

8. **Computers in Transportation** Your project team has been accepted to present a business proposal to a group of potential investors. Because the presentation will take place in San Francisco, CA, you will need to transport people and ship some materials to that location. Form a team of three people and determine how to use technology to ship materials and how to make travel arrangements. One team member should research the steps required to use a Web site to make flight reservations, one team member should determine the steps necessary to print a UPS shipping label from his or her computer and track the package while it is en route, and another team member should find directions from San Francisco International Airport to a nearby hotel.

Learn How To

The Learn How To activities step you through fundamental technology skills when using a computer. The Learn How To exercises enable you to become more proficient with these skills.

Premium Activity: To relate this Learn How To activity to your everyday life, see a visual demonstration of the activity, and complete a short assessment, visit the Computer Concepts CourseMate Web site at www.cengagebrain.com and then navigate to the Chapter 1 Learn How To resource for this book.

Learn How To 1: Start and Close a Program

You can start any program by using the Start button. Complete these steps to start the Web browser program called Internet Explorer:

1. Click the Start button ( ) at the left of the Windows taskbar on the bottom of the screen to display the Start menu.
2. Click All Programs on the Start menu to display the All Programs list (Figure 1-45).
3. Click the Internet Explorer in the All Programs list to start Internet Explorer (Figure 1-46).

An item in the All Programs list might have an open folder icon next to it. When this occurs, click the item and another list will appear. Click the program name in this list to start the program. Some program names might appear on the Start menu itself. If so, click any of these names to start the corresponding program.

The Start menu displays the names of the programs recently opened on the computer. You can start any of these programs by clicking the name of the program.

To close a program, click the Close button ( ) in the upper-right corner of the window. If you have created but not saved a document, Windows will ask if you want to save the document. If you do not want to save it, click the No button in the displayed dialog box. If you want to save it, refer to Learn How To 1 in Chapter 3 on page 188.

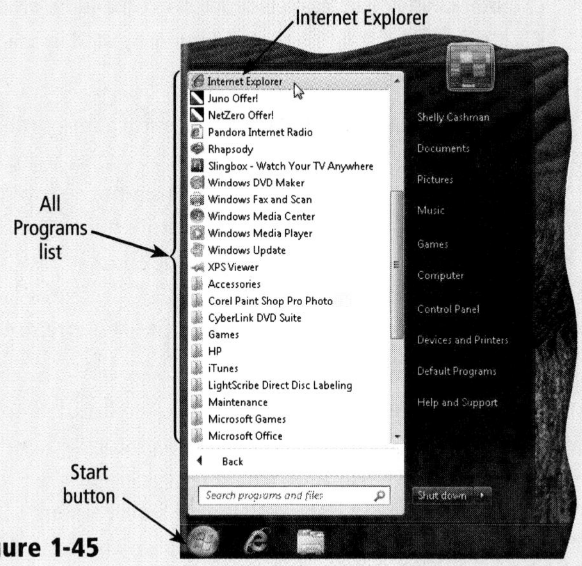

Figure 1-45

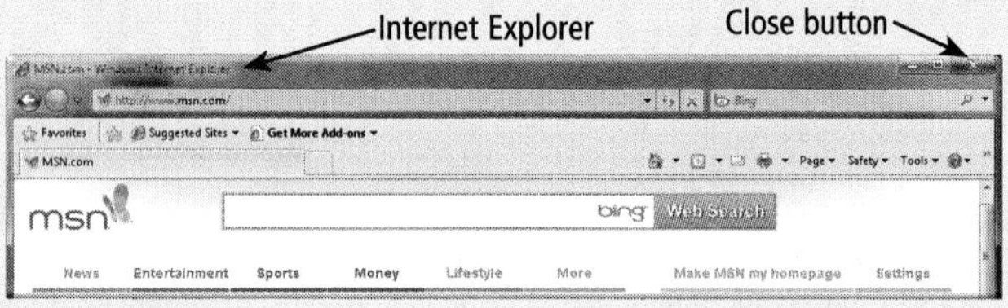

Figure 1-46

Exercises

1a. Using the Start button, start the program named WordPad found in the Accessories list in the All Programs list. WordPad is a word processing program. Type the following: `To start a program, click the program name in the All Programs list` and then type your name. Print the document, and then submit the printout to your instructor.

1b. Close the WordPad program. If you are asked if you want to save changes to the document, click the Don't Save button. Start the WordPad program again, type some new text, and then close the WordPad program. When the dialog box is displayed, click the Cancel button. What happened? Now, close the WordPad window without saving the document. Submit your answer to your instructor.

2. Using the Start menu, start the e-mail program on the computer. What is the name of the e-mail program? In the program window, what menu names are displayed on the menu bar at the top of the window? Close the e-mail program. Submit your answers to your instructor.

Learn How To 2: Create and Use Your Own Blog

A blog can contain any information you wish to place in it. For example, blogs contain addresses, thoughts, diaries, and anything else a person or group wants to share.

Once you have created a blog, you can update it. A variety of services available on the Web can help you create and maintain your blog. One widely used service is called Blogger. To create a blog using Blogger, complete the following steps:

1. Start your Web browser, type `blogger.com` in the Address bar, and then press the ENTER key to display the Blogger home page (Figure 1-47).
2. Click the CREATE A BLOG button.

Learn How To

3. Enter the data required on the 'Create Blogger Account' page. Your e-mail address and password will allow you to change and manage your blog. Your Display name is the name that will be shown on the blog as its author. Many people use their own names, but others use pseudonyms as their "pen names" so that they are not readily identifiable.
4. Click the Continue arrow and then enter your Blog title and Blog address. These are the names and addresses everyone will use to view your blog.
5. Click the Continue arrow to display the 'Choose a template' screen.
6. Choose a template for your blog and then click the Continue arrow to create your blog.
7. When the 'Your blog has been created!' screen appears, click the START BLOGGING arrow.
8. When the screen appears, you can post items for or view your blog, specify settings, and change the layout.
9. When you are finished, click the Sign out link at the top right of the screen to log out.
10. To edit your blog and add or change information on it, visit the Blogger home page, sign in by entering your user name and password, and then make changes.
11. Others can view your blog by entering its address in the browser's Address bar and then pressing the ENTER key.

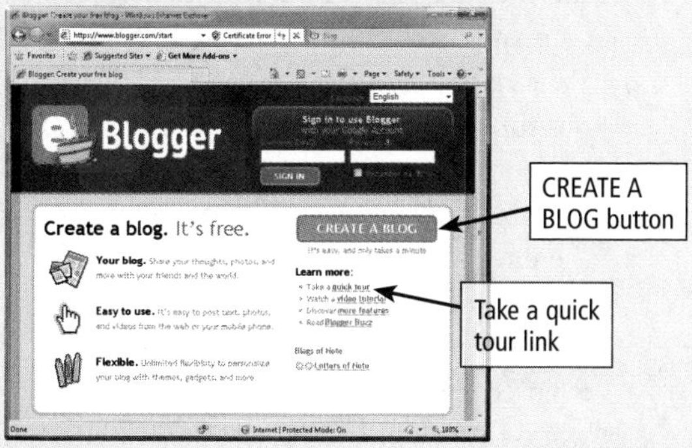

Figure 1-47

Exercises

1. Start your Web browser and visit blogger.com. Click the 'Take a quick tour' link and go through all the screens that explain about a blog. What did you learn that you did not know? What type of blog do you find most compelling — a group or an individual blog? Why? Submit your answers to your instructor.
2. Optional: Create your own blog. Carefully name it and begin your posts at this time. What is your blog name and address? What is its primary purpose? Is it an individual or group blog? Write a paragraph containing the answers to these questions and any other information you feel is pertinent. Submit this paragraph to your instructor.

Learn How To 3: Use the Computer Concepts CourseMate Web Site for Discovering Computers

The Computer Concepts CourseMate Web site for Discovering Computers provides a variety of activities, exercises, and other resources. To use the site, you first must create a student account and then register this book, as described in the following steps:

1. Start the Web browser, type the Web address of `www.cengagebrain.com` in the browser Address bar, and then press the ENTER key to display the CengageBrain home page.
2. If you do not have an account, follow the on-screen instructions to sign up for a new account. If you have an account, log in with your user name and password.
3. Register this book by entering its Access Code in the appropriate text box and then clicking the corresponding button.
4. To open the resources for this book, click the button corresponding to Computer Concepts CourseMate Web site for Discovering Computers.

Exercise

1a. With a student account created and this book registered, type `www.cengagebrain.com` in the Address bar of your browser, press the ENTER key to display the CengageBrain home page, and then log in to your student account with your user name and password.

1b. Open the resources for this book by clicking the button corresponding to Computer Concepts CourseMate Web site for Discovering Computers.

1c. Select Chapter 1 and then click each resource listed below the chapter title to display the content associated with the selected resource.

1d. Write a report that describes the use of each of the Chapter 1 resources for this book. Which resource do you think will prove the most valuable to you when using the book and the Web site? Why? Which will be the least useful? Why? Submit your report to your instructor.

STUDENT ASSIGNMENTS

Web Research

The Web Research exercises broaden your understanding of the chapter concepts by presenting questions that require you to search the Web for answers.

1 Search Sleuth

Use one of the search engines listed in Figure 2-10 in Chapter 2 on page 85 or your own favorite search engine to find the answers to the following questions. Copy and paste the Web address from the Web page where you found the answer. Some questions may have more than one answer. If required, submit your answers to your instructor. (1) What company was the first to sell a USB flash drive? (2) What is the significance of the Universal symbol on Apple's Mac application programs? (3) Which retailers offer to dispose of old computers and other electronic products properly to help protect the environment? (4) What are three Illustrative Grant Commitments the Bill & Melinda Gates Foundation has made? (5) According to *Fortune*, at what company do MBA students most want to work when they graduate? (6) Who created the first set of icons for the Macintosh computer? What sound does her Clarus the Dogcow make? (7) What company manufactured the first notebook computer, the UltraLite, in 1989?

2 Green Computing

Computer usage requires electricity, whether to power the system unit and monitor, recharge batteries, or print. In addition, the computer manufacturing process depletes natural resources and often uses toxic chemicals. As you learned in this chapter, many environmentally conscious people practice green computing by attempting to reduce electricity and environmental waste. Examine your computing practices, and determine 10 ways that you can use less power on your computing equipment at home, work, and school. Consider how often you use the printer and the types of documents you print. Examine your monitor, system unit, and printer. Do you see any notation indicating they are environmentally sound? Do they hibernate or go into a power save mode when not being used? Write a 50-word summary of the green computing practices in your life.

3 Social Networking

One of the more popular social networking Web sites is Facebook. This quickly growing service differentiates itself from other online social networks by having widespread privacy controls. In addition, its development platform, called f8, allows developers to create programs (called applications) that users can add to a Web page. Hostels, for example, lets world travelers research and rate hostels and includes photos and descriptions. Visit the Facebook site (facebook.com), click the About link at the bottom of the page, and then read about Facebook's features. What are three of Facebook's top features? What information is given in the recent Facebook blog posts? Visit the AppRate Web site (apprate.com) and then summarize three Facebook application reviews and ratings.

4 Blogs

Blogs profiling the music industry discuss new technologies, legal issues, podcasts, and business news. Visit the CNET blog (news.cnet.com/tech-blogs) and then read and summarize at least three of the articles in the Most Recent Posts section. Locate the Crave, Gaming and Culture, and Green Tech features and then read and summarize at least one story from each blog. Then visit the iLounge (ilounge.com) Web site and read reviews of at least three new products for the iPhone. Would you purchase any of the products discussed? What books and buyer's guides are available to download from the Library? Which iPod cases and speakers received favorable reviews? Read and summarize at least three stories and associated comments in the News section.

5 Ethics in Action

The Internet has increased the ease with which students can plagiarize material for research paper assignments. Teachers are using online services, such as Turnitin and PlagiarismDetect.com, to help detect plagiarized papers and to help students understand how to cite sources correctly. Visit the Turnitin Web site (turnitin.com) and then write a summary of how this service is used. How does this service attempt to prevent plagiarism through the Turnitin Write Cycle? How prevalent is plagiarism on your campus? What is your school's official policy on disciplining students who submit plagiarized papers? Does your school have an honor code? If required, submit your summary to your instructor.

Critical Thinking

The Critical Thinking exercises challenge your assessment and decision-making skills by presenting real-world situations associated with the chapter concepts. The Collaboration exercise should be completed with a team.

To evaluate the situations below, use personal experiences and available resources such as articles on the Web or in print, blogs, podcasts, videos, television, user guides, other individuals, and electronics and computer stores. You may need to use multiple resources to form conclusions and make recommendations.

1. **Class Discussion — Reactions to Computer Problems** Virtually everyone who works with computers has experienced problems with computer software. Problems can range from not being able to install the software on your computer to installed software producing unanticipated results. Depending on the situation and time these problems occur, it can result in a great amount of user stress. Some people compare these types of problems to a craftsman's tools malfunctioning in the middle of a project. On the other hand, many people feel reactions to computer software problems tend to be more extreme than reactions to problems with other tools they use. Evaluate situations in which you have seen people react to computer software problems. Discuss how these users can reduce their frustration when dealing with such problems.

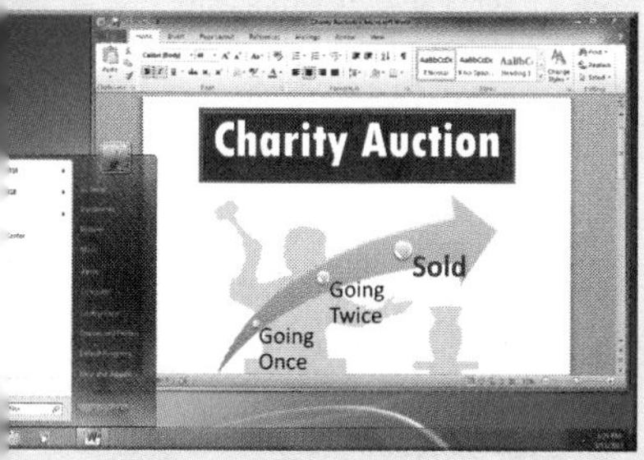

2. **Class Presentation — Technology in Education** You are a member of your local school district's board of education. During the past year, the number of computers purchased by the district increased by 85 percent, while the supply of library books declined by almost 10 percent. School officials claim that computers extend learning opportunities and develop the computer literacy needed in today's technological world. Yet, some parents complain that computer purchases represent frivolous, status-seeking spending. Notebook computers are purchased for teachers, while textbooks and library books are too old, too worn, and too scarce. Analyze how computers are being used in schools, and then present your recommendation of the percentage of the instructional materials budget that should be spent on computers versus the percentage that should be spent on library books and textbooks. Note the factors that influenced your decision.

3. **Research — Energy Efficiency** Increases in fuel prices result in increases in energy prices. When this occurs, many individuals and companies look at purchasing energy-efficient computers. These energy-efficient computers require less energy to operate and often look and perform similarly to equivalent computers that are not as energy efficient. Find two computers of identical configuration, where the only difference is energy consumption. How much energy does the energy-efficient computer save? Are energy-efficient computers more or less expensive? Will the difference in cost (if any) alter your preference to purchase an energy-efficient computer instead of one that is not energy efficient? What other ways might you be able to configure your computer to save energy? Compile your findings into a brief report and then submit it to your instructor.

Collaboration

4. **Recommending Technology Solutions** People use computers in a variety of fields, including education, finance, government, health care, science, publishing, travel, and manufacturing. Although the way people use computers varies, each use of a computer involves computer hardware, computer software, and normally some type of communications capability over networks, such as the Internet. Form a three-member team and choose a field in which you all are interested. Assign one member of your team to investigate hardware used in the field, another member to investigate software used in the field, and the third member to investigate communications capabilities used in the field. Each team member should develop a list of related items that may be used in the selected field. After the team's investigation, characterize a hypothetical business or organization in the field. Based on your investigation, recommend specific hardware, software, and networking capabilities that would be best for the business or organization. Each team member should provide an explanation for each selected item. Be sure to include comparisons of specific items. Prepare a report and/or presentation summarizing your investigations, describing the hypothetical business or organization, and outlining and supporting your recommendations.

Timeline

Milestones in Computer History

Visit the Computer Concepts CourseMate Web site at www.cengagebrain.com and then navigate to the Timeline Feature resource for this book.

1937 Dr. John V. Atanasoff and Clifford Berry design and build the first electronic digital computer. Their machine, the Atanasoff-Berry-Computer, or ABC, provides the foundation for advances in electronic digital computers.

1943 During World War II, British scientist Alan Turing designs the Colossus, an electronic computer created for the military to break German codes. The computer's existence is kept secret until the 1970s.

1945 John von Neumann poses in front of the electronic computer built at the Institute for Advanced Study. This computer and its von Neumann architecture served as the prototype for subsequent stored program computers worldwide.

1946 Dr. John W. Mauchly and J. Presper Eckert, Jr. complete work on the first large-scale electronic, general-purpose digital computer. The ENIAC (Electronic Numerical Integrator And Computer) weighs 30 tons, contains 18,000 vacuum tubes, occupies a 30 × 50 foot space, and consumes 160 kilowatts of power.

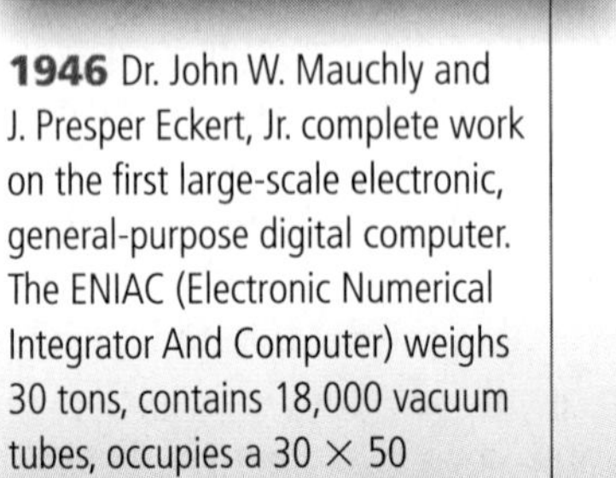

1947 William Shockley, John Bardeen, and Walter Brattain invent the transfer resistance device, eventually called the transistor. The transistor would revolutionize computers, proving much more reliable than vacuum tubes.

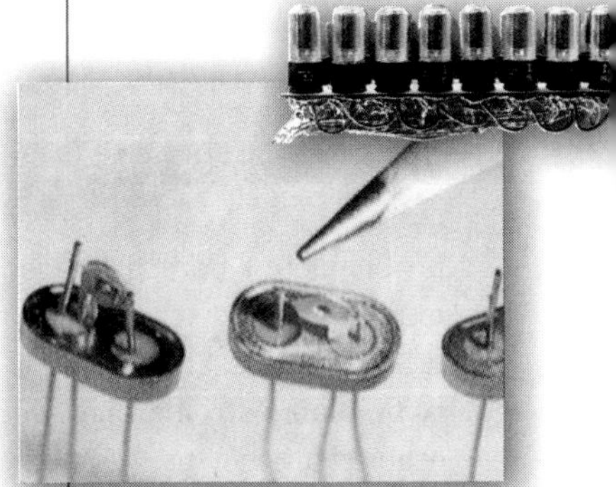

1951 The first commercially available electronic digital computer, the UNIVAC I (UNIVersal Automatic Computer), is introduced by Remington Rand. Public awareness of computers increases when the UNIVAC correctly predicts that Dwight D. Eisenhower will win the presidential election.

1952 Dr. Grace Hopper considers the concept of reusable software in her paper, "The Education of a Computer." The paper describes how to program a computer with symbolic notation instead of detailed machine language.

1957 The IBM 305 RAMAC computer is the first to use magnetic disk for external storage. The computer provides storage capacity similar to magnetic tape that previously was used but offers the advantage of semi-random access capability.

1959 More than 200 programming languages have been created.

1959 IBM introduces two smaller, desk-sized computers: the IBM 1401 for business and the IBM 1620 for scientists.

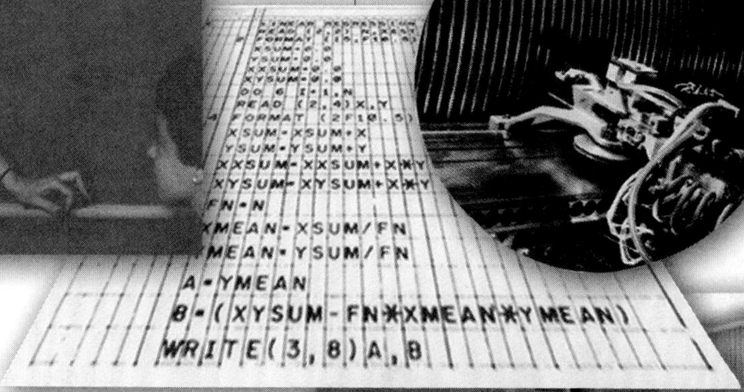

1957 FORTRAN (FORmula TRANslation), an efficient, easy-to-use programming language, is introduced by John Backus.

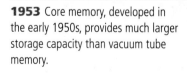

1953 Core memory, developed in the early 1950s, provides much larger storage capacity than vacuum tube memory.

1953 The IBM model 650 is one of the first widely used computers. The computer is so successful that IBM manufactures more than 1,000. IBM will dominate the mainframe market for the next decade.

1958 Jack Kilby of Texas Instruments invents the integrated circuit, which lays the foundation for high-speed computers and large-capacity memory. Computers built with transistors mark the beginning of the second generation of computer hardware.

1960 COBOL, a high-level business application language, is developed by a committee headed by Dr. Grace Hopper.

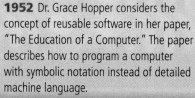

1964

1964 The number of computers has grown to 18,000. Third-generation computers, with their controlling circuitry stored on chips, are introduced. The IBM System/360 computer is the first family of compatible machines, merging science and business lines.

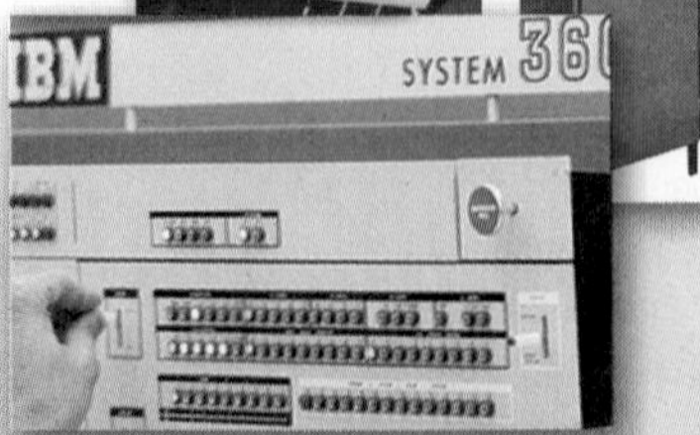

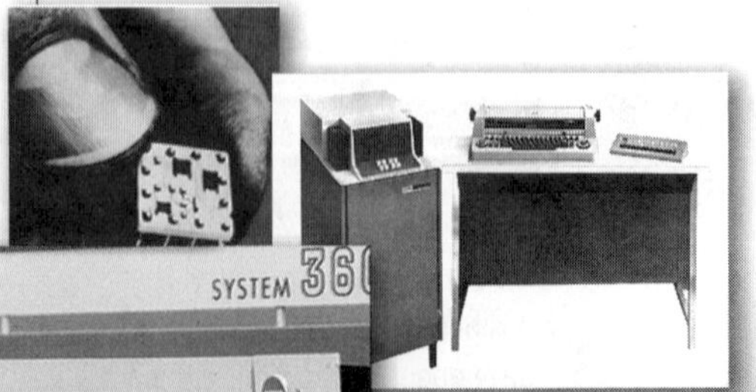

1964 IBM introduces the term word processing for the first time with its Magnetic Tape/Selectric Typewriter (MT/ST). The MT/ST was the first reusable storage medium that allowed typed material to be edited without having to retype the document.

1965

1965 Dr. John Kemeny of Dartmouth leads the development of the BASIC programming language.

1965 Digital Equipment Corporation (DEC) introduces the first minicomputer, the PDP-8. The machine is used extensively as an interface for time-sharing systems.

1968

1968 In a letter to the editor titled, "GO TO Statements Considered Harmful," Dr. Edsger Dijkstra introduces the concept of structured programming, developing standards for constructing computer programs.

1968 Computer Science Corporation (CSC) becomes the first software company listed on the New York Stock Exchange.

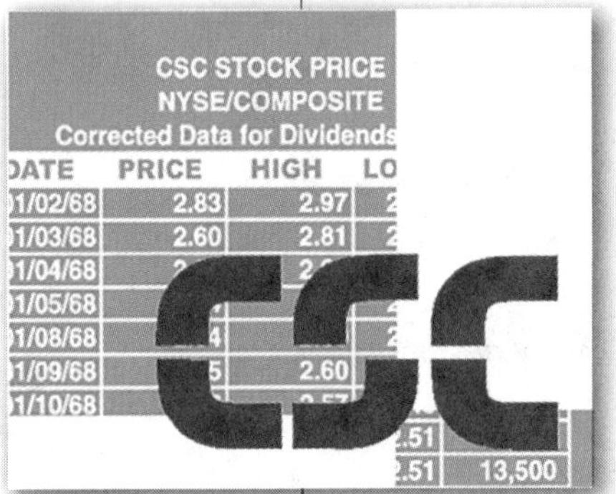
CSC STOCK PRICE
NYSE/COMPOSITE
Corrected Data for Dividends
DATE PRICE HIGH
01/02/68 2.83 2.97
01/03/68 2.60 2.81
01/04/68
01/05/68
01/08/68
01/09/68 2.60
01/10/68
2.51
2.51 13,500
CSC

1968 Alan Shugart at IBM demonstrates the first regular use of an 8-inch floppy disk.

1969

1969 Under pressure from the industry, IBM announces that some of its software will be priced separately from the computer hardware, allowing software firms to emerge in the industry.

IBM

1969 The ARPANET network is established, which eventually grows to become the Internet.

ARPANET

1970

1970 Fourth-generation computers, built with chips that use LSI (large-scale integration) arrive. While the chips used in 1965 contained up to 1,000 circuits, the LSI chip contains as many as 15,000.

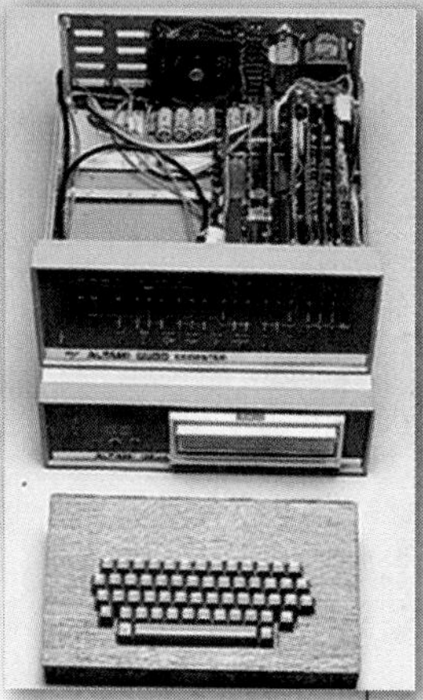

1975 MITS, Inc. advertises one of the first microcomputers, the Altair. The Altair is sold in kits for less than $400 and within the first three months 4,000 orders are taken.

1975 Ethernet, the first local area network (LAN), is developed at Xerox PARC (Palo Alto Research Center) by Robert Metcalfe.

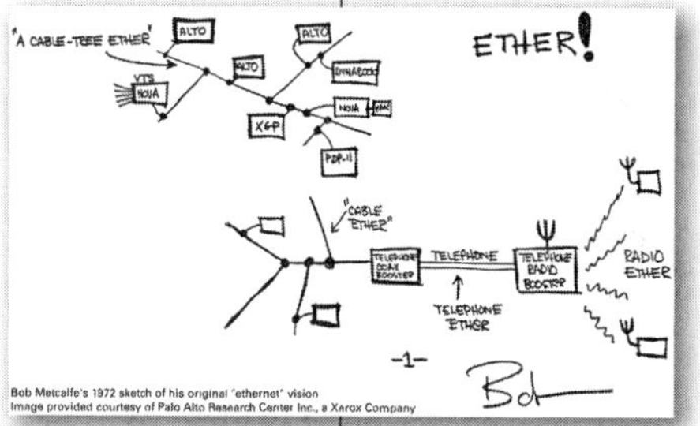

Bob Metcalfe's 1972 sketch of his original "ethernet" vision
Image provided courtesy of Palo Alto Research Center Inc., a Xerox Company

1979 The first public online information services, CompuServe and the Source, are founded.

1979 VisiCalc, a spreadsheet program written by Bob Frankston and Dan Bricklin, is introduced.

1981 The IBM PC is introduced, signaling IBM's entrance into the personal computer marketplace. The IBM PC quickly garners the largest share of the personal computer market and becomes the personal computer of choice in business.

1971 1975 1976 1979 1980 1981

1971 Dr. Ted Hoff of Intel Corporation develops a microprocessor, or microprogrammable computer chip, the Intel 4004.

1976 Steve Jobs and Steve Wozniak build the first Apple computer. A subsequent version, the Apple II, is an immediate success. Adopted by elementary schools, high schools, and colleges, for many students, the Apple II is their first contact with the world of computers.

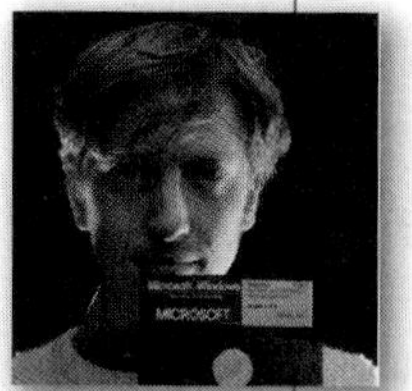

1980 IBM offers Microsoft Corporation cofounder, Bill Gates, the opportunity to develop the operating system for the soon-to-be announced IBM personal computer. With the development of MS-DOS, Microsoft achieves tremendous growth and success.

1980 Alan Shugart presents the Winchester hard disk, revolutionizing storage for personal computers.

1981 The first computer virus, Elk Cloner, is spread via Apple II floppy disks, which contained the operating system. A short rhyme would appear on the screen when the user pressed Reset after the 50th boot of an infected disk.

1982 3,275,000 personal computers are sold, almost 3,000,000 more than in 1981.

3.275 Million

1982 Compaq, Inc. is founded to develop and market IBM-compatible PCs.

1982 Hayes introduces the 300 bps smart modem. The modem is an immediate success.

1984 Apple introduces the Macintosh computer, which incorporates a unique, easy-to-learn, graphical user interface.

Apple

1984 Hewlett-Packard announces the first LaserJet printer for personal computers.

1982

1983

1984

1986

1983 Instead of choosing a person for its annual award, *TIME* magazine names the computer Machine of the Year for 1982, acknowledging the impact of computers on society.

1983 Lotus Development Corporation is founded. Its spreadsheet software, Lotus 1-2-3, which combines spreadsheet, graphics, and database programs in one package, becomes the best-selling program for IBM personal computers.

1986 Microsoft has public stock offering and raises approximately $61 million.

1989 While working at CERN, Switzerland, Tim Berners-Lee invents the World Wide Web.

WWW

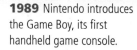

1991 Kodak announces the first digital SLR (single-lens reflex) camera. The Kodak DCS 100 is developed mostly for photojournalism purposes and stores the photos and batteries in a separate unit.

1989 Nintendo introduces the Game Boy, its first handheld game console.

1991 World Wide Web Consortium releases standards that describe a framework for linking documents on different computers.

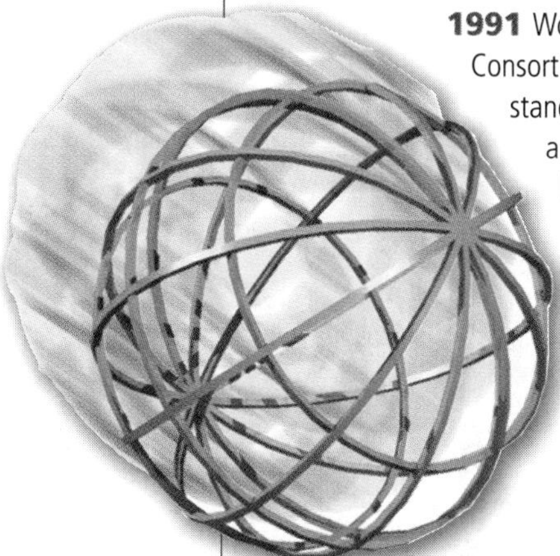

1988 Microsoft surpasses Lotus Development Corporation to become the world's top software vendor.

1989 The Intel 486 becomes the world's first 1,000,000 transistor microprocessor. It executes 15,000,000 instructions per second — four times as fast as its predecessor, the 80386 chip.

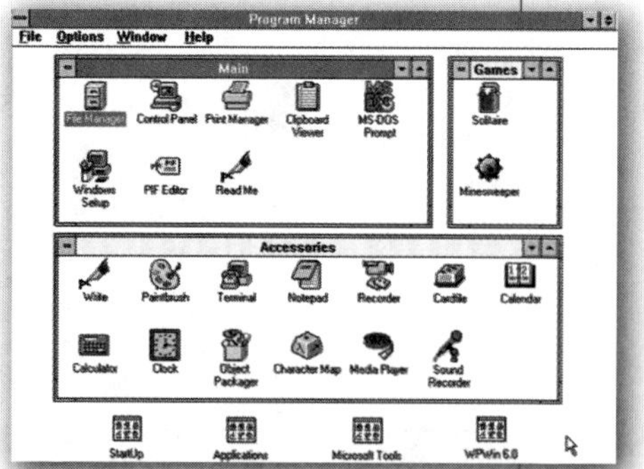

1992 Microsoft releases Windows 3.1, the latest version of its Windows operating system. Windows 3.1 offers improvements such as TrueType fonts, multimedia capability, and object linking and embedding (OLE). In two months, 3,000,000 copies of Windows 3.1 are sold.

1993 Several companies introduce computers using the Pentium processor from Intel. The Pentium chip contains 3.1 million transistors and is capable of performing 112,000,000 instructions per second.

1993 The U.S. Air Force completes the Global Positioning System by launching its 24th Navstar satellite into orbit. Today, GPS receivers can be found in cars, notebook computers, and smart phones.

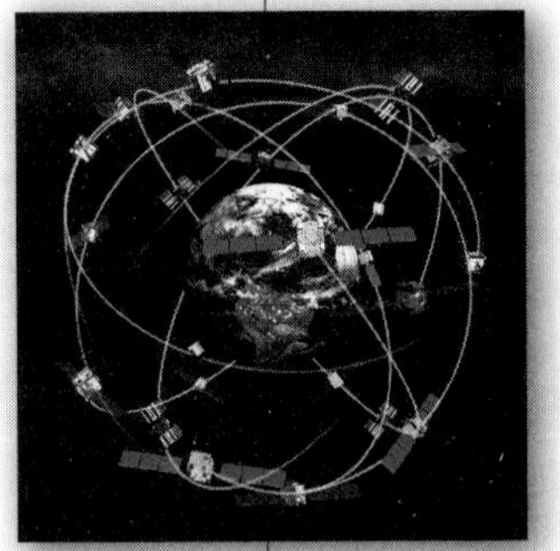

1993

1993 Microsoft releases Microsoft Office 3 Professional, the first version of Microsoft Office for the Windows operating system.

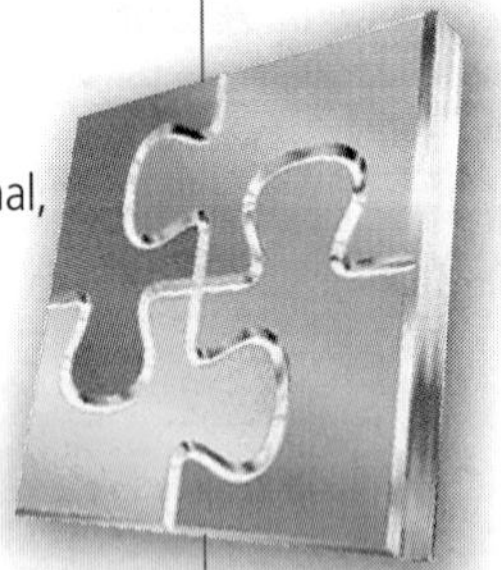

1993 The White House launches its Web site, which includes an interactive citizens' handbook and White House history and tours.

1994 Jim Clark and Marc Andreessen found Netscape and launch Netscape Navigator 1.0, a Web browser.

1994 Linus Torvalds creates the Linux kernel, a UNIX-like operating system that he releases free across the Internet for further enhancement by other programmers.

1994 Apple introduces the first digital camera intended for consumers. The Apple QuickTake 100 is connected to home computers using a serial cable.

1994

1994 Yahoo!, a popular search engine and portal, is founded by two Stanford Ph.D. students as a way to keep track of their personal interests on the Internet. Currently, Yahoo! has approximately 12,000 employees and more than 500 million unique visitors to its Web site.

1994 Amazon is founded and later begins business as an online bookstore. Amazon eventually expands to sell products of all types and facilitates the buying and selling of new and used goods. Today, Amazon has approximately 17,000 employees.

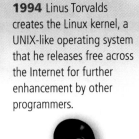

1995 Sun Microsystems launches Java, an object-oriented programming language that allows users to write one program for a variety of computer platforms.

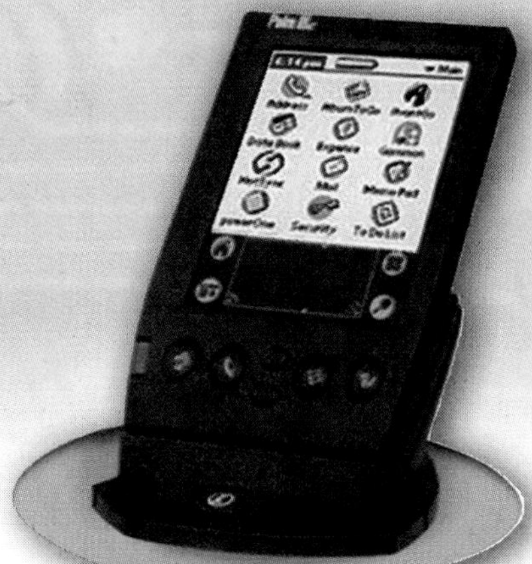

1996 U.S. Robotics introduces the PalmPilot, an inexpensive user-friendly personal digital assistant (PDA).

1996 Microsoft releases Windows NT 4.0, an operating system for client-server networks.

1995

1996

1997

1995 Microsoft releases Windows 95, a major upgrade to its Windows operating system. Windows 95 consists of more than 10,000,000 lines of computer instructions developed by 300 person-years of effort.

1997 Intel introduces the Pentium II processor with 7.5 million transistors. The new processor, which incorporates MMX technology, processes video, audio, and graphics data more efficiently and supports programs such as movie editing, gaming, and more.

1995 eBay, an online auction Web site, is founded. Providing an online venue for people to buy and sell goods, it quickly becomes the world's largest online marketplace as it approaches 100 million active users worldwide.

1997 Microsoft releases Internet Explorer 4.0 and seizes a key place in the Internet arena.

1998 Google files for incorporation and is now the most used search engine, capturing more than 60 percent of the market over other search engines.

1998 Apple Computer introduces the iMac, the next version of its popular Macintosh computer. The iMac wins customers with its futuristic design, see-through case, and easy setup.

1999 Microsoft introduces Office 2000, its premier productivity suite, offering new tools for users to create content and save it directly to a Web site without any file conversion or special steps.

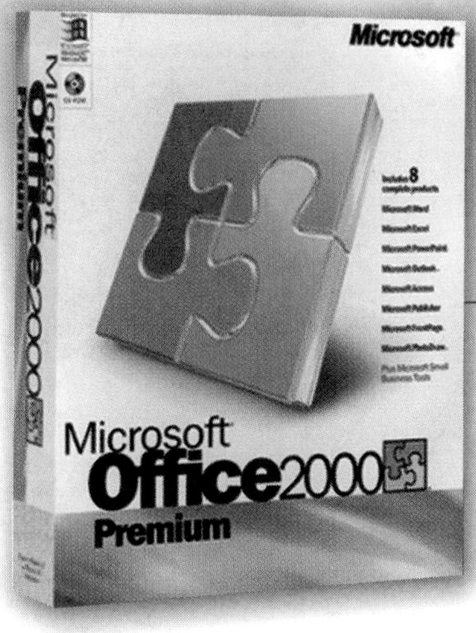

1999 Open source software, such as the Linux operating system and the Apache Web server created by unpaid volunteers, begin to gain wide acceptance among computer users.

1999 Intel introduces the Pentium III processor. This processor succeeds the Pentium II and can process 3-D graphics more quickly. The Pentium III processor contains between 9.5 and 44 million transistors.

1999

1998

1998 E-commerce booms. Companies such as Amazon.com, Dell, and E*TRADE spur online shopping, allowing buyers to obtain a variety of goods and services.

1998 Microsoft ships Windows 98, an upgrade to Windows 95. Windows 98 offers improved Internet access, better system performance, and support for a new generation of hardware and software.

1999 Governments and businesses frantically work to make their computers Y2K (Year 2000) compliant, spending more than $500 billion worldwide.

2000 Shawn Fanning, 19, and his company, Napster, turn the music industry upside down by developing software that allows computer users to swap music files with one another without going through a centralized file server.

napster™

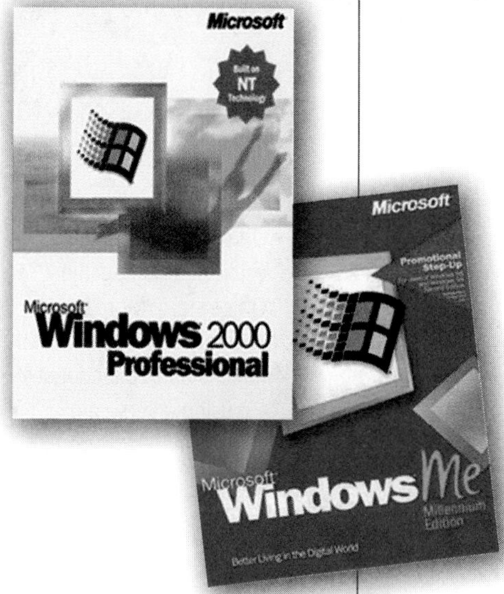

2000 Microsoft ships Windows 2000 and Windows Me. Windows 2000 offers improved behind-the-scenes security and reliability.

2000

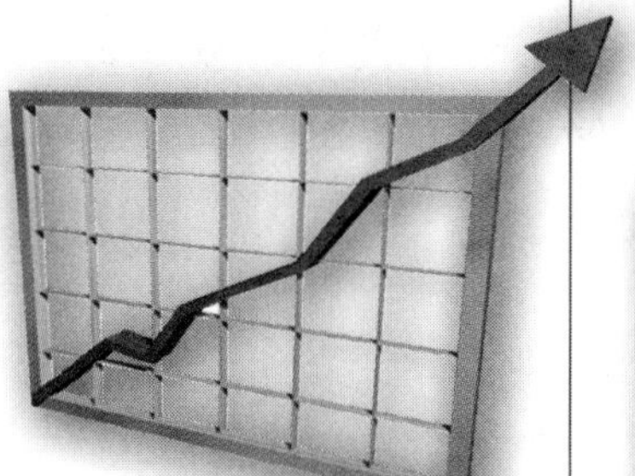

2000 E-commerce achieves mainstream acceptance. Annual e-commerce sales exceed $100 billion, and Internet advertising expenditures reach more than $5 billion.

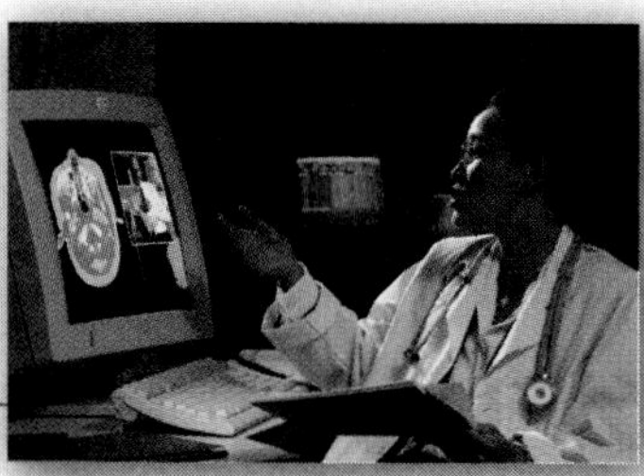

2000 Telemedicine uses satellite technology and video conferencing to broadcast consultations and to perform distant surgeries. Robots are used for complex and precise tasks.

2000 Dot-com companies (Internet based) go out of business at a record pace — nearly one per day — as financial investors withhold funding due to the companies' unprofitability.

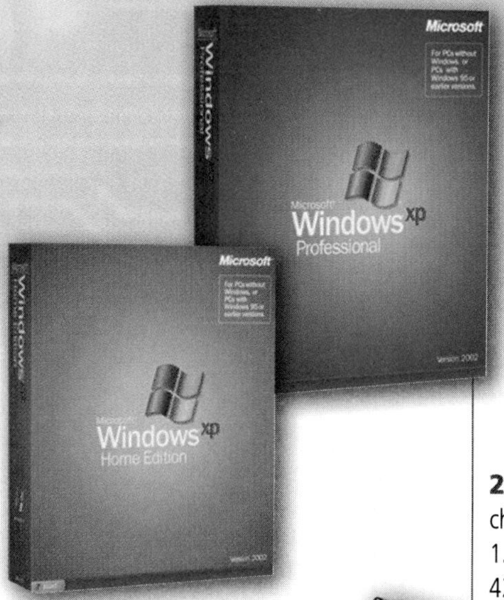

2001 Microsoft releases major operating system updates with Windows XP for personal computers and servers. Windows XP is significantly more reliable than previous versions, features a 32-bit computing architecture, and offers a new look and feel.

2001 Intel unveils its Pentium 4 chip with clock speeds starting at 1.4 GHz. The Pentium 4 includes 42 million transistors.

2001

2001 Microsoft introduces Office XP, the next version of the world's leading suite of productivity software. Features include speech and handwriting recognition, smart tags, and task panes.

2001 Wikipedia, a free online encyclopedia, is introduced. Additional wikis begin to appear on the Internet, enabling people to share information in their areas of expertise. Although some might rely on wikis for research purposes, the content is not always verified for accuracy.

2002 After several years of negligible sales, the Tablet PC is reintroduced to meet the needs of a more targeted audience.

2002 Digital video cameras, DVD burners, easy-to-use video editing software, and improvements in storage capabilities allow the average computer user to create Hollywood-like videos with introductions, conclusions, rearranged scenes, music, and voice-over.

2002

Microsoft .net

2002 Microsoft launches its .NET strategy, which is a new environment for developing and running software applications featuring ease of development of Web-based services.

2002 DVD burners begin to replace CD burners (CD-RW). DVDs can store up to eight times as much data as CDs. Uses include storing home movies, music, photos, and backups.

2002 Intel ships its revamped Pentium 4 chip with the 0.13 micron processor and Hyper-Threading (HT) Technology, operating at speeds of 3.06 GHz. This new development eventually will enable processors with a billion transistors to operate at 20 GHz.

2003 Wireless computers and devices, such as keyboards, mouse devices, home networks, and wireless Internet access points become commonplace.

2003 Microsoft ships Office 2003, the latest version of its flagship Office suite. More than 400 million people in 175 nations and 70 languages are using a version of Office.

2003

2003 In an attempt to maintain their current business model of selling songs, the Recording Industry Association of America (RIAA) files more than 250 lawsuits against individual computer users who offer copyrighted music over peer-to-peer networks.

myspace.com
a place for friends™

2003 MySpace, an online social network, is founded. MySpace allows users to share information, photos, and videos, as well as stay in touch with their friends and make new friends. MySpace eventually grows to nearly 200 million users, making it one of the more popular and successful online social networks.

2004 Companies such as RealNetworks, Microsoft, Sony, and Walmart stake out turf in the online music store business started by Apple Computer.

2004 USB flash drives become a cost-effective way to transport data and information from one computer to another.

USB flash drive

2004 Flat-panel LCD monitors overtake bulky CRT monitors as the popular choice of computer users.

2004 106 million, or 53 percent, of the 200 million online population in America accesses the Internet via broadband.

2004 Major retailers begin requiring suppliers to include radio frequency identification (RFID) tags or microchips with antennas, which can be as small as one-third of a millimeter across, in the goods they sell.

2004 The smart phone overtakes the PDA as the mobile device of choice.

facebook

2004 Facebook, an online social network originally available only to college students, is founded. Facebook eventually opens registration to all people and immediately grows to more than 110 million users with more than 10 billion photos, 30 million of which are uploaded daily.

2004

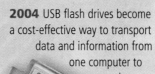

2004 Linux, the open source operating system, makes major inroads into the server market as a viable alternative to Microsoft Windows Server 2003, Sun's Solaris, and the UNIX operating systems.

2004 Sony unveils its PlayStation Portable (PSP). This handheld game console is the first to use optical discs.

2004 Mozilla releases its first version of the Firefox Web browser. Firefox provides innovative features that enhance the Web browsing experience for users, including tabbed browsing and a Search box. Firefox quickly gains popularity and takes market share away from Microsoft's Internet Explorer.

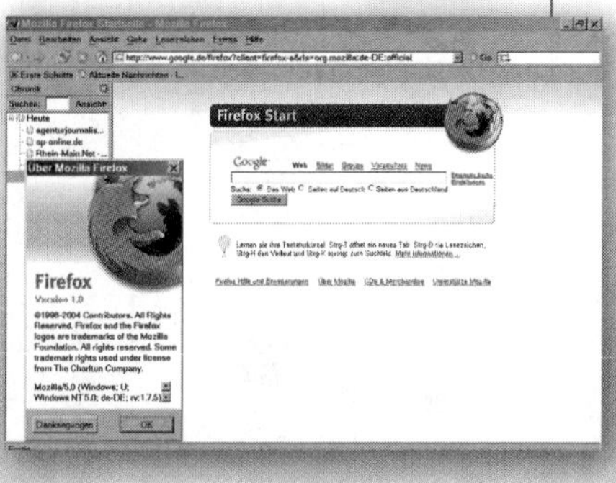

2004 Apple Computer introduces the sleek iMac G5. The new computer's display device contains the system unit.

Video iPod

2005 Apple releases the latest version of its popular pocket-sized iPod portable media player. First it played songs, then photos, then podcasts, and now, in addition, up to 150 hours of music videos and television shows on a 2.5" color display.

2005 YouTube, an online community for video sharing, is founded. YouTube includes content such as home videos, movie previews, and clips from television shows. In November 2006, Google acquires YouTube.

YouTube™

2005 Microsoft introduces Visual Studio 2005. The product includes Visual Basic, Visual C#, Visual J#, Visual C++, and SQL Server.

Spyware **Pharming** **Spam** **Phishing** **Spim** **Spit**

2005 Spam, spyware, phishing, pharming, spim, and spit take center stage, along with viruses, as major nuisances to the 801 million computer users worldwide.

2005

2005 Microsoft unveils Windows XP Media Center Edition 2005. This operating system focuses on delivering media content such as music, digital photos, movies, and television.

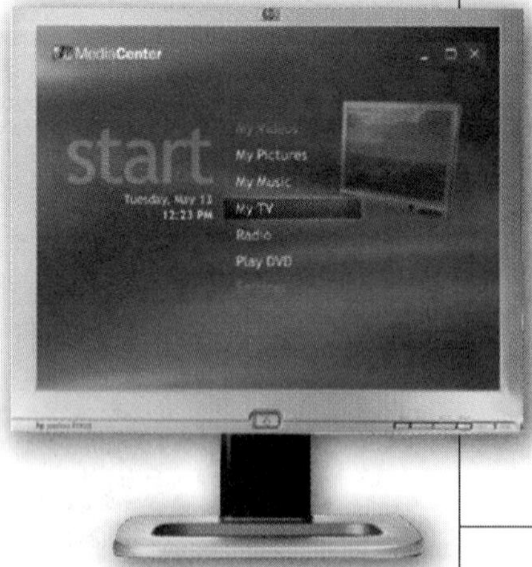

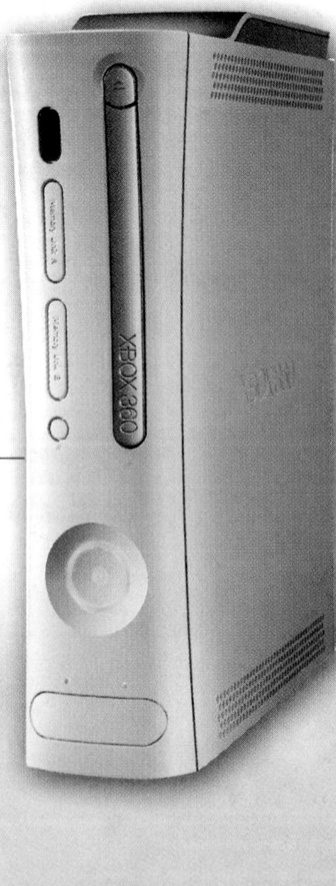

2005 Microsoft releases the Xbox 360, its latest game console. Features include the capability to play music, display photos, and network with computers and other Xbox gamers.

2005 Blogging and podcasting become mainstream methods for distributing information via the Web.

Blogging
Podcasting

2006 Sony launches its PlayStation 3. New features include a Blu-ray Disc player, high-definition capabilities, and always-on online connectivity.

2006 Microsoft and Mozilla release new versions of their respective Web browsers. Microsoft's Internet Explorer 7 and Mozilla's Firefox 2 offer easier browsing through the use of tabs and allow search capabilities directly from the toolbar.

2006 Web 2.0, a term coined in 2004, becomes a household term with the increase in popularity of online social networks, wikis, and Web applications.

2006 Text, picture, and video messaging continue to increase as popular communications methods. In addition to people sending informal messages to each other, businesses and other institutions use messaging to allow people to vote in polls, receive targeted advertisements, and view news updates.

2006 Nintendo Wii is introduced and immediately becomes a leader in game consoles. The Wii is being used in revolutionary ways, such as training surgeons.

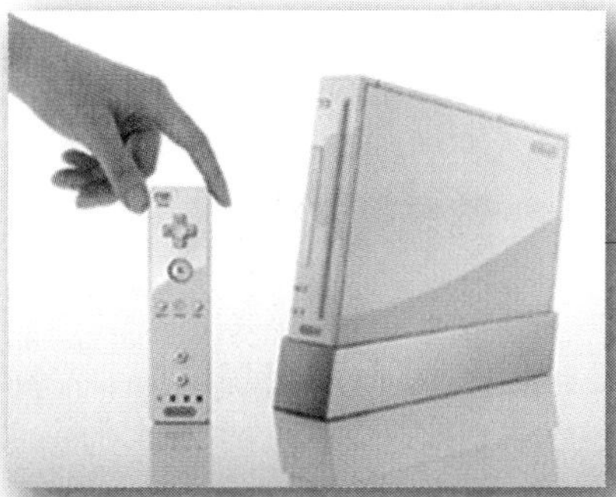

2006 Intel introduces its Core 2 Duo processor family. Boasting record-breaking performance while using less power, the family consists of five desktop computer processors and five mobile computer processors. The desktop processor includes 291 million transistors, yet uses 40 percent less power than the Pentium processor.

2006

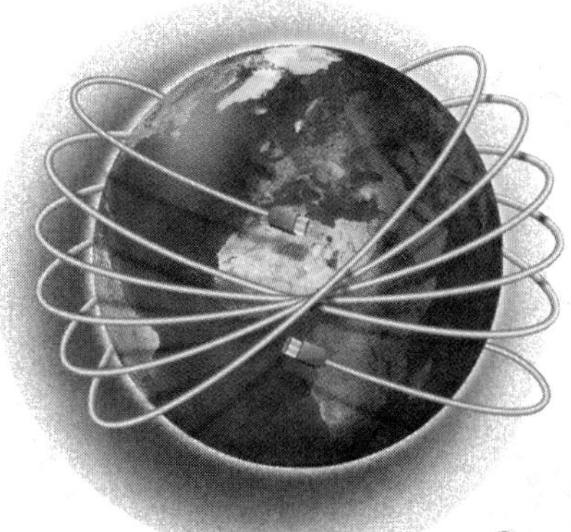

2006 IBM produces the fastest supercomputer, Blue Gene/L. It can perform approximately 28 trillion calculations in the time it takes you to blink your eye, or about one-tenth of a second.

2006 Nintendo releases the Nintendo DS Lite, a handheld game console with new features such as dual screens and improved graphics and sound.

2006 Apple begins selling Macintosh computers with Intel microprocessors.

2007 Intel introduces Core 2 Quad, a four-core processor made for dual-processor servers and desktop computers. The larger number of cores allows for more energy-efficient performance and optimizes battery performance in notebook computers.

2007 Video blogs, or vlogs, grow in popularity along with YouTube. Vlogs allow users to video their message instead of entering text via a regular blog. The growth in the popularity of vlogs is attributed to several factors, including the use of video portable media players. Podcasting also increases in popularity for the same reasons. A podcast is distinguished from other digital audio formats by its capability to be downloaded automatically.

2007 Apple introduces the iPhone and sells 270,000 phones in the first 2 days. iPhone uses iTouch technology that allows you to make a call simply by tapping a name or number in your address book. In addition, it stores and plays music like an iPod. Also, Apple sells its one billionth song on iTunes.

2007 VoIP (Voice over Internet Protocol) providers expand usage to include Wi-Fi phones. The phones enable high-quality service through a Wireless-G network and high-speed Internet connection.

2007 Apple releases its Mac OS X version 10.5 "Leopard" operating system, available in a desktop version and server version. The system includes a significantly revised desktop, with a semitransparent menu bar and an updated search tool that incorporates the same visual navigation interface as iTunes.

2007

2007 Wi-Fi hotspots are popular in a variety of locations. People bring their computers to coffeehouses, fast food restaurants, or bookstores to access the Internet wirelessly, either free or for a small fee.

2007 Blu-ray Discs increase in popularity, overcoming and replacing HD DVD in less than one year. A Blu-ray Disc can store approximately 9 hours of high-definition (HD) video on a 50 GB disc or approximately 23 hours of standard-definition (SD) video.

2007 Half of the world's population uses cell phones. More and more people are using a cell phone in lieu of a landline in their home.

2007 Microsoft releases Office 2007. New features include the most significant update to the user interface in more than a decade, including the introduction of the Ribbon, which replaces the toolbars in most of the programs, and the capability to save documents in XML and PDF formats.

Windows Vista

2007 Microsoft ships the latest version of its widely used operating system, Windows Vista. Vista offers the Basic interface and the Aero interface, which offers several graphical features, including transparent windows. Internet Explorer 7 is included with Windows Vista.

2008 Microsoft introduces Windows Server 2008, the successor to Windows Server 2003.

2008 Bill Gates retires from Microsoft. He continues as chairman and advisor on key development projects.

2008 Dell offers a hybrid computer. Smaller than a desktop computer but larger than a notebook computer, these hybrid computers contain features comparable to their larger counterparts and can work more easily in a home entertainment environment.

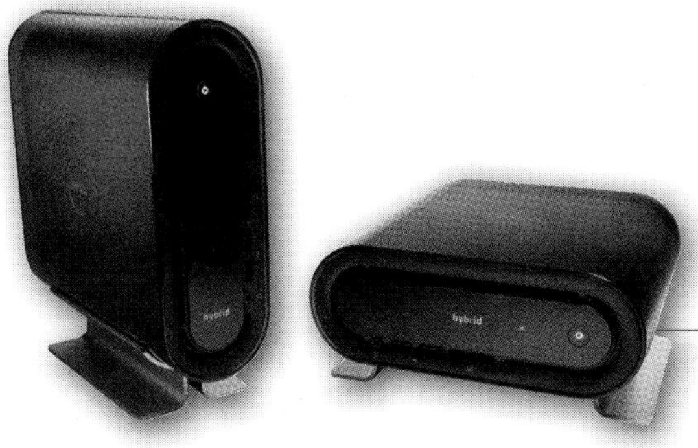

2008 Netflix, an online movie rental company, and TiVo, a company manufacturing digital video recorders (DVRs), make Netflix movies and television episodes available on TiVo (DVRs).

2008

2008 WiMAX goes live! The advantage of this technology is the capability to access video, music, voice, and video calls wherever and whenever desired. Average download speeds are between 2 Mbps and 4 Mbps. By year's end, Sprint has approximately 100 million users on its network.

2008 Computer manufacturers begin to offer solid state drives (SSDs) instead of hard disks, mostly in notebook computers. Although SSDs have a lower storage capacity, are more expensive, and slightly more susceptible to failure, they are significantly faster.

2008 Google releases its new Web browser. Google Chrome uses an entirely unique interface and offers other features such as dynamic tabs, crash control, and application shortcuts.

2008 Smart phones become smarter. Smart phones introduced this year include enhanced features such as touch screens with multi-touch technology, mobile TV, tactile feedback, improved graphics, GPS receivers, and better cameras.

2008 Mozilla releases Firefox 3, the latest version of its Web browser. Firefox 3 offers greater security, a more user-friendly interface, and other improvements to enhance the Web browsing experience.

2009 In June 2009, federal law requires that all full-power television stations broadcast only in digital format. Analog television owners are required to purchase a converter box to view over-the-air digital programming.

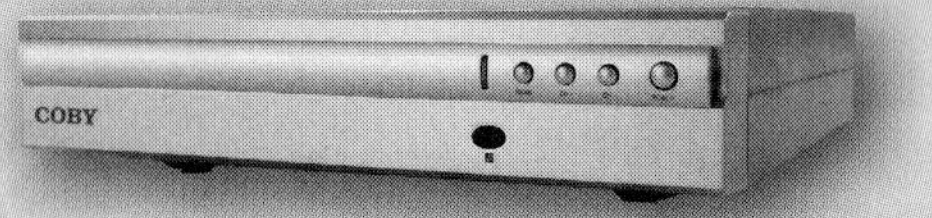

2009 Web applications continue to increase in popularity. Web applications make it easier to perform tasks such as word processing, photo editing, and tax preparation without installing software on your computer.

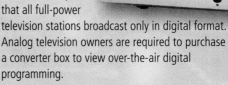

2010 Kinect for Xbox 360 changes the way people play video games. Game players now can interact with the game with a series of sensors, as well as a camera, tracking their movements in 3-D.

2009 Microsoft releases Internet Explorer 8, also known as IE8. IE8 offers new features such as InPrivate Browsing, Accelerators, and support for WebSlices.

2009 Microsoft releases the newest version of its Windows operating system, Windows 7. This version provides greater stability and security; a more flexible, user-friendly interface; and requires fewer computing resources to operate.

2010

2009

2009 Intel releases the Core i5 and Core i7 line of processors. These processors offer increased performance for some of the more demanding tasks. Intel also enhances its Core processor family by releasing multi-core processors, designed to increase the number of instructions that can be processed at a given time.

2010 AMD develops a 12-core processor, which contains two 6-core processors, each on an individual chip. Power consumption is similar to that of a 6-core processor but offers reduced clock speed.

2009 Computers and mobile devices promote fitness by offering games and programs to help users exercise and track their progress. These games and programs also are used to assist with physical rehabilitation.

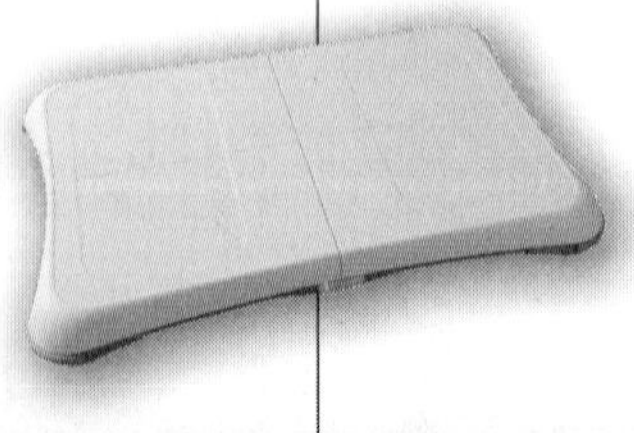

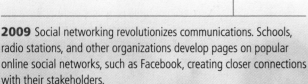

2010 Microsoft releases Office 2010, the latest version of its Office suite. This version is available in multiple editions and continues to help people work more efficiently. Office Web apps, available free to Windows Live users, offer online access to scaled-down versions of Word, PowerPoint, Excel, and OneNote.

2009 Social networking revolutionizes communications. Schools, radio stations, and other organizations develop pages on popular online social networks, such as Facebook, creating closer connections with their stakeholders.

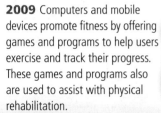

2010 Adobe releases the latest version of its design suite, Adobe CS5. This new suite has many performance and interface enhancements over previous versions and takes advantage of new technologies such as multi-touch.

2011 Individuals and enterprises increase their focus on green computing. Computer manufacturers not only sell more energy-efficient hardware, they also provide easy ways in which customers can recycle their old computers and devices.

2010 Hard disk capacity continues to increase at an exponential rate, with the largest hard disks storing more than 2.5 TB of data and information. Solid state storage also is becoming more popular, with storage capacities increasing and prices decreasing.

2010 Apple releases the iPad, a revolutionary mobile device with a 9.7-inch multi-touch screen. The iPad boasts up to 10 hours of battery life, connects wirelessly to the Internet, and is capable of running thousands of apps.

2011 Netbooks prove to be an attractive alternative to traditional notebook computers. Netbooks are smaller and lighter than traditional notebook computers, while providing nearly the same functionality.

2010

2011

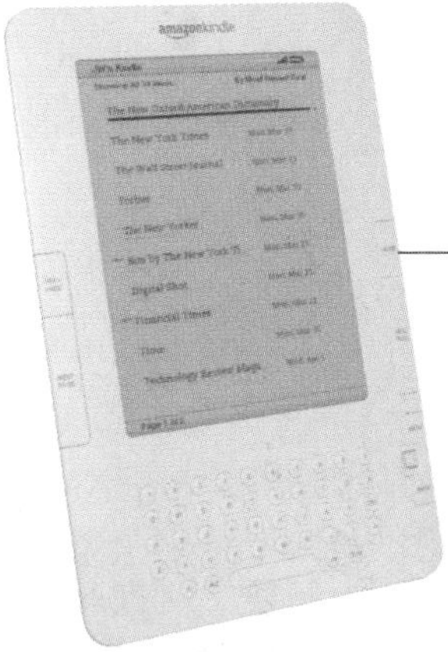

2011 E-books and e-book readers explode in popularity. Many novels, textbooks, and other publications now are available digitally and can be read on an e-book reader, computer, or mobile device.

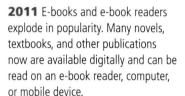

2011 Decreases in storage costs and increases in Internet connection speeds persuade more users to use cloud storage for their data. Cloud storage also provides users with the convenience of accessing their files from almost anywhere.

2011 A new generation of Web browsers is released to support HTML5, enabling Web pages to contain more vivid, dynamic content.

2011 More than 200 types of mobile devices are using Google Android, an operating system originally designed for mobile devices.

Chapter Two

The Internet and World Wide Web

Objectives

After completing this chapter, you will be able to:

1 Discuss the evolution of the Internet

2 Identify and briefly describe various broadband Internet connections and state differences between broadband Internet connections and dial-up connections

3 Describe the types of Internet access providers: Internet service providers, online service providers, wireless Internet service providers

4 Describe the purpose of an IP address and its relationship to a domain name

5 Explain the purpose of a Web browser and identify the components of a Web address

6 Describe how to use a search engine to search for information on the Web and differentiate between a search engine and a subject directory

7 Describe the types of Web sites: portal, news, informational, business/marketing, blog, wiki, online social network, educational, entertainment, advocacy, Web application, content aggregator, and personal

8 Explain how Web pages use graphics, animation, audio, video, virtual reality, and plug-ins

9 Identify and briefly describe the steps required for Web publishing

10 Describe the types of e-commerce: business-to-consumer, consumer-to-consumer, and business-to-business

11 Explain how e-mail, mailing lists, instant messaging, chat rooms, VoIP, newsgroups and message boards, and FTP work

12 Identify the rules of netiquette

The Internet

One of the major reasons business, home, and other users purchase computers is for Internet access. The Internet is a widely used research tool, providing society with access to global information and instant communications. Further, access to the Internet can occur anytime from a computer anywhere: at home, at work, at school, in a restaurant, on an airplane, and at a park.

The **Internet**, also called the *Net*, is a worldwide collection of networks that links millions of businesses, government agencies, educational institutions, and individuals. Each of the networks on the Internet provides resources that add to the abundance of goods, services, and information accessible via the Internet.

Today, more than one billion home and business users around the world access a variety of services on the Internet, some of which are shown in Figure 2-1. The World Wide Web, or simply the Web, and e-mail are two of the more widely used Internet services. Other services include chat rooms, instant messaging, and VoIP (Voice over Internet Protocol). To enhance your understanding of these Internet services, the chapter begins by discussing the history of the Internet and how the Internet works and then explains each of these services.

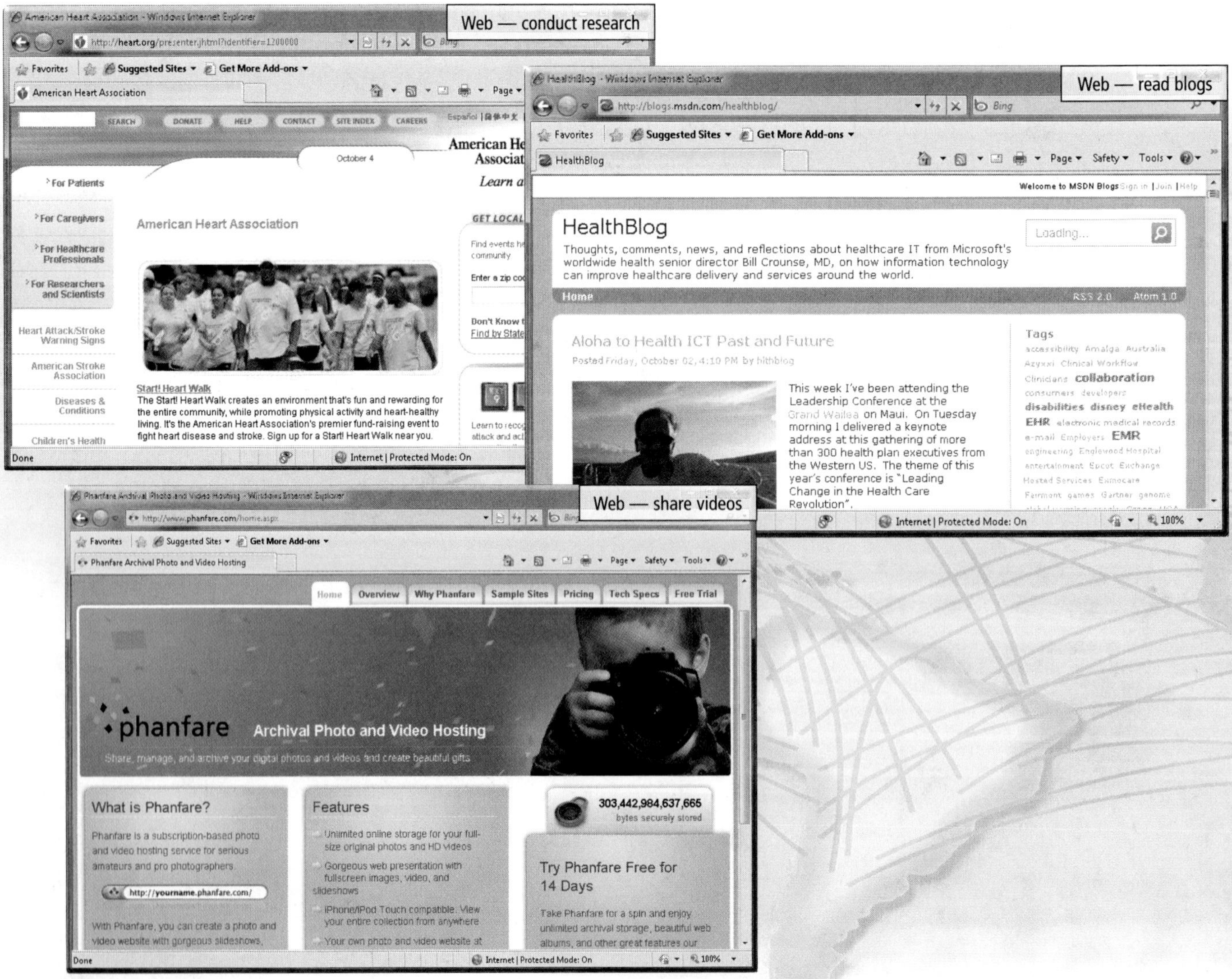

Figure 2-1 People around the world use a variety of Internet services in daily activities. Internet services allow home and business users to access the Web for activities such as conducting research, reading blogs, or sharing videos; to send e-mail messages; or to converse with others using chat rooms, instant messaging, or VoIP.

Evolution of the Internet

The Internet has its roots in a networking project started by the Pentagon's Advanced Research Projects Agency (*ARPA*), an agency of the U.S. Department of Defense. ARPA's goal was to build a network that (1) allowed scientists at different physical locations to share information and work together on military and scientific projects and (2) could function even if part of the network were disabled or destroyed by a disaster such as a nuclear attack. That network, called *ARPANET*, became functional in September 1969, linking scientific and academic researchers across the United States.

The original ARPANET consisted of four main computers, one each located at the University of California at Los Angeles, the University of California at Santa Barbara, the Stanford Research Institute, and the University of Utah. Each of these computers served as a host on the network. A *host*, more commonly known today as a server, is any computer that provides services and connections to other computers on a network. Hosts often use high-speed communications to transfer data and messages over a network.

As researchers and others realized the great benefit of using ARPANET to share data and information, ARPANET underwent phenomenal growth. By 1984, ARPANET had more than 1,000 individual computers linked as hosts. Today, more than 550 million hosts connect to the Internet.

Some organizations connected entire networks to ARPANET to take advantage of its high-speed communications. In 1986, the National Science Foundation (NSF) connected its huge network of five supercomputer centers, called *NSFnet*, to ARPANET. This configuration of complex networks and hosts became known as the Internet.

Until 1995, NSFnet handled the bulk of the communications activity, or **traffic**, on the Internet. In 1995, NSFnet terminated its network on the Internet and resumed its status as a research network.

Today, the Internet consists of many local, regional, national, and international networks. Numerous corporations, commercial firms, and other companies such as IBM provide networks to handle Internet traffic. Both public and private organizations own networks on the Internet. These networks, along with telephone companies such as Verizon and AT&T, cable and satellite companies, and the government, all contribute toward the internal structure of the Internet.

Each organization on the Internet is responsible only for maintaining its own network. No single person, company, institution, or government agency controls or owns the Internet. The World Wide Web Consortium (*W3C*), however, oversees research and sets standards and guidelines for many areas of the Internet. The mission of the W3C is to contribute to the growth of the Web. More than 350 organizations from around the world are members of the W3C, advising, defining standards, and addressing other issues.

W3C

For more information, visit the Computer Concepts CourseMate Web site at www.cengagebrain.com, navigate to the Chapter 2 Web Link resource for this book, and then click W3C.

Internet2

Internet2 is a not-for-profit research and development project that connects more than 200 universities and 115 companies via a high-speed private network. Founded in 1996, the goal of Internet2 is to develop and test advanced network technologies that will benefit Internet users in the short-term future. These technologies require an extremely high-speed network that exceeds the capabilities of today's Internet and networks. Examples of previous Internet2 projects that are now mainstream include telemedicine, digital libraries (online books, magazines, music, movies, speeches, etc.), and faster Internet services. Current Internet2 projects include interactive high-definition video and enhanced detection and resolution of network problems.

Connecting to the Internet

Many home and small business users connect to the Internet via high-speed *broadband* Internet service. With broadband Internet service, your computer or mobile device usually is connected to the Internet the entire time it is powered on. Examples of broadband Internet service include cable, DSL, fiber, radio signals, and satellite.

- *Cable Internet service* provides high-speed Internet access through the cable television network via a cable modem.
- *DSL* (digital subscriber line) provides high-speed Internet connections using regular copper telephone lines.
- *Fiber to the Premises* (*FTTP*) uses fiber-optic cable to provide high-speed Internet access to home and business users.
- *Fixed wireless* provides high-speed Internet connections using a dish-shaped antenna on your house or business to communicate with a tower location via radio signals.
- A *cellular radio network* offers high-speed Internet connections to devices with built-in compatible technology or computers with wireless modems.
- A **Wi-Fi** (wireless fidelity) network uses radio signals to provide high-speed Internet connections to compatible or properly equipped wireless computers and devices.
- *Satellite Internet service* provides high-speed Internet connections via satellite to a satellite dish that communicates with a satellite modem.

Employees and students typically connect their computers to the Internet through a business or school network. The business or school network connects to a high-speed broadband Internet service.

Many home users set up a Wi-Fi network, which sends signals to a communications device that is connected to a high-speed Internet service such as cable or DSL. Instead of using broadband Internet service, however, some home users connect to the Internet via dial-up access, which is a slower-speed technology. *Dial-up access* takes place when the modem in your computer connects to the Internet via a standard telephone line that transmits data and information using an analog (continuous wave pattern) signal. Users may opt for dial-up access because of its lower price or because broadband access is not available in their area.

Mobile users access the Internet using a variety of Internet services. Most hotels and airports provide wired or wireless Internet connections as a service to travelers. Wireless Internet services, such as Wi-Fi networks, allow mobile users to connect easily to the Internet with notebook computers, smart phones, and other mobile devices while away from a telephone, cable, or other wired connection. Many public locations, such as airports, hotels, schools, shopping malls, and coffee shops, are *hot spots* that provide Wi-Fi Internet connections to users with mobile computers or devices. At public locations, you may be required to agree to terms of service, obtain a password (for example, from the hotel's front desk), or perform some other action in order to connect to the Internet. Some cities provide free Wi-Fi Internet connections to all residents.

FAQ 2-1

How popular is broadband?

According to a study performed by Pew Internet & American Life Project, 63 percent of American adults have broadband Internet connections at home. Adoption of broadband connections increases during good economic times, while some may hesitate to make the switch during an economic downturn. It is believed that once the price of a broadband connection decreases, and broadband is available in more rural areas, its popularity will increase further.

For more information, visit the Computer Concepts CourseMate Web site at www.cengagebrain.com, navigate to the Chapter 2 FAQ resource for this book, and then click Broadband.

Access Providers

An **access provider** is a business that provides individuals and organizations access to the Internet free or for a fee. For example, some Wi-Fi networks provide free access while others charge a per use fee. Other access providers often charge a fixed amount for an Internet connection, offering faster speeds or more services for higher rates. Typical monthly rates range from about $5 to $24 per month for dial-up, $13 to $70 for DSL, $20 to $75 for cable, $40 to $150 for FTTP, $30 to $80 for fixed wireless, $60 to $80 for cellular networks, and $50 to $120 for satellite. Many Internet access providers offer services such as news, weather, financial data, games, travel guides, e-mail, photo communities, and online storage to hold digital photos and other files. (A *file* is a named unit of storage.)

Access providers are categorized as regional or national ISPs, online service providers, and wireless Internet service providers (Figure 2-2).

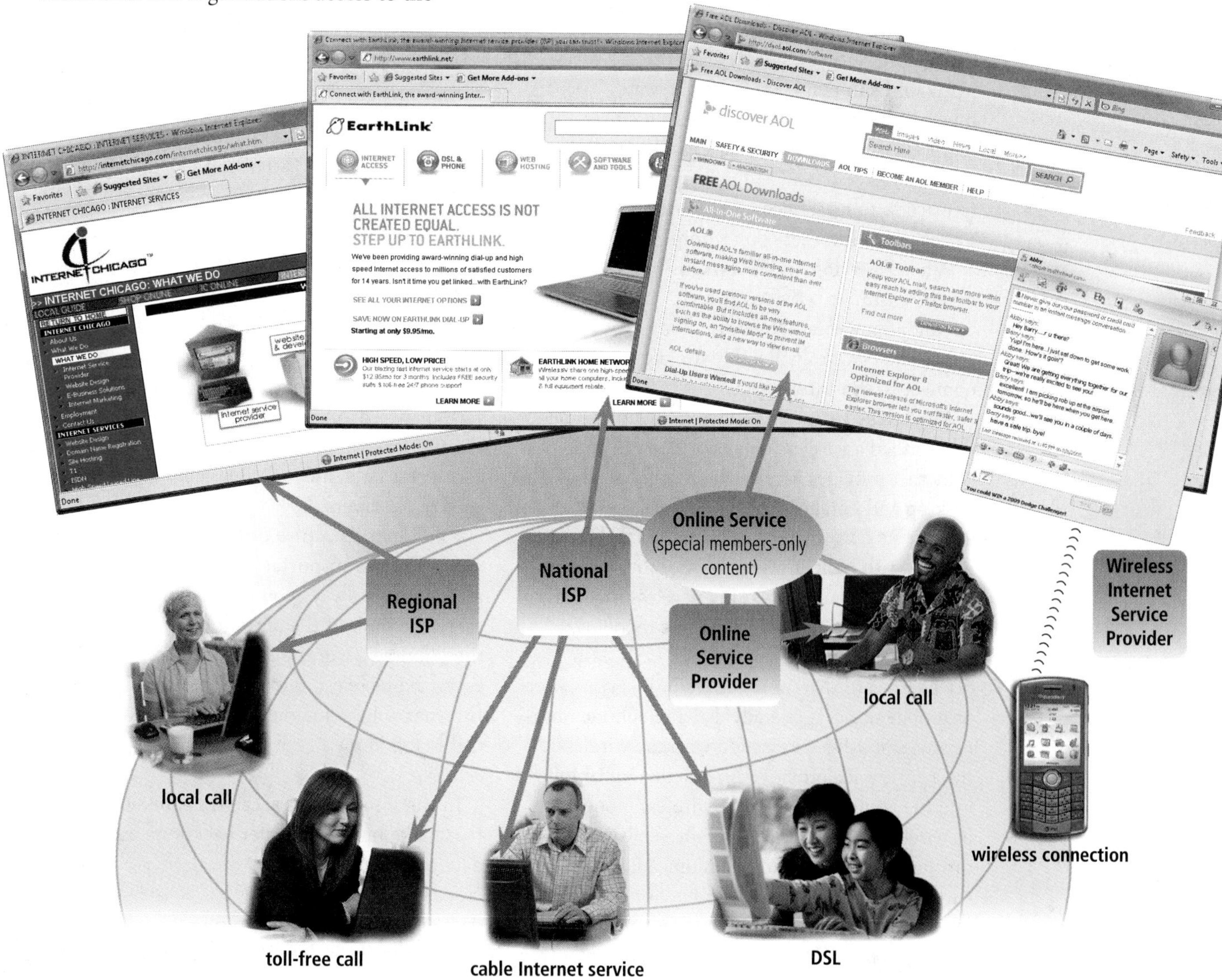

Figure 2-2 Common ways to access the Internet are through a regional or national Internet service provider, an online service provider, or a wireless Internet service provider.

An **ISP (Internet service provider)** is a regional or national access provider. A *regional ISP* usually provides Internet access to a specific geographic area. A *national ISP* is a business that provides Internet access in cities and towns nationwide. For dial-up access, some national ISPs provide both local and toll-free telephone numbers. Due to their larger size, national ISPs usually offer more services and have a larger technical support staff than regional ISPs. Examples of national ISPs are AT&T and EarthLink.

In addition to providing Internet access, an **online service provider (OSP)** also has many members-only features such as instant messaging or their own customized version of a Web browser. The two more popular OSPs are AOL (America Online) and MSN (Microsoft Network). AOL differs from many OSPs in that it provides gateway functionality to the Internet, meaning it regulates the Internet services to which members have access. AOL also provides free access to its services to any user with a broadband Internet connection.

When selecting an ISP or OSP for dial-up access, ensure it provides at least one local telephone number. Otherwise, long-distance telephone charges will apply for the time you connect to the Internet.

A **wireless Internet service provider**, sometimes called a wireless data provider, is a company that provides wireless Internet access to desktop and notebook computers and mobile devices, such as smart phones and portable media players, with built-in wireless capability (such as Wi-Fi) or to computers using wireless modems or wireless access devices. Wireless modems, which usually are in the form of a USB flash drive or a card that inserts in a slot in a computer or mobile device, generally dial a telephone number to establish a connection with the wireless Internet service provider. An antenna on or built into the computer or device, wireless modem, or wireless access device typically sends signals through the airwaves to communicate with a wireless Internet service provider. Some examples of wireless Internet service providers include AT&T, Boingo Wireless, Sprint Broadband Direct, T-Mobile, and Verizon Wireless.

Wireless Modems

For more information, visit the Computer Concepts CourseMate Web site at www.cengagebrain.com, navigate to the Chapter 2 Web Link resource for this book, and then click Wireless Modems.

? FAQ 2-2

What types of Web sites do mobile Internet users visit?

More than 87 million individuals subscribe to a wireless Internet service provider. Mobile Internet users most frequently visit weather, entertainment, and e-mail Web sites. The chart below illustrates various types of Web sites and their associated increase in traffic resulting from mobile Internet users.

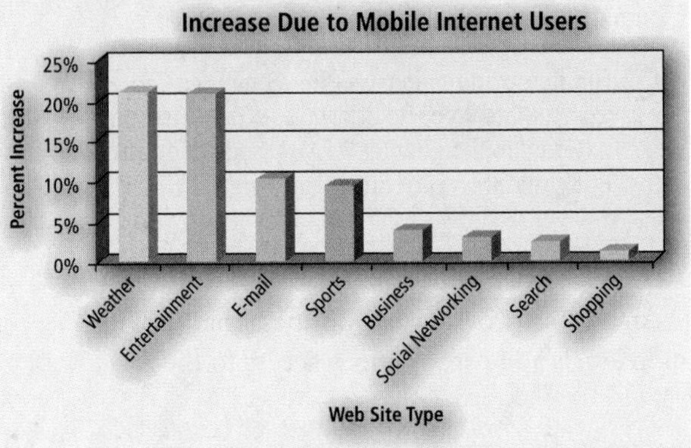

Source: ClickZ

For more information, visit the Computer Concepts CourseMate Web site at www.cengagebrain.com, navigate to the Chapter 2 FAQ resource for this book, and then click Mobile Internet.

How Data and Information Travel the Internet

Computers connected to the Internet work together to transfer data and information around the world using servers and clients and various wired and wireless transmission media. On the Internet, your computer is a client that can access data, information, and services on a variety of servers.

The inner structure of the Internet works much like a transportation system. Just as interstate highways connect major cities and carry the bulk of the automotive traffic across the country, several main transmission media carry the heaviest amount of traffic on the Internet. These major carriers of network traffic are known collectively as the *Internet backbone*.

In the United States, the transmission media that make up the Internet backbone exchange data and information at several different major cities across the country. That is, they transfer data and information from one network to another until reaching the final destination (Figure 2-3).

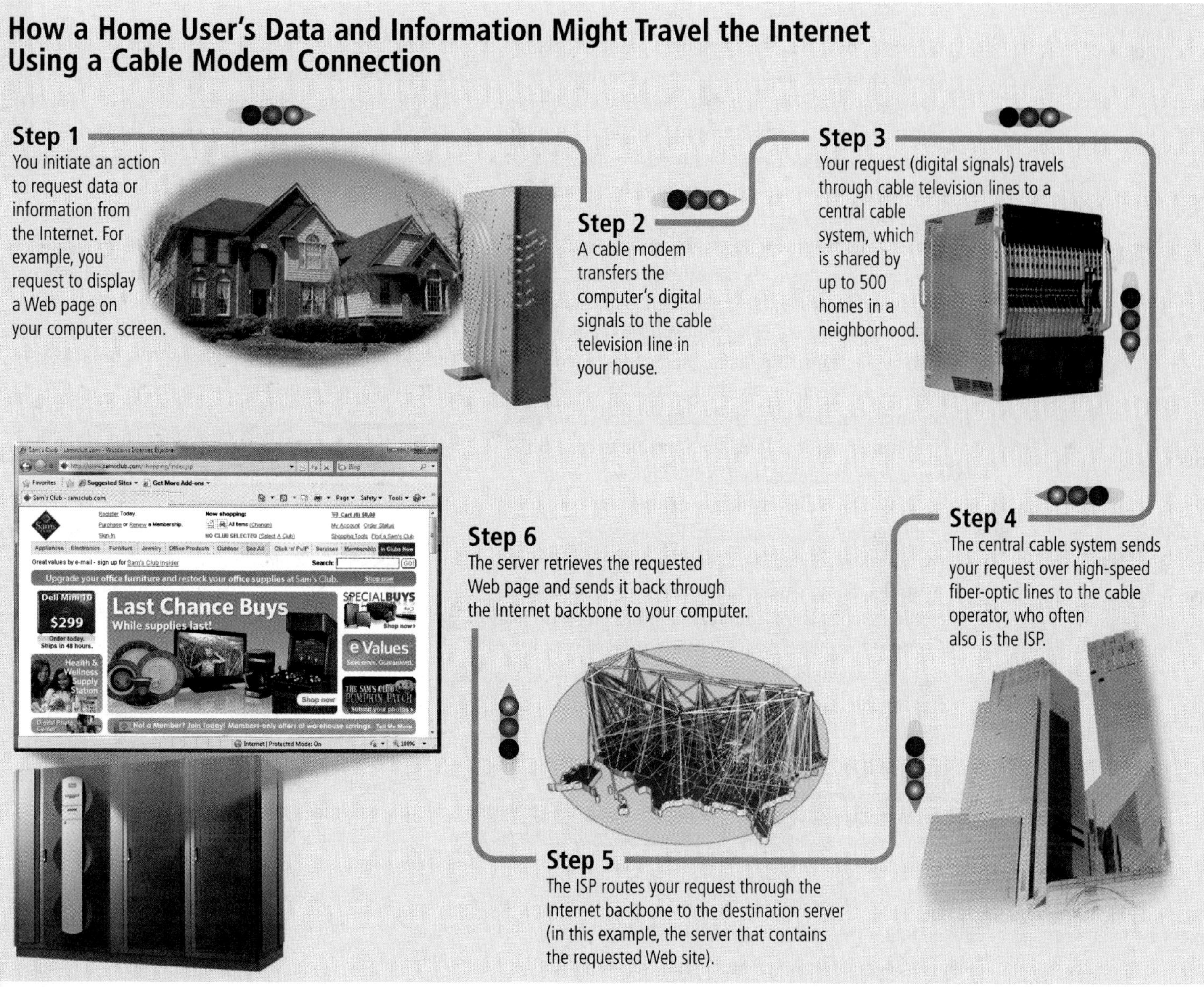
How a Home User's Data and Information Might Travel the Internet Using a Cable Modem Connection
Step 1
You initiate an action to request data or information from the Internet. For example, you request to display a Web page on your computer screen.
Step 2
A cable modem transfers the computer's digital signals to the cable television line in your house.
Step 3
Your request (digital signals) travels through cable television lines to a central cable system, which is shared by up to 500 homes in a neighborhood.
Step 4
The central cable system sends your request over high-speed fiber-optic lines to the cable operator, who often also is the ISP.
Step 5
The ISP routes your request through the Internet backbone to the destination server (in this example, the server that contains the requested Web site).
Step 6
The server retrieves the requested Web page and sends it back through the Internet backbone to your computer.
Last Chance Buys
While supplies last!
$299
SPECIALBUYS
e Values

Figure 2-3 This figure shows how a home user's data and information might travel the Internet using a cable modem connection.

Internet Addresses

The Internet relies on an addressing system much like the postal service to send data and information to a computer at a specific destination. An **IP address**, short for Internet Protocol address, is a number that uniquely identifies each computer or device connected to the Internet. The IP address usually consists of four groups of numbers, each separated by a period. The number in each group is between 0 and 255. For example, the numbers 72.14.207.99 are an IP address. In general, the first portion of each IP address identifies the network and the last portion identifies the specific computer.

These all-numeric IP addresses are difficult to remember and use. Thus, the Internet supports the use of a text name that represents one or more IP addresses. A **domain name** is the text version of an IP address. Figure 2-4 shows an IP address and its associated domain name. As with an IP address, the components of a domain name are separated by periods.

The text in the domain name up to the first period identifies the type of Internet server. In Figure 2-4, for example, the www indicates a Web server.

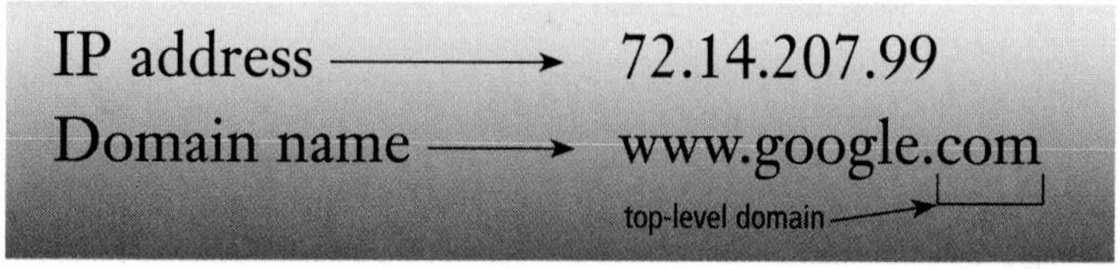
IP address → 72.14.207.99
Domain name → www.google.com
top-level domain

Figure 2-4 The IP address and domain name for the Google Web site.

Every domain name contains a *top-level domain* (*TLD*), which is the last section of the domain name. A generic TLD (*gTLD*), such as the com in Figure 2-4 on the previous page, identifies the type of organization associated with the domain. The Internet server and gTLD portions of a domain name often are not required.

The organization that assigns and controls top-level domains is the Internet Corporation for Assigned Names and Numbers (*ICANN* pronounced EYE-can). Figure 2-5 lists some gTLDs. For TLDs such as biz, com, info, name, net, and org, you register for a domain name from a *registrar*, which is an organization that sells and manages domain names.

For international Web sites outside the United States, the domain name also includes a country code TLD (*ccTLD*), which is a two-letter country code, such as au for Australia. For example, www.philips.com.au is the domain name for Philips Australia. Some smaller countries have granted use of their ccTLDs for commercial purposes, such as tv (Tuvalu) for the television/entertainment industry.

The *domain name system* (*DNS*) is the method that the Internet uses to store domain names and their corresponding IP addresses. When you specify a domain name, a **DNS server** translates the domain name to its associated IP address so that data and information can be routed to the correct computer. A DNS server is an Internet server that usually is associated with an Internet access provider. For a more technical discussion about DNS servers, read the High-Tech Talk article on page 382.

The growth of the Internet has led to a shortage of IP addresses. Thus, a new IP addressing scheme, called *IPv6*, may increase the number of available IP addresses. For a more technical discussion about Internet addresses and IPv6, read the High-Tech Talk article on page 110.

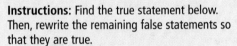

Examples of Generic Top-Level Domains

Generic TLD	Intended Purpose
aero	Aviation community members
biz	Businesses of all sizes
cat	Catalan cultural community
com	Commercial organizations, businesses, and companies
coop	Business cooperatives such as credit unions and rural electric co-ops
edu	Educational institutions
gov	Government agencies
info	Business organizations or individuals providing general information
jobs	Employment or human resource businesses
mil	Military organizations
mobi	Delivery and management of mobile Internet services
museum	Accredited museums
name	Individuals or families
net	Network providers or commercial companies
org	Nonprofit organizations
pro	Certified professionals such as doctors, lawyers, and accountants
tel	Internet communications
travel	Travel industry

Figure 2-5 In addition to the generic TLDs listed above, ICANN continually evaluates proposals for new TLDs.

QUIZ YOURSELF 2-1

Instructions: Find the true statement below. Then, rewrite the remaining false statements so that they are true.

1. An access provider is a business that provides individuals and organizations access to the Internet free or for a fee.
2. A wireless Internet service provider is a number that uniquely identifies each computer or device connected to the Internet.
3. An IP address, such as www.google.com, is the text version of a domain name.
4. Satellite Internet service provides high-speed Internet access through the cable television network via a cable modem.
5. The World Wide Web Consortium (W3C) oversees research and owns the Internet.

Quiz Yourself Online: To further check your knowledge of pages 74 through 80, visit the Computer Concepts CourseMate Web site at www.cengagebrain.com, navigate to the Chapter 2 Quiz Yourself resource for this book, and then click Objectives 1 – 4.

The World Wide Web

Although many people use the terms World Wide Web and Internet interchangeably, the World Wide Web actually is a service of the Internet. While the Internet was developed in the late 1960s, the World Wide Web emerged in the early 1990s. Since then, it has grown phenomenally to become one of the more widely used Internet services.

The **World Wide Web** (*WWW*), or **Web**, consists of a worldwide collection of electronic documents. Each electronic document on the Web is called a **Web page**, which can contain text, graphics, animation, audio, and video. Additionally, Web pages usually have built-in connections to other documents.

Some Web pages are static (fixed); others are dynamic (changing). Visitors to a *static Web page* all see the same content. With a *dynamic Web page*, by contrast, visitors can customize some or all of the viewed content such as desired stock quotes, weather for a region, or ticket availability for flights.

A **Web site** is a collection of related Web pages and associated items, such as documents and pictures, stored on a Web server. A **Web server** is a computer that delivers requested Web pages to your computer. The same Web server can store multiple Web sites. Some industry experts use the term **Web 2.0** to refer to Web sites that provide a means for users to share personal information (such as social networking Web sites), allow users to modify Web site content (such as wikis, which are discussed later in this chapter), and have application software built into the site for visitors to use (such as e-mail and word processing programs). Read Looking Ahead 2-1 for a look at Web 3.0.

> **LOOKING AHEAD 2-1**
>
> ### Web 3.0 to Reinvent the Virtual World
>
> The Web has evolved through versions 1.0 and 2.0, and work is underway to develop *Web 3.0*, also known as the *Semantic Web*. Some researchers predict that this next generation of the Web will perform practically any task imaginable. For example, your computer will be able to scan a Web page much as you do to look for specific useful information. If you need the location of the nearest eye doctor and the time when your brother's flight from Chicago actually will land, Web 3.0 first will provide those facts and then search your calendar, checking to see if your schedule allows time for the doctor's appointment before picking up your brother at the airport. In essence, the Web will become one huge searchable database, and automated agents of every type will retrieve the data we need to live productive lives.
>
> For more information, visit the Computer Concepts CourseMate Web site at www.cengagebrain.com, navigate to the Chapter 2 Looking Ahead resource for this book, and then click Web 3.0.

Browsing the Web

A **Web browser**, or **browser**, is application software that allows users to access and view Web pages or access Web 2.0 programs. To browse the Web, you need a computer or mobile device that is connected to the Internet and has a Web browser. The more widely used Web browsers for personal computers are Internet Explorer, Firefox, Opera, Safari, and Google Chrome.

With an Internet connection established, you start a Web browser. The browser retrieves and displays a starting Web page, sometimes called the browser's home page (Figure 2-6). The initial home

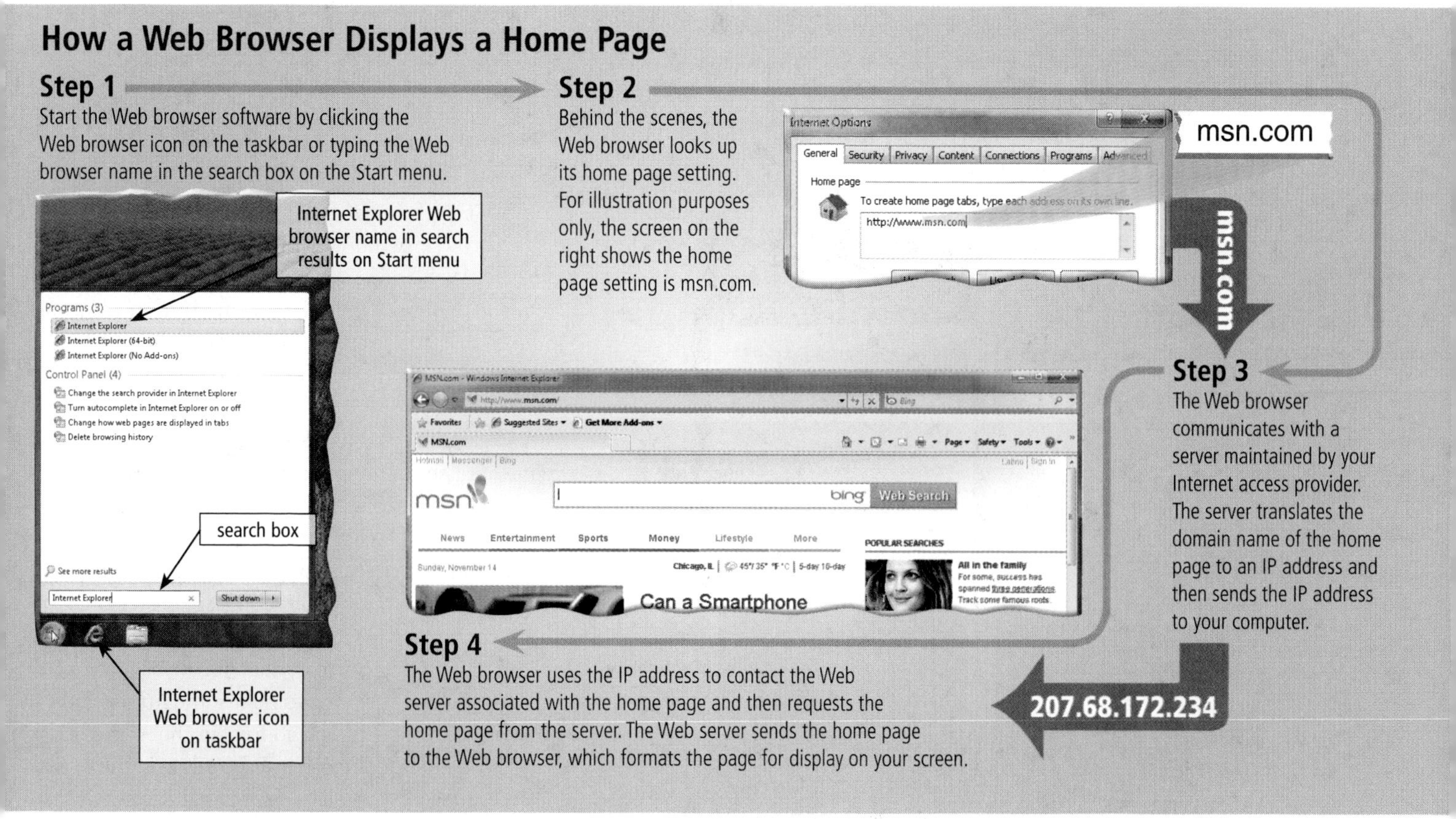
How a Web Browser Displays a Home Page
Step 1
Start the Web browser software by clicking the Web browser icon on the taskbar or typing the Web browser name in the search box on the Start menu.
Internet Explorer Web browser name in search results on Start menu
search box
Internet Explorer Web browser icon on taskbar
Step 2
Behind the scenes, the Web browser looks up its home page setting. For illustration purposes only, the screen on the right shows the home page setting is msn.com.
msn.com
msn.com
Step 3
The Web browser communicates with a server maintained by your Internet access provider. The server translates the domain name of the home page to an IP address and then sends the IP address to your computer.
207.68.172.234
Step 4
The Web browser uses the IP address to contact the Web server associated with the home page and then requests the home page from the server. The Web server sends the home page to the Web browser, which formats the page for display on your screen.

Figure 2-6 This figure shows how a Web browser displays a home page.

page that is displayed is one selected by your Web browser. You can change your browser's home page at anytime.

Another use of the term, **home page**, refers to the first page that a Web site displays. Similar to a book cover or a table of contents for a Web site, the home page provides information about the Web site's purpose and content. Many Web sites, such as iGoogle, allow you to personalize the home page so that it contains areas of interest to you. The home page usually contains links to other documents, Web pages, or Web sites. A **link**, short for *hyperlink*, is a built-in connection to another related Web page or part of a Web page.

Internet-enabled mobile devices such as smart phones use a special type of browser, called a *microbrowser*, which is designed for their small screens and limited computing power. Many Web sites design Web pages specifically for display on a microbrowser (Figure 2-7).

For a computer or mobile device to display a Web page, the page must be downloaded. **Downloading** is the process of a computer or device receiving information, such as a Web page, from a server on the Internet. While a browser downloads a Web page, it typically displays an animated logo or icon in the browser window. The animation stops when the download is complete. The time required to download a Web page varies depending on the speed of your Internet connection and the amount of graphics involved.

iPhone

For more information, visit the Computer Concepts CourseMate Web site at www.cengagebrain.com, navigate to the Chapter 2 Web Link resource for this book, and then click iPhone.

Figure 2-7 Sample microbrowser screen shown on this iPhone.

FAQ 2-3

Which Web browser currently has the highest market share?

Windows Internet Explorer (IE) currently is the most popular browser, with approximately 68 percent of the market share. The chart below illustrates the market share of the more popular Web browsers.

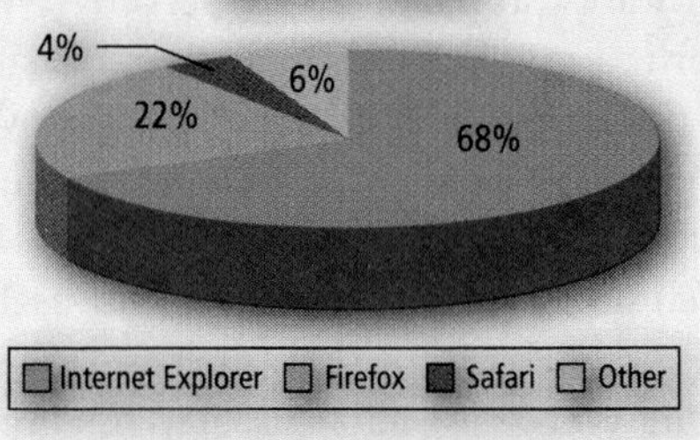

Source: Market Share by Net Applications

For more information, visit the Computer Concepts CourseMate Web site at www.cengagebrain.com, navigate to the Chapter 2 FAQ resource for this book, and then click Browser Market Share.

Web Addresses

A Web page has a unique address, called a **URL** (*Uniform Resource Locator*) or **Web address**. For example, the home page for the United States National Park Service Web site has http://www.nps.gov as its Web address. A Web browser retrieves a Web page using its Web address.

If you know the Web address of a Web page, you can type it in the Address bar at the top of the browser window. For example, if you type the Web address http://www.nps.gov/grsm/planyourvisit/wildlifeviewing.htm in the Address bar and then press the ENTER key, the browser downloads and displays the Web page shown in Figure 2-8.

A Web address consists of a protocol, domain name, and sometimes the path to a specific Web page or location on a Web page. Many Web page addresses begin with http://. The *http*, which stands for *Hypertext Transfer Protocol*, is a set of rules that defines how pages transfer on the Internet.

To help minimize errors, many browsers and Web sites do not require you enter the http:// and www portions of the Web address in the Address bar. If you enter an incorrect Web address, the browser may display a list of similar addresses or related Web sites from which you can select.

When you enter the Web address, http://www.nps.gov/grsm/planyourvisit/wildlifeviewing.htm in the Web browser, it sends a request to the Web server that contains the nps.gov Web site. The server then retrieves the Web page named wildlifeviewing.htm that is located in the grsm/planyourvisit path and delivers it to your browser, which then displays the Web page on the screen.

To save time, many users create bookmarks for their frequently visited Web pages. A *bookmark*, or *favorite*, is a saved Web address that you access by clicking its name in a list. That is, instead of entering a Web address to display a Web page, you can click a previously saved bookmark.

When you enter a Web address in a browser, you request, or *pull*, information from a Web server. Some Web servers also can *push* content to your computer at regular intervals or whenever updates are made to the site. For example, some Web servers provide the capability of displaying current sporting event scores or weather reports on your computer screen.

For information about useful Web sites and their associated Web addresses, read the Making Use of the Web feature that follows this chapter.

Navigating Web Pages

Most Web pages contain hypertext or hypermedia links. *Hypertext* refers to links in text-based documents, whereas *hypermedia* combines text-based links with graphic, audio, and video links. Links allow you to obtain information in a nonlinear way. That is, instead of accessing topics in a specified order, you move directly to a topic of interest. Branching from one related topic to another in a nonlinear fashion is what makes links so powerful. Some people use the phrase, **surfing the Web**, to refer to the activity of using links to explore the Web.

Figure 2-8 After entering http://www.nps.gov/grsm/planyourvisit/wildlifeviewing.htm as the Web address in the Address bar, this Web page at the United States National Park Service Web site is displayed.

A link can be text or an image. Text links may be underlined and/or displayed in a color different from other text on the Web page. Pointing to, or positioning the pointer on, a link on the screen typically changes the shape of the pointer to a small hand with a pointing index finger. Pointing to a link also sometimes causes the link to change in appearance or play a sound. For example, an underline may disappear, the text may change color, the image may change, etc. The Web page shown in Figure 2-9 contains a variety of link types, with the pointer on one of the links.

Each link on a Web page corresponds to a Web address or a document. To activate a link, you *click* it, that is, point to the link and then press the left mouse button. Clicking a link causes the Web page or document associated with the link to be displayed on the screen. The linked object might be on the same Web page, a different Web page at the same Web site, or a separate Web page at a different Web site in another city or country. To remind you visually that you have clicked a link, a text link often changes color after you click it.

Most current Web browsers support **tabbed browsing**, where the top of the browser displays a tab (similar to a file folder tab) for each Web page you open (shown in Figure 2-9). To move from one open Web page to another, you click the tab in the Web browser. Tabbed browsing allows users to have multiple home pages that automatically open when the browser starts. You also can organize tabs in a group, called a tab group, and save the group as a favorite, so that at any time you can display all tabs at once.

Because some Web sites attempt to track your browsing habits or gather personal information, some current Web browsers include a feature that allows you to disable and/or more tightly control the dissemination of your browsing habits and personal information. Read Ethics & Issues 2-1 for a related discussion.

Tabbed Browsing

For more information, visit the Computer Concepts CourseMate Web site at www.cengagebrain.com, navigate to the Chapter 2 Web Link resource for this book, and then click Tabbed Browsing.

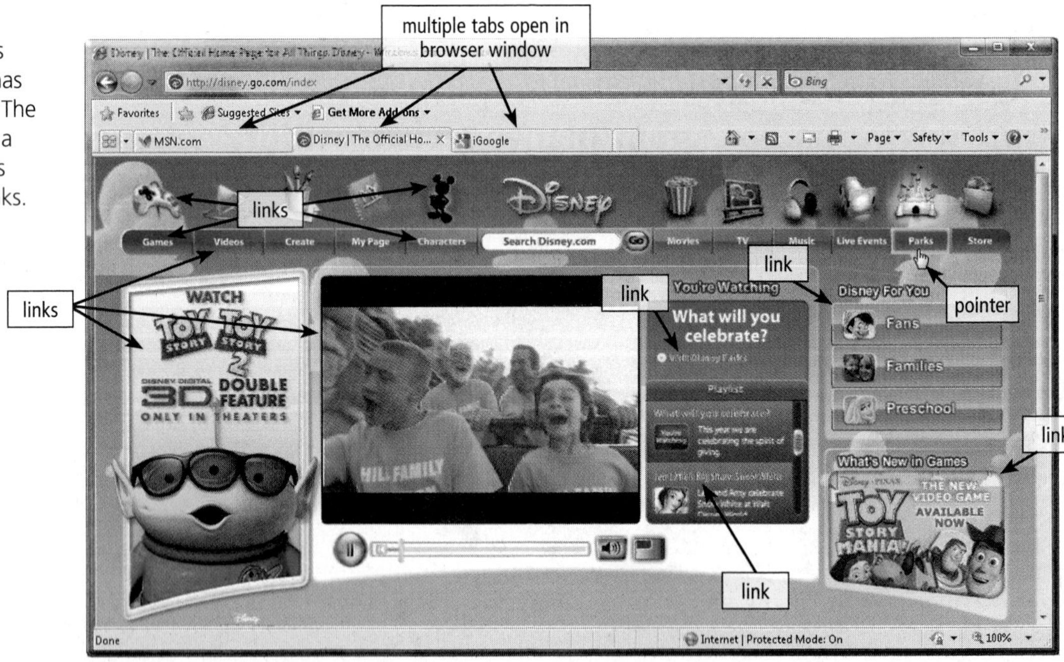

Figure 2-9 This browser window has several open tabs. The current tab shows a Web page that has various types of links.

Ethics & Issues

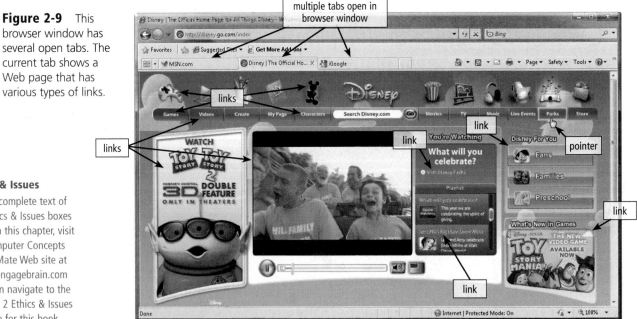

For the complete text of the Ethics & Issues boxes found in this chapter, visit the Computer Concepts CourseMate Web site at www.cengagebrain.com and then navigate to the Chapter 2 Ethics & Issues resource for this book.

ETHICS & ISSUES 2-1

Should the Government Allow You to Sign Up for a Do-Not-Track List?

When you visit a Web site that includes an advertisement, someone probably is recording the fact that you visited that Web site and viewed the advertisement with your browser. Over time, companies that specialize in tracking who views which online advertisements can amass an enormous amount of information about your online Web surfing habits. Through tracking the Web sites a user visits, the products they buy, and the articles they read, a company may attempt to profile the visitor's beliefs, associations, and habits. Although a user may think he or she is anonymous while navigating the Web, the company can attempt through various means to link the user's true identity with the user's online profile. The company can sell online profiles, with or without the user's true identity, to other advertisers or organizations. Some privacy groups have called for the government to allow consumers to sign up for a do-not-track list modeled after the popular do-not-call list.

Should organizations be allowed to track your Web surfing habits? Why or why not? Should organizations be allowed to associate your real identity with your online identity and profit from the information? Should the government force companies to give you the option of not being tracked? Why or why not? What are the benefits and dangers of online tracking?

Searching the Web

The Web is a worldwide resource of information. A primary reason that people use the Web is to search for specific information, including text, pictures, music, and video.

The first step in successful searching is to identify the main idea or concept in the topic about which you are seeking information. Determine any synonyms, alternate spellings, or variant word forms for the topic. Then, use a search tool to locate the information.

Two types of search tools are search engines and subject directories. A **search engine** is a program that finds Web sites, Web pages, images, videos, news, maps, and other information related to a specific topic. A **subject directory** classifies Web pages in an organized set of categories, such as sports or shopping, and related subcategories.

Some Web sites offer the functionality of both a search engine and a subject directory. The table in Figure 2-10 lists the Web addresses of several popular general-purpose search engines and subject directories.

Widely Used Search Tools

Search Tool	Web Address	Search Engine	Subject Directory
A9	a9.com	X	
AlltheWeb	alltheweb.com	X	
AltaVista	altavista.com	X	
AOL Search	search.aol.com	X	
Ask	ask.com	X	
Bing	bing.com	X	
Cuil (pronounced cool)	cuil.com	X	
Dogpile	dogpile.com	X	
Excite	excite.com	X	X
Gigablast	gigablast.com	X	X
Google	google.com	X	X
Lycos	lycos.com	X	
MSN	msn.com	X	X
Open Directory Project	dmoz.org	X	X
WebCrawler	webcrawler.com	X	
Yahoo!	yahoo.com	X	X

Figure 2-10 Popular search engines and subject directories.

Search Engines A search engine is helpful in locating information for which you do not know an exact Web address or are not seeking a particular Web site. Thousands of search engines are available. Some search through Web pages for all types of information. Other search engines can restrict their searches to a specific type of information, such as the following items:

- Images — pictures, diagrams, and drawings.
- Videos — home videos, music videos, television programs, and movie clips.
- Audio — music, songs, recordings, and sounds.
- Publications — news articles, journals, and books.
- Maps — maps of a business or address, or driving directions to a destination.
- People or Businesses — addresses and telephone numbers.
- Blogs — specific opinions and ideas of others.

Search engines require that you enter a word or phrase, called **search text** or *search query*, that describes the item you want to find. Each word in the search text is known as a *keyword*. Your search text can be broad, such as spring break destinations, or more specific, such as Walt Disney World. Search engines often respond with thousands of results, whose content varies depending on the type of information you are seeking. Some results are links to Web pages or articles; other results are media, such as images or videos. You may find that many items that appear in the search results have little or no bearing on the item you are seeking. You can eliminate the superfluous items in your search results by carefully crafting search text that limits the search.

If you misspell search text, many search engines identify alternative search text. Some also provide suggested keywords, links, and/or images as you begin typing your search text.

Figure 2-11 shows one way to use the Google search engine to search for the text, Aspen Colorado ski resorts. The results of the search, called *hits*, shown in Step 3 include nearly 150,000 links to Web pages that reference Aspen Colorado ski resorts. Each hit in the list has a link that, when clicked, displays an associated Web site or Web page. Most search engines sequence the hits based on how close the words in the search text are to one another in the titles and descriptions of the hits. Thus, the first few links probably contain more relevant information. Read Ethics & Issues 2-2 for a related discussion.

How to Use a Search Engine

Step 1
Type the search engine's Web address (in this case, google.com) in the Address bar in the Web browser.

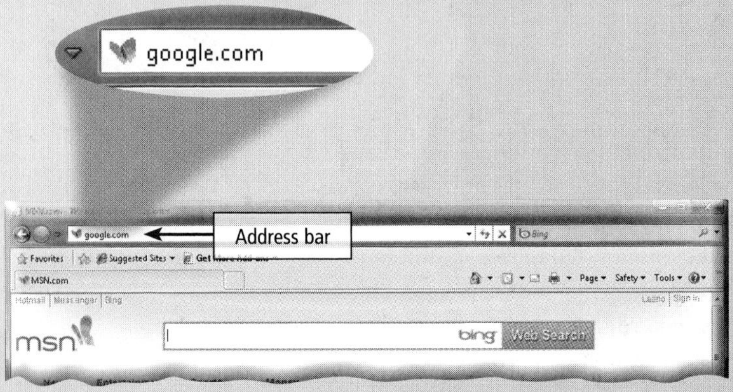

Step 2
Press the ENTER key. When the Google home page is displayed, type **Aspen Colorado ski resorts** as the search text and then point to the Google Search button.

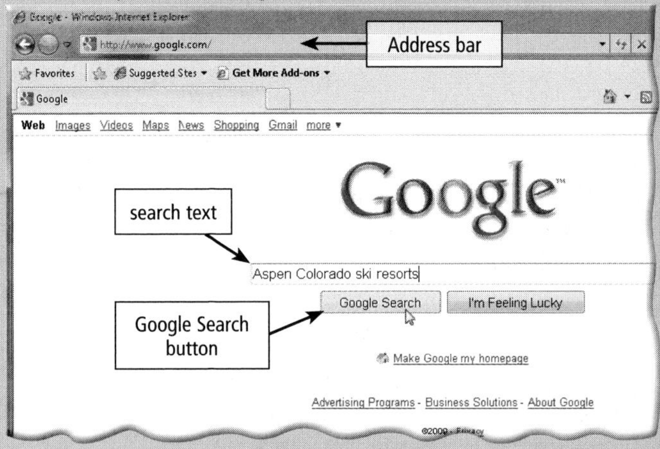

Step 3
Click the Google Search button. When the results of the search are displayed, scroll through the links and read the descriptions. Point to the Aspen Snowmass link.

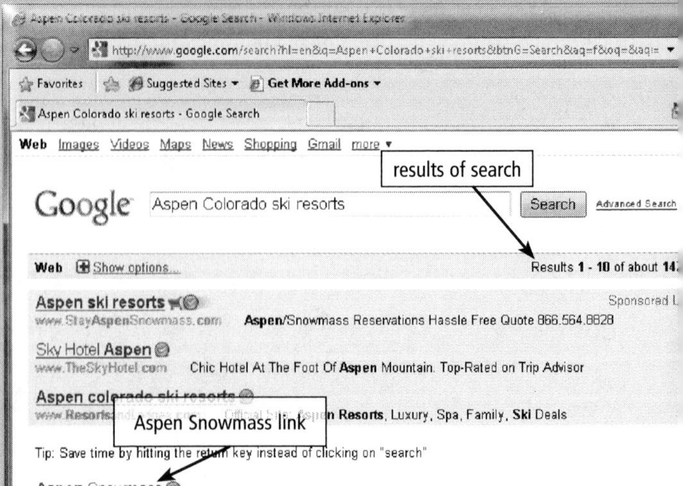

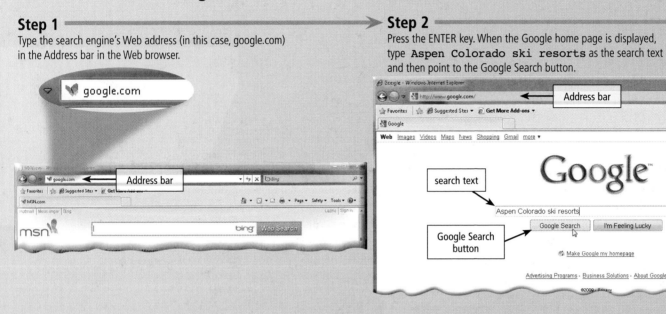

Step 4
Click the Aspen Snowmass link to display a Web page with a description and links to skiing in Aspen.

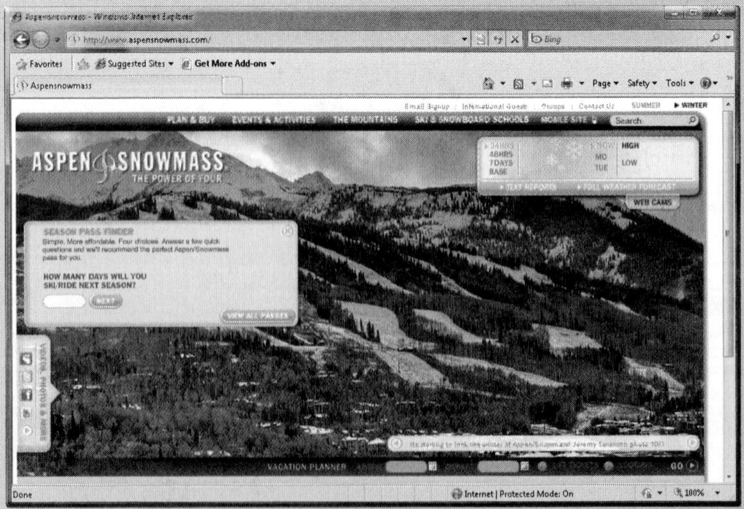

Figure 2-11 This figure shows how to use a search engine.

Some Web browsers contain an Instant Search box that, when filled in, uses a predefined or default search engine to perform searches (Figure 2-12). Using the Instant Search box eliminates the steps of displaying the search engine's Web page prior to entering the search text.

If you enter a phrase with spaces between the words in the search text, most search engines display results (hits) that include all of the words, except for common words (e.g., to, the, and). The table in Figure 2-13 lists some operators you can include in your search text to refine your search. Instead of using operators to refine your search text, many search engines have an Advanced Search feature that displays a form that assists with refining your search.

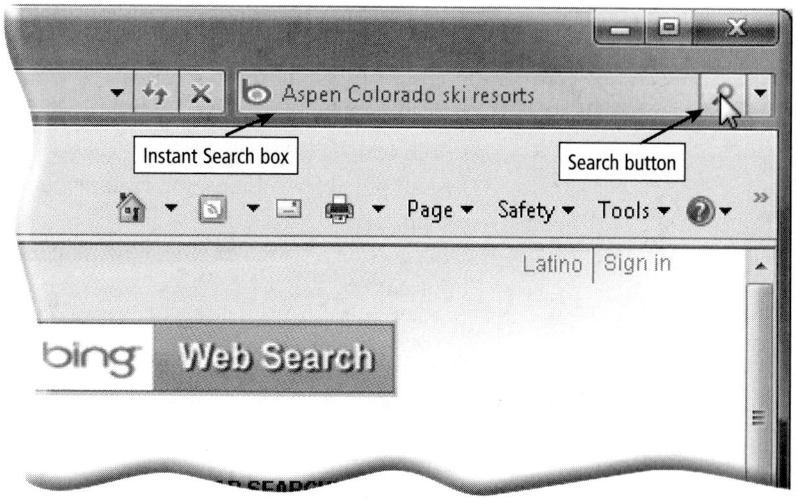

Figure 2-12 Using the Instant Search box combines Steps 1 and 2 in Figure 2-11.

ETHICS & ISSUES 2-2

Is It Ethical to Manipulate Search Engine Results?

Search engines attempt to present the most relevant and popular results to users when they perform searches. Search engines use special software to create indexes of topics from as many Web sites as possible. One key piece of information used by search engines to determine the relevance and popularity of a Web site is to examine how many other Web pages link to the Web site. Some individuals and groups take advantage of that fact and attempt to skew search results by creating hundreds or thousands of Web sites that link to a Web site that is the target of the effort. The practice of attempting to skew search engine results is known as *Google bombing*. One example of this is political activists Google bombing their opponents. When a person searches for a particular word or phrase with a negative connotation, the search results become skewed to return results about a political opponent of the Google bomber. A Google bomb can promote a product or service, or disparage a competing product or service. Google bombing often is used in a humorous manner. Comedians and television personalities sometimes request that their audience engage in some particular Google bomb. Opponents of Google bombing state that the practice lessens the public's trust in search engines and causes the search engines to be less accurate.

Is Google bombing ethical? Why or why not? How should Google bombers be handled? Why? Can Google bombing be stopped? Why or why not? Is there an ethical difference between Google bombs that attack a rival and those that are self-promoting? Why?

Search Engine Operators

Operator	Description	Examples	Explanation
Space or +	Display hits that include specific words.	art + music art music	Results have both words art and music — in any order.
OR	Display hits that include only one word from a list.	dog OR puppy dog OR puppy OR canine	Results have either the word dog or puppy. Results have the word dog or puppy or canine.
( )	Combine hits that include specific words with those that include only one word from a list.	Kalamazoo Michigan (pizza OR subs)	Results have both words Kalamazoo Michigan and either the word, pizza, or the word, subs.
-	Exclude a word from the search results.	automobile -convertible	Results include automobile but do not include convertible.
" "	Search for an exact phrase in a certain order.	"19th century literature"	Results have the exact phrase, 19th century literature.
*	Substitute characters in place of the asterisk.	writer*	Results include any word that begins with writer (e.g., writer, writers, writer's).

Figure 2-13 Use search engine operators to help refine a search.

Other techniques you can use to improve your searches include the following:

- Use specific nouns.
- Put the most important terms first in the search text.
- List all possible spellings, for example, email, e-mail.
- Before using a search engine, read its Help information.
- If the search is unsuccessful with one search engine, try another.

FAQ 2-4

How many words do people typically use in search text?

According to research performed by OneStat, Internet users most often use only two words in their search text. The chart to the right illustrates the percentage of searches performed with search text of various lengths.

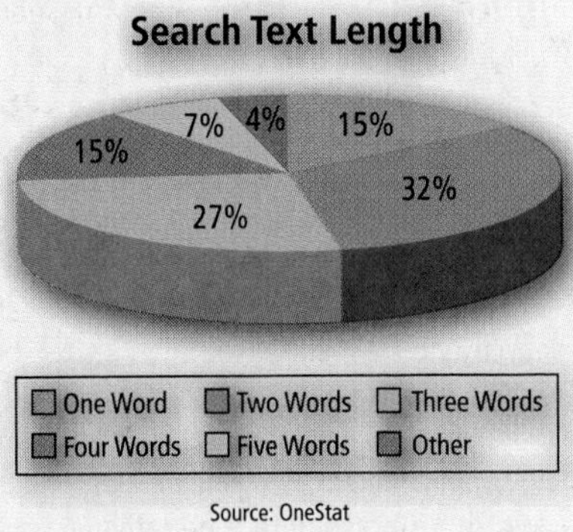

For more information, visit the Computer Concepts CourseMate Web site at www.cengagebrain.com, navigate to the Chapter 2 FAQ resource for this book, and then click Search Text.

Some search engines that work with navigation devices are location based, meaning they display results related to the device's current geographical position. For example, your mobile device can display all gas stations within a certain distance of your current location.

Many search engines use a program called a *spider* to build and maintain lists of words found on Web sites. When you enter search text, the search engine scans this prebuilt list for hits. The more sophisticated the search engine combined with precise search criteria, the more rapid the response and effective the search.

To learn more about searching for information, complete the Learn How To 2 activity on pages 120 and 121.

Subject Directories A subject directory provides categorized lists of links arranged by subject (Figure 2-14). Using this search tool, you locate a particular topic by clicking links through different levels, moving from the general to the specific. Each time you click a category link, the subject directory displays a list of subcategory links, from which you again choose. You continue in this fashion until the search tool displays a list of Web pages about the desired topic.

The major disadvantage with a subject directory is that users have difficulty deciding which categories to choose as they work through the menus of links presented.

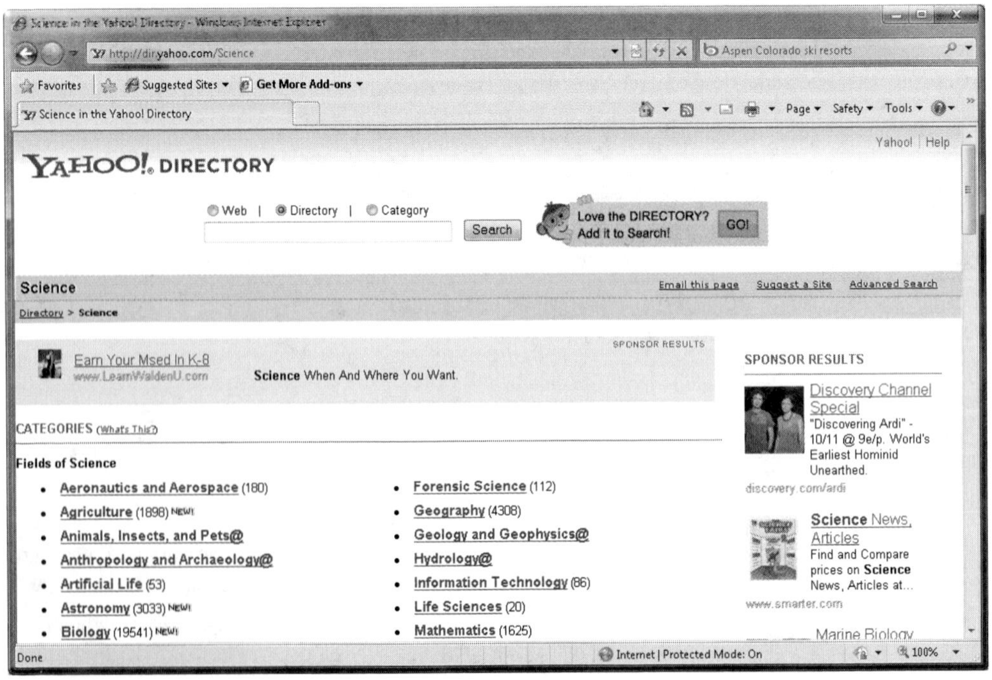

Figure 2-14 A subject directory provides categorized lists of links.

Types of Web Sites

Thirteen types of Web sites are portal, news, informational, business/marketing, blog, wiki, online social network, educational, entertainment, advocacy, Web application, content aggregator, and personal (Figure 2-15). Many Web sites fall in more than one of these categories.

Portal A **portal** is a Web site that offers a variety of Internet services from a single, convenient location (Figure 2-15a). Most portals offer these free services: search engine; news; sports and weather; Web publishing; reference tools such as yellow pages, stock quotes, and maps; shopping; and e-mail and other communications services.

Many portals have online communities. An **online community** is a Web site that joins a specific group of people with similar interests or relationships. These communities may offer online photo albums, chat rooms, and other services to facilitate communications among members.

Popular portals include AltaVista, AOL, Excite, GO.com, iGoogle, Lycos, MSN, and Yahoo!. A *wireless portal* is a portal designed for Internet-enabled mobile devices.

News A news Web site contains newsworthy material including stories and articles relating to current events, life, money, sports, and the weather (Figure 2-15b). Many magazines and newspapers sponsor Web sites that provide summaries of printed articles, as well as articles not included in the printed versions. Newspapers and television and radio stations are some of the media that maintain news Web sites.

Informational An informational Web site contains factual information (Figure 2-15c). Many United States government agencies have informational Web sites providing information such as census data, tax codes, and the congressional budget. Other organizations provide information such as public transportation schedules and published research findings.

Business/Marketing A business/marketing Web site contains content that promotes or sells products or services (Figure 2-15d). Nearly every enterprise has a business/marketing Web site. Allstate Insurance Company, Dell Inc., General Motors Corporation, Kraft Foods Inc., and Walt Disney Company all have business/marketing Web sites. Many of these enterprises also allow you to purchase their products or services online.

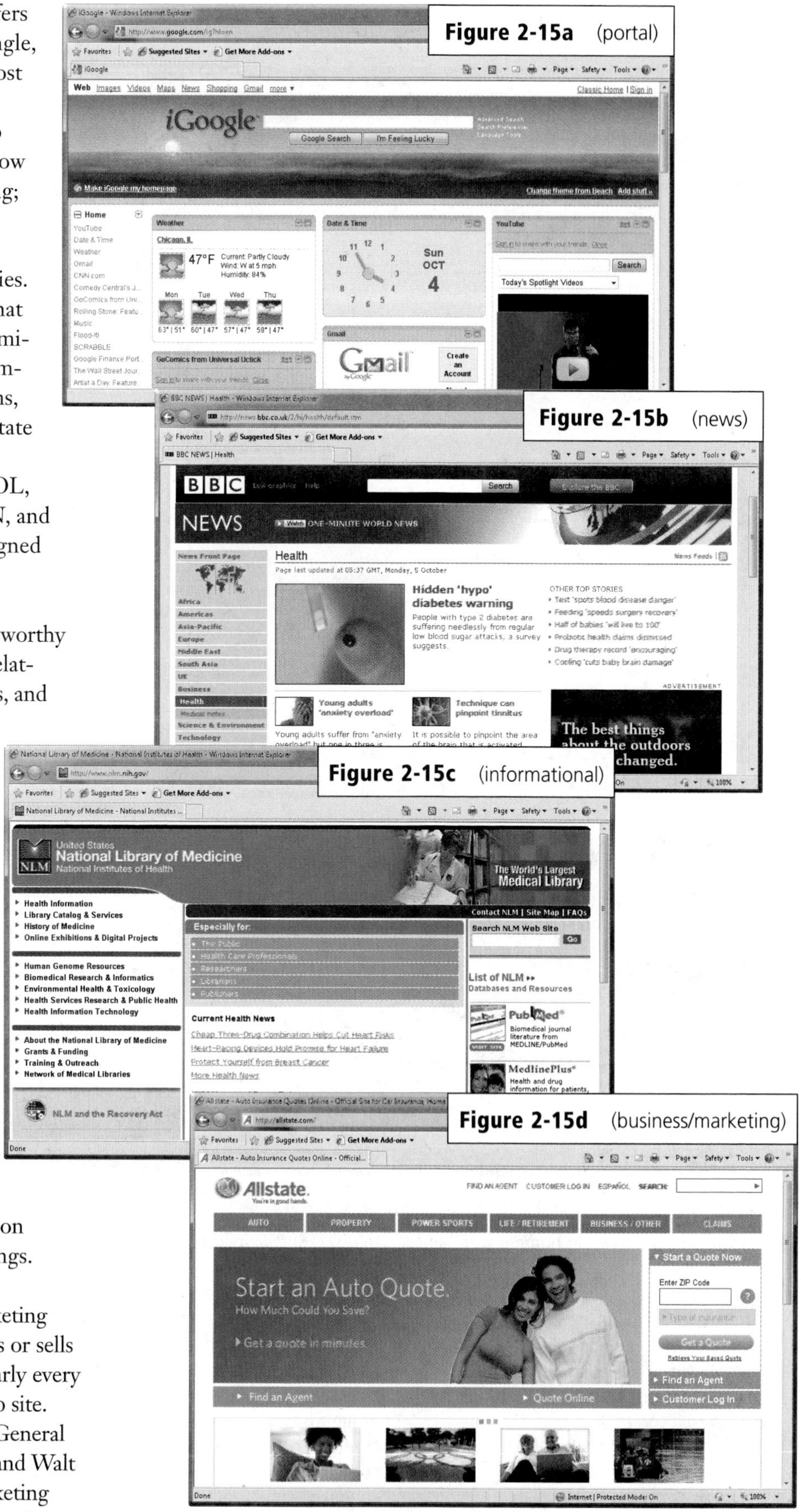

Figure 2-15 Types of Web sites. *(continued on next page)*

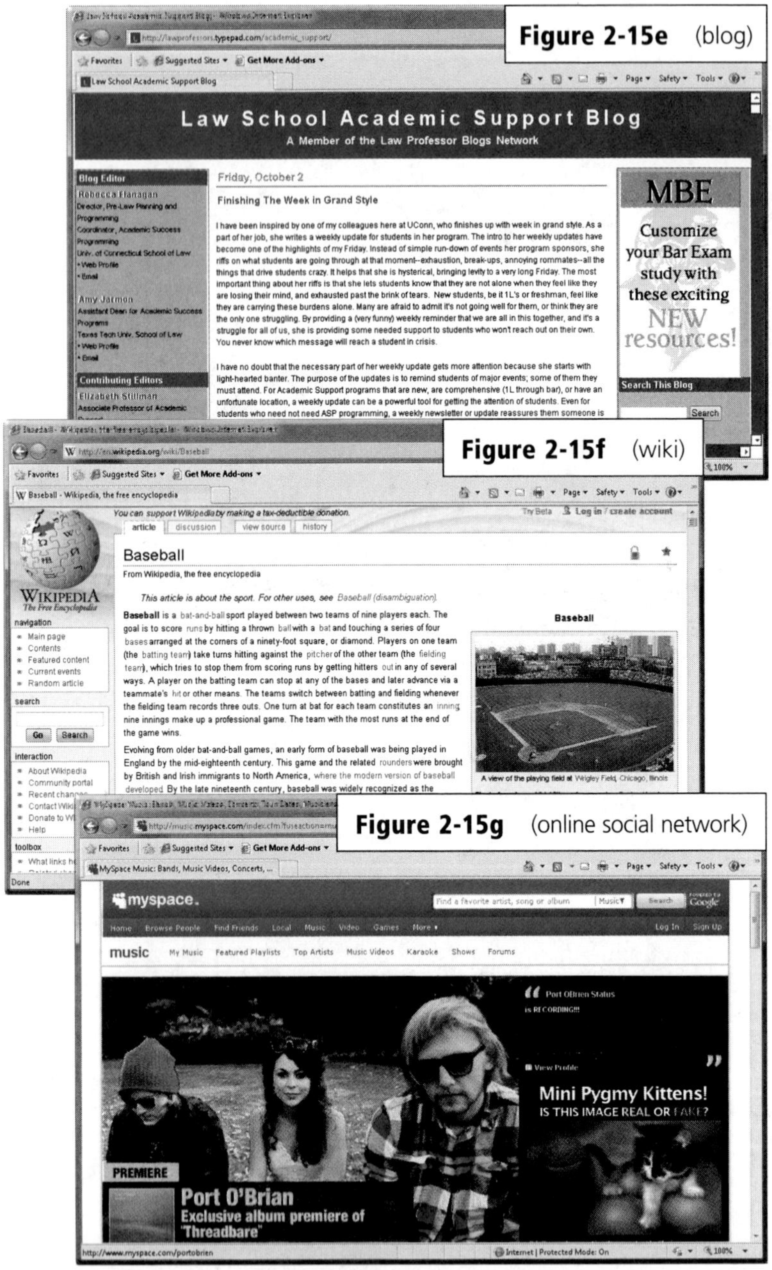

Figure 2-15 Types of Web sites. *(continued)*

Blog A **blog**, short for *Weblog*, is an informal Web site consisting of time-stamped articles, or posts, in a diary or journal format, usually listed in reverse chronological order (Figure 2-15e). A blog that contains video clips is called a **video blog**, or *vlog*. A **microblog** allows users to publish short messages, usually between 100 and 200 characters, for others to read. Twitter is a popular microblog. The term *blogosphere* refers to the worldwide collection of blogs, and the *vlogosphere* refers to all vlogs worldwide.

Blogs reflect the interests, opinions, and personalities of the author, called the *blogger* or *vlogger* (for vlog author), and sometimes site visitors.

Blogs have become an important means of worldwide communications. Businesses create blogs to communicate with employees, customers, and vendors. Teachers create blogs to collaborate with other teachers and students. Home users create blogs to share aspects of their personal life with family, friends, and others.

Wiki A **wiki** is a collaborative Web site that allows users to create, add to, modify, or delete the Web site content via their Web browser. Many wikis are open to modification by the general public. Wikis usually collect recent edits on a Web page so that someone can review them for accuracy. The difference between a wiki and a blog is that users cannot modify original posts made by the blogger. A popular wiki is Wikipedia, a free Web encyclopedia (Figure 2-15f). Read Ethics & Issues 2-3 for a related discussion.

Online Social Network An **online social network**, also called a **social networking Web site**, is a Web site that encourages members in its online community to share their interests, ideas, stories, photos, music, and videos with other registered users (Figure 2-15g). Most include chat rooms, newsgroups, and other communications services.

ETHICS & ISSUES 2-3

Should You Trust a Wiki for Academic Research?

As wikis have grown in number, size, and popularity, some educators and librarians have shunned the sites as valid sources of research. While many wikis are tightly controlled with a limited number of contributors and expert editors, these usually focus on narrowly-defined, specialized topics. Most large online wikis, such as Wikipedia, often involve thousands of editors, many of whom remain anonymous. Recently, television station reporters purposefully vandalized entries on Wikipedia for John Lennon and Elvis Presley in an attempt either to discredit Wikipedia or to test how quickly corrections are made. Editors quickly corrected the information. In other situations, rival political factions falsified or embellished wiki entries in an attempt to give their candidate an advantage. Some wiki supporters argue that most wikis provide adequate controls to correct false or misleading content quickly and to punish those who submit it. One popular wiki now requires an experienced editor to verify changes made to certain types of articles. Some propose that wikis should be used as a starting point for researching a fact, but that the fact should be verified using traditional sources.

Should wikis be allowed as valid sources for academic research? Why or why not? Would you submit a paper to your instructor that cites a wiki as a source? An encyclopedia? Why or why not? What policies could wikis enforce that could garner more confidence from the public? If a wiki provided verification of the credentials of the author, would you trust the wiki more? Why or why not?

Popular social networking Web sites include MySpace and Facebook, with Facebook alone boasting more than 300 million active users. In some social networking Web sites, such as Second Life, users assume an imaginary identity and interact with other users in a role-playing type of environment.

A **media sharing Web site** is a specific type of online social network that enables members to share media such as photos, music, and videos. Flickr, Fotki, and Webshots are popular photo sharing communities; PixelFish and YouTube are popular video sharing communities.

Educational An educational Web site offers exciting, challenging avenues for formal and informal teaching and learning (Figure 2-15h). On the Web, you can learn how airplanes fly or how to cook a meal. For a more structured learning experience, companies provide online training to employees; and colleges offer online classes and degrees. Instructors often use the Web to enhance classroom teaching by publishing course materials, grades, and other pertinent class information.

Entertainment An entertainment Web site offers an interactive and engaging environment (Figure 2-15i). Popular entertainment Web sites offer music, videos, sports, games, ongoing Web episodes, sweepstakes, chat rooms, and more. Sophisticated entertainment Web sites often partner with other technologies. For example, you can cast your vote about a topic on a television show.

Advocacy An advocacy Web site contains content that describes a cause, opinion, or idea (Figure 2-15j). These Web sites usually present views of a particular group or association. Sponsors of advocacy Web sites include the Democratic National Committee, the Republican National Committee, the Society for the Prevention of Cruelty to Animals, and the Society to Protect Human Rights.

Web Application A **Web application**, or *Web app*, is a Web site that allows users to access and interact with software through a Web browser on any computer or device that is connected to the Internet. Some Web applications provide free access to their software (Figure 2-15k). Others offer part of their software free and charge for access to more comprehensive features or when a particular action is requested. Examples of Web applications include Google Docs (word processing, spreadsheets, presentations), TurboTax Online (tax preparation), and Windows Live Hotmail (e-mail).

Figure 2-15 Types of Web sites. *(continued on next page)*

Content Aggregator A *content aggregator* is a business that gathers and organizes Web content and then distributes, or feeds, the content to subscribers for free or a fee (Figure 2-15l). Examples of distributed content include news, music, video, and pictures. Subscribers select content in which they are interested. Whenever the selected content changes, it is downloaded automatically (pushed) to the subscriber's computer or mobile device.

RSS 2.0, which stands for *Really Simple Syndication*, is a specification that some content aggregators use to distribute content to subscribers. *Atom* is another specification sometimes used by content aggregators to distribute content. Some current browsers include a feature, such as Internet Explorer's *WebSlices*, that enables content aggregators to mark sections of their Web pages as feeds to which users can subscribe.

Personal A private individual or family not usually associated with any organization may maintain a personal Web site or just a single Web page (Figure 2-15m). People publish personal Web pages for a variety of reasons. Some are job hunting. Others simply want to share life experiences with the world.

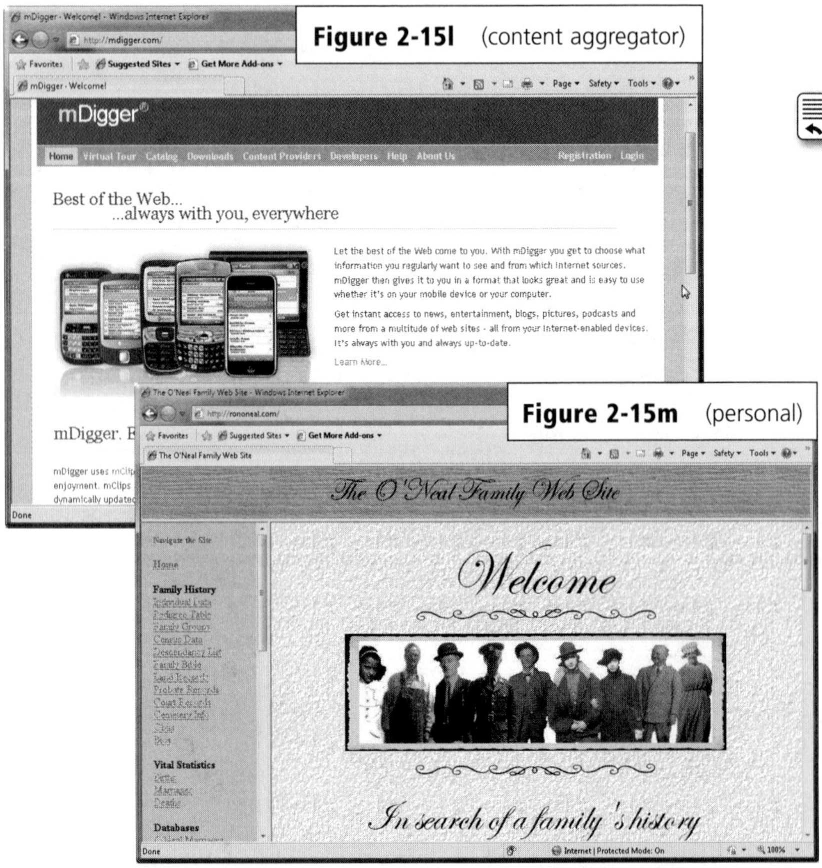

Figure 2-15l (content aggregator)

Figure 2-15m (personal)

Figure 2-15 Types of Web sites. *(continued)*

Evaluating a Web Site

Do not assume that information presented on the Web is correct or accurate. Any person, company, or organization can publish a Web page on the Internet. No one oversees the content of these Web pages. Figure 2-16 lists guidelines for assessing the value of a Web site or Web page before relying on its content.

Criteria for Evaluating a Web Site's Content

Evaluation Criteria	Reliable Web Sites
Affiliation	A reputable institution should support the Web site without bias in the information.
Audience	The Web site should be written at an appropriate level.
Authority	The Web site should list the author and the appropriate credentials.
Content	The Web site should be well organized and the links should work.
Currency	The information on the Web page should be current.
Design	The pages at the Web site should download quickly, be visually pleasing, and easy to navigate.
Objectivity	The Web site should contain little advertising and be free of preconceptions.

Figure 2-16 Criteria for evaluating a Web site's content.

Multimedia on the Web

Most Web pages include more than just formatted text and links. The more exciting Web pages use multimedia. **Multimedia** refers to any application that combines text with graphics, animation, audio, video, and/or virtual reality. Multimedia brings a Web page to life, increases the types of information available on the Web, expands the Web's potential uses, and makes the Internet a more entertaining place to explore. Multimedia Web pages often require specific hardware and software and take more time to download because they contain large graphics files and video or audio clips. Many Web sites have an option that allows visitors to disable multimedia, for example, if they have a slower-speed Internet connection.

The sections that follow discuss how the Web uses graphics, animation, audio, video, and virtual reality.

Graphics A **graphic**, or *graphical image*, is a digital representation of nontext information such as a drawing, chart, or photo. Today, many Web pages use colorful graphical designs and images to convey messages (Figure 2-17).

The Web contains countless images about a variety of subjects. You can download many of these images at no cost and use them for noncommercial purposes. Recall that downloading is the process of transferring an object from the Web to your computer. For example, you can insert images into greeting cards, announcements, and other documents. Read Innovative Computing 2-1 to find out how astronomers share graphics of the universe.

Of the graphics formats that exist on the Web (Figure 2-18), the two more common are JPEG and GIF formats. *JPEG* (pronounced JAY-peg) is a format that compresses graphics to reduce their file size, which means the file takes up less storage space. Smaller file sizes result in faster downloading of Web pages because small files transmit faster than large files. The more compressed the file, the smaller the image and the lower the quality. The goal with JPEG graphics is to reach a balance between image quality and file size. Digital photos often use the JPEG format.

GIF (pronounced jiff) graphics also use compression techniques to reduce file sizes. The GIF format works best for images that have only a few distinct colors, such as company logos. The newer *PNG* (pronounced ping) graphics format improves upon the GIF format, and thus may eventually replace the GIF format.

The BMP and TIFF formats listed in Figure 2-18 may require special viewer software, and they have larger file sizes. Thus, these formats are not used on the Web as frequently as JPEG, GIF, and PNG formats.

Figure 2-17 This Web page uses colorful graphical designs and images to convey its messages.

INNOVATIVE COMPUTING 2-1

View the Wonders of Space through the WorldWide Telescope

The phrase, reach for the stars, takes on a new meaning when using Microsoft's *WorldWide Telescope*. Users can access the Telescope from a Web browser or download free software. They then can view a variety of multimedia, including high-resolution graphics from telescopes located on Earth and in space, with Web 2.0 services to allow people to explore the final frontier from their computers.

Users can pan and zoom around the night sky by looking through a specific telescope, such as the Hubble Space Telescope, and view the universe in the past, present, or future. In addition, they can browse graphics of a specific planet, the Milky Way Galaxy, black holes, and other celestial bodies in our solar system, galaxy, and beyond. They also can select different wavelengths, such as X-ray or visible light, to search for objects. Astronomers and educators also have created narrated tours of the sky to help interpret the images.

For more information, visit the Computer Concepts CourseMate Web site at www.cengagebrain.com, navigate to the Chapter 2 Innovative Computing resource for this book, and then click WorldWide Telescope.

Graphics Formats Used on the Web

Abbreviation	Name	Uses
BMP	Bitmap	Desktop background, scanned images
GIF	Graphics Interchange Format	Simple diagrams, shapes, images with few colors
JPEG	Joint Photographic Experts Group	Digital camera photos
PNG	Portable Network Graphics	Web graphics
TIFF	Tagged Image File Format	Photos used by printing industry

Figure 2-18 The Web uses graphics file formats for images.

Some Web sites use thumbnails on their pages because graphics can be time-consuming to display. A *thumbnail* is a small version of a larger graphic. You usually can click a thumbnail to display a larger image (Figure 2-19).

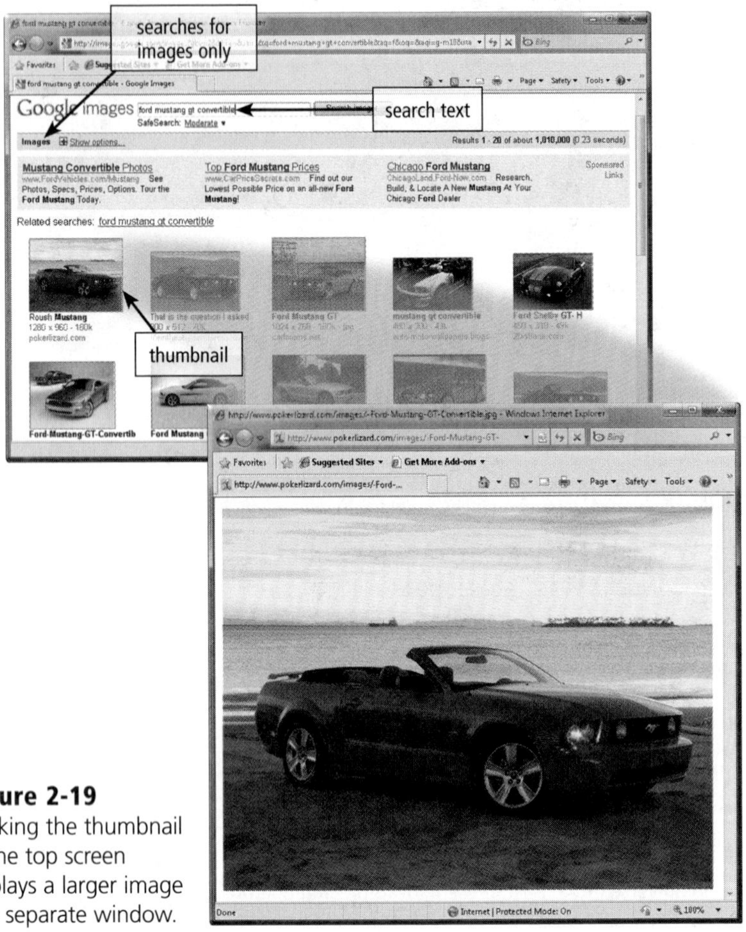

Figure 2-19
Clicking the thumbnail in the top screen displays a larger image in a separate window.

Animation Many Web pages use **animation**, which is the appearance of motion created by displaying a series of still images in sequence. Animation can make Web pages more visually interesting or draw attention to important information or links. For example, text that animates by scrolling across the screen can serve as a ticker to display stock updates, news, sports scores, weather, or other information. Web-based games often use animation.

Web page developers add animation to Web pages using a variety of techniques. Web page authoring programs, such as Adobe Flash and Microsoft Expression Web, enable Web site developers to combine animation and interactivity in Web pages. Developers unfamiliar with Web page authoring programs can create an *animated GIF*, which combines several GIF images in a single GIF file.

Audio On the Web, you can listen to audio clips and live audio. **Audio** includes music, speech, or any other sound. Simple applications consist of individual audio files available for download to a computer or device. Once downloaded, you can play (listen to) the contents of these files. Some common Web audio file formats are listed in Figure 2-20. Audio files are compressed to reduce their file sizes. For example, the **MP3** format reduces an audio file to about one-tenth its original size, while preserving much of the original quality of the sound.

Some music publishers have Web sites that allow users to download sample tracks free to persuade them to buy all the songs contained on the CD. Others allow a user to purchase and download an entire CD (Figure 2-21). It is legal to download copyrighted music only if the song's copyright holder has granted permission for users to download and play the song.

To listen to an audio file on your computer, you need special software called a **player**. Most current operating systems contain a player, for example, Windows Media Player. Some audio files, however, might require you to download a player. Players available for download include iTunes and RealPlayer. You can download the players free from the Web; some are plug-ins, which are discussed later in this chapter.

Some applications on the Web use streaming audio. **Streaming** is the process of transferring data in a continuous and even flow. Streaming allows users to access and use a file while it is transmitting. For example, *streaming audio* enables you to listen to music as it downloads to your computer. Many radio and television stations use streaming audio to broadcast music, interviews, talk shows, sporting events, music videos, news, live concerts, and other segments.

Podcasting is another popular method of distributing audio. A *podcast* is recorded audio, usually an MP3 file, stored on a Web site that can be downloaded to a computer or a portable media player such as an iPod. Examples of podcasts include music, radio shows, news stories, classroom lectures, political messages, and television commentaries. Podcasters register their podcasts with content aggregators. Subscribers select podcast feeds they want to be downloaded automatically whenever they connect. Most smart phone users who subscribe to a wireless Internet service provider can listen to streaming audio and podcasts.

Audio Web File Formats

Format	Description	Format	Description
AAC	Advanced Audio Coding	WAV	Windows waveform
AIFF	Audio Interchange File Format	WMA	Windows Media Audio (part of Windows Media framework)
ASF	Advanced Streaming (or Systems) Format (part of Windows Media framework)	RA	RealAudio sound file (supported by RealPlayer)
MP3	Moving Pictures Experts Group Audio Layer 3 (MPEG-3)	QT	QuickTime audio, video, or 3-D animation
Ogg	Free, unpatented audio and video format		

Figure 2-20 Popular Web audio file formats.

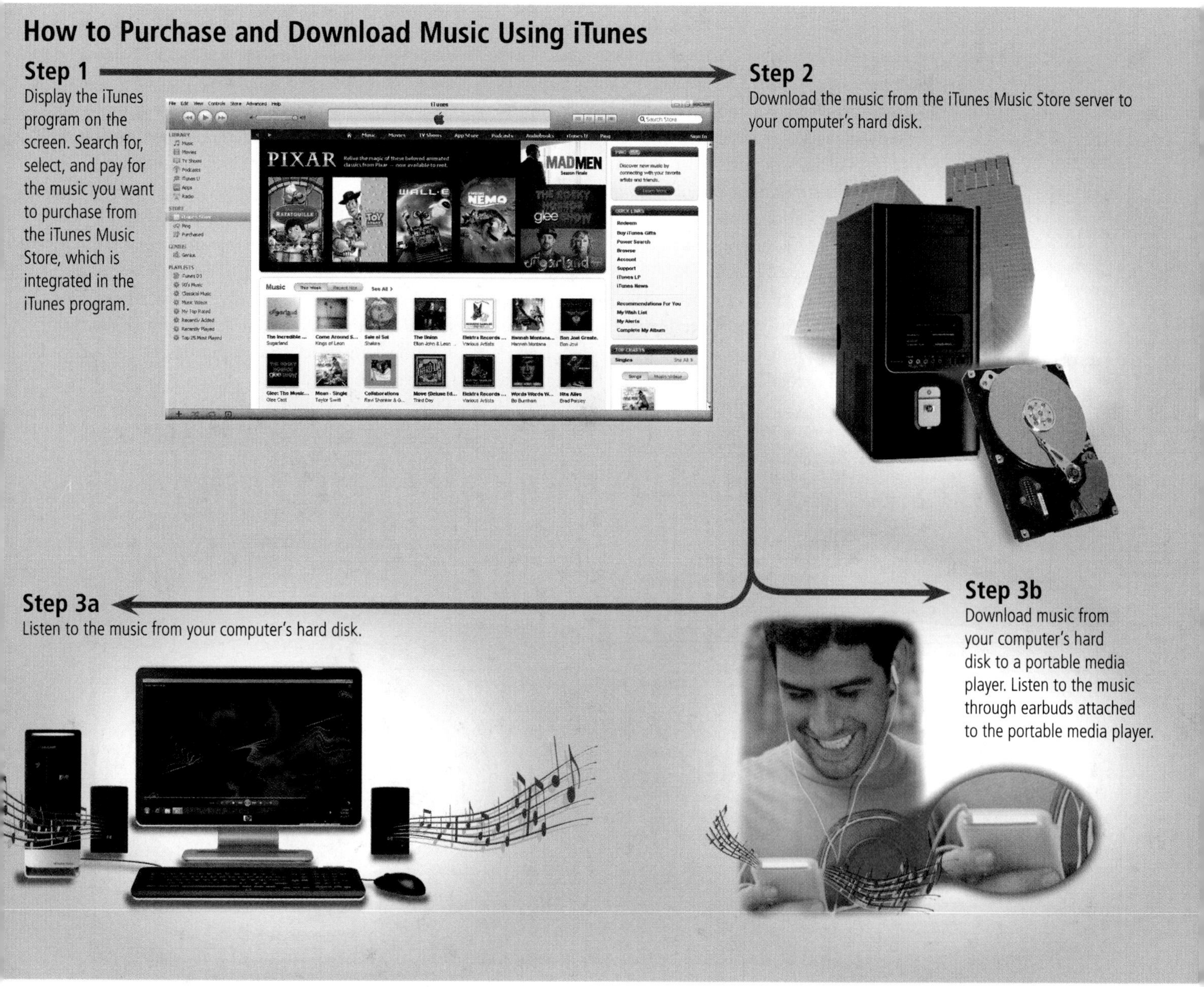
How to Purchase and Download Music Using iTunes
Step 1
Display the iTunes program on the screen. Search for, select, and pay for the music you want to purchase from the iTunes Music Store, which is integrated in the iTunes program.
PIXAR
MADMEN
Step 2
Download the music from the iTunes Music Store server to your computer's hard disk.
Step 3a
Listen to the music from your computer's hard disk.
Step 3b
Download music from your computer's hard disk to a portable media player. Listen to the music through earbuds attached to the portable media player.

Figure 2-21 This figure shows how to purchase and download music using iTunes.

Video On the Web, you can view video clips or watch live video. **Video** consists of images displayed in motion. Most video also has accompanying audio. You can use the Internet to watch live and/or prerecorded coverage of your favorite television programs or enjoy a live performance of your favorite vocalist. You can upload, share, or view video clips at a video sharing Web site such as YouTube (Figure 2-22). Educators, politicians, and businesses are using video blogs and video podcasts to engage students, voters, and consumers.

Simple video applications on the Web consist of individual video files, such as movie or television clips, that you must download completely before you can play them on the computer. Video files often are compressed because they are quite large in size. These clips also are short in length, usually less than 10 minutes, because they can take a long time to download. The Moving Pictures Experts Group (*MPEG*) defines a popular video compression standard, a widely used one called *MPEG-4* or *MP4*. Another popular video format is Adobe Flash.

As with streaming audio, *streaming video* allows you to view longer or live video images as they download to your computer. Widely used standards supported by most Web browsers for transmitting streaming video data on the Internet are AVI (Audio Video Interleaved), QuickTime, Windows Media Format, and RealVideo. Like RealAudio, RealVideo is supported by RealPlayer.

YouTube

For more information, visit the Computer Concepts CourseMate Web site at www.cengagebrain.com, navigate to the Chapter 2 Web Link resource for this book, and then click YouTube.

FAQ 2-5

How are social networking Web sites and Internet video affecting Internet traffic?

A report from Cisco Systems states that Internet traffic will double every two years until 2012. The volume of Internet traffic is increasing mostly because of Internet videos and social networking. In addition, the increased use of video conferencing by business users also accounts for the increase in traffic.

For more information, visit the Computer Concepts CourseMate Web site at www.cengagebrain.com, navigate to the Chapter 2 FAQ resource for this book, and then click Internet Traffic.

Virtual Reality **Virtual reality** (**VR**) is the use of computers to simulate a real or imagined environment that appears as a three-dimensional (3-D) space. VR involves the display of 3-D images that users explore and manipulate interactively.

Using special VR software, a Web developer creates an entire 3-D environment that contains infinite space and depth, called a *VR world*. A VR world, for example, might show a house for sale. Potential buyers walk through rooms in the VR house by moving an input device forward, backward, or to the side.

Figure 2-22 A video of a horse race.

Games and simulations on optical disc or on the Web often use VR (Figure 2-23). Many practical applications of VR also exist. Science educators create VR models of molecules, organisms, and other structures for students to examine. Companies use VR to showcase products or create advertisements. Architects create VR models of buildings and rooms so that clients can see how a completed construction project will look before it is built.

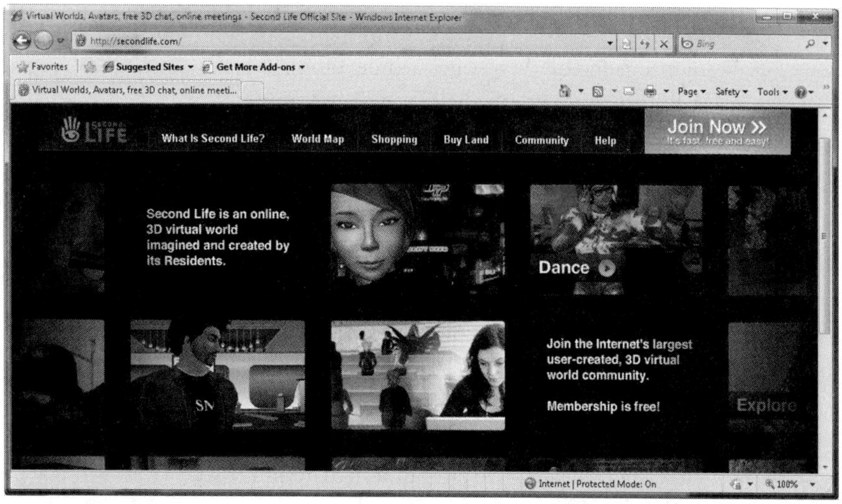

Figure 2-23 Residents (users) of the Second Life online social network interact with other online residents (users) in a VR world.

Plug-ins Most Web browsers have the capability of displaying basic multimedia elements on a Web page. Sometimes, a browser might need an additional program, called a plug-in. A **plug-in**, or *add-on*, is a program that extends the capability of a browser. You can download many plug-ins at no cost from various Web sites (Figure 2-24). Some plug-ins run on all sizes of personal computers and mobile devices. Others have special versions for mobile devices.

Web Publishing

Before the World Wide Web, the means to share opinions and ideas with others easily and inexpensively was limited to the media, classroom, work, or social environments. Generating an advertisement or publication that could reach a massive audience required much expense. Today, businesses and individuals convey information to millions of people by creating their own Web pages. The content of the Web pages ranges from news stories to product information to blogs.

Popular Plug-Ins

Plug-In Application	Description	Web Address
Acrobat Reader	View, navigate, and print Portable Document Format (PDF) files — documents formatted to look just as they look in print	adobe.com
Flash Player	View dazzling graphics and animation, hear outstanding sound and music, display Web pages across an entire screen	adobe.com
Java	Enable Web browser to run programs written in Java, which add interactivity to Web pages	java.com
QuickTime	View animation, music, audio, video, and VR panoramas and objects directly on a Web page	apple.com
RealPlayer	Listen to live and on-demand near-CD-quality audio and newscast-quality video, stream audio and video content for faster viewing, play MP3 files, create music CDs	real.com
Shockwave Player	Experience dynamic interactive multimedia, 3-D graphics, and streaming audio	adobe.com
Silverlight	Experience high-definition video, high-resolution interactive multimedia, and streaming audio and video	microsoft.com
Windows Media Player	Listen to live and on-demand audio, play or edit WMA and MP3 files, burn CDs, and watch DVD movies	microsoft.com

Figure 2-24 Most plug-ins can be downloaded free from the Web.

Web publishing is the development and maintenance of Web pages. To develop a Web page, you do not have to be a computer programmer. For the small business or home user, Web publishing is fairly easy as long as you have the proper tools. To learn more about how to publish a document on the Web, complete the Learn How To 3 activity on page 121.

The five major steps in Web publishing are as follows:

1. **Plan a Web site.**
   Think about issues that could affect the design of the Web site. Identify the purpose of the Web site and the characteristics of the people whom you want to visit the Web site. Determine ways to differentiate your Web site from other similar ones.
2. **Analyze and design a Web site.**
   Design the layout of elements of the Web site such as links, text, graphics, animation, audio, video, and virtual reality. Required hardware may include a digital camera, Web cam, scanner, sound card, and microphone.
3. **Create a Web site.**
   Use a word processing program to create basic Web pages that contain text and graphics. Use Web page authoring software to create more sophisticated Web sites that include text, graphics, animation, audio, video, and special effects. For advanced features such as managing users, passwords, chat rooms, and e-mail, you may need to purchase specialized Web site management software.
4. **Deploy a Web site.**
   Transfer the Web pages from your computer to a Web server. Many Internet access providers offer their customers storage space on a Web server. Another option is a Web hosting service, which provides storage space on a Web server for a reasonable monthly fee. To help others locate your Web page, register your Web address with various search engines to ensure your site will appear in the hit lists for searches for certain keywords.
5. **Maintain a Web site.**
   Visit the Web site regularly to ensure the Web site contents are current and all links work properly.

Web Page Authoring Software

For more information, visit the Computer Concepts CourseMate Web site at www.cengagebrain.com, navigate to the Chapter 2 Web Link resource for this book, and then click Web Page Authoring Software.

QUIZ YOURSELF 2-2

Instructions: Find the true statement below. Then, rewrite the remaining false statements so that they are true.

1. A blog is a Web site that uses a regularly updated journal format to reflect the interests, opinions, and personalities of the author and sometimes site visitors.
2. You can assume that information on the Web is correct and accurate.
3. Audio and video files are downloaded to reduce their file sizes.
4. Popular portals include iTunes, RealPlayer, and Windows Media Player.
5. The more widely used search engines for personal computers are Internet Explorer, Firefox, Opera, Safari, and Google Chrome.
6. To develop a Web page, you have to be a computer programmer.
7. To improve your Web searches, use general nouns and put the least important terms first in the search text.

Quiz Yourself Online: To further check your knowledge of pages 80 through 98, visit the Computer Concepts CourseMate Web site at www.cengagebrain.com, navigate to the Chapter 2 Quiz Yourself resource for this book, and then click Objectives 5 – 9.

E-Commerce

E-commerce, short for *electronic commerce*, is a business transaction that occurs over an electronic network such as the Internet. Anyone with access to a computer or mobile device, an Internet connection, and a means to pay for purchased goods or services can participate in e-commerce. Some people use the term *m-commerce* (mobile commerce) to identify e-commerce that takes place using mobile devices.

Popular uses of e-commerce by consumers include retail, finance, travel, entertainment, and health. Users can purchase just about any product or service on the Web, including groceries, flowers, books, computers, music, movies, cars, airline tickets, and concert tickets. They also can pay bills, invest in stocks, make airline reservations, reserve a hotel or car, and fill prescriptions.

Three types of e-commerce are business-to-consumer, consumer-to-consumer, and business-to-business. *Business-to-consumer (B2C) e-commerce* consists of the sale of goods and services to the general public. For example,

Apple has a B2C Web site. Instead of visiting a retail store to purchase an iPod, customers can order one directly from Apple's Web site.

A customer (consumer) visits an online business through an **electronic storefront**, which contains product descriptions, images, and a shopping cart. The **shopping cart** allows the customer to collect purchases. When ready to complete the sale, the customer enters personal data and the method of payment, which should be through a secure Internet connection. *E-retail*, short for electronic retail, occurs when businesses use the Web to sell products (Figure 2-25).

FAQ 2-6

Is it safe to shop online?

Not always. Although 78 percent of shoppers find online shopping convenient, about 75 percent of surveyed individuals are hesitant to enter their personal or credit card information online. It always is best to conduct online transactions with well-established companies. If possible, research these companies and read about others' online shopping experiences before making a purchase. If you never have heard of a particular online business, do not entrust them with your credit card information.

For more information, visit the Computer Concepts CourseMate Web site at www.cengagebrain.com, navigate to the Chapter 2 FAQ resource for this book, and then click Online Shopping.

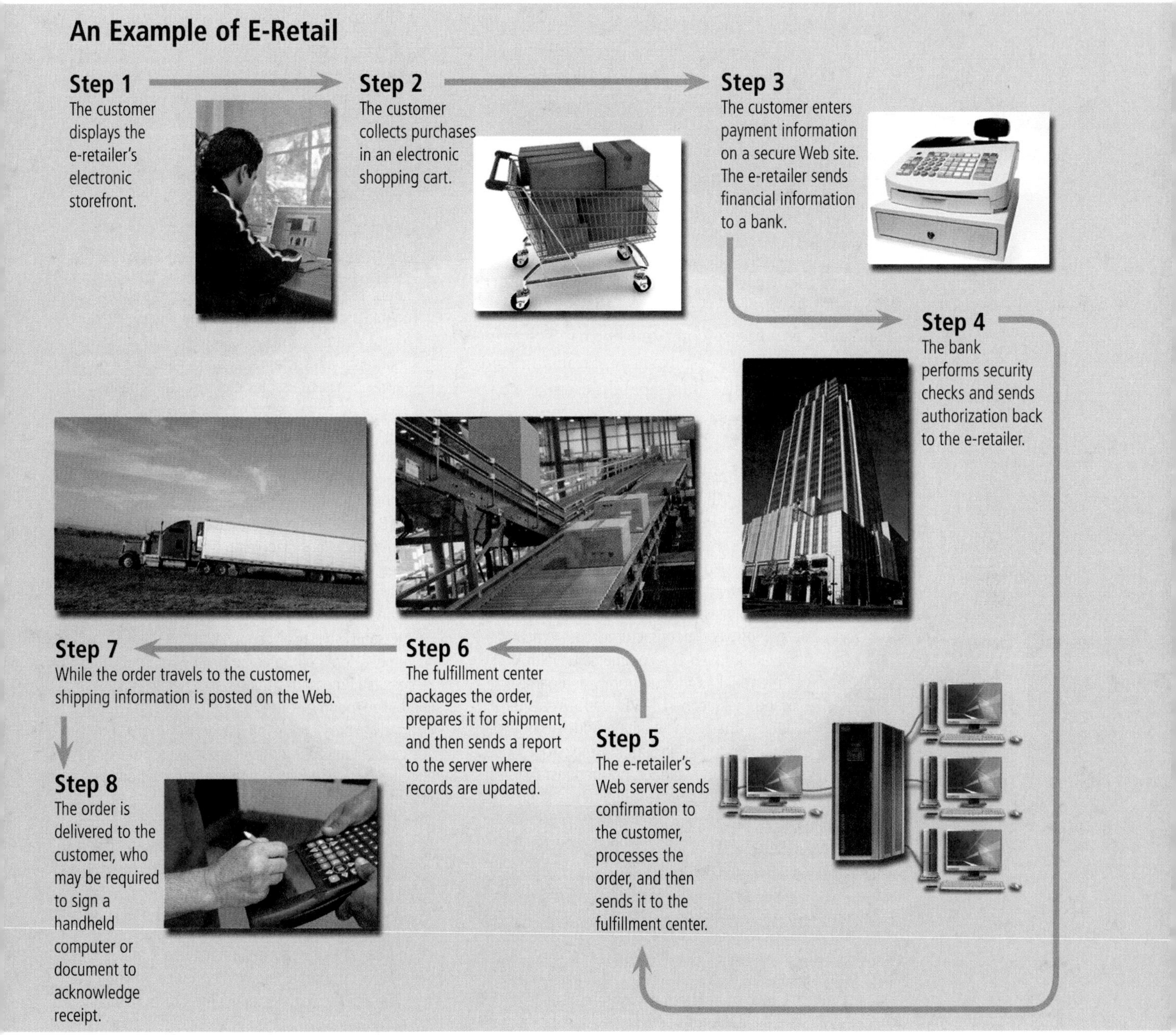
An Example of E-Retail
Step 1
The customer displays the e-retailer's electronic storefront.
Step 2
The customer collects purchases in an electronic shopping cart.
Step 3
The customer enters payment information on a secure Web site. The e-retailer sends financial information to a bank.
Step 4
The bank performs security checks and sends authorization back to the e-retailer.
Step 5
The e-retailer's Web server sends confirmation to the customer, processes the order, and then sends it to the fulfillment center.
Step 6
The fulfillment center packages the order, prepares it for shipment, and then sends a report to the server where records are updated.
Step 7
While the order travels to the customer, shipping information is posted on the Web.
Step 8
The order is delivered to the customer, who may be required to sign a handheld computer or document to acknowledge receipt.

Figure 2-25 This figure shows an example of e-retail.

Consumer-to-consumer (C2C) e-commerce occurs when one consumer sells directly to another, such as in an online auction. With an **online auction**, users bid on an item being sold by someone else. The highest bidder at the end of the bidding period purchases the item. eBay is one of the more popular online auction Web sites.

As an alternative to entering credit card, bank account, or other financial information online, some shopping and auction Web sites allow consumers to use an online payment service such as PayPal or Google Checkout. To use an online payment service, you create an account that is linked to your credit card or funds at a financial institution. When you make a purchase, you use your online payment service account, which transfers money for you without revealing your financial information. Read Innovative Computing 2-2 to find out how shoppers can experience 3-D online stores.

Google Checkout

For more information, visit the Computer Concepts CourseMate Web site at www.cengagebrain.com, navigate to the Chapter 2 Web Link resource for this book, and then click Google Checkout.

Most e-commerce, though, actually takes place between businesses, which is called *business-to-business (B2B) e-commerce*. Businesses often provide goods and services to other businesses, such as online advertising, recruiting, credit, sales, market research, technical support, and training. For example, some MasterCard and Visa credit card companies provide corporations with Web-based purchasing, tracking, and transaction downloading capabilities.

INNOVATIVE COMPUTING 2-2

Shopping Becomes a Virtual Experience

Part of retail shopping at the mall or the grocery store is the ability to browse aisles, view labels, and compare products side by side. Online shoppers may be able to share these shopping experiences in three-dimensional environments complete with shelving, signs, overhead lighting, and outdoor plazas.

Software manufacturer Kinset, Inc. is leading the 3-D e-commerce development. Taking its cue from video games and the Second Life VR world Web site, Kinset has launched its product to big-name retailers, including Brookstone. Shoppers download and then install this software, connect to the Internet, and then begin their shopping experience.

When shoppers position their mouse pointer over an item, the information about the product is displayed. Pressing a specific key adds the item to a shopping cart, and another key brings the shopper to the checkout screen.

For more information, visit the Computer Concepts CourseMate Web site at www.cengagebrain.com, navigate to the Chapter 2 Innovative Computing resource for this book, and then click Online Shopping.

Other Internet Services

The Web is only one of the many services on the Internet. The Web and other Internet services have changed the way we communicate. We use computers and mobile devices to send e-mail messages to the president, have a discussion with experts about the stock market, chat with someone in another country about genealogy, and talk about homework assignments with classmates via instant messages. Many times, these communications take place completely in writing — without the parties ever meeting each other. Read Ethics & Issues 2-4 for a related discussion.

The following pages discuss these Internet services: e-mail, mailing lists, instant messaging, chat rooms, VoIP (Voice over IP), newsgroups and message boards, and FTP (File Transfer Protocol).

ETHICS & ISSUES 2-4

Should You Be Judged by Your Internet Communications?

Internet features, such as e-mail, instant messages, and chat, have become some of today's most popular methods of communications. Millions of people around the world send and receive various forms of Internet messages. The Internet links the geographically distanced, connects the economically separated, enables the physically challenged, and encourages the publicly timid. Almost all office workers are prolific users of Internet communications because their job depends on a great deal of collaboration with co-workers, management, vendors, and other departments.

Because of the ease of use of such forms of communications, people are writing more than ever before — but is it good writing? The carefully crafted letters of an era gone by, handwritten in beautiful penmanship, have been replaced by messages stylistically equivalent to notes on the refrigerator. The immediacy of the Internet often results in messages that are ill conceived, casually spelled, poorly worded, grammatically flawed, and tritely expressed. Despite experts suggesting that users always should proofread messages carefully before sending them, communications often are misinterpreted or come across as being rude.

Should employers require that employees adhere to e-mail authoring policies? In general, has e-mail's impact on communications been positive or negative? Why? Would you judge somebody by the quality of his or her e-mail message? Why or why not? Could someone's professional reputation be enhanced or hindered by the quality and effectiveness of his or her Internet communications?

E-Mail

E-mail (short for *electronic mail*) is the transmission of messages and files via a computer network. E-mail was one of the original services on the Internet, enabling scientists and researchers working on government-sponsored projects to communicate with colleagues at other locations. Today, e-mail is a primary communications method for both personal and business use.

You use an **e-mail program** to create, send, receive, forward, store, print, and delete e-mail messages. Outlook and Windows Live Mail are two popular desktop e-mail programs; Gmail and Windows Live Hotmail are two popular free e-mail Web applications. The steps in Figure 2-26 illustrate how to send an e-mail message using Outlook.

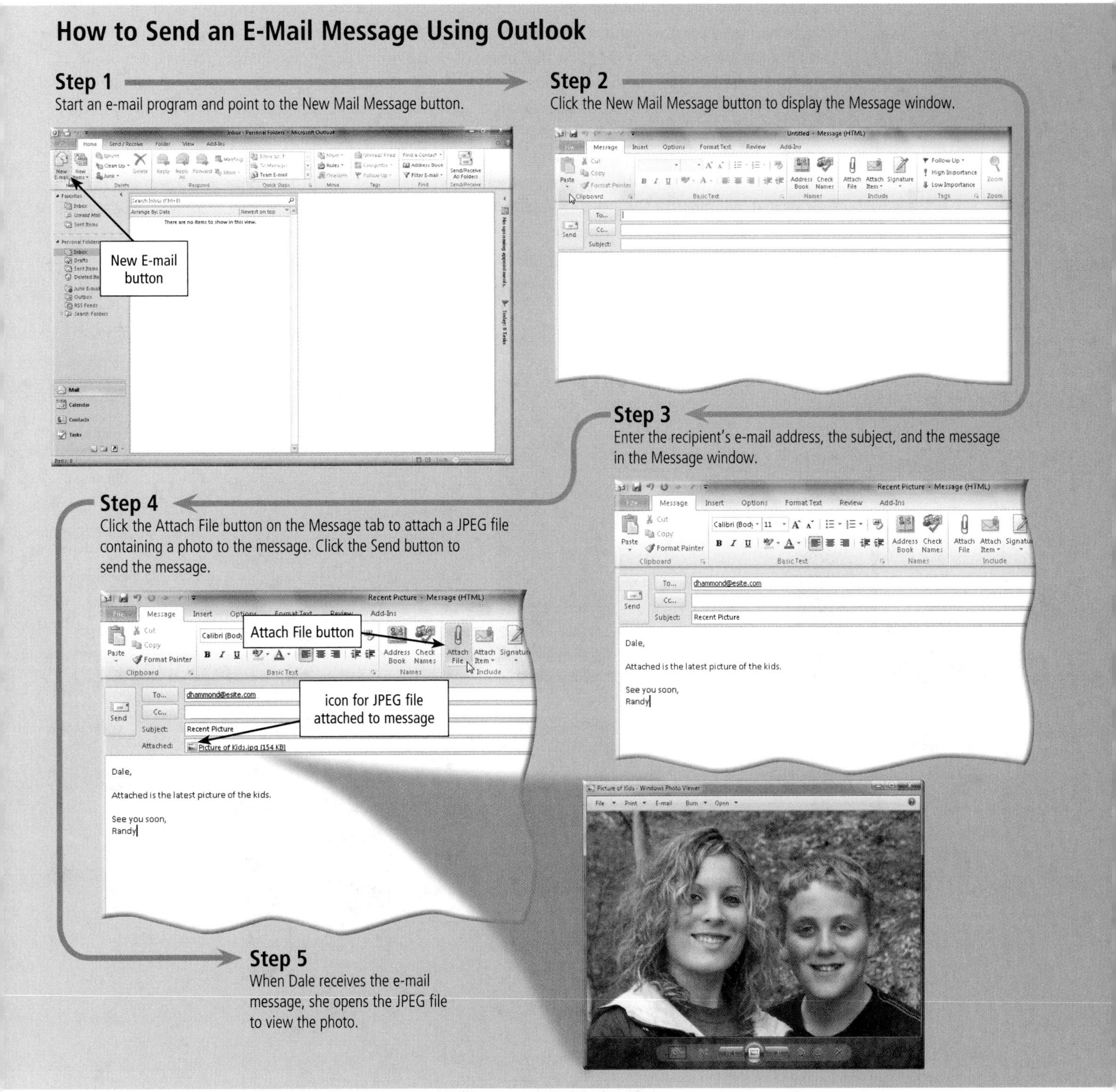
How to Send an E-Mail Message Using Outlook
Step 1
Start an e-mail program and point to the New Mail Message button.
New E-mail button
Step 2
Click the New Mail Message button to display the Message window.
Step 3
Enter the recipient's e-mail address, the subject, and the message in the Message window.
dhammond@esite.com
Recent Picture
Dale,
Attached is the latest picture of the kids.
See you soon,
Randy
Step 4
Click the Attach File button on the Message tab to attach a JPEG file containing a photo to the message. Click the Send button to send the message.
Attach File button
icon for JPEG file attached to message
Step 5
When Dale receives the e-mail message, she opens the JPEG file to view the photo.

Figure 2-26 This figure shows how to send an e-mail message using Outlook.

The message can be simple text or can include an attachment such as a word processing document, a graphic, an audio clip, or a video clip. To learn more about how to attach a file to an e-mail message, complete the Learn How To 1 activity on page 120.

Just as you address a letter when using the postal system, you address an e-mail message with the e-mail address of your intended recipient. Likewise, when someone sends you a message, he or she must have your e-mail address. An **e-mail address** is a combination of a user name and a domain name that identifies a user so that he or she can receive Internet e-mail.

A **user name** is a unique combination of characters, such as letters of the alphabet and/or numbers, that identifies a specific user. Your user name must be different from the other user names in the same domain. For example, a user named Kiley Barnhill whose server has a domain name of esite.com might want to select kbarnhill as her user name. If esite.com already has a kbarnhill (for Ken Barnhill), Kiley will have to select a different user name, such as kileybarnhill or k_barnhill.

Sometimes, organizations decide user names for new users. In many cases, however, users select their own user names, often selecting a nickname or any other combination of characters for their user name. Many users select a combination of their first and last names so that others can remember it easily.

In an Internet e-mail address, an @ (pronounced at) symbol separates the user name from the domain name. Your service provider supplies the domain name. A possible e-mail address for Kiley Barnhill would be kbarnhill@esite.com, which would be read as follows: K Barnhill at e site dot com. Most e-mail programs allow you to create an **address book**, or contacts folder, which contains a list of names and e-mail addresses.

Figure 2-27 illustrates how an e-mail message may travel from a sender to a receiver using a desktop e-mail program. When you send an

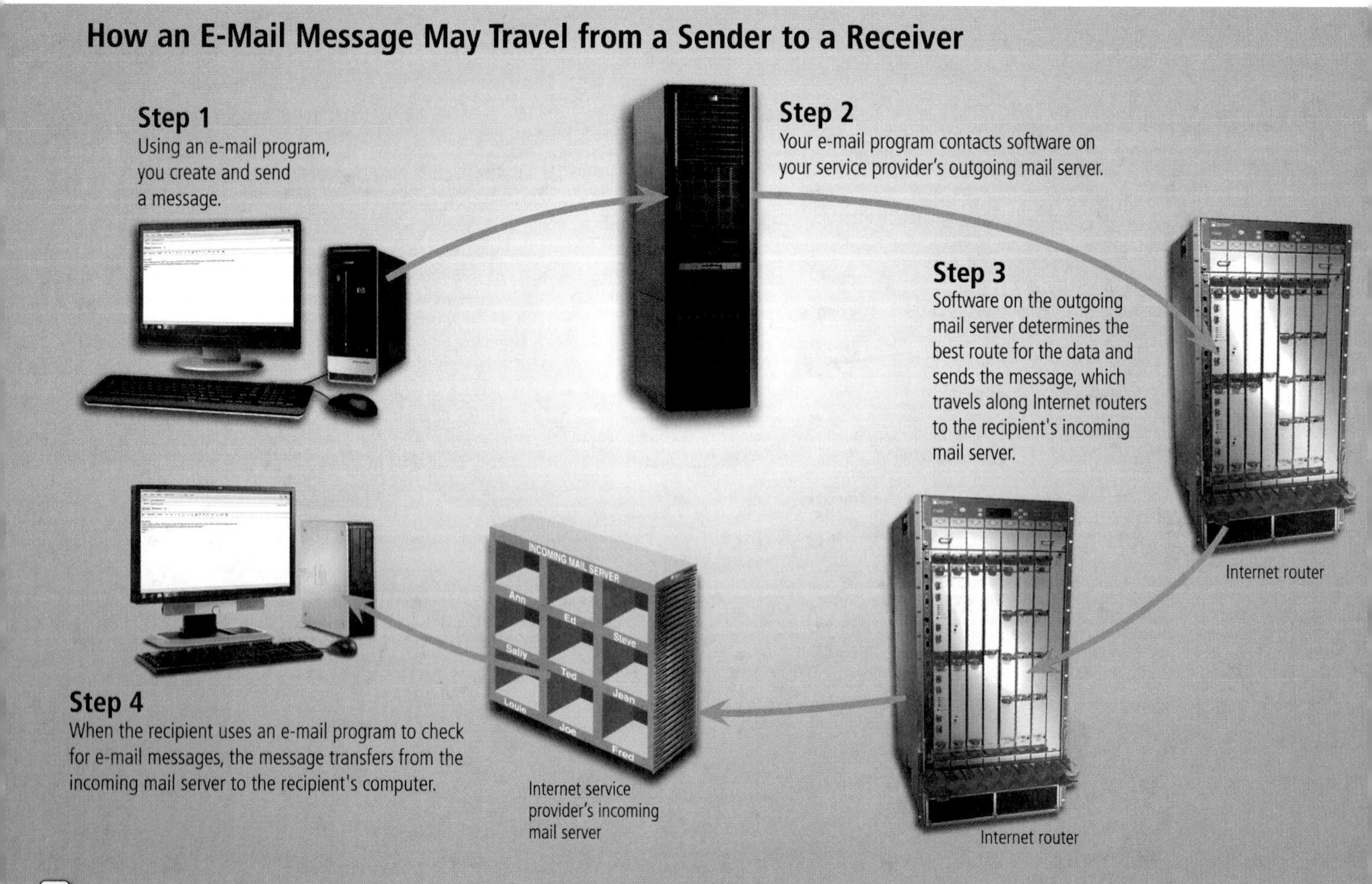
How an E-Mail Message May Travel from a Sender to a Receiver
Step 1
Using an e-mail program, you create and send a message.
Step 2
Your e-mail program contacts software on your service provider's outgoing mail server.
Step 3
Software on the outgoing mail server determines the best route for the data and sends the message, which travels along Internet routers to the recipient's incoming mail server.
Internet router
Internet router
INCOMING MAIL SERVER
Ann
Ed
Steve
Sally
Ted
Jean
Louis
Joe
Fred
Internet service provider's incoming mail server
Step 4
When the recipient uses an e-mail program to check for e-mail messages, the message transfers from the incoming mail server to the recipient's computer.

Figure 2-27 This figure shows how an e-mail message may travel from a sender to a receiver.

e-mail message, an outgoing mail server that is operated by your Internet access provider determines how to route the message through the Internet and then sends the message. *SMTP* (simple mail transfer protocol) is a communications protocol used by some outgoing mail servers.

As you receive e-mail messages, an incoming mail server — also operated by your Internet access provider — holds the messages in your mailbox until you use your e-mail program to retrieve them. *POP3*, the latest version of POP (*Post Office Protocol*), is a communications protocol used by some incoming mail servers. Most e-mail programs have a mail notification alert that informs you via a message and/or sound when you receive new mail.

Mailing Lists

A **mailing list**, also called an e-mail list or distribution list, is a group of e-mail names and addresses given a single name. When a message is sent to a mailing list, every person on the list receives a copy of the message in his or her mailbox. For example, your credit card company may add you to its mailing list in order to send you special offers. To add your e-mail name and address to a mailing list, you **subscribe** to it (Figure 2-28). To remove your name, you **unsubscribe** from the mailing list.

Thousands of mailing lists exist about a variety of topics in areas of entertainment, business, computers, society, culture, health, recreation, and education. Many vendors use mailing lists to communicate with their customer base.

? FAQ 2-7

Can my computer get a virus through e-mail?

Yes. A *virus* is a computer program that can damage files and the operating system. One way that virus authors attempt to spread a virus is by sending virus-infected e-mail attachments. If you receive an e-mail attachment, you should use an antivirus program to verify that it is virus free.

For more information, read the High-Tech Talk article on page 178 and the section about viruses and antivirus programs in Chapter 8; and visit the Computer Concepts CourseMate Web site at www.cengagebrain.com, navigate to the Chapter 2 FAQ resource for this book, and then click Viruses.

E-Mail

For more information, visit the Computer Concepts CourseMate Web site at www.cengagebrain.com, navigate to the Chapter 2 Web Link resource for this book, and then click E-Mail.

Figure 2-28 When you join a mailing list, you and all others on the mailing list receive e-mail messages from the Web site.

Instant Messaging

Instant messaging (IM) is a real-time Internet communications service that notifies you when one or more people are online and then allows you to exchange messages or files or join a private chat room with them. **Real time** means that you and the people with whom you are conversing are online at the same time. Some IM services support voice and video conversations (Figure 2-29). Many IM services also can alert you to information such as calendar appointments, stock quotes, weather, or sports scores. They also allow you to send photos

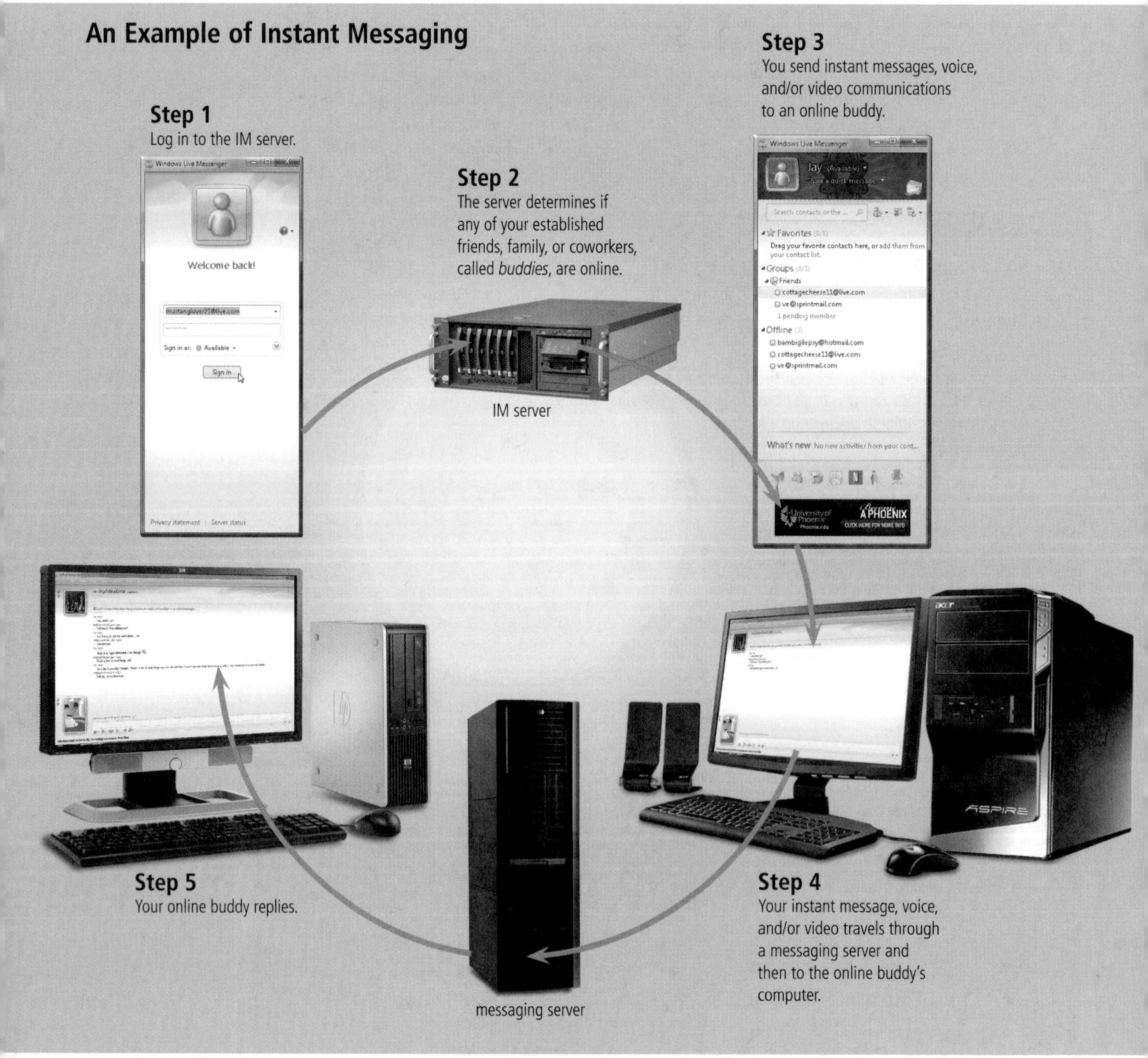
An Example of Instant Messaging
Step 1
Log in to the IM server.
Step 2
The server determines if any of your established friends, family, or coworkers, called *buddies*, are online.
IM server
Step 3
You send instant messages, voice, and/or video communications to an online buddy.
Step 4
Your instant message, voice, and/or video travels through a messaging server and then to the online buddy's computer.
messaging server
Step 5
Your online buddy replies.
Windows Live Messenger
Welcome back!
Sign in
Favorites
Groups
Friends
Offline
What's new

Figure 2-29 This figure shows an example of instant messaging.

or other documents to a recipient, listen to streaming music, and play games with another online party. For IM to work, both parties must be online at the same time. Also, the receiver of a message must be willing to accept messages.

To use IM, you may have to install *instant messenger* software on the computer or mobile device, such as a smart phone, you plan to use. Some operating systems, such as Windows, include an instant messenger. Popular IM software includes AIM (AOL Instant Messenger), Google Talk, MySpace IM, Windows Live Messenger, and Yahoo! Messenger.

Few IM programs follow IM standards. To ensure successful communications, all individuals on the contact list need to use the same or a compatible instant messenger.

FAQ 2-8

How popular are various online communications methods?

A research study conducted by Ipsos revealed that e-mail is expected to remain the preferred method of online communications during the next several years, at least. Methods of online communications expected to become more popular in the future include (listed from most popular to least popular) video conferencing, instant messaging, and text messaging.

For more information, visit the Computer Concepts CourseMate Web site at www.cengagebrain.com, navigate to the Chapter 2 FAQ resource for this book, and then click Online Communications.

Chat Rooms

A **chat** is a real-time typed conversation that takes place on a computer. A **chat room** is a location on an Internet server that permits users to chat with each other. Anyone in the chat room can participate in the conversation, which usually is specific to a particular topic.

As you type on your keyboard, a line of characters and symbols is displayed on the computer screen. Others connected to the same chat room server also see what you have typed (Figure 2-30). Some chat rooms support voice chats and video chats, in which people hear or see each other as they chat.

To start a chat session, you connect to a chat server through a program called a *chat client*. Today's browsers usually include a chat client. If yours does not, you can download a chat client from the Web. Some Web sites allow users to conduct chats without a chat client.

Once you have installed a chat client, you can create or join a conversation on the chat server to which you are connected. The chat room should indicate the discussion topic. The person who creates a chat room acts as the operator and has responsibility for monitoring the conversation and disconnecting anyone who becomes disruptive. Operator status can be shared or transferred to someone else.

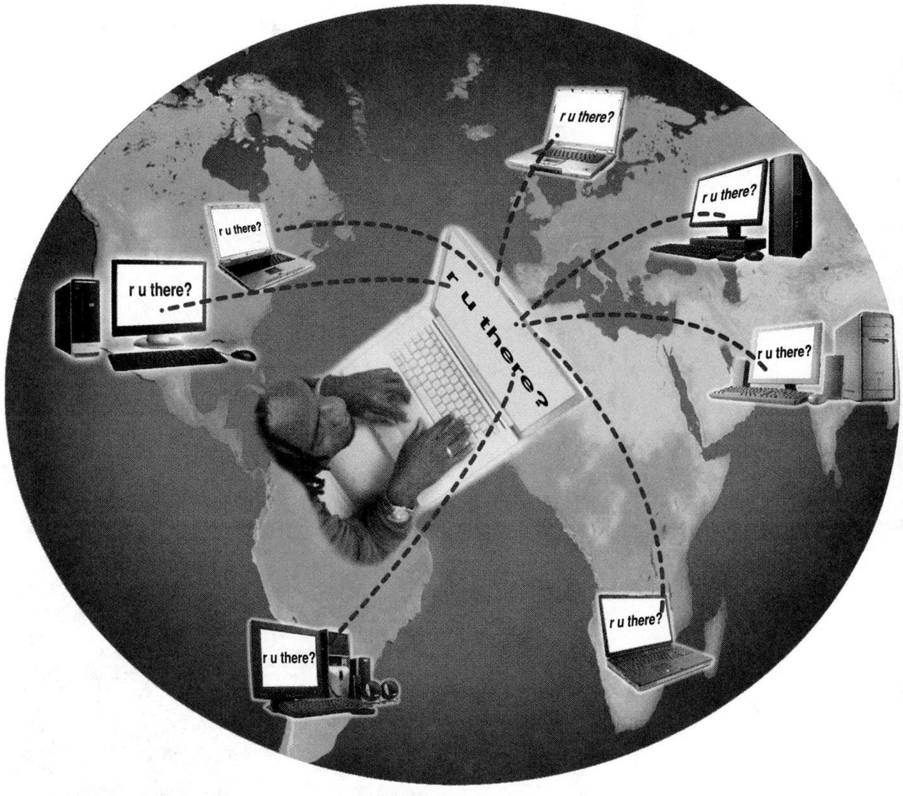

Figure 2-30 As you type, the words and symbols you enter are displayed on the computer screens of other people in the same chat room. To save time many chat and IM users type abbreviations and acronyms for phrases, such as 'r u there?', which stands for 'Are you there?'.

Chat Rooms

For more information, visit the Computer Concepts CourseMate Web site at www.cengagebrain.com, navigate to the Chapter 2 Web Link resource for this book, and then click Chat Rooms.

VoIP

VoIP, (*Voice over IP*, or Internet Protocol) also called *Internet telephony*, enables users to speak to other users over the Internet. That is, VoIP uses the Internet (instead of the public switched telephone network) to connect a calling party to one or more local or long-distance called parties.

To place an Internet telephone call, you need a high-speed Internet connection (such as a DSL or cable modem); Internet telephone service; a microphone or telephone, depending on the Internet telephone service; and Internet telephone software or a VoIP router, or a telephone adapter, depending on the Internet telephone service. VoIP services also are available on some mobile devices that have wireless Internet service. Calls to other parties with the same Internet telephone service often are free, while calls that connect to the telephone network typically cost about $15 to $35 per month.

As you speak in a microphone connected to your computer or a telephone connected to the VoIP router or telephone adapter, the Internet telephone software and the computer's sound card or the VoIP router or telephone adapter convert your spoken words (analog signals) to digital signals and then transmit the digitized audio over the Internet to the called parties. Software and equipment at the receiving end reverse the process so that the receiving parties can hear what you have said. Figure 2-31 illustrates one possible configuration for VoIP.

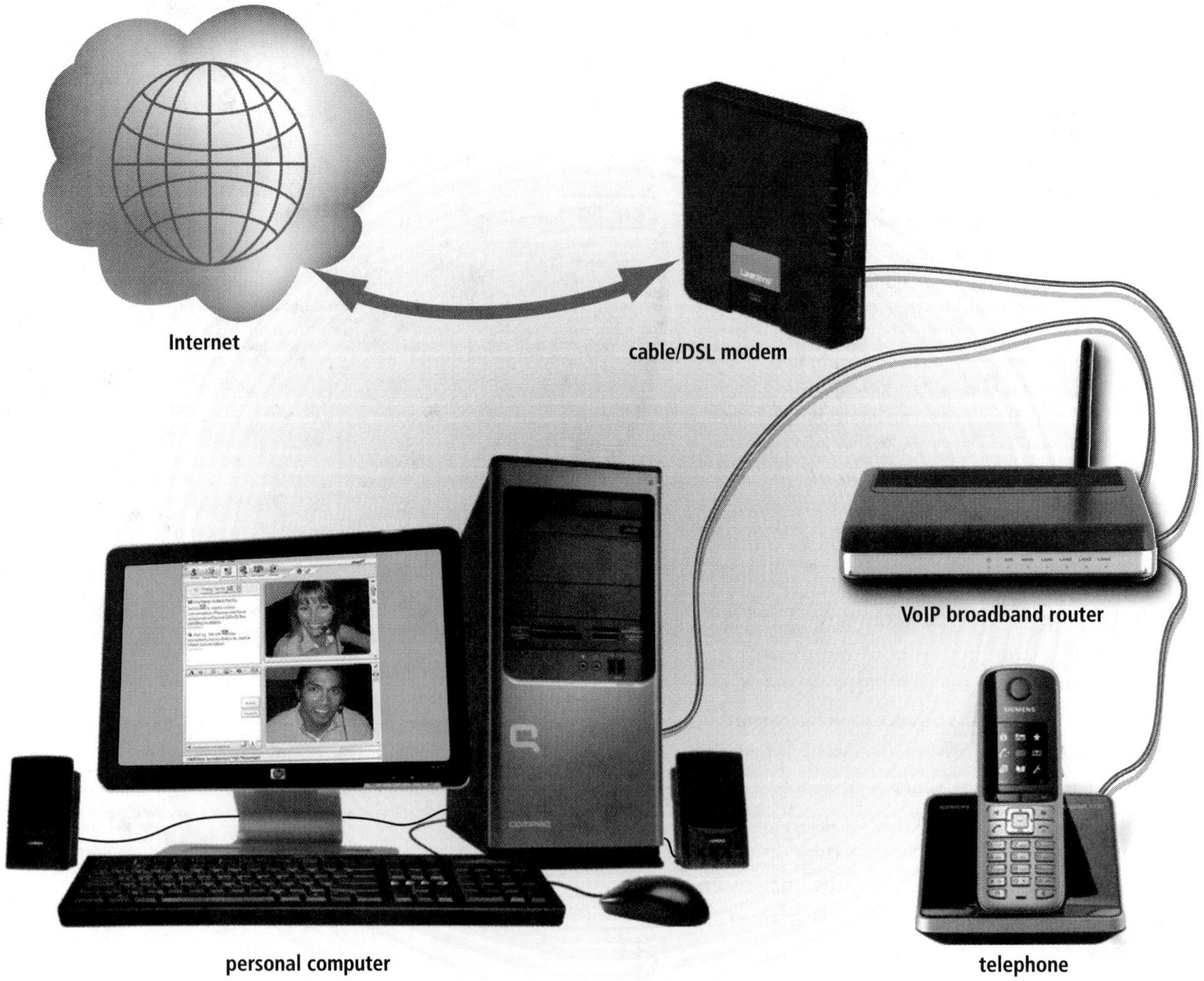

Figure 2-31 One type of equipment configuration for a user making a call via VoIP.

Newsgroups and Message Boards

A **newsgroup** is an online area in which users have written discussions about a particular subject (Figure 2-32). To participate in a discussion, a user posts a message, called an article, to the newsgroup, and other users in the newsgroup read and reply to the message. A *thread* or *threaded discussion* consists of the original article and all subsequent related replies.

A computer that stores and distributes newsgroup messages is called a news server. Some newsgroups require you to enter a user name and password to participate in the discussion. For example, a newsgroup for students taking a college course may require a user name and password to access the newsgroup. This ensures that only students in the course participate in the discussion.

To participate in a newsgroup, typically you use a program called a *newsreader*. Windows Live Mail includes a newsreader. Some Web sites, such as Google Groups, that sponsor newsgroups have a built-in newsreader.

A popular Web-based type of discussion group that does not require a newsreader is a **message board**. Many Web sites use message boards instead of newsgroups because they are easier to use.

FTP

FTP (File Transfer Protocol) is an Internet standard that permits file uploading and downloading with other computers on the Internet. Uploading is the opposite of downloading; that is, **uploading** is the process of transferring documents, graphics, and other objects from your computer to a server on the Internet. Web page authors, for example, often use FTP to upload their Web pages to a Web server.

Many operating systems include FTP capabilities. If yours does not, you can download FTP programs from the Web, usually for a small fee.

An *FTP server* is a computer that allows users to upload and/or download files using FTP. An FTP site is a collection of files including text, graphics, audio clips, video clips, and program files that reside on an FTP server. Many FTP sites have *anonymous FTP*, whereby anyone can transfer some, if not all, available files. Some FTP sites restrict file transfers to those who have authorized accounts (user names and passwords) on the FTP server.

Large files on FTP sites often are compressed to reduce storage space and download time. Before you can use a compressed (zipped) file, you must uncompress (unzip) it. Chapter 8 discusses utilities that zip and unzip files.

FTP

For more information, visit the Computer Concepts CourseMate Web site at www.cengagebrain.com, navigate to the Chapter 2 Web Link resource for this book, and then click FTP.

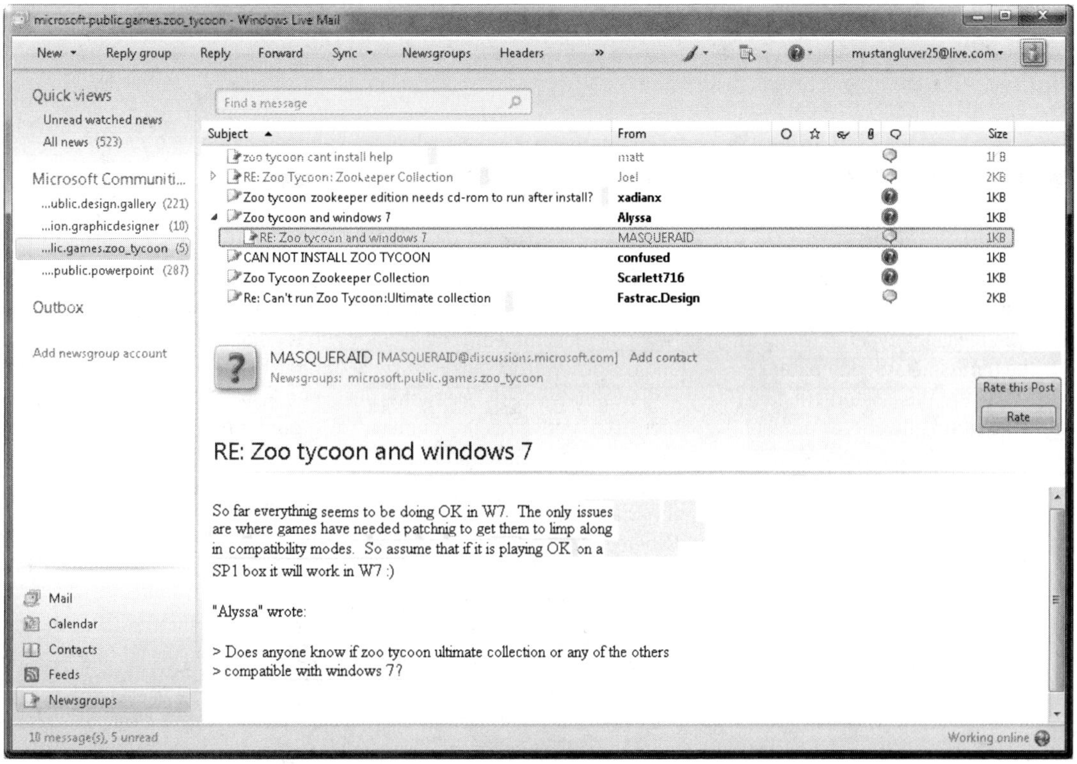

Figure 2-32 Users in a newsgroup read and reply to other users' messages.

Netiquette

Netiquette, which is short for Internet etiquette, is the code of acceptable behaviors users should follow while on the Internet; that is, it is the conduct expected of individuals while online. Netiquette includes rules for all aspects of the Internet, including the World Wide Web, e-mail, instant messaging, chat rooms, FTP, and newsgroups and message boards. Figure 2-33 outlines some of the rules of netiquette. Read Ethics & Issues 2-5 for a related discussion.

NETIQUETTE — Golden Rule: Treat others as you would like them to treat you.

1. In e-mail, chat rooms, and newsgroups:
   - Keep messages brief. Use proper grammar, spelling, and punctuation.
   - Be careful when using sarcasm and humor, as it might be misinterpreted.
   - Be polite. Avoid offensive language.
   - Read the message before you send it.
   - Use meaningful subject lines.
   - Avoid sending or posting *flames,* which are abusive or insulting messages. Do not participate in *flame wars,* which are exchanges of flames.
   - Avoid sending spam, which is the Internet's version of junk mail. *Spam* is an unsolicited e-mail message or newsgroup posting sent to many recipients or newsgroups at once.
   - Do not use all capital letters, which is the equivalent of SHOUTING!
   - Use **emoticons** to express emotion. Popular emoticons include

:)	Smile	:|	Indifference	:o	Surprised
:(	Frown	:\	Undecided		

   - Use abbreviations and acronyms for phrases:

btw	by the way
imho	in my humble opinion
fyi	for your information
ttfn	ta ta for now
fwiw	for what it's worth
tyvm	thank you very much

   - Clearly identify a *spoiler,* which is a message that reveals a solution to a game or ending to a movie or program.
2. Read the *FAQ* (frequently asked questions), if one exists. Many newsgroups and Web pages have an FAQ.
3. Do not assume material is accurate or up-to-date. Be forgiving of other's mistakes.
4. Never read someone's private e-mail.

Figure 2-33 Some of the rules of netiquette.

ETHICS & ISSUES 2-5

Would Banning Anonymous Comments Reduce Cyberbullying?

Recently, several high-profile cases highlighted the issue of cyberbullying. *Cyberbullying* is the harassment of computer users, often teens and preteens, through various forms of Internet communications. The behavior typically occurs via e-mail, instant messaging, and chat rooms, and can result in a traumatic experience for the recipient. The bullying may be in the form of threats, spreading of rumors, or humiliation. Usually, the perpetrators of cyberbullying remain anonymous. Many people believe that the anonymous nature of the Internet directly leads to this unscrupulous behavior. Some government officials and advocacy groups have asked for laws that would ban anonymous comments in chat rooms and require that Internet access providers verify and record the true identity of all users. Others have proposed that it be illegal to sign up for an e-mail account or instant messaging account with a fake screen name. Opponents of such plans claim that anonymity and privacy are too important to give up. They state, for example, that the right to be critical of the government in an anonymous forum is a basic right. The rights of everyone should not be infringed upon due to bad behavior of a small group of people.

Would banning anonymous comments reduce cyberbullying? Why or why not? What are the positive and negative aspects of the freedom to remain anonymous on the Internet? What other measures can be taken to reduce cyberbullying? What role can parents play in reducing cyberbullying?

Cyberbullying

For more information, visit the Computer Concepts CourseMate Web site at www.cengagebrain.com, navigate to the Chapter 2 Web Link resource for this book, and then click Cyberbullying.

QUIZ YOURSELF 2-3

Instructions: Find the true statement below. Then, rewrite the remaining false statements so that they are true.

1. A chat room is a location on an Internet server that permits users to chat with each other.
2. An e-mail address is a combination of a user name and an e-mail program that identifies a user so that he or she can receive Internet e-mail.
3. Business-to-consumer e-commerce occurs when one consumer sells directly to another, such as in an online auction.
4. FTP is an Internet standard that permits file reading and writing with other computers on the Internet.
5. Spam uses the Internet (instead of the public switched telephone network) to connect a calling party to one or more called parties.
6. Netiquette is the code of unacceptable behaviors while on the Internet.
7. VoIP enables users to subscribe to other users over the Internet.

Quiz Yourself Online: To further check your knowledge of pages 98 through 108, visit the Computer Concepts CourseMate Web site at www.cengagebrain.com, navigate to the Chapter 2 Quiz Yourself resource for this book, and then click Objectives 10 – 12.

Chapter Summary

This chapter presented the history and structure of the Internet. It discussed the World Wide Web at length, including topics such as browsing, navigating, searching, Web publishing, and e-commerce. It also introduced other services available on the Internet, such as e-mail, mailing lists, instant messaging, chat rooms, VoIP, newsgroups and message boards, and FTP. Finally, the chapter listed rules of netiquette.

Computer Usage @ Work

Entertainment

Do you wonder how music on the radio sounds so perfectly in tune, how animated motion pictures are created, or how one controls lighting during a concert? Not only does the entertainment industry rely on computers to advertise and sell their services on the Internet, computers also assist in other aspects, including audio and video composition, lighting control, computerized animation, and computer gaming.

As mentioned in this chapter, entertainment Web sites provide music and movies you can purchase and download to your computer or mobile device; live news broadcasts, performances, and sporting events; games you can play with other online users; and much more.

As early as 1951, computers were used to record and play music. Today, computers play a much larger role in the music industry. For example, if you are listening to a song on the radio and notice that not one note is out of tune, it is possible that software was used to change individual notes without altering the rest of the song.

Many years ago, creating cartoons or animated motion pictures was an extremely time-consuming task because artists were responsible for sketching thousands of drawings by hand. Currently, artists use computers to create these drawings in a fraction of the time, which significantly can reduce the time and cost of development.

Computers also are used in the game industry. While some game developers create games from scratch, others might use game engines that simplify the development process. For example, LucasArts created the GrimE game engine, which is designed to create adventure games.

During a concert, lighting technicians use computer programs to turn lights off and on, change color, or change location at specified intervals. In fact, once a performance begins, the technicians often merely are standing by, monitoring the computer as it performs most of the work. A significant amount of time and effort, however, is required to program the computer to perform its required tasks during a live show.

The next time you listen to a song, watch a movie, play a game, or attend a concert, think about the role computers play in contributing to your entertainment.

For more information, visit the Computer Concepts CourseMate Web site at www.cengagebrain.com, navigate to the Chapter 2 Computer Usage @ Work resource for this book, and then click Entertainment.

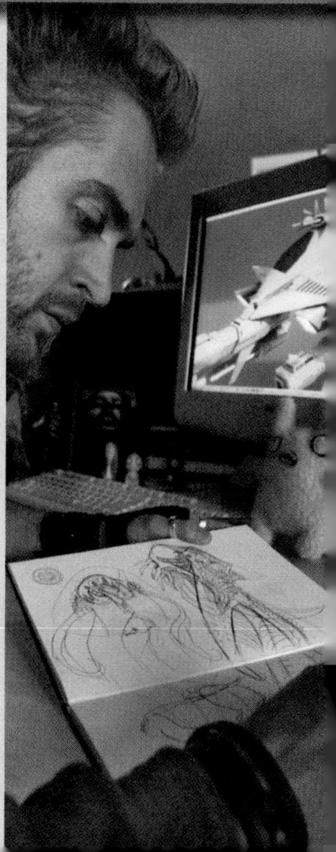

High-Tech Talk

A Computer's Internet Protocol (IP) Address

Every computer on the Internet has a unique address, called an IP address, that distinguishes it from other computers on the Internet. Currently, two versions of IP addresses exist: IPv4 (Internet Protocol Version 4) and IPv6 (Internet Protocol Version 6). An IPv4 address has two parts that identify a specific computer: one part to identify the network where that computer resides and a second part to pinpoint the specific computer or host within that network. An IPv6 address has three parts: a global prefix to identify the network, a subnet to identify the location within the network, and the interface ID to identify the specific computer or host (Figure 2-34). Today, IPv4 addresses are more commonly used. For this reason, the terms IP address and IPv4 address are used interchangeably.

A typical IPv4 address — such as 72.14.207.99 — has four groups of numbers that range from 0 through 255. This form of the IP address sometimes is called a *dotted decimal number* or *dotted quad*. The four groups of numbers in the dotted quad are called octets, because they each have 8 bits when viewed in binary form for a total of 32 bits in the IP address. For instance, the binary form of 72.14.207.99 is 01001000.00001110.11001111.01100011. For more information about how the binary system works, see Appendix C.

Because each of the 8 bits can be 1 or 0, the total possible combinations per octet are 2^8, or 256. Combining the four octets of an IP address provides a possible 2^{32} or 4,294,967,296 unique values. The actual number of available addresses is about 3 billion, because some values are reserved for special use and are, therefore, off limits.

IP addresses, which are assigned by InterNIC (The Internet's Network Information Center), belong to one of three network classes: A, B, or C. In a Class A network, the first octet of the IPv4 address is assigned a number between 1 and 127. Large enterprises typically are assigned a Class A network, which can contain more than 16 million hosts; this allows network administrators to assign a value of their choice to the remaining three octets. Class B networks contain a number between 128 and 191 in the first octet. The second octet also is fixed, but the organization can assign values of its choice to the third and fourth octets. Class B networks have more than 65,000 hosts. Class C networks begin with a value between 192 and 223 and allow only the fourth octet to be customized. Class C networks can have only 254 hosts. Class D and E networks also exist, although they rarely are used.

To request data such as a Web page from a computer on the Internet, you need only an IP address. For instance, if you type the IPv4 address 72.14.207.99 in your Web browser's Address bar, the browser will display the home page on the machine hosting the Google Web site. Remembering an IP address is difficult at best — so you probably would just type the domain name, www.google.com, in the browser. The browser then contacts a domain name server (DNS) to resolve the human-readable domain name into a machine-readable IP address. Each domain name server houses a simple database that maps domain names to IP addresses. The DNS would resolve the human-readable domain name, www.google.com, into a machine-readable IP address, 72.14.207.99.

Domain names are helpful because they are easier for people to remember than IP addresses. You can learn more about a domain using the whois form at the Network Solutions Web site (www.netsol.com and then click the WHOIS link). If you type a domain name, such as google.com, the form displays the registration information for that domain, including its IP address.

Like all other computers, your computer must have an IP address to connect to the Internet or another computer that has an IP address. Servers generally have *static IP addresses*, because they usually are connected to the Internet and their IP addresses do not change often. When you connect to the Internet using your home computer, you most likely are using a temporary or *dynamic IP address*. Your access provider uses the *Dynamic Host Configuration Protocol (DHCP)* to assign your computer a temporary dynamic IP address from a pool of IP addresses. The dynamic IP address is unique only for that session. Once you disconnect, the DHCP server releases that IP address back in the IP address pool so that it can assign it to the next requesting computer. Even if you immediately reconnect, the DHCP server might not assign you the same IP address. Using DHCP and dynamic IP addresses means an Internet access provider needs only one IP address for each modem it supports, rather than one for each of its millions of customers.

Billions of IP addresses sounds like a lot. But, because so many computers and other devices connected to the Internet need unique IP addresses, a growing shortage of IP addresses exists. The newer IP addressing scheme is IPv6, also called IPng (IP Next Generation, which) will lengthen IP addresses from 32 bits to 128 bits and increase the number of available IP addresses to a whopping 3.4×10^{38}, or 340,000,000,000,000,000,000,000,000,000,000,000,000. Software is available that will install IPv6 on most current computers, although many networks and Internet service providers do not yet require its use. In fact, it could be many years before IPv6 completely replaces IPv4.

Do you want to know the IP address currently assigned to your computer? Click the Start button on the Windows taskbar and then click Control Panel. Click Network and Internet and then click View Network Status and Tasks. Finally, click View status and then click Details.

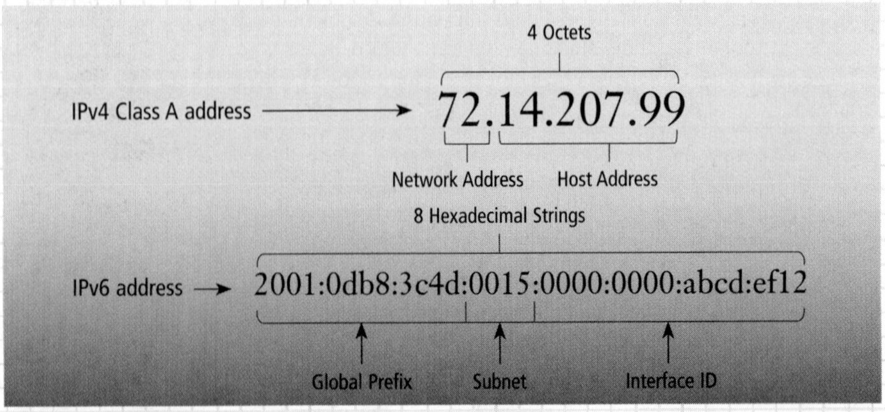

Figure 2-34 Components of IPv4 and IPv6 addresses.

For more information, visit the Computer Concepts CourseMate Web site at www.cengagebrain.com, navigate to the Chapter 2 High-Tech Talk resource for this book, and then click IP Addresses.

Companies on the Cutting Edge

GOOGLE Popular Search Engine and Services

Google founders Sergey Brin and Larry Page have done very little advertising, but their Web site has become a household word, largely on favorable word-of-mouth reviews. They launched the Web site in 1998 in a friend's garage with the goal of providing the best possible experience for their loyal users who are looking for information presented clearly and quickly.

Google regularly scans more than one trillion Web pages in search of unique phrases and terms. Its thousands of connected computers deliver organized search results for the hundreds of millions of queries users input daily. Recently, the company updated its Google Earth product to allow users to explore the Moon, and also updated its popular advertising product, AdWords. Among its other services are Google Docs and YouTube.

eBAY World's Largest Online Marketplace

Millions of products are traded daily on *eBay* auctions, whether it is across town or across the globe. The more than 88 million registered worldwide shoppers generate at least $1.8 billion in annual revenue through purchases on the main Web site, eBay, along with items on Shopping.com, tickets on StubHub, classifieds on Kijiji, and other e-commerce venues.

The shoppers likely pay for their merchandise using PayPal, another eBay service. This merchant service allows buyers to transfer money from savings accounts or use their credit card without having to expose the account number to the seller. Other eBay companies are Rent.com, which offers listings for apartments and houses, and Shopping.com, which allows consumers to find and compare products. Recently, eBay introduced a program to more easily identify its top-rated sellers. It also invited buyers and sellers to become members of the eBay Green Team, which encourages and promotes environmentally friendly business practices.

For more information, visit the Computer Concepts CourseMate Web site at www.cengagebrain.com and then navigate to the Chapter 2 Companies on the Cutting Edge resource for this book.

Technology Trailblazers

TIM BERNERS-LEE Creator of the World Wide Web

Being the creator of the World Wide Web is an impressive item on any resume, and it certainly helped *Tim Berners-Lee* become the 3Com Founders Professor of Engineering at the Massachusetts Institute of Technology in 2008. As a professor in the electrical engineering and computer science departments, he researches social and technical collaboration on the Internet.

Berners-Lee's interest in sharing information via Web servers, browsers, and Web addresses developed in 1989 while working at CERN, the European Organization for Nuclear Research, in Geneva, Switzerland. He continued to improve his design of a program that tracked random associations for several years and then became the director of the World Wide Web Consortium (W3C), a forum to develop Web standards, in 1994.

Recently, Queen Elizabeth bestowed the Order of Merit – the highest civilian honor – upon the British-born Berners-Lee.

MARK ZUCKERBERG Facebook Founder and CEO

As one of the youngest self-made billionaires in history, *Mark Zuckerberg* could have his choice of the finest things in life. Instead, he lives very modestly and walks to Facebook's Palo Alto headquarters.

Both Microsoft and AOL had recruited Zuckerberg during his senior year in high school in New Hampshire. He declined their job offers and decided to attend Harvard. In college, he and some friends developed several projects, laying the foundation that led to Facebook's eventual start. Harvard administrators claimed these Web sites violated students' privacy. He, however, had instant success launching Facebook from his dorm room, and the Web site's popularity quickly spread to other Ivy League and Boston-area colleges and then worldwide. He left his studies at Harvard University in 2004 and moved to California.

Today, Zuckerberg says he spends the majority of his time running the $15 billion company on very little sleep.

For more information, visit the Computer Concepts CourseMate Web site at www.cengagebrain.com and then navigate to the Chapter 2 Technology Trailblazers resource for this book.

Chapter Review

The Chapter Review reinforces the main concepts presented in this chapter.

To listen to an audio version of this Chapter Review, visit the Computer Concepts CourseMate Web site at www.cengagebrain.com and then navigate to the Chapter 2 Chapter Review resource for this book.

1. **How Did the Internet Evolve?** The **Internet**, also called the *Net*, is a worldwide collection of networks that links millions of businesses, government agencies, educational institutions, and individuals. The Internet has its roots in *ARPANET*, a network started in 1969 to link scientific and academic researchers across the United States. In 1986, the National Science Foundation connected its huge network, called *NSFnet*, to ARPANET, creating a configuration of complex networks and hosts that became known as the Internet. Today, more than 550 million *host* computers connect to the Internet.

2. **What Are the Various Types of Internet Connections, and What Are the Differences between Broadband and Dial-Up Connections?** Many home and small business users opt to connect to the Internet via high-speed *broadband* Internet connections. *DSL* (digital subscriber line) provides Internet connections using regular copper telephone lines. *Cable Internet service* provides high-speed Internet access through the cable television network via a cable modem. *Fiber to the Premises* (*FTTP*) uses fiber-optic cable to provide high-speed Internet access. *Fixed wireless* provides high-speed Internet connections using a dish-shaped antenna to communicate via radio signals. A *cellular radio network* offers high-speed Internet connections to devices with built-in compatible technology or computers with wireless modems. A **Wi-Fi** network uses radio signals. *Satellite Internet service* provides high-speed Internet connections via satellite. Some homes and small businesses connect to the Internet with dial-up access. *Dial-up access*, which is slower-speed technology, takes place when the modem in your computer connects to the Internet via a standard telephone line that transmits data and information using an analog (continuous wave) pattern.

3. **What Are the Types of Internet Access Providers?** An **access provider** is a business that provides access to the Internet free or for a fee. An **ISP** (**Internet service provider**) is a regional or national access provider. An **online service provider** (**OSP**) provides Internet access in addition to members-only features. A **wireless Internet service provider** provides wireless Internet access to desktop and notebook computers and mobile devices with built-in wireless capabilities (such as Wi-Fi) or to computers using wireless modems or wireless access devices.

4. **What Is the Purpose of an IP Address, and What Is Its Relationship to a Domain Name?** An **IP address** (Internet Protocol address) is a number that uniquely identifies each computer or device connected to the Internet. The Internet relies on IP addresses to send data to computers at specific locations. The IP address usually consists of four groups of numbers, each separated by a period. A **domain name** is the text version of an IP address.

Visit the Computer Concepts CourseMate Web site at www.cengagebrain.com, navigate to the Chapter 2 Quiz Yourself resource for this book, and then click Objectives 1 – 4.

5. **What Is the Purpose of a Web Browser, and What Are the Components of a Web Address?** A **Web browser**, or **browser**, is application software that allows users to access and view Web pages or access Web 2.0 programs. With an Internet connection established, you start a Web browser, which then retrieves and displays a starting Web page, sometimes called a **home page**. The home page usually contains links to other Web pages. A **link**, short for *hyperlink*, is a built-in connection to another related Web page or part of a Web page. A **Web page** has a unique address called a **URL** (*Uniform Resource Locator*), or **Web address**. A Web address consists of a protocol, a domain name, and sometimes the path to a specific Web page or location on a Web page.

6. **How Do You Use a Search Engine to Search for Information on the Web, and What Is the Difference between a Search Engine and a Subject Directory?** A **search engine** is a program that finds Web sites, Web pages, images, videos, news, maps, and other information related to a specific topic. To use a search engine, you enter a word or phrase, called **search text** or a *search query*, that describes the item you want to find. Each word in the search text is known as a *keyword*. The search engine displays a list of *hits*. When clicked, each hit displays an associated Web site or Web page. A **subject directory** classifies Web pages in an organized set of categories and related subcategories. By clicking links, you move through levels to display a list of Web pages about a desired topic.

Chapter Review

7. **What Are the Types of Web Sites?** A **portal** is a Web site that offers a variety of Internet services from a single location. A news Web site contains newsworthy material. An informational Web site contains factual information. A business/marketing Web site promotes or sells products or services. A **blog**, short for *Weblog*, is an informal Web site consisting of time-stamped articles, or posts, in a diary or journal format, usually listed in reverse chronological order. A **wiki** is a collaborative Web site that allows users to create, add to, modify, or delete the Web site content via their Web browser. An **online social network**, or **social networking Web site**, encourages members to share their interests, ideas, stories, photos, music, and videos with other registered users. An educational Web site offers avenues for teaching and learning. An entertainment Web site provides an interactive and engaging environment. An advocacy Web site describes a cause, opinion, or idea. A **Web application**, or *Web app*, is a Web site that allows users to access and interact with software through a Web browser or any computer or device connected to the Internet. A *content aggregator* is a business that gathers and organizes Web content and then distributes, or feeds, the content to subscribers for free or a fee. A personal Web site is maintained by a private individual or family.

8. **How Do Web Pages Use Graphics, Animation, Audio, Video, Virtual Reality, and Plug-Ins?** Some Web pages use **multimedia**, which combines text with graphics, animation, audio, video, and/or virtual reality. A **graphic** is a digital representation of nontext information such as a drawing, chart, or photo. **Animation** is the appearance of motion created by displaying a series of still images in sequence. **Audio** includes music, speech, or any other sound. **Video** consists of full-motion images played back at various speeds. **Virtual reality** (**VR**) is the use of computers to simulate an environment that appears as three-dimensional space. A **plug-in**, or *add-on*, is a program that extends a browser's capability to display multimedia elements.

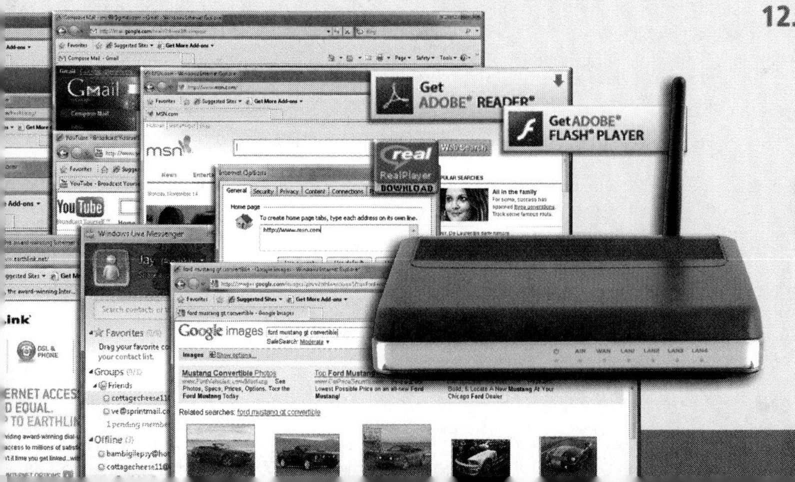

9. **What Are the Steps Required for Web Publishing?** **Web publishing** is the development and maintenance of Web pages. The five major steps to Web publishing are: (1) plan a Web site, (2) analyze and design a Web site, (3) create a Web site, (4) deploy a Web site, and (5) maintain a Web site.

Visit the Computer Concepts CourseMate Web site at www.cengagebrain.com, navigate to the Chapter 2 Quiz Yourself resource for this book, and then click Objectives 5 – 9.

10. **What Are the Types of E-Commerce?** **E-commerce**, short for *electronic commerce*, is a business transaction that occurs over an electronic network such as the Internet. *Business-to-consumer (B2C) e-commerce* consists of the sale of goods and services to the general public. *Consumer-to-consumer (C2C) e-commerce* occurs when one consumer sells directly to another, such as in an **online auction**. *Business-to-business (B2B) e-commerce* takes place between businesses that exchange goods and services.

11. **How Do E-Mail, Mailing Lists, Instant Messaging, Chat Rooms, VoIP, Newsgroups and Message Boards, and FTP Work?** **E-mail** (short for *electronic mail*) is the transmission of messages and files via a computer network. A **mailing list** is a group of e-mail names and addresses given a single name, so that everyone on the list receives a message sent to the list. **Instant messaging** (**IM**) is a **real-time** Internet communications service that notifies you when one or more people are online. A **chat room** is a location on an Internet server that permits users to conduct real-time typed conversations. **VoIP** (*Voice over IP*, or Internet Protocol), also called *Internet telephony*, enables users to speak to other users over the Internet, instead of the public switched telephone network. A **newsgroup** is an online area in which users have written discussions about a particular subject. A **message board** is a Web-based type of discussion group that is easier to use than a newsgroup. **FTP** (*File Transfer Protocol*) is an Internet standard that permits file **uploading** and **downloading** with other computers on the Internet.

12. **What Are the Rules of Netiquette?** **Netiquette**, which is short for Internet etiquette, is the code of acceptable behaviors users should follow while on the Internet. Netiquette rules include: keep messages short, be polite, avoid sending *flames* or *spam*, use **emoticons** and acronyms, clearly identify a *spoiler*, read the *FAQ*, do not assume material is accurate or up-to-date, and never read someone's private e-mail.

Visit the Computer Concepts CourseMate Web site at www.cengagebrain.com, navigate to the Chapter 2 Quiz Yourself resource for this book, and then click Objectives 10 – 12.

Key Terms

You should know the Primary Terms and be familiar with the Secondary Terms. The list below helps focus your study.

To see an example of and a definition for each term, and to access current and additional information from the Web, visit the Computer Concepts CourseMate Web site at www.cengagebrain.com and then navigate to the Chapter 2 Key Terms resource for this book.

Primary Terms

(shown in bold-black characters in the chapter)

access provider (77)
address book (102)
animation (94)
audio (94)
blog (90)
browser (81)
chat (105)
chat room (105)
DNS server (80)
domain name (79)
downloading (82)
e-commerce (98)
electronic storefront (99)
e-mail (101)
e-mail address (102)
e-mail program (101)
emoticons (108)
FTP (107)
graphic (93)
home page (82)
instant messaging (IM) (104)
Internet (74)
IP address (79)
ISP (Internet service provider) (78)
link (82)
mailing list (103)
media sharing Web site (91)
message board (107)
microblog (90)
MP3 (94)
multimedia (92)
netiquette (108)
newsgroup (107)
online auction (100)
online community (89)
online service provider (OSP) (78)
online social network (90)
player (94)
plug-in (97)
portal (89)
real time (104)
RSS 2.0 (92)
search engine (85)
search text (85)
shopping cart (99)
social networking Web site (90)
streaming (94)
subject directory (85)
subscribe (103)
surfing the Web (83)
tabbed browsing (84)
traffic (76)
unsubscribe (103)
uploading (107)
URL (82)
user name (102)
video (96)
video blog (90)
virtual reality (VR) (96)
VoIP (106)
Web (80)
Web 2.0 (81)
Web address (82)
Web application (91)
Web browser (81)
Web page (80)
Web publishing (98)
Web server (81)
Web site (81)
Wi-Fi (76)
wiki (90)
wireless Internet service provider (78)
World Wide Web (80)

blog (90)

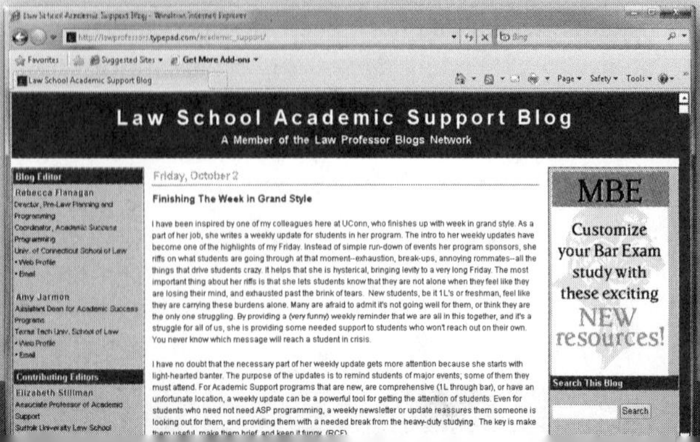

Secondary Terms

(shown in italic characters in the chapter)

add-on (97)
animated GIF (94)
anonymous FTP (107)
ARPA (75)
ARPANET (75)
Atom (92)
blogger (90)
blogosphere (90)
bookmark (83)
broadband (76)
buddies (104)
business-to-business (B2B) e-commerce (100)
business-to-consumer (B2C) e-commerce (98)
cable Internet service (76)
ccTLD (80)
cellular radio network (76)
chat client (105)
click (84)
consumer-to-consumer (C2C) e-commerce (100)
content aggregator (92)
dial-up access (76)
domain name system (DNS) (80)
DSL (76)
dynamic Web page (81)
electronic commerce (98)
electronic mail (101)
e-retail (99)
FAQ (108)
favorite (83)
Fiber to the Premises (FTTP) (76)
file (77)
fixed wireless (76)
flame wars (108)
flames (108)
FTP server (107)
GIF (93)
graphical image (93)
gTLD (80)
hits (86)
host (75)
hot spots (76)
http (82)
hyperlink (82)
hypermedia (83)
hypertext (83)
Hypertext Transfer Protocol (82)
ICANN (80)
instant messenger (105)
Internet backbone (78)
Internet telephony (106)
IPv6 (80)
JPEG (93)
keyword (85)
m-commerce (98)
microbrowser (82)
MP4 (96)
MPEG (96)
MPEG-4 (96)
national ISP (78)
Net (74)
newsreader (107)
NSFnet (75)
PNG (93)
podcast (94)
POP3 (103)
Post Office Protocol (103)
pull (83)
push (83)
Really Simple Syndication (92)
regional ISP (78)
registrar (80)
satellite Internet service (76)
search query (85)
SMTP (103)
spam (108)
spider (88)
spoiler (108)
static Web page (81)
streaming audio (94)
streaming video (96)
thread (107)
threaded discussion (107)
thumbnail (94)
top-level domain (TLD) (80)
Uniform Resource Locator (82)
vlog (90)
vlogger (90)
vlogosphere (90)
Voice over IP (106)
VR world (96)
W3C (76)
Web app (91)
Weblog (90)
WebSlices (92)
wireless portal (89)
WWW (80)

Checkpoint

The Checkpoint exercises test your knowledge of the chapter concepts. The page number containing the answer appears in parentheses after each exercise. The Beyond the Book exercises will help broaden your understanding of the concepts presented in this chapter.

To complete the Checkpoint exercises interactively, visit the Computer Concepts CourseMate Web site at www.cengagebrain.com and then navigate to the Chapter 2 Checkpoint resource for this book.

True/False

Mark T for True and F for False.

_____ 1. A single government agency owns and controls the Internet. (76)

_____ 2. DSL provides high-speed Internet connections through the cable television network. (76)

_____ 3. In general, the first portion of each IP address identifies the network and the last portion identifies the specific computer. (79)

_____ 4. A Web 2.0 Web site can never allow users to modify Web site content. (81)

_____ 5. A Web page has a unique address, called a URL or Web address. (82)

_____ 6. Hypertext combines text-based links with graphic, audio, and video links. (83)

_____ 7. The major disadvantage with a subject directory is that users have difficulty deciding which categories to choose as they work through the menus of links presented. (88)

_____ 8. Most social networking Web sites include chat rooms, newsgroups, and other communications services. (90)

_____ 9. Streaming disallows users from accessing and using a file while it is transmitting. (94)

_____ 10. A plug-in is a program that extends the capability of an add-on. (97)

_____ 11. Most e-commerce actually takes place between consumers, which is called consumer-to-consumer e-commerce. (100)

_____ 12. Flames are abusive or insulting messages. (108)

Multiple Choice

Select the best answer.

1. _____ offers high-speed Internet connections to devices with built-in compatible technology or computers with wireless modems. (76)
   a. Cable Internet service
   b. A digital subscriber line
   c. A cellular radio network
   d. Fiber to the Premises (FTTP)

2. As with an IP address, the components of a domain name are separated by _____. (79)
   a. commas
   b. periods
   c. colons
   d. semicolons

3. _____ combines text-based links with graphic, audio, and video links. (83)
   a. Hypertext
   b. Multi-linking
   c. Hypermedia
   d. Tabbed browsing

4. All of the following techniques can be used to improve Web searches except _____. (88)
   a. put the most important terms last
   b. read a search engine's Help information
   c. list all possible spellings
   d. if a search is unsuccessful, try another search engine

5. A _____ is a Web site that allows users to post short text updates, usually between 100 and 200 characters. (90)
   a. microblog
   b. wiki
   c. portal
   d. podcast

6. A(n) _____ is a small version of a larger graphic. (94)
   a. thumbnail
   b. MP3
   c. wiki
   d. portal

7. _____ is the process of transferring documents, graphics, and other objects from your computer to a server on the Internet. (107)
   a. Downloading
   b. Social networking
   c. Uploading
   d. Blogging

8. _____ is the code of acceptable behaviors users should follow while on the Internet. (108)
   a. Post Office Protocol
   b. The Golden Rule
   c. Netiquette
   d. An FAQ

Checkpoint

Matching

Match the terms with their definitions.

____ 1. gTLD (80)
____ 2. ccTLD (80)
____ 3. DNS Server (80)
____ 4. IPv6 (80)
____ 5. link (82)
____ 6. search engine (85)
____ 7. MP3 (94)
____ 8. player (94)
____ 9. video (96)
____ 10. VoIP (106)

a. built-in connection to another related Web page or part of a Web page
b. a two-letter country code for international Web sites outside the United States
c. enables users to speak to other users over the Internet
d. format that reduces an audio file to about one-tenth its original size
e. new IP addressing scheme that may increase the number of available IP addresses
f. translates the domain name to its associated IP address
g. software used to listen to an audio file on a computer
h. identifies the type of organization associated with a domain
i. program that finds Web sites, Web pages, images, videos, news, maps, and other information related to a specific topic
j. full-motion images that are played back at various speeds

Short Answer

Write a brief answer to each of the following questions.

1. Describe three different types of broadband Internet services. __________ What is the difference between a regional ISP and a national ISP? __________
2. How is a static Web page different from a dynamic Web page? __________ What is a Web site? __________
3. What is a Web application? __________What are some features and examples of Web applications? __________
4. What are three types of specifications used by content aggregators to distribute content? __________ How might you evaluate the accuracy of a Web site? __________
5. What is Web publishing? __________ What are the five major steps in Web publishing? __________

Beyond the Book

Follow the book element instructions below; then present your findings (brief report, presentation, discussion, or other means).

1. Ethics & Issues — Select an Ethics & Issues in this chapter (84, 87, 90, 100, 108), find a recent newspaper/magazine article that supports one point of view presented, and then evaluate the article.
2. Computer Usage @ Work — Use the Web or a recent newspaper/magazine to locate three additional unique usages of computer technology in the entertainment industry (109). What makes the use of these technologies unique to the entertainment industry?
3. Companies on the Cutting Edge and Technology Trailblazers — Use the Web or a recent business newspaper/magazine to locate an interesting fact about Google, eBay, Tim Berners-Lee, or Mark Zuckerberg that was not presented in the chapter (111).
4. High-Tech Talk — Locate a recent newspaper/magazine article that discusses topics related to A Computer's Internet Protocol (IP) Address (110). Would you recommend the article you found? Why or why not?
5. FAQs and Web Links — Use the Web or a recent newspaper/magazine to locate three additional facts about an FAQ (77, 78, 82, 88, 96, 99, 103, 105) and Web Link (76, 78, 82, 84, 96, 98, 100, 103, 105, 107, 108) that were not presented in the chapter.
6. Looking Ahead — Use the Web or a recent newspaper/magazine to discover additional uses of the technology presented in Web 3.0 to Reinvent the Virtual World (81).
7. Innovative Computing — Use the Web or a recent newspaper/magazine to locate two additional interesting facts about View the Wonders of Space through the WorldWide Telescope (93) and Shopping Becomes a Virtual Experience (100).
8. Making Use of the Web — Visit three of the Research Web Sites (126) and outline the information on each Web site and the possible uses for each Web site.

Learn It Online

The Learn It Online exercises are interactive Web exercises designed to reinforce and expand your understanding of the chapter concepts. The descriptions below briefly summarize each exercise.

To complete the Learn It Online exercises, visit the Computer Concepts CourseMate Web site at www.cengagebrain.com, navigate to the Chapter 2 resources for this book, click the link for the exercise you want to complete, and then read the instructions.

1 At the Movies — Tell Your Stories via Vlog
Watch a movie to learn about how to post your thoughts to a vlog and then answer questions about the movie.

2 Video and Audio: You Review It — VoIP
Search for, choose, and write a review of a video, podcast, or vodcast that discusses Voice over IP.

3 Student Edition Labs — Connecting to the Internet, Getting the Most out of the Internet, and E-mail
Enhance your understanding and knowledge about the Internet and e-mail by completing the Connecting to the Internet, Getting the Most out of the Internet, and E-mail Labs.

4 Practice Test
Take a multiple choice test that checks your knowledge of the chapter concepts and review the resulting study guide.

5 Who Wants To Be a Computer Genius^2?
Play the Shelly Cashman Series version of this popular game by answering questions to find out if you are a computer genius. Panic buttons are available to provide assistance during game play.

6 Wheel of Terms
Identify important key terms presented in this chapter by playing the Shelly Cashman Series version of this popular game.

7 You're Hired!
Embark on the path to a career in computers by answering questions and solving puzzles related to concepts discussed in this chapter.

8 Crossword Puzzle Challenge
Complete an interactive crossword puzzle to reinforce concepts presented in this chapter.

9 Windows Exercises
Step through the Windows 7 exercises to learn about Internet properties, dial-up networking connections, and using Help to understand the Internet.

10 Exploring Computer Careers
Read about a career as a Web developer, search for related employment advertisements, and then answer related questions.

11 Web Apps — Windows Live Hotmail
Learn how to sign up for a free e-mail account, add a contact to your address book, and send an e-mail message.

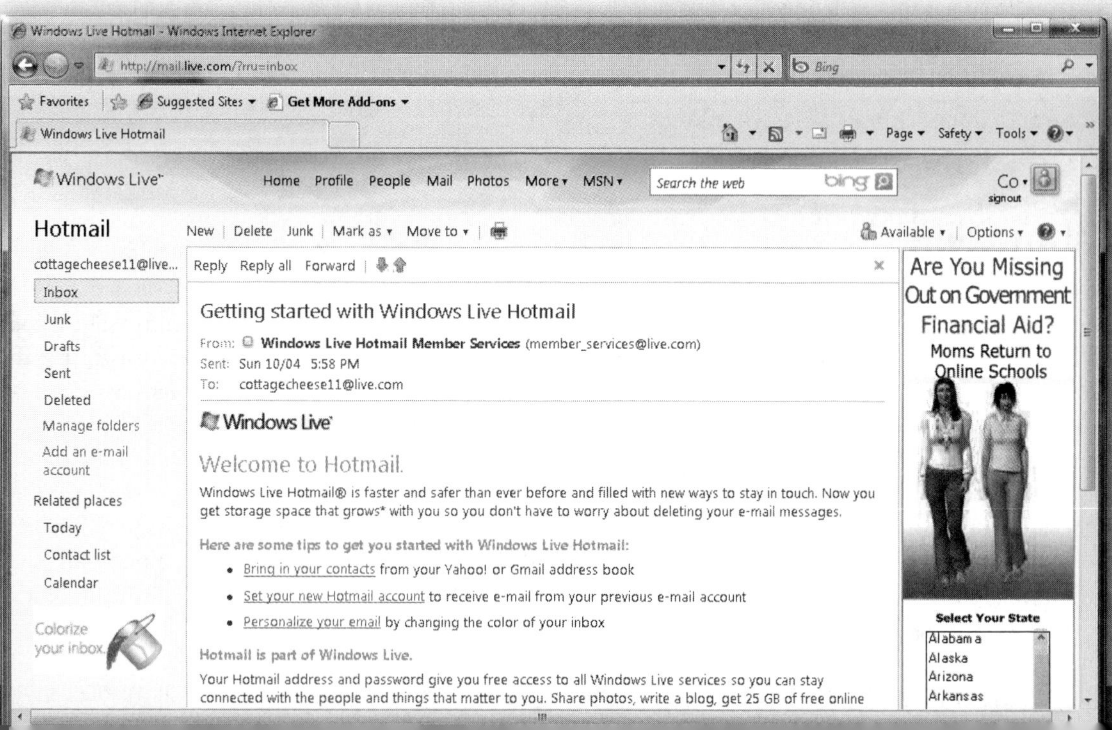

Problem Solving @ Home

The Problem Solving @ Home exercises extend your knowledge of the chapter concepts by seeking solutions to practical computer problems that you may encounter at home or school. The Collaboration exercise should be completed with a team.

In the real world, practical problems often can be solved in multiple ways. Provide one solution to each of the following problems using available resources, such as articles on the Web or in print, blogs, podcasts, videos, television, user guides, other individuals, and electronics and computer stores. You may need to use multiple resources to obtain an answer. Present your solutions in the form requested by your instructor (brief report, presentation, discussion, or other means).

1. **Page Not Displayed** When you type the Web address of your favorite news Web site in the Address bar of the Web browser, you immediately see an error message stating that the Web page cannot be displayed. You did not have problems accessing the Internet yesterday. Before calling technical support, how will you attempt to troubleshoot the problem?

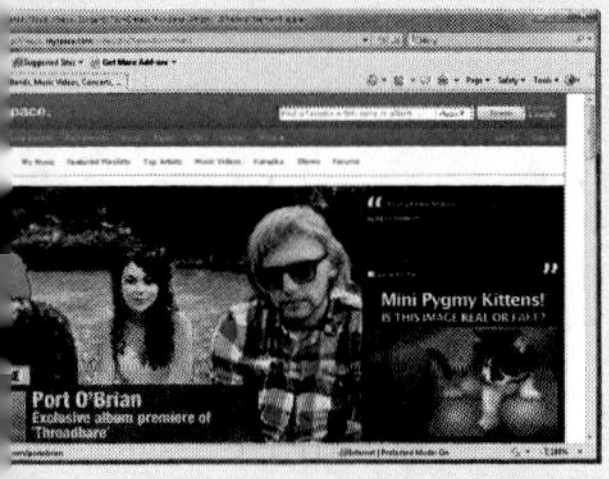

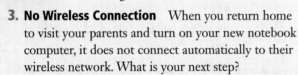

2. **Slow Internet Connection** You just installed VoIP telephone service in your house. Each time you are on the telephone, however, you notice that your Internet connection slows down significantly. What could be causing this?
3. **No Wireless Connection** When you return home to visit your parents and turn on your new notebook computer, it does not connect automatically to their wireless network. What is your next step?
4. **Eliminating Pop-Ups** Each time you attempt to visit a Web site, many pop-up windows open on your computer. In fact, you sometimes close up to 10 windows that automatically appear. You used to browse the Web without this nuisance, but it is worsening by the day. What steps will you take to eliminate these pop-up windows?
5. **Incorrect Home Page** After starting your Web browser, you notice that your home page has changed. You display the Internet Options dialog box to change your home page back to its previous setting, close your browser, and then start the browser again. Surprisingly, your Web browser still navigates to a Web site other than the one you chose. What is your next step?
6. **Images Not Being Displayed** When you navigate to a Web page, you notice that no images are displaying. You successfully have viewed Web pages with images in the past and are not sure why images suddenly are not displayed. What steps will you take to view the images?
7. **Incorrect Search Engine** A class project requires that you conduct research on the Web. After typing the Web address for Google's home page and pressing the ENTER key, your Web browser redirects you to a different search engine. What could be wrong?
8. **Unsolicited Friend Requests** You recently signed up for an account on the MySpace social networking Web site. When you log in periodically, you find that people you do not know are requesting to be your friend. How should you respond?
9. **New Browser Windows** While browsing the Web, each time you click a link, the link's destination opens in a new browser window. You prefer to have each link open in a new tab so that your taskbar does not become cluttered. How will you resolve this?

Collaboration

10. **Finding Trustworthy Sources** Your history professor asked all of the students in her class to write a five-page paper about the Boston Tea Party. Instead of using books, you decide to find all of the relevant information you need on the Internet. After reading this chapter, you realize that not all Internet sources may be trustworthy, and that you must search the Internet for accurate Web sites. Form a team of three people and use various search engines to search for Web sites that discuss the Boston Tea Party. One team member should use the Google search engine, one team member should use the Yahoo! search engine, and one team member should use the Bing search engine. Which search engine displayed the most results overall? Which search engine returned the most relevant, trustworthy results? What search text did everyone use to narrow the search results to the most relevant Web sites? Did any of the search engines recommend alternate search text that might help to find relevant information?

Problem Solving @ Work

The Problem Solving @ Work exercises extend your knowledge of the chapter concepts by seeking solutions to practical computer problems that you may encounter at work. The Collaboration exercise should be completed with a team.

In the real world, practical problems often can be solved in multiple ways. Provide one solution to each of the following problems using available resources, such as articles on the Web or in print, blogs, podcasts, videos, television, user guides, other individuals, and electronics and computer stores. You may need to use multiple resources to obtain an answer. Present your solutions in the form requested by your instructor (brief report, presentation, discussion, or other means).

1. **Plug-In Required** Upon viewing a Web page, a message appears stating that you do not have the proper plug-in required to view the page's multimedia content. What is your next step?
2. **Blocked Instant Messenger** Today, you started a new job. After setting up your new computer, you download your favorite IM (instant messaging) program successfully and without issue. After attempting to enter your user name and password, however, the program does not connect to the IM service. You are certain that your user name and password are correct, so what else might be causing this?
3. **Access Denied** During your lunch hour, you decide to search the Web for possible vacation destinations. After visiting several airline and hotel Web sites, you attempt to visit the Web site for a Caribbean resort. Much to your surprise, the Web browser informs you that the Web site has been blocked. Why might this happen?
4. **Sporadic E-Mail Message Delivery** The e-mail program on your computer has been delivering new messages only every hour, on the hour. Historically, new e-mail messages would arrive and be displayed immediately upon being sent by the sender. Furthermore, your coworkers claim that they sometimes do not receive your e-mail messages until hours after they are sent. What might be the problem?
5. **E-Mail Message Formatting** A friend sent an e-mail message containing a photo to your e-mail account at work. Upon receiving the e-mail message, the photo does not display. You also notice that e-mail messages never display any formatting, such as different fonts, font sizes, and font colors. What might be causing this?
6. **Automatic Response** When you return from vacation, a colleague informs you that when she sent e-mail messages to your e-mail address, she would not always receive your automatic response stating that you were out of the office. Why might your e-mail program not respond automatically to every e-mail message received?
7. **Suspicious Web Site Visits** The director of your company's Information Technology department has sent you an e-mail message stating that you have been spending an excessive amount of time viewing Web sites not related to your job. You periodically visit Web sites not related to work, but only on breaks, which the company allows. How does he know your Web browsing habits? How will you respond to this claim?

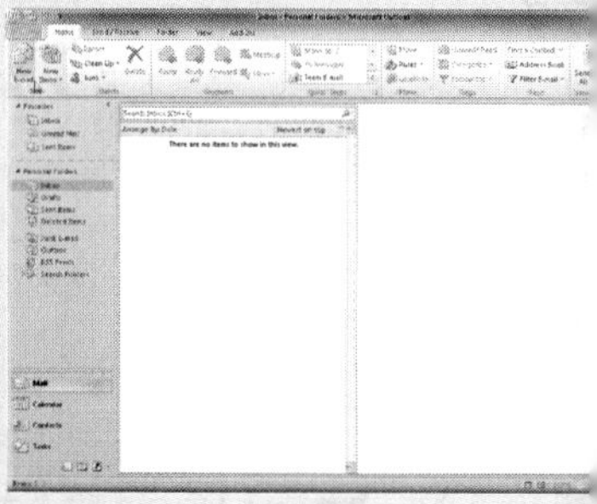

8. **Wrong Web Site** When attempting to visit your friend's Web site from your office computer, another Web site displays in its place. What might be wrong? What steps can you take so that you can visit his Web site?

Collaboration

9. **Computers in Entertainment** The drama department at a local high school is considering developing a movie and has asked for your help. The drama teacher would like to incorporate technology wherever possible, in hopes that it would decrease the costs of the movie's production. Form a team of three people to help determine what technology can be used to assist in the movie's production. One team member should research the type of technology that can be used during the filming process. Another team member should research the types of hardware and software available for editing footage, and the third team member should research the hardware and software requirements for creating the media to distribute the finished product.

STUDENT ASSIGNMENTS

Learn How To

The Learn How To activities step you through fundamental technology skills when using a computer. The Learn How To exercises enable you to become more proficient with these skills.

Premium Activity: To relate this Learn How To activity to your everyday life, see a visual demonstration of the activity, and complete a short assessment, visit the Computer Concepts CourseMate Web site at www.cengagebrain.com and then navigate to the Chapter 2 Learn How To resource for this book.

Learn How To 1: Attach a File to an E-Mail Message

When you send an e-mail message, it sometimes is necessary to attach a file to supplement the body of the e-mail message. Most e-mail programs allow you to attach a file to your e-mail messages easily, but many do not allow you to attach files exceeding a specified size limit (which varies by your e-mail service). You can attach a file to an e-mail message by completing the following steps:

1. Start your e-mail program and compose a new e-mail message to your recipient. Make sure that you have a descriptive subject and that you explain in the e-mail message that you are attaching a file.
2. To attach a file, locate and click the Attach File button or link. If you are unable to locate this button, you may find an icon with a picture of a paperclip or a menu command to attach a file. Some e-mail programs also may have a text box in the new message window with an adjacent Browse button. In this case, click the Browse button.
3. Locate and click the file you wish to attach and then click the Open (or Insert or Select) button (Figure 2-35).
4. Verify that your e-mail message contains the attachment and then click the Send button.

When the recipient opens the e-mail message, he or she also will be able to open the attachment.

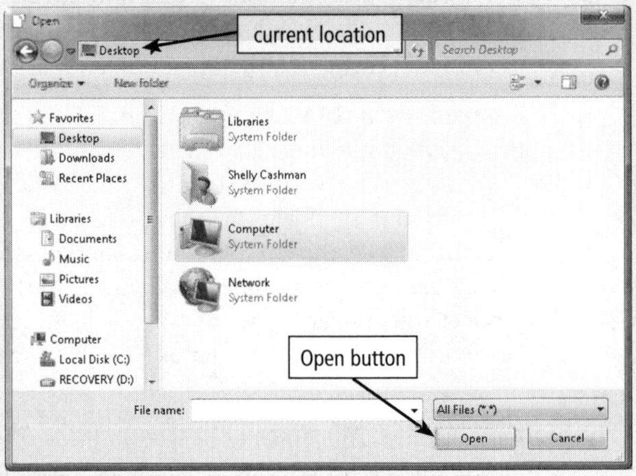

Figure 2-35

Exercises

1. Start your e-mail program. Compose a new e-mail message to your instructor, and attach a file containing your current course schedule. Verify that your message has been received and then close your e-mail program.
2. Locate three free e-mail Web applications. How many file attachments do these e-mail programs allow you to attach to one e-mail message? Is a maximum file size specified for an e-mail attachment? Can you pay to upgrade your e-mail account so that these restrictions are lifted? Submit these answers to your instructor.

Learn How To 2: Search the Web for Driving Directions, Addresses, and Telephone Numbers

In addition to searching the Web for information using search engines such as Google and Yahoo!, some Web sites are designed specifically to search for other information such as driving directions, addresses, and telephone numbers.

Search for Driving Directions

1. Start your Web browser, type `mapquest.com` in the Address bar, press the ENTER key to display the MapQuest home page, and then click the Directions tab.
2. Type the starting address (or intersection), city, state, and ZIP code (if you know it) in the appropriate text boxes in the Starting Location area of the Directions page.
3. Type the ending address (or intersection), city, state, and ZIP code (if you know it) in the appropriate text boxes in the Ending Location area of the Directions page.
4. Click the Get Directions button to display the driving directions.

Search for the Address and Telephone Number of a Business

1. If necessary, start your Web browser. Type `yellowpages.com` in the Address bar, and then press the ENTER key to display the Yellow Pages Local Directory home page.
2. Type the name of the business in the Find text box, and type the city, state, and ZIP (if you know it) in the Location text box.
3. Click the FIND button to display the search results.
4. Close your Web browser.

Learn How To

Exercises

1. If necessary, start Internet Explorer by clicking the Start button, and then click Internet Explorer on the Start menu. Type `mapquest.com` in the Address bar, and then press the ENTER key. Search for driving directions between your address and the address of a friend or family member. How many miles are between the two addresses? How long would it take you to drive from your address to the other address? Write a paragraph explaining whether you would or would not use MapQuest to retrieve driving directions. Submit this paragraph to your instructor.
2. Use the Web to search for another Web site that provides driving directions. Use the Web site to search for directions between the same two locations from Exercise 1. Are the driving directions the same as the ones that MapQuest provided? If not, why might they be different? Which Web site did you use? Do you prefer this Web site to MapQuest? Why or why not? Write a paragraph with your answers and submit it to your instructor.
3. Think about a company for which you would like to work. In your Web browser, display the Yellow Pages Web page (yellowpages.com) and then search for the address and telephone number of this company. If Yellow Pages does not display the desired information, what other Web sites might you be able to use to search for the address and telephone number for a company?

Learn How To 3: Publish Your Resume on the Web

Publishing your resume on the Web is a great way to distribute your resume to multiple people. To publish your resume on the Web, complete the following steps:

1. Using Microsoft Word, create a new resume or open an existing resume that you wish to publish on the Web. When you have finished creating the resume, click the Office Button and then click Save As on the menu.
2. Click the Desktop button in the Save As dialog box, type `resume` in the File name text box, click Web page in the 'Save as type' list, and then click the Save button.
3. Quit Microsoft Word.
4. Start your Web browser and then type `50Webs.com` in the Address bar. When the Web page is displayed, click one of the SIGN UP buttons (Figure 2-36).
5. Select the free Web hosting plan, click the 'Use a subdomain' option button, and then click the NEXT button.
6. Type the required information to sign up for the free plan. Make note of the subdomain you choose for your Web site. For example, if you type resume as your subdomain, your Web site address will be http://resume.50webs.com.
7. Click the check box to agree to the Terms and Conditions, and then click the Signup button. 50Webs will send your user name and password to the e-mail address you specified while signing up.
8. Click the Start button and then click Computer on the Start menu. In the Address bar, type `ftp://subdomain.50webs.com` (where subdomain should be replaced with the name of the subdomain you chose in Step 6). Type your user name and password in the Log On As dialog box, and then click the Log On button.
9. Double-click your Web site folder, and then drag your resume file from the desktop to the window containing your Web site files. If a resume_files folder exists on your desktop, you also should drag that folder to the window containing your Web site files.
10. In your Web browser, type `http://subdomain.50webs.com/resume.htm` (subdomain should be replaced with your chosen subdomain from Step 6).

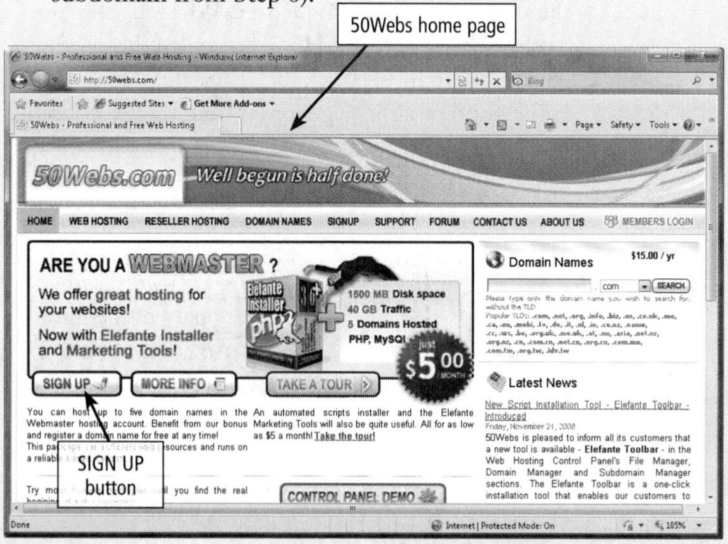

Figure 2-36

Exercise

1. Use Microsoft Word to create a Web page that you would like others to see when they visit your new Web site. Include your name, e-mail address, and any other information that you would not object to making public. Save the file as a Web page using the file name, index.htm. Upload the file to the 50Webs.com Web server and then send the Web page address to your instructor.

Web Research

The Web Research exercises broaden your understanding of the chapter concepts by presenting questions that require you to search the Web for answers.

1 Search Sleuth

Use one of the search engines listed in Figure 2-10 in Chapter 2 on page 85 or your own favorite search engine to find the answers to the following questions. Copy and paste the Web address from the Web page where you found the answer. Some questions may have more than one answer. If required, submit your answers to your instructor. (1) What were the title, date of publication, and purpose of the Internet Engineering Task Force's RFC 1 document? (2) What is the mission of the World Wide Web Consortium (W3C)? (3) What topic does the film *Adina's Deck* address? (4) What are the current figures on the Reporters Without Borders' Press Freedom Barometer? (5) What was eBay's original name, and what was the first item offered for auction? (6) Why did ConnectU sue Facebook in 2008 and 2004? (7) What is the cost to use Google's 411 service?

2 Green Computing

EcoSearch is a search engine dedicated to supporting the Earth's natural resources. Visit this Web site (ecosearch.org), use your word processing program to answer the following questions, and then, if required, submit your answers to your instructor. (1) From what company do the search results come? (2) Click the Learn More link on the page. What charities does EcoSearch support? (3) How can you get involved to help EcoSearch? (4) Click the EcoSearch Home link at the bottom of the page to return to the EcoSearch home page. In the text box, type `ecosearch donate profits` and then click the Search button. Click several of the resulting links and review the information. Write a 50-word summary of the information, including what percent of EcoSearch proceeds is donated to charities and how much money EcoSearch expects to donate each year.

3 Social Networking

MySpace is considered one of the pioneering Web sites that helped popularize the online social networking phenomenon. Calling itself "a place for friends," it allows the millions of registered members to create profiles for free and then invite friends to join their networks. The growth of this Web site has helped it emerge as one of the more popular search engines. Visit the MySpace site (myspace.com), type the name of your favorite musical artist or group in the search text box, and then click the Search button. How many search results were found? Visit some of these profiles. Which music videos, playlists, and ringtones are featured? How do you create and edit your own playlists and add a song to your profile? Then click the Safety Tips link at the bottom of the page and read the guidelines for posting information and reporting inappropriate content. Summarize the music profiles you viewed and the guidelines. If required, submit your summary to your instructor.

4 Blogs

Many of the best blogs in the blogosphere have received awards for their content and design. For example, loyal blogging fans nominate and vote for their favorite blogs by visiting the Blogger's Choice Awards Web site (bloggerschoiceawards.com). Visit this Web site, click the Best Blog Design, Best Blog About Blogging, and Best Education Blog links, and view some of the blogs receiving the largest number of votes. Then visit other award sites, including the Interactive Media Awards (interactivemediaawards .com), Bloggies (bloggies.com), and the Best of Blogs (thebestofblogs.com). Which blogs, if any, received multiple awards on the different Web sites? Who casts the votes? What criteria are used to judge these blogs?

5 Ethics in Action

Some Internet access providers have admitted they monitored their users' Web surfing activities without giving notice of this eavesdropping practice. Embarq and Charter Communications secretly tested advertising technology to gather data about specific Web searches and then display advertisements relating to these searches. Privacy experts claim these Internet access providers' practices violate federal privacy laws, including the wiretapping statute. Locate news articles discussing the Internet access providers' Web eavesdropping. Then locate Web sites that oppose this practice. Summarize the views of the advertisers and the privacy proponents. If required, submit your summary to your instructor.

Critical Thinking

The Critical Thinking exercises challenge your assessment and decision-making skills by presenting real-world situations associated with the chapter concepts. The Collaboration exercise should be completed with a team.

To evaluate the situations below, use personal experiences and available resources such as articles on the Web or in print, blogs, podcasts, videos, television, user guides, other individuals, and electronics and computer stores. You may need to use multiple resources to form conclusions and make recommendations.

1. **Class Discussion — Browser Comparison**
Although Internet Explorer may be the most widely used Web browser, it is not the only Web browser in use. Evaluate and compare reviews of other Web browsers such as Google Chrome, Safari, or Firefox with Internet Explorer. Discuss the major differences between the browsers you researched and Internet Explorer. Examples of differences might include the number and types of features, how they display Web pages, and the speed at which they perform. Include in your discussion which browser you would recommend and the reasons for your recommendation.

2. **Class Presentation — Brick-and-Click Businesses** Many retailers, such as Best Buy, Barnes and Noble, and Toys R Us, are brick-and-click businesses. That is, they allow customers to conduct complete transactions at a physical location as well as online at a Web site. Choose a local brick-and-click business in which you have shopped at the physical location and then visit the Web site of the same business. Compare the type, availability, and cost (include tax and shipping) of products or services available. Analyze the advantages and disadvantages of dealing with the physical location versus the Web site of a brick-and-click business and then present your recommendation of whether you would rather shop at the physical location or at the Web site. Note the factors that influenced your decision. Next, locate a company that only conducts business online, but sells the same products as the brick-and-click business. How do the prices compare? Would you prefer to shop using this Web site instead?

3. **Research — Acceptable Use Policy** Most schools and businesses provide free Internet access to students and employees while they are at school or at work. While the school's or business's intention is for the Internet to be used for academic or work-related purposes, employees and students often find it easy to become involved with other activities on the Internet not related to their job or academics, which can degrade Internet access for others, or lead to poor job performance. For these reasons, many schools and businesses create an Acceptable Use Policy that outlines how students and employees should use the Internet. It also may outline consequences for unauthorized Internet use. Locate two Acceptable Use Policies that are published online. Compare these two policies, find two additional Acceptable Use Policies online, and then create a policy you believe would be fair to employees of a small business. Be sure to include guidelines for Internet use during breaks, use of IM programs, and the use of Web sites that are not related to their job.

Collaboration

4. **Web Site Evaluation** You are vice president of operations for a major luxury hotel chain. You and three teammates want to start a new chain of discount hotels called Sleepy Hollow. You have made a plan that includes opening hotels initially in Seattle, Kansas City, Nashville, and Dallas. You plan to offer comfortable rooms, wireless Internet access, a business center, and a hot breakfast buffet. Besides offering reservations over the telephone, you want to develop a Web site that will allow customers to negotiate a nightly rate as their check-in time approaches. With your teammates, evaluate existing major hotel Web sites by listing the advantages and disadvantages of each. Assign each member the task of evaluating two of the following hotel chains: Marriot, Hilton, Holiday Inn, Ramada, Super 8, Motel 6, Days Inn, and Radisson. Team members should print the home page of the hotel chain to which they are assigned and evaluate their respective hotels' Web sites, paying particular attention to the following areas: (1) design of the Web site, (2) ease of use, (3) reservations, (4) awards programs, (5) special offers, (6) online Help, (7) information about the hotel, and (8) contact information for the hotel. Prepare a report and/or presentation summarizing your evaluations and ranking the sites in terms of their effectiveness. Be sure to include brief explanations supporting your rankings.

Making Use of the Web

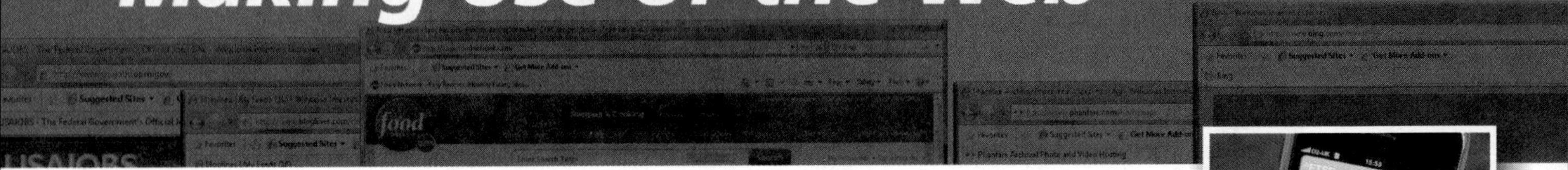

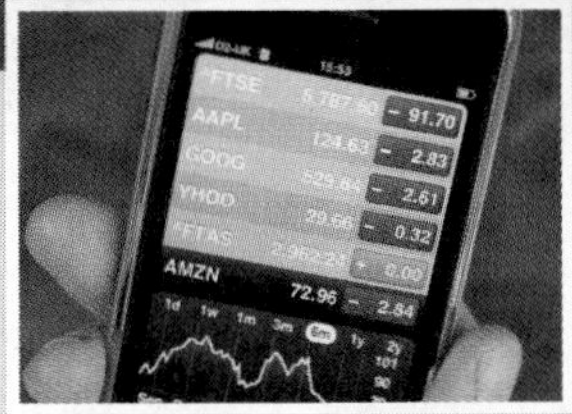

INFORMATION LITERACY IS DEFINED as having the practical skills needed to evaluate information critically from print and electronic resources and to use this information accurately in daily life. Locating Web sites may be profitable for your educational and professional careers, as the resources may help you research class assignments and make your life more fulfilling and manageable.

Because the Web does not have an organizational structure to assist you in locating reliable material, you may need additional resources to guide you in searching. To help you find useful Web sites, this Special Feature describes specific information about a variety of Web pages, and it includes tables of Web addresses so that you can get started. The material is organized in several areas of interest.

Web Exercises at the end of each area will reinforce the material and help you discover Web sites that may add a treasure trove of knowledge to your life.

Areas of Interest	
Fun and Entertainment	Shopping and Auctions
Research	Weather, Sports, and News
Blogs	Learning
Online Social Networks and Media Sharing	Science
Travel	Health
Environment	Careers
Finance	Literature and Arts
Government	

Fun and Entertainment

That's Entertainment

Rock 'n' Roll on the Web

Consumers place great significance on buying entertainment products for fun and recreation. Nearly 10 percent of the United States's economy is spent on attending concerts and buying optical discs, reading materials, sporting goods, and toys.

Many Web sites supplement our cravings for fun and entertainment. For example, you can see and hear the musicians inducted into the Rock and Roll Hall of Fame and Museum. If you need an update on your favorite reality-based television program or a preview of an upcoming movie, E! Online and Entertainment Weekly provide the latest features about actors and actresses. The Internet Movie Database contains reviews of more than one million titles (Figure 1).

Watch the surfers riding the waves and romp with pandas at the San Diego Zoo. Web cams can display live video on Web pages, taking armchair travelers across the world for views of natural attractions, monuments, and cities. Many Web sites featuring Web cams are listed in the table in Figure 2.

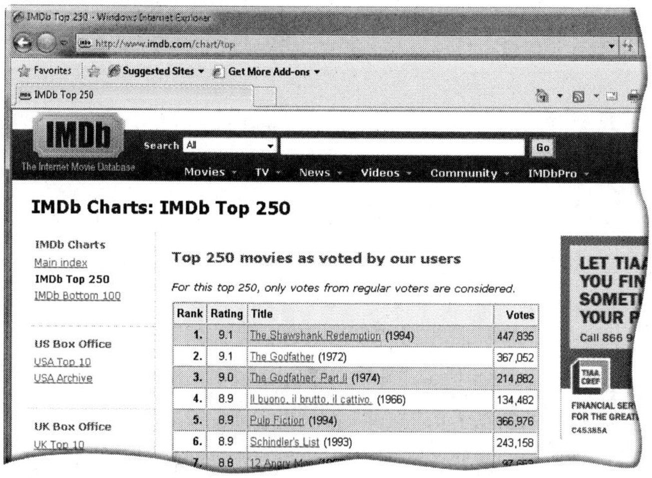

Figure 1 Visitors exploring the Internet Movie Database will find the latest news about their favorite television programs and movies.

Fun and Entertainment Web Sites

Entertainment	Web Address
allmusic	allmusic.com
E! Online	eonline.com
Entertainment Weekly's EW	ew.com/ew
Games.com	games.com
Internet Movie Database	imdb.com
Old Time Radio (OTR) — Radio Days: A Radio History	otr.com
Rock and Roll Hall of Fame and Museum	rockhall.com
World Radio Network	wrn.org
Yahoo! Entertainment	entertainment.yahoo.com
Web Cams	**Web Address**
Camvista	camvista.com
Discovery Kids — Live Cams	kids.discovery.com/cams/cams.html
EarthCam — Webcam Network	earthcam.com
ESRL/GMD Mauna Loa Live Camera	esrl.noaa.gov/gmd/obop/mlo/livecam/index.html
Gatorland	gatorland.com/gatorcam.php
Geocaching — The Official Global GPS Cache Hunt Site	geocaching.com
Panda Cam San Diego Zoo	sandiegozoo.org/zoo/ex_panda_station.html
WebCam Central	camcentral.com
Wild Birds Unlimited Bird FeederCam	wbu.com/feedercam_home.html

For more information about fun and entertainment Web sites, visit the Computer Concepts CourseMate Web site at www.cengagebrain.com and then navigate to the Making Use of the Web Feature resource for this book.

Figure 2 When you visit Web sites offering fun and entertainment resources, you can be both amused and informed.

Fun and Entertainment Web Exercises

1. **Visit the Geocaching site listed in Figure 2.** Find the geocaches within five miles of your home or school and then print a map showing their locations. Then, visit the Discovery Kids — Live Cams Web site and view one of the animal cams in the Live Cams. What do you observe? Visit another Web site listed in Figure 2 and describe the view. What are the benefits of having Web cams at these locations throughout the world?

2. **What are your favorite movies?** Use the Internet Movie Database Web site listed in Figure 2 to search for information about two films, and write a brief description of the biographies of the major stars and director for each movie. Then, visit one of the entertainment Web sites and describe three of the featured stories. At the Rock and Roll Hall of Fame and Museum Web site, view the information about The Beatles and one of your favorite musicians. Write a paragraph describing the information available about these rock stars.

Research

Search and Ye Shall Find

Information on the Web

A recent Web Usability survey conducted by the Nielsen Norman Group found that 88 percent of people who connect to the Internet use a search engine as their first online action. Search engines require users to type words and phrases that characterize the information being sought. Bing (Figure 3), Google, and AltaVista are some of the more popular search engines. The key to effective searching on the Web is composing search queries that narrow the search results and place the more relevant Web sites at the top of the results list.

Keep up with the latest computer and related product developments by viewing online dictionaries and encyclopedias that add to their collections on a regular basis. Shopping for a new computer can be a daunting experience, but many online guides can help you select the components that best fit your needs and budget. If you are not confident in your ability to solve a problem alone, turn to online technical support. Web sites often provide streaming how-to video lessons, tutorials, and real-time chats with experienced technicians. Hardware and software reviews, price comparisons, shareware, technical questions and answers, and breaking technology news are found on comprehensive portals. Figure 4 lists popular research Web sites.

Figure 3 The Bing Web site provides a search engine for images, videos, shopping, news, maps, and travel.

Research Web Sites

Research	Web Address
A9.com	a9.com
AccessMyLibrary	accessmylibrary.com
AltaVista	altavista.com
Answers.com	answers.com
Ask	ask.com
Bing	bing.com
ChaCha	chacha.com
CNET	cnet.com
eHow	ehow.com
Google	google.com
HotBot	hotbot.com
Librarians' Internet Index	lii.org
PC911	pcnineoneone.com
Switchboard	switchboard.com
Webopedia	webopedia.com
ZDNet	zdnet.com

For more information about research Web sites, visit the Computer Concepts CourseMate Web site at www.cengagebrain.com and then navigate to the Making Use of the Web Feature resource for this book.

Figure 4 Web users can find information by using research Web sites.

Research Web Exercises

1. Visit two of the research Web sites listed in Figure 4 to find three Web sites that review the latest digital cameras from Kodak and Canon. Make a table listing the research Web sites, the located Web site names, and the cameras' model numbers, suggested retail price, and features.

2. Visit the Webopedia Web site. Search this site for five terms of your choice. Create a table with two columns: one for the term and one for the Web definition. Then, create a second table listing five recently added or updated words and their definitions on this Web site. Next, visit the CNET Web site to choose the components you would buy if you were building a customized desktop computer and notebook computer. Create a table for both computers, listing the computer manufacturer, processor model name or number and manufacturer, clock speed, RAM, cache, number of expansion slots, and number of bays.

Blogs

Express Yourself

Blogosphere Growing Swiftly

Internet users are feeling the need to publish their views, and they are finding Weblogs, or blogs for short, the ideal vehicle. The blogosphere began as an easy way for individuals to express their opinions on the Web. Today, this communications vehicle has become a powerful tool, for individuals, groups, and corporations are using blogs to promote their ideas and advertise their products. It is not necessary to have a background in Web design to be able to post to a blog.

Bloggers generally update their Web sites frequently to reflect their views. Their posts range from a paragraph to an entire essay and often contain links to other Web sites. The more popular blogs discuss politics, lifestyles, and technology.

Individuals easily may set up a blog free or for a fee, using Web sites such as Blogger, Bloglines (Figure 5), and TypePad. In addition, online social networks may have a built-in blogging feature. Be cautious of the information you post on your blog, especially if it is accessible to everyone online.

Corporate blogs, such as The GM FastLane Blog, discuss all aspects of the company's products, whereas all-encompassing blogs, such as the MetaFilter Community Weblog and others in Figure 6, are designed to keep general readers entertained and informed.

Blogs are affecting the manner in which people communicate, and some experts predict they will one day become our primary method of sharing information.

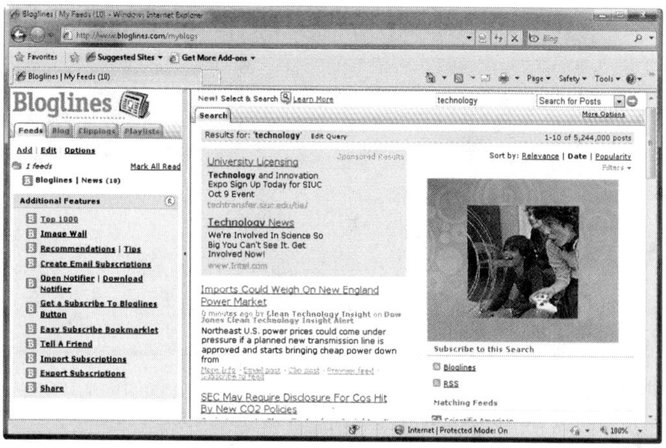

Figure 5 Bloglines keeps readers abreast of the latest technology, entertainment, and political news in the blogosphere.

Blogs Web Sites

Blog	Web Address
A List Apart	alistapart.com
Blog.com	blog.com
Blog Flux	topsites.blogflux.com
Blogger	blogger.com
Bloglines	bloglines.com
Blogstream	blogstream.com
Davenetics*Remote Control Revolutionary	davenetics.com
Geek News Central	geeknewscentral.com
GM FastLane Blog	fastlane.gmblogs.com
kottke.org	kottke.org
MetaFilter Community Weblog	metafilter.com
Rocketboom	rocketboom.com
TreeHugger	treehuggertv.com
Twitter	twitter.com
TypePad	typepad.com

For more information about blogs Web sites, visit the Computer Concepts CourseMate Web site at www.cengagebrain.com and then navigate to the Making Use of the Web Feature resource for this book.

Figure 6 These blogs offer information about technology, news, politics, and entertainment.

Blogs Web Exercises

1. **Visit three of the blog Web sites listed in Figure 6.** Make a table listing the blog name, its purpose, the author, its audience, and advertisers, if any, who sponsor the blog. Then, write a paragraph that describes the information you found on each of these blogs.

2. **Many Internet users read the technology blogs to keep abreast of the latest developments.** Visit the Geek News Central and Bloglines blogs listed in Figure 6 and write a paragraph describing the top story in each blog. Read the posted comments, if any. Then, write another paragraph describing two other stories found on these blogs that cover material you have discussed in this course. Write a third paragraph discussing which one is more interesting to you. Would you add reading blogs to your list of Internet activities? Why or why not?

Online Social Networks and Media Sharing

Check Out My New Photos

Online Social Networks and Media Sharing Web Sites Gain Popularity

Do you ever wonder what your friends are doing? What about your friends' friends? The popularity of online social networks has increased dramatically in recent years. Online social networks, such as those listed in Figure 7, allow you to create a personalized profile that others are able to view online. These profiles may include information about you such as your hometown, your age, your hobbies, and pictures. You also may create links to your friends' pages, post messages for individual friends, or bulletins for all of your friends to see. Online social networks are great places to keep in touch with your friends and to network with professionals for business purposes.

If you would like to post pictures and videos and do not require the full functionality of an online social network, you might consider a media sharing Web site, which is a type of online social network. Media sharing Web sites such as YouTube and Phanfare (Figure 8) allow you to post media, including photos and videos, for others to view, print, and/or download. Media sharing Web sites, which may be free or charge a fee, provide a quick, efficient way to share photos of your last vacation or videos of your family reunion.

Online Social Networks and Media Sharing

Online Social Networks	Web Address
Club Penguin	clubpenguin.com
Facebook	facebook.com
LinkedIn	linkedin.com
MySpace — a place for friends	myspace.com
orkut	orkut.com
Windows Live Spaces	spaces.live.com
Media Sharing	**Web Address**
flickr	flickr.com
Phanfare	phanfare.com
Photobucket	photobucket.com
Picasa	picasa.com
Shutterfly	shutterfly.com
Yahoo! Video	video.yahoo.com
YouTube	youtube.com

For more information about online social networks and media sharing Web sites, visit the Computer Concepts CourseMate Web site at www.cengagebrain.com and then navigate to the Making Use of the Web Feature resource for this book.

Figure 7 Online social networks and media sharing Web sites are popular ways to keep in touch with friends, meet new people, and share media.

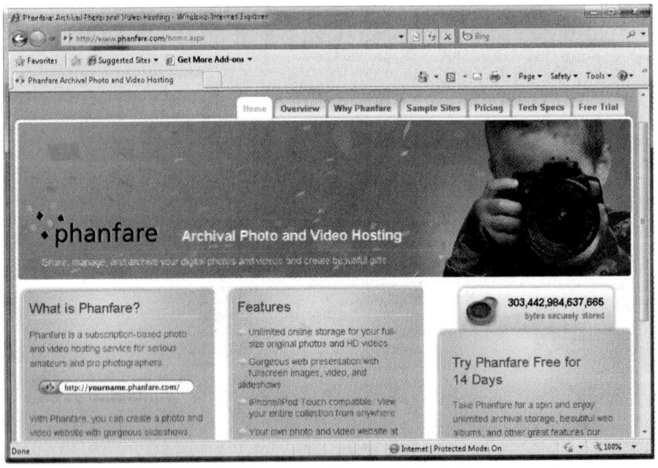

Figure 8 The Phanfare Web site allows users to share their photo and video files with people throughout the world.

Online Social Networks and Media Sharing Web Exercises

1. **Many individuals now use online social networks.** Visit two online social networks listed in Figure 7. (If you are attempting to access an online social network from your classroom and are unable to do so, your school may have restricted use of social networking Web sites.) Compare and contrast these two sites by performing the following actions and recording your findings. First, create a profile on each of these sites. If you find a Web site that charges a fee to sign up, choose another Web site. How easy is the sign-up process? Does either Web site ask for any personal information you are uncomfortable sharing? If so, what information? Once you sign up, make a list of five of your closest friends, and search for their profiles on each of these two sites. Which site contains more of your friends? Browse each site and make a list of its features. In your opinion, which site is better? Explain why.

2. **Media sharing Web sites make it extremely easy to share photos and videos with friends, family, and colleagues.** Before choosing a media sharing Web site to use, you should do some research. Visit two media sharing Web sites in Figure 7. Is there a fee to post media to these Web sites? If so, how much? Are these Web sites supported by advertisements? Locate the instructions for posting media to these Web sites. Are the instructions straightforward? Do these Web sites impose a limit on the number and/or size of media files you can post? Summarize your responses to these questions in two or three paragraphs.

Travel

Get Packing!

Explore the World without Leaving Home

When you are ready to arrange your next travel adventure or just want to explore destination possibilities, the Internet provides ample resources to set your plans in motion.

To discover exactly where your destination is on this planet, cartography Web sites, including MapQuest and Yahoo! Maps, allow you to pinpoint your destination. View your exact destination using satellite imagery with Google Maps and Bing Maps (Figure 9).

Some excellent starting places are general travel Web sites such as Expedia Travel, Cheap Tickets, Orbitz, and Travelocity. Many airline Web sites allow you to reserve hotel rooms, activities, and rental cars while booking a flight. These all-encompassing Web sites, including those in Figure 10, have tools to help you find the lowest prices and details about flights, car rentals, cruises, and hotels. Comprehensive online guidebooks can provide useful details about maximizing your vacation time while saving money.

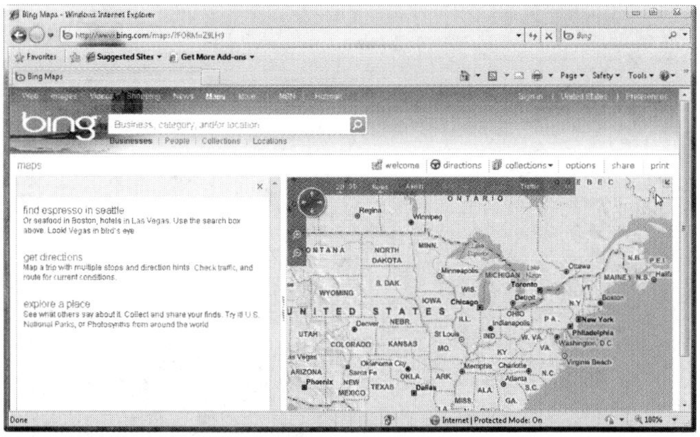

Figure 9 Bing Maps provides location information and satellite imagery for many regions on this planet.

Travel Web Sites

General Travel	Web Address
CheapTickets	cheaptickets.com
Expedia Travel	expedia.com
Kayak	kayak.com
Orbitz	orbitz.com
SideStep	sidestep.com
Travelocity	travelocity.com
Cartography	**Web Address**
Bing Maps	bing.com/maps
Google Maps	maps.google.com
MapQuest	mapquest.com
Maps.com	maps.com
Yahoo! Maps	maps.yahoo.com
Travel and City Guides	**Web Address**
Frommer's Travel Guides	frommers.com
GoPlanit	goplanit.com
U.S.-Parks US National Parks Travel Guide	www.us-parks.com
Virtual Tourist	virtualtourist.com

For more information about travel Web sites, visit the Computer Concepts CourseMate Web site at www.cengagebrain.com and then navigate to the Making Use of the Web Feature resource for this book.

Figure 10 These travel resources Web sites offer travel information to exciting destinations throughout the world.

Travel Web Exercises

1. **Visit one of the cartography Web sites listed in Figure 10** and obtain the directions from your campus to one of these destinations: the Washington Monument in Washington, D.C.; the Statue of Liberty on Ellis Island in New York; Disneyland in Anaheim, California; or the Grand Old Opry in Nashville, Tennessee. How many miles is it to your destination? What is the estimated driving time? Use the Google Maps Web site to obtain an overhead image of this destination. Then, visit one of the general travel Web sites listed in the table and plan a flight from the nearest major airport to one of the four destinations for the week after finals and a return trip one week later. Which airline, flight numbers, and departure and arrival times did you select?

2. **Visit one of the travel and city guides Web sites listed in Figure 10,** and choose a destination for a getaway this coming weekend. Write a one-page paper giving details about this location, such as popular hotels and lodging, expected weather, population, local colleges and universities, parks and recreation, ancient and modern history, and tours. Include a map or satellite photo of this place. Why did you select this destination? How would you travel there and back? What is the breakdown of expected costs for this weekend, including travel expenditures, meals, lodging, and tickets to events and activities? Which Web addresses did you use to complete this exercise?

Environment

The Future of the Planet

Making a Difference for Earth

From the rain forests of Africa to the marine life in the Pacific Ocean, the fragile ecosystem is under extreme stress. Many environmental groups have developed informative Web sites, including those listed in Figure 11, in attempts to educate worldwide populations and to increase resource conservation. The Environmental Defense Fund Web site (Figure 12) contains information for people who would like to help safeguard the environment.

On an international scale, the Environmental Sites on the Internet Web page developed by the Royal Institute of Technology in Stockholm, Sweden, has been rated as one of the better ecological Web sites. Its comprehensive listing of environmental concerns range from aquatic ecology to wetlands.

The U.S. federal government has a number of Web sites devoted to specific environmental concerns. For example, the U.S. Environmental Protection Agency (EPA) provides pollution data, including ozone levels and air pollutants, for specific areas. Its AirData Web site displays air pollution emissions and monitoring data from the entire United States and is the world's most extensive collection of air pollution data.

Environment Web Sites

Name	Web Address
Central African Regional Program for the Environment (CARPE)	carpe.umd.edu
Earthjustice	earthjustice.org
EarthTrends: Environmental Information	earthtrends.wri.org
Environmental Defense Fund	edf.org
Environmental Sites on the Internet	www.ima.kth.se/im/envsite/envsite.htm
EPA AirData — Access to Air Pollution Data	epa.gov/air/data
Global Warming	globalwarming.org
Green Computing Impact Organization	gcio.org
GreenNet	gn.apc.org
New American Dream	newdream.org
University of Wisconsin — Milwaukee Environmental Health and Safety Resources	uwm.edu/Dept/EHSRM/EHSLINKS
USGS Branch of Quality Systems	bqs.usgs.gov/acidrain

For more information about environment Web sites, visit the Computer Concepts CourseMate Web site at www.cengagebrain.com and then navigate to the Making Use of the Web Feature resource for this book.

Figure 11 Environment Web sites provide vast resources for ecological data and action groups.

Figure 12 A visit to the Environmental Defense Fund Web site provides practical advice about protecting the environment.

Environment Web Exercises

1. **The New American Dream Web site encourages consumers to reduce the amount of junk mail sent to their homes.** Using the table in Figure 11, visit the Web site to learn how many trees are leveled each year to provide paper for these mailings and how many garbage trucks are needed to haul this waste. Read the letters used to eliminate names from bulk mail lists. To whom would you mail these letters? How long does it take to stop these unsolicited letters?

2. **Visit the EPA AirData Web site.** What is the highest ozone level recorded in your state this past year? Where are the nearest air pollution monitoring Web sites, and what are their levels? Where are the nearest sources of air pollution? Read two reports about two different topics, such as acid rain and air quality, and summarize their findings. Include information about who sponsored the research, who conducted the studies, when the data was collected, and the impact of this pollution on the atmosphere, water, forests, and human health. Whom would you contact for further information regarding the data and studies?

Finance

Money Matters

Cashing In on Financial Advice

You can manage your money with advice from financial Web sites that offer online banking, tax help, personal finance, and small business and commercial services.

If you do not have a personal banker or a financial planner, consider a Web adviser to guide your investment decisions. The MSN Money Web site (Figure 13) provides financial news and investment information.

If you are ready to ride the ups and downs of the Dow and the NASDAQ, an abundance of Web sites listed in Figure 14, including Reuters and Morningstar, can help you select companies that fit your interests and financial needs.

Claiming to be the fastest, easiest tax publication on the planet, the Internal Revenue Service Web site contains procedures for filing tax appeals and contains IRS forms, publications, and legal regulations.

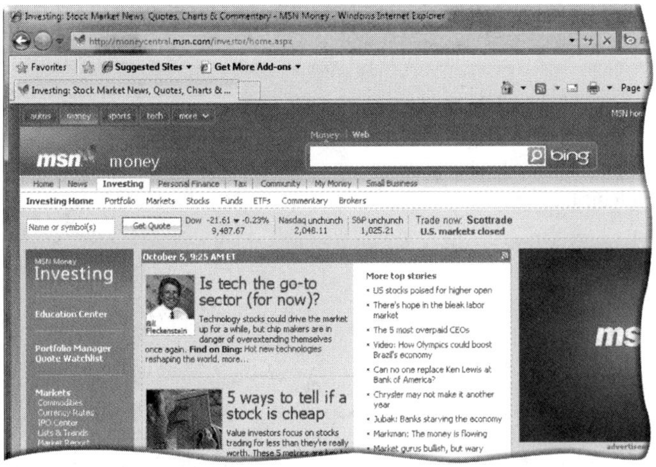

Figure 13 The MSN Money Web site contains features related to college and family finances.

Finance Web Sites

Advice and Education	Web Address
Bankrate	bankrate.com
ING Direct	ingdirect.com
LendingTree	lendingtree.com
Loan.com	loan.com
The Motley Fool	fool.com
MSN Money	moneycentral.msn.com
Wells Fargo	wellsfargo.com
Yahoo! Finance	finance.yahoo.com
Stock Market	**Web Address**
E*TRADE	us.etrade.com
Financial Engines	financialengines.com
Merrill Lynch	ml.com
Morningstar	morningstar.com
Reuters	reuters.com/investing
Valic	valic.com
Vanguard	vanguard.com
Taxes	**Web Address**
H&R Block	hrblock.com
Internal Revenue Service	www.irs.gov
Jackson Hewitt	jacksonhewitt.com
Liberty Tax Service	libertytax.com

For more information about finance Web sites, visit the Computer Concepts CourseMate Web site at www.cengagebrain.com and then navigate to the Making Use of the Web Feature resource for this book.

Figure 14 Financial resources Web sites offer general information, stock market analyses, and tax advice, as well as guidance and money-saving tips.

Finance Web Exercises

1. **Visit three advice and education Web sites listed in Figure 14** and read their top business world reports. Write a paragraph about each, summarizing these stories. Which stocks or mutual funds do these Web sites predict as being sound investments today? What are the current market indexes for the DJIA (Dow Jones Industrial Average), S&P 500, and NASDAQ, and how do these figures compare with the previous day's numbers?

2. **Using two of the stock market Web sites listed in Figure 14,** search for information about Microsoft, Apple, and one other software vendor. Write a paragraph about each of these stocks describing the revenues, net incomes, total assets for the previous year, current stock price per share, highest and lowest prices of each stock during the past year, and other relevant investment information.

Government

Stamp of Approval

Making a Federal Case for Useful Information

When it is time to buy stamps to mail your correspondence, you no longer need to wait in long lines at your local post office. The U.S. Postal Service has authorized several organizations to sell stamps online.

You can recognize U.S. Government Web sites on the Internet by their gov top-level domain. For example, the extensive Library of Congress Web site is loc.gov (Figure 15). Government and military Web sites offer a wide range of information. The Time Service Department Web site will provide you with the correct time. If you are looking for a federal document, FedWorld lists thousands of documents distributed by the government on its Web site. For access to the names of your congressional representatives, visit the extensive HG.org Web site. Figure 16 shows some of the more popular U.S. Government Web sites.

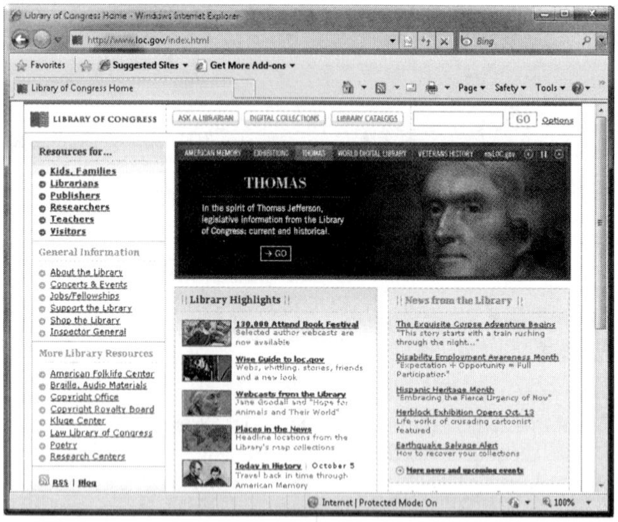

Figure 15 The Library of Congress Web site has resources about American history, world culture, and digital preservation.

Government Resources Web Sites

Postage	Web Address
Endicia	endicia.com
Pitney Bowes	pb.com
Stamps.com	stamps.com
Government	**Web Address**
FedWorld	www.fedworld.gov
HG.org — Worldwide Legal Directories	hg.org
Library of Congress	loc.gov
National Agricultural Library	nal.usda.gov
Smithsonian Institution	smithsonian.org
THOMAS (Library of Congress)	thomas.loc.gov
Time Service Department	tycho.usno.navy.mil
U.S. Department of Education	ed.gov
United States Department of the Treasury	treas.gov
U.S. Government Printing Office	www.access.gpo.gov
United States National Library of Medicine	nlm.nih.gov
United States Patent and Trademark Office	uspto.gov
USAJOBS	usajobs.opm.gov
The White House	whitehouse.gov

For more information about government Web sites, visit the Computer Concepts CourseMate Web site at www.cengagebrain.com and then navigate to the Making Use of the Web Feature resource for this book.

Figure 16 These Web sites offer information about buying U.S.-approved postage online and researching federal agencies.

Government Web Exercises

1. **View the three postage Web sites listed in Figure 16.** Compare and contrast the available services on each one. Consider postage cost, necessary equipment, shipping services, security techniques, and tracking capability. Explain why you would or would not like to use this service.

2. **Visit the HG.org Web site listed in Figure 16.** What are the names, addresses, and phone numbers of your two state senators and your local congressional representative? On what committees do they serve? Who is the chief justice of the Supreme Court, and what has been this justice's opinion on two recently decided cases? Who are the members of the president's cabinet? Then, visit two other Web sites listed in Figure 16. Write a paragraph about each Web site describing its content and features.

Shopping and Auctions

Bargains Galore

Let Your Mouse Do Your Shopping

From groceries to clothing to computers, you can buy just about everything you need with just a few clicks of your mouse. More than one-half of Internet users will make at least one online purchase this year. Books, computer software and hardware, and music are the hottest commodities.

The two categories of Internet shopping Web sites are those with physical counterparts, such as Walmart and Fry's Electronics (Figure 17), and those with only a Web presence, such as Amazon and Buy. Popular Web shopping sites are listed in Figure 18.

Another method of shopping for the items you need, and maybe some you really do not need, is to visit auction Web sites, including those listed in Figure 18. Categories include antiques and collectibles, automotive, computers, electronics, music, sports, sports cards and memorabilia, and toys. Online auction Web sites can offer unusual items, including *Star Wars* memorabilia or a round of golf with Jack Nicklaus. eBay is one of thousands of Internet auction Web sites and is the world's largest personal online trading community. In addition, craigslist is a free online equivalent of classified advertisements.

Figure 17 Fry's is a popular electronic retailer that sells a variety of products.

Shopping and Auctions Web Sites

Auctions	Web Address
craigslist	craigslist.org
eBay	ebay.com
Sotheby's	sothebys.com
uBid	ubid.com
U.S. Treasury — Seized Property Auctions	ustreas.gov/auctions
Books and Music	**Web Address**
Amazon	amazon.com
Barnes & Noble	bn.com
BookFinder	bookfinder.com
Computers and Electronics	**Web Address**
BestBuy	bestbuy.com
Buy	buy.com
Fry's Electronics	frys.com
Miscellaneous	**Web Address**
drugstore	drugstore.com
Google Product Search	google.com/products
SmashBuys	smashbuys.com
Walmart	walmart.com

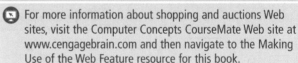

For more information about shopping and auctions Web sites, visit the Computer Concepts CourseMate Web site at www.cengagebrain.com and then navigate to the Making Use of the Web Feature resource for this book.

Figure 18 Making online purchases can help ease the burden of driving to and fighting the crowds in local malls.

Shopping and Auctions Web Exercises

1. Visit two of the computers and electronics and two of the miscellaneous Web sites listed in Figure 18. Write a paragraph describing the features these Web sites offer compared with the same offerings from stores. In another paragraph, describe any disadvantages of shopping at these Web sites instead of actually visiting a store. Then, describe their policies for returning unwanted merchandise and for handling complaints.

2. Using one of the auction Web sites listed in Figure 18, search for two objects pertaining to your hobbies. For example, if you are a sports fan, you can search for a complete set of Upper Deck cards. If you are a car buff, search for your dream car. Describe these two items. How many people have bid on these items? Who are the sellers? What are the opening and current bids?

Weather, Sports, and News

What's News?

Weather, Sports, and News Web Sites Score Big Hits

Rain or sun? Hot or cold? Weather is the leading online news item, with at least 10,000 Web sites devoted to this field. Millions of people view The Weather Channel Web site (Figure 19) each month.

Baseball may be the national pastime, but sports aficionados yearn for everything from auto racing to cricket. The Internet has millions of pages of multimedia sports news, entertainment, and merchandise.

The Internet has emerged as a major source for news, with more than one-third of Americans going online at least once a week and 15 percent going online daily for reports of major news events. Many of these viewers are using RSS (Really Simple Syndication) technology to be notified when new stories about their favorite topics are available on the Internet. Popular weather, sports, and news Web sites are listed in Figure 20.

Figure 19 Local, national, and international weather conditions and details about breaking weather stories are available on The Weather Channel Web site.

Weather, Sports, and News Web Sites

Weather	Web Address
AccuWeather	accuweather.com
Infoplease Weather	infoplease.com/weather.html
Intellicast	www.intellicast.com
National Weather Service	www.crh.noaa.gov
The Weather Channel	weather.com
Sports	**Web Address**
CBS Sports	cbssports.com
ESPN	espn.com
NASCAR	nascar.com
International Olympic Committee	www.olympic.org
Sporting News Radio	radio.sportingnews.com
Yahoo! Sports	sports.yahoo.com
News	**Web Address**
FactCheck	factcheck.org
Geek.com	geek.com
Google News	news.google.com
MSNBC	msnbc.com
Onlinenewspapers	onlinenewspapers.com
privacy.org	privacy.org
SiliconValley	siliconvalley.com
starting page	startingpage.com/html/news.html
USA TODAY	usatoday.com
Washington Post	washingtonpost.com

For more information about weather, sports, and news Web sites, visit the Computer Concepts CourseMate Web site at www.cengagebrain.com and then navigate to the Making Use of the Web Feature resource for this book.

Figure 20 Keep informed about the latest weather, sports, and news events with these Web sites.

Weather, Sports, and News Web Exercises

1. Visit two of the sports Web sites in Figure 20 and write a paragraph describing the content these Web sites provide concerning your favorite sport. Visit Google News and then search for stories about this sports team or athlete. Then, create a customized news page with stories about your sports interests. Include RSS feeds to get regularly updated summaries on this subject.

2. Visit the Onlinenewspapers and starting page Web sites listed in Figure 20 and select two newspapers from each site. Write a paragraph describing the top national news story featured in each of these four Web pages. Then, write another paragraph describing the top international news story displayed at each Web site. In the third paragraph, discuss which of the four Web sites is the most interesting in terms of story selection, photos, and Web page design.

Learning

Yearn to Learn

Discover New Worlds Online

While you may believe your education ends when you finally graduate from college, learning is a lifelong process. You can increase your technological knowledge by visiting several Web sites (Figure 21) with tutorials about building your own Web sites, the latest news about the Internet, and resources for visually impaired users.

Learning Web Sites

Learning How To's	Web Address
Bartleby: Great Books Online	bartleby.com
AT&T Knowledge Network Explorer	www.kn.pacbell.com/wired
BBC Learning	bbc.co.uk/learning
CBT Nuggets	cbtnuggets.com
HowStuffWorks	howstuffworks.com
Internet Public Library	ipl.org
Learn the Net	learnthenet.com
ScienceMaster	sciencemaster.com
Search Engine Watch	searchenginewatch.com
Wiredguide	wiredguide.com
Cooking	**Web Address**
Betty Crocker	bettycrocker.com
Chef2Chef	chef2chef.net
Food Network	foodnetwork.com

For more information about learning Web sites, visit the Computer Concepts CourseMate Web site at www.cengagebrain.com and then navigate to the Making Use of the Web Feature resource for this book.

Figure 21 The information gleaned from these Web sites can help you learn about many aspects of our existence.

The HowStuffWorks Web site has won numerous awards for its clear, comprehensive articles that demystify aspects of our everyday life. It includes ratings and reviews of products written by *Consumer Guide* editors.

A consortium of colleges maintains the Internet Public Library, which includes subject collections, reference materials, and a reading room filled with magazines and books. Volunteer librarians will answer your personal questions asked in its Ask an IPL Librarian form.

Enhancing your culinary skills can be a rewarding endeavor. No matter if you are a gourmet chef or a weekend cook, you will be cooking in style with the help of online resources, including those listed in Figure 21.

Have you ever wondered how to make a key lime pie? How about learning how to cook some easy, low-calorie dishes? Are you seeking advice from expert chefs? The Food Network Web site (Figure 22) is filled with information related to cooking, grilling, and healthy eating.

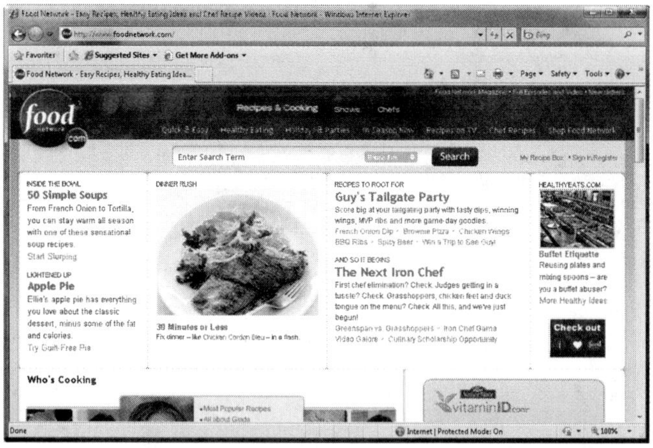

Figure 22 The Food Network Web site provides access to healthy recipes, grilling tips, and cookware.

Learning Web Exercises

1. **Using one of the Learning How To's Web sites listed in Figure 21,** search for information about installing memory in a computer. Write a paragraph about your findings. Then, review the material in the HowStuffWorks Web site listed in Figure 21, and write a paragraph describing articles on this Web site that are pertinent to your major.

2. **Visit one of the cooking Web sites listed in Figure 21** and find two recipes or cooking tips that you can use when preparing your next meal. Write a paragraph about each one, summarizing your discoveries. Which Web sites allow you to create your own online recipe book? What are the advantages and disadvantages of accessing these Web sites on the new appliances and gadgets that might someday be in your kitchen?

Science

E = mc²

Rocket Science on the Web

For some people, space exploration is a hobby. Building and launching model rockets allow these at-home scientists to participate in exploring the great frontier of space. For others, space exploration is their life. Numerous Web sites, including those in Figure 23, provide in-depth information about the universe.

Science Web Sites

Periodicals	**Web Address**
Archaeology Magazine	archaeology.org
Astronomy Magazine	astronomy.com
New Scientist	newscientist.com
OceanLink	oceanlink.info
Science Magazine	sciencemag.org
Scientific American	sciam.com
Resources	**Web Address**
National Science Foundation (NSF)	nsf.gov
Science.gov: USA.gov for Science	science.gov
Thomson Reuters	scientific.thomson.com/free/
Science Community	**Web Address**
American Scientist	amsci.org
Federation of American Scientists	fas.org
NASA	www.nasa.gov
Sigma Xi, The Scientific Research Society	sigmaxi.org

For more information about science Web sites, visit the Computer Concepts CourseMate Web site at www.cengagebrain.com and then navigate to the Making Use of the Web Feature resource for this book.

Figure 23 Resources available on the Internet offer a wide range of subjects for enthusiasts who want to delve into familiar and unknown territories in the world of science.

NASA's Web site contains information about rockets, space exploration, the International Space Station, space transportation, and communications. Other science resources explore space-related questions about astronomy, physics, the earth sciences, microgravity, and robotics.

Rockets and space are not the only areas to explore in the world of science. Where can you find the latest pictures taken with the Hubble Space Telescope? Do you know how climate change is affecting the human body? You can find the answers to these questions and many others through the New Scientist Web site (newscientist.com) shown in Figure 24.

The National Science Foundation's Web site features overviews of current topics and an extensive Multimedia Gallery with audio and video files, photos, and paintings.

Science.gov is an outstanding resource for scientific databases and thousands of authoritative science Web sites. The U.S. government science information provided offers 200 million pages of research, with search results ranked by relevance and sorted by topic and year.

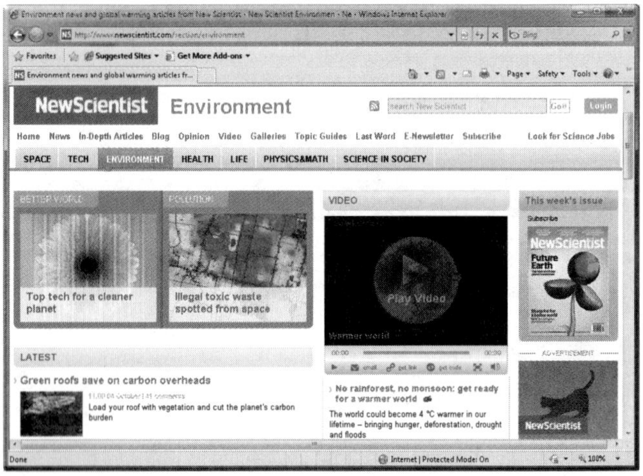

Figure 24 The New Scientist Web site covers news about space exploration, the environment, and technology.

Science Web Exercises

1. **Visit the National Science Foundation Web site listed in the table in Figure 23.** What are the topics of the latest science news and special reports? Which speeches and lectures are featured? What are the titles of image, video, and audio files in the Multimedia Gallery?

2. **Visit the NASA Web site listed in the table in Figure 23.** Click the Missions link and then click the Mission Calendar link. When are the next two launches scheduled? What are the purposes of these missions? Click the Careers @ NASA topic and then write a paragraph describing the internships, cooperative programs, and summer employment opportunities. Then, view two of the science community Web sites listed in Figure 23 and write a paragraph about each of these Web sites describing the information each contains.

Health

No Pain, All Gain

Store Personal Health Records Online

More than 75 million consumers use the Internet yearly to search for health information, so using the Web to store personal medical data is a natural extension of the Internet's capabilities. Internet health services and portals are available to store your personal health history, including prescriptions, lab test results, doctor visits, allergies, and immunizations.

Google Health allows users to create a health profile, import medical records, and locate medical services and doctors. Web sites such as healthfinder.gov (Figure 25) provide free wellness information to consumers. Wise consumers, however, verify the online information they read with their personal physician.

In minutes, you can register with a health Web site by choosing a user name and password. Then, you create a record to enter your medical history. You also can store data for your emergency contacts, primary care physicians, specialists, blood type, cholesterol levels, blood pressure, and insurance plan. No matter where you are in the world, you and medical personnel can obtain records via the Internet or fax machine. Some popular online health databases are shown in Figure 26.

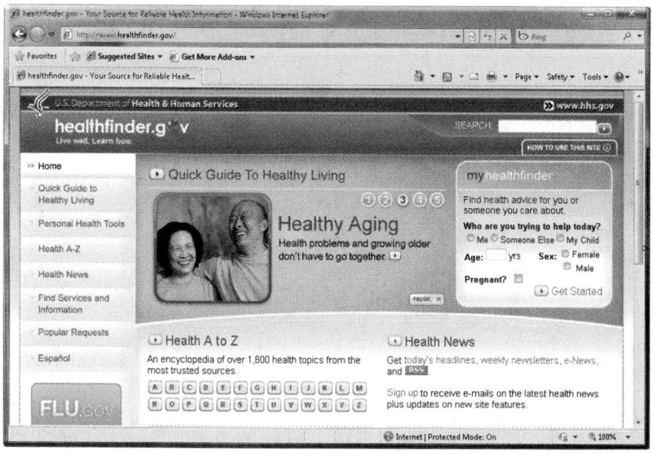

Figure 25 The healthfinder.gov Web site provides advice and tools to prevent illnesses and check drug interactions.

Health Web Sites

Medical History	Web Address
Google Health	google.com/health
Lifestar	mylifestarphr.com
Medem	medem.com
PersonalMD	personalmd.com
Practice Solutions	practicesolutions.ca
Records for Living, Inc — Personal Health and Living Management	recordsforliving.com
WebMD	webmd.com
General Health	**Web Address**
Consumer and Patient Health Information Section (CAPHIS)	caphis.mlanet.org/consumer
Centers for Disease Control and Prevention	cdc.gov
familydoctor	familydoctor.org
healthfinder	healthfinder.gov
KidsHealth	kidshealth.org
LIVESTRONG.COM	livestrong.com
MedlinePlus	medlineplus.gov
PE Central: Health and Nutrition Web Sites	pecentral.org/websites/healthsites.html
Physical Activity Guidelines	health.gov/paguidelines

For more information about health Web sites, visit the Computer Concepts CourseMate Web site at www.cengagebrain.com and then navigate to the Making Use of the Web Feature resource for this book.

Figure 26 These health Web sites allow you to organize your medical information and store it in an online database and also obtain information about a variety of medical conditions and treatments.

Health Web Exercises

1. **Access one of the health Web sites listed in Figure 26.** Register yourself or a family member and then enter the full health history. Create an emergency medical card if the Web site provides the card option. Submit this record and emergency card to your instructor. If you feel uncomfortable disclosing medical information for yourself or a family member, you may enter fictitious information.

2. **Visit three of the health Web sites listed in Figure 26.** Describe the features of each. Which of the three is the most user-friendly? Why? Describe the privacy policies of these three Web sites. Submit your analysis of these Web sites to your instructor.

Careers

In Search of the Perfect Job

Web Helps Career Hunt

While your teachers give you valuable training to prepare you for a career, they rarely teach you how to begin that career. You can broaden your horizons by searching the Internet for career information and job openings.

First, examine some of the job search Web sites. These resources list thousands of openings in hundreds of fields, companies, and locations. For example, the USAJOBS Web site, shown in Figure 27, allows you to find information for Federal jobs. This information may include the training and education required, salary data, working conditions, job descriptions, and more. In addition, many companies advertise careers on their Web sites.

When a company contacts you for an interview, learn as much about it and the industry as possible before the interview. Many of the Web sites listed in Figure 28 include detailed company profiles and links to their corporate Web sites.

Figure 27 The USAJOBS Web site is the official location for federal jobs and information for job seekers.

Career Web Sites

Job Search	Web Address
BestJobsUSA	bestjobsusa.com
CareerBuilder	careerbuilder.com
Careerjet	careerjet.com
CareerNET	careernet.com
CAREERXCHANGE	careerxchange.com
CollegeGrad.com	collegegrad.com
EmploymentGuide.com	employmentguide.com
Job.com	job.com
Job Bank USA	jobbankusa.com
Job-Hunt	job-hunt.org
Monster	monster.com
USAJOBS	www.usajobs.gov
VolunteerMatch	volunteermatch.org
Yahoo! HotJobs	hotjobs.yahoo.com
Company/Industry Information	**Web Address**
Careers.org	careers.org
Forbes	forbes.com/leadership/careers
Fortune	fortune.com
Hoover's	hoovers.com
Occupational Outlook Handbook	stats.bls.gov/oco

For more information about career Web sites, visit the Computer Concepts CourseMate Web site at www.cengagebrain.com and then navigate to the Making Use of the Web Feature resource for this book.

Figure 28 Career Web sites provide a variety of job openings and information about major companies worldwide.

Careers Web Exercises

1. **Use two of the job search Web sites listed in Figure 28 to find three companies with job openings in your field.** Make a table listing the Web site name, position available, description, salary, location, desired education, and desired experience.

2. **It is a good idea to acquire information before graduation about the industry in which you would like to work.** Are you interested in the automotive manufacturing industry, the restaurant service industry, or the financial industry? Use two of the company/industry information Web sites listed in Figure 28 to research a particular career related to your major. Write a paragraph naming the Web sites and the specific information you found, such as the nature of the work, recommended training and qualifications, employment outlook, and earnings. Then, use two other Web sites to profile three companies with positions available in this field. Write a paragraph about each of these companies, describing the headquarters' location, sales and earnings for the previous year, total number of employees, working conditions, benefits, and competitors.

Literature and Arts

Find Some Culture

Get Ready to Read, Paint, and Dance

Brush up your knowledge of Shakespeare, grab a canvas, and put on your dancing shoes. Literature and arts Web sites, including those in Figure 29, are about to sweep you off your cyberfeet.

Literature and Arts Web Sites

Literature	Web Address
Bartleby	bartleby.com
Bibliomania	bibliomania.com
The Complete Review	www.complete-review.com
eNotes	enotes.com
Fantastic Fiction	fantasticfiction.co.uk
Literary History	literaryhistory.com
Nobel Prize in Literature	nobelprize.org/nobel_prizes/literature/laureates/1909/press.html
Project Gutenberg	gutenberg.org
Project MUSE	muse.jhu.edu
Arts	**Web Address**
absolutearts	absolutearts.com
The Children's Museum of Indianapolis	childrensmuseum.org
ARTINFO Gallery Guide	artinfo.com/galleryguide/
The Getty	getty.edu
Louvre Museum	louvre.fr
Montreal Museum of Fine Arts	mmfa.qc.ca
Museumstuff.com	museumstuff.com
The Museum of Online Museums	coudal.com/moom
National Gallery of Art	nga.gov

For more information about literature and arts Web sites, visit the Computer Concepts CourseMate Web site at www.cengagebrain.com and then navigate to the Making Use of the Web Feature resource for this book.

Figure 29 Discover culture throughout the world by visiting these literature and arts Web sites.

The full text of hundreds of books is available online from the Bibliomania and Project Gutenberg Web sites. The Complete Review provides summaries, reviews, and Web links about a variety of books and their authors. The Bartleby Web site features biographies, definitions, quotations, dictionaries, and indexes.

When you are ready to absorb more culture, you can turn to various art Web sites. Many museums have images of their collections online. Among them are the Getty Museum in Los Angeles, the Montreal Museum of Fine Arts, and the Louvre Museum in Paris (Figure 30).

The absolutearts Web site focuses on contemporary art and includes video interviews with artists, art history research, and artists' blogs.

The Museum of Online Museums Web site provides links to museum and gallery Web sites, such as the Museum of Modern Art, The Bauhaus Archive, and The Art Institute of Chicago.

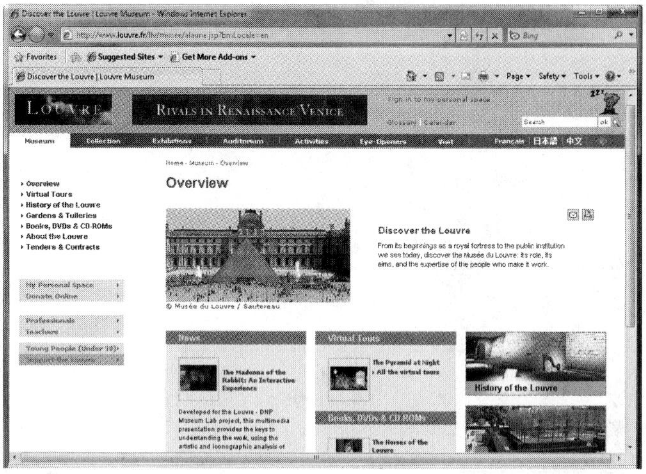

Figure 30 Permanent and temporary exhibitions, educational activities, and a bookstore are featured on the Louvre Museum Web site.

Literature and Arts Web Exercises

1. **Visit the Literary History Web site listed in Figure 29** and view one author in the Twentieth Century Literature, Nineteenth Century Literature, British Poets, and African American Literature sections. Read two literary criticism articles about each of the four authors and write a paragraph describing which of these authors is the most interesting to you. What are the advantages and disadvantages of reading literary criticism electronically?

2. **Using the arts Web sites listed in Figure 29,** search for three temporary exhibitions in galleries throughout the world. Describe the venues, the artists, and the works. Which permanent collections are found in these museums? Some people shop for gifts in the museums' stores. View and describe three items for sale.

Chapter Three

Application Software

Objectives

After completing this chapter, you will be able to:

1 Identify the four categories of application software

2 Differentiate among the seven forms through which software is available: packaged software, custom software, Web application, open source software, shareware, freeware, and public-domain software

3 Explain how the operating system and utility programs work with application software

4 Describe characteristics of a user interface

5 Identify the key features of widely used business programs: word processing, spreadsheet, database, presentation, note taking, personal information manager, business software for phones, business software suite, project management, accounting, document management, and enterprise computing

6 Identify the key features of widely used graphics and multimedia programs: computer-aided design, professional desktop publishing, professional paint/image editing, professional photo editing, professional video and audio editing, multimedia authoring, and Web page authoring

7 Identify the key features of widely used home, personal, and educational programs: personal finance, legal, tax preparation, personal desktop publishing, personal paint/image editing, personal photo editing and photo management, clip art/image gallery, personal video and audio editing, travel and mapping, reference and educational, and entertainment

8 Discuss the advantages of and ways to access Web applications

9 Identify the types of application software used in communications

10 Describe the learning aids available for application software

Application Software

With the proper software, a computer is a valuable tool. Software allows users to create letters, memos, reports, and other documents; develop multimedia presentations; design Web pages and diagrams; draw and alter images; record and enhance audio and video clips; prepare and file taxes; play single player or multiplayer games; compose e-mail messages and instant messages; and much more. To accomplish these and many other tasks, users work with application software. **Application software** consists of programs designed to make users more productive and/or assist them with personal tasks. Application software has a variety of uses:

1. To make business activities more efficient
2. To assist with graphics and multimedia projects
3. To support home, personal, and educational tasks
4. To facilitate communications

The table in Figure 3-1 categorizes popular types of application software by their general use. Although many types of communications software exist, the ones listed in Figure 3-1 are application software oriented.

The categories of application software in Figure 3-1 are not mutually exclusive. Software listed in one category may be used in other categories. For example, desktop publishing programs, which are categorized as graphics and multimedia software, often are used for business or personal reasons.

Application software is available in a variety of forms: packaged, custom, Web application, open source, shareware, freeware, and public domain.

- **Packaged software** is mass-produced, copyrighted retail software that meets the needs of a wide variety of users, not just a single user or company. Packaged software is available in retail stores or on the Web. Figure 3-1 shows some images of packaged software.
- **Custom software** performs functions specific to a business or industry. Sometimes a company cannot find packaged software that meets its unique requirements. In this case, the company may use programmers to develop tailor-made custom software, which usually costs more than packaged software.
- A **Web application** is a Web site that allows users to access and interact with software from any computer or device that is connected to the Internet. Many Web sites provide free access to their programs; some charge a fee. Types of Web applications include e-mail, word processing, tax preparation, and game programs. Web applications are discussed in more depth later in this chapter.

Four Categories of Application Software

Business	Graphics and Multimedia	Home/Personal/Educational
• Word Processing	• Computer-Aided Design (CAD)	• Software Suite (for Personal Use)
• Spreadsheet	• Desktop Publishing (for the Professional)	• Personal Finance
• Database	• Paint/Image Editing (for the Professional)	• Legal
• Presentation	• Photo Editing (for the Professional)	• Tax Preparation
• Note Taking	• Video and Audio Editing (for the Professional)	• Desktop Publishing (for Personal Use)
• Personal Information Manager (PIM)	• Multimedia Authoring	• Paint/Image Editing (for Personal Use)
• Business Software for Phones	• Web Page Authoring	• Photo Editing and Photo Management (for Personal Use)
• Business Software Suite		• Clip Art/Image Gallery
• Project Management		• Video and Audio Editing (for Personal Use)
• Accounting		• Home Design/Landscaping
• Document Management		• Travel and Mapping
• Enterprise Computing		• Reference and Educational
		• Entertainment

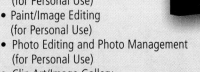

Communications

• Web Browser	• E-Mail	• Instant Messaging	• Chat Room	• Text, Picture, Video Messaging	
• RSS Aggregator	• Blogging	• Newsgroup/Message Board	• FTP	• VoIP	• Video Conferencing

Figure 3-1 The four major categories of popular application software are outlined in this table. Communications software often is bundled with other application or system software.

- **Open source software** is software provided for use, modification, and redistribution. This software has no restrictions from the copyright holder regarding modification of the software's internal instructions and its redistribution. Open source software usually can be downloaded from the Internet, often at no cost.
- **Shareware** is copyrighted software that is distributed at no cost for a trial period. To use a shareware program beyond that period, you send payment to the program developer. Shareware developers trust users to send payment if software use extends beyond the stated trial period. In some cases, a scaled-down version of the software is distributed free, and payment entitles the user to the fully functional product.
- **Freeware** is copyrighted software provided at no cost by an individual or a company that retains all rights to the software. Thus, programmers typically cannot incorporate freeware in applications they intend to sell. The word, free, in freeware indicates the software has no charge.
- **Public-domain software** has been donated for public use and has no copyright restrictions. Anyone can copy or distribute public-domain software to others at no cost.

Thousands of shareware, freeware, and public-domain programs are available on the Internet for users to download. Examples include communications, graphics, and game programs. These programs usually have fewer capabilities than packaged programs. Some packaged programs have trial versions, which you can use at no charge for a limited time, to see if the software meets your needs.

After you purchase or download software, you install it. During installation, the program may ask you to register and/or activate the software. (To learn more about installing software, complete the Learn How To 2 activity on pages 188 and 189.) Registering the software is optional and usually involves submitting your name and other personal information to the software manufacturer or developer. Registering the software often entitles you to product support. *Product activation* is a technique that some software manufacturers use to ensure the software is not installed on more computers than legally licensed. Usually, the software does not function or has limited functionality until you activate it via the Internet or telephone. Thus, activation is a required process for programs requesting it. You can activate some software more than once, for example, to run a program on both a desktop and notebook computer. Registering and/or activating the software also usually entitles you to free program updates for a specified time period, such as a year.

The Role of System Software

System software serves as the interface between the user, the application software, and the computer's hardware (Figure 3-2). To use application software, such as a word processing program, your computer must be running system software — specifically,

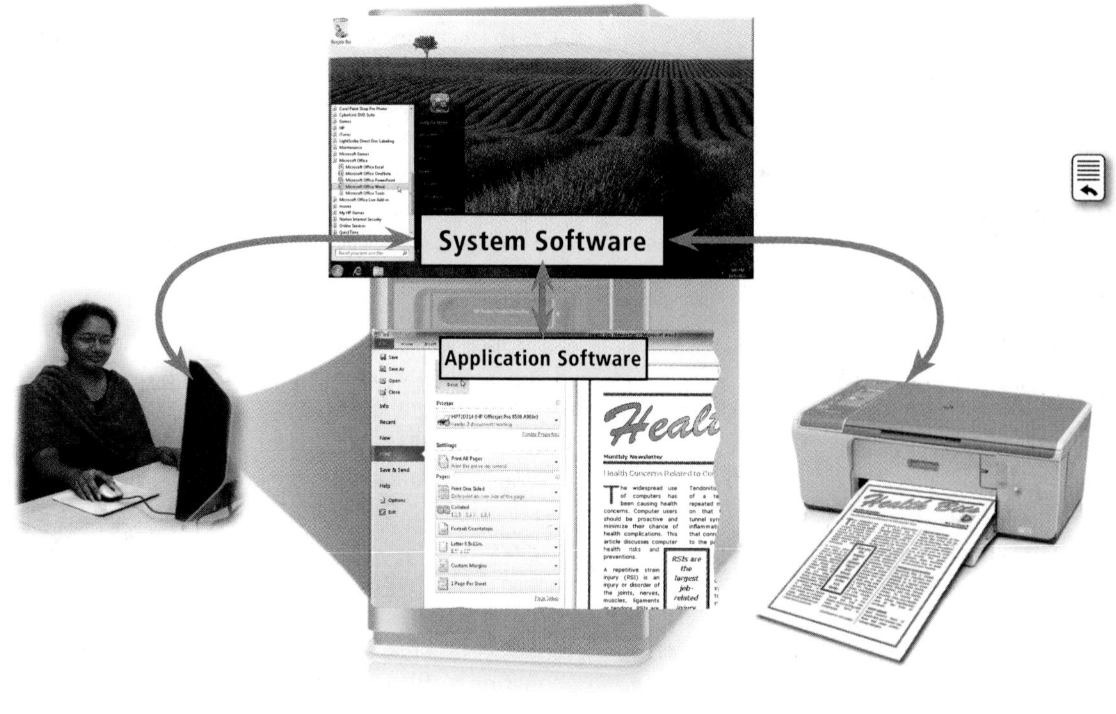

Figure 3-2 A user does not communicate directly with the computer hardware. Instead, system software is the interface between the user, the application software, and the hardware. For example, when a user instructs the application software to print a document, the application software sends the print instruction to the system software, which in turn sends the print instruction to the hardware.

an operating system. Three popular personal computer operating systems are Windows, Mac OS, and Linux.

Each time you start a computer, the operating system is *loaded* (copied) from the computer's hard disk into memory. Once the operating system is loaded, it coordinates all the activities of the computer. This includes starting application software and transferring data among input and output devices and memory. While the computer is running, the operating system remains in memory.

Utility Programs A utility program is a type of system software that assists users with controlling or maintaining the operation of a computer, its devices, or its software. Utility programs typically offer features that provide an environment conducive to successful use of application software. For example, utility programs protect a computer against malicious software and unauthorized intrusions, manage files and disks, compress files, play media files, and burn optical discs. (To learn more about how to compress files, complete the Learn How To 3 activity on page 189.)

One of the more important utility programs protects a computer against malicious software, or *malware*, which is a program that acts without a user's knowledge and deliberately alters the computer's operations. A computer virus is a type of malicious software. For a technical discussion about viruses and other malicious software, read the High-Tech Talk article on page 178. Chapter 8 discusses system software and utility programs in more depth.

Antivirus Programs
For more information, visit the Computer Concepts CourseMate Web site at www.cengagebrain.com, navigate to the Chapter 3 Web Link resource for this book, and then click Antivirus Programs.

FAQ 3-1

How many viruses exist on the Internet?

More than one million viruses exist on the Internet. This statistic stresses the importance of protecting your computer from various threats on the Internet, as well as practicing safe Web browsing habits. Not only is it possible to get a computer virus from downloading and opening an infected file or by opening an infected e-mail message, you also can fall victim to a computer virus simply by visiting a malicious Web site.

For more information, visit the Computer Concepts CourseMate Web site at www.cengagebrain.com, navigate to the Chapter 3 FAQ resource for this book, and then click Computer Viruses.

Working with Application Software

To use application software, you must instruct the operating system to start the program. The steps in Figure 3-3 illustrate one way to start and interact with the Paint program, which is included with the Windows operating system. The following paragraphs explain the steps in Figure 3-3.

Personal computer operating systems often use the concept of a desktop to make the computer easier to use. The **desktop** is an on-screen work area that has a graphical user interface. Step 1 of Figure 3-3 shows icons, a button, a pointer, and a menu on the Windows desktop. An **icon** is a small image displayed on the screen that represents a program, a document, or some other object. A **button** is a graphical element that you activate to cause a specific action to occur. One way to activate a button is to click it. To **click** a button on the screen requires moving the pointer to the button and then pressing and releasing a button on the mouse (usually the left mouse button). The **pointer** is a small symbol displayed on the screen that moves as you interact with the mouse or other pointing device. Common pointer shapes are an I-beam (I), a block arrow ( ), and a pointing hand ( ).

The Windows desktop contains a Start button on the lower-left corner of the taskbar. When you click the Start button, the Start menu is displayed on the desktop. A **menu** contains a list of commands from which you make selections. A **command** is an instruction that causes a program to perform a specific action.

As illustrated in Steps 1 and 2 of Figure 3-3, when you click the Start button and then click the All Programs command on the Start menu, the All Programs list is displayed on the Start menu. Clicking the Accessories folder in the All Programs list displays the Accessories list.

To start a program, you can click its program name on a menu or in a list. This action instructs the operating system to start the program, which means the program's instructions load from a storage medium (such as a hard disk) into memory. For example, when you click Paint in the Accessories list, Windows loads the Paint program instructions from the computer's hard disk into memory.

Once loaded into memory, the program appears in a window on the desktop (Step 3 of Figure 3-3). A **window** is a rectangular area of the screen that displays data and information. The top of a window has a **title bar**, which is a horizontal space that contains the window's name.

With the program loaded, you can create a new file or open an existing one. A *file* is a named collection of stored data, instructions, or information. A file can contain text, images, audio, and video. To distinguish among various files, each file has a file name. A *file name* is a unique combination of letters of the alphabet, numbers, and other characters that identifies a file. The title bar of the document window usually displays a document's file name. Step 4 of Figure 3-3 shows the contents of the file, Baby Buffalo, displaying in the Paint window. The file contains an image photographed with a digital camera.

In some cases, when you instruct a program to perform an activity such as print, the program displays a dialog box. A *dialog box* is a window that provides information, presents available options, or requests a response. Dialog boxes, such as the one shown in Step 5 of Figure 3-3, often contain option buttons, text boxes, check boxes, and command buttons. In this case, clicking the Print button in the dialog box instructs the computer to print the photo.

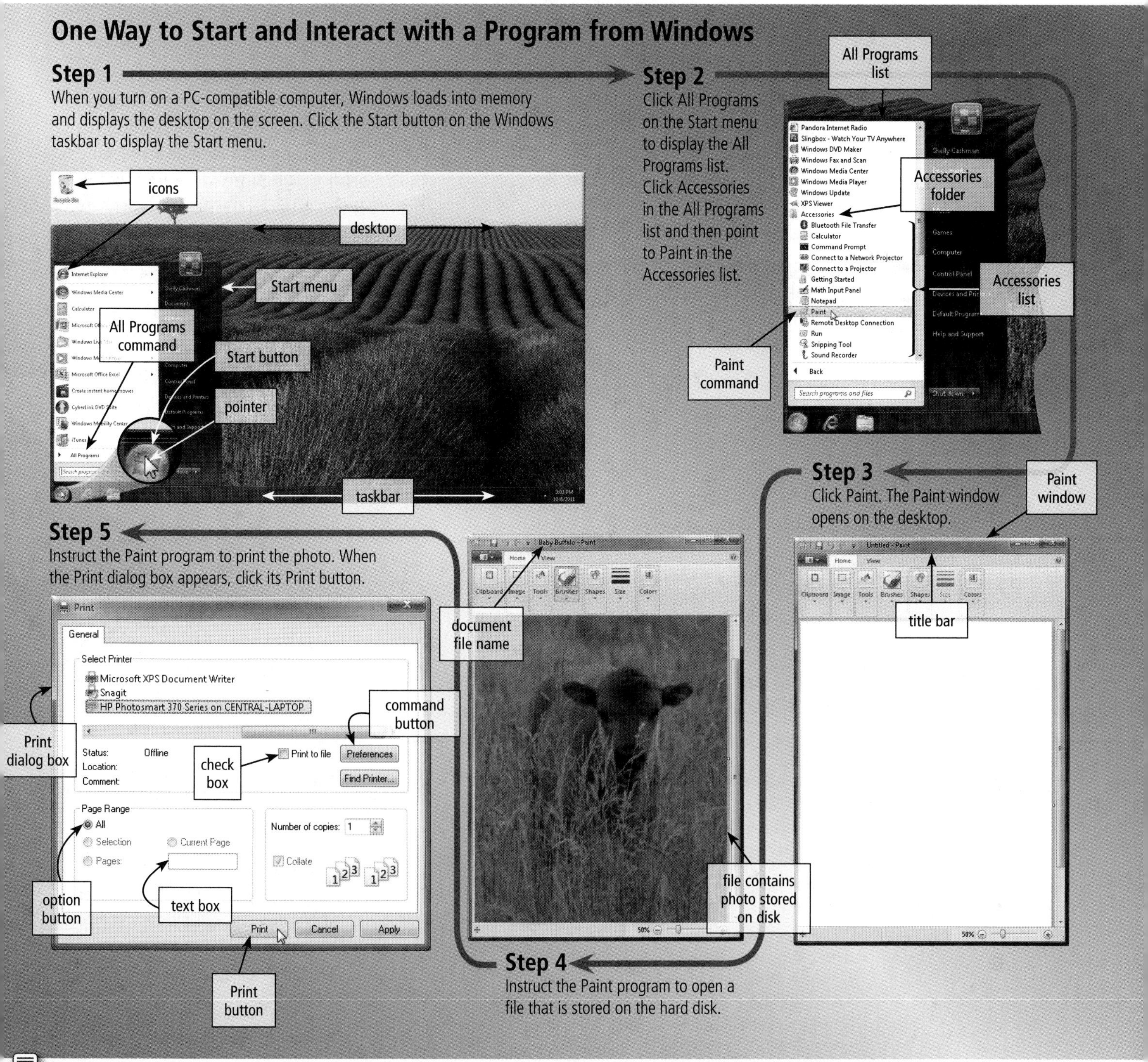
One Way to Start and Interact with a Program from Windows
Step 1
When you turn on a PC-compatible computer, Windows loads into memory and displays the desktop on the screen. Click the Start button on the Windows taskbar to display the Start menu.
icons
desktop
Start menu
All Programs command
Start button
pointer
taskbar
Step 2
Click All Programs on the Start menu to display the All Programs list. Click Accessories in the All Programs list and then point to Paint in the Accessories list.
All Programs list
Accessories folder
Accessories list
Paint command
Step 3
Click Paint. The Paint window opens on the desktop.
Paint window
title bar
Step 4
Instruct the Paint program to open a file that is stored on the hard disk.
document file name
file contains photo stored on disk
Step 5
Instruct the Paint program to print the photo. When the Print dialog box appears, click its Print button.
Print dialog box
command button
check box
option button
text box
Print button
Print
General
Select Printer
Microsoft XPS Document Writer
Snagit
HP Photosmart 370 Series on CENTRAL-LAPTOP
Status: Offline
Location:
Comment:
Print to file
Preferences
Find Printer...
Page Range
All
Selection
Current Page
Pages:
Number of copies: 1
Collate
Print
Cancel
Apply

Figure 3-3 This figure shows one way to start and interact with a program from Windows.

✔ QUIZ YOURSELF 3-1

Instructions: Find the true statement below. Then, rewrite the remaining false statements so that they are true.

1. Application software is used to make business activities more efficient; assist with graphics and multimedia projects; support home, personal, and educational tasks; and facilitate communications.
2. Public-domain software is mass-produced, copyrighted retail software that meets the needs of a wide variety of users, not just a single user or company.
3. To use system software, your computer must be running application software.
4. When a program is started, its instructions load from memory into a storage medium.

Quiz Yourself Online: To further check your knowledge of pages 142 through 145, visit the Computer Concepts CourseMate Web site at www.cengagebrain.com, navigate to the Chapter 3 Quiz Yourself resource for this book, and then click Objectives 1 – 4.

Business Software

Business software is application software that assists people in becoming more effective and efficient while performing their daily business activities. Business software includes programs such as word processing, spreadsheet, database, presentation, note taking, personal information manager, business software for phones, business software suites, project management, accounting, document management, and enterprise computing software. Figure 3-4 lists popular programs for each of these categories.

Popular Business Programs

Application Software	Manufacturer	Program Name
Word Processing	Microsoft	Word
	Apple	Pages
	Corel	WordPerfect
Spreadsheet	Microsoft	Excel
	Apple	Numbers
	Corel	Quattro Pro
Database	Microsoft	Access
	Corel	Paradox
	Oracle	Oracle Database
	Sun	MySQL
Presentation	Microsoft	PowerPoint
	Apple	Keynote
	Corel	Presentations
Note Taking	Microsoft	OneNote
	Agilix	GoBinder
	Corel	Grafigo
	SnapFiles	KeyNote
Personal Information Manager (PIM)	Microsoft	Outlook
	Google	Calendar
	IBM	Lotus Organizer
	Palm	Desktop
	Mozilla	Thunderbird
Business Software for Phones	CNetX	Pocket SlideShow
	DataViz	Documents To Go
	Microsoft	Word Mobile Excel Mobile PowerPoint Mobile Outlook Mobile
	Mobile Systems	MobiSystems Office Suite
	Ultrasoft	Money
Business Software Suite (for the Professional)	Microsoft	Office Office for Mac
	Apple	iWork
	Google	Google Docs
	Sun	OpenOffice.org StarOffice
	Corel	WordPerfect Office
	IBM	Lotus SmartSuite
Project Management	CS Odessa	ConceptDraw PROJECT
	Microsoft	Project
	Oracle	Primavera SureTrak Project Manager
Accounting	Intuit	QuickBooks
	Microsoft	Accounting
	Sage Software	Peachtree
Document Management	Adobe	Acrobat
	Enfocus	PitStop
	Nuance	PDF Converter
Enterprise Computing	Oracle	PeopleSoft Enterprise Human Capital Management
	Sage Software	Sage MAS 500
	MSC Software	MSC.SimManager
	Oracle	Oracle Manufacturing
	SAP	mySAP Customer Relationship Management
	NetSuite	NetERP
	Syntellect	Syntellect Interaction Management Suite

Figure 3-4 Popular business software.

The following sections discuss the features and functions of business software. Word processing and spreadsheet software have a heavier emphasis because of their predominant use.

Word Processing Software

Word processing software is one of the more widely used types of application software. **Word processing software**, sometimes called a *word processor*, allows users to create and manipulate documents containing mostly text and sometimes graphics (Figure 3-5). Millions of people use word processing software every day to develop documents such as letters, memos, reports, mailing labels, newsletters, and Web pages.

A major advantage of using word processing software is that users easily can change what they have written. For example, you can insert, delete, or rearrange words, sentences, paragraphs, or entire sections. Word processing software also has many features to make documents look professional and visually appealing. For example, you can change the shape, size, and color of characters; apply special effects such as three-dimensional shadows; and organize text in newspaper-style columns. When using colors, however, they print as black or gray unless you have a color printer.

Most word processing software allows users to incorporate graphical images, such as digital photos and clip art, in documents. **Clip art** is a collection of electronic drawings, photos, and other images. Word processing software usually includes public-domain images. You can find additional public-domain and proprietary images on the Web or purchase them on optical disc. In Figure 3-5, a user inserted an image of a baseball player in the document. With word processing software, you easily can modify the appearance of an image after inserting it in the document.

With word processing software, you can define the size of the paper on which to print and specify the *margins* — that is, the portion of the page outside the main body of text, including the top, the bottom, and both sides of the paper. A feature, called *wordwrap*, allows users to type words in a paragraph continually without pressing the ENTER key at the end of each line. When you modify paper size or margins, the word processing software automatically rewraps text so that it fits in the adjusted paper size and margins.

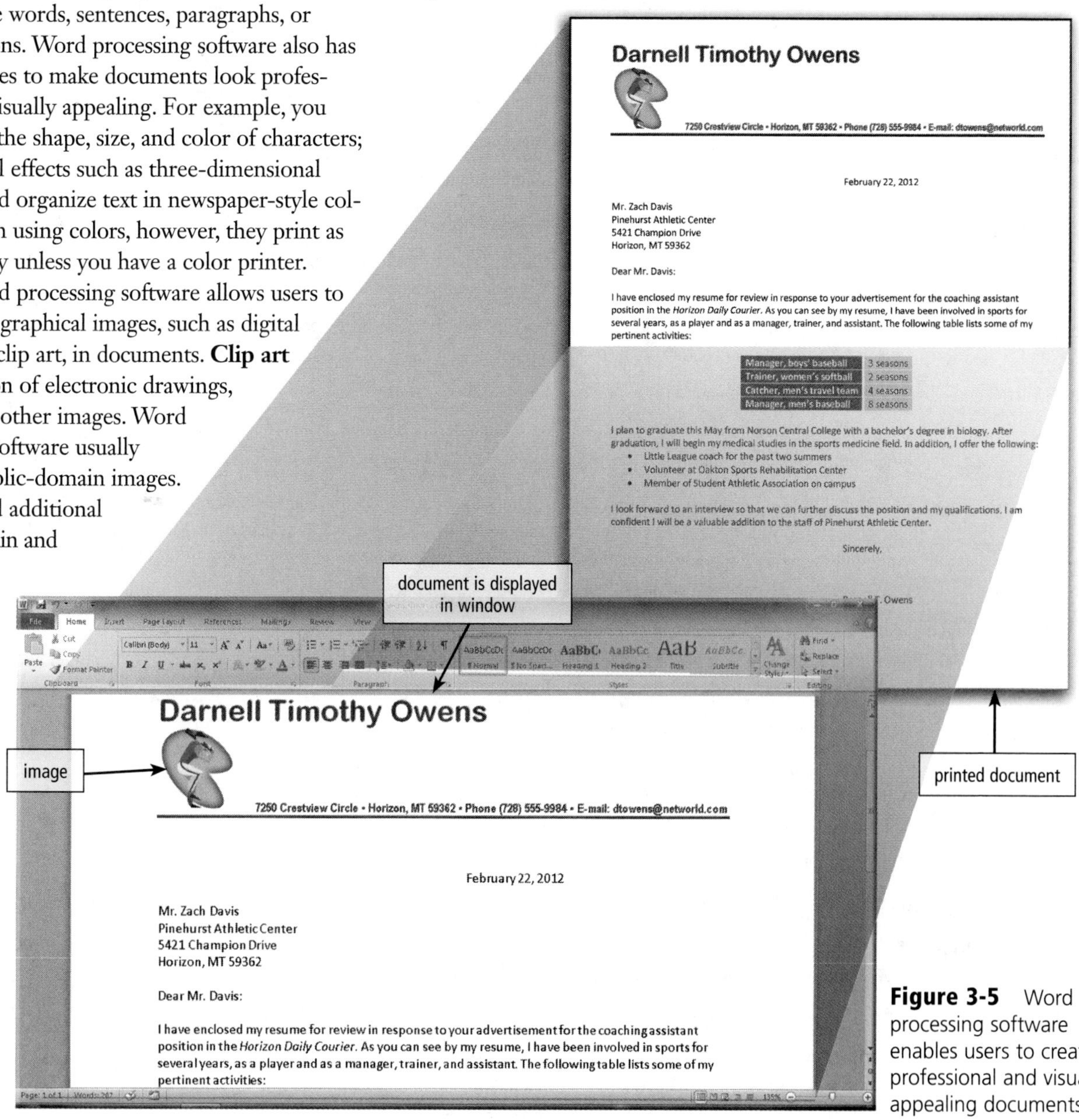

Figure 3-5 Word processing software enables users to create professional and visually appealing documents.

As you type more lines of text than can be displayed on the screen, the top portion of the document moves upward, or scrolls, off the screen. *Scrolling* is the process of moving different portions of the document on the screen into view.

Word processing software typically includes a *spelling checker*, which reviews the spelling of individual words, sections of a document, or the entire document. The spelling checker compares the words in the document with an electronic dictionary that is part of the word processing software. You can customize the electronic dictionary by adding words such as personal names. Some word processing programs also check for contextual spelling errors, such as a misuse of homophones (words pronounced the same but have different spellings or meanings, such as one and won).

Word processing software also enables you to insert headers and footers in a document. A *header* is text that appears at the top of each page, and a *footer* is text that appears at the bottom of each page. Page numbers, company names, report titles, and dates are examples of items included in headers and footers.

In addition to these basic capabilities, most current word processing programs provide numerous additional features, which are listed in the table in Figure 3-6.

Word Processing Software

For more information, visit the Computer Concepts CourseMate Web site at www.cengagebrain.com, navigate to the Chapter 3 Web Link resource for this book, and then click Word Processing Software.

Additional Word Processing Features	
AutoCorrect	As you type words, the AutoCorrect feature corrects common spelling and capitalization errors.
AutoFormat	As you type, the AutoFormat feature automatically applies formatting to the text. For example, it automatically numbers a list or converts a Web address to a hyperlink.
Collaboration	Collaboration allows multiple users to enter comments in a document and read and reply to each other's comments.
Columns	Most word processing software can arrange text in two or more columns to look like text in a newspaper or magazine. The text from the bottom of one column automatically flows to the top of the next column.
Grammar Checker	The grammar checker proofreads documents for grammar, writing style, sentence structure errors, and reading statistics.
Ink Input	Supports input from a digital pen. Word processing software that supports ink input incorporates user's handwritten text and drawings in a word processing document. Ink input is popular on Tablet PCs.
Macros	A *macro* is a sequence of keystrokes and instructions that a user records and saves. When you want to execute the same series of instructions, execute the macro instead.
Mail Merge	Creates form letters, mailing labels, and envelopes.
Reading Layout	For users who prefer reading on the screen, reading layout increases the readability and legibility of an on-screen document by hiding unnecessary buttons and increasing the size of displayed characters.
Research	Allows you to search through various forms of Internet reference information — based on selected text in a document. Research services available include a thesaurus, English and bilingual dictionaries, encyclopedias, and Web sites that provide information such as stock quotes, news articles, and company profiles.
Search and Replace	The search feature finds all occurrences of a certain character, word, or phrase. The replace feature, which usually works in conjunction with the search feature, substitutes existing characters or words with new ones.
Smart Tags	*Smart tags* automatically appear on the screen when you perform a certain action. For example, typing an address causes a smart tag to appear. Clicking this smart tag provides options to display a map of the address or driving directions to or from the address.
Tables	Tables organize information into rows and columns.
Templates	A *template* is a document that contains the formatting necessary for a specific document type. Templates usually exist for memos, fax cover sheets, and letters. In addition to templates provided with the software, users have access to many online templates through the manufacturer's Web site.
Thesaurus	With a thesaurus, a user looks up a synonym (word with the same meaning) for a word in a document.
Tracking Changes	If multiple users work with a document, the word processing software highlights or color-codes changes made by various users.
Voice Recognition	With some word processing programs, users can speak into the computer's microphone and watch the spoken words appear on the screen as they talk. Users edit and format the document by speaking or spelling an instruction.
Web Page Development	Most word processing software allows users to create, edit, format, and convert documents so that they can be displayed on the Web.

Figure 3-6 Many additional features of word processing software.

Developing a Document

With application software, such as a word processing program, users create, edit, format, save, and print documents. During the process of developing a document, users likely will switch back and forth among all of these activities.

When you **create** a document, you enter text or numbers, insert images, and perform other tasks using an input device such as a keyboard, mouse, digital pen, or microphone. If you are using Microsoft Word to design a flyer, for example, you are creating a document.

To **edit** a document means to make changes to its existing content. Common editing tasks include inserting, deleting, cutting, copying, and pasting. Inserting text involves adding text to a document. Deleting text means that you are removing text or other content. Cutting is the process of removing a portion of the document and storing it in a temporary storage location, sometimes called a *clipboard*. A clipboard also contains items that you copy (duplicate) in a document. *Pasting* is the process of transferring an item from a clipboard to a specific location in a document. Read Ethics & Issues 3-1 for a related discussion.

When users **format** a document, they change its appearance. Formatting is important because the overall look of a document significantly can affect its ability to communicate clearly. Examples of formatting tasks are changing the font, font size, and font style.

A **font** is a name assigned to a specific design of characters. Two basic types of fonts are serif and sans serif. A *serif font* has short decorative lines at the upper and lower ends of some characters. Sans means without. Thus, a *sans serif font* does not have the short decorative lines at the upper and lower ends of the characters. Cambria is an example of a serif font. Calibri is an example of a sans serif font.

Font size indicates the size of the characters in a particular font. Font size is gauged by a measurement system called points. A single *point* is about 1/72 of an inch in height. The text you are reading in this book is about 10 point. Thus, each character is about 5/36 (10/72) of an inch in height. A *font style* adds emphasis to a font. Bold, italic, underline, and color are examples of font styles. Figure 3-7 illustrates fonts, font sizes, and font styles.

Ethics & Issues

For the complete text of the Ethics & Issues boxes found in this chapter, visit the Computer Concepts CourseMate Web site at www.cengagebrain.com and then navigate to the Chapter 3 Ethics & Issues resource for this book.

ETHICS & ISSUES 3-1

How Should Schools Deal with Internet Plagiarism?

A high school teacher failed 28 students for plagiarizing, or copying, material from the Internet. When parents complained, the school board passed the students, and the teacher resigned. Word processing software and the Internet make plagiarism easier than ever. Students can use term paper Web sites, such as CheatHouse.com or Research Papers Online, to copy complete papers on a variety of topics. According to one survey, half of those who responded said that cheating does not or may not matter in the long run, and 60 percent had plagiarized in the past. Students who plagiarize blame peer pressure, classroom competition, the "busy work" nature of some assignments, and the permissive attitude that pervades the Internet. Teachers have several tools to catch plagiarists, including a variety of Internet-based services, such as Turnitin, that compare suspected papers to papers found on the Internet and produce an originality report highlighting text that may have been copied. Some instructors, however, are reluctant to investigate the integrity of a student's work and possibly ruin an academic career.

How should educators deal with plagiarism? Should a school's response to plagiarism depend on such factors as the material copied, the assignment for which it was copied, or the reason it was copied? Why or why not? How would you feel if a paper you wrote was used by a service such as Turnitin to be used as a benchmark against other student's papers? Why? Should schools nationwide be required to use a service such as Turnitin in an attempt to stop cheating? Why or why not?

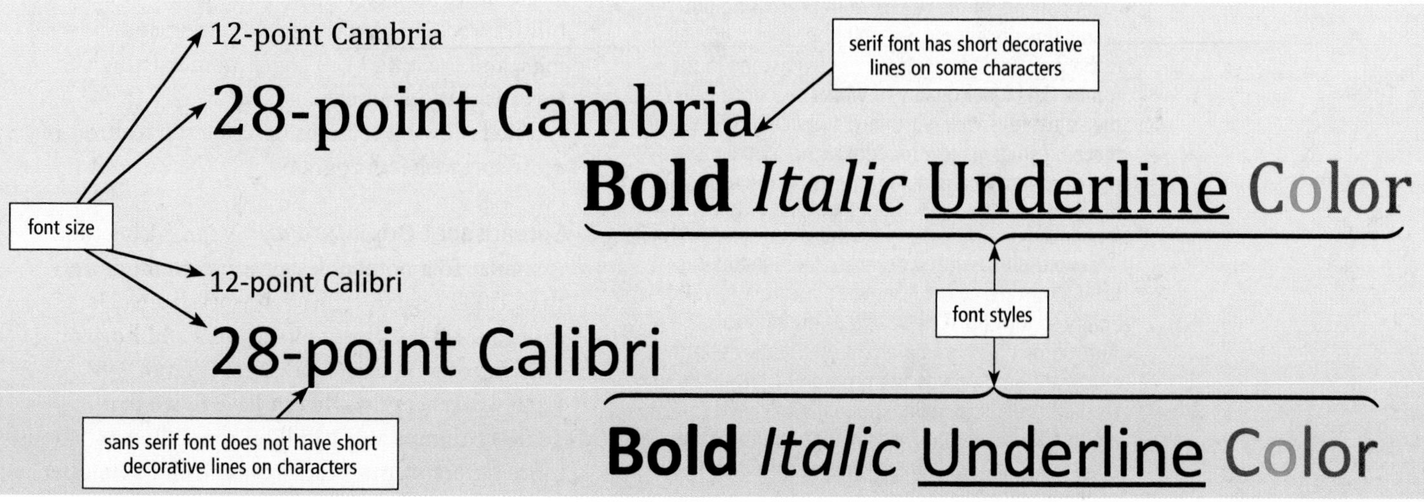

Figure 3-7 The Cambria and Calibri fonts are shown in two font sizes and a variety of font styles.

During the process of creating, editing, and formatting a document, the computer holds it in memory. To keep the document for future use requires that you save it. When you **save** a document, the computer transfers the document from memory to a storage medium such as a USB flash drive or hard disk. Once saved, a document is stored permanently as a file on the storage medium. To learn more about how to save a file, complete the Learn How To 1 activity on page 188.

When you **print** a document, the computer places the contents of the document on paper or some other medium. You can print the same document many times, with each copy looking just like the first. Instead of printing a document and physically distributing it, some users e-mail the document to others on a network such as the Internet. Read Ethics & Issues 3-2 for a related discussion.

ETHICS & ISSUES 3-2

Are Word Processing Programs Making Students Lazy?

Today, word processing programs fix spelling and grammar mistakes, automatically format documents with templates, help correctly reference works cited in a document, and seem to do everything short of generating an idea for a document. Some educators believe that the proliferation of word processing automation is cheating students of the fundamental ability to perform these tasks on their own. Research shows that as word processing programs became more popular over the past years, the quality of written work done without the aid of this software has dropped dramatically. Opponents of using word processing software for assignments point out the quality of e-mail and instant messages is markedly worse than works written with the aid of modern word processing programs.

Proponents of the use of word processing programs for educational use point out that automation is the way writing should be done now and in the future. The higher quality of works produced using the software is well worth not sacrificing time toward teaching students less modern tactics. Students are more productive and able to focus on the topics at hand, rather than worry about spelling errors.

Are word processing programs making students lazy? Why or why not? Should educators have the ability to turn off time-saving features, such as the AutoCorrect and grammar checker features, in their students' word processing programs? Why? Do students need the ability manually to check spelling and grammar, format a document, and reference cited works in a document, in the same way that students still learn multiplication and long division? Why or why not?

FAQ 3-2

How often should I save a document?

Saving at regular intervals ensures that the majority of your work will not be lost in the event of a power loss or system failure. Many programs have an AutoSave feature that automatically saves open documents at specified time intervals, such as every 10 minutes.

For more information, visit the Computer Concepts CourseMate Web site at www.cengagebrain.com, navigate to the Chapter 3 FAQ resource for this book, and then click Saving Documents.

Spreadsheet Software

Spreadsheet software is another widely used type of application software. **Spreadsheet software** allows users to organize data in rows and columns and perform calculations on the data. These rows and columns collectively are called a *worksheet*. For years, people used paper to organize data and perform calculations by hand. In an electronic worksheet, you organize data in the same manner, and the computer performs the calculations more quickly and accurately (Figure 3-8). Because of spreadsheet software's logical approach to organizing data, many people use this software to organize and present non-financial data, as well as financial data.

Like word processing software, most spreadsheet software has basic features to help users create, edit, and format worksheets. Spreadsheet software also incorporates many of the features found in word processing software such as macros, checking spelling, changing fonts and font sizes, adding colors, tracking changes, inserting audio and video clips, providing research capabilities, recognizing handwritten text and drawings, and creating Web pages from existing spreadsheet documents.

The following sections describe the features of most spreadsheet programs.

Spreadsheet Organization A spreadsheet file is similar to a notebook that can contain more than 1,000 related individual worksheets. Data is organized vertically in columns and horizontally in rows on each worksheet (Figure 3-8). Each worksheet usually can have more than 16,000 columns and 1 million rows. One or more letters identify each column, and a number identifies each row. Only a small fraction of the

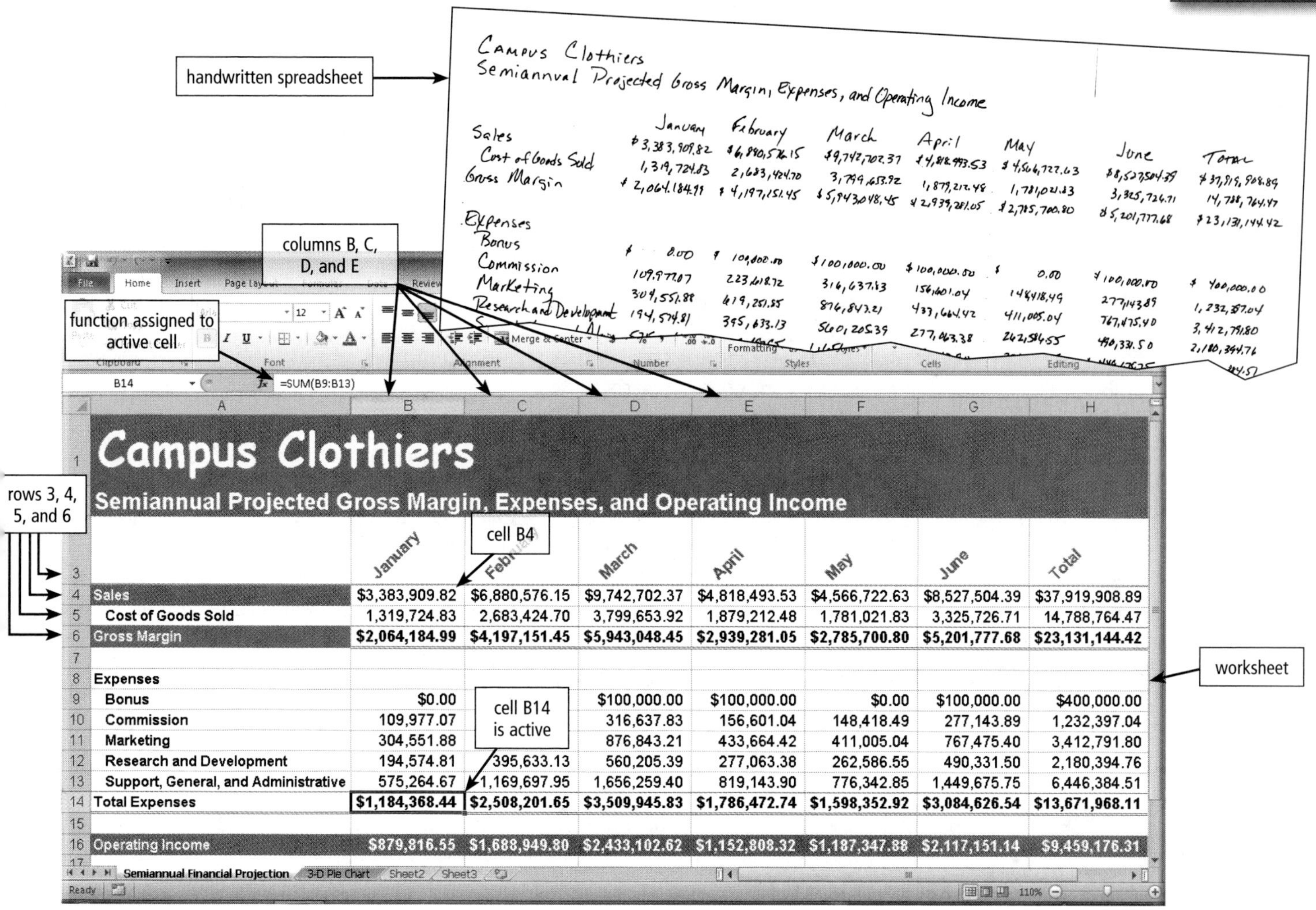

Figure 3-8 With spreadsheet software, you create worksheets that contain data arranged in rows and columns, and you perform calculations on the data in the worksheets.

columns and rows are visible on the screen at one time. Scrolling through the worksheet displays different parts of it on the screen.

A *cell* is the intersection of a column and row. Each worksheet has more than 17 billion cells in which you can enter data. The spreadsheet software identifies cells by the column and row in which they are located. For example, the intersection of column B and row 4 is referred to as cell B4. As shown in Figure 3-8, cell B4 contains the number, $3,383,909.82, which represents the sales for January.

Cells can contain three types of data: labels, values, and formulas. The text, or *label*, entered in a cell identifies the worksheet data and helps organize the worksheet. Using descriptive labels, such as Gross Margin and Total Expenses, helps make a worksheet more meaningful.

Calculations Many of the worksheet cells shown in Figure 3-8 contain a number, called a *value*, that can be used in a calculation. Other cells, however, contain formulas that generate values. A *formula* performs calculations on the data in the worksheet and displays the resulting value in a cell, usually the cell containing the formula. When creating a worksheet, you can enter your own formulas. In Figure 3-8, for example, cell B14 could contain the formula =B9+B10+B11+B12+B13, which would add together (sum) the contents of cells B9, B10, B11, B12, and B13. That is, this formula calculates the total expenses for January. A more efficient way to sum the contents of cells, however, is to use a special type of formula, called a function.

A *function* is a predefined formula that performs common calculations such as adding the values in a group of cells or generating a

Spreadsheet Software

For more information, visit the Computer Concepts CourseMate Web site at www.cengagebrain.com, navigate to the Chapter 3 Web Link resource for this book, and then click Spreadsheet Software.

value such as the time or date. For example, the function =SUM(B9:B13) instructs the spreadsheet program to add all of the numbers in cells B9 through B13. Figure 3-9 lists functions commonly included in spreadsheet programs.

Spreadsheet Functions

Financial	
FV (rate, number of periods, payment)	Calculates the future value of an investment
NPV (rate, range)	Calculates the net present value of an investment
PMT (rate, number of periods, present value)	Calculates the periodic payment for an annuity
PV (rate, number of periods, payment)	Calculates the present value of an investment
RATE (number of periods, payment, present value)	Calculates the periodic interest rate of an annuity
Date and Time	
DATE	Returns the current date
NOW	Returns the current date and time
TIME	Returns the current time
Mathematical	
ABS (number)	Returns the absolute value of a number
INT (number)	Rounds a number down to the nearest integer
LN (number)	Calculates the natural logarithm of a number
LOG (number, base)	Calculates the logarithm of a number to a specified base
ROUND (number, number of digits)	Rounds a number to a specified number of digits
SQRT (number)	Calculates the square root of a number
SUM (range)	Calculates the total of a range of numbers
Statistical	
AVERAGE (range)	Calculates the average value of a range of numbers
COUNT (range)	Counts how many cells in the range have numeric entries
MAX (range)	Returns the maximum value in a range
MIN (range)	Returns the minimum value in a range
STDEV (range)	Calculates the standard deviation of a range of numbers
Logical	
IF (logical test, value if true, value if false)	Performs a test and returns one value if the result of the test is true and another value if the result is false

Figure 3-9 Functions typically found in spreadsheet software.

Recalculation One of the more powerful features of spreadsheet software is its capability of recalculating the rest of the worksheet when data in a worksheet changes. In Figure 3-8 on the previous page, for example, if you change the bonus for January from $0.00 to $100,000.00, the total expenses in cell B14 automatically change from $1,184,368.44 to $1,284,368.44.

Spreadsheet software's capability of recalculating data also makes it a valuable budgeting, forecasting, and decision making tool. Most spreadsheet software includes *what-if analysis* tools, where you change certain values in a spreadsheet to reveal the effects of those changes.

Charting Another standard feature of spreadsheet software is *charting*, which depicts the data in graphical form. A visual representation of data through charts often makes it easier for users to see at a glance the relationship among the numbers.

Three popular chart types are line charts, column charts, and pie charts. Figure 3-10 shows examples of these charts that were plotted using the five types of expenses for each of the months shown in the worksheet in Figure 3-8 on the previous page. A *line chart* shows a trend during a period of time, as indicated by a rising or falling line. For example, a line chart could show the total expenses for each of the six months. A *column chart*, also called a *bar chart*, displays bars of various lengths to show the relationship of data. The bars can be horizontal, vertical, or stacked on top of one another. For example, a column chart might show the total expenses, with each bar representing a different category of expense in a given month. A *pie chart*, which has the shape of a round pie cut into slices, shows the relationship of parts to a whole. For example, you might use a pie chart to show the percentage each expense category contributed to the total expenditures.

When you modify data in a worksheet, any associated charts automatically update to reflect the worksheet changes. Charts, as well as any other part of a worksheet, can be linked to or embedded in a word processing document.

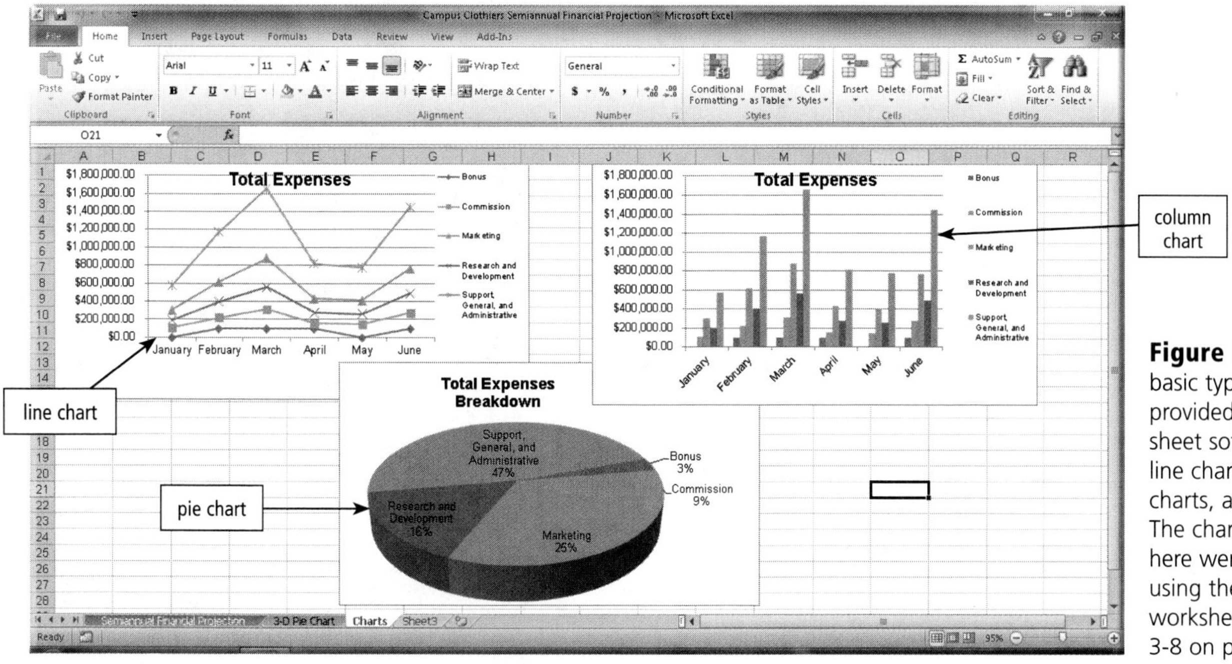

Figure 3-10 Three basic types of charts provided with spreadsheet software are line charts, column charts, and pie charts. The charts shown here were created using the data in the worksheet in Figure 3-8 on page 151.

Database Software

A **database** is a collection of data organized in a manner that allows access, retrieval, and use of that data. In a manual database, you might record data on paper and store it in a filing cabinet. With a computerized database, such as the one shown in Figure 3-11, the computer stores the data in an electronic format on a storage medium such as a hard disk.

Database software is application software that allows users to create, access, and manage a database. Using database software, you can add, change, and delete data in a database; sort and retrieve data from the database; and create forms and reports using the data in the database.

With most personal computer database programs, a database consists of a collection

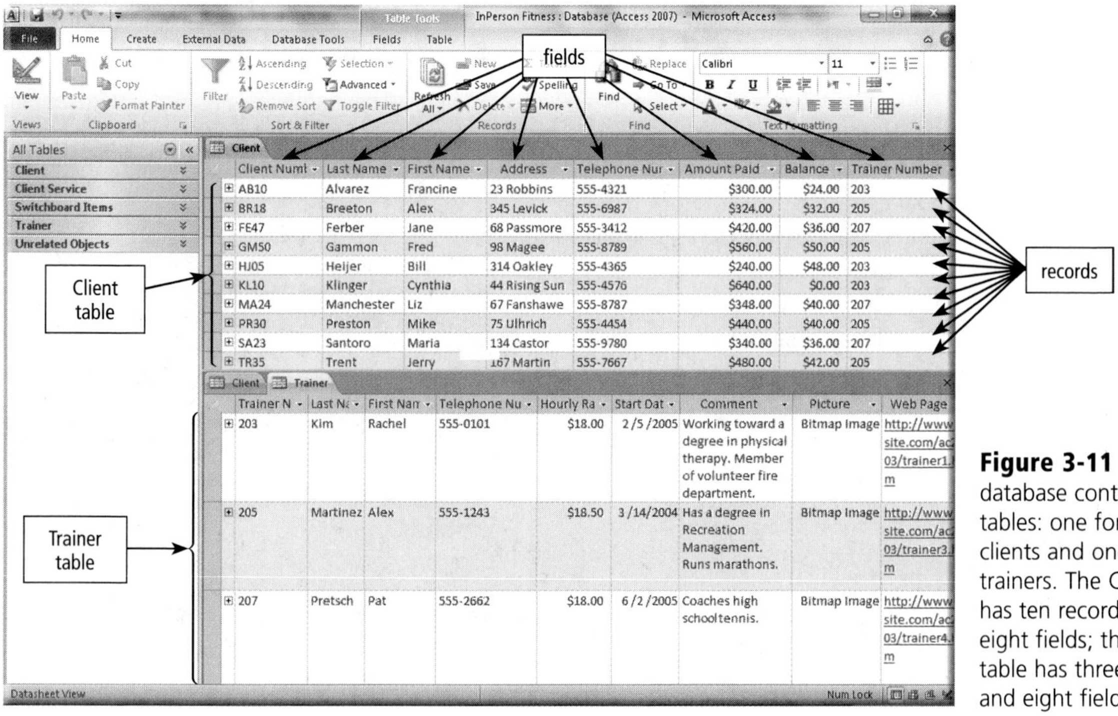

Figure 3-11 This database contains two tables: one for the clients and one for the trainers. The Client table has ten records and eight fields; the Trainer table has three records and eight fields.

of tables, organized in rows and columns. Each row, called a *record*, contains data about a given person, product, object, or event. Each column, called a *field*, contains a specific category of data within a record.

The Fitness database shown in Figure 3-11 on the previous page consists of two tables: a Client table and a Trainer table. The Client table contains ten records (rows), each storing data about one client. The client data is grouped into eight fields (columns): Client Number, Last Name, First Name, Address, Telephone Number, Amount Paid, Balance, and Trainer Number. The Balance field, for instance, contains the balance due from the client. The Client and Trainer tables relate to one another through a common field, Trainer Number.

Database Software

For more information, visit the Computer Concepts CourseMate Web site at www.cengagebrain.com, navigate to the Chapter 3 Web Link resource for this book, and then click Database Software.

Users run queries to retrieve data. A *query* is a request for specific data from the database. For example, a query might request clients whose balance is greater than $45. Database software can take the results of a query and present it in a window on the screen or send it to the printer.

? FAQ 3-3

How big is the largest database?

According to a recent survey, the world's largest database holds more than 6 quadrillion characters. The size of the largest database is expected to rise significantly during the next several years.

For more information, visit the Computer Concepts CourseMate Web site at www.cengagebrain.com, navigate to the Chapter 3 FAQ resource for this book, and then click Enterprise Databases.

Presentation Software

Presentation software is application software that allows users to create visual aids for presentations to communicate ideas, messages, and other information to a group. The presentations can be viewed as slides, sometimes called a *slide show*, that are displayed on a large monitor or on a projection screen (Figure 3-12).

Presentation software typically provides a variety of predefined presentation formats that define complementary colors for backgrounds, text, and graphical accents on the slides. This software also provides a variety of layouts for each individual slide such as a title slide, a two-column slide, and a slide with clip art, a picture, a chart, a table, or a diagram (Figure 3-13). In addition, you can enhance any

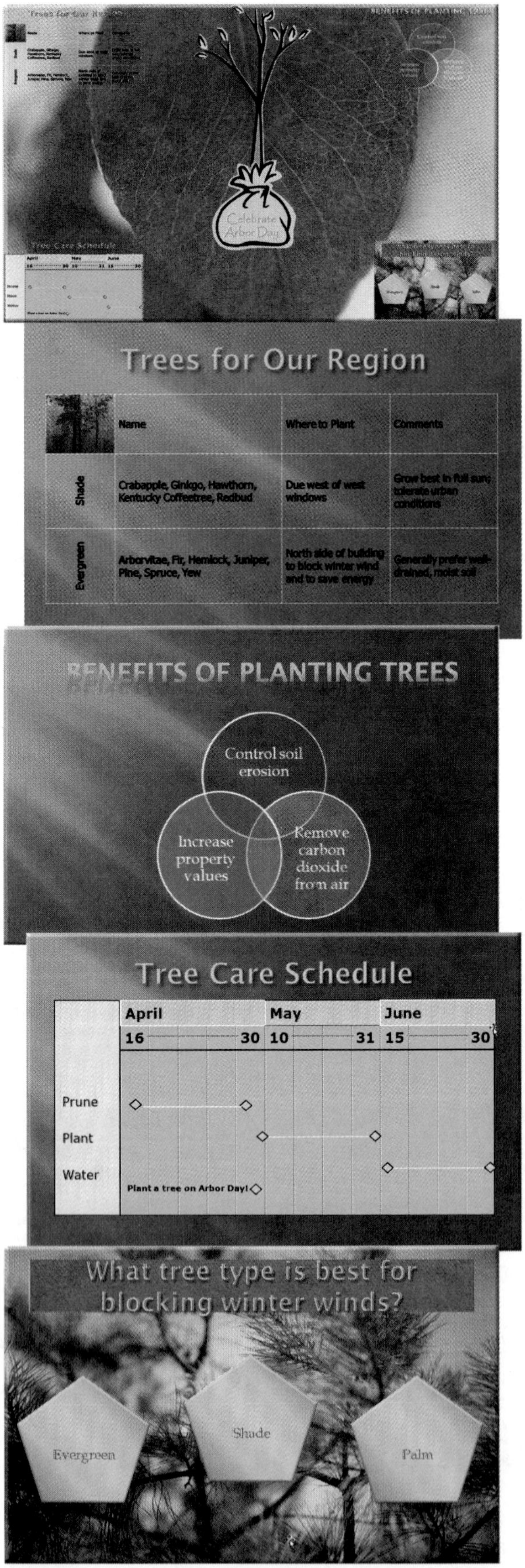

Figure 3-12 This presentation created with presentation software consists of five slides.

text, charts, and graphical images on a slide with 3-D, animation, and other special effects such as shading, shadows, and textures.

When building a presentation, users can set the slide timing so that the presentation automatically displays the next slide after a preset delay. Presentation software allows you to apply special effects to the transition between slides. One slide, for example, might fade away as the next slide appears.

To help organize the presentation, you can view thumbnail versions of all the slides similarly to how 35mm slides look on a photographer's light table.

Presentation software typically includes a clip gallery that provides images, photos, video clips, and audio clips to enhance multimedia presentations. Users with an artistic ability can create their own graphics using paint/image editing software (discussed later in the chapter) and then *import* (bring in) the graphics into a slide. Some audio and video editing programs work with presentation software, providing users with an easy means to record and insert video, music, and audio commentary in a presentation.

You can view or print a finished presentation in a variety of formats, including an outline of text from each slide, audience handouts that show completed slides, and speaker notes for each slide. Current presentation software enables users to work with multiple monitors, for example, displaying the presentation on one monitor and the speaker notes on another.

Presentation software incorporates some of the features found in word processing software such as checking spelling, formatting, providing research capabilities, recognizing handwritten text and drawings, and creating Web pages from existing slide shows.

Presentation Software

For more information, visit the Computer Concepts CourseMate Web site at www.cengagebrain.com, navigate to the Chapter 3 Web Link resource for this book, and then click Presentation Software.

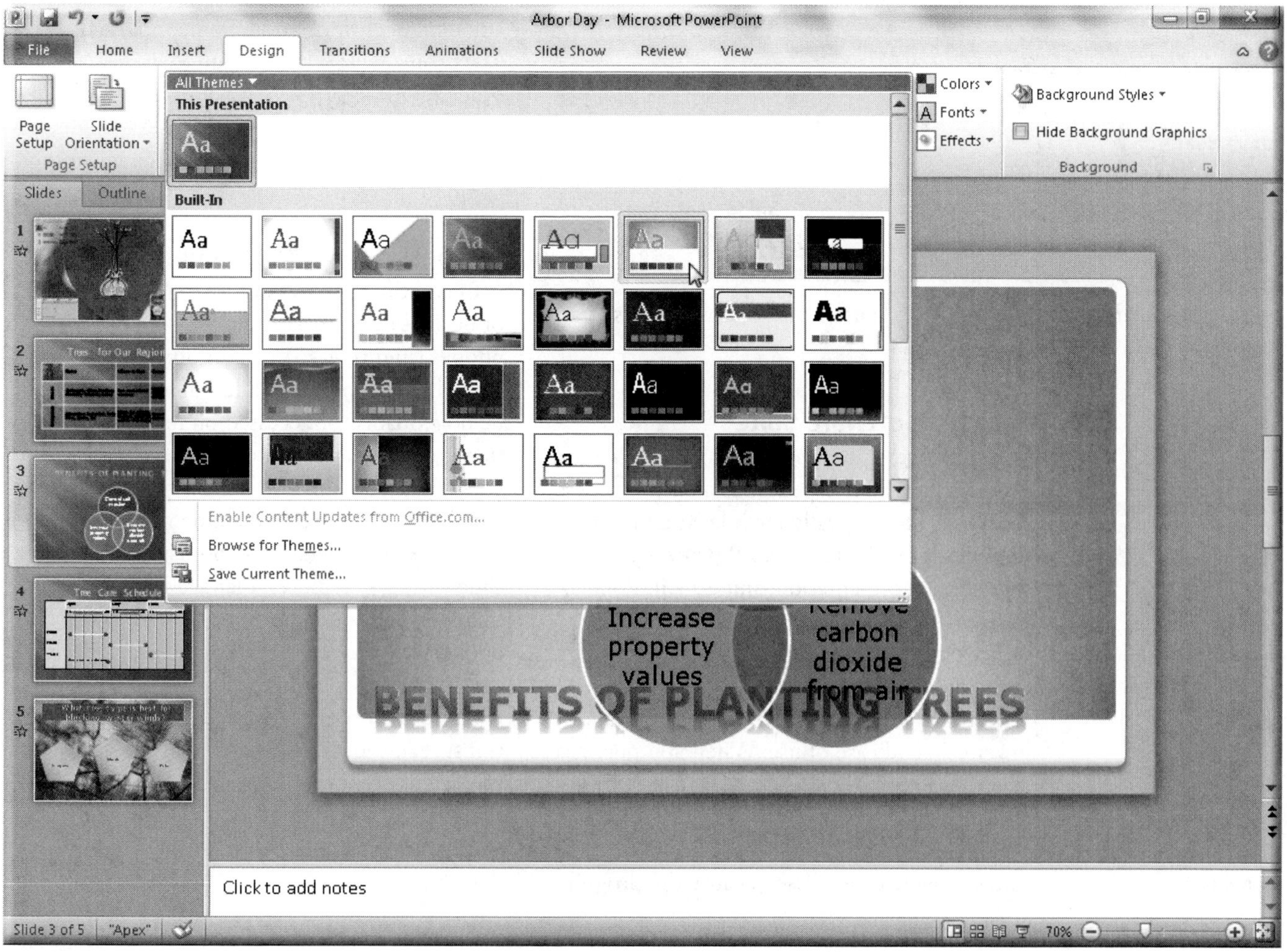

Figure 3-13 In presentation software, users can change the design and layout of any slide in a presentation.

Note Taking Software

Note taking software is application software that enables users to enter typed text, handwritten comments, drawings, or sketches anywhere on a page and then save the page as part of a notebook (Figure 3-14). The software can convert handwritten comments to typed text or store the notes in handwritten form. Users also can include audio recordings as part of their notes.

Users find note taking software convenient during meetings, class lectures, conferences, in libraries, and other settings that previously required a pencil and tablet of paper for recording thoughts and discussions.

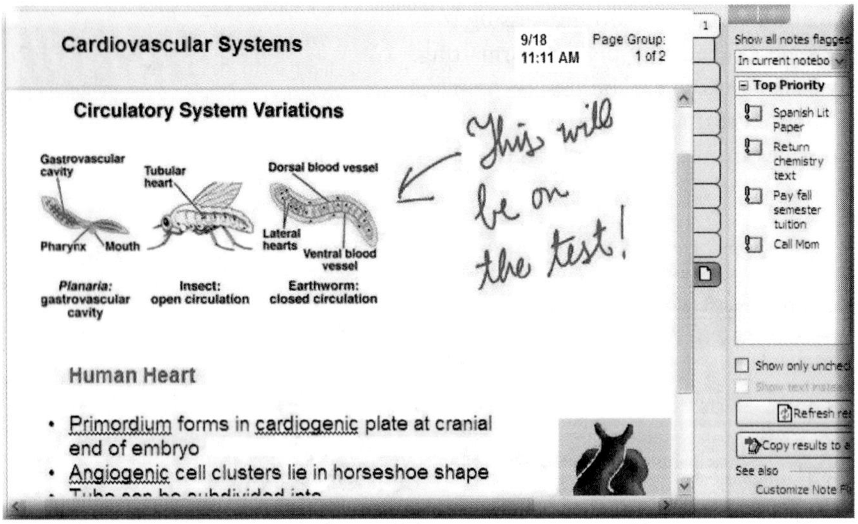

Figure 3-14 With note taking software, mobile users can handwrite notes, draw sketches, and type text.

Business Software Suite

A **software suite** is a collection of individual programs available together as a unit. Business software suites typically include, at a minimum, the following programs: word processing, spreadsheet, presentation, and e-mail. Popular business software suites include Microsoft Office, Apple iWork, Corel WordPerfect Office, and Google Docs.

Microsoft Office

For more information, visit the Computer Concepts CourseMate Web site at www.cengagebrain.com, navigate to the Chapter 3 Web Link resource for this book, and then click Microsoft Office.

Software suites offer two major advantages: lower cost and ease of use. When you purchase a collection of programs as a software suite, the suite usually costs significantly less than purchasing the programs individually. Software suites provide ease of use because the programs in the suite normally use a similar interface and share features such as clip art and spelling checker. For example, once you learn how to print using the software suite's word processing program, you can apply the same skill to the spreadsheet and presentation programs in the suite.

Personal Information Manager Software

A **personal information manager (PIM)** is application software that includes an appointment calendar, address book, notepad, and other features to help users organize personal information. With a PIM, you can take information previously tracked in a weekly or daily calendar, and organize and store it on your computer.

Mobile devices such as smart phones and PDAs include, among many other features, PIM functionality. You can synchronize, or coordinate, information so that both the mobile device and your personal computer and/or organization's server have the latest version of any updated information. Some mobile devices synchronize with the computer wirelessly. With others, you connect the mobile device to the computer with a cable, or you insert the device in a cradle, which has a cable that plugs in the computer.

Business Software for Phones

In addition to PIM software, a huge variety of business and other software is available for phones (Figure 3-15). Some software is preloaded on the phone, while other programs can be downloaded or accessed on memory cards that you insert in a slot on the device.

Business software available for phones enables users to create documents and worksheets, manage databases and lists, create slide shows, take notes, manage budgets and finances, view and edit photos, read electronic books, plan travel routes, compose and read e-mail messages, send instant messages, send text and picture messages, view maps and directions, read the latest news articles, and browse the Web. Many of the programs discussed in this chapter have scaled-down versions that work with smart phones and other mobile devices.

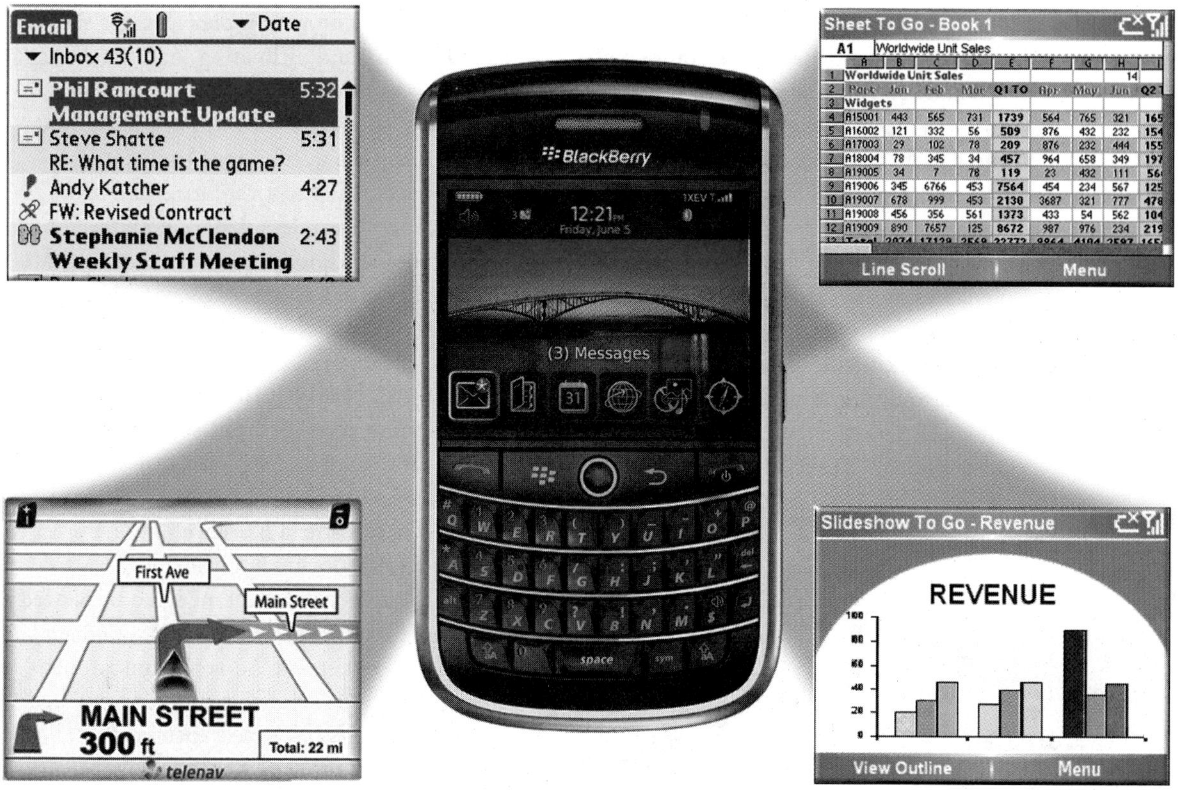

Figure 3-15 In addition to appointment, calendar, address book, and notepad, current phones include business and other software such as e-mail, spreadsheet, presentation, and travel and mapping.

Project Management Software

Project management software allows a user to plan, schedule, track, and analyze the events, resources, and costs of a project. Project management software helps users manage project variables, allowing them to complete a project on time and within budget. An engineer, for example, might use project management software to manage new product development to schedule timing of market analysis, product design, marketing, and public relations activities. A customer service manager might use this software to schedule the process of administering customer surveys, evaluating responses, and presenting recommendations (Figure 3-16).

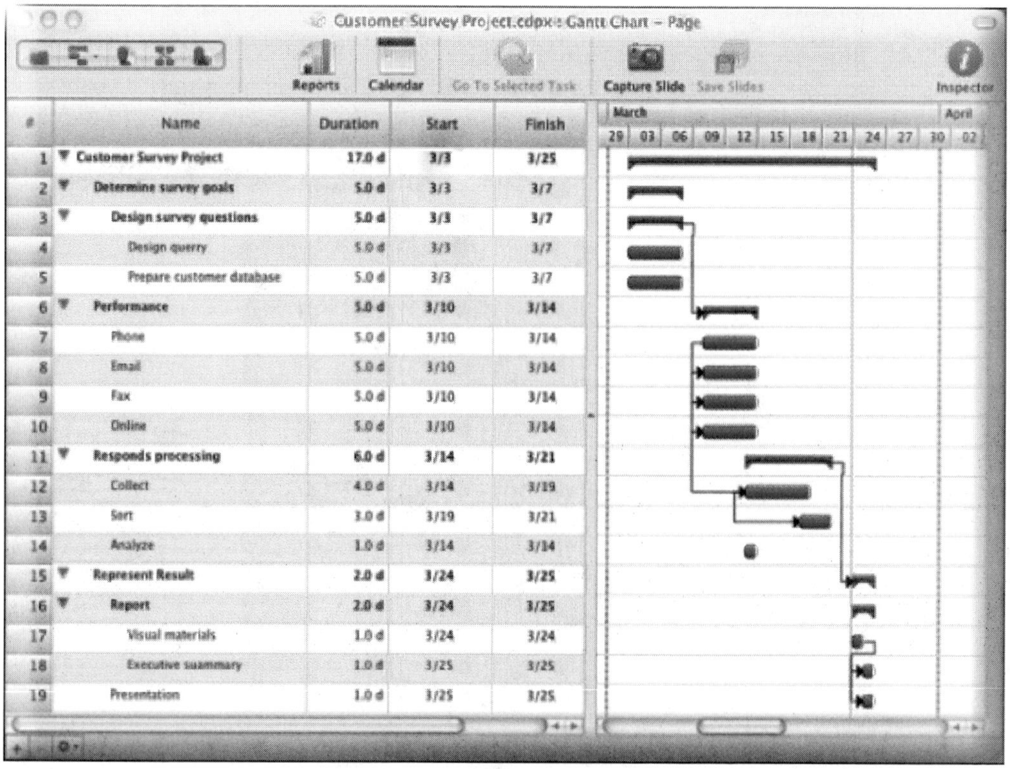

Figure 3-16 With project management software, you can plan and schedule a project.

Accounting Software

Accounting software helps companies record and report their financial transactions (Figure 3-17). With accounting software, business users perform accounting activities related to the general ledger, accounts receivable, accounts payable, purchasing, invoicing, and payroll functions. Accounting software also enables business users to write and print checks, track checking account activity, and update and reconcile balances on demand.

Most accounting software supports online credit checks, invoicing, bill payment, direct deposit, and payroll services. Some accounting software offers more complex features such as job costing and estimating, time tracking, multiple company reporting, foreign currency reporting, and forecasting the amount of raw materials needed for products. The cost of accounting software for small businesses ranges from less than one hundred to several thousand dollars. Accounting software for large businesses can cost several hundred thousand dollars.

Document Management Software

Document management software provides a means for sharing, distributing, and searching through documents by converting them into a format that can be viewed by any user. The converted document, which mirrors the original document's appearance, can be viewed and printed without the software that created the original document. Some document management software allows users to edit and add comments to the converted document.

A popular file format that document management software uses to save converted documents is *PDF* (Portable Document Format), developed by Adobe Systems. Because of the widespread use of PDF files, some current business programs such as Microsoft Office include a feature that allows users to save their documents as PDF files. To view and print a PDF file, you need Acrobat Reader software (Figure 3-18), which can be downloaded free from Adobe's Web site.

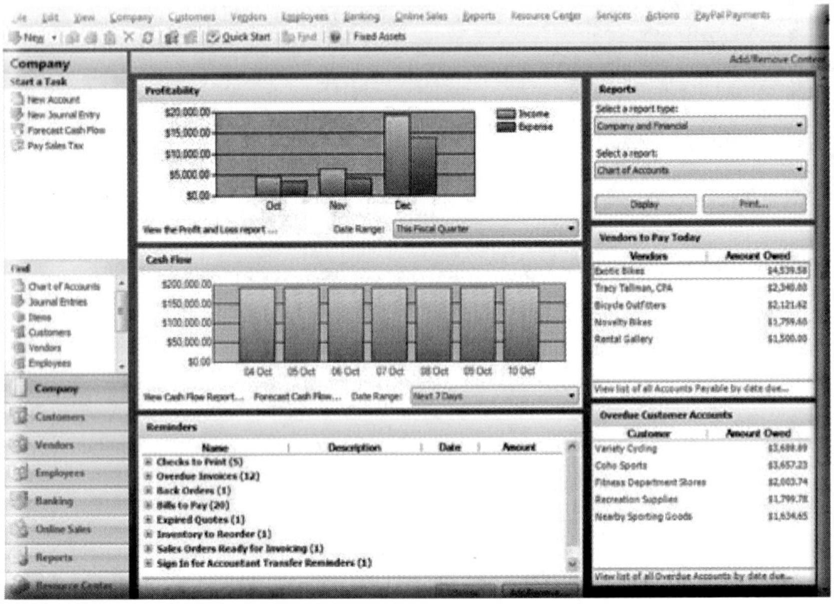

Figure 3-17 Accounting software helps companies record and report their financial transactions.

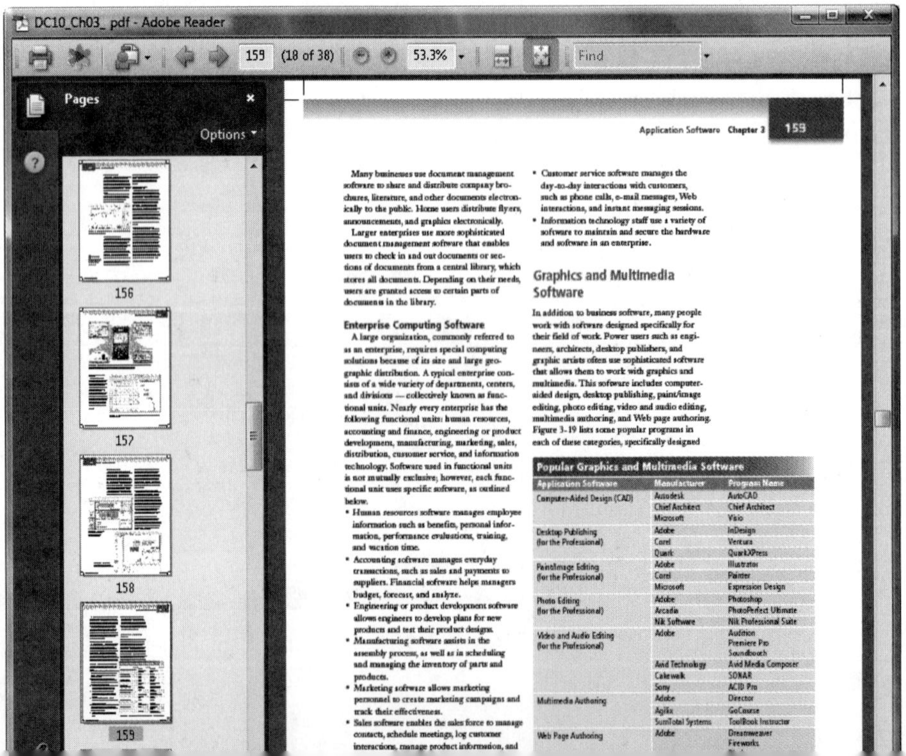

Figure 3-18 With Adobe Reader, you can view any PDF file, such as the page from this book shown in this figure.

Many businesses use document management software to share and distribute company brochures, literature, and other documents electronically to the public. Home users distribute flyers, announcements, and graphics electronically.

Larger enterprises use more sophisticated document management software that enables users to check in and out documents or sections of documents from a central library, which stores all documents. Depending on their needs, users are granted access to certain parts of documents in the library.

Enterprise Computing Software

A large organization, commonly referred to as an enterprise, requires special computing solutions because of its size and large geographic distribution. A typical enterprise consists of a wide variety of departments, centers, and divisions — collectively known as functional units. Nearly every enterprise has the following functional units: human resources, accounting and finance, engineering or product development, manufacturing, marketing, sales, distribution, customer service, and information technology. Software used in functional units is not mutually exclusive; however, each functional unit uses specific software, as outlined below.

- Human resources software manages employee information such as benefits, personal information, performance evaluations, training, and vacation time.
- Accounting software manages everyday transactions, such as sales and payments to suppliers. Financial software helps managers budget, forecast, and analyze.
- Engineering or product development software allows engineers to develop plans for new products and test their product designs.
- Manufacturing software assists in the assembly process, as well as in scheduling and managing the inventory of parts and products.
- Marketing software allows marketing personnel to create marketing campaigns and track their effectiveness.
- Sales software enables the sales force to manage contacts, schedule meetings, log customer interactions, manage product information, and take customer orders.
- Distribution software analyzes and tracks inventory and manages product shipping status.
- Customer service software manages the day-to-day interactions with customers, such as phone calls, e-mail messages, Web interactions, and instant messaging sessions.
- Information technology staff use a variety of software to maintain and secure the hardware and software in an enterprise.

Graphics and Multimedia Software

In addition to business software, many people work with software designed specifically for their field of work. Power users such as engineers, architects, desktop publishers, and graphic artists often use sophisticated software that allows them to work with graphics and multimedia. This software includes computer-aided design, desktop publishing, paint/image editing, photo editing, video and audio editing, multimedia authoring, and Web page authoring. Figure 3-19 lists some popular programs in each of these categories, specifically designed

Popular Graphics and Multimedia Software

Application Software	Manufacturer	Program Name
Computer-Aided Design (CAD)	Autodesk	AutoCAD
	Chief Architect	Chief Architect
	Microsoft	Visio
Desktop Publishing (for the Professional)	Adobe	InDesign
	Corel	Ventura
	Quark	QuarkXPress
Paint/Image Editing (for the Professional)	Adobe	Illustrator
	Corel	Painter
	Microsoft	Expression Design
Photo Editing (for the Professional)	Adobe	Photoshop
	Arcadia	PhotoPerfect Ultimate
	Nik Software	Nik Professional Suite
Video and Audio Editing (for the Professional)	Adobe	Audition Premiere Pro Soundbooth
	Avid Technology	Avid Media Composer
	Cakewalk	SONAR
	Sony	ACID Pro
Multimedia Authoring	Adobe	Director
	Agilix	GoCourse
	SumTotal Systems	ToolBook Instructor
Web Page Authoring	Adobe	Dreamweaver Fireworks Flash
	Microsoft	Expression Web SharePoint Designer

Figure 3-19 Popular graphics and multimedia programs — for the professional.

for professional or more technically astute users. These programs often cost several hundred dollars or more.

Many graphics and multimedia programs incorporate user-friendly interfaces and/or have scaled-down versions, making it possible for the home and small business users to create documents using these programs. The following sections discuss the features and functions of graphics and multimedia software. Read Innovative Computing 3-1 to find out how fireworks shows can be produced using multimedia software.

INNOVATIVE COMPUTING 3-1

Fireworks Software Creates a Real Blast

The "oohs" and "aahs" you hear at a fireworks show may be in response to the music and pyrotechnics synchronized with special multimedia software. Major fireworks productions on Independence Day and at theme parks are choreographed with programs designed to fire each shell, sometimes only one-hundredth of a second apart, at a specific beat of the music.

A 20-minute show can take 4 months to plan. Show choreographers estimate they spend at least four hours planning the firing order for each minute of music, not including testing and setting up the equipment. When the fireworks show operator starts the program, the computer sends a signal to the firing module, which connects to each shell.

The multimedia software can cost from $2,000 to $8,000, while the firing hardware that the computer synchronizes wirelessly or with wires can cost between $30,000 and $50,000.

For more information, visit the Computer Concepts CourseMate Web site at www.cengagebrain.com, navigate to the Chapter 3 Innovative Computing resource for this book, and then click Fireworks.

Graphics Software

For more information, visit the Computer Concepts CourseMate Web site at www.cengagebrain.com, navigate to the Chapter 3 Web Link resource for this book, and then click Graphics Software.

Computer-Aided Design

Computer-aided design (CAD) software is a sophisticated type of application software that assists a professional user in creating engineering, architectural, and scientific designs. For example, engineers create design plans for vehicles and security systems. Architects design building structures and floor plans (Figure 3-20). Scientists design drawings of molecular structures.

CAD software eliminates the laborious manual drafting that design processes can require. Three-dimensional CAD programs allow designers to rotate designs of 3-D objects to view them from any angle. Some CAD software even can generate material lists for building designs.

Figure 3-20 Architects use CAD software to design building structures.

Desktop Publishing Software (for the Professional)

Desktop publishing (DTP) software enables professional designers to create sophisticated documents that contain text, graphics, and many colors (Figure 3-21). Professional DTP software is ideal for the production of high-quality color documents such as textbooks, corporate newsletters, marketing literature, product catalogs, and annual reports.

Although many word processing programs have some of the capabilities of DTP software, professional designers and graphic artists use DTP software because it supports page layout. *Page layout* is the process of arranging text and graphics in a document

Figure 3-21 Professional designers and graphic artists use DTP software to produce sophisticated publications such as a printed magazine article.

on a page-by-page basis. DTP software includes color libraries to assist in color selections for text and graphics. A *color library* is a standard set of colors used by designers and printers to ensure that colors will print exactly as specified. Designers and graphic artists can print finished publications on a color printer, take them to a professional printer, or post them on the Web in a format that can be viewed by those without DTP software.

Paint/Image Editing Software (for the Professional)

Graphic artists, multimedia professionals, technical illustrators, and desktop publishers use paint software and image editing software to create and modify graphical images such as those used in DTP documents and Web pages. **Paint software**, also called *illustration software*, allows users to draw pictures (Figure 3-22), shapes, and other graphical images with various on-screen tools such as a pen, brush, eyedropper, and paint bucket.

Image editing software provides the capabilities of paint software and also includes the capability to enhance and modify existing images and pictures. Modifications can include adjusting or enhancing image colors, adding special effects such as shadows and glows, creating animations, and *image stitching*, which is the process of combining multiple images into a larger image.

Figure 3-22 This graphic artist uses paint software to draw characters in a computer game.

Photo Editing Software (for the Professional)

Professional photo editing software is a type of image editing software that allows photographers, videographers, engineers, scientists, and other high-volume digital photo users to edit and customize digital photos (Figure 3-23). Professional photo editing software allows users to save images in a wide variety of file formats. With professional photo editing software, users can retouch photos, crop images, remove red-eye, change image shapes, color-correct images, straighten images, remove or rearrange objects in a photo, and apply filters. Read Ethics & Issues 3-3 for a related discussion.

Figure 3-23 With professional photo editing software, users can edit and customize digital photos, such as by adjusting lighting as shown here.

Video and Audio Editing Software (for the Professional)

Video editing software allows professionals to modify a segment of a video, called a clip. For example, users can reduce the length of a video clip, reorder a series of clips, or add special effects such as words that move horizontally across the screen.

Video editing software typically includes audio editing capabilities. **Audio editing software** lets users modify audio clips, produce studio-quality soundtracks, and add audio to video clips (Figure 3-24). Audio editing software usually includes *filters*, which are designed to enhance audio quality. For example, a filter might remove a distracting background noise from the audio clip. Most television shows and movies are created or enhanced using video and audio editing software.

Multimedia Authoring Software

Multimedia authoring software allows users to combine text, graphics, audio, video, and animation in an interactive application (Figure 3-25). With this software, users control the placement of text and images and the duration of sounds, video, and animation. Once created, multimedia presentations often take the form of interactive computer-based presentations or Web-based presentations designed to facilitate learning, demonstrate product functionality, and elicit direct-user participation. Training centers, educational institutions, and online magazine publishers all use multimedia authoring software to develop interactive applications. These applications may be available on an optical disc, over a local area network, or via the Internet.

ETHICS & ISSUES 3-3

Altering Digital Photos — Art or Fraud?

In several recent high-profile cases, major news sources have published purposefully altered photos. The alterations were more than just touching up a bad-hair day; rather, they were attempts to alter the facts. Typically, those responsible for the deception are fired from their jobs. Many commercial artists, photojournalists, and creators of cartoons, book covers, and billboards use photo editing software to alter photos. Real estate agents increasingly are being found to alter photos of homes for online listings. With software, an artist can convert photos to a digital form that can be colorized, stretched, squeezed, texturized, or otherwise altered. For example, tabloid newspapers or dubious online sources may alter a photo by switching a head on a body in a photo with someone else's head. In another situation, several major news sources were duped by a country into publishing pictures of a faked missile test.

The National Press Photographers Association, however, has expressed reservations about digital altering and endorses the following: "As [photo] journalists we believe the guiding principle of our profession is accuracy; therefore, we believe it is wrong to alter the content of a photo in any way ... that deceives the public." Yet, some insist that the extent to which a photo "deceives the public" is in the eye of the beholder.

Is it ethical to alter digital photos? Why or why not? Does the answer depend on the reason for the alteration, the extent of the alteration, or some other factor? If some alteration is accepted, can photographic integrity still be guaranteed? Why or why not?

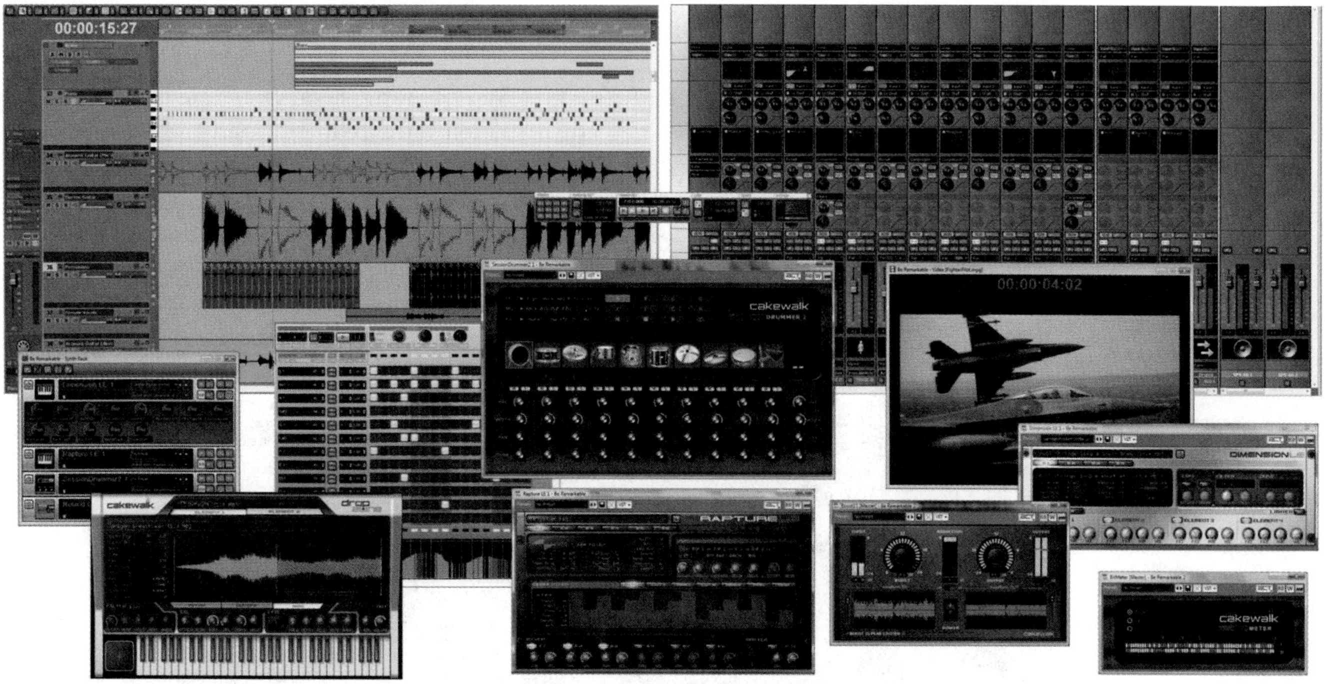

Figure 3-24 With audio editing software, users modify audio clips.

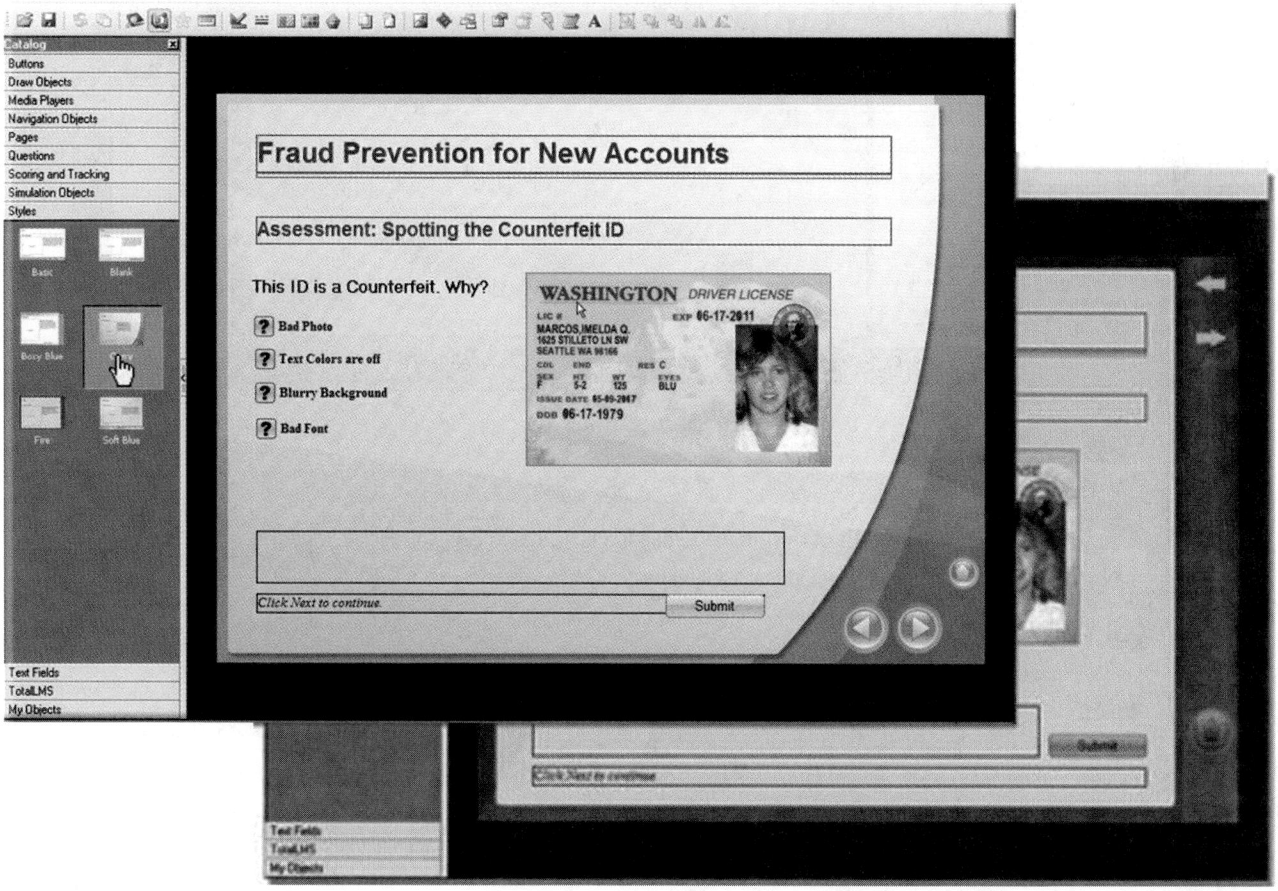

Figure 3-25 Multimedia authoring software allows you to create dynamic presentations that include text, graphics, video, sound, and animation.

Web Page Authoring Software

Web page authoring software helps users of all skill levels create Web pages that include graphical images, video, audio, animation, and other special effects with interactive content (Figure 3-26). In addition, many Web page authoring programs allow users to organize, manage, and maintain Web sites.

Application software, such as Word and Excel, often includes Web page authoring features. This allows home and small business users to create basic Web pages using application software they already own. For more sophisticated Web pages, users work with Web page authoring software. Many Web page developers also use multimedia authoring software along with, or instead of, Web page authoring software for Web page development.

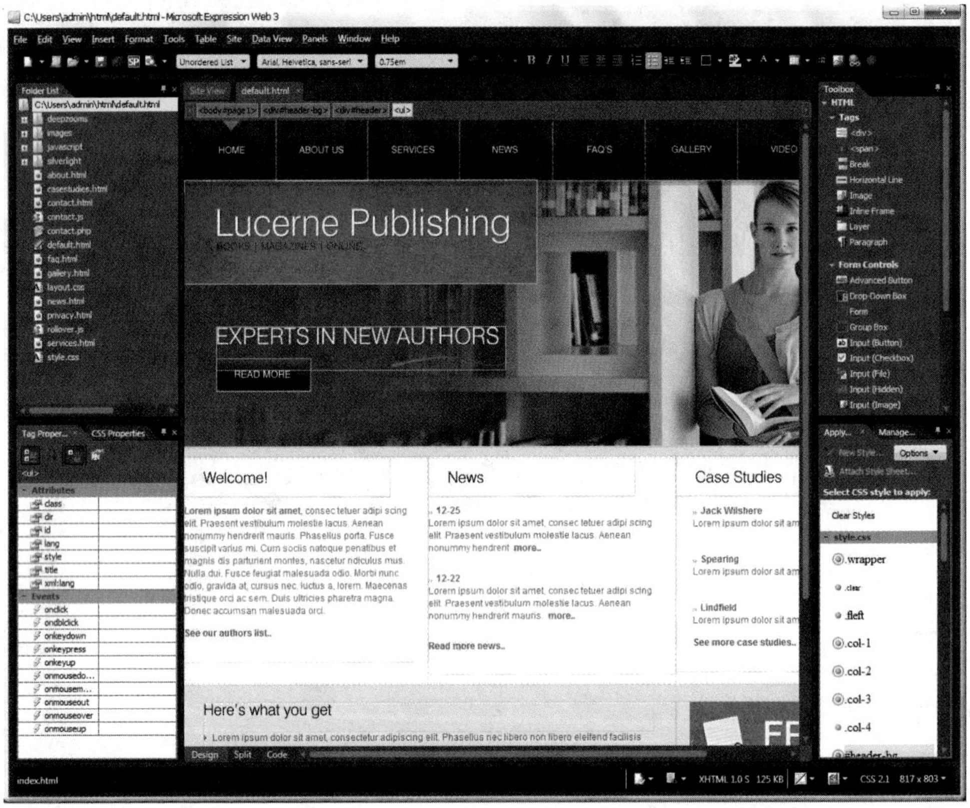

Figure 3-26 With Web page authoring software, users create sophisticated Web pages.

Web Page Authoring Software
For more information, visit the Computer Concepts CourseMate Web site at www.cengagebrain.com, navigate to the Chapter 3 Web Link resource for this book, and then click Web Page Authoring Software.

✔ QUIZ YOURSELF 3-2

Instructions: Find the true statement below. Then, rewrite the remaining false statements so that they are true.

1. Audio editing software typically includes video editing capabilities.
2. Enterprise computing software provides the capabilities of paint software and also includes the capability to modify existing images.
3. Millions of people use spreadsheet software every day to develop documents such as letters, memos, reports, mailing labels, newsletters, and Web pages.
4. Professional accounting software is ideal for the production of high-quality color documents such as textbooks, corporate newsletters, marketing literature, product catalogs, and annual reports.
5. Database software is application software that allows users to create visual aids for presentations to communicate ideas, messages, and other information to a group.
6. Popular CAD programs include Microsoft Office, Apple iWork, Corel WordPerfect Office, and Google Docs.
7. Web page authoring software helps users of all skill levels create Web pages.

Quiz Yourself Online: To further check your knowledge of pages 146 through 164, visit the Computer Concepts CourseMate Web site at www.cengagebrain.com, navigate to the Chapter 3 Quiz Yourself resource for this book, and then click Objectives 5 – 6.

Software for Home, Personal, and Educational Use

A large amount of application software is designed specifically for home, personal, and educational use. Most of the programs in this category are relatively inexpensive, often priced less than $100 and sometimes free. Figure 3-27 lists popular programs for many of these categories. The following pages discuss the features and functions of this application software.

Popular Programs for Home/Personal/Educational Use

Application Software	Manufacturer	Program Names
Personal Finance	IGG Software	iBank
	Intuit	Quicken
Legal	Broderbund	Home and Business Lawyer; WillWriter
	Cosmi	Perfect Attorney
	Nolo	Quicken Legal Business; Quicken WillMaker
Tax Preparation	2nd Story Software	TaxACT
	H&R Block	TaxCut
	Intuit	TurboTax
Desktop Publishing (for Personal Use)	Broderbund	The Print Shop; PrintMaster
	Microsoft	Publisher
Paint/Image Editing (for Personal Use)	Corel	CorelDRAW; Painter Essentials
	The GIMP Team	The Gimp
Photo Editing and Photo Management (for Personal Use)	Adobe	Photoshop Elements; Photoshop Express
	Corel	Paint Shop Pro Photo; Ulead PhotoImpact; MediaOne Plus
	Yahoo!	Flickr
	Google	Picasa
	Microsoft	Windows Live Photo Gallery
	Roxio	PhotoShow
Clip Art/Image Gallery	Broderbund	ClickArt
	Nova Development	Art Explosion
	CoolArchive	CoolArchive
Video and Audio Editing (for Personal Use)	Corel	VideoStudio
	Microsoft	Windows Live Movie Maker
	Pinnacle Systems	Studio
	Roxio	Buzz
Home Design/Landscaping	Broderbund	Instant Architect
	Chief Architect	Better Homes and Gardens Home Designer
	IMSI/Design	TurboFLOORPLAN
Travel and Mapping	DeLorme	Street Atlas
	Microsoft	Streets & Trips
	Google	Earth; Maps
Reference	Fogware Publishing	Merriam-Webster Collegiate Dictionary & Thesaurus
	Encyclopedia Britannica	Britannica Ultimate Reference Suite

Figure 3-27 Many popular programs are available for home, personal, and educational use.

Personal Finance Software

Personal finance software is a simplified accounting program that helps home users and small office/home office users balance their checkbooks, pay bills, track personal income and expenses (Figure 3-28), set up budgets, manage home inventory, track investments, and evaluate financial plans. Personal finance software helps determine where, and for what purpose, you are spending money so that you can manage your finances. Reports can summarize transactions by category (such as dining), by payee (such as the electric company), or by time (such as the last two months). Financial planning features include analyzing home and personal loans, preparing income taxes, and managing retirement savings.

Most of these personal finance programs also offer a variety of online services, which require access to the Internet. For example, users can track investments online, compare insurance rates from leading insurance companies, and bank online. **Online banking** offers access to account balances, provides bill payment services, and allows you to download monthly transactions and statements from the Web directly to your computer.

FAQ 3-4

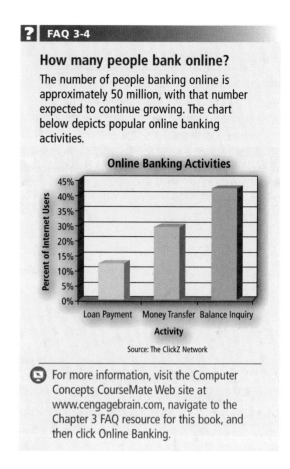

How many people bank online?

The number of people banking online is approximately 50 million, with that number expected to continue growing. The chart below depicts popular online banking activities.

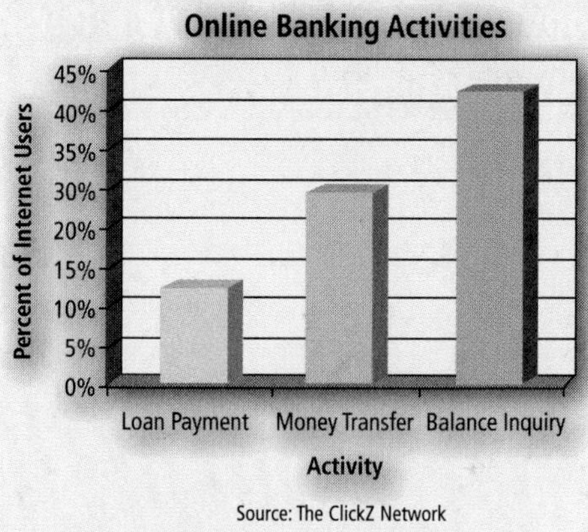

For more information, visit the Computer Concepts CourseMate Web site at www.cengagebrain.com, navigate to the Chapter 3 FAQ resource for this book, and then click Online Banking.

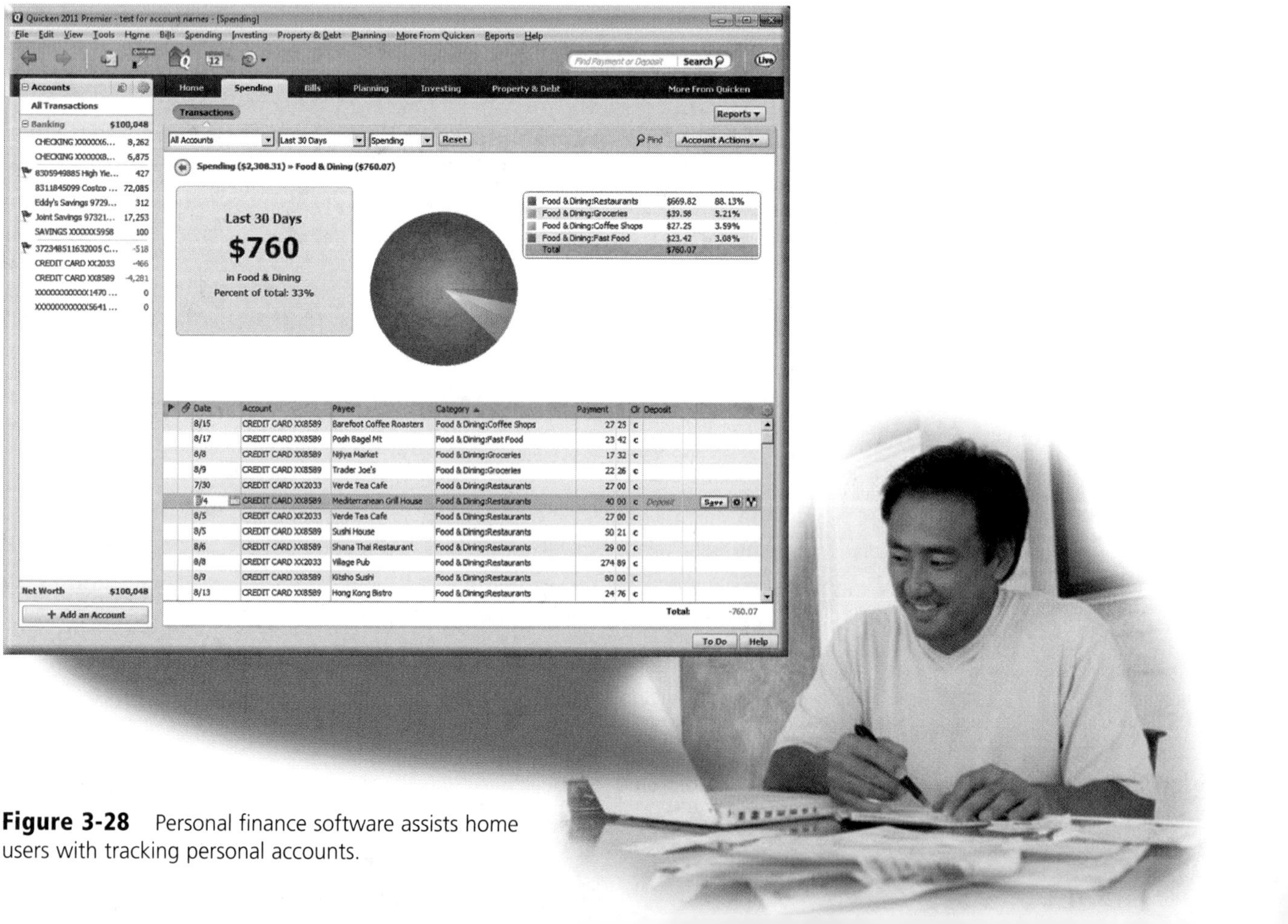

Figure 3-28 Personal finance software assists home users with tracking personal accounts.

Legal Software

Legal software assists in the preparation of legal documents and provides legal information to individuals, families, and small businesses (Figure 3-29). Legal software provides standard contracts and documents associated with buying, selling, and renting property; estate planning; marriage and divorce; and preparing a will or living trust. By answering a series of questions or completing a form, the legal software tailors the legal document to specific needs.

Once the legal document is created, you can file the paperwork with the appropriate agency, court, or office; or take the document to your attorney for his or her review and signature.

FAQ 3-5

Should I use legal software instead of hiring an attorney?

Although legal software may be approved for creating certain legal documents and can help save time and money in their preparation, you should check with your local bar association for the document's legality before using it.

For more information, visit the Computer Concepts CourseMate Web site at www.cengagebrain.com, navigate to the Chapter 3 FAQ resource for this book, and then click Legal Software.

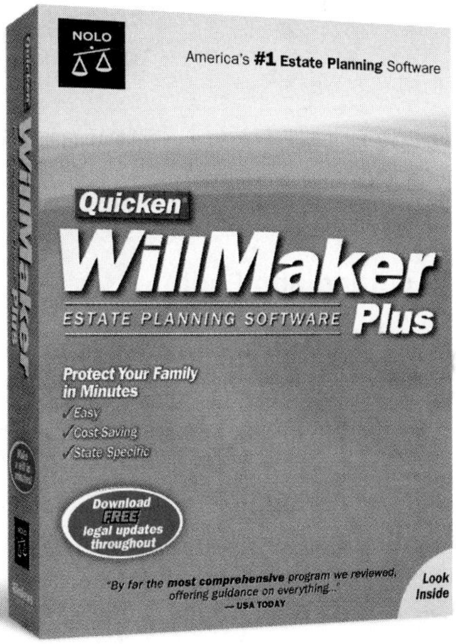

Figure 3-29 Legal software provides legal information to individuals, families, and small businesses and assists in record keeping and the preparation of legal documents.

Tax Preparation Software

Tax preparation software, which is available both as packaged software and as Web applications, can guide individuals, families, or small businesses through the process of filing federal taxes (Figure 3-30). These programs forecast tax liability and offer money-saving tax tips, designed to lower your tax bill. After you answer a series of questions and complete basic forms, the software creates and analyzes your tax forms to search for potential errors and deduction opportunities. Once the forms are complete, you can print any necessary paperwork, and then they are ready for filing. Instead of mailing forms through the postal service, the IRS allows taxpayers to file their state and federal tax returns online, called *e-filing*.

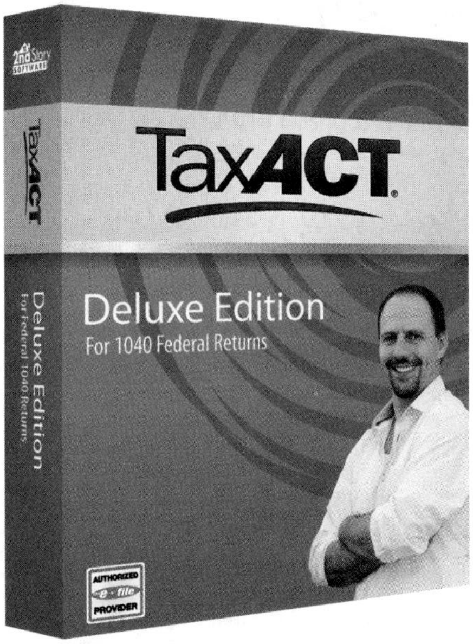

Figure 3-30 Tax preparation software guides individuals, families, or small businesses through the process of filing federal taxes.

Tax Preparation Software

For more information, visit the Computer Concepts CourseMate Web site at www.cengagebrain.com, navigate to the Chapter 3 Web Link resource for this book, and then click Tax Preparation Software.

Desktop Publishing Software (for Personal Use)

Instead of using professional DTP software (as discussed earlier in this chapter), many home and small business users work with simpler, easy-to-understand DTP software designed for smaller-scale desktop publishing projects. **Personal DTP software** helps home and small business users create newsletters, brochures, flyers (Figure 3-31), advertisements, postcards, greeting cards, letterhead, business cards, banners, calendars, logos, and Web pages.

Although many word processing programs include DTP features, users often prefer to create DTP documents using DTP software because of its enhanced features. For example, personal DTP programs provide hundreds of thousands of graphical images. You also can import (bring in) your own digital photos into the documents. These programs typically guide you through the development of a document by asking a series of questions, offering numerous predefined layouts, and providing standard text you can add to documents. Then, you can print a finished publication on a color printer or post it on the Web in a format that can be viewed by those without DTP software.

Many personal DTP programs also include paint/image editing software and photo editing and photo management software.

Desktop Publishing Software

For more information, visit the Computer Concepts CourseMate Web site at www.cengagebrain.com, navigate to the Chapter 3 Web Link resource for this book, and then click Desktop Publishing Software.

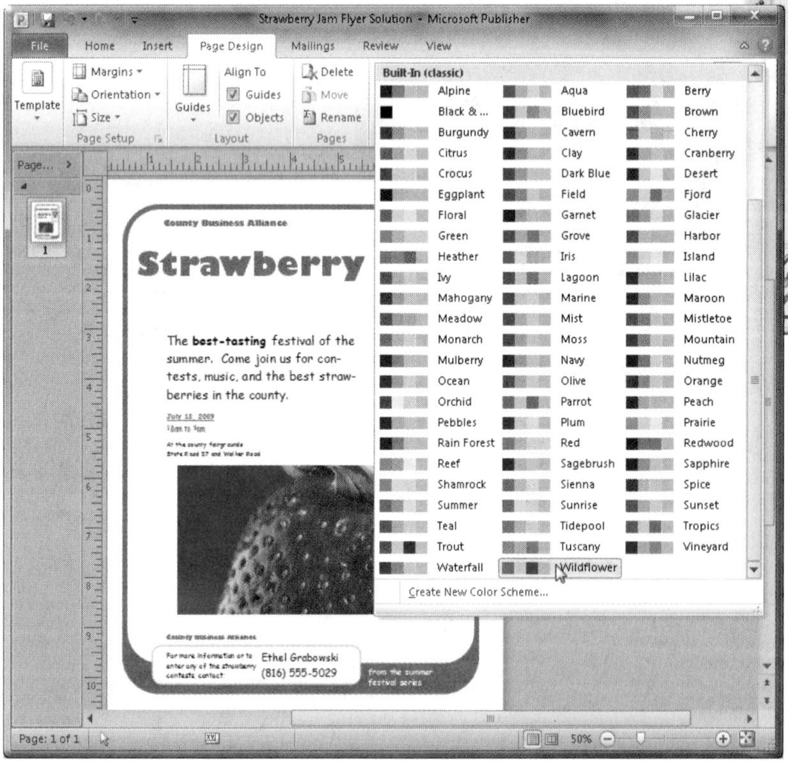

Figure 3-31 With desktop publishing software, home and small business users can create flyers.

Paint/Image Editing Software (for Personal Use)

Personal paint/image editing software provides an easy-to-use interface, usually with more simplified capabilities than its professional counterpart, including functions tailored to meet the needs of the home and small business user.

As with the professional versions, personal paint software includes various simplified tools that allow you to draw pictures (Figure 3-32), shapes, and other images. Personal image editing software provides the capabilities of paint software and the ability to modify existing graphics and photos. These programs also include many templates to assist you in adding images to documents such as greeting cards, banners, calendars, signs, labels, business cards, and letterhead. Some operating systems include a basic paint/image editing program.

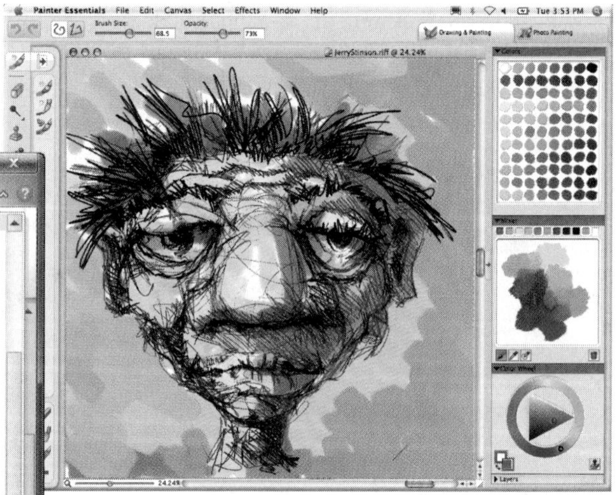

Figure 3-32 Home users can purchase affordable paint/image editing programs that enable them to draw images.

Photo Editing and Photo Management Software

Instead of professional photo editing software, many home and small business users work with easier-to-use personal photo editing software, which is available both as packaged software and as Web applications. **Personal photo editing software** allows users to edit digital photos by removing red-eye, erasing blemishes, restoring aged photos, adding special effects, enhancing image quality, or creating electronic photo albums. When you purchase a digital camera, it usually includes photo editing software (Figure 3-33). Some digital cameras

Figure 3-33 As shown here, home users can adjust color on their digital photos with personal photo editing software.

even have basic photo editing software built in so that you can edit the image directly on the camera. You can print edited photos on labels, calendars, business cards, and banners, or you can post them on the Web. Some photo editing software allows users to send digital photos to an online print service, which will deliver high-resolution printed images through the postal service or allow you to pick them up at a local store. Many online print services also have a photo community where users can post photos on the Web for others to view and purchase, if desired.

With *photo management software*, you can view, organize, sort, catalog, print, and share digital photos. Some photo editing software includes photo management functionality (Figure 3-34).

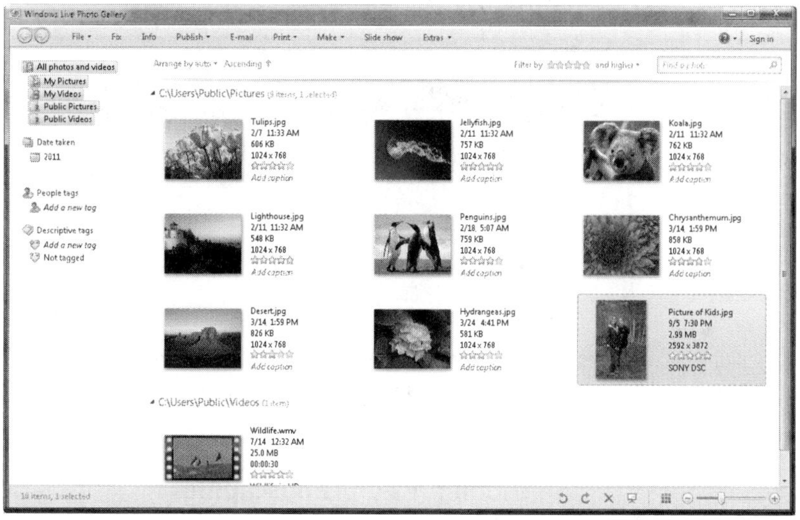

Figure 3-34 Photo management software enables you quickly to view thumbnails of all your digital photos.

Clip Art/Image Gallery

Application software often includes a **clip art/image gallery**, which is a collection of clip art and photos. Some programs have links to additional clips available on the Web or are available as Web applications. You also can purchase clip art/image gallery software that contains thousands of images (Figure 3-35).

In addition to clip art, many clip art/image galleries provide fonts, animations, sounds, video clips, and audio clips. You can use the images, fonts, and other items from the clip art/image gallery in all types of documents, including word processing, desktop publishing, spreadsheet, and presentations.

Figure 3-35 Clip art/image gallery software contains thousands of images.

Video and Audio Editing Software (for Personal Use)

Many home users work with easy-to-use video and audio editing software, which is much simpler to use than its professional counterpart, for small-scale movie making projects (Figure 3-36). With these programs, home users can edit home movies, add music or other sounds to the video, and share their movies on the Web. Some operating systems include video editing and audio editing software.

Figure 3-36 With personal video and audio editing software, home users can edit their home movies.

Home Design/Landscaping Software

Homeowners or potential homeowners can use **home design/landscaping software** to assist them with the design, remodeling, or improvement of a home, deck, or landscape (Figure 3-37).

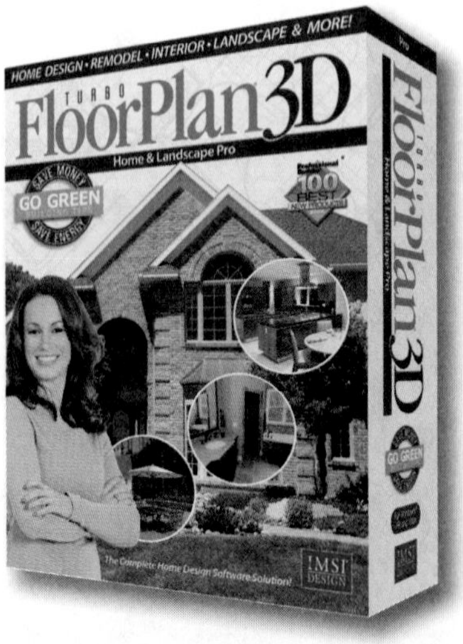

Figure 3-37 Home design/landscaping software can help you design or remodel a home, deck, or landscape.

Home design/landscaping software includes hundreds of predrawn plans that you can customize to meet your needs. These programs show changes to home designs and landscapes, allowing homeowners to preview proposed modifications. Once designed, many home design/landscaping programs print a materials list outlining costs and quantities for the entire project.

Travel and Mapping Software

Travel and mapping software enables users to view maps, determine route directions, and locate points of interest (Figure 3-38). Using travel and mapping software, which is available both as packaged software and as Web applications, you can display maps by searching for an address, postal code, telephone number, or point of interest (such as airports, lodging, and historical sites). This software often provides driving directions when a user enters a starting and destination point. Most programs also allow you to download construction reports and calculate mileage, time, and expenses. Many are compatible with mobile devices such as smart phones and portable media players. Many navigation devices, including those in vehicles, have travel and mapping software. Read Looking Ahead 3-1 for a look at the next generation of navigation software.

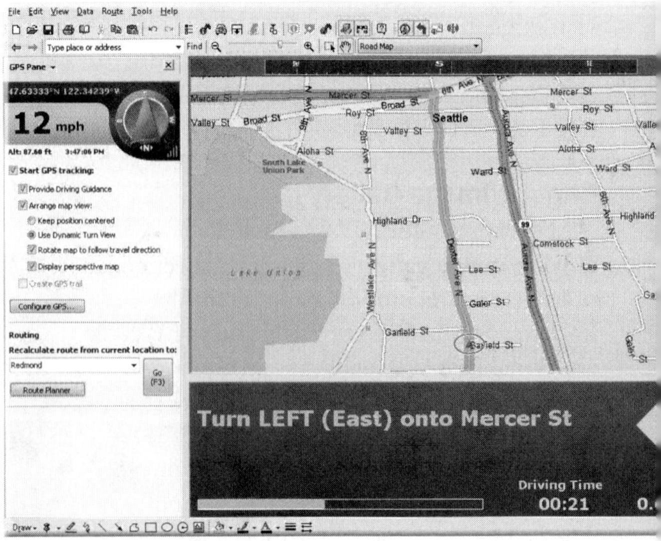

Figure 3-38 This software provides turn-by-turn directions, along with estimated travel times.

LOOKING AHEAD 3-1

Sensors Help Drivers Find Their Way

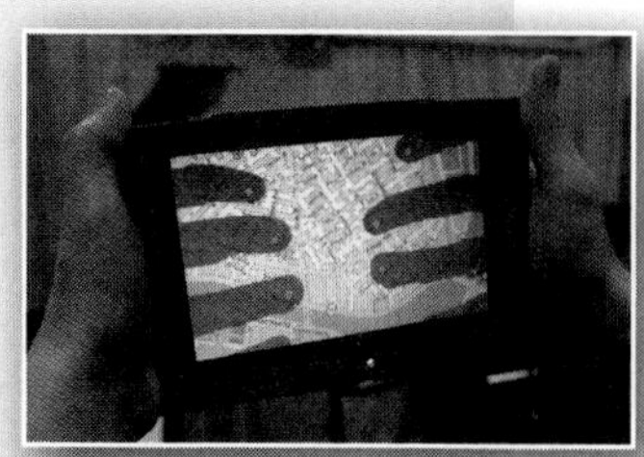

Navigating through town may become less burdensome with products under development at Microsoft. Current devices are touted as being small enough to fit in a pocket, but this size can be a hindrance for people with large hands. When they attempt to place their fingers on the touch screen to press the commands, their fingers cover information they are trying to see. Microsoft's prototype LucidTouch solves this problem by allowing users to place their hands underneath the device, in-between it and a camera attached to the back. The camera captures an image of their hands, and the device overlays a semitransparent shadow of their fingers on the screen.

Microsoft also is developing sensors for a cell phone that collect data as a driver passes through town. These accelerometers sense speed, braking, and even when the driver hits a pothole, and the cell phone's microphone can detect the car's horn. Another potential use of Microsoft's sensors in cell phones is to monitor the behavior and health status of the elderly so that they can lead independent lives.

For more information, visit the Computer Concepts CourseMate Web site at www.cengagebrain.com, navigate to the Chapter 3 Looking Ahead resource for this book, and then click Mapping.

Reference and Educational Software

Reference software provides valuable and thorough information for all individuals. Popular reference software includes encyclopedias, dictionaries, and health/medical guides.

Educational software is software that teaches a particular skill. Educational software exists for just about any subject, from learning how to type (Figure 3-39) to learning how to cook. Preschool to high-school learners use educational software to assist them with subjects such as reading and math or to prepare them for class or college entrance exams. Educational software often includes games and other content to make the learning experience more fun.

Many educational programs use a computer-based training approach. **Computer-based training (CBT)**, also called computer-aided instruction (CAI), is a type of education in which students learn by using and completing exercises with instructional software. CBT typically consists of self-directed, self-paced instruction about a topic. Beginning athletes, for example, use CBT programs to learn the intricacies of baseball, football, soccer, tennis, and golf. The military and airlines use CBT simulations to train pilots to fly in various conditions and environments (Figure 3-40).

Figure 3-39 Educational software can teach a skill.

Figure 3-40 Military pilots use CBT simulations for flight training.

Entertainment Software

Entertainment software for personal computers, game consoles, and mobile devices includes interactive games, videos, and other programs designed to support a hobby or provide amusement and enjoyment. For example, you might use entertainment software to play games individually (Figure 3-41) or with others online, make a family tree, or fly an aircraft. Many games are available as Web applications, allowing you to play individually or with other online players.

Game Software

For more information, visit the Computer Concepts CourseMate Web site at www.cengagebrain.com, navigate to the Chapter 3 Web Link resource for this book, and then click Game Software.

FAQ 3-6

How popular is entertainment software?

The popularity of entertainment software has increased greatly during the past few years. More than 65 percent of American households play computer or video games. Further, more than 36 percent play games on a mobile device such as a smart phone or PDA.

For more information, visit the Computer Concepts CourseMate Web site at www.cengagebrain.com, navigate to the Chapter 3 FAQ resource for this book, and then click Entertainment Software.

Figure 3-41 Entertainment software can provide hours of recreation on personal computers, game consoles, and mobile devices.

Web Applications

As discussed earlier in this chapter, users can purchase application software from a software vendor, retail store, or Web-based business. Users typically install purchased application software on a computer before they run it. Installed software has two disadvantages: (1) it requires disk space on your computer, and (2) it can be costly to upgrade as vendors release new versions. As an alternative, some users opt to access Web applications.

As previously mentioned, a Web application, or *Web app*, is a Web site that allows users to access and interact with software from any computer or device that is connected to the Internet. Users often interact with Web applications, directly at the Web site, referred to as the host, through their Web browser. Some Web sites, however, require you download the software to your local computer or device. Web application hosts often store users' data and information on their servers, which sometimes is called *cloud storage*. Users concerned with data security may shy away from this type of Web application. Thus, some Web applications provide users with an option of storing data locally on their own personal computer or mobile device.

Many of the previously discussed types of application software are available as Web applications. Figure 3-42 identifies the more popular Web applications. In addition, thousands of games are available as Web applications. Read Ethics & Issues 3-4 for a related discussion.

Many Web application hosts provide free access to their software, such as Google Docs shown in Figure 3-43. Others, such as Google Earth, offer part of their Web application free and charge for access to a more comprehensive program. Some Web applications, such as online tax preparation programs, allow you to use the Web application free and pay a fee when a certain action occurs. For example, you can prepare your tax return free, but if you elect to print it or file it electronically, you pay a minimal fee.

Experts often use the term Web 2.0 to describe Web applications. Recall that Web 2.0 refers to Web sites that provide users with a means to share personal information, allow users to modify Web site content, and/or have application software built into the site for visitors to use.

Popular Web Applications

Program Name	Type of Application Software
Britannica.com	Reference
Dictionary.com	Reference
Flickr	Photo Editing and Photo Management
Gmail	E-Mail
Google Docs	Productivity Suite
Google Earth	Travel and Mapping
Google Maps	Travel and Mapping
MSN Encarta	Reference
Office Web Apps	Productivity Suite
Photoshop Express	Photo Editing
Picnik	Photo Editing
TaxACT Online	Tax Preparation
TurboTax Online	Tax Preparation
Windows Live Calendar	Personal Information Manager
Windows Live Hotmail	E-Mail
YouSendIt	File Transfer and E-Mail

Figure 3-42 Some popular Web applications. For practice using Web applications, complete the last Learn It Online exercise in each chapter.

ETHICS & ISSUES 3-4

Should Online Mapping Services Make You Feel More Secure or More Vulnerable?

Most Internet users find that online maps, such as Google Maps and Bing Maps, provide tremendous convenience and reliability. Instead of searching the house or car for maps or making phone calls for directions, a quick Web search results in a readable map with exact directions. Sometimes, even photos of the route and location are available. Some parents and advocacy groups, however, claim that the services allow predators to locate potential victims quickly. Google Maps, for example, provides photos for neighborhoods of entire cities. The opponents of the services believe that predators may find potential victims in the photos or find likely locations where a crime may be easier to commit. Opponents of this point of view state that mapping services allow known predators and high-crime areas to be more readily identified. The services, therefore, increase personal security because the location of known predators can be pinpointed before the predators find victims. The services also provide much more positive value than any potential problems that they create, and, therefore, should thrive.

Do online mapping services make you feel more secure or more vulnerable? Why? Should parents and neighborhood associations have the legal right to have photos and personal information removed from mapping services? Why or why not? Would you feel comfortable if a service such as Google Maps showed a photo of you walking your normal route from home to work or school? Why?

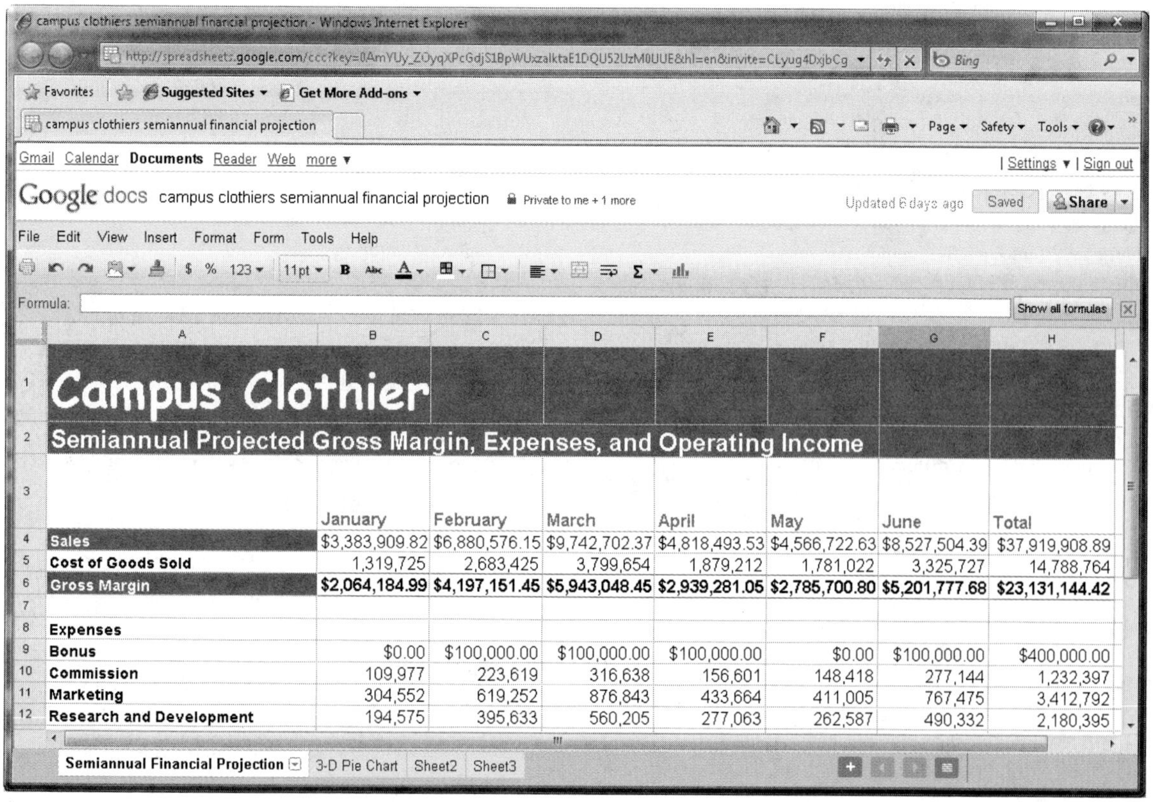

Figure 3-43 The spreadsheet shown here in Google Docs is the same Microsoft Excel spreadsheet that is shown in Figure 3-8 on page 151. Differences between the two figures are due to different features in the two programs.

Google Docs

For more information, visit the Computer Concepts CourseMate Web site at www.cengagebrain.com, navigate to the Chapter 3 Web Link resource for this book, and then click Google Docs.

Application Software for Communications

One of the main reasons people use computers is to communicate and share information with others. Some communications software is considered system software because it works with hardware and transmission media. Other communications software makes users more productive and/or assists them with personal tasks, and thus, is considered application software. Chapter 2 presented a variety of application software for communications, which is summarized in the table in Figure 3-44.

FAQ 3-7

Does text messaging improve typing skills?

Although some individuals are able to send text messages from their phones quickly, the differences in layout between a phone keypad and a standard computer keyboard might not allow for their typing skills to improve at the same rate. Some individuals are able to send text messages more quickly than they can type. In fact, a 20-year-old college student won $50,000 in a text messaging competition when he typed more than 125 characters in 50 seconds with no mistakes.

For more information, visit the Computer Concepts CourseMate Web site at www.cengagebrain.com, navigate to the Chapter 3 FAQ resource for this book, and then click Text Messaging.

Application Software for Communications

Web Browser
- Allows users to access and view Web pages on the Internet
- Requires a Web browser program
  - Integrated in some operating systems
  - Available for download on the Web free or for a fee

E-Mail
- Messages and files sent via a network such as the Internet
- Requires an e-mail program
  - Integrated in many software suites and operating systems
  - Available free at portals on the Web
  - Included with paid Internet access service
  - Can be purchased separately from retailers

Instant Messaging
- Real-time exchange of messages, files, audio, and/or video with another online user
- Requires instant messenger software
  - Integrated in some operating systems
  - Available for download on the Web, usually at no cost
  - Included with some paid Internet access services

Chat Room
- Real-time, online typed conversation
- Requires chat client software
  - Integrated in some operating systems and Web browsers
  - Available for download on the Web, usually at no cost
  - Included with some paid Internet access services
  - Built into some Web sites

Text, Picture, Video Messaging
- Short text, picture, or video messages sent and received, mainly on mobile devices
- Requires text, picture, video messenger software
  - Integrated in most mobile devices
  - Available for download on the Web, usually at no cost, for personal computers

RSS Aggregator
- Keeps track of changes made to Web sites by checking RSS feeds
- Requires RSS aggregator program
  - Integrated in some e-mail programs and Web browsers
  - Available for download on the Web, usually at no cost

Blogging
- Time-stamped articles, or posts, in a diary or journal format, usually listed in reverse chronological order
- Blogger needs *blog software*, or *blogware*, to create/maintain blog
  - Some Web sites do not require installation of blog software

Newsgroup/Message Board
- Online area where users have written discussions
- Newsgroup may require a newsreader program
  - Integrated in some operating systems, e-mail programs, and Web browsers

FTP
- Method of uploading and downloading files with other computers on the Internet
- May require an FTP program
  - Integrated in some operating systems
  - Available for download on the Web for a small fee

VoIP (Internet Telephony)
- Allows users to speak to other users over the Internet
- Requires Internet connection, Internet telephone service, microphone or telephone, and Internet telephone software or telephone adapter

Video Conferencing
- Meeting between geographically separated people who use a network such as the Internet to transmit video/audio
- Requires video conferencing software, a microphone, speakers, and sometimes a video camera attached to your computer

Figure 3-44 A summary of application software for home and business communications.

Learning Tools for Application Software

Learning how to use application software effectively involves time and practice. To assist in the learning process, many programs include an integrated Help feature. **Online Help** is the electronic equivalent of a user manual (Figure 3-45a). When working with a program, you can use online Help to ask a question or access the Help topics in subject or alphabetical order. Most online Help also links to Web sites that offer *Web-based Help*, which provides updates and more comprehensive resources to respond to technical issues about software (Figure 3-45b). Read Innovative Computing 3-2 to find out about a digital learning resource that can supplement the classroom experience.

If you want to learn more about a particular program from a printed manual, many books are available to help you learn to use the features of personal computer programs. These books typically are available in bookstores and software stores.

Many colleges and schools provide training on several of the programs discussed in this chapter. For more information, contact your local school for a list of class offerings.

Figure 3-45a (online Help)

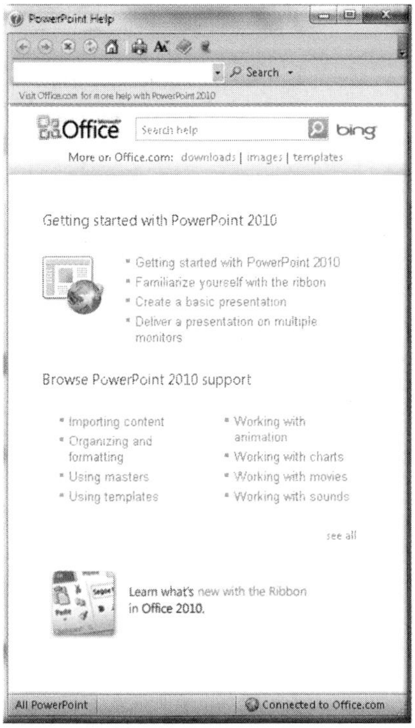

Figure 3-45b (Web-based Help)

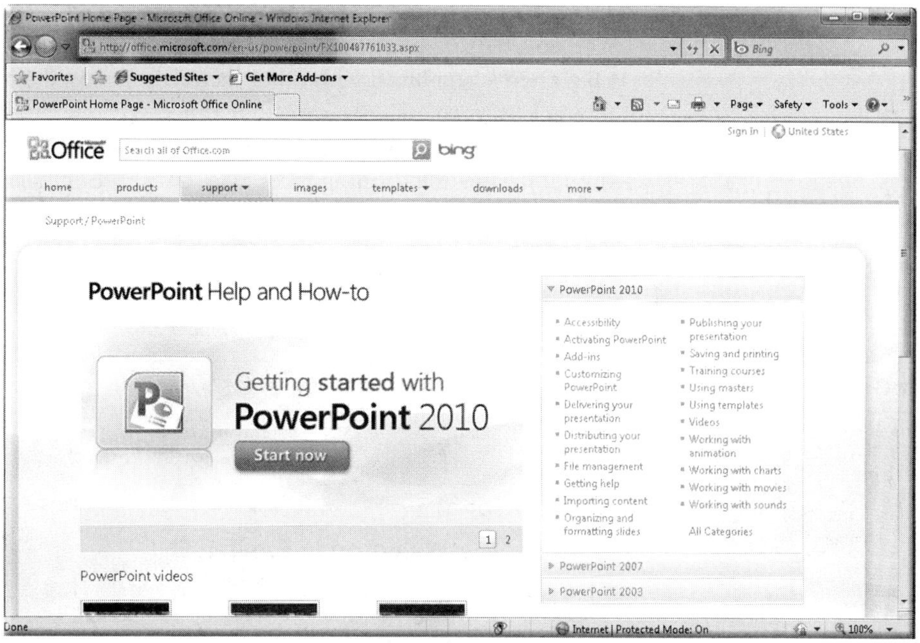

Figure 3-45 Many programs include online Help and Web-based Help.

INNOVATIVE COMPUTING 3-2

iTunes U Supplements Classroom Learning

Your reliable study partner can join you at the gym, on the bus, at dinner, and anywhere you want to go. *iTunes U* is a digital learning resource with a direct connection to lectures, demonstrations, and performances that enrich the classroom experience.

Professors and other educators develop multimedia content for iTunes U, and other organizations add their resources to the Beyond Campus area. For example, PBS, New York's Museum of Modern Art, and the Smithsonian have shared their collections and interviews. All you need to access this treasure trove of free resources is a computer or mobile device and Internet access. You can watch and listen to the iTunes U content on your computer, iPod, and iPhone.

iTunes U content has been downloaded more than four million times since the Web site's inception in 2007. Popular lectures are on the topics of black holes, Mozart, copyright law, and Greek. A world literature lecture was viewed 74,000 times in one month.

For more information, visit the Computer Concepts CourseMate Web site at www.cengagebrain.com, navigate to the Chapter 3 Innovative Computing resource for this book, and then click iTunes U.

Web-Based Training

Web-based training (*WBT*) is a type of CBT (computer-based training) that uses Internet technology and consists of application software on the Web. Similar to CBT, WBT typically consists of self-directed, self-paced instruction about a topic. WBT is popular in business, industry, and schools for teaching new skills or enhancing existing skills of employees, teachers, or students. When using a WBT product, students actively become involved in the learning process instead of remaining passive recipients of information.

Many Web sites offer WBT to the general public. Such training covers a wide range of topics, from how to change a flat tire to creating documents in Word. Many of these Web sites are free. Others require registration and payment to take the complete Web-based course.

WBT often is combined with other materials for distance learning and e-learning. **Distance learning** (**DL**) is the delivery of education at one location while the learning takes place at other locations. DL courses provide time, distance, and place advantages for students who live far from a college campus or work full time. These courses enable students to attend class from anywhere in the world and at times that fit their schedules. Many national and international companies offer DL training. These training courses eliminate the costs of airfare, hotels, and meals for centralized training sessions.

E-learning, short for electronic learning, is the delivery of education via some electronic method such as the Internet, networks, or optical discs. To enhance communications, e-learning systems also may include video conferencing, e-mail, blogs, wikis, newsgroups, chat rooms, and groupware.

E-learning providers often specialize in presenting instructors with the tools for preparation, distribution, and management of DL courses (Figure 3-46). These tools enable instructors to create rich, educational Web-based training sites and allow the students to interact with a powerful Web learning environment. Through the training site, students can check their progress, take practice tests, search for topics, send e-mail messages, and participate in discussions and chats.

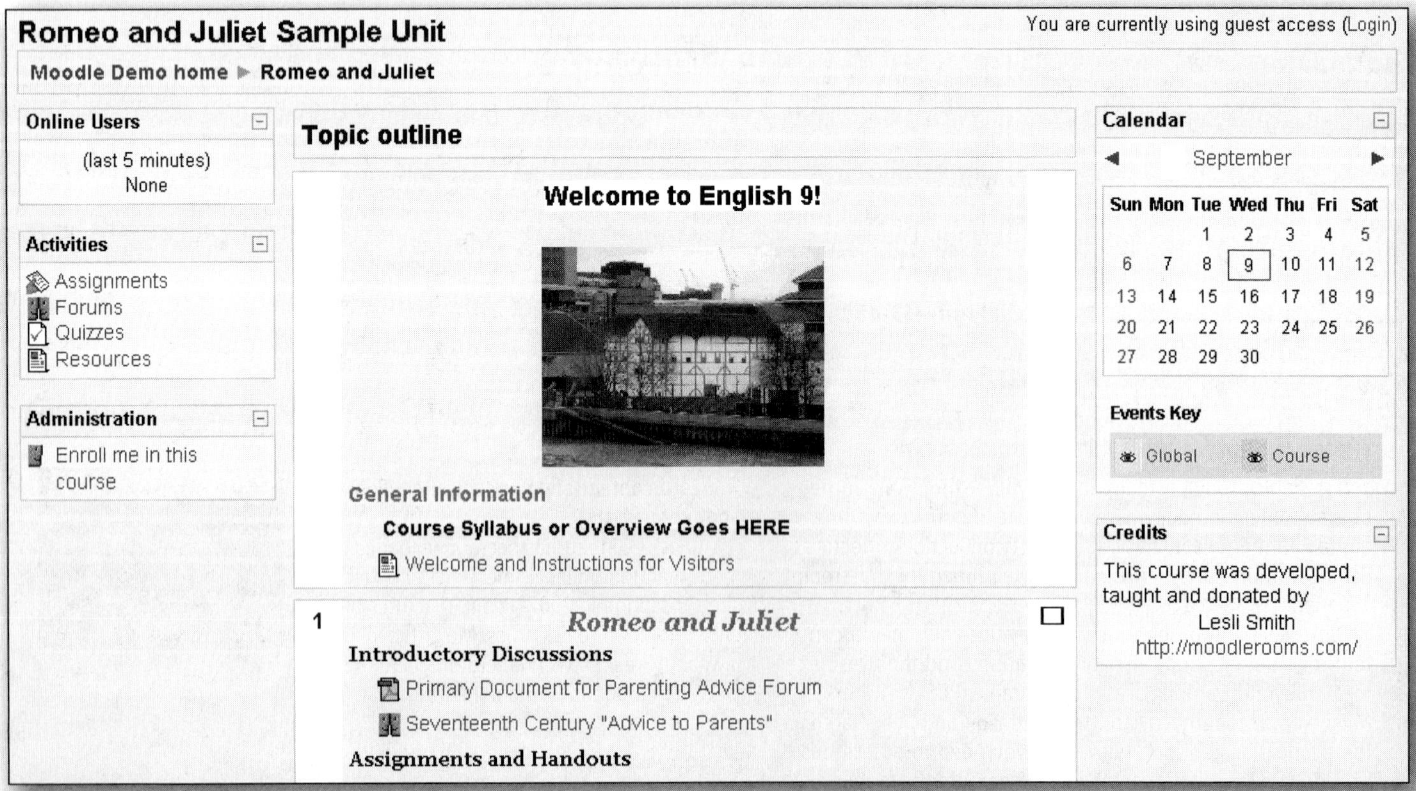

Figure 3-46 E-learning systems enable instructors to post course materials for their students.

QUIZ YOURSELF 3-3

Instructions: Find the true statement below. Then, rewrite the remaining false statements so that they are true.

1. All Web application hosts provide free access to their software.
2. Computer-based training is a type of Web-based training that uses Internet technology and consists of application software on the Web.
3. E-mail and Web browsers are examples of communications software that are considered application software.
4. Legal software is a simplified accounting program that helps home users and small office/home office users balance their checkbooks, pay bills, track investments, and evaluate financial plans.
5. Personal DTP software is a popular type of image editing software that allows users to edit digital photos.

Quiz Yourself Online: To further check your knowledge of pages 165 through 176, visit the Computer Concepts CourseMate Web site at www.cengagebrain.com, navigate to the Chapter 3 Quiz Yourself resource for this book, and then click Objectives 7 – 10.

Chapter Summary

This chapter illustrated how to start and interact with application software. It then presented an overview of a variety of business software, graphics and multimedia software, and home/personal/educational software.

The chapter also discussed Web applications and application software for communications. Lastly, learning tools for application software and Web-based training were presented.

Computer Usage @ Work

Construction

Walking the streets, you stop to admire a new skyscraper with the most striking architectural features you ever have seen. You think to yourself that those responsible for designing the building are nothing less than brilliant. While a great deal of work goes into the design and construction of a building, computers and technology also play an important role in the process. In fact, the role of computers not only saves time and provides for more accurate results, it also allows us to preview how a building will look before construction even begins.

As mentioned in the chapter, computer-aided design (CAD) software is a sophisticated type of application software that assists a professional user in creating engineering, architectural, and scientific plans. During the preliminary design process, architects and design firms use CAD software to design the appearance and layout of a new building and can provide clients with a three-dimensional walkthrough of a building so that they can determine whether the proposed design will meet their needs. Later, the program can be used to include the placement of support beams, walls, roof shape, and so on, and also conform to building code.

CAD software also allows engineers in various fields, such as mechanical and electrical, to design separate layers in a structure. The software then can superimpose the designs to check for interactions and conflicts, such as if a structural beam in one layer covers a drain in another layer. The CAD software makes it easy to modify and correct the structure before it is built, which can save time and money during the construction process. This software also eliminates most, if not all, of the manual drafting required.

Engineers use computers to determine the type of foundation required to support the building and its occupants; the heating, ventilating, and air conditioning (HVAC); and the electrical requirements, as well as how the building may withstand external threats such as hurricanes and tornadoes.

During construction, contractors and builders are able to use computer software to estimate accurately the amount of materials and time required to complete the job. Without computers, determining materials and time required is a cumbersome and time-consuming task.

The next time you notice a building under construction, stop to think about how computer technology has increased the efficiency of the design and construction process.

For more information, visit the Computer Concepts CourseMate Web site at www.cengagebrain.com, navigate to the Chapter 3 Computer Usage @ Work resource for this book, and then click Construction.

High-Tech Talk

Computer Viruses: Delivery, Infection, and Avoidance

Klez. Melissa. Mydoom. Nimda. Like the common cold, virtually countless variations of computer viruses exist. Unlike the biological viruses that cause the common cold, people create computer viruses. To create a virus, an unscrupulous programmer must code and then test the virus code to ensure the virus can replicate itself, conceal itself, monitor for certain events, and then deliver its *payload* — the destructive event or prank the virus was created to deliver. Despite the many variations of viruses, most have two phases to their execution: infection and delivery.

To start the infection phase, the virus must be activated. Today, the most common way viruses spread is by people running infected programs disguised as e-mail attachments. During the infection phase, viruses typically perform three actions:

1. First, a virus replicates by attaching itself to program files. A *macro virus* hides in the macro language of a program, such as Word. A *boot sector virus* targets the master boot record and executes when the computer starts. A *file virus* attaches itself to program files. The file virus, Win32.Hatred, for example, replicates by first infecting Windows executable files for the Calculator, Notepad, Help, and other programs on the hard disk. The virus then scans the computer to locate .exe files on other drives and stores this information in the system registry. The next time an infected file is run, the virus reads the registry and continues infecting another drive.
2. Viruses also conceal themselves to avoid detection. A *stealth virus* disguises itself by hiding in fake code sections, which it inserts within working code in a file. A *polymorphic virus* actually changes its code as it infects computers. The Win32.Hatred virus uses both concealment techniques. The virus writes itself to the last file section, while modifying the file header to hide the increased file size. It also scrambles and encrypts the virus code as it infects files.
3. Finally, viruses watch for a certain condition or event and activate when that condition or event occurs. The event might be starting the computer or reaching a date on the system clock. A *logic bomb* activates when it detects a specific condition (say, a name deleted from the employee list). A *time bomb* is a logic bomb that activates on a particular date or time. Win32.Hatred, for instance, unleashes its destruction when the computer clock hits the seventh day of any month. If the triggering condition does not exist, the virus simply replicates.

During the delivery phase, the virus unleashes its payload, which might be a harmless prank that displays a meaningless message — or it might be destructive, corrupting or deleting data and files. When the Win32.Hatred virus triggers, it displays the author's message and then covers the screen with black dots. The virus also deletes several antivirus files as it infects the system. The most dangerous viruses do not have an obvious payload; instead they quietly modify files. A virus, for example, could change numbers randomly in an inventory program or introduce delays to slow a computer. One way antivirus software detects computer viruses is by monitoring files for unknown changes, particularly in file size. Because many computer viruses alter system and data files — files that should not change in size — changes in file sizes often are a key indication of an infection.

Other kinds of electronic annoyances exist in addition to viruses. While often called viruses, worms, Trojan horse programs, and rootkits actually are part of a broader category called *malicious-logic programs* or *malware*.

- A *worm*, such as the CodeRed or Sircam worm, resides in active memory and replicates itself over a network to infect machines, using up the system resources and possibly shutting the system down.
- A *Trojan horse* is a destructive program disguised as a real program, such as a screen saver. When a user runs a seemingly innocent program, a Trojan horse hiding inside can capture information, such as user names and passwords, from your system or open up a backdoor that allows a hacker remotely to control your computer. Unlike viruses, Trojan horses do not replicate themselves.
- A *rootkit* is a program that easily can hide and allow someone to take full control of your computer from a remote location, often for nefarious purposes. For example, a rootkit can hide in a folder on your computer, and the folder will appear empty. This is because the rootkit has instructed your computer not to display the contents of the folder. Rootkits can be very dangerous and often require special software to detect and remove. Rootkits are becoming more common. In fact, a recent study has shown that more than 20 percent of computers in the United States are infected with a rootkit. It is extremely important that you use caution when installing software from unknown sources.

Every computer user is susceptible to a computer virus. Studies show that an unprotected computer can be infected by a virus within minutes after being connected to the Internet. Due to the increasing threat of viruses attacking your computer, it is more important than ever to protect your computer from viruses. Figure 3-47 lists steps you can follow to protect your computer from a virus infection.

Steps to Virus Protection
1. Install the latest Microsoft updates.
2. Purchase a reputable antivirus program.
3. After installing an antivirus program, scan your entire computer to be sure it is free of malware.
4. Update your antivirus definitions regularly.
5. Be suspicious of any and all unsolicited e-mail attachments.
6. Stay informed about viruses and virus hoaxes.
7. Install a personal firewall program.
8. Download software only if you are sure the Web site is legitimate.
9. Avoid as best you can visiting unscrupulous Web sites.

Figure 3-47 Guidelines to keep your computer virus free.

For more information, visit the Computer Concepts CourseMate Web site at www.cengagebrain.com, navigate to the Chapter 3 High-Tech Talk resource for this book, and then click Computer Viruses.

Companies on the Cutting Edge

ADOBE SYSTEMS Design Software Leader

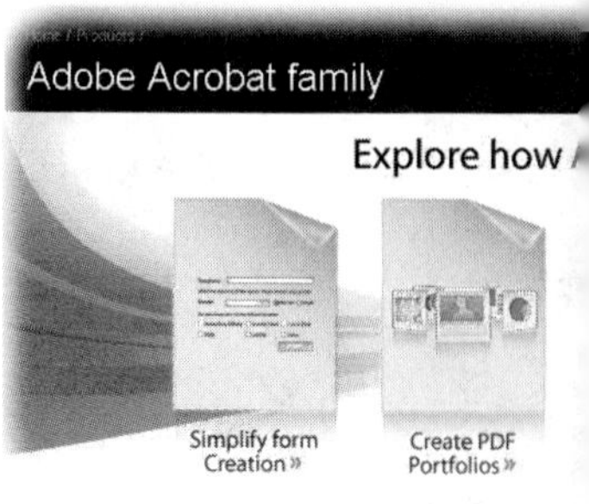

Practically all creative professionals involved with art and photography have a copy of Adobe Photoshop on their computer, and the leading computer manufacturers ship their products with a copy of Adobe Reader installed. The worldwide presence of *Adobe Systems* software attests to the company's success in developing programs that help people communicate effectively.

Charles Geschke and John Warnock founded the company in 1982 and named it after a creek that ran behind Warnock's house in California. Creative Suite contains the fundamental tools that help photographers, designers, and publishers develop and maintain their documents and Web sites, and it includes Dreamweaver, Flash, Fireworks, Contribute, InDesign, Illustrator, and Photoshop.

Recently, Adobe was voted one of the 100 Best Companies to Work For.

MICROSOFT Computer Technology Innovator

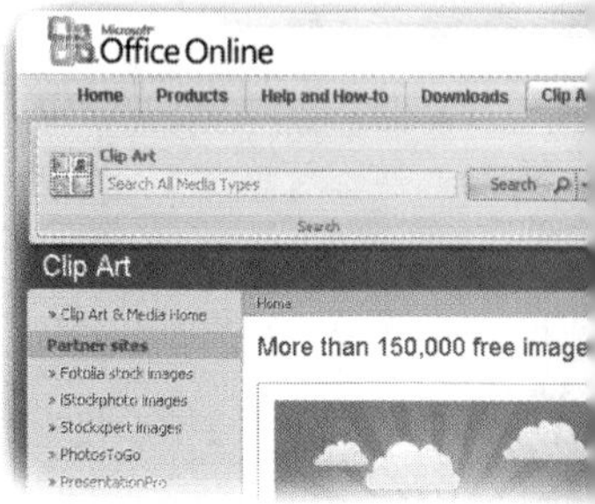

Internet users view *Microsoft*'s Web site more than 2.4 million times each day, attesting to the company's presence as the largest software company in the world. Its Office and Internet Explorer programs dominate the computer industry, and it also has assets in the MSNBC cable television network, the Encarta multimedia encyclopedia, SharePoint, and gaming software, including Flight Simulator and Zoo Tycoon. Microsoft also manufactures hardware, such as the Xbox, Zune, mouse devices, keyboards, fingerprint readers, Web cams, and game controllers.

When Microsoft was incorporated in 1975, the company had three programmers, one product, and revenues of $16,000. The company now employs more than 92,000 people and has annual revenues in excess of $58 billion. Windows 7 is the latest version of Microsoft's flagship operating system.

For more information, visit the Computer Concepts CourseMate Web site at www.cengagebrain.com and then navigate to the Chapter 3 Companies on the Cutting Edge resource for this book.

Technology Trailblazers

DAN BRICKLIN VisiCalc Developer

Dan Bricklin introduced wikiCalc in 2007 as a free software tool for Web pages that have data in lists and tables. This program is an offshoot of a prototype program he had developed 30 years earlier, named VisiCalc, that performed a series of calculations automatically when numbers were entered.

Bricklin and a friend founded a company, Software Arts, to develop VisiCalc, short for Visible Calculator. They programmed the software using Apple Basic on an Apple II computer. This small program was the first type of application software that provided a reason for businesses to buy Apple computers. It included many features found in today's spreadsheet software.

Bricklin founded a small consulting company, Software Garden, to develop and market software such as wikiCalc. The company also distributes resources to help programmers learn about licensing their products and about open source software.

MASAYOSHI SON Softbank President and CEO

In the 1970s, *Masayoshi Son* was convinced that the microchip was going to change people's lives. As an economics major at the University of California, Berkeley, each day he attempted to develop one original use for computer technology. One of these ideas made him a millionaire: a multilingual pocket translating device that he sold to Sharp Corporation.

At age 23, Son founded Softbank, which is one of Japan's largest telecommunications and media corporations. He now is one of the richest men in the world with a net worth of $3.7 billion.

Recently, Softbank partnered with Apple to develop a version of the iPhone for the Japanese market. In addition, Son's company collaborated with Tiffany & Co. to manufacture 10 cell phones, each worth more than $910,000, with 400 diamonds weighing more than 20 karats total.

For more information, visit the Computer Concepts CourseMate Web site at www.cengagebrain.com and then navigate to the Chapter 3 Technology Trailblazers resource for this book.

Chapter Review

The Chapter Review reinforces the main concepts presented in this chapter.

To listen to an audio version of this Chapter Review, visit the Computer Concepts CourseMate Web site at www.cengagebrain.com and then navigate to the Chapter 3 Chapter Review resource for this book.

1. What Are the Four Categories of Application Software? **Application software** consists of programs designed to make users more productive and/or assist them with personal tasks. The major categories of application software are business software; graphics and multimedia software; home, personal, and educational software; and communications software.

2. What Are the Seven Forms through Which Software Is Available? Application software is available in a variety of forms. **Packaged software** is mass-produced, copyrighted retail software that meets the needs of a variety of users. **Custom software** performs functions specific to a business or industry. A **Web application** is a Web site that allows users to access and interact with software from any computer or device that is connected to the Internet. **Open source software** is provided for use, modification, and redistribution. **Shareware** is copyrighted software that is distributed free for a trial period. **Freeware** is copyrighted software provided at no cost by an individual or a company that retains all rights to the software. **Public-domain software** is free software donated for public use and has no copyright restrictions.

3. How Do the Operating System and Utility Programs Work with Application Software? To use application software, your computer must be running *system software*, specifically an operating system. The system software serves as the interface between the user, the application software, and the computer's hardware. Each time you start a computer, the operating system is *loaded* (copied) from the computer's hard disk into memory. Once loaded, it coordinates all the computer's activities, including starting application software and transferring data among input/output devices and memory. A utility program is a type of system software that assists users with controlling or maintaining the operations of a computer, its devices, or its software.

4. What Are the Characteristics of a User Interface? Personal computer operating systems often use the concept of a **desktop**, which is an on-screen work area that has a graphical user interface. One way to start a program in Windows is to move the **pointer** to the Start **button** on the taskbar and **click** the Start button by pressing and releasing a button on the mouse. Then, click the program name on the **menu** or in a list. Once loaded into memory, the program is displayed in a **window** on the desktop.

Visit the Computer Concepts CourseMate Web site at www.cengagebrain.com, navigate to the Chapter 3 Quiz Yourself resource for this book, and then click Objectives 1 – 4.

5. What Are the Key Features of Widely Used Business Programs? **Business software** assists people in becoming more effective and efficient while performing daily business activities. Business software includes the following programs. **Word processing software**, sometimes called a *word processor*, allows users to **create** a document by entering text and inserting images, **edit** the document by making changes, and **format** the document by changing its appearance. **Spreadsheet software** allows users to organize data in rows and columns, perform calculations, recalculate when data changes, and chart the data. **Database software** allows users to create, access, and manage a **database**, which is a collection of data organized to allow access, retrieval, and use of that data. **Presentation software** allows users to create a *slide show* that is displayed on a monitor or projection screen. **Note taking software** enables users to enter typed text, handwritten comments, drawings, or sketches on a page and then save the page as part of a notebook. A **personal information manager (PIM)** includes features to help users organize personal information. In addition to PIM software, a huge variety of business and other software for phones is available. A **software suite** is a collection of individual programs available together as a unit. At a minimum, business software suites include word processing, spreadsheet, e-mail, and presentation programs. **Project management software** allows users to plan, schedule, track, and analyze the events, resources, and costs of a project. **Accounting software** helps companies record and report their financial transactions. **Document management software** provides a means for sharing, distributing, and searching through documents by converting them into a format that can be viewed by any user.

6. What Are the Key Features of Widely Used Graphics and Multimedia Programs? Graphics and multimedia software includes the following programs. **Computer-aided design (CAD) software** assists in creating engineering, architectural, and scientific designs. **Desktop publishing (DTP) software** enables professional designers to create sophisticated

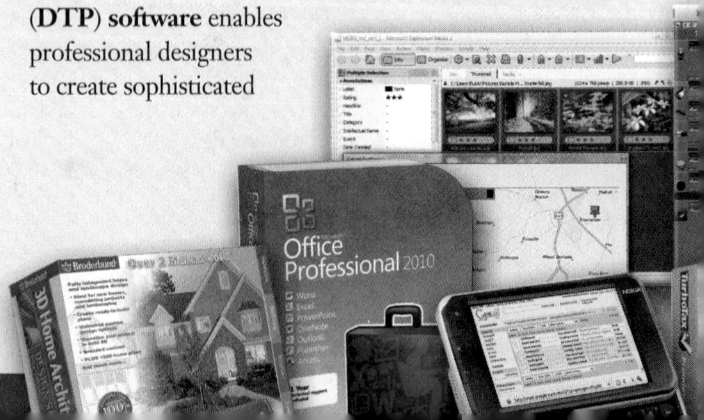

Chapter Review

documents that contain text, graphics, and colors. **Paint software**, also called *illustration software*, lets users draw graphical images with various on-screen tools. **Image editing software** provides the capabilities of paint software and includes the capability to enhance and modify existing images. **Professional photo editing software** is a type of image editing software that allows high-volume digital photo users to edit and customize digital photos. **Video editing software** allows professionals to modify segments of a video. **Audio editing software** lets users modify audio clips, produce studio-quality soundtracks, and add audio to video clips. **Multimedia authoring software** allows users to combine text, graphics, audio, video, and animation in an interactive application. **Web page authoring software** helps users of all skill levels create Web pages that include graphical images, video, audio, animation, and other special effects with interactive content.

Visit the Computer Concepts CourseMate Web site at www.cengagebrain.com, navigate to the Chapter 3 Quiz Yourself resource for this book, and then click Objectives 5 – 6.

7. **What Are the Key Features of Widely Used Home, Personal, and Educational Programs?** Software for home, personal, and educational use includes the following programs. **Personal finance software** is an accounting program that helps users balance their checkbooks, pay bills, track income and expenses, track investments, and evaluate financial plans. **Legal software** assists in the preparation of legal documents. **Tax preparation software** guides users through filing federal taxes. **Personal DTP software** helps users create newsletters, brochures, flyers, advertisements, greeting and business cards, logos, and Web pages. **Personal paint/image editing software** provides an easy-to-use interface with functions tailored to meet the needs of home and small business users. **Personal photo editing software** is a type of image editing software used to edit digital photos. *Photo management software* helps users view, organize, sort, catalog, and share digital photos. Application software often includes a **clip art/image gallery**, which is a collection of clip art and photos. Video and audio editing software is used to edit home movies, add music or other sounds, and share movies on the Web. **Home design/landscaping software** assists with the design, remodeling, or improvement of a home or landscape. **Travel and mapping software** enables users to view maps, determine route directions, and locate points of interest. **Reference software** provides valuable and thorough information for all individuals. **Educational software** teaches a particular skill. **Entertainment software** includes interactive games, videos, and other programs to support hobbies or provide amusement.

8. **What Are the Advantages of and Ways to Access Web Applications?** A Web application, or *Web app*, requires less disk space on a computer than installed software and is less costly to upgrade. Users often interact with Web applications directly at the Web site, referred to as the host, through their Web browser. Some Web sites require that you download the software to your computer or device.

9. **What Are the Types of Application Software Used in Communications?** Application software for communications includes Web browsers to access and view Web pages; e-mail programs to transmit messages via a network; instant messaging software for real-time exchange of messages or files; chat room software to have real-time, online typed conversations; text, picture, and video messaging software; RSS aggregator program to keep track of changes made to Web sites; *blog software*, or *blogware*, to create and maintain a blog; newsgroup/message board programs that allow online written discussions; FTP programs to upload and download files on the Internet; VoIP (Internet telephony), which allows users to speak to other users over the Internet; and video conferencing software for meetings on a network.

10. **What Learning Aids Are Available for Application Software?** To assist in the learning process, many programs offer Help features. **Online Help** is the electronic equivalent of a user manual. Most online Help links to *Web-based Help*, which provides updates and more comprehensive resources. Popular in business, industry, and schools, **Web-based training** (*WBT*) is a type of computer-based training that uses Internet technology and consists of application software on the Web.

Visit the Computer Concepts CourseMate Web site at www.cengagebrain.com, navigate to the Chapter 3 Quiz Yourself resource for this book, and then click Objectives 7 – 10.

Key Terms

You should know the Primary Terms and be familiar with the Secondary Terms. The list below helps focus your study.

To see an example of and a definition for each term, and to access current and additional information from the Web, visit the Computer Concepts CourseMate Web site at www.cengagebrain.com and then navigate to the Chapter 3 Key Terms resource for this book.

Primary Terms

(shown in bold-black characters in the chapter)

accounting software (158)
application software (142)
audio editing software (162)
business software (146)
button (144)
click (144)
clip art (147)
clip art/image gallery (169)
command (144)
computer-aided design (CAD) software (160)
computer-based training (CBT) (171)
create (149)
custom software (142)
database (153)
database software (153)
desktop (144)
desktop publishing (DTP) software (160)
distance learning (DL) (176)
document management software (158)
edit (149)
educational software (171)
entertainment software (172)
font (149)
font size (149)
format (149)
freeware (143)
home design/landscaping software (170)
icon (144)
image editing software (161)
legal software (167)
menu (144)
multimedia authoring software (162)
note taking software (156)
online banking (166)
online Help (175)
open source software (143)
packaged software (142)
paint software (161)
personal DTP software (167)
personal finance software (166)
personal information manager (PIM) (156)
personal paint/image editing software (168)
personal photo editing software (168)
pointer (144)
presentation software (154)
print (150)
professional photo editing software (162)
project management software (157)
public-domain software (143)
reference software (171)
save (150)
shareware (143)
software suite (156)
spreadsheet software (150)
tax preparation software (167)
title bar (144)
travel and mapping software (170)
video editing software (162)
Web application (142)
Web page authoring software (164)
Web-based training (176)
window (144)
word processing software (147)

Secondary Terms

(shown in italic characters in the chapter)

bar chart (152)
blog software (174)
blogware (174)
cell (151)
charting (152)
clipboard (149)
cloud storage (172)
color library (161)
column chart (152)
dialog box (145)
e-filing (167)
e-learning (176)
field (154)
file (144)
file name (145)
filters (162)
font style (149)
footer (148)
formula (151)
function (151)
header (148)
illustration software (161)
image stitching (161)
import (155)
label (151)
line chart (152)
loaded (144)
macro (148)
malware (144)
margins (147)
page layout (160)
pasting (149)
PDF (158)
photo management software (169)
pie chart (152)
point (149)
product activation (143)
query (154)
record (154)
sans serif font (149)
scrolling (148)
serif font (149)
slide show (154)
smart tags (148)
spelling checker (148)
system software (143)
template (148)
value (151)
WBT (176)
Web app (172)
Web-based Help (175)
what-if analysis (152)
word processor (147)
wordwrap (147)
worksheet (150)

computer-aided design (CAD) software (160)

Checkpoint

The Checkpoint exercises test your knowledge of the chapter concepts. The page number containing the answer appears in parentheses after each exercise. The Beyond the Book exercises will help broaden your understanding of the concepts presented in this chapter.

To complete the Checkpoint exercises interactively, visit the Computer Concepts CourseMate Web site at www.cengagebrain.com and then navigate to the Chapter 3 Checkpoint resource for this book.

True/False Mark T for True and F for False.

_____ 1. The categories of application software are mutually exclusive. (142)

_____ 2. Public-domain software is available to the public for a fee. (143)

_____ 3. To click a button on the screen requires moving the pointer to the button and then pressing and holding down a button on the mouse (usually the right mouse button). (144)

_____ 4. A dialog box is a window that provides information, presents available options, or requests a response. (145)

_____ 5. A font is a name assigned to a specific design of characters. (149)

_____ 6. In a spreadsheet program, a function is a predefined formula that performs common calculations such as adding the values in a group of cells or generating a value such as the time or date. (151)

_____ 7. Computer-aided design (CAD) software is a sophisticated type of application software that assists a professional user in creating engineering, architectural, and scientific designs. (160)

_____ 8. Image stitching is the process of adjusting or enhancing image colors and/or adding special effects such as shadows and glows. (161)

_____ 9. Although many word processing programs include desktop publishing (DTP) software features, users often prefer to create DTP documents using DTP software because of its enhanced features. (168)

_____ 10. Some Web sites require you to download software in order to run their Web applications. (172)

_____ 11. Some communications software is considered system software because it works with hardware and transmission media. (174)

_____ 12. An RSS aggregator includes time-stamped articles, or posts, in a diary or journal format, usually listed in reverse chronological order. (174)

Multiple Choice Select the best answer.

1. _____ is mass-produced, copyrighted retail software that meets the needs of a wide variety of users, not just a single user or company. (142)
   a. Packaged software b. A Web application
   c. Open source software d. Custom software

2. _____ is a collection of individual programs available together as a unit. (156)
   a. A software suite b. Shareware
   c. Packaged software d. Custom software

3. _____ allows a user to plan, schedule, track, and analyze the events, resources, and costs of a project. (157)
   a. Accounting software
   b. Project management software
   c. CAD software
   d. Document management software

4. _____ software provides a means for sharing, distributing, and searching through documents by converting them into a format that can be viewed by any user. (158)
   a. Database
   b. Portable Document Format (PDF)
   c. Document management
   d. Word processing

5. _____ helps home and small business users create newsletters, brochures, advertisements, postcards, greeting cards, letterhead, business cards, banners, calendars, logos, and Web pages. (168)
   a. Blogware
   b. A personal information manager
   c. Personal DTP software
   d. Note taking software

6. With _____, you can view, organize, sort, catalog, print, and share digital photos. (169)
   a. spreadsheet software
   b. photo management software
   c. clip art
   d. desktop publishing software

7. A(n) _____ is an online area where users have written discussions. (174)
   a. FTP program
   b. text message
   c. newsgroup/message board
   d. Web browser

8. _____ is the electronic equivalent of a user manual. (175)
   a. Web-based training b. Online Help
   c. E-learning d. Distance learning

STUDENT ASSIGNMENTS

Checkpoint

Matching Match the terms with their definitions.

____ 1. button (144)	a. popular file format that document management software uses to save converted documents
____ 2. window (144)	b. the process of transferring an item from a clipboard to a specific location in a document
____ 3. title bar (144)	c. Web site that allows users to access and interact with software from any computer or device that is connected to the Internet
____ 4. pasting (149)	d. intersection of a row and column in a spreadsheet
____ 5. cell (151)	e. rectangular area of the screen that displays data and information
____ 6. database (153)	f. small symbol on the screen that moves as you move the mouse
____ 7. PDF (158)	g. simplified accounting program that helps home users and small office/home office users balance their checkbooks, pay bills, track personal income and expenses, set up budgets, manage home inventory, track investments, and evaluate financial plans
____ 8. personal finance software (166)	h. text that appears at the bottom of every page
____ 9. online banking (166)	i. graphical image activated to cause a specific action to occur
____ 10. Web app (172)	j. horizontal space that contains the window's name
	k. offers access to account balances, provides bill payment services, and allows you to download monthly transactions and statements from the Web directly to your computer
	l. collection of data organized in a manner that allows access, retrieval, and use of that data

Short Answer Write a brief answer to each of the following questions.

1. Describe some types of utility programs. ____________ What is malware? ____________
2. What are the features of presentation software? ____________ What types of media might a person use to enhance a presentation? ____________
3. How is travel and mapping software used? ____________ What are some examples of reference software? ____________
4. What is computer-based training (CBT)? ____________ List a few examples of CBT usage. ____________
5. Describe how many Web sites utilize Web-based training. ____________ What are some ways that e-learning enhances communications? ____________

Beyond the Book Follow the book element instructions below; present your findings (brief report, presentation, discussion, or other means).

1. Ethics & Issues — Select an Ethics & Issues in this chapter (149, 150, 162, 173), find a recent newspaper/magazine article that supports one point of view presented, and then evaluate the article.
2. Computer Usage @ Work — Use the Web or a recent newspaper/magazine to locate three additional unique usages of computer technology in the construction industry (177). What makes the use of these technologies unique to the construction industry?
3. Companies on the Cutting Edge and Technology Trailblazers — Use the Web or a recent business newspaper/magazine to locate an interesting fact about Adobe Systems, Microsoft, Dan Bricklin, or Masayoshi Son that was not presented in the chapter (179).
4. High-Tech Talk — Locate a recent newspaper/magazine article that discusses topics related to Computer Viruses (178). Would you recommend the article you found? Why or why not?
5. FAQs and Web Links — Use the Web or a recent newspaper/magazine to locate three additional facts about an FAQ (144, 150, 154, 166, 167, 172, 174) and Web Link (144, 148, 151, 154, 155, 156, 160, 164, 167, 168, 172, 173) that were not presented in the chapter.
6. Looking Ahead — Use the Web or a recent newspaper/magazine to discover additional uses of the technology presented in Sensors Help Drivers Find Their Way (171).
7. Innovative Computing — Use the Web or a recent newspaper/magazine to locate two additional interesting facts about Fireworks Software Creates a Real Blast (160) and iTunes U Supplements Classroom Learning (175).
8. Making Use of the Web — Visit three of the Blogs sites (127) and outline the information on each Web site and the possible uses for each Web site.
9. Digital Communications — Select a topic discussed in the Digital Communications feature (192) and then present a current issue related to the topic found on the Web or in a magazine article.

Learn It Online

The Learn It Online exercises are interactive Web exercises designed to reinforce and expand your understanding of the chapter concepts. The descriptions below briefly summarize each exercise.

To complete the Learn It Online exercises, visit the Computer Concepts CourseMate Web site at www.cengagebrain.com, navigate to the Chapter 3 resources for this book, click the link for the exercise you want to complete, and then read the instructions.

1 At the Movies — MediaCell Video Converter
Watch a movie to learn how to use the MediaCell Video Converter and then answer questions about the movie.

2 Video and Audio: You Review It — Video Editing Software
Search for, choose, and write a review of a video, podcast, or vodcast that discusses video editing software.

3 Student Edition Labs — Word Processing, Spreadsheets, Databases, and Presentation Software
Enhance your understanding and knowledge about business application software by completing the Word Processing, Spreadsheets, Databases, and Presentation Software Labs.

4 Practice Test
Take a multiple choice test that checks your knowledge of the chapter concepts and review the resulting study guide.

5 Who Wants To Be a Computer Genius^2?
Play the Shelly Cashman Series version of this popular game by answering questions to find out if you are a computer genius. Panic buttons are available to provide assistance during game play.

6 Wheel of Terms
Identify important key terms presented in this chapter by playing the Shelly Cashman Series version of this popular game.

7 You're Hired!
Embark on the path to a career in computers by answering questions and solving puzzles related to concepts discussed in this chapter.

8 Crossword Puzzle Challenge
Complete an interactive crossword puzzle to reinforce concepts presented in this chapter.

9 Windows Exercises
Step through the Windows 7 exercises to learn about working with application programs, creating a word processing document, using WordPad Help, and business software products.

10 Exploring Computer Careers
Read about a career as a help desk specialist, search for related employment advertisements, and then answer related questions.

11 Web Apps — Britannica.com
Learn how to browse world history and search for various encyclopedia articles using Britannica.com.

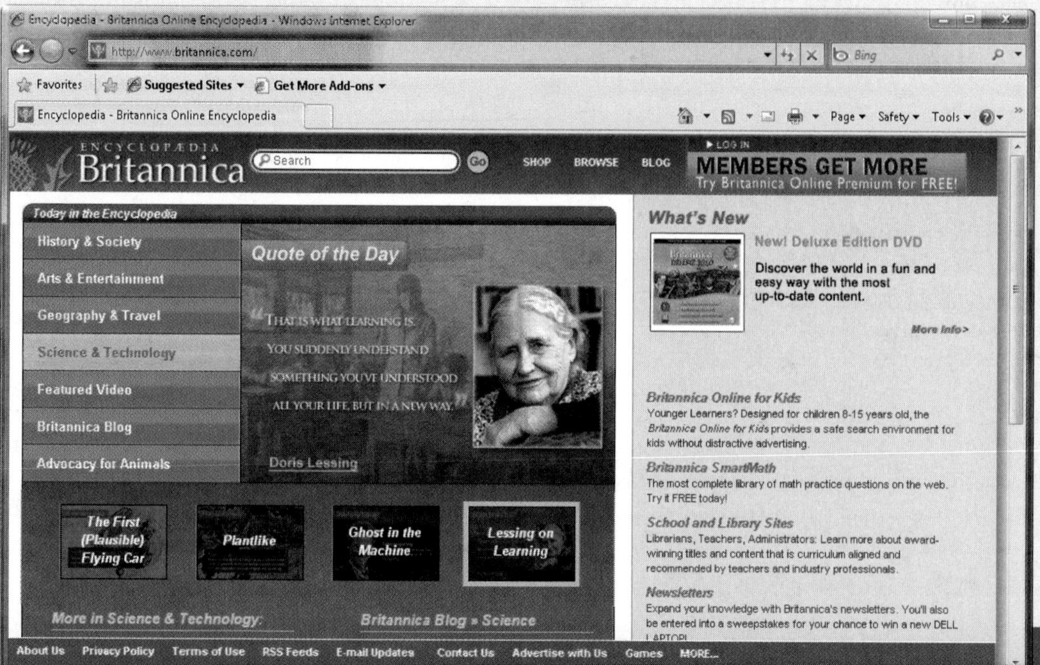

Problem Solving @ Home

The Problem Solving @ Home exercises extend your knowledge of the chapter concepts by seeking solutions to practical computer problems that you may encounter at home or school. The Collaboration exercise should be completed with a team.

In the real world, practical problems often can be solved in multiple ways. Provide one solution to each of the following problems using available resources, such as articles on the Web or in print, blogs, podcasts, videos, television, user guides, other individuals, and electronics and computer stores. You may need to use multiple resources to obtain an answer. Present your solutions in the form requested by your instructor (brief report, presentation, discussion, or other means).

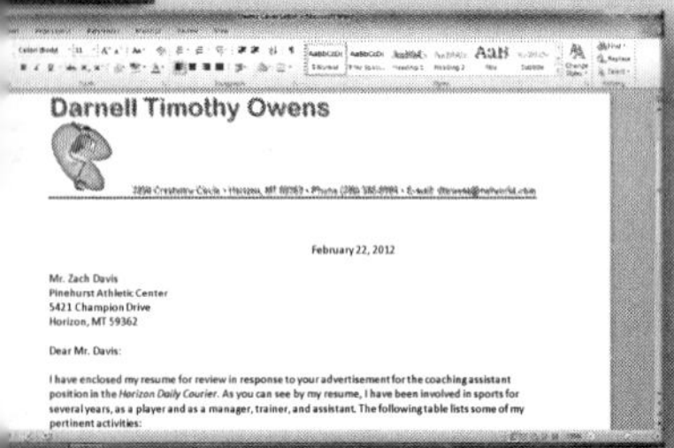

1. **Program Not Responding** While working with a document, Microsoft Word suddenly fails to recognize when you click the mouse or type on the keyboard. The title bar also indicates that the program is not responding. What could be wrong?

2. **Incorrect Calculations** As a teacher's assistant at a local high school, you keep track of students' grades in Microsoft Excel. At semester's end, you use a formula to calculate the final letter grade for each student. The final letter grades, however, do not calculate properly. What might be causing the error?

3. **Unable to Save** You have been using Microsoft Access to maintain a database of your optical discs. Upon attempting to open the database, you receive a message on the screen stating that only a read-only copy of the database could be opened, which means that you are unable to save any changes. What is your next step?

4. **Smart Phone Not Synchronizing** You regularly connect your smart phone to your computer to synchronize your e-mail messages, contacts, and calendar. The last few times you tried to connect the smart phone, the computer did not respond. Before placing a call to technical support, what steps can you take so that the computer will recognize your smart phone?

5. **Unwanted Page** A local charity in which you are active has asked you to design a one-page brochure. Each time you print the brochure, it prints the first page correctly, but a blank second page also comes out. What steps will you take to eliminate the blank second page?

6. **Audio Not Playing** You are attempting for the first time to transfer video from your video recorder directly to your computer. When you save the file on your computer and play it back, the video quality is acceptable, but there is no audio. What is the first step you will take to troubleshoot this problem?

7. **Unusual File Size** You are using photo editing software to remove red eye from a photo. After successfully removing the red eye, you save the file and notice that the size of the file nearly has doubled. What might be causing this?

8. **Program Crashing on Exit** Each time you attempt to quit Microsoft Excel by clicking the Close button, the program does not quit, and the title bar indicates that it is not responding. When you click the Close button again, a dialog box is displayed that states Microsoft Excel has encountered a problem. What steps will you take to solve this problem?

Collaboration

9. **Poor Computer Performance** While working on a class project with a group of friends, you notice that your computer is running exceptionally slowly. In addition, you notice that the light identifying hard disk activity is flashing almost constantly. Your first instincts are that the computer is low on hard disk space, the computer might have a virus, or too many programs are running on the computer. Form a team of three people and begin searching for information about how to isolate the problem. One team member should look for free, up-to-date virus scanning software to scan the computer for viruses, another team member should research ways to find programs that are running (that might not be displayed on the taskbar), and one team member should create a list of ways to free up space on the hard disk. Compile your answers and submit them to your instructor.

Problem Solving @ Work

The Problem Solving @ Work exercises extend your knowledge of the chapter concepts by seeking solutions to practical computer problems that you may encounter at work. The Collaboration exercise should be completed with a team.

In the real world, practical problems often can be solved in multiple ways. Provide one solution to each of the following problems using available resources, such as articles on the Web or in print, blogs, podcasts, videos, television, user guides, other individuals, and electronics and computer stores. You may need to use multiple resources to obtain an answer. Present your solutions in the form requested by your instructor (brief report, presentation, discussion, or other means).

1. **Missing Font** A coworker has sent you a document that was created in Microsoft Word. She asks you to format the heading of the document with a specific font; however, the font name does not appear in your list of fonts. What steps will you take to retrieve the font?
2. **Incorrect File Format** You have been working from your home office creating your company's annual report in Microsoft Word. Upon attempting to open the annual report on a computer at your company's office, an error message is displayed stating that the file format cannot be recognized. What might have caused this?
3. **Insufficient Permission** When reviewing a document in your company's document management system, you attempt to correct a typographical error for the next person who views the file. The document management system prohibits this action and informs you that you do not have the proper permission. What will you do to resolve this problem?
4. **Software Activation Required** Your company has purchased a new netbook to allow you to work from home. After using the computer for about one month, Windows informs you that it must be activated to continue functioning. Why is this happening, and what are your next steps?
5. **Trial Version Expired** New job responsibilities require that you use Adobe Photoshop to create a new company logo. Your boss has been unable to purchase the latest version of the software for you, and recommends that you download and install the trial version until she is able to purchase the software. The trial period now has expired and you are unable to use the program. How might you be able to continue using the software?

6. **Web-Based Training Difficulties** You have signed up for Web-based training that is designed to teach you how to use your company's new accounting system. During your training, you notice that the Web-based training Web site is not keeping track of your progress. Consequently, you have to start from the beginning of the training program each time you log in to the Web site. What might be causing this?
7. **Installation Media Required** Each time you start Microsoft Excel and attempt to use one of its advanced features, a dialog box appears asking you to insert the installation disc. You are unable to locate the installation disc. What are your next steps so that you can use the advanced features of Microsoft Excel?

Collaboration

8. **Computers in Construction** As a student in a drafting class, your instructor has challenged you to design your dream home by using application software wherever possible. Form a team of three people that will determine how to accomplish this objective. One team member should compare and contrast two programs that can be used to create a two-dimensional floor plan, another team member should compare and contrast two computer-aided design programs that can create a more detailed design of the house, and the third team member should compare and contrast two programs that can assist with other aspects of the design process such as landscaping and interior design.

Learn How To

The Learn How To activities step you through fundamental technology skills when using a computer. The Learn How To exercises enable you to become more proficient with these skills.

Premium Activity: To relate this Learn How To activity to your everyday life, see a visual demonstration of the activity, and complete a short assessment, visit the Computer Concepts CourseMate Web site at www.cengagebrain.com and then navigate to the Chapter 3 Learn How To resource for this book.

Learn How To 1: Save a File in Application Software

When you use application software, usually you either will create a new file or modify an existing file. If you turn off your computer or lose electrical power while working on the file, the file will not be retained. In order to retain the file, you must save it.

To save a new file, you must complete several tasks:

1. Initiate an action indicating you want to save the file, such as selecting Save on the File menu.
2. Designate where the file should be stored. This includes identifying both the device (such as drive C) and the folder or library.
3. Specify the name of the file.
4. Click the Save button to save the file.

Tasks 2 through 4 normally can be completed using a dialog box such as the one shown in Figure 3-48.

If you close a program prior to saving a new or modified file, the program may display a dialog box asking if you want to save the file. If you click the Yes button, a modified file will be saved using the same file name in the same location. Saving a new file requires that you complete tasks 2 through 4.

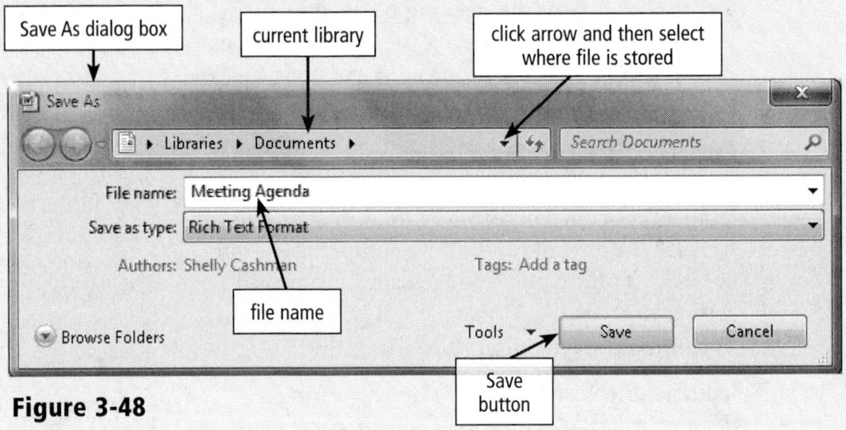

Figure 3-48

Exercise

1a. Start the WordPad program from the Accessories list in the All Programs list. Type `Saving a file is the best insurance against losing work.`

1b. Click the Save button on the Quick Access Toolbar. What dialog box is displayed? Where will the file be saved? What is the default file name? If you wanted to save the file on the desktop, what would you do? Click the Cancel button in the dialog box. Submit your answers to your instructor.

1c. Click the Close button in the WordPad window. What happened? Click the Yes button in the WordPad dialog box. What happened? Connect a USB flash drive to one of the computer's USB ports. Select the USB flash drive as the location for saving the file. Save the file with the name, Chapter 3 Learn How To 1. What happened? Submit your answers to your instructor.

Learn How To 2: Install and Uninstall Application Software

When you purchase application software, you must install the software on the computer where you want to run it. The exact installation process varies with each program, but generally you must complete the following steps:

1. Insert the optical disc containing the application software into a drive.
2. The opening window will appear. If the optical disc contains more than one program, choose the program you want to install. Click the Continue or Next button.
3. Some file extractions will occur and then an Install Wizard will begin. You normally must accomplish the following steps by completing the directions within the wizard:
   a. Accept the terms of the license agreement.
   b. Identify where on your computer the software will be stored. The software usually selects a default location on drive C, and you normally will accept the default location.
   c. Select any default options for the software.
   d. Click a button to install the software.
4. A Welcome/Help screen often will be displayed. Click a button to finish the installation process.

At some point, you may want to remove software. Most software includes an uninstall program that will remove the program and all its software components. To uninstall a program, complete the following steps:

1. Click the Start button on the Windows taskbar.
2. Click Control Panel on the Start menu.

Learn How To

3. Click 'Uninstall a program' to open the Programs and Features window (Figure 3-49).
4. Select the program that you wish to remove. In Figure 3-49, Adobe Acrobat Professional is selected as the program to remove.
5. Click the Uninstall/Change button.
6. A dialog box will be displayed informing you that the software is being prepared for uninstall. You then will be informed that the process you are following will remove the program. You will be asked if you want to continue.

To uninstall the program, click the Yes button. The program will be removed from the computer.

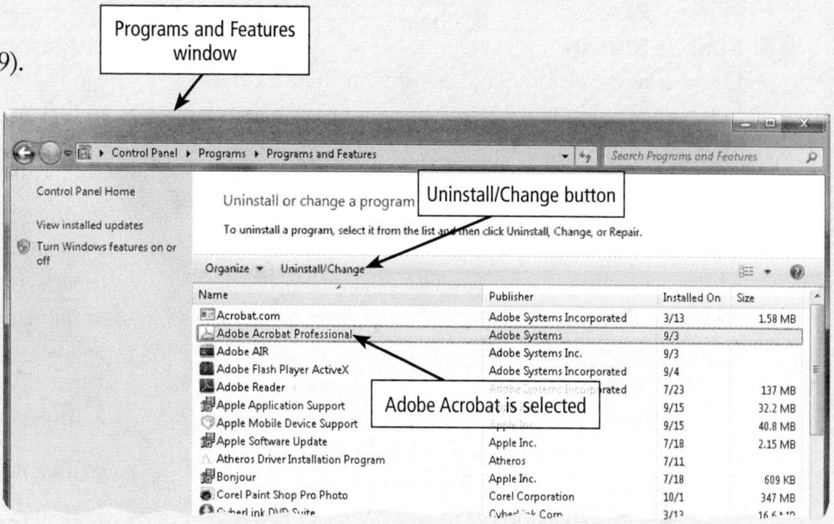

Figure 3-49

Exercises

1. Optional: Insert the optical disc containing the software you want to install into a drive and follow the instructions for installing the software. **Warning: If you are using a computer other than your own, particularly in a school laboratory, do not perform this exercise unless you have specific permission from your instructor.**
2. Optional: Follow the steps above to uninstall software you want to remove. Be aware that if you uninstall software, the software will not be available for use until you reinstall it. **Warning: If you are using a computer other than your own, particularly in a school laboratory, do not perform this exercise unless you have specific permission from your instructor.**

Learn How To 3: Zip/Compress a File

When you zip or compress one or more files in Windows, it attempts to shrink the file size(s) by reducing the amount of unneeded space. Compressing a file is particularly useful when you attach files to an e-mail message and wish to keep the file size as small as possible. It also is useful when you compress multiple files simultaneously, because Windows compresses the multiple files into a single file. You can compress a file or folder by completing the following steps:

1. Locate the file(s) or folder(s) you want to compress. If the files or folders you wish to compress are located in multiple locations, it might be helpful to first move them so that they are in a single location.
2. Select the file(s) or folder(s) you would like to compress. If you are selecting multiple files or folders, click the first one and then hold down the CTRL key while you select the remaining files and/or folders. Once you are finished making your selections, release the CTRL key.
3. Right-click the selection to display a shortcut menu, point to Send to on the shortcut menu to display the Send to submenu (Figure 3-50), and then click Compressed (zipped) folder to create the compressed folder.
4. If necessary, type a new name for the compressed folder and then press the ENTER key.

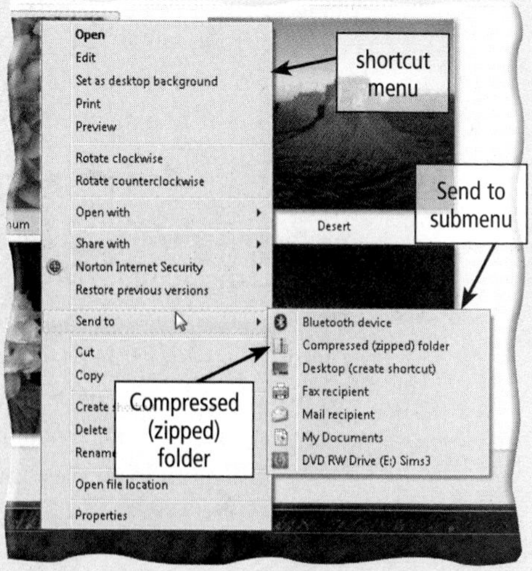

Figure 3-50

Exercise

1. To better organize your hard disk, you decide to compress files you rarely use, but would like to keep as a backup. Click the Start button to display the Start menu, click Pictures to display the Pictures library, and then double-click the Sample Pictures folder to display sample pictures included with Windows 7. Select three pictures and compress them into one compressed folder. Use your first initial and last name as the name of the new compressed folder and then e-mail the folder to your instructor.

STUDENT ASSIGNMENTS

Web Research

The Web Research exercises broaden your understanding of the chapter concepts by presenting questions that require you to search the Web for answers.

1 Search Sleuth

Use one of the search engines listed in Figure 2-10 in Chapter 2 on page 85 or your own favorite search engine to find the answers to the following questions. Copy and paste the Web address from the Web page where you found the answer. Some questions may have more than one answer. If required, submit your answers to your instructor. (1) What company did Bruce Artwick form in 1977, and what game did it license to Microsoft in 1982? (2) In what year did the United States Department of Revenue first provide tax forms and booklets in Adobe PDF format on its Web site? (3) What is the latest security incident listed on the United States Computer Emergency Readiness Team (US-CERT) Web site? (4) What is the name of the sans serif font the German Bauhaus movement developed in 1928? (5) What United States president's speech did Peter Norvig turn into a lighthearted PowerPoint presentation?

2 Green Computing

A typical desktop computer and 17-inch monitor that always are turned on release 750 pounds of carbon dioxide in one year, which is the same amount of carbon dioxide released by a car driven 820 miles. Power management software helps conserve a computer's electricity consumption while maintaining acceptable performance. The programs determine when a computer is inactive and, in turn, power down the computer. Use one of the search engines listed in Figure 2-10 in Chapter 2 on page 85 or your own favorite search engine to find information about power management software. What average return-on-investment do they promise? What features do they have, such as generating reports and exempting critical programs from powering down? What is their cost? Powering down the computer stresses critical components, such as the CPU and memory, so does this practice actually result in more waste because these parts must be replaced? Write a report summarizing your findings, and include a table of links to Web sites that you viewed.

3 Social Networking

Career-minded professionals have turned to LinkedIn as a resource for online networking. The more than 45 million registered users, who represent each of the FORTUNE 500 companies, create public profiles that recruiters scour in search of new talent. Users can link to work contacts who, in turn, give access to their work contacts. Visit the LinkedIn Web site (linkedin.com), click the What is LinkedIn? link at the top of the page, and then read the information about reconnecting with current and former colleagues and classmates, job hunting, and obtaining advice from experts. Click the LinkedIn Jobs link at the bottom of the page, type a keyword describing the type of job you would like to have, and then browse the listings. What tips for finding jobs does LinkedIn provide? Summarize the listings and job information you read.

4 Blogs

Vehicle buyers know that the Internet provides a wealth of information that helps direct them toward the best vehicle for their needs. Those consumers who research blogs can obtain price, safety, performance, and maintenance facts and then employ savvy negotiation techniques that help them make the purchase confidently. Visit several automotive blogs, including those from Popular Mechanics (popularmechanics.com/blogs/automotive_news), Autoblog (autoblog.com), Autoblog Green (autobloggreen.com), Autopia (blog.wired.com/cars), and Ask Patty — Car Advice for Women (caradvice.askpatty.com). What new hybrid, luxury, and high-performance vehicles are profiled? Which are promoted as being environmentally friendly? Write a report summarizing the vehicle information you read.

5 Ethics in Action

A hacker is someone who tries to access a computer or network illegally. Although hacking activity sometimes is a harmless prank, at times it causes extensive damage. Some hackers say their activities allow them to test their skills. Others say their activities are a form of civil disobedience that forces companies to make their products more secure. View online sites such as The Ethical Hacker Network (ethicalhacker.net) that provide information about when hackers provide some benefit to the Internet society. Write a report summarizing your findings, and include a table of links to Web sites that provide additional details.

Critical Thinking

The Critical Thinking exercises challenge your assessment and decision-making skills by presenting real-world situations associated with the chapter concepts. The Collaboration exercise should be completed with a team.

To evaluate the situations below, use personal experiences and available resources such as articles on the Web or in print, blogs, podcasts, videos, television, user guides, other individuals, and electronics and computer stores. You may need to use multiple resources to form conclusions and make recommendations.

1. **Class Discussion — Selecting a Spreadsheet Program** Your manager at Dean's Office Supply Outlet intends to choose a spreadsheet program that the entire company will use. He prefers to learn about software using trade books — written textbooks that explain the features of a program and how to use it — rather than using online Help or tutorials. Evaluate the spreadsheet trade books available in online bookstores. Visit an online bookstore and other Web sites that sell books to evaluate the spreadsheet trade books for Microsoft Excel, Lotus, Quattro Pro, and StarOffice Calc. Discuss how difficult it would be to learn each program using the trade books at hand. Include in your discussion which trade book you think is the best. Also discuss which program you would buy if you were going to purchase software solely on the basis of the related trade books. Include the reasons for your recommendation.

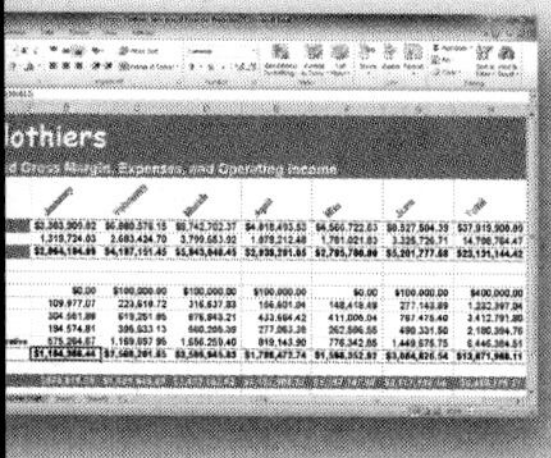

2. **Class Presentation — Entertainment Software Recommendations** Karl's Game Den sells new and used computer video games. Karl recently purchased a large quantity of children's games; however, they are not selling as he expected. You recently read that 60 percent of entertainment software purchases are made by males, and the average age of frequent purchasers is 35. You suggest that Karl may be selling to the wrong demographic. Use the Web and/or print media to evaluate the top five selling games in the United States. Determine if males and females favor different types of software, and if software developers adapt their products accordingly. Based on your findings, present your recommendation on what types of games and how many Karl should stock. Discuss the importance of why software developers should modify educational/entertainment software to meet the interests of different groups.

3. **Research — Application Software Comparison** Web applications are becoming increasingly popular, and some people prefer the convenience of using a Web application instead of application software installed on their computer. For example, some prefer to use Google Docs (a Web application) to Microsoft Word. Your boss notices this trend, and asks you whether it will benefit the company to use Web applications instead of application software. Compare application software installed on your computer with a comparable Web application. Are any security risks associated with using the application software? How do the features compare between a Web application and the application software? Would you recommend using a Web application to application software? Why?

Collaboration

4. **Educational Software Effectiveness** The new superintendent of Lisle Elementary School District 205 has recommended that educational software play a major role in the learning process at every grade level. In her presentation to the school board, she claimed that educational software is available for a wide variety of skills and subjects. She also indicated that educational software enables students to learn at their own pace, shows infinite patience, and usually offers an entertaining approach. The president of the school board is not so sure. Unlike human instructors, educational software often does not recognize unique problems, fails to address individual goals, and provides limited feedback. Form a three-member team and investigate the use of educational software. Each member of your team should visit a software vendor's Web site or an educational cooperative's Web site, and list the advantages and disadvantages of using educational software. Select a program on the Web or from your school's education department library and use it. Note the subject being taught, the audience to which the software is directed, the approach used, and any special features. Would you recommend the program you chose? Why or why not? Be sure to consider such factors as initial cost, upgrade costs, online Help, and technical support in your recommendation. Then, meet with your team, discuss your findings, prepare a presentation, and share it with your class.

Digital Communications

DIGITAL COMMUNICATIONS, which factor largely in many people's personal and business lives, include any transmission of information from one computer or mobile device to another (Figure 1). This feature covers many forms of digital communications: e-mail; text messaging, instant messaging, and picture/video messaging; digital voice communications; blogs and wikis; online social networks, chat rooms, and Web conferences; and content sharing.

Figure 1 People use a variety of methods in their personal and business lives to engage in digital communications.

With the Internet, cell phone networks, and other wireless networks increasing in size and speed, digital communications have become more and more prevalent. The most common devices used to communicate digitally are desktop computers, mobile computers, smart phones, and other mobile devices.

Successful use of digital communications involves selecting both the proper communications device and the proper mode of communication for a given situation. For example, under what circumstances might sending a text message from a smart phone be more appropriate than sending an e-mail message from a desktop computer? The answer to this question also may depend on whether the situation involves personal or business communications. Each computer or mobile device and communications method has advantages and disadvantages that you should consider.

The following pages describe how people use different types of digital communications in their personal and business lives to enhance collaboration and increase productivity. The final section of the feature includes an example of how you might use digital communications.

digital voice communications

video messaging with smart phone

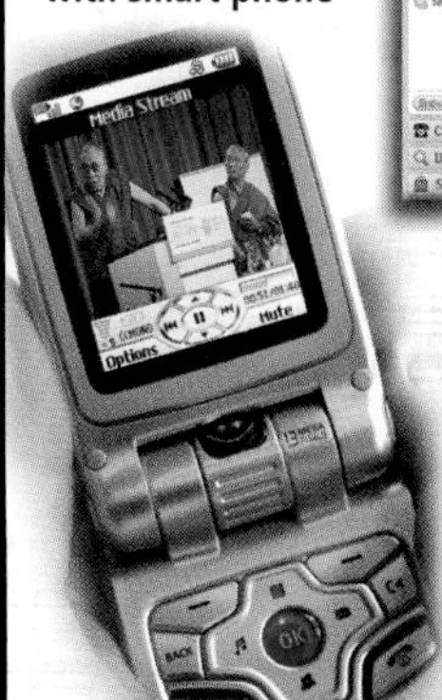

blog

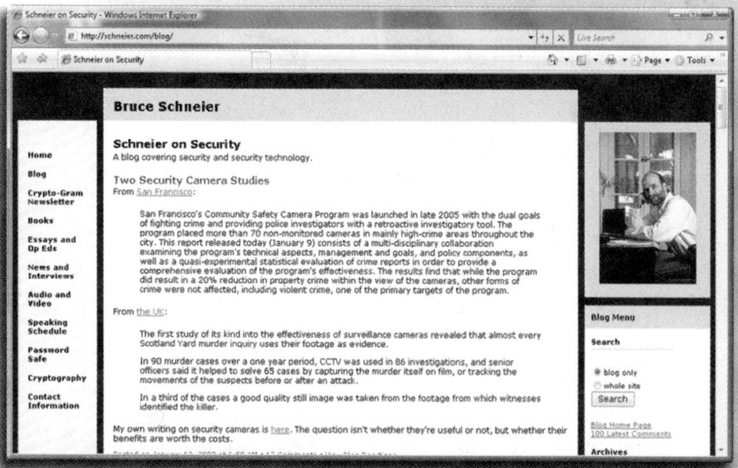

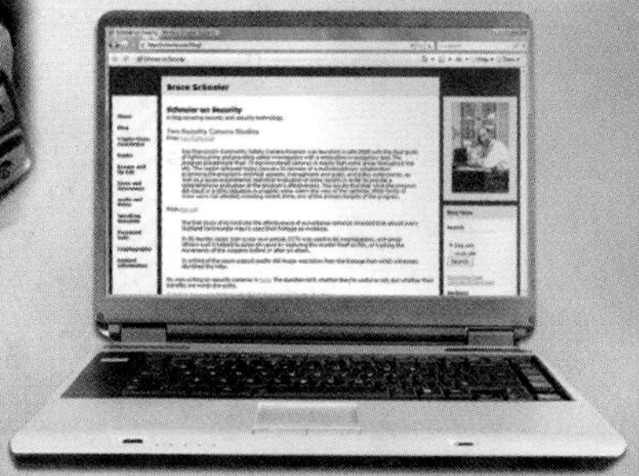

mobile computer

online social network

wiki

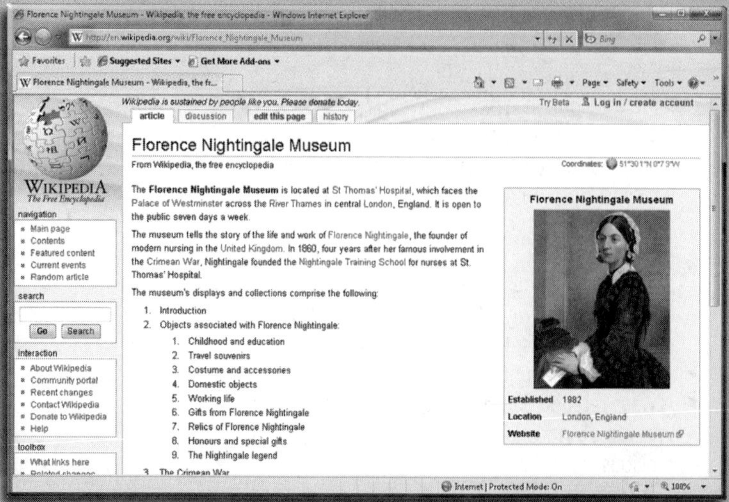

SPECIAL FEATURE

E-Mail

E-mail is the transmission of messages and files via a computer network. E-mail quickly has become one of the more widely used forms of digital communications. Although e-mail is primarily a text-based form of digital communications, it also can be used to share photos, videos, and other types of files by attaching files to e-mail messages.

E-Mail: The Personal Perspective

With a computer or mobile device connected to the Internet, you can use e-mail to keep in contact with friends, family, stores, companies, schools, and government agencies. Some people maintain several different e-mail addresses for use in different situations. Figure 2 lists some advantages, disadvantages, and good practices of personal e-mail use. Some e-mail programs are application programs that run on your computer, while others are Web applications (shown in Figure 3).

Personal E-Mail Use

Advantages
- One of the most preferred methods of online communications.
- Available on nearly any computer or mobile device with Internet access.
- Send files, called attachments, via e-mail messages to others.
- Fast, reliable, and proven technology.
- Allows messages to be sent anywhere free of charge or inexpensively.
- Allows communications with more than one person at a time.
- Provides an electronic forum for communications in which the originator has time to consider a thought before it is sent or spoken, unlike face-to-face meetings or telephone conversations.

Disadvantages
- Number of messages received can become overwhelming and unmanageable.
- Spam can overwhelm your e-mail inbox.
- Message tone can be misunderstood.
- Many computer viruses and other malicious programs are transmitted via e-mail messages.

Good practices
- Keep messages as short as possible.
- Check with the recipient before sending attachments, especially large attachments.
- Respond to messages promptly.
- Use a reputable Internet access provider that uses a spam filter, which is a program that detects and removes spam, and use an e-mail program that includes a spam filter.
- Never respond to unsolicited advertisements or spam.
- Informal language and shortcuts are acceptable when communicating with friends and family (e.g., suitable to use HRU? as a shortcut for How are you?).
- Always include a Subject line.
- Always reread your message and edit it before sending it.
- When replying to questions or comments included with a previous message, include the original message.

Figure 2 Personal e-mail remains one of the more popular reasons to use the Internet.

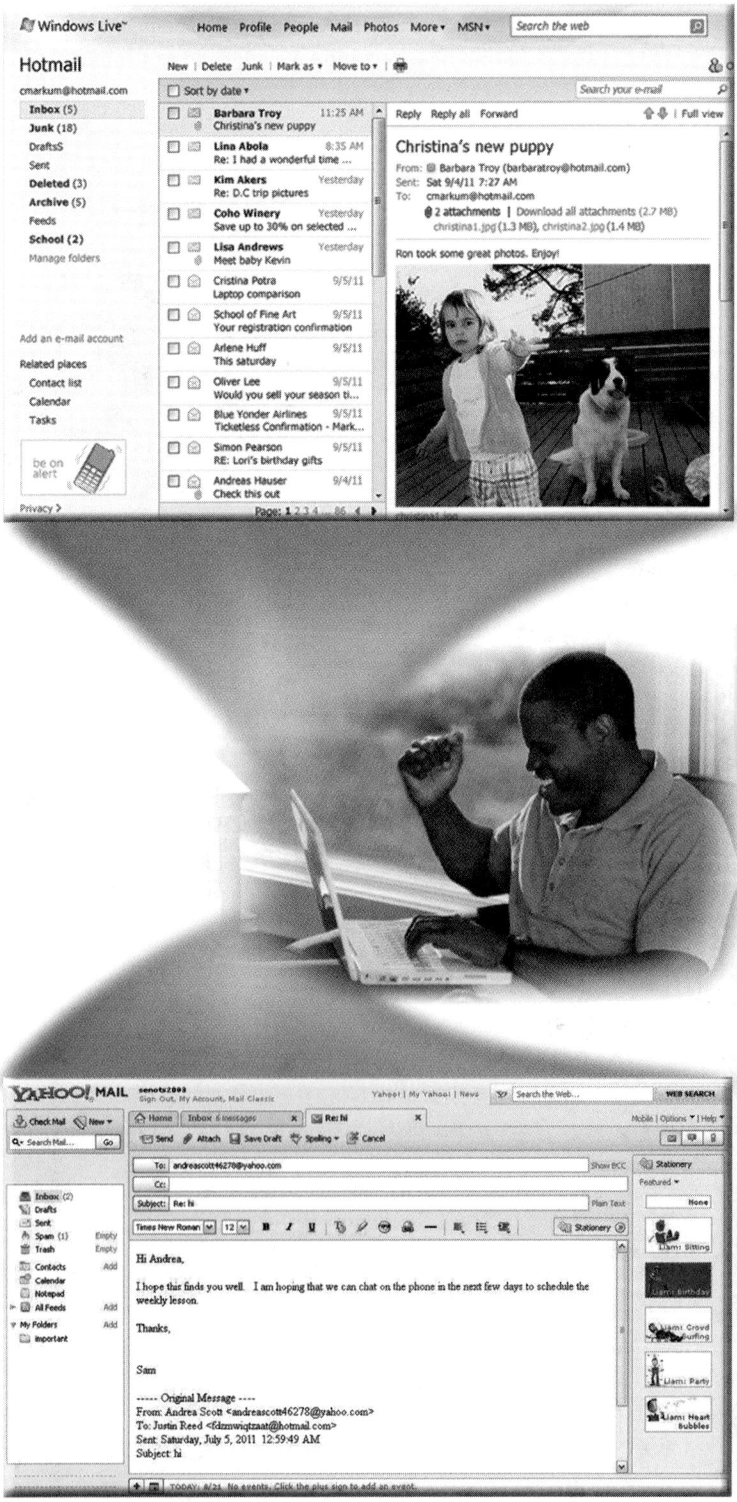

Figure 3 Many home users work with e-mail Web applications.

E-Mail: The Business Perspective

Nearly all businesses use e-mail for internal communications among employees and external communications with customers and business partners. E-mail gradually has replaced typed and copied memos, letters, and faxes while increasing the reliability, cost effectiveness, and speed of the communications. Figure 4 indicates some advantages, disadvantages, and good practices of e-mail use in business. Many of the notes listed in Figure 2 also apply to e-mail communications in business. Figure 5 shows an example of the inbox of a business e-mail program user and an example of an appropriate business e-mail message.

E-Mail Use in Business

Advantages

- Easily archive, or store long-term, all e-mail messages sent from or received by the business.
- Generally can guarantee delivery of any e-mail message that is sent within the business.
- A replacement for memos, letters, faxes, and other internal and external business communications when permitted by company policy.
- Communicate with someone who is not available at the time you need to communicate.

Disadvantages

- Volume of e-mail messages often becomes overwhelming.
- Often leads to overcommunication, which can result in important information being lost because it is ignored.
- Sometimes leads to avoidance of personal contact, such as a meeting or telephone call.

Good practices

- Because most companies archive, or save, all e-mail messages, use e-mail when you want a permanent record of a communication.
- Understand your company's e-mail policies. Many companies prohibit sending personal e-mail messages from a business computer.
- Never include any language that would be considered inappropriate in a business environment.
- Check your e-mail inbox regularly.
- Follow your company's or department's guidelines for formatting messages and including contact information and any appropriate disclaimers.
- In most cases, it is appropriate to send larger attachments in business e-mail messages as compared to those permissible in personal messages.
- Avoid sending messages to many people simultaneously or replying to large groups of people. For example, it is almost always inappropriate to send a message to the entire company.
- Avoid using e-mail messages when the content involves sensitive issues, such as a negotiation, legal matter, or employee review.
- When you need to know that the recipient has read your e-mail message, use the return receipt feature of your e-mail program to receive automatic notification as soon as the message is read.

Figure 4 Most businesses provide written policies and guidelines regarding use of e-mail programs.

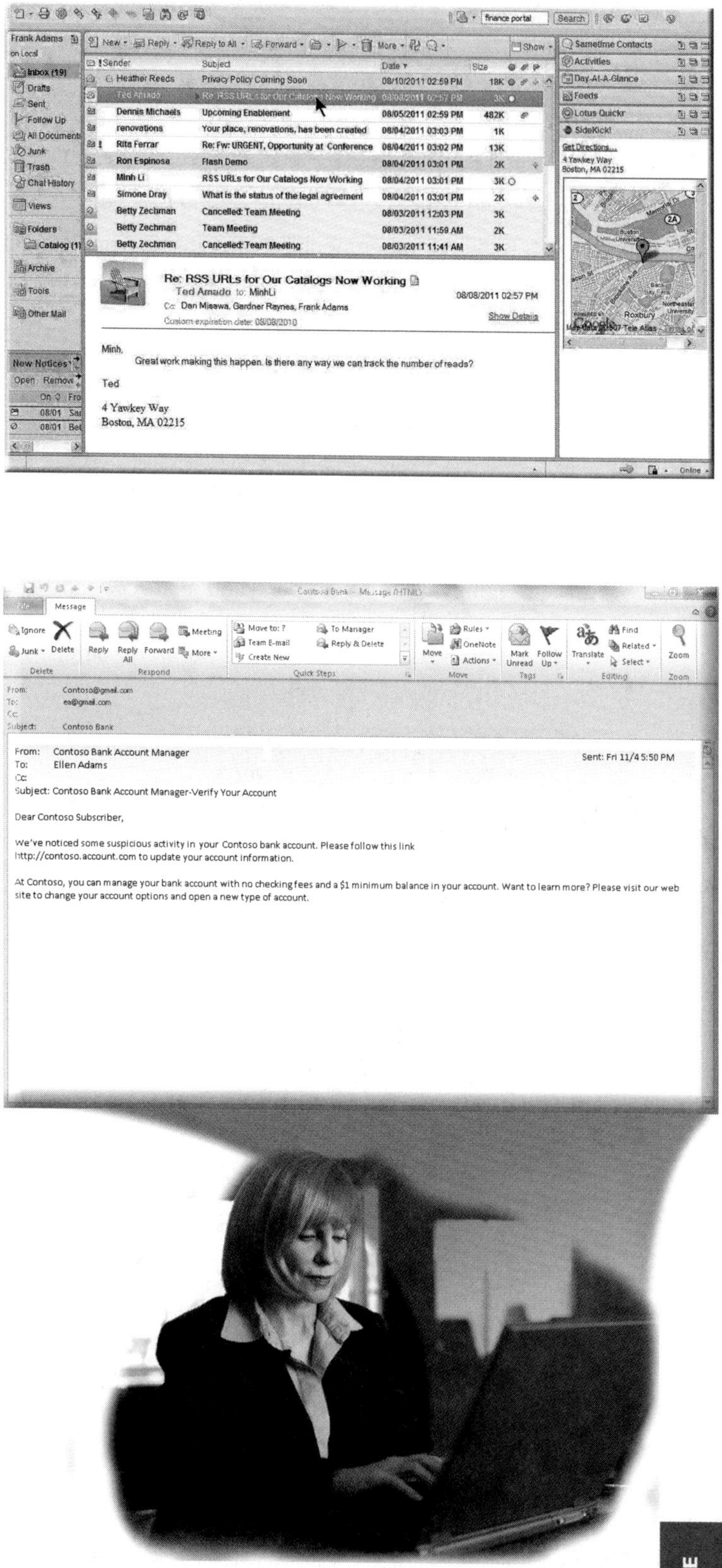

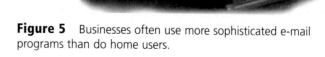

Figure 5 Businesses often use more sophisticated e-mail programs than do home users.

Text Messaging, Instant Messaging, and Picture/Video Messaging

Text messaging, instant messaging, and picture/video messaging allow you to exchange short messages and small multimedia files with other online users. Text messaging is a wireless messaging service that allows users to send and receive short notes on a smart phone or other mobile device. Instant messaging is a real-time Internet communications service that notifies a user when one or more people are online and allows the user to exchange messages or files or join a private chat room with those people. Picture messaging is a wireless messaging service that allows users to send and receive photos and sound files, as well as short text messages, to and from a mobile device or computer. Video messaging is a wireless messaging service that allows users to send and receive short video clips, usually up to 30 seconds, in addition to all picture messaging services.

Text Messaging, Instant Messaging, and Picture/Video Messaging: The Personal Perspective

Text messaging, instant messaging, and picture/video messaging typically are used on smart phones. Instant messaging often is used on desktop and notebook computers.

Virtually instantaneous communication is possible with the various forms of messaging. Figure 6 indicates some advantages, disadvantages, and good practices of using text messaging, instant messaging, and picture/video messaging in your personal life. Figure 7 shows some examples of people using messaging.

Personal Text Messaging, Instant Messaging, and Picture/Video Messaging Use

Advantages
- Virtually instantaneous form of digital communications.
- Fast, reliable, and popular method of digital communications.
- Useful when you prefer an immediate response from the recipient.
- Allows you to carry on several conversations at any time.

Disadvantages
- Can be addictive in nature.
- Receiving a constant stream of messages can be distracting.
- May be very expensive on mobile devices.
- Text messaging: Overuse may result in repetitive stress injuries (RSIs).

Good practices
- Know the person with whom you are exchanging messages.
- Keep in mind that any text, picture, or video you send can be sent to others by the recipient.
- When messaging with a new contact, do not share personal information quickly.
- Always reread your text messages and preview your pictures and videos before you send them.
- Respect the status of others when they indicate they are busy.
- Instant messaging: If the program allows you to indicate your status to others, such as "Busy" or "Do not disturb," use these indicators to let others know when you are unavailable.
- Picture/video messaging: When sending picture/video messages, make sure the content is appropriate.

Figure 6 People use various types of messaging for different reasons. (Where noted, some bullet points apply only to particular technologies.)

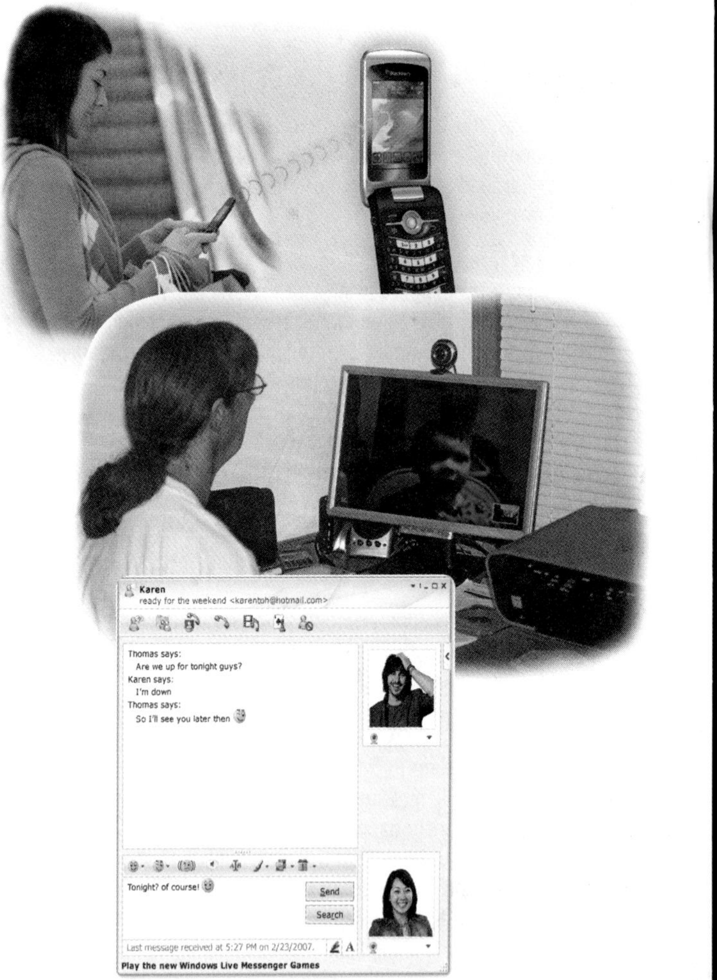

Figure 7 Many people interact with messaging software both at home and while away from home or work.

Text Messaging, Instant Messaging, and Picture/Video Messaging: The Business Perspective

Businesses typically use more secure, feature-rich messaging programs that allow all messages to be archived. Archiving of messages often is required by law and allows old messages to be available for future reference. Messaging allows colleagues to collaborate, or work together, online. Figure 8 indicates some advantages, disadvantages, and good practices of text messaging, instant messaging, and picture/video messaging use in business. Many of the notes listed in Figure 6 also apply to the various forms of messaging in business. Figure 9 shows an example of business-level instant messaging software and video messaging at job sites.

Text Messaging, Instant Messaging, and Picture/Video Messaging Use in Business

Advantages

- When used properly, greatly increases collaboration and communications because users have instantaneous access to each other.
- All messages can be archived for retrieval at a later date or for meeting legal requirements.
- Immediate contact with customers when allowed by company policy and agreed to by the customer.
- Collaboration with geographically separated colleagues.
- Instant messaging: Some programs allow conferences of several people at one time, eliminating the need for scheduling meeting rooms or conference calls.
- Picture/video messaging: Provides instant views of remote locations, such as work sites or company assets.

Disadvantages

- Despite policies, business conversations often lead to personal conversations.
- Often leads to over-reliance on simply messaging a colleague for an answer to a question rather than determining the answer on your own.
- Can lead to a significant decline in important face-to-face contact with coworkers, customers, and business partners.
- Instant messaging: Because all messages can be archived, it can lead to difficult situations when inappropriate content is shared.

Good practices

- When beginning a messaging conversation, make your point quickly and keep messages concise.
- Separate your personal messaging habits from your business messaging habits, avoiding use of emoticons and shortcuts, such as "brb" as a shortcut for "Be right back."
- Use proper spelling, grammar, and punctuation, and avoid colloquialisms.
- Be aware of cultural differences that might arise during casual conversations.
- Acknowledge the end of a messaging conversation.
- Follow your company's policies regarding the type of information that can be conveyed in a message and with whom you may engage in messaging.
- Always try to meet or telephone a person to introduce yourself before sending a first message to him or her.
- Review all messages you send to colleagues to make sure that the contents are appropriate for the workplace.

Figure 8 Businesses use a variety of messaging methods to allow employees to collaborate in a timely and secure manner. (Where noted, some bullet points apply only to particular technologies.)

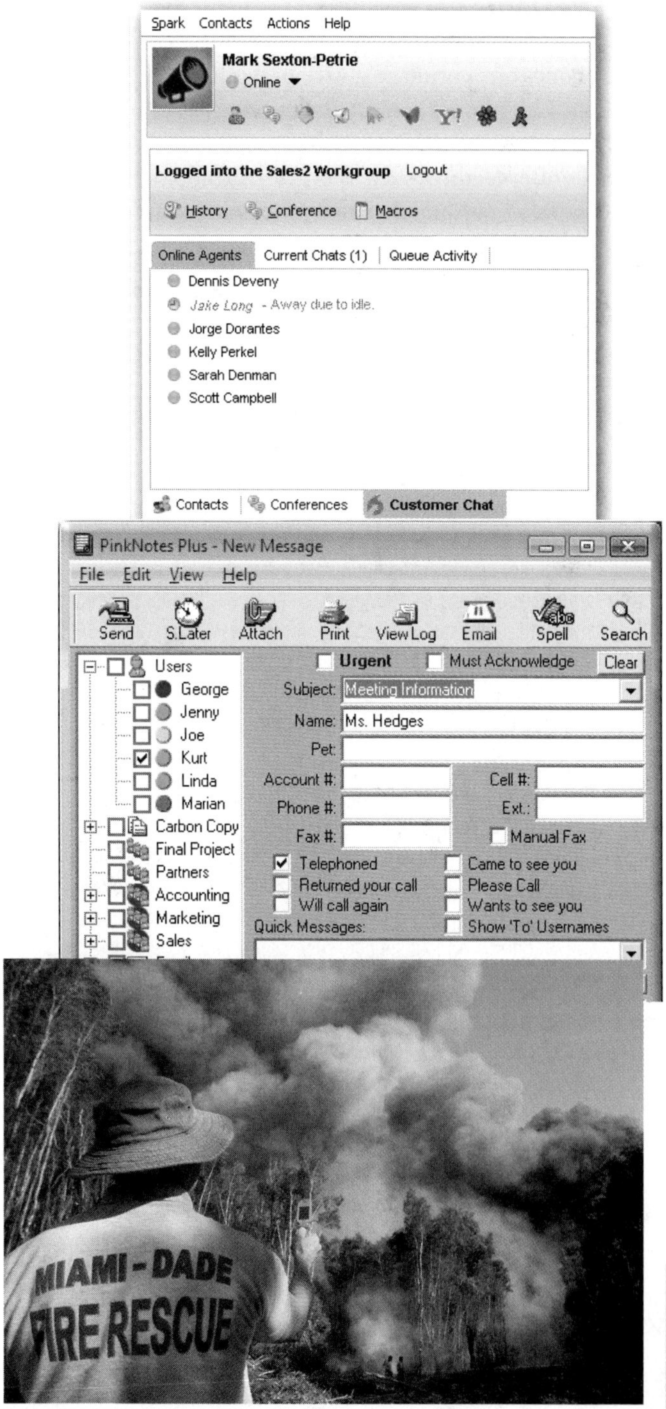

Figure 9 Business users employ instant messaging and video messaging to communicate ideas and multimedia information quickly.

Digital Voice Communications

Digital voice communications includes the use of cell phones, smart phones, and VoIP (Voice over IP). VoIP is a technology that allows users to speak to other users via the Internet. VoIP can be used as a replacement for the traditional telephone at work or in the home.

Digital Voice Communications: The Personal Perspective

With more than 200 million in use in the United States, cell phones are a primary source of digital voice communications. Cell phones can act as a suitable replacement for the traditional, wired, public switched telephone network. Smart phones offer features such as e-mail, text messaging, picture/video messaging, and playing or streaming multimedia.

Figure 10 indicates some advantages, disadvantages, and good practices of digital voice communications in your personal life. Figure 11 shows some examples of digital voice communications, including visual voice mail, which is a service that automatically translates voice mail into text messages or allows you to download voice messages to your smart phone and listen to them at your convenience.

Personal Digital Voice Communications Use

Advantages
- Increase productivity through greater and more timely communications.
- Both cell phones and VoIP offer more choice in providers than the public switched telephone network.
- Cell phones: Widespread coverage of cell phone networks provides voice communications nearly everywhere in the United States.
- Cell phones: Have been instrumental in saving lives in emergency situations.
- VoIP: Often offers free features, such as voice mail, unlimited in-country long distance calling, three-way calling, and call forwarding.
- VoIP: Typically is less expensive for both local and long distance calls than the public switched telephone network.

Disadvantages
- Cell phones: In some situations, such as while driving a car, can contribute to accidents.
- VoIP: Not as strictly regulated as the public switched telephone network, meaning that the quality of service may be lower.
- With many VoIP providers and some cell phone providers, connecting to a local service, such as 911 for emergencies, may be difficult or cumbersome.

Good practices
- Cell phones: Use a headset if you must use a cell phone while driving. Be aware of laws in your area that prohibit or limit cell phone use while driving.
- Cell phones: When using in public, be mindful of and courteous to those around you.
- Cell phones: Be aware of rules or policies at some locations, such as schools, medical facilities, or religious facilities.
- Cell phones: In public locations, use an alternative ring method, such as a vibration setting, to avoid interrupting others.

Figure 10 Cell phones and other forms of digital voice communications have become an essential means of communications throughout the world. (Where noted, some bullet points apply only to particular technologies.)

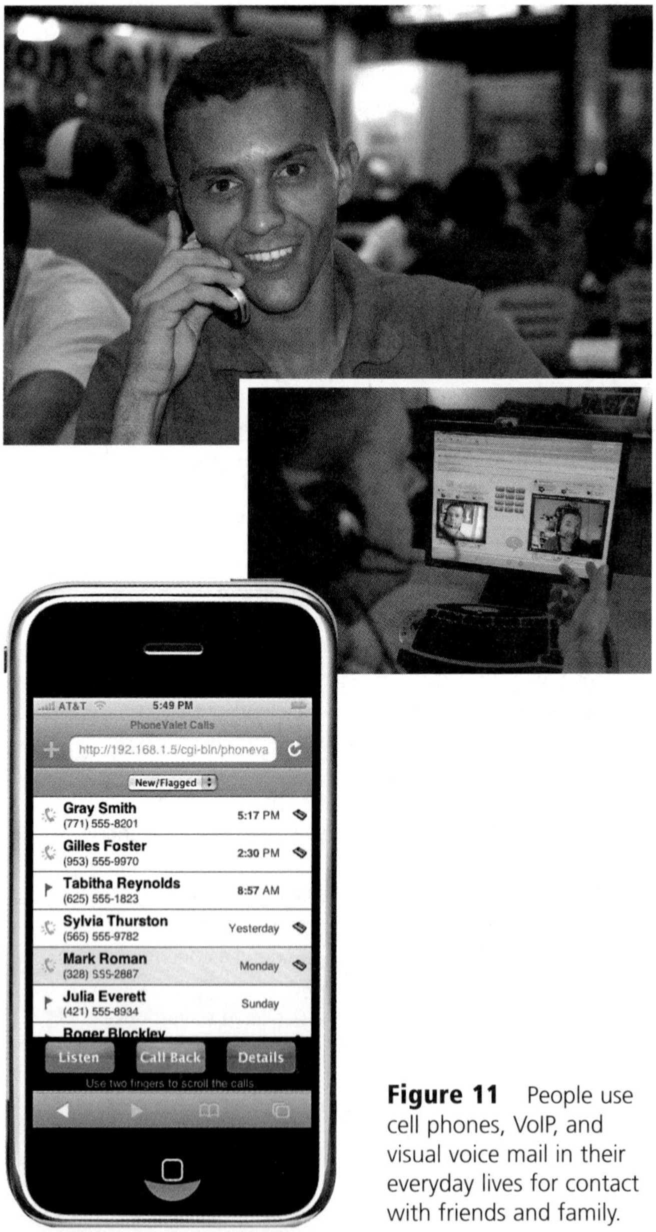

Figure 11 People use cell phones, VoIP, and visual voice mail in their everyday lives for contact with friends and family.

Digital Voice Communications: The Business Perspective

Businesses embrace digital voice communications because of increased collaboration and productivity, cost savings, and mobility. Figure 12 lists many of the advantages, disadvantages, and good practices of digital voice communications use in business. Many of the notes listed in Figure 10 also apply to the various forms of digital voice communications in business. Figure 13 shows an example of a simple VoIP system.

Digital Voice Communications Use in Business

Advantages

- Increased communications and collaboration can result in increased productivity and cost savings.
- Cell phones: Ability to contact a person almost anywhere at any time.
- VoIP: With some systems, employees can listen to and manage their voice messages on their personal computer.
- VoIP: A computer is not necessary to use a VoIP system.
- VoIP: Allows large companies to consolidate communications between geographically diverse locations.
- VoIP: Implement as an alternative to the public switched telephone network because VoIP allows businesses to use their existing network more efficiently and provides more features than the public switched telephone network.

Disadvantages

- With many VoIP providers and some cell phone providers, connecting to a local service, such as 911 for emergencies, may be difficult or cumbersome.
- The quality of calls may change at times due to excessive network usage.
- Cell phones: Misuse often leads to rude behavior or disruption of meetings.
- Cell phones: Using a cell phone provided by an employer for personal calls may have undesirable tax consequences.
- VoIP: Large companies may find it expensive and difficult to manage.
- VoIP: Unlike a public switched telephone network, many VoIP systems and equipment will not function during a power outage.

Good practices

- Cell phones: Follow company policy regarding the use for business communications. Limit personal calls on your cell phone during business hours.
- Cell phones: Disable the ringer when in meetings or during important discussions.
- Cell phones: Resist the need to answer every call at all times, such as when you are on breaks or when you are not at work.
- Cell phones: Avoid speaking loudly on the phone when walking through others' work areas.
- VoIP: When possible, use a VoIP telephone rather than a cell phone because it generally is less expensive for the company on a per-call basis.

Figure 12 Digital voice communications are used when a more personal form of communications than e-mail or messaging is required in real time. (Where noted, some bullet points apply only to particular technologies.)

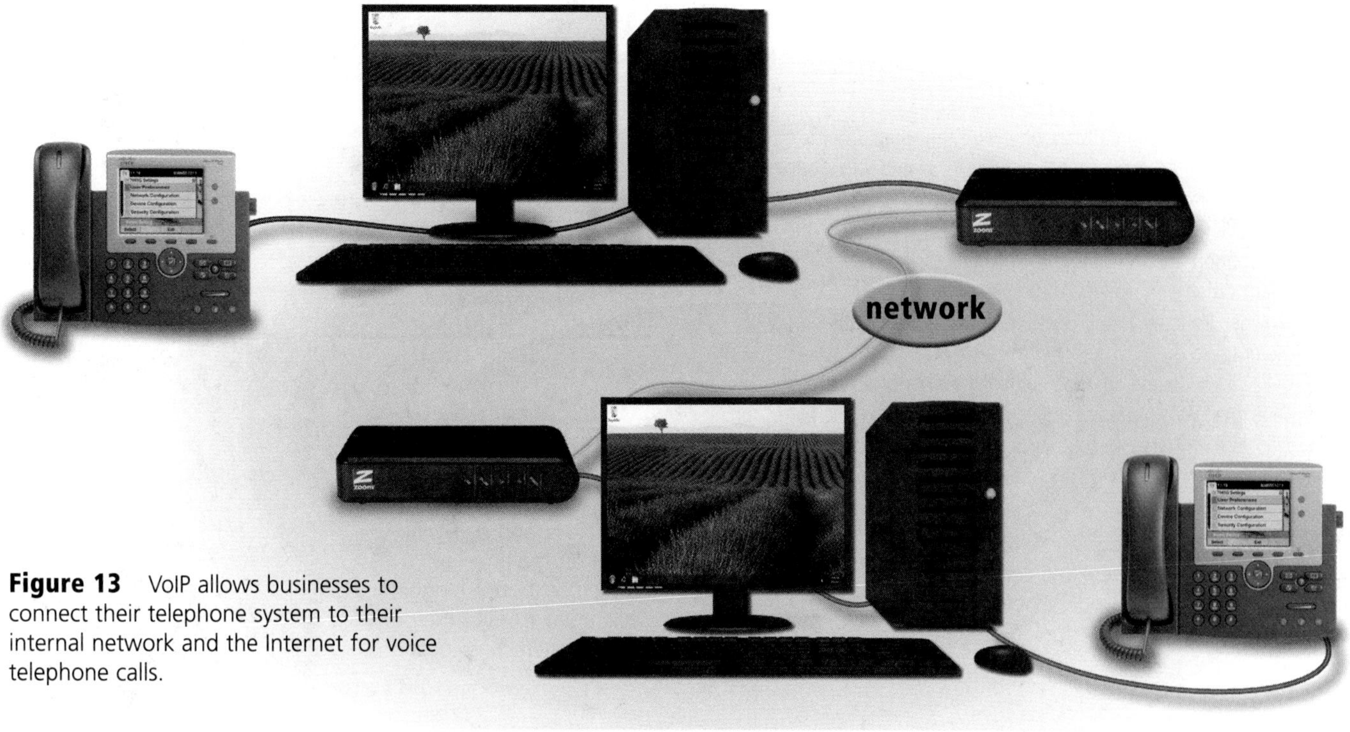

Figure 13 VoIP allows businesses to connect their telephone system to their internal network and the Internet for voice telephone calls.

Blogs and Wikis

A **blog** is an informal Web site consisting of time-stamped articles, or posts, in a diary or journal format, usually listed in reverse chronological order. A **wiki** is a collaborative Web site that allows users to create, add to, modify, or delete the Web site content via their Web browser.

Blogs and Wikis: The Personal Perspective

Blog topics often include family life, social life, a personal project, or events during a vacation. You might read and contribute to a wiki regarding classical guitar techniques if your hobbies included playing classical guitar. While blogs can be modified only by the author, a wiki can be authored and edited by any user. Another difference between blogs and wikis is that blog entries typically are not included in search results from search engines, such as Google, while wiki entries are recognized by search engine queries. Figure 14 indicates some advantages, disadvantages, and good practices of using blogs and wikis in your personal life. Figure 15 shows examples of blog and wiki entries.

Personal Blog and Wiki Use

Advantages

- Some blogs and wikis provide secure access so that only a select group of qualified or desired individuals are allowed to read and write entries.
- Blogs: Easy, accessible, and often free method of keeping a group of people informed about events.
- Blogs: Easy way to keep up with an acquaintance or expand your knowledge about political or social points of view.
- Blogs: Often can be read or written using Internet-enabled mobile devices.
- Wikis: Provide free access to concise, almost encyclopedic, information about nearly any topic.

Disadvantages

- Vulnerable to fraudulent or biased entries placed by businesses or special interest groups in an effort to sway public opinion.
- Blogs: Often are biased towards a particular point of view.
- Blogs: Some blogging Web sites are often sources of malicious programs.
- Wikis: Publicly accessible wikis sometimes are vulnerable to vandalism or subject to errors.

Good practices

- Blogs: When writing a blog, be aware that the contents of your blog may be accessible publicly and associated with your identity for a long time.
- Blogs: When reading blogs, be aware of the source of the information and evaluate the credibility of the source.
- Wikis: When performing research using a wiki, check any provided sources and, if possible, check the editorial history of the entries.
- Wikis: If you locate an error, notify the author or editor of the wiki page, or, if possible, edit the page yourself to make the correction.
- Wikis: When possible, contribute your own knowledge to wikis that interest you, being sure to follow the guidelines of the wiki.

Figure 14 While blogs and wikis provide a great deal of information sharing, users and contributors alike should be aware of the risks involved. (Where noted, some bullet points apply only to particular technologies.)

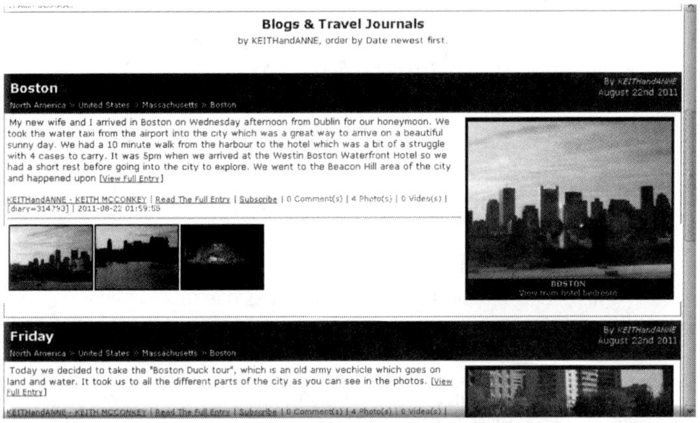

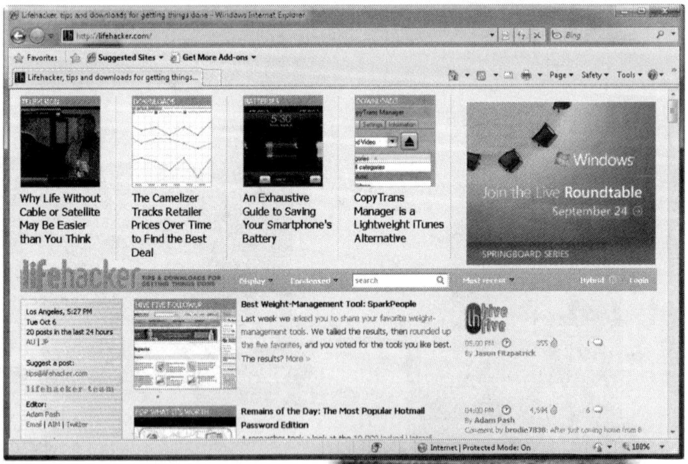

Figure 15 Blogs and wikis allow people to share their knowledge, experience, viewpoints, and personal events on the Internet. People use mobile blogging while away from home or while in interesting locations.

Blogs and Wikis: The Business Perspective

Many businesses use blogs and wikis to share knowledge within the company. One large company claims to maintain more than 300,000 blogs and wikis internally. A key reason that blogs and wikis are so popular in business is that they can be written, read, and searched easily. As the company's resident expert regarding a particular topic, an employee may blog to keep others informed about topics relating to that expertise. A business-oriented wiki may contain a wealth of historical knowledge for a particular department in the company. Figure 16 indicates some advantages, disadvantages, and good practices of using blogs and wikis in business. Many of the notes listed in Figure 14 also apply to using blogs and wikis in business. Figure 17 shows examples of typical business-oriented blog and wiki entries.

Blog and Wiki Use in Business

Advantages

- Provide easy access to gained knowledge and experience.
- Easily can be searched by employees.
- Some may be made available to customers, business partners, or the general public.
- Blogs: Publicly accessible blogs often are used as an effective means to promote products or services.

Disadvantages

- Mistakes, inaccuracies, and inconsistencies in entries can lead to lost productivity and increased costs.
- Internal company blogs and wikis often contain proprietary company information that easily can be leaked to competitors or the press.
- Blogs: When contributing to a blog, some employees become engrossed with capturing every detail of their job.
- Wikis: Information often may become old, or stale, if it is not updated regularly.

Good practices

- Search your company's blogs and wikis for information before telephoning, instant messaging, or e-mailing a colleague with a question.
- If you do not find an answer to a question on your company's blogs or wikis, then contribute to a blog or wiki once you find the answer.
- When contributing to a blog or wiki entry, read your company's policies regarding content, formatting, and style. Some companies employ full-time bloggers and writers who can help you contribute a valuable entry.
- When contributing to a blog or wiki entry, stay on topic and create links within your entry to other related or relevant Web pages, including other blog and wiki entries.
- Blogs: When engaging in personal blogging, do not discredit your employer or potential future employers; many people have lost their jobs as a result of engaging in such behavior.
- Blogs: When engaging in personal blogging, be careful not to divulge proprietary company information.

Figure 16 Business blog and wiki use typically is governed by more guidelines and rules than those for personal blogs and wikis. (Where noted, some bullet points apply only to particular technologies.)

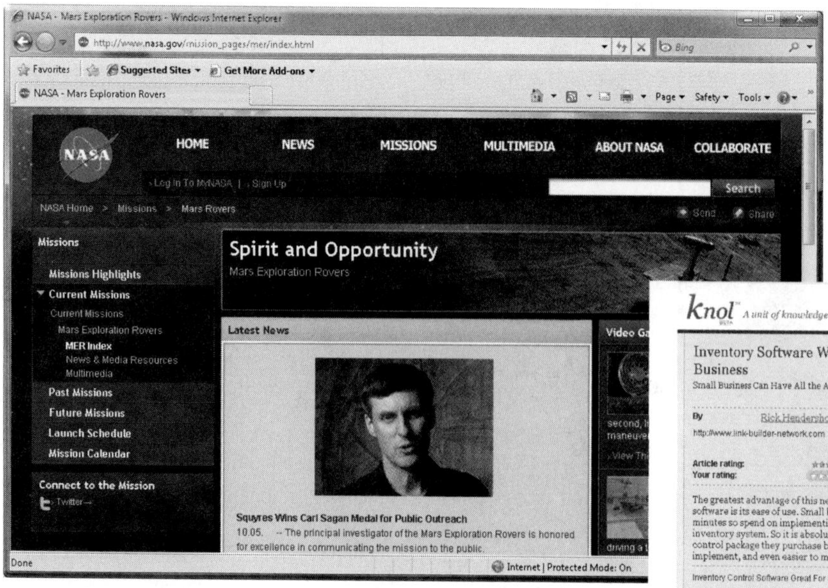

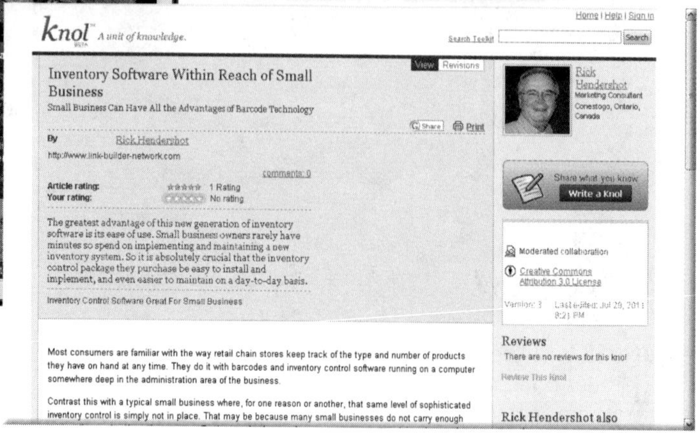

Figure 17 Increasingly more businesses use blogs and wikis to allow employees to share information with each other, customers, and business partners.

Online Social Networks, Chat Rooms, and Web Conferences

An **online social network** is a Web site that encourages members in its online community to share their interest, ideas, stories, photos, music, and videos with other registered users. A **chat room** is a location on the Internet that permits users to chat with one another. A **Web conference** allows two or more people to engage in an online meeting and often allows the attendees to access programs and digital content, such as documents, audio, and video, during the meeting.

Online Social Networks, Chat Rooms, and Web Conferences: The Personal Perspective

The popularity of online social networks such as Facebook continues to skyrocket. Most online social networks allow you to maintain a personal Web site that you can share with other registered users who, after being invited, may view or contribute content to your site. Those invited to your online social network often are known as friends. While chat rooms have decreased in popularity over the years, people often use them for targeted discussions about specific topics. Web conferences often are used by consumers to obtain technical support or assistance from companies and government agencies or in educational settings to engage in online learning. Figure 18 shows an example of an online social network and a virtual chat room.

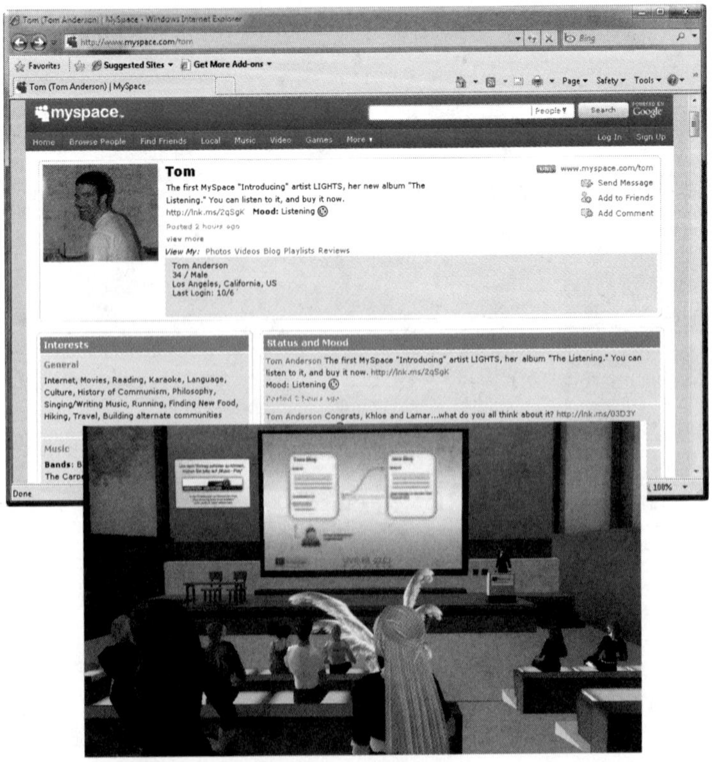

Figure 18 Online social networks and virtual chat rooms allow groups of people with similar interests or lifestyles to enjoy real-time communications.

Figure 19 indicates some advantages, disadvantages, and good practices of using online social networks, chat rooms, and Web conferences in your personal life.

Personal Use of Online Social Networks, Chat Rooms, and Web Conferences

Advantages

- Online social networks/chat rooms: Easily find friends throughout the world with similar interests or traits.
- Online social networks/chat rooms: Can expand your knowledge about political or social points of view.
- Web conferences: Use Web conferencing when offered by a company for technical support issues because the tenor of the interaction is more personal than a telephone call.
- Web conferences: Often effectively provides the necessary communications to avoid a visit to a store location or a visit from a repair technician.

Disadvantages

- Online social networks/chat rooms: Some people are susceptible to overusing these forms of communications in lieu of real, in-person contacts and relationships. Overuse of these forms of communications may lead to addiction.
- Online social networks/chat rooms: People often hide their real identity to lure others into revealing too much personal information.
- Online social networks/chat rooms: Several high-profile incidents occurred in which people engaged in illegal activity using online social networks and chat rooms.

Good practices

- Online social networks: When submitting information, be aware that the information may be accessible publicly and associated with your identity for a long time.
- Online social networks: While many online social networks encourage the practice, do not try to gather too many friends in your social network. Some experts believe that a functional social network is limited to a maximum of 150 people.
- Chat rooms/Web conferences: Be as polite and courteous as you would be to someone in person.

Figure 19 People use online social networks, chat rooms, and Web conferences as a means of extending their social lives beyond their physical surroundings. (Where noted, some bullet points apply only to particular technologies.)

Online Social Networks, Chat Rooms, and Web Conferences: The Business Perspective

Online social networks, chat rooms, and Web conferences allow business users to interact and collaborate as teams. While online social networks have not been as popular as other forms of digital communications in business, their use is showing promise for many companies and groups who use it for business purposes. One company claims to have signed up more than five million business users for its business-oriented online social network. Chat rooms and Web conferences often serve as forums for online meetings. Figure 20 indicates some advantages, disadvantages, and good practices of using online social networks, chat rooms, and Web conferences in business. Many of the notes listed in Figure 6 on page 196 and Figure 19 also apply to these forms of digital communication in business. Figure 21 shows an example of a business-oriented online social network, chat room, and Web conference.

Online Social Network, Chat Room, and Web Conference Use in Business

Advantages

- Online social networks: Encourage people to collaborate with others with whom they typically would not collaborate.
- Online social networks/chat rooms: Often can be accessed using Internet-enabled mobile devices, providing instant collaboration almost anywhere.
- Online social networks/chat rooms: Provide forums for meeting potential customers, employers, and employees.
- Web conferences: Programs often allow application program sharing, which means that all participants can view the contents of one or more participant's computer screen.
- Online social networks/chat rooms: Some are located internally within a company and allow only employees access to the sites.
- Online social networks/chat rooms: Some are subscription-based and allow people to interact freely with others in related fields or industries.

Disadvantages

- Employees often over-rely on these means of online digital communications and do not interact with others in more personal ways.
- Online social networks: Can be cumbersome and expensive to maintain.

Good practices

- When engaging in online social networks, chat rooms, and Web conferences outside of your company, be careful not to divulge proprietary company information.
- Always maintain a professional demeanor. Often, those who use this technology in their personal lives are quick to behave more casually than is appropriate in a business setting.
- Divulge only that information about yourself that is relevant to the reasons you are participating in an online social network or chat room.

Figure 20 Businesses have embraced online social networks, chat rooms, and Web conferences to drive collaboration among geographically separated teams, employees, and other business contacts. (Where noted, some bullet points apply only to particular technologies.)

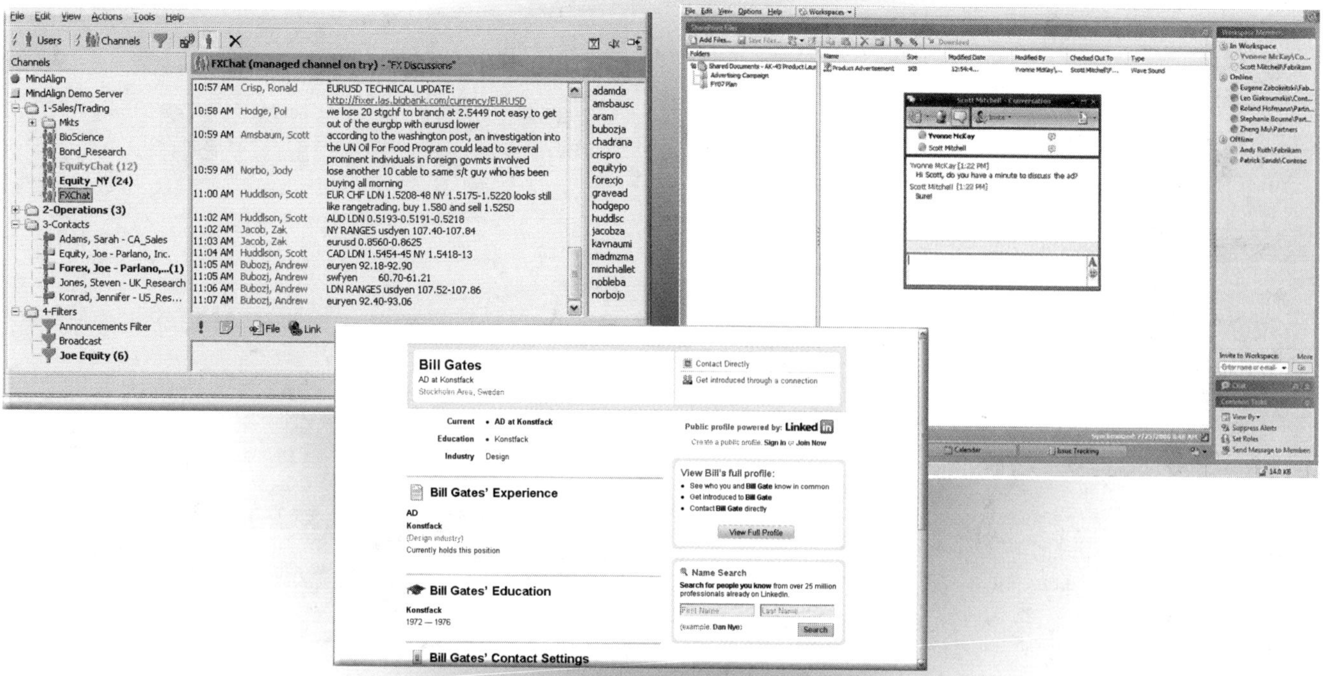

Figure 21 Businesses use online social networks, chat rooms, and Web conferences to allow employees and teams to communicate more effectively.

Content Sharing

Content sharing provides a means by which rich content, such as audio, video, photos, and documents, can be communicated digitally.

Content Sharing: The Personal Perspective

The prolific spread of digital cameras and digital video cameras combined with ever-increasing speeds of home and mobile Internet connections has resulted in the explosive growth of media sharing Web sites, such as YouTube and Flickr. In addition to sharing media, people are sharing documents, spreadsheets, and other content on Web sites. Figure 22 indicates some advantages, disadvantages, and good practices of content sharing in your personal life. Figure 23 shows some examples of a video sharing Web site, a photo sharing group Web site, and a personal photo sharing Web site.

Personal Content Sharing Use

Advantages

- Ability to view broadcasts of events that may not be available through traditional broadcasts in your area.
- Media sharing Web sites provide almost limitless information and entertainment at little or no cost.
- Some services allow you to edit your content or the content of others directly on the site using a Web application.
- View or listen to live broadcasts of sporting events.
- View or listen to news stories.
- Much like online social networks, media sharing Web sites can provide a sense of community to a group of geographically separated individuals.

Disadvantages

- You may find it difficult to locate media and content that interests you.
- When sharing video and photos on a media sharing Web site, you may be giving up some of your rights to the media.
- Many people have been embarrassed by content posted by others to media sharing Web sites.

Good practices

- Before placing your content on a media sharing Web site, make a good effort to edit the content for brevity and clarity. For example, make certain that audio is clear in a video, and use photo editing software to remove red-eye.
- Take advantage of the fact that most media and content sharing Web sites allow you to limit who can access your media and content.
- Before you allow somebody to record video of you or take your picture, remember that the video or photo may end up on a media sharing Web site.
- Before placing your multimedia content on a media sharing Web site, check the terms of the service agreement and make certain you agree to give up certain legal rights to your multimedia content.
- Do not post pictures or videos that are protected by a copyright.

Figure 22 While most people act as consumers of content shared on the Internet, some share their own content.

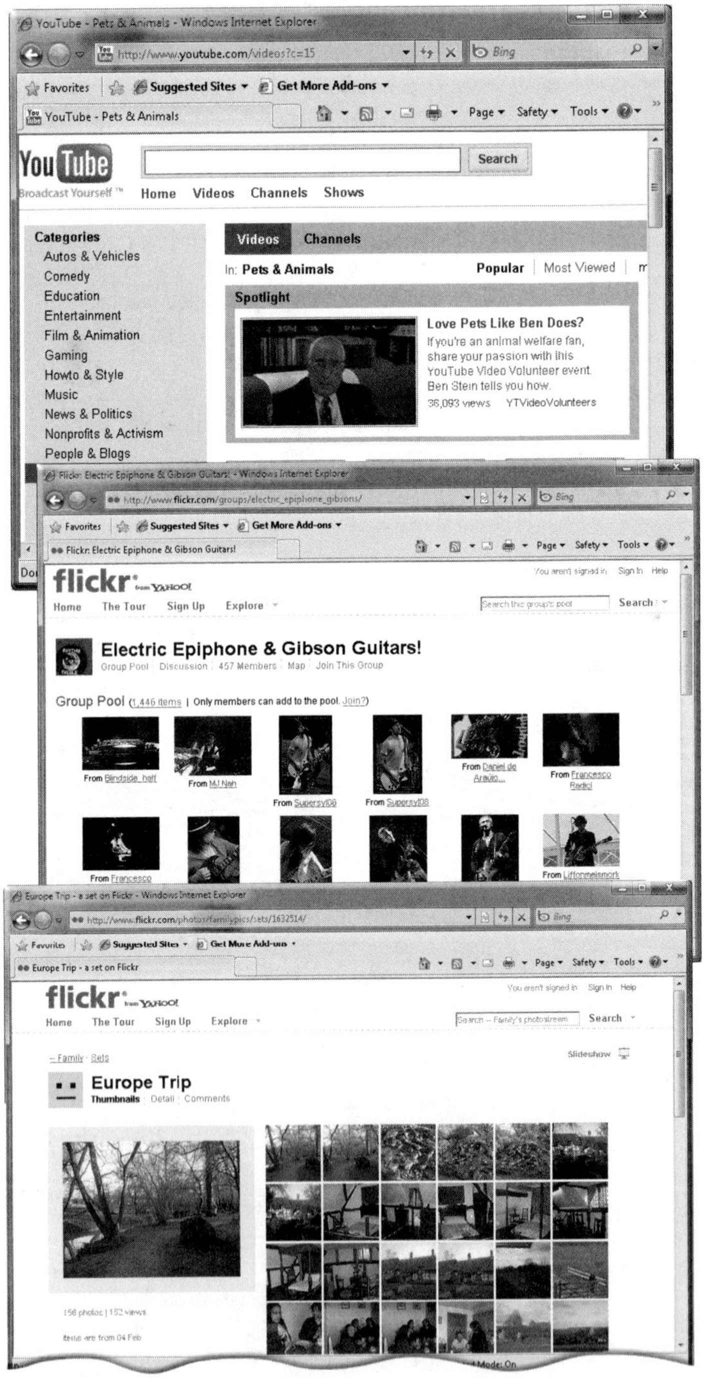

Figure 23 People share and view content on the Internet in a number of ways.

Content Sharing: The Business Perspective

Media sharing Web sites allow business to interact creatively with employees, customers, and prospective customers. Video conferencing is the oldest form of real-time multimedia content sharing in business. Figure 24 outlines some advantages, disadvantages, and good practices of content sharing in business. Many of the notes listed in Figure 22 also apply to content sharing in business. Figure 25 shows examples of content shared in an educational setting and a document management system, which allows for secure storage and management of a company's documents.

Content Sharing Use in Business

Advantages

- Multimedia sharing sites allow companies to archive video conferences, advertisements, employee photos, and other multimedia content.
- Executives and managers create podcasts or vodcasts to spread their vision or message. Vodcasts are podcasts that contain video and usually audio.
- Video conferences allow geographically separate people to transmit audio and video and engage in a meeting remotely.
- Most business-based content sharing software provides for enhanced collaboration by making the content accessible and searchable.
- Multimedia content, such as videos and photos, can be stored in a document management system to archive information about important projects or events.

Disadvantages

- Production and distribution of multimedia content often is more expensive than traditional methods.
- Security on business content sharing systems often frustrates employees who are denied access to information without special approval.

Good practices

- Unless you have permission, do not share company-owned photos and videos on publicly available media sharing Web sites, such as YouTube or Flickr.
- When viewing or sharing photos and videos in the workplace, be certain that the content is appropriate for the workplace. Some businesses have a media department that manages all of the company's multimedia content.

Figure 24 Businesses provide secure content sharing repositories and real-time multimedia.

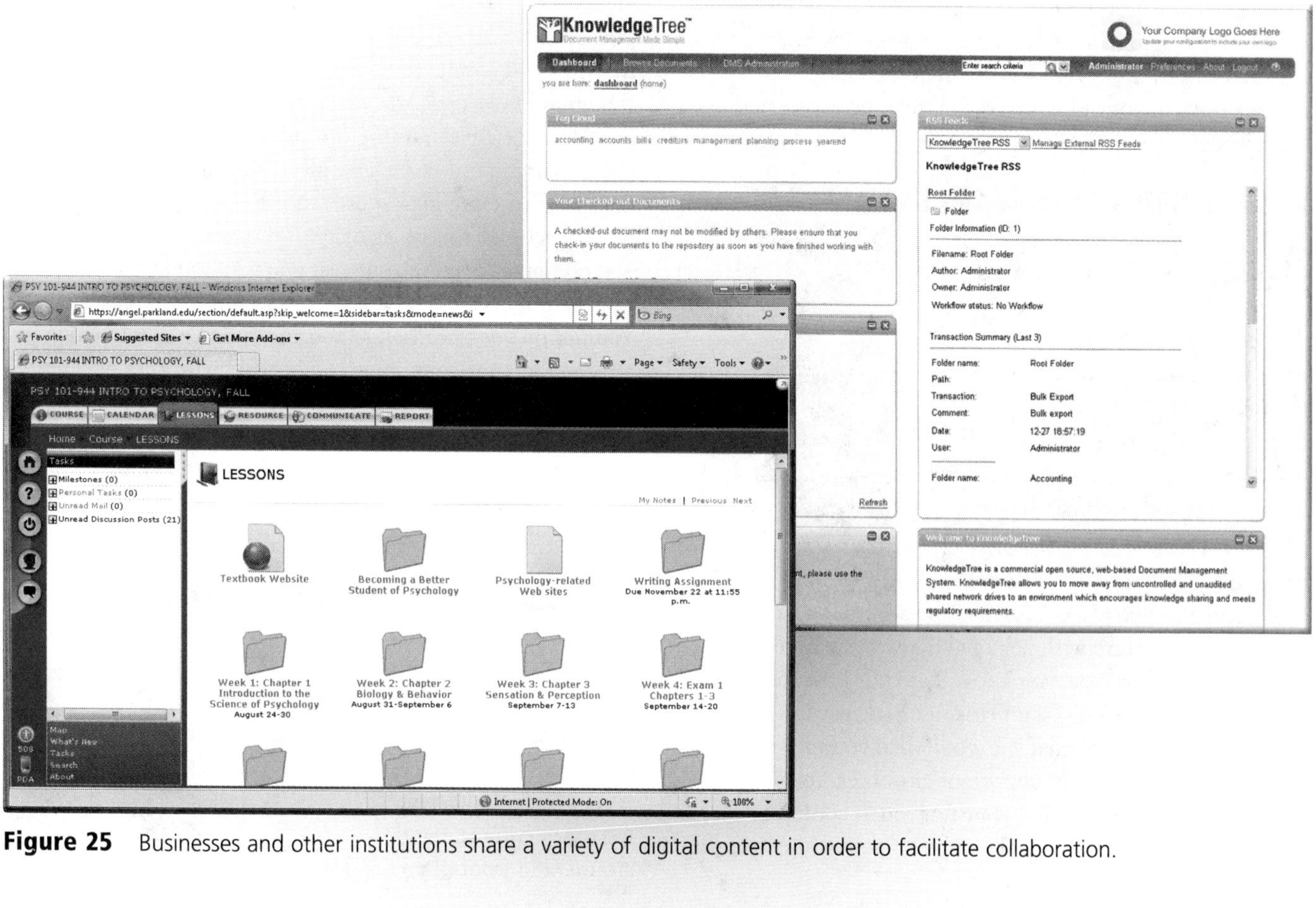

Figure 25 Businesses and other institutions share a variety of digital content in order to facilitate collaboration.

Digital Communications in Your Life

Many people use various forms of digital communications in both their personal and business lives. Imagine you are working in your chosen field and making decisions every day regarding how to communicate best with family, friends, and business contacts. The following scenario presents several situations and decisions regarding digital communications made during a single day.

8:15 a.m.

SITUATION: Before leaving for work, you remember that you are expecting an e-mail confirmation from your travel agent regarding plans for a trip to a friend's birthday party. You also need to send thank-you notes to your past instructors regarding letters of recommendation that they wrote to help you secure the new job.

RESOLUTION: E-mail is a good tool when instant communication is not necessary. Personal business, such as travel arrangements, is negotiated or confirmed easily via e-mail messages, resulting in a permanent record of the communication.

You receive the e-mail message on your personal computer from your travel agent with the news that your trip is booked. You then quickly send e-mail messages to your past instructors with informal thank-you notes, being sure to include links to your blog where you maintain a journal of experiences at your first job.

8:47 a.m.

SITUATION: While riding the bus to work, you drown out the noise of the crowd by using your smart phone to access wirelessly the newest song from your favorite band. The phone number of an incoming call appears on the smart phone's display, and you recognize it as your boss's phone number. Should you take the call?

RESOLUTION: Many people feel uncomfortable answering business calls while on personal time or in a public place. The decision whether to allow work life to interfere with personal life varies with each individual. In your case, you know that your boss calls your cell phone only for important reasons. You answer the call and your boss explains that she would like you to join a video conference with an important customer. You jump at the chance to be involved in your first video conference later in the day. After hanging up the phone, you resume listening to your song.

9:11 a.m.

SITUATION: After arriving at work, your first task is to check e-mail messages. Working at an international firm means that e-mail is a round-the-clock method of communication with coworkers, customers, and business partners. You have more than 30 new e-mail messages since you last checked your e-mail inbox at 5:00 p.m. yesterday.

RESOLUTION: Business e-mail programs usually include several methods for organizing and managing your e-mail inbox. As you view your inbox, a few items have red exclamation marks next to them, indicating that the sender marked them as urgent. Your e-mail program also allows you to mark e-mail messages in your inbox with colored flags, and you have developed a procedure for using these flags. You quickly flag the urgent items with a red flag, meaning that you will handle these immediately after you flag the remaining messages. You flag messages from customers with a yellow flag. By skimming the subject and first few lines of the remaining messages, you place blue, green, and black flags next to some messages. You use the colors to code messages based on the priority of the messages.

Good practices often suggest you respond by telephone to urgent messages or messages from important customers. You put on your headset, and, using your VoIP telephone attached to your computer, you begin the process of calling some of the people whose messages you marked with red and yellow flags. When you are finished talking on the telephone, you respond to several of the other messages, being careful to use a spelling checker and properly format each response before sending it. By 9:45 a.m., your inbox is empty.

10:00 a.m.

SITUATION: By the time you arrive at your office's video conferencing room, five other coworkers already have gathered. After sitting down, you see a large monitor and a camera in front of you.

Instinctively, you check your hair, just as a group of people in another conference room in London appears on the monitor. Your boss whispers that your shirt is a bit bright for the video conference. As the meeting begins, you are asked to introduce yourself. You were not expecting to appear on camera today, but you proceed to introduce yourself and the meeting begins. During the meeting, the cell phone in your pocket buzzes a number of times. Should you take the call?

RESOLUTION: At first, most people find video conferences to be uncomfortable experiences. In comparison to a typical meeting, some people tend to fidget more, tap their fingers, or speak more nervously in a video conference. People tend to recognize those actions when they view others on a monitor in a video conference, so experts suggest keeping these types of actions to a minimum.

You ignore the cell phone calls during the meeting. You have learned that meetings are a time to stay focused and that you would not be invited to the meeting if your presence was not important to someone else. You plan to check your visual voice mail on your cell phone later.

12:19 p.m.

SITUATION: Excited but relieved to be finished with the video conference, you go out for lunch and check your visual voice mail. Your cell phone translates the messages to text so that you can read them on your cell phone rather than listening to them. One personal message from a friend reminds you to sign up for a new online social network. On your way back to the office, you spot a new advertisement for a product from one of your company's competitors. You use your cell phone to take a picture of the advertisement.

RESOLUTION: You instantly use your cell phone to send a picture message to your coworker in your company's marketing department. The coworker sends you a text message thanking you for the advertisement, which she had not seen yet and will be valuable for her research. Later, you decide to sign up for that online social networking Web site recommended by your friend using your work computer. Your company has a liberal attitude toward employees using computers in the office for limited personal use. You also quickly use your cell phone to add an entry to your blog regarding your first video conference today.

3:15 p.m.

SITUATION: Your cell phone rings, indicating that you have a new text message. At the moment, you are engaged in a brief discussion in a colleague's office. When the cell phone rings again, you look at its display and realize that the message is from an important customer. Should you exchange text messages with a customer?

RESOLUTION: Text messaging offers portability and is appropriate for short business and personal contact when responses are not time sensitive. Most businesses restrict employees' use of text messaging to interact with customers or business partners because the messages often are not logged or archived. While looking at the display, you realize that the message is not of a sensitive nature, so you excuse yourself and send a text message to the customer stating that you will research her question. Back at your desk, you search for the answer to the customer's question in your department's wiki. You find that the answer is to send a particular document to the customer that is located in the company's content management system. You locate the document and send it to the customer as an attachment to an e-mail message. Minutes later, you receive a text message from the customer thanking you for the quick reply.

9:15 p.m.

SITUATION: As you end the day at home, you log on to the online social network that you joined earlier in the day. When you add your friend to your list of contacts, you notice that she currently is logged on. You start your instant messaging program and begin instant messaging with your friend. Your friend reminds you that you still have a home page on another online social network from your days in school.

RESOLUTION: You log on to the old online social network that you used when you were in school. You decide to close your home page and ask that the site delete it. People often forget that once they put content on an online social network, in a blog, or on a wiki that it may remain there forever unless they delete or edit it. Periodically, consider checking how others might perceive you based on content you have placed on the Internet.

Digital Communications: Summary

Digital communications are a huge part of our personal and business lives. We make decisions each day when choosing the appropriate method of communication at the right time in the right place. The methods of digital communications involve both the advantages and the disadvantages of instant, archived, and distant collaboration with others.

Chapter Four

The Components of the System Unit

Objectives

After completing this chapter, you will be able to:

1 Differentiate among various styles of system units on desktop computers, notebook computers, and mobile devices

2 Identify chips, adapter cards, and other components of a motherboard

3 Describe the control unit and arithmetic logic unit components of a processor, and explain the four steps in a machine cycle

4 Identify characteristics of various personal computer processors on the market today, and describe the ways processors are cooled

5 Define a bit and describe how a series of bits represents data

6 Explain how program instructions transfer in and out of memory

7 Differentiate among the various types of memory: RAM, cache, ROM, flash memory, and CMOS

8 Describe the purpose and types of expansion slots and adapter cards, and differentiate among slots for various removable flash memory devices

9 Differentiate between a port and a connector, and explain the differences among a USB port, FireWire port, Bluetooth port, SCSI port, eSATA port, IrDA port, serial port, and MIDI port

10 Describe the types of buses in a computer: front side bus, backside bus, and expansion buses (PCI bus, PCIe bus, AGP, USB, FireWire bus, and PC Card bus)

11 Explain the purpose of a power supply and describe how it keeps cool

12 Understand how to clean a system unit on a computer or mobile device

The System Unit

Whether you are a home user or a business user, you most likely will purchase a new computer or upgrade an existing computer at some time in the future. Thus, you should understand the purpose of each component in a computer. As Chapter 1 discussed, a computer includes devices used for input, processing, output, storage, and communications. Many of these components are part of the system unit.

The **system unit** is a case that contains electronic components of the computer used to process data. System units are available in a variety of shapes and sizes. The case of the system unit, sometimes called the *chassis*, is made of metal or plastic and protects the internal electronic components from damage. All computers and mobile devices have a system unit (Figure 4-1).

On desktop personal computers, the electronic components and most storage devices are part of the system unit. Other devices, such as the keyboard, mouse, microphone, monitor, printer, USB flash drive, scanner, Web cam, and speakers, normally occupy space outside the system unit. An all-in-one desktop personal computer is an exception, which houses the monitor and the system unit in the same case. The trend is toward a smaller *form factor*, or size and shape, of the desktop personal computer system unit.

On most notebook computers, including netbooks, the keyboard and pointing device

Figure 4-1 All sizes of computers and mobile devices have a system unit.

often occupy the area on the top of the system unit, and the display attaches to the system unit by hinges. The location of the system unit on a Tablet PC varies, depending on the design of the Tablet PC. With the slate Tablet PC (shown in Figure 4-35 on page 236), which typically does not include a keyboard, the system unit is behind the display. On a convertible Tablet PC (shown in lower-left corner of Figure 4-1), by contrast, the system unit is positioned below a keyboard, providing functionality similar to a traditional notebook computer or netbook. The difference is the display attaches to the system unit with a swivel-type hinge, which enables a user to rotate the display and fold it down over the keyboard to look like a slate Tablet PC. The system unit on an Ultra-Mobile PC, a smart phone, and a PDA usually consumes the entire device. On these mobile computers and devices, the display often is built into the system unit.

With game consoles, the input and output devices, such as controllers and a television, reside outside the system unit. On handheld game consoles, portable media players, and digital cameras, by contrast, the packaging around the system unit houses the input devices and display.

At some point, you might have to open the system unit on a desktop personal computer to replace or install a new electronic component. For this reason, you should be familiar with the electronic components of a system unit. Figure 4-2 identifies some of these components, which include the processor, memory, adapter cards, drive bays, and the power supply.

The processor interprets and carries out the basic instructions that operate a computer. Memory typically holds data waiting to be processed and instructions waiting to be executed. The electronic components and circuitry of the system unit, such as the processor and memory, usually are part of or are connected to a circuit

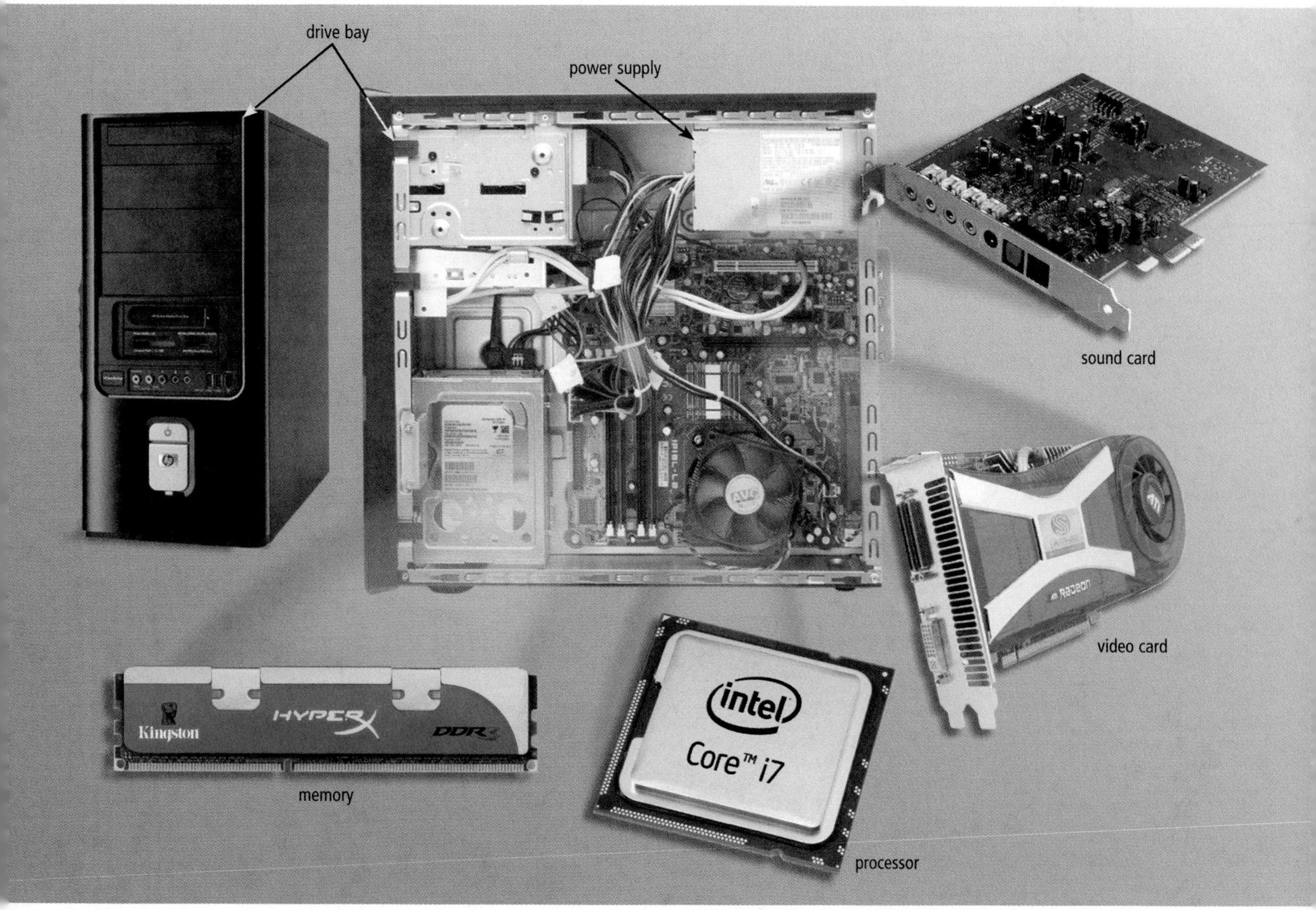

Figure 4-2 The system unit on a typical personal computer consists of numerous electronic components, some of which are shown in this figure. The sound card and video card are two types of adapter cards.

board called the motherboard. Many current motherboards also integrate sound, video, and networking capabilities.

Adapter cards are circuit boards that provide connections and functions not built into the motherboard or expand on the capability of features integrated into the motherboard. For example, a sound card and a video card are two types of adapter cards found in some desktop personal computers today.

Devices outside the system unit often attach to ports on the system unit by a connector on a cable. These devices may include a keyboard, mouse, microphone, monitor, printer, scanner, USB flash drive, card reader/writer, Web cam, and speakers. A drive bay holds one or more disk drives. The power supply converts electricity from a power cord plugged in a wall outlet into a form that can be used by the computer.

FAQ 4-1

How many PCs are in use worldwide?

A recent study shows that more than one billion personal computers are in use worldwide, with 58 percent of these computers in the United States, Europe, and Japan. This number, expected to double by 2014, is growing rapidly because of developing markets.

For more information, visit the Computer Concepts CourseMate Web site at www.cengagebrain.com, navigate to the Chapter 4 FAQ resource for this book, and then click Personal Computer Use.

The Motherboard

The **motherboard**, sometimes called a *system board*, is the main circuit board of the system unit. Many electronic components attach to the motherboard; others are built into it. Figure 4-3 shows a photo of a current desktop personal computer motherboard and identifies its slots for adapter cards, the processor chip, and memory. Memory chips are installed on memory cards (modules) that fit in a slot on the motherboard.

A computer **chip** is a small piece of semiconducting material, usually silicon, on which integrated circuits are etched. An *integrated circuit* contains many microscopic pathways capable of carrying electrical current. Each integrated circuit can contain millions of elements such as resistors, capacitors, and transistors. A *transistor*, for example, can act as an electronic switch that opens or closes the circuit for electrical charges. Today's computer chips contain millions or billions of transistors. Most chips are no bigger than one-half-inch square. Manufacturers package chips so that the chips can be attached to a circuit board, such as a motherboard or an adapter card. Specific types of processor, memory, and other chips are discussed later in the chapter. Read Innovative Computing 4-1 to find out about chips implanted in animals.

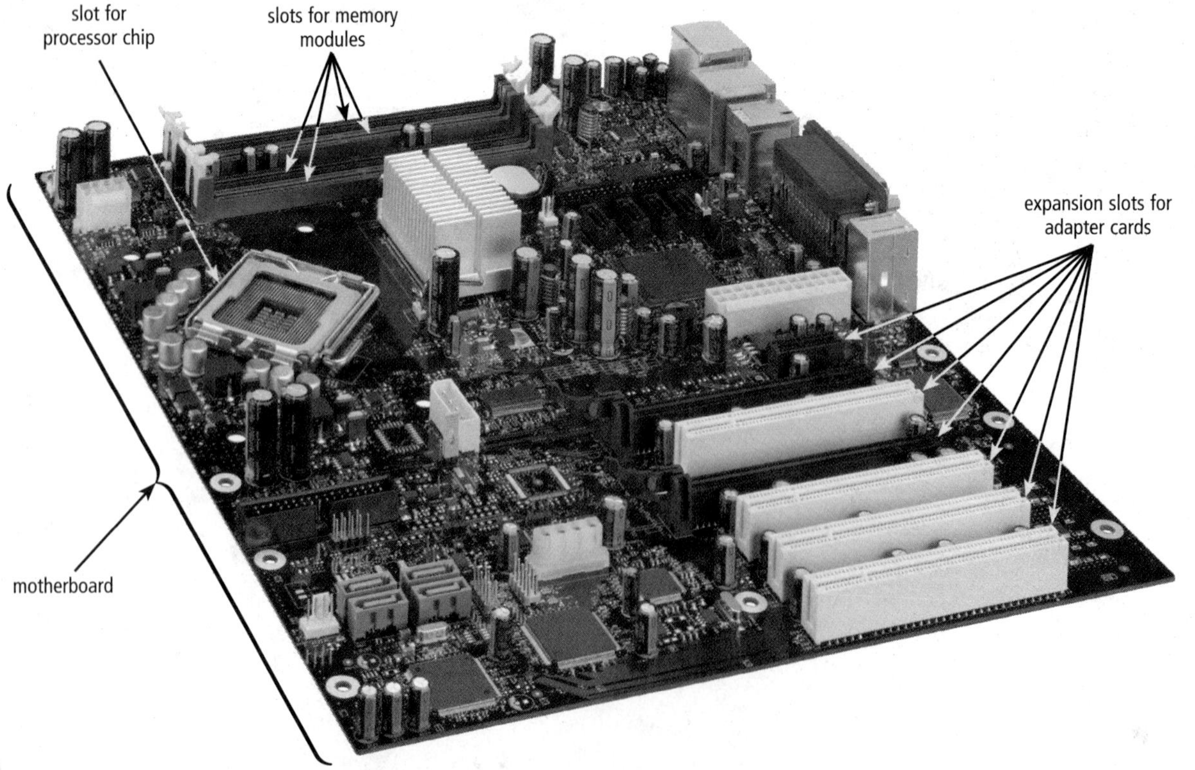

Figure 4-3 Many electronic components attach to the motherboard in a desktop personal computer, including a processor chip, memory modules, and adapter cards.

INNOVATIVE COMPUTING 4-1

Chip Implants Identify Animals

When Fido and Fluffy run away, their safe return home may be based on data stored on a chip that veterinarians have implanted under the skin, usually at the neck or shoulder blades. Other animals can be chipped, including horses, birds, and livestock.

Each chip is numbered uniquely and registered to the owner's name and address. This chip, sometimes called a microchip because it is the size of a grain of rice, contains an antenna and transponder encased in a glass tube. The antenna receives low-frequency radio waves when a scanning device passes over the chip, and the transponder sends a signal with the chip's number back to the scanner.

Shelters and animal control centers routinely scan runaway pets for chips in an attempt to reunite animals with their owners, and some animal hospitals scan pets to determine whether they have been reported lost or stolen. Most shelters require pets to have the implant before the animals are adopted. In addition, breeders, farmers, and animal associations implant the chips to thwart thieves. Researchers also use this technology to track migration of wild animals and fish.

For more information, visit the Computer Concepts CourseMate Web site at www.cengagebrain.com, navigate to the Chapter 4 Innovative Computing resource for this book, and then click ID Chips.

Processor

The **processor**, also called the **central processing unit (CPU)**, interprets and carries out the basic instructions that operate a computer. The processor significantly impacts overall computing power and manages most of a computer's operations. On larger computers, such as mainframes and supercomputers, the various functions performed by the processor extend over many separate chips and often multiple circuit boards. On a personal computer, all functions of the processor usually are on a single chip. Some computer and chip manufacturers use the term *microprocessor* to refer to a personal computer processor chip.

Most processor chip manufacturers now offer multi-core processors. A processor core, or simply core, contains the circuitry necessary to execute instructions. The operating system views each processor core as a separate processor. A **multi-core processor** is a single chip with two or more separate processor cores. Two common multi-core processors are dual-core and quad-core. A **dual-core processor** is a chip that contains two separate processor cores. Similarly, a **quad-core processor** is a chip with four separate processor cores.

Each processor core on a multi-core processor generally runs at a slower clock speed than a single-core processor, but multi-core processors typically increase overall performance. For example, although a dual-core processor does not double the processing speed of a single-core processor, it can approach those speeds. The performance increase is especially noticeable when users are running multiple programs simultaneously such as antivirus software, spyware remover, e-mail program, instant messaging, media player, disc burning software, and photo editing software. Multi-core processors also are more energy efficient than separate multiple processors, requiring lower levels of power consumption and emitting less heat in the system unit.

Processors contain a control unit and an arithmetic logic unit (ALU). These two components work together to perform processing operations. Figure 4-4 illustrates how other devices connected to the computer communicate

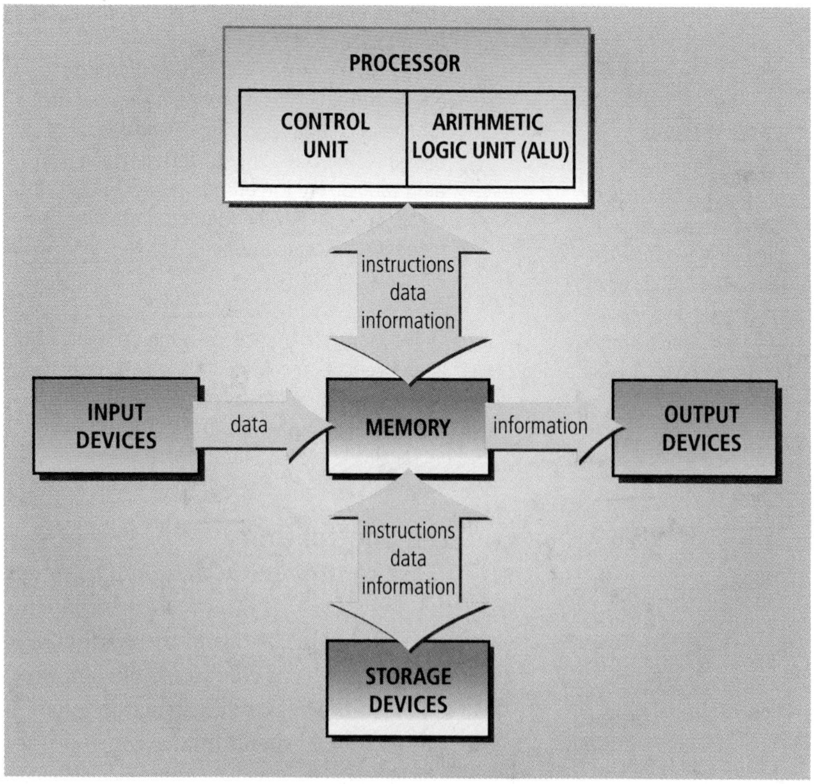

Figure 4-4 Most devices connected to the computer communicate with the processor to carry out a task. When a user starts a program, for example, its instructions transfer from a storage device to memory. Data needed by programs enters memory from either an input device or a storage device. The control unit interprets and executes instructions in memory, and the ALU performs calculations on the data in memory. Resulting information is stored in memory, from which it can be sent to an output device or a storage device for future access, as needed.

with the processor to carry out a task. Read Innovative Computing 4-2 to find out how processors control robots.

INNOVATIVE COMPUTING 4-2

Robots Assist with Everyday Tasks

Be prepared to see a new type of gardener, house cleaner, and receptionist because robots are becoming mainstream. Robotic technology will handle mundane chores as well as provide companionship in both professional and personal worlds.

Approximately 40 percent of the world's robots reside in Japan, where 32 of these machines work alongside every 1,000 workers employed in manufacturing settings. The Japanese accept robots as human replacements and view them as friendly helpers. The machines can greet patients in doctors' offices, print maps when people ask for directions, mow lawns, and check oil and gas pipelines for leaks. They also can feed hospitalized patients and provide companionship for homebound people as well as toddlers.

The United States' military and foreign armed forces are using robots as unmanned drones in combat and search-and-rescue missions. The Department of Defense is planning to increase the unmanned technology's presence with soft, bendable robots that can maneuver through openings smaller than their actual dimensions.

For more information, visit the Computer Concepts CourseMate Web site at www.cengagebrain.com, navigate to the Chapter 4 Innovative Computing resource for this book, and then click Robots.

ETHICS & ISSUES 4-1

Can Computers Think?

Since the dawn of the computing age, people have wondered if a computer ever would be capable of thought. As computer processors and software become more powerful, the question is debated more hotly. People who believe computers can think argue that, if a person had a conversation with a computer and was convinced the computer was really human, then the computer is intelligent. This criteria is known as the Turing Test, named after British mathematician Alan Turing who proposed the test in 1950. If a computer can pass a modern version of the Turing Test, it is considered to be intelligent, and it may win the prestigious $100,000 Loebner Prize. While the $100,000 prize has yet to be claimed, an annual event awards $2,000 to the most human-like computer chat partner.

Opponents to those who believe computers may one day think claim that, if a question written in a foreign language was submitted to a person who can read and write the language and a person who cannot read or write the language but has a list of questions and appropriate answers, it might be impossible to tell the response of one person from the other. But, the person who cannot read or write the language really does not understand it, any more than a computer really can think. Opponents also claim that research towards the Turing Test is a distraction from more beneficial research. Besides, computers lack at least two essential components of human thinking — common sense and emotion.

Can computers think? Why or why not? If computers cannot think now, might they be able to think in the future? Why? How important are common sense and emotion in the ability to think? Are any benefits to be gained if a computer can pass the Turing Test? Why?

Ethics & Issues

For the complete text of the Ethics & Issues boxes found in this chapter, visit the Computer Concepts CourseMate Web site at www.cengagebrain.com and then navigate to the Chapter 4 Ethics & Issues resource for this book.

The Control Unit

The **control unit** is the component of the processor that directs and coordinates most of the operations in the computer. The control unit has a role much like a traffic cop: it interprets each instruction issued by a program and then initiates the appropriate action to carry out the instruction. Types of internal components that the control unit directs include the arithmetic/logic unit, registers, and buses, each discussed later in this chapter. Read Ethics & Issues 4-1 for a related discussion.

Control Unit

For more information, visit the Computer Concepts CourseMate Web site at www.cengagebrain.com, navigate to the Chapter 4 Web Link resource for this book, and then click Control Unit.

The Arithmetic Logic Unit

The **arithmetic logic unit** (*ALU*), another component of the processor, performs arithmetic, comparison, and other operations.

Arithmetic operations include basic calculations such as addition, subtraction, multiplication, and division. *Comparison operations* involve comparing one data item with another to determine whether the first item is greater than, equal to, or less than the other item. Depending on the result of the comparison, different actions may occur. For example, to determine if an employee should receive overtime pay, software instructs the ALU to compare the number of hours an employee worked during the week with the regular time hours allowed (e.g., 40 hours). If the hours worked exceed 40, for example, software instructs the ALU to perform calculations that compute the overtime wage.

Machine Cycle

For every instruction, a processor repeats a set of four basic operations, which comprise a *machine cycle* (Figure 4-5): (1) fetching, (2) decoding, (3) executing, and, if necessary, (4) storing. *Fetching* is the process of obtaining a program instruction or data item from memory. The term *decoding* refers to the process of translating the instruction into signals the computer can execute. *Executing* is the process of carrying out the commands. *Storing*, in this context, means writing the result to memory (not to a storage medium).

In some computers, the processor fetches, decodes, executes, and stores only one instruction at a time. In these computers, the processor waits until an instruction completes all four stages of the machine cycle (fetch, decode, execute, and store) before beginning work on the next instruction.

Most of today's personal computers support a concept called pipelining. With *pipelining*, the processor begins fetching a second instruction before it completes the machine cycle for the first instruction. Processors that use pipelining are faster because they do not have to wait for one instruction to complete the machine cycle before fetching the next. Think of a pipeline as an assembly line. By the time the first instruction is in the last stage of the machine cycle, three

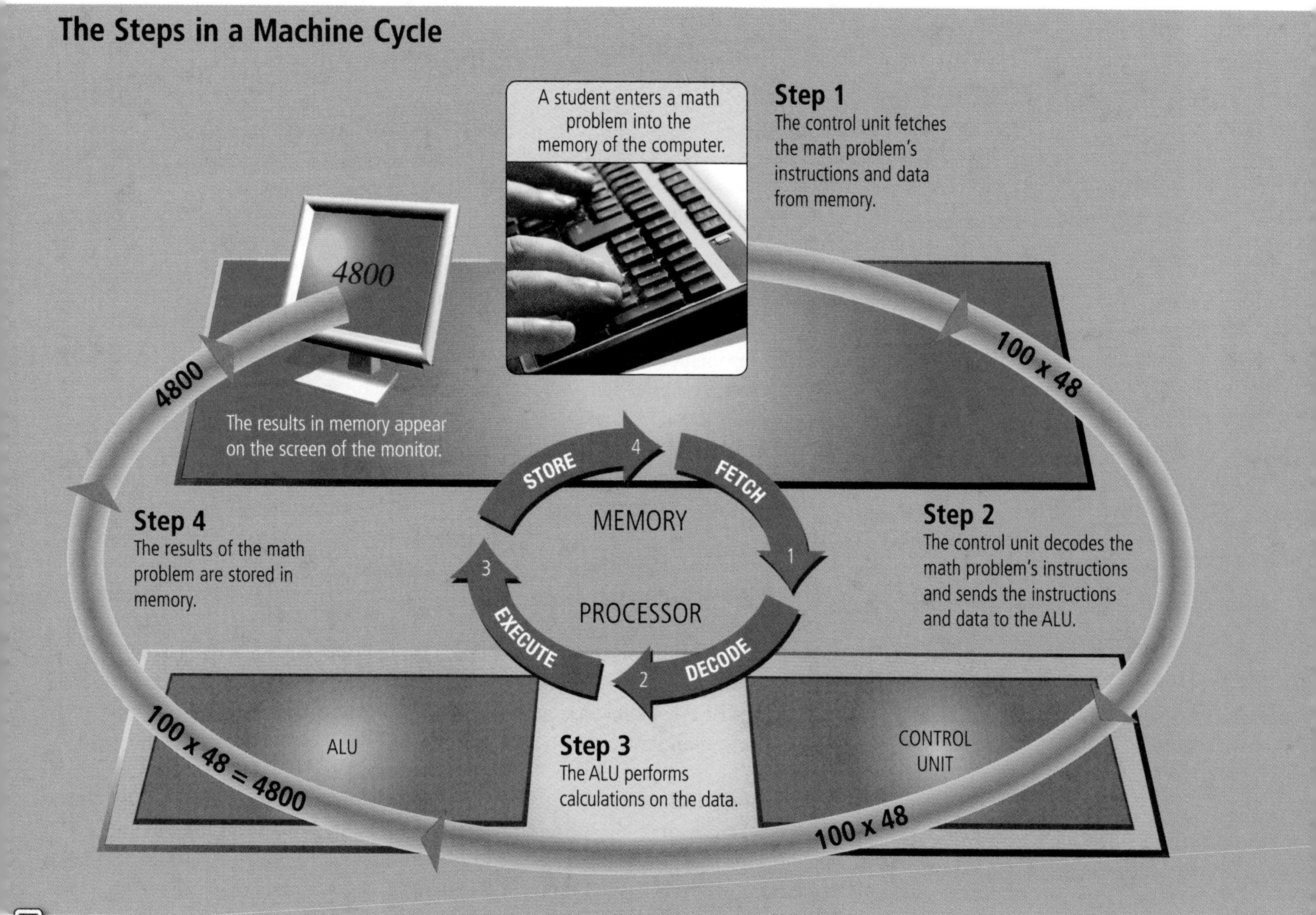

Figure 4-5 This figure shows the steps in a machine cycle.

other instructions could have been fetched and started through the machine cycle (Figure 4-6).

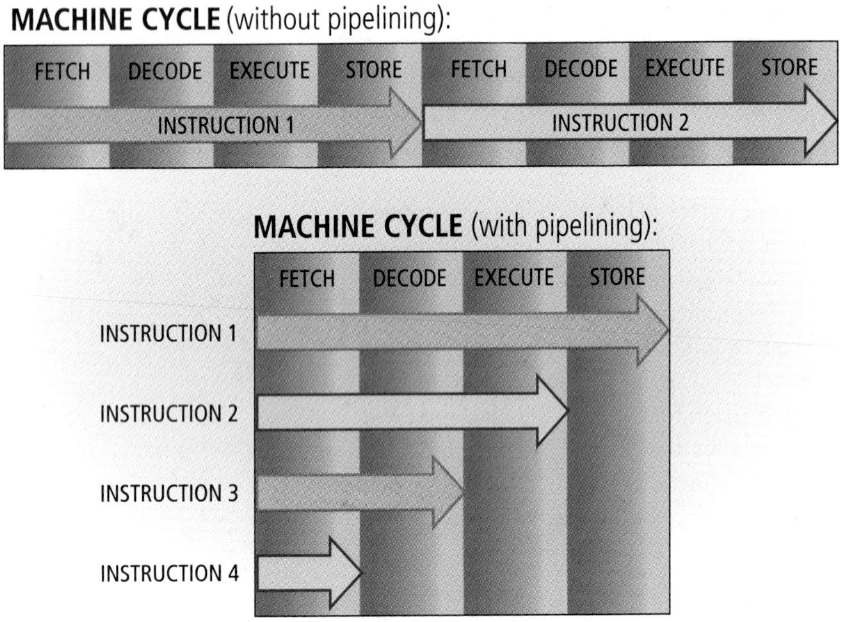

Figure 4-6 With pipelining, the processor fetches a second instruction before the first instruction is completed. The result is faster processing.

Registers

A processor contains small, high-speed storage locations, called *registers*, that temporarily hold data and instructions. Registers are part of the processor, not part of memory or a permanent storage device. Processors have many different types of registers, each with a specific storage function. Register functions include storing the location from where an instruction was fetched, storing an instruction while the control unit decodes it, storing data while the ALU computes it, and storing the results of a calculation.

The System Clock

The processor relies on a small quartz crystal circuit called the **system clock** to control the timing of all computer operations. Just as your heart beats at a regular rate to keep your body functioning, the system clock generates regular electronic pulses, or ticks, that set the operating pace of components of the system unit.

Each tick equates to a *clock cycle*. In the past, processors used one or more clock cycles to execute each instruction. Processors today often are *superscalar*, which means they can execute more than one instruction per clock cycle.

The pace of the system clock, called the **clock speed**, is measured by the number of ticks per second. Current personal computer processors have clock speeds in the gigahertz range. Giga is a prefix that stands for billion, and a *hertz* is one cycle per second. Thus, one **gigahertz (GHz)** equals one billion ticks of the system clock per second. A computer that operates at 3 GHz has 3 billion (giga) clock cycles in one second (hertz).

The faster the clock speed, the more instructions the processor can execute per second. The speed of the system clock has no effect on devices such as a printer or disk drive. The speed of the system clock is just one factor that influences a computer's performance. Other factors, such as the type of processor chip, amount of cache, memory access time, bus width, and bus clock speed, are discussed later in this chapter.

? FAQ 4-2

Does the system clock also keep track of the current date and time?

No, a separate battery-backed chip, called the *real-time clock*, keeps track of the date and time in a computer. The battery continues to run the real-time clock even when the computer is off.

For more information, visit the Computer Concepts CourseMate Web site at www.cengagebrain.com, navigate to the Chapter 4 FAQ resource for this book, and then click Computer Clock.

Comparison of Personal Computer Processors

The leading manufacturers of personal computer processor chips are Intel and AMD. These manufacturers often identify their processor chips by a model name or model number (Figure 4-7). High-performance personal computers today may use a processor in the Intel **Core** family. Less expensive, basic personal computers may use a brand of Intel processor in the **Pentium** or **Celeron** family. The **Xeon** and **Itanium** families of processors are ideal for workstations and low-end servers.

AMD is the leading manufacturer of *Intel-compatible processors*, which have an internal design similar to Intel processors, perform the same functions, and can be as powerful, but often are less expensive.

In the past, chip manufacturers listed a processor's clock speed in marketing literature and advertisements. As previously mentioned, though, clock speed is only one factor that impacts processing speed in today's computers. To help consumers evaluate various processors, manufacturers such as Intel and AMD now use a numbering scheme that more accurately reflects the processing speed of their chips.

Processor chips include technologies to improve processing performance, for example, to improve performance of multimedia and 3-D graphics. Most of Intel's processor chips also include *vPro technology*, which provides the capability to track computer hardware and software, diagnose and resolve computer problems, and secure computers from outside threats. Read Ethics & Issues 4-2 for a related discussion.

As mentioned earlier, many personal computer processors are multi-core, with the processor cores working simultaneously on related instructions. These related instructions, called a thread, can be independent or part of a larger task. Software written to support multiple threads, called a *multi-threaded program*, runs much faster than those in nonthreaded environments.

Processors for traditional notebook computers and Tablet PCs also include technology to optimize and extend battery life, enhance security, and integrate wireless capabilities. For example, Intel's *Centrino 2* mobile technology, which may have a Pro designator depending on its capabilities, integrates wireless functionality in notebook computers and Tablet PCs. Netbooks, smart phones, and other smaller mobile devices often use more compact processors that consume less power, yet offer high performance.

Multi-Core Processors

For more information, visit the Computer Concepts CourseMate Web site at www.cengagebrain.com, navigate to the Chapter 4 Web Link resource for this book, and then click Multi-Core Processors.

Comparison of Currently Available Personal Computer Processors

	Name	Multi-Core Availability	Manufacturer
SERVER PROCESSORS	Xeon	8 Core, 6 Core, Quad Core, Dual Core	Intel
	Itanium	Quad Core, Dual Core	Intel
	Opteron	6 Core, Quad Core	AMD
DESKTOP PERSONAL COMPUTER PROCESSORS	Core i7 Extreme	6 Core, Quad Core	Intel
	Core i7	6 Core, Quad Core	Intel
	Core i5	Quad Core, Dual Core	Intel
	Core i3	Dual Core	Intel
	Celeron	Dual Core	Intel
	Phenom	6 Core, Quad Core, Triple Core	AMD
	Athlon	Quad Core, Triple Core, Dual Core	AMD
	Sempron		AMD
NOTEBOOK COMPUTER PROCESSORS	Core i7 Extreme	Quad Core	Intel
	Core i7	Quad Core, Dual Core	Intel
	Core i5 and i3	Dual Core	Intel
	Atom		Intel
	Phenom	Quad Core, Triple Core, Dual Core	AMD
	Turion	Dual Core	AMD
	Athlon	Dual Core	AMD
	Sempron		AMD

Figure 4-7 Most of today's processors are multi-core.

ETHICS & ISSUES 4-2

Is Government Search and Seizure of Computers Ethical?

In the interest of national security, the Department of Homeland Security may search and seize any mobile computer or device from people arriving in the United States. The sometimes random searches may be done without a warrant or even a reason. Additionally, the government has taken computers from schools and libraries in a similar manner. Computers and mobile devices might be taken away for an off-site inspection for any amount of time. Sometimes, the devices are not returned and little or no reason is given for the seizure.

At airports and other points of entry to the country, the government considers computers and mobile devices to be containers, just as a piece of luggage is a container. Computers, therefore, can be searched and seized similarly to luggage without reasonable suspicion. Opponents claim that the data on a computer is like memories stored in the brain. They claim that the government should be able to inspect the hardware, but not the contents of memory or a hard disk. Librarians and school administrators claim that the government is invading the privacy of patrons and students.

Is government search and seizure of computers without a warrant ethical? Why or why not? Would you allow a government employee to inspect the data on your mobile computer or device? Why or why not? If memories, thoughts, or intentions in one's mind could someday be deciphered by a computer at a security checkpoint, should the government be allowed to scan them? Why?

Another type of processor, called *system-on-a-chip*, integrates the functions of a processor, memory, and a video card on a single chip. Lower-priced personal computers, Tablet PCs, networking devices, portable media players, and game consoles sometimes have a system-on-a-chip processor. The goal of system-on-a-chip manufacturers is to create processors that have faster clock speeds, consume less power, are small, and are cost effective.

Buying a Personal Computer

If you are ready to buy a new computer, the processor you select should depend on how you plan to use the computer (Figure 4-8). To realize greater processing performance, you may want to choose a multi-core processor.

Instead of buying an entirely new computer, you might be able to upgrade your processor to increase the computer's performance. Be certain the processor you buy is compatible with your computer's motherboard; otherwise, you will have to replace the motherboard, too. Replacing a processor is a fairly simple process, whereas replacing a motherboard is much more complicated.

For detailed personal computer and mobile device purchasing guidelines, read the Buyer's Guide feature that follows Chapter 8. Read Ethics & Issues 4-3 for a related discussion.

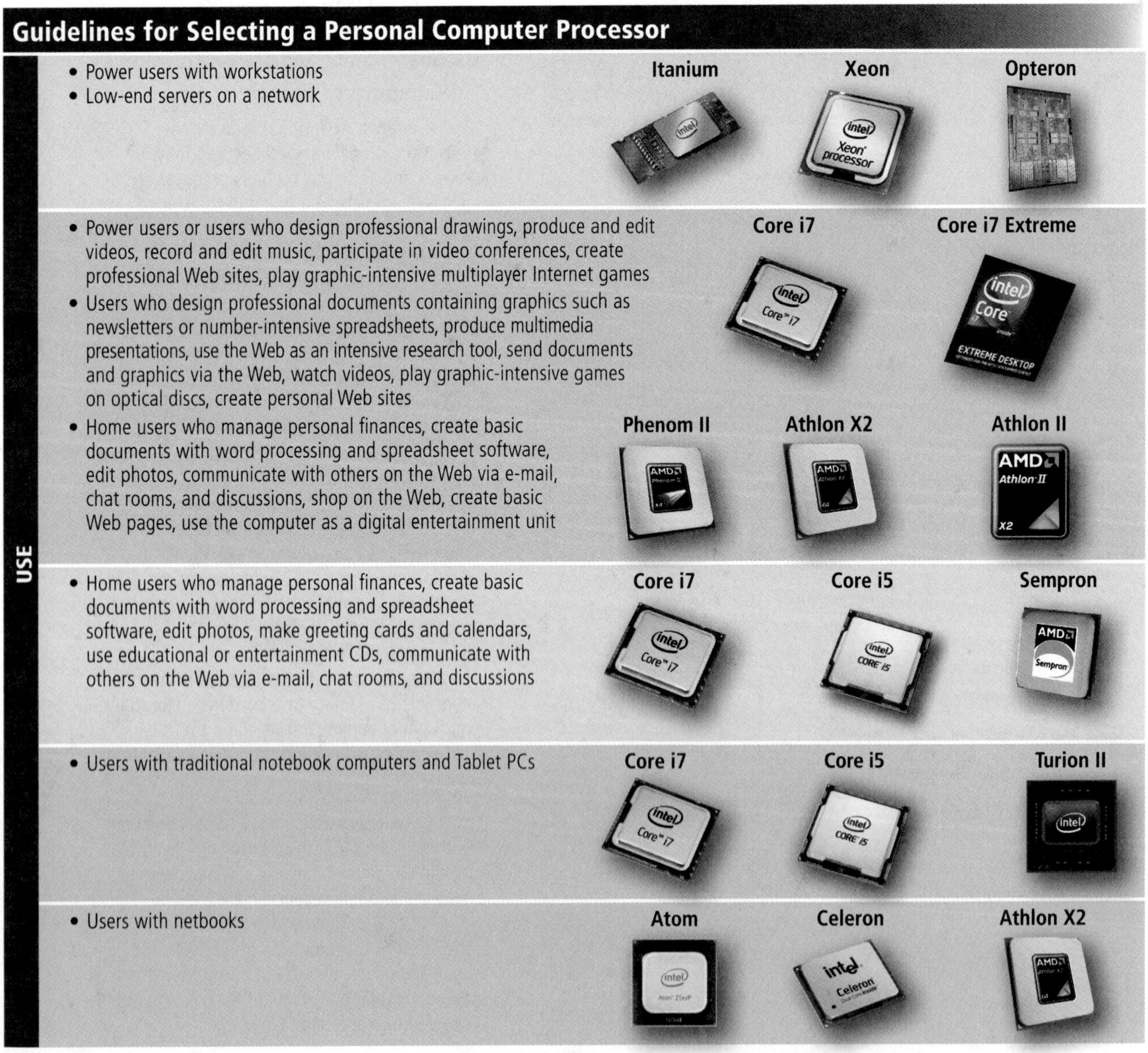
Guidelines for Selecting a Personal Computer Processor
USE
• Power users with workstations
• Low-end servers on a network
Itanium
Xeon
Opteron
• Power users or users who design professional drawings, produce and edit videos, record and edit music, participate in video conferences, create professional Web sites, play graphic-intensive multiplayer Internet games
• Users who design professional documents containing graphics such as newsletters or number-intensive spreadsheets, produce multimedia presentations, use the Web as an intensive research tool, send documents and graphics via the Web, watch videos, play graphic-intensive games on optical discs, create personal Web sites
Core i7
Core i7 Extreme
• Home users who manage personal finances, create basic documents with word processing and spreadsheet software, edit photos, communicate with others on the Web via e-mail, chat rooms, and discussions, shop on the Web, create basic Web pages, use the computer as a digital entertainment unit
Phenom II
Athlon X2
Athlon II
• Home users who manage personal finances, create basic documents with word processing and spreadsheet software, edit photos, make greeting cards and calendars, use educational or entertainment CDs, communicate with others on the Web via e-mail, chat rooms, and discussions
Core i7
Core i5
Sempron
• Users with traditional notebook computers and Tablet PCs
Core i7
Core i5
Turion II
• Users with netbooks
Atom
Celeron
Athlon X2

Figure 4-8 Determining which processor to obtain when you purchase a computer depends on computer usage.

ETHICS & ISSUES 4-3

Should Mobile Computers and Devices Be Banned from the Classroom?

Instead of student faces, the view for today's instructors often is a sea of bent necks as students use their notebook computers, netbooks, Tablet PCs, smart phones, and portable media players during lectures. Many students have found that mobile computers and devices provide an ideal place to take notes, make recordings of lectures, and perform lecture-related research. Other students have found that mobile computers and devices provide endless entertainment, instant messaging, and other activities unrelated to course work during a lecture. Some instructors and students find that this inappropriate use of computers during a lecture to be distracting, especially if the computer or device makes sounds such as keyboard clicks or screen taps. Even when used for note taking, some feel that mobile computers are incompatible with a good learning experience. One law professor describes the mobile computers' raised computer screens as a picket fence between an instructor and the student, as students attempt to capture every nuance of the lecture on their computers. This professor is one of a growing number of instructors who have banned the use of mobile computers and devices during lectures. Classroom rules vary by instructor, with some choosing to disallow listening to music, sending text messages, or using a cell phone.

Are mobile computers and devices too distracting in the classroom? Why? Should instructors, departments, or entire schools be able to ban mobile computers and devices in the classroom? Why or why not? What are proper and improper uses of mobile computers and devices in the classroom? Why? Is the use of a mobile computer and devices more of a distraction than taking notes or doodling in a notebook pad during class? Why or why not?

FAQ 4-3

Which PC vendors are the most popular with consumers?

Hewlett-Packard (HP) has the highest market share worldwide at approximately 20 percent, with Dell in second place with nearly 13 percent market share. HP accounts for nearly 21 percent of PC sales in the United States. The chart to the right compares the worldwide market share for various PC vendors.

For more information, visit the Computer Concepts CourseMate Web site at www.cengagebrain.com, navigate to the Chapter 4 FAQ resource for this book, and then click PC Vendor Market.

Processor Cooling

Processor chips generate quite a bit of heat, which could cause the chip to burn up. Although the computer's main fan generates airflow, many of today's personal computer processors require additional cooling. Heat sinks/pipes and liquid cooling technologies often are used to help dissipate processor heat.

A *heat sink* is a small ceramic or metal component with fins on its surface that absorbs and disperses heat produced by electrical components such as a processor (Figure 4-9). Some heat sinks are packaged as part of a processor chip. Others are installed on the top or the side of the chip. Because a heat sink consumes extra space, a smaller device called a *heat pipe* cools processors in notebook computers, including netbooks and Tablet PCs.

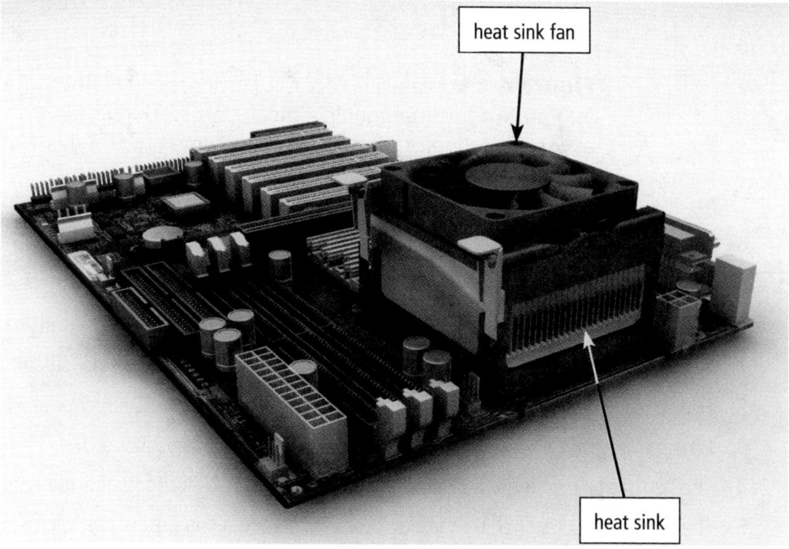

Figure 4-9 A heat sink, which in this photo is attached to the top of a processor, prevents the chip from overheating. The heat sink fan, which attaches to the top of the heat sink, helps distribute air dissipated by the heat sink.

Some computers use liquid cooling technology to reduce the temperature of a processor. *Liquid cooling technology* uses a continuous flow of fluid(s), such as water and glycol, in a process that transfers the heated fluid away from the

Liquid Cooling
For more information, visit the Computer Concepts CourseMate Web site at www.cengagebrain.com, navigate to the Chapter 4 Web Link resource for this book, and then click Liquid Cooling.

processor to a radiator-type grill, which cools the liquid, and then returns the cooled fluid to the processor (Figure 4-10).

Some mobile computers and devices often have Low Voltage or Ultra Low Voltage (ULV) processors, which have such low power demands that they do not require additional cooling.

Figure 4-10 With liquid cooling technology, heat transfers from a processor through a copper plate, which is attached to the processor and also to tubing that contains liquid. The liquid travels away from the processor to a radiator-type grill, where it is cooled before travelling back to the plate attached to the processor.

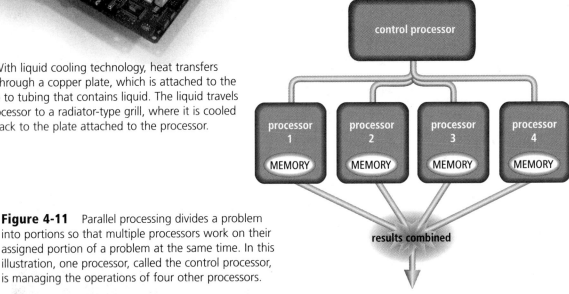

Parallel Processing

Parallel processing is a method that uses multiple processors simultaneously to execute a single program or task (Figure 4-11). Parallel processing divides a single problem into portions so that multiple processors work on their assigned portion of the problem at the same time. Parallel processing requires special software that recognizes how to divide the problem and then bring the results back together again.

Some personal computers implement parallel processing with dual-core processors or multi-core processors. Others have two or more separate processor chips, respectively called dual processor or multiprocessor computers.

Massively parallel processing is large scale parallel processing that involves hundreds or thousands of processors. Supercomputers use massively parallel processing for applications such as artificial intelligence and weather forecasting.

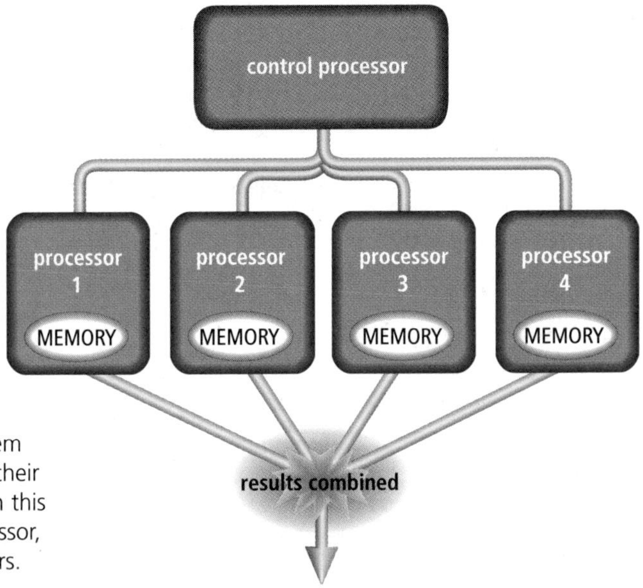

Figure 4-11 Parallel processing divides a problem into portions so that multiple processors work on their assigned portion of a problem at the same time. In this illustration, one processor, called the control processor, is managing the operations of four other processors.

✓ QUIZ YOURSELF 4-1

Instructions: Find the true statement below. Then, rewrite the remaining false statements so that they are true.

1. A computer chip is a small piece of semiconducting material, usually silicon, on which integrated circuits are etched.
2. Four basic operations in a machine cycle are: (1) comparing, (2) decoding, (3) executing, and, if necessary, (4) pipelining.
3. Processors contain a motherboard and an arithmetic logic unit (ALU).
4. The central processing unit, sometimes called a system board, is the main circuit board of the system unit.
5. The leading processor chip manufacturers for personal computers are Microsoft and AMD.
6. The pace of the system clock, called the clock speed, is measured by the number of ticks per minute.
7. The system unit is a case that contains mechanical components of the computer used to process data.

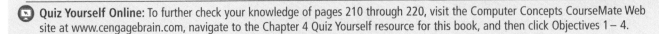

Quiz Yourself Online: To further check your knowledge of pages 210 through 220, visit the Computer Concepts CourseMate Web site at www.cengagebrain.com, navigate to the Chapter 4 Quiz Yourself resource for this book, and then click Objectives 1 – 4.

Data Representation

To understand how a computer processes data, you should know how a computer represents data. People communicate through speech by combining words into sentences. Human speech is **analog** because it uses continuous (wave form) signals that vary in strength and quality. Most computers are **digital**. They recognize only two discrete states: on and off. This is because computers are electronic devices powered by electricity, which also has only two states: on and off.

The two digits, 0 and 1, easily can represent these two states (Figure 4-12). The digit 0 represents the electronic state of off (absence of an electronic charge). The digit 1 represents the electronic state of on (presence of an electronic charge).

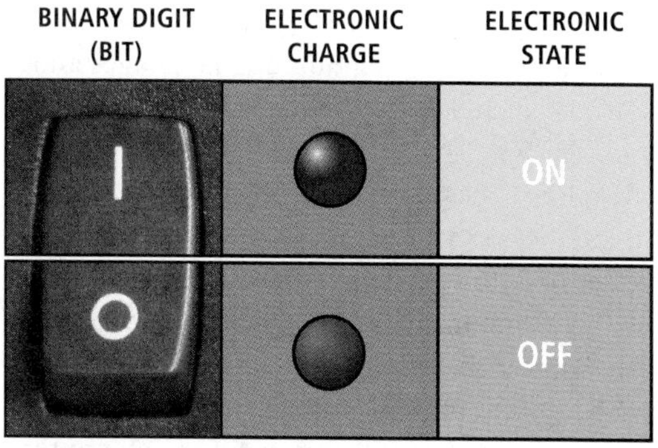

Figure 4-12 A computer circuit represents the 0 or the 1 electronically by the presence or absence of an electronic charge.

When people count, they use the digits in the decimal system (0 through 9). The computer, by contrast, uses a binary system because it recognizes only two states. The **binary system** is a number system that has just two unique digits, 0 and 1, called bits. A **bit** (short for *binary digit*) is the smallest unit of data the computer can process. By itself, a bit is not very informative.

When 8 bits are grouped together as a unit, they form a **byte**. A byte provides enough different combinations of 0s and 1s to represent 256 individual characters. These characters include numbers, uppercase and lowercase letters of the alphabet, punctuation marks, and others, such as the letters of the Greek alphabet.

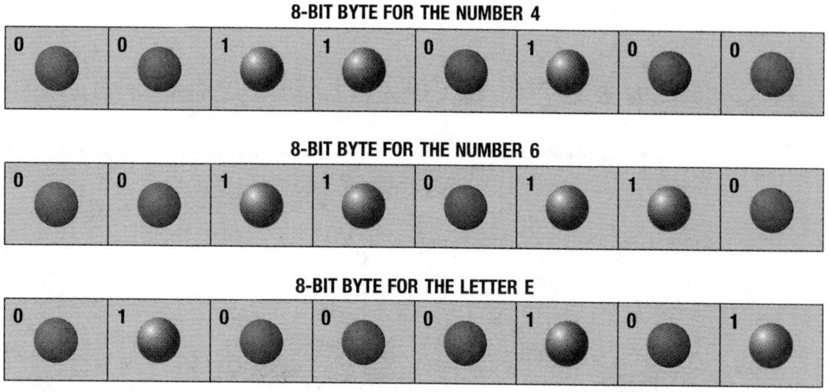

Figure 4-13 Eight bits grouped together as a unit are called a byte. A byte represents a single character in the computer.

The combinations of 0s and 1s that represent characters are defined by patterns called a coding scheme. In one coding scheme, the number 4 is represented as 00110100, the number 6 as 00110110, and the capital letter E as 01000101 (Figure 4-13). *ASCII* (pronounced ASK-ee), which stands for American Standard Code for Information Interchange, is the most widely used coding scheme to represent data (Figure 4-14).

ASCII	SYMBOL	ASCII	SYMBOL
00110000	0	01001110	N
00110001	1	01001111	O
00110010	2	01010000	P
00110011	3	01010001	Q
00110100	4	01010010	R
00110101	5	01010011	S
00110110	6	01010100	T
00110111	7	01010101	U
00111000	8	01010110	V
00111001	9	01010111	W
01000001	A	01011000	X
01000010	B	01011001	Y
01000011	C	01011010	Z
01000100	D	00100001	!
01000101	E	00100010	"
01000110	F	00100011	#
01000111	G	00100100	$
01001000	H	00100101	%
01001001	I	00100110	&
01001010	J	00101000	(
01001011	K	00101001	)
01001100	L	00101010	*
01001101	M	00101011	+

Figure 4-14 ASCII is a widely used coding scheme.

The ASCII coding scheme is sufficient for English and Western European languages but is not large enough for Asian and other languages that use different alphabets. *Unicode* is a 16-bit coding scheme that has the capacity of representing more than 65,000 characters and symbols. The Unicode coding scheme is capable of representing almost all the world's current written languages, as well as classic and historical languages. To allow for expansion, Unicode reserves 30,000 codes for future use and 6,000 codes for private use. Unicode is implemented in several operating systems, including Windows, Mac OS, and Linux. Unicode-enabled programming languages and software include Java, XML, Microsoft Office, and Oracle.

Coding schemes make it possible for humans to interact with a digital computer that processes only bits. When you press a key on a keyboard, a chip in the keyboard converts the key's electronic signal into a special code that is sent to the system unit. Then, the system unit converts the code into a binary form the computer can process and stores it in memory. Every character is converted to its corresponding byte. The computer then processes the data as bytes, which actually is a series of on/off electrical states. When processing is finished, software converts the byte into a human-recognizable number, letter of the alphabet, or special character that is displayed on a screen or is printed (Figure 4-15). All of these conversions take place so quickly that you do not realize they are occurring.

Standards, such as those defined by ASCII and Unicode, also make it possible for components in computers to communicate with each other successfully. By following these and other standards, manufacturers can produce a component and be assured that it will operate correctly in a computer. Appendix C at the back of this book discusses the ASCII and Unicode schemes in more depth, along with the parity bit and number systems.

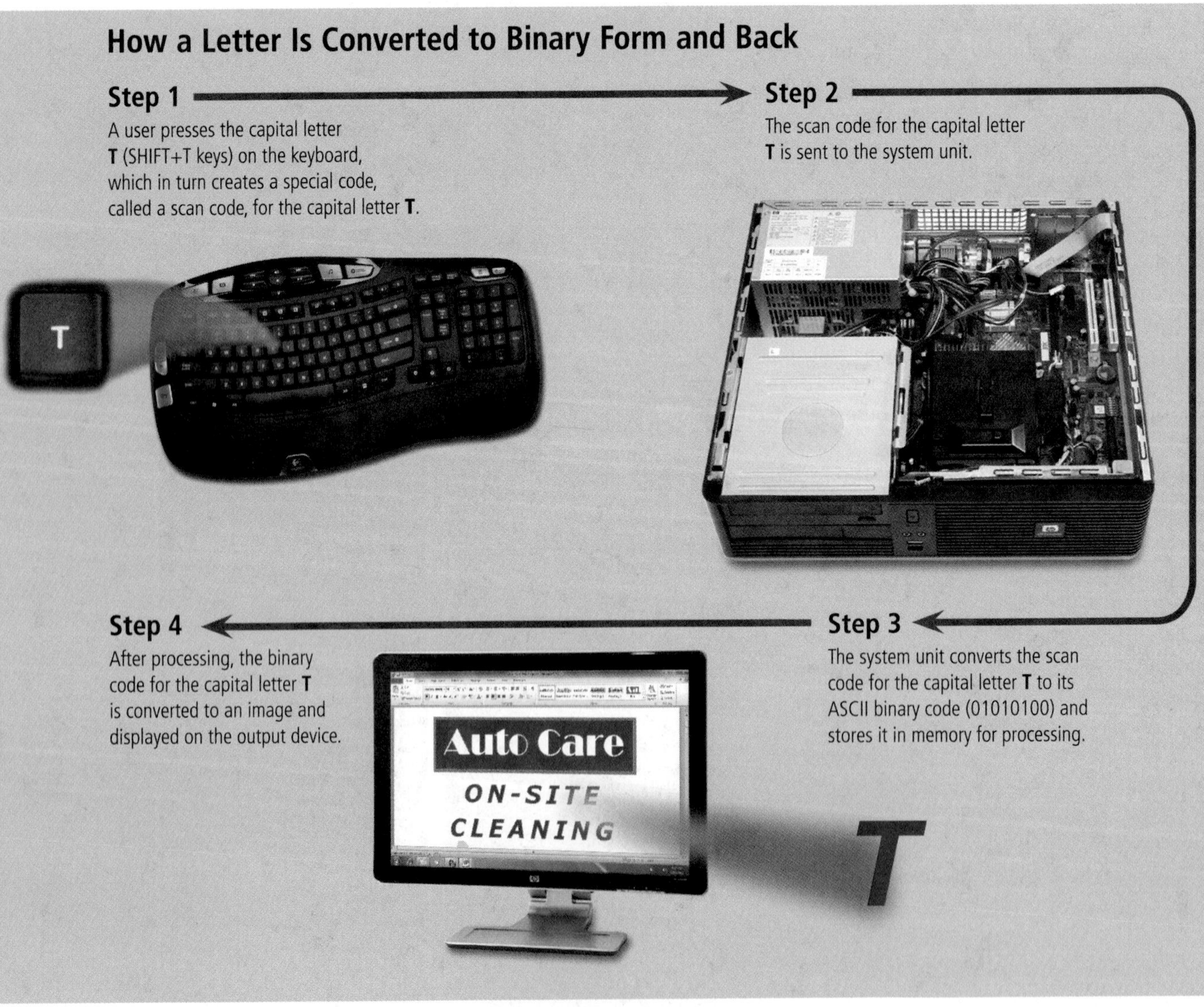
How a Letter Is Converted to Binary Form and Back
Step 1
A user presses the capital letter T (SHIFT+T keys) on the keyboard, which in turn creates a special code, called a scan code, for the capital letter T.
T
Step 2
The scan code for the capital letter T is sent to the system unit.
Step 3
The system unit converts the scan code for the capital letter T to its ASCII binary code (01010100) and stores it in memory for processing.
Step 4
After processing, the binary code for the capital letter T is converted to an image and displayed on the output device.
Auto Care
ON-SITE
CLEANING
T

Figure 4-15 This figure shows how a letter is converted to binary form and back.

Memory

Memory consists of electronic components that store instructions waiting to be executed by the processor, data needed by those instructions, and the results of processing the data (information). Memory usually consists of one or more chips on the motherboard or some other circuit board in the computer.

Memory stores three basic categories of items: (1) the operating system and other system software that control or maintain the computer and its devices; (2) application programs that carry out a specific task such as word processing; and (3) the data being processed by the application programs and resulting information. This role of memory to store both data and programs is known as the *stored program concept*.

Bytes and Addressable Memory

A byte (character) is the basic storage unit in memory. When application program instructions and data are transferred to memory from storage devices, the instructions and data exist as bytes. Each byte resides temporarily in a location in memory that has an *address*. An address simply is a unique number that identifies the location of a byte in memory. The illustration in Figure 4-16 shows how seats in an opera house are similar to addresses in memory: (1) a seat, which is identified by a unique seat number, holds one person at a time, and a location in memory, which is identified by a unique address, holds a single byte; and (2) both a seat, identified by a seat number, and a byte, identified by an address, can be empty. To access data or instructions in memory, the computer references the addresses that contain bytes of data.

Figure 4-16 Seats in an opera house are similar to addresses in memory: a seat holds one person at a time, and a location in memory holds a single byte; and both a seat and a byte can be empty.

Memory Sizes

Manufacturers state the size of memory (Figure 4-17) and storage devices in terms of the number of bytes the chip or device has available for storage. Recall that storage devices hold data, instructions, and information for future use, while most memory holds these items temporarily. A **kilobyte** (**KB** or **K**) is equal to exactly 1,024 bytes. To simplify memory and storage definitions, computer users often round a kilobyte down to 1,000 bytes. For example, if a memory chip can store 100 KB, it can hold approximately 100,000 bytes (characters). A **megabyte** (**MB**) is equal to approximately 1 million bytes. A **gigabyte** (**GB**) equals approximately 1 billion bytes. A **terabyte** (**TB**) is equal to approximately 1 trillion bytes.

Memory Sizes

Term	Abbreviation	Approximate Number of Bytes	Exact Number of Bytes	Approximate Number of Pages of Text
Kilobyte	KB or K	1 thousand	1,024	1/2
Megabyte	MB	1 million	1,048,576	500
Gigabyte	GB	1 billion	1,073,741,824	500,000
Terabyte	TB	1 trillion	1,099,511,627,776	500,000,000

Figure 4-17 Terms commonly used to define memory sizes.

Types of Memory

The system unit contains two types of memory: volatile and nonvolatile. When the computer's power is turned off, *volatile memory* loses its contents. *Nonvolatile memory*, by contrast, does not lose its contents when power is removed from the computer. Thus, volatile memory is temporary and nonvolatile memory is permanent. RAM is the most common type of volatile memory. Examples of nonvolatile memory include ROM, flash memory, and CMOS. The following sections discuss these types of memory.

RAM

Users typically are referring to RAM when discussing computer memory. **RAM** (*random access memory*), also called *main memory*, consists of memory chips that can be read from and written to by the processor and other devices. When you turn on power to a computer, certain operating system files (such as the files that determine how the desktop appears) load into RAM from a storage device such as a hard disk. These files remain in RAM as long as the computer has continuous power. As additional programs and data are requested, they also load into RAM from storage.

The processor interprets and executes a program's instructions while the program is in RAM. During this time, the contents of RAM may change (Figure 4-18). RAM can accommodate multiple programs simultaneously.

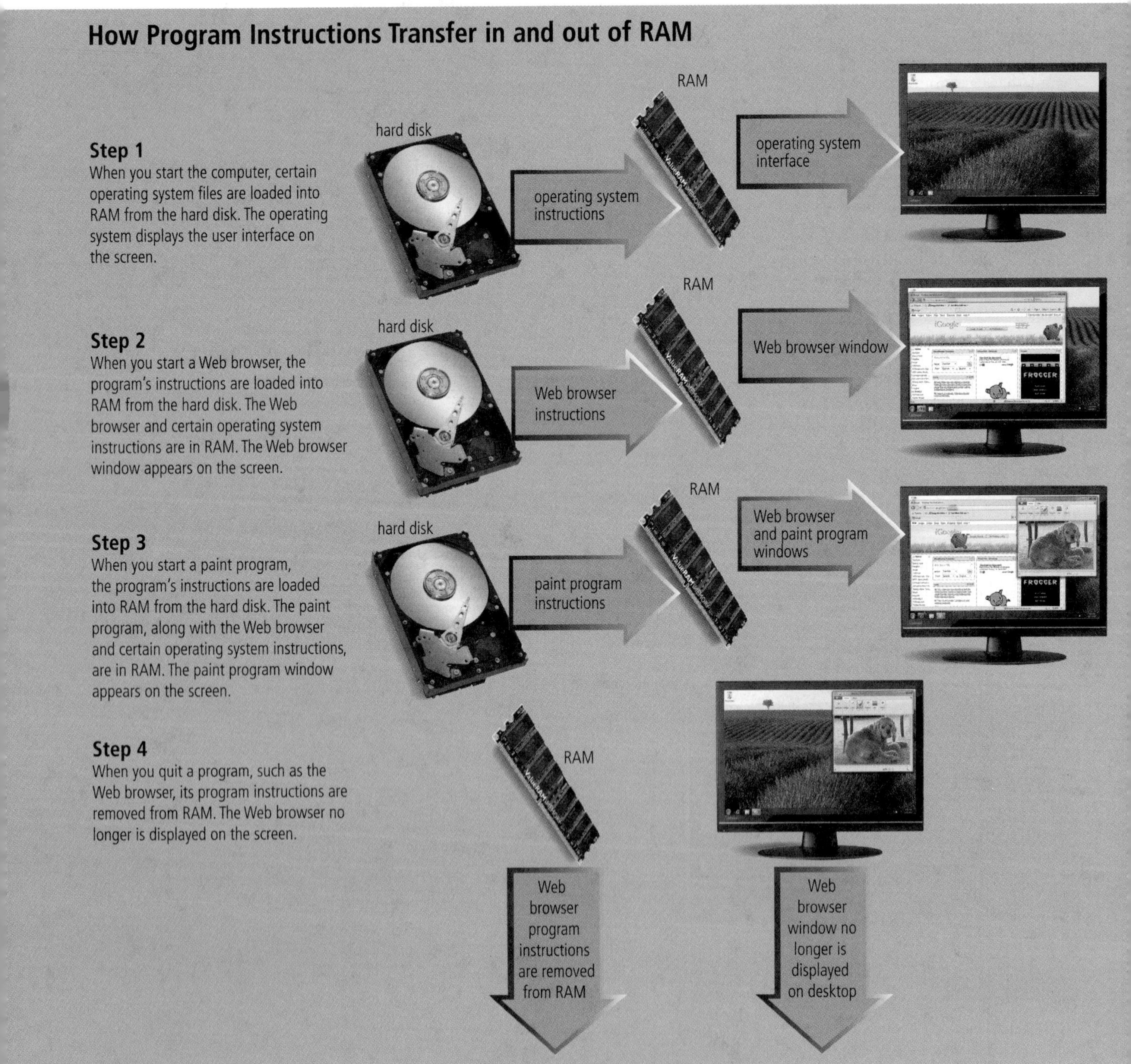
How Program Instructions Transfer in and out of RAM
Step 1
When you start the computer, certain operating system files are loaded into RAM from the hard disk. The operating system displays the user interface on the screen.
hard disk
operating system instructions
RAM
operating system interface
Step 2
When you start a Web browser, the program's instructions are loaded into RAM from the hard disk. The Web browser and certain operating system instructions are in RAM. The Web browser window appears on the screen.
hard disk
Web browser instructions
RAM
Web browser window
Step 3
When you start a paint program, the program's instructions are loaded into RAM from the hard disk. The paint program, along with the Web browser and certain operating system instructions, are in RAM. The paint program window appears on the screen.
hard disk
paint program instructions
RAM
Web browser and paint program windows
Step 4
When you quit a program, such as the Web browser, its program instructions are removed from RAM. The Web browser no longer is displayed on the screen.
RAM
Web browser program instructions are removed from RAM
Web browser window no longer is displayed on desktop

Figure 4-18 This figure shows how program instructions transfer in and out of RAM.

Most RAM is volatile, which means it loses its contents when the power is removed from the computer. For this reason, you must save any data, instructions, and information you may need in the future. Saving is the process of copying data, instructions, and information from RAM to a storage device such as a hard disk.

Three basic types of RAM chips exist: dynamic RAM, static RAM, and magnetoresistive RAM.

- *Dynamic RAM* (*DRAM* pronounced DEE-ram) chips must be re-energized constantly or they lose their contents. Many variations of DRAM chips exist, most of which are faster than the basic DRAM (Figure 4-19). Most personal computers today use some form of SDRAM chips or RDRAM chips.
- *Static RAM* (*SRAM* pronounced ESS-ram) chips are faster and more reliable than any variation of DRAM chips. These chips do not have to be re-energized as often as DRAM chips, thus, the term static. SRAM chips, however, are much more expensive than DRAM chips. Special applications such as cache use SRAM chips. A later section in this chapter discusses cache.
- A newer type of RAM, called *magnetoresistive RAM* (*MRAM* pronounced EM-ram), stores data using magnetic charges instead of electrical charges. Manufacturers claim that MRAM has greater storage capacity, consumes less power, and has faster access times than electronic RAM. Also, MRAM retains its contents after power is removed from the computer, which could prevent loss of data for users. As the cost of MRAM declines, experts predict MRAM could replace both DRAM and SRAM.

RAM chips usually reside on a **memory module**, which is a small circuit board. **Memory slots** on the motherboard hold memory modules (Figure 4-20). Three types of memory modules are SIMMs, DIMMs, and RIMMs. A *SIMM* (*single inline memory module*) has pins on opposite sides of the circuit board that connect together to form a single set of contacts. With a *DIMM* (*dual inline memory module*), by contrast, the pins on opposite sides of the circuit board do not connect and thus form two sets of contacts. SIMMs and DIMMs typically hold SDRAM chips. A *RIMM* (*Rambus inline memory module*) houses RDRAM chips. For a more technical discussion about RAM, read the High-Tech Talk article on page 242 at the end of this chapter. To learn more about how to install RAM in a computer, complete the Learn How To 1 activity on pages 252 and 253.

RAM

For more information, visit the Computer Concepts CourseMate Web site at www.cengagebrain.com, navigate to the Chapter 4 Web Link resource for this book, and then click RAM.

DRAM Variations

Name	Comments
SDRAM (Synchronous DRAM)	• synchronized to the system clock • much faster than DRAM
DDR SDRAM (Double Data Rate SDRAM)	• transfers data twice, instead of once, for each clock cycle • faster than SDRAM
DDR2	• second generation of DDR • faster than DDR
DDR3	• third generation of DDR • designed for computers with multi-core processors • faster than DDR2
RDRAM (Rambus DRAM)	• uses pipelining techniques • much faster than SDRAM

Figure 4-19 This table shows variations of DRAM chips.

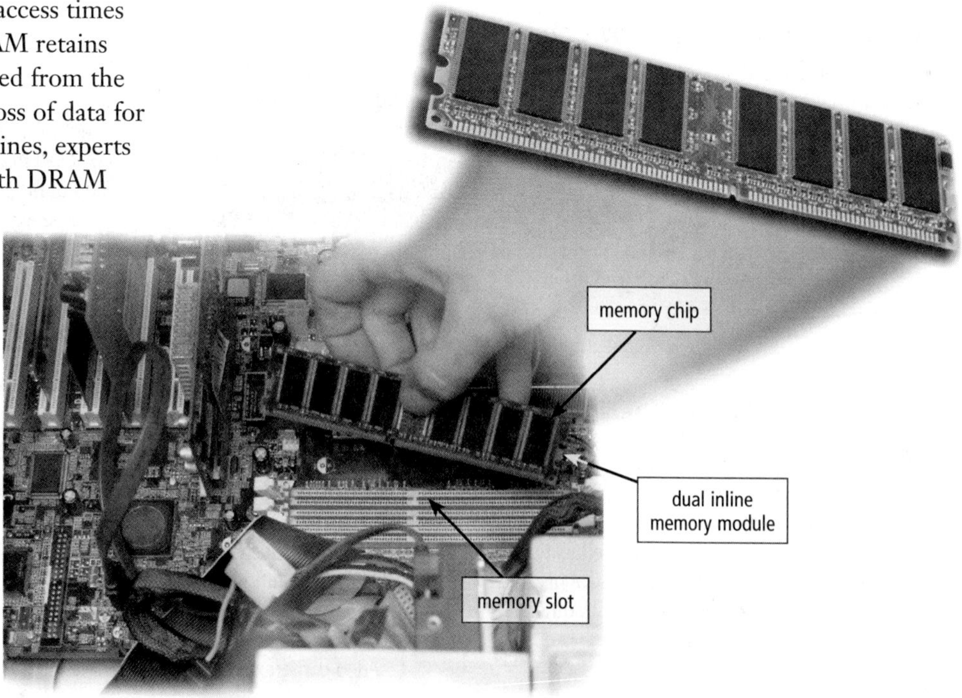

Figure 4-20 This photo shows a memory module being inserted in a motherboard.

RAM Configurations The amount of RAM necessary in a computer often depends on the types of software you plan to use. A computer executes programs that are in RAM. Think of RAM as the workspace on the top of your desk. Just as the top of your desk needs a certain amount of space to hold papers, a computer needs a certain amount of memory to store programs, data, and information. The more RAM a computer has, the faster the computer will respond.

Retail software typically indicates the minimum amount of RAM it requires. If you want the software to perform optimally, usually you need more than the minimum specifications for the software.

Figure 4-21 lists guidelines for the amount of RAM for various types of users. Advertisements normally list the type of processor and the amount of RAM in the computer. The amount of RAM in computers purchased today ranges from 1 GB to 128 GB. (A computer with more than 4 GB of RAM should have a 64-bit processor, which is discussed later in this chapter, and an operating system that can utilize the RAM.) In an advertisement, manufacturers typically specify the maximum amount of RAM a computer can hold, for example, 4 GB expandable to 32 GB. Read Ethics & Issues 4-4 for a related discussion.

FAQ 4-4

Can I add more RAM to my computer?

Check your computer documentation to see how much RAM you can add. RAM modules are relatively inexpensive and usually include easy-to-follow installation instructions. Be sure to purchase RAM that is compatible with your brand and model of computer.

For more information, visit the Computer Concepts CourseMate Web site at www.cengagebrain.com, navigate to the Chapter 4 FAQ resource for this book, and then click Upgrading RAM.

ETHICS & ISSUES 4-4

How Much Technology Should Be Provided to Students and Teachers?

Around the country and around the world, local and national governments have begun to supply schoolchildren with inexpensive notebook computers, including netbooks. Many school districts in the United States purchase notebook computers for each student and hope to recoup some of the cost by purchasing lower-cost CD-based textbooks. The United Nations endorses a plan known as *One Laptop per Child* to supply $100 notebook computers to developing countries, some of which already pledged to purchase millions of the devices for schoolchildren. The device, which recharges with a hand crank, includes Wi-Fi networking and a simple, intuitive user interface.

Supporters of these plans maintain that computer literacy and electronic communications are vital skills in today's world, and students should be introduced to computers as early in their school years as possible. Others claim that when students use notebook computers, instructors tend to lecture less, requiring students to engage in more research and independent study. Many people oppose plans to equip every student with a computer because they say that the technology detracts from traditional educational subjects, such as basic reading and math. Some believe that the best approach is to maintain dedicated computer lab rooms rather than allow computers in the classroom. Computers require maintenance, support, and instructional time to teach students how to use the devices. Young children may lack the responsibility to care for and use the computers properly.

Should schools supply computers to all students or teachers or both? Why or why not? What is the appropriate grade level at which to require computer literacy? Why? Should computers be relegated to a dedicated lab room? Why or why not?

RAM	2 GB or less	2 GB to 8 GB	8 GB and up
Use	Home and business users managing personal finances; using standard application software such as word processing; using educational or entertainment optical discs; communicating with others on the Web	Users requiring more advanced multimedia capabilities; running number-intensive accounting, financial, or spreadsheet programs; using voice recognition; working with videos, music, and digital imaging; creating Web sites; participating in video conferences; playing Internet games	Power users creating professional Web sites; running sophisticated CAD, 3-D design, or other graphics-intensive software

Figure 4-21 Determining how much RAM you need depends on the programs you intend to run on your computer.

Cache

Most of today's computers improve their processing times with **cache** (pronounced cash). Two types of cache are memory cache and disk cache. This chapter discusses memory cache. Chapter 7 discusses disk cache.

Memory cache helps speed the processes of the computer because it stores frequently used instructions and data. Most personal computers today have two types of memory cache: L1 cache and L2 cache. Some also have L3 cache.

- *L1 cache* is built directly in the processor chip. L1 cache usually has a very small capacity, ranging from 8 KB to 128 KB. The more common sizes for personal computers are 32 KB or 64 KB.
- *L2 cache* is slightly slower than L1 cache but has a much larger capacity, ranging from 64 KB to 16 MB. When discussing cache, most users are referring to L2 cache. Current processors include *advanced transfer cache (ATC)*, a type of L2 cache built directly on the processor chip. Processors that use ATC perform at much faster rates than those that do not use it.

  Personal computers today typically have from 512 KB to 12 MB of advanced transfer cache. Servers and workstations have from 12 MB to 16 MB of advanced transfer cache.
- *L3 cache* is a cache on the motherboard that is separate from the processor chip. L3 cache exists only on computers that use L2 advanced transfer cache. Personal computers often have up to 8 MB of L3 cache; servers and workstations have from 8 MB to 24 MB of L3 cache.

Cache speeds up processing time because it stores frequently used instructions and data. When the processor needs an instruction or data, it searches memory in this order: L1 cache, then L2 cache, then L3 cache (if it exists), then RAM — with a greater delay in processing for each level of memory it must search (Figure 4-22). If the instruction or data is not found in memory, then it must search a slower speed storage medium such as a hard disk or optical disc.

Windows users can increase the size of cache through *Windows ReadyBoost*, which can allocate available storage space on removable flash memory devices as additional cache. Examples of removable flash memory include USB flash drives, CompactFlash cards, and SD (Secure Digital) cards. Removable flash memory is discussed in more depth later in the book.

Windows ReadyBoost
For more information, visit the Computer Concepts CourseMate Web site at www.cengagebrain.com, navigate to the Chapter 4 Web Link resource for this book, and then click Windows ReadyBoost.

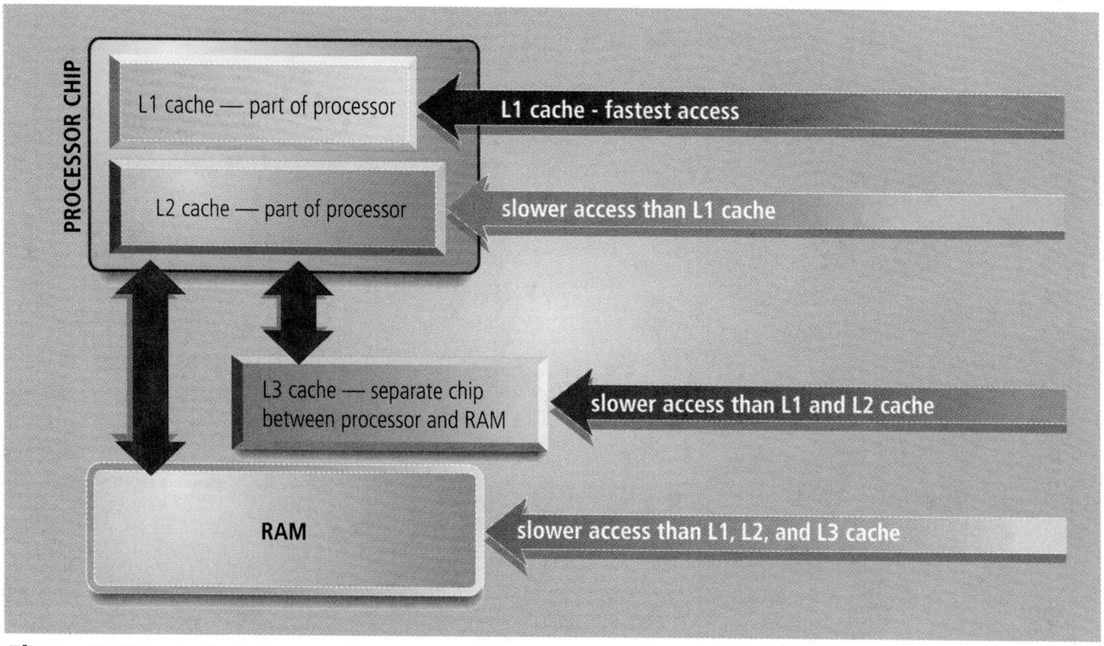

Figure 4-22 Cache helps speed processing times when the processor requests data, instructions, or information.

ROM

Read-only memory (**ROM** pronounced rahm) refers to memory chips storing permanent data and instructions. The data on most ROM chips cannot be modified — hence, the name read-only. ROM is nonvolatile, which means its contents are not lost when power is removed from the computer. In addition to computers, many devices contain ROM chips. For example, ROM chips in printers contain data for fonts.

Manufacturers of ROM chips often record data, instructions, or information on the chips when they manufacture the chips. These ROM chips, called **firmware**, contain permanently written data, instructions, or information.

A *PROM* (*programmable read-only memory*) *chip* is a blank ROM chip on which a programmer can write permanently. Programmers use *microcode* instructions to program a PROM chip. Once a programmer writes the microcode on the PROM chip, it functions like a regular ROM chip and cannot be erased or changed.

A variation of the PROM chip, called an *EEPROM* (electrically erasable programmable read-only memory) *chip*, allows a programmer to erase the microcode with an electric signal.

ROM

For more information, visit the Computer Concepts CourseMate Web site at www.cengagebrain.com, navigate to the Chapter 4 Web Link resource for this book, and then click ROM.

Flash Memory

Flash memory is a type of nonvolatile memory that can be erased electronically and rewritten, similar to EEPROM. Most computers use flash memory to hold their startup instructions because it allows the computer easily to update its contents. For example, when the computer changes from standard time to daylight savings time, the contents of a flash memory chip (and the real-time clock chip) change to reflect the new time.

Flash memory chips also store data and programs on many mobile computers and devices, such as smart phones, portable media players, PDAs, printers, digital cameras, automotive devices, digital voice recorders, and pagers. When you enter names and addresses in a smart phone or PDA, a flash memory chip stores the data. Some portable media players store music on flash memory chips (Figure 4-23); others store music on tiny hard disks or flash memory cards. Flash memory cards contain flash memory on a removable device instead of a chip.

How a Portable Media Player Might Store Music in Flash Memory

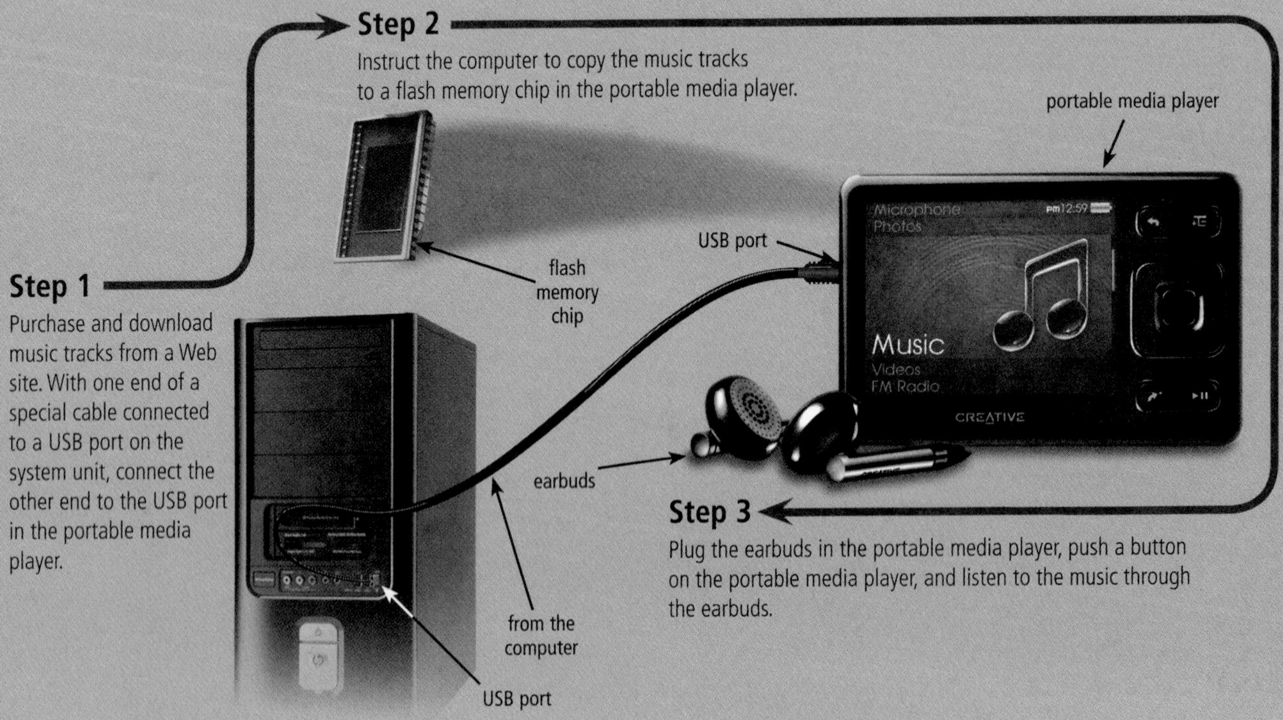
Step 1
Purchase and download music tracks from a Web site. With one end of a special cable connected to a USB port on the system unit, connect the other end to the USB port in the portable media player.
Step 2
Instruct the computer to copy the music tracks to a flash memory chip in the portable media player.
portable media player
USB port
flash memory chip
earbuds
from the computer
USB port
Step 3
Plug the earbuds in the portable media player, push a button on the portable media player, and listen to the music through the earbuds.
Music
Videos
FM Radio
CREATIVE

Figure 4-23 This figure shows how a portable media player might store music in flash memory.

FAQ 4-5

How much music can I store on a portable media player?

Portable media players that store music on flash memory chips can hold up to 16,000 songs. Portable media players with tiny hard disks have a much greater storage capacity — from 1,000 to more than 80,000 songs.

For more information, visit the Computer Concepts CourseMate Web site at www.cengagebrain.com, navigate to the Chapter 4 FAQ resource for this book, and then click Portable Media Players.

CMOS

Some RAM chips, flash memory chips, and other memory chips use **complementary metal-oxide semiconductor (CMOS** pronounced SEE-moss) technology because it provides high speeds and consumes little power. CMOS technology uses battery power to retain information even when the power to the computer is off. Battery-backed CMOS memory chips, for example, can keep the calendar, date, and time current even when the computer is off. The flash memory chips that store a computer's startup information often use CMOS technology.

Memory Access Times

Access time is the amount of time it takes the processor to read data, instructions, and information from memory. A computer's access time directly affects how fast the computer processes data. Accessing data in memory can be more than 200,000 times faster than accessing data on a hard disk because of the mechanical motion of the hard disk.

Today's manufacturers use a variety of terminology to state access times (Figure 4-24). Some use fractions of a second, which for memory occurs in nanoseconds. A **nanosecond** (abbreviated *ns*) is one billionth of a second. A nanosecond is extremely fast (Figure 4-25). In fact, electricity travels about one foot in a nanosecond.

Other manufacturers state access times in MHz; for example, 800 MHz DDR2 SDRAM. If a manufacturer states access time in megahertz, you can convert it to nanoseconds by dividing 1 billion ns by the megahertz number. For example, 800 MHz equals approximately 1.25 ns (1,000,000,000/800,000,000).

The access time (speed) of memory contributes to the overall performance of the computer. Standard SDRAM chips can have access times up to 133 MHz (about 7.5 ns), and access times of the DDR SDRAM chips reach 266 MHz, DDR2 chips reach 800 MHz, and DDR3 chips reach 1600 MHz. The higher the megahertz, the faster the access time; conversely, the lower the nanoseconds, the faster the access time. The faster RDRAM chips can have access times up to 1600 MHz (about 0.625 ns). ROM access times range from 25 to 250 ns.

While access times of memory greatly affect overall computer performance, manufacturers and retailers usually list a computer's memory in terms of its size, not its access time. Thus, an advertisement might describe a computer as having 2 GB of SDRAM upgradeable to 4 GB.

Access Time Terminology

Term	Abbreviation	Speed
Millisecond	ms	One-thousandth of a second
Microsecond	µs	One-millionth of a second
Nanosecond	ns	One-billionth of a second
Picosecond	ps	One-trillionth of a second

Figure 4-24 Access times are measured in fractions of a second. This table lists the terms used to define access times.

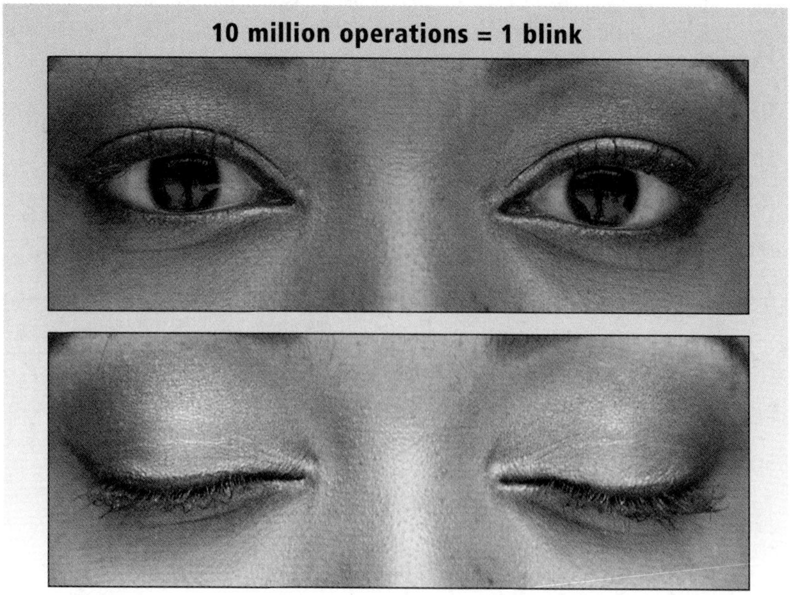

Figure 4-25 It takes about one-tenth of a second to blink your eye, which is the equivalent of 100 million nanoseconds. In the time it takes to blink your eye, a computer can perform some operations 10 million times.

✔ QUIZ YOURSELF 4-2

Instructions: Find the true statement below. Then, rewrite the remaining false statements so that they are true.

1. A computer's memory access time directly affects how fast the computer processes data.
2. A gigabyte (GB) equals approximately 1 trillion bytes.
3. Memory cache helps speed the processes of the computer because it stores seldom used instructions and data.
4. Most computers are analog, which means they recognize only two discrete states: on and off.
5. Most RAM retains its contents when the power is removed from the computer.
6. Read-only memory (ROM) refers to memory chips storing temporary data and instructions.

Quiz Yourself Online: To further check your knowledge of pages 221 through 229, visit the Computer Concepts CourseMate Web site at www.cengagebrain.com, navigate to the Chapter 4 Quiz Yourself resource for this book, and then click Objectives 5 – 7.

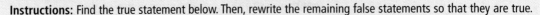

Expansion Slots and Adapter Cards

An **expansion slot** is a socket on the motherboard that can hold an adapter card. An **adapter card**, sometimes called an *expansion card*, is a circuit board that enhances functions of a component of the system unit and/or provides connections to peripherals. A **peripheral** is a device that connects to the system unit and is controlled by the processor in the computer. Examples of peripherals are modems, disk drives, printers, scanners, and keyboards.

Figure 4-26 lists currently used types of adapter cards. Sometimes, all functionality is built in the adapter card. With others, a cable connects the adapter card to a device, such as a digital video camera, outside the system unit. Some are a card that you insert in a slot on the computer. Figure 4-27 shows an adapter card being inserted in an expansion slot on a personal computer motherboard.

Some motherboards include all necessary capabilities and do not require adapter cards. Other motherboards may require adapter cards to provide capabilities such as sound and video. A **sound card** enhances the sound-generating capabilities of a personal computer by allowing sound to be input through a microphone and output through external speakers or headphones. A **video card**, also called a *graphics card*, converts computer output into a video signal that travels through a cable to the monitor, which displays an image on the screen.

Video Cards
For more information, visit the Computer Concepts CourseMate Web site at www.cengagebrain.com, navigate to the Chapter 4 Web Link resource for this book, and then click Video Cards.

Types of Adapter Cards

Adapter Card	Purpose
CableCARD	Allows viewing of digital cable television channels
Disk controller	Connects disk drives
FireWire	Connects to FireWire devices
HDTV tuner	Allows viewing of HDTV broadcasts on the monitor
MIDI	Connects musical instruments
Modem	Connects other computers through telephone lines, cable television lines, or other transmission media
Network	Connects other computers and peripherals
PC-to-TV converter	Connects a television
Sound	Connects speakers or a microphone
TV tuner	Allows viewing of television channels on the monitor
USB	Connects to USB devices
Video	Connects a monitor
Video capture	Connects an analog video camera or VCR

Figure 4-26 Currently used adapter cards and their functions.

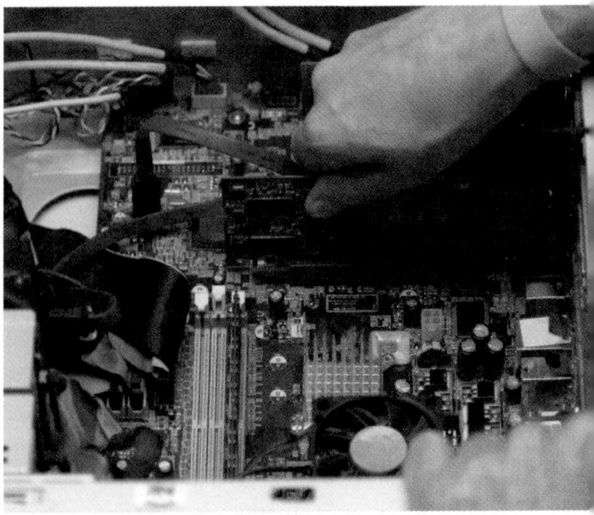

Figure 4-27 An adapter card being inserted in an expansion slot on the motherboard of a personal computer.

Today's computers support **Plug and Play**, which means the computer automatically can configure adapter cards and other peripherals as you install them. Having Plug and Play support means you can plug in a device, turn on the computer, and then immediately begin using the device.

Removable Flash Memory

Unlike adapter cards that require you to open the system unit and install the card on the motherboard, you can change a removable flash memory device without having to open the system unit or restart the computer. This feature, called *hot plugging*, allows you to insert and remove the removable flash memory and other devices while the computer is running. Removable flash memory includes memory cards, USB flash drives, and PC Cards/ExpressCard modules (Figure 4-28).

- A **memory card** is a removable flash memory device, usually no bigger than 1.5" in height or width, that you insert and remove from a slot in a personal computer, game console, mobile device, or card reader/writer. Many mobile and consumer devices, such as smart phones, digital cameras, and portable media players use memory cards. Some printers and computers have built-in card readers/writers or slots that read memory cards. In addition, you can purchase an external card reader/writer that attaches to any computer.
- A *USB flash drive* is a flash memory storage device that plugs in a USB port on a computer or mobile device. (A later section discusses USB ports.)
- Many desktop computers, traditional notebook computers, and Tablet PCs have a **PC Card slot** or an **ExpressCard slot**, which is a special type of expansion slot that holds a PC Card or an ExpressCard module, respectively. Most netbooks do not have a PC Card slot or ExpressCard slot. A **PC Card** is a thin, credit card-sized removable flash memory device that primarily is used today to enable traditional notebook computers and Tablet PCs to access the Internet wirelessly. ExpressCard modules, about one-half the size of PC Cards, are the next generation of PC Cards. An **ExpressCard module**, which can be used as a removable flash memory device, adds memory, communications, multimedia, and security capabilities to computers.

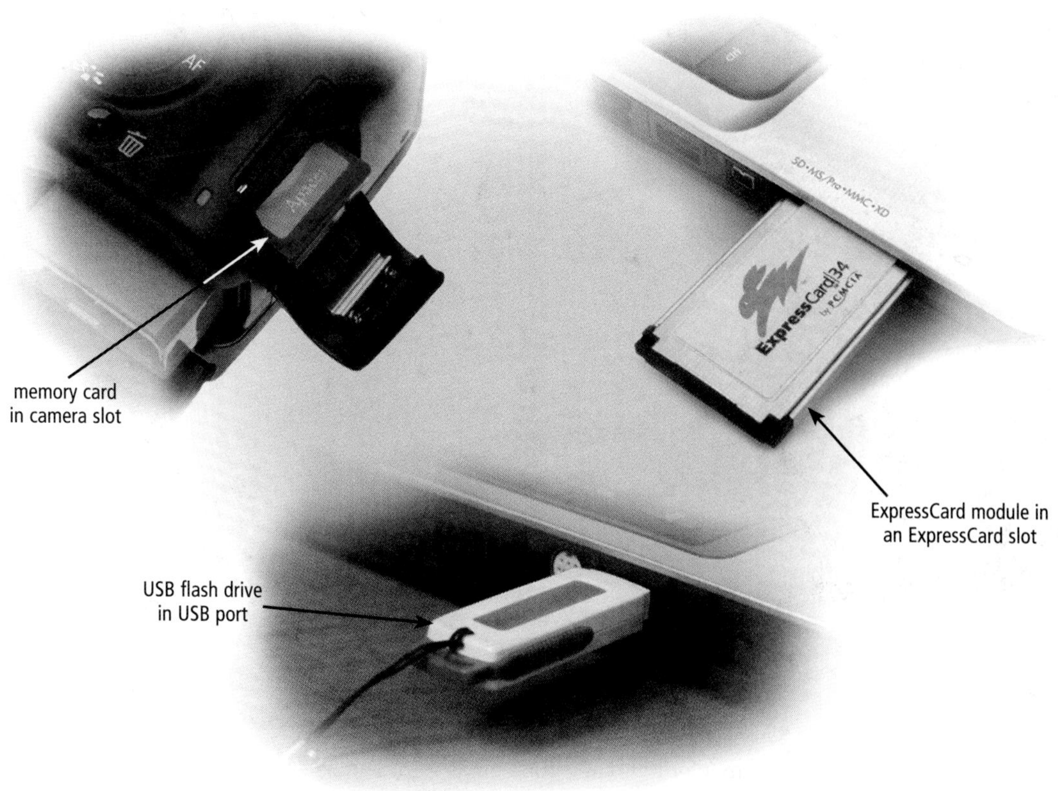

Figure 4-28 Examples of removable flash memory in use.

Ports and Connectors

A **port** is the point at which a peripheral attaches to or communicates with a system unit so that the peripheral can send data to or receive information from the computer. An external device, such as a keyboard, monitor, printer, mouse, and microphone, often attaches by a cable to a port on the system unit. Instead of port, the term **jack** sometimes is used to identify audio and video ports. The front and back of a system unit on a desktop personal computer contain many ports (Figure 4-29). On notebook computers, including netbooks and Tablet PCs, the ports are on the back, front, and/or sides (Figure 4-30).

Digital Audio Port

For more information, visit the Computer Concepts CourseMate Web site at www.cengagebrain.com, navigate to the Chapter 4 Web Link resource for this book, and then click Digital Audio Port.

A **connector** joins a cable to a port. A connector at one end of a cable attaches to a port on the system unit, and a connector at the other end of the cable attaches to a port on the peripheral. Most connectors and ports are available in one of two genders: male or female. Male connectors and ports have one or more exposed pins, like the end of an electrical cord you plug in the wall. Female connectors and ports have matching holes to accept the pins on a male connector or port, like an electrical wall outlet.

Sometimes, you cannot attach a new peripheral to the computer because the port on the system unit is the same gender as the connector on the cable. In this case, purchasing a gender changer solves this problem. A *gender changer* is a device that enables you to join a port and a connector that are both female or both male.

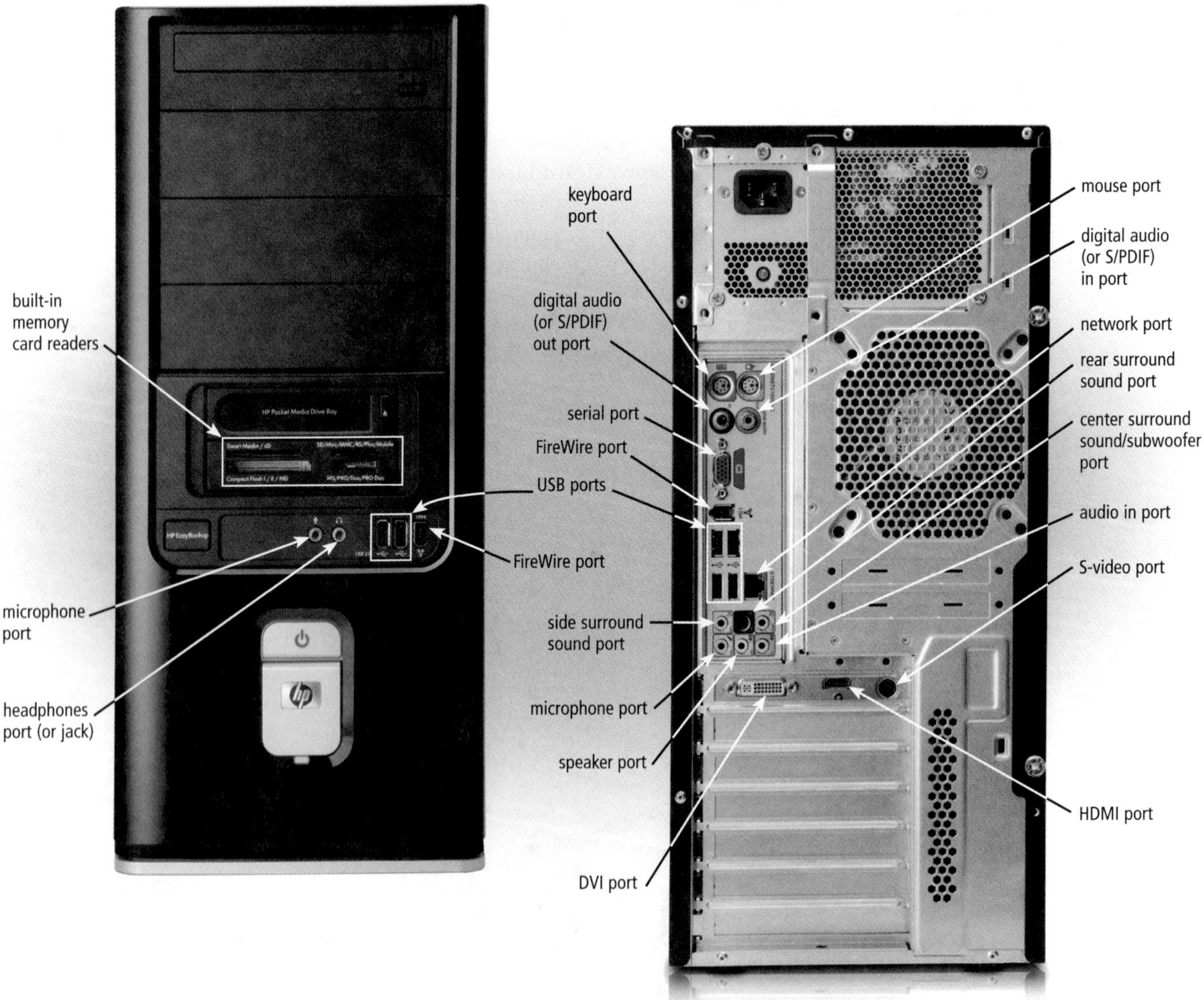

Figure 4-29 A system unit on a desktop personal computer has many ports on its front and back.

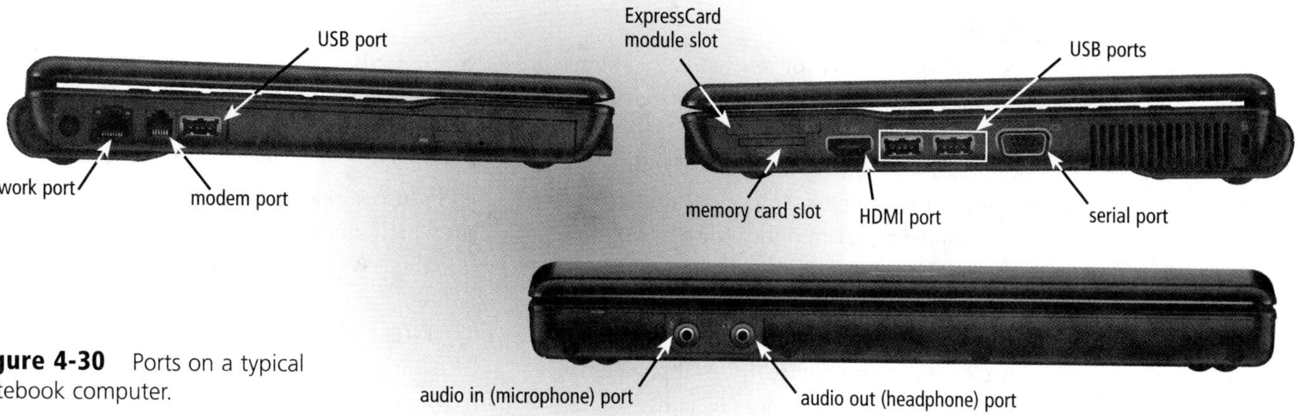

Figure 4-30 Ports on a typical notebook computer.

Manufacturers often identify cables by their connector types to assist you with purchasing a cable to connect a computer to a peripheral port. Figure 4-31 shows the different types of ports you may find on a system unit. Notice that many are color-coded to help you match the connector to the correct port. Some system units include these ports when you buy the computer. You add other ports by inserting adapter cards on the motherboard. Certain adapter cards have ports that allow you to attach a peripheral to the adapter card.

The next section discusses the more widely used ports.

Port Types

Type	Picture	Type	Picture	Type	Picture
Audio in		HDMI port		Serial	
Cable TV		Headphones		Side surround sound	
Center surround sound/subwoofer		Keyboard		S/PDIF in	
Composite video in		Microphone		S/PDIF out	
Digital Video Interface (DVI)		Monitor		Speaker	
eSATA port		Mouse		S-video	
FireWire		Network		Telephone line in	
FM reception		Rear surround sound		USB	

Figure 4-31 Examples of different types of ports on a system unit.

USB Ports

A **USB port**, short for *universal serial bus port*, can connect up to 127 different peripherals together with a single connector. Devices that connect to a USB port include the following: mouse, printer, digital camera, scanner, speakers, portable media player, optical disc drive, smart phone, PDA, game console, and removable hard disk. Personal computers typically have six to eight USB ports on the front and/or back of the system unit (Figure 4-29 on page 232). USB ports on mobile devices usually are smaller than those on personal computers. Figure 4-32 shows a variety of USB ports and connectors.

USB 2.0, also called *Hi-Speed USB*, is a more advanced and faster USB, with speeds 40 times higher than that of its predecessor. *USB 3.0* is approximately 10 times faster than USB 2.0. Both USB 2.0 and USB 3.0 are *backward compatible*, which means they support older USB devices as well as USB 2.0 or USB 3.0 devices. Keep in mind, though, that older USB devices do not run any faster in a newer USB port.

To attach multiple peripherals using a single USB port, you can use a USB hub. A **USB hub** is a device that plugs in a USB port on the system unit and contains multiple USB ports in which you plug cables from USB devices. USB hubs are self-powered or bus-powered. A self-powered USB hub draws power from an electrical outlet, whereas a bus-powered USB hub draws power from the USB bus in the computer. (The USB bus is discussed later in the chapter.) Some devices will work only with a self-powered hub.

USB Ports

For more information, visit the Computer Concepts CourseMate Web site at www.cengagebrain.com, navigate to the Chapter 4 Web Link resource for this book, and then click USB Ports.

USB Connectors and Ports

	Connector	Port	Where Used
Type A			Desktop computers, traditional notebook computers, netbooks, and Tablet PCs
Type B			Peripherals (printers, scanners, external hard disks, etc.)
Mini-B			Mobile devices (cameras, phones, handheld game consoles)

Figure 4-32 A variety of USB ports and connectors are available.

Some USB hubs are wireless. That is, a receiver plugs into a USB port on the computer and the USB hub communicates wirelessly with the receiver.

USB also supports hot plugging and Plug and Play, which means you can attach peripherals while the computer is running.

FireWire Ports

Previously called an *IEEE 1394 port*, a **FireWire port** is similar to a USB port in that it can connect multiple types of devices that require faster data transmission speeds, such as digital video cameras, digital VCRs, color printers, scanners, digital cameras, and DVD drives, to a single connector. A FireWire port allows you to connect up to 63 devices together. The three latest versions, FireWire 800, FireWire 1600, and FireWire 3200, have speeds faster than the original FireWire 400.

You can use a FireWire hub to attach multiple devices to a single FireWire port. A **FireWire hub** is a device that plugs in a FireWire port on the system unit and contains multiple FireWire ports in which you plug cables from FireWire devices. The FireWire port supports Plug and Play.

Other Ports

Some ports not included in typical computers but sometimes used are Bluetooth, SCSI, eSATA, IrDA, serial, and MIDI. For a computer to have these ports, you often must customize the computer purchase order.

Bluetooth Port **Bluetooth** technology uses radio waves to transmit data between two devices. Bluetooth devices have to be within about 33 feet of each other. Many computers, peripherals, smart phones, PDAs, cars, and other consumer electronics are Bluetooth-enabled, which means they contain a small chip that allows them to communicate with other Bluetooth-enabled computers and devices. Bluetooth headsets allow smart phone users to connect their telephone to a headset wirelessly.

If you have a computer that is not Bluetooth enabled, you can purchase a *Bluetooth wireless port adapter* that will convert an existing USB port into a Bluetooth port (Figure 4-33). Also available are Bluetooth PC Cards and ExpressCard modules for traditional notebook computers and Tablet PCs, and Bluetooth cards for smart phones and PDAs.

Figure 4-33 A Bluetooth wireless port adapter, such as the one shown here, converts a USB port into a Bluetooth port.

FAQ 4-6

Can I simultaneously use multiple wireless devices in my house?

Not always. Because some wireless devices may communicate using the same frequency range, they may interfere with each other. For example, a Bluetooth device temporarily may stop working while your cordless phone is in use, or your carbon monoxide detector may sound when your cell phone rings.

For more information, visit the Computer Concepts CourseMate Web site at www.cengagebrain.com, navigate to the Chapter 4 FAQ resource for this book, and then click Wireless Devices.

SCSI Port A special high-speed parallel port, called a **SCSI port**, allows you to attach SCSI (pronounced skuzzy) peripherals such as disk drives and printers. *SAS (serial-attached SCSI)* is a newer type of SCSI that transmits at much faster speeds than parallel SCSI. Depending on the type of *SCSI*, which stands for small computer system interface, you can daisy chain up to either 7 or 15 devices together. Some computers include a SCSI port. Others have a slot that supports a SCSI card.

eSATA Port An **eSATA port**, or *external SATA port*, allows you to connect an external SATA (Serial Advanced Technology Attachment) hard disk to a computer. SATA hard disks are popular because of their fast data transmission speeds. eSATA connections provide up to six times faster data transmission speeds than external hard disks attached to a computer's USB or FireWire port.

IrDA Port Some devices can transmit data via infrared light waves. For these wireless devices to transmit signals to a computer, both the computer and the device must have an **IrDA port** (Figure 4-34). These ports conform to standards developed by the *IrDA* (Infrared Data Association).

To ensure nothing obstructs the path of the infrared light wave, you must align the IrDA port on the device with the IrDA port on the computer, similarly to the way you operate a television remote control. Devices that use IrDA ports include a smart phone, PDA, keyboard, mouse, and printer. Several of these devices use a high-speed IrDA port, sometimes called a *fast infrared port*.

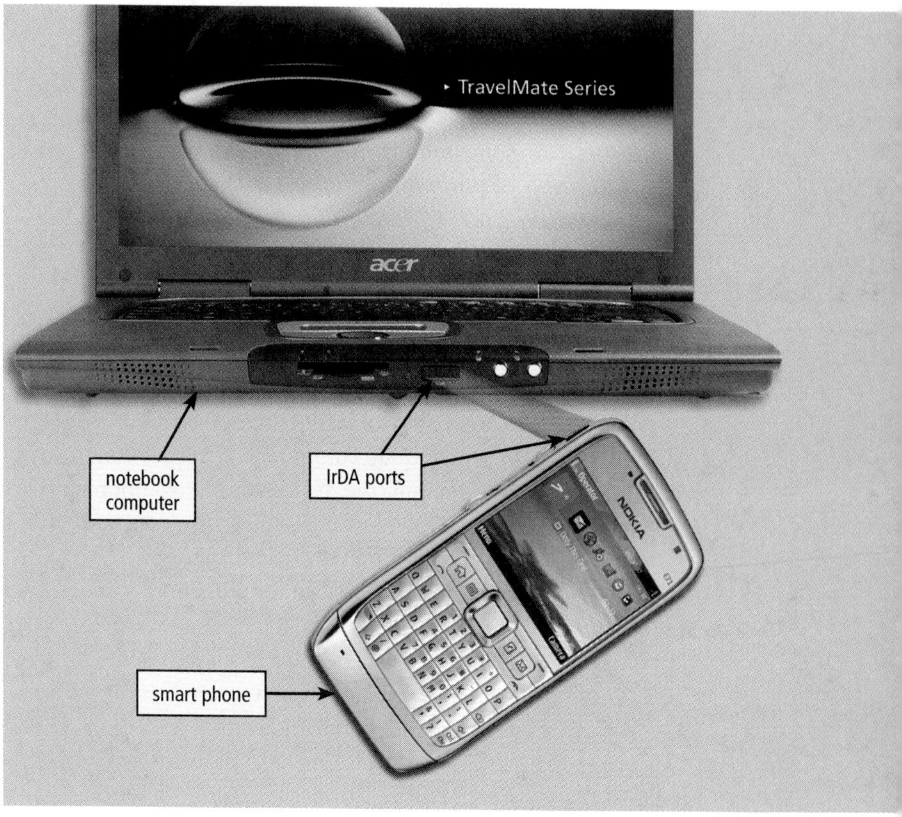

Figure 4-34 Many devices communicate wirelessly with desktop or notebook computers through IrDA ports.

Serial Ports A **serial port** is a type of interface that connects a device to the system unit by transmitting data one bit at a time. Some modems that connect the system unit to a telephone line use a serial port because the telephone line expects the data in a specific frequency.

MIDI Port A special type of serial port that connects the system unit to a musical instrument, such as an electronic keyboard, is called a **MIDI port**. Short for *Musical Instrument Digital Interface*, MIDI (pronounced MID-dee) is the electronic music industry's standard that defines how devices, such as sound cards and synthesizers, represent sounds electronically. A *synthesizer*, which can be a peripheral or a chip, creates sound from digital instructions.

A system unit with a MIDI port has the capability of recording sounds that have been created by a synthesizer and then processing the sounds (the data) to create new sounds. Nearly every sound card supports the MIDI standard, so that you can play and manipulate on one computer sounds that originally were created on another computer.

Port Replicators and Docking Stations

Instead of connecting peripherals directly to ports on a mobile computer, some mobile users prefer the flexibility of port replicators and docking stations. A *port replicator* is an external device that provides connections to peripherals through ports built into the device. The mobile user accesses peripherals by connecting the port replicator to a USB port or a special port on the mobile computer. Port replicators sometimes disable ports on the mobile computer to prevent conflicts among the devices on the computer and port replicator.

A docking station is similar to a port replicator, but it has more functionality. A *docking station*, which is an external device that attaches to a mobile computer or device, contains a power connection and provides connections to peripherals; it usually also includes slots for memory cards, optical disc drives, and other devices (Figure 4-35). With the mobile computer or device in the docking station, users can work with a full-sized keyboard, a mouse, and other desktop peripherals from their traditional notebook computer, netbook, or Tablet PC. Read Looking Ahead 4-1 for a look at the next generation of notebook computers.

Docking Station

For more information, visit the Computer Concepts CourseMate Web site at www.cengagebrain.com, navigate to the Chapter 4 Web Link resource for this book, and then click Docking Station.

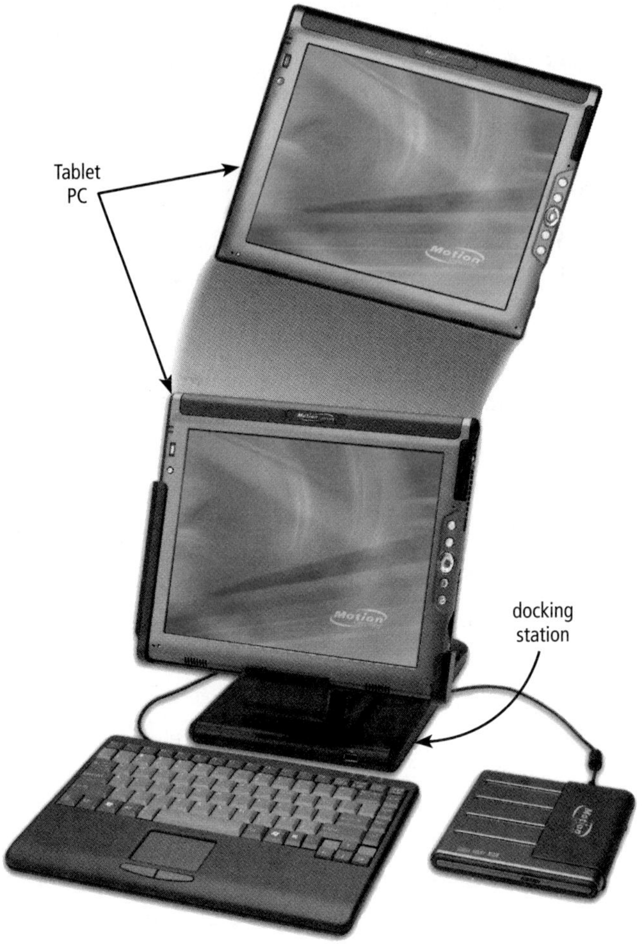

Figure 4-35 To use a slate Tablet PC while working at a desk, insert the Tablet PC in a docking station. Devices such as a keyboard and an optical disc drive can be plugged in the docking station.

LOOKING AHEAD 4-1

Bendable Notebook Computers Will Slip in Your Pocket

Today's notebook computers are light and compact, but they will be enormous compared to what is being planned for the retail marketplace in the next 10 years. Top designers at Lenovo and Intel are designing flexible machines weighing less than one pound that are thin enough to fold and place in a pocket. Battery life will be nearly one week, and the 256-core processors will make current computers with quad-core processors seem like they are running at a snail's pace.

Notebook computer users will speak into a microphone, touch the screen, or type on a virtual keyboard that does not have actual keys but can give feedback that a letter or number has been selected. Thin screens will roll out to any size needed and will be viewed easily outdoors. Users with sight impairments can coat their screens with a synthetic material that will create 3-D shapes for such tactile uses as reading Braille letters and blueprints.

For more information, visit the Computer Concepts CourseMate Web site at www.cengagebrain.com, navigate to the Chapter 4 Looking Ahead resource for this book, and then click Future Notebooks.

Buses

As explained earlier in this chapter, a computer processes and stores data as a series of electronic bits. These bits transfer internally within the circuitry of the computer along electrical channels. Each channel, called a **bus**, allows the various devices both inside and attached to the system unit to communicate with each other. Just as vehicles travel on a highway to move from one destination to another, bits travel on a bus (Figure 4-36).

Buses are used to transfer bits from input devices to memory, from memory to the processor, from the processor to memory, and from memory to output or storage devices. Buses consist of two parts: a data bus and an address bus. The *data bus* is used to transfer actual data and the *address bus* is used to transfer information about where the data should reside in memory.

The size of a bus, called the *bus width*, determines the number of bits that the computer can transmit at one time. For example, a 32-bit bus can transmit 32 bits (4 bytes) at a time. On a 64-bit bus, bits transmit from one location to another 64 bits (8 bytes) at a time. The larger the number of bits handled by the bus, the faster the computer transfers data. Using the highway analogy again, assume that one lane on a highway can carry one bit. A 32-bit bus is like a 32-lane highway. A 64-bit bus is like a 64-lane highway.

If a number in memory occupies 8 bytes, or 64 bits, the computer must transmit it in two separate steps when using a 32-bit bus: once for the first 32 bits and once for the second 32 bits. Using a 64-bit bus, the computer can transmit the number in a single step, transferring all 64 bits at once. The wider the bus, the fewer number of transfer steps required and the faster the transfer of data. Most personal computers today use a 64-bit bus.

In conjunction with the bus width, many computer professionals refer to a computer's word size. **Word size** is the number of bits the processor can interpret and execute at a given time. That is, a 64-bit processor can manipulate 64 bits at a time. Computers with a larger word size can process more data in the same amount of time than computers with a smaller word size. In most computers, the word size is the same as the bus width.

Every bus also has a clock speed. Just like the processor, manufacturers state the clock speed for a bus in hertz. Recall that one megahertz (MHz) is equal to one million ticks per second. Today's processors usually have a bus clock speed of 400, 533, 667, 800, 1066, 1333, or 1600 MHz. The higher the bus clock speed, the faster the transmission of data, which results in programs running faster.

A computer has these basic types of buses: a system bus, possibly a backside bus, and an expansion bus. A *system bus*, also called the *front side bus (FSB)*, is part of the motherboard and connects the processor to main memory. A *backside bus (BSB)* connects the processor to cache. An *expansion bus* allows the processor to communicate with peripherals. When computer professionals use the term bus by itself, they usually are referring to the system bus.

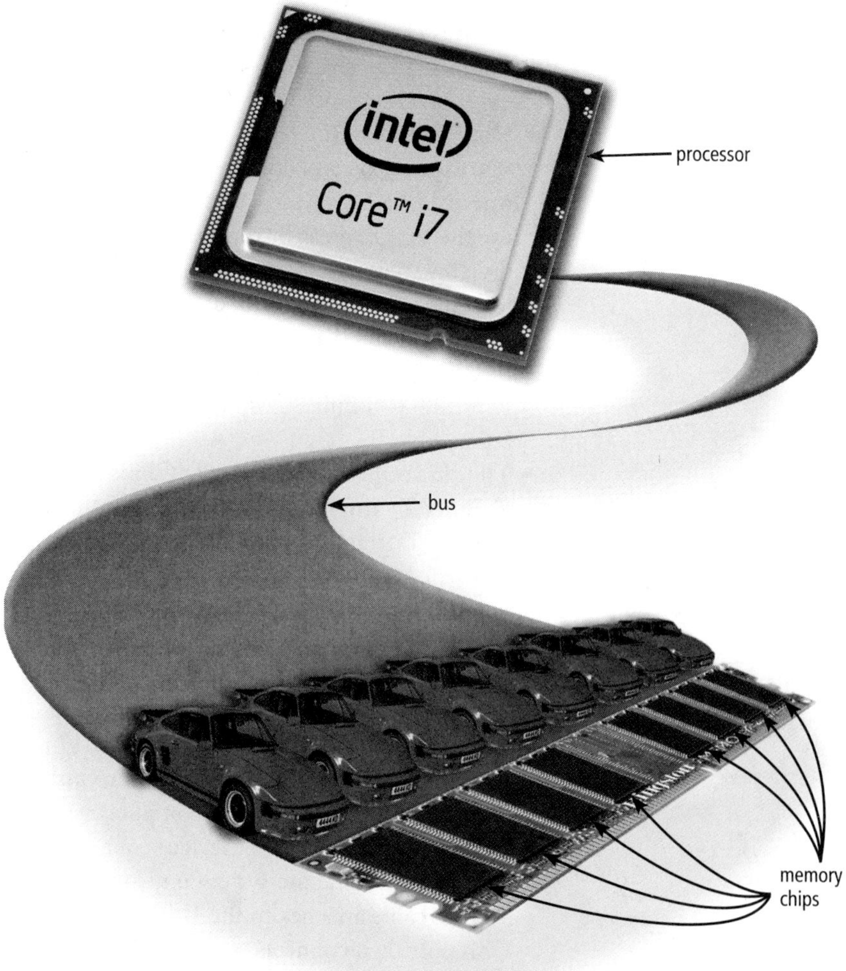

Figure 4-36 Just as vehicles travel on a highway, bits travel on a bus. Buses are used to transfer bits from input devices to memory, from memory to the processor, from the processor to memory, and from memory to output or storage devices.

Expansion Bus

Some peripherals outside the system unit connect to a port on an adapter card, which is inserted in an expansion slot on the motherboard. This expansion slot connects to the expansion bus, which allows the processor to communicate with the peripheral attached to the adapter card. Data transmitted to memory or the processor travels from the expansion slot via the expansion bus and the system bus.

The types of expansion buses on a motherboard determine the types of cards you can add to the computer. Thus, you should understand expansion buses commonly found in today's personal computers: PCI bus, PCI Express bus, AGP bus, USB, FireWire bus, and PC Card bus.

- The *PCI bus* (Peripheral Component Interconnect bus) is a high-speed expansion bus that connects higher speed devices. Types of cards you can insert in a PCI bus expansion slot include video cards, sound cards, SCSI cards, and high-speed network cards.
- The *PCI Express (PCIe) bus* is an expansion bus that expands on and doubles the speed of the original PCI bus. Nearly all video cards today use the PCI Express bus, as well as many hard disks and network cards. The ExpressCard technology used in traditional notebook computers and Tablet PCs also works with the PCI Express bus. Experts predict the PCI Express bus eventually will replace the PCI bus completely.
- The *Accelerated Graphics Port (AGP)* is a bus designed by Intel to improve the speed with which 3-D graphics and video transmit. With an AGP video card in an AGP bus slot, the AGP bus provides a faster, dedicated interface between the video card and memory. Newer processors support AGP technology.
- The USB (universal serial bus) and *FireWire bus* are buses that eliminate the need to install cards in expansion slots. In a computer with a USB, for example, USB devices connect to each other outside the system unit, and then a single cable attaches to the USB port. The USB port then connects to the USB, which connects to the PCI bus on the motherboard. The FireWire bus works in a similar fashion. With these buses, expansion slots are available for devices not compatible with USB or FireWire.
- The expansion bus for a PC Card is the *PC Card bus*. With a PC Card inserted in a PC Card slot, data travels on the PC Card bus to the PCI bus.

FireWire

For more information, visit the Computer Concepts CourseMate Web site at www.cengagebrain.com, navigate to the Chapter 4 Web Link resource for this book, and then click FireWire.

Bays

After you purchase a desktop or notebook computer, you may want to install an additional storage device, such as a disk drive, in the system unit. A **bay** is an opening inside the system unit in which you can install additional equipment. A bay is different from a slot on the motherboard, which is used for the installation of adapter cards. A **drive bay** is a rectangular opening that typically holds disk drives. Other bays house card readers and widely used ports such as USB, FireWire, and audio ports.

An *external bay* allows a user to access openings in the bay from outside the system unit (Figure 4-37). Optical disc drives are examples of devices installed in external bays. An *internal bay* is concealed entirely within the system unit. Hard disk drives are installed in internal bays.

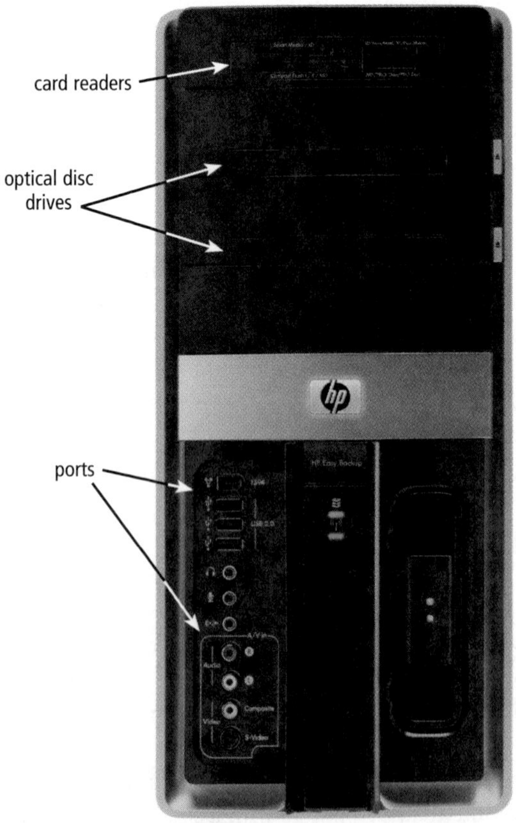

Figure 4-37 External bays usually are located beside or on top of one another.

Power Supply

Many personal computers plug in standard wall outlets, which supply an alternating current (AC) of 115 to 120 volts. This type of power is unsuitable for use with a computer, which requires a direct current (DC) ranging from 5 to more than 15 volts. The **power supply** is the component of the system unit that converts the wall outlet AC power into DC power. Different motherboards and computers require different wattages on the power supply. Notebook computers, including netbooks and Tablet PCs, can run using either batteries or a power supply. If a power supply is not providing the necessary power, the computer will not function properly.

Built into the power supply is a fan that keeps the power supply cool. Some have variable speed fans that change speed or stop running, depending on temperature in the system unit. Many newer computers have additional fans near certain components in the system unit such as the processor, hard disk, and ports. Some users install more fans to help dissipate heat generated by the components of the system unit. Mobile users may place their notebook computer on a cooling pad to help disperse the computer's heat.

Some external peripherals such as a cable modem, speakers, or a printer have an **AC adapter**, which is an external power supply. One end of the AC adapter plugs in the wall outlet and the other end attaches to the peripheral. The AC adapter converts the AC power into DC power that the peripheral requires.

FAQ 4-7

How many fans are in a system unit?

Most system units have at least three fans: one in the power supply, one in the case, and one on the processor heat sink. In addition, you also may find a fan on a video card or other adapter card. While some computers contain fans that are designed to be quiet or operate in a quiet mode, others allow you to turn off noisy fans until they are needed. You also can purchase utility programs that slow or stop the fan until the temperature reaches a certain level.

For more information, visit the Computer Concepts CourseMate Web site at www.cengagebrain.com, navigate to the Chapter 4 FAQ resource for this book, and then click Computer Fans.

Putting It All Together

Many components of the system unit influence the speed and power of a computer, including the type of processor and the amount of RAM. The table in Figure 4-38 lists the suggested minimum processor and RAM requirements based on the needs of various types of computer users.

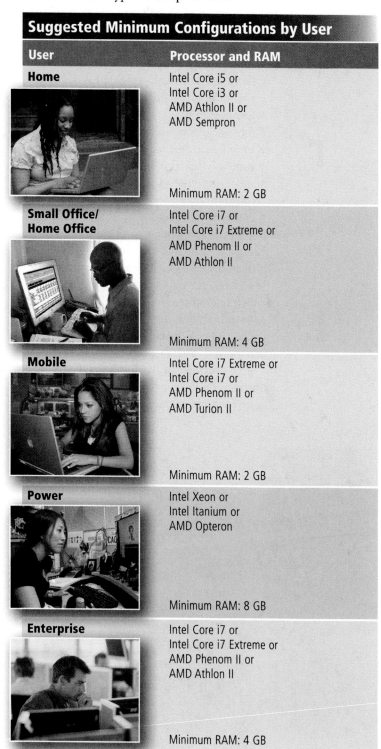

Suggested Minimum Configurations by User

User	Processor and RAM
Home 	Intel Core i5 or Intel Core i3 or AMD Athlon II or AMD Sempron Minimum RAM: 2 GB
Small Office/ Home Office 	Intel Core i7 or Intel Core i7 Extreme or AMD Phenom II or AMD Athlon II Minimum RAM: 4 GB
Mobile 	Intel Core i7 Extreme or Intel Core i7 or AMD Phenom II or AMD Turion II Minimum RAM: 2 GB
Power 	Intel Xeon or Intel Itanium or AMD Opteron Minimum RAM: 8 GB
Enterprise 	Intel Core i7 or Intel Core i7 Extreme or AMD Phenom II or AMD Athlon II Minimum RAM: 4 GB

Figure 4-38 Suggested processor and RAM configurations by user.

Keeping Your Computer or Mobile Device Clean

Over time, the system unit collects dust — even in a clean environment. Built up dust can block airflow in a computer or mobile device, which can cause it to overheat, corrode, or even stop working. By cleaning your computer or mobile device once or twice a year, you can help extend its life. This preventive maintenance task requires a few basic products (Figure 4-39):

- can of compressed air — removes dust and lint from difficult-to-reach areas; removes sticky liquid spilled on keyboards
- lint-free antistatic wipes and swabs
- screen cleaning solution or 50/50 mix of rubbing alcohol and water (do not use ammonia-based solutions)
- small computer vacuum (or small attachments on your house vacuum)
- antistatic wristband — to avoid damaging internal components with static electricity
- small screwdriver (may be required to open the case or remove adapter cards)

Before cleaning the exterior of a computer or mobile device, turn it off, and if necessary, unplug it from the electrical outlet, remove its battery, and disconnect all cables from the ports. Use compressed air to blow away dust from any openings on the computer or device case, such as drives, slots, ports, and fan vents. Then, use an antistatic wipe to clean the exterior of the case and a cleaning solution on a soft cloth to clean the screen.

If you do not feel comfortable cleaning the inside of a desktop or notebook computer case, you can have a local professional or computer company clean it for you (read Ethics & Issues 4-5 for a related discussion). Or, if you are familiar with electronics, you can clean it yourself. While working inside the case, be sure to wear an antistatic wristband. Use the antistatic wipes to clean inside the walls of the case. Vacuum as much dust as possible from the interior of the case, including the wires, chips, adapter cards, and fan blades. Release short blasts of compressed air in areas the vacuum cannot reach. If the motherboard and adapter cards still look dirty, gently clean them with lint-free wipes or swabs lightly dampened with alcohol. When finished, write down the date you cleaned the computer so that you have a record for your next cleaning.

Figure 4-39 With a few products, this computer user keeps his computer clean.

ETHICS & ISSUES 4-5

Should Computer Repair Technicians Be Required to Have a Private Investigator License?

Recently, a state government passed legislation that requires computer repair technicians to obtain a private investigator license if they review or analyze data on computers that they repair. One reason the law was written is that business managers and parents often take computers to technicians to analyze the computer usage habits of employees and children. In this sense, the technician is performing an investigation. To obtain a private investigator license, one must obtain a criminal justice degree or serve as an apprentice for a private investigator. The process takes up to three years and is expensive. Violating the law, however, may result in jail time and a large fine. Many smaller computer repair companies claim that, if enforced, the law certainly will put them out of business. Larger companies sometimes have employees with private investigator licenses. Critics of the law claim that the law is overly broad. For example, parents should have the right to take a computer to a technician to see what their children have been doing on the computer.

Should computer repair technicians be required to have a private investigator license? Why or why not? Should the government consider a different type of certification for computer repair technicians who must review or analyze customer data in the course of their job? If so, what should be required for the certification?

FAQ 4-8

Is it safe to open my computer case?

Yes, as long as you are careful and wear an antistatic wristband. Before opening the case, though, check with the computer manufacturer to be sure you will not void a warranty if you clean the computer or install additional components. Also, do not handle any internal components unless you intend to repair or replace them, as unnecessary handling may decrease the life of the component(s).

For more information, visit the Computer Concepts CourseMate Web site at www.cengagebrain.com, navigate to the Chapter 4 FAQ resource for this book, and then click Computer Cases.

QUIZ YOURSELF 4-3

Instructions: Find the true statement below. Then, rewrite the remaining false statements so that they are true.

1. A bus is the point at which a peripheral attaches to or communicates with a system unit so that the peripheral can send data to or receive information from the computer.
2. An AC adapter is a socket on the motherboard that can hold an adapter card.
3. Built into the power supply is a heater that keeps components of the system unit warm.
4. eSATA ports can connect up to 127 different peripherals together with a single connector.
5. The higher the bus clock speed, the slower the transmission of data.
6. When cleaning the inside of the system unit, wear an antistatic wristband to avoid damaging internal components with static electricity.

Quiz Yourself Online: To further check your knowledge of pages 230 through 240, visit the Computer Concepts CourseMate Web site at www.cengagebrain.com, navigate to the Chapter 4 Quiz Yourself resource for this book, and then click Objectives 8 – 12.

Chapter Summary

Chapter 4 presented the components of the system unit; described how memory stores data, instructions, and information; and discussed the sequence of operations that occur when a computer executes an instruction. The chapter included a comparison of various personal computer processors on the market today. It also discussed how to clean the exterior and interior of a system unit.

Computer Usage @ Work

Sports

While watching your local football team play an out-of-state game on television, you watch various player and game statistics appear on the screen, alerting you to how many yards the offense must travel before making a first down. The camera then focuses on the large, colorful, high-resolution scoreboard at the stadium. While sports such as football have been around for many decades, the integration of computers has added significantly to the viewing experience.

While watching a baseball game, you notice that the scoreboard shows the number of balls and strikes for the player at bat, as well as the speed of each pitch. Behind home plate, an electronic radar gun calculates and records the speed of each pitch. This recorded data, along with the umpire's call (ball or strike) and the player's performance at bat (hit, home run, strike out, etc.) are entered in a computer, which updates the player's batting average automatically. During this entire time, the video display on the stadium's scoreboard plays audio and video to entertain the fans. The computer storing the player and game statistics, audio, and video communicates with the scoreboard and video display using either a wired or wireless connection. (If the computer communicates using wires, the scoreboard and video display connect directly to a port on a system unit. Recall from the chapter that a port is the point at which a peripheral attaches to or communicates with a system unit.) At the same time, these computers send updated scores and statistics to Web pages and mobile devices.

Computers not only are used to keep track of athlete statistics and communicate with scoreboards, but also in NASCAR to help measure a vehicle's performance before a race. Sensors installed on a car can measure throttle inputs, airflow over the body, the distance between the car's frame and the track, and more. The NASCAR teams then can modify the car so that it achieves maximum performance during a race.

Overall, computers add enjoyment to various sporting events for many individuals. While waiting for a pitcher to throw the next ball or for a football team to start its next play, keep in mind that the integration of computers entertains you with interesting statistics and replays between the action.

For more information, visit the Computer Concepts CourseMate Web site at www.cengagebrain.com, navigate to the Chapter 4 Computer Usage @ Work resource for this book, and then click Sports.

High-Tech Talk

Random Access Memory (RAM): The Genius of Memory

Inside your computer, RAM takes the form of separate microchip modules that plug in slots on the computer's motherboard. These slots connect through a line (bus) or set of electrical paths to the computer's processor. Before you turn on a computer, its RAM is a blank slate. As you start and use your computer, the operating system files, programs, and any data currently being used by the processor are written to and stored in RAM so that the processor can access them quickly.

How is this data written to and stored in RAM? In the most common form of RAM, dynamic random access memory (DRAM), *transistors* (in this case, acting as switches) and a *capacitor* (as a data storage element) create a *memory cell*, which represents a single bit of data.

Memory cells are etched onto a silicon wafer in a series of columns (bitlines) and rows (wordlines), known as an *array*. The intersection of a column and row constitutes the *address* of the memory cell (Figure 4-40). Each memory cell has a unique address that can be found by counting across columns and then counting down by row. The address of a character consists of a series of memory cell addresses put together.

To write data to RAM, the processor sends the memory controller the address of a memory cell in which to store data. The *memory controller* organizes the request and sends the column and row address in an electrical charge along the appropriate address lines, which are very thin electrical lines etched into the RAM chip. This causes the transistors along those address lines to close.

These transistors act as a switch to control the flow of electrical current in an either closed or open circuit. While the transistors are closed, the software sends bursts of electricity along selected data lines. When the electrical charge traveling down the data line reaches an address line where a transistor is closed, the charge flows through the closed transistor and charges the capacitor.

A capacitor works as electronic storage that holds an electrical charge. Each charged capacitor along the address line represents a 1 bit. An uncharged capacitor represents a 0 bit. The combination of 1s and 0s from eight data lines forms a single byte of data.

The capacitors used in dynamic RAM, however, lose their electrical charge. The processor or memory controller continuously has to recharge all of the capacitors holding a charge (a 1 bit) before the capacitor discharges. During this *refresh operation*, which happens automatically thousands of times per second, the memory controller reads memory and then immediately rewrites it. This refresh operation is what gives dynamic RAM its name. Dynamic RAM has to be refreshed continually, or it loses the charges that represent bits of data. A specialized circuit called a counter tracks the refresh sequence to ensure that all of the rows are refreshed.

The process of reading data from RAM uses a similar, but reverse, series of steps. When the processor gets the next instruction it is to perform, the instruction may contain the address of a memory cell from which to read data. This address is sent to the memory controller. To locate the memory cell, the memory controller sends the column and row address in an electrical charge down the appropriate address lines.

This electrical charge causes the transistors along the address line to close. At every point along the address line where a capacitor is holding a charge, the capacitor discharges through the circuit created by the closed transistors, sending electrical charges along the data lines.

A specialized circuit called a *sense amplifier* determines and amplifies the level of charge in the capacitor. A capacitor charge over a certain voltage level represents the binary value 1; a capacitor charge below that level represents a 0. The sensed and amplified value is sent back down the address line to the processor.

As long as a computer is running, data continuously is being written to and read from RAM. As soon as you shut down a computer, RAM loses its data. The next time you turn on a computer, operating system files and other data are again loaded into RAM and the read/write process starts all over.

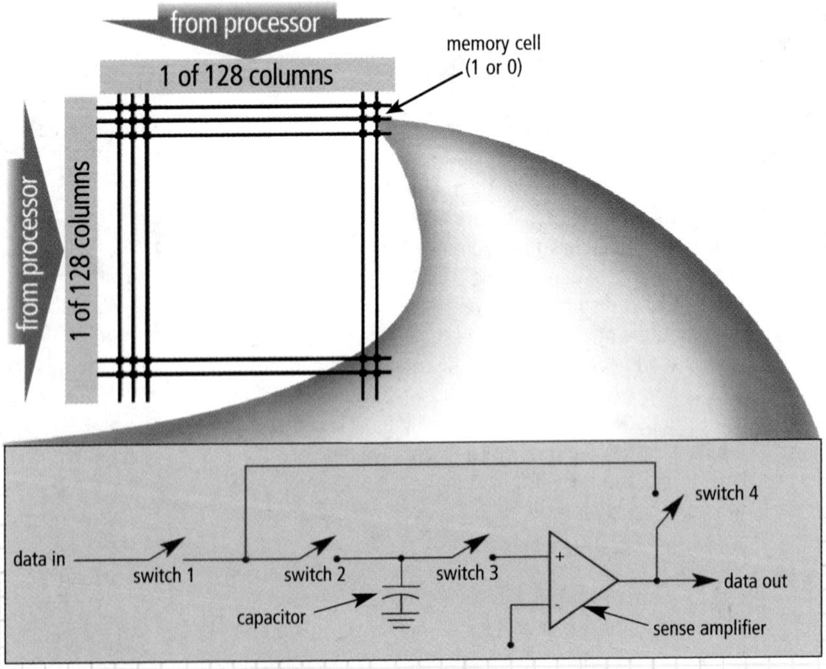

Figure 4-40 An illustration of one type of DRAM. When writing data, switches 1 and 2 in the circuit are closed and switches 3 and 4 are open. When reading data, switches 2, 3, and 4 in the circuit are closed and switch 1 is open. Most DRAM chips actually have arrays of memory cells (upper-left corner of figure) that are 16 rows deep.

For more information, visit the Computer Concepts CourseMate Web site at www.cengagebrain.com, navigate to the Chapter 4 High-Tech Talk resource for this book, and then click Memory.

Companies on the Cutting Edge

NVIDIA Visual Computing Technologies Leader

Serious gamers relish software with ultra-realistic graphics, while film producers need high-definition graphics. Both of these creative types of people likely have used a system unit equipped with an *NVIDIA* processor.

NVIDIA's technological specialty is developing high-performance processors that help generate graphics for personal computers, game consoles, and mobile devices. In the film and entertainment worlds, Sony Pictures, Sportvision, and Weather Central rely on NVIDIA's processor chips to produce imagery and animation. In medicine, the company's processors helped researchers to design a device that stabilizes the heart during bypass surgery and also to develop virtual reality simulations that help burn victims undergoing therapy.

Recently, NVIDIA's CUDA technology was used to enhance the historic *Apollo 11* video of Neil Armstrong walking on the moon.

INTEL World's Leading Chip Manufacturer

Turbochargers have a place in high-performance sports cars, but they have a new home residing in *Intel's* processors. Some of the company's chips have a turbo mode, which turns cores on and off depending upon when programs demand more processing power, all while conserving energy.

The company's chips have set the standard for personal computers since 1980 when IBM chose the Intel 8080 chip for its new product. Intel now is the world's largest chip manufacturer, with its processors found in approximately 80 percent of the world's personal computers.

Recently, Intel completed its acquisition of Wind River Systems, Inc., a leading software vendor in embedded devices. This acquisition will allow Intel to reach customers outside the traditional PC and server market.

For more information, visit the Computer Concepts CourseMate Web site at www.cengagebrain.com and then navigate to the Chapter 4 Companies on the Cutting Edge resource for this book.

Technology Trailblazers

JACK KILBY Integrated Circuit Inventor

Jack Kilby is credited with being one of the more influential people in the world. He was awarded more than 60 patents during his lifetime, but none changed society as much as the one for his integrated circuit, or microchip, that made microprocessors possible. His Nobel Prize in physics, awarded in 2005, recognized his part in the invention of the integrated circuit.

Kilby started his work with miniature electrical components at Centralab, where he developed transistors for hearing aids. He then took a research position with Texas Instruments and developed a working model of the first integrated circuit, which was patented in 1959. Kilby applied this invention to various industrial, military, and commercial applications, including the first pocket calculator. Kilby died in 2005, but his legacy lives on.

GORDON MOORE Intel Cofounder

Moore's Law is a prediction made in 1965 by one of Intel's founders, *Gordon Moore*, that the number of transistors and resistors placed on a computer chip would double every year. This doubling would have a proportional increase in computing power and decrease in cost. This forecast proved amazingly accurate for 10 years, and then Moore revised the estimate to doubling every two years. A recent breakthrough in chip technology using *photolithography*, which uses light to imprint circuits on a chip, could perpetuate his estimate.

Moore cofounded Intel in 1968 with the conviction that silicon chips would change the world. His lifelong interest in technology is continuing with his contributions to the Large Binocular Telescope, the world's most technologically advanced optical telescope, in southeastern Arizona.

For more information, visit the Computer Concepts CourseMate Web site at www.cengagebrain.com and then navigate to the Chapter 4 Technology Trailblazers resource for this book.

Chapter Review

The Chapter Review reinforces the main concepts presented in this chapter.

To listen to the audio version of this Chapter Review, visit the Computer Concepts CourseMate Web site at www.cengagebrain.com and then navigate to the Chapter 4 Chapter Review resource for this book.

1. How Are Various Styles of System Units on Desktop Computers, Notebook Computers, and Mobile Devices Different? The **system unit** is a case that contains electronic components of the computer used to process data. On desktop personal computers, most storage devices also are part of the system unit. On most notebook computers, including netbooks, the keyboard and pointing device often occupy the area on top of the system unit, and the display attaches to the system unit by hinges. The location of the system unit on a Tablet PC varies, depending on the design of the Tablet PC. On mobile computers and devices, the display often is built into the system unit. With game consoles, the input and output devices, such as controllers and a television, reside outside the system unit. On handheld game consoles, portable media players, and digital cameras by contrast, the packaging around the system unit houses the input devices and display.

2. What Are Chips, Adapter Cards, and Other Components of the Motherboard? The **motherboard**, sometimes called a *system board*, is the main circuit board of the system unit. The motherboard contains many electronic components including a processor chip, memory chips, expansion slots, and adapter cards. A computer **chip** is a small piece of semiconducting material, usually silicon, on which integrated circuits are etched. Expansion slots hold adapter cards that provide connections and functions not built into the motherboard.

3. What Are the Control Unit and Arithmetic Logic Unit Components of a Processor, and What Are the Four Steps in a Machine Cycle? The **processor**, also called the **central processing unit** (**CPU**), interprets and carries out the basic instructions that operate a computer. Processors contain a **control unit** that directs and coordinates most of the operations in the computer and an **arithmetic logic unit** (*ALU*) that performs arithmetic, comparison, and other operations. The *machine cycle* is a set of four basic operations — *fetching, decoding, executing,* and *storing* — that the processor repeats for every instruction.

4. What Are the Characteristics of Various Personal Computer Processors, and How Are Processors Cooled? A **multi-core processor** is a single chip with two or more separate processor cores. Two common multi-core processors are dual-core and quad-core. A **dual-core processor** is a chip that contains two separate processor cores. A **quad-core processor** is a chip with four or more separate processor cores. Intel produces the **Core** processor family for high-performance personal computers, the **Pentium** and **Celeron** processor families for basic personal computers, and the **Xeon** and **Itanium** processor families for workstations and low-end servers. AMD manufactures *Intel-compatible processors*, which have an internal design similar to Intel processors. Some devices have a *system-on-a-chip* processor that integrates the functions of a processor, memory, and a video card on a single chip. Heat sinks/pipes and liquid cooling technologies are used to dissipate processor heat. A *heat sink* is a small ceramic or metal component that absorbs and disperses heat. A smaller device called a *heat pipe* cools processors in notebook computers, including netbooks and Tablet PCs. Some computers use *liquid cooling technology*, which uses a continuous flow of fluid(s) to transfer heated fluid away from the processor.

Visit the Computer Concepts CourseMate Web site at www.cengagebrain.com, navigate to the Chapter 4 Quiz Yourself resource for this book, and then click Objectives 1 – 4.

5. What Is a Bit, and How Does a Series of Bits Represent Data? Most computers are **digital** and recognize only two discrete states: off and on. To represent these states, computers use the **binary system**, which is a number system that has just two unique digits — 0 (for off) and 1 (for on) — called bits. A **bit** (short for *binary digit*), is the smallest unit of data a computer can process. Grouped together as a unit, 8 bits form a **byte**, which provides enough different combinations of 0s and 1s to represent 256 individual characters. The combinations are defined by patterns, called coding schemes, such as *ASCII* and *Unicode*.

6. How Do Program Instructions Transfer in and out of Memory? When a program starts, the program's instructions and data are transferred to memory from storage devices. The program and operating system instructions are in memory, and the program's window appears on the screen. When you quit the program, the program instructions are removed from memory, and the program no longer is displayed on the screen.

Chapter Review

7. What Are the Various Types of Memory? **Memory** usually consists of one or more chips on the motherboard or some other circuit board in the computer. The system unit contains volatile and nonvolatile memory. *Volatile memory* loses its contents when the computer's power is turned off. *Nonvolatile memory* does not lose its contents when the computer's power is turned off. RAM is the most common type of volatile memory. ROM, flash memory, and CMOS are examples of nonvolatile memory. **RAM** (*random access memory*), also called *main memory*, consists of memory chips that can be read from and written to by the processor and other devices. **ROM (read-only memory)** refers to memory chips storing permanent data and instructions that usually cannot be modified. **Flash memory** can be erased electronically and rewritten. **CMOS (complementary metal-oxide semiconductor)** technology uses battery power to retain information even when the power to the computer is turned off.

Visit the Computer Concepts CourseMate Web site at www.cengagebrain.com, navigate to the Chapter 4 Quiz Yourself resource for this book, and then click Objectives 5 – 7.

8. What Are the Purpose and Types of Expansion Slots and Adapter Cards, and What Are the Different Slots for Flash Memory Devices? An **expansion slot** is a socket on the motherboard that can hold an adapter card. An **adapter card**, sometimes called an *expansion card*, is a circuit board that enhances functions of a component of the system unit and/or provides a connection to a **peripheral**. A **sound card** enhances the sound-generating capabilities of a personal computer. A **video card**, also called a *graphics card*, converts computer output into a video signal that displays an image on the screen. A **memory card** is a removable flash memory device that you insert and remove from a slot in a personal computer, a game console, a mobile device, or card reader/writer. A *USB flash drive* plugs in a USB port on a computer or mobile device. A **PC Card slot** or an **ExpressCard slot** holds a **PC Card** or **ExpressCard module**.

9. What Is the Difference between a Port and a Connector, and What Are the Differences among the Various Types of Ports? A **port** is the point at which a peripheral attaches to or communicates with a system unit so that it can send data to or receive information from the computer. A **connector** joins a cable to a port. A **USB port**, short for *universal serial bus port*, can connect up to 127 different peripherals together with a single connector. A **FireWire port** can connect multiple types of devices that require faster data transmission speeds. **Bluetooth** technology uses radio waves to transfer data between two devices. A **SCSI port** attaches the system unit to SCSI peripherals, such as disk drives and printers. An **eSATA port** connects an external SATA hard disk to a computer. An **IrDA port** allows wireless devices to transmit signals to a computer via infrared light waves. A **serial port** transmits data one bit at a time. A **MIDI port** connects the system unit to a musical instrument.

10. What Are the Types of Buses in a Computer? A **bus** is an electrical channel along which bits transfer within the circuitry of a computer, allowing devices both inside and attached to the system unit to communicate. The *data bus* transfers actual data, and the *address bus* transfers information about where the data should reside in memory. The size of a bus, called the *bus width*, determines the number of bits that the computer can transmit at one time. The larger the bus width, the faster the computer transfers data. A computer has a *system bus*, or *front side bus* (*FSB*); possibly a *backside bus* (*BSB*); and an *expansion bus*.

11. What Is the Purpose of a Power Supply, and How Does It Keep Cool? A **power supply** is the component of the system unit that converts wall outlet AC power into DC power for the computer to use. A fan built directly into the power supply keeps it cool. Some have variable speed fans, and many newer computers have additional fans near components in the system unit. Notebook computers, including netbooks and Tablet PCs, can be placed on a cooling pad to help disperse heat.

12. How Do You Clean a System Unit on a Personal Computer or Mobile Device? Before cleaning the exterior of a computer or mobile device, turn it off, and if necessary, unplug it from the electrical outlet, remove the battery, and disconnect all cables from the ports. Use compressed air to blow away dirt from any openings on the case, such as drives, slots, ports, and fan vents. Use an antistatic wipe to clean the exterior of the case and a cleaning solution on a soft cloth to clean the screen. While working inside the case, be sure to wear an antistatic wristband. If you do not feel comfortable cleaning the inside of the case, you can have a professional or computer company clean it for you. Use a vacuum and compressed air to remove dust inside the case.

Visit the Computer Concepts CourseMate Web site at www.cengagebrain.com, navigate to the Chapter 4 Quiz Yourself resource for this book, and then click Objectives 8 – 12.

Key Terms

You should know the Primary Terms and be familiar with the Secondary Terms. The list below helps focus your study.

To see an example of and a definition for each term, and to access current and additional information from the Web, visit the Computer Concepts CourseMate Web site at www.cengagebrain.com and then navigate to the Chapter 4 Key Terms resource for this book.

Primary Terms

(shown in bold-black characters in the chapter)

AC adapter (239)
access time (229)
adapter card (230)
analog (221)
arithmetic logic unit (214)
bay (238)
binary system (221)
bit (221)
Bluetooth (234)
bus (237)
byte (221)
cache (227)
Celeron (216)
central processing unit (CPU) (213)
chip (212)
clock speed (216)
complementary metal-oxide semiconductor (CMOS) (229)
connector (232)
control unit (214)
Core (216)
digital (221)
drive bay (238)
dual-core processor (213)
eSATA port (235)
expansion slot (230)
ExpressCard module (231)
ExpressCard slot (231)
FireWire hub (234)
FireWire port (234)
firmware (228)
flash memory (228)
gigabyte (GB) (223)
gigahertz (GHz) (216)
IrDA port (235)
Itanium (216)
jack (232)
kilobyte (KB or K) (223)
megabyte (MB) (223)
memory (223)
memory cache (227)
memory card (231)
memory module (225)
memory slots (225)
MIDI port (235)
motherboard (212)
multi-core processor (213)
nanosecond (229)
PC Card (231)
PC Card slot (231)
Pentium (216)
peripheral (230)
Plug and Play (231)
port (232)
power supply (239)
processor (213)
quad-core processor (213)
RAM (224)
read-only memory (ROM) (228)
SCSI port (235)
serial port (235)
sound card (230)
system clock (216)
system unit (210)
terabyte (TB) (223)
USB hub (234)
USB port (234)
video card (230)
word size (237)
Xeon (216)

motherboard (212)

Secondary Terms

(shown in italic characters in the chapter)

Accelerated Graphics Port (AGP) (238)
address (223)
address bus (237)
advanced transfer cache (ATC) (227)
ALU (214)
arithmetic operations (214)
ASCII (221)
backward compatible (234)
backside bus (BSB) (237)
binary digit (221)
Bluetooth wireless port adapter (234)
bus width (237)
Centrino 2 (217)
chassis (210)
clock cycle (216)
comparison operations (214)
data bus (237)
DDR SDRAM (225)
DDR2 (225)
DDR3 (225)
decoding (215)
DIMM (dual inline memory module) (225)
docking station (236)
dynamic RAM (DRAM) (225)
EEPROM chip (228)
executing (215)
expansion bus (237)
expansion card (230)
external bay (238)
external SATA port (235)
fast infrared port (235)
fetching (215)
FireWire bus (238)
form factor (210)
front side bus (FSB) (237)
gender changer (232)
graphics card (230)
heat pipe (219)
heat sink (219)
hertz (216)
Hi-Speed USB (234)
hot plugging (231)
IEEE 1394 port (234)
integrated circuit (212)
Intel-compatible processors (216)
internal bay (238)
IrDA (235)
L1 cache (227)
L2 cache (227)
L3 cache (227)
liquid cooling technology (219)
machine cycle (215)
magnetoresistive RAM (MRAM) (225)
main memory (224)
massively parallel processing (220)
microcode (228)
microprocessor (213)
multi-threaded program (217)
Musical Instrument Digital Interface (235)
nonvolatile memory (223)
ns (229)
parallel processing (220)
PC Card bus (238)
PCI bus (238)
PCI Express (PCIe) bus (238)
pipelining (215)
port replicator (236)
PROM (programmable read-only memory) chip (228)
random access memory (224)
RDRAM (225)
registers (216)
RIMM (Rambus inline memory module) (225)
SAS (serial-attached SCSI) (235)
SCSI (235)
SDRAM (225)
SIMM (single inline memory module) (225)
static RAM (SRAM) (225)
stored program concept (223)
storing (215)
superscalar (216)
synthesizer (236)
system board (212)
system bus (237)
system-on-a-chip (218)
transistor (212)
Unicode (221)
universal serial bus port (234)
USB 2.0 (234)
USB 3.0 (234)
USB flash drive (231)
volatile memory (223)
vPro technology (217)
Windows ReadyBoost (227)

Checkpoint

The Checkpoint exercises test your knowledge of the chapter concepts. The page number containing the answer appears in parentheses after each exercise. The Beyond the Book exercises will help broaden your understanding of the concepts presented in this chapter.

To complete the Checkpoint exercises interactively, visit the Computer Concepts CourseMate Web site at www.cengagebrain.com and then navigate to the Chapter 4 Checkpoint resource for this book.

True/False Mark T for True and F for False.

_____ 1. The system unit is a case that contains electronic components of the computer used to process data. (210)

_____ 2. The processor holds data waiting to be processed and instructions waiting to be executed. (213)

_____ 3. The speed of the system clock is just one factor that influences a computer's performance. (216)

_____ 4. Replacing a motherboard is a fairly complicated process, whereas replacing a processor is much simpler. (218)

_____ 5. A byte is the smallest unit of data the computer can process. (221)

_____ 6. When the computer's power is turned off, volatile memory loses its contents. (223)

_____ 7. Current processors include advanced transfer cache (ATC), a type of L2 cache built directly on the processor chip. (227)

_____ 8. Read-only memory refers to memory chips storing permanent data and instructions. (228)

_____ 9. Hi-Speed USB is a more advanced and faster USB, with speeds 100 times higher than that of its predecessor. (234)

_____ 10. USB 3.0 is more than 10 times faster than USB 2.0. (234)

_____ 11. Both USB 2.0 and USB 3.0 are backward compatible, which means they do not support older USB devices. (234)

_____ 12. SAS (serial-attached SCSI) is a newer type of SCSI that transmits more reliably, but at slower speeds, than parallel SCSI. (235)

Multiple Choice Select the best answer.

1. The processor also is called the _____. (213)
   a. motherboard
   b. central processing unit (CPU)
   c. adapter card
   d. chip

2. The _____ is the component of the processor that directs and coordinates most of the operations in the computer. (214)
   a. control unit
   b. arithmetic logic unit
   c. register
   d. machine cycle

3. A processor contains small, high-speed storage locations, called _____, that temporarily hold data and instructions. (216)
   a. flash drives
   b. registers
   c. jacks
   d. heat sinks

4. Supercomputers use _____ for applications such as artificial intelligence and weather forecasting. (220)
   a. system-on-a-chip technology
   b. massively parallel processing
   c. SCSI
   d. Accelerated Graphics Ports

5. ROM chips, called _____, contain permanently written data, instructions, or information. (228)
   a. memory cache
   b. registers
   c. firmware
   d. transistors

6. A(n) _____ is an external device that provides connections to peripherals through ports built into the device. (236)
   a. expansion bus
   b. port replicator
   c. docking station
   d. synthesizer

7. A(n) _____, which is an external device that attaches to a mobile computer or device, contains a power connection and provides connections to peripherals; it usually also includes slots for memory cards, optical disc drives, and other devices. (236)
   a. docking station
   b. port replicator
   c. peripheral
   d. expansion bus

8. A(n) _____ is part of the motherboard and connects the processor to main memory. (237)
   a. expansion bus
   b. system clock
   c. memory module
   d. front side bus

STUDENT ASSIGNMENTS

Checkpoint

Matching
Match the terms with their definitions.

____ 1. motherboard (212)
____ 2. processor (213)
____ 3. vPro technology (217)
____ 4. heat sink (219)
____ 5. memory (223)
____ 6. Windows ReadyBoost (227)
____ 7. flash memory (228)
____ 8. access time (229)
____ 9. USB hub (234)
____ 10. backside bus (237)

a. interprets and carries out the basic instructions that operate a computer
b. small ceramic or metal component with fins on its surface that absorbs and disperses heat produced by electrical components such as a processor
c. amount of time it takes the processor to read data, instructions, and information from memory
d. electronic components that store instructions, data, and results of processed data
e. can allocate available space on removable flash memory devices as additional cache
f. provides the capability to track computer hardware and software, diagnose and resolve computer problems, and secure computers from outside threats
g. nonvolatile memory that can be erased electronically and rewritten
h. main circuit board of the system unit
i. device that plugs in a USB port on the system unit and contains multiple USB ports in which you plug cables from USB devices
j. connects the processor to cache

Short Answer
Write a brief answer to each of the following questions.

1. What are two types of designs of Tablet PCs? __________ What are the differences in the designs of the two types of Tablet PCs? __________
2. What is the motherboard? __________ What is a computer chip? __________
3. What are the four basic operations in a machine cycle? __________ What are some functions of registers? __________
4. What types of devices might be Bluetooth enabled? __________ Describe three ways in which a computer can become Bluetooth enabled. __________
5. What is compressed air used for with regards to caring for your computer? __________ How should you prepare for cleaning your computer? __________

Beyond the Book
Follow the book element instructions below; present your findings (brief report, presentation, discussion, or other means).

1. Ethics & Issues — Select an Ethics & Issues in this chapter (214, 217, 219, 226, 240), find a recent newspaper/magazine article that supports one point of view presented, and then evaluate the article.
2. Computer Usage @ Work — Use the Web or a recent newspaper/magazine to locate three additional unique usages of computer technology in sports (241). What makes the use of these technologies unique to sports?
3. Companies on the Cutting Edge and Technology Trailblazers — Use the Web or a recent business newspaper/magazine to locate an interesting fact about NVIDIA, Intel, Jack Kilby, or Gordon Moore that was not presented in the chapter (243).
4. High-Tech Talk — Locate a recent newspaper/magazine article that discusses topics related to Random Access Memory (RAM) (242). Would you recommend the article you found? Why or why not?
5. FAQs and Web Links — Use the Web or a recent newspaper/magazine to locate three additional facts about an FAQ (212, 216, 219, 226, 229, 235, 239, 241) and Web Link (214, 217, 220, 225, 227, 228, 230, 232, 234, 236, 238) that were not presented in the chapter.
6. Looking Ahead — Use the Web or a recent newspaper/magazine to discover additional uses of the technology presented in Bendable Notebook Computers Will Slip in Your Pocket (236).
7. Innovative Computing — Use the Web or a recent newspaper/magazine to locate two additional interesting facts about Chip Implants Identify Animals (213) and Robots Assist with Everyday Tasks (214).
8. Making Use of the Web — Visit three of the Online Social Networks and Media Sharing sites (128) and outline the information on each Web site and the possible uses for each Web site.

Learn It Online

The Learn It Online exercises are interactive Web exercises designed to reinforce and expand your understanding of the chapter concepts. The descriptions below briefly summarize each exercise.

To complete the Learn It Online exercises, visit the Computer Concepts CourseMate Web site at www.cengagebrain.com, navigate to the Chapter 4 resources for this book, click the link for the exercise you want to complete, and then read the instructions.

1 At the Movies — The Leopard with a Time Machine

Watch a movie to learn about Apple Computer's "Time Machine" software, which allows users to travel through time by scrolling through different windows that represent days, to help them find the files that they need and then answer questions about the movie.

2 Video and Audio: You Review It — Bluetooth Technology

Search for, choose, and write a review of a video, podcast, or vodcast that discusses Bluetooth technology.

3 Student Edition Labs — Understanding the Motherboard and Binary Numbers

Enhance your understanding and knowledge about the motherboard and binary numbers by completing the Understanding the Motherboard and Binary Numbers Labs.

4 Practice Test

Take a multiple choice test that checks your knowledge of the chapter concepts and review the resulting study guide.

5 Who Wants To Be a Computer Genius^2?

Play the Shelly Cashman Series version of this popular game by answering questions to find out if you are a computer genius. Panic buttons are available to provide assistance during game play.

6 Wheel of Terms

Identify important key terms presented in this chapter by playing the Shelly Cashman Series version of this popular game.

7 You're Hired!

Embark on the path to a career in computers by answering questions and solving puzzles related to concepts discussed in this chapter.

8 Crossword Puzzle Challenge

Complete an interactive crossword puzzle to reinforce concepts presented in this chapter.

9 Windows Exercises

Step through the Windows 7 exercises to learn about installing new hardware, setting the system clock, using Calculator to perform number system conversion, and power management.

10 Exploring Computer Careers

Read about a career as a computer engineer, search for related employment advertisements, and then answer related questions.

11 Web Apps — Google Docs

Learn how to create, edit, and share documents, presentations, and spreadsheets using Google Docs.

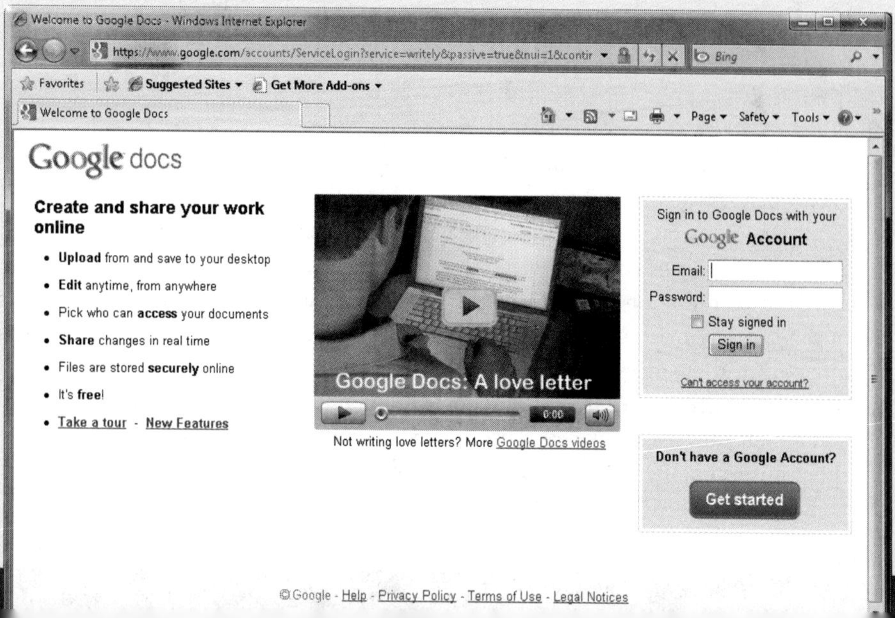

Problem Solving @ Home

The Problem Solving @ Home exercises extend your knowledge of the chapter concepts by seeking solutions to practical computer problems that you may encounter at home or school. The Collaboration exercise should be completed with a team.

In the real world, practical problems often can be solved in multiple ways. Provide one solution to each of the following problems using available resources, such as articles on the Web or in print, blogs, podcasts, videos, television, user guides, other individuals, and electronics and computer stores. You may need to use multiple resources to obtain an answer. Present your solutions in the form requested by your instructor (brief report, presentation, discussion, or other means).

1. **Malfunctioning Speakers** While working on a homework assignment, you decide to listen to one of your favorite music CDs through your computer speakers. The media player program on your computer automatically starts when you insert the CD. Although it looks like the CD is playing, no sound is coming from your speakers. What might be causing this? What is the first step that you will take to correct this problem?
2. **Optical Disc Drive Stuck** While using your computer, you attempt to open the optical disc drive to insert an installation disc for a program you wish to install. The drive, however, does not open when you press the eject button. The drive opened a few minutes prior, when you removed a music CD. What steps will you take to open the drive before calling technical support?

3. **Removing Germs** While recovering from an illness, you realize that by using your computer during your illness, you probably left some germs behind on the keyboard and mouse. How will you clean these devices so that your family members will not become sick?
4. **Computer Will Not Boot** To remedy your computer's slow performance, you installed additional memory. After the installation, you close your computer case, connect the power and all peripheral devices, and turn on the computer. Although your computer turns on, it beeps in rapid succession, it is not responding, and the operating system does not start. What might be causing this?
5. **Numerous Memory Types** You have decided to purchase additional memory for your computer in order to better support the latest version of the Windows operating system. At the local computer store, you notice that not only are different types of memory for sale, but different sizes are available. What will you do to ensure that you get the proper memory for your computer?
6. **Missing Songs** During the past several months, you downloaded more than 1,000 songs to your portable media player. Tonight, when you turn on your portable media player, it is not able to locate any of your songs and an error message displays on the screen. What might be causing this?
7. **Uncommon Memory Card Size** Recently, you purchased a smart phone that is capable of storing pictures, music, and videos on a memory card. The memory card, which you purchased separately, works with your smart phone, but you cannot find a slot on your computer's card reader that will accept the card. Furthermore, you have been unable to find a card reader that can accept this particular type of memory card. Given your predicament, how can you transfer the pictures from your memory card to your computer?

Collaboration

8. **Configuring New Computers** Three of your friends have asked you to configure a new computer for each of them. Each friend has $2,000 budgeted for the computer. One friend likes to play video games, another wants to purchase a computer for his home office (where he works as a travel agent), and the third would like a notebook computer that he can use for schoolwork. You ask two classmates to assist you with this task. Form a team of three people and search for computers that will meet the needs of your three friends. One team member configures a computer for the gamer, another team member configures a computer for the travel agent, and the last team member configures a computer for the student. No team member should exceed the $2,000 budget while configuring a computer that best suits each user's needs. Finally, all team members should discuss the differences among the three computers. Compile the team's findings and submit them to your instructor.

Problem Solving @ Work

The Problem Solving @ Work exercises extend your knowledge of the chapter concepts by seeking solutions to practical computer problems that you may encounter at work. The Collaboration exercise should be completed with a team.

In the real world, practical problems often can be solved in multiple ways. Provide one solution to each of the following problems using available resources, such as articles on the Web or in print, blogs, podcasts, videos, television, user guides, other individuals, and electronics and computer stores. You may need to use multiple resources to obtain an answer. Present your solutions in the form requested by your instructor (brief report, presentation, discussion, or other means).

1. **Update Issue** You just installed some Microsoft updates on your computer, which is running the latest version of the Windows operating system. The updates required you to reboot your computer immediately following their installation. When the desktop appears, the sizes of the icons and other elements on your screen have increased. Why might the update have caused this? What could you do to return the screen elements to their original sizes?
2. **Printer Port Problem** A colleague received a new printer and has delivered her old printer to your desk for your use. When attempting to plug the printer in a port on the back of your computer, you see that the connector will not fit in any of the available ports. You also notice that even the ports that are in use will not accept the connector. What steps will you take so that you can use the printer?
3. **USB Device Not Working** You purchased a new USB external hard disk so that you can take work home. After plugging the hard disk in a USB port on your computer, the other USB devices stopped working, and the external hard disk does not work. You return to the store to exchange the hard disk, but the same problem occurs with the new device. Why might this be happening? What steps will you take to resolve this problem?
4. **Noisy Fan** After moving to a new office, you turn on your computer for the first time and hear a buzzing sound inside the case. You turn off your computer, the noise winds down, and you wait several minutes before turning the computer back on. When you turn on your computer again, however, the noise resumes. What could be causing this?

5. **Slots Unavailable** Your computer is running slowly, and technical support informs you that they will install additional memory to help boost your computer's performance. A technician removes your computer, returns it one hour later, and informs you that no slots are available to accommodate additional memory. What might the technician be able to do to increase your computer's memory?
6. **Incorrect System Date and Time** While using your computer, you notice that the date and time are incorrect. You correct the date and time settings, continue using your computer, and then power it off before leaving work. When you arrive to work the next morning and turn on the computer, the date and time once again are incorrect. What might be causing this, and what is the first step you might take to solve this problem?
7. **Dirty Fan** While using your computer, you notice that the fan that removes the hot air from the inside of the computer has stopped running. You immediately turn off your computer to prevent it from overheating and notice that the fan is coated with dust. How will you clean the fan?

Collaboration

8. **Computers in Sports** You serve as an assistant coach for your former high school's football team. The head coach, who has a computer that is more than five years old, informs you that he would like to create a program that will allow him to keep track of his players' statistics. For instance, he would like to track the quarterback's number of passing yards, rushing yards, and completions. Form a team of three people to determine the requirements for implementing his request. One team member will research the types of application software that can track this data, another team member will determine the specifications for a computer capable of running the software and storing the data, and the other team member will determine the best way to collect the data during the game.

STUDENT ASSIGNMENTS

Learn How To

The Learn How To activities step you through fundamental technology skills when using a computer. The Learn How To exercises enable you to become more proficient with these skills.

Learn How To 1: Purchase and Install Memory in a Computer

One of the less expensive and more effective ways to speed up a computer, make it capable of processing more programs at the same time, and enable it to handle graphics, gaming, and other high-level programs is to increase the amount of memory. The process of increasing memory is accomplished in two phases — purchasing the memory and installing the memory. To purchase memory for a computer, complete the following steps:

1. Determine the amount of memory currently in the computer. The amount of memory in your computer is displayed in the Welcome Center when Windows starts.
2. Determine the maximum amount of memory your computer can contain. This value can change for different computers, based primarily on the number of slots on the motherboard available for memory and the size of the memory modules you can place in each slot. On most computers, different size memory modules can be inserted in slots. A computer, therefore, might allow a 128 MB, 256 MB, 512 MB, 1 GB, or 2 GB memory module to be inserted in each slot. To determine the maximum memory for a computer, in many cases you can multiply the number of memory slots on the computer by the maximum size memory module that can be inserted in each slot.

   For example, if a computer contains four memory slots and is able to accept memory modules of 128 MB, 256 MB, 512 MB, 1 GB, or 2 GB in each of its memory slots, the maximum amount of memory the computer can contain is 8 GB (4 x 2 GB).

   You can find the number of slots and the allowable sizes of each memory module by contacting the computer manufacturer, looking in the computer's documentation, or contacting sellers of memory such as Kingston (kingston.com) or Crucial (crucial.com) on the Web. These sellers have documentation for most computers, and even programs you can download to run on your computer that will specify how much memory your computer currently has and how much you can add.
3. Determine how much memory you want to add, which will be somewhere between the current memory and the maximum memory allowed on the computer.
4. Determine the current configuration of memory on the computer. For example, if a computer with four memory slots contains 1 GB of memory, it could be using one memory module of 1 GB in a single slot and the other three slots would be empty; two memory modules of 512 MB each in two slots with two slots empty; one memory module of 512 MB and two memory modules of 256 MB each in three slots with one slot empty; or four memory modules of 256 MB each in four slots with no slots empty. You may be required to look inside the system unit to make this determination. The current memory configuration on a computer will determine what new memory modules you should buy to increase the memory to the amount determined in Step 3.

   You also should be aware that a few computers require memory to be installed in matching pairs. This means a computer with four slots could obtain 1 GB of memory with two memory modules of 512 MB in two slots, or four memory modules of 256 MB in four slots.
5. Determine the number of available memory slots on your computer and the number and size memory modules you must buy to fulfill your requirement. Several scenarios can occur (in the following examples, assume you can install memory one module at a time).
   a. Scenario 1: The computer has one or more open slots. In this case, you might be able to purchase a memory module that matches the amount of memory increase you desire. For example, if you want to increase memory by 2 GB, you should purchase a 2 GB memory module for insertion in the open slot. Generally, you should buy the maximum size module you can for an open slot. So, if you find two empty slots and wish to increase memory by 2 GB, it is smarter to buy one 2 GB module and leave one empty slot rather than buy two 1 GB memory modules and use both slots. This allows you to increase memory again without removing currently used modules.
   b. Scenario 2: The computer has no open slots. For example, a computer containing 2 GB of memory could have four slots each containing 512 MB memory modules. If you want to increase the memory on the computer to 4 GB, you will have to remove some of the 512 MB memory modules and replace them with the new memory modules you purchase. In this example, you want to increase the memory by 2 GB. You would have several options: (1) You could replace all four 512 MB memory modules with 1 GB memory modules; (2) You could

Learn How To

replace all four 512 MB memory modules with two 2 GB memory modules; (3) You could replace one 512 MB memory module with a 1 GB memory module, and replace a second 512 MB module with a 2 GB memory module. Each of these options results in a total memory of 4 GB. The best option will depend on the price of memory and whether you anticipate increasing the memory size at a later time. The least expensive option probably would be number 3.

c. Scenario 3: Many combinations can occur. You may have to perform calculations to decide the combination of modules that will work for the number of slots on the computer and the desired additional memory.

6. Determine the type of memory to buy for the computer. Computer memory has many types and configurations, and it is critical that you buy the kind of memory for which the computer was designed. It is preferable to buy the same type of memory that currently is found in the computer. That is, if the memory is DDR3 SDRAM with a certain clock speed, then that is the type of additional memory you should place in the computer. The documentation for the computer should specify the memory type. In addition, the Web sites cited in Step 2, and others as well, will present a list of memory modules that will work with your computer. Enough emphasis cannot be placed on the fact that the memory you buy must be compatible with the type of memory usable on your computer. Because so many types and configurations exist, you must be especially diligent to ensure you purchase the proper memory for your computer.
7. Once you have determined the type and size of memory to purchase, buy it from a reputable dealer. Buying poor or mismatched memory is a major reason for a computer's erratic performance and is a difficult problem to troubleshoot.

After purchasing the memory, you must install it on your computer. Complete the following steps to install memory:

1. Unplug the computer, and remove all electrical cords and device cables from the ports on the computer. Open the case of the system unit. You may want to consult the computer's documentation to determine the exact procedure.
2. Ground yourself so that you do not generate static electricity that can cause memory or other components within the system unit to be damaged. To do this, wear an antistatic wristband you can purchase inexpensively in a computer or electronics store; or, before you touch any component within the system unit, touch an unpainted metal surface. If you are not wearing an antistatic wristband, periodically touch an unpainted metal surface to dissipate any static electricity.
3. Within the system unit, find the memory slots on the motherboard. The easiest way to do this is look for memory modules that are similar to those you purchased. The memory slots often are located near the processor. If you cannot find the slots, consult the documentation. A diagram often is available to help you spot the memory slots.
4. Insert the memory module in the next empty slot. Orient the memory module in the slot to match the modules currently installed. A notch or notches on the memory module will ensure you do not install the module backwards.

   If your memory module is a DIMM, insert the module straight down into grooves on the clips and then apply gentle pressure (see Figure 4-20 on page 225). If your memory is SIMM, insert the module at a 45 degree angle and then rotate it to a vertical position until the module snaps into place.
5. If you must remove one or more memory modules before inserting the new memory, carefully release the clips before lifting the memory module out of the memory slot.
6. Plug in the machine and replace all the device cables without replacing the cover.
7. Start the computer. In most cases, the new memory will be recognized and the computer will run normally. If an error message appears, determine the cause of the error.
8. Replace the computer cover.

Exercises

1. Assume you have a computer that contains 1 GB of memory. It contains four memory slots. Each slot can contain 128 MB, 256 MB, 512 MB, 1 GB, or 2 GB memory modules. Two of the slots contain 512 MB memory modules. What memory chip(s) would you buy to increase the memory on the computer to 4 GB? What is the maximum memory on the computer? Submit your answers to your instructor.
2. Assume you have a computer that contains 2 GB of memory. It contains four memory slots. Each slot can contain 128 MB, 256 MB, 512 MB, 1 GB, or 2 GB memory modules. Currently, each slot contains a 512 MB memory module. What combinations of memory modules will satisfy your memory upgrade to 8 GB? Visit a Web site to determine which of these combinations is the least expensive. Submit your answers and recommendations to your instructor.

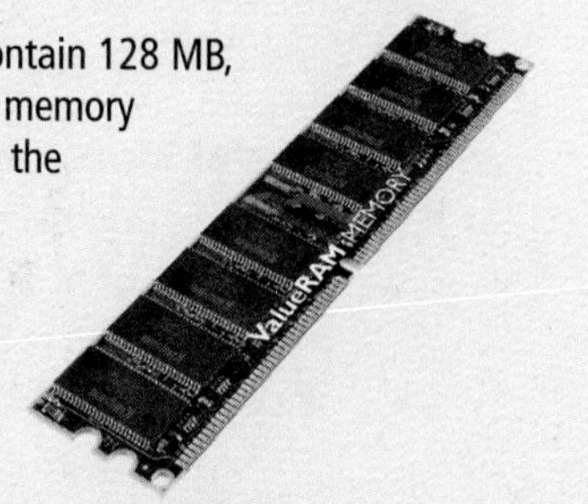

Web Research

The Web Research exercises broaden your understanding of the chapter concepts by presenting questions that require you to search the Web for answers.

1 Search Sleuth

Use one of the search engines listed in Figure 2-10 Chapter 2 on page 85 or your own favorite search engine to find the answers to the following questions. Copy and paste the Web address from the Web page where you found the answer. Some questions may have more than one answer. If required, submit your answers to your instructor. (1) In nanometers, what is the current size of a quad-core processor? (2) What company holds the trademark for the term, FireWire? (3) What is the relationship between the names of the Itanium processors and the steamship *Titanic*? (4) What Intel chip powered the Busicom calculator? (5) What is the admission price to visit the Intel Museum in Santa Clara, California? (6) What term did Dr. Werner Buchholz coin while designing the IBM Stretch computer?

2 Green Computing

Greenpeace International's *Guide to Greener Electronics* ranks the major technology hardware companies in their manufacturing and recycling efforts. The goal is to urge these computer, television, mobile devices, and game console manufacturers to reduce the use of toxic chemicals and to implement recycling policies. View the *Guide* (greenpeace.org/electronics) and then use your word processing program to answer the following questions. Then, if required, submit your answers to your instructor. (1) The Guide has been updated every three months since June 2006. What is the version of this most current Guide? (2) Which company is at the top of the list for its better toxic waste, recycling, and climate change practices? What is this company's score, and why did this company receive this ranking? (3) Which company received the lowest ranking? Why? (4) What criteria are used to score the manufacturers? (5) Review the Toxics News links and read the article discussing the rankings from the previous year. Compare the companies' rankings between the past year and the current year. (6) What are Greenpeace's definitions of PVC-free and BFR-free?

3 Social Networking

Business creativity helps drive innovation and invention of new products. Oddpodz is an online meeting place for creative people to share ideas with like-minded professionals. This Web site includes a blog, a marketplace for unique products, job postings, and a forum to discuss current topics. Visit the Oddpodz Web site (Oddpodz.com) and then read the FAQs to get an overview of the Web site. Browse the company profiles in the Creative Services Marketplace. Read the profiles of some new members, who are called citizens, and view some of the creative projects featured. Read several articles in the Cylibrary about advice given to plan a business. Review topics in the blog, especially those discussing current advertising campaigns. Summarize the information you read and viewed.

4 Blogs

Technology news blogs offer information about new products, trends, and issues facing information technology professionals. Visit several technology blogs, including those from CNET (news.cnet.com), Geekzone (geekzone.co.nz/blogindex.asp), Good Morning Silicon Valley (blogs.siliconvalley.com/gmsv), Lifehacker (lifehacker.com), TechnoClicks (technoclicks.com), and WordPress (wordpress.com/tag/technology/). What are bloggers discussing? What top news stories are featured? What products are reviewed? What questions are members asking about computer chips, flash memory, Bluetooth, and green computing products? Which stories have generated more than 20 comments?

5 Ethics in Action

Law enforcement agencies use handheld wireless devices to access commercial databases. For example, Massachusetts state police stationed at Logan International Airport use the LocatePLUS Holdings Corporation's database, which has information on 98 percent of Americans. Police say accessing this information helps them perform their jobs more efficiently. Privacy experts, in contrast, say that information collected for one purpose, such as checking credit or registering motor vehicles, should not be available in other contexts. View online sites that provide information about commercial databases for sale. Write a report summarizing your findings, and include a table of links to Web sites that provide additional details.

Critical Thinking

The Critical Thinking exercises challenge your assessment and decision-making skills by presenting real-world situations associated with the chapter concepts. The Collaboration exercise should be completed with a team.

To evaluate the situations below, use personal experiences and available resources such as articles on the Web or in print, blogs, podcasts, videos, television, user guides, other individuals, and electronics and computer stores. You may need to use multiple resources to form conclusions and make recommendations.

1. **Class Discussion — Technology Purchases** You are the purchasing manager at TechnoInk, a company that specializes in designing and producing logos for local high school and college sports teams. The company has 35 nonnetworked computers that are used throughout the company for common business applications. The computers are four years old, and you would like to replace them. The director of information technology agrees, but he has reservations. Evaluate and compare the cost of new computers, comparing the major features found on system units at three different price levels: less than $1,000; $1,000 to $1,750; and greater than $1,750. Discuss the major features of system units at the various price levels and which computer you would recommend. Include in your discussion recommendations on which system units would meet the company's needs most economically.

2. **Class Presentation — Mac vs. PC** Universal Computing, Inc. has decided to upgrade several hundred PCs used in their offices nationwide. The information technology department has recommended that the company again purchase PCs for approximately $1,500 each. The system units would include Intel Core 2 Quad processors with speeds of 2.4 GHz with 2 GB of RAM. From her days in college, the CFO (chief financial officer) has preferred Apple computers and currently uses an Apple iMac at home. She has hired you as a consultant to analyze purchasing iMacs versus purchasing PCs in the same price range and with similar capabilities. Use the Web and/or print media to select a comparable iMac. Obtain answers to the following questions by analyzing your findings, so that you can present a recommendation on which computer to purchase. Which one starts faster? Which one opens files faster? Which one displays Web pages faster? Is the iMac in the same price range as the PC? Include in your presentation any other advantages and disadvantages of each.

3. **Research — Computer Upgrades** Your boss would like to save money by asking employees to begin performing simple computer upgrades, such as installing additional memory modules, themselves. Your boss informed you that some computers might be easier to upgrade than other computers. For example, smaller form factor computers sometimes can be more difficult to upgrade than towers. Notebook computers, including netbooks and Tablet PCs, can be more difficult to upgrade than desktop computers. Some might find it more difficult to upgrade a Mac than to upgrade a PC because the components inside the system unit are arranged differently. Use the Web to locate copyright-free pictures of the inside of various types of system units. Be sure to include both large and small system units on Macs, PCs, and notebook computers. What type of computer would you find easiest to upgrade? What challenges might you face upgrading a smaller computer? Prepare a brief report for your instructor with your findings, and be sure to include the pictures in your report.

Collaboration

4. **Computers in the Military** Computers have become an integral part of military operations. Many military research projects use simulators that resemble civilian computer games. Your company has been contacted by the Department of Defense for a research project. Form a four-member team, and then form two two-member groups. Assign each group one of the following topics to research: 1) How have notebook computers changed the combat environment, and how have these military uses impacted the design of the personal computer? 2) How can the utilization of microchips worn by soldiers, or wearable computers, be integrated into civilian use? Meet with your team and discuss your findings. Then, prepare a presentation to include both topics and share with your class. Include in your presentation any advantages or disadvantages of introducing these technologies into public use. Discuss any legal ramifications that may arise.

Chapter Five

Input

Objectives

After completing this chapter, you will be able to:

1 Define input and differentiate among a program, command, and user response

2 Identify the keys and buttons commonly found on desktop computer keyboards, and describe how keyboards for mobile computers and devices differ from desktop computer keyboards

3 Describe different mouse types and explain how to use a mouse

4 Describe various types of touch screens and explain how a touch-sensitive pad works

5 Describe various types of pen input, and identify other types of input for smart phones

6 Summarize the purpose of various game controllers: gamepads, joysticks and wheels, light guns, dance pads, and motion-sensing game controllers

7 Explain how resolution affects the quality of a picture captured on a digital camera

8 Describe the uses of voice recognition, Web cams, and video conferencing

9 Discuss how various scanners and reading devices work: optical scanners, optical readers, bar code readers, RFID readers, magnetic stripe card readers, MICR readers, and data collection devices

10 Summarize the various biometric devices: fingerprint reader, face recognition system, hand geometry system, voice verification system, signature verification system, and iris recognition system

11 Discuss how POS terminals, automated teller machines, and DVD kiosks work

12 Identify alternative input devices for physically challenged users

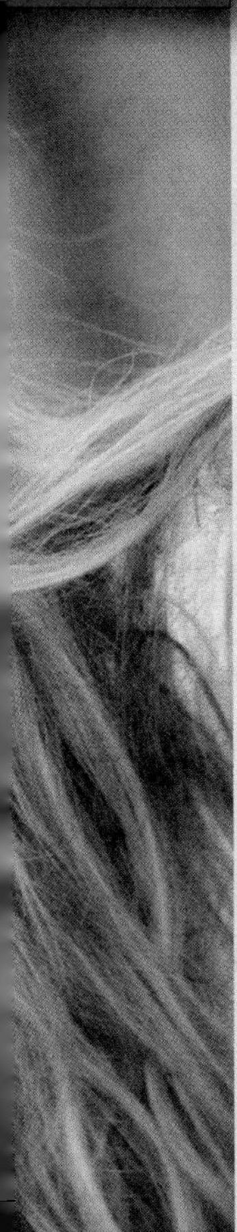

What Is Input?

Input is any data and instructions entered into the memory of a computer. As shown in Figure 5-1, people have a variety of options for entering data and instructions into a computer.

As discussed in Chapter 1, *data* is a collection of unprocessed items, including text, numbers, images, audio, and video. Once data is in memory, the computer interprets and executes instructions to process the data into information. Instructions entered into the computer can be in the form of programs, commands, and user responses.

- A *program* is a series of related instructions that tells a computer what tasks to perform and how to perform them. When a programmer writes a program, he or she enters the program into the computer by using a keyboard, mouse, or other input device. The programmer then stores the program in a file that a user can

Figure 5-1 Users can enter data and instructions into a computer in a variety of ways.

execute (run). When a user runs a program, the computer loads the program from a storage medium into memory. Thus, a program is entered into a computer's memory.

- Programs respond to commands that a user issues. A *command* is an instruction that causes a program to perform a specific action. Users issue commands by pressing keys on the keyboard, clicking a mouse button, speaking into a microphone, or touching an area on a screen.
- A *user response* is an instruction a user issues by replying to a question displayed by a program. A response to the question instructs the program to perform certain actions. Assume the program asks the question, Is the time card correct? If you answer Yes, the program processes the time card. If you answer No, the program gives you the opportunity to modify the time card entries.

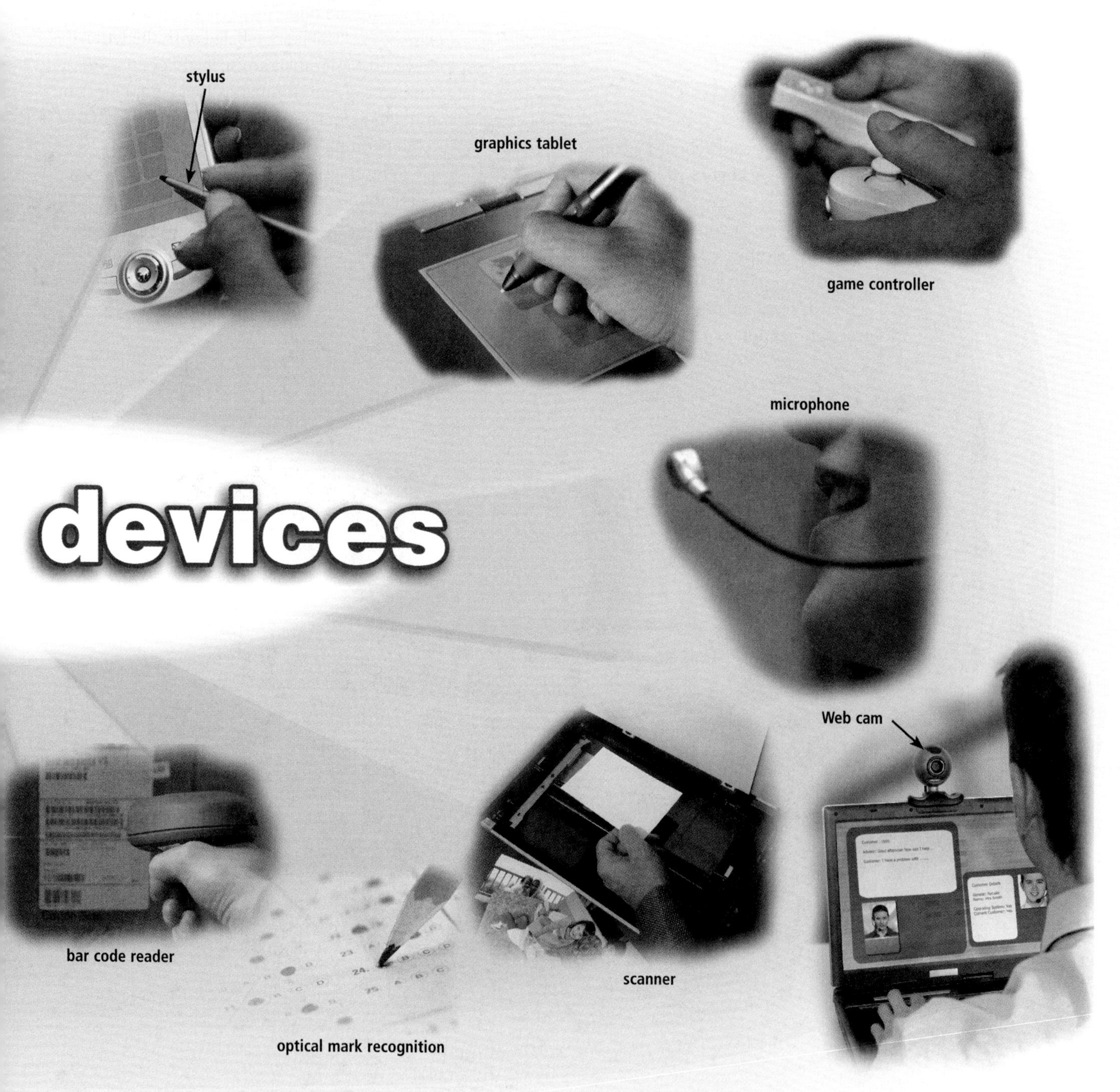

What Are Input Devices?

An **input device** is any hardware component that allows users to enter data and instructions (programs, commands, and user responses) into a computer. Depending on the application and your particular requirements, the input device selected may vary. The following pages discuss a variety of input devices.

Storage devices, such as disk drives, serve as both input and output devices. Chapter 7 discusses storage devices.

The Keyboard

Many people use a keyboard as one of their input devices. A **keyboard** is an input device that contains keys users press to enter data and instructions into a computer (Figure 5-2).

Desktop computer keyboards typically have from 101 to 105 keys. All desktop computer keyboards have a typing area that includes the letters of the alphabet, numbers, punctuation marks, and other basic keys. Many desktop computer keyboards also have a numeric keypad on the right side of the keyboard. A keyboard also contains other keys that allow users to enter data and instructions into the computer. Read Ethics & Issues 5-1 for a related discussion.

Most of today's desktop computer keyboards are enhanced keyboards. An *enhanced keyboard* has twelve or more function keys along the top; it also has two CTRL keys, two ALT keys, and a set of arrow and additional keys between the typing area and the numeric keypad (Figure 5-2). *Function keys*, which are labeled with the letter F followed by a number, are special keys programmed to issue commands to a computer. The command associated with a function key may vary, depending on the program with which you are interacting. For example, the F3 key may issue one command to an operating system and an entirely different command to a word processing program. To issue commands, users often can press a function key in combination with other special keys (SHIFT, CTRL, ALT, and others).

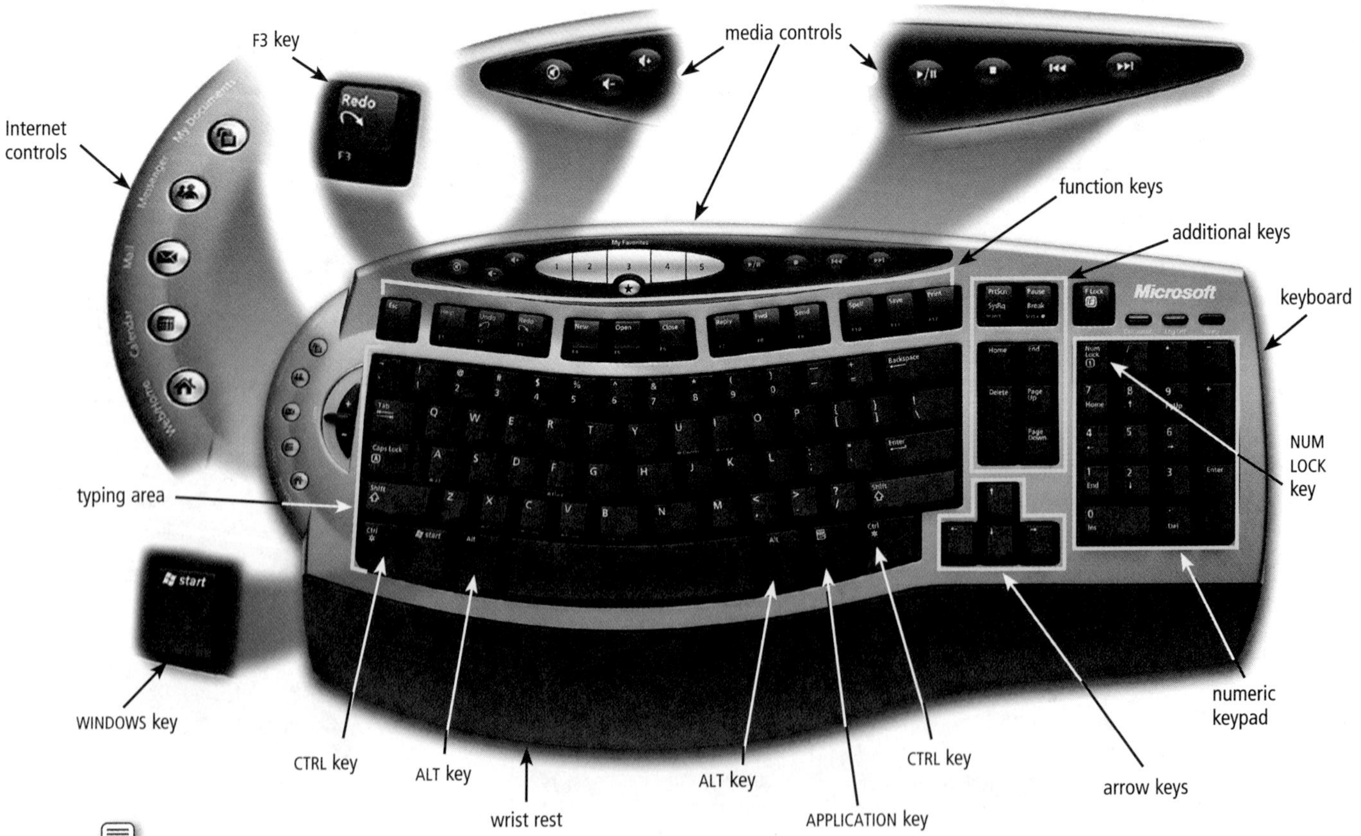

Figure 5-2 On a desktop computer keyboard, you type using keys in the typing area and on the numeric keypad.

? FAQ 5-1

What is the rationale for the arrangement of keys in the typing area?

The keys originally were arranged to reduce the frequency of key jams on old mechanical typewriters. Called a *QWERTY keyboard*, the first letters on the top alphabetic line spell QWERTY. A *Dvorak keyboard*, by contrast, places frequently typed letters in the middle of the typing area. Despite the Dvorak keyboard's logical design, most people and computers use a QWERTY keyboard.

For more information, visit the Computer Concepts CourseMate Web site at www.cengagebrain.com, navigate to the Chapter 5 FAQ resource for this book, and then click Keyboards.

Keyboards also often have a WINDOWS key(s) and an APPLICATION key. When pressed, the WINDOWS key displays the Windows Start menu, and the APPLICATION key displays an item's shortcut menu.

Nearly all keyboards have toggle keys. A *toggle key* is a key that switches between two states each time a user presses the key. When you press the NUM LOCK key, for example, it locks the numeric keypad so that you can use the keypad to type numbers. When you press the NUM LOCK key again, the numeric keypad unlocks so that the same keys can serve to move around a document. Many keyboards have status lights that light up when you activate a toggle key.

Users can press the arrow keys and other keys such as PAGE UP and PAGE DOWN on the keyboard to move the insertion point left, right, up, or down. The **insertion point**, also known as a *cursor* in some programs, is a symbol on the screen, usually a blinking vertical bar, that indicates where the next character you type will appear (Figure 5-3).

Keyboards with media control buttons allow you to control your media player program, access the computer's optical disc drive, and adjust speaker volume. Internet control buttons allow you to open an e-mail program, start a Web browser, and search the Internet. Some keyboards have USB ports so that you can plug a USB device directly in the keyboard instead of in the system unit. Some keyboards include a fingerprint reader and/or smart card reader, each of which is discussed later in this chapter.

A *gaming keyboard* is a keyboard designed specifically for users who enjoy playing games on the

Figure 5-3 In most programs, such as Word, the insertion point is a blinking vertical bar. You use the keyboard or other input device to move the insertion point. The pointer, another symbol that is displayed on the screen, is controlled using a pointing device such as a mouse.

ETHICS & ISSUES 5-1

Keyboard Monitoring — Privacy Risk?

Do you have a feeling that someone is watching everything you type on your computer at work? Are you concerned about your teenager's conversations in Internet chat rooms? Keyboard monitoring software can dispel your doubts. When installed on a computer, *keyboard monitoring software*, also called a *keylogger*, records every keystroke in a hidden file, which later can be accessed by supplying the correct password. With keyboard monitoring software, you can see everything that was typed on a computer keyboard. Some programs also store a record of software used, Web sites visited, user logons, and periodic screen shots. The software can run completely undetected; in fact, recently computer hackers have installed keyloggers in a malicious attempt to capture people's user names and passwords as they sign on to banking and financial Web sites. With keyboard monitoring software, you can discover that an employee is providing sensitive information to a competitor or recognize that your teenager has made a potentially dangerous contact in a chat room. Businesses sometimes use keyboard monitoring software to analyze the efficiency of data entry personnel. Recently, courts ruled that law-enforcement agencies secretly can install keyboard monitoring software on suspects' computers if a proper search warrant is obtained. Many maintain, however, that keyboard monitoring software is an invasion of privacy, even in the workplace, and some states have outlawed the secret installation of such software.

Should keyboard monitoring software ever be used? If so, when? Some marketers of keyboard monitoring software recommend computer users be informed that the software is installed. Is this a good idea? Why or why not?

computer. Gaming keyboards typically include programmable keys so that gamers can customize the keyboard to the game being played. The keys on gaming keyboards light up so that the keys are visible in all lighting conditions. Some have small displays that show important game statistics, such as time or targets remaining.

Desktop computer keyboards often attach via a cable to a USB port on the system unit. Some keyboards, however, do not have any wires connecting the keyboard to the system unit. A *wireless keyboard*, or *cordless keyboard*, is a battery-powered device that transmits data to the system unit using wireless technology, such as radio waves (Bluetooth) or infrared light waves (IrDA).

Keyboard Ergonomics

Many keyboards have a rectangular shape with the keys aligned in straight, horizontal rows. Users who spend a lot of time typing on these keyboards sometimes experience repetitive strain injuries (RSI) of their wrists and hands. For this reason, some manufacturers offer ergonomic keyboards. An *ergonomic keyboard* has a design that reduces the chance of wrist and hand injuries (Figure 5-4). Even keyboards that are not ergonomically designed attempt to offer a user more comfort by including a wrist rest or palm rest (Figure 5-2 on page 260).

Ergonomics
For more information, visit the Computer Concepts CourseMate Web site at www.cengagebrain.com, navigate to the Chapter 5 Web Link resource for this book, and then click Ergonomics.

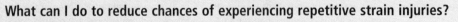

Figure 5-4 An ergonomic keyboard.

The goal of **ergonomics** is to incorporate comfort, efficiency, and safety in the design of the workplace. Employees can be injured or develop disorders of the muscles, nerves, tendons, ligaments, and joints from working in an area that is not designed ergonomically.

Keyboards for Mobile Computers and Mobile Devices

On notebook computers and some handheld computers, smart phones, and other mobile devices the keyboard is built in the top of the system unit. To fit in these mobile computers and devices, the keyboards usually are smaller and have fewer keys than desktop computer keyboards. A typical notebook computer keyboard usually has only about 85 keys. To provide all of the functionality of a desktop computer keyboard, manufacturers design many of the keys to serve two or three purposes.

A variety of options are available for typing on a smart phone (Figure 5-5). Many can display an on-screen keyboard, where you press the on-screen keys using a stylus or your finger. Some smart phones have one key for each letter of the alphabet, often called a mini-keyboard. Other phones have keypads that contain fewer keys than there are letters in the alphabet. For these phones, each key on the keypad represents multiple characters, which are identified on the key. That is, the 2 key on the phone's keypad displays the letters a, b, and c on the key's face. On many phones, you cycle through the number, letters, and other symbols associated with a particular key by pressing a key on the keypad multiple times. For example, to type the word, hi, on a phone keypad, you would press the 4 key twice to display the letter h, pause momentarily to advance the cursor, and then press the 4 key three times to display the letter i.

Some phones use *predictive text input*, where you press one key on the keypad for each letter in a word, and software on the phone predicts the word you want. Predictive text input saves users time when entering text using the phone's keypad.

? FAQ 5-2

What can I do to reduce chances of experiencing repetitive strain injuries?

If possible, use an ergonomic keyboard. Do not rest your wrists on the edge of a desk; use a wrist rest. Keep your forearms and wrists level so that your wrists do not bend. Take a break and do hand exercises every 15 minutes. Keep your shoulders, arms, hands, and wrists relaxed while you work. Maintain good posture. Keep feet flat on the floor, with one foot slightly in front of the other. Immediately stop using the computer if you begin to experience pain or fatigue.

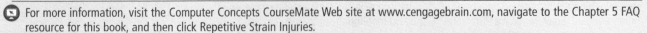

For more information, visit the Computer Concepts CourseMate Web site at www.cengagebrain.com, navigate to the Chapter 5 FAQ resource for this book, and then click Repetitive Strain Injuries.

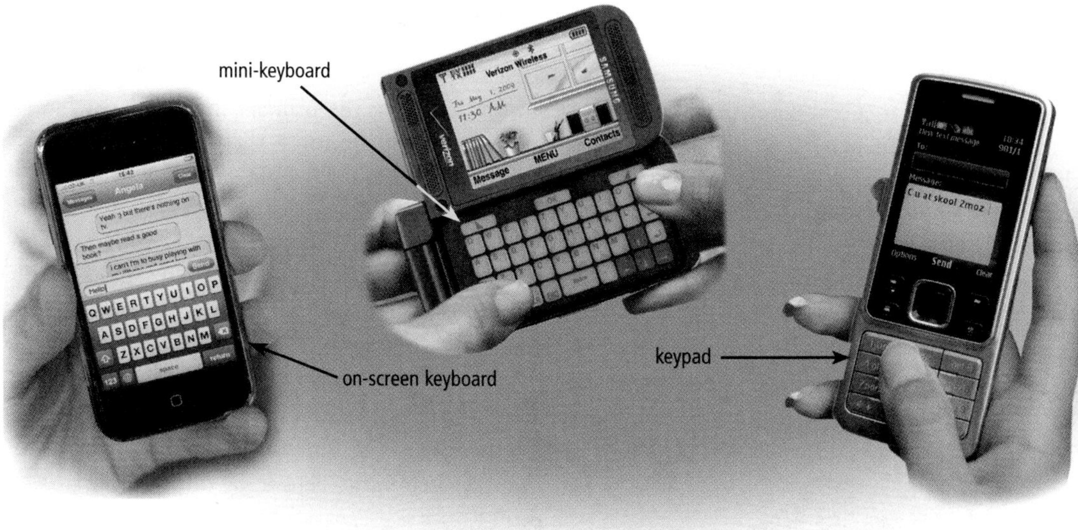

Figure 5-5 Users have a variety of options for typing on a phone.

Pointing Devices

A **pointing device** is an input device that allows a user to control a pointer on the screen. In a graphical user interface, a **pointer** is a small symbol on the screen (Figure 5-3 on page 261) whose location and shape change as a user moves a pointing device. A pointing device can be used to move the insertion point; select text, graphics, and other objects; and click buttons, icons, links, and menu commands. The following sections discuss the mouse and other pointing devices.

Mouse

A **mouse** is a pointing device that fits under the palm of your hand comfortably. The mouse is the most widely used pointing device on desktop computers.

With a mouse, users control the movement of the pointer, often called a *mouse pointer* in this case. As you move a mouse, the pointer on the screen also moves. Generally, you use the mouse to move the pointer on the screen to an object such as a button, a menu, an icon, a link, or text. Then, you press a mouse button to perform a certain action associated with that object. The top and sides of a mouse have one to four buttons; some also have a small wheel. The bottom of a mouse is flat and contains a mechanism that detects movement of the mouse.

Most desktop computer users today have some type of *optical mouse*, which uses devices that emit and sense light to detect the mouse's movement. Some use optical sensors, and others use a laser. The latter, often referred to as a *laser mouse* (Figure 5-6), usually is more expensive than the former. You can place an optical mouse on nearly all types of flat surfaces. Some newer models combine both optical sensors and laser, enabling users to place the mouse on rougher surfaces such as carpeting and park benches. Further, some mouse devices are more sensitive than others for users requiring more precision such as graphic artists, engineers, or game players.

The mobile user who makes presentations may prefer a mouse that has additional buttons for running a slide show and controlling media, similar to a remote control. A newer type of mouse, called an *air mouse*, is a motion-sensing mouse that, in addition to the typical buttons, allows you to control objects, media players, and slide shows by moving the mouse in predetermined directions

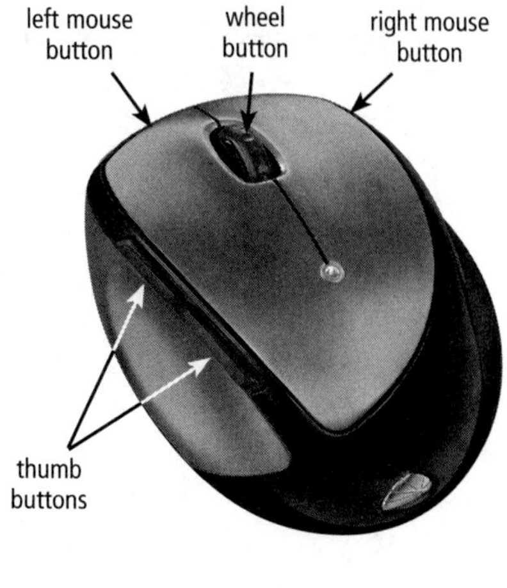

Figure 5-6 This mouse uses a laser to detect movement of the mouse. It also includes buttons you push with your thumb that enable forward and backward navigation through Web pages.

through the air (Figure 5-7). For example, raising the mouse up might increase the volume on your media player.

A mouse connects to a computer in several ways. Many types connect with a cable that attaches to a USB port or a mouse port on the system unit. A *wireless mouse*, or *cordless mouse*, is a battery-powered device that transmits data using wireless technology, such as radio waves (Bluetooth) or infrared light waves (IrDA). Some users prefer a wireless mouse because it frees up desk space and eliminates the clutter of a cord.

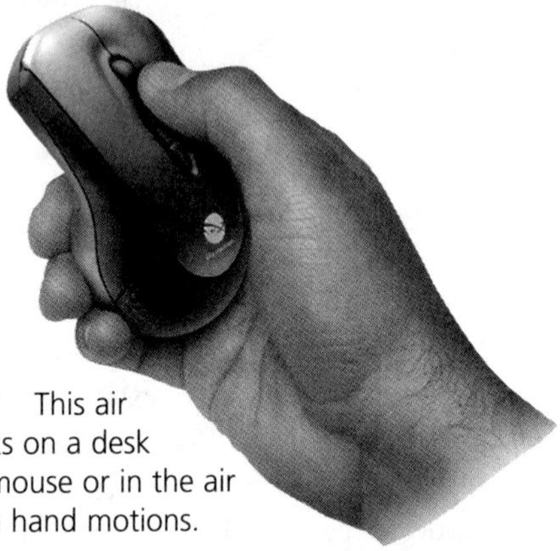

Figure 5-7 This air mouse works on a desk like a laser mouse or in the air by detecting hand motions.

Using a Mouse

Windows users work with a mouse that has at least two buttons. For a right-handed user, the left button usually is the primary mouse button, and the right mouse button is the secondary mouse button. Left-handed people, however, can reverse the function of these buttons.

The table in Figure 5-8 explains how to perform a variety of mouse operations. Some programs also use keys in combination with the mouse to perform certain actions. For example, when you hold down the CTRL key while rolling the wheel, text on the screen becomes larger or smaller based on the direction you roll the wheel. The function of the mouse buttons and the wheel varies depending on the program. Read Ethics & Issues 5-2 for a related discussion.

Some programs support *mouse gestures*, where the user performs certain operations by holding a mouse button while moving the mouse in a particular pattern. For example, moving the mouse down and to the left may close all open windows. Mouse gestures minimize the amount of time users spend navigating through menus or toolbars because users can perform these tasks by simply moving (gesturing) the mouse.

Mouse Operations

Operation	Mouse Action	Example
Point	Move the mouse until the pointer on the desktop is positioned on the item of choice.	Position the pointer on the screen.
Click	Press and release the primary mouse button, which usually is the left mouse button.	Select or deselect items on the screen or start a program or program feature.
Right-click	Press and release the secondary mouse button, which usually is the right mouse button.	Display a shortcut menu.
Double-click	Quickly press and release the left mouse button twice without moving the mouse.	Start a program or program feature.
Triple-click	Quickly press and release the left mouse button three times without moving the mouse.	Select a paragraph.
Drag	Point to an item, hold down the left mouse button, move the item to the desired location on the screen, and then release the left mouse button.	Move an object from one location to another or draw pictures.
Right-drag	Point to an item, hold down the right mouse button, move the item to the desired location on the screen, and then release the right mouse button.	Display a shortcut menu after moving an object from one location to another.
Rotate wheel	Roll the wheel forward or backward.	Scroll vertically (up and down).
Free-spin wheel	Whirl the wheel forward or backward so that it spins freely on its own.	Scroll through hundreds of pages in seconds.
Press wheel	Press the wheel button while moving the mouse.	Scroll continuously.
Tilt wheel	Press the wheel toward the right or left.	Scroll horizontally (left and right).
Press thumb button	Press the button on the side of the mouse with your thumb.	Move forward or backward through Web pages and/or control media, games, etc.

Figure 5-8 Common mouse operations.

ETHICS & ISSUES 5-2

Are Employers Responsible for Computer-Related Repetitive Strain Injuries?

When you consider the causes of workplace injuries, you might not put clicking a mouse or use of a cell phone in the same category with lifting a bag of concrete, but perhaps you should. According to the chairman of a National Academy of Sciences panel that investigated workplace injuries, every year one million Americans lose workdays because of repetitive strain injuries (RSIs), including the latest malady known as cell phone elbow. RSI is caused when muscle groups perform the same actions over and over again. Once, RSIs were common among factory workers who performed the same tasks on an assembly line for hours a day. Today, these injuries, which often result from prolonged use of a computer mouse and keyboard or overuse of cell phones and other mobile devices, are the largest job-related injury and illness problem in the United States and are almost completely avoidable with proper computer and mobile device use. OSHA proposed standards whereby employers would have to establish programs to prevent workplace injuries with respect to computer use. Yet, Congress rejected the standards, accepting the argument that the cost to employers would be prohibitive and unfair. Some argue that it is each employee's responsibility to be aware of preventative measures against RSI.

Should the government establish laws regarding computer use? Why or why not? Are employees, employers, or the government responsible for repetitive strain injuries? Why? Who should be responsible for the costs of prevention and medical care? Why?

Other Pointing Devices

The mouse is the most widely used pointing device today. Some users, however, work with other pointing devices. These include the trackball, touchpad, pointing stick, touch screen, touch-sensitive pads, stylus, pen, signature capture pad, and graphics tablet. The following sections discuss each of these pointing devices.

Trackball

A **trackball** is a stationary pointing device with a ball on its top or side (Figure 5-9). The ball in most trackballs is about the size of a Ping-Pong ball.

To move the pointer using a trackball, you rotate the ball with your thumb, fingers, or the palm of your hand. In addition to the ball, a trackball usually has one or more buttons that work just like mouse buttons.

A trackball requires frequent cleaning because it picks up oils from fingers and dust from the environment. For users who have limited desk space, however, a trackball is a good alternative to a mouse because the device is stationary.

Figure 5-9 A trackball.

Touchpad

A **touchpad** is a small, flat, rectangular pointing device that is sensitive to pressure and motion (Figure 5-10). To move the pointer using a touchpad, slide your fingertip across the surface of the pad. Some touchpads have one or more buttons around the edge of the pad that work like mouse buttons. On most touchpads, you also can tap the pad's surface to imitate mouse operations such as clicking. Touchpads are found most often on notebook computers, including netbooks and many Tablet PCs.

Ethics & Issues
For the complete text of the Ethics & Issues boxes found in this chapter, visit the Computer Concepts CourseMate Web site at www.cengagebrain.com and then navigate to the Chapter 5 Ethics & Issues resource for this book.

Figure 5-10 Most notebook computers have a touchpad that allows users to control the movement of the pointer.

Pointing Stick

A **pointing stick** is a pressure-sensitive pointing device shaped like a pencil eraser that is positioned between keys on a keyboard (Figure 5-11). To move the pointer using a pointing stick, you push the pointing stick with a finger. The pointer on the screen moves in the direction you push the pointing stick. By pressing buttons below the keyboard, users can click and perform other mouse-type operations with a pointing stick. A pointing stick does not require any additional desk space.

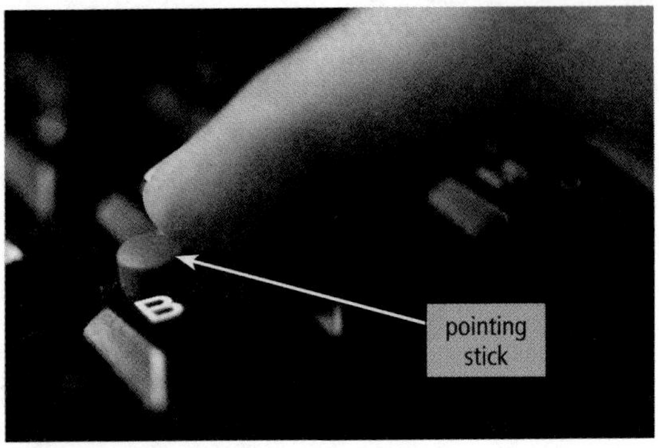

Figure 5-11 Some notebook computers include a pointing stick to allow a user to control the movement of the pointer.

Touch Screens and Touch-Sensitive Pads

A **touch screen** is a touch-sensitive display device. Touch screens that recognize multiple points of contact at the same time are known as *multi-touch*. Users can interact with touch screens by touching areas of the screen. Because touch screens require a lot of arm or hand movements, you do not enter large amounts of data using a touch screen. Instead, you touch words, pictures, numbers, letters, or locations identified on the screen. Some touch screens also respond to finger motions such as sliding your finger to drag an object or pinching your fingers to zoom in or out. The latest version of the Windows operating system provides increased support for computers with touch screens. Support for touch screen makes it easier for users to interact with the operating system.

Multi-Touch Screens

For more information, visit the Computer Concepts CourseMate Web site at www.cengagebrain.com, navigate to the Chapter 5 Web Link resource for this book, and then click Multi-Touch Screens.

Some models of desktop computers and notebook computers, including netbooks and Tablet PCs, and many mobile devices have touch screens (Figure 5-12). With some smart phones, portable media players, and other mobile devices, for example, you can touch the screen to perform tasks such as dialing phone numbers, entering text, and making on-screen selections. Some handheld game consoles also have touch screens.

A *kiosk*, which is a freestanding computer, usually includes a touch screen (Figure 5-13). For example, travelers use kiosks in airports to print tickets ordered online and in hotels for easy check in and check out. To allow easy access of your bank account from a car, many ATMs have touch screens.

Figure 5-12 Computers and mobile devices have touch screens.

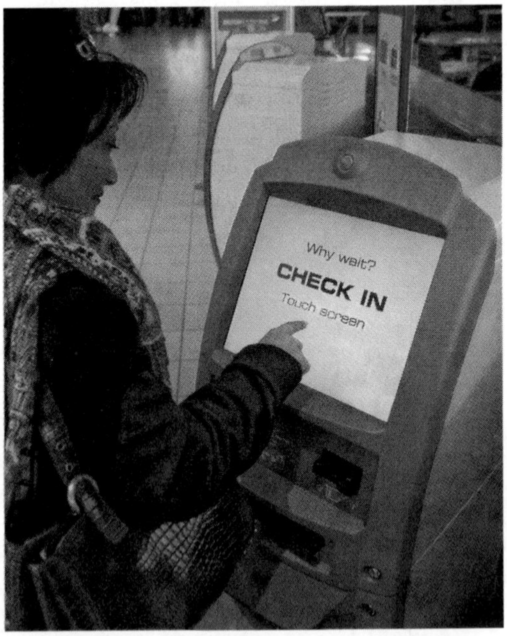

Figure 5-13 This traveler checks in using an airport kiosk.

A recently developed touch screen, called *Microsoft Surface*, is a 30-inch tabletop display that allows one or more people to interact with the screen using their fingers or hands (Figure 5-14). The Microsoft Surface display also allows devices that are not digital, such as an everyday paintbrush, to be used as an input device. Restaurants, hotels, and other public locations provide Microsoft Surface tables to enhance guest services.

Figure 5-14 Guests explore photos of hotel amenities by touching and dragging them across the Microsoft Surface display.

Touch-Sensitive Pads

Portable media players that do not have touch screens typically have a *touch-sensitive pad*, which is an input device that enables users to scroll through and play music, view pictures, watch videos or movies, adjust volume, and/or customize settings. Touch-sensitive pads typically contain buttons and/or wheels that are operated with a thumb or finger. For example, users rotate a *Click Wheel* to browse through the portable media player's song, picture, or movie lists and press the Click Wheel's buttons to play or pause media, display a menu, and perform other actions (Figure 5-15). To learn more about how to download songs to a portable media player, complete the Learn How To 2 activity on pages 298 and 299.

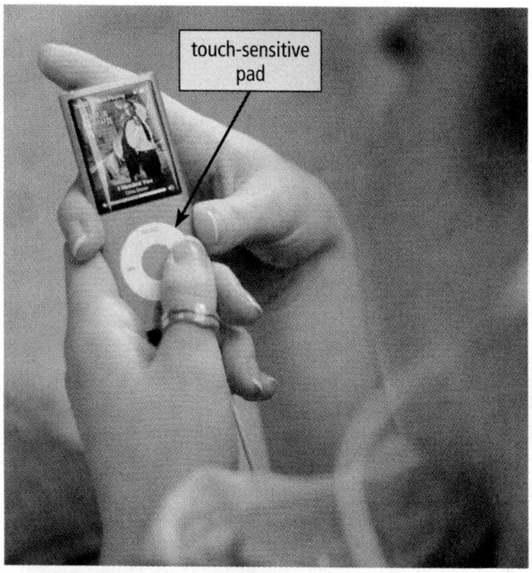

Figure 5-15 You use your thumb to rotate or press buttons on a Click Wheel.

FAQ 5-3

Which companies sell the most portable media players?

Apple has dominated the portable media player market for several years. A recent study shows that Apple holds 71 percent of the market share, with SanDisk in second place at 11 percent of the market. The chart to the right illustrates the market share for the top four portable media player manufacturers.

For more information, visit the Computer Concepts CourseMate Web site at www.cengagebrain.com, navigate to the Chapter 5 FAQ resource for this book, and then click Portable Media Players.

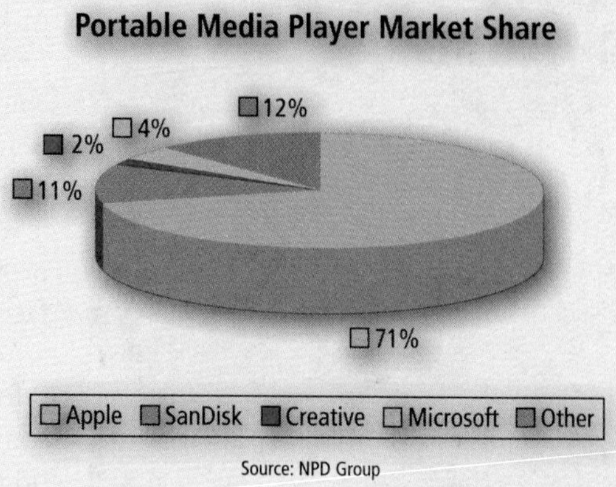

Pen Input

With **pen input**, you touch a stylus or digital pen on a flat surface to write, draw, or make selections. The flat surface may be a screen on a monitor or mobile device, a signature capture pad, or a graphics tablet (Figure 5-16). A **stylus** is a small metal or plastic device that looks like a tiny ink pen but uses pressure instead of ink. A **digital pen**, which is slightly larger than a stylus, typically provides more functionality than a stylus, featuring electronic erasers and programmable buttons. Most digital pens, often simply called pens, are pressure-sensitive.

Some desktop and mobile computers and nearly all mobile devices have touch screens that recognize pen input and thus include a pressure-sensitive digital pen or stylus. Computers and mobile devices often use *handwriting recognition software*, which is a program that translates the handwritten letters and symbols created on the screen with the stylus or pen into characters that the computer or device can process.

To capture a handwritten signature, a user writes his or her name on a **signature capture pad** with a stylus or pen that is attached to the device. Software then transmits the signature via a cable connected to a port on the computer. Signature capture pads often include a magnetic stripe card reader and work with POS terminals, both discussed later in the chapter.

To use pen input on a computer that does not have a touch screen, you can attach a graphics tablet to the computer. A **graphics tablet** is a flat, rectangular, electronic, plastic board. Architects, mapmakers, designers, artists, and home users create drawings by using a pressure-sensitive pen on a graphics tablet. Each location on the graphics tablet corresponds to a specific location on the screen. When drawing on the tablet with a pen, the tablet detects and converts the movements into digital signals that are sent in the computer. Large-scale applications sometimes refer to the graphics tablet as a *digitizer*.

Signature Capture Pads
For more information, visit the Computer Concepts CourseMate Web site at www.cengagebrain.com, navigate to the Chapter 5 Web Link resource for this book, and then click Signature Capture Pads.

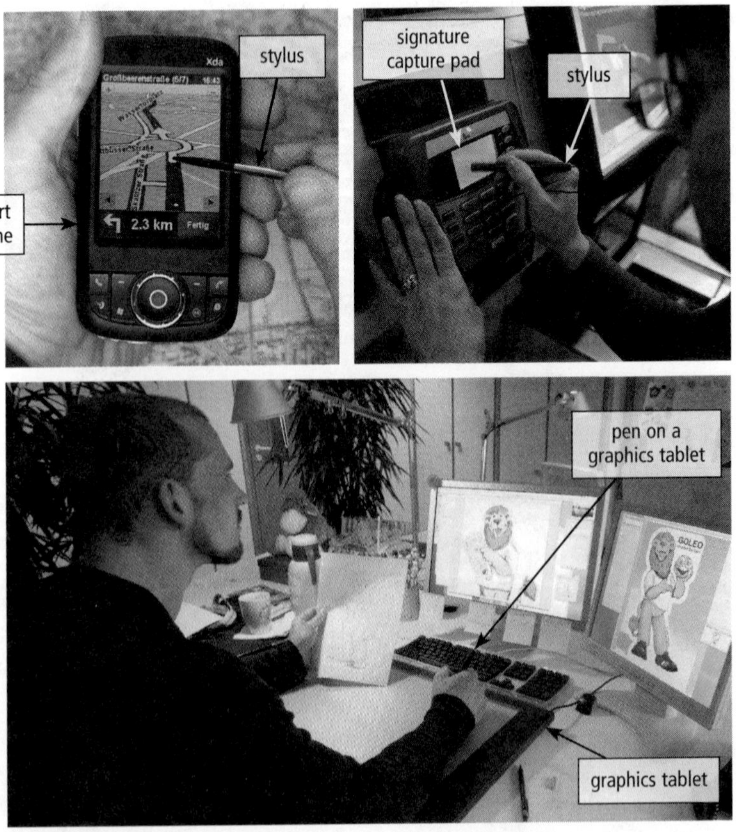

Figure 5-16 You use a stylus or a pen to write, draw, or make selections on a screen, signature capture pad, or graphics tablet.

Other Input for Smart Phones

Previously discussed input devices such as mini-keyboards, keypads, touch screens, and a stylus are used with smart phones. In addition to these input methods, a variety of alternatives for input is available for smart phones (Figure 5-17).

You can talk directly into the smart phone's microphone or into a Bluetooth headset that wirelessly communicates with the phone. Some smart phones have digital cameras that take pictures and touch-sensitive pads that enable you to interact with media, such as music and photos. Others receive navigation signals to provide users with maps and directions. You can purchase a more elaborate stylus that has a ballpoint pen at one end and a stylus at the other.

Instead of typing on a phone's keyboard or keypad, users can enter text via a *portable keyboard*, which is a full-sized keyboard that communicates with a smart phone or PDA. Some portable keyboards physically attach to and remove from the device; others are wireless. Another option is an optical keyboard that projects an image of a keyboard on a flat surface (Figure 5-18).

You also can transfer, or synchronize, data and information from a computer to a phone. With some phones, you synchronize wirelessly; with others, you attach the phone to the computer via a cable or a cradle that has a cable connected to the computer.

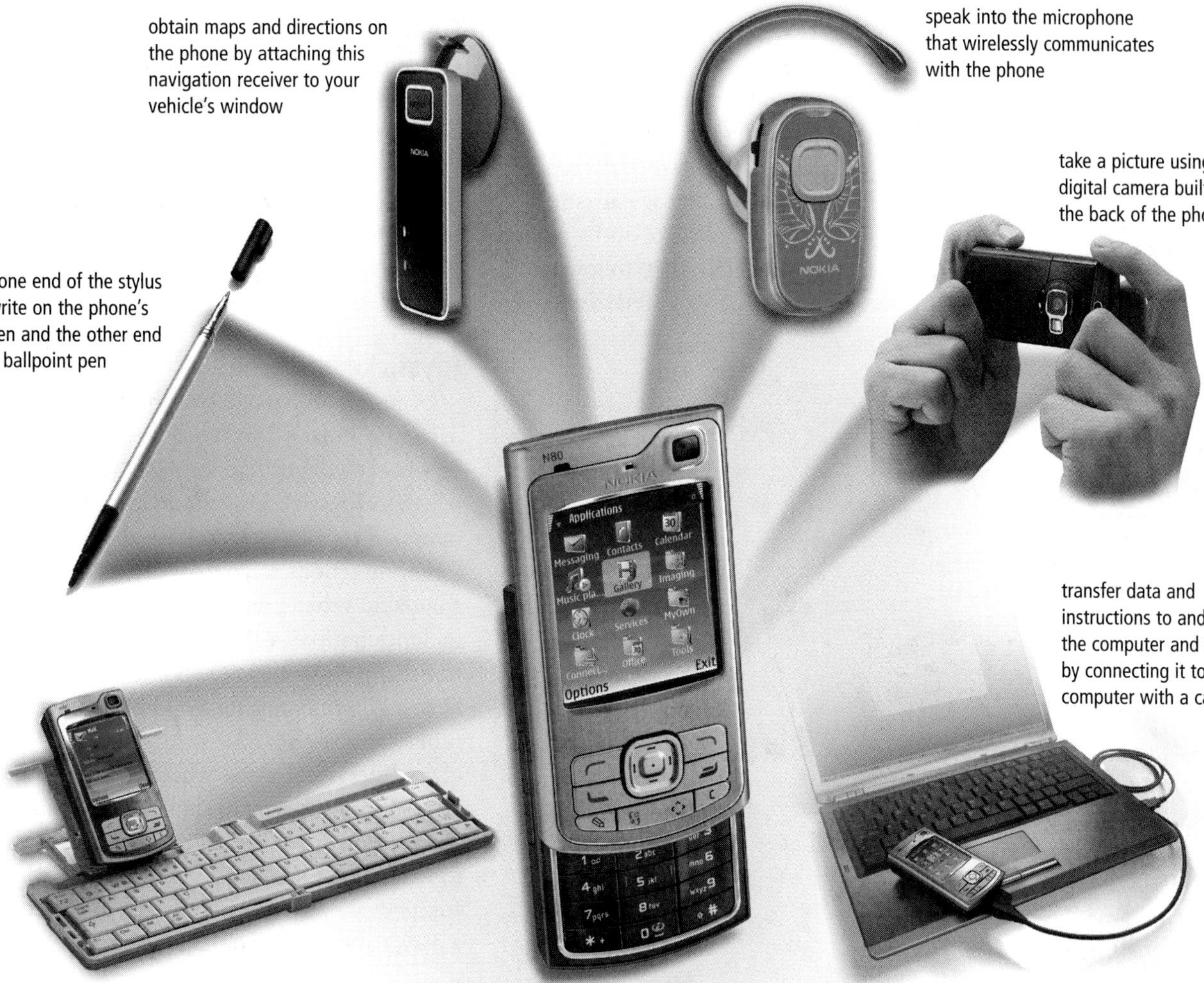

obtain maps and directions on the phone by attaching this navigation receiver to your vehicle's window
speak into the microphone that wirelessly communicates with the phone
take a picture using the digital camera built into the back of the phone
use one end of the stylus to write on the phone's screen and the other end as a ballpoint pen
transfer data and instructions to and from the computer and phone by connecting it to the computer with a cable
enter text-based messages via a wireless keyboard

Figure 5-17 Besides a touch screen and basic stylus, users have a variety of other options for entering data and instructions into a smart phone.

Figure 5-18 The characters you type on this full-sized optical keyboard appear on your smart phone.

FAQ 5-4

What security issues affect mobile computers or devices?

Mobile computers and mobile devices are susceptible to virus threats when you download infected Web pages or open infected e-mail messages. Another risk involves wireless networks, which provide a means for others to connect to your computer or device without your knowledge. One wireless service provider reported that in one year, it cleaned more than 100,000 infections from mobile devices. Once users connect to your computer or device, they may be able to add to, change, or remove your data.

For more information, visit the Computer Concepts CourseMate Web site at www.cengagebrain.com, navigate to the Chapter 5 FAQ resource for this book, and then click Security Threats and Mobile Devices.

Game Controllers

Game Controllers
For more information, visit the Computer Concepts CourseMate Web site at www.cengagebrain.com, navigate to the Chapter 5 Web Link resource for this book, and then click Game Controllers.

Video games and computer games use a **game controller** as the input device that directs movements and actions of on-screen objects. Game controllers include gamepads, joysticks and wheels, light guns, dance pads, and a variety of motion-sensing controllers. The following sections discuss a variety of game controllers (Figure 5-19).

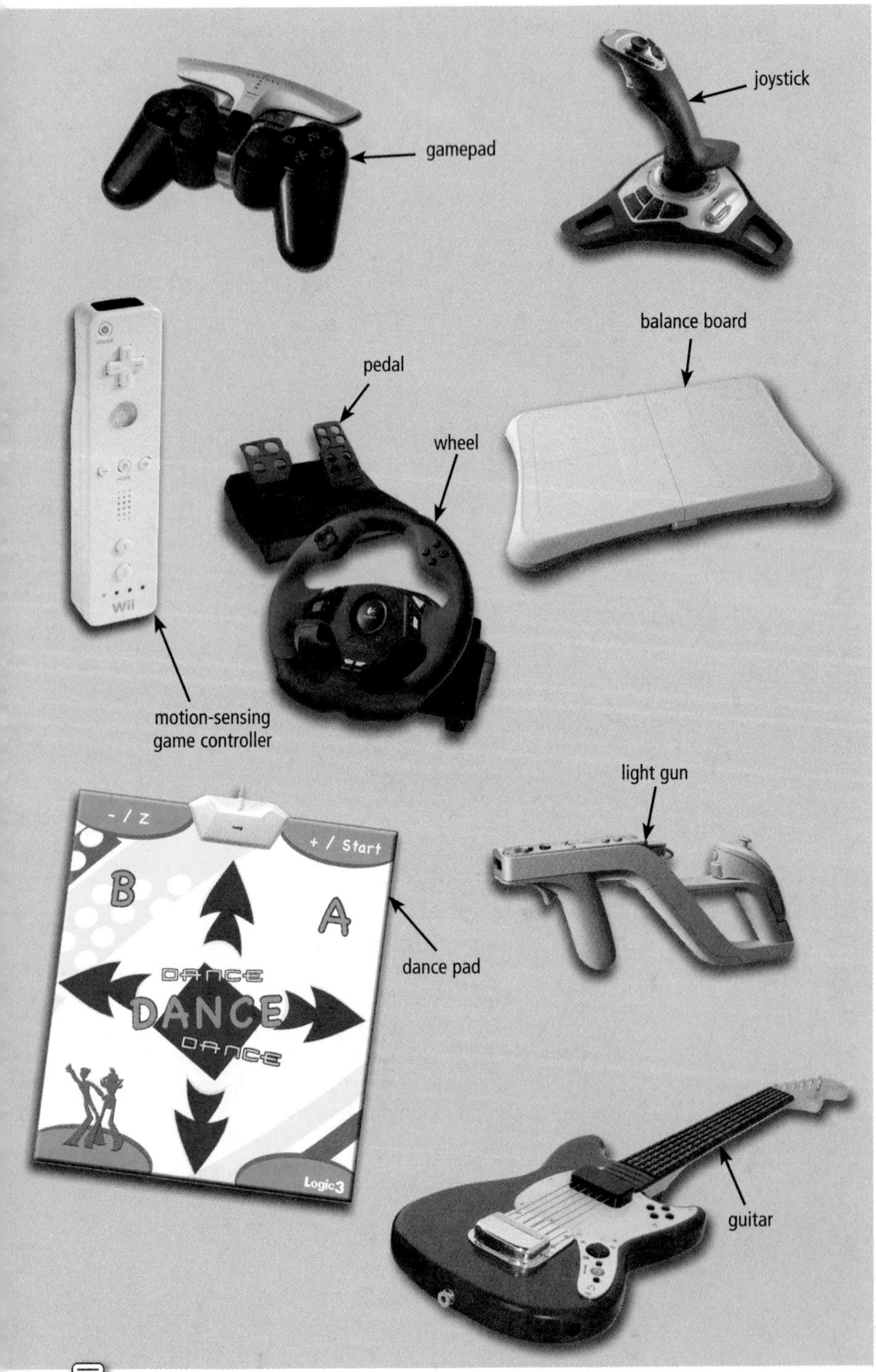

Figure 5-19 A variety of game controllers.

Gamepads

A **gamepad**, which is held with both hands, controls the movement and actions of players or objects in video games or computer games. On the gamepad, users press buttons with their thumbs or move sticks in various directions to trigger events. Gamepads communicate with a game console or a personal computer via wired or wireless technology.

Joysticks and Wheels

Users running game software or flight and driving simulation software often use a joystick or wheel to control an airplane, vehicle, or player. A **joystick** is a handheld vertical lever mounted on a base. You move the lever in different directions to control the actions of the simulated vehicle or player. The lever usually includes buttons, called triggers, that you press to initiate certain events. Some joysticks also have additional buttons you press to perform other actions.

A **wheel** is a steering-wheel-type input device. Users turn the wheel to simulate driving a car, truck, or other vehicle. Most wheels also include foot pedals for acceleration and braking actions. Joysticks and wheels typically attach via a cable to a personal computer or game console.

Light Guns

A **light gun** is used to shoot targets and moving objects after you pull the trigger on the weapon. Instead of emitting light, most light guns work by detecting light. When the user pulls the trigger, the screen uses one of several techniques to send light, which is received by a receptor in the barrel of the gun. Light guns typically attach via a cable to a game console or personal computer.

Dance Pads

A **dance pad** is a flat electronic device divided into panels that users press with their feet in response to instructions from a music video game. These games test the user's ability to step on the correct panel at the correct time, following a pattern that is synchronized with the rhythm or beat of a song. Dance pads communicate with a game console or a personal computer via wired or wireless technology.

Motion-Sensing Game Controllers

Motion-sensing game controllers allow the user to guide on-screen elements by moving a handheld input device in predetermined directions through the air. Some are sold with a particular type of game; others are general purpose. Sports games, for example, use motion-sensing game controllers, such as baseball bats and golf clubs, as their input device. These types of controllers communicate with a game console or a personal computer via wired or wireless technology.

A popular general-purpose, motion-sensing game controller is Nintendo's Wii Remote. Shaped like a television remote control and operated with one hand, the *Wii Remote* is a motion-sensing input device that uses Bluetooth wireless technology to communicate with the Wii game console. Users point the Wii Remote in different directions and rotate it to control on-screen players, vehicles, and other objects.

Other Game Controllers

Other popular game controllers include musical instruments and balance boards. Controllers that resemble musical instruments, such as guitars, drums, and keyboards, work with music video games that enable game players to create sounds and music by playing the instrument. Fitness games often communicate with a balance board, which is shaped like a weight scale and contains sensors that measure a game player's balance and weight (read Ethics & Issues 5-3 for a related discussion). Musical instrument and balance board controllers communicate with game consoles via wired or wireless technology.

ETHICS & ISSUES 5-3

Are Video Game Makers Qualified to Provide Medical Advice?

Video games historically have been considered a couch-potato activity. Recently, however, some video games began providing full workout regimens, including push-ups, sit-ups, yoga, jogging, and even hula hoop. Virtual trainers provide encouragement and guidance. Some critics find fault with these systems, claiming that neither the video game makers nor the games themselves have been evaluated by medical personnel, and as such, are not as qualified as a legitimate human trainer. One game estimated the age of a triathlete to be more than 10 years older than her actual age. Other game players reported that after an hour of an advanced workout with a game, the game reported that only a few calories were burned. In another situation, a game noted that a child was obese, which resulted not only in hurt feelings, but also a lawsuit. Some medical experts note that games do not take a participant's medical history into account when evaluating or recommending activities to a participant. Proponents of fitness-related games state that as long as the games encourage people to be more active, the games are doing what they were designed to do. The games are popular with the elderly and with children who might otherwise not get much physical activity.

Are video game makers qualified to provide medical advice? Why or why not? Can fitness-related video games provide a quality workout similar to an experience at a gym? Why or why not? As long as the games make people more active, should the games' shortcomings be ignored? Why?

QUIZ YOURSELF 5-1

Instructions: Find the true statement below. Then, rewrite the remaining false statements so that they are true.

1. A keyboard is an output device that contains keys users press to enter data in a computer.
2. A stylus is a flat, rectangular, electronic, plastic board.
3. A trackball is a small, flat, rectangular pointing device commonly found on notebook computers, including netbooks and many Tablet PCs.
4. Input is any data or instructions entered into the memory of a computer.
5. Operations you can perform with a wheel include point, click, right-click, double-click, triple-click, drag, right-drag, rotate wheel, free-spin wheel, press wheel button, tilt wheel, and press thumb button.

Quiz Yourself Online: To further check your knowledge of pages 258 through 271, visit the Computer Concepts CourseMate Web site at www.cengagebrain.com, navigate to the Chapter 5 Quiz Yourself resource for this book, and then click Objectives 1 – 6.

Digital Cameras

As discussed in Chapter 1, a **digital camera** is a mobile device that allows users to take pictures and store the photographed images digitally, instead of on traditional film. While many digital cameras look like a traditional camera, many mobile devices such as smart phones, PDAs, and portable media players often have a built-in digital camera. Mobile users such as real estate agents, insurance agents, general contractors, and photojournalists use digital cameras so that they immediately can view photographed images on the camera. Home and business users have digital cameras to save the expense of film developing, duplication, and postage.

The three basic types of digital cameras are studio cameras, field cameras, and point-and-shoot cameras. The most expensive and highest quality of the three is a *studio camera*, which is a stationary camera used for professional studio work. Often used by photojournalists, a *field camera* is a portable camera that has many lenses and other attachments. As with the studio camera, a field camera can be quite expensive. A *point-and-shoot camera* is much more affordable and lightweight and provides acceptable quality photographic images for the home or small business user. Figure 5-20 illustrates how one make of a point-and-shoot digital camera works.

Often users prefer to *download*, or transfer a copy of, the images from the digital camera to the computer's hard disk. With some digital cameras, images download through a cable that connects the digital camera (or the camera's docking station) to a USB port or a FireWire port on the system unit. For cameras that store photos on a memory card, simply insert the media in a reading/writing device that communicates wirelessly or attaches to a port on the system unit.

When you copy photos to the hard disk in a computer, the photos are available for editing with photo editing software, printing, faxing, sending via e-mail, including in another document, or posting to a Web site or photo community for everyone to see. Many users add

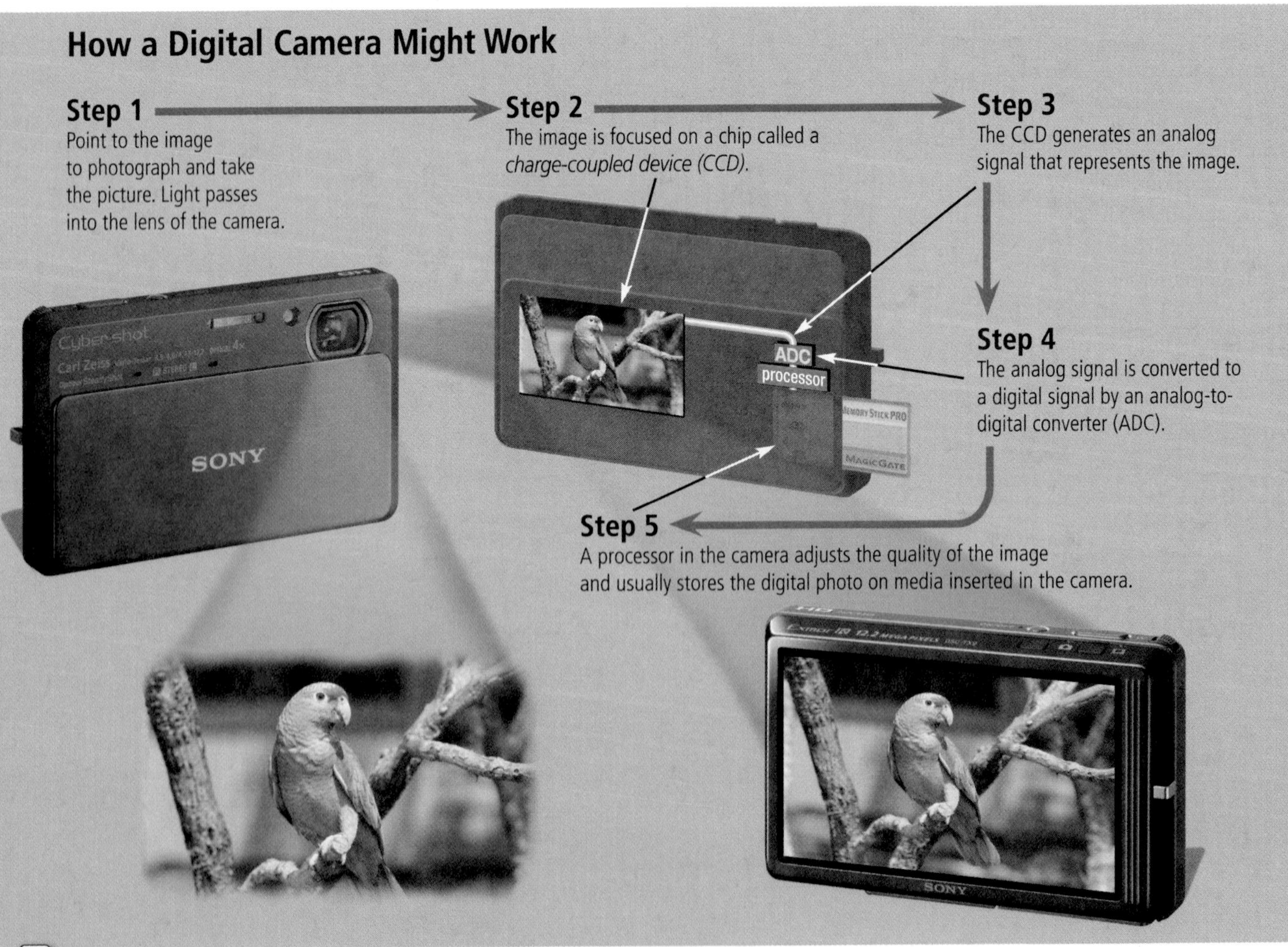

How a Digital Camera Might Work
Step 1
Point to the image to photograph and take the picture. Light passes into the lens of the camera.
Step 2
The image is focused on a chip called a *charge-coupled device (CCD)*.
Step 3
The CCD generates an analog signal that represents the image.
Step 4
The analog signal is converted to a digital signal by an analog-to-digital converter (ADC).
Step 5
A processor in the camera adjusts the quality of the image and usually stores the digital photo on media inserted in the camera.
ADC
processor
SONY
Cyber-shot

Figure 5-20 This figure shows how a digital camera might work.

photos to greeting cards, a computerized photo album, a family newsletter, certificates, and awards.

Digital Camera Photo Quality

One factor that affects the quality of digital camera photos is its resolution. **Resolution** is the number of horizontal and vertical pixels in a display device. A *pixel* (short for picture element) is the smallest element in an electronic image (Figure 5-21). The greater the number of pixels the camera uses to capture a picture, the better the quality of the picture. Thus, the higher the resolution, the better the picture quality, but the more expensive the camera.

Digital camera resolutions range from approximately 4 million to more than 16 million pixels (*MP*). A camera with a 7.1 MP (7,100,000 pixels) resolution will provide a better quality than one with a 4 MP resolution. As a general rule, a 4 MP camera is fine for photos sent via e-mail or posted on the Web. For good quality printed photos, users should have a 5 MP camera for 4 × 6 inch photos, a 6 MP camera for 8 × 10 photos, and 7 MP or greater camera for larger size prints or more professional results.

Manufacturers often use pixels per inch to represent a digital camera's resolution. *Pixels per inch* (*ppi*) is the number of pixels in one inch of screen display. For example, a 2304 × 1728 (pronounced 2304 by 1728) ppi camera has 2,304 pixels per vertical inch and 1,728 pixels per horizontal inch. Multiplying these two numbers together gives an approximate total number of pixels. For example, 2304 times 1728 equals approximately 4 million, or 4 MP. If just one number is stated, such as 1600 ppi, then both the vertical and horizontal numbers are the same.

Many digital cameras provide a means to adjust the ppi to the desired resolution. With a lower ppi, you can capture and store more images in the camera. For example, a camera set at 1280 × 960 ppi might capture and store 61 photos, if it has sufficient storage capacity. The number of photos may reduce to 24 on the same camera set at 2592 × 1944 ppi, because each photo consumes more storage space.

The actual photographed resolution is known as the *optical resolution*. Some manufacturers state *enhanced resolution*, instead of, or in addition to, optical resolution. Optical resolution is different from enhanced resolution. The enhanced resolution usually is higher because it uses a special formula to add pixels between those generated by the optical resolution. Be aware that some manufacturers compute a digital camera's megapixels from the enhanced resolution, instead of optical resolution.

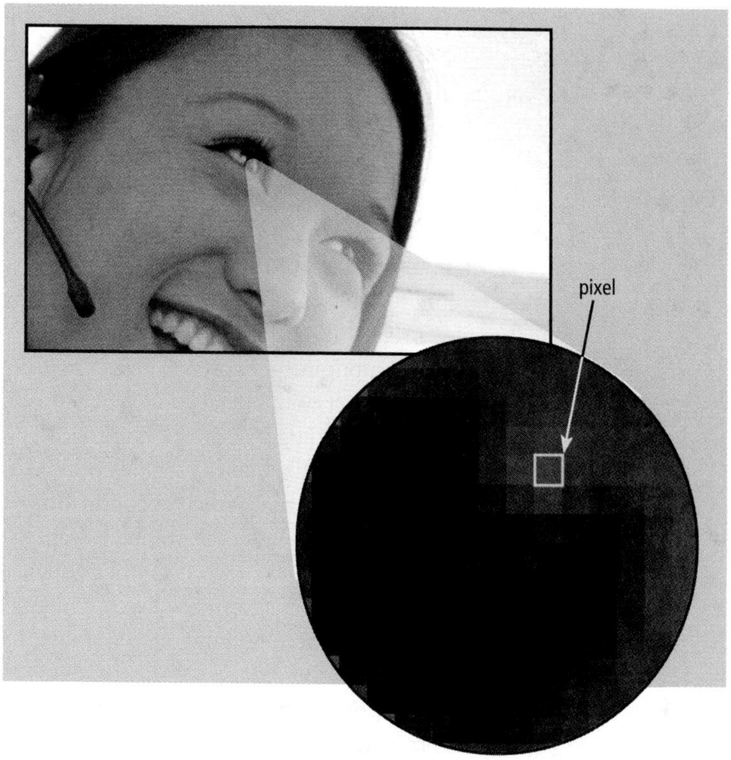

Figure 5-21 A pixel is a single point in an electronic image.

Another measure of a digital camera's photo quality is the number of bits it stores in a pixel. Each pixel consists of one or more bits of data. The more bits used to represent a pixel, the more colors and shades of gray that can be represented. One bit per pixel is enough for simple one-color images. For multiple colors and shades of gray, each pixel requires more than one bit of data. A point-and-shoot camera should be at least 24 bit.

? FAQ 5-5

Why do some advertisements state camera resolution as dpi?

Some advertisements incorrectly use dpi to mean the same as ppi. The acronym *dpi*, which stands for *dots per inch*, is a measure of a print resolution. For screen resolution, the proper measurement term is ppi (pixels per inch).

For more information, visit the Computer Concepts CourseMate Web site at www.cengagebrain.com, navigate to the Chapter 5 FAQ resource for this book, and then click Resolution.

Voice Input

Voice input is the process of entering input by speaking into a microphone. The microphone may be a stand-alone peripheral that sits on top of a desk, or built in the computer or device, or in a headset. Some external microphones have a cable that attaches to a port on the sound card on the computer. Others communicate using wireless technology such as Bluetooth.

Uses of voice input include instant messaging that supports voice conversations, chat rooms that support voice chats, VoIP, and voice recognition. Recall that VoIP (Voice over IP) enables users to speak to other users over the Internet. **Voice recognition**, also called *speech recognition*, is the computer's capability of distinguishing spoken words. Other popular voice recognition programs for personal computers include IBM ViaVoice and Dragon Naturally Speaking (Figure 5-22).

Voice recognition programs recognize a vocabulary of preprogrammed words, which can range from two words to millions of words. The automated telephone system at your bank may ask you to answer questions by speaking the words Yes or No into the telephone. A voice recognition program on your computer, by contrast, may recognize up to two million words. Some current cell phones and other mobile devices allow you to store voice commands such as "Call Tom at home." Operating systems, such as Windows, also include voice recognition capabilities. Keep in mind that the best voice recognition programs are 90 to 95 percent accurate, which means the software may interpret as many as one in ten words incorrectly.

Figure 5-22 With voice recognition software, users can dictate text and enter instructions to the computer by speaking into a microphone.

Audio Input

Voice input is part of a larger category of input called audio input. **Audio input** is the process of entering any sound into the computer such as speech, music, and sound effects. To enter high-quality sound into a personal computer, the computer must have a sound card. Users enter sound into a computer via devices such as microphones, tape players, CD/DVD/Blu-ray Disc players, or radios, each of which plugs in a port on the sound card. Read Innovative Computing 5-1 to find out how software can help you accompany your own songs.

Some users also record live music and other sound effects into a computer by connecting external music devices such as an electronic keyboard (Figure 5-23), guitar, drums, harmonica, and microphones to a port on the system unit. When purchasing a music device, check its specifications for the type(s) of ports to which it connects. Ports that connect music devices to the system unit include USB, FireWire, MIDI, and S/PDIF, each illustrated in the previous chapter.

Music production software allows users to record, compose, mix, and edit music and sounds. For example, you can change the speed, add notes, or rearrange the score to produce an entirely new arrangement.

Figure 5-23 An electronic keyboard can be connected to a computer, allowing users to record and store music in the computer.

INNOVATIVE COMPUTING 5-1

Create Your Vocal Accompaniment Automatically

You never will sing alone again if you use Microsoft's MySong software. This ground-breaking program selects piano chords automatically to accompany vocal melodies. As a result, soloists and composers will hear full musical arrangements for their creations without having to write one note.

MySong was developed in Microsoft's research lab and at the University of Washington. The programmers asked a person to sing a melody. Then, the researchers created a file of musical notes from the sung melody. Finally, they used an algorithm to match chords with fragments of the melody. Several chord sequences are generated so that the singer can choose the style of accompaniment, such as jazzy or happy.

The software developers intended that novice singers use MySong as a basis to learn how accompaniments are written. In addition, they thought the software would help experienced songwriters explore some possible chords and styles for songs.

For more information, visit the Computer Concepts CourseMate Web site at www.cengagebrain.com, navigate to the Chapter 5 Innovative Computing resource for this book, and then click MySong.

Video Input

Video input is the process of capturing full-motion images and storing them on a computer's storage medium such as a hard disk or optical disc.

Some video devices record video using analog signals. Computers, by contrast, use digital signals. To enter video from an analog device into a personal computer, the analog signal must be converted to a digital signal. To do this, you plug a video camera or other analog video device in a video capture port on the system unit. One type of adapter card that has a video capture port is a *video capture card*, which converts an analog video signal into a digital signal that a computer can process. Most new computers are not equipped with a video capture card because not all users have the need for this type of adapter card.

A **digital video (DV) camera**, by contrast, records video as digital signals instead of analog signals. Many DV cameras can capture still frames, as well as motion. To transfer recorded images to a hard disk or optical disc, users connect DV cameras directly to a USB port or a FireWire port on the system unit. Thus, the computer does not need a video capture card. Simply connect the video device to the computer and begin transferring images. After saving the video on a storage medium, such as a hard disk or optical disc, you can play it or edit it using video editing software on a computer (Figure 5-24).

Figure 5-24 Home users can transfer videos to their computers and then use video editing software to edit the video.

Web Cams

A **Web cam**, also called a *PC video camera*, is a type of digital video camera that enables a home or small business user to capture video and still images, send e-mail messages with video attachments, add live images to instant messages, broadcast live images over the Internet, and make video telephone calls. During a *video telephone call*, both parties see each other as they communicate over the Internet. The cost of Web cams usually is less than $100.

Attached to the computer's USB port or FireWire port, a Web cam usually sits on top of a desktop computer monitor (shown in Figure 5-1 on page 259). Many notebook computers have built-in Web cams, such as the one in Figure 5-25.

You can configure some Web cams to display their output on a Web page. This use of a Web cam attracts Web site visitors by showing images that change regularly. Home or small business users might use Web cams to show a work in-progress, weather and traffic information, employees at work, or as a security system.

Some Web sites have live Web cams that display still pictures and update the displayed image at a specified time or time intervals, such as 15 seconds. A *streaming cam* has the illusion of moving images because it sends a continual stream of still images. To learn more about how to install and use a Web cam, complete the Learn How To 1 activity on page 298.

Web Cams

For more information, visit the Computer Concepts CourseMate Web site at www.cengagebrain.com, navigate to the Chapter 5 Web Link resource for this book, and then click Web Cams.

Figure 5-25 This student uses a notebook computer, which has a built-in Web cam, to watch a video of a lecture for her online class.

Video Conferencing

A **video conference** is a meeting between two or more geographically separated people who use a network or the Internet to transmit audio and video data (Figure 5-26). To participate in a video conference using a computer, you need video conferencing software or use a video conferencing Web application, along with a microphone, speakers, and a video camera attached to or built in to a computer. Examples of video conferencing software include CUworld, Live Meeting, and WebEx.

As you speak, members of the meeting hear your voice on their speakers. Any image in front of the video camera, such as a person's face, appears in a window on each participant's screen. A *whiteboard* is another window on the screen that displays notes and drawings simultaneously on all participants' screens. This window provides multiple users with an area on which they can write or draw.

As the costs of video conferencing hardware and software decrease, increasingly more business meetings, corporate training, and educational classes will be conducted as video conferences. Read Innovative Computing 5-2 to find out how patients conference with their health care providers.

INNOVATIVE COMPUTING 5-2

Monitor Health Status Remotely

As people age, they need to monitor their health regularly. The need for managing and treating their personal medical status is even more critical when their conditions include diabetes or congestive heart failure. Intel has developed the Health Guide to allow patients to measure their own vital signs, interact with health care professionals, and receive information without leaving their homes.

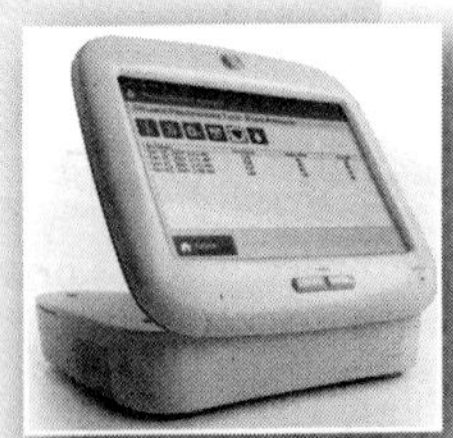

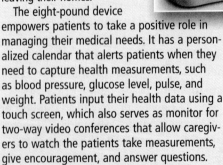

The eight-pound device empowers patients to take a positive role in managing their medical needs. It has a personalized calendar that alerts patients when they need to capture health measurements, such as blood pressure, glucose level, pulse, and weight. Patients input their health data using a touch screen, which also serves as monitor for two-way video conferences that allow caregivers to watch the patients take measurements, give encouragement, and answer questions.

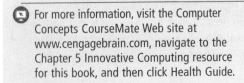

For more information, visit the Computer Concepts CourseMate Web site at www.cengagebrain.com, navigate to the Chapter 5 Innovative Computing resource for this book, and then click Health Guide.

Figure 5-26 To save on travel expenses, many large businesses are turning to video conferencing.

Scanners and Reading Devices

Some input devices save users time by eliminating manual data entry. With these devices, users do not type, speak, or write into the computer. Instead, these devices capture data from a *source document*, which is the original form of the data. Examples of source documents include time cards, order forms, invoices, paychecks, advertisements, brochures, photos, inventory tags, or any other document that contains data to be processed.

Devices that can capture data directly from a source document include optical scanners, optical readers, bar code readers, RFID readers, magnetic stripe card readers, and magnetic-ink character recognition readers. The following pages discuss each of these devices.

Optical Scanners

An *optical scanner*, usually called a **scanner**, is a light-sensing input device that reads printed text and graphics and then translates the results into a form the computer can process. Four types of scanners are flatbed, pen, sheet-fed, and drum (Figure 5-27).

✔ QUIZ YOURSELF 5-2

Instructions: Find the true statement below. Then, rewrite the remaining false statements so that they are true.

1. A digital camera allows users to take pictures and store the photographed images digitally, instead of on traditional film.
2. DV cameras record video as analog signals.
3. Video games and computer games use a Web cam as the input device that directs movements and actions of on-screen objects.
4. Many smart phones today have a built-in camera so that users easily can type text.
5. The lower the resolution of a digital camera, the better the photo quality, but the more expensive the camera.

Quiz Yourself Online: To further check your knowledge of pages 272 through 277, visit the Computer Concepts CourseMate Web site at www.cengagebrain.com, navigate to the Chapter 5 Quiz Yourself resource for this book, and then click Objectives 7 – 8.

Types of Scanners

Scanner	Method of Scanning and Use	Scannable Items
Flatbed 	• Similar to a copy machine • Scanning mechanism passes under the item to be scanned, which is placed on a glass surface	• Single-sheet documents • Bound material • Photos • Some models include trays for slides, transparencies, and negatives
Pen or Handheld 	• Move pen over text to be scanned, then transfer data to computer • Ideal for mobile users, students, and researchers • Some connect to a smart phone	• Any printed text
Sheet-Fed 	• Item to be scanned is pulled into a stationary scanning mechanism • Smaller than a flatbed scanner • A model designed specifically for photos is called a *photo scanner*	• Single-sheet documents • Photos • Slides (with an adapter) • Negatives
Drum 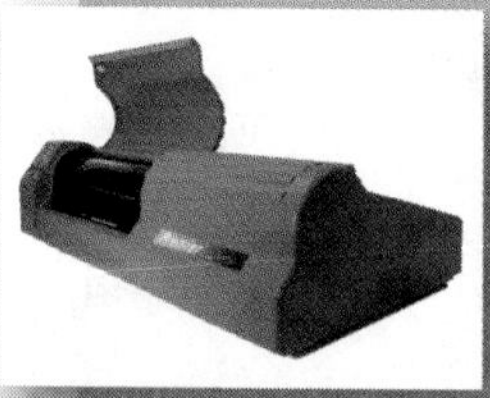	• Item to be scanned rotates around stationary scanning mechanism • Very expensive • Used in large businesses	• Single-sheet documents • Photos • Slides • Negatives

Figure 5-27 This table describes the various types of scanners.

A **flatbed scanner** works in a manner similar to a copy machine except it creates a file of the document in memory instead of a paper copy (Figure 5-28). Once you scan a document or picture, you can display the scanned object on the screen, modify its appearance, store it on a storage medium, print it, fax it, attach it to an e-mail message, include it in another document, or post it on a Web site or photo community for everyone to see.

As with a digital camera, the quality of a scanner is measured by the number of bits it stores in a pixel and the number of pixels per inch, or resolution. The higher each number, the better the quality, but the more expensive the scanner. Most of today's affordable color desktop scanners for the home or small business range from 30 to 48 bits and have an optical resolution ranging from 600 to 9600 ppi. Commercial scanners designed for power users range from 9600 to 14,000 ppi.

Many scanners include *OCR (optical character recognition) software*, which can read and convert text documents into electronic files. OCR software is useful if you need to modify a document but do not have the original word processing file. For example, if you scan a business report with a flatbed scanner and do not use OCR software, you cannot edit the report because the scanner saves the report as an image. This is because the scanner does not differentiate between text and graphics. OCR software, however, would convert the scanned image into a text file that you could edit, for example, with a word processing program.

Businesses often use scanners for *image processing*, which consists of capturing, storing, analyzing, displaying, printing, and manipulating images. Image processing allows users to convert paper documents such as reports, memos, and procedure manuals into electronic images. Users distribute and publish these electronic documents on networks and the Internet.

Business users typically store and index electronic documents with an image processing system. An *image processing system* is similar to an electronic filing cabinet that provides access to exact reproductions of the original documents. Local governments, for example, use image processing systems to store property deeds and titles to provide the public and professionals, such as lawyers and loan officers, quick access to electronic documents.

? FAQ 5-6

How can I improve the quality of scanned documents?

Place a blank sheet of paper behind translucent papers, newspapers, and other see-through types of paper. If the original image is crooked, draw a line on the back at the bottom of the image. Use that mark to align the original on the scanner. Use photo editing software to fix imperfections in images.

For more information, visit the Computer Concepts CourseMate Web site at www.cengagebrain.com, navigate to the Chapter 5 FAQ resource for this book, and then click Scanning.

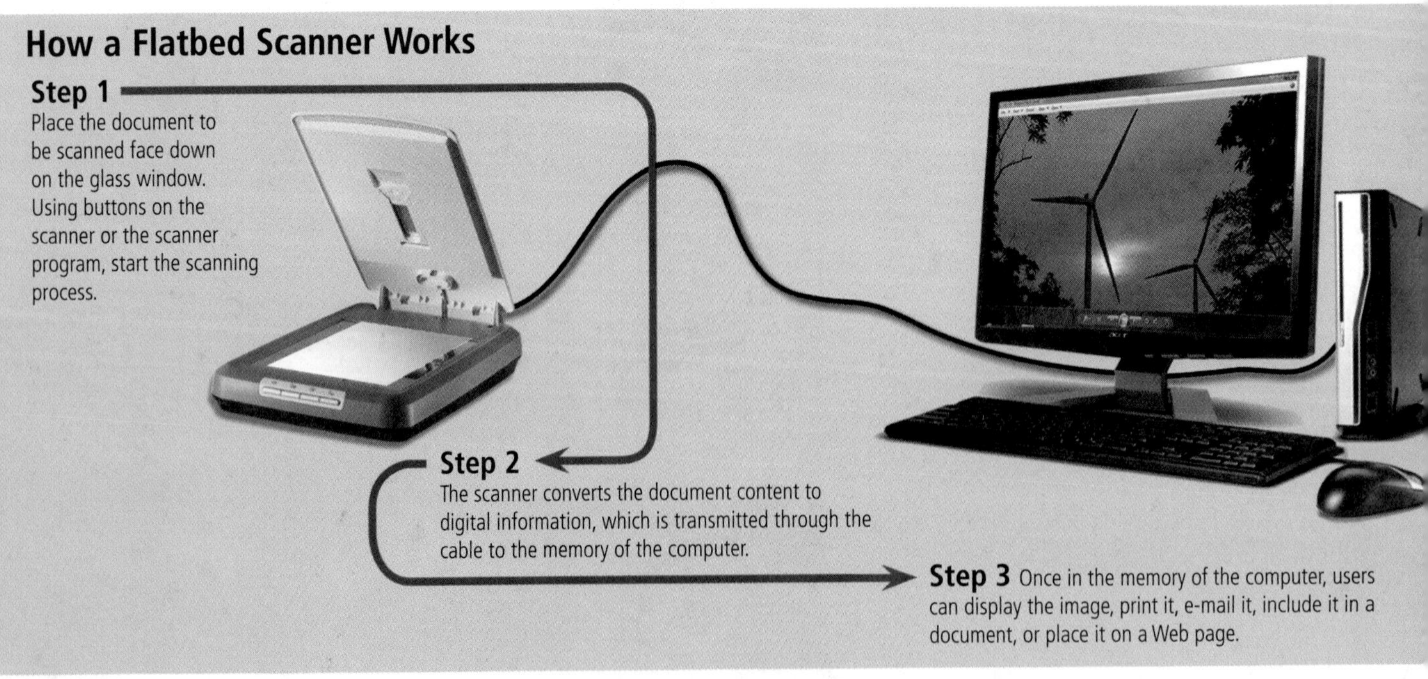

How a Flatbed Scanner Works
Step 1
Place the document to be scanned face down on the glass window. Using buttons on the scanner or the scanner program, start the scanning process.
Step 2
The scanner converts the document content to digital information, which is transmitted through the cable to the memory of the computer.
Step 3 Once in the memory of the computer, users can display the image, print it, e-mail it, include it in a document, or place it on a Web page.

Figure 5-28 This figure shows how a flatbed scanner works.

Optical Readers

An *optical reader* is a device that uses a light source to read characters, marks, and codes and then converts them into digital data that a computer can process. Two technologies used by optical readers are optical character recognition and optical mark recognition.

Optical Character Recognition **Optical character recognition (OCR)** is a technology that involves reading typewritten, computer-printed, or hand-printed characters from ordinary documents and translating the images into a form that the computer can process. Most **OCR devices** include a small optical scanner for reading characters and sophisticated software to analyze what is read.

OCR devices range from large machines that can read thousands of documents per minute to handheld wands that read one document at a time. OCR devices read printed characters in an OCR font. A widely used OCR font is called OCR-A (Figure 5-29). During the scan of a document, an OCR device determines the shapes of characters by detecting patterns of light and dark. OCR software then compares these shapes with predefined shapes stored in memory and converts the shapes into characters the computer can process.

Many companies use OCR characters on turnaround documents. A **turnaround document** is a document that you return (turn around) to the company that creates and sends it. For example, when consumers receive a bill, they often tear off a portion of the bill and send it back to the company with their payment (Figure 5-30). The portion of the bill they return usually has their payment amount, account number, and other information printed in OCR characters.

Figure 5-29 A portion of the characters in the OCR-A font. Notice how characters such as the number 0 and the letter O are shaped differently so that the reading device easily can distinguish between them.

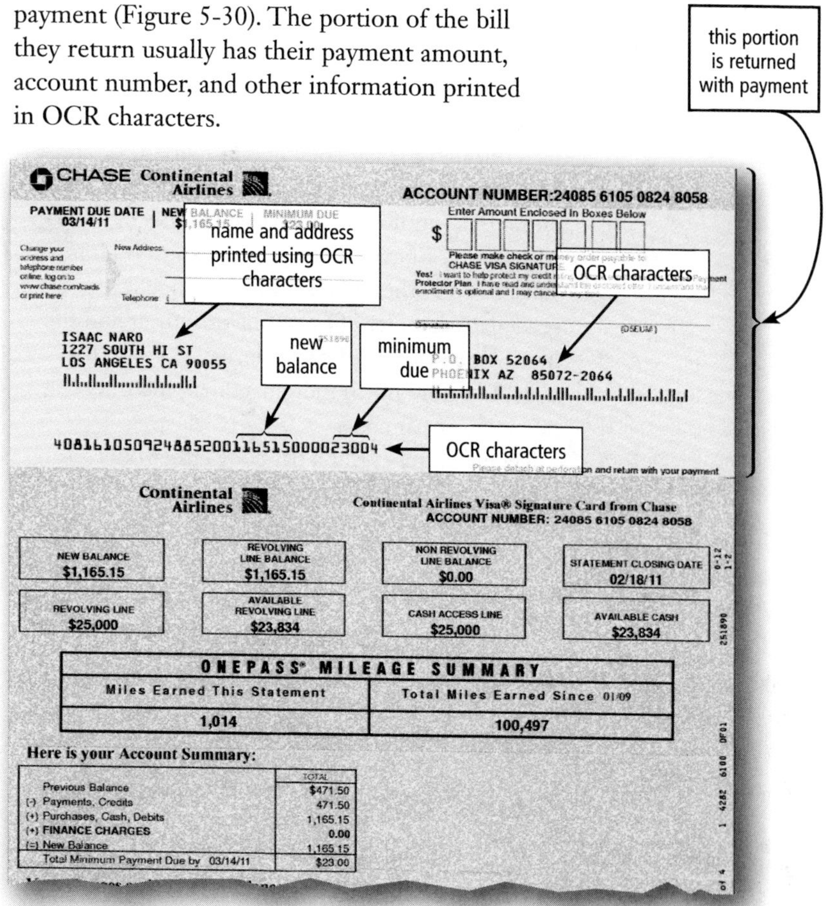

Figure 5-30 OCR characters frequently are used with turnaround documents. With this bill, you tear off the top portion and return it with a payment.

Optical Mark Recognition **Optical mark recognition (OMR)** is a technology that reads hand-drawn marks such as small circles or rectangles (Figure 5-31). A person places these marks on a form, such as a test, survey, or questionnaire answer sheet. With a test, the OMR device first scans the answer key sheet to record correct answers based on patterns of light. The OMR device then scans the remaining documents and matches their patterns of light against the answer key sheet.

Figure 5-31 This person uses a pencil to darken in boxes on this document that can be read by an OMR device.

Bar Code Readers

A **bar code reader**, also called a **bar code scanner**, is an optical reader that uses laser beams to read bar codes by using light patterns that pass through the bar code lines (Figure 5-32). A **bar code** is an identification code that consists either of a set of vertical lines and spaces of different widths or a two-dimensional pattern of dots, squares, and other images. The bar code represents data that identifies the manufacturer and the item. A newer type of bar code, called a 2-D bar code, can store much more data than the traditional linear bar code.

Bar Code Readers
For more information, visit the Computer Concepts CourseMate Web site at www.cengagebrain.com, navigate to the Chapter 5 Web Link resource for this book, and then click Bar Code Readers.

Manufacturers print a bar code either on a product's package or on a label that is affixed to a product. A variety of products such as groceries, books, clothing, vehicles, mail, and packages have bar codes. Some airports now are accepting electronic boarding passes by using a bar code reader to scan a bar code that is displayed on the screen of a smart phone or PDA. Each industry uses its own type of bar code. The United States Postal Service (USPS) uses a POSTNET bar code. Retail and grocery stores use the *UPC* (*Universal Product Code*) bar code.

Figure 5-32 A bar code reader uses laser beams to read bar codes on products such as food and boarding passes.

RFID Readers

RFID (*radio frequency identification*) is a technology that uses radio signals to communicate with a tag placed in or attached to an object, an animal, or a person. RFID tags, which contain a memory chip and an antenna, are available in many shapes and sizes and sometimes are embedded in glass, labels, or cards. Some RFID tags are as small as a grain of sand; others are the size of a luggage tag. An **RFID reader** reads information on the tag via radio waves. RFID readers can be handheld devices or mounted in a stationary object such as a doorway.

Many retailers see RFID as an alternative to bar code identification because it does not require direct contact or line-of-site transmission. Each product in a store would contain a tag that identifies the product (Figure 5-33). As consumers remove products from the store shelves and walk through a checkout area, an RFID reader reads the tag(s) and communicates with a computer that calculates the amount due, eliminating the need for checking out each item.

Other uses of RFID include tracking times of runners in a marathon; tracking location of soldiers, employee wardrobes, airline baggage, and misplaced or stolen goods; checking lift tickets of skiers; managing inventory; gauging pressure and temperature of tires on a vehicle; checking out library books; and tracking payment as vehicles pass through booths on tollway systems. Read Ethics & Issues 5-4 for a related discussion.

ETHICS & ISSUES 5-4

Will RFID Track Your Every Move?

The rapid growth of RFID worries some privacy advocates. RFID (radio frequency identification) uses a tiny computer chip that can be mounted on a tag attached to a product, sewn into an article of clothing, or even attached to a document. For merchants, RFID can help to locate items in a warehouse and identify items that need to be replenished. For consumers, RFID can supply detailed product information, and someday let buyers bypass check-out lines and take purchases directly from the store, with the item's cost charged to their card. The federal government started a program to include RFID chips on all passports. Privacy advocates worry, however, that RFID could obliterate a person's anonymity. They fear that with an RFID reader, any individual or organization could track a person's movements and make that information available to marketers or government agencies. Several researchers have shown that current RFID passports can be copied and forged. Further, some fear that the RFID chip in a passport could be copied by a hidden RFID reader and then used for nefarious purposes such as faking one's identity. To protect privacy, privacy advocates insist that merchants should be forced to disable RFID transmitters as soon as buyers leave a store. They also recommend that RFID-enabled documents, such as passports, be kept in special containers made of material that will not allow the chip to be read until it is removed from the container.

Would you be comfortable purchasing a product that includes RFID? Why or why not? Should buyers be allowed to request that RFID transmitters be disabled after they make a purchase, or should merchants be required to render transmitters inoperative when the product leaves the store? Why? Would you feel comfortable carrying a form of identification that is RFID-enabled? Why or why not?

Figure 5-33 RFID readers read information stored on an RFID tag and then communicate this information to computers, which instantaneously compute payments and update inventory records. In this example, the RFID tag is embedded in a label attached to the tire.

Magnetic Stripe Card Readers

A **magnetic stripe card reader**, often called a *magstripe reader*, reads the magnetic stripe on the back of credit cards, entertainment cards, bank cards, and other similar cards. The stripe, which is divided in three horizontal tracks, contains information identifying you and the card issuer (Figure 5-34). Some information stored in the stripe includes your name, account number, the card's expiration date, and a country code.

Information on magnetic card stripes is used to make payments, authenticate users, record attendance, and provide access to secure areas. When a consumer swipes a credit card through a magstripe reader, for example, it reads the information stored on the magnetic stripe on the card. If the magstripe reader rejects the card, it is possible that the magnetic stripe on the card is scratched, dirty, or erased. Exposure to a magnet or magnetic field can erase the contents of a card's magnetic stripe.

In many cases, a magstripe reader is part of a signature capture pad and/or a point-of-sale terminal. Point-of-sale terminals are discussed later in this chapter.

Figure 5-34 A magnetic stripe card reader reads information encoded on the stripe on the back of your credit card.

MICR Readers

MICR (*magnetic-ink character recognition*) devices read text printed with magnetized ink. An **MICR reader** converts MICR characters into a form the computer can process. The banking industry almost exclusively uses MICR for check processing. Each check in your checkbook has precoded MICR characters beginning at the lower-left edge (Figure 5-35). The MICR characters represent the bank routing number, the customer account number, and the check number. These numbers may appear in a different order than the ones shown in the sample in Figure 5-35.

When a bank receives a check for payment, it uses an MICR inscriber to print the amount of the check in MICR characters in the lower-right corner. The check then is sorted or routed to the customer's bank, along with thousands of others. Each check is inserted in an MICR reader, which sends the check information — including the amount of the check — to a computer for processing. When you balance your checkbook, verify that the amount printed in the lower-right corner is the same as the amount written on the check; otherwise, your statement will not balance.

The banking industry has established an international standard not only for bank numbers, but also for the font of the MICR characters. This standardization makes it possible for people to write checks in other countries.

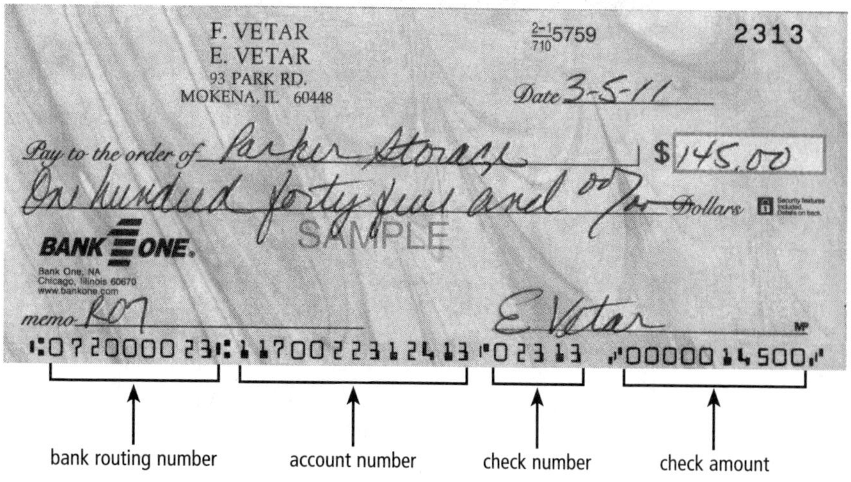

Figure 5-35 The MICR characters preprinted on the check represent the bank routing number, the customer account number, and the check number. The amount of the check in the lower-right corner is added after the check is cashed.

Data Collection Devices

Instead of reading or scanning data from a source document, a *data collection device* obtains data directly at the location where the transaction or event takes place. For example, employees use bar code readers, handheld computers, or other mobile devices to collect data wirelessly (Figure 5-36). These types of data collection devices are used in restaurants, grocery stores, factories, warehouses, the outdoors, or other locations where heat, humidity, and cleanliness are not easy to control. For example, factories and retail stores use data collection devices to take inventory and order products.

Data collection devices and many mobile computers and devices have the capability of wirelessly transmitting data over a network or the Internet. Increasingly more users today send data wirelessly to central office computers using these devices.

Figure 5-36 A warehouse employee uses this rugged handheld computer, which includes a bar code reader, that wirelessly transmits information about the scanned item to the store's inventory system.

Biometric Input

Biometrics is the technology of authenticating a person's identity by verifying a personal characteristic. Biometric devices grant users access to programs, systems, or rooms by analyzing some biometric identifier. A *biometric identifier* is a physiological (related to physical or chemical activities in the body) or behavioral characteristic. Examples include fingerprints, hand geometry, facial features, voice, signatures, and eye patterns.

A *biometric device* translates a personal characteristic (the input) into a digital code that is compared with a digital code stored in the computer. If the digital code in the computer does not match the personal characteristic's code, the computer denies access to the individual.

The most widely used biometric device today is a fingerprint reader. A **fingerprint reader**, or scanner, captures curves and indentations of a fingerprint (Figure 5-37). The reader can be set up to perform different functions for different fingers; for example, one finger starts a program and another finger shuts down the computer. With the cost of fingerprint readers often less than $100, home and small business users install fingerprint readers to authenticate users before they can access a personal computer. External fingerprint readers usually plug into a USB port. To save on desk space, some newer keyboards and notebook computers have a fingerprint reader attached to them, which allows users to log on to programs and Web sites via their fingerprint instead of entering a user name and password. For a technical discussion about fingerprint readers, read the High-Tech Talk article on page 288.

A *face recognition system* captures a live face image and compares it with a stored image to determine if the person is a legitimate user. Some buildings use face recognition systems to secure access to rooms. Law enforcement, surveillance systems, and airports use face recognition to protect the public. Some notebook computers use this security technique to safeguard a computer. The computer will not start unless the user is legitimate. These programs are becoming more sophisticated and can recognize

Figure 5-37 A fingerprint reader.

people with or without glasses, makeup, or jewelry, and with new hairstyles. Read Ethics & Issues 5-5 for a related discussion.

Biometric devices measure the shape and size of a person's hand using a *hand geometry system* (Figure 5-38). Because their cost is more than $1,000, larger companies use these systems as time and attendance devices or as security devices. Colleges use hand geometry systems to verify students' identities. Day-care centers and hospital nurseries use them to verify parents who pick up their children.

A *voice verification system* compares a person's live speech with their stored voice pattern. Larger organizations sometimes use voice verification systems as time and attendance devices. Many companies also use this technology for access to sensitive files and networks. Some financial services use voice verification systems to secure telephone banking transactions.

A *signature verification system* recognizes the shape of your handwritten signature, as well as measures the pressure exerted and the motion used to write the signature. Signature verification systems use a specialized pen and tablet.

High security areas use iris recognition systems. The camera in an *iris recognition system* uses iris recognition technology to read patterns in the iris of the eye (Figure 5-39). These patterns are as unique as a fingerprint. Iris recognition systems are quite expensive and are used by government security organizations, the military, and financial institutions that deal with highly sensitive data. Some organizations use *retinal scanners*, which work similarly but instead scan patterns of blood vessels in the back of the retina.

Biometric Input
For more information, visit the Computer Concepts CourseMate Web site at www.cengagebrain.com, navigate to the Chapter 5 Web Link resource for this book, and then click Biometric Input.

Figure 5-38 A hand geometry system verifies this student's identity before he is allowed access to the school gymnasium.

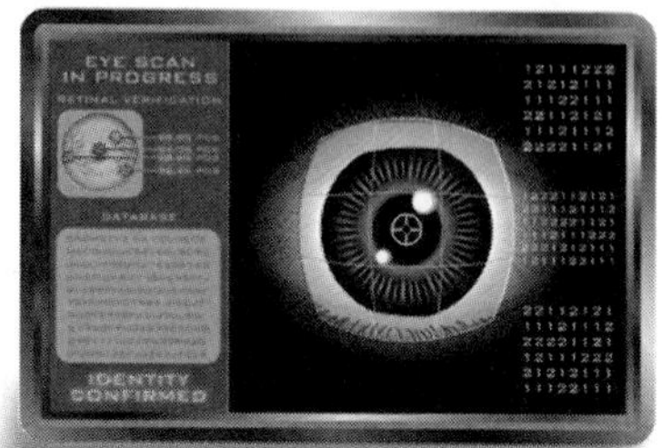

Figure 5-39 An iris recognition system.

ETHICS & ISSUES 5-5

How Often Should You Be Monitored in Public Locations?

Customers with yearly passes for a theme park in Japan enjoy a unique method of entering the park. A biometric face recognition system recognizes the customer's face and allows the visitor entry into the park. At large sporting events, airports, and other public areas, face recognition systems scan visitors' faces and compare the visitors' faces to wanted or known criminals. Those who match a known criminal's face are detained so that authorities can make a final determination if the person should be removed from the location or arrested. Some local governments support placing face recognition systems on streets and scanning everybody who walks by. Supporters state the use of these systems, rather than authorities trying to recognize criminals, is more efficient in finding wanted criminals and allows law enforcement personnel to focus their efforts elsewhere. Opponents of the systems claim that they are an invasion of privacy and even may violate the fourth amendment to the Constitution, which provides protection from unreasonable searches. They also claim that the systems result in an increase in innocent people being detained because the systems are imperfect. In fact, at one large sporting event, more than a dozen people were detained, but none was found to be a match to a known criminal.

Would you mind constant monitoring by face recognition systems? Why? Which types of criminals should face recognition systems be used to locate? Why? How would you react if you were improperly detained due to a mistake made by a face recognition system?

Terminals

A *terminal* is a computer, usually with limited processing power, that enables users to send data to and/or receive information from a host computer. The host computer processes the data and then, if necessary, sends information (output) back to the terminal. The host computer usually is a server or mainframe.

Special-purpose terminals perform specific tasks and contain features uniquely designed for use in a particular industry. Three widely used special-purpose terminals are point-of-sale (POS) terminals, automated teller machines, and DVD kiosks.

Point-of-Sale Terminals

The location in a retail or grocery store where a consumer pays for goods or services is the point of sale (POS). Most retail stores use a **POS terminal** to record purchases, process credit or debit cards, and update inventory.

In a grocery store, the POS terminal is a combination of an electronic cash register, bar code reader, and printer (Figure 5-40). When the checkout clerk or customer scans the bar code on the food product, the computer uses the manufacturer and item numbers to look up the price of the item and the complete product name in a database. Then, the price of the item in the database shows on the display device, the name of the item and its price print on a receipt, and the item being sold is recorded so that the inventory can be updated. Thus, the output from a POS terminal serves as input to other computers to maintain sales records, update inventory, verify credit, and perform other activities associated with the sales transactions that are critical to running the business. Some POS terminals are Web-enabled, which allows updates to inventory at geographically separate locations.

Many POS terminals handle credit card or debit card payments and thus also include a magstripe reader. Some have a fingerprint reader that is linked to a payment method such as a checking account or credit card. After swiping your card through the reader or reading your fingerprint, the POS terminal connects to a system that authenticates the purchase. Once the transaction is approved, the terminal prints a receipt for the customer.

Figure 5-40 Many grocery stores offer self-serve checkouts, where the consumers themselves use the POS terminals to scan purchases, scan their store saver card and coupons, and then pay for the goods.

Automated Teller Machines

An **automated teller machine** (**ATM**) is a self-service banking machine that connects to a host computer through a network (Figure 5-41). Banks place ATMs in convenient locations, including grocery stores, convenience stores, retail outlets, shopping malls, sports and concert venues, and gas stations, so that customers conveniently can access their bank accounts.

Using an ATM, people withdraw cash, deposit money, transfer funds, or inquire about an account balance. Some ATMs have a touch screen; others have special buttons or keypads for entering input. To access a bank account, you insert a plastic bankcard in the ATM's magstripe reader. The ATM asks you to enter a password, called a *personal identification number* (*PIN*), which verifies that you are the holder of the bankcard. When your transaction is complete, the ATM prints a receipt for your records.

Figure 5-41 An ATM is a self-service banking terminal that allows customers to access their bank accounts.

DVD Kiosks

A **DVD kiosk** is a self-service DVD rental machine that connects to a host computer through a network (Figure 5-42). The DVD kiosks, some of which can hold more than 600 DVDs, are located nationwide at retail stores, fast-food restaurants, grocery stores, airports, and other convenient public locations.

A DVD kiosk is associated with a particular vendor. To rent a movie online, for example, a customer visits the vendor's Web site, establishes an account or connects to an existing account, selects the desired movie, and then chooses a nearby DVD kiosk where the movie will be picked up. Customers also usually can select movies directly on the DVD kiosk via a touch screen or some other input device on the kiosk. After presenting identifying information and swiping a credit card through the reader, the DVD kiosk dispenses the rented movie to the customer. When finished viewing the movie, the customer returns it to any of the vendor's nationwide DVD kiosks, at which time the customer's account is charged a fee based on the time elapsed.

Figure 5-42 A DVD kiosk is a self-service DVD rental machine.

Putting It All Together

When you purchase a computer, you should have an understanding of the input devices included with the computer, as well as those you may need that are not included. Many factors influence the type of input devices you may use: the type of input desired, the hardware and software in use, and the desired cost. The type of input devices you require depends on your intended use. Figure 5-43 outlines several suggested input devices for specific computer users.

Suggested Input Devices by User

User	Input Device
Home 	• Enhanced keyboard or ergonomic keyboard • Mouse • Stylus for smart phone or other mobile device • Game controller(s) • 30-bit 600 × 1200 ppi color scanner • 7 MP digital camera • Headphones that include a microphone (headset) • Web cam • Fingerprint reader
Small Office/ Home Office 	• Enhanced keyboard or ergonomic keyboard • Mouse • Stylus and portable keyboard for smart phone or other mobile device, or digital pen for Tablet PC • 36-bit 600 × 1200 ppi color scanner • 8 MP digital camera • Headphones that include a microphone (headset) • Web cam
Mobile 	• Wireless mouse for notebook computer • Touchpad or pointing stick on notebook computer • Stylus and portable keyboard for smart phone or other mobile device, or digital pen for Tablet PC • 7 or 8 MP digital camera • Headphones that include a microphone (headset) • Fingerprint reader for notebook computer
Power 	• Enhanced keyboard or ergonomic keyboard • Mouse • Stylus and portable keyboard for smart phone or other mobile device • Pen for graphics tablet • 48-bit 1200 × 1200 ppi color scanner • 9 to 12 MP digital camera • Headphones that include a microphone (headset) • Web cam
Enterprise 	• Enhanced keyboard or ergonomic keyboard • Mouse • Stylus and portable keyboard for smart phone or other mobile device, or digital pen for Tablet PC • Touch screen • 42-bit 1200 × 1200 ppi color scanner • 9 to 12 MP digital camera • OCR/OMR readers, bar code readers, MICR reader, or data collection devices • Microphone • Video camera for video conferences • Fingerprint reader or other biometric device

Figure 5-43 This table recommends suggested input devices.

Input Devices for Physically Challenged Users

The ever-increasing presence of computers in everyone's lives has generated an awareness of the need to address computing requirements for those who have or may develop physical limitations. The **Americans with Disabilities Act (ADA)** requires any company with 15 or more employees to make reasonable attempts to accommodate the needs of physically challenged workers.

Besides voice recognition, which is ideal for blind or visually impaired users, several other input devices are available. A *keyguard* is a metal or plastic plate placed over the keyboard that allows users to rest their hands on the keyboard without accidentally pressing any keys. A keyguard also guides a finger or pointing device so that a user presses only one key at a time.

Keyboards with larger keys also are available (Figure 5-44). Still another option is the *on-screen keyboard*, in which a graphic of a standard keyboard is displayed on the user's screen.

Figure 5-44 A keyboard with larger keys.

Various pointing devices are available for users with motor disabilities. Small trackballs that the user controls with a thumb or one finger can be attached to a table, mounted to a wheelchair, or held in the user's hand. Another option for people with limited hand movement is a *head-mounted pointer* to control the pointer or insertion point (Figure 5-45). To simulate the functions of a mouse button, a user works with switches that control the pointer. The switch might be a hand pad, a foot pedal, a receptor that detects facial motions, or a pneumatic instrument controlled by puffs of air.

Two exciting developments in this area are gesture recognition and computerized implant devices. Both in the prototype stage, they attempt to provide users with a natural computer interface. With *gesture recognition*, the computer will detect human motions. Computers with gesture recognition capability have the potential to recognize sign language, read lips, track facial movements, or follow eye gazes. For paralyzed or speech impaired individuals, a doctor will implant a computerized device into the brain. This device will contain a transmitter. As the user thinks thoughts, the transmitter will send signals to the computer. Read Looking Ahead 5-1 for a look at a tongue-powered input device.

Gesture Recognition

For more information, visit the Computer Concepts CourseMate Web site at www.cengagebrain.com, navigate to the Chapter 5 Web Link resource for this book, and then click Gesture Recognition.

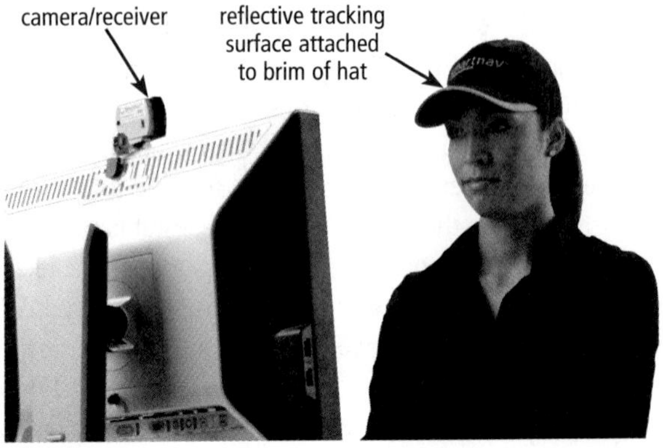

Figure 5-45 A camera/receiver mounted on the monitor tracks the position of the head-mounted pointer, which is reflective material that this user is wearing on the brim of her hat. As the user moves her head, the pointer on the screen also moves.

LOOKING AHEAD 5-1

Tongue May Become Joystick to Control Devices

Thousands of people are paralyzed from the neck down due to spinal cord damage, but they have full control of their tongue because it is controlled by a cranial nerve, not the spinal cord. For these people, Georgia Institute of Technology's Tongue Drive System may be the input device that helps them control their lives.

In the Georgia Tech prototype, the tongue serves as a joystick. A magnet less than one-eighth of an inch wide is surgically implanted under the tip of the tongue, and when a person moves his or her tongue, sensors on each cheek record the magnet's movements in one of six directions: left, right, forward, backward, single-click, and double-click. This data is sent to a receiver on top of the person's head, which, in turn, transmits a signal wirelessly to a computer that controls an electronic device. For example, if the tongue moves forward and to the left, lights in the room could turn on or a wheelchair could roll forward.

In a future development of the Tongue Drive System, an individual tooth could be designated as a specific letter, so teeth could function, in effect, as a keyboard.

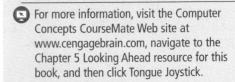

For more information, visit the Computer Concepts CourseMate Web site at www.cengagebrain.com, navigate to the Chapter 5 Looking Ahead resource for this book, and then click Tongue Joystick.

✔ QUIZ YOURSELF 5-3

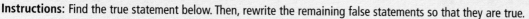

Instructions: Find the true statement below. Then, rewrite the remaining false statements so that they are true.

1. A fingerprint reader captures curves and indentations of a signature.
2. After swiping a credit card through an MICR reader, a POS terminal connects to a system that authenticates the purchase.
3. ATMs ask you to enter a password, called a biometric identifier, which verifies that you are the holder of the bankcard.
4. Four types of source documents are flatbed, pen, sheet-fed, and drum.
5. Retail and grocery stores use the POSTNET bar code.
6. RFID is a technology that uses laser signals to communicate with a tag placed in an object, an animal, or a person.
7. The Americans with Disabilities Act (ADA) requires any company with 15 or more employees to make reasonable attempts to accommodate the needs of physically challenged workers.

Quiz Yourself Online: To further check your knowledge of pages 277 through 286, visit the Computer Concepts CourseMate Web site at www.cengagebrain.com, navigate to the Chapter 5 Quiz Yourself resource for this book, and then click Objectives 9 – 12.

Chapter Summary

Input is any data and instructions you enter into the memory of a computer. This chapter described the various techniques of entering input and several commonly used input devices. Topics presented included the keyboard, mouse, and other pointing devices; touch screens; pen input; other input for smart phones; game controllers; digital cameras; voice input; video input; scanners and reading devices; biometric input; terminals; and input devices for physically challenged users.

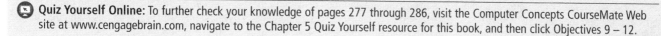

Computer Usage @ Work

Hospitality

Before technology use became widespread in the hospitality industry, the service that customers received was personal but inefficient. For example, most hotel reservations and transactions were recorded manually on paper, which was a time-consuming process. As technology evolved and became more prominent in the hospitality industry, hotels and restaurants began running their businesses more efficiently.

Many hotels now rely on technology to reduce the number of people-hours necessary to perform tasks. For instance, some individuals shop for and reserve hotel rooms online. Many hotel Web sites allow potential guests to take virtual tours of their rooms and read about available amenities. When someone books a reservation online, the information automatically transfers to the hotel's reservation system without intervention from the hotel staff. When guests arrive, an employee verifies their reservation and might hand them an electronic key that opens their room during their stay. After they check out, the key no longer opens the door to that room. During a hotel stay, guests might wish to charge various hotel purchases to their room, which often happens electronically using POS terminals in the hotel's stores and restaurants. An up-to-the-minute listing of all room charges usually is available through the hotel room's television, as well as when the guests check out. Without this technology, employees would complete these transactions manually, which can introduce inaccuracies, causing the hotel to lose money.

In addition to hotels, many restaurants rely on computers for routine tasks. When a server takes a customer's order at a restaurant, the server might enter the order in a computer; the order then is sent directly to a monitor or printer in the kitchen. In this instance, computers can increase accuracy by not requiring cooks and chefs to decipher handwriting. In addition, these computers also store the correct prices for menu items, eliminating the potential for servers to charge customers an incorrect price. When the customer has finished his or her meal, the server prints a check. If the customer pays by credit card, the computer also might process the credit card transaction.

Computers significantly have changed the experience patrons have at restaurants, hotels, and other areas in the hospitality industry. The increased accuracy and efficiency often results in greater guest satisfaction, which can increase sales and justify the investment in the technology.

For more information, visit the Computer Concepts CourseMate Web site at www.cengagebrain.com, navigate to the Chapter 5 Computer Usage @ Work resource for this book, and then click Hospitality.

High-Tech Talk

Biometrics: Personalized Security

Biometric authentication is based on the measurement of an individual's unique physiological and behavioral characteristics. The most common measurements, described earlier in this chapter, such as fingerprints, hand geometry, facial features, and eye patterns are physiological biometrics. Some of the more novel measurements, such as body odor, brain wave patterns, DNA, ear shape, sweat pores, and vein patterns also fall into the category of physiological biometrics. Voice scan and signature scan are examples of behavioral biometrics.

Any biometric technology process involves two basic steps — enrollment and matching. To illustrate these steps, this High-Tech Talk uses the most common biometric technology, finger-scan technology.

ENROLLMENT Enrollment is the process in which a user presents the fingerprint data to be stored in a template for future use, as shown in the top of Figure 5-46. This initial template is called the *enrollment template*. Creating the enrollment template involves four basic steps: (1) acquire fingerprint, (2) extract fingerprint feature, (3) create enrollment template, and (4) store enrollment template. The enrollment template usually is created only after the user has submitted several samples of the same fingerprint. Most fingerprint images will have false details, usually caused by cuts, scars, or even dirt, which must be filtered out.

The first step, acquire fingerprint, presents a major challenge to finger-scan technology. The quality of a fingerprint may vary substantially from person to person and even finger to finger. The two main methods of acquiring images are optical and silicon. With optical technology, a camera is used to register the fingerprint image against a plastic or glass platen (scanner). Silicon technology uses a silicon chip as a platen, which usually produces a higher quality fingerprint image than optical devices.

The second step, extract fingerprint feature, involves thinning the ridges of the raw image to a minuscule size and then converting the characteristics to binary format. Fingerprints are comprised of ridges and valleys that have unique patterns, such as arches, loops, and swirls. Irregularities and discontinuities in these ridges and valleys are known as *minutiae*. Minutiae are the distinctive characteristics upon which most finger-scan technology is based. The fingerprint-feature extraction process used is highly sophisticated, patented, and a closely-held vendor secret.

In the third step, the binary format is used to create the enrollment template. The fourth and final step involves storing the template on a storage device, such as a hard disk or smart card for future use when the same person attempts to be authenticated.

MATCHING Matching is the process of comparing a match template to an enrollment template. A *match template* is created when the user attempts to gain access through a fingerprint reader. Some biometric systems also include *liveness detection*, which verifies that a living person is creating the match template. For example, a fingerprint reader with liveness detection might monitor a pulse. Most computer and network systems are set up so that the person also must claim an identity, such as a user name, along with the fingerprint. In this case, the match template is compared directly to the enrollment template for that user name. Other systems, such as those used for criminal investigations, will search the entire enrollment template database for a match.

The match template is created in the same fashion as the enrollment template described earlier. Rather than storing the match template on disk, however, it is compared to the user's stored enrollment template, as shown in the bottom of Figure 5-46. The result of the matching process is a score. The score is compared against a threshold. The threshold is a predefined number that can be adjusted depending on the desired level of security.

The scoring process leads to the decision process. The decision process will produce one of three actions: (1) the threshold has been exceeded, thereby resulting in a match; (2) the threshold has not been met, thereby resulting in a nonmatch; or (3) the data may have been insufficient, resulting in the system requesting a new sample from the user to begin a new comparison.

Finger-scan technology has grown to become the centerpiece of the biometric industry, and even is becoming more common as an authentication method on desktop and notebook computers.

For more information, visit the Computer Concepts CourseMate Web site at www.cengagebrain.com, navigate to the Chapter 5 High-Tech Talk resource for this book, and then click Biometrics.

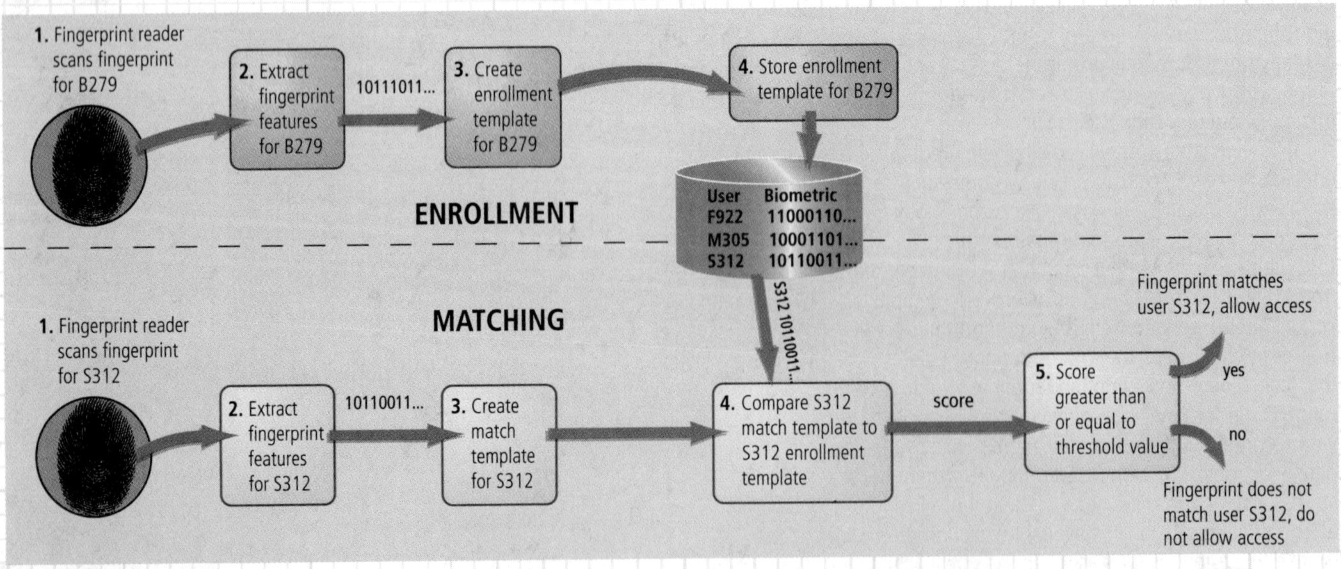

Figure 5-46 The two steps in biometric technology.

Companies on the Cutting Edge

LOGITECH Personal Interface Products Leader

Design and innovation drive the development of *Logitech* products, and the company continues to win top industry awards for its imaginative personal peripheral, Internet communications, home entertainment, gaming, and digital music devices. Logitech has sold millions of mouse devices and wireless products in practically every country in the world.

Stanford computer science students Daniel Borel and Pierluigi Zappacosta, along with Giacomo Marini, founded Logitech in 1981 at Borel's father-in-law's farm in Apples, Switzerland. The company's name is derived from logiciel, which is the French word for software.

Many of Logitech's latest ventures have capitalized on consumers' growing interest in their digital homes. Recently, Logitech announced its one millionth Logitech Vid customer after only three months of being available publicly. Logitech Vid is Logitech's free video conferencing software.

NOKIA Mobile Technology Leader

Approximately four billion people worldwide are using mobile devices, and chances are a majority of them are using a *Nokia* product. This Finnish company is ranked as the number one brand in Asia and Europe and is recognized in the Best Global Brands list as the fifth most valuable brand in the world.

Nokia has a long history in the field of communications. The company began when miner Fredrik Idestam built a wood pulp mill on the Nokianvirta River in Finland in the 1860s and began manufacturing paper. He called his company Nokia Ab. In the next 100 years, the company merged with companies that manufactured rubber and cables. Nokia then focused on the telecommunications industry and became the world's leader in manufacturing mobile phones and cameras.

Recently, Nokia introduced the Nokia Booklet 3G, a netbook boasting a 12-hour battery life. This netbook, slightly thicker than two centimeters, runs the Windows operating system and includes such features as a Web cam, Bluetooth, and an integrated GPS receiver.

For more information, visit the Computer Concepts CourseMate Web site at www.cengagebrain.com and then navigate to the Chapter 5 Companies on the Cutting Edge resource for this book.

Technology Trailblazers

SATORU IWATA Nintendo CEO and President

Being paid to play video games sounds like a dream job, but that activity is all in a day's work for *Satoru Iwata*, Nintendo's fourth president and CEO. The Japanese-born gamer began his career at Nintendo in 2000 as the leader of the company's corporate planning division. Before coming to Nintendo, Iwata served as the coordinator of software production at HAL Laboratory, Inc., where he helped develop the Balloon Flight, EarthBound, and Kirby games. He also freelanced at Nintendo during that time by assisting with some video game development.

At Nintendo, Iwata is credited with leading the GameCube and the Wii technologies. He also has overseen the Zelda, Mario, and Animal Crossing game series. He is commended for persuading third-party companies, including Sega and Electronic Arts, to continue to develop software for the DS and Wii gaming systems.

DOUGLAS ENGELBART Creator of the Mouse

The ubiquitous mouse is a staple for desktop computers, but its evolution to becoming the most widely used pointing device was a slow process. *Douglas Engelbart* conceived the idea of the mouse in 1950 to help humans work more efficiently. Fourteen years later he developed the first prototype with the goal of making it easier for people to move a cursor around a computer screen. In 1974, engineers at Xerox refined Engelbart's prototype and showed the redesigned product to Apple's Steve Jobs, who applied the concept to his graphical Macintosh computer. The final product did not gain worldwide acceptance for another 10 years.

Engelbart is continuing his pursuits of helping people work smarter. His Bootstrap Institute is a California-based company that promotes collaboration, creativity, and competition to solve problems.

For more information, visit the Computer Concepts CourseMate Web site at www.cengagebrain.com and then navigate to the Chapter 5 Technology Trailblazers resource for this book.

Chapter Review

The Chapter Review reinforces the main concepts presented in this chapter.

To listen to the audio version of this Chapter Review, visit the Computer Concepts CourseMate Web site at www.cengagebrain.com and then navigate to the Chapter 5 Chapter Review resource for this book.

1. **What Is Input, and What Are the Differences among a Program, a Command, and a User Response?** **Input** is any *data* or instructions entered into the memory of a computer. A *program* is a series of related instructions that tells a computer what tasks to perform and how to perform them. A *command* is an instruction that causes a program to perform a specific action. A user issues a *user response* by replying to a question displayed by a program to perform certain actions.

2. **What Keys Are Commonly Found on Desktop Computer Keyboards, and How Do Keyboards for Mobile Computers and Devices Differ from Desktop Computer Keyboards?** A **keyboard** is an input device that contains keys users press to enter data and instructions into a computer. Computer keyboards have a typing area that includes letters of the alphabet, numbers, punctuation marks, and other basic keys. Most keyboards also have *function keys* programmed to issue commands; *toggle keys* that switch between two states when pressed; and keys used to move the **insertion point**, or *cursor*, on the screen. A *gaming keyboard* is a keyboard designed specifically for users who enjoy playing games on the computer. On notebook computers and some other mobile devices, the keyboard is built into the top of the system unit. To fit in these mobile computers and devices, the keyboards usually are smaller and have fewer keys than desktop computer keyboards.

3. **What Are Different Mouse Types, and How Do You Use a Mouse?** A **mouse** is a **pointing device** that fits under the palm of your hand. An *optical mouse* uses devices that emit and sense light to detect the mouse's movement. A *laser mouse* uses a laser and is more expensive than an optical mouse. An *air mouse* allows you to control objects, media players, and slide shows by moving the mouse in predetermined directions through the air. A *wireless mouse*, or *cordless mouse*, transmits data using wireless technology. As you move a mouse, the *mouse pointer* moves on the screen. You then press a mouse button (usually the left) to *click* objects. Some programs support *mouse gestures*, where users can perform certain actions by holding a mouse button while moving the mouse in a particular pattern.

4. **What Are the Various Types of Touch Screens, and How Does a Touch-Sensitive Pad Work?** A **touch screen** is a touch-sensitive display device. Touch screens that recognize multiple points of contact at the same time are known as *multi-touch*. Users interact with touch screens by touching areas of the screen such as pictures, numbers, letters, or locations identified on the screen. A *kiosk* is a freestanding computer that usually includes a touch screen. *Microsoft Surface* is a 30-inch tabletop display that allows one or more people to interact with the screen using their fingers or hands. A *touch-sensitive pad* is an input device that enables users to scroll through and play music, view pictures, watch videos or movies, adjust volume, and/or customize settings on a portable media player or other mobile device.

5. **What Are the Various Types of Pen Input, and What Are Other Types of Input for Smart Phones?** With **pen input**, you touch a stylus or digital pen on a flat surface, such as a screen on a monitor or mobile device, a signature capture pad, or a graphics tablet, to write, draw, or make selections. A **stylus** is a small metal or plastic device that looks like a tiny ink pen but uses pressure instead of ink. A **digital pen**, which is slightly larger than a stylus, features electronic erasers and programmable buttons. *Handwriting recognition software* is a program that translates handwritten letters and symbols into characters a computer or mobile device can process. A **signature capture pad** captures signatures written with a stylus or pen attached to a device. Some smart phones have digital cameras that have touch-sensitive pads. Others have a *portable keyboard* or optical keyboard built in.

6. **What Are the Purposes of Gamepads, Joysticks and Wheels, Light Guns, Dance Pads, and Motion-Sensing Game Controllers?** A **gamepad** controls the movement and actions of players or objects in video games or computer games. A **joystick** is a handheld vertical lever that you move to control a simulated vehicle or player. A **wheel** is a steering-wheel-type device that you turn to simulate driving a vehicle. A **light gun** is used to shoot targets as you pull the trigger on the

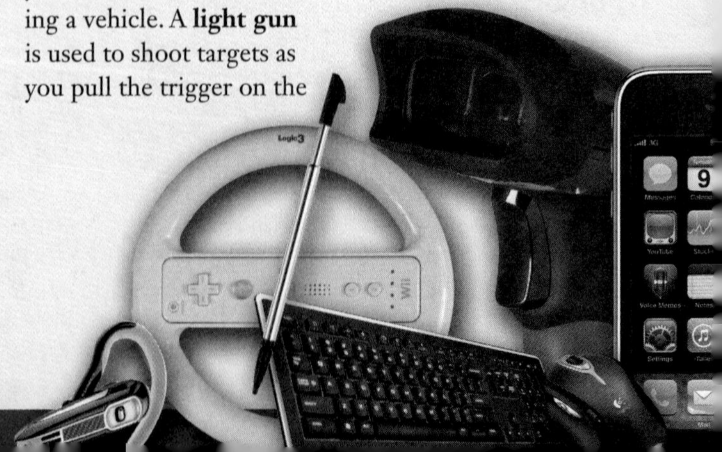

Chapter Review

weapon. A **dance pad** is an electronic device, divided into panels, that users press with their feet. *Motion-sensing game controllers*, such as the *Wii Remote*, guide on-screen elements by moving a handheld input device in predetermined directions through the air.

Visit the Computer Concepts CourseMate Web site at www.cengagebrain.com, navigate to the Chapter 5 Quiz Yourself resource for this book, and then click Objectives 1 – 6.

7. How Does Resolution Affect the Quality of a Picture Captured on a Digital Camera? A **digital camera** allows users to take pictures and store the photographed images digitally. **Resolution** is the number of horizontal and vertical pixels in a display device. The greater the number of pixels the camera uses to capture a picture, the better the quality of the picture. Thus, the higher the resolution, the better the picture quality, but the more expensive the camera.

8. How Are Voice Recognition, Web Cams, and Video Conferencing Used? **Voice recognition**, also called *speech recognition*, is the computer's capability of distinguishing spoken words. A **Web cam**, also called a *PC video camera*, is a digital video camera that enables users to capture video and still images and then send or broadcast the images over the Internet. A **video conference** is a meeting between two or more geographically separated people who use a network or the Internet to transmit audio and video data.

Visit the Computer Concepts CourseMate Web site at www.cengagebrain.com, navigate to the Chapter 5 Quiz Yourself resource for this book, and then click Objectives 7 – 8.

9. How Do the Various Types of Scanners and Reading Devices Work? A **scanner**, or *optical scanner*, is a light-sensing input device that reads printed text and graphics and translates the results into a form the computer can process. A **flatbed scanner** works in a manner similar to a copy machine except it creates a file of the document. An *optical reader* uses a light source to read characters, marks, and codes and converts them into digital data that a computer can process. **Optical character recognition (OCR)** reads characters from ordinary documents. **Optical mark recognition (OMR)** reads hand-drawn marks such as small circles or rectangles. A **bar code reader**, or **bar code scanner**, is an optical reader that uses laser beams to read a **bar code**, or identification code. **RFID** (*radio frequency identification*) uses radio signals to communicate with an embedded tag placed in or attached to an object, an animal, or a person. A **magnetic stripe card reader**, also called a *magstripe reader*, reads the magnetic stripe on the back of credit cards and other similar cards. **MICR** (*magnetic-ink character recognition*) reads text printed with magnetized ink.

10. What Are Various Biometric Devices? A *biometric device* translates a personal characteristic into digital code that is compared with a digital code stored in the computer to identify an individual. A **fingerprint reader** captures curves and indentations of a fingerprint. A *face recognition system* captures a live face image and compares it with a stored image. A *hand geometry system* measures the shape and size of a hand. A *voice verification system* compares live speech with a stored voice pattern. A *signature verification system* recognizes the shape of a signature. An *iris recognition system* reads patterns in the iris of the eye. *Retinal scanners* scan patterns of blood vessels in the back of the retina.

11. How Do POS Terminals, Automated Teller Machines, and DVD Kiosks Work? A *terminal* is a computer, usually with limited processing power, that enables users to send data to and/or receive information from a host computer. POS terminals, ATMs, and DVD kiosks are special-purpose terminals. A **POS** (point-of-sale) **terminal** records purchases, processes credit or debit cards, and updates inventory. An **automated teller machine** (**ATM**) is a self-service banking machine that connects to a host computer through a network. A **DVD kiosk** is a self-service DVD rental machine that connects to a host computer through a network.

12. What Are Alternative Input Devices for Physically Challenged Users? Voice recognition is ideal for visually impaired users. A *keyguard* is a plate placed over the keyboard that allows users with limited hand mobility to rest their hands and press only one key at a time. Keyboards with larger keys or an *on-screen keyboard* displayed on a user's screen also are available. A small trackball or a *head-mounted pointer* helps users with limited hand movement to control the pointer or insertion point. Two developments in the prototype stage are *gesture recognition* and computerized implant devices.

Visit the Computer Concepts CourseMate Web site at www.cengagebrain.com, navigate to the Chapter 5 Quiz Yourself resource for this book, and then click Objectives 9 – 12.

Key Terms

You should know the Primary Terms and be familiar with the Secondary Terms. The list below helps focus your study.

To see an example of and a definition for each term, and to access current and additional information from the Web, visit the Computer Concepts CourseMate Web site at www.cengagebrain.com and then navigate to the Chapter 5 Key Terms resource for this book.

Primary Terms

(shown in bold-black characters in the chapter)

Americans with Disabilities Act (ADA) (286)
audio input (274)
automated teller machine (ATM) (284)
bar code (280)
bar code reader (280)
bar code scanner (280)
dance pad (270)
digital camera (272)
digital pen (268)
digital video (DV) camera (275)
DVD kiosk (285)
ergonomics (262)
fingerprint reader (282)
flatbed scanner (278)
game controller (270)
gamepad (270)
graphics tablet (268)
input (258)
input device (260)
insertion point (261)
joystick (270)
keyboard (260)
light gun (270)
magnetic stripe card reader (281)
MICR (281)
MICR reader (281)
mouse (263)
OCR devices (279)
optical character recognition (OCR) (279)
optical mark recognition (OMR) (279)
pen input (268)
pointer (263)
pointing device (263)
pointing stick (266)
POS terminal (284)
resolution (273)
RFID (280)
RFID reader (280)
scanner (277)
signature capture pad (268)
stylus (268)
touch screen (266)
touchpad (265)
trackball (265)
turnaround document (279)
video conference (276)
video input (275)
voice input (274)
voice recognition (274)
Web cam (275)
wheel (270)

Secondary Terms

(shown in italic characters in the chapter)

air mouse (263)
biometric device (282)
biometric identifier (282)
biometrics (282)
charge-coupled device (CCD) (272)
Click Wheel (267)
command (259)
cordless keyboard (262)
cordless mouse (264)
cursor (261)
data (258)
data collection device (282)
digitizer (268)
download (272)
enhanced keyboard (260)
enhanced resolution (273)
ergonomic keyboard (262)
face recognition system (282)
field camera (272)
function keys (260)
gaming keyboard (261)
gesture recognition (286)
hand geometry system (283)
handwriting recognition software (268)
head-mounted pointer (286)
image processing (278)
image processing system (278)
iris recognition system (283)
keyguard (286)
kiosk (266)
laser mouse (263)
magnetic-ink character recognition (281)
magstripe reader (281)
Microsoft Surface (267)
motion-sensing game controllers (271)
mouse gestures (264)
mouse pointer (263)
MP (273)
multi-touch (266)
music production software (274)
OCR (optical character recognition) software (278)
on-screen keyboard (286)
optical mouse (263)
optical reader (279)
optical resolution (273)
optical scanner (277)
PC video camera (275)
personal identification number (PIN) (284)
photo scanner (277)
pixel (273)
pixels per inch (ppi) (273)
point-and-shoot camera (272)
portable keyboard (268)
predictive text input (262)
program (258)
radio frequency identification (280)
retinal scanners (283)
signature verification system (283)
source document (277)
speech recognition (274)
streaming cam (276)
studio camera (272)
terminal (284)
toggle key (261)
touch-sensitive pad (267)
UPC (Universal Product Code) (280)
user response (259)
video capture card (275)
video telephone call (275)
voice verification system (283)
whiteboard (276)
Wii Remote (271)
wireless keyboard (262)
wireless mouse (264)

trackball (265)

Checkpoint

The Checkpoint exercises test your knowledge of the chapter concepts. The page number containing the answer appears in parentheses after each exercise. The Beyond the Book exercises will help broaden your understanding of the concepts presented in this chapter.

To complete the Checkpoint exercises interactively, visit the Computer Concepts CourseMate Web site at www.cengagebrain.com and then navigate to the Chapter 5 Checkpoint resource for this book.

True/False Mark T for True and F for False.

_____ 1. Once data is in memory, the computer interprets and executes instructions to process the data into information. (258)

_____ 2. An input device is any hardware component that allows users to enter data and instructions into a computer. (260)

_____ 3. The command associated with a function key performs the same task within each program with which you are interacting. (260)

_____ 4. A touchpad is a small, flat, rectangular pointing device that is sensitive to pressure and motion. (265)

_____ 5. Touch-sensitive pads typically contain buttons and/or wheels that are operated with a thumb or finger. (267)

_____ 6. To capture a signature, a user speaks his or her name into a signature capture pad. (268)

_____ 7. Resolution is the smallest element in an electronic image. (273)

_____ 8. A whiteboard is a meeting between two or more geographically separated people who use a network or the Internet to transmit audio and video data. (276)

_____ 9. Scanners capture data from a target document, which is the original form of the data. (277)

_____ 10. A flatbed scanner works in a manner similar to a copy machine except it creates a file of the document in memory instead of a paper copy. (278)

_____ 11. A DVD kiosk is a self-service DVD rental machine that connects to a host computer through a network. (285)

_____ 12. A keyguard is a metal or plastic plate placed over the keyboard that allows users to rest their hands on the keyboard without accidentally pressing any keys. (286)

Multiple Choice Select the best answer.

1. A(n) _____ has a design that reduces the chance of wrist and hand injuries. (262)
   a. gaming keyboard
   b. cordless keyboard
   c. ergonomic keyboard
   d. function key

2. Some phones use _____, where you press one key on the keypad for each letter in a word and software on the phone predicts the word you want. (262)
   a. predictive text input
   b. text messaging
   c. ergonomics
   d. optical character recognition (OCR)

3. Touch screens that recognize multiple points of contact at the same time are known as _____. (266)
   a. touch-sensitive pads
   b. multi-touch
   c. graphics tablets
   d. digitizers

4. Architects, mapmakers, designers, artists, and home users create drawings and sketches on a _____. (268)
   a. trackball b. terminal
   c. graphics tablet d. touchpad

5. _____ is the computer's capability of distinguishing spoken words. (274)
   a. Voice input
   b. VoIP
   c. MIDI
   d. Voice recognition

6. _____ allows users to record, compose, mix, and edit music and sounds. (274)
   a. Kiosks
   b. Voice input
   c. Music production software
   d. Voice recognition

7. RFID is a technology that uses _____ to communicate with a tag placed in or attached to an object, an animal, or a person. (280)
   a. a thin wire b. pixels
   c. radio signals d. light waves

8. With _____, the computer will detect human motions. (286)
   a. a head-mounted pointer
   b. an on-screen keyboard
   c. gesture recognition
   d. a computerized implant

STUDENT ASSIGNMENTS

Checkpoint

Matching
Match the terms with their definitions.

_____ 1. insertion point (261)	a. freestanding computer that usually includes a touch screen
_____ 2. gaming keyboard (261)	b. symbol on the screen that indicates where the next character typed will appear
_____ 3. ergonomics (262)	c. obtains data directly at the location where the transaction or event takes place
_____ 4. trackball (265)	d. incorporates comfort, efficiency, and safety in the design of the workplace
_____ 5. pointing stick (266)	e. pressure-sensitive pointing device shaped like a pencil eraser that is positioned between keys on a keyboard
_____ 6. kiosk (266)	f. controls the movement and actions of players or objects in video games or computer games
_____ 7. game controller (270)	g. keyboard designed specifically for users who enjoy playing games on the computer
_____ 8. gamepad (270)	h. used by video games and computer games as the input device that directs movements and actions of on-screen objects
_____ 9. video capture card (275)	i. converts an analog video signal to a digital signal that a computer can process
_____ 10. data collection device (282)	j. stationary pointing device with a ball on its top or side

Short Answer
Write a brief answer to each of the following questions.

1. What are three different types of mouse devices? __________ What makes them different from each other? __________
2. Name at least five mouse operations. __________ Describe and give examples of each of the mouse operations that you chose. __________
3. What is OCR (optical character recognition)? __________ What is OMR (optical mark recognition)? __________
4. What is the most widely used biometric device today? __________ Describe how the device works. __________
5. What is the Americans with Disabilities Act (ADA)? __________ How might gesture recognition and computerized implant devices help physically challenged users in the future? __________

Beyond the Book
Follow the book element instructions below; present your findings (brief report, presentation, discussion, or other means).

1. Ethics & Issues — Select an Ethics & Issues in this chapter (261, 265, 271, 280, 283), find a recent newspaper/magazine article that supports one point of view presented, and then evaluate the article.
2. Computer Usage @ Work — Use the Web or a recent newspaper/magazine to locate three additional unique usages of computer technology in the hospitality industry (287). What makes the use of these technologies unique to the hospitality industry?
3. Companies on the Cutting Edge and Technology Trailblazers — Use the Web or a recent business newspaper/magazine to locate an interesting fact about Logitech, Nokia, Satoru Iwata, or Douglas Engelbart that was not presented in the chapter (289).
4. High-Tech Talk — Locate a recent newspaper/magazine article that discusses topics related to Biometrics (288). Would you recommend the article you found? Why or why not?
5. FAQs and Web Links — Use the Web or a recent business newspaper/magazine to locate three additional facts about an FAQ (261, 262, 267, 269, 273, 278) and Web Link (262, 266, 268, 270, 276, 280, 283, 286) that were not presented in the chapter.
6. Looking Ahead — Use the Web or a recent newspaper/magazine to discover additional uses of the technology presented in Tongue May Become Joystick to Control Devices (286).
7. Innovative Computing — Use the Web or a recent newspaper/magazine to locate two additional interesting facts about Create Your Vocal Accompaniment Automatically (275) and Monitor Health Status Remotely (276).
8. Making Use of the Web — Visit three of the Travel sites (129) and outline the information on each Web site and the possible uses for each Web site.

Learn It Online

The Learn It Online exercises are interactive Web exercises designed to reinforce and expand your understanding of the chapter concepts. The descriptions below briefly summarize each exercise.

To complete the Learn It Online exercises, visit the Computer Concepts CourseMate Web site at www.cengagebrain.com, navigate to the Chapter 5 resources for this book, click the link for the exercise you want to complete, and then read the instructions.

1 At the Movies — Video Editing on Your Computer
Watch a movie to learn about simple editing tips for converting raw video footage into interesting videos.

2 Video and Audio: You Review It — Voice Recognition
Search for, choose, and write a review of a video, podcast, or vodcast that discusses voice recognition.

3 Student Edition Labs — Working with Audio and Working with Video
Enhance your understanding and knowledge about working with audio and video by completing the Working with Audio and Working with Video Labs.

4 Practice Test
Take a multiple choice test that checks your knowledge of the chapter concepts and review the resulting study guide.

5 Who Wants To Be a Computer Genius²?
Play the Shelly Cashman Series version of this popular game by answering questions to find out if you are a computer genius. Panic buttons are available to provide assistance during game play.

6 Wheel of Terms
Identify important key terms presented in this chapter by playing the Shelly Cashman Series version of this popular game.

7 You're Hired!
Embark on the path to a career in computers by answering questions and solving puzzles related to concepts discussed in this chapter.

8 Crossword Puzzle Challenge
Complete an interactive crossword puzzle to reinforce concepts presented in this chapter.

9 Windows Exercises
Step through the Windows 7 exercises to learn about locating information about your computer, customizing the keyboard, using the mouse and keyboard to interact with a Web application, mouse keys, and using the on-screen keyboard.

10 Exploring Computer Careers
Read about a career as a data entry clerk, search for related employment advertisements, and then answer related questions.

11 Web Apps — Flickr.com
Learn how to use the Internet to upload and share photos, search for photos, and edit photos online using Flickr.com.

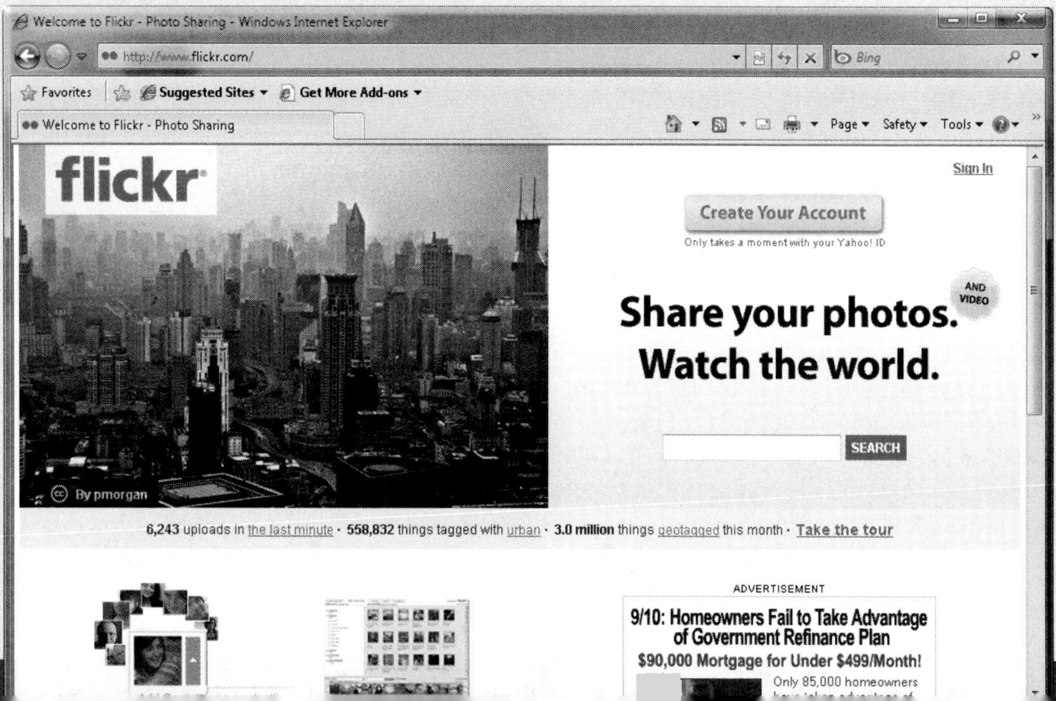

Problem Solving @ Home

The Problem Solving @ Home exercises extend your knowledge of the chapter concepts by seeking solutions to practical computer problems that you may encounter at home or school. The Collaboration exercise should be completed with a team.

In the real world, practical problems often can be solved in multiple ways. Provide one solution to each of the following problems using available resources, such as articles on the Web or in print, blogs, podcasts, videos, television, user guides, other individuals, and electronics and computer stores. You may need to use multiple resources to obtain an answer. Present your solutions in the form requested by your instructor (brief report, presentation, discussion, or other means).

1. **No Media Controls** You have purchased a new keyboard for your three-year-old computer. When you connect the keyboard to your computer's USB port, you are able to type, but the media controls do not work. What could be the problem?
2. **Unresponsive Keyboard** When you turn on your computer, a message appears on your display that says, "Keyboard Error." You press the ENTER key to bypass the message and continue the startup process, but nothing happens. How will you attempt to troubleshoot the problem before calling technical support?
3. **Arrow Keys Functioning Differently** While typing a report in Microsoft Word, you attempt to use the arrow keys on the keyboard to move the insertion point around the document. When you press the UP and DOWN ARROW keys, instead of moving the insertion point up or down, these keys scroll the entire Word window up and down. What could be causing this?
4. **Optical Mouse Problems** During the past several months, it has become increasingly difficult to use your optical mouse to move the mouse pointer around the screen. For example, when you move the mouse from left to right, the mouse pointer appears to jump randomly around the screen. What could be causing this?
5. **Mouse Keys Reversed** While using your friend's computer, you click the Start button with the left mouse button. Instead of the Start menu, a shortcut menu is displayed. You explain the problem to your friend, and he informs you that he would like this behavior to be corrected. What are your next steps?
6. **Touch Screen Problems** At your bank, you notice that the bank has installed a new ATM with a touch screen. When you insert your bank card to begin the transaction, the ATM asks for your personal identification number (PIN). When you attempt to enter your PIN using the touch screen, you find that the ATM is not recognizing your input. What are your next steps?
7. **Incorrect Calculation** Having resolved the ATM touch screen problem in Exercise 6 (above), you are able to access your bank account using the ATM. You now are ready to deposit the checks that you have been accumulating. This new ATM does not require an envelope; all you do is insert the stack of checks. The ATM reads the amount for which each check is written, totals the amounts, and then displays the sum. You are certain, however, that the ATM is miscalculating your deposit. What are your next steps?

Collaboration

8. **Restaurant Automation** You work in the restaurant industry, and your boss decides that he would like to install new computers that will be used to relay orders to the kitchen. Once a server has taken a customer's order, he or she will enter the order into a computer and then the order will appear on a display device in the kitchen. The computers also will print a check for each guest, as well as allow the managers to generate sales reports at the end of each shift. In a team of three people, determine the input devices that will be necessary for the computers to perform the above tasks. The team should consider how the servers enter orders and how the managers will instruct the computers to print the sales reports. Compile the team's findings into a report and present it to your instructor.

Problem Solving @ Work

The Problem Solving @ Work exercises extend your knowledge of the chapter concepts by seeking solutions to practical computer problems that you may encounter at work. The Collaboration exercise should be completed with a team.

In the real world, practical problems often can be solved in multiple ways. Provide one solution to each of the following problems using available resources, such as articles on the Web or in print, blogs, podcasts, videos, television, user guides, other individuals, and electronics and computer stores. You may need to use multiple resources to obtain an answer. Present your solutions in the form requested by your instructor (brief report, presentation, discussion, or other means).

1. **Fingerprint Not Recognized** To increase security, your company now requires employees to log into their computers using a fingerprint reader instead of entering a user name and password. This past weekend, you cut the finger you use to log in, and your computer now does not recognize your fingerprint. As a result, you are unable to access your computer. What are your next steps?
2. **No Audio** While hosting a video conference from your company's conference room with various remote locations, attendees at one of the locations inform you that they no longer can receive audio from your location. The other locations can hear you without a problem. What could be causing this?
3. **Fuzzy Pictures** Your boss has asked you to take pictures of the office building for the company's new Web site. You take the pictures with a digital camera and then view them on the computer. It appears, however, that distant objects appear fuzzy in the pictures you took. What could be causing this? Why did the pictures not appear fuzzy on the digital camera's display?
4. **Keyboard Not Working** The Bluetooth keyboard for your computer suddenly has stopped working. You have changed the batteries, but the keyboard still does not work. You are sure that the batteries are new, and these same batteries also work in your Bluetooth mouse. What might be wrong with the keyboard, and how can you correct the problem?
5. **Unreadable Bar Code** Your company tracks inventory by placing decals with bar codes on all items that are worth more than $1,000 and then uses a bar code reader to track all items. While performing a semiannual inventory check, you encounter a bar code that the bar code reader is unable to scan. What are your next steps?
6. **Liquid on Keyboard** While enjoying lunch at your desk, you inadvertently spill water on your keyboard. You immediately shut down your computer and unplug it from the wall to prevent further damage. What are your next steps?
7. **Malfunctioning Touchpad** When you attempt to navigate the Windows desktop using the touchpad on your notebook computer, the mouse pointer does not move. The left and right touchpad buttons, however, appear to function without issue. When you connect a mouse to the computer, the pointer moves properly. What might be wrong with the touchpad?

8. **Access Denied** Your company uses security badges with embedded RFID tags to authenticate the rooms to which employees have access. When arriving at work one morning, you wave your badge in front of the RFID reader, but the front door does not open. In addition, a red light blinks on the RFID reader. What are your next steps?

Collaboration

9. **Computers in Hospitality** You work for a bed and breakfast that has 12 guest rooms. You currently record reservations in an appointment book and use traditional door keys to grant access to rooms. Occasionally, your guests check out and forget to turn in their keys. For this reason, you must change the lock to that room so that former guests cannot enter the rooms after their stay has ended. You want to use technology to automate the room keys and other processes at the bed and breakfast. Form a team of three people. One team member should research solutions for a computerized reservation system. Another team member should research solutions for implementing an electronic lock solution, and the last team member should research the costs of creating a Web site that allows guests to reserve rooms online.

STUDENT ASSIGNMENTS

Learn How To

The Learn How To activities step you through fundamental technology skills when using a computer. The Learn How To exercises enable you to become more proficient with these skills.

Premium Activity: To relate this Learn How To activity to your everyday life, see a visual demonstration of the activity, and complete a short assessment, visit the Computer Concepts CourseMate Web site at www.cengagebrain.com and then navigate to the Chapter 5 Learn How To resource for this book.

Learn How To 1: Install and Use a Web Cam

A Web cam is a digital video camera that allows you to capture video and still images. The videos can be used in live instant messages or for live images over the Internet. Recordings of the videos can be included on Web pages or in e-mail messages as attachments. In addition, some cameras include software that enables you to establish a visual security environment where the camera can be used to detect and record movement in its general vicinity.

Using a Web cam requires two phases: 1) purchasing and installing the Web cam, and 2) using the Web cam to transmit live video or to record video or digital images.

To purchase and install a Web cam, complete the following steps:

1. Determine how you want to use the camera in order to decide the quality of camera you require and the camera software you need. Web cams range in price from about $25 to more than $125, and vary in picture quality, features, and accompanying software. If you are not sure of all features and prices, search the Web to determine the best camera for your use.
2. After making your purchase, you will find that most cameras are accompanied by an optical disc containing the software that enables the camera to communicate and work with the computer. Often, the instructions with the device will specify that you should place the optical disc in an optical disc drive and follow the on-screen instructions to install the software on the computer.
3. After the software is installed, you likely will be instructed to connect the camera to the computer. You do so by connecting the USB or FireWire cable first to the camera and then to a USB or FireWire port on your computer. When the camera is connected, you will be able to start the camera software from either the All Programs list or the desktop.

Once you have started the camera software, you will be able to use the camera for any of the tasks you require. Each camera and its accompanying software will allow you to create a video, use instant messaging to send live video to your instant messaging contacts, and other uses as well. In addition, you often will be able to control the quality of your video output by modifying brightness, contrast, and clarity. With many cameras, you will be able to zoom in and out and, from your keyboard, enter commands to move the camera lens left, right, up, and down.

On some cameras, you can use a feature called *face tracking*, where the camera will remain focused on your face even when you move. This feature allows you to be more natural and not be concerned with always making sure you are placed exactly right for the camera.

As you can see, once you have purchased and installed a Web cam, you will open an entirely new world of communications right from your computer.

Exercises

1. Assume you have decided to purchase a Web cam to use for instant messaging. Search the Web to find the highest rated cameras available for purchase that can be used for your purposes. What is the most expensive camera you found? The least expensive? What features distinguish the two? Based on your use of the camera for instant messaging, what camera would you choose to buy? Why? Submit your answers to your instructor.
2. Optional: Purchase a Web cam or borrow one from a friend. Install the camera software on a computer. **Warning: If you are using a computer that is not your own, complete this exercise only with the owner's permission.** Connect the camera to the computer. Practice with the camera and the accompanying software. What features does the software provide? Which feature do you find the most compelling? Which features could you do without? Record a video of yourself answering these questions. Submit the video to your instructor.

Learn How To 2: Download Songs to a Portable Media Player

The methods by which you can download a song to a portable media player vary depending upon the type of portable media player you own. Some portable media players connect to your computer, often using a USB connection, and appear as a removable disk in Windows. Some use flash memory mobile media, such as SD cards, that you remove from the portable media player, and then insert into your computer's card reader. Some portable

Learn How To

media players, such as the iPod Touch, can connect to wireless networks and download songs from the Internet without requiring a connection to a computer; others connect directly to your computer and require a special program, such as iTunes, to add songs. This Learn How To exercises describes how to download songs to an iPod from a CD, how to download music to an iPod using iTunes, and how to transfer files to a portable media player that connects directly to your computer.

Using iTunes to Add Songs from a CD to Your iTunes Library

1. If necessary, download and install the latest version of iTunes, which is available at Apple's Web site (apple.com).
2. Click the Start button, click All Programs, click the iTunes folder in the All Programs list, and then click iTunes in the iTunes folder (Figure 5-47).

Figure 5-47

3. If you have not done so already, connect your iPod to a USB port on your computer. When iTunes displays the name of your iPod in the left pane of the iTunes window indicating that your iPod is connected, insert a music CD into an optical disc drive on your computer. **Check the CD's copyright notice before completing the following steps to make sure that you are authorized to copy the CD.**
4. iTunes will download the track names from the CD automatically and display a dialog box asking if you would like to import the entire CD. Click the Yes button to import all songs from the CD. If you wish to select individual songs from the CD, click the No button and select the songs you wish to import.
5. Once the import process is complete, click the Eject button to eject the CD. The songs now are in your iTunes library.
6. If your playlist does not synchronize automatically, right-click the name of your playlist and then click Sync on the shortcut menu. Once the synchronization process is complete, the files are stored on your iPod.

Using iTunes to Add Songs from the iTunes Store

1. If necessary, start iTunes and connect your iPod to your computer.
2. Click iTunes Store in the left pane of the iTunes window to display items available for purchase.
3. Locate the song you wish to purchase in the iTunes Store. If you are looking for a particular song, use the Search iTunes Store box at the top of the iTunes window.
4. Once you locate a song to download, click the Buy Song button. If necessary, enter the information for your iTunes account. If a dialog box is displayed asking if you are sure that you want to buy the song, click the Buy button. iTunes will download the song and charge the credit card or gift card associated with your iTunes account.
5. If your playlist does not synchronize automatically, right-click the name of your playlist and then click Sync on the shortcut menu. Once the synchronization process is complete, the files are stored on your iPod.

Adding a Music File on a Computer to a Portable Media Player

1. Connect your portable media player to an available port on the computer. If the portable media player does not connect to the computer with a cable, remove the memory card from the portable media player and insert it into the card reader on the computer.
2. When Windows displays the AutoPlay dialog box, click the Open device to view files using Windows Explorer button to display a window containing the contents of the portable media player.
3. Locate the song on the computer that you wish to copy to the portable media player and then drag the file to the window containing the contents of the portable media player.
4. Close any open windows and disconnect the portable media player from the computer.

Exercise

1. Locate a music CD that you own and use a program such as Windows Media Player to save the songs as digital files on your hard disk. Once you transfer the songs to your hard disk, connect your portable media player and then transfer the songs from the hard disk to the portable media player. How long did it take to transfer the music from the CD to the computer to the portable media player? Is there an easier way to accomplish this task?

Web Research

The Web Research exercises broaden your understanding of the chapter concepts by presenting questions that require you to search the Web for answers.

1 Search Sleuth

Use one of the search engines listed in Figure 2-10 in Chapter 2 on page 85 or your own favorite search engine to find the answers to the following questions. Copy and paste the Web address from the Web page where you found the answer. Some questions may have more than one answer. If required, submit your answers to your instructor. (1) Which Haruhi Suzumiya games have been released for the Nintendo Wii? (2) What two companies worked in partnership with Kodak to develop kiosks with digital image-making software? (3) Who holds U.S. Patent 4,384,288 issued in 1983 for RFID technology? (4) What object did Tom Cranston, Fred Longstaff, and Kenyton Taylor use as the ball in their trackball, which they invented in 1952? (5) How is the term, disability, defined in the Americans with Disabilities Act? (6) Who are the current MIDI Manufacturers Association (MMA) Executive Board members, and what companies do they represent? (7) Walter Cronkite and Stevie Wonder used the first production version of which machine? (8) According to the Smart Card Alliance, what is the maximum distance a contactless smart card operates?

2 Green Computing

Digital cameras use more battery power than film cameras because they operate electronic image sensors, LCD viewfinders, and flashes. They also write images to storage devices. The battery packs discharge whether you snap photos or not, but you can help extend your digital camera's battery life by following some conservation tips. View online Web sites, including The Battery Bank (batterybank.net), MalekTips (malektips.com/digital_camera_battery_help_and_tips.html), and Associated Content (associatedcontent.com) that provide information about charging battery packs, using cameras, and storing batteries. How do nickel cadmium (Ni-Cd), nickel metal hydride (Ni-MH), and lithium ion (Li-ion) batteries differ in charging time and discharge? How should batteries be stored if cameras are used infrequently? How does conditioning affect "memory effect"? Write a report summarizing your findings, and include a table of links to Web sites that provide additional details.

3 Social Networking

Google's social networking Web site, orkut, enjoys immense popularity in countries outside the United States, with one-half the registered users from Brazil. It won a Pepsi & MTV Youth Icon award for being the largest social networking forum among young users in India. Launched in 2004, the Web site is named after its creator, Orkut Büyükkökten, who is a Turkish software engineer at Google. Visit the orkut Web site (orkut.com) and then click the About orkut link at the bottom of the home page. Click the Demographics link. Which age group has the largest number of registered users? Click the Blog link at the bottom of the page and read several of the entries. Click the Safety Center link and read the Policies, Privacy Features, Security Features, and General Safety Resources sections. Summarize the information you read and viewed.

4 Blogs

Whether you are listening to the radio, watching television, or drinking a beverage at the local coffee shop, the world of sports is likely to surface. People are passionate about their favorite athletes and sporting events, from the community Little League game to the NFL Super Bowl. Visit several sports blogs, including those from Fanblogs (fanblogs.com), BC Sports (blogcritics.org/sports), Deadspin (deadspin.com), Full Throttle (fullthrottle.cranialcavity.net), ESPN (sports.espn.go.com/espn/blog), and Fox Sports (community.foxsports.com/blogs). What are the more popular discussions? Which college football and basketball teams are featured? Who are the professional athletes receiving much discussion? Which NASCAR teams are analyzed?

5 Ethics in Action

Some reports suggest that the Echelon global surveillance system is monitoring more than three billion e-mail messages, telephone calls, and faxes per day. The National Security Agency is forbidden to monitor U.S. citizens, but privacy experts contend that at least 90 percent of U.S. communications is gathered and reviewed. View online sites that provide information about Echelon, including FAS Intelligence Resource Program (fas.org/irp/program/process/echelon.htm) and YouTube videos about Echelon Spy Satellites. Write a report summarizing your findings, and include a table of links to Web sites that provide additional details.

Critical Thinking

The Critical Thinking exercises challenge your assessment and decision-making skills by presenting real-world situations associated with the chapter concepts. The Collaboration exercise should be completed with a team.

To evaluate the situations below, use personal experiences and available resources such as articles on the Web or in print, blogs, podcasts, videos, television, user guides, other individuals, and electronics and computer stores. You may need to use multiple resources to form conclusions and make recommendations.

1. **Class Discussion — Bar Codes vs. RFID** You work in the Efficiency Analysis department of one of the largest retail companies in the world, with multiple stores in every state and many other countries. For the past 25 years, the company has used bar code readers at checkout counters that scan the bar code on products to determine from a database the price to charge customers. The company is considering replacing the bar code readers with radio frequency identification, or RFID. The reader receives the code identifying the product via a chip with an antenna that is part of the box or label on the outside of the product. Analyze and discuss the impact such a change would have on the company, its suppliers, and its customers.

2. **Class Presentation — Carpal Tunnel Syndrome** While attending college part-time for the past two years, you have worked as a data entry clerk for Salmon Mirror. Recently, you began to feel an unusual pain in your right wrist. Your doctor diagnosed the problem as carpal tunnel syndrome, which is the most well-known of a series of musculoskeletal disorders that fall under the umbrella of repetitive strain injuries (RSIs). Your doctor made several recommendations to relieve the pain, one of which was to find a new job. Before you begin job hunting, however, you want to learn more about this debilitating injury. Use the Web and/or print media to investigate carpal tunnel syndrome. Prepare a presentation to include information about carpal tunnel syndrome warning signs, risk factors, suggestions about proper workstation ergonomics, and procedures for healing the injury.

3. **Research — Advantages of Video Conferencing** An electronics company where you are employed as an analyst spends hundreds of thousands of dollars each year on travel to the multiple locations where they operate around the country. In an effort to curb the ever-increasing costs of travel, the chief financial officer has asked you to research the feasibility of adopting video conferencing at all of its major locations. Use the Web and/or print media to determine the advantages and disadvantages of video conferencing. Prepare a brief report that answers the following questions. Can the technology replace all or most face-to-face meetings? What are the costs of common video conferencing systems and the recurring costs their use incurs? Compare those costs to the cost of travel for a team of three people making six trips per year between New York and Los Angeles, including hotel, rental car, airline, and food expenses.

Collaboration

4. **Professional Photography**
You currently work for a small professional photography company that wants to transition from using traditional film cameras to using digital cameras. The company, however, does not want to sacrifice quality because of this change, and they want to keep the cost associated with purchasing new digital cameras reasonable. Your boss has asked you, along with two coworkers, to look for digital cameras that will meet the company's needs for a reasonable price. One team member should research the resolution requirements for the camera, as well as the prices of various digital cameras with that resolution. It might be necessary to research other photography Web sites to determine the acceptable resolution for professional photography. Another team member should determine the type of memory card the cameras should support. Be sure to select a camera that uses a memory card that can hold as many high-quality photos as possible. The third team member should research the type of lens and optical zoom that are required to take professional pictures. The team should compile its findings and make a recommendation to the instructor about which digital camera will meet the needs of the business.

Chapter Six

Output

Objectives

After completing this chapter, you will be able to:

1 Describe the types of output: text, graphics, audio, and video

2 Explain the characteristics of various display devices: LCD monitors, LCD screens, plasma monitors, and CRT monitors

3 Describe the factors that affect the quality of an LCD monitor or LCD screen: resolution, response time, brightness, dot pitch, and contrast ratio

4 Describe various ways to print

5 Differentiate between a nonimpact printer and an impact printer

6 Summarize the characteristics of ink-jet printers, photo printers, laser printers, multifunction peripherals, thermal printers, mobile printers, label and postage printers, and plotters and large-format printers

7 Describe the uses and characteristics of speakers, headphones, and earbuds

8 Identify the purpose and features of data projectors, interactive whiteboards, and force-feedback game controllers and tactile output

9 Identify output options for physically challenged users

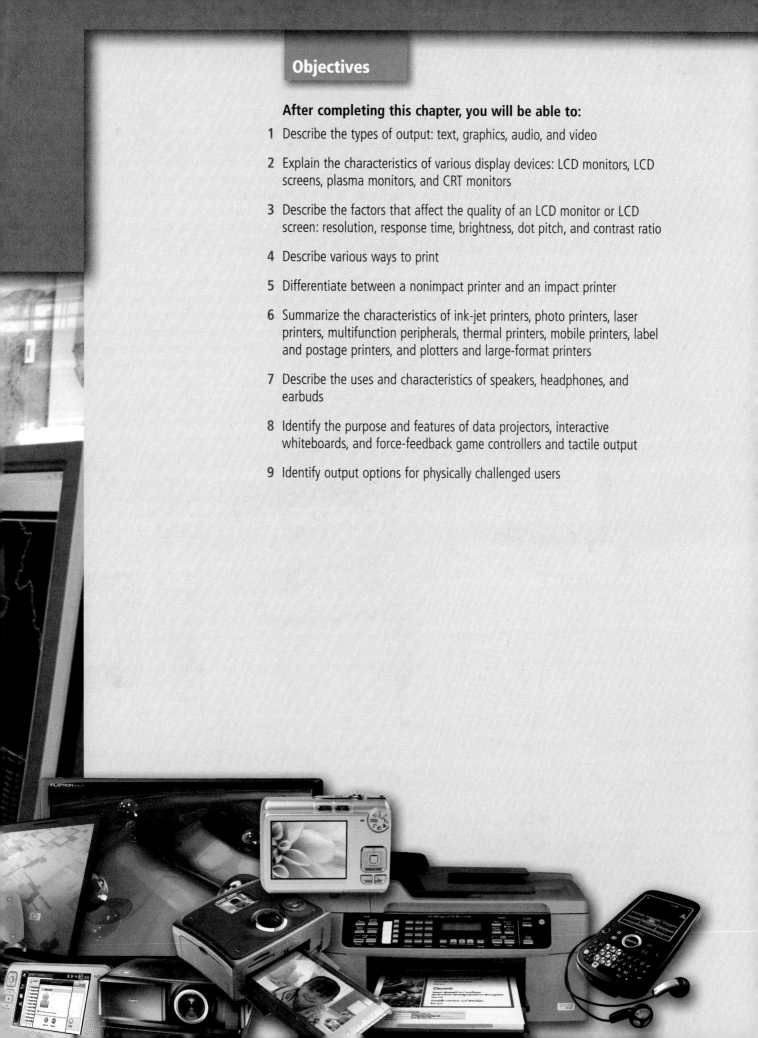

What Is Output?

Output is data that has been processed into a useful form. That is, computers process data (input) into information (output). The form of output varies, depending on the hardware and software being used and the requirements of the user. Monitors, traditional notebook computers, netbooks, Tablet PCs, portable media players, smart phones, digital cameras, and other mobile devices have screens that allow users to view documents, Web sites, e-mail messages, photos, videos, and movies. Many printers enable users to print color documents and photos. Through the computer's speakers, headphones, or earbuds, users listen to sounds, music, and voice messages.

While working with a computer, a user encounters four basic types of output: text, graphics, audio, and video (Figure 6-1). Very often, a single form of output, such as a Web page, includes more than one of these types of output.

- Text — Examples of output that primarily contain text are memos, letters, press releases, reports, classified advertisements, envelopes, mailing labels, and text messages. On the Web, users view and print many other types of text-based output. These include blogs, news and magazine articles, books, television show transcripts, stock quotes, speeches, and lectures.
- Graphics — Many forms of output include graphics to enhance visual appeal and convey information. Business letters have logos. Reports include charts. Newsletters use drawings, clip art, and photos. Users print high-quality photos taken with a digital camera. Many Web sites use animated graphics, such as blinking icons, scrolling messages, or simulations.

Figure 6-1 Four types of output are text, graphics, audio, and video.

- Audio — Users download their favorite songs from iTunes and listen to the music while working on the computer. Software such as games, encyclopedias, and simulations often have musical accompaniments for entertainment and audio clips, such as narrations and speeches, to enhance understanding. On the Web, users tune into radio and television stations and listen to audio clips, podcasts, or live broadcasts of interviews, talk shows, sporting events, news, music, and concerts. They also use the Internet to conduct real-time conversations with friends, coworkers, or family members, just as if they were speaking on the telephone.
- Video — As with audio, software and Web sites often include video clips to enhance understanding. Vodcasts and video blogs, for example, add a video component to the traditional podcast and blog. Users watch a live or prerecorded news report, view a replay while attending a live sporting event, observe weather conditions, or enjoy a live performance of their favorite musician or musical group on a computer or mobile device. Instead of renting a movie, users can download movie content from a Web site for a fee and then watch the entire movie on a computer or mobile device. Attaching a video camera to the computer allows users to watch home movies on the computer. They also can attach a television's antenna or cable to the computer and watch a television program on the computer screen.

An **output device** is any type of hardware component that conveys information to one or more people. Commonly used output devices include display devices; printers; speakers, headphones, and earbuds; data projectors; interactive whiteboards; and force-feedback game controllers and tactile output. This chapter discusses each of these output devices.

Display Devices

A **display device**, or simply *display*, is an output device that visually conveys text, graphics, and video information. Information on a display device, sometimes called *soft copy*, exists electronically and appears for a temporary period. Read Ethics & Issues 6-1 for a related discussion.

Display devices consist of a screen and the components that produce the information on the screen. Desktop computers typically use a monitor as their display device. A **monitor** is a display device that is packaged as a separate peripheral. Some monitors have a tilt-and-swivel base that allows users to adjust the angle of the screen to minimize neck strain and reduce glare from overhead lighting. With some, you can rotate the screen. Adjustable monitor stands allow you to adjust the height of the monitor. Monitor controls permit users to adjust the brightness, contrast, positioning, height, and width of images. Some have integrated speakers and/or a built-in Web cam.

Most mobile computers and devices integrate the display and other components into the same physical case. Some have touch screens. Traditional notebook computers and netbooks have a display that attaches with a hinge to the system unit. Tablet PCs are available with two types of displays: one that attaches with a hinge and one built into the top of the case. Some smart phone and digital camera displays also attach with a hinge to the device. On other smart phones and most PDAs, portable media players, digital cameras, and handheld game consoles, the display is built into the case. Newer vehicles integrate a display in the dashboard, enabling drivers to control audio, video, navigation, temperature, and other settings.

Ethics & Issues

For the complete text of the Ethics & Issues boxes found in this chapter, visit the Computer Concepts CourseMate Web site at www.cengagebrain.com and then navigate to the Chapter 6 Ethics & Issues resource for this book.

Most display devices show text, graphics, and video information in color. Some, however, are monochrome. *Monochrome* means the information appears in one color (such as white, amber, green, black, blue, or gray) on a different color background (such as black or grayish-white). Some mobile devices use monochrome displays because they require less battery power.

Two types of display devices are flat-panel displays and CRT monitors. A *flat-panel display* is a lightweight display device with a shallow depth and flat screen that typically uses LCD (liquid crystal display) or gas plasma technology. Types of flat-panel displays include LCD monitors, LCD screens, and plasma monitors. All flat-panel displays and some CRT monitors have a flat screen. The term, flat screen, means the screen is not curved. The following sections discuss a variety of display devices.

FAQ 6-1

What can I do to ease eyestrain while using my computer?

Position the computer screen about 20 degrees below eye level. Clean the screen regularly. Blink your eyes every five seconds. Adjust the room lighting. Face into an open space beyond the computer screen. Use larger fonts or zoom a display. Take an eye break every 30 minutes: look into the distance and focus on an object for 20 to 30 seconds, roll your eyes in a complete circle, and then close your eyes for at least 30 seconds. If you wear glasses, ask your doctor about computer glasses.

For more information, visit the Computer Concepts CourseMate Web site at www.cengagebrain.com, navigate to the Chapter 6 FAQ resource for this book, and then click Eye Strain.

ETHICS & ISSUES 6-1

Are Digital Billboards a Public Safety Hazard?

A company that sells advertising space on billboards recently upgraded seven static billboards in an area to digital billboards at a cost of more than $3 million. In the first year alone, the seven billboards nearly paid for themselves by increasing advertising revenue tenfold from $300,000 to $3 million per year. *Digital billboards* display advertisements that often change every six seconds and can include video content. While advertising industry funded research shows no correlation between the location of digital billboards and vehicle accidents, other research proves otherwise. Supporters of the billboards claim that the billboards are no more of a distraction than anything else visible near a roadway. Some research shows a significant increase in accident rates where digital billboards replace static billboards. Government agencies that control zoning issues for the billboards often are torn between the tax and lease revenue generated by the billboards and the need for public safety. Some states and municipalities have banned digital billboards, while others welcome them. The billboards often display public service advertisements, Amber Alerts, or other valuable information.

Are digital billboards any more of a distraction than other driving distractions? Why or why not? Should the government regulate digital billboards? What types of regulations, if any, should governments apply to digital billboards, and which level of government should regulate them? Have you seen a digital billboard, and, if so, do you feel that the billboard was distracting?

LCD Monitors and LCD Screens

An **LCD monitor** is a desktop monitor that uses a liquid crystal display to produce images. These monitors produce sharp, flicker-free images. LCD monitors have a small footprint; that is, they do not take up much desk space. For additional space savings, some LCD monitors are wall mountable. LCD monitors are available in a variety of sizes, with the more common being 19, 20, 22, 24, 26, 27, and 30 inches — some are 45 or 65 inches. Most are *widescreen*, which are wider than they are tall (Figure 6-2). You measure a monitor the same way you measure a television, that is, diagonally from one corner to the other.

Determining which size monitor to purchase depends on your intended use. A large monitor allows you to view more information on the screen at once, but usually is more expensive. You may want to invest in a 30-inch monitor if you use multiple programs at one time or do a lot of research on the Web. Users working with intense graphics programs, such as desktop publishing and engineering, typically have larger monitors.

For an even wider screen area, some users position two or more monitors side by side or stacked. For example, the left monitor can show the left side of a wide document, such as a spreadsheet, with the right monitor showing the right side. Or, you can run multiple programs simultaneously with some programs showing on one monitor and other program(s) on a second monitor (Figure 6-3). Users of side-by-side or stacked monitors include music editors, video editors, network administrators, gamers, researchers, Web developers, graphic designers, and engineers.

Mobile computers and mobile devices have built-in LCD screens (Figure 6-4). Many are widescreen; some are touch screen.

Notebook computer screens are available in a variety of sizes, with the more common

Widescreen LCD Monitors

For more information, visit the Computer Concepts CourseMate Web site at www.cengagebrain.com, navigate to the Chapter 6 Web Link resource for this book, and then click Widescreen LCD Monitors.

Figure 6-2 This widescreen LCD monitor has built-in speakers.

Figure 6-3 Users sometimes have multiple monitors stacked or side by side to increase their viewing area.

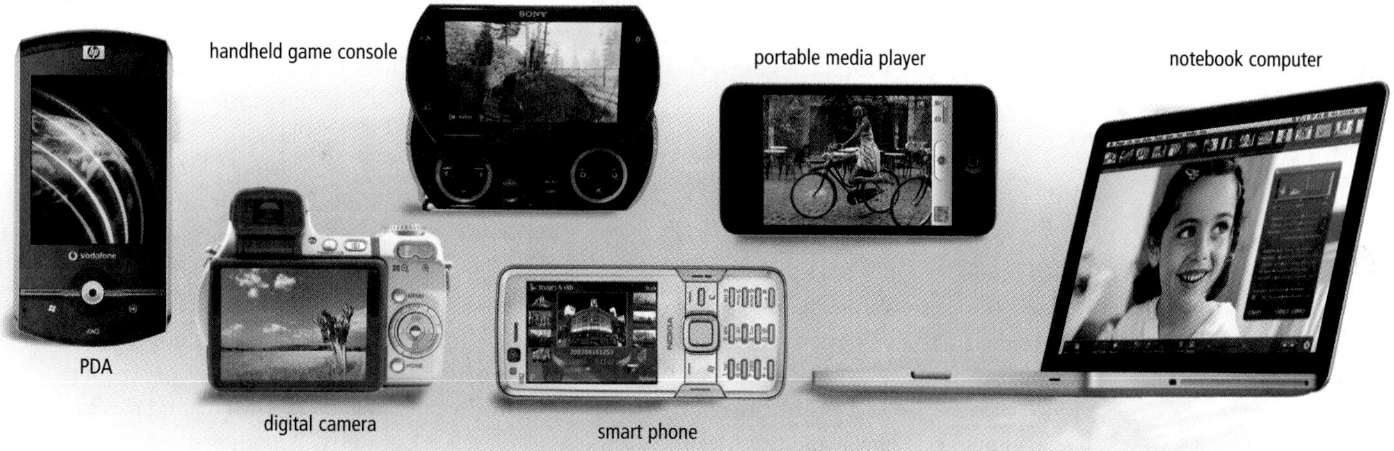

Figure 6-4 Many people use their computers and mobile devices to view photos or watch downloaded videos and home movies. To learn about creating and uploading videos to YouTube, complete the Learn How To 1 activity on pages 340 and 341.

being 14.1, 15.4, 17, and 20.1 inches. Netbook screens typically range in size from 7 inches to 12.1 inches, and Tablet PC screens range from 8.4 inches to 14.1 inches. Portable media players usually have screen sizes from 1.5 inches to 3.5 inches. On smart phones, screen sizes range from 2.5 inches to 4.1 inches. Digital camera screen sizes usually range from 2.5 inches to 4 inches. Read Innovative Computing 6-1 to find out about another use of LCD screens.

INNOVATIVE COMPUTING 6-1

Get the Picture with Digital Frames

Put away your photo albums filled with vacation pictures, baby portraits, and wedding reception candids. With *digital photo frames*, you constantly can display all the photos that capture the best times of your life.

Digital photo frames are becoming mainstream as they drop in price and increase in quality. A correlation exists between price, photo quality, and features, so the higher priced frames generally have clearer displays with accurate color. They also have adjustments for brightness, contrast, tint, and color and may use rechargeable batteries instead of electricity to power the display and dissolve from one photo to the next. Look for frames with a resolution of at least 640 × 480.

Some frames integrate Wi-Fi so that you can send your photos to the frame via your home network or download them from photo sharing Web sites. Once the photos are stored, you can add transitions and set the mood by timing the presentation to your favorite songs.

For more information, visit the Computer Concepts CourseMate Web site at www.cengagebrain.com, navigate to the Chapter 6 Innovative Computing resource for this book, and then click Digital Frames.

LCD Technology

A **liquid crystal display (LCD)** uses a liquid compound to present information on a display device. Computer LCDs typically contain fluorescent tubes that emit light waves toward the liquid-crystal cells, which are sandwiched between two sheets of material. When an electrical charge passes through the cells, the cells twist. This twisting causes some light waves to be blocked and allows others to pass through, creating images on the display.

LCD monitors and LCD screens typically produce color using either active-matrix or passive-matrix technology. An *active-matrix display*, also known as a *TFT (thin-film transistor) display*, uses a separate transistor to apply charges to each liquid crystal cell and thus displays high-quality color that is viewable from all angles. A newer type of TFT technology, called *organic LED (OLED)*, uses organic molecules that produce an even brighter, easier-to-read display than standard TFT displays. OLEDs are less expensive to produce, consume less power, and can be fabricated on thin, flexible surfaces. A newer use of OLED technology is in the *head-mounted display* (HMD), which is a display in a helmet, goggles, or glasses. HMDs are used by pilots, military and law enforcement personnel, engineers, scientists, travelers, and video game players. Some newer LCD screens, known as LCD LED screens, use LEDs to light the screen. LCD LED screens offer better picture quality than traditional LCD screens. LCD LED screens also are thinner and consume approximately 40 percent less power than LCD screens.

A *passive-matrix display* uses fewer transistors, requires less power, and is less expensive than an active-matrix display. The color on a passive-matrix display often is not as bright as an active-matrix display. Users view images on a passive-matrix display best when working directly in front of it.

LCD Quality

The quality of an LCD monitor or LCD screen depends primarily on its resolution, response time, brightness, dot pitch, and contrast ratio.

- **Resolution** is the number of horizontal and vertical pixels in a display device. For example, a monitor that has a 1440 × 900 resolution displays up to 1440 pixels per horizontal row and 900 pixels per vertical row, for a total of 1,296,000 pixels to create a screen image. Recall that a *pixel* (short for picture element) is a single point in an electronic image. A higher resolution uses a greater number of pixels and thus provides a smoother, sharper, and clearer image. As you increase the resolution, however, some items on the screen appear smaller (Figure 6-5).

  With LCD monitors and screens, resolution generally is proportional to the size of the device. For example, a widescreen 19-inch LCD monitor typically has a resolution of 1440 × 900, while a widescreen 22-inch LCD monitor has a resolution of 1680 × 1050. LCDs are geared for a specific resolution, called the *native resolution*. Although you can change the resolution to any setting, for optimal results, use the monitor's native resolution setting.
- *Response time* of an LCD monitor or screen is the time in milliseconds (ms) that it takes to turn a pixel on or off. LCD monitors' and screens' response times range from 3 to 16 ms. The lower the number, the faster the response time.

Figure 6-5a (screen resolution at 1024 × 768)

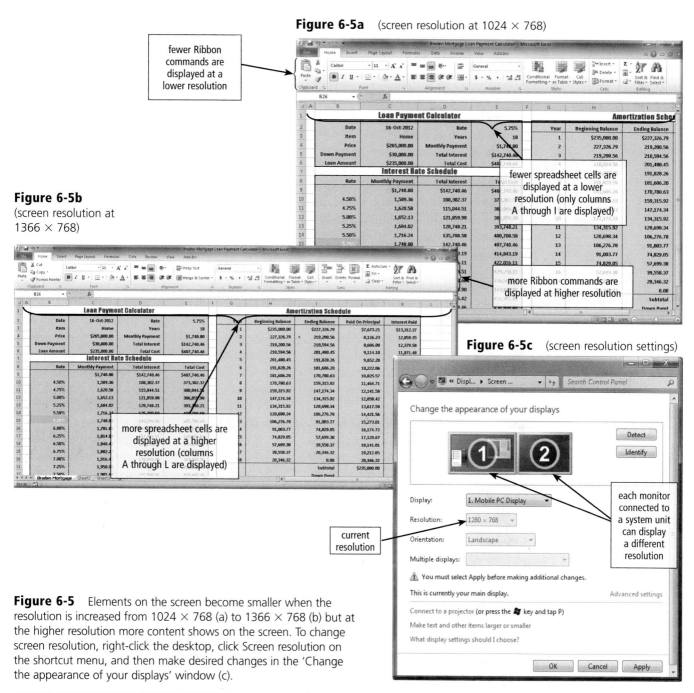

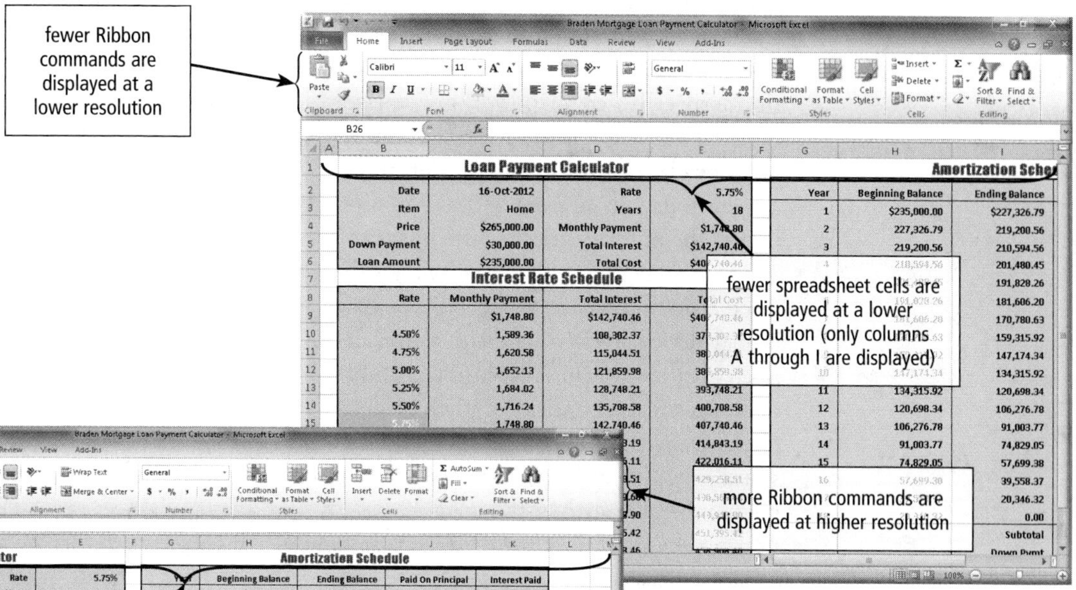

Figure 6-5b (screen resolution at 1366 × 768)

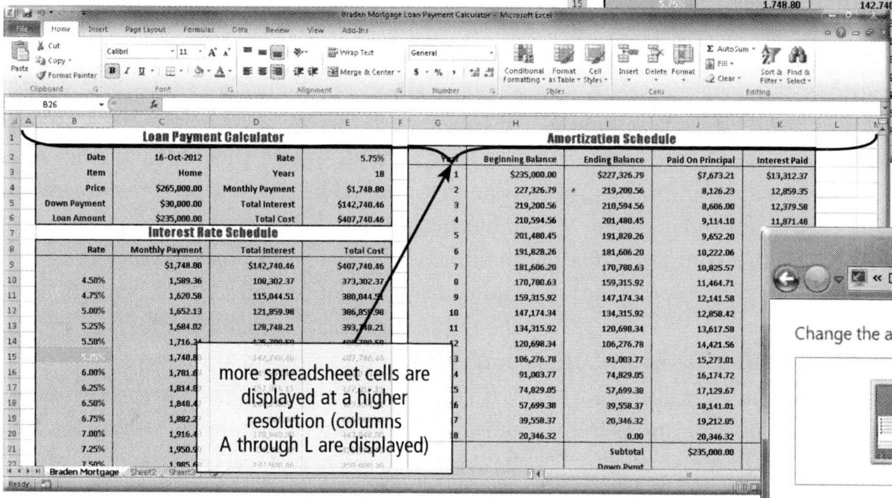

Figure 6-5c (screen resolution settings)

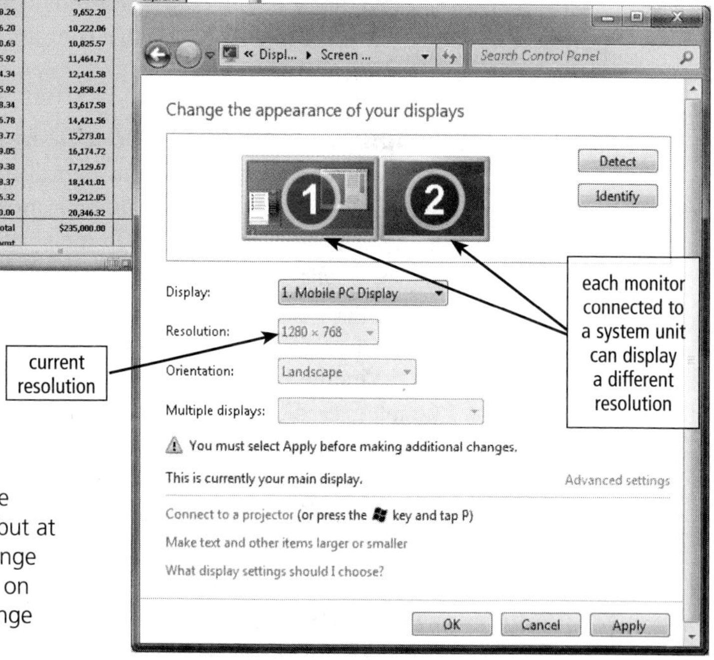

Figure 6-5 Elements on the screen become smaller when the resolution is increased from 1024 × 768 (a) to 1366 × 768 (b) but at the higher resolution more content shows on the screen. To change screen resolution, right-click the desktop, click Screen resolution on the shortcut menu, and then make desired changes in the 'Change the appearance of your displays' window (c).

? FAQ 6-2

Which screen resolution currently is the most popular?

A recent study has shown that more than 93 percent of computer users configure their display device with a 1024 x 768 resolution or higher. The chart to the right lists some common resolutions, along with the percentage of users for each resolution.

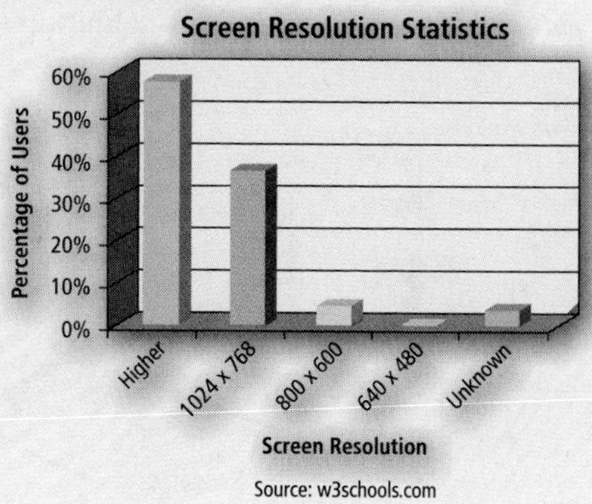

For more information, visit the Computer Concepts CourseMate Web site at www.cengagebrain.com, navigate to the Chapter 6 FAQ resource for this book, and then click Screen Resolution.

- Brightness of an LCD monitor or LCD screen is measured in nits. A *nit* is a unit of visible light intensity equal to one candela (formerly called candlepower) per square meter. The *candela* is the standard unit of luminous intensity. LCD monitors and screens today range from 250 to 550 nits. The higher the nits, the brighter the images.
- *Dot pitch*, sometimes called *pixel pitch*, is the distance in millimeters between pixels on a display device. Text created with a smaller dot pitch is easier to read. Advertisements normally specify a monitor's dot pitch or pixel pitch. Average dot pitch on LCD monitors and screens should be .30 mm or lower. The lower the number, the sharper the image.
- *Contrast ratio* describes the difference in light intensity between the brightest white and darkest black that can be displayed on an LCD monitor. Contrast ratios today range from 500:1 to 2000:1. Higher contrast ratios represent colors better.

Graphics Chips, Ports, and LCD Monitors

A cable on a monitor plugs in a port on the system unit, which enables communications from a graphics chip. This chip, called the *graphics processing unit (GPU)*, controls the manipulation and display of graphics on a display device. The graphics processing unit either is integrated on the motherboard or resides on a video card (graphics card) in a slot in the motherboard. Video cards usually contain a fan or heat sink to keep this and other chips from overheating.

LCD monitors use a digital signal to produce a picture. To display the highest quality images, an LCD monitor should plug in a DVI port, an HDMI port, or a DisplayPort. A *DVI (Digital Video Interface) port* enables digital signals to transmit directly to the LCD monitor. An *HDMI (High-Definition Media Interface) port* combines DVI with high-definition (HD) television and video. The *DisplayPort* is an alternative to DVI that also supports HDMI. Current models of system units either have an integrated DVI chip or contain a video card that has one or more DVI ports, HDMI ports, and/or DisplayPorts. They also may have a standard monitor port and an *S-video port*, allowing users to connect external analog devices such as a television, DVD/Blu-ray Disc player, or video recorder, to the computer (Figure 6-6).

DVI

For more information, visit the Computer Concepts CourseMate Web site at www.cengagebrain.com, navigate to the Chapter 6 Web Link resource for this book, and then click DVI.

Over the years, several video standards have been developed to define the resolution, number of colors, and other display properties. The table in Figure 6-7 identifies some video standards available today, along with their typical resolution and aspect ratio. The *aspect ratio* defines a display's width relative to its height. A 2:1 aspect ratio, for example, means the display is twice as wide as it is tall. The aspect ratio for widescreen monitors is 16:10. Some display devices support multiple video standards. For a display device to show images as defined by a video standard, both the display device and graphics processing unit must support the same video standard.

The number of colors a graphics processing unit displays is determined by bit depth. The *bit depth*, also called *color depth*, is the number of bits used to store information about each pixel. For example, a video card with a 24-bit depth uses 24 bits to store information about each pixel. Thus, this video card can display 2^{24} or 16.7 million colors. The greater the number of bits, the better the resulting image. Today's video cards use a pipelining technique that enables them to display in excess of one billion colors.

A video card or motherboard, in the case of integrated video, must have enough video memory to generate the resolution and number

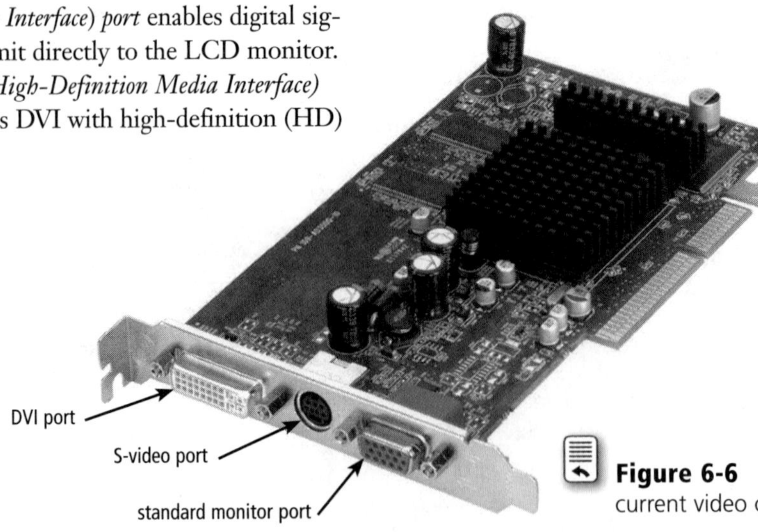

Figure 6-6 Ports on a current video card.

Popular Video Standards

Video Standard		Typical Resolution	Aspect Ratio
SVGA	Super Video Graphics Array	800 × 600	4:3
XGA	Extended Graphics Array	1024 × 768	4:3
SXGA	Super XGA	1280 × 1024	5:4
WXGA	Wide XGA	1280 × 1024 or 1366 × 768	16:10 or 16:9
UXGA	Ultra XGA	1600 × 1200	4:3
WSXGA	Wide Super XGA	1680 × 1050	16:10
WUXGA	Wide Ultra XGA	1920 × 1200	16:10
WQXGA	Wide Quad XGA	2560 × 1600	16:10

Figure 6-7 Wide (widescreen) video standard formats are preferable for users who watch movies and play video games on the computer.

of colors you want to display. This memory, which often is between 128 MB and 512 MB on typical video cards, stores information about each pixel. Users with intense graphics or gaming requirements may opt for more video memory, such as 1 GB. For a more technical discussion about the manipulation and display of graphics on a display device, read the High-Tech Talk article on page 330.

Plasma Monitors

A **plasma monitor** is a display device that uses gas plasma technology, which sandwiches a layer of gas between two glass plates (Figure 6-8). When voltage is applied, the gas releases ultraviolet (UV) light. This UV light causes the pixels on the screen to glow and form an image.

Plasma monitors offer screen sizes up to 150 inches wide and richer colors than LCD monitors but are more expensive. Like LCD monitors, plasma monitors can hang directly on a wall.

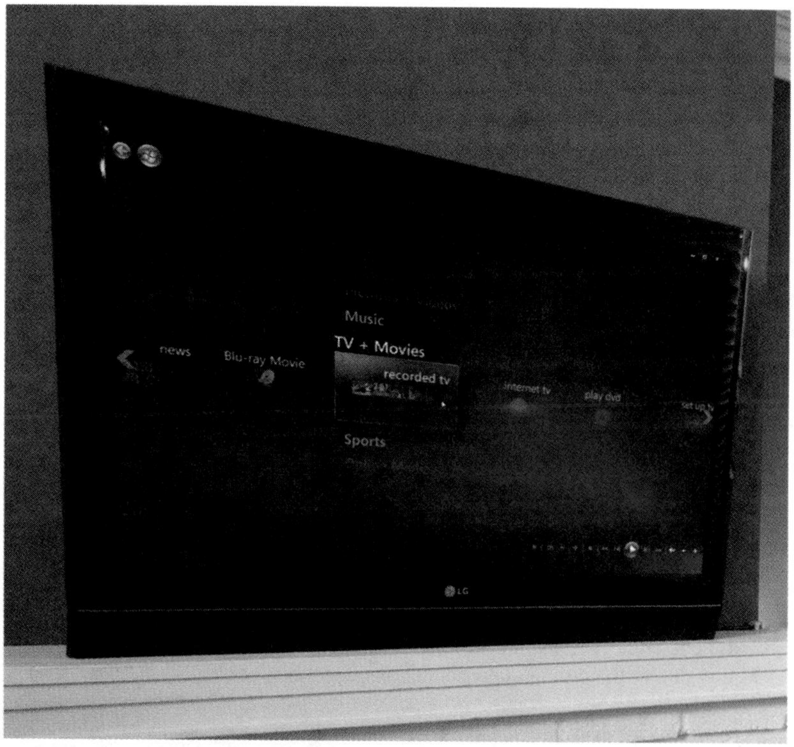

Figure 6-8 Large plasma monitors can measure up to 150 inches wide.

FAQ 6-3

What type of video content do users view on display devices?

Music videos and newscasts are the most widely viewed video content on display devices, as shown in the chart to the right.

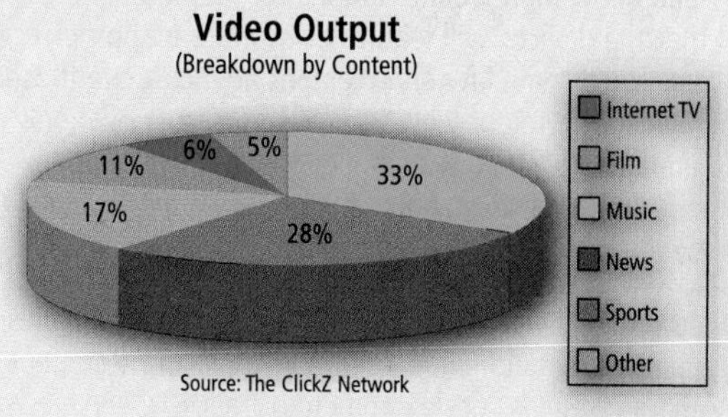

For more information, visit the Computer Concepts CourseMate Web site at www.cengagebrain.com, navigate to the Chapter 6 FAQ resource for this book, and then click Video Output Content.

Televisions

Home users sometimes use their television as a display device. Connecting a computer to an analog television requires a converter that translates the digital signal from the computer into an analog signal that the television can display. The best analog televisions have a resolution of only 520 × 400 pixels. Thus, users are turning to *digital television (DTV)* for crisper, higher-quality output on their LCD or plasma televisions.

Digital television signals provide two major advantages over analog signals. First, digital signals produce a higher-quality picture. Second, many programs can be broadcast on a single digital channel, whereas only one program can be broadcast on an analog channel. Today, all broadcast stations must transmit digital signals, as mandated by the FCC. Read Ethics & Issues 6-2 for a related discussion.

HDTV (*high-definition television*) is the most advanced form of digital television, working with digital broadcast signals, transmitting digital sound, supporting wide screens, and providing resolutions up to 1920 × 1080 pixels. With HDTV, the broadcast signals are digitized when they are sent via over-the-air (OTA) broadcasts from local television networks, satellite, or cable. To receive the HDTV signals via OTA broadcasts, you need a VHF/UHF antenna; via satellite, you need an HDTV-compatible satellite receiver/tuner; and via cable, you need an HDTV-compatible cable box.

With game consoles, such as Microsoft's Xbox 360, Nintendo's Wii, and Sony's PlayStation 3, the output device often is a television (Figure 6-9). Users plug one end of a cable in the game console and the other end in the video port on the television. Home users often prefer the larger television displays for game playing, watching movies, and browsing the Internet on a television connected to a game console.

ETHICS & ISSUES 6-2

Should People Be Allowed to Watch Inappropriate Movies in Public?

While seated with their small child on a cross-country flight, parents are shocked when the person seated across from them begins to watch a violent movie projected from a handheld device onto the seatback in front of them. Situations like this occur every day, and the problem continues to grow due to the proliferation of multimedia-enabled mobile devices, such as cell phones and portable media players. The situation, however, promises to become more controversial as new miniature digital projectors become prevalent. The new generation of digital projectors allows any multimedia-enabled mobile device to display a movie on any flat surface, such as the side of a home or the inside wall of a restaurant. Manufacturers of such devices claim that they enhance productivity for business people because the devices are smaller and allow more venue options for multimedia presentations. Others feel that the devices will lead to even more inappropriate content in public view. While some law-enforcement agencies cite those who engage in such behavior with minor violations of laws, most overlook the issue. Some people engaging in the behavior claim First Amendment free speech rights as the reason that they should be allowed to view their movies when and wherever they like.

Should people be allowed to view what some consider inappropriate movies in public? Why or why not? Who should judge what is inappropriate content and why? In what way should business or governments, if at all, assert control over what can be viewed in a business establishment or in public?

FAQ 6-4

What is the largest high-definition display to date?

The new Dallas Cowboys stadium in Texas has a more than 11,000 square foot display, measuring about 160 feet wide and 70 feet tall.

For more information, visit the Computer Concepts CourseMate Web site at www.cengagebrain.com, navigate to the Chapter 6 FAQ resource for this book, and then click Largest High-Definition Display.

Figure 6-9 Video game players often use a television as their game console's output device.

CRT Monitors

A **CRT monitor** is a desktop monitor that contains a cathode-ray tube (Figure 6-10). A *cathode-ray tube* (*CRT*) is a large, sealed glass tube. The front of the tube is the screen. Tiny dots of phosphor material coat the screen on a CRT. Inside the CRT, an electron beam moves back and forth across the back of the screen. This causes the dots on the front of the screen to glow, which produces an image on the screen.

CRT monitors have a much larger footprint than do LCD monitors; that is, they take up more desk space and thus are not used much today. A CRT monitor's *viewable size* is the diagonal measurement of the actual viewing area provided by the screen in the CRT monitor. A 21-inch monitor, for example, may have a viewable size of 20 inches.

Figure 6-10 The popularity of CRT monitors is declining.

QUIZ YOURSELF 6-1

Instructions: Find the true statement below. Then, rewrite the remaining false statements so that they are true.

1. A lower resolution uses a greater number of pixels and thus provides a smoother image.
2. An output device is any type of software component that conveys information to one or more people.
3. Documents often include text to enhance their visual appeal and convey information.
4. Types of pixels include LCD monitors, LCD screens, and plasma monitors.
5. You measure a monitor diagonally from one corner to the other.

Quiz Yourself Online: To further check your knowledge of pages 304 through 313, visit the Computer Concepts CourseMate Web site at www.cengagebrain.com, navigate to the Chapter 6 Quiz Yourself resource for this book, and then click Objectives 1 – 3.

Printers

A **printer** is an output device that produces text and graphics on a physical medium such as paper. Printed information, called *hard copy*, exists physically and is a more permanent form of output than that presented on a display device (soft copy).

A hard copy, also called a *printout*, is either in portrait or landscape orientation (Figure 6-11). A printout in *portrait orientation* is taller than it

Figure 6-11a (portrait orientation)

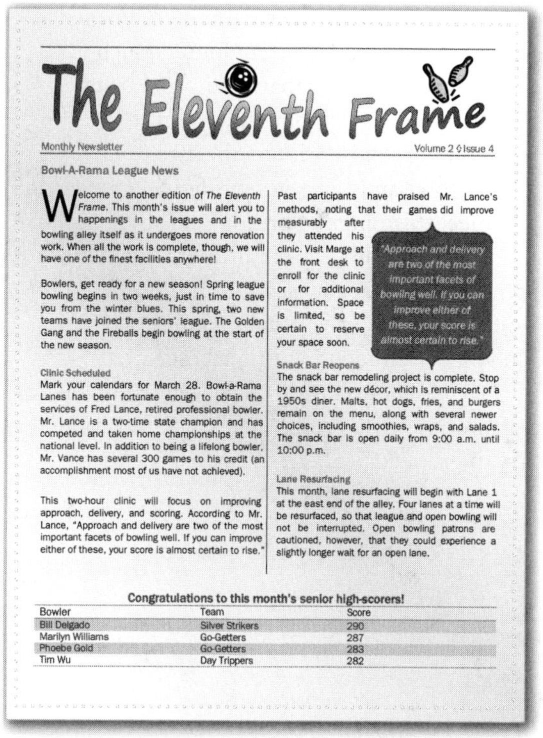

The Eleventh Frame

Monthly Newsletter — Volume 2 ◊ Issue 4

Bowl-A-Rama League News

Welcome to another edition of *The Eleventh Frame*. This month's issue will alert you to happenings in the leagues and in the bowling alley itself as it undergoes more renovation work. When all the work is complete, though, we will have one of the finest facilities anywhere!

Bowlers, get ready for a new season! Spring league bowling begins in two weeks, just in time to save you from the winter blues. This spring, two new teams have joined the seniors' league. The Golden Gang and the Fireballs begin bowling at the start of the new season.

Clinic Scheduled

Mark your calendars for March 28. Bowl-a-Rama Lanes has been fortunate enough to obtain the services of Fred Lance, retired professional bowler. Mr. Lance is a two-time state champion and has competed and taken home championships at the national level. In addition to being a lifelong bowler, Mr. Vance has several 300 games to his credit (an accomplishment most of us have not achieved).

This two-hour clinic will focus on improving approach, delivery, and scoring. According to Mr. Lance, "Approach and delivery are two of the most important facets of bowling well. If you can improve either of these, your score is almost certain to rise."

Past participants have praised Mr. Lance's methods, noting that their games did improve measurably after they attended his clinic. Visit Marge at the front desk to enroll for the clinic or for additional information. Space is limited, so be certain to reserve your space soon.

"Approach and delivery are two of the most important facets of bowling well. If you can improve either of these, your score is almost certain to rise."

Snack Bar Reopens

The snack bar remodeling project is complete. Stop by and see the new décor, which is reminiscent of a 1950s diner. Malts, hot dogs, fries, and burgers remain on the menu, along with several newer choices, including smoothies, wraps, and salads. The snack bar is open daily from 9:00 a.m. until 10:00 p.m.

Lane Resurfacing

This month, lane resurfacing will begin with Lane 1 at the east end of the alley. Four lanes at a time will be resurfaced, so that league and open bowling will not be interrupted. Open bowling patrons are cautioned, however, that they could experience a slightly longer wait for an open lane.

Congratulations to this month's senior high-scorers!

Bowler	Team	Score
Bill Delgado	Silver Strikers	290
Marilyn Williams	Go-Getters	287
Phoebe Gold	Go-Getters	283
Tim Wu	Day Trippers	282

Figure 6-11b (landscape orientation)

Figure 6-11 Portrait orientation is taller than it is wide. Landscape orientation is wider than it is tall.

is wide, with information printed across the shorter width of the paper. A printout in *landscape orientation* is wider than it is tall, with information printed across the widest part of the paper. Letters, reports, and books typically use portrait orientation. Spreadsheets, slide shows, and graphics often use landscape orientation. To learn about controlling printing on a computer, complete the Learn How To 2 activity on page 341. Read Looking Ahead 6-1 for a look at a future type of paper.

Home computer users might print fewer than a hundred pages a week. Small business computer users might print several hundred pages a day. Users of mainframe computers, such as large utility companies that send printed statements to hundreds of thousands of customers each month, require printers that are capable of printing thousands of pages per hour.

To meet this range of printing needs, many different types and styles of printers exist with varying speeds, capabilities, and printing methods. Figure 6-12 presents a list of questions to help you determine the printer best suited to your needs. The following pages will help you to answer these questions by discussing various ways to produce printed output, as well as many different types of printers.

1. What is my budget?
2. How fast must my printer print?
3. Do I need a color printer?
4. What is the cost per page for printing?
5. Do I need multiple copies of documents?
6. Will I print graphics?
7. Do I want to print photos?
8. Do I want to print directly from a memory card?
9. What types of paper does the printer use?
10. What sizes of paper does the printer accept?
11. Do I want to print on both sides of the paper?
12. How much paper can the printer tray hold?
13. Will the printer work with my computer and software?
14. How much do supplies such as ink, toner, and paper cost?
15. Can the printer print on envelopes?
16. How many envelopes can the printer print at a time?
17. How much do I print now, and how much will I be printing in a year or two?
18. Will the printer be connected to a network?
19. Do I want wireless printing capability?

Figure 6-12 Questions to ask when purchasing a printer.

LOOKING AHEAD 6-1

Reusable Paper May Become a Disappearing Act

If you want that stack of papers on your desk to disappear, Xerox may have the solution. The company is developing paper that allows print on it to disappear in a short period of time, generally no more than one day.

The paper's molecular compound changes color when it is exposed to a particular wavelength of light. The paper changes from light to dark or vice versa based on exposure to ultraviolet light in much the same way that eyeglasses with photochromatic lenses darken when a wearer moves from inside to outside a building on a sunny day. In addition, when the Xerox paper is heated, the print disappears immediately.

Although the erasable paper will cost three times more than conventional paper, it can be reused approximately 30 times. Xerox estimates that 40 percent of paper is looked at only once and then discarded, so the erasable paper product should reduce drastically the 20 trillion pieces of paper that will be used by 2018.

For more information, visit the Computer Concepts CourseMate Web site at www.cengagebrain.com, navigate to the Chapter 6 Looking Ahead resource for this book, and then click Erasable Paper.

Producing Printed Output

Until a few years ago, printing a document required connecting a computer to a printer with a cable. Although many users today continue to print using this method, a variety of printing options are available, as shown in Figure 6-13.

Today, wireless printing technology makes the task of printing from a notebook computer, smart phone, or digital camera much easier. As discussed in Chapter 4, two wireless technologies for printing are Bluetooth and infrared. With *Bluetooth printing*, a computer or other device transmits output to a printer via radio waves. The computer or other device and the printer do not have to be aligned with each other; rather, they need to be within an approximate 30-foot range. With *infrared printing*, a printer communicates with a computer or other device using infrared light waves. To print from a smart phone, for example, a user lines up the IrDA port on the smart phone with the IrDA port on the printer.

Instead of downloading photos from a digital camera to a computer, users can print these digital photos using a variety of techniques. Some cameras connect directly to a printer via a cable. Others store photos on memory cards that can be removed and inserted in the printer. Some printers have a docking station, into which the user inserts the camera to print photos stored in the camera.

Finally, many home and business users print to a central printer on a network. Their computer may communicate with the network printer via cables or wirelessly.

Nonimpact Printers

A **nonimpact printer** forms characters and graphics on a piece of paper without actually striking the paper. Some spray ink, while others use heat or pressure to create images.

Commonly used nonimpact printers are ink-jet printers, photo printers, laser printers, thermal printers, mobile printers, label and postage printers, plotters, and large-format printers. The following pages discuss each of these printer types.

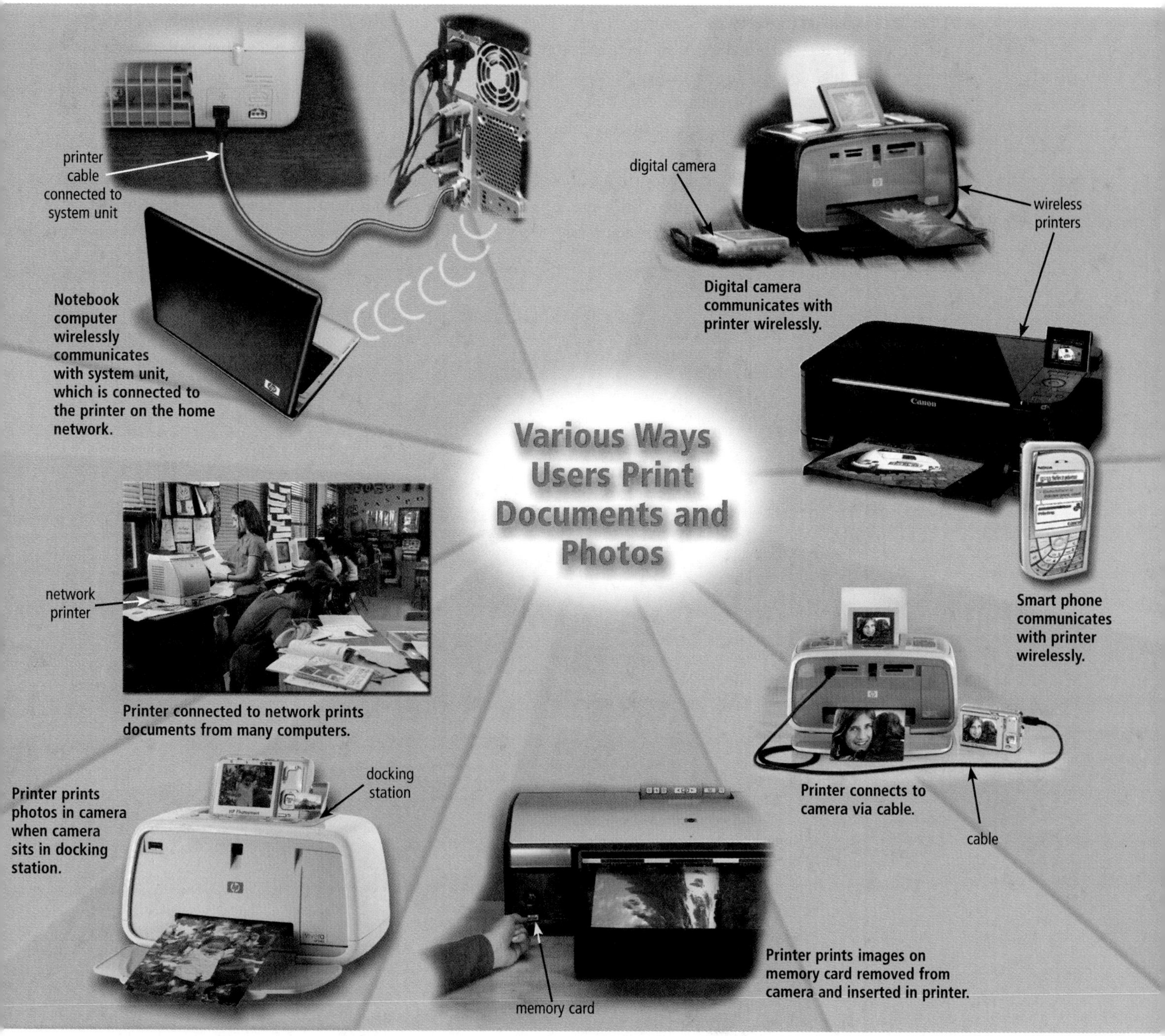

Figure 6-13 Users print documents and photos using a variety of printing methods.

Ink-Jet Printers

An **ink-jet printer** is a type of nonimpact printer that forms characters and graphics by spraying tiny drops of liquid ink onto a piece of paper. Ink-jet printers have become a popular type of color printer for use in the home. A reasonable quality ink-jet printer costs less than $100.

Ink-jet printers produce text and graphics in both black-and-white and color on a variety of paper types (Figure 6-14). These printers normally use individual sheets of paper stored in one or two removable or stationary trays. Ink-jet printers accept papers in many sizes, ranging from 3 × 5 inches to 8½ × 14 inches. Available paper types include plain paper, ink-jet paper, photo paper, glossy paper, and banner paper. Most ink-jet printers can print photographic-quality images on any of these types of paper.

Ink-jet printers also print on other materials such as envelopes, labels, index cards, greeting card paper (card stock), transparencies, and iron-on T-shirt transfers. Many ink-jet printers include software for creating greeting cards, banners, business cards, and letterhead.

As with many other input and output devices, one factor that determines the quality of an ink-jet printer is its resolution. Printer resolution is measured by the number of *dots per inch* (*dpi*) a printer can print. With an ink-jet printer, a dot is a drop of ink. A higher dpi means the drops of ink are smaller. Most ink-jet printers can print from 1200 to 4800 dpi.

As shown in Figure 6-15, the higher the dpi, the better the print quality. The difference in quality becomes noticeable when the size of the printed image increases. That is, a wallet-sized image printed at 1200 dpi may look similar in quality to one printed at 2400 dpi. When you increase the size of the image, to 8 × 10 for example, the printout of the 1200 dpi resolution may look grainier than the one printed using a 2400 dpi resolution.

Figure 6-14 Ink-jet printers are a popular type of color printer used in the home.

The speed of an ink-jet printer is measured by the number of pages per minute (ppm) it can print. Most ink-jet printers print from 12 to 36 ppm. Graphics and colors print at a slower rate. For example, an ink-jet printer may print 36 ppm for black text and only 27 ppm for color and/or graphics.

The print head mechanism in an ink-jet printer contains ink-filled cartridges. Each cartridge has fifty to several hundred small ink holes, or nozzles. The steps in Figure 6-16 illustrate how a drop of ink appears on a page. The ink propels through any combination of the nozzles to form a character or image on the paper.

300 dpi
600 dpi
1200 dpi

Figure 6-15 You will notice a higher quality output with printers that can print at a higher dpi.

When the cartridge runs out of ink, you simply replace the cartridge. Most ink-jet printers use two or more ink cartridges: one containing black ink and the other(s) containing colors. Some color cartridges contain a variety of ink colors; others contain only a single color. Consider the number of ink cartridges a printer requires, along with the cost of the cartridges, when purchasing a printer. Cartridges with black ink cost $10 to $40 each. Color ink cartridge prices range from $15 to $45 each. The number of pages a single cartridge can print varies by manufacturer and the type of documents you print. For example, black ink cartridges typically print from 200 to 800 pages, and color ink cartridges from 125 to 450 pages. To reduce the expense of purchasing cartridges, some users opt to purchase refilled cartridges or have empty cartridges refilled by a third party vendor.

Ink-Jet Printers

For more information, visit the Computer Concepts CourseMate Web site at www.cengagebrain.com, navigate to the Chapter 6 Web Link resource for this book, and then click Ink-Jet Printers.

How an Ink-Jet Printer Works

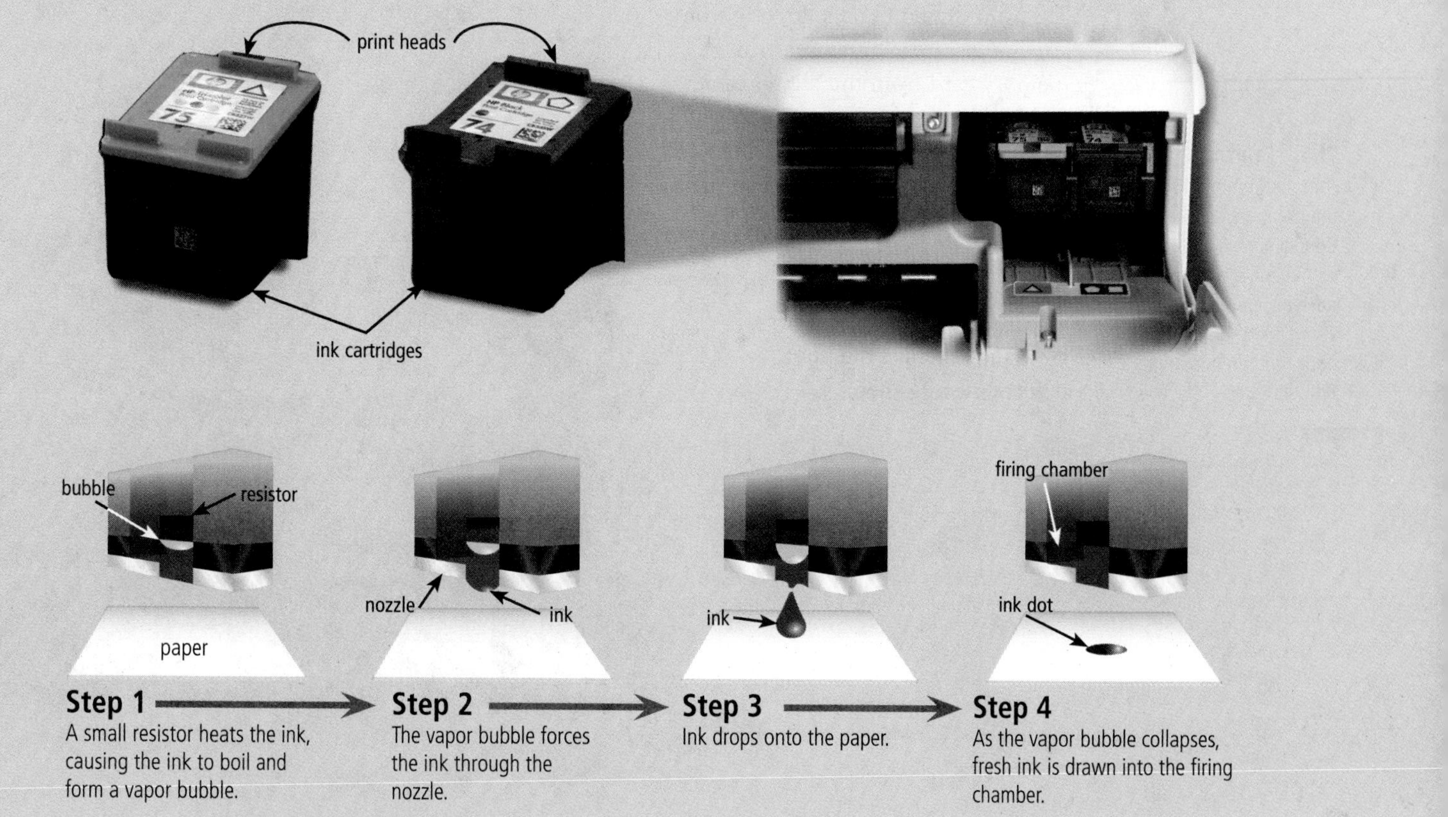
print heads
ink cartridges
bubble
resistor
paper
nozzle
ink
ink
firing chamber
ink dot
Step 1
A small resistor heats the ink, causing the ink to boil and form a vapor bubble.
Step 2
The vapor bubble forces the ink through the nozzle.
Step 3
Ink drops onto the paper.
Step 4
As the vapor bubble collapses, fresh ink is drawn into the firing chamber.

Figure 6-16 This figure shows how an ink-jet printer works.

Photo Printers

A **photo printer** is a color printer that produces photo-lab-quality pictures (Figure 6-17). Some photo printers print just one or two sizes of photos, for example, 3 × 5 inches and 4 × 6 inches. Others print up to letter size, legal size, or even larger. Some even print panoramic photos. Generally, the more sizes the printer prints, the more expensive the printer.

Many photo printers use ink-jet technology. With models that can print letter-sized documents, users connect the photo printer to their computer and use it for all their printing needs. For a few hundred dollars, this type of photo printer is ideal for the home or small business user. Other photo printer technologies are discussed later in the chapter.

Most photo printers are PictBridge enabled, so that you can print photos without a computer. *PictBridge* is a standard technology that allows you to print photos directly from a digital camera by connecting a cable from the digital camera to a USB port on the printer.

Photo printers also usually have a built-in card slot(s) so that the printer can print digital photos directly from a memory card. Simply remove the memory card from the digital camera and insert it in the printer's card slot. Then, push buttons on the printer to select the desired photo, specify the number of copies, and indicate the size of the printed photo. Some photo printers have built-in LCD color screens, allowing users to view and enhance the photos before printing them.

Photo Printers

For more information, visit the Computer Concepts CourseMate Web site at www.cengagebrain.com, navigate to the Chapter 6 Web Link resource for this book, and then click Photo Printers.

FAQ 6-5

How long do photos printed on a photo or ink-jet printer last?

Recent studies indicate that depending on the combination of paper and ink you use to print photos, some photos might begin to fade after several months. To ensure that your photos retain the best possible quality, you should use high-quality paper, as well as ink that is supplied by the printer's manufacturer.

For more information, visit the Computer Concepts CourseMate Web site at www.cengagebrain.com, navigate to the Chapter 6 FAQ resource for this book, and then click Photo Paper.

Figure 6-17 Photo printers print in a range of sizes.

Laser Printers

A **laser printer** is a high-speed, high-quality nonimpact printer (Figure 6-18). Laser printers are available in both black-and-white and color models. A laser printer for personal computers ordinarily uses individual 8½ × 11-inch sheets of paper stored in one or more removable trays that slide in the printer case. Some laser printers have built-in trays that accommodate different sizes of paper, while others require separate trays for letter- and legal-sized paper. Most laser printers have a manual feed slot where you can insert individual sheets and envelopes.

Laser printers print text and graphics in high-quality resolutions, usually 1200 dpi for black-and-white printers and up to 2400 dpi for color printers. While laser printers usually cost more than ink-jet printers, many models are available at affordable prices for the home user. Laser printers usually print at faster speeds than ink-jet printers. Printer manufacturers state that a laser printer for the home and small office user typically prints black-and-white text at speeds of 15 to 62 ppm. Color laser printers print 8 to 40 ppm. Laser printers for large business users print more than 150 ppm.

Depending on the quality, speed, and type of laser printer, the cost ranges from a few hundred to a few thousand dollars for the home and small office user, and several hundred thousand dollars for the large business user. Color laser printers are slightly higher priced than otherwise equivalent black-and-white laser printers.

When printing a document, laser printers process and store the entire page before they actually print it. For this reason, laser printers sometimes are called page printers. Storing a page before printing requires that the laser printer has a certain amount of memory in the device. The more memory in the printer, the faster it usually can print.

Depending on the amount of graphics you intend to print, a laser printer for the small business user can have up to 1 GB of memory and an 80 GB hard disk. To print a full-page 1200-dpi photo, for instance, you might need 64 MB of memory in the printer. If the printer does not have enough memory to print the photo, either it will print as much of the photo as its memory will allow, or it will display an error message and not print any of the photo.

Laser printers use software that enables them to interpret a *page description language (PDL)*, which tells the printer how to arrange the contents of a printed page. When you purchase a laser printer, it comes with at least one of two common page description languages: PCL or PostScript. Developed by HP, a leading printer manufacturer, *PCL (Printer Control Language)* is a standard printer language that supports the fonts and layout used in standard office documents. Professionals in the desktop publishing and graphic art fields commonly use *PostScript* because it is designed for complex documents with intense graphics and colors.

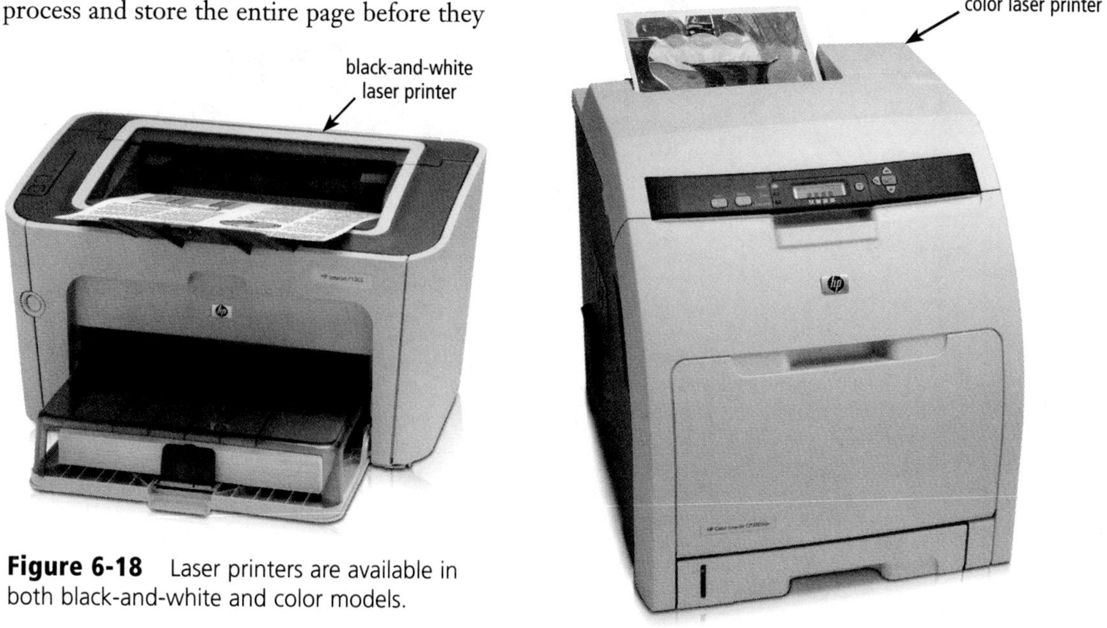

Figure 6-18 Laser printers are available in both black-and-white and color models.

Operating in a manner similar to a copy machine, a laser printer creates images using a laser beam and powdered ink, called *toner*. The laser beam produces an image on a special drum inside the printer. The light of the laser alters the electrical charge on the drum wherever it hits. When this occurs, the toner sticks to the drum and then transfers to the paper through a combination of pressure and heat (Figure 6-19).

When the toner runs out, you replace the toner cartridge. Toner cartridge prices range from $40 to more than $200 for about 5,000 printed pages.

Laser Printers
For more information, visit the Computer Concepts CourseMate Web site at www.cengagebrain.com, navigate to the Chapter 6 Web Link resource for this book, and then click Laser Printers.

FAQ 6-6

How do I dispose of toner cartridges?

Do not throw them in the garbage. The housing contains iron, metal, and aluminum that is not biodegradable. The ink toner inside the cartridges contains toxic chemicals that pollute water and soil if discarded in dumps. Instead, recycle empty toner cartridges. Many stores that sell new toner cartridges also allow you to recycle your old ones. Recycling programs in which some schools and organizations participate offer discounts or cash to customers who bring in depleted cartridges. If you are unable to find a recycling program in your area, contact your printer manufacturer to see if it has a recycling program.

For more information, visit the Computer Concepts CourseMate Web site at www.cengagebrain.com, navigate to the Chapter 6 FAQ resource for this book, and then click Recycling Toner Cartridges.

Multifunction Peripherals

A **multifunction peripheral** (MFP), also called an *all-in-one device*, is a single device that looks like a printer or a copy machine but provides the functionality of a printer, scanner, copy machine, and perhaps a fax machine (Figure 6-20). A fax machine is a device that codes and encodes documents so that they can be transmitted over telephone lines. The documents can contain text, drawings or photos, or can be handwritten.

The features of these devices vary. For example, some use color ink-jet printer technology, while others include a black-and-white or color laser printer.

Small offices and home office (SOHO) users have multifunction peripherals because these devices require less space than having a separate printer, scanner, copy machine, and fax machine. Another advantage of these devices is they are significantly less expensive than if you purchase each device separately. If the device breaks down, however, you lose all four functions, which is the primary disadvantage.

How a Black-and-White Laser Printer Works

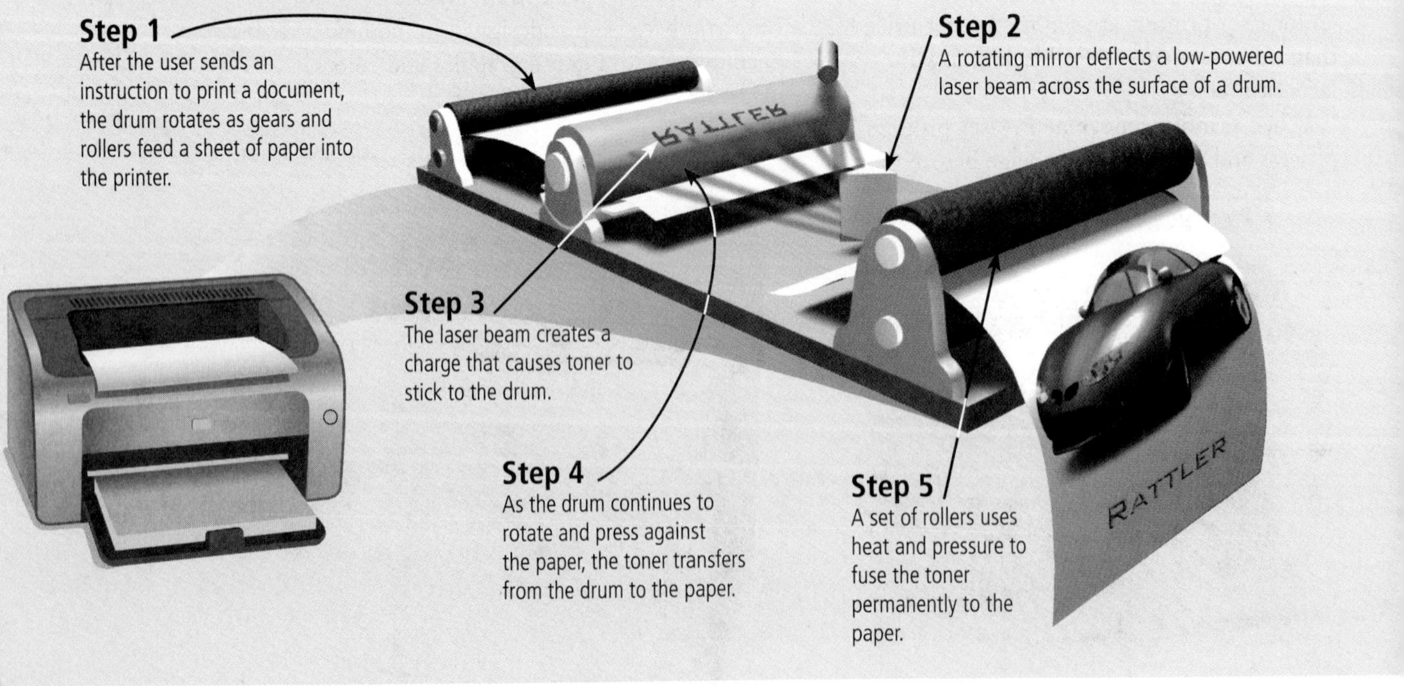

Step 1
After the user sends an instruction to print a document, the drum rotates as gears and rollers feed a sheet of paper into the printer.
Step 2
A rotating mirror deflects a low-powered laser beam across the surface of a drum.
Step 3
The laser beam creates a charge that causes toner to stick to the drum.
Step 4
As the drum continues to rotate and press against the paper, the toner transfers from the drum to the paper.
Step 5
A set of rollers uses heat and pressure to fuse the toner permanently to the paper.
RATTLER

Figure 6-19 This figure shows how a black-and-white laser printer works.

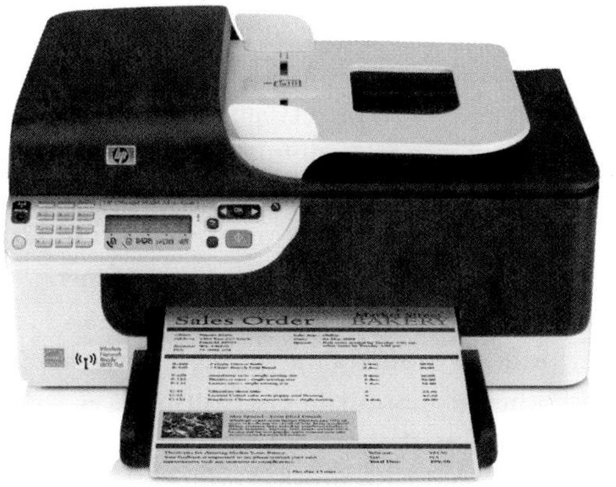

Figure 6-20 This multifunction peripheral is a color printer, scanner, copy machine, and fax machine.

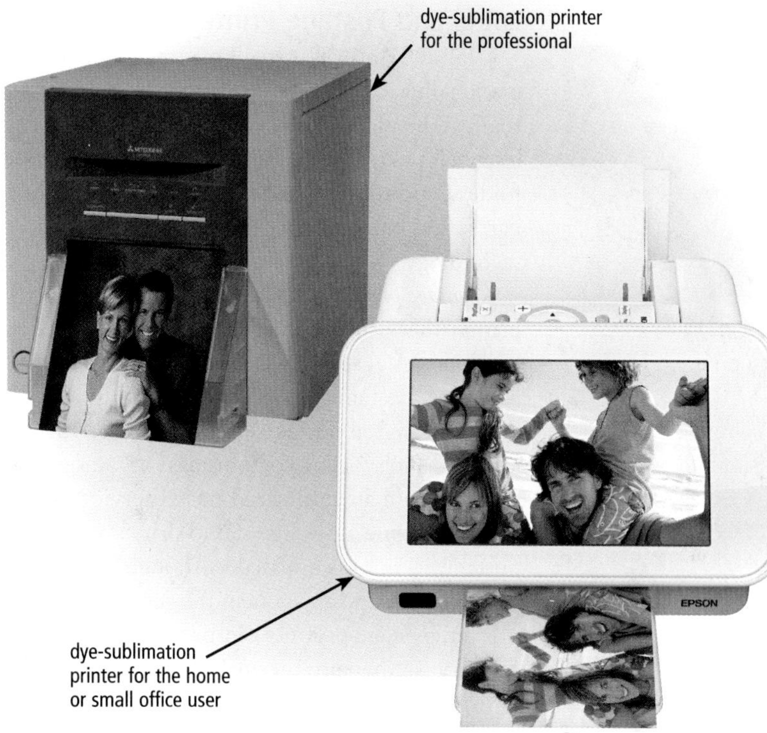

Figure 6-21 The printers shown in this figure use dye-sublimation technology to create photographic-quality output.

Thermal Printers

A **thermal printer** generates images by pushing electrically heated pins against heat-sensitive paper. Basic thermal printers are inexpensive, but the print quality is low and the images tend to fade over time. Self-service gas pumps often print gas receipts using a built-in lower-quality thermal printer. Many point-of-sale terminals in retail and grocery stores also print purchase receipts on thermal paper.

Two special types of thermal printers have high print quality and can print at much faster rates than ink-jet and laser printers. A *thermal wax-transfer printer* generates rich, nonsmearing images by using heat to melt colored wax onto heat-sensitive paper. Thermal wax-transfer printers are more expensive than ink-jet printers, but less expensive than many color laser printers.

A *dye-sublimation printer*, sometimes called a *digital photo printer*, uses heat to transfer colored dye to specially coated paper. Most dye-sublimation printers create images that are of photographic quality (Figure 6-21). Professional applications requiring high image quality, such as photography studios, medical labs, and security identification systems, use dye-sublimation printers. These high-end printers cost thousands of dollars and print images in a wide range of sizes. Most dye-sublimation printers for the home or small business user, by contrast, typically print images in only one or two sizes and are much slower than their professional counterparts. These lower-end dye-sublimation printers are comparable in cost to a photo printer based on ink-jet technology. Some are small enough for the mobile user to carry the printer in a briefcase.

Mobile Printers

A **mobile printer** is a small, lightweight, battery-powered printer that allows a mobile user to print from a notebook computer, smart phone, or other mobile device while traveling (Figure 6-22). Barely wider than the paper on which they print, mobile printers fit easily in a briefcase alongside a notebook computer.

Mobile printers mainly use ink-jet, thermal, thermal wax-transfer, or dye-sublimation technology. Many of these printers connect to a USB port. Others have a built-in wireless port through which they communicate with the computer wirelessly.

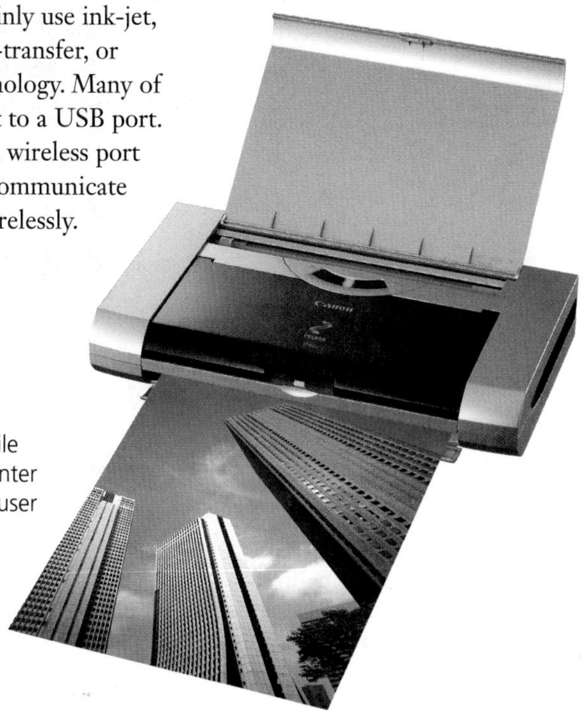

Figure 6-22 A mobile printer is a compact printer that allows the mobile user to print from a mobile computer or device.

Figure 6-23
A label printer.

Label and Postage Printers

A **label printer** is a small printer that prints on an adhesive-type material (Figure 6-23) that can be placed on a variety of items such as envelopes, packages, optical discs, photos, file folders, and toys. Most label printers also print bar codes. Label printers typically use thermal technology.

A *postage printer* is a special type of label printer that prints postage stamps. Some have built-in digital scales for weighing letters and packages. Postage printers allow users to buy and print digital postage, often called *Internet postage*, which means you purchase an amount of postage from an authorized postal service Web site. Each time a postage stamp prints, your postage account is updated. Although you can print Internet postage on an ink-jet or photo printer, postage printers can be more economical because they use thermal technology instead of ink cartridges.

Large-Format Printers
For more information, visit the Computer Concepts CourseMate Web site at www.cengagebrain.com, navigate to the Chapter 6 Web Link resource for this book, and then click Large-Format Printers.

Plotters and Large-Format Printers

Plotters are sophisticated printers used to produce high-quality drawings such as blueprints, maps, and circuit diagrams. These printers are used in specialized fields such as engineering and drafting and usually are very costly. Current plotters use a row of charged wires (called styli) to draw an electrostatic pattern on specially coated paper and then fuse toner to the pattern. The printed image consists of a series of very small dots, which provides high-quality output.

Using ink-jet printer technology, but on a much larger scale, a **large-format printer** creates photo-realistic-quality color prints. Graphic artists use these high-cost, high-performance printers for signs, posters, and other professional quality displays (Figure 6-24).

Plotters and large-format printers can accommodate paper with widths up to 98 inches because blueprints, maps, signs, posters and other such drawings and displays can be quite large. Some plotters and large-format printers use individual sheets of paper, while others take large rolls.

Impact Printers

An **impact printer** forms characters and graphics on a piece of paper by striking a mechanism against an inked ribbon that physically contacts the paper. Impact printers characteristically are noisy because of this striking activity. These printers commonly produce *near letter quality* (*NLQ*) output, which is print quality slightly less clear than what is acceptable for business letters. Companies may use impact printers for routine jobs such

Figure 6-24 Graphic artists use large-format printers to print signs, posters, and other professional quality displays.

as printing labels. Impact printers are ideal for printing multipart forms because they easily print through many layers of paper. Factories, warehouses, and retail counters may use impact printers because these printers withstand dusty environments, vibrations, and extreme temperatures. Two commonly used types of impact printers are dot-matrix printers and line printers.

A **dot-matrix printer** produces printed images when tiny wire pins on a print head mechanism strike an inked ribbon (Figure 6-25). When the ribbon presses against the paper, it creates dots that form characters and graphics. Most dot-matrix printers use *continuous-form paper*, in which thousands of sheets of paper are connected together end to end. The pages have holes along the sides to help feed the paper through the printer.

The speed of a dot-matrix printer is measured by the number of characters per second (cps) it can print. The speed of most dot-matrix printers ranges from 375 to 1100 characters per second (cps), depending on the desired print quality.

A **line printer** is a high-speed impact printer that prints an entire line at a time. The speed of a line printer is measured by the number of lines per minute (lpm) it can print. Some line printers print as many as 3,000 lpm. Mainframes, servers, or networked applications, such as manufacturing, distribution, or shipping, often use line printers. These printers typically use 11 × 17-inch continuous-form paper.

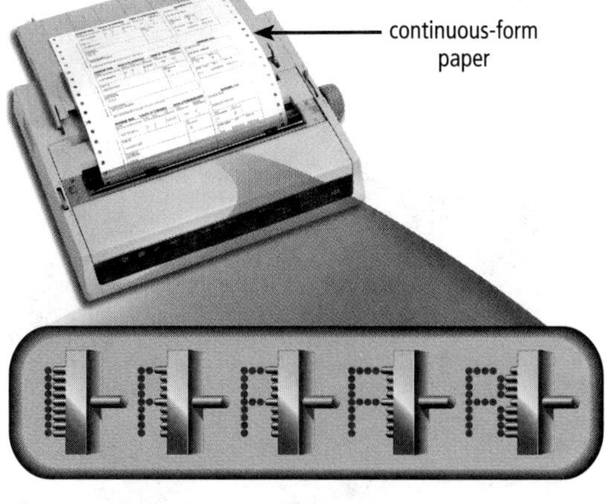

Figure 6-25 A dot-matrix printer produces printed images when tiny pins strike an inked ribbon.

QUIZ YOURSELF 6-2

Instructions: Find the true statement below. Then, rewrite the remaining false statements so that they are true.

1. A laser printer generates images by pushing electrically heated pins against heat-sensitive paper.
2. A photo printer creates images using a laser beam and powdered ink, called toner.
3. An ink-jet printer is a type of impact printer that forms characters and graphics by spraying tiny drops of liquid nitrogen onto a piece of paper.
4. Printed information is called soft copy.
5. With Bluetooth printing, a computer or other device transmits output to a printer via radio waves.

Quiz Yourself Online: To further check your knowledge of pages 313 through 323, visit the Computer Concepts CourseMate Web site at www.cengagebrain.com, navigate to the Chapter 6 Quiz Yourself resource for this book, and then click Objectives 4 – 6.

Speakers, Headphones, and Earbuds

An **audio output device** is a component of a computer that produces music, speech, or other sounds, such as beeps. Three commonly used audio output devices are speakers, headphones, and earbuds.

Most personal computers and mobile devices have a small internal speaker that usually emits only low-quality sound. Thus, many users attach surround sound **speakers** or speaker systems to their computers, including game consoles and mobile devices, to generate higher-quality sounds for playing games, interacting with multimedia presentations, listening to music, and viewing movies (Figure 6-26).

Figure 6-26 Most personal computer users attach high-quality surround sound speaker systems to their computers.

Most surround sound computer speaker systems include one or two center speakers and two or more *satellite speakers* that are positioned so that sound emits from all directions. Speakers typically have tone and volume controls, allowing users to adjust settings. To boost the low bass sounds, surround sound speaker systems also include a *subwoofer*.

Surround sound systems are available in a variety of configurations. For example, a 2.1 speaker system contains two speakers and a subwoofer. A 5.1 speaker system has four satellite speakers, a center speaker, and a subwoofer. A 6.1 speaker system has four satellite speakers, a front center speaker, a rear center speaker, and a subwoofer. A 7.1 speaker system has four satellite speakers, two side speakers, a center speaker, and a subwoofer.

In many cases, a cable connects the speakers or the subwoofer to a port on the sound card. With wireless speakers, however, a transmitter connects to the sound card, which wirelessly communicates with the speakers. To take full advantage of high-end surround sound speaker systems, be sure the sound card in the computer is compatible with the speaker system.

Audio resolution, which is the number of bytes that represent sound in a given time, is stated as a bit rate such as 8-bit, 16-bit, or 24-bit. A sound card using 8-bit resolution, for example, represents a sound with any 1 of 256 values (2^8), and a 16-bit sound card uses any 1 of 65,536 values (2^{16}). Higher resolutions result in better sound quality. With 8-bit resolution, the sound quality is similar to an AM radio; 16-bit resolution yields optical disc-quality sound; and 24-bit resolution is used for high-quality digital audio editing.

Many users opt for a wireless music system, which includes a USB transmitter that plugs in a computer, a receiver that connects to a television or stereo system, and a remote control. With this system, you can play any optical disc or media file on your computer and transmit the audio to a home or office stereo or television at a distance of up to about 330 feet. You also can plug a portable media player, such as an iPod, into the computer to hear its songs on the stereo or television speakers.

Earbuds

For more information, visit the Computer Concepts CourseMate Web site at www.cengagebrain.com, navigate to the Chapter 6 Web Link resource for this book, and then click Earbuds.

When using speakers, anyone in listening distance can hear the output. In a computer laboratory or other crowded environment, speakers might not be practical. Instead, users can listen through wireless headphones or earbuds or plug the device in a port on the sound card, in a speaker, or on the front of the system unit. With headphones or earbuds, only the individual wearing the headphones or earbuds hears the sound from the computer. The difference is that **headphones** cover or are placed outside of the ear (Figure 6-27), whereas **earbuds**, or *earphones* (shown in Figure 6-1 on page 304), rest inside the ear canal. Both headphones and earbuds usually include noise-cancelling technology to reduce the interference of sounds from the surrounding environment.

A *headset* is a device that functions as both headphones and a microphone. Computer and smart phone users wear a headset to free their hands for typing and other activities while talking or listening to audio output.

Portable media players usually include a set of earbuds. As an alternative, you can listen to audio from the portable media player through speakers in a vehicle or on a stereo system at home or work. Or, you can purchase speakers specifically designed to play audio from a portable media player (Figure 6-28).

Figure 6-27 In a crowded environment where speakers are not practical, users can wear headphones to hear audio output.

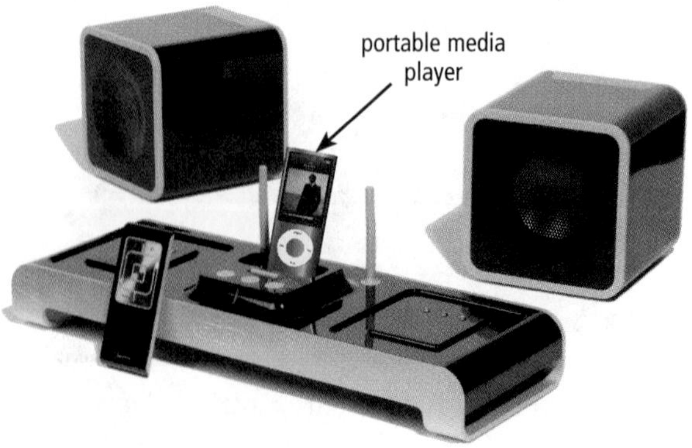

Figure 6-28 Instead of listening to your portable media player through earbuds, you can purchase separate speakers for the device, such as the wireless speakers shown here.

Electronically produced voice output is growing in popularity. **Voice output** occurs when you hear a person's voice or when the computer talks to you through the speakers on the computer. In some programs, the computer can speak the contents of a document through voice output.

On the Web, you can listen to (or download and then listen to) interviews, talk shows, sporting events, news, recorded music, and live concerts from many radio and television stations. Some Web sites and programs, such as media players, dedicate themselves to providing voice output, such as those that allow you to listen to and then purchase and download songs.

Very often, voice output works with voice input. For example, when you call an airline to check the status of gates, terminals, and arrival times, your voice interacts with a computer-generated voice output. Another example is *VoIP*, which allows users to speak and listen to others over the Internet using their desktop computer, mobile computer, or mobile device.

Sophisticated programs enable the computer to converse with you. Talk into the microphone and say, "I'd like today's weather report." The computer replies, "For which city?" You reply, "Chicago." The computer says, "Sunny and 80 degrees."

Other Output Devices

In addition to display devices, printers, and speakers, other output devices are available for specific uses and applications such as data projectors, interactive whiteboards, and force-feedback game controllers and tactile output.

Data Projectors

A **data projector** is a device that takes the text and images displaying on a computer screen and projects them on a larger screen so that an audience can see the image clearly (Figure 6-29). For example, many classrooms use data projectors so that all students easily can see an instructor's presentation on the screen. Read Ethics & Issues 6-3 for a related discussion.

Some data projectors are large devices that attach to a ceiling or wall in an auditorium. Some operating systems allow projectors to be part of the network, which enables a presenter to operate the projector remotely via a network connection. Others, designed for the mobile user, are small portable devices that can be transported easily. Two types of smaller, lower-cost units are LCD projectors and DLP projectors.

An *LCD projector*, which uses liquid crystal display technology, attaches directly to a computer, and uses its own light source to display the information shown on the computer screen.

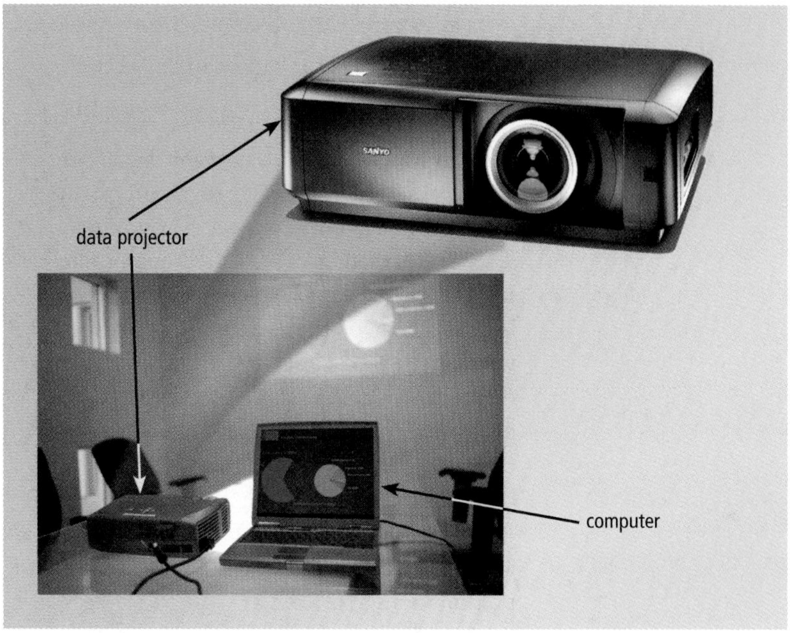

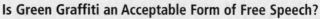

Figure 6-29 A data projector projects an image from a computer screen on a larger screen so that an audience easily can see the image.

ETHICS & ISSUES 6-3

Is Green Graffiti an Acceptable Form of Free Speech?

Around the world, activists paint protest graffiti across historical landmarks and public structures, such as the Coliseum of Rome or the Brooklyn Bridge. Artists paint their works across skyscrapers. More and more, however, the "paint" is in the form of light or laser beams, not the traditional, indelible spray paint. Use of digital projectors or laser beams is part of the growing practice known as *green graffiti*. When used for graffiti, the practice also is known as laser tagging. Sometimes, the devices used for green graffiti also are used for creative advertising. Proponents of green graffiti state that the practice is an environmentally friendly form of free speech and is no more damaging than writing "Wash Me" with one's finger on a dusty car. Opponents claim that the graffiti is as much an eyesore as traditional graffiti, especially when the message or art interferes with the view of landmarks and other interesting vistas.

Is green graffiti an acceptable form of free speech? Why or why not? Should protesters and artists be required to receive permission from the owners or caretakers of their venues before they engage in the practice? Why or why not? If you spent a large sum of money on a vacation to see a historic location only to find it covered in green graffiti on the evening of your visit, how would you react? Would you engage in green graffiti to make a political statement or create art? Is green graffiti an acceptable form of advertising? Why or why not?

Because LCD projectors tend to produce lower-quality images, users often prefer DLP projectors for their sharper, brighter images.

A *digital light processing* (*DLP*) *projector* uses tiny mirrors to reflect light, which produces crisp, bright, colorful images that remain in focus and can be seen clearly even in a well-lit room. Some newer televisions use DLP instead of LCD or plasma technology.

As an alternative to data projectors, some users work with an LCD or plasma display.

Interactive Whiteboards

An **interactive whiteboard** is a touch-sensitive device, resembling a dry-erase board, that displays the image on a connected computer screen. A presenter controls the computer program by clicking a remote control, touching the whiteboard, drawing on or erasing the whiteboard with a special digital pen and eraser, or writing on a special tablet. Notes written on the interactive whiteboard can be saved directly on the computer. Interactive whiteboards are used frequently in classrooms as a teaching tool (Figure 6-30), during meetings as a collaboration tool, and to enhance delivery of presentations.

SMART Board
For more information, visit the Computer Concepts CourseMate Web site at www.cengagebrain.com, navigate to the Chapter 6 Web Link resource for this book, and then click SMART Board.

Three basic technologies exist for displaying computer images on an interactive whiteboard: (1) front projection: separate projector displays an image from the computer screen on the interactive whiteboard; (2) rear projection: a projector built into the back of the interactive whiteboard displays an image from the computer screen on the whiteboard; and (3) an interactive whiteboard fits over an LCD screen or a plasma display. Front projection and rear projection interactive whiteboards, which are hung on the wall or mounted on a stand, range in size from 48 to 94 inches. A widely used interactive whiteboard is the SMART Board.

Force-Feedback Game Controllers and Tactile Output

As discussed in Chapter 5, joysticks, wheels, gamepads, and motion-sensing game controllers are input devices used to control movement and actions of a player or object in computer games, simulations, and video games. Today's joysticks, wheels, gamepads, and motion-sensing game controllers also include *force feedback*, which is a technology that sends resistance to the device in response to actions of the user (Figure 6-31). For example, as you use the simulation software to drive from a smooth road onto a gravel alley, the steering wheel trembles or vibrates, making the driving experience as realistic as possible.

Figure 6-30 Teachers and students can write directly on an interactive whiteboard, or they can write on a wireless slate that communicates with the whiteboard.

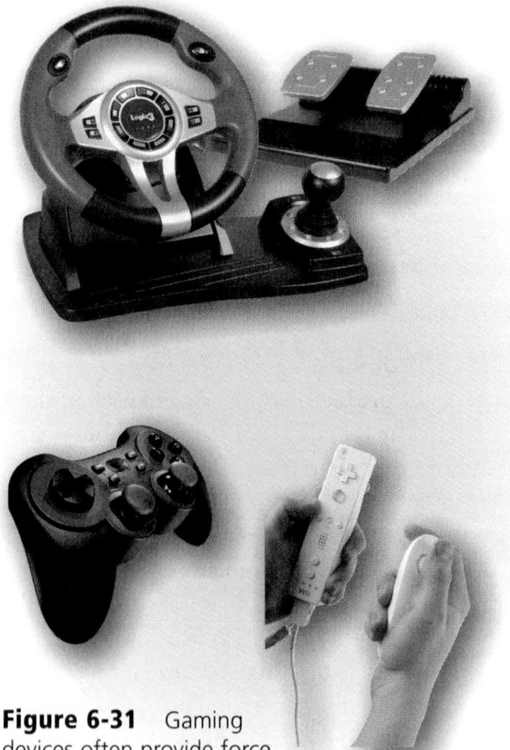

Figure 6-31 Gaming devices often provide force feedback, giving the user a realistic experience.

These devices also are used in practical training applications such as in the military and aviation.

Some input devices, such as a mouse, and mobile devices, such as a smart phone, include *tactile output* that provides the user with a physical response from the device. For example, users may sense a bumping feeling on their hand while scrolling through a smart phone's contact list.

Putting It All Together

Many factors influence the type of output devices you should use: the type of output desired, the hardware and software in use, and the anticipated cost. Figure 6-32 outlines several suggested monitors, printers, and other output devices for various types of computer users.

Suggested Output Devices by User

User	Monitor	Printer	Other
Home 	• 19- or 20-inch LCD monitor, or 17-inch LCD screen on notebook computer	• Ink-jet color printer; or • Photo printer	• Speakers • Headphones or earbuds or headset • Force-feedback game controller or tactile output
Small Office/Home Office 	• 20- or 22-inch LCD monitor • LCD screen smart phone or other mobile device	• Multifunction peripheral; or • Ink-jet color printer; or • Laser printer (black-and-white or color) • Label printer • Postage printer	• Speakers
Mobile 	• 17-inch LCD screen on notebook computer • 8.9-inch screen on a netbook • LCD screen on smart phone or other mobile device	• Mobile color printer • Ink-jet color printer; or • Laser printer for in-office use (black-and-white or color) • Photo printer	• Headphones or earbuds or headset • DLP data projector
Power 	• 30-inch LCD monitor	• Laser printer (black-and-white or color) • Plotter or large-format printer; or • Photo printer; or • Dye-sublimation printer	• Speakers • Headphones or earbuds or headset
Enterprise 	• 20- or 22-inch LCD monitor • LCD screen on smart phone or other mobile device	• High-speed laser printer • Laser printer, color • Line printer (for large reports from a mainframe) • Label printer	• Speakers • Headphones or earbuds or headset • Networked DLP data projector • Interactive whiteboard

Figure 6-32 This table recommends suggested output devices for various types of users.

Output Devices for Physically Challenged Users

As Chapter 5 discussed, the growing presence of computers has generated an awareness of the need to address computing requirements for those with physical limitations. Read Ethics & Issues 6-4 for a related discussion.

For users with mobility, hearing, or vision disabilities, many different types of output devices are available. Hearing-impaired users, for example, can instruct programs to display words instead of sounds. With the latest Windows operating systems, users also can set options to make programs easier to use. The Magnifier, for example, enlarges text and other items in a window on the screen (Figure 6-33).

ETHICS & ISSUES 6-4

Should Web Sites Be Held Accountable for Accessibility Levels for Physically Challenged People?

The World Wide Web Consortium (W3C) has published accessibility guidelines for Web sites. The guidelines specify measures that Web site designers can take to increase accessibility for physically challenged users. Among its guidelines, the W3C urges Web site designers to provide equivalent text for audio or visual content, include features that allow elements to be activated and understood using a variety of input and output devices, and make the user interface follow principles of accessible design. A recent report found that most Web sites do not meet all of the W3C guidelines. This failure is disappointing, because many physically challenged users could benefit from the Web's capability to bring products and services into the home. Ironically, a survey discovered that more than 50 percent of the Web sites hosted by disability organizations also fail to meet the W3C guidelines. Critics contend that these Web sites neglect the needs of their users and fail to lead by example. The Web site supporters contend, however, that many sponsoring organizations lack the funding necessary to comply with the guidelines.

Should the government require that all Web sites meet the W3C accessibility guidelines? Why or why not? Do Web sites hosted by disability organizations have a moral obligation to meet the guidelines? Why? What can be done to encourage people and organizations to make their Web sites more accessible?

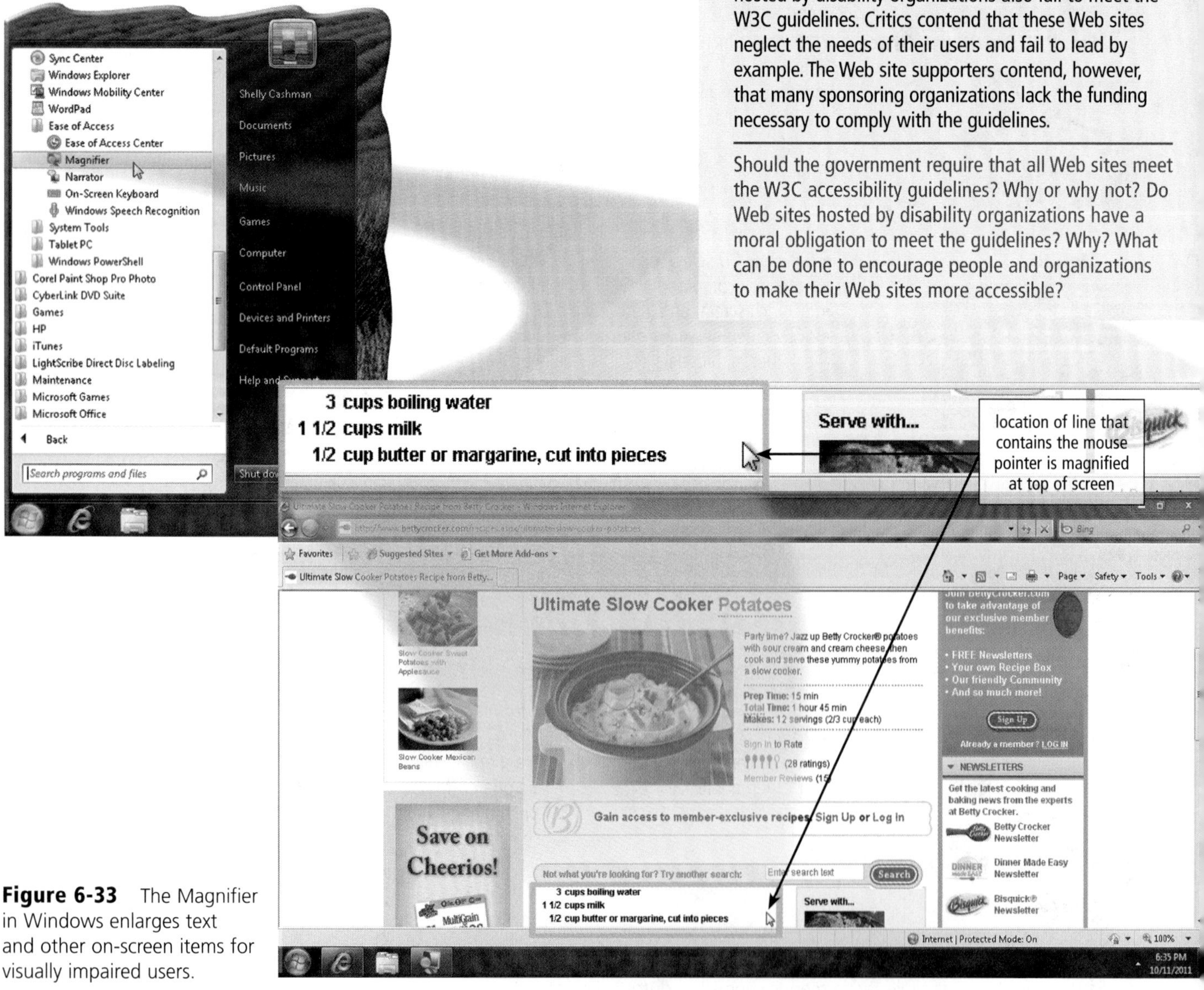

Figure 6-33 The Magnifier in Windows enlarges text and other on-screen items for visually impaired users.

Visually impaired users can change Windows settings, such as increasing the size or changing the color of the text to make the words easier to read. Instead of using a monitor, blind users can work with voice output via Windows Narrator. That is, the computer reads the information that is displayed on the screen. Another alternative is a *Braille printer*, which prints information on paper in Braille (Figure 6-34).

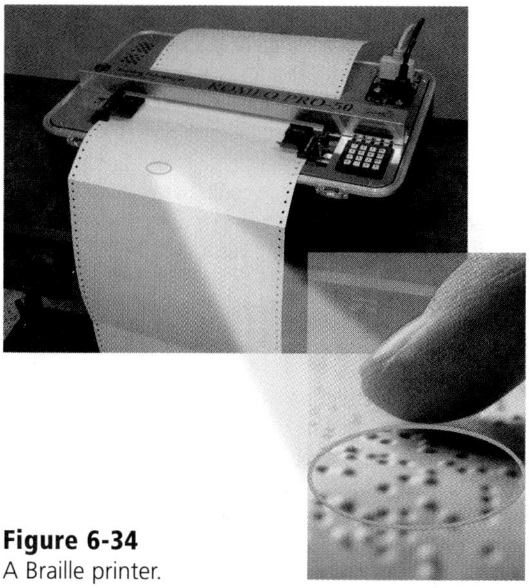

Figure 6-34
A Braille printer.

QUIZ YOURSELF 6-3

Instructions: Find the true statement below. Then, rewrite the remaining false statements so that they are true.

1. A digital light processing (DLP) projector uses tiny lightbulbs to reflect light.
2. Many personal computer users attach surround sound printer systems to their computers to generate a higher-quality sound.
3. Multifunction peripherals require less space than having a separate printer, scanner, copy machine, and fax machine.
4. Some game controllers and mobile devices include real-time action, which is a technology that sends resistance to the device in response to actions of the user.

Quiz Yourself Online: To further check your knowledge of pages 323 through 329, visit the Computer Concepts CourseMate Web site at www.cengagebrain.com, navigate to the Chapter 6 Quiz Yourself resource for this book, and then click Objectives 7 – 9.

Chapter Summary

Computers process and organize data (input) into information (output). This chapter described the various methods of output and several commonly used output devices. Output devices presented were display devices; printers; speakers, headphones, and earbuds; data projectors; interactive whiteboards; and force-feedback game controllers and tactile output.

Computer Usage @ Work

Space Exploration

Watching the television closely, you hear the announcer count the seconds until the spacecraft lifts off from its launch pad: "Three, two, one, and we have liftoff." The engines ignite and the glow from the burning fuel illuminates the night sky as it begins its journey toward the International Space Station. As you sit back and watch, mesmerized by the thought that a group of astronauts are accomplishing something of which you only could dream, hundreds of individuals and computers are working behind the scenes to ensure a safe mission.

Because space exploration is fraught with danger, it is extremely important that all decisions be made with precision and that personnel become aware of problems before the problems become too serious. For instance, space vehicles contain a plethora of sensors that measure environmental variables such as temperature, velocity, position, and altitude. If the sensors return readings outside an acceptable range, computers correct any problems or notify mission managers as necessary. Employees work around the clock monitoring the output from the spacecraft sensors while it is in flight and communicating to astronauts any actions required to ensure a continued safe mission.

In addition to keeping the spacecraft safe while in orbit, computers also help guide the spacecraft into and out of orbit. To reach the International Space Station, spacecraft can be launched safely only during specified launch time frames. Once the spacecraft is launched, it must travel in a precise direction at an exact velocity to ensure a successful mission. As the mission nears completion and a capsule containing the astronauts reenters the atmosphere, onboard computers position the capsule precisely so that the extreme temperatures at the reentry interface do not cause catastrophic damage. Furthermore, these onboard computers help to ensure that the capsule touches down in a safe location.

With billions of dollars spent on space travel, computers play a vital role in guaranteeing the safety of the space vehicle, the astronauts, and those of us on Earth.

For more information, visit the Computer Concepts CourseMate Web site at www.cengagebrain.com, navigate to the Chapter 6 Computer Usage @ Work resource for this book, and then click Space Exploration.

High-Tech Talk

3-D Graphics: Creating a Realistic Experience

Three-dimensional (3-D) graphics, which appear to have height, width, and depth, give realistic qualities to objects in computer programs, particularly computer games. Although you view computer games on a two-dimensional (2-D) computer screen, modern technology creates a 3-D experience by adding the appearance of depth. A game programmer can give single objects or an entire virtual world a 3-D appearance.

Creating a 3-D appearance first requires that you create a wireframe. A *wireframe* is a series of lines, curves, and shapes arranged to resemble an object in a 3-D world (Figure 6-35a). Most 3-D wireframes, for example, consist of a series of polygons. A completed wireframe enables you to identify the shape of the object, although it appears to be hollow. To transform the appearance of the 3-D object from hollow to solid, you add a surface to the wireframe (Figure 6-35b). Some 3-D graphics are composed of more than one wireframe. When adding a surface, it is important to make the object look as realistic as possible by adding color, texture, and reflectance. *Reflectance* refers to the amount of light the object's surface reflects.

With the surface added to a wireframe, you next consider how the object will be lit from one or more lighting sources. Some people create 3-D graphics using a technique called ray-tracing. *Ray-tracing* involves drawing an imaginary path that rays of light follow as they leave their source and then land on an object. The light intensity will be greater on some portions of the object and less on other portions. In addition, the object also might cast a shadow once it is lit from a particular angle.

When creating a 3-D world, the next considerations are perspective and depth of field. *Perspective* refers to differences in how objects appear in relation to one another when they are close to you, versus farther away. Objects appearing close may seem to be spaced apart. As they move farther away from you, they become closer to one another. A technique for calculating which objects appear in front of or behind one another is called the *Z-Buffer*, named after the imaginary axis from the screen to the distant horizon. *Depth of field* gives the appearance that objects farther from you are less focused than closer objects.

Anti-aliasing is the final technique in creating 3-D objects that appear in a 3-D world. *Anti-aliasing* makes curved and diagonal lines appear straight. When computers render graphics with curved and diagonal lines, they often appear jagged. Anti-aliasing inserts additional colored pixels that give the appearance of a smooth edge. All these techniques combined create a realistic 3-D graphic (Figure 6-35c).

The complex nature of 3-D technology requires more computing power in order to render a graphic in an acceptable period of time. For example, computer gamers often buy computers designed for gaming so that a lack of performance does not slow their game. Gaming computers often have faster processors, several gigabytes of RAM, and one or more video cards containing at least 256 MB of RAM. These video cards also might support *DirectX*, which is a programming interface that allows game programmers direct access to enhanced hardware features. For some computer games to work properly, they require a video card that supports a specific version of DirectX. For example, if a game is programmed using the DirectX 11 standard, the video card also must support DirectX 11 for the game to work.

Although game programmers spend many hours creating 3-D graphics for programs such as computer games, the results are rewarding when a player faces an experience so realistic that it is difficult to differentiate between the game and reality.

For more information, visit the Computer Concepts CourseMate Web site at www.cengagebrain.com, navigate to the Chapter 6 High-Tech Talk resource for this book, and then click 3-D Graphics.

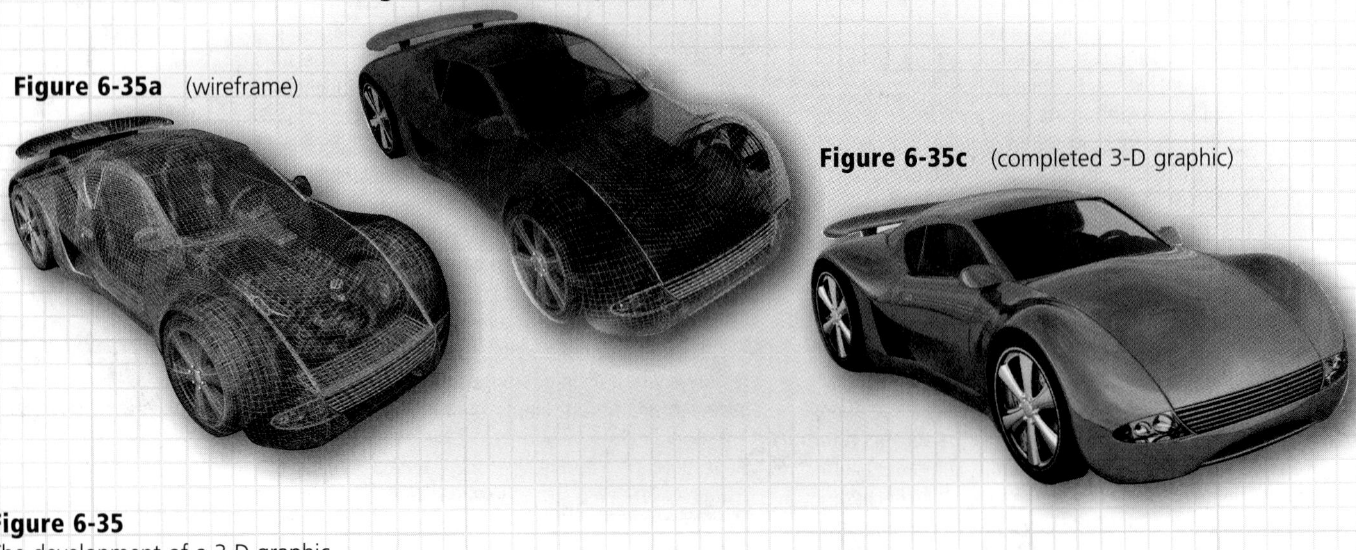

Figure 6-35b (adding surface)

Figure 6-35a (wireframe)

Figure 6-35c (completed 3-D graphic)

Figure 6-35
The development of a 3-D graphic.

Companies on the Cutting Edge

HP Hardware and Software Products Leader

One of the more famous real estate parcels in the United States is the birthplace of the Silicon Valley: the garage where Stanford University friends William Hewlett and David Packard developed various electronic products. Their first success in 1938 was an oscillator used to test sound equipment.

Today *HP* (*Hewlett-Packard*) has become the world's top manufacturer of ink-jet and laser printers, multifunction peripherals, desktop and notebook computers, and servers. It also is a leading software company with products for networking and storage management.

In 2009, HP introduced the first workstation with a six-core AMD Opteron processor, delivering high productivity for multi-threaded programs. HP also ranked ninth in the 2009 FORTUNE 500 ranking.

SAMSUNG ELECTRONICS Top Consumer Electronics Manufacturer

Products branded as "Wow, Simple, Inclusive" are part of *SAMSUNG Electronics*' presence as the world's leading consumer electronics company. Based in Seoul, South Korea, SAMSUNG manufactures more than 60 categories of products including flash memory, plasma monitors, mobile devices, laser printers, and home appliances.

The company was founded in 1969 and originally manufactured electronic home appliances such as televisions, refrigerators, washers, and air conditioners. It merged with Samsung Semiconductor & Communications in 1988 and has grown to become the world's second largest cell phone manufacturer.

The company introduced the world's slimmest watch-phone device in 2009. This device features a full touch screen that allows users to stay connected. By 2013, Samsung Electronics plans to be a leading eco-friendly company.

For more information, visit the Computer Concepts CourseMate Web site at www.cengagebrain.com and then navigate to the Chapter 6 Companies on the Cutting Edge resource for this book.

Technology Trailblazers

STEVE JOBS Apple and Pixar Cofounder

Apricot orchards once grew in the area known today as California's Silicon Valley. *Steve Jobs* was raised in this area, but he has found his fruit of choice to be an Apple. As Apple's CEO, Jobs continues to use his charismatic personality and motivational skills to lead the company and lists himself on patent applications as the coinventor of more than 100 Apple products.

Jobs cofounded Apple in 1976 in his parents' garage with Steve Wozniak. Five years later, he was worth $200 million and on the cover of *Time* magazine at the age of 26. By that time he had helped build the first desktop personal computer, marketed an innovative operating system, and cofounded the Apple Computer Corporation.

Jobs also cofounded Pixar Animation Studios, which merged with The Walt Disney Company in 2006. Pixar and its employees have received more than 100 awards and nominations.

URSULA BURNS Xerox Chairman and CEO

When *Ursula Burns* was nominated to chair Xerox Corporation in 2010, two milestones were reached: she became the first African-American woman to lead a major American company and the first woman to succeed another woman in that role.

She began working at Xerox 30 years earlier as a mechanical engineering summer intern. After earning her bachelor's and master's degrees in that field, she worked in various areas of the corporation, including office network printing, global research, product development, manufacturing, and planning. When Burns was named Xerox's president in 2007, her leadership role expanded to include the information technology, corporate marketing, and human resources departments.

Forbes and *Fortune* have named Burns as one of the most powerful women in the world. She serves as advisor to several educational and community organizations, including FIRST (For Inspiration and Recognition of Science and Technology) and the White House's STEM (Science, Technology, Engineering, and Math) program.

For more information, visit the Computer Concepts CourseMate Web site at www.cengagebrain.com and then navigate to the Chapter 6 Technology Trailblazers resource for this book.

Chapter Review

The Chapter Review reinforces the main concepts presented in this chapter.

To listen to an audio version of this Chapter Review, visit the Computer Concepts CourseMate Web site at www.cengagebrain.com and then navigate to the Chapter 6 Chapter Review resource for this book.

1. **What Are the Four Types of Output?** **Output** is data that has been processed into a useful form. Computers process data (input) into information (output). Four categories of output are text, graphics, audio, and video. An **output device** is any hardware component that conveys information to one or more people. Commonly used output devices include display devices; printers; speakers, headphones, and earbuds; data projectors; interactive whiteboards; and force-feedback game controllers and tactile output.

2. **What Are the Characteristics of Various Display Devices?** A **display device**, or simply *display*, is an output device that visually conveys text, graphics, and video information and consists of a screen and the components that produce the information on the screen. Desktop computers typically use a **monitor** as their display device; most mobile computers and devices integrate the display into the same physical case. LCD monitors, LCD screens, and plasma monitors are types of flat-panel displays. A *flat-panel display* is a lightweight display device with a shallow depth that typically uses LCD or gas plasma technology. An **LCD monitor** is a desktop monitor that uses a liquid crystal display to produce images. A **plasma monitor** is a display device that uses gas plasma technology, which substitutes a layer of gas for the liquid crystal material in an LCD monitor. A **CRT monitor** is a desktop monitor that contains a *cathode-ray tube* (*CRT*). CRT monitors take up more desk space and thus are not used much today.

3. **What Factors Affect the Quality of an LCD monitor or LCD screen?** The quality of an LCD monitor or LCD screen depends primarily on its resolution, response time, brightness, dot pitch, and contrast ratio. **Resolution** is the number of horizontal and vertical pixels in a display device; a higher resolution uses a greater number of pixels and provides a sharper image. *Response time* is the time in milliseconds that it takes to turn a pixel on or off. Brightness of an LCD monitor or LCD screen is measured in nits; the higher the nits, the brighter the image. A *nit* is a unit of visible light intensity equal to one *candela* per square meter. *Dot pitch*, or *pixel pitch*, is the distance in millimeters between pixels on a display device. *Contrast ratio* describes the difference in light intensity between the brightest white and darkest black that can be displayed on a monitor.

Visit the Computer Concepts CourseMate Web site at www.cengagebrain.com, navigate to the Chapter 6 Quiz Yourself resource for this book, and then click Objectives 1 – 3.

4. **What Are the Various Ways to Print?** Users can print by connecting a computer to a printer with a cable that plugs in a port on the computer. *Bluetooth printing* uses radio waves to transmit output to a printer. With *infrared printing*, a computer or other device communicates with the printer via infrared light waves. Some digital cameras connect directly to a printer via a cable; others store images on memory cards that can be removed and inserted in the printer. Networked computers can communicate with the network printer via cables or wirelessly.

5. **How Is a Nonimpact Printer Different from an Impact Printer?** A **printer** is an output device that produces text and graphics on a physical medium, such as paper. A **nonimpact printer** forms characters and graphics on a piece of paper without actually striking the paper. Some spray ink, while others use heat or pressure to create images. Commonly used nonimpact printers are ink-jet printers, photo printers, laser printers, thermal printers, mobile printers, label and postage printers, plotters, and large-format printers. An **impact printer** forms characters and graphics on a piece of paper by striking a mechanism against an inked ribbon that physically contacts the paper. These printers commonly produce *near letter quality* (*NLQ*) output, which is print quality slightly less clear than what is acceptable for business letters. Two commonly used types of impact printers are a **dot-matrix printer** and a **line printer**.

6. **What Are Ink-Jet Printers, Photo Printers, Laser Printers, Multifunction Peripherals, Thermal Printers, Mobile Printers, Label and Postage Printers, and Plotters and Large-Format Printers?** An **ink-jet printer** is a type of nonimpact printer that forms characters and graphics by spraying tiny drops of liquid ink onto a piece of paper. One factor that influences the quality of an ink-jet printer is its resolution. Printer resolution is measured

Chapter Review

by the number of *dots per inch* (*dpi*) a printer can print. A **photo printer** is a color printer that produces photo-lab-quality pictures. A **laser printer** is a high-speed, high-quality nonimpact printer that operates in a manner similar to a copy machine, creating images using a laser beam and powdered ink, called *toner*. Laser printers usually print at faster speeds than ink-jet printers. A **multifunction peripheral** (MFP), or *all-in-one device*, is a single device that looks like a printer or a copy machine but provides the functionality of a printer, scanner, copy machine, and perhaps a fax machine. Some MFPs use color ink-jet printer technology; others include a black-and-white or color laser printer. The primary disadvantage of these devices is that if the device breaks down, you lose all four functions. A **thermal printer** generates images by pushing electrically heated pins against heat-sensitive paper. They are inexpensive, but the print quality is low and the images tend to fade over time. A **mobile printer** is a small, lightweight, battery-powered printer that allows a mobile user to print from a notebook computer or other mobile device. A **label printer** is a small printer that prints on an adhesive-type material that can be placed on a variety of items. Most label printers also print bar codes. A *postage printer* is a special type of label printer that has a built-in scale and prints postage stamps. **Plotters** are sophisticated printers used to produce high-quality drawings, such as blueprints, maps, and circuit diagrams. A **large-format printer** uses ink-jet technology on a large scale to create photo-realistic-quality color prints.

Visit the Computer Concepts CourseMate Web site at www.cengagebrain.com, navigate to the Chapter 6 Quiz Yourself resource for this book, and then click Objectives 4 – 6.

7. What Are the Uses and Characteristics of Speakers, Headphones, and Earbuds? Speakers, headphones, and earbuds are three commonly used audio output devices. An **audio output device** is a component of a computer that produces music, speech, or other sounds. Many personal computer users add stereo **speakers** to their computers, including game consoles and mobile devices, to generate higher-quality sounds. With headphones or earbuds, only the individual wearing the headphones or earbuds hears the sound from the computer. The difference is that **headphones** cover or are placed outside of the ear, whereas **earbuds**, or *earphones*, rest inside the ear canal. A *headset* is a device that functions as both headphones and a microphone, so that users' hands are free for typing or other activities while listening to audio output.

8. What Are the Purposes and Features of Data Projectors, Interactive Whiteboards, and Force-Feedback Game Controllers and Mobile Devices? A **data projector** is a device that takes the text and images displaying on a computer screen and projects them onto a larger screen so that an audience of people can see the image clearly. An *LCD projector* attaches directly to a computer and uses its own light source to display information shown on the computer screen. A *digital light processing* (*DLP*) *projector* uses tiny mirrors to reflect light. An **interactive whiteboard** is a touch-sensitive device, resembling a dry-erase board, that displays the image on a connected computer screen. Joysticks, wheels, gamepads, and motion-sensing game controllers are input devices used to control actions of a player or object in computer games, simulations, and video games. Today's joysticks, wheels, gamepads, and motion-sensing game controllers also include *force feedback*, which is a technology that sends resistance to the device in response to actions of the user. Some input devices include *tactile output* that provides the user with a physical response from the device.

9. What Output Options Are Available for Physically Challenged Users? Hearing-impaired users can instruct programs to display words instead of sound. The Magnifier in Windows enlarges text and other items in a window on the screen. Visually impaired users can enlarge items on the screen and change other settings, such as increasing the size or changing the color of text to make words easier to read. Blind users can work with voice output instead of a monitor via Windows Narrator. Another alternative is a *Braille printer*, which prints information in Braille on paper.

Visit the Computer Concepts CourseMate Web site at www.cengagebrain.com, navigate to the Chapter 6 Quiz Yourself resource for this book, and then click Objectives 7 – 9.

STUDENT ASSIGNMENTS

Key Terms

You should know the Primary Terms and be familiar with the Secondary Terms. The list below helps focus your study.

To see an example of and a definition for each term, and to access current and additional information from the Web, visit the Computer Concepts CourseMate Web site at www.cengagebrain.com and then navigate to the Chapter 6 Key Terms resource for this book.

Primary Terms

(shown in bold-black characters in the chapter)

audio output device (323)
CRT monitor (313)
data projector (325)
display device (306)
dot-matrix printer (323)
earbuds (324)
HDTV (312)
headphones (324)
impact printer (322)
ink-jet printer (316)
interactive whiteboard (326)
label printer (322)
large-format printer (322)
laser printer (319)
LCD monitor (307)
line printer (323)
liquid crystal display (LCD) (308)
mobile printer (321)
monitor (306)
multifunction peripheral (320)
nonimpact printer (315)
output (304)
output device (305)
photo printer (318)
plasma monitor (311)
plotters (322)
printer (313)
resolution (308)
speakers (323)
thermal printer (321)
voice output (325)

photo printer (318)

Secondary Terms

(shown in italic characters in the chapter)

active-matrix display (308)
all-in-one device (320)
aspect ratio (310)
bit depth (310)
Bluetooth printing (314)
Braille printer (329)
candela (310)
cathode-ray tube (CRT) (313)
color depth (310)
continuous-form paper (323)
contrast ratio (310)
digital light processing (DLP) projector (326)
digital photo printer (321)
digital television (DTV) (312)
display (306)
DisplayPort (310)
dot pitch (310)
dots per inch (dpi) (316)
DVI (Digital Video Interface) port (310)
dye-sublimation printer (321)
earphones (324)
flat-panel display (306)
force feedback (326)
graphics processing unit (GPU) (310)
hard copy (313)
HDMI (High-Definition Media Interface) port (310)
head-mounted display (308)
headset (324)
high-definition television (312)
infrared printing (314)
Internet postage (322)
landscape orientation (314)
LCD projector (325)
monochrome (306)
native resolution (308)
near letter quality (NLQ) (322)
nit (310)
organic LED (OLED) (308)
page description language (PDL) (319)
passive-matrix display (308)
PCL (Printer Control Language) (319)
PictBridge (318)
pixel (308)
pixel pitch (310)
portrait orientation (313)
postage printer (322)
PostScript (319)
printout (313)
response time (308)
satellite speakers (324)
soft copy (306)
subwoofer (324)
S-video port (310)
SVGA (311)
SXGA (311)
tactile output (327)
TFT (thin-film transistor) display (308)
thermal wax-transfer printer (321)
toner (320)
UXGA (311)
viewable size (313)
VoIP (325)
widescreen (307)
WQXGA (311)
WSXGA (311)
WUXGA (311)
WXGA (311)
XGA (311)

Checkpoint

The Checkpoint exercises test your knowledge of the chapter concepts. The page number containing the answer appears in parentheses after each exercise. The Beyond the Book exercises will help broaden your understanding of the concepts presented in this chapter.

To complete the Checkpoint exercises interactively, visit the Computer Concepts CourseMate Web site at www.cengagebrain.com and then navigate to the Chapter 6 Checkpoint resource for this book.

True/False Mark T for True and F for False.

_____ 1. The form of output generated by a computer varies depending on the hardware and software being used and the requirements of the user. (304)

_____ 2. Information on a display device sometimes is called soft copy. (306)

_____ 3. Most mobile computers and devices do not integrate the display and other components into the same physical case. (306)

_____ 4. Widescreen LCD monitors are wider than they are tall. (307)

_____ 5. Brightness describes the difference in light intensity between the brightest white and darkest black that can be displayed on an LCD monitor. (310)

_____ 6. An HDMI (High-Definition Media Interface) port combines S-video with high-definition (HD) television and video. (310)

_____ 7. With game consoles, the output device often is a television. (312)

_____ 8. A printout in landscape orientation is taller than it is wide. (313)

_____ 9. With Bluetooth printing, a computer or other device transmits output to a printer via infrared light waves. (314)

_____ 10. An all-in-one device is a single device that looks like a printer or a copy machine but provides the functionality of a printer, scanner, copy machine, and perhaps a fax machine. (320)

_____ 11. An impact printer forms characters and graphics on a piece of paper without actually striking the paper. (322)

_____ 12. A headset is a device that functions as both headphones and a Web cam. (324)

_____ 13. An LCD projector uses tiny mirrors to reflect light, which produces crisp, bright, colorful images that remain in focus and can be seen clearly even in a well lit room. (326)

Multiple Choice Select the best answer.

1. Examples of output that primarily contain text-based documents are _____. (304)
   a. drawings, clip art, and photos
   b. music, narrations, and speeches
   c. home movies and live performances
   d. letters, reports, and e-mail messages

2. _____ uses organic molecules that produce an even brighter, easier-to-read display than standard TFT displays. (308)
   a. HDTV b. OLED
   c. LCD d. LED

3. The _____ is an alternative to DVI that also supports HDMI. (310)
   a. DisplayPort
   b. Digital Video Interface
   c. S-video port
   d. standard monitor port

4. A CRT monitor's viewable size is the _____ measurement of the actual viewing area provided by the screen in the monitor. (313)
   a. horizontal b. vertical
   c. three-dimensional d. diagonal

5. Ink-jet printer resolution is measured by the number of _____ a printer can print. (316)
   a. pages per minute (ppm) b. pixels per inch (ppi)
   c. lines per minute (lpm) d. dots per inch (dpi)

6. The primary disadvantage of multifunction peripherals is that _____. (320)
   a. they require more space than having separate devices
   b. if the multifunction peripheral breaks down, all functions are lost
   c. they are significantly more expensive than purchasing each device separately
   d. all of the above

7. A(n) _____ is a touch-sensitive device, resembling a dry-erase board, that displays the image on a connected computer screen. (326)
   a. flatbed scanner b. data projector
   c. interactive whiteboard d. video conference

8. _____ is a technology that sends resistance to a device in response to actions of the user. (326)
   a. An interactive whiteboard b. A CRT
   c. A dance pad d. Force feedback

STUDENT ASSIGNMENTS

Checkpoint

Matching

Match the terms with their definitions.

____ 1. display device (306)	a. printed information that exists physically and is a more permanent form of output
____ 2. LCD monitor (307)	b. component of a computer that produces music, speech, or other sounds, such as beeps
____ 3. head-mounted display (HMD) (308)	c. defines a display's width relative to its height
____ 4. nit (310)	d. an output device that visually conveys text, graphics, and video information
____ 5. candela (310)	e. forms characters and graphics on a piece of paper without actually striking the paper
____ 6. aspect ratio (310)	f. standard unit of luminous intensity
____ 7. hard copy (313)	g. a display in a helmet, goggles, or glasses
____ 8. nonimpact printer (315)	h. unit of visible light intensity equal to one candela per square meter
____ 9. audio output device (323)	i. provides the user with a physical response from a device
____ 10. tactile output (327)	j. a desktop monitor that uses a liquid crystal display to produce images

Short Answer

Write a brief answer to each of the following questions.

1. How does resolution affect images displayed on a monitor? __________ How does resolution relate to the size of an LCD monitor or screen? __________
2. Describe some of the features of HDTV. __________ How do game console users set up the output for the consoles? __________
3. What are two types of wireless printing technology? __________ How do they differ in how they communicate with a computer or other device? __________
4. How does an ink-jet printer work? __________ What are the differences between dye-sublimation printers used by professionals as compared to home or small business users? __________
5. What might be included with a surround sound system for a computer? __________ What is audio resolution, and what are three examples of audio resolutions? __________

Beyond the Book

Follow the book element instructions below; present your findings (brief report, presentation, discussion, or other means).

1. Ethics & Issues — Select an Ethics & Issues in this chapter (306, 312, 325, 328), find a recent newspaper/magazine article that supports one point of view presented, and then evaluate the article.
2. Computer Usage @ Work — Use the Web or a recent newspaper/magazine to locate three additional unique usages of computer technology in the space exploration industry (329). What makes the use of these technologies unique to the space exploration industry?
3. Companies on the Cutting Edge and Technology Trailblazers — Use the Web or a recent business newspaper/magazine to locate an interesting fact about HP, SAMSUNG Electronics, Steve Jobs, or Anne Mulcahy that was not presented in the chapter (331).
4. High-Tech Talk — Locate a recent newspaper/magazine article that discusses topics related to 3-D Graphics (330). Would you recommend the article you found? Why or why not?
5. FAQs and Web Links — Use the Web or a recent newspaper/magazine to locate three additional facts about an FAQ (306, 309, 311, 312, 318, 320) and Web Link (307, 310, 317, 318, 320, 322, 324, 326) that were not presented in the chapter.
6. Looking Ahead — Use the Web or a recent newspaper/magazine to discover additional uses of the technology presented in Reusable Paper May Become a Disappearing Act (314).
7. Innovative Computing — Use the Web or a recent newspaper/magazine to locate two additional interesting facts about Get the Picture with Digital Frames (308).
8. Making Use of the Web — Visit three of the Environment sites (130) and outline the information on each Web site and the possible uses for each Web site.
9. Digital Video Technology — Select a topic from the Digital Video Technology feature (344) and then create a presentation about the topic using the Web or a newspaper/magazine article.

Learn It Online

The Learn It Online exercises are interactive Web exercises designed to reinforce and expand your understanding of the chapter concepts. The descriptions below briefly summarize each exercise.

To complete the Learn It Online exercises, visit the Computer Concepts CourseMate Web site at www.cengagebrain.com, navigate to the Chapter 6 resources for this book, click the link for the exercise you want to complete, and then read the instructions.

1 At the Movies — SID: Size Matters
Watch a movie to learn about 100-inch HD screens and dual-imaging screens making appearances at a technology trade show and applications of two-way viewing, and then answer questions about the movie.

2 Video and Audio: You Review It — HDTV
Search for, choose, and write a review of a video, podcast, or vodcast that discusses HDTV.

3 Student Edition Labs — Peripheral Devices and Working with Graphics
Enhance your understanding and knowledge about the motherboard and binary numbers by completing the Peripheral Devices and Working with Graphics Labs.

4 Practice Test
Take a multiple choice test that checks your knowledge of the chapter concepts and review the resulting study guide.

5 Who Wants To Be a Computer Genius^2?
Play the Shelly Cashman Series version of this popular game by answering questions to find out if you are a computer genius. Panic buttons are available to provide assistance during game play.

6 Wheel of Terms
Identify important key terms presented in this chapter by playing the Shelly Cashman Series version of this popular game.

7 You're Hired!
Embark on the path to a career in computers by answering questions and solving puzzles related to concepts discussed in this chapter.

8 Crossword Puzzle Challenge
Complete an interactive crossword puzzle to reinforce concepts presented in this chapter.

9 Windows Exercises
Step through the Windows 7 exercises to learn about your computer, Accessibility options, Magnifier, and adjusting the sound on a computer.

10 Exploring Computer Careers
Read about a career as a graphic designer/illustrator, search for related employment advertisements, and then answer related questions.

11 Web Apps — YouSendIt
Learn how to use YouSendIt to create an e-mail message with an attachment and add options such as premium delivery, password-protected secure delivery, certified delivery with tracking, and return receipt.

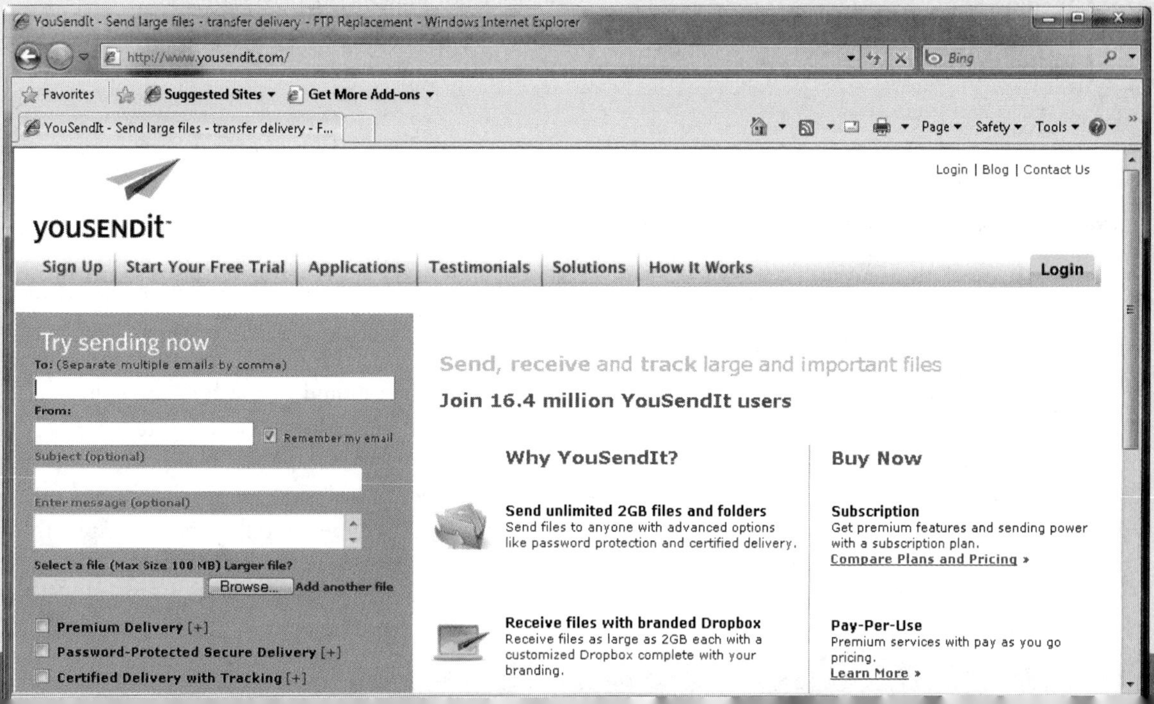

Problem Solving @ Home

The Problem Solving @ Home exercises extend your knowledge of the chapter concepts by seeking solutions to practical computer problems that you may encounter at home or school. The Collaboration exercise should be completed with a team.

In the real world, practical problems often can be solved in multiple ways. Provide one solution to each of the following problems using available resources, such as articles on the Web or in print, blogs, podcasts, videos, television, user guides, other individuals, and electronics and computer stores. You may need to use multiple resources to obtain an answer. Present your solutions in the form requested by your instructor (brief report, presentation, discussion, or other means).

1. **Smeared Printouts** Each time you print a picture on photo paper using your photo printer, the photo comes out of the printer smeared. What is one step you can take that might prevent the ink from smearing while the photo is printing?
2. **Damaged Monitor** You have just moved into a new house. After unpacking your notebook computer and turning it on, you notice that the center of the screen contains a dark spot, about the size of a quarter. You try cleaning the monitor, but the dark spot does not go away. What might have caused this?
3. **Image Not Displaying** When you turn on your computer and monitor, the monitor's power light is flashing orange and no image is displayed. Normally, when your monitor is on, an image is displayed, and the power light is green. What might be wrong?
4. **Monitor Not Working** You just purchased a second monitor for your computer. When you plug in the monitor, turn on the computer, and start Windows, the new monitor does not display an image. What steps will you take to display an image correctly on your new, second monitor?
5. **Incorrect Resolution** You installed a new video card that supports higher resolutions. After installing the video card and turning on the computer, the components of the Windows desktop (taskbar, icons, and gadgets) appear larger than normal. You attempt to change the resolution, but Windows will not allow the resolution to be set any higher than 640×480. You know that your new video card can support higher resolutions. What are your next steps?
6. **Paper Loading Incorrectly** Having depleted your supply of business cards, you decide to print temporary business cards to use until you receive the new cards from your company. You use Microsoft Publisher to design your business cards and then print them on business card paper. When you print the cards, however, the printer loads the paper unevenly. As a result, the printing on the business cards is crooked. What steps will you take to correct this?
7. **Dim Screen** While using your notebook computer, the screen suddenly becomes dim. You set the brightness to its highest setting before it dimmed, and wonder why it suddenly changed. After resetting the brightness to its highest setting, you continue working. What might have caused the screen to dim?
8. **Malfunctioning Earbud** While listening to music on your portable media player, one side of your earbuds suddenly stops working. What might have caused this?

Collaboration

9. **Allocating Printers** You and two of your classmates volunteered at a new private school in your community. A local technology company has donated five printers to the school, including a color laser printer, a black-and-white laser printer, a line printer, and two ink-jet printers. The school, however, is having difficulty deciding where the printers should be placed to be the most effective. The school has asked you and your classmates to recommend locations for the printers. In a team of three people, determine where these printers should be placed in a small private school. One team member should research where color and black-and-white laser printers might be used most effectively, one team member should investigate where line printers would be used, and one team member should provide a recommendation regarding where the ink-jet printers should be placed. After each team member has completed his or her research, the teammates should present their findings to each other and offer any suggestions or recommendations. Then, compile the team's findings in a report and submit it to your instructor.

Problem Solving @ Work

The Problem Solving @ Work exercises extend your knowledge of the chapter concepts by seeking solutions to practical computer problems that you may encounter at work. The Collaboration exercise should be completed with a team.

In the real world, practical problems often can be solved in multiple ways. Provide one solution to each of the following problems using available resources, such as articles on the Web or in print, blogs, podcasts, videos, television, user guides, other individuals, and electronics and computer stores. You may need to use multiple resources to obtain an answer. Present your solutions in the form requested by your instructor (brief report, presentation, discussion, or other means).

1. **Junk Faxes** Your company has a fax machine that sometimes receives faxes advertising low software prices and low mortgage rates at various times throughout the day. These faxes not only are a nuisance, they also are wasting toner and paper. What actions might you take to eliminate or minimize this problem?
2. **Misaligned Printer** While working at your job fulfilling orders in a warehouse, you notice that each time an invoice prints on the dot-matrix printer, the customer and order information does not align properly with the rows and columns on the preprinted forms. What steps will you take to correct this?
3. **Problem with Printouts** You have printed slide handouts on your color printer to distribute during a presentation you are giving later in the day. When you retrieve the printouts from the printer, you notice that the colors do not look right. In fact, anything that was a shade of blue on your monitor did not print on handout. What might be wrong?
4. **Speaker Interference** You work in a cubicle located in a room containing several other cubicles. Whenever a nearby coworker's cell phone rings, a strange sound comes from your computer speakers. You turn the speaker volume lower, but still hear the sound. Why might this be happening? What can you do to resolve the problem?
5. **Unrecognizable Characters** You and your coworkers print to a printer connected to the company network. You started to print a 40-page document, but realized immediately that the document needed one more change, so you cancelled the print job. After making the change and printing the document again, you walk to the printer and find the printer printing many pages with unrecognizable characters. What might be wrong?
6. **Printer Not Ready** While attempting to print an expense report to submit to your supervisor, your computer displays an error message stating that your printer is not ready. What could be causing this?
7. **Monitors Reversed** You have two monitors set up on your desk at work: the monitor on the left is your primary monitor and displays the taskbar, and you typically use the monitor on the right to display your e-mail program. When you arrive at work and log into Windows, you realize that the monitor on the right is now the primary monitor. What might have happened?

8. **Printer Error** Your printer is displaying an error message stating that the toner needs to be replaced; however, the print quality is acceptable each time you print a document. Why might the printer ask you to change the toner when it still is printing acceptable copies?

Collaboration

9. **Computers in Space Exploration** The space tourism industry is gaining worldwide attention. Many more people might express interest in experiencing outer space if prices become more reasonable and safety concerns are minimized. Computers help ensure safety by helping the space vehicles to fly with great precision, but human intervention also is necessary. Form a team of three people and determine how computer output can provide enough information to ensure a safe experience. One team member should research current space exploration and data returned from space vehicles that proves useful. Another team member should research how space vehicles collect this data and present it in a useful form, and the other team member should think of additional ways that computer output can assist in space exploration. Write a brief report summarizing your findings.

Learn How To

The Learn How To activities step you through fundamental technology skills when using a computer. The Learn How To exercises enable you to become more proficient with these skills.

Premium Activity: To relate this Learn How To activity to your everyday life, see a visual demonstration of the activity, and complete a short assessment, visit the Computer Concepts CourseMate Web site at www.cengagebrain.com and then navigate to the Chapter 6 Learn How To resource for this book.

Learn How To 1: Make a Video and Upload It to YouTube

As digital video cameras become smaller and more affordable, many individuals are choosing to create digital recordings of everyday events. In the past, video cameras were bulky, expensive, and required big VCR tapes. Video cameras now are digital and small enough to take anywhere. They also have the capability to transfer video footage to a computer, allowing you to reuse tapes. The increase in individuals storing videos on their computer has prompted companies to develop media sharing Web sites, such as YouTube, for people to post their videos online for others to view. This is especially helpful when you would like to share a video of a memorable event, such as your child's first steps, with a relative across the country who was unable to experience it in person.

Transferring a Video from a Digital Video Camera to a Computer

1. Connect the digital video camera to the computer using the provided USB or FireWire cable. If the camera does not have a cable and stores the digital video on a memory card, remove the memory card from the camera and then insert it into your computer.
2. You can transfer the video from a digital video camera to a computer in one or more of the following ways, depending upon the type of camera you own:
   a. Start the program that came with the digital video camera and follow the manufacturer's instructions for importing the video to a hard disk.
   b. When the digital video camera or memory card is displayed as a removable disk in Windows, copy the video file(s) to the hard disk.
   c. Open Windows Live Movie Maker and click the 'Import from device' command on the Movie Maker menu to import video from the digital video camera.
3. Your video should be less than 10 minutes, less than 2 GB in size, and one of the following file formats: .AVI, .MOV, .WMV, or .MPG. If your video does not meet these requirements, you either should create your video again or use software such as Windows Live Movie Maker to change its file format or reduce its length or size.
4. Double-click the video on the computer to make sure that it plays in its entirety and that you can hear audio.
5. If you would like to free space on the digital camera's media, delete the original video file(s) from the digital video camera or memory card.
6. Disconnect the digital video camera from the computer or remove the memory card from the computer.

Log into YouTube

1. Start a Web browser, type `youtube.com` in the Address bar, and then press the ENTER key to display the YouTube — Broadcast Yourself Web page.
2. Click the Sign In link.
3. Type your user name and password, and then click the Sign In button. If you do not have a YouTube account, click the Sign up for YouTube! link and follow the instructions to sign up for a new YouTube account.

Upload the Video

1. Click the Upload button to display the Video File Upload Web page.
2. Click the Upload Video button to display the 'Select file to upload' dialog box. Locate the video on your computer that you wish to upload and then click the Open button.
3. If necessary, change the title of the video to one you prefer.
4. Enter the description and tags for this video. If you would like to make it easy for people to find your video, enter a detailed description and several tags.
5. Select a video category from the Category drop-down list.
6. If you want to make the video private, click the 'Private (Viewable by you and up to 25 people)' option button.
7. Click the Save Changes button.
8. YouTube will save your changes once the video is finished uploading.

View the Video

1. Point to your user name at the top of the Video File Upload Web page and then click My Videos.
2. Click the Play button to preview the video. Once the video has finished playing, click the Sign Out link to sign out of YouTube.

Learn How To

Exercise

1. Use a digital video camera to create a short video that is less than 20 seconds in length. Save the video to your computer and then sign into YouTube. Upload the video you just created (if you do not have a digital video camera, upload a sample video that is included with Windows or another video on your computer that is not protected by copyright). Once the video has finished uploading, preview it and then send the Web address to your instructor.

Learn How To 2: Control Printing on Your Computer

When you print using a computer, you control printing at two different points: first, before the printing actually begins, and second, after the document has been sent to the printer and either is physically printing or is waiting to be printed. To set the parameters for printing and then print the document, complete the following steps:

1. Click File on the menu bar of the program that will be used for printing and then click Print on the File menu to display the Print dialog box (Figure 6-36). The Print dialog box will vary somewhat depending on the program used. If you are using a program without a menu bar, locate and click the Print command.
2. In the Print dialog box, make the selections for which printer will be used, which pages will be printed, the number of copies to be printed, and any other choices available. For further options, click the Preferences button (or, sometimes, the Properties button) or click the Options button.
3. Click the OK button or the Print button. The document to be printed is sent to a print queue, which is an area on disk storage from which documents actually are printed.

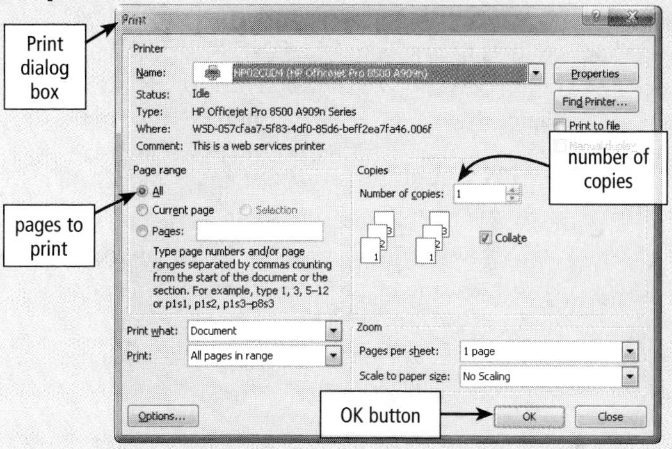

Figure 6-36

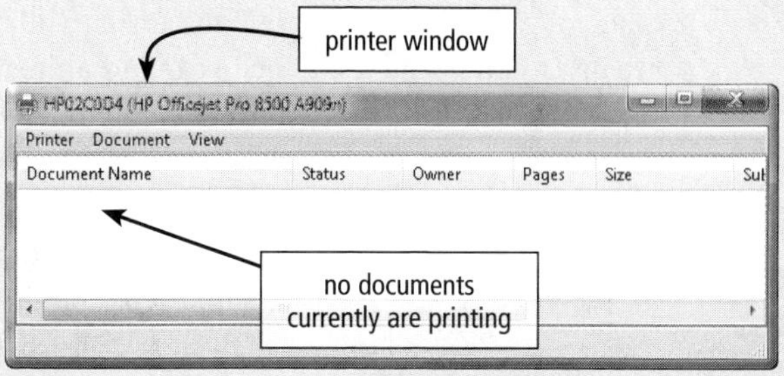

Figure 6-37

When you click the Print button to send the document to the print queue, a printer icon may appear on the Windows taskbar. To see the print queue and control the actual printing of documents on the printer, complete the following steps:

1. If the printer icon appears on the Windows taskbar, double-click it; otherwise, click the Start button on the Windows taskbar, click Control Panel on the Start menu, click the Devices and Printers link, and then double-click the printer icon with the checkmark. The checkmark indicates the default printer. A window opens with the name of the printer on the title bar (Figure 6-37). All documents either printing or waiting to be printed are listed in the window. The Status column indicates whether the document is printing or waiting. In addition, the owner of the file, number of pages, size, date and time submitted, and printer port are listed.
2. If you click Printer on the menu bar in the printer window, you can set printing preferences from the Printer menu. In addition, you can pause all printing and cancel all printing jobs from the Printer menu.
3. If you select a document in the document list and then click Document on the menu bar, you can cancel the selected document for printing, or you can pause the printing for the selected document. To continue printing for the selected document, click Document on the menu bar and then click Resume on the Document menu.

Exercises

1. Start WordPad from the Accessories list. Type `Click Print on the File menu to display the Print dialog box.`
2. Display the Print dialog box and then click the Preferences button. What choices do you have in the Layout sheet? Close the Printing Preferences dialog box. How do you select the number of copies you want to print? How would you print pages 25–35 of a document? Submit your answers to your instructor.

STUDENT ASSIGNMENTS

Web Research

The Web Research exercises broaden your understanding of the chapter concepts by presenting questions that require you to search the Web for answers.

1 Search Sleuth

Use one of the search engines listed in Figure 2-10 in Chapter 2 on page 85 or your own favorite search engine to find the answers to the following questions. Copy and paste the Web address from the Web page where you found the answer. Some questions may have more than one answer. If required, submit your answers to your instructor. (1) Which countries have adopted the ENERGY STAR program? (2) What is the function of a Bayer filter in a digital camera? (3) What invention relating to the printing industry did Lord Kelvin patent in 1867? (4) Which output devices did Donald Bitzer design for the PLATO IV computer assisted instruction system at the University of Illinois? (5) Which television network was the first to broadcast a high-definition signal in 1997? (6) Which country has imposed a maximum limit of 100 decibels on all headphones and earbuds sold?

2 Green Computing

Nearly all printer toner and ink-jet cartridges are made of recyclable or reusable materials. Millions are discarded in the trash each year and ultimately reach landfills. One method of reducing the environmental impact of disposing these oil-based products is to buy locally remanufactured cartridges and to

refill empty cartridges yourself at office supply stores. View online Web sites that provide information about recycling printer cartridges. Which stores give a credit toward a purchase for returning an empty cartridge? What is the cost of refilling a cartridge compared to buying a comparable new cartridge? What steps are involved in the cartridge remanufacturing process? Do schools in your community sponsor a fundraising opportunity for recycling cartridges? Write a report summarizing your findings, and include a table of links to Web sites that provide additional details.

3 Social Networking

Each day, more than 100,000 people register for Friendster, which is one of the top three online social networking Web sites in the world. The San Francisco-based company is popular in more than 75 countries, particularly in Asia. Its mobile Web site, m.friendster.com, allows the more than 110 million registered users to receive and send messages using their smart phones. Visit the Friendster Web site (friendster.com). Follow the instructions to create a Friendster account, log in, and then click the Explore link at the top of the home page. Who are some musicians, athletes, and artists featured in the Fan Profiles section? Click the Classifieds link and then select a city in the Location area. What types of computer listings are shown in the Services area? Click the About Us link at the bottom of the page and then click the Testimonials link. What do members like about Friendster? Summarize the information you read and viewed.

4 Blogs

One of the foremost online music entertainment companies is MTV Networks. Its Web sites feature music and entertainment from throughout the world, including Europe, Asia, and Latin America. MTV has a news blog (newsroom.mtv.com) and a video games blog (multiplayerblog.mtv.com). Visit these two sites and read the blogs. What are the top news stories? Which games are reviewed? VH1.com and CMT.com are the Networks' more popular Web sites, and each has its own blog: blog.vh1.com and blog.cmt.com. Visit these sites and read the blogs. Who is the intended audience? Which musicians and celebrities are featured in the first three posts?

5 Ethics in Action

"Netomania" is not a recognized disorder, but this popular name for Internet Addiction Disorder (IAD) may be affecting some Internet users who spend many hours gaming, blogging, shopping, and social networking. People may be addicted when they spend up to 10 hours a day online, they occasionally binge for extended Internet sessions, and they suffer withdrawal symptoms when they have not been online for some time. Some researchers, however, believe the Internet problem is just a symptom of other psychiatric disorders, such as manic depression. View online sites that provide information about IAD, including the Center for Internet Addiction Recovery (netaddiction.com). Write a report summarizing your findings, and include a table of links to Web sites that provide additional details.

Critical Thinking

The Critical Thinking exercises challenge your assessment and decision-making skills by presenting real-world situations associated with the chapter concepts. The Collaboration exercise should be completed with a team.

To evaluate the situations below, use personal experiences and available resources such as articles on the Web or in print, blogs, podcasts, videos, television, user guides, other individuals, and electronics and computer stores. You may need to use multiple resources to form conclusions and make recommendations.

1. Class Discussion — Music in the Workplace
Your company is purchasing new computers for all employees, and your supervisor asks you if it is necessary to purchase a set of speakers with each computer. Standard job duties do not require speakers, but employees enjoy listening to music quietly at their desk. The added cost of including speakers with the new computers is minimal, but your supervisor is concerned that listening to music while working can decrease job performance. Do you feel that listening to music can increase or decrease your job performance? Is the increase in employee morale worth the cost of purchasing speakers? Could the speakers from employees' old computers work on their new computers? If your supervisor chooses not to include speakers, how else would you recommend he spend the money to improve the computers?

2. Class Presentation — Printer Comparison
Printing requirements vary greatly among users. The local insurance agency where you are employed part time is having their IT person shop for a printer. The owner is aware that you are taking a computer class and has asked you to assist her in deciding which printer to buy. Figure 6-12 on page 314 lists several questions to consider when choosing a printer. Use what you learned in class to answer the questions posed in Figure 6-12. Answer each question according to what you believe to be your employer's needs. Then, use the Web and/or print media to research at least two printers that meet the requirements. Prepare a presentation that identifies the printers you researched, describes their features, and evaluates their advantages and disadvantages. Include in your presentation a recommendation for which printer you would buy and reasons supporting your recommendation.

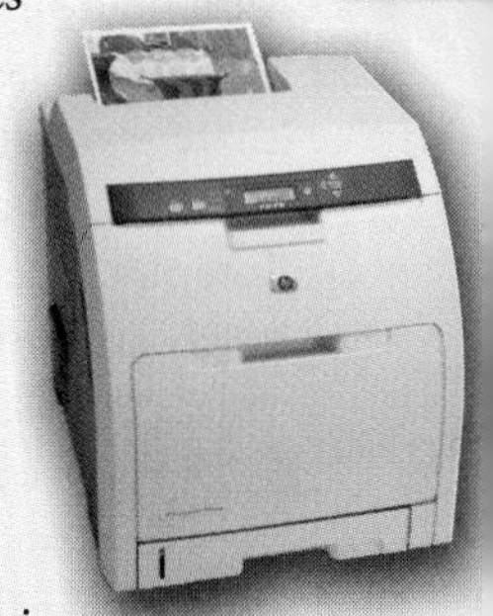

3. Research — Recurring Costs for Plotters
While printers produce an image on a page from top to bottom, plotters can draw on any part of a page at random and then move on to any other part. This capability, coupled with their capacity to use large sheets of paper, make plotters particularly valuable to people who produce maps or blueprints. A local engineering firm that has used hand drawings for the past 50 years has hired you to assist the head of their drafting department in purchasing three 42-inch plotters with a maximum print length of 300 feet and at least 1200 × 600 dpi. Use the Web and/or print media to research both the initial and recurring costs (ink, paper, maintenance, etc.) of plotters that meet the stated requirements from three different manufacturers. Include in your research how long each plotter takes to produce an image and other noteworthy information. What are the advantages or disadvantages of using a plotter compared to simply creating a drawing by hand? Prepare a report summarizing your findings.

Collaboration

4. Recommending Output Devices
Three accountants at the company where you work want to branch off independently and open a small accounting office with approximately 20 to 25 employees. They have hired your team as consultants to help with the setup. The goal is to determine the type of output devices they will need within the office. Consider the types and number of printers, types and number of display devices, audio devices, microphones, LCD projectors, accommodations or specialized devices for the physically challenged, and whether multifunction peripherals are needed. Form a three-member team and assign each team member one or more categories of output devices. Each team member should use the Web and/or print media to research his or her assignments. Prepare a presentation that combines all team members' findings. List the advantages and disadvantages of the various devices. Include your team's recommendations on which devices would be appropriate and a short explanation of why the team selected each device.

Digital Video Technology

Everywhere you look, people are capturing moments they want to remember. They shoot movies of their vacations, birthday parties, activities, accomplishments, sporting events, weddings, and more. Because of the popularity of digital video cameras and mobile devices with built-in digital cameras, increasingly more people desire to capture their memories digitally, instead of on film. As shown in Figure 1, people have the ability to modify and share the digital videos they create. When you use special hardware and/or software, you can copy, manipulate, and distribute digital videos using your personal computer and the Internet. Amateurs can achieve professional quality results by using more sophisticated hardware and software. This feature describes how to select a video camera, record a video, transfer and manage videos, edit a video, and distribute a video.

Digital recordings deliver significant benefits over film-based movie making. With digital video cameras, recordings reside on storage media such as a hard disk, optical disc, or memory card. Unlike film, storage media can be reused, which reduces costs, saves time, and provides immediate results. Digital technology allows greater control over the creative process, both while recording video and in the editing process. You can check results immediately after recording video to determine whether it meets your expectations. If you are dissatisfied with a video, you can erase it and recapture it, again and again. Today, many mobile devices, such as smart phones and PDAs, allow you to capture video.

Figure 1 A variety of input, output, and storage devices are used by home users to process and edit digital video.

As shown in Figure 1, digital video cameras and mobile devices function as input devices when they transmit video to a personal computer. You can transmit video by connecting the video camera or mobile device to your personal computer using a USB or FireWire port, or by placing the storage media used on the camera or mobile device in the computer. Some cameras and devices also can transmit wirelessly to a computer or to the media sharing Web sites.

When you transmit video that was captured with a digital video camera or mobile device to a computer, you can edit the video using video editing software. If desired, you often can preview the video during the editing process on a television. Finally, you save the finished result to the desired media, such as an optical disc or, perhaps, e-mail the edited video or post it to a media sharing Web site. In this example, an optical disc drive also can be used to input video from an optical disc. Also in the example shown in Figure 1, a mobile device that includes a video camera sends a video directly to a media sharing Web site.

Digital video technology allows you to input, edit, manage, publish, and share your videos using a personal computer. With digital video technology, you can transform home videos into Hollywood-style movies by enhancing the videos with scrolling titles and transitions, cutting out or adding scenes, and adding background music and voice-over narration. The following sections outline the steps involved in the process of using digital video technology.

1 Select a Video Camera

Video cameras record in either analog or digital format. **Analog formats** include 8mm, Hi8, VHS-C, and Super VHS-C. **Digital formats** include Mini-DV, MICROMV, Digital8, DVD, Blu-ray, and HDV (high-definition video format). Some digital video cameras record on an internal hard disk. Others may allow you to record directly on an optical disc drive. Digital video cameras fall into three general categories: high-end consumer,

consumer, and webcasting and monitoring (Figure 2). Consumer digital video cameras are by far the most popular type among consumers. High-end consumer models may support the Blu-ray or HDV standards. A video recorded in high-definition can be played back on a high-definition display. Many mobile devices allow you to record video that you later can transmit to your computer or e-mail from the device. Some devices allow you to upload video directly to video sharing Web sites. Digital video cameras provide more features than analog video cameras, such as a higher level of zoom, better sound, or greater control over color and lighting.

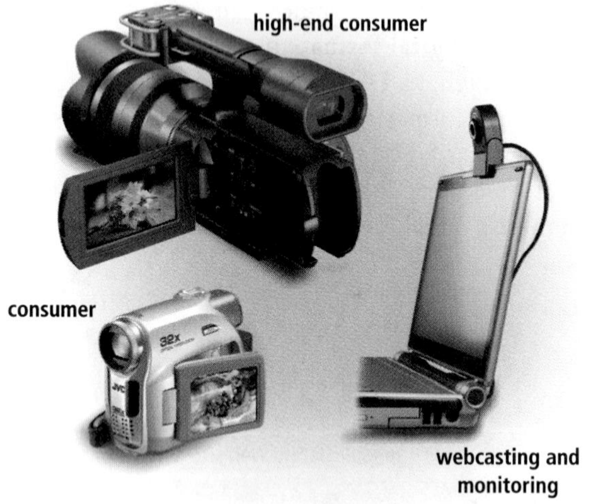

Figure 2 The high-end consumer digital video camera can produce professional-grade results. The consumer digital video camera produces amateur-grade results. The webcasting and monitoring digital video camera is appropriate for webcasting and security monitoring.

2 Record a Video

Most video cameras provide you with a choice of recording programs, which sometimes are called automatic settings. Each recording program includes a different combination of camera settings, so that you can adjust the exposure and other functions to match the recording environment. Usually, several different programs are available, such as point-and-shoot, point-and-shoot with manual adjustment, sports, portrait, spotlit scenes, and low light. You also have the ability to select special digital effects, such as fade, wipe, and black and white. If you are recording outside on a windy day, then you can enable the windscreen to prevent wind noise. If you are recording home videos or video meant for a Web site, then the point-and-shoot recording program is sufficient.

3 Transfer and Manage Videos

After recording the video, the next step is to transfer the video to your personal computer or to the Internet. Most video cameras connect directly to a USB or FireWire port on a personal computer (Figure 3). Transferring video with a digital camera or mobile device is easy, because the video already is in a digital format that the computer can recognize. Many mobile devices include a special cable used to connect the device to a personal computer or allow you to transfer the videos to a media sharing Web site or your own Web site.

Some people own analog format video tapes that require additional hardware to convert the analog signals to a digital format before the video can be manipulated on a personal computer. The additional hardware includes a special video capture card using a standard RCA video cable or an S-video cable (Figure 4). *S-video* cables provide sharper images and greater overall quality. A personal computer also can record video to an optical disc, or it can be connected to an external DVD/Blu-ray Disc recorder to record videos. Video conversion services often specialize in converting older analog video to a variety of digital formats.

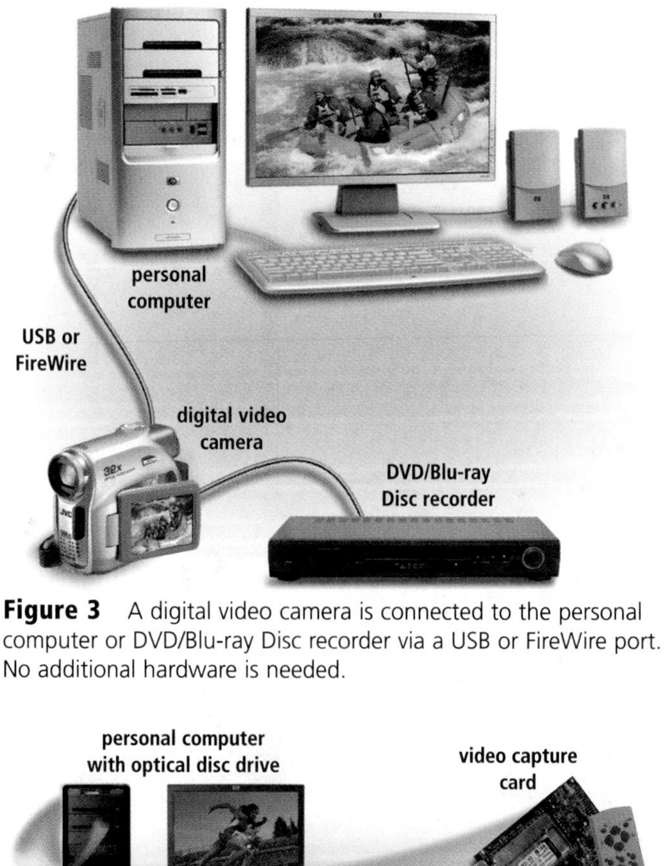

Figure 3 A digital video camera is connected to the personal computer or DVD/Blu-ray Disc recorder via a USB or FireWire port. No additional hardware is needed.

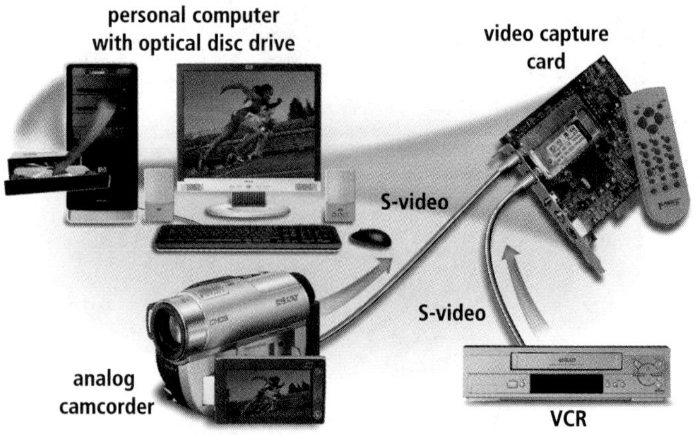

Figure 4 An analog camcorder or VCR is connected to the personal computer via an S-video port on a video capture card.

When transferring video, plan to use approximately 15 to 30 GB of hard disk storage per hour of digital video. High-definition formats may require much more storage per hour. A typical video project requires about four times the amount of raw footage as the final product. At the high end, therefore, a video that lasts an hour may require up to 120 GB of storage for the raw footage, editing process, and final video. This storage requirement can vary depending on the software you use to copy the video from the video camera to the hard disk and the format you select to save the video. For example, Microsoft's Windows Live Movie Maker can save 15 hours of video in 10 GB when creating video for playback on a computer, but saves only 1 hour of video in 10 GB when creating video for playback on a DVD. A high-definition video file may require more than 10 GB per hour.

The video transfer requires application software on the personal computer (Figure 5). The Windows Live Movie Maker software, available as a free download from Microsoft's Web site, allows you to transfer the video from a video camera. Depending on the length of video and the type of connection used, the video may take a long time to transfer. Make certain that no other programs are running on your personal computer while transferring the video.

The frame rate of a video refers to the number of frames per second (fps) that are captured in the video. The most widely used frame rate is 30 fps. A smaller frame rate results in a smaller file size for the video, but playback of the video will not be as smooth as one recorded with a higher frame rate.

When transferring video, the software may allow you to choose a file format and a codec to store the video. A video **file format** holds the video information in a manner specified by a vendor, such as Apple or Microsoft. Six of the more popular file formats are listed in Figure 6. The 3GP format is widely used on mobile devices.

Figure 5 Some video editing software allows you to transfer a video from any video source to a hard disk.

File formats support codecs to encode the audio and video into the file formats. A **codec** specifies how the audio and video is compressed and stored within the file. A particular file format may be able to store audio and video in a number of different codecs. Figure 7 shows some options available for specifying a file format and video quality settings in a video capture program. The file format and codec you choose often is based on what you plan to do with the movie. For example, if you plan to upload your video to the YouTube video sharing Web site, the best choices are DivX and MPEG-4 file formats. Many users find that they are unable to play their own or others' videos, and the problem often is that the proper codec is not installed on the user's personal computer. Video conversion software often allows the user to convert a video in a less popular format to a better supported format. Many of these programs are available as freeware.

After transferring the video to a personal computer or the Internet, and before manipulating the video, you should store the video files in appropriate folders, named correctly, and backed up. Most video transfer application software helps manage these tasks.

Popular Video File Formats

File Format	File Extensions
Apple QuickTime	.MOV or .QT
DivX	.DIVX
Microsoft Windows Media Video	.WMV or .ASF
MPEG-4 Part 4	.MP4
Real RealMedia	.RM or .RAM
3GP	.3GP or .3G2

Figure 6 Apple, DivX, Microsoft, and Real offer the more popular video file formats.

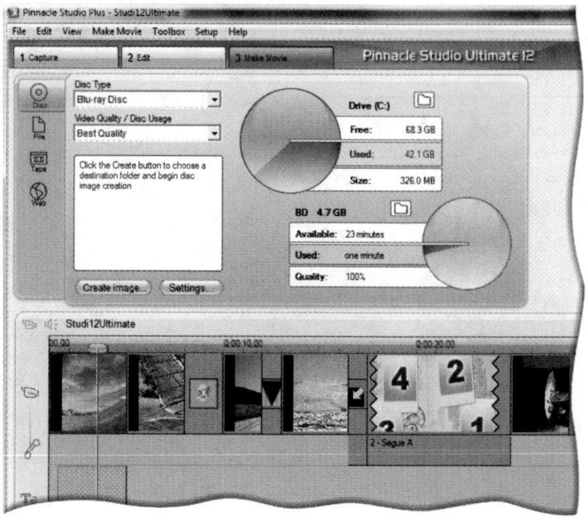

Figure 7 Video editing software allows you to specify a combination of file format and video quality settings when saving a video.

4 Edit a Video

Once the video is stored on your hard disk or the Internet, the next step is to edit, or manipulate, the video. If you used a video capture card to transfer analog video to the computer (Figure 4 on page 346), the files may require extra initial processing. Some Web sites allow you to perform minor editing and other tasks on the Web site. When you use a video capture card, some of the video frames may be lost in the transfer process. Some video editing programs allow you to fix this problem with **frame rate correction** tools.

The first step in the editing process is to split the video into smaller pieces, or *scenes*, that you can manipulate more easily. This process is called *splitting*. Most video software automatically splits the video into scenes, thus sparing you the task. After splitting, you should delete unwanted scenes or portions of scenes. This process is called *pruning*.

After creating the scenes you want to use in the final production, you edit each individual scene. You can *crop*, or change the size of, scenes. That is, you may want to delete the top or a side of a scene that is irrelevant. You also can resize the scene. For example, you may be creating a video that will be displayed on a media sharing Web site. Making a smaller video, such as 320 × 200 pixels instead of 640 × 480 pixels, results in a smaller file that transmits faster over the Internet. Some media sharing Web sites recommend smaller video resolutions, such as 320 × 200 pixels, and some will perform the conversion for you automatically.

If a video has been recorded over a long period, using different cameras or under different lighting conditions, the video may need color correction. *Color correction tools* analyze your video and match brightness, colors, and other attributes of video clips to ensure a smooth look to the video (Figure 8).

You can add logos, special effects, or titles to scenes. You can place a company logo or personal logo in a video to identify yourself or the company producing the video. Logos often are added on the lower-right corner of a video and remain for the duration of the video. Special effects include warping, changing from color to black and white, morphing, or zoom motion. *Morphing* is a special effect in which one video image is transformed into another image over the course of several frames of video, creating the illusion of metamorphosis. You usually add titles at the beginning and ending of a video to give the video context. A training video may have titles throughout the video to label a particular scene, or each scene may begin with a title.

The next step in editing a video is to add audio effects, including voice-over narration and background music. Many video editing programs allow you to add additional tracks, or *layers*, of sound to a video in addition to the sound that was

Figure 8 Color correction tools in video editing software allow a great deal of control over the mood of your video creation.

recorded on the video camera or mobile device. You also can add special audio effects.

The final step in editing a video is to combine the scenes into a complete video (Figure 9). This process involves ordering scenes and adding transition effects between scenes. Video editing software allows you to combine scenes and separate each scene with a transition. *Transitions* include fading, wiping, blurry, bursts, ruptures, erosions, and more.

5 Distribute the Video

After editing the video, the final step is to distribute it or save it on an appropriate medium. You can save video in a variety of formats. Video recorded on a mobile device often requires conversion to a more widely accepted format.

Video also can be stored in digital formats in any of several optical disc formats or on a media sharing Web site. *Optical disc creation software*, which often is packaged with video editing software, allows you to create, or *master*, optical discs. You can add interactivity to your optical disc creations. For example, you can allow viewers to jump to certain scenes using a menu.

You also can save your video creation in electronic format for distribution over the Web, via e-mail, or to a mobile device. Some cameras include a button that allows users to upload directly to a media sharing Web site. Popular media sharing Web sites, such as YouTube (Figure 10), have recommendations for the best file format and codecs to use for video that you upload to them (Figure 11). Your video editing software must support the file format and codec you want to use. For example, Apple's iMovie software typically saves files in the QuickTime file format.

Professionals use hardware and software that allow them to create a film version of digital video that can be played in movie theaters. This technology is becoming increasingly popular. The cost of professional video editing software ranges from thousands to hundreds of thousands of dollars. Video editing software for the home user is available for a few hundred dollars or less. Some Hollywood directors believe that eventually all movies will be recorded and edited digitally.

After creating your final video for distribution or for your personal video collection, you should back up the final video file. You can save your scenes for inclusion in other video creations or create new masters using different effects, transitions, and ordering of scenes.

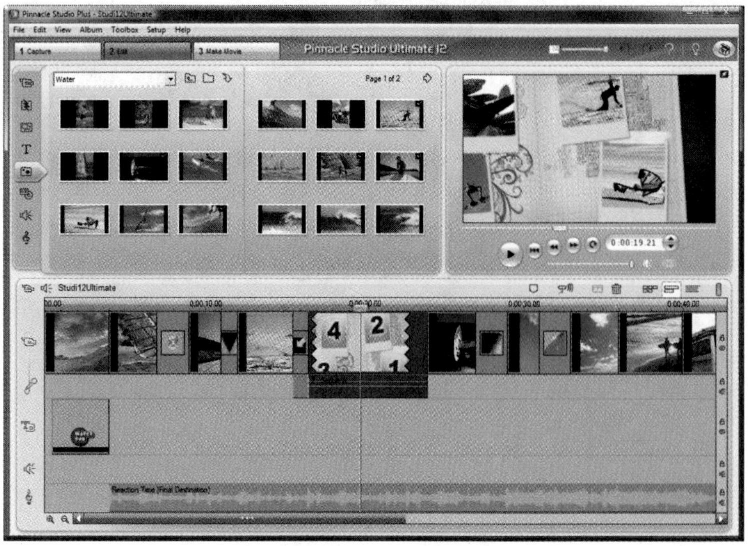

Figure 9 Scenes are combined into a sequence on the bottom of the screen.

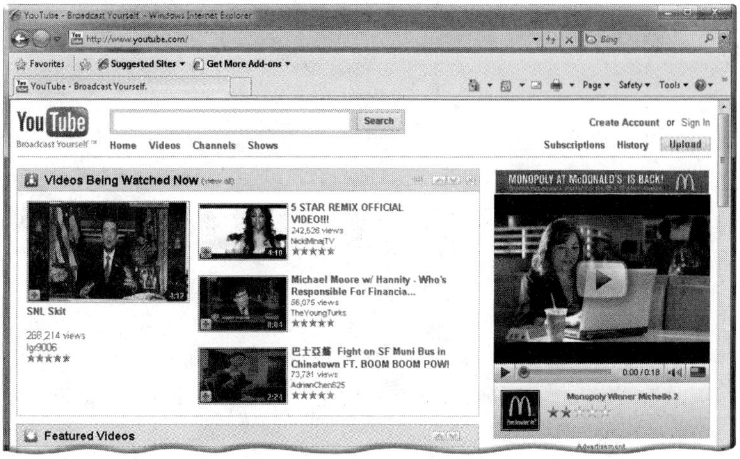

Figure 10 Media sharing Web sites allow you to share your videos with acquaintances or the entire world.

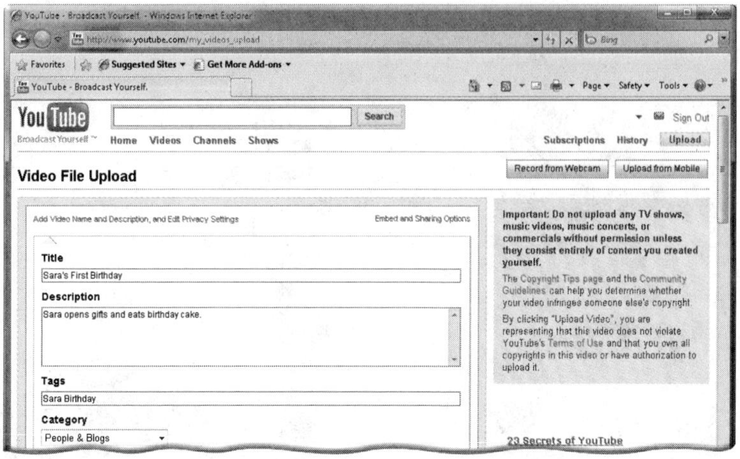

Figure 11 Media sharing Web sites, such as YouTube, provide tools that simplify the process of uploading videos to the site.

Chapter Seven

Storage

Objectives

After completing this chapter, you will be able to:

1 Differentiate between storage devices and storage media

2 Describe the characteristics of an internal hard disk including capacity, platters, read/write heads, cylinders, sectors and tracks, revolutions per minute, transfer rate, and access time

3 Discuss the purpose of network attached storage devices, external and removable hard disks, and hard disk controllers

4 Describe the various types of flash memory storage: solid state drives, memory cards, USB flash drives, and ExpressCard modules

5 Describe cloud storage and explain its advantages

6 Describe the characteristics of optical discs

7 Differentiate among various types of optical discs: CDs, archive discs and Picture CDs, DVDs, and Blu-ray Discs

8 Identify the uses of tape, magnetic stripe cards, smart cards, microfilm and microfiche, and enterprise storage

Storage

Storage holds data, instructions, and information for future use. Every computer stores system software and application software. To start up, a computer locates an operating system (system software) in storage, usually a hard disk, and loads it into memory (RAM). When a user issues a command to start application software, such as a word processing program or a Web browser, the operating system locates the program in storage, such as on a hard disk or optical disc, and loads it into memory (RAM).

In addition to programs, users store a variety of data and information on mainframe computers, servers, desktop computers, notebook computers (including netbooks and Tablet PCs), smart phones, portable media players, and other mobile devices. For example, all types of users store digital photos; appointments, schedules, and contact/address information; correspondence, such as letters and e-mail messages; tax records; and Web pages.

A home user also might store budgets, bank statements, a household inventory, records of stock purchases, tax information, homework assignments, recipes, music, and videos. In addition or instead, a business user stores reports, financial records, travel records, customer

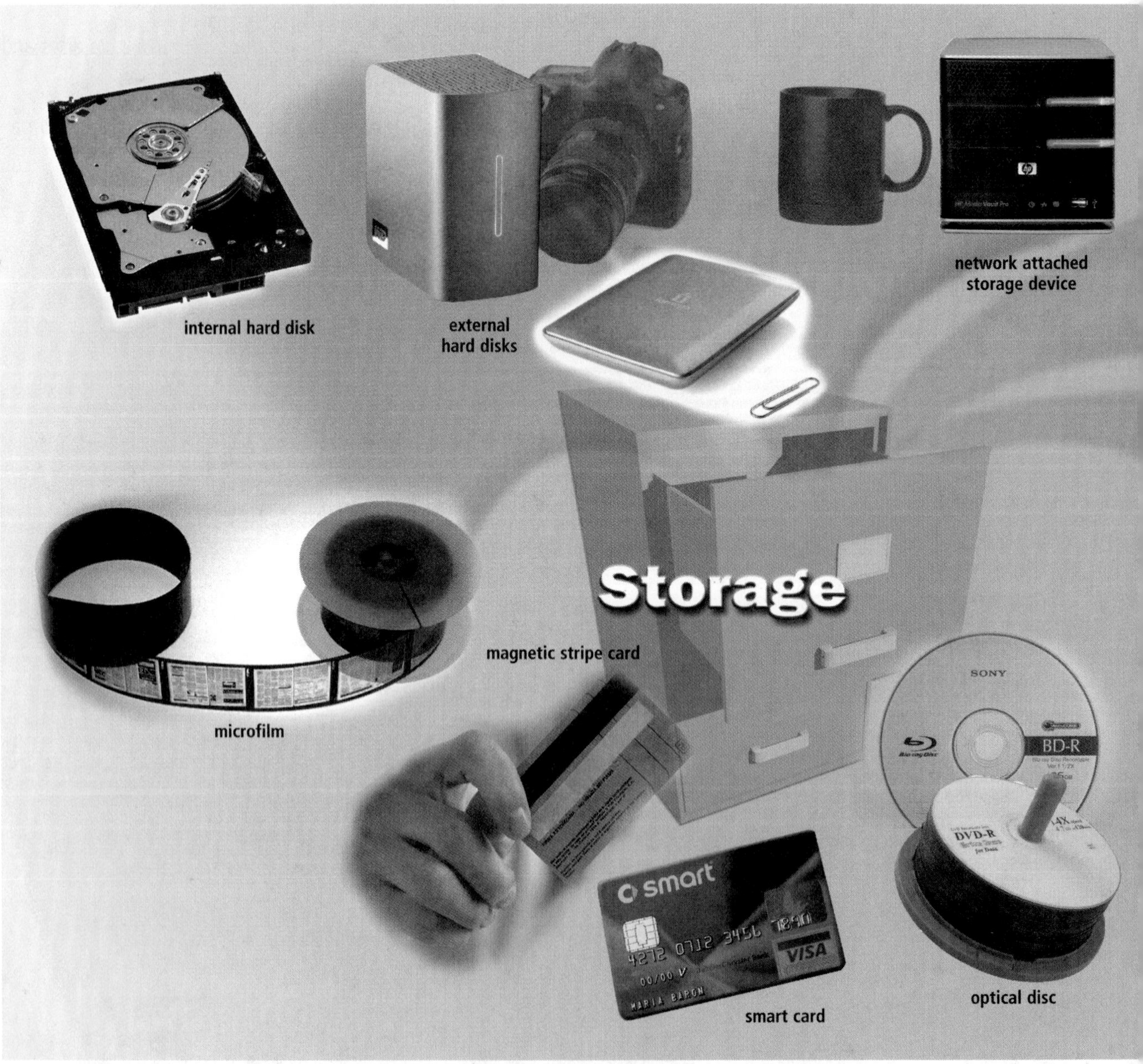

Figure 7-1 A variety of storage options.

orders and invoices, vendor payments, payroll records, inventory records, presentations, quotations, and contracts. Other users store diagrams, drawings, blueprints, designs, marketing literature, corporate newsletters, and product catalogs.

Storage requirements among users vary greatly. Home users, small office/home office users, and mobile users typically have much smaller storage requirements than enterprise users. For example, a home user may need 320 GB (billion bytes) of storage, while enterprises may require 50 PB (quadrillion bytes).

A **storage medium** (media is the plural), also called *secondary storage*, is the physical material on which a computer keeps data, instructions, and information. Examples of storage media are hard disks, solid state drives, memory cards, USB flash drives, ExpressCard modules, optical discs, smart cards, magnetic stripe cards, and microfilm. Cloud storage is another storage option, in which the actual storage media used is transparent to the user. Figure 7-1 shows a variety of storage options. Memory (RAM), by contrast, typically consists of one or more chips on the motherboard or some other circuit board in the computer.

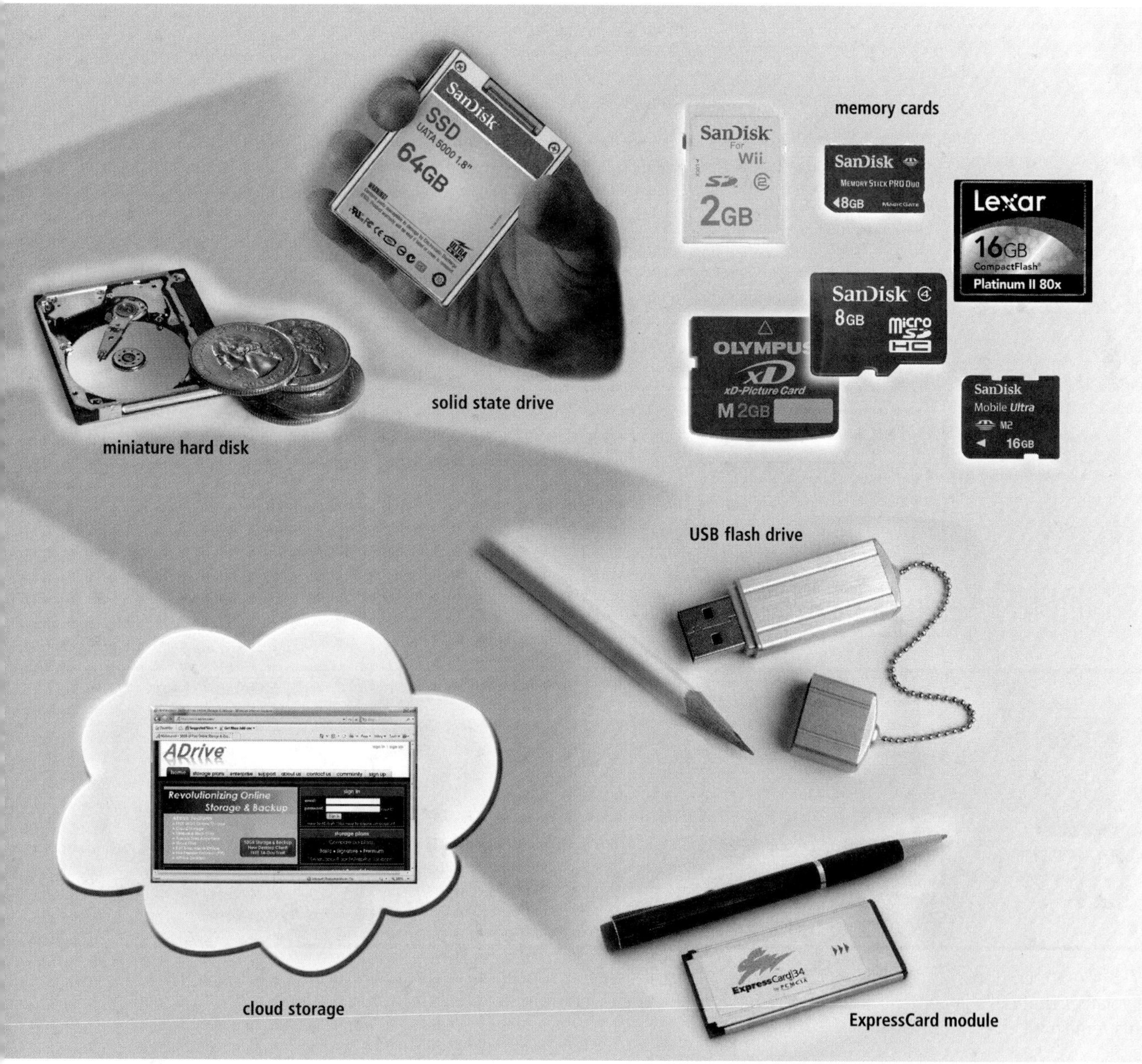

Capacity is the number of bytes (characters) a storage medium can hold. Figure 7-2 identifies the terms manufacturers use to define the capacity of storage media. For example, a reasonably priced USB flash drive can store up to 4 GB of data (approximately four billion bytes) and a typical hard disk has 320 GB (approximately 320 billion bytes) of storage capacity.

Items on a storage medium remain intact even when power is removed from the computer. Thus, a storage medium is nonvolatile. Most memory (i.e., RAM), by contrast, holds data and instructions temporarily and thus is volatile. Figure 7-3 illustrates the concept of volatility. For an analogy, think of a filing cabinet that holds file folders as a storage medium, and the top of your desk as memory. When you want to work with a file, you remove it from the filing cabinet (storage medium) and place it on your desk (memory). When you are finished with the file, you remove it from your desk (memory) and return it to the filing cabinet (storage medium).

A **storage device** is the computer hardware that records and/or retrieves items to and from storage media. **Writing** is the process of transferring data, instructions, and information from memory to a storage medium. **Reading** is the process of transferring these items from a storage medium into memory. When storage devices write data on storage media, they are creating

Storage Terms

Storage Term	Approximate Number of Bytes	Exact Number of Bytes
Kilobyte (KB)	1 thousand	2^{10} or 1,024
Megabyte (MB)	1 million	2^{20} or 1,048,576
Gigabyte (GB)	1 billion	2^{30} or 1,073,741,824
Terabyte (TB)	1 trillion	2^{40} or 1,099,511,627,776
Petabyte (PB)	1 quadrillion	2^{50} or 1,125,899,906,842,624
Exabyte (EB)	1 quintillion	2^{60} or 1,152,921,504,606,846,976
Zettabyte (ZB)	1 sextillion	2^{70} or 1,180,591,620,717,411,303,424
Yottabyte (YB)	1 septillion	2^{80} or 1,208,925,819,614,629,174,706,176

Figure 7-2 The capacity of a storage medium is measured by the number of bytes it can hold.

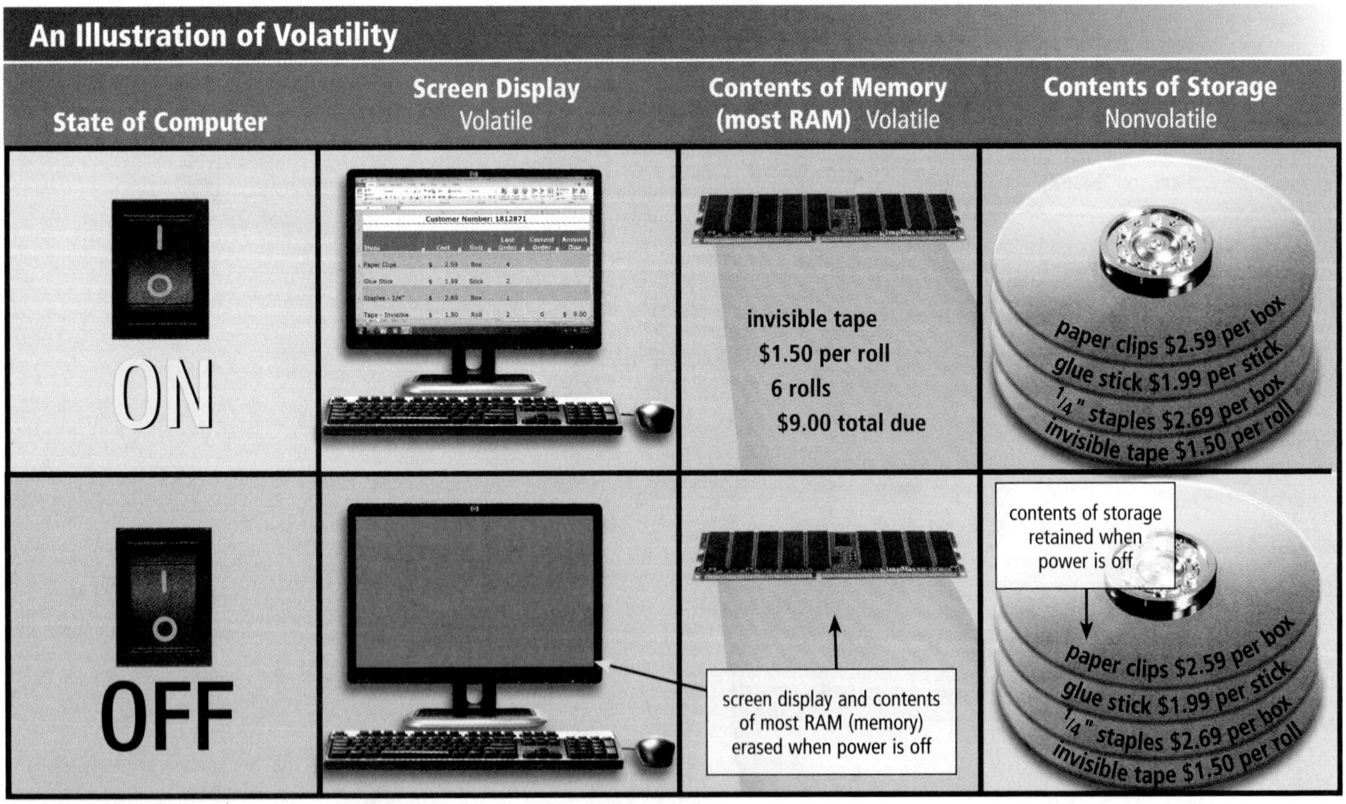

Figure 7-3 A screen display is considered volatile because its contents disappear when power is removed. Likewise, most RAM chips are volatile. That is, their contents are erased when power is removed from the computer. Storage, by contrast, is nonvolatile. Its contents remain when power is off.

output. Similarly, when storage devices read from storage media, they function as a source of input. Nevertheless, they are categorized as storage devices, not as input or output devices.

The speed of storage devices and memory is defined by access time. **Access time** measures (1) the amount of time it takes a storage device to locate an item on a storage medium or (2) the time required to deliver an item from memory to the processor. The access time of storage devices is slow, compared with the access time of memory. Memory (chips) accesses items in billionths of a second (nanoseconds). Storage devices, by contrast, access items in thousandths of a second (milliseconds) or millionths of a second (microseconds).

Instead of, or in addition to access time, some manufacturers state a storage device's transfer rate because it affects access time. *Transfer rate* is the speed with which data, instructions, and information transfer to and from a device. Transfer rates for storage are stated in *KBps* (kilobytes per second), *MBps* (megabytes per second), and *GBps* (gigabytes per second).

Numerous types of storage media and storage devices exist to meet a variety of users' needs. Figure 7-4 shows how different types of storage media and memory compare in terms of transfer rates and uses. This chapter discusses these and other storage media.

faster transfer rates

		Stores...
Memory	Memory (most RAM)	Items waiting to be interpreted and executed by the processor
Storage	Hard Disk	Operating system; application software; user data and information, including photos, music, and videos; backups
	Memory Cards and USB Flash Drives	Digital photos or files to be transported
	Optical Discs	Software, movies, music
	Tape	Backups

slower transfer rates

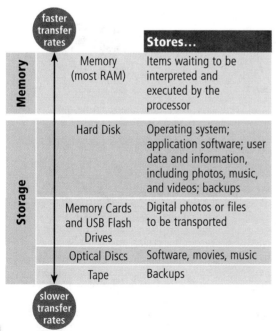

Figure 7-4 A comparison of different types of storage media and memory in terms of relative speed and uses. Memory is faster than storage but is expensive and not practical for all storage requirements. Storage is less expensive but is slower than memory.

Hard Disks

A **hard disk**, also called a *hard disk drive* or hard drive, is a storage device that contains one or more inflexible, circular platters that use magnetic particles to store data, instructions, and information. Depending on how the magnetic particles are aligned, they represent either a 0 bit or a 1 bit. Recall from Chapter 4 that a bit (binary digit) is the smallest unit of data a computer can process. Thus, the alignment of the magnetic particles represents the data.

The system unit on most desktop and notebook computers contains at least one hard disk. The entire device is enclosed in an airtight, sealed case to protect it from contamination. A hard disk that is mounted inside the system unit sometimes is called a *fixed disk* because it is not portable (Figure 7-5). With respect to a storage medium, the term *portable* means you can remove the medium from one computer and carry it to another computer. Portable hard disks are discussed later in this chapter.

Current personal computer hard disks have storage capacities from 160 GB to 2 TB and more. Home users store documents, spreadsheets, presentations, databases, e-mail messages,

Figure 7-5 The hard disk in a desktop personal computer is enclosed inside an airtight, sealed case inside the system unit. (In this and other hard disk photos in the book, the top plate is removed from the hard disk for illustration purposes.)

Web pages, digital photos, music, videos, and software on hard disks. Businesses also store correspondence, reports, financial records, customer orders and invoices, payroll records, inventory records, contracts, marketing literature, schedules, and Web sites.

Traditionally, hard disks stored data using *longitudinal recording*, which aligned the magnetic particles horizontally around the surface of the disk. With *perpendicular recording*, by contrast, hard disks align the magnetic particles vertically, or perpendicular to the disk's surface, making much greater storage capacities possible. Figure 7-6 shows the difference between longitudinal and perpendicular recording. Experts estimate that hard disks using perpendicular recording provide storage capacities about 10 times greater than disks that use longitudinal recording.

Hard disks are read/write storage media. That is, you can read from and write on a hard disk any number of times. If the computer contains only one hard disk, the operating system designates it as drive C. Additional hard disks are assigned the next available drive letter. Some people use a second hard disk to duplicate the contents of the first hard disk, in case the first is damaged or destroyed. Read Ethics & Issues 7-1 for a related discussion.

Perpendicular Recording

For more information, visit the Computer Concepts CourseMate Web site at www.cengagebrain.com, navigate to the Chapter 7 Web Link resource for this book, and then click Perpendicular Recording.

FAQ 7-1

To what degree are hard disk capacities increasing?

Hard disk capacities have increased at an exponential rate. Advancements in technology, such as perpendicular recording and enhanced read/write heads that can read and write denser areas on the platter, have resulted in a hard disk's capability of storing increasing amounts of data and information in a fixed amount of space. The chart below illustrates that the maximum hard disk size is growing.

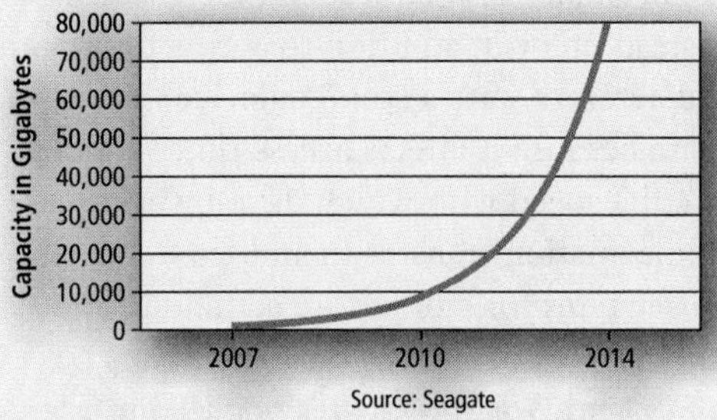

For more information, visit the Computer Concepts CourseMate Web site at www.cengagebrain.com, navigate to the Chapter 7 FAQ resource for this book, and then click Hard Disk Capacity.

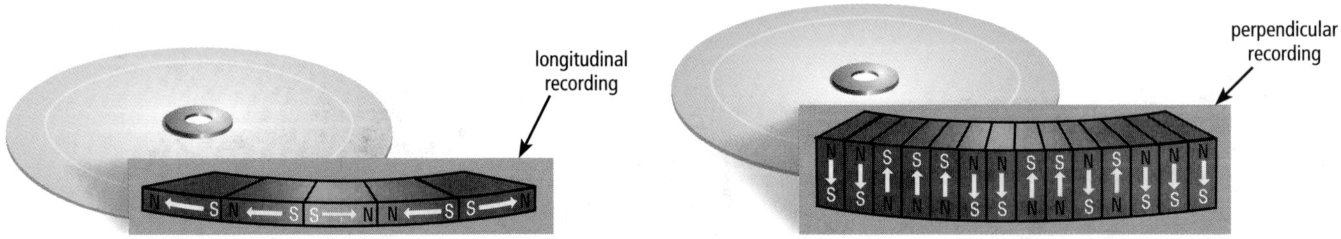

Figure 7-6 Magnetic particles are aligned horizontally in longitudinal recording and vertically in perpendicular recording.

ETHICS & ISSUES 7-1

Should the Government Require Hard Disks to Be Cleaned?

An IT professional recently purchased a hard disk on an auction Web site only to find private banking records of several million people. Fortunately, the purchaser notified authorities, rather than use the data for nefarious purposes. In other incidents, taxpayer data and secret police tactics appeared on hard disks purchased on auction Web sites, donated to charitable organizations, or recovered from discarded computers. Most people do not realize that deleting files from a computer does not render the data permanently inaccessible. Deleted files can be recovered easily by a smart criminal or digital forensics examiner.

Experts recommend that special utility software, known as a *wiping utility*, be used to clean the contents of a hard disk before it leaves possession of the owner. The government sets various disk wiping standards. For example, one standard requires that the software wipe the drive seven times, while a more stringent standard requires fourteen. Experts also recommend the use of full disk encryption, which is the process of encoding data and information into an unreadable form. Others recommend that any hard disk that at any time contained sensitive information be destroyed by a service company that specializes in hard disk destruction. Some companies now offer a service that allows you to keep a hard disk if it fails while covered by a warranty. Typically, companies require that you return the damaged hard disk when you receive the replacement. Some people are not comfortable with this service, for fear of confidential information on the damaged hard disk falling into the wrong hands.

Should the government require that hard disks on sold, donated, or discarded computers be cleaned, encrypted, or destroyed? Why or why not? Would you make an extra effort to clean or encrypt the contents of hard disks on sold, donated, or discarded computers? Why or why not?

Characteristics of a Hard Disk

Characteristics of a hard disk include its capacity, platters, read/write heads, cylinders, sectors and tracks, revolutions per minute, transfer rate, and access time. Figure 7-7 shows characteristics of a sample 1 TB hard disk that uses perpendicular recording. The following paragraphs discuss each of these characteristics.

The capacity of a hard disk is determined from whether it uses longitudinal or perpendicular recording, the number of platters it contains, and the composition of the magnetic coating on the platters. A *platter* is made of aluminum, glass, or ceramic and is coated with an alloy material that allows items to be recorded magnetically on its surface. The coating usually is three millionths of an inch thick.

Before any data can be read from or written on a hard disk, the disk must be formatted. **Formatting** is the process of dividing the disk into tracks and sectors (Figure 7-8), so that the operating system can store and locate data and information on the disk. A *track* is a narrow recording band that forms a full circle on the surface of the disk. The disk's storage locations consist of pie-shaped sections, which break the tracks into small arcs called *sectors*. On a hard disk, a sector typically stores up to 512 bytes of data. Sometimes, a sector has a flaw and cannot store data. When you format a disk, the operating system marks these bad sectors as unusable.

For reading and writing purposes, sectors are grouped into clusters. A *cluster* is the smallest unit of disk space that stores data and information. Each cluster, also called an *allocation unit*, consists

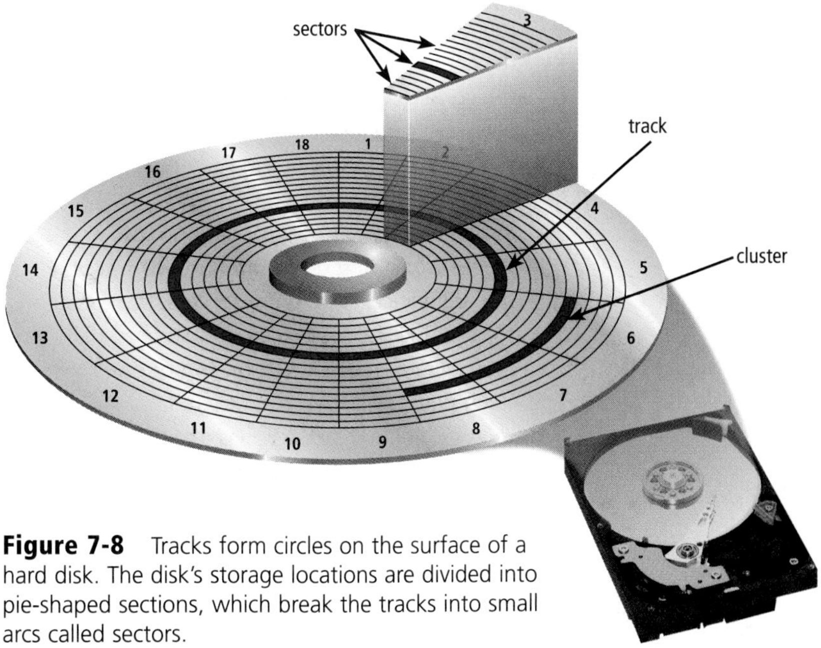

Figure 7-8 Tracks form circles on the surface of a hard disk. The disk's storage locations are divided into pie-shaped sections, which break the tracks into small arcs called sectors.

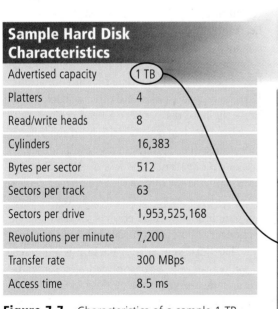

Sample Hard Disk Characteristics	
Advertised capacity	1 TB
Platters	4
Read/write heads	8
Cylinders	16,383
Bytes per sector	512
Sectors per track	63
Sectors per drive	1,953,525,168
Revolutions per minute	7,200
Transfer rate	300 MBps
Access time	8.5 ms

1 TB disk can store any of the following:
- 500,000,000 pages of text
- 285,000 digital photos
- 250,000 songs
- 120 hours of digital video

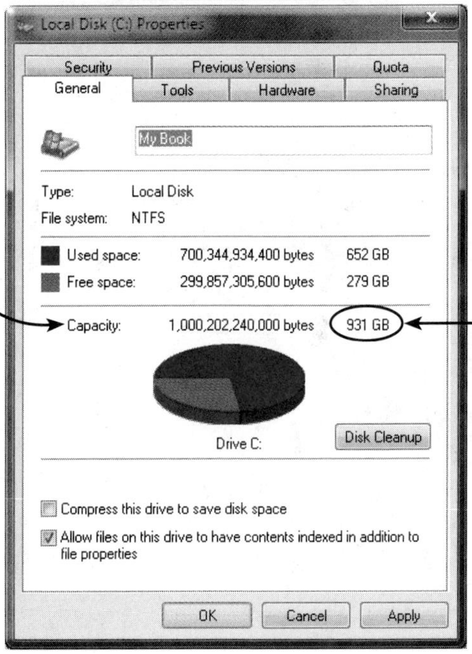

actual disk capacity

Figure 7-7 Characteristics of a sample 1 TB hard disk. The actual disk's capacity sometimes is different from the advertised capacity because of bad sectors on the disk.

of two to eight sectors (the number varies depending on the operating system). Even if a file consists of only a few bytes, it uses an entire cluster. Each cluster holds data from only one file. One file, however, can span many clusters.

On desktop computers, platters most often have a *form factor*, or size, of approximately 3.5 inches in diameter; on notebook computers, mobile devices, and some servers, the form factor is 2.5 inches or less. A typical hard disk has multiple platters stacked on top of one another. Each platter has two read/write heads, one for each side. The hard disk has arms that move the read/write heads to the proper location on the platter (Figure 7-9). A *read/write head* is the mechanism that reads items and writes items in the drive as it barely touches the disk's recording surface.

The location of the read/write heads often is referred to by its cylinder. A *cylinder* is the vertical section of a track that passes through all platters (Figure 7-10). A single movement of the read/write head arms accesses all the platters in a cylinder. If a hard disk has two platters

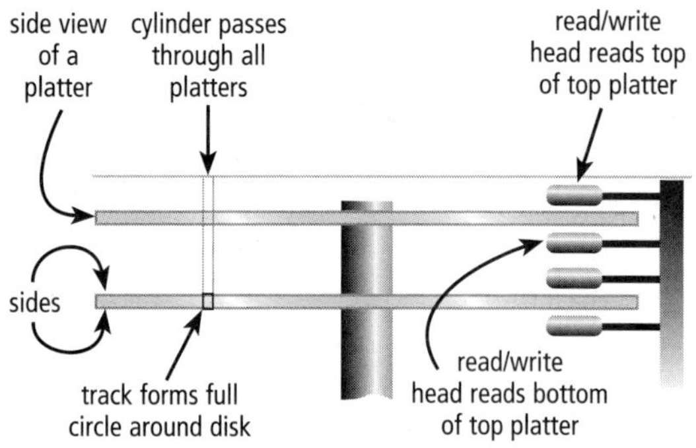

Figure 7-10 A cylinder is the vertical section of track through all platters on a hard disk.

(four sides), each with 1,000 tracks, then it will have 1,000 cylinders with each cylinder consisting of 4 tracks (2 tracks for each platter).

While the computer is running, the platters in the hard disk rotate at a high rate of speed. This spinning, which usually is 5,400 to 15,000 *revolutions per minute* (*rpm*), allows nearly instant access to all tracks and sectors on the platters. The platters may continue to spin until power is removed from the computer, or more commonly today, they stop spinning or slow down after a specified time to save power. The spinning motion creates a cushion of air between the platter and its read/write head. This cushion ensures that the read/write head floats above the platter instead of making direct contact with the platter surface. The distance between the read/write head and the platter is about two millionths of one inch.

As shown in Figure 7-11, this close clearance leaves no room for any type of contamination. Dirt, hair, dust, smoke, and other particles could cause the hard disk to have a head crash. A *head crash* occurs when a read/write head touches the surface of a platter, usually resulting in a loss of data or sometimes loss of the entire disk. Although current internal hard disks are built to withstand shocks and are sealed tightly to keep out contaminants, head crashes occasionally do still occur. Thus, it is crucial that you back up your hard disk regularly. A **backup** is a duplicate of a file, program, or disk placed on a separate storage medium that you can use in case the original is lost, damaged, or destroyed. Chapter 8 discusses backup techniques.

Depending on the type of hard disk, transfer rates range from 15 MBps to 320 MBps. Access time for today's hard disks ranges from about 3 to 12 ms (milliseconds).

How a Hard Disk Works
Step 1
The circuit board controls the movement of the head actuator and a small motor.
Step 2
A small motor spins the platters while the computer is running.
Step 3
When software requests a disk access, the read/write heads determine the current or new location of the data.
Step 4
The head actuator positions the read/write head arms over the correct location on the platters to read or write data.

Figure 7-9 This figure shows how a hard disk works.

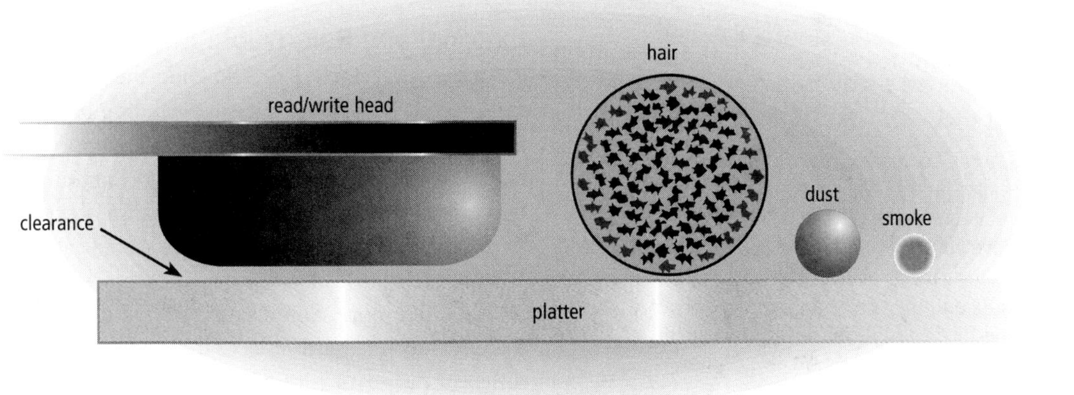

Figure 7-11 The clearance between a disk read/write head and the platter is about two millionths of an inch. A smoke particle, dust particle, human hair, or other contaminant could render the disk unusable.

Hard disks improve their access time by caching, specifically using disk cache. *Disk cache* (pronounced cash), sometimes called a buffer, consists of a memory chip(s) on a hard disk that stores frequently accessed items such as data, instructions, and information (Figure 7-12). Disk cache and memory cache work in a similar fashion. When a processor requests data, instructions, or information from the hard disk, the hard disk first checks its disk cache — before moving any mechanical parts to access the platters. If the requested item is in disk cache, the hard disk sends it to the processor. If the hard disk does not find the requested item in the disk cache, then the processor must wait for the hard disk to locate and transfer the item from the disk to the processor. Hard disks today contain between 2 MB and 64 MB of disk cache. The greater the disk cache, the faster the hard disk.

Density is the number of bits in an area on a storage medium. A higher density means more storage capacity.

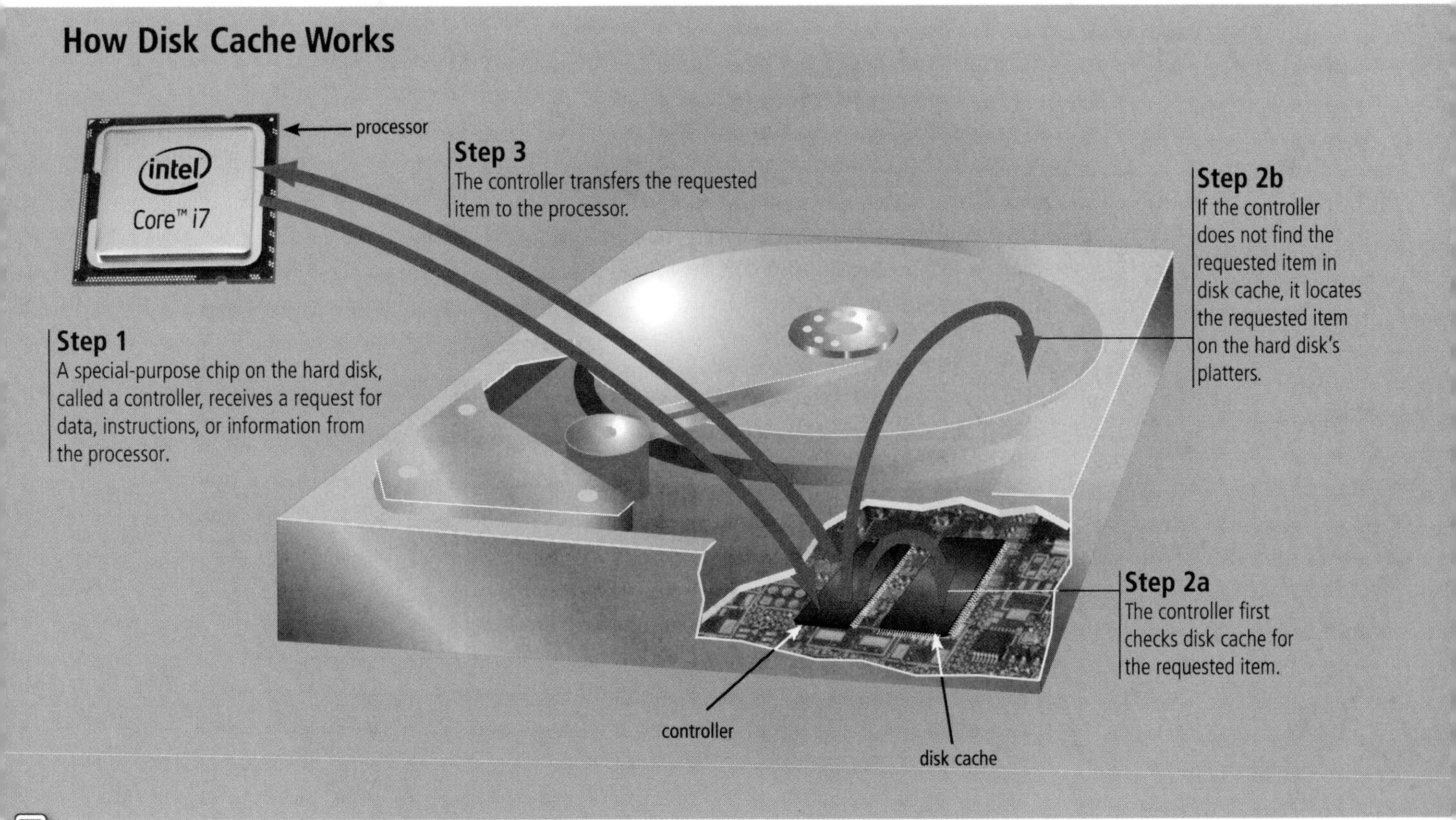

How Disk Cache Works
processor
intel
Core™ i7
Step 3
The controller transfers the requested item to the processor.
Step 2b
If the controller does not find the requested item in disk cache, it locates the requested item on the hard disk's platters.
Step 1
A special-purpose chip on the hard disk, called a controller, receives a request for data, instructions, or information from the processor.
Step 2a
The controller first checks disk cache for the requested item.
controller
disk cache

Figure 7-12 This figure shows how disk cache works.

FAQ 7-2

Can files be recovered from a failed hard disk?

Yes. Some companies, such as DriveSavers, specialize in retrieving data and information from hard disks that have failed mechanically or have sustained other damage to the physical media. These services can cost more than $1,000, and they do not guarantee recovery of specific lost files. For this reason, it still is critical that you back up important files.

For more information, visit the Computer Concepts CourseMate Web site at www.cengagebrain.com, navigate to the Chapter 7 FAQ resource for this book, and then click Hard Disk Recovery.

RAID

Some personal computer manufacturers provide a hard disk configuration that connects multiple smaller disks into a single unit that acts like a single large hard disk. A group of two or more integrated hard disks is called a **RAID** (redundant array of independent disks). RAID is an ideal storage solution for users who must have the data available when they attempt to access it.

NAS

A **network attached storage** (*NAS*) device is a server connected to a network with the sole purpose of providing storage (Figure 7-13). Any user or device connected to the network can access files on the NAS device. These devices often use a RAID configuration. In the past, enterprises were the primary users of NAS. With the introduction of smaller, less expensive NAS devices, however, some home and small business users opt to add up to 6 TB or more of hard disk storage space to their network with a NAS device.

Network Attached Storage

For more information, visit the Computer Concepts CourseMate Web site at www.cengagebrain.com, navigate to the Chapter 7 Web Link resource for this book, and then click Network Attached Storage.

Figure 7-13 A network attached storage device.

External and Removable Hard Disks

An **external hard disk,** shown in the top photo in Figure 7-14, is a separate freestanding hard disk that connects with a cable to a USB port or FireWire port on the system unit or communicates wirelessly. As with the internal hard disk, the entire hard disk is enclosed in an airtight, sealed case. External hard disks have storage capacities of up to 4 TB and more. Some external hard disk units include multiple hard disks that you can use for different purposes, if desired.

A **removable hard disk** is a hard disk that you insert and remove from a drive. Sometimes the drive is built in the system unit. Others are external devices that connect with a cable to a USB port or FireWire port on the system unit. A removable hard disk drive, shown in the bottom photo in Figure 7-14, reads from and writes on the removable hard disk. Removable hard disks have storage capacities up to 1 TB or more.

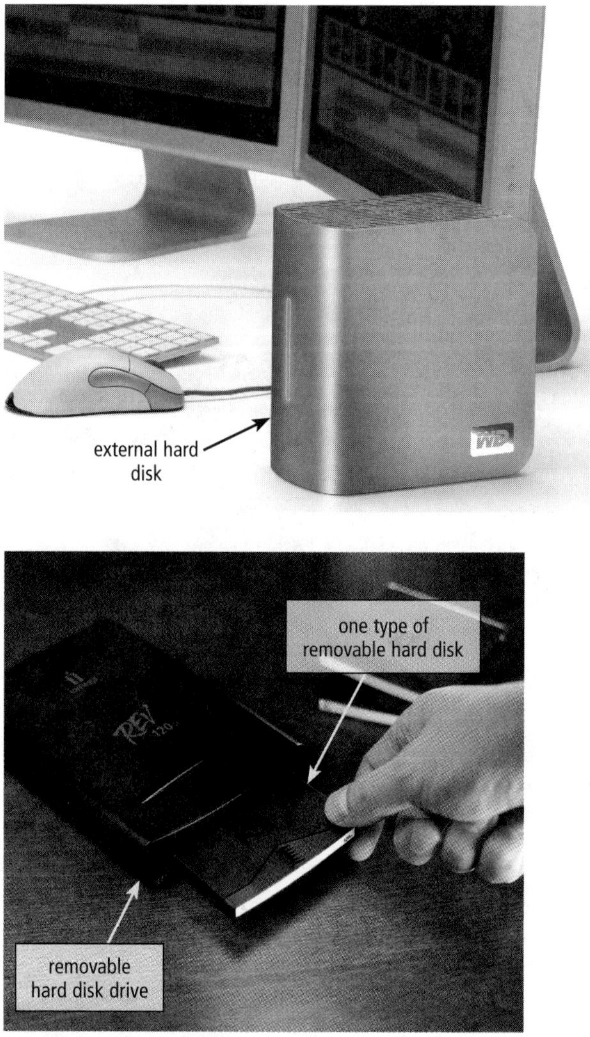

Figure 7-14 Examples of external and removable hard disks.

Although the transfer rate of external and removable hard disks usually is slower than that of internal hard disks, they do offer many advantages over internal hard disks (fixed disks):

- Transport a large number of files
- Back up important files or an entire internal hard disk (several external hard disk models allow you to back up simply by pushing a button on the disk)
- Easily store large audio and video files
- Secure your data; for example, at the end of a work session, remove the hard disk and lock it up, leaving no data in the computer
- Add storage space to a notebook computer, including netbooks and Tablet PCs
- Add storage space to a desktop computer without having to open the system unit or connect to a network

Miniature Hard Disks

Both internal and external hard disks are available in miniature sizes. These tiny hard disks have form factors of 1.8 inch, 1 inch, and 0.85 inch. Devices such as portable media players, digital cameras, and smart phones often have internal miniature hard disks, which provide greater storage capacities than flash memory (Figure 7-15). External hard disks that are smaller in size and capacity, which also contain miniature hard disks, are sometimes called a *pocket hard drive* because they enable mobile users easily to transport photos and other files from one computer to another (Figure 7-16).

When a device containing a miniature hard disk is connected to a computer, the user can read from and write on the device as a separate drive. Miniature hard disks have storage capacities that range from 1 GB to 320 GB. Miniature hard disks with the greater storage capacities typically use perpendicular recording.

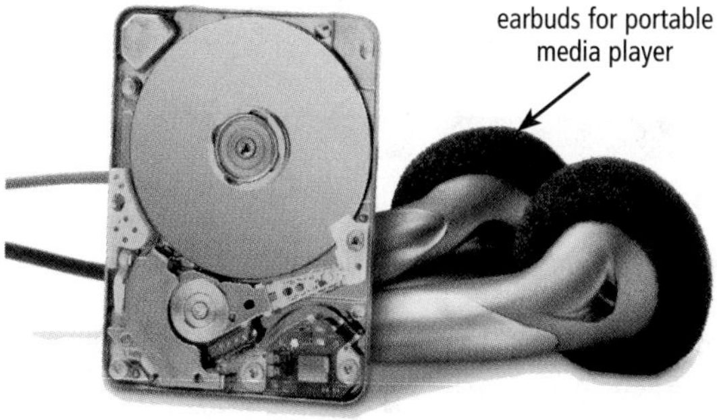

Figure 7-15 This miniature hard disk is used in portable media players and other small devices, enabling users to store music, videos, movies, and any other type of files on the disk.

Figure 7-16 Users easily can transport data from one computer to another with a pocket hard drive.

Hard Disk Controllers

A *disk controller* consists of a special-purpose chip and electronic circuits that control the transfer of data, instructions, and information from a disk to and from the system bus and other components in the computer. That is, it controls the interface between the hard disk and the system bus. A disk controller for a hard disk, called the hard disk controller, may be part of a hard disk or the motherboard, or it may be a separate adapter card inside the system unit.

In their personal computer advertisements, vendors usually state the type of hard disk interface supported by the hard disk controller. Thus, you should understand the types of available hard disk interfaces. In addition to USB and FireWire, which can function as external hard disk interfaces, four other types of hard disk interfaces for use in personal computers are SATA, EIDE, SCSI, and SAS.

- *SATA* (*Serial Advanced Technology Attachment*) uses serial signals to transfer data, instructions, and information. The primary advantage of SATA interfaces is their cables are thinner, longer, more flexible, and less susceptible to interference than cables used by hard disks that use parallel signals. SATA interfaces have data transfer rates of up to 300 MBps and higher. In addition to hard disks, SATA interfaces support connections to optical disc drives. External disks can use the *eSATA* (external SATA) interface, which is much faster than USB and FireWire.
- *EIDE* (*Enhanced Integrated Drive Electronics*) is a hard disk interface that uses parallel signals to transfer data, instructions, and information. EIDE interfaces can support up to four hard disks at 137 GB per disk. These interfaces have data transfer rates up to 133 MBps. EIDE interfaces also provide

eSATA

For more information, visit the Computer Concepts CourseMate Web site at www.cengagebrain.com, navigate to the Chapter 7 Web Link resource for this book, and then click eSATA.

connections for optical disc drives and tape drives. Some manufacturers market their EIDE interfaces as Fast ATA or Ultra ATA.
- *SCSI* interfaces, which also use parallel signals, can support up to eight or fifteen peripheral devices. Supported devices include hard disks, optical disc drives, tape drives, printers, scanners, network cards, and much more. Recall from Chapter 4 that SCSI is an acronym for Small Computer System Interface. Some computers have a built-in SCSI interface, while others use an adapter card to add a SCSI interface. SCSI interfaces provide up to 640 MBps data transfer rates.
- *SAS* (*serial-attached SCSI*) is a newer type of SCSI that uses serial signals to transfer data, instructions, and information. Advantages of SAS over parallel SCSI include thinner, longer cables; reduced interference; less expensive; support for many more connected devices at once; and faster speeds. SAS interfaces have data transfer rates of 750 MBps and higher. In addition to hard disks, SAS interfaces support connections to optical disc drives, printers, scanners, digital cameras, and other devices. SAS interfaces usually are compatible with devices that have parallel SCSI and SATA interfaces. Experts predict that SAS eventually will replace parallel SCSI.

Maintaining Data Stored on a Hard Disk

Most manufacturers guarantee their hard disks to last approximately three to five years. Many last much longer with proper care. To prevent the loss of items stored on a hard disk, you regularly should perform preventive maintenance such as defragmenting or scanning the disk for errors. To learn more about how to maintain a hard disk, complete the Learn How To 1 activity on pages 392 and 393. Chapter 8 discusses these and other utilities in depth.

QUIZ YOURSELF 7-1

Instructions: Find the true statement below. Then, rewrite the remaining false statements so that they are true.

1. Disk recording consists of a memory chip(s) on a hard disk that stores frequently accessed items.
2. Hard disks contain one or more inflexible, circular platters that magnetically store data, instructions, and information.
3. SATA is a hard disk interface that uses parallel signals to transfer data, instructions, and information.
4. Storage media is the computer hardware that records and/or retrieves items to and from a storage device.
5. Users can move an internal hard disk from computer to computer as needed by connecting the disk to a USB port or FireWire port on the system unit.

Quiz Yourself Online: To further check your knowledge of pages 352 through 362, visit the Computer Concepts CourseMate Web site at www.cengagebrain.com, navigate to the Chapter 7 Quiz Yourself resource for this book, and then click Objectives 1 – 3.

Flash Memory Storage

As discussed in Chapter 4, flash memory is a type of nonvolatile memory that can be erased electronically and rewritten. Flash memory chips are a type of *solid state media*, which means they consist entirely of electronic components, such as integrated circuits, and contain no moving parts. The lack of moving parts makes flash memory storage more durable and shock resistant than other types of media such as magnetic hard disks or optical discs.

Types of flash memory storage include solid state drives, memory cards, USB flash drives, and ExpressCard modules.

FAQ 7-3

How can I improve the performance of my hard disk?

Windows includes many tools that can be used to improve the performance of your hard disk, including Disk Cleanup and Disk Defragmenter. Disk Cleanup removes unused files from a hard disk so that the computer does not have to spend time searching through and accessing unneeded files, and Disk Defragmenter reorganizes the data on a hard disk so that the data can be accessed more quickly. The next chapter further describes these two tools.

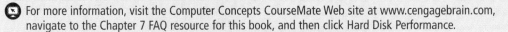

For more information, visit the Computer Concepts CourseMate Web site at www.cengagebrain.com, navigate to the Chapter 7 FAQ resource for this book, and then click Hard Disk Performance.

Solid State Drives

A **solid state drive (SSD)** is a storage device that typically uses flash memory to store data, instructions, and information (Figure 7-17). With available form factors of 3.5 inches, 2.5 inches, and 1.8 inches, SSDs are used in all types of computers including servers, desktop computers, and mobile computers and devices such as portable media players and digital video cameras. Storage capacities of current SSDs range from 16 GB to 256 GB and more.

SSDs have several advantages over magnetic hard disks.

- Access times of SSDs are about 0.1 ms, which is more than 80 times faster than a hard disk.
- Transfer rates of SSDs are faster than comparable hard disks. For example, SSD transfer rates range from 80 to 100 MBps, while transfer rates of a typical 2.5-inch hard disk is about 60 MBps.
- SSDs generate less heat and consume less power than hard disks.
- Manufacturers claim that SSDs will last more than 50 years, which is much greater than the 3 to 5 year hard disk stated lifespan.

The disadvantages of SSDs are they currently have a higher failure rate than hard disks, and their cost is much higher per gigabyte. As the price of SSDs drops, experts estimate that increasingly more users will purchase computers and devices that use this media.

? FAQ 7-4

Are data transfer speeds on solid state technology increasing?

IBM's Project Quicksilver is breaking new ground by achieving data transfer speeds of more than one million input/output operations per second. Significant increases in data transfer speeds on solid state devices eventually may result in more solid state storage devices replacing storage devices with moving components, such as hard disks and optical disc drives.

For more information, visit the Computer Concepts CourseMate Web site at www.cengagebrain.com, navigate to the Chapter 7 FAQ resource for this book, and then click Project Quicksilver.

Solid State Drives

For more information, visit the Computer Concepts CourseMate Web site at www.cengagebrain.com, navigate to the Chapter 7 Web Link resource for this book, and then click Solid State Drives.

Figure 7-17 As the price of SSDs drops, experts estimate that increasingly more users will purchase computers and devices that use this media.

Memory Cards

Memory cards enable mobile users easily to transport digital photos, music, or files to and from mobile devices and computers or other devices. As mentioned in Chapter 4, a **memory card** is a removable flash memory device, usually no bigger than 1.5 inches in height or width, that you insert and remove from a slot in a computer, mobile device, or card reader/writer (Figure 7-18).

Common types of memory cards include *CompactFlash* (*CF*), *Secure Digital* (*SD*), *Secure Digital High Capacity* (*SDHC*), *microSD*, *microSDHC*, *xD Picture Card*, *Memory Stick*, and *Memory Stick Micro* (*M2*). The table in Figure 7-19 compares storage capacities and uses of these media.

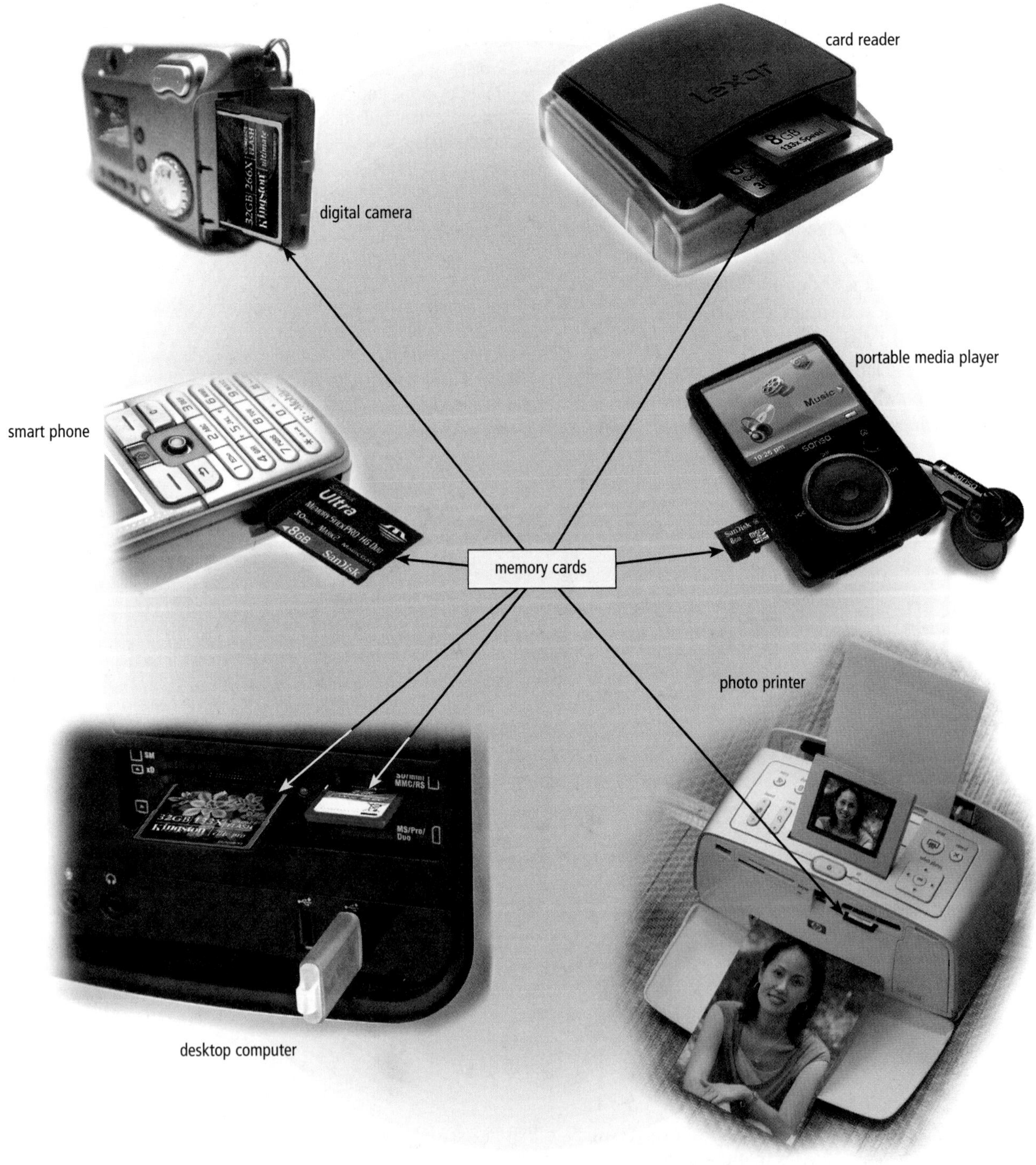

Figure 7-18 Many types of computers and devices have slots for memory cards.

Depending on the device, manufacturers claim memory cards can last from 10 to 100 years. Transfer rates range from about 1 MBps to 20 MBps or more, depending on the device. Memory cards are quite expensive compared to other storage media with equivalent capacity. For example, the cost of a 16 GB CompactFlash card can be the same as a 1 TB external hard disk.

To view, edit, or print images and information stored on memory cards, you transfer the contents to your desktop computer or other device. Some printers have slots to read memory cards. If your computer or printer does not have a built-in slot, you can purchase a *card reader/writer*, which is a device that reads and writes data, instructions, and information stored on memory cards. Card reader/writers usually

SDHC Cards

For more information, visit the Computer Concepts CourseMate Web site at www.cengagebrain.com, navigate to the Chapter 7 Web Link resource for this book, and then click SDHC Cards.

Various Memory Cards

Media Type		Storage Capacity	Use
CompactFlash (CF)		512 MB to 100 GB	Digital cameras, smart phones, PDAs, photo printers, portable media players, notebook computers, desktop computers
Secure Digital (SD)		512 MB to 8 GB	Digital cameras, digital video cameras, smart phones, PDAs, photo printers, portable media players
SDHC		4 to 32 GB	Digital cameras
microSD		1 to 2 GB	Smart phones, portable media players, handheld game consoles, handheld navigation devices
microSDHC		4 to 16 GB	Smart phones, portable media players, handheld game consoles, handheld navigation devices
xD Picture Card		256 MB to 2 GB	Digital cameras, photo printers
Memory Stick PRO Duo	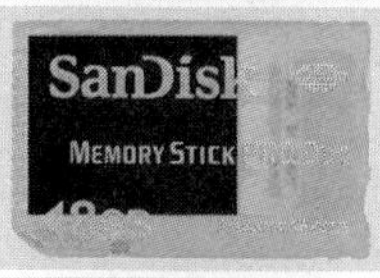	1 to 16 GB	Digital cameras, smart phones, handheld game consoles
Memory Stick Micro (M2)		1 to 16 GB	Smart phones

Figure 7-19 A variety of memory cards.

connect to the USB port or FireWire port on the system unit. The type of card you have will determine the type of card reader/writer needed. Figure 7-20 shows how one type of memory card works with a card reader/writer. Read Ethics & Issues 7-2 for a related discussion.

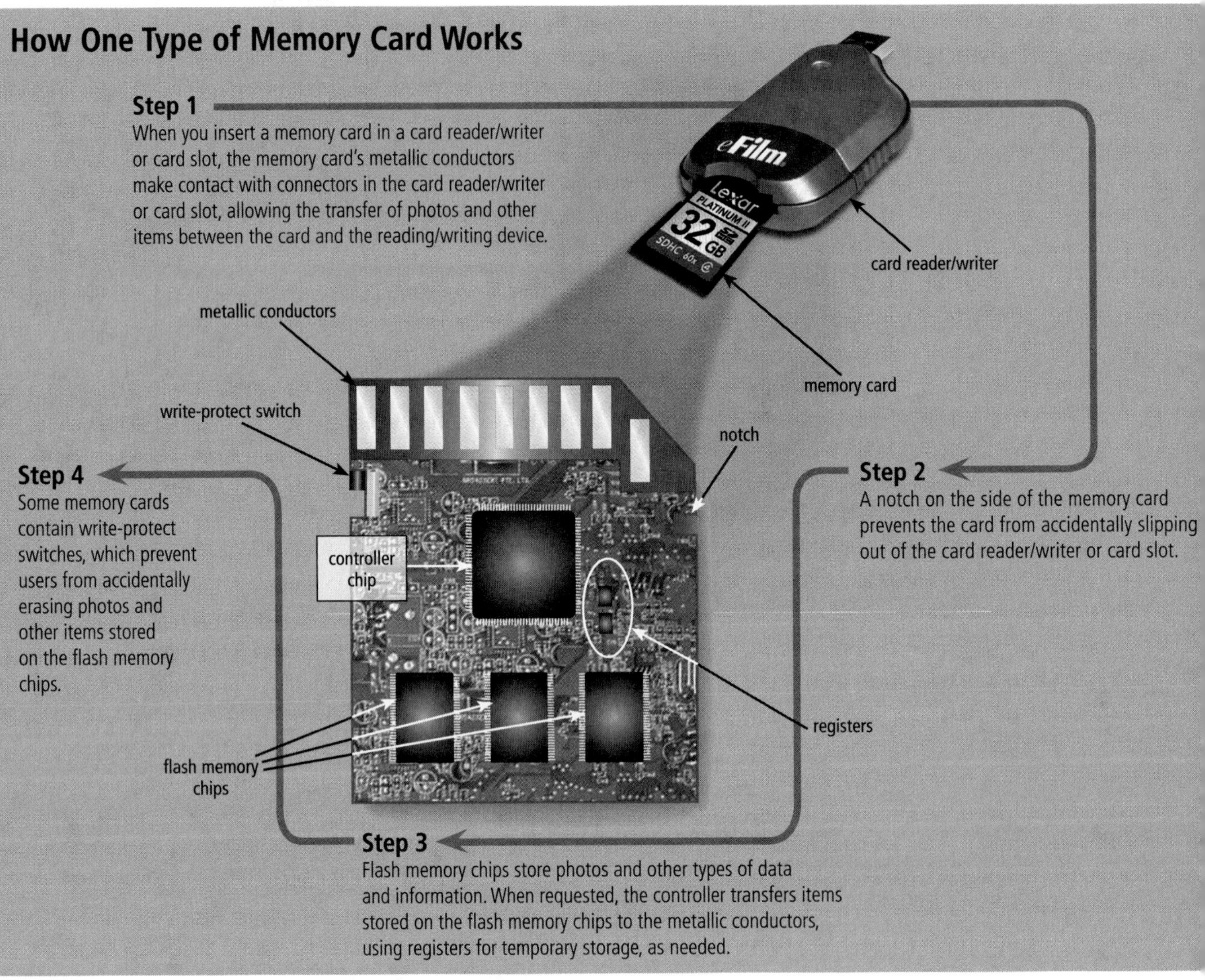
How One Type of Memory Card Works
Step 1
When you insert a memory card in a card reader/writer or card slot, the memory card's metallic conductors make contact with connectors in the card reader/writer or card slot, allowing the transfer of photos and other items between the card and the reading/writing device.
eFilm
Lexar
PLATINUM II
32 GB
SDHC 60x
card reader/writer
metallic conductors
memory card
write-protect switch
notch
Step 2
A notch on the side of the memory card prevents the card from accidentally slipping out of the card reader/writer or card slot.
Step 4
Some memory cards contain write-protect switches, which prevent users from accidentally erasing photos and other items stored on the flash memory chips.
controller chip
registers
flash memory chips
Step 3
Flash memory chips store photos and other types of data and information. When requested, the controller transfers items stored on the flash memory chips to the metallic conductors, using registers for temporary storage, as needed.

Figure 7-20 This figure shows how one type of memory card works.

ETHICS & ISSUES 7-2

Is the Large Variety of Options for Flash Memory Mobile Media Good?

When you buy a new mobile device, such as a cell phone, digital camera, or GPS device, you probably consider how much flash memory you will be able to use on the device. Too often, though, people do not consider the type of flash memory mobile media that the device supports. With more than 50 types of memory cards and USB flash drives available, consumers find their devices cannot share media, resulting in frustration and additional costs for adapters and readers. One company sells a card reader that reads 56 types of memory cards and USB flash drives. While companies in the flash memory mobile media business failed at developing a smaller set of standards in the past, a new attempt by some companies looks promising for frustrated consumers. The proposed standard, known as *Universal Flash Storage* (*UFS*), would be faster, use less power, allow for higher capacities, and eliminate the need for the array of adapters and readers currently used by consumers. Some analysts remain skeptical, noting that many of the larger manufacturers do not support the standard and that the effort, therefore, is doomed to fail. These manufacturers claim that more choices for consumers are good, and multiple standards are necessary to support various device storage capacities and usages of flash memory.

Is the large variety of options for flash memory mobile media an advantage or disadvantage for consumers? Why? Should manufacturers join forces to develop fewer standards, or should the free market be allowed to run its course over time with the best formats winning the format war? Why?

USB Flash Drives

As discussed in Chapter 4, a **USB flash drive**, sometimes called a *thumb drive*, is a flash memory storage device that plugs in a USB port on a computer or mobile device (Figure 7-21). USB flash drives are convenient for mobile users because they are small and lightweight enough to be transported on a keychain or in a pocket. With a USB flash drive, users easily transfer documents, photos, music, and videos from one computer to another. Current USB flash drives have data transfer rates of about 12 MBps and storage capacities ranging from 512 MB to 100 GB, with the latter being extremely expensive.

A special type of USB flash drive, called a *U3 smart drive*, includes pre-installed software accessed through a Windows-type interface. Some USB flash drives include fingerprint readers, restricting access to authenticated users.

The drive designation of a USB flash drive usually follows alphabetically after all other disks. For example, if the computer has one internal hard disk (drive C) and an optical disc drive (drive D) and no other disk drives, then the USB flash drive probably will be drive E.

? FAQ 7-5

Can airport security screening equipment damage or erase the data on my mobile media or hard disk?

The Transportation Security Administration's Web site states that their screening (X-ray) equipment will not damage or erase the data stored on flash memory mobile media, optical discs, or hard disks. Although your media is equally safe whether you carry it onto the airplane or leave it in checked baggage, packing it with your carry-on items is a better safeguard against physical damage. If you are uneasy about your media passing through the airport screening equipment, you may be able to request that the items be manually (hand) searched. It is important to note that the equipment used to screen checked baggage will not harm electronic media, but it may damage undeveloped film. As a safeguard, you should carry all film onto the airplane and request a manual search.

For more information, visit the Computer Concepts CourseMate Web site at www.cengagebrain.com, navigate to the Chapter 7 FAQ resource for this book, and then click Airport Screening Equipment.

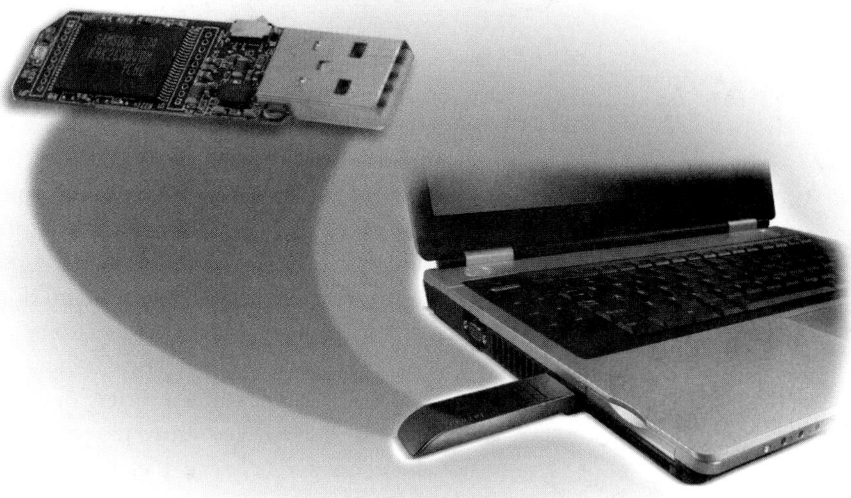

Figure 7-21 A close-up of the flash memory and circuitry inside a USB flash drive.

ExpressCard Modules

As discussed in Chapter 4, an **ExpressCard module** is a removable device, about 75 mm long and 34 mm wide or L-shaped with a width of 54 mm, that fits in an ExpressCard slot (Figure 7-22). ExpressCard modules can be used to add memory, storage, communications, multimedia, and security capabilities to a computer. Developed by the PCMCIA (Personal Computer Memory Card International Association), ExpressCard modules commonly are used in notebook computers.

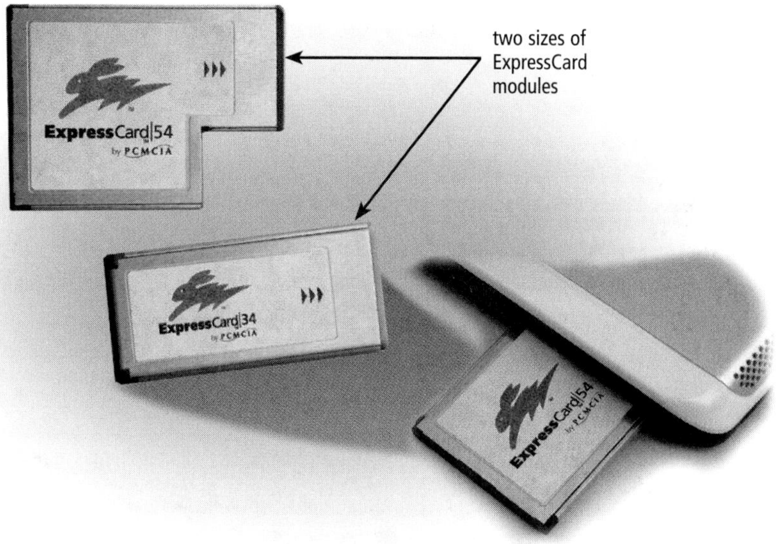

Figure 7-22 ExpressCard modules are available in two sizes.

Cloud Storage

Some users choose cloud storage instead of storing data locally on a hard disk or other media. **Cloud storage** is an Internet service that provides storage to computer users (Figure 7-23).

Types of services offered by cloud storage providers vary. Some provide storage for specific types of files, such as photos or e-mail messages, whereas others store any type of file. Many cloud storage providers offer additional services such as encryption, passwords, Web applications, and Web services. Figure 7-24 identifies a variety of cloud storage providers. Read Innovative Computing 7-1 to find out about another type of cloud storage.

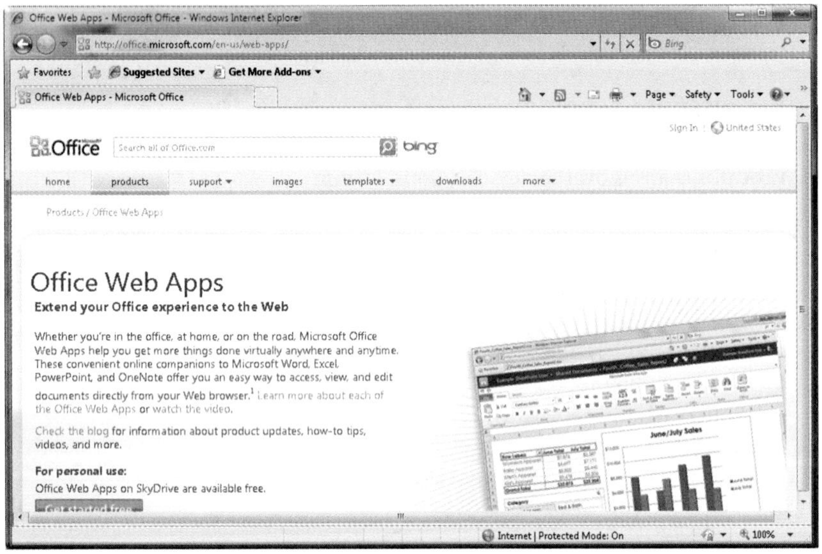

Figure 7-23 An example of one Web site that provides cloud storage.

INNOVATIVE COMPUTING 7-1

Digital Books Are a Good Read

It is time to dust off your library card because thousands of libraries are stocking their digital shelves with electronic books that you can download from anywhere you have computer access. Just locate a participating library's Web site, download the desired book files to your personal computer, and then transfer the files to your portable media player or smart phone. For patrons who do not want to download files, some libraries are lending a Playaway, which is a small device that stores 80 hours of digitized audio books.

Another set of books is available for reading at the British Library's Online Gallery. Software called Turning the Pages allows readers to browse some of the rarest books in the world and magnify details on the pages. The books include the *Gutenberg Bible*, Lewis Carroll's original *Alice in Wonderland*, and *The Diamond Sutra*, the oldest book in existence, printed in China in 868 A.D.

For more information, visit the Computer Concepts CourseMate Web site at www.cengagebrain.com, navigate to the Chapter 7 Innovative Computing resource for this book, and then click Online Libraries.

Cloud Storage Providers

Web Site Names	Type of Storage Provided	Other Services
Box.net, IDrive, Windows Live SkyDrive	Backup or additional storage for any type of file	
Flickr, Picasa	Digital photos	Photo editing and photo management
YouTube	Digital videos	
Facebook, MySpace	Digital photos, digital videos, messages, and personal information	Social networking
Google Docs, Office Web Apps	Documents, spreadsheets, presentations	Productivity suite
Gmail, Windows Live Hotmail, Yahoo! Mail	E-mail messages	
Amazon EC2, Amazon S3, Nirvanix	Enterprise-level storage	Web services, data center services

Figure 7-24 Some of the more widely used cloud storage providers.

Cloud storage is available for all sizes of users, with various degrees of storage services available for home and business users. Cloud storage fee arrangements vary, depending on the user's storage requirements. For example, one cloud storage service provides 25 GB of storage free to registered users; another charges $5 per month for 150 GB of storage. For enterprises, cloud storage services typically charge for storage on a per gigabyte basis, such as 15 cents per gigabyte. Some also charge an additional per gigabyte fee for data transferred to and from the cloud storage service. Read Ethics & Issues 7-3 for a related discussion.

Users subscribe to cloud storage for a variety of reasons:

- To access files on the Internet from any computer or device that has Internet access
- To store large audio, video, and graphics files on the Internet instantaneously, instead of spending time downloading to a local hard disk or other media
- To allow others to access their files on the Internet so that others can listen to an audio file, watch a video clip, or view a photo — instead of e-mailing the file to them
- To view time-critical data and images immediately while away from the main office or location; for example, doctors can view X-ray images from another hospital, home, or office, or while on vacation
- To store offsite backups of data (Chapter 8 presents this and other backup strategies)
- To provide data center functions, relieving enterprises of this task

Cloud Storage

For more information, visit the Computer Concepts CourseMate Web site at www.cengagebrain.com, navigate to the Chapter 7 Web Link resource for this book, and then click Cloud Storage.

ETHICS & ISSUES 7-3

Is Data Stored in the Cloud Free from Prying Eyes?

At an ever increasing rate, companies and individuals store Web sites and data in the cloud. For example, those who utilize Web-based e-mail store their sent and received e-mail messages in the e-mail provider's cloud environment. Those who use corporate or private e-mail servers do not store their communications in the cloud. Important legal rulings highlight the differences between the two approaches for storing e-mail messages. Law enforcement agencies consider e-mail stored in the cloud to belong to the company that owns the cloud service, often an Internet access provider.

E-mail stored on a private e-mail server, however, is the property of the company or individual who owns the server. When the law enforcement officials need to read someone's e-mail on a private e-mail server, they must obtain a warrant that outlines exactly the information being sought. In the cloud, however, law enforcement officials simply may need to request the information from the company that owns the cloud service. The user might not be notified of the search until up to 90 days later; further, the search may occur without limitations and may include continuous monitoring of an individual's e-mail. While the government takes a liberal approach to viewing one's e-mail in the cloud, individuals who secretly read others' e-mail messages may be subject to felony computer crimes.

Should data kept in the cloud be treated the same way legally as items that are kept in one's home? Why? Should the government be able to access your data in the cloud without your knowledge or permission? Why or why not? What types and amount of personal data are you comfortable storing in the cloud? Why?

QUIZ YOURSELF 7-2

Instructions: Find the true statement below. Then, rewrite the remaining false statements so that they are true.

1. Cloud storage is a storage device that typically uses flash memory to store data, instructions, and information.
2. A USB flash drive is a flash memory storage device that plugs in a parallel port on a computer or mobile device.
3. Flash memory cards are a type of magnetic media, which means they consist entirely of electronic components and contain no moving parts.
4. An ExpressCard module is a removable device that fits in an ExpressCard slot.

Quiz Yourself Online: To further check your knowledge of pages 362 through 369, visit the Computer Concepts CourseMate Web site at www.cengagebrain.com, navigate to the Chapter 7 Quiz Yourself resource for this book, and then click Objectives 4 – 5.

Optical Discs

An *optical disc* is a type of storage media that consists of a flat, round, portable disc made of metal, plastic, and lacquer that is written and read by a laser. (The spelling, disk, is used for magnetic and flash memory media, and disc is used for optical media.) Optical discs used in personal computers are 4.75 inches in diameter and less than one-twentieth of an inch thick. Smaller computers, game consoles, and mobile devices, however, often use *mini discs* that have a diameter of 3 inches or less.

Optical discs primarily store software, data, digital photos, movies, and music. Some optical disc formats are read only, meaning users cannot write (save) on the media. Others are read/write, which allows users to save on the disc just as they save on a hard disk.

Nearly every personal computer today has some type of optical disc drive installed in a drive bay. On some, you push a button to slide out a tray, insert the disc, and then push the same button to close the tray; others are slot loaded, which means you insert the disc in a narrow opening on the drive (Figure 7-25). When you insert the disc, the operating system automatically may start the program, music, or video on the disc.

Figure 7-25
A slot-loaded optical disc drive.

With some discs, you can read and/or write on one side only. Manufacturers usually place a silk-screened label on the top layer of these single-sided discs. You insert a single-sided disc in the drive with the label side up. Other discs are double-sided. Simply remove the disc from the drive, flip it over, and reinsert it in the drive to use the other side of the disc. Double-sided discs often have no label; instead, each side of the disc is identified with small writing around the center of the disc. Some drives use *LightScribe technology*, which works with specially coated optical discs, to etch labels directly on the disc (as opposed to placing an adhesive label on the disc).

The drive designation of an optical disc drive usually follows alphabetically after that of all the hard disks. For example, if the computer has one internal hard disk (drive C) and an external hard disk (drive D), then the first optical disc drive is drive E. A second optical disc drive would be drive F.

Optical discs store items by using microscopic pits (indentations) and lands (flat areas) that are in the middle layer of the disc (Figure 7-26).

How a Laser Reads Data on an Optical Disc

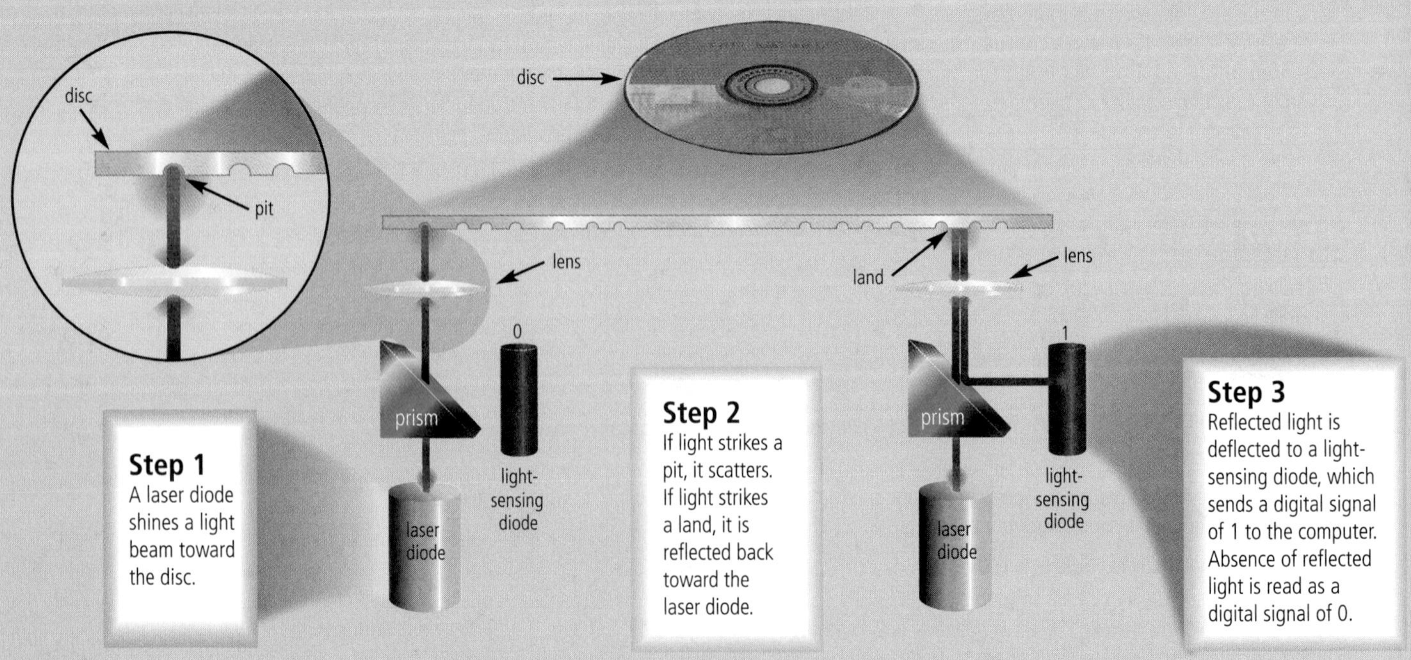

disc
pit
disc
lens
0
prism
light-sensing diode
laser diode
land
lens
1
prism
light-sensing diode
laser diode
Step 1
A laser diode shines a light beam toward the disc.
Step 2
If light strikes a pit, it scatters. If light strikes a land, it is reflected back toward the laser diode.
Step 3
Reflected light is deflected to a light-sensing diode, which sends a digital signal of 1 to the computer. Absence of reflected light is read as a digital signal of 0.

Figure 7-26 This figure shows how a laser reads data on an optical disc.

A high-powered laser light creates the pits. A lower-powered laser light reads items from the disc by reflecting light through the bottom of the disc. The reflected light is converted into a series of bits the computer can process. A land causes light to reflect, which is read as binary digit 1. Pits absorb the light; this absence of light is read as binary digit 0.

Optical discs commonly store items in a single track that spirals from the center of the disc to the edge of the disc. As with a hard disk, this single track is divided into evenly sized sectors on which items are stored (Figure 7-27).

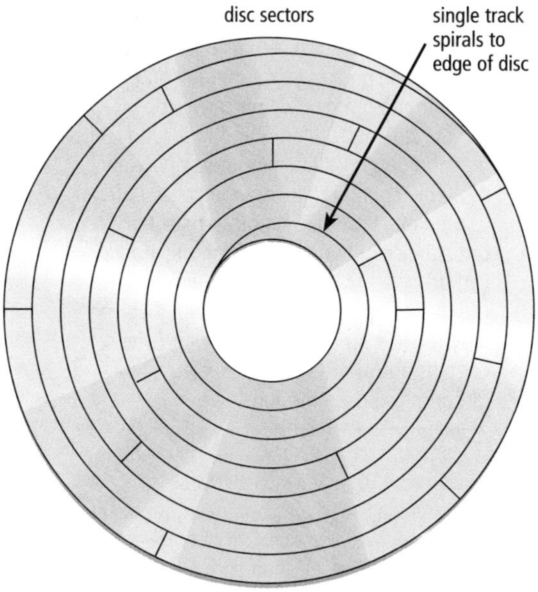

Figure 7-27 An optical disc typically stores data, instructions, and information in a single track that spirals from the center of the disc to the edge of the disc.

Care of Optical Discs

Manufacturers claim that a properly cared for high-quality optical disc will last 5 years but could last up to 100 years. Figure 7-28 offers some guidelines for the proper care of optical discs. Never bend a disc; it may break. Do not expose discs to extreme temperatures or humidity. The ideal temperature range for disc storage is 50 to 70 degrees Fahrenheit. Stacking discs, touching the underside of discs, or exposing them to any type of contaminant may scratch a disc. Place an optical disc in its protective case, called a *jewel box,* when you are finished using it and store in an upright (vertical) position.

FAQ 7-6

Can I clean a disc?

Yes, you can remove dust, dirt, smudges, and fingerprints from the surface of an optical disc. Moisten a nonabrasive cloth with warm water or rubbing alcohol (do not use ammonia-based solutions) and then wipe the disc in straight lines from the center outward. You also can repair scratches on the surface with a specialized disc repair kit.

For more information, visit the Computer Concepts CourseMate Web site at www.cengagebrain.com, navigate to the Chapter 7 FAQ resource for this book, and then click Cleaning and Repairing Discs.

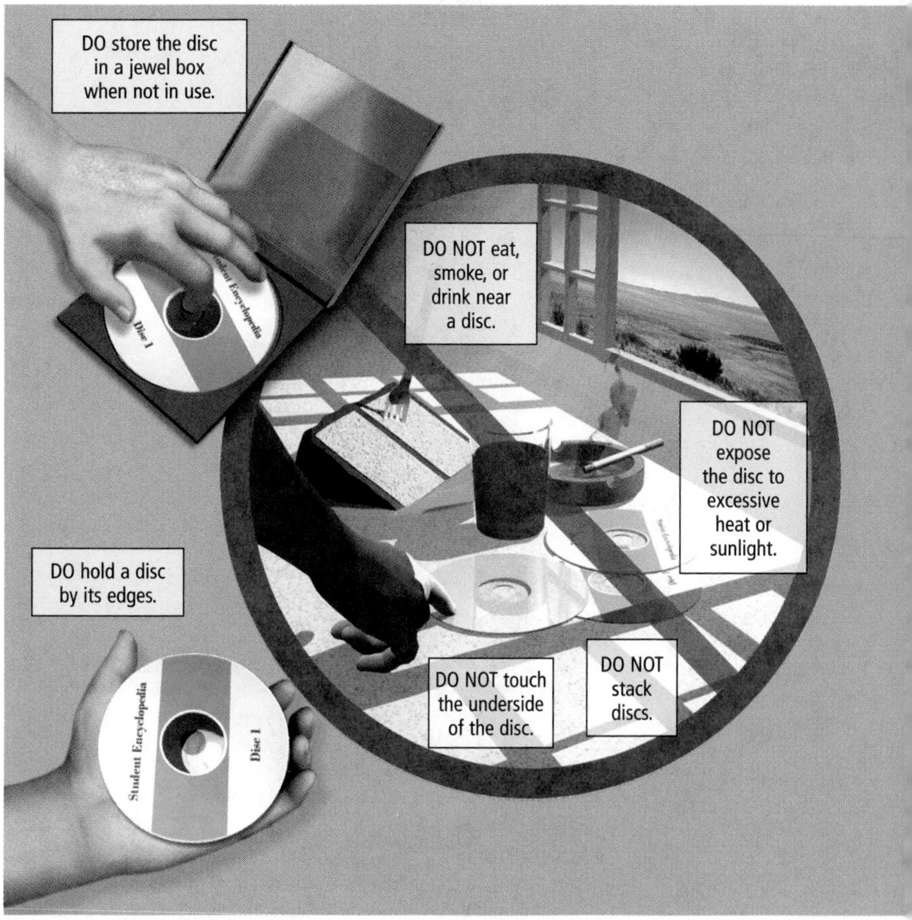

Figure 7-28 Some guidelines for the proper care of optical discs.

Types of Optical Discs

Many different formats of optical discs exist today. Figure 7-29 identifies a variety of optical disc formats and specifies whether a user can read from the disc, write to the disc, and/or erase the disc. The following sections describe characteristics unique to each of these disc formats. Read Innovative Computing 7-2 to find out about a new use for optical discs.

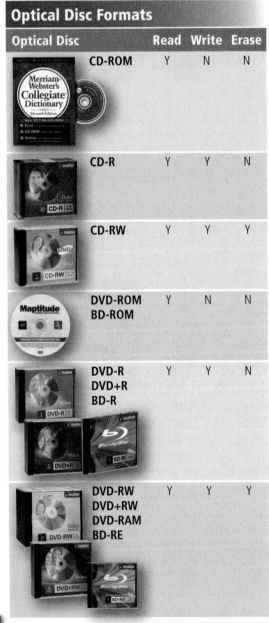

Optical Disc Formats

	Optical Disc	Read	Write	Erase
	CD-ROM	Y	N	N
	CD-R	Y	Y	N
	CD-RW	Y	Y	Y
	DVD-ROM BD-ROM	Y	N	N
	DVD-R DVD+R BD-R	Y	Y	N
	DVD-RW DVD+RW DVD-RAM BD-RE	Y	Y	Y

Figure 7-29 Manufacturers sell CD-ROM, DVD-ROM, and BD-ROM media prerecorded (written) with audio, video, and software. Users cannot change the contents of these discs. Users, however, can purchase the other formats of optical discs as blank media and record (write) their own data, instructions, and information on these discs.

INNOVATIVE COMPUTING 7-2

The Perfect Gift for Buying and Marketing

The one-size-fits-all gift card is the gift of choice for more than 60 percent of shoppers. Consumers now find store racks filled with a wide variety of cards, and marketers are searching for unique methods of persuading consumers to buy a particular merchant's gift card instead of a competitor's card.

One way to stand out from the rest is to use a multimedia card on an optical disc. EnXnet has developed an interactive gift card for companies to use as a marketing tool, one being a physical therapy and personal training provider. The card is distributed to doctors, athletes, and fans who can play the disc on their computers and view printable coupons, videos, and special offers.

Marketers are finding other uses for the optical disc gift cards. For example, hotels can use the product as a room key. When the guests open their hotel doors, they can play the key on their computer and view content about the hotel, exclusive online discounts, and promotions.

For more information, visit the Computer Concepts CourseMate Web site at www.cengagebrain.com, navigate to the Chapter 7 Innovative Computing resource for this book, and then click Optical Discs.

CDs

A **CD-ROM**, or *compact disc read-only memory*, is a type of optical disc that users can read but not write (record) or erase — hence, the name read-only. Manufacturers write the contents of standard CD-ROMs. A standard CD-ROM is called a *single-session disc* because manufacturers write all items on the disc at one time. Software manufacturers often distribute their programs using CD-ROMs (Figure 7-30).

A typical CD-ROM holds from 650 MB to 1 GB of data, instructions, and information. To read a CD-ROM, insert the disc in a **CD-ROM drive** or a CD-ROM player. Because audio CDs and CD-ROMs use the same laser technology, you may be able to use a CD-ROM drive to listen to an audio CD while using the computer.

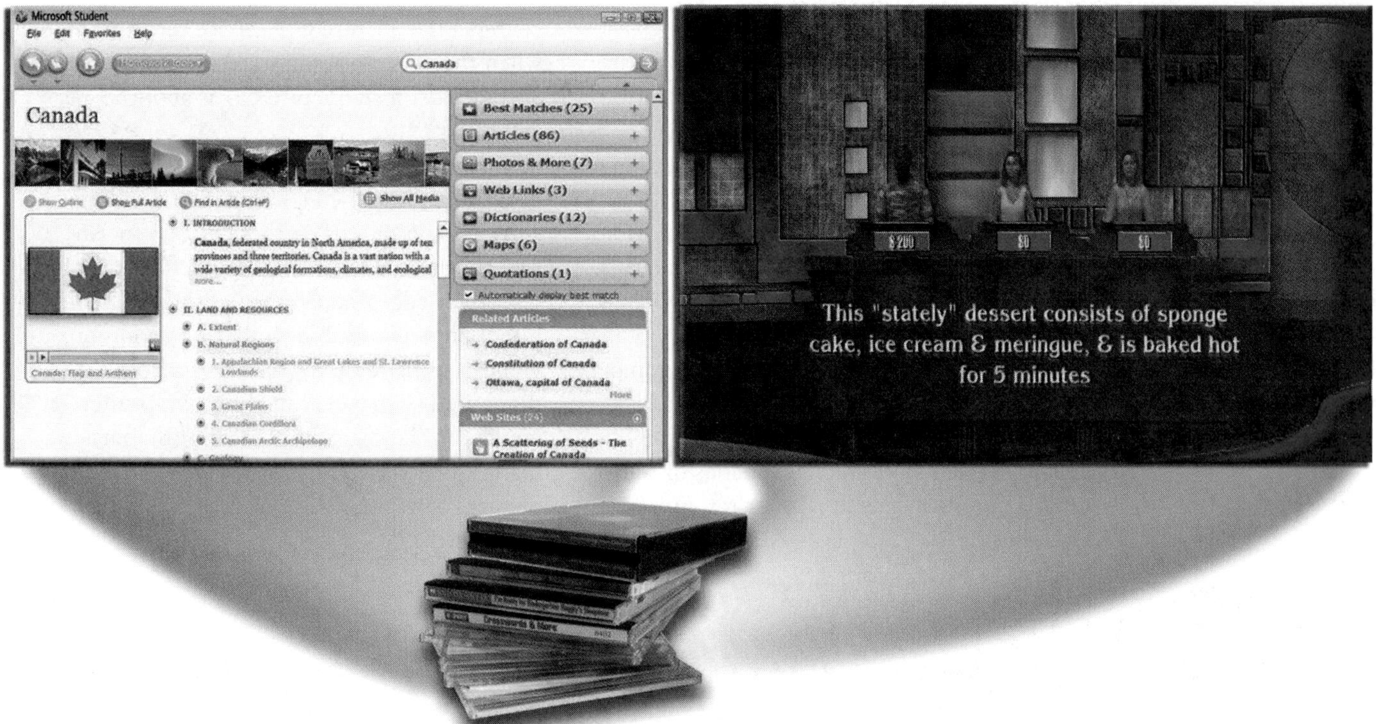

Figure 7-30 Encyclopedias, games, simulations, and many other programs are distributed on CD-ROM.

The speed of a CD-ROM drive determines how fast it installs programs and accesses the disc. Original CD-ROM drives were single-speed drives with transfer rates of 150 KBps. Manufacturers measure all optical disc drives relative to this original CD-ROM drive. They use an X to denote the original transfer rate of 150 KBps. For example, a 48X CD-ROM drive has a data transfer rate of 7,200 (48 × 150) KBps, or 7.2 MBps.

Current CD-ROM drives have transfer rates, or speeds, ranging from 48X to 75X or faster. The higher the number, the faster the CD-ROM drive. Faster CD-ROM drives are more expensive than slower drives.

CD-Rs and CD-RWs A **CD-R** (*compact disc-recordable*) is a multisession optical disc on which users can write, but not erase, their own items such as text, graphics, and audio. *Multisession* means you can write on part of the disc at one time and another part at a later time. Each part of a CD-R, however, can be written on only one time, and the disc's contents cannot be erased.

A **CD-RW** (*compact disc-rewritable*) is an erasable multisession disc you can write on multiple times. CD-RW overcomes the major disadvantage of CD-R because it allows users to write and rewrite data, instructions, and information on the CD-RW disc multiple times — instead of just once. Reliability of the disc tends to drop, however, with each successive rewrite.

To write on a CD-RW disc, you must have CD-RW software and a **CD-RW drive**. These drives have write speeds of 52X or more, rewrite speeds of 32X or more, and read speeds of 52X or more. Manufacturers state the speeds in this order; that is, write speed, rewrite speed, and read speed is stated as 52/32/52. Most CD-RW drives can read audio CDs, CD-ROMs, CD-Rs, and CD-RWs.

Many personal computers today include either a CD-R or CD-RW drive, or a combination drive that includes CD-R or CD-RW capabilities, as a standard feature so that users can burn their own discs. The process of writing on an optical disc is called *burning*. Some operating systems, such as Windows, include the capability of burning discs.

A popular use of CD-RW and CD-R discs is to create audio CDs. For example, users can record their own music and save it on a CD, purchase and download songs from the Web, or rearrange tracks on a purchased music CD. The process of copying audio and/or video data from a purchased disc and saving it on digital media is called *ripping*.

Archive Discs and Picture CDs

Many people use archive discs or Picture CDs to preserve their photos. When you post and share photos online on a photo sharing community, you can choose to save your collection of online photos on an archive disc (Figure 7-31). An **archive disc** stores photos from an online photo center in the jpg file format, usually at a maximum resolution of 7200 pixels per photo. The cost of archive discs is determined by the number of photos being stored. One service, for example, charges $9.99 for the first hundred pictures.

A Kodak **Picture CD** is a single-session CD-ROM that stores digital versions of film using a jpg file format at a lower resolution, typically 1024 × 1536 pixels. Many photo centers offer Picture CD service for consumers when they drop off film to be developed. The average cost for a Picture CD is about $3 per roll of film.

Most optical disc drives can read an archive disc and a Picture CD. Using photo editing software and photos on these discs, you can remove red eye, crop the photo, enhance colors, trim away edges, adjust the lighting, and edit just about any aspect of a photo. In addition, you can print copies of the photos from the disc on glossy paper with an ink-jet printer. If you do not have a printer to print the images, many stores have kiosks at which you can print pictures from an archive disc, a Picture CD, or other media.

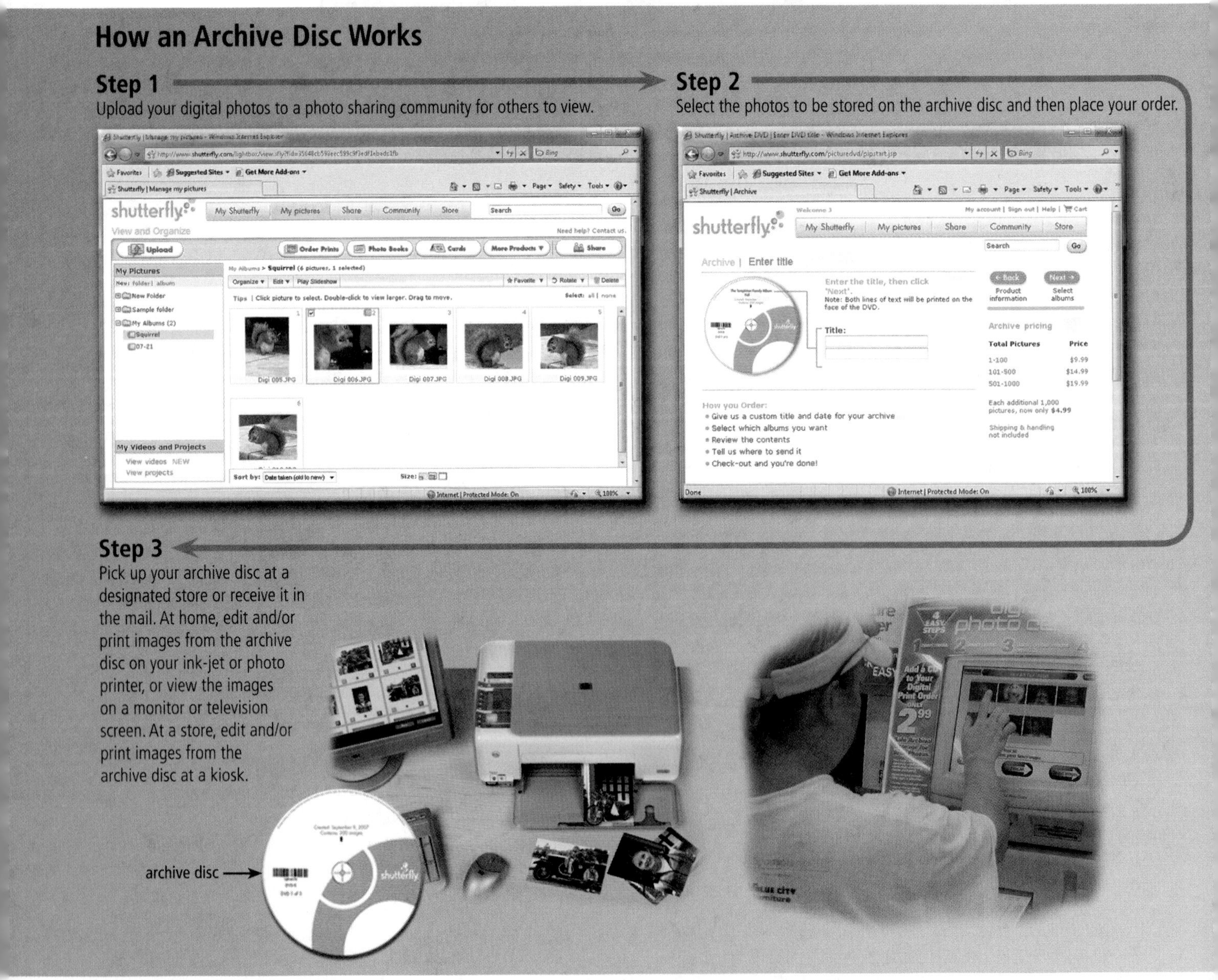

How an Archive Disc Works
Step 1
Upload your digital photos to a photo sharing community for others to view.
Step 2
Select the photos to be stored on the archive disc and then place your order.
Step 3
Pick up your archive disc at a designated store or receive it in the mail. At home, edit and/or print images from the archive disc on your ink-jet or photo printer, or view the images on a monitor or television screen. At a store, edit and/or print images from the archive disc at a kiosk.
archive disc

Figure 7-31 This figure shows how an archive disc works.

DVDs and Blu-ray Discs

Although the size and shape of a CD and DVD are similar, a DVD stores data, instructions, and information in a slightly different manner and thus achieves a higher storage capacity. DVD quality also far surpasses that of CDs because images are stored at higher resolution.

Widely used DVDs are capable of storing 4.7 GB to 17 GB, depending on the storage techniques used. The first storage technique involves making the disc denser by packing the pits closer together. The second involves using two layers of pits. For this technique to work, the lower layer of pits is semitransparent so that the laser can read through it to the upper layer. This technique doubles the capacity of the disc. Finally, some DVDs are double-sided.

A **DVD-ROM** (*digital versatile disc-read-only memory* or *digital video disc-read-only memory*) is a high-capacity optical disc on which users can read but not write or erase. Manufacturers write the contents of DVD-ROMs and distribute them to consumers. DVD-ROMs store movies, music, music videos, huge databases, and complex software (Figure 7-32).

To read a DVD-ROM, you need a **DVD-ROM drive** or DVD player. Most DVD-ROM drives also can read audio CDs, CD-ROMs, CD-Rs, and CD-RWs. DVD-ROM drives can read DVDs at speeds of 16X or more and CDs at speeds of 52X or more. Some drives, called DVD/CD-RW drives, are combination drives that read and write DVD and CD media. Many of today's computers include these combination drives.

A newer, more expensive DVD format is Blu-ray, which has a higher capacity and better quality than standard DVDs, especially for high-definition audio and video. A *Blu-ray Disc-ROM (BD-ROM)* has storage capacities of 100 GB, with expectations of exceeding 200 GB in the future. Blu-ray Disc (BD) drives and players are backward compatible with DVD and CD formats. Some game consoles include a Blu-ray drive. Original Blu-ray Disc drives had read speeds of 4.5 MBps, designated as 1X. Current read/write speeds of Blu-ray Discs range from 9 MBps (2X) to 36 Mbps (8X) in the future. Figure 7-33 compares the current storage capacities of DVD and Blu-ray media.

Another high density format, called HD VMD, recently emerged as a competitor to Blu-ray. With future technology, an *HD VMD (Versatile Multilayer Disc)* potentially will contain up to 20 layers, each with a capacity of 5 GB. Current HD VMDs have capacities of 40 GB and more.

A mini-DVD that has grown in popularity is the UMD, which works specifically with the PlayStation Portable (PSP) handheld game console. The *UMD* (Universal Media Disc), which has a diameter of about 2.4 inches, can store up to 1.8 GB of games, movies, or music (Figure 7-34). Similarly, the mini Blu-ray Disc, which is used primarily in digital video recorders, stores approximately 7.5 GB.

Blu-ray

For more information, visit the Computer Concepts CourseMate Web site at www.cengagebrain.com, navigate to the Chapter 7 Web Link resource for this book, and then click Blu-ray.

DVD and Blu-ray Storage Capacities

Sides	Layers	DVD	Blu-ray
1	1	4.7 GB	25 GB
1	2	8.5 GB	50 GB
2	1	9.4 GB	50 GB
2	2	17 GB	100 GB

Figure 7-33 Storage capacities of DVDs and Blu-ray Discs.

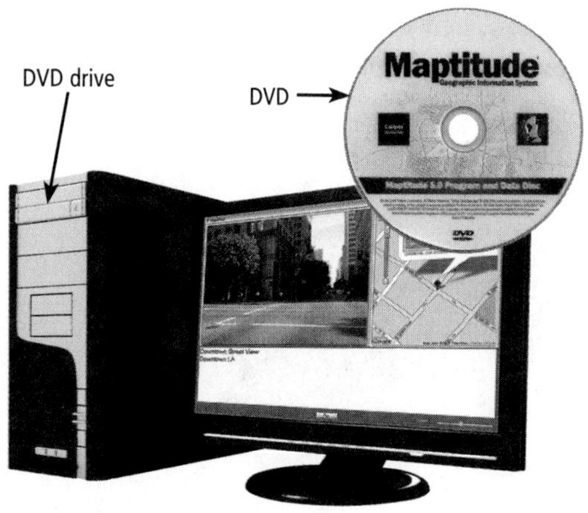

Figure 7-32 A DVD-ROM is a high-capacity optical disc.

Figure 7-34 The PSP handheld game console plays games stored on a UMD.

Recordable and Rewritable DVDs Many types of recordable and rewritable DVD formats are available. *DVD-R* and *DVD+R* are competing DVD-recordable formats, each with up to 4.7 GB storage capacity. Similarly, *BD-R* is a high-capacity DVD-recordable format. Each of these formats allows users to write on the disc once and read (play) it many times.

Instead of recordable DVDs, however, most users work with rewritable DVDs because these discs can be written on multiple times and also erased. Three competing rewritable DVD formats, each with storage capacities up to 4.7 GB per side are **DVD-RW, DVD+RW**, and **DVD+RAM**. Likewise, *BD-RE* is a high-capacity rewritable DVD format. To write on these discs, you must have a compatible drive or recorder. Rewritable drives usually can read a variety of DVD and CD media. Before investing in equipment, check to be sure it is compatible with the media on which you intend to record.

? FAQ 7-7

Is it a good idea to transfer movies from older media, such as VHS, to an optical disc or cloud storage?

Older media, especially magnetic disks and tapes, have a relatively short lifespan and can be damaged easily. For this reason, many people prefer to transfer their older recordings to newer storage media, such as an optical disc or cloud storage. While it might be safe to copy movies to which you own the rights entirely, you should check applicable copyright laws in your area before making a copy of a movie to which someone else owns the rights.

For more information, visit the Computer Concepts CourseMate Web site at www.cengagebrain.com, navigate to the Chapter 7 FAQ resource for this book, and then click Transferring Movies.

Other Types of Storage

In addition to the previously discussed types of storage, other options are available for specific uses and applications. These include tape, magnetic stripe cards and smart cards, microfilm and microfiche, and enterprise storage.

Tape

One of the first storage media used with mainframe computers was tape. **Tape** is a magnetically coated ribbon of plastic capable of storing large amounts of data and information at a low cost. Tape no longer is used as a primary method of storage. Instead, business users utilize tape most often for long-term storage and backup.

Comparable to a tape recorder, a **tape drive** reads and writes data and information on a tape. Although older computers used reel-to-reel tape drives, today's tape drives use tape cartridges. A *tape cartridge* is a small, rectangular, plastic housing for tape (Figure 7-35). Tape cartridges that contain quarter-inch-wide tape are slightly larger than audiocassette tapes. Business users sometimes back up personal computer hard disks to tape, often using an external tape drive. On larger computers, tape cartridges are mounted in a separate cabinet called a *tape library*. Often, a tape robot automatically retrieves tape cartridges, which are identified by location or bar code. Transfer rates of tape drives range from 1.25 MBps to 6 MBps.

Tape storage requires *sequential access*, which refers to reading or writing data consecutively. As with a music tape, you must forward or rewind the tape to a specific point to access a specific piece of data. For example, to access item W requires passing through items A through V sequentially.

Hard disks, flash memory storage, and optical discs all use direct access. *Direct access*, also called *random access*, means that the device can locate a particular data item or file immediately, without having to move consecutively through items stored in front of the desired data item or file. When writing or reading specific data, direct access is much faster than sequential access.

Figure 7-35 A tape drive and a tape cartridge.

Magnetic Stripe Cards and Smart Cards

A **magnetic stripe card** is a credit card, entertainment card, bank card, or other similar card, with a stripe that contains information identifying you and the card (shown in Figure 7-1 on page 352). Information stored in the stripe includes your name, account number, and the card's expiration date. A magnetic stripe card reader reads information stored on the stripe.

A **smart card**, which is similar in size to a credit card or ATM card, stores data on a thin microprocessor embedded in the card. Smart cards contain a processor and have input, process, output, and storage capabilities. When you insert the smart card in a specialized card reader, the information on the smart card is read and, if necessary, updated. Some credit cards are smart cards, and some store biometric data such as fingerprints to authenticate a user (Figure 7-36).

Uses of smart cards include storing medical records, vaccination data, and other health care and identification information; tracking information, such as employee attendance or customer purchases; storing a prepaid amount of money, such as for student purchases on campus; and authenticating users, such as for Internet purchases or building access. In addition, a smart card can double as an ID card. Read Ethics & Issues 7-4 for a related discussion.

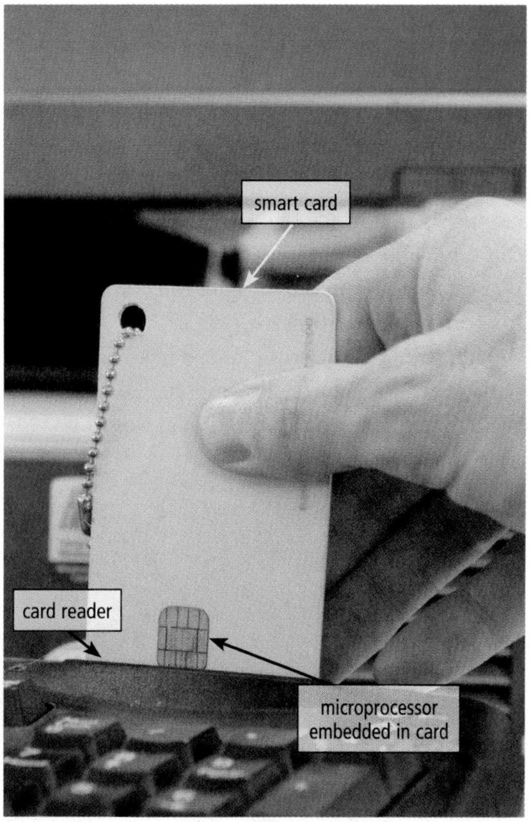

Figure 7-36 This user inserts the smart card to access the computer.

Smart Cards

For more information, visit the Computer Concepts CourseMate Web site at www.cengagebrain.com, navigate to the Chapter 7 Web Link resource for this book, and then click Smart Cards.

ETHICS & ISSUES 7-4

Should the World Become a Cashless Society?

Do you toss your loose change in a jar with the hopes of making a special purchase with the savings someday? This habit may become futile if the world goes cashless. Some forecasters say that the world is moving toward a cashless society. One form of payment that could end the need for cash is the smart card, which can store a dollar amount on a thin microprocessor and update the amount whenever a transaction is made. Advocates claim that smart cards would eliminate muggings and robberies, make it difficult to purchase illegal goods, and reduce taxes by identifying tax cheats. Also, payment using biometrics, such as fingerprints, is becoming more common. Several high-profile security breaches at credit reporting and credit card companies, however, have heightened concerns over privacy. In a recent survey, most Americans said that they would not use a smart card even if privacy was guaranteed. Another survey shows that most Americans believe that fingerprints are a trustworthy form of identification. A cash purchase usually is anonymous. Yet, a smart card purchase preserves a record of the transaction that could become available to other merchants, advertisers, government agencies, or hackers.

Should the world become a cashless society? Why or why not? Would you be comfortable using a smart card or fingerprint instead of cash for all transactions? Why?

Ethics & Issues

For the complete text of the Ethics & Issues boxes found in this chapter, visit the Computer Concepts CourseMate Web site at www.cengagebrain.com and then navigate to the Chapter 7 Ethics & Issues resource for this book.

Microfilm and Microfiche

Microfilm and microfiche store microscopic images of documents on roll or sheet film. **Microfilm** is a 100- to 215-foot roll of film. **Microfiche** is a small sheet of film, usually about 4 × 6 inches. A *computer output microfilm recorder* is the device that records the images on the film. The stored images are so small that you can read them only with a microfilm or microfiche reader (Figure 7-37).

Microfilm and microfiche use is widespread, with many companies allowing you to search through and view microfilm images online. Libraries use these media to store back issues of newspapers, magazines, and genealogy records. Some large organizations use microfilm and microfiche to archive inactive files. Some banks use them to store transactions and canceled checks. The U.S. Army uses them to store personnel records.

The use of microfilm and microfiche provides a number of advantages. They greatly reduce the amount of paper firms must handle. They are inexpensive and have the longest life of any storage media (Figure 7-38). Read Looking Ahead 7-1 for a look at long-term storage.

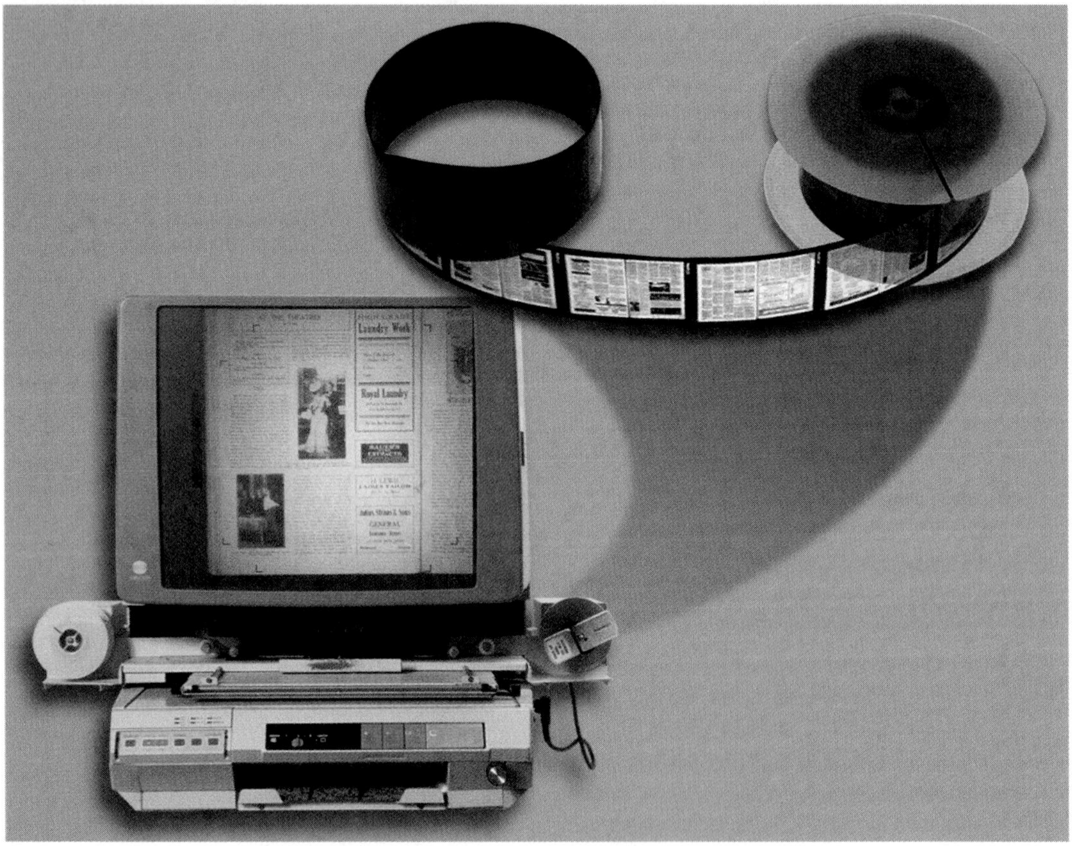

Figure 7-37 Images on microfilm can be read only with a microfilm reader.

Media Life Expectancies* **(when using high-quality media)**

Media Type	Guaranteed Life Expectancy	Potential Life Expectancy
Magnetic disks	3 to 5 years	20 to 30 years
Optical discs	5 to 10 years	50 to 100 years
Solid state drives	50 years	140 years
Microfilm	100 years	500 years

* according to manufacturers of the media

Figure 7-38 Microfilm is the medium with the longest life.

LOOKING AHEAD 7-1

Rosetta Project a Storage Solution

The Rosetta Stone unlocked the secret of understanding Egyptian hieroglyphics. Created in 186 B.C., the carved stone contains translations of one hieroglyphic passage into three languages. Today, more than 2,500 human languages exist, but 50 to 90 percent of them are expected to become extinct by the end of this century. In an effort to preserve these languages using long-term storage technology, thousands of people collaborated on the Rosetta Project to create the Rosetta Disk.

Measuring only 3 inches wide, the nickel Rosetta Disk contains 15,000 etched pages documenting more than 1,000 known languages in the world. Each page is .019 inches wide, approximately the width of 5 human hairs. The pages are readable when the Disk is magnified 1,000 times. For protection, the Disk is housed in a 4-inch spherical container.

Five prototype Disks were created. The original Disk is attached to the European Space Agency's Rosetta Space Probe that was launched in 2004 and is expected to land on a comet in 2014. The Probe will measure the comet's molecular composition and then orbit the sun for millions of years.

For more information, visit the Computer Concepts CourseMate Web site at www.cengagebrain.com, navigate to the Chapter 7 Looking Ahead resource for this book, and then click Long-Term Storage.

Enterprise Storage

A large business, commonly referred to as an enterprise, has hundreds or thousands of employees in offices across the country or around the world. Enterprises use computers and computer networks to manage and store huge volumes of data and information about customers, suppliers, and employees (Figure 7-39).

To meet their large-scale needs, enterprises use special hardware geared for heavy use, maximum availability, and maximum efficiency. One or more servers on the network have the sole purpose of providing storage to connected users. For high-speed storage access, entire networks are dedicated exclusively to connecting devices that provide storage to other servers. (For a technical discussion about a particular type of Internet server, read the High-Tech Talk article on page 382.) In an enterprise, some storage systems can provide more than 185 TB of storage capacity. Optical disc servers hold hundreds of optical discs.

An enterprise's storage needs usually grow daily. Thus, the storage solutions an enterprise chooses must be able to store its data and information requirements today and tomorrow.

Enterprise Storage

For more information, visit the Computer Concepts CourseMate Web site at www.cengagebrain.com, navigate to the Chapter 7 Web Link resource for this book, and then click Enterprise Storage.

Figure 7-39 An enterprise uses high-capacity storage devices.

Categories of Users

User	Typical Storage Devices
Home 	• 500 GB hard disk • Cloud storage • Optical disc drive • Card reader/writer • USB flash drive
Small Office/Home Office 	• 1 TB hard disk • Cloud storage • Optical disc drive • External hard disk for backup • USB flash drive
Mobile 	• 250 GB hard disk • Cloud storage • Optical disc drive • Card reader/writer • Portable hard disk for backup • USB flash drive
Power 	• 2.5 TB hard disk • Cloud storage • Optical disc drive • Portable hard disk for backup • USB flash drive
Enterprise 	• Desktop Computer - 1 TB hard disk - Optical disc drive - Smart card reader - Tape drive - USB flash drive • Server or Mainframe - Network storage server - 40 TB hard disk system - Optical disc server - Microfilm or microfiche

Figure 7-40 Recommended storage devices for various users.

Putting It All Together

Many factors influence the type of storage devices you should use: the amount of data, instructions, and information to be stored; the hardware and software in use; and the desired cost. The table in Figure 7-40 outlines several suggested storage devices for various types of computer users. Read Ethics & Issues 7-5 for a related discussion.

ETHICS & ISSUES 7-5

Who Should Be Looking at Your Medical Records?

A medical transcriber based in a foreign country and hired by a U.S. medical center threatened to post private medical records to the Internet if she was not paid more. With the widespread use of computers and an explosion in data storage capacity around the world, private information, such as medical records, requires increased diligence by companies, governments, and individuals to maintain this privacy. The government would like most Americans' health care records available in privacy-protected electronic format by 2014. Although these records will be stored by a corporation or the government, individuals probably will have complete control, or ownership, of these electronic records.

The Health Insurance Portability and Accountability Act (HIPAA) sets rigorous standards for medical record privacy. The law does not cover financial records, education records, or employment records — each of which may contain medical information about you. Your medical information also may be examined by insurance companies, government agencies, the Medical Information Bureau (MIB), employers, and the courts. You also inadvertently may pass on medical information to direct marketers when you participate in informal health screenings or surveys. Some people have found that discussing medical conditions via Internet chat rooms or newsgroups has resulted in unwanted attention, and they later regret the disclosures. Proponents of greater electronic access to medical records claim that more access means that physicians can be better prepared when they see patients, physicians will make fewer errors, and insurance companies can better root out fraud.

Should more limits be placed on what other people can do with your medical information? Why or why not? What are the advantages of increased access to medical records? What are the disadvantages?

QUIZ YOURSELF 7-3

Instructions: Find the true statement below. Then, rewrite the remaining false statements so that they are true.

1. A CD-RW is a type of optical disc on which users can read but not write (record) or erase.
2. A DVD-RAM is a single-session disc that stores digital versions of film using a jpg file format.
3. DVDs have the same storage capacities as CDs.
4. Optical discs are written and read by mirrors.
5. Single session means you can write on part of the disc at one time and another part at a later time.
6. Microfilm and microfiche have the longest life of any media.

Quiz Yourself Online: To further check your knowledge of pages 370 through 380, visit the Computer Concepts CourseMate Web site at www.cengagebrain.com, navigate to the Chapter 7 Quiz Yourself resource for this book, and then click Objectives 6 – 8.

Chapter Summary

Storage holds data, instructions, and information, which includes pictures, music, and videos, for future use. Users depend on storage devices to provide access to their storage media for years and decades to come.

This chapter identified and discussed various storage media and storage devices. Storage media covered included internal hard disks; external and removable hard disks; solid state drives; memory cards; USB flash drives; ExpressCard modules; cloud storage; CDs, DVDs, and Blu-ray Discs; tape; smart cards; and microfilm and microfiche.

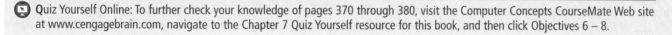

Computer Usage @ Work

Meteorology

With the television tuned to the local weather station, you anxiously are awaiting to see the projected path of a hurricane in the tropics. Having experienced hurricanes in the past, you rely heavily on the accuracy of weather forecasts so that you can adequately prepare if a storm travels through the area. Computers allow meteorologists to better estimate the severity and path of storms, enabling people to make potentially life-saving preparations.

The National Hurricane Center uses multiple computer models to determine a storm's path. These models consider factors such as the storm's current strength, the effects of nearby weather systems, the storm's central pressure, and whether the storm may travel over land. These models also may consider previous storms that traveled a similar path. Historical weather and storm data are stored on large storage devices by the National Weather Service. While these models are not 100 percent accurate, they do ensure that everyone who may be affected by the storm has enough time to prepare.

Violent, rotating thunderstorms potentially can spawn tornadoes, which sometimes cause catastrophic damage. For this reason, it is important for everyone to closely watch or listen to the weather during the storm. Meteorologists can monitor weather systems on multiple radars and send additional severe weather warnings automatically to weather radios. Computer technology enables these messages to be broadcast automatically only to weather radios in areas that may be affected.

In addition to computers helping us stay safe during severe storms, they also assist with day-to-day weather forecasting. Several years ago, meteorologists could predict the weather for only a few days into the future. Beyond that point, the forecast was very uncertain. Meteorologists presently are able to predict the weather, including temperature and chance of precipitation, one week or more into the future with much greater accuracy because computers create models using historical weather data and behavior to predict the future path of various weather systems.

News and weather stations also post their weather forecasts online. In fact, several Web sites have interactive radars that allow visitors to zoom in and view how weather is affecting their immediate neighborhood.

The meteorology field has made significant advancements because of computer technologies. Weather forecasts are more meaningful, which not only helps us prepare on land but also helps to protect those traveling by air or by sea.

For more information, visit the Computer Concepts CourseMate Web site at www.cengagebrain.com, navigate to the Chapter 7 Computer Usage @ Work resource for this book, and then click Meteorology.

High-Tech Talk

DNS Servers: How Devices on the Internet Easily Locate Each Other

Domain name system (DNS) servers, also called name servers, play an important role for Internet users who visit Web sites and send e-mail messages. DNS is a service on the Internet that converts domain names into Internet protocol (IP) addresses. Recall that a domain name is the text version of an IP address; for example, www.google.com is the domain name for the IP address of 72.14.207.99. Because the DNS stores IP addresses for each domain name, it is one of the largest databases stored across servers worldwide. In fact, some view DNS databases as nothing more than large address books. The absence of DNS servers would require users to remember IP addresses for Web sites.

To visit a Web site on the Internet, you begin by starting a Web browser and typing the Web address (which includes a domain name) in the Address bar. Once you press the ENTER key, the Web browser initiates a request for the IP address associated with the Web address. If the DNS server on your network or your Internet access provider's network knows the IP address, it will answer the request. Otherwise, it will ask another DNS server for this information or return an error message indicating that the domain name does not exist. If a DNS server is able to return an IP address to the Web browser, the Web browser contacts the Web server located at that IP address and requests a Web page. In some cases, DNS servers cache IP addresses for frequently requested domain names for a specified period of time, called the *Time To Live* (TTL). Because IP addresses are cached for certain domain names, it can take several days or more for updates to be reflected on DNS servers worldwide. For example, if the google.com Web server (accessible at www.google.com) is replaced with a new Web server with a new IP address, it might take several days for other DNS servers to acquire the new IP address.

If a DNS server does not know the IP address for a requested domain name, it will contact a root name server. A *root name server* stores a list of IP addresses for all DNS servers that handle a specific top-level domain, such as com or edu. For example, if you are attempting to reach www.google.com and your DNS server does not know the IP address, the root name server forwards the request to one of the DNS servers that handle the top-level domain of com. Your request will travel from one root server to the next until one can fulfill it. At that time, it requests the IP address associated with the Web address – in this case, www.google.com – from the COM root name server. Figure 7-41 illustrates a simple example of a DNS request.

The DNS has built-in redundancy. Network administrators typically set up multiple DNS servers on their network so that if one becomes overburdened or stops functioning, the other one(s) can continue filling requests. Similarly, multiple root name servers exist for each top-level domain.

Domain name servers also play an important role in e-mail communications. If you send an e-mail message to kbarnhill@esite.com, the DNS servers will locate the mail exchange (MX) record for the esite.com domain. The *MX record* identifies the location, or IP address, of the SMTP server accepting e-mail messages.

DNS servers often process billions of requests each day; each time you send an e-mail message or view a Web site, you are creating a request for a DNS server. While the average user might generate around 20 requests each day, those who primarily work with computers may generate hundreds of requests per day. Consequently, the millions of users connected to the Internet at any given time are generating billions of DNS requests each day.

For more information, visit the Computer Concepts CourseMate Web site at www.cengagebrain.com, navigate to the Chapter 7 High-Tech Talk resource for this book, and then click DNS Servers.

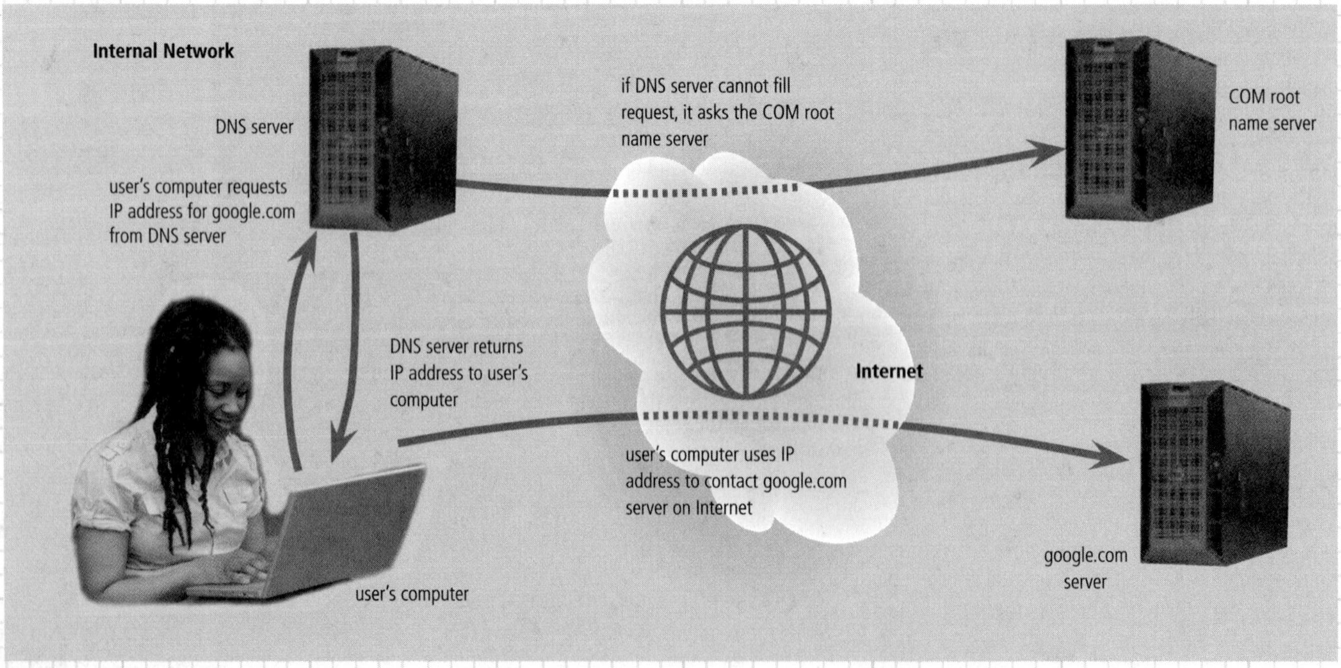

Figure 7-41 A simple DNS request.

Companies on the Cutting Edge

SEAGATE TECHNOLOGY Storage Solutions Supplier

The average household with a broadband Internet connection will need nearly 1 TB of storage for its personal media collections, and *Seagate* has the storage solutions for practically every digital need. The company offers more than 40 products for the personal computing, consumer electronics, and enterprise computing fields.

Seagate has been at the forefront of the digital storage world since it developed the first 5.25-inch hard disk for the personal computer in 1980. In 2008 it shipped its one billionth hard disk, making the company's production for the past 30 years a total of 79 million terabytes. Seagate expects to ship its two billionth hard disk by 2013.

Seagate recently introduced the FreeAgent DockStar network adapter. This device allows users to access their digital media from anywhere in the world and share these files with anyone. The FreeAgent DockStar network adapter also enables users to link their digital content to online social networks such as Facebook, Twitter, and MySpace.

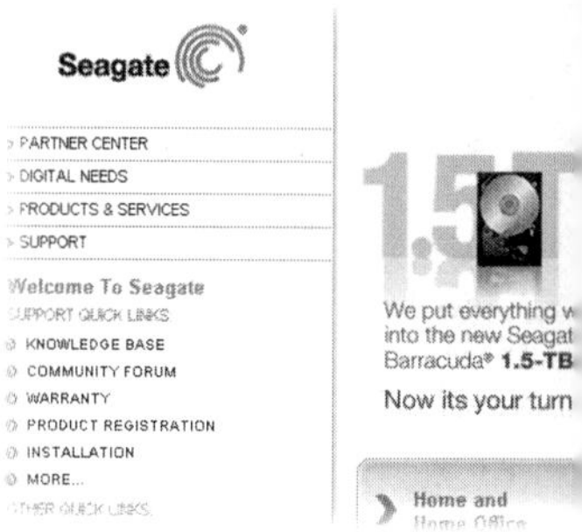

SANDISK CORPORATION Flash Memory Storage Supplier

The number of flash memory card formats is growing, and only one company has the rights to design, develop, manufacture, and market every one of them: *SanDisk*. The company is the world's largest supplier of flash memory storage products and also has lines of portable media players.

The company was founded in 1988, and one of its earliest flash drives was used on a U.S. space shuttle three years later. Today SanDisk is developing rewritable 3-D memory products that will store data vertically, and company executives believe this technology will replace flash products in the next decade.

SanDisk recently introduced the world's fastest 32 GB SDHC card. The 32 GB SanDisk Extreme SDHC card boasts read and write speeds of 30 megabytes per second. The increased speeds enable photographers to take pictures quickly without having to wait long for the card to record the images. In addition, computer users also are able to transfer data to and from the card quickly.

For more information, visit the Computer Concepts CourseMate Web site at www.cengagebrain.com and then navigate to the Chapter 7 Companies on the Cutting Edge resource for this book.

Technology Trailblazers

AL SHUGART Storage Expert

Al Shugart said that his real goal in life was to have fun, and he spent his life doing the things that gave him the most pleasure. The day after receiving his bachelor's degree in engineering physics in 1951, he landed a job at IBM doing what he loved to do: fixing broken items and developing new technology. He was promoted to supervisor of the product development team that developed the first removable hard disk drive.

Shugart then left IBM, became vice president of Memorex, and then started Shugart Associates and began developing floppy disks. In 1979 he founded Seagate Technology with a friend. As his company grew to become the world's largest hard disk manufacturer, he had fun placing his dog, Ernest, on the ballot for a Congressional seat.

Shugart served as president and CEO of Al Shugart International, a venture capital firm in California, until his death in 2006.

MARK DEAN IBM Inventor

Web 2.0 applications demand large, inexpensive storage, and *Mark Dean* is hard at work helping to meet this need. As vice president of IBM's Almaden Research Center lab in California, Dean is responsible for developing innovative products.

Dean joined IBM after graduating from Stanford University with a degree in electrical engineering. He led a team that developed the first CMOS microprocessor to operate at one gigahertz and has more than 40 patents or patents pending that are used in more than 40 million personal computers manufactured each year. Three of his patents are among the nine registered for the architecture of the original personal computer.

Dean is the first African-American to be appointed to IBM Fellow, the company's highest level of technical merit. He also was inducted in the National Inventors Hall of Fame.

For more information, visit the Computer Concepts CourseMate Web site at www.cengagebrain.com and then navigate to the Chapter 7 Technology Trailblazers resource for this book.

Chapter Review

The Chapter Review reinforces the main concepts presented in this chapter.

To listen to an audio version of this Chapter Review, visit the Computer Concepts CourseMate Web site at www.cengagebrain.com and then navigate to the Chapter 7 Chapter Review resource for this book.

1. How Are Storage Devices Different from Storage Media? A **storage medium** is the physical material on which a computer keeps data, instructions, and information. The number of bytes (characters) a storage medium can hold is its **capacity**. A **storage device** is the computer hardware that records and/or retrieves items to and from storage media. **Writing** is the process of transferring items from memory to a storage medium, and **reading** is the process of transferring these items from a storage medium into memory.

2. What Are the Characteristics of an Internal Hard Disk? A **hard disk**, also called a *hard disk drive* or hard drive, is a storage device that contains one or more inflexible, circular platters that use magnetic particles to store data, instructions, and information. Traditionally, hard disks stored data using *longitudinal recording*, which aligned the magnetic particles horizontally. With *perpendicular recording*, hard disks align the particles vertically, making much greater storage capacities possible. The capacity of a hard disk is determined from whether it uses longitudinal or perpendicular recording, the number of platters it contains, and the composition of the magnetic coating on the platters. A *platter* is made of aluminum, glass, or ceramic and is coated with a material that allows items to be recorded magnetically on its surface. Each platter has two read/write heads, one for each side. The location of a *read/write head* often is referred to by its *cylinder*, which is the vertical section of a track that passes through all platters. **Formatting** is the process of dividing the disk into tracks and sectors. A *track* is a narrow recording band that forms a full circle on the surface of the disk. The disk's storage locations are divided into pie-shaped sections, which break the tracks into small arcs called *sectors*. While the computer is running, the platters in the hard disk rotate at 5,400 to 15,000 *revolutions per minute* (*rpm*), which allows nearly instant access to all tracks and sectors on the platters. *Transfer rate* is the speed with which data, instructions, and information transfer to and from a storage device. **Access time** measures the amount of time it takes a storage device to locate an item on a storage medium, or the time required to deliver an item from memory to the processor.

3. What Is the Purpose of Network Attached Storage Devices, External and Removable Hard Disks, and Hard Disk Controllers? A **network attached storage** (*NAS*) device is a server connected to a network with the sole purpose of providing storage. NAS devices often use a **RAID** configuration. An **external hard disk** is a separate freestanding hard disk that connects with a cable to a USB or FireWire port on the system unit or communicates wirelessly. External hard disks have storage capacities up to 4 TB and more. A **removable hard disk** can be inserted or removed from a built-in or external drive. Removable hard disks have storage capacities up to 1 TB. A *disk controller* consists of a special-purpose chip and electronic circuits that control the transfer of data, instructions, and information from a disk to and from the system bus and other components in a computer. A hard disk controller may be part of the hard disk on the motherboard, or it may be a separate adapter card inside the system unit.

Visit the Computer Concepts CourseMate Web site at www.cengagebrain.com, navigate to the Chapter 7 Quiz Yourself resource for this book, and then click Objectives 1 – 3.

4. What Are the Various Types of Flash Memory Storage? Flash memory chips are a type of *solid state media*, which means they consist entirely of electronic components and contain no moving parts. A **solid state drive (SSD)** typically uses flash memory to store data, instructions, and information. A **memory card** is a removable flash memory device that you insert and remove from a slot in a computer, mobile device, or *card reader/writer*. Common memory cards include *CompactFlash* (*CF*), *Secure Digital* (*SD*), *Secure Digital High Capacity* (*SDHC*), *microSD*, *microSDHC*, *xD Picture Card*, *Memory Stick*, and *Memory Stick Micro* (*M2*). A **USB flash drive**, sometimes called a *thumb drive*, is a flash memory storage device that plugs in a port on a computer or mobile

Chapter Review

device. An **ExpressCard module** is a removable device that fits in an ExpressCard slot. ExpressCard modules can add memory, storage, communications, or other capabilities to a computer.

5. **What Is Cloud Storage, and What Are Its Advantages?** **Cloud storage** is an Internet service that provides storage for computer users. Available for all sizes of users, with various degrees of storage services available for home and business users, cloud storage fees vary, depending on the user's storage requirements. Advantages include accessing files on the Internet from any computer or device with Internet access; storing large audio, video, and graphics files on the Internet instantaneously; allowing others to access their files on the Internet; viewing time-critical data and images immediately; storing off-site backups of data; and providing data center functions.

Visit the Computer Concepts CourseMate Web site at www.cengagebrain.com, navigate to the Chapter 7 Quiz Yourself resource for this book, and then click Objectives 4 – 5.

6. **What Are the Characteristics of Optical Discs?** An *optical disc* is a type of storage media that consists of a flat, round, portable disc made of metal, plastic, and lacquer that is written and read by a laser. Optical discs, which primarily store software, data, digital photos, movies, and music, contain microscopic pits (indentations) and lands (flat areas) in their middle layer. Optical discs commonly store items in a single track that spirals from the center of the disc to its edge. Like a hard disk, the single track is divided into evenly sized sectors.

7. **How Are the Various Types of Optical Discs Different?** A **CD-ROM**, or *compact disc read-only memory*, is a type of optical disc that uses laser technology to store items. Users can read the contents of standard CD-ROMs but cannot erase or modify their contents. A **CD-R** (*compact disc-recordable*) is a *multisession* disc on which users can record their own items, such as text, graphics, and audio. Each part of a CD-R can be written on only one time, and the disc's contents cannot be erased. A **CD-RW** (*compact disc-rewritable*) is an erasable disc that can be written on multiple times. An **archive disc** stores photos from an online photo center in the jpg file format. A **Picture CD** is a *single-session* CD-ROM that stores digital versions of film using the jpg format at a lower resolution than an archive disc. A **DVD-ROM** (*digital versatile disc-read-only memory* or *digital video disc-read-only memory*) is a high capacity optical disc that you can read but not write on or erase. A newer, more expensive DVD format is *Blu-ray Disc-ROM* (*BD-ROM*), with higher capacity and better quality than standard DVDs. Many types of recordable and rewritable DVD formats are available. *DVD-R* and *DVD+R* are DVD-recordable formats. *BD-R* is a high-capacity DVD-recordable format. **DVD-RW**, **DVD+RW**, and **DVD+RAM** are rewritable DVD formats that allow users to erase and record multiple times. *BD-RE* is a high-capacity rewritable DVD format.

8. **How Are Tape, Magnetic Stripe Cards, Smart Cards, Microfilm and Microfiche, and Enterprise Storage Used?** **Tape** is a magnetically coated ribbon of plastic capable of storing large amounts of data and information at a low cost. A **tape drive** reads and writes data and information on tape. Business users utilize tape most often for long-term storage and backup. A **magnetic stripe card** is a credit card, entertainment card, bank card, or other similar card with a stripe that contains information identifying you and the card. A magnetic stripe card reader reads the information stored on the stripe. A **smart card**, which is similar in size to a credit or ATM card, stores data on a thin microprocessor embedded in the card. A smart card reader reads the information on the smart card and updates it if necessary. **Microfilm** is a 100- to 215-foot roll of film. **Microfiche** is a small sheet of film, usually about 4 × 6 inches. Microfilm and microfiche reduce the amount of paper firms must handle, are inexpensive, and have the longest life of any storage media. Enterprises use computers, servers, and networks to manage and store huge volumes of data and information. In an enterprise, some storage systems can provide more than 185 TB of storage, and optical disc servers hold hundreds of optical discs.

Visit the Computer Concepts CourseMate Web site at www.cengagebrain.com, navigate to the Chapter 7 Quiz Yourself resource for this book, and then click Objectives 6 – 8.

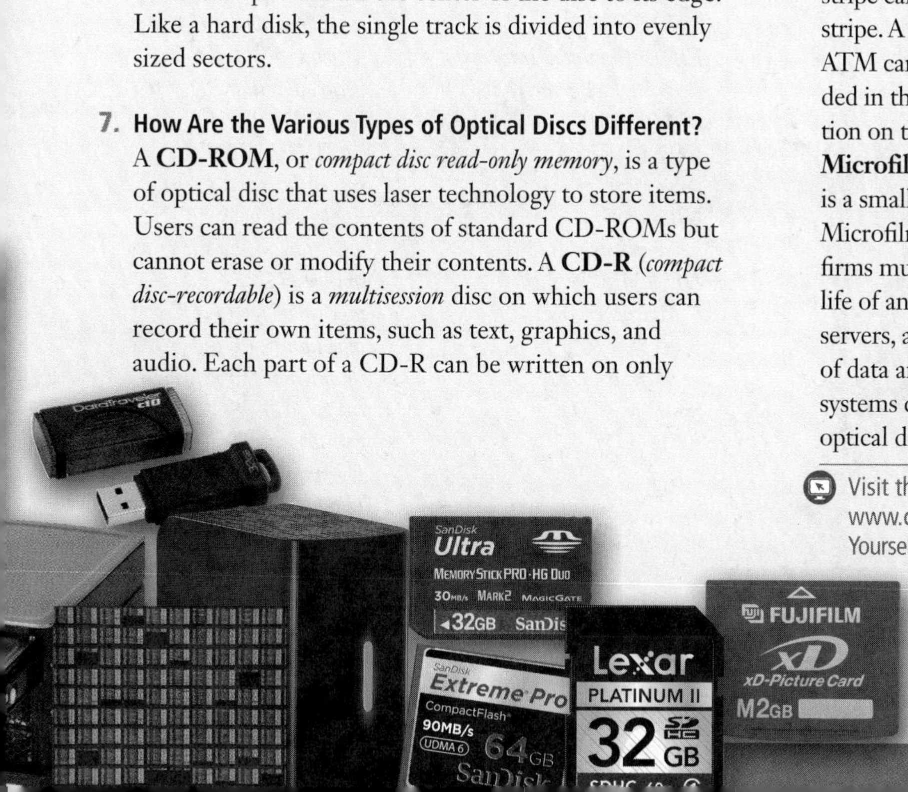

Key Terms

You should know the Primary Terms and be familiar with the Secondary Terms. The list below helps focus your study.

To see an example of and a definition for each term, and to access current and additional information from the Web, visit the Computer Concepts CourseMate Web site at www.cengagebrain.com and then navigate to the Chapter 7 Key Terms resource for this book.

Primary Terms

(shown in bold-black characters in the chapter)

access time (355)
archive disc (374)
backup (358)
capacity (354)
CD-R (373)
CD-ROM (372)
CD-ROM drive (372)
CD-RW (373)
CD-RW drive (373)
cloud storage (368)
DVD+RAM (376)
DVD-ROM (375)
DVD-ROM drive (375)
DVD+RW (376)
DVD-RW (376)
ExpressCard module (367)
external hard disk (360)
formatting (357)
hard disk (355)
magnetic stripe card (377)
memory card (364)
microfiche (378)
microfilm (378)
network attached storage (360)
Picture CD (374)
RAID (360)
reading (354)
removable hard disk (360)
smart card (377)
solid state drive (SSD) (363)
storage device (354)
storage medium (353)
tape (376)
tape drive (376)
USB flash drive (367)
writing (354)

external hard disk (360)

Secondary Terms

(shown in italic characters in the chapter)

allocation unit (357)
BD-R (376)
BD-RE (376)
Blu-ray Disc-ROM (BD-ROM) (375)
burning (373)
card reader/writer (365)
cluster (357)
compact disc read-only memory (372)
compact disc-recordable (373)
compact disc-rewritable (373)
CompactFlash (CF) (364)
computer output microfilm recorder (378)
cylinder (358)
density (359)
digital versatile disc-read-only memory (375)
digital video disc-read-only memory (375)
direct access (376)
disk cache (359)
disk controller (361)
DVD+R (376)
DVD-R (376)
EIDE (Enhanced Integrated Drive Electronics) (361)
eSATA (361)
fixed disk (355)
form factor (358)
GBps (355)
hard disk drive (355)
HD VMD (Versatile Multilayer Disc) (375)
head crash (358)
jewel box (371)
KBps (355)
LightScribe technology (370)
longitudinal recording (356)
MBps (355)
Memory Stick (364)
Memory Stick Micro (M2) (364)
microSD (364)
microSDHC (364)
mini discs (370)
multisession (373)
NAS (360)
optical disc (370)
perpendicular recording (356)
platter (357)
pocket hard drive (361)
portable (355)
random access (376)
read/write head (358)
revolutions per minute (rpm) (358)
ripping (373)
SAS (serial-attached SCSI) (362)
SATA (Serial Advanced Technology Attachment) (361)
SCSI (362)
secondary storage (353)
sectors (357)
Secure Digital (SD) (364)
Secure Digital High Capacity (SDHC) (364)
sequential access (376)
single-session disc (372)
solid state media (362)
storage (352)
tape cartridge (376)
tape library (376)
thumb drive (367)
track (357)
transfer rate (355)
U3 smart drive (367)
UMD (375)
xD Picture Card (364)

Checkpoint

The Checkpoint exercises test your knowledge of the chapter concepts. The page number containing the answer appears in parentheses after each exercise. The Beyond the Book exercises will help broaden your understanding of the concepts presented in this chapter.

To complete the Checkpoint exercises interactively, visit the Computer Concepts CourseMate Web site at www.cengagebrain.com and then navigate to the Chapter 7 Checkpoint resource for this book.

True/False Mark T for True and F for False.

_____ 1. A storage medium, also called secondary storage, is the physical material on which a computer keeps data, instructions, and information. (353)

_____ 2. Reading is the process of transferring data, instructions, and information from memory to a storage medium. (354)

_____ 3. Formatting is the process of dividing the disk into clusters and cylinders. (357)

_____ 4. A cluster can hold data from many files. (358)

_____ 5. A typical hard disk contains only one platter. (358)

_____ 6. A removable hard disk is a separate, freestanding hard disk that connects with a cable to a port on the system unit or communicates wirelessly. (360)

_____ 7. microSD and miniSDHC are common types of removable hard disks. (364)

_____ 8. ExpressCard modules can be used to add memory, storage, communications, multimedia, and security capabilities to a computer. (367)

_____ 9. The process of writing on an optical disc is called ripping. (373)

_____ 10. HD VMDs have a capacity of 40 GB and more. (375)

_____ 11. BD-R is an older low-capacity DVD-recordable format. (376)

_____ 12. Rewritable drives usually can read one type of media. (376)

_____ 13. Direct access means that the device can locate a particular data item or file immediately, without having to move consecutively through items stored in front of the desired data item or file. (376)

Multiple Choice Select the best answer.

1. _____ is the speed with which data, instructions, and information transfer to and from a device. (355)
   a. Access time
   b. Transfer rate
   c. Formatting
   d. Reading

2. Traditionally, hard disks stored data using _____, which aligned the magnetic particles horizontally around the surface of the disk. (356)
   a. LightScribe technology
   b. RAID
   c. longitudinal recording
   d. perpendicular recording

3. A group of two or more integrated hard disks is called a _____. (360)
   a. backup
   b. disk cache
   c. portable hard disk
   d. RAID

4. Users subscribe to a cloud storage service to _____. (369)
   a. save time by storing large files instantaneously
   b. allow others to access their files
   c. store offsite backups of data
   d. all of the above

5. A(n) _____ is a type of storage media that consists of a flat, round, portable disc made of metal, plastic, and lacquer that is written and read by a laser. (370)
   a. optical disc
   b. hard disk
   c. memory card
   d. thumb drive

6. _____ technology works with specially coated optical discs to etch labels directly on the disc. (370)
   a. SCSI
   b. SATA
   c. LightScribe
   d. LightSaber

7. On larger computers, tape cartridges are mounted in a separate cabinet called a(n) _____. (376)
   a. SATA (Serial Advanced Technology Attachment)
   b. tape library
   c. tape cartridge
   d. HD VMD

8. A _____ card is a credit card, entertainment card, bank card, or other similar card, with a stripe that contains information identifying you and the card. (377)
   a. Secure Digital High Capacity
   b. magnetic stripe
   c. Secure Digital
   d. microSDHC

STUDENT ASSIGNMENTS

Checkpoint

Matching

Match the terms with their definitions.

____ 1. capacity (354)
____ 2. cluster (357)
____ 3. cylinder (358)
____ 4. head crash (358)
____ 5. backup (358)
____ 6. disk cache (359)
____ 7. disk controller (361)
____ 8. eSATA (361)
____ 9. solid state media (362)
____ 10. solid state drive (363)

a. vertical section of a track that passes through all platters
b. external disk interface that is much faster than USB and FireWire
c. smallest unit of disk space that stores data and information
d. special-purpose chip and electronic circuits that control the transfer of items to and from the system bus
e. occurs when a read/write head touches the surface of a platter on a hard disk
f. duplicate of a file, program, or disk placed on a separate storage medium that you can use in case the original is lost, damaged, or destroyed
g. a storage device that typically uses flash memory to store data, instructions, and information
h. the number of bytes (characters) a storage medium can hold
i. media which consist entirely of electronic components, such as integrated circuits, and contain no moving parts
j. memory chips that the processor uses to store frequently accessed items

Short Answer

Write a brief answer to each of the following questions.

1. What is network attached storage? ____________ How much hard disk storage can home and small business users add to their network with a NAS device? ____________
2. What are the advantages of SAS (serial-attached SCSI)? ____________ What types of devices can be connected to SAS interfaces? ____________
3. How is a single-session disc different from a multisession disc? ____________ What is the purpose of archive discs and Picture CDs? ____________
4. Why do users use memory cards? ____________ Name five types of memory cards and describe some of the characteristics of each card. ____________
5. What is one difference between microfilm and microfiche? ____________ What are some uses of microfilm and microfiche? ____________

Beyond the Book

Follow the book element instructions below; present your findings (brief report, presentation, discussion, or other means).

1. Ethics & Issues — Select an Ethics & Issues in this chapter (356, 366, 369, 377, 380), find a recent newspaper/magazine article that supports one point of view presented, and then evaluate the article.
2. Computer Usage @ Work — Use the Web or a recent newspaper/magazine to locate three additional unique usages of computer technology in the meteorology field (381). What makes the use of these technologies unique to the meteorology field?
3. Companies on the Cutting Edge and Technology Trailblazers — Use the Web or a recent business newspaper/magazine to locate an interesting fact about Seagate Technology, SanDisk Corporation, Al Shugart, or Mark Dean that was not presented in the chapter (383).
4. High-Tech Talk — Locate a recent newspaper/magazine article that discusses topics related to DNS Servers (382). Would you recommend the article you found? Why or why not?
5. FAQs and Web Links — Use the Web or a recent newspaper/magazine to locate three additional facts about an FAQ (356, 360, 362, 363, 367, 371, 376) and Web Link (356, 360, 361, 363, 365, 369, 375, 377, 379) that were not presented in the chapter.
6. Looking Ahead — Use the Web or a recent newspaper/magazine to discover additional uses of the technology presented in Rosetta Project a Storage Solution (379).
7. Innovative Computing — Use the Web or a recent newspaper/magazine to locate two additional interesting facts about Digital Books Are a Good Read (368) and The Perfect Gift for Buying and Marketing (372).
8. Making Use of the Web — Visit three of the Finance sites (131) and outline the information on each Web site and the possible uses for each Web site.

Learn It Online

The Learn It Online exercises are interactive Web exercises designed to reinforce and expand your understanding of the chapter concepts. The descriptions below briefly summarize each exercise.

To complete the Learn It Online exercises, visit the Computer Concepts CourseMate Web site at www.cengagebrain.com, navigate to the Chapter 7 resources for this book, click the link for the exercise you want to complete, and then read the instructions.

1 At the Movies — Thumb-drive (USB Flash Drive) Encryption
Watch a movie to learn how people who store personal and confidential information on USB flash drives can use third-party programs to password-protect the files so that others cannot access them, and then answer questions about the movie.

2 Video and Audio: You Review It — Blu-ray Disc-ROM (BD-ROM)
Search for, choose, and write a review of a video, podcast, or vodcast that discusses Blu-ray Disc-ROMs.

3 Student Edition Labs — Maintaining a Hard Drive (Hard Disk) and Managing Files and Folders
Enhance your understanding and knowledge about maintaining a hard disk and managing files and folders by completing the Maintaining a Hard Drive and Managing Files and Folders Labs.

4 Practice Test
Take a multiple choice test that checks your knowledge of the chapter concepts and review the resulting study guide.

5 Who Wants To Be a Computer Genius²?
Play the Shelly Cashman Series version of this popular game by answering questions to find out if you are a computer genius. Panic buttons are available to provide assistance during game play.

6 Wheel of Terms
Identify important key terms presented in this chapter by playing the Shelly Cashman Series version of this popular game.

7 You're Hired!
Embark on the path to a career in computers by answering questions and solving puzzles related to concepts discussed in this chapter.

8 Crossword Puzzle Challenge
Complete an interactive crossword puzzle to reinforce concepts presented in this chapter.

9 Windows Exercises
Step through the Windows 7 exercises to learn about the Recycle Bin, working with files, the hard disk, and Disk Cleanup.

10 Exploring Computer Careers
Read about a career as a computer technician, search for related employment advertisements, and then answer related questions.

11 Web Apps — TurboTax Online
Learn how to use TurboTax Online to create an account, start a new tax return from scratch, review your tax return, and then print and file your tax return.

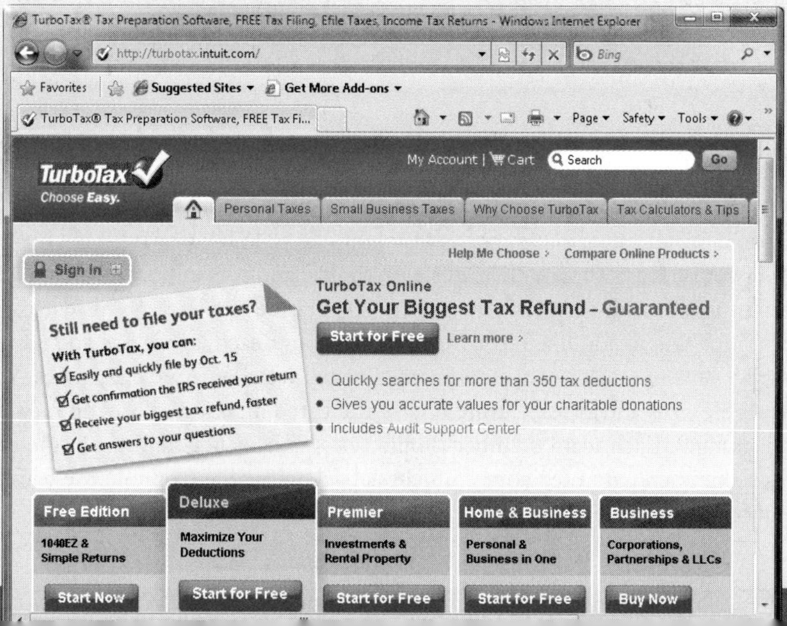

Problem Solving @ Home

The Problem Solving @ Home exercises extend your knowledge of the chapter concepts by seeking solutions to practical computer problems that you may encounter at home or school. The Collaboration exercise should be completed with a team.

In the real world, practical problems often can be solved in multiple ways. Provide one solution to each of the following problems using available resources, such as articles on the Web or in print, blogs, podcasts, videos, television, user guides, other individuals, and electronics and computer stores. You may need to use multiple resources to obtain an answer. Present your solutions in the form requested by your instructor (brief report, presentation, discussion, or other means).

1. **Old Movies** During the past two decades, you have been recording home movies on VHS tapes. It is becoming more difficult to locate blank VHS tapes, and you are worried that if your current VCR breaks, it will be hard to find a new one. A friend suggests that you copy these movies to an optical disc. What steps will you take to convert these movies?
2. **Possible Head Crash** When you turn on your computer, you hear a clicking sound coming from inside the computer. Furthermore, you realize that Windows is not starting automatically. You talk to a friend who said that your hard disk might have experienced a head crash. What might have caused this?

3. **Missing Cable** You are attempting to install a new 1 TB hard disk in your computer. You have found the empty bay for the new hard disk, but you cannot locate the cable that connects it to the computer. What are your next steps?
4. **Different Disk Capacity** After successfully connecting the secondary hard disk that you purchased, you turn on your computer. You click the Computer icon in Windows and then display the properties for the new hard disk. To your surprise, the hard disk capacity that Windows displays is lower than the capacity of the hard disk you have purchased. What might be wrong?
5. **No Space Available** You are attempting to copy some files to an optical disc. After starting the program to burn an optical disc and attempting to start the copy process, the program informs you that not enough space is available on the optical disc. The optical disc that is in the drive is brand new and contains no files of any type. What could be causing this?
6. **Memory Card Problems** For the past two years, you have been using the same Secure Digital (SD) memory card to take pictures with your digital camera. When you insert the SD memory card in your computer's card reader to transfer the pictures, your computer does not display the contents of the card. When you put the card back into your digital camera, you can see that the pictures still are stored on the card. What might be wrong?
7. **Unreadable Credit Card** Lately, the magnetic stripe readers at some store check-out registers are having increasing difficulty reading your credit card. In fact, many merchants now enter your credit card information manually, because the card cannot be read. What might be the problem?

Collaboration

8. **Backup Strategies** You and two of your coworkers have been tasked with determining an effective backup strategy for your company. Specifically, your supervisor would like to know what storage medium is best for the backed up data. You work for a company that sells electronics, and it is important that all data is backed up at the end of each business day. You inform your supervisor that he can back up his data to a hard disk, an optical disc, or cloud storage. He would like more information about each, as well as your recommendation about which medium best suits the needs of the company. Form a team of three classmates. Each team member should research the pros and cons of using one of the three mentioned backup media (hard disk, optical disc, and cloud storage). Each team member should report his or her findings to the other members. As a team, formulate a recommendation for your company's backup media. Compile the team's findings in a report and then submit it to your instructor.

Problem Solving @ Work

The Problem Solving @ Work exercises extend your knowledge of the chapter concepts by seeking solutions to practical computer problems that you may encounter at work. The Collaboration exercise should be completed with a team.

In the real world, practical problems often can be solved in multiple ways. Provide one solution to each of the following problems using available resources, such as articles on the Web or in print, blogs, podcasts, videos, television, user guides, other individuals, and electronics and computer stores. You may need to use multiple resources to obtain an answer. Present your solutions in the form requested by your instructor (brief report, presentation, discussion, or other means).

1. **Disc Will Not Eject** You just installed the newest version of Microsoft Office on your computer. When you attempt to eject the installation disc from the slot-loaded optical disc drive, the disc will not eject from the drive, and you still can hear it spinning inside. You want to remove this disc so that you can insert another disc with photos from the last company party. What steps will you take before calling technical support?
2. **Low Disk Space** While using your computer, Windows displays a message in the notification area indicating that you are very low on disk space. You have not installed any programs or saved any files recently. What could be causing this?
3. **RAID Failure** Your office computer has two hard disks configured as a redundant array of independent disks (RAID) to increase performance. Windows reports that there is a problem with the RAID configuration; specifically, one of your hard disks might be ready to fail. What are your next steps?
4. **Moving Files between Computers** A company policy dictates that employees are not allowed to connect USB flash drives to their office computers for fear of infecting the computer with a virus. After spending the weekend creating PowerPoint presentations for a meeting, you are unsure of how to transfer these files to your office computer. What are your next steps?
5. **Disk Not Recognized** The information technology manager at your company has purchased external hard disks for employees to use to back up their files. When you connect the external hard disk to the USB port on your computer, the computer displays a message stating that it cannot recognize the device. What might you do to correct this problem?
6. **File Will Not Open** Your computer is unable to open a file on an optical disc that you just inserted into the optical disc drive. You have been able to access other files on the same disc, but one file in particular is not opening. What might be causing this?

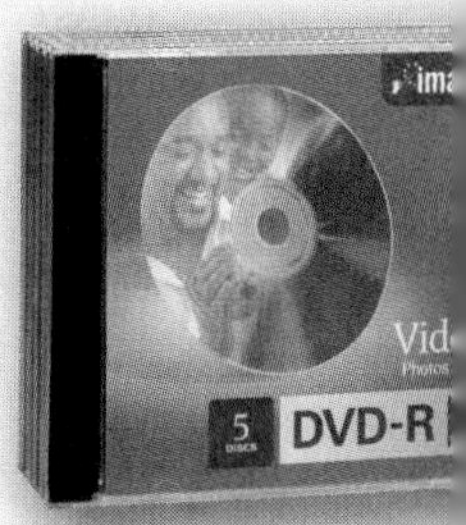

7. **Backing Up Data** It has been several years since your office computer was upgraded, and you just received an e-mail message stating that you finally will receive a new computer next week. The e-mail message also stated that all employees will be responsible for backing up their data. What files will you back up?
8. **Optical Disc Problem** Your colleague gives you an optical disc containing some video files. When you insert the disc in your computer, the disc burning software asks if you would like to finalize the disc. How will you respond?

Collaboration

9. **Computers in Meteorology** Your environmental sciences instructor is teaching a lesson about how computers have advanced the meteorology field. Form a team of three people to prepare a brief report about how computers and meteorology are connected. One team member should research how meteorologists predicted weather patterns before computer use became mainstream. Another team member should create a timeline illustrating when and how computers were introduced to the meteorology field, and the third team member should research the types of computer hardware and software required for a typical news station to forecast and present the weather.

Learn How To

The Learn How To activities step you through fundamental technology skills when using a computer. The Learn How To exercises enable you to become more proficient with these skills.

Premium Activity: To relate this Learn How To activity to your everyday life, see a visual demonstration of the activity, and complete a short assessment, visit the Computer Concepts CourseMate Web site at www.cengagebrain.com and then navigate to the Chapter 7 Learn How To resource for this book.

Learn How To 1: Maintain a Hard Disk

A computer's hard disk is used for the majority of storage requirements. It is important, therefore, to ensure that each hard disk on a computer is operating at peak efficiency.

Three tasks that maximize disk operations are detecting and repairing disk errors by using the Check Disk utility program; removing unused or unnecessary files and folders by using the Disk Cleanup utility program; and consolidating files and folders into contiguous storage areas using the Disk Defragmenter utility program.

A. Check Disk

To detect and repair disk errors using the Check Disk utility program, complete the following steps:

1. Click the Start button on the Windows taskbar and then click Computer on the Start menu.
2. When the Computer window opens, right-click the hard disk icon for drive C (or any other hard disk you want to select) and then click Properties on the shortcut menu.
3. In the Properties dialog box, if necessary, click the Tools tab to display the Tools sheet. The Tools sheet contains buttons to start the Check Disk program, the Defragment program, and the Backup program (Figure 7-42).
4. Click the Check now button to display the Check Disk dialog box.
5. To do a complete scan of the disk and correct any errors that are found, place a checkmark in the 'Scan for and attempt recovery of bad sectors' check box, and then click the Start button. Four phases of checking the disk will occur. While the checking is in progress, the disk being checked cannot be used for any purpose whatsoever; furthermore, once it has started, the process cannot be stopped. If the Check Disk program cannot check the disk because it is in use, you can schedule the disk check to run next time you start the computer.
6. When the four phases are complete (this may take more than one-half hour, depending on the size of the hard disk and how many corrections must occur), a dialog box is displayed with the message, Disk Check Complete. Click the OK button in the dialog box.

B. Cleanup Disk

After checking the disk, your next step can be to clean up the disk by removing any programs and data that are not required for the computer. To do so, complete the following steps:

1. Click the General tab (Figure 7-42) in the disk drive Properties dialog box to display the General sheet.
2. Click the Disk Cleanup button in the General sheet to display the Disk Cleanup Options dialog box.
3. The Disk Cleanup dialog box is displayed and contains a message that indicates the amount of space that can be freed up is being calculated.
4. After the calculation is complete, the Disk Cleanup dialog box specifies the amount of space that can be freed up and the files to delete, some of which are selected automatically (Figure 7-43). Select those items from which you wish to delete files.

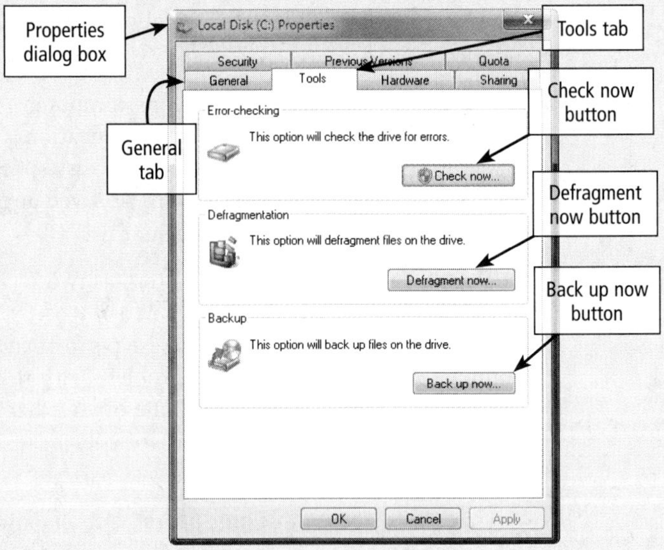

Figure 7-42

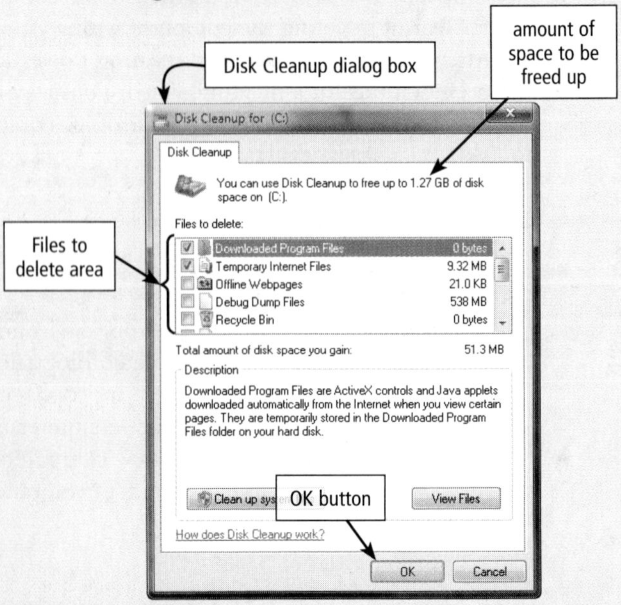

Figure 7-43

Learn How To

5. Click the OK button in the Disk Cleanup dialog box.
6. A dialog box asks if you are sure you want to perform these actions. Click the Delete Files button. The Disk Cleanup dialog box illustrates the progress of the cleanup. When the cleanup is complete, the dialog box closes.

C. Defragment Disk

The next step in disk maintenance is to defragment all the files on the disk. When a file is stored on disk, the data in the file sometimes is stored contiguously, and other times is stored in a noncontiguous manner. When a file is stored in a noncontiguous manner, it can take significantly longer to find and retrieve data from the file. One of the more useful utilities to speed up disk operations, therefore, is the defragmentation program, which combines all files so that no files are stored in a noncontiguous manner. To use the defragmentation program, complete the following steps:

1. If necessary, click the Tools tab (Figure 7-42) in the Properties dialog box for the hard disk to be defragmented.
2. Click the Defragment now button in the Tools sheet to open the Disk Defragmenter window (Figure 7-44). This window displays the Disk Defragmenter schedule, when Disk Defragmenter was run last, and when Disk Defragmenter is scheduled to run next.
3. Click the Defragment disk button to begin the defragmentation process. During the defragmentation process, the Stop operation button replaces the Defragment disk button. The defragmentation process can consume more than one hour in some cases. You can cancel the operation at any time by clicking the Stop operation button in the Disk Defragmenter window.
4. When the process is complete, the Defragment disk button will replace the Stop operation button.
5. Click the Close button to close the Disk Defragmenter window.

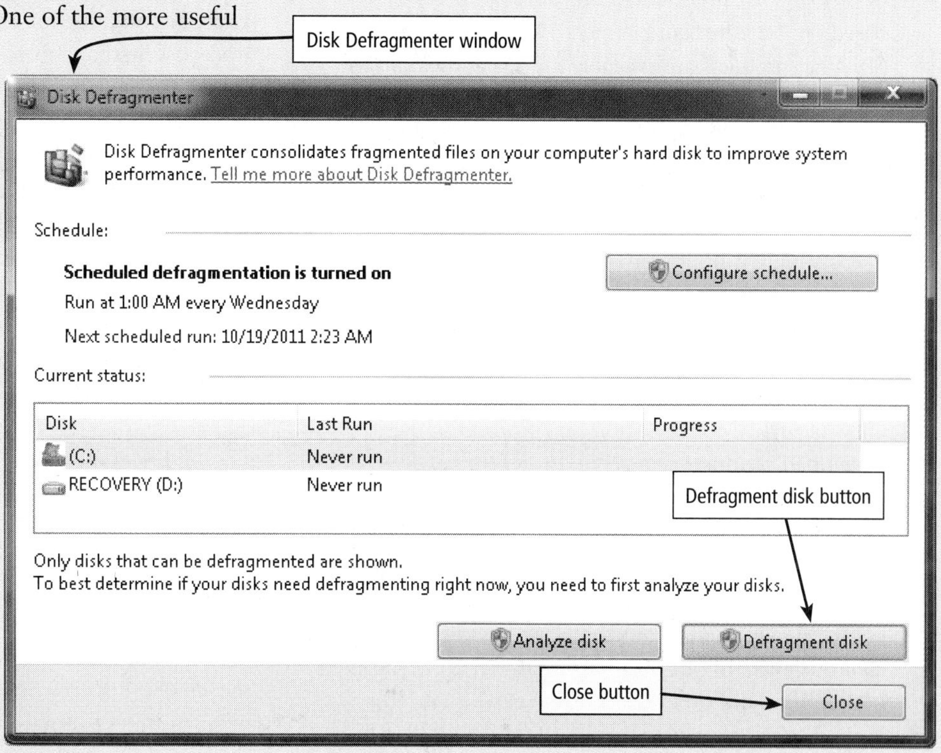

Figure 7-44

Exercises

Caution: The exercises for this chapter that require actual disk maintenance are optional. If you are performing these exercises on a computer that is not your own, obtain explicit permission to complete these exercises. Keep in mind that these exercises can require significant computer time and the computer may be unusable during this time.

1. Display the Properties dialog box for a hard disk found on the computer. Display the Tools sheet. Click the Check now button and then place a check mark in the 'Scan for and attempt recovery of bad sectors' check box. Click the Start button. How long did it take to complete the check of the hard disk? Were any errors discovered and corrected? Submit your answers to your instructor.
2. Display the Properties dialog box for a hard disk found on the computer. Display the General sheet. What is the capacity of the hard disk? How much space is used? How much free space is available? Click the Disk Cleanup button. How much space can be freed up if you use the Disk Cleanup program? Click the OK button to clean up the disk. How long did it take to perform the disk cleanup? Submit your answers to your instructor.
3. Display the Properties dialog box for a hard disk found on the computer. Display the Tools sheet. Click the Defragment now button. In the Disk Defragmenter window, click the Defragment disk button. How could you tell when the defragmentation process completes? How long did defragmentation require? Submit your answers to your instructor.

Web Research

The Web Research exercises broaden your understanding of the chapter concepts by presenting questions that require you to search the Web for answers.

1 Search Sleuth

Use one of the search engines listed in Figure 2-10 in Chapter 2 on page 85 or your own favorite search engine to find the answers to the following questions. Copy and paste the Web address from the Web page where you found the answer. Some questions may have more than one answer. If required, submit your answers to your instructor. (1) What album did Hillsong United release in 2008 on a flash drive embedded in a rubber wristband? (2) What country uses the MyKad smart card for national identification? (3) What product did HP develop in 2004 based on the efforts of engineer Daryl Anderson? (4) What products are available for sale at the SanDisk Plaza? (5) For what storage medium are phase change alloys used? (6) What company introduced using a hard disk for accounting projects in 1956?

2 Green Computing

Data storage is doubling every 18 months according to some computer industry experts, and consumers and businesses are turning to environmentally sound methods of backing up and storing files. Accessing hard disks consumes 80 percent of a storage system's electrical consumption, so companies have developed products that reduce a system's energy usage. Businesses invest in cooling systems that dissipate the heat generated when servers and storage hardware operate. Locate Web sites that describe these products and how they operate efficiently to conserve energy. How much energy savings do they claim to make in one year? To what extent are carbon dioxide and other greenhouse gases reduced? How do they maximize the use of power and cooling resources? Review your search results and then write a 50-word summary of your findings.

3 Social Networking

Privacy on social networking Web sites such as MySpace and Facebook is an international concern, and the Electronic Privacy Information Center (epic.org/privacy/socialnet) features news, policies, and resources discussing safeguarding and controlling personal information. At least one-fourth of hiring managers admit to researching job applicants' "digital dirt" by searching social networks and blogs, and some employers search social networking Web sites for profiles of current employees. Visit the Reputation Defender (reputationdefender.com) and Defend My Name (defendmyname.com) Web sites and read about the services offered. Then view the standards posted on the MySpace and Facebook Web sites regarding privacy and allowable content. Summarize the information you read and viewed.

4 Blogs

Exercise and nutrition advice is available from experts who post firsthand experiences in their blogs. These authorities may be people who share a particular experience, such as losing weight or training for a marathon, or who have specialized training in the fitness field. For example, noted author Lou Schuler discusses nutrition, weight training, and issues of particular interest to men (malepatternfitness.com). Other popular fitness blogs are featured by The Families.com (fitness.families.com/blog) and Diet-Blog (diet-blog.com). Athlete Blog Central (yardbarker.com/athletes) lists blogs that professional and amateur athletes and their fans write. Visit these sites and read the posts. Which stories received more than 25 comments? Which food, exercises, and programs are featured?

5 Ethics in Action

The United States Federal Bureau of Investigation used a controversial program until January 2005 to monitor and store the e-mail and Internet activity of suspected criminals. Originally called Carnivore, the surveillance program was renamed DCS1000. The program was designed to track the activities of potential terrorists, spies, drug traffickers, and organized crime ring members. FBI agents needed to obtain a court order to monitor an individual, but privacy advocates claim the software tracked people not covered under the court order. View online sites that provide information about DCS1000 or Carnivore, including HowStuffWorks (howstuffworks.com/carnivore.htm). What commercial software has replaced Carnivore? Write a report summarizing your findings, and include a table of links to Web sites that provide additional details.

Critical Thinking

The Critical Thinking exercises challenge your assessment and decision-making skills by presenting real-world situations associated with the chapter concepts. The Collaboration exercise should be completed with a team.

To evaluate the situations below, use personal experiences and available resources such as articles on the Web or in print, blogs, podcasts, videos, television, user guides, other individuals, and electronics and computer stores. You may need to use multiple resources to form conclusions and make recommendations.

1. Class Discussion — Cloud Storage
The owner of the motorcycle repair shop where you are employed as a part-time office manager is seeking alternatives to continually upgrading the company's computers. After attending a seminar about how small businesses can make use of the Internet, she asked you to look into the feasibility of using cloud storage, rather than purchasing additional storage for the company's computer. Analyze and discuss the advantages and disadvantages of using cloud storage. Include in your discussion a comparison between Box.net and Windows Live SkyDrive cloud storage offerings. Which company offers the best arrangement? Why?

2. Class Presentation — Increasing Storage Capacity
An old aphorism claims, "You never can have too much money." Many computer users support a similar maxim, "You never can have too much storage." Your manager at MJ National Bank where you are employed as an analyst, however, would prefer other options to buying more hardware to meet the bank's storage needs. She wants you to investigate alternative ways to increase storage capacity. Use the Web and/or print media to learn more about hard disk partitions and data compression as a means of increasing storage capacity. Evaluate the differences among various data compression algorithms. Prepare a presentation that shows how partitions and compression increase the capacity of hard disks. Include the following in your presentation: What kind of data compression is most suitable for storage devices? What are the most well known data compression algorithms? How can compression ratios of different algorithms be compared? What are some formats for data compression archives?

3. Research — Permanently Removing Data
Many companies and government agencies make extensive efforts to protect the data and information stored on their computers. When a computer reaches the end of its useful life, it either is recycled or thrown away. Although the obsolete computer does not perform well, if at all, the data on the hard disk often is intact. For this reason, companies and government agencies take precautionary measures to remove the data and information so that someone else cannot recover it and use it for malicious purposes. Use the Internet to find ways that some companies currently destroy their data before discarding their computers. Next, locate at least three programs that permanently can destroy data on a hard disk. Finally, prepare a report recommending to your instructor which method or program is the best for destroying data so that nobody can recover it.

Collaboration

4. Computers in Telemarketing Your team has been assigned to perform IT research for a new local magazine-subscription telemarketing company that is about to open for business. The company's business plan calls for 150 telemarketers to make a minimum of 100 calls a day. If a telemarketer does not meet the minimum number of calls, then he or she is required to finish the calls from home. The company plans to buy used computers for each telemarketer to use at home. The company also must decide on the type of storage device to provide the telemarketers so that when they have to make calls from home, they have a way to take the necessary data home with them. Senior management has narrowed down their choice to three storage devices — rewritable optical discs, cloud storage, or USB flash drives. Form a three-member team. Each team member should choose and research a different storage device. Using the Web and/or print media, each team member should evaluate the advantages and disadvantages of their chosen device. Include features such as capacity, access time, durability of media, ease of transporting between home and office, and cost. As a team, merge your findings and prepare a presentation to share your recommendations with your class.

Chapter Eight

Operating Systems and Utility Programs

Objectives

After completing this chapter, you will be able to:

1 Define system software and identify the two types of system software

2 Describe each of these functions of an operating system: starting and shutting down a computer, providing a user interface, managing programs, managing memory, coordinating tasks, configuring devices, establishing an Internet connection, monitoring performance, providing file management and other utilities, updating automatically, controlling a network, and administering security

3 Summarize the startup process on a personal computer

4 Summarize the features of several stand-alone operating systems: Windows, Mac OS, UNIX, and Linux

5 Briefly describe various server operating systems: Windows Server, UNIX, Linux, Solaris, and NetWare

6 Summarize the features of several embedded operating systems: Windows Embedded CE, Windows Phone, Palm OS, iPhone OS, BlackBerry, Google Android, Embedded Linux, and Symbian OS

7 Explain the purpose of several utility programs: file manager, search utility, image viewer, uninstaller, disk cleanup, disk defragmenter, backup and restore utilities, screen saver, personal firewall, antivirus programs, spyware and adware removers, Internet filters, file compression, media player, disc burning, and personal computer maintenance

System Software

When you purchase a personal computer, it usually has system software installed on its hard disk. **System software** consists of the programs that control or maintain the operations of the computer and its devices. System software serves as the interface between the user, the application software, and the computer's hardware.

Two types of system software are operating systems and utility programs. This chapter discusses the operating system and its functions, as well as several types of utility programs for personal computers.

Operating Systems

An **operating system (OS)** is a set of programs containing instructions that work together to coordinate all the activities among computer hardware resources. Most operating systems perform similar functions that include starting and shutting down a computer, providing a user interface, managing programs, managing memory, coordinating tasks, configuring devices, establishing an Internet connection, monitoring performance, providing file management and other utilities, and automatically updating itself and certain utility programs. Some operating

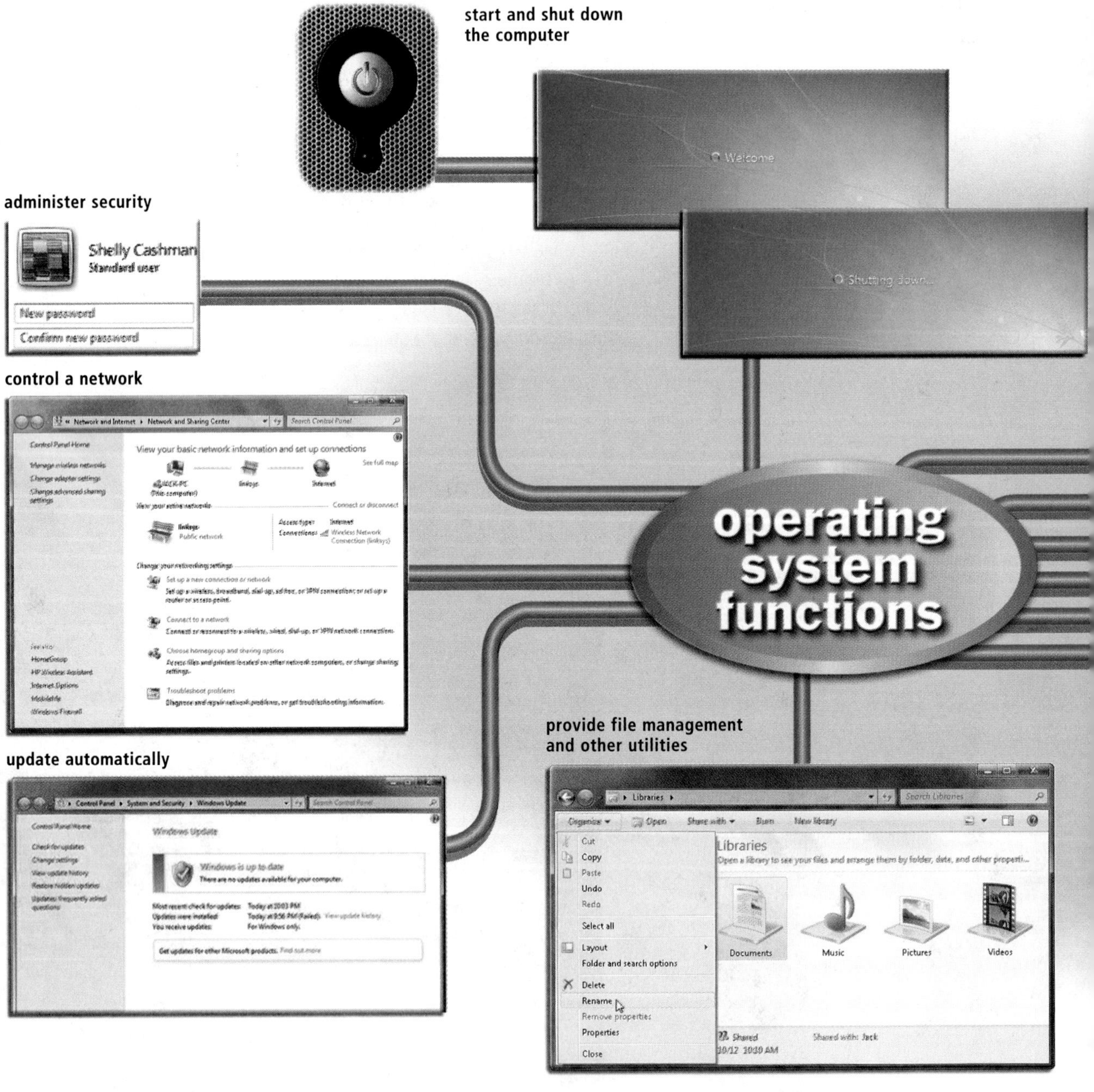

Figure 8-1 Most operating systems perform similar functions, which are illustrated with the latest version of Windows in this figure.

systems also allow users to control a network and administer security (Figure 8-1).

Although an operating system can run from an optical disc and/or flash memory mobile media, in most cases, the operating system is installed and resides on the computer's hard disk. On handheld computers and many mobile devices such as smart phones, the operating system may reside on a ROM chip.

Different sizes of computers typically use different operating systems because operating systems generally are written to run on a specific type of computer. For example, a mainframe computer does not use the same operating system as a personal computer. Even the same types of computers, such as desktop computers, may not use the same operating system. Some, however, can run multiple operating systems. When purchasing application software, you must ensure that it works with the operating system installed on your computer or mobile device.

The operating system that a computer uses sometimes is called the *platform*. With purchased application software, the package or specifications identify the required platform (operating system). A *cross-platform* program is one that runs the same on multiple operating systems.

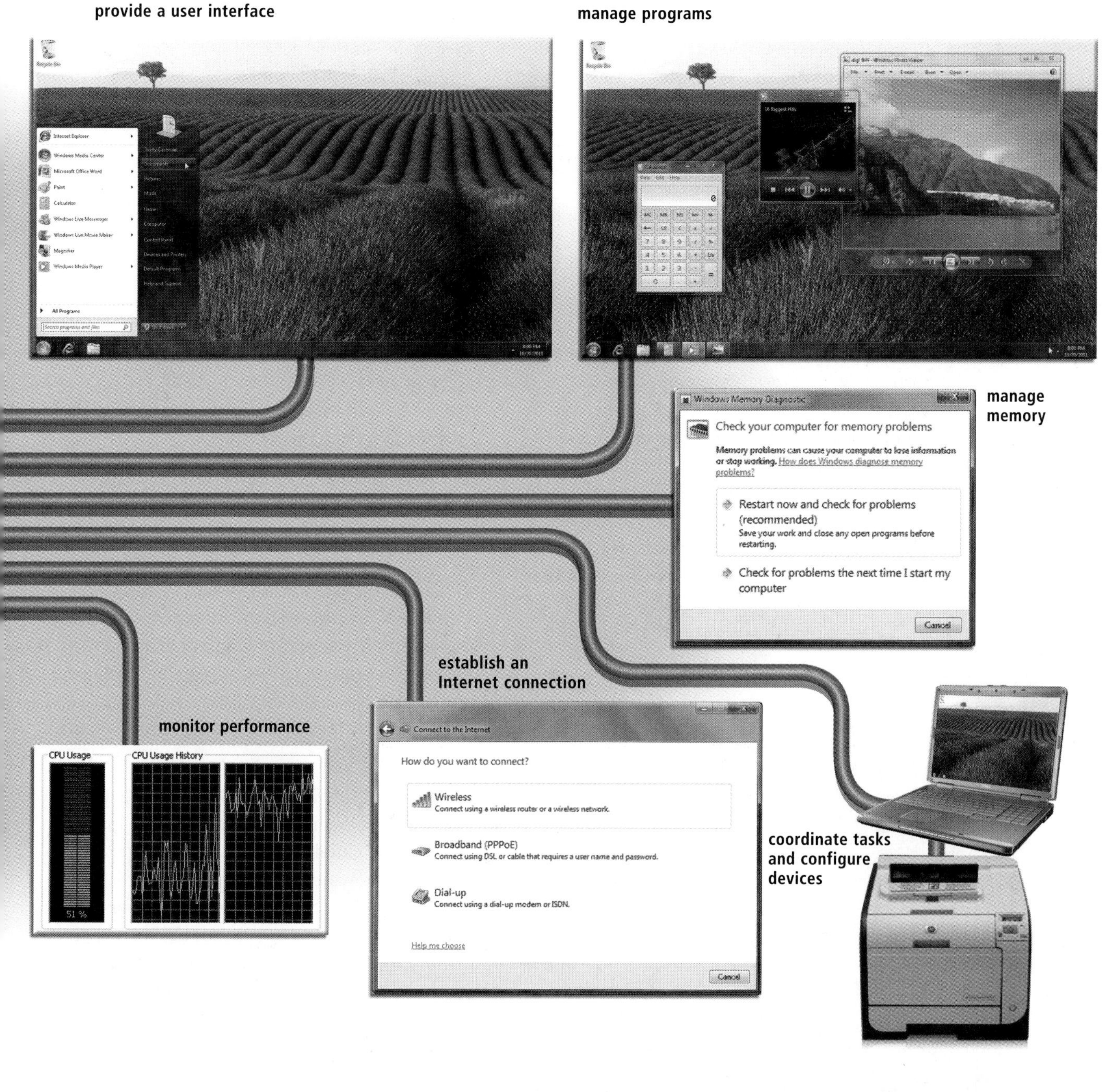

Operating System Functions

Many different operating systems exist, designed for all types of computers. Regardless of the size of the computer, however, most operating systems provide similar functions. The following sections discuss functions common to most operating systems. The operating system handles many of these functions automatically, without requiring any instructions from a user.

Starting and Shutting Down a Computer

The process of starting or restarting a computer is called **booting**. When turning on a computer that has been powered off completely, you are performing a **cold boot**. A **warm boot**, by contrast, is the process of using the operating system to restart a computer. A warm boot properly closes any running processes and programs; however, it does not save any unsaved work. Thus, always remember to save your work before rebooting (restarting) a computer.

With Windows, you can perform a warm boot by clicking the Start button on the taskbar, clicking the arrow next to the Shut down button on the Start menu, and then clicking Restart (Figure 8-2).

When you install new software or update existing software, often an on-screen prompt instructs you to restart the computer. In this case, a warm boot is appropriate. If the computer stops responding, try pressing and holding down the power button to turn off the computer. As a last resort, remove power from the computer and then restart the computer. On newer computers, pressing the power button momentarily is the same as a warm boot, whereas pressing and holding the power button does not properly close running processes and programs.

Each time you boot a computer, the kernel and other frequently used operating system instructions are loaded, or copied, from storage into the computer's memory (RAM). The *kernel* is the core of an operating system that manages memory and devices, maintains the computer's clock, starts programs, and assigns the computer's resources, such as devices, programs, data, and information. The kernel is *memory resident*, which means it remains in memory while the computer is running. Other parts of the operating system are *nonresident*, that is, these instructions remain on a storage medium until they are needed.

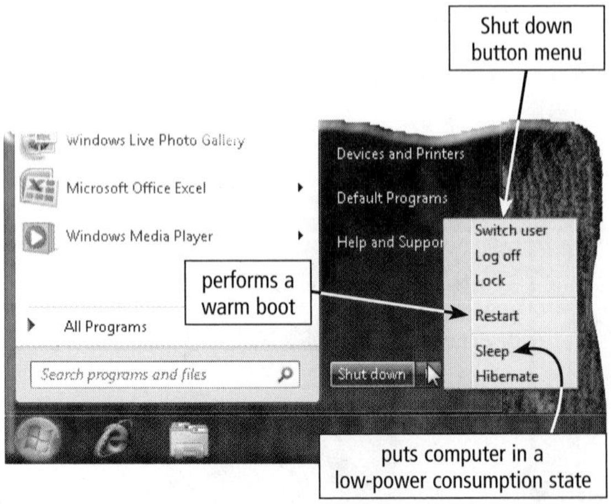

Figure 8-2 To reboot a running computer, click the Shut down button arrow and then click Restart.

When you boot a computer, a series of messages may appear on the screen. The actual information displayed varies depending on the make and type of the computer and the equipment installed. The boot process, however, is similar for large and small computers.

The steps in the following paragraphs explain what occurs during a cold boot on a personal computer using the Windows operating system. The steps in Figure 8-3 illustrate and correspond to the steps discussed in the following paragraphs.

Step 1: When you turn on the computer, the power supply sends an electrical signal to the components in the system unit.

Step 2: The charge of electricity causes the processor chip to reset itself and find the ROM chip(s) that contains the BIOS. The **BIOS** (pronounced BYE-ose), which stands for *basic input/output system*, is firmware that contains the computer's startup instructions.

Step 3: The BIOS executes a series of tests to make sure the computer hardware is connected properly and operating correctly. The tests, collectively called the *power-on self test (POST)*, check the various system components including the buses, system clock, adapter cards, RAM chips, mouse, keyboard, and drives. As the POST executes, LEDs (tiny lights) flicker on devices such as the disk drives and keyboard. Beeps also may sound, and messages may appear on the screen.

Step 4: The POST results are compared with data in a CMOS chip. As discussed in Chapter 4, CMOS is a technology that uses battery power to retain information when the computer is off. The CMOS chip stores configuration information about the computer, such as the amount of memory; type of disk drives, keyboard, and monitor; the current date and time; and other startup information. It also detects any new devices connected to the computer. If any problems are identified, the computer may beep, display error messages, or cease operating — depending on the severity of the problem.

Step 5: If the POST completes successfully, the BIOS searches for specific operating system files called *system files*. The BIOS may look first to see if a USB flash drive plugged in a USB port or a disc in an optical disc drive contains the system files, or it may look directly on drive C (the designation usually given to the first hard disk) for the system files.

Step 6: Once located, the system files load into memory (RAM) from storage (usually the hard disk) and execute. Next, the kernel of the operating system loads into memory. Then, the operating system in memory takes control of the computer.

Step 7: The operating system loads system configuration information. In the latest Windows versions, the *registry* consists of several files that contain the system configuration information. Windows constantly accesses the registry during the computer's operation for information such as installed hardware and software devices and individual user preferences for mouse speed, passwords, and other information. In addition, the Windows registry constantly checks credentials of users to verify they have the necessary privileges to run programs.

Necessary operating system files are loaded into memory. On some computers, the operating system verifies that the person attempting to use the computer is a legitimate user. Finally, the Windows desktop and icons are displayed on the screen. The operating system executes programs in the *Startup folder*, which contains a list of programs that open automatically when you boot the computer.

Windows Registry

For more information, visit the Computer Concepts CourseMate Web site at www.cengagebrain.com, navigate to the Chapter 8 Web Link resource for this book, and then click Windows Registry.

How a PC Boots

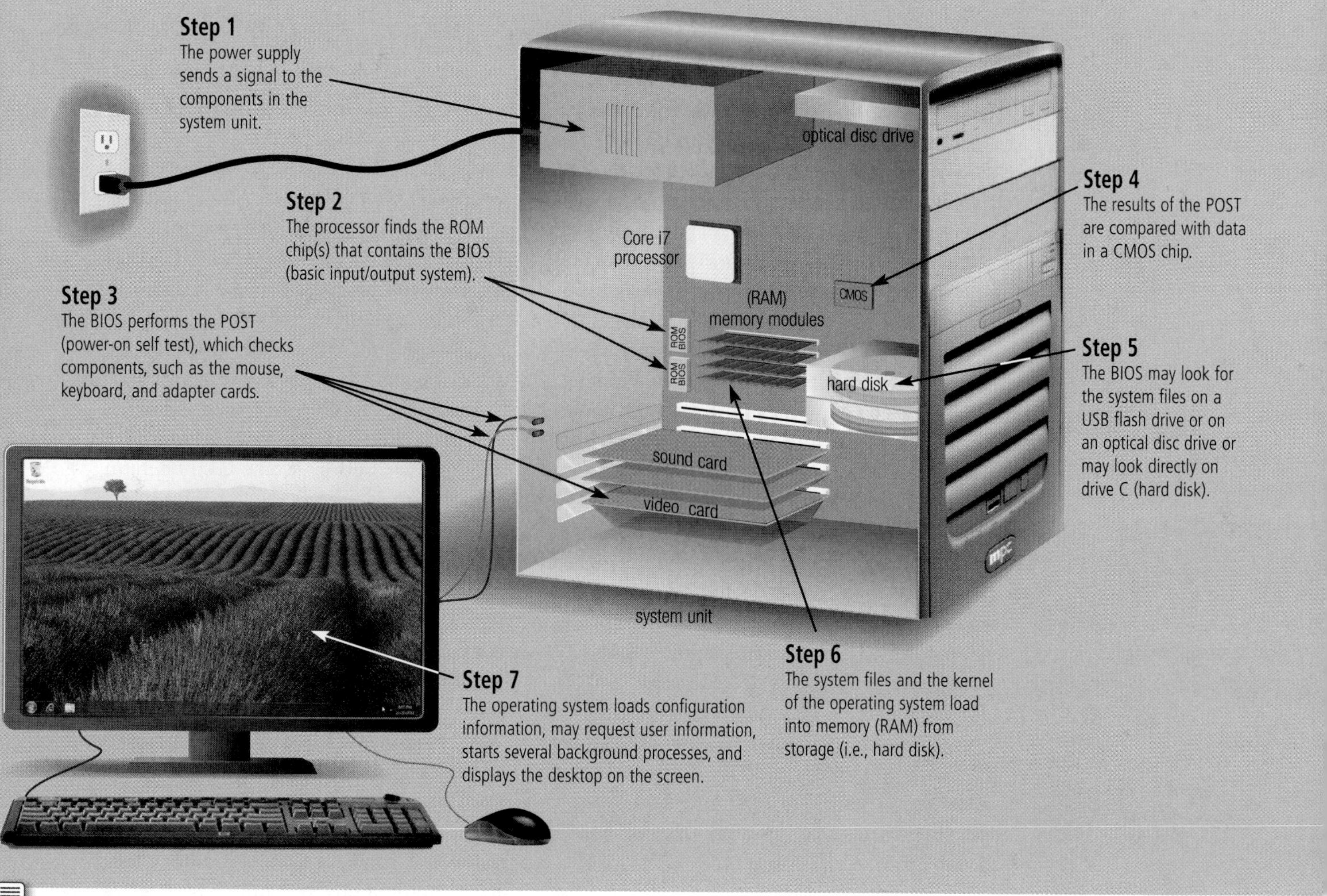

Step 1
The power supply sends a signal to the components in the system unit.
Step 2
The processor finds the ROM chip(s) that contains the BIOS (basic input/output system).
Step 3
The BIOS performs the POST (power-on self test), which checks components, such as the mouse, keyboard, and adapter cards.
Step 4
The results of the POST are compared with data in a CMOS chip.
Step 5
The BIOS may look for the system files on a USB flash drive or on an optical disc drive or may look directly on drive C (hard disk).
Step 6
The system files and the kernel of the operating system load into memory (RAM) from storage (i.e., hard disk).
Step 7
The operating system loads configuration information, may request user information, starts several background processes, and displays the desktop on the screen.
optical disc drive
Core i7 processor
CMOS
(RAM) memory modules
ROM BIOS
ROM BIOS
hard disk
sound card
video card
system unit

Figure 8-3 This figure shows how a PC boots.

Boot Disk A **boot drive** is the drive from which your personal computer boots (starts). In most cases, drive C (the hard disk) is the boot drive. Sometimes a hard disk becomes damaged and the computer cannot boot from the hard disk, or you may want to preview an operating system without installing it. In these cases, you can boot from a special disk, called a **boot disk** or a **recovery disk**, that contains a few system files that will start the computer. When the word, Live, is used with a type of media, such as Live CD or Live USB, this usually means the media can be used to boot the computer.

When you purchase a computer, it usually includes a boot disk in the form of an optical disc. If you do not have a boot disk, the operating system may provide a means to create one. With the latest versions of Windows, the installation disc is itself a boot disk, which you can use to start Windows in the event you cannot boot from the hard disk.

Shut Down Options Although some users leave their computers running continually and never turn them off, others choose to shut them down. Shut down options including powering off the computer, placing the computer in sleep mode, and hibernating the computer. Both sleep mode and hibernate, which store the current state of all open programs and documents, are designed to save time when you resume working on the computer. *Sleep mode* saves any open documents and programs to RAM, turns off all unneeded functions, and then places the computer in a low-power state. If, for some reason, power is removed from a computer that is in sleep mode, any unsaved work could be lost. *Hibernate*, by contrast, saves any open documents and programs to a hard disk before removing power from the computer.

The function of the Power button on a computer or mobile device varies, and users typically are able to configure its default behavior. When you press the Power button on a desktop computer, for example, it may place the computer in sleep mode or hibernate it. Pressing and holding down the Power button may remove all power from the computer. Closing the lid on a notebook computer may place the computer in a low-power state. The operating system also usually presents shut down options in menus, dialog boxes, or other means.

Sleep Mode

For more information, visit the Computer Concepts CourseMate Web site at www.cengagebrain.com, navigate to the Chapter 8 Web Link resource for this book, and then click Sleep Mode.

FAQ 8-1

Can shut down features wear out hardware by forcing the computer to turn on and off several times each day?

No. In fact, today's computers can be turned on and off more than 40,000 times before they fail. If the lifespan of a computer is 5 years, the computer would have to turn on and off nearly 22 times per day to become susceptible to failure after 5 years.

For more information, visit the Computer Concepts CourseMate Web site at www.cengagebrain.com, navigate to the Chapter 8 FAQ resource for this book, and then click Power Management.

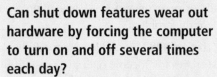

Providing a User Interface

You interact with software through its user interface. That is, a **user interface** controls how you enter data and instructions and how information is displayed on the screen. Two types of user interfaces are graphical and command-line. Operating systems often use a combination of these interfaces to define how a user interacts with a computer.

Graphical User Interface Most users today work with a graphical user interface. With a *graphical user interface* (*GUI*), you interact with menus and visual images such as buttons and other graphical objects to issue commands. Many current GUI operating systems incorporate features similar to those of a Web browser, such as links and navigation buttons (i.e., Back button and Forward button). Some GUI operating systems provide access to command-line interfaces, which are discussed in the next section.

Windows, for example, offers two different GUIs, depending on your hardware configuration. Computers with less than 1 GB of RAM work with the Windows 7 Basic interface (Figure 8-4a). Computers with more than 1 GB of RAM that have the required hardware may be able to work with the Windows 7 Aero interface, also known as *Windows Aero* (Figure 8-4b), which provides an enhanced visual look, additional navigation options, and animation.

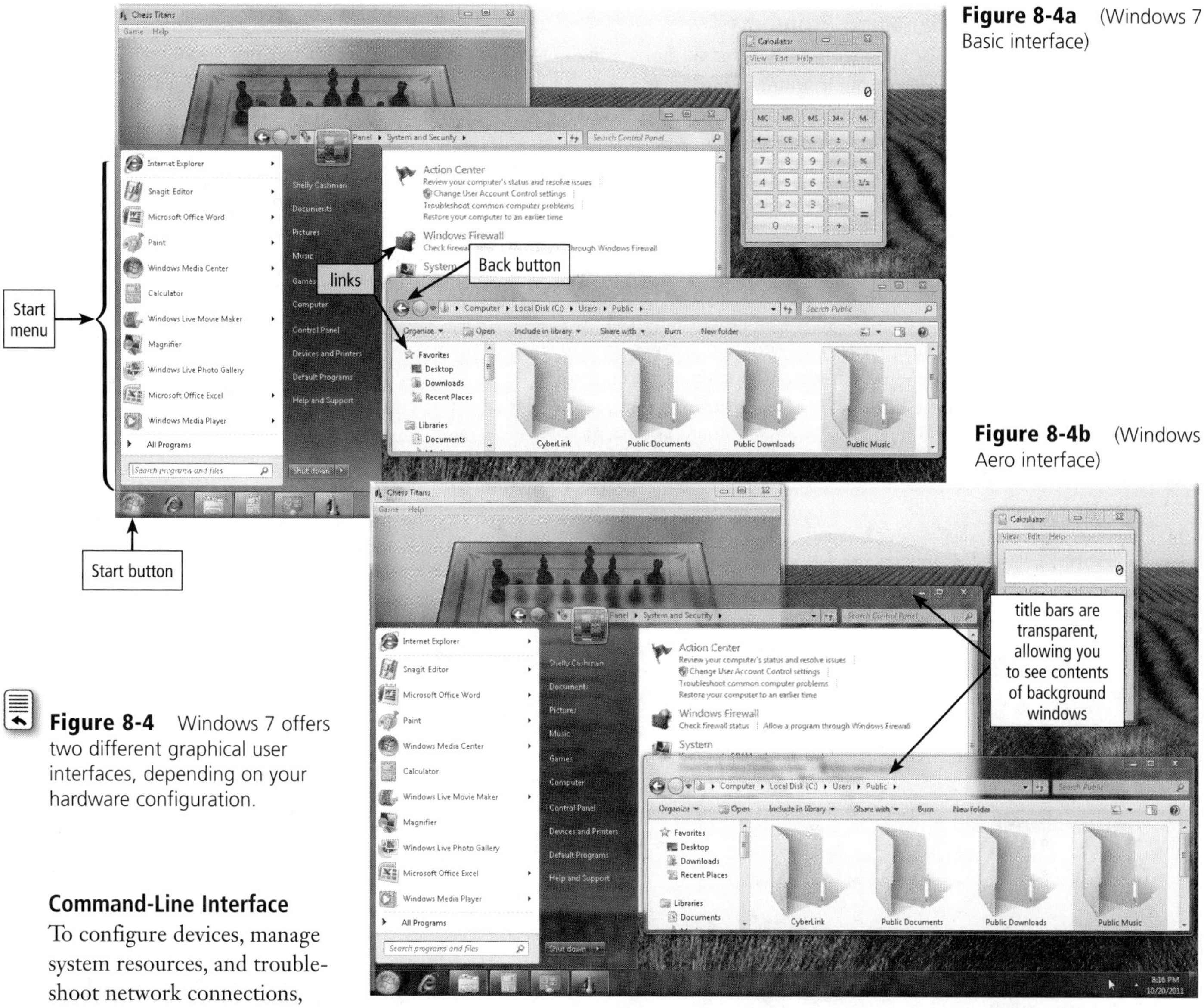

title bars are transparent, allowing you to see contents of background windows

Figure 8-4a (Windows 7 Basic interface)

Figure 8-4b (Windows 7 Aero interface)

Figure 8-4 Windows 7 offers two different graphical user interfaces, depending on your hardware configuration.

Command-Line Interface

To configure devices, manage system resources, and troubleshoot network connections, network administrators and other advanced users work with a command-line interface. In a *command-line interface*, a user types commands or presses special keys on the keyboard (such as function keys or key combinations) to enter data and instructions (Figure 8-5).

Some people consider command-line interfaces difficult to use because they require exact spelling, grammar, and punctuation. Minor errors, such as a missing period, generate an error message. Command-line interfaces, however, give a user more control to manage detailed settings. When working with a command-line interface, the set of commands entered into the computer is called the *command language*.

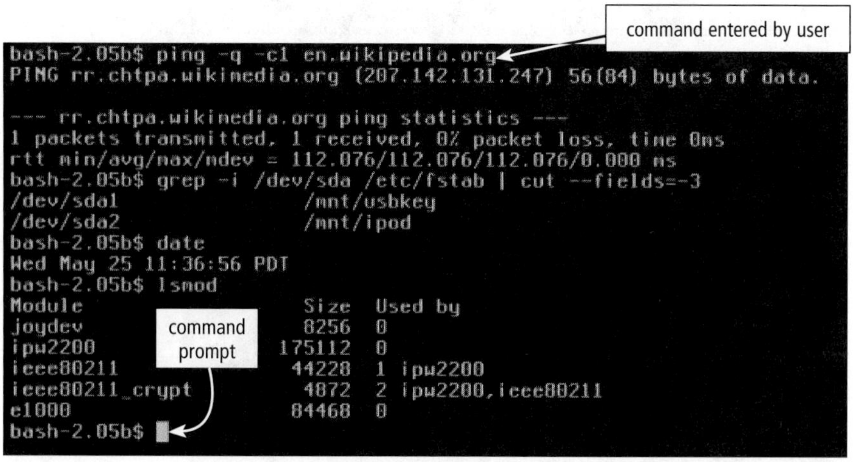
command entered by user
bash-2.05b$ ping -q -c1 en.wikipedia.org
PING rr.chtpa.wikimedia.org (207.142.131.247) 56(84) bytes of data.
--- rr.chtpa.wikimedia.org ping statistics ---
1 packets transmitted, 1 received, 0% packet loss, time 0ms
rtt min/avg/max/mdev = 112.076/112.076/112.076/0.000 ms
bash-2.05b$ grep -i /dev/sda /etc/fstab | cut --fields=-3
/dev/sda1 /mnt/usbkey
/dev/sda2 /mnt/ipod
bash-2.05b$ date
Wed May 25 11:36:56 PDT
bash-2.05b$ lsmod
Module Size Used by
joydev 8256 0
ipw2200 175112 0
ieee80211 44228 1 ipw2200
ieee80211_crypt 4872 2 ipw2200,ieee80211
e1000 84468 0
bash-2.05b$
command prompt

Figure 8-5 A command-line interface requires you enter exact spelling, grammar, and punctuation.

Managing Programs

Some operating systems support a single user and only one running program at a time. Others support thousands of users running multiple programs. How an operating system handles programs directly affects your productivity.

A *single user/single tasking* operating system allows only one user to run one program at a time. For example, if you are working in a graphics program and want to check e-mail messages, you must quit the graphics program before you can run the e-mail program. Early systems were single user/single tasking. Smart phones and other mobile devices, however, often use a single user/single tasking operating system. Most other operating systems today are multitasking.

A *single user/multitasking* operating system allows a single user to work on two or more programs that reside in memory at the same time. Using the example just cited, if you are working with a single user/multitasking operating system, you do not have to quit the graphics program to run the e-mail program. Both programs can run concurrently. Users today typically run multiple programs concurrently. It is common to have an e-mail program and Web browser open at all times, while working with application programs such as word processing or graphics.

When a computer is running multiple programs concurrently, one program is in the foreground and the others are in the background. The one in the *foreground* is the active program, that is, the one you currently are using. The other programs running but not in use are in the *background*. In Figure 8-6, the Windows

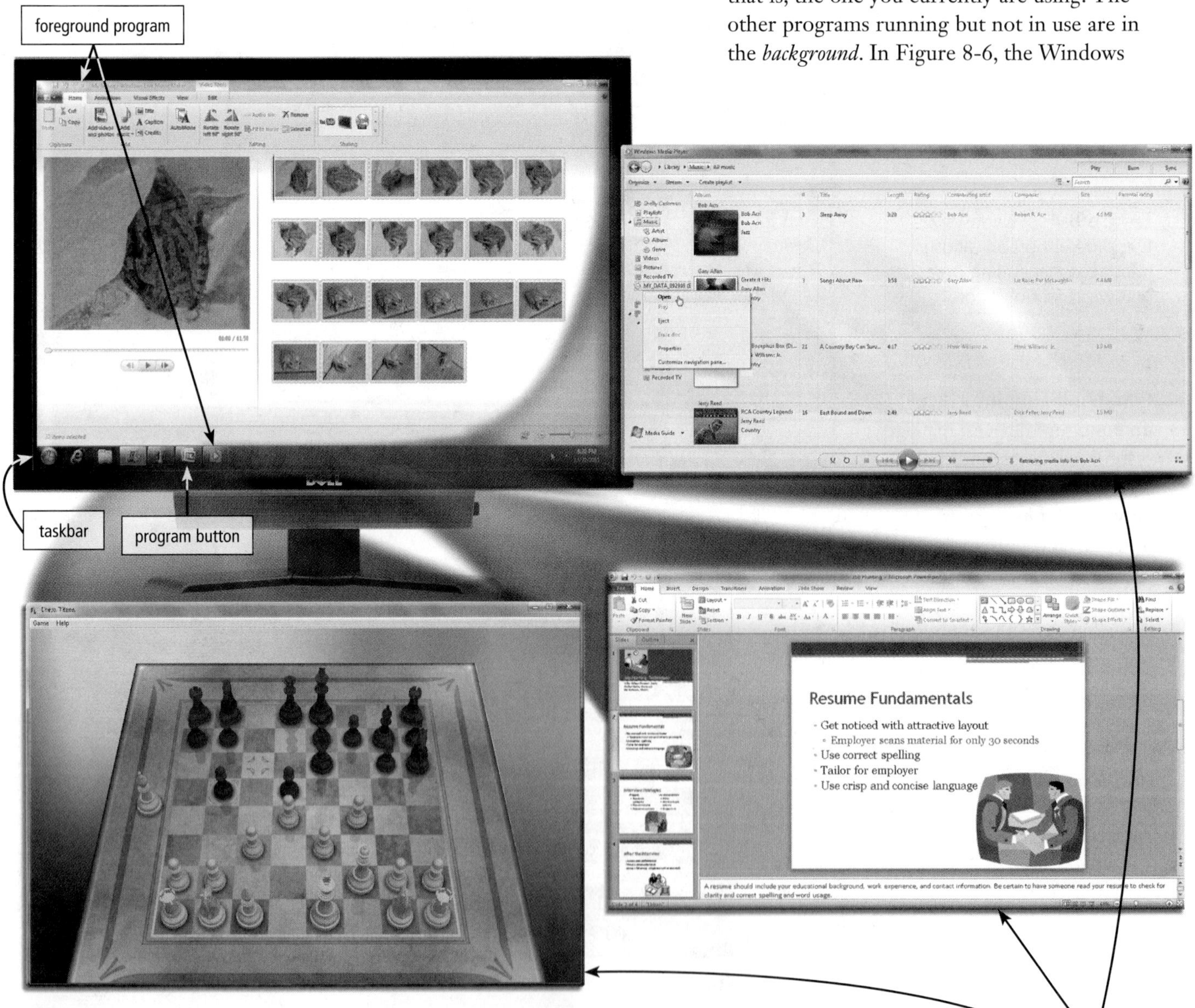

Figure 8-6 The foreground program, Windows Live Movie Maker, is displayed on the desktop. The other programs (Windows Media Player, Microsoft PowerPoint, and Chess Titans) are in the background.

Live Movie Maker program is in the foreground, and three other programs are running in the background (Windows Media Player, Microsoft PowerPoint and Chess Titans). For example, Windows Media Player can play music while you create a movie.

The foreground program typically displays on the desktop, and the background programs are hidden partially or completely behind the foreground program. You easily can switch between foreground and background programs. To make a program active (in the foreground) in Windows, click its program button on the taskbar. This causes the operating system to place all other programs in the background.

In addition to application programs, an operating system manages other processes. These processes include utilities or routines that provide support to other programs or hardware. Some are memory resident. Others run as they are required. Figure 8-7 shows a list of some processes running on a Windows computer. The list contains the applications programs running, as well as other programs and processes.

Some operating systems use preemptive multitasking to prevent any one process from monopolizing the computer's resources. With *preemptive multitasking*, the operating system interrupts a program that is executing and passes control to another program waiting to be executed. An advantage of preemptive multitasking is the operating system regains control if one program stops operating properly.

A *multiuser* operating system enables two or more users to run programs simultaneously. Networks, servers, mainframes, and supercomputers allow hundreds to thousands of users to connect at the same time, and thus are multiuser.

A *multiprocessing* operating system supports two or more processors running programs at the same time. Multiprocessing involves the coordinated processing of programs by more than one processor. Multiprocessing increases a computer's processing speed.

A computer with separate processors also can serve as a fault-tolerant computer. A *fault-tolerant computer* continues to operate when one of its components fails, ensuring that no data is lost. Fault-tolerant computers have duplicate components such as processors, memory, and disk drives. If any one of these components fails, the computer switches to the duplicate component and continues to operate. Airline reservation systems, communications networks, automated teller machines, and other systems that must be operational at all times use fault-tolerant computers.

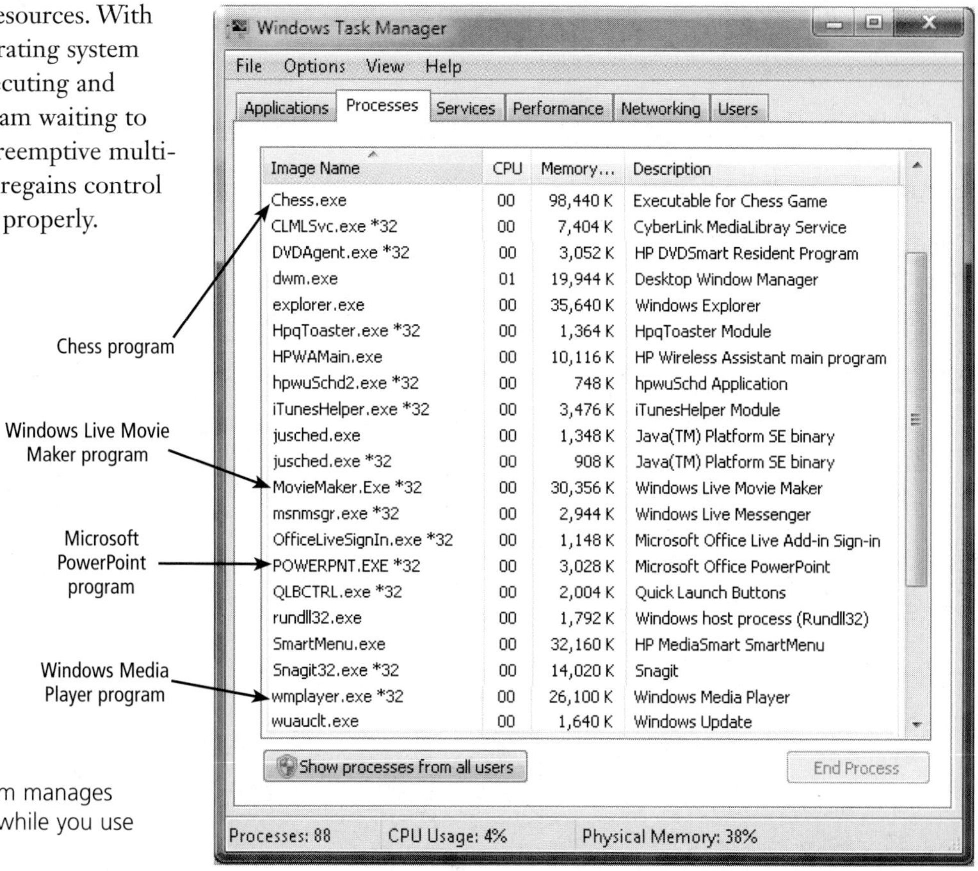

Figure 8-7 An operating system manages multiple programs and processes while you use the computer.

Managing Memory

The purpose of **memory management** is to optimize the use of random access memory (RAM). As Chapter 4 discussed, RAM consists of one or more chips on the motherboard that hold items such as data and instructions while the processor interprets and executes them. The operating system allocates, or assigns, data and instructions to an area of memory while they are being processed. Then, it carefully monitors the contents of memory. Finally, the operating system releases these items from being monitored in memory when the processor no longer requires them.

If you have multiple programs running simultaneously, it is possible to run out of RAM. For example, assume an operating system requires 512 MB of RAM, an antivirus program — 256 MB of RAM, a Web browser — 128 MB of RAM, a business software suite — 512 MB of RAM, and a photo editing program — 256 MB of RAM. With all these programs running simultaneously, the total RAM required would be 1664 MB of RAM (512 + 256 + 128 + 512 + 256). If the computer has only 1 GB of RAM, the operating system may have to use virtual memory to solve the problem.

With **virtual memory**, the operating system allocates a portion of a storage medium, usually the hard disk, to function as additional RAM (Figure 8-8). As you interact with a program, part of it may be in physical RAM, while the rest of the program is on the hard disk as virtual memory. Because virtual memory is slower than RAM, users may notice the computer slowing down while it uses virtual memory.

The area of the hard disk used for virtual memory is called a *swap file* because it swaps (exchanges) data, information, and instructions between memory and storage. A *page* is the amount of data and program instructions that can swap at a given time. The technique of swapping items between memory and storage, called *paging*, is a time-consuming process for the computer.

When an operating system spends much of its time paging, instead of executing application software, it is said to be *thrashing*. If application software, such as a Web browser, has stopped responding and the hard disk's LED blinks repeatedly, the operating system probably is thrashing.

Instead of using a hard disk as virtual memory, Windows users can increase the size of memory through *Windows ReadyBoost*, which can allocate

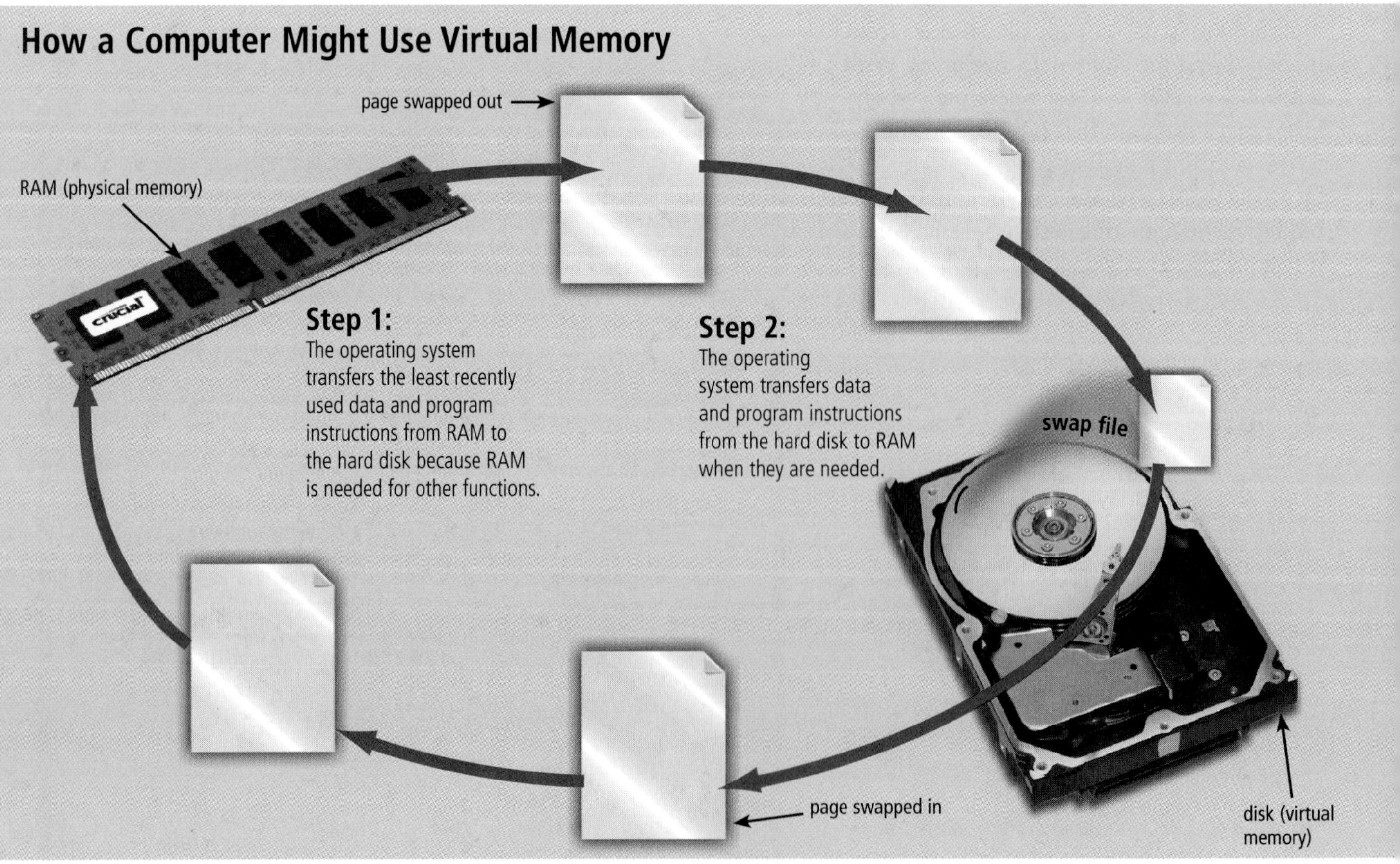
How a Computer Might Use Virtual Memory
page swapped out
RAM (physical memory)
Step 1:
The operating system transfers the least recently used data and program instructions from RAM to the hard disk because RAM is needed for other functions.
Step 2:
The operating system transfers data and program instructions from the hard disk to RAM when they are needed.
swap file
page swapped in
disk (virtual memory)

Figure 8-8 This figure shows how a computer might use virtual memory.

available storage space on removable flash memory devices as additional memory cache. Users notice better peformance with Windows ReadyBoost versus hard disk virtual memory because the operating system accesses a flash memory device, such as a USB flash drive or SD memory card, more quickly than it accesses a hard disk.

FAQ 8-2

How can I stop a computer from thrashing?

Try to quit the program that stopped responding. If the computer does not respond and continues to thrash, do a warm boot. When the computer reboots, check whether the available hard disk space is less than 200 MB. If it is, remove unnecessary files from the hard disk and if possible uninstall seldom used programs. Defragment the hard disk (discussed later in this chapter). If thrashing continues to occur, you may need to install more RAM in the computer.

For more information, visit the Computer Concepts CourseMate Web site at www.cengagebrain.com, navigate to the Chapter 8 FAQ resource for this book, and then click Optimizing Memory.

Coordinating Tasks

The operating system determines the order in which tasks are processed. A task, or job, is an operation the processor manages. Tasks include receiving data from an input device, processing instructions, sending information to an output device, and transferring items from storage to memory and from memory to storage.

A mulituser operating system does not always process tasks on a first-come, first-served basis. Sometimes, one user may have a higher priority than other users. In this case, the operating system adjusts the schedule of tasks.

Sometimes, a device already may be busy processing one task when it receives a second task. This occurs because the processor operates at a much faster rate of speed than peripheral devices. For example, if the processor sends five documents to a printer, the printer can print only one document at a time and store as many documents as its memory can handle.

While waiting for devices to become idle, the operating system places items in buffers. A **buffer** is a segment of memory or storage in which items are placed while waiting to be transferred from an input device or to an output device.

The operating system commonly uses buffers with printed documents. This process, called **spooling**, sends documents to be printed to a buffer instead of sending them immediately to the printer. If a printer does not have its own internal memory or if its memory is full, the operating system's buffer holds the documents waiting to print while the printer prints from the buffer at its own rate of speed. By spooling documents to a buffer, the processor can continue interpreting and executing instructions while the printer prints. This allows users to work on the computer for other activities while a printer is printing. Multiple documents line up in a **queue** (pronounced Q) in the buffer. A program, called a *print spooler*, intercepts documents to be printed from the operating system and places them in the queue (Figure 8-9).

Spooling

For more information, visit the Computer Concepts CourseMate Web site at www.cengagebrain.com, navigate to the Chapter 8 Web Link resource for this book, and then click Spooling.

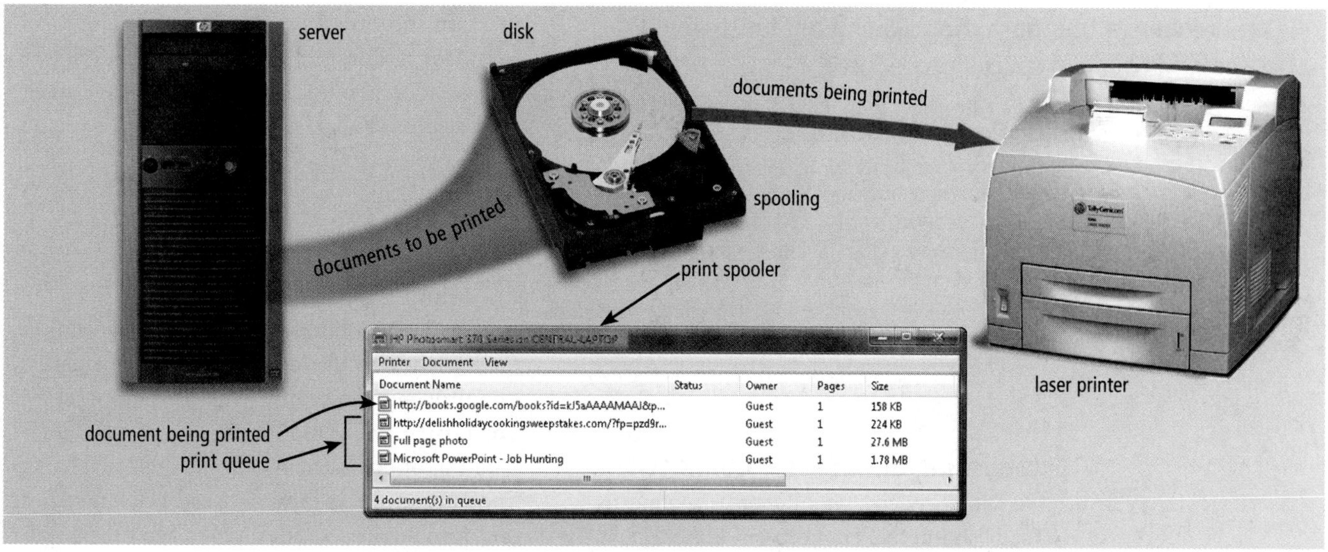

Figure 8-9 Spooling increases both processor and printer efficiency by placing documents to be printed in a buffer on disk before they are printed. This figure illustrates three documents in the queue with one document printing.

Configuring Devices

A **driver**, short for *device driver*, is a small program that tells the operating system how to communicate with a specific device. Each device on a computer, such as the mouse, keyboard, monitor, printer, card reader/writer, and scanner, has its own specialized set of commands and thus requires its own specific driver. When you boot a computer, the operating system loads each device's driver. These devices will not function without their correct drivers.

If you attach a new device to a computer, such as a printer or scanner, its driver must be installed before you can use the device. Today, most devices and operating systems support Plug and Play. As discussed in Chapter 4, **Plug and Play** means the operating system automatically configures new devices as you install them. Specifically, it assists you in the device's installation by loading the necessary drivers automatically and checking for conflicts with other devices. With Plug and Play, a user plugs in a device, turns on the computer, and then uses the device without having to configure the system manually. Devices that connect to a USB port on the system unit typically are Plug and Play.

Manufacturers often update a device's driver. For example, the update may enable the device to work with a new operating system, or it may improve the reliability of the device. You can visit the manufacturer's Web site to determine if a driver has been updated. In some cases, you may be notified that a driver has been updated. Always be sure to install updated drivers.

Plug and Play

For more information, visit the Computer Concepts CourseMate Web site at www.cengagebrain.com, navigate to the Chapter 8 Web Link resource for this book, and then click Plug and Play.

? FAQ 8-3

Can I remove a USB flash drive when I am finished with it, or should I follow a special procedure?

Before removing an external storage device from the USB port, you first should close all programs and files you have opened from the device. To avoid any chance of losing some or all data on the device, operating systems usually provide a means to ensure you can remove the device safely. In Windows, for example, if the Safely Remove Hardware and Eject Media icon appears on the taskbar, click it (or right-click the drive in the Computer window) and then click the appropriate Eject command on the menu.

For more information, visit the Computer Concepts CourseMate Web site at www.cengagebrain.com, navigate to the Chapter 8 FAQ resource for this book, and then click USB Flash Drives.

Establishing an Internet Connection

Operating systems typically provide a means to establish Internet connections. For example, Windows automatically configures some broadband Internet connections as soon as you connect to the broadband line. Otherwise, Windows includes a Set Up a Connection or Network wizard that guides users through the process of setting up a connection between a computer and an Internet access provider (Figure 8-10).

Some operating systems also include a Web browser and an e-mail program, enabling you to begin using the Web and communicate with others as soon as you set up the Internet connection. Some also include utilities to protect computers from unauthorized intrusions and unwanted software such as viruses and spyware.

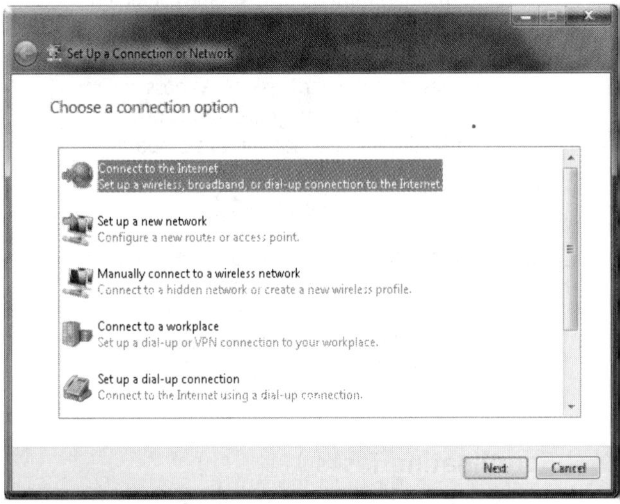

Figure 8-10 To connect to a network using Windows, click the Start button, click Control Panel, click Network and Internet, click Network and Sharing Center, and then click 'Set up a new connection or network' to open the window shown here.

Monitoring Performance

Operating systems typically contain a performance monitor. A **performance monitor** is a program that assesses and reports information about various computer resources and devices (Figure 8-11). For example, users can monitor the processor, disks, network, and memory usage.

The information in performance reports helps users and administrators identify a problem with resources so that they can try to resolve any problems. If a computer is running extremely slow, for example, the performance monitor may determine that the computer's memory is being used to its maximum. Thus, you might consider installing additional memory in the computer. Read Looking Ahead 8-1 for a look at a future type of health-based performance monitor.

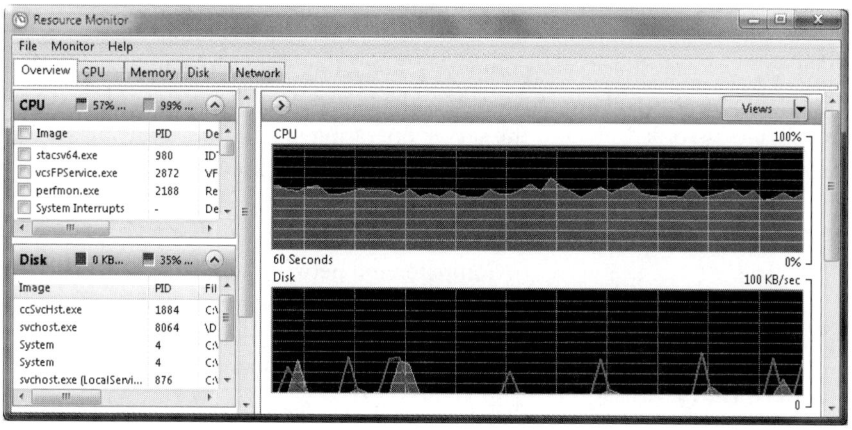

Figure 8-11 The Windows Resource Monitor above is tracking CPU (processor), disk, network, and memory usage.

Providing File Management and Other Utilities

Operating systems often provide users with the capability of managing files, searching for files, viewing images, securing a computer from unauthorized access, uninstalling programs, cleaning up disks, defragmenting disks, diagnosing problems, backing up files and disks, and setting up screen savers. A later section in the chapter discusses these and other utilities in depth. To learn about installing and maintaining a computer, complete the Learn How To 1 exercise on page 440.

Updating Software Automatically

Many popular programs, including most operating systems, include an **automatic update** feature that automatically provides updates to the program. With an operating system, these updates can include fixes to program *bugs*, or errors, enhancements to security, modifications to device drivers, access to new or expanded components such as desktop themes or games, and even updates to application software on the computer such as a Web browser or an e-mail program (Figure 8-12).

Many software makers provide free downloadable updates, sometimes called a *service pack*, to users who have registered and/or activated their software. With operating systems, the automatic update feature automatically alerts users when an update is

LOOKING AHEAD 8-1

Contact Lenses Monitor Glaucoma

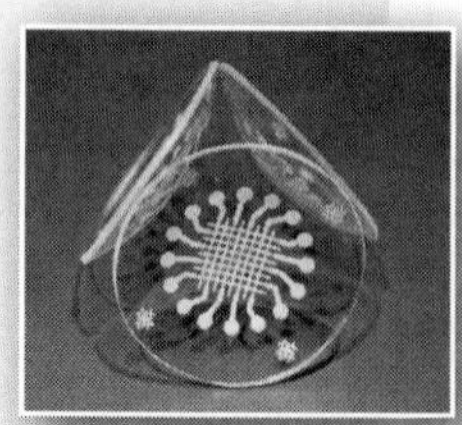

The future looks good for contact lenses that will help study and treat glaucoma. Biomedical engineers at the University of California – Davis are developing lenses that measure eye pressure and then flow if the readings are abnormal.

Glaucoma occurs when the fluid pressure inside the eye increases. This intraocular pressure can result in total blindness if the optic nerve, which sends messages from the eyes to the brain, is damaged. Doctors can measure the amount of pressure and then perform surgery to correct the blockage in the back of the eye that prevents the fluid from draining. As an alternative to the pressure measurement, the new contact lenses can perform the fluidic resistance evaluation for the drainage network of the eye, which prevents dangerously high levels in the early glaucomatous eyes.

Lasers, too, are expected to become part of a doctor's means of detecting glaucoma. A high-resolution laser can measure 28 million areas of the optic nerve, and then software can create a 3-D view of the eye and assess signs of the disease.

For more information, visit the Computer Concepts CourseMate Web site at www.cengagebrain.com, navigate to the Chapter 8 Looking Ahead resource for this book, and then click Contact Lenses.

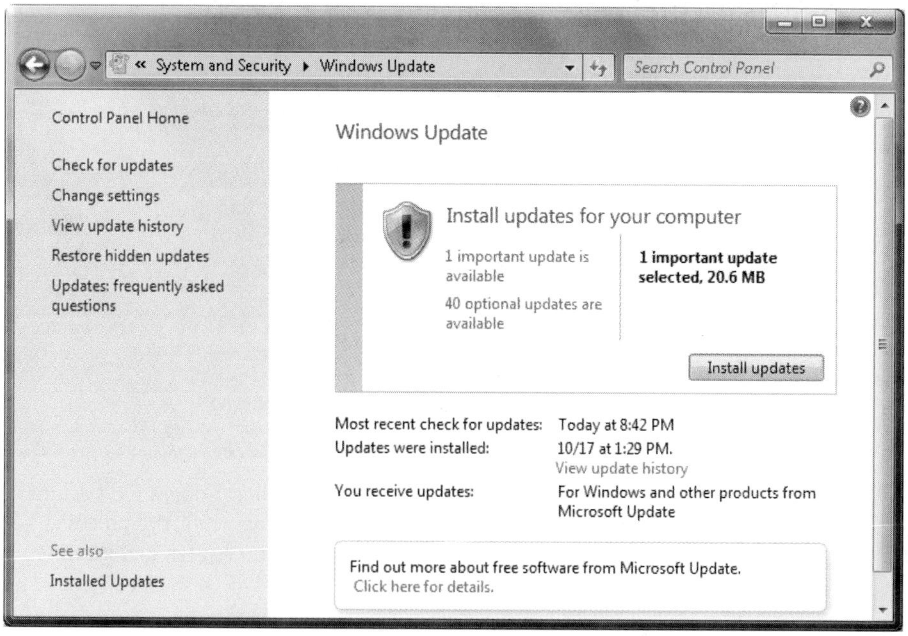

Figure 8-12 With Windows Update, you can download and install important operating system and utility updates.

available; further, it can be configured to download and install the update automatically. Read Ethics & Issues 8-1 for a related discussion. Users without an Internet connection usually can order the updates on an optical disc for a minimal shipping fee. To learn about keeping Windows up-to-date, complete the Learn How To 3 exercise on pages 440 and 441.

ETHICS & ISSUES 8-1

Is Operating System Automatic Update Software Dangerous?

When the feature is enabled, Microsoft Windows automatically downloads updates to a computer. One recent automatic update was installed even on computers that had the feature disabled. Microsoft claimed that the update was harmless and was for the benefit of its customers. Only later did some customers realize that this stealth update caused serious problems. Ironically, one problem was that updates no longer could be installed on the affected computers. Customers not only were furious about the problems, but many were angry that Microsoft was making changes to computers without the knowledge of the owners of the computers. One of the consequences of the ensuing outrage was that many people turned off the automatic update feature on their computers, fearing that future updates might cause even more damage. This action may backfire because these users may not receive critical security updates. Many people believe that Microsoft should be more forthcoming about its automatic update feature.

Should software companies be able to send automatic updates to your computer without your knowledge? Why or why not? How should software companies be held accountable when automatic software updates cause serious problems? Why? Who should determine actions to be taken against software companies that cause serious problems with automatic updates? Why?

Ethics & Issues

For the complete text of the Ethics & Issues boxes found in this chapter, visit the Computer Concepts CourseMate Web site at www.cengagebrain.com and then navigate to the Chapter 8 Ethics & Issues resource for this book.

Controlling a Network

Some operating systems are designed to work with a server on a network. A **server operating system** is an operating system that organizes and coordinates how multiple users access and share resources on a network. Resources include hardware, software, data, and information. For example, a server operating system allows multiple users to share a printer, Internet access, files, and programs.

Some operating systems have network features built into them. In other cases, the server operating system is a set of programs separate from the operating system on the client computers that access the network. When not connected to the network, the client computers use their own operating system. When connected to the network, the server operating system may assume some of the operating system functions.

The *network administrator*, the person overseeing network operations, uses the server operating system to add and remove users, computers, and other devices to and from the network. The network administrator also uses the server operating system to install software and administer network security.

Administering Security

Computer and network administrators typically have an *administrator account* that enables them to access all files and programs on the computer or network, install programs, and specify settings that affect all users on a computer or network. Settings include creating user accounts and establishing permissions. These *permissions* define who can access certain resources and when they can access those resources.

For each user, the computer or network administrator establishes a user account, which enables a user to access, or **log on** to, a computer or a network (Figure 8-13). Each user account typically consists of a user name and password. A **user name**, or **user ID**, is a unique combination of characters, such as letters of the alphabet or numbers, that identifies one specific user. Many users select a combination of their first and last names as their user name. A user named Henry Baker might choose H Baker as his user name.

A **password** is a private combination of characters associated with the user name that allows access to certain computer resources. Some operating systems allow the computer or network administrator to assign passwords to files and commands, restricting access to only authorized users.

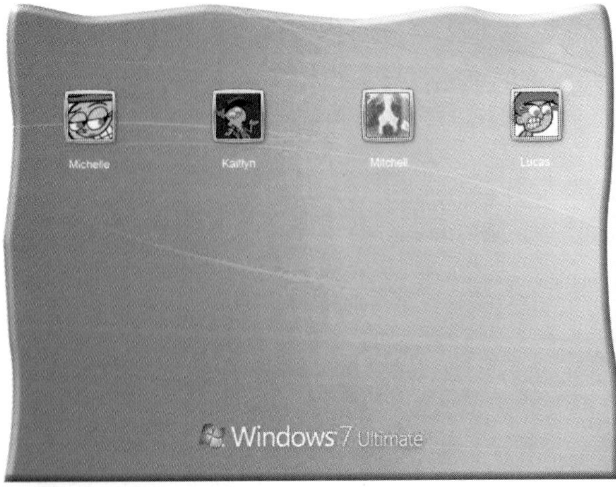

Figure 8-13 Most multiuser operating systems allow each user to log on, which is the process of entering a user name and a password into the computer.

To prevent unauthorized users from accessing computer resources, keep your password confidential. While users type a password, most computers hide the actual password characters by displaying some other characters, such as asterisks (*) or dots. After entering a user name and password, the operating system compares the user's entry with a list of authorized user names and passwords. If the entry matches the user name and password kept on file, the operating system grants the user access. If the entry does not match, the operating system denies access to the user.

The operating system records successful and unsuccessful logon attempts in a file. This allows the computer or network administrator to review who is using or attempting to use the computer. The administrators also use these files to monitor computer usage.

To protect sensitive data and information further as it travels over a network, the operating system may encrypt it. *Encryption* is the process of encoding data and information into an unreadable form. Administrators can specify that data be encrypted as it travels over a network to prevent unauthorized users from reading the data. When an authorized user attempts to read the data, it automatically is decrypted, or converted back into a readable form.

FAQ 8-4

What are the guidelines for selecting a good password?

Choose a password that is easy to remember, and that no one could guess. Do not use any part of your first or last name, your spouse's or child's name, telephone number, street address, license plate number, Social Security number, birthday, and so on. Be sure your password is at least eight characters long, mixed with uppercase and lowercase letters, numbers, and special characters. You also should avoid using single-word passwords that are found in the dictionary. Security experts also recommend using a *passphrase*, which is similar to a password, but comprised of several words separated by spaces.

For more information, visit the Computer Concepts CourseMate Web site at www.cengagebrain.com, navigate to the Chapter 8 FAQ resource for this book, and then click Passwords.

QUIZ YOURSELF 8-1

Instructions: Find the true statement below. Then, rewrite the remaining false statements so that they are true.

1. A buffer is a small program that tells the operating system how to communicate with a specific device.
2. A cold boot is the process of using the operating system to restart a computer.
3. A password is a public combination of characters associated with the user name that allows access to certain computer resources.
4. Firmware that contains the computer's startup instructions is called the kernel.
5. The program you currently are using is in the background, and the other programs running but not in use are in the foreground.
6. Two types of system software are operating systems and application programs.
7. With virtual memory, the operating system allocates a portion of a storage medium, usually the hard disk, to function as additional RAM.

Quiz Yourself Online: To further check your knowledge of pages 398 through 411, visit the Computer Concepts CourseMate Web site at www.cengagebrain.com, navigate to the Chapter 8 Quiz Yourself resource for this book, and then click Objectives 1 – 3.

Types of Operating Systems

Many of the first operating systems were device dependent and proprietary. A *device-dependent* program is one that runs only on a specific type or make of computer. *Proprietary software* is privately owned and limited to a specific vendor or computer model. Some operating systems still are device dependent. The trend today, however, is toward *device-independent* operating systems that run on computers provided by a variety of manufacturers. The advantage of device-independent operating systems is you can retain existing application software and data files even if you change computer models or vendors.

When you purchase a new computer or mobile device, it typically has an operating system preinstalled. As new versions of the operating system are released, users upgrade their existing computers and mobile devices to incorporate features of the new version. Purchasing an operating system upgrade usually costs less than purchasing the entire operating system.

New versions of an operating system usually are backward compatible. That is, they recognize and work with application software written for an earlier version of the operating system (or platform). The application software, by contrast, may or may not be upward compatible, meaning it may or may not run on new versions of the operating system.

The three basic categories of operating systems that exist today are stand-alone, server, and embedded. The table in Figure 8-14 lists specific names of operating systems in each category. The following pages discuss a variety of operating systems.

Categories of Operating Systems

Category	Operating System Name
Stand-alone	• DOS • Early Windows versions (Windows 3.x, Windows 95, Windows NT Workstation, Windows 98, Windows 2000 Professional, Windows Millennium Edition, Windows XP, Windows Vista) • Windows 7 • Mac OS X • UNIX • Linux
Server	• Early Windows Server versions (Windows NT Server, Windows 2000 Server, Windows Server 2003) • Windows Server 2008 • UNIX • Linux • Solaris • NetWare
Embedded	• Windows Embedded CE • Windows Phone 7 • Palm OS • iPhone OS • BlackBerry • Google Android • Embedded Linux • Symbian OS

Figure 8-14 Examples of stand-alone, server, and embedded operating systems. Some stand-alone operating systems include the capability of configuring small home or office networks.

FAQ 8-5

Which operating systems have the most market share?

The Windows operating system family currently dominates the operating system market with more than 93 percent market share. The Mac operating system is in second place with nearly 5 percent market share. The chart to the right illustrates the market share for various operating systems.

For more information, visit the Computer Concepts CourseMate Web site at www.cengagebrain.com, navigate to the Chapter 8 FAQ resource for this book, and then click Operating System Market Share.

Operating System Market Share

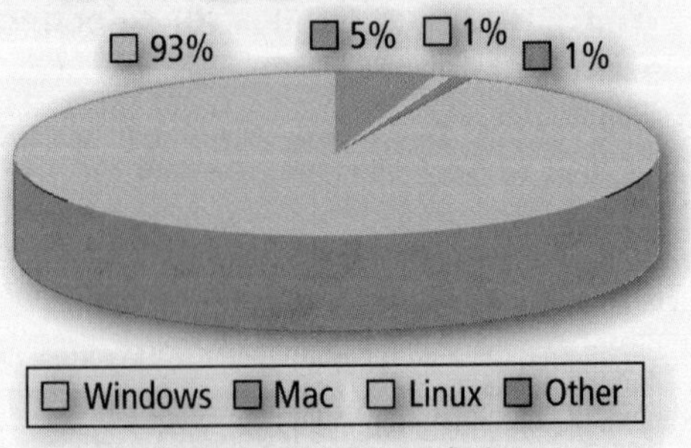

Source: Market Share by Net Applications

Stand-Alone Operating Systems

A **stand-alone operating system** is a complete operating system that works on a desktop computer, notebook computer, or mobile computing device. Some stand-alone operating systems are called *client operating systems* because they also work in conjunction with a server operating system. Client operating systems can operate with or without a network. Other stand-alone operating systems include networking capabilities, allowing the home and small business user to set up a small network.

Examples of currently used stand-alone operating systems are Windows 7, Mac OS X, UNIX, and Linux. The following pages briefly discuss these operating systems.

Windows 7

In the mid-1980s, Microsoft developed its first version of Windows, which provided a graphical user interface (GUI). Since then, Microsoft continually has updated its Windows operating system, incorporating innovative features and functions with each subsequent version (Figure 8-15). **Windows 7** is Microsoft's fastest, most efficient operating system to date, offering quicker program start up, built-in

Highlights of Stand-Alone Windows Versions

Windows Version	Year Released	Highlights
Windows 3.x	1990	• Provided a GUI • An operating environment only — worked in combination with DOS
Windows NT 3.1	1993	• Client OS that connected to a Windows NT Advanced Server • Interface similar to Windows 3.x
Windows 95	1995	• True multitasking operating system • Improved GUI • Included support for networking, Plug and Play technology, longer file names, and e-mail
Windows NT Workstation 4.0	1996	• Client OS that connected to a Windows NT Server • Interface similar to Windows 95 • Network integration
Windows 98	1998	• Upgrade to Windows 95 • More integrated with the Internet; included *Internet Explorer* (a Web browser) • Faster system startup and shut down, better file management, support for multimedia technologies (e.g., DVDs), and USB connectivity
Windows Millennium Edition	2000	• Upgrade to Windows 98 • Designed for the home user who wanted music playing, video editing, and networking capabilities
Windows 2000 Professional	2000	• Upgrade to Windows NT Workstation 4.0 • Complete multitasking client OS designed for business personal computers • Certified device drivers, faster performance, adaptive Start menu, image viewer, enhanced for mobile users
Windows XP	2001	• Upgrade to Windows Millennium Edition called Windows XP Home Edition • Upgrade to Windows 2000 Professional called Windows XP Professional • Windows XP Tablet PC Edition designed for Tablet PC users • Windows XP Media Center Edition designed for PCs used for home entertainment • Windows XP Professional x64 Edition designed for workstations that use 64-bit processors • Improved interface and increased performance in all editions
Service Pack 2	2004	• More built-in security technologies, improved firewall utility, and automatic blocking of Internet pop-up advertisements
Service Pack 3	2008	• Improved security and Network Access Protection restricts computers that do not meet specified requirements
Windows Vista	2006/2007	• Upgrade to Windows XP • Easier to navigate user interface, simplified customization techniques, and improved performance and reliability • Enhanced administration of user accounts and improved firewall • New Instant Search improves searching capabilities • New Documents Explorer, Pictures Explorer, and Music Explorer improve organizing capabilities
Service Pack 1	2008	• Improved Instant Search feature, increased support for devices and drivers, compatibility with more application software, and enhanced security
Service Pack 2	2009	• Support for new hardware, increased performance, and increased security
Windows 7	2009	• Upgrade to Windows Vista • Improved desktop interface and navigation • Simplified home and wireless networking • Enhanced searching capabilities • Improved performance for both desktop and notebook computers • Support for touch screen computers • Access to free, downloadable programs through the Windows Live Web site

Figure 8-15 Microsoft has released many versions of Windows.

diagnostics, automatic recovery, improved security, enhanced searching and organizing capabilities, and an easy-to-use interface (Figure 8-16).

Windows 7 includes several programs to enhance user experiences. Home and small office users easily can set up a network and secure it from hackers with *Windows Firewall.* With *Windows DVD Maker*, users easily can create DVDs from digital videos. *Windows Media Player* allows users to listen to Internet radio stations, play MP3 and other music formats, copy music and data to CDs, and watch movies.

Using the *Desktop Gadget Gallery*, users can display a variety of gadgets on the Windows desktop. A *gadget*, also known as a *widget*, is a mini-program with minimal functionality that connects to another program or provides information. Examples of gadgets included with Windows 7 include a calendar, clock, CPU meter, currency converter, news headlines, picture puzzle, picture slide show, weather, and a Windows Media Center gadget.

Most users choose one of these Windows 7 editions: Windows 7 Starter, Windows 7 Home Premium, Windows 7 Ultimate, or Windows 7 Professional.

Windows 7

For more information, visit the Computer Concepts CourseMate Web site at www.cengagebrain.com, navigate to the Chapter 8 Web Link resource for this book, and then click Windows 7.

- *Windows 7 Starter*, designed for netbooks and other small notebook computers, uses the Windows 7 Basic interface and allows users easily to search for files, connect to printers and devices, browse the Internet, join home networks, and connect to wireless networks. This edition of Windows typically is preinstalled on new computers and not available for purchase in retail stores.
- *Windows 7 Home Premium* includes all the capabilities of Windows 7 Starter and also includes Windows Aero with its *Aero Flip 3D* feature (Figure 8-17). It also provides tools to create and edit high-definition movies, record and watch television shows, connect to a game console, and read from and write on Blu-ray Discs.
- *Windows 7 Ultimate*, which includes all features of Windows 7 Home Premium, provides additional features designed to keep your files secure and support for 35 languages.
- With *Windows 7 Professional*, users in all sizes of businesses are provided a secure operating environment that uses Windows Aero where they easily can search for files, protect their computers from unauthorized intruders and unwanted programs, use improved backup technologies, securely connect to Wi-Fi networks, quickly view messages on a powered-off, specially equipped notebook computer, easily share documents and collaborate with other users, and watch and record live television.

Additional Windows 7 features are summarized in Figure 8-18. To run Windows 7 Home Premium, your computer must have at least 1 GB of RAM. If you are installing Windows on a 64-bit computer, 2 GB of RAM is required. Windows 7 adapts to the hardware configuration on which it is installed. Thus, two users with the same edition of Windows 7 may experience different functionality and interfaces.

Figure 8-16 Windows 7 has a new interface, easier navigation and searching techniques, and improved security.

Figure 8-17 With Windows 7 Aero Flip 3D, users flip through windows by rolling the wheel on their mouse.

Additional Windows 7 Features	
Reliability and Performance	• Low-powered Sleep state allows you to resume work quickly when you return to the computer • Programs start faster with Windows SuperFetch technology • Automatically detects and fine-tunes performance problems • Built-in hardware diagnostics detect and repair problems automatically • Automatically recovers from failures, including restoring an unbootable computer to a usable state
Security	• User Account Control allows administrators to restrict permissions • Protects users from dangerous Web sites • Improved firewall and *Windows Defender* protects your computer from external threats • Parental controls allow parents to monitor and control computer usage
Information Management	• Improved and redesigned windows help users locate files by showing thumbnails that preview content • Use Search to locate files based on file name or any other property saved with the file • Coordinate your schedule with others' schedules in *Windows Calendar* • Use the *Snipping Tool* to copy screen elements to a file on your computer • Easily share files with other users
Appearance and Navigation	• Easy-to-navigate user interface with translucent windows • Display a preview of windows open in a particular program when you point to that program button on the taskbar • Windows Snap and Aero Shake make it easier to manage the appearance of open windows • Jump Lists make it easier to open recent files quickly in their respective program • *Windows Touch* supports computers with multi-touch technology
Communications and the Internet	• Enhanced Internet Explorer • Free access to *Windows Live Essentials*, which includes programs such as *Windows Live Messenger* for instant messaging, *Windows Live Photo Gallery* for photo editing and sharing, *Windows Live Mail* for e-mail, *Windows Live Writer* for blogging, and *Windows Live Movie Maker* for video editing and sharing • Consistent and secure wireless network connections • Speech recognition allows you to interact with the computer by voice

Figure 8-18 Some additional features of Windows 7.

Mac OS X

Since it was released in 1984 with Macintosh computers, Apple's **Macintosh operating system** has set the standard for operating system ease of use and has been the model for most of the new GUIs developed for non-Macintosh systems. The latest version, **Mac OS X**, is a multitasking operating system available only for computers manufactured by Apple (Figure 8-19).

Mac OS X includes features from previous versions of the Macintosh operating system such as large photo-quality icons, built-in networking support, e-mail, chat, online shopping, enhanced speech recognition, optical disc burning, and enhanced multimedia capabilities. In addition, Mac OS X includes these features:

- New desktop search technology
- Dashboard, a desktop area for mini-programs called widgets
- Built-in, fast Web browser
- Parental controls
- Improved backup utility, called Time Machine
- Accessibility interface reads e-mail messages
- 3-D personal video and audio conferencing
- Filter to eliminate junk e-mail messages
- Contact lists synchronized with Bluetooth-enabled smart phone or other mobile device
- Latest version of QuickTime to listen to music and view videos on the Internet
- Easy networking of computers and devices
- Windows network connection and shared Windows documents

Mac OS X

For more information, visit the Computer Concepts CourseMate Web site at www.cengagebrain.com, navigate to the Chapter 8 Web Link resource for this book, and then click Mac OS X.

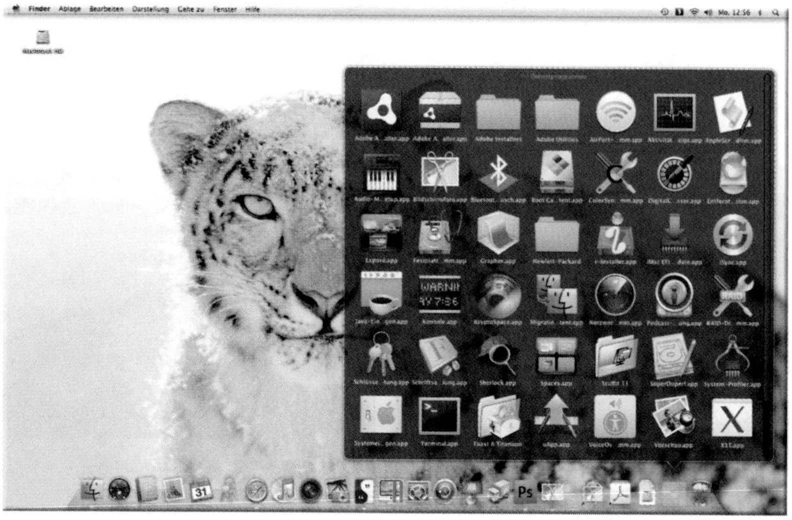

Figure 8-19 Mac OS X is the operating system used with Apple Macintosh computers.

UNIX

UNIX (pronounced YOU-nix) is a multitasking operating system developed in the early 1970s by scientists at Bell Laboratories. Bell Labs (a subsidiary of AT&T) was prohibited from actively promoting UNIX in the commercial marketplace because of federal regulations. Bell Labs instead licensed UNIX for a low fee to numerous colleges and universities, where UNIX obtained a wide following. UNIX was implemented on many different types of computers. After deregulation of the telephone companies in the 1980s, UNIX was licensed to many hardware and software companies.

Several versions of this operating system exist, each slightly different. When programmers move application software from one UNIX version to another, they sometimes have to rewrite some of the programs. Although some versions of UNIX have a command-line interface, most versions of UNIX offer a graphical user interface (Figure 8-20).

Today, a version of UNIX is available for most computers of all sizes. Power users often work with UNIX because of its flexibility and power. Manufacturers such as Sun and IBM sell personal computers and workstations with a UNIX operating system.

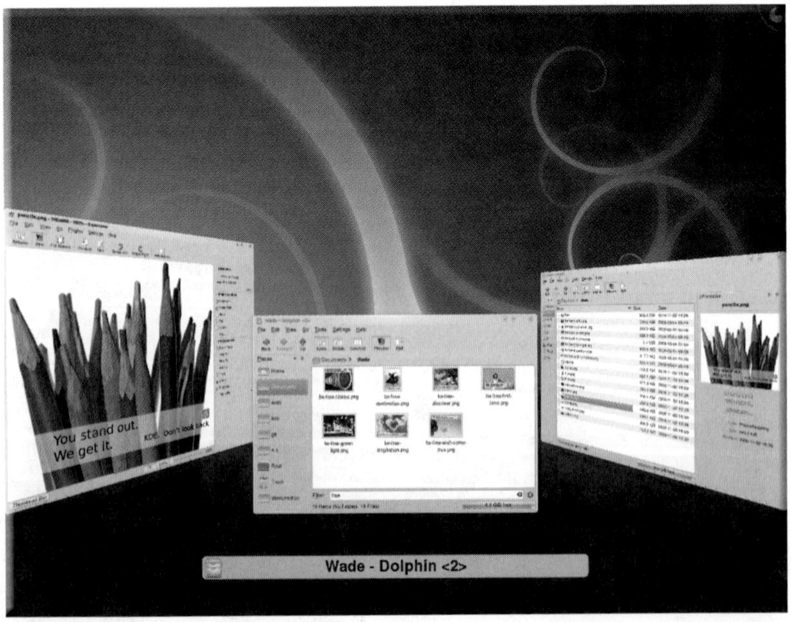

Figure 8-20 Many versions of UNIX have a graphical user interface.

Linux

Linux is one of the faster growing operating systems. **Linux** (pronounced LINN-uks), introduced in 1991, is a popular, multitasking UNIX-type operating system. In addition to the basic operating system, Linux also includes many free programming languages and utility programs.

Linux is not proprietary software like the operating systems discussed thus far. Instead, Linux is *open source software*, which means its code is provided for use, modification, and redistribution. It has no restrictions from the copyright holder regarding modification of the software's internal instructions and redistribution of the software. Many programmers have donated time to modify and redistribute Linux to make it the best possible version of UNIX. Promoters of open source software state two main advantages: users who modify the software share their improvements with others, and customers can personalize the software to meet their needs. Read Ethics & Issues 8-2 for a related discussion.

Linux is available in a variety of forms, known as distributions. Some distributions of Linux are command-line. Others are GUI (Figure 8-21).

ETHICS & ISSUES 8-2

Closed Source vs. Open Source Operating Systems

One of the features that make Linux different from other operating systems is that Linux is open source and its source code, along with any changes, remains public. Often, when closed source operating system developers refuse to share some or all of the operating system code, third-party software developers become hindered when developing application software for the operating system. Supporters of open source maintain that source code should be open to the public so that it can be scrutinized, corrected, and enhanced. In light of concerns about security and fears of possible virus problems, however, some people are not sure open source software is a good idea. Besides, they argue, companies and programmers should be able to control, and profit from, the operating systems they create. On the other hand, open source software can be scrutinized for errors by a much larger group of people and changes can be made immediately, resulting in better software.

Are open source operating systems a good idea? Why or why not? How can the concerns about open source operating systems be addressed? What might be some of the advantages and disadvantages of open versus closed source operating systems? Does the open source model lead to better software? Why or why not?

Figure 8-21 This distribution of Linux has a graphical user interface.

Linux

For more information, visit the Computer Concepts CourseMate Web site at www.cengagebrain.com, navigate to the Chapter 8 Web Link resource for this book, and then click Linux.

The two most popular GUIs available for Linux are GNOME and KDE. Some companies such as Red Hat market software that runs on their own distribution of Linux. Many application programs, utilities, and plug-ins have Linux distributions, including OpenOffice.org, StarOffice, Mozilla, Yahoo! Messenger, RealPlayer, QuickTime, and Acrobat Reader.

Users obtain Linux in a variety of ways. Some download it free from the Web. Others purchase it from vendors such as Red Hat or IBM, who bundle their own software with the operating system. Linux optical discs are included in many Linux books and also are available for purchase from vendors. Some retailers such as Dell will preinstall Linux on a new computer's hard disk on request. If you want to preview the Linux operating system, you can obtain a Live CD or Live USB.

Server Operating Systems

As discussed earlier in this chapter, a server operating system is an operating system that is designed specifically to support a network. A server operating system typically resides on a server. The client computers on the network rely on the server(s) for resources.

Many of the stand-alone operating systems discussed in the previous section function as clients and work in conjunction with a server operating system. Some of these stand-alone operating systems do include networking capability; however, server operating systems are designed specifically to support all sizes of networks, including medium- to large-sized businesses and Web servers. Examples of server operating systems include Windows Server 2008, UNIX, Linux, Solaris, and NetWare.

Windows Server 2008

Windows Server 2008 is an upgrade to Windows Server 2003. Windows Server 2008, which includes features of previous Windows Server versions, offers the following capabilities:

- Improved Web server management, enabling users to share data
- Enhanced server security
- Network Access Protection restricts computers that do not meet specified requirements
- Protection against malicious software attacks
- Shares many technologies with Windows
- Client support using Windows, Mac OS, UNIX, and Linux

To meet the needs of all sizes of businesses, the **Windows Server 2008 family** includes many editions, with the more common listed below:

- *Windows Server 2008 Standard* for the typical small- to medium-sized business network
- *Windows Server 2008 Enterprise* for medium- to large-sized businesses, including those with e-commerce operations
- *Windows Server 2008 Datacenter* for businesses with huge volumes of transactions and large-scale databases

- *Windows Web Server 2008* for Web server and Web hosting businesses
- *Windows Server 2008 for Itanium-Based Systems* for computers with 64-bit processors that function as a Web server

Most editions of Windows Server 2008 include Hyper-V, which is a virtualization technology. *Virtualization* is the practice of sharing or pooling computing resources, such as servers. Through virtualization, for example, operating systems such as Windows Server 2008 can separate a physical server into several virtual servers. Each virtual server then can perform an independent, separate function, such as running a different operating system.

Virtualization
For more information, visit the Computer Concepts CourseMate Web site at www.cengagebrain.com, navigate to the Chapter 8 Web Link resource for this book, and then click Virtualization.

UNIX

In addition to being a stand-alone operating system, UNIX also is a server operating system. That is, UNIX is capable of handling a high volume of transactions in a multiuser environment and working with multiple processors using multiprocessing. For this reason, some computer professionals call UNIX a *multipurpose operating system* because it is both a stand-alone and server operating system. Many Web servers use UNIX as their operating system.

Linux

Some network servers use Linux as their operating system. Thus, Linux also is a multipurpose operating system. With Linux, a network administrator can configure the network, administer security, run a Web server, and process e-mail. Clients on the network can run Linux, UNIX, or Windows. Distributions of Linux include the Mozilla Web browser.

Solaris

Solaris, a version of UNIX developed by Sun Microsystems, is a server operating system designed specifically for e-commerce applications. Solaris manages high-traffic accounts and incorporates security necessary for Web transactions. Client computers often use a desktop program, such as GNOME desktop, that communicates with the Solaris operating system.

NetWare

Novell's *NetWare* is a server operating system designed for client/server networks. NetWare has a server portion that resides on the network server and a client portion that resides on each client computer connected to the network. NetWare supports open source software and runs on all types of computers from mainframes to personal computers. Client computers also can have their own stand-alone operating system such as a Windows, Mac OS, or Linux.

Embedded Operating Systems

The operating system on mobile devices and many consumer electronics, called an **embedded operating system**, resides on a ROM chip. Popular embedded operating systems today include Windows Embedded CE, Windows Phone 7, Palm OS, iPhone OS, BlackBerry, Google Android, embedded Linux, and Symbian OS. The following sections discuss these operating systems, most of which work on smart phones. Read Ethics & Issues 8-3 for a related discussion.

ETHICS & ISSUES 8-3

Should the Smart Phone Industry Adopt a Standard?

When you purchase a new personal computer, typically you choose between a Windows or Mac operating system. When you purchase a smart phone, however, you probably spend little time considering the operating system running on the phone. More than 10 operating systems currently run the functions of an increasing number of available smart phones. The many choices result in considerable frustration for third-party program developers who want their programs to operate on all possible smart phones. Today, developers must rewrite code, often in different programming languages, to provide their programs on a variety of phones. The situation results in *user lockdown*, meaning that users of smart phones often are forced to stay with the same brand of mobile phone, because changing to a different brand results in losing access to their favorite programs. Third-party program developers, consumers, and enterprises increasingly demand that the industry create a standard operating system for smart phones. They state that smart phone manufacturers would retain control of the phones' graphical user interface, input and output technology, and built-in utility programs in order to differentiate their phones from the competition. The manufacturers claim, however, that competition eventually will solve the issue.

Should the smart phone industry adopt a standard development platform? Why or why not? Should competition, a group of companies, or a standards-setting body decide the best operating system for smart phones? Why?

Windows Embedded CE

Windows Embedded CE is a scaled-down Windows operating system designed for use on communications, entertainment, and computing devices with limited functionality. Examples of devices that use Windows Embedded CE include VoIP telephones, industrial control devices, digital cameras, point-of-sale terminals, automated teller machines, digital photo frames, fuel pumps, security robots, handheld navigation devices, portable media players, ticket machines, and computerized sewing machines (Figure 8-22).

Windows Embedded CE is a GUI that supports color, sound, multitasking, multimedia, e-mail, Internet access, and Web browsing. A built-in file viewer allows users to view files created in popular programs such as Word, Excel, and PowerPoint.

Devices equipped with Windows Embedded CE can communicate wirelessly with computers and other devices using Bluetooth or other wireless technologies, as long as the device is equipped with the necessary communications hardware.

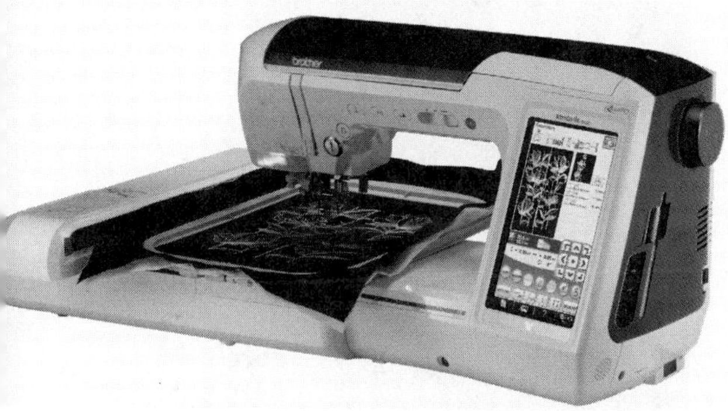

Figure 8-22 This sewing machine uses Windows Embedded CE to assist with stitching quilts, garments, crafts, decorations, and embroidery.

Windows Phone 7

Windows Phone 7, which is a successor to Windows Mobile, includes functionality, programs, and a user interface designed for specific types of smart phones (Figure 8-23). Windows Phone 7 supports multi-touch screens, which are touch screens that recognize multiple points of contact at the same time.

With the Windows Phone 7 operating system and a compatible device, users have access to all the basic PIM (personal information manager) functions such as contact lists, schedules, tasks, calendars, and notes. Information on the mobile device easily synchronizes with a personal computer or prints on a printer using a cable or a wireless technology.

Windows Phone 7 also provides numerous additional features that allow users to check e-mail, browse the Web, listen to music, take pictures or record video, watch a video, send and receive text messages and instant messages, record a voice message, manage finances, view a map, read an e-book, or play a game. Many programs, such as Word, Excel, Outlook, and Internet Explorer, have scaled-down versions that run with Windows Phone 7. Some devices with Windows Phone 7 also support voice input.

Figure 8-23 A smart phone that uses the Windows Phone 7 operating system, which uses tiles on the home screen to link to various programs and functions.

Palm OS

A competing operating system to Windows Phone 7 is *Palm OS*, which runs on smart phones (Figure 8-24) and PDAs. With Palm OS devices, users manage schedules and contacts, phone messages, notes, task and address lists, and appointments. Information on the mobile device easily synchronizes with a personal computer or prints on a printer using a cable or a wireless technology.

Many Palm OS devices allow users to connect wirelessly to the Internet; browse the Web; send and receive e-mail messages, text messages, and instant messages; listen to music; record voice messages; and view digital photos. Most have touch screens. The latest version of Palm OS allows for biometric identification and supports the use of smart cards.

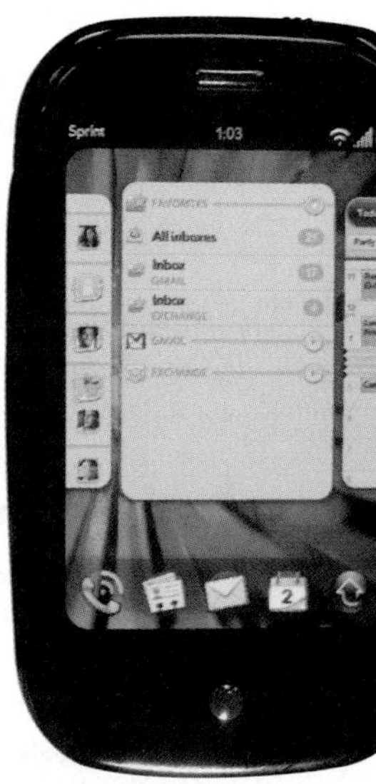

Figure 8-24 A smart phone that uses the Palm OS operating system.

iPhone OS

iPhone OS, developed by Apple, is an operating system for the iPhone and iPod touch, Apple's smart phone (Figure 8-25) and touch screen portable media player, respectively. These devices are multi-touch, meaning they recognize multiple points of contact. This feature enables users to interact with iPhone OS devices using finger motions such as tapping a button on the screen, sliding your finger to drag an object, and pinching or unpinching your fingers to zoom in or out.

With the iPhone OS, users can manage contacts and notes, send and receive e-mail and text messages, take pictures, record videos, record voice messages, view a compass, connect to the Internet wirelessly and browse the Web, check stocks, access maps and obtain directions, listen to music, watch movies and videos, and display photos. It also provides Wi-Fi access to the iTunes Music Store.

Figure 8-25 The iPhone OS runs on Apple's iPhone.

iPhone OS
For more information, visit the Computer Concepts CourseMate Web site at www.cengagebrain.com, navigate to the Chapter 8 Web Link resource for this book, and then click iPhone OS.

BlackBerry

The *BlackBerry* operating system runs on handheld devices supplied by RIM (Research In Motion). BlackBerry devices provide PIM capabilities such as managing schedules, contacts, and appointments, as well as phone capabilities. They also provide wireless functionality that includes sending e-mail messages, text messages, and instant messages; connecting to the Internet and browsing the Web; and accessing Bluetooth devices. Some BlackBerry devices allow users to take pictures, play music, and access maps and directions.

Information on the device easily synchronizes wirelessly with a computer or other BlackBerry device. Many BlackBerry devices include a mini-keyboard; some have touch screens (Figure 8-26). For a technical discussion about touch screens, read the High-Tech Talk article on page 430.

Figure 8-26 A smart phone that uses the BlackBerry operating system.

BlackBerry
For more information, visit the Computer Concepts CourseMate Web site at www.cengagebrain.com, navigate to the Chapter 8 Web Link resource for this book, and then click BlackBerry.

Google Android

Google Android is an operating system designed by Google for mobile devices. Used on more than 20 different types of mobile devices, Google Android allows programmers to design programs specifically for devices supporting this operating system. Google Android contains features such as access to e-mail accounts, an alarm clock, video capture, access to Google Apps, Wi-Fi access, and easy Web browsing.

Embedded Linux

Embedded Linux is a scaled-down Linux operating system designed for smart phones, PDAs, portable media players, Internet telephones, and many other types of devices and computers requiring an embedded operating system. Devices with embedded Linux offer calendar and address book and other PIM functions, touch screens, and handwriting recognition. Many also allow you to connect to the Internet, take pictures, play videos, listen to music, and send e-mail and instant messages. Devices that use embedded Linux synchronize with desktop computers using a variety of technologies including Bluetooth.

Symbian OS

Symbian OS is an open source multitasking operating system designed for smart phones. In addition to making phone calls, users of Symbian OS can maintain contact lists; save appointments; browse the Web; and send and receive text and picture messages, e-mail messages, and faxes using a smart phone. Users enter data by pressing keys on the keypad or keyboard, touching the screen, writing on the screen with a stylus, or speaking into the smart phone. Symbian OS allows users to communicate wirelessly.

QUIZ YOURSELF 8-2

Instructions: Find the true statement below. Then, rewrite the remaining false statements so that they are true.

1. BlackBerry devices use Palm OS as their operating system.
2. Examples of embedded operating systems include Windows Server 2008, UNIX, Linux, Solaris, and NetWare.
3. Windows 7 Starter uses Windows Aero.
4. Mac OS X is a multitasking operating system available only for computers manufactured by Apple.
5. Aero Flip 3D is a UNIX-type operating system that is open source software.

Quiz Yourself Online: To further check your knowledge of pages 411 through 421, visit the Computer Concepts CourseMate Web site at www.cengagebrain.com, navigate to the Chapter 8 Quiz Yourself resource for this book, and then click Objectives 4 – 6.

Utility Programs

A **utility program**, also called a **utility**, is a type of system software that allows a user to perform maintenance-type tasks, usually related to managing a computer, its devices, or its programs. Most operating systems include several built-in utility programs (Figure 8-27). Users often buy stand-alone utilities, however, because they offer improvements over those included with the operating system.

Functions provided by utility programs include the following: managing files, searching for files, viewing images, uninstalling programs, cleaning up disks, defragmenting disks, backing up files and disks, setting up screen savers, securing a computer from unauthorized access, protecting against viruses, removing spyware and adware, filtering Internet content, compressing files, playing media files, burning optical discs, and maintaining a personal computer. The following sections briefly discuss each of these utilities. Read Innovative Computing 8-1 to find out about utility programs that can help you recover deleted files.

INNOVATIVE COMPUTING 8-1

Utility Programs Locate Deleted Files

If you delete a file mistakenly from a USB flash drive, removable flash memory device, or hard disk, you easily can recover that erased file with utility programs. A few of the more popular utility programs have names that explain their purpose: Recuva, Recover My Files, FreeUndelete, FileMakerRecovery, R-Studio, and Recovery Toolbox. Most can be downloaded from the Web, often free of charge.

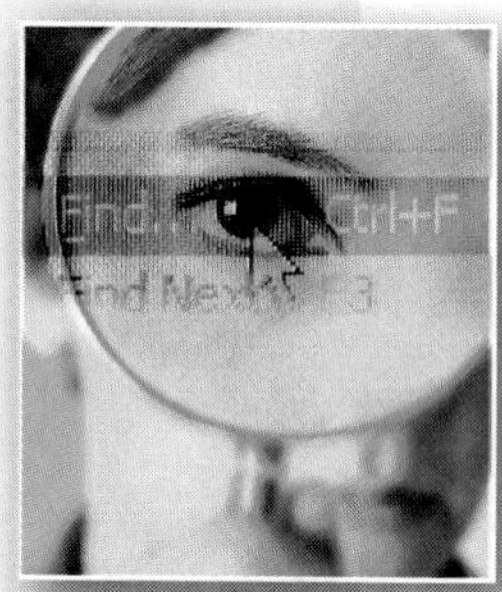

Data recovery experts offer advice on actions to take immediately when you realize you have erased files, even if you have emptied the Recycle Bin. Although the file name does not appear in the list of files on that storage medium, the file actually remains intact on the storage medium. The computer marks the space on the disk as free so that another file can overwrite the contents of the deleted file. As long as you do not save any file, no matter how small, the utility program generally can locate the marked space and then retrieve the contents of the file.

For more information, visit the Computer Concepts CourseMate Web site at www.cengagebrain.com, navigate to the Chapter 8 Innovative Computing resource for this book, and then click Recovering Deleted Files.

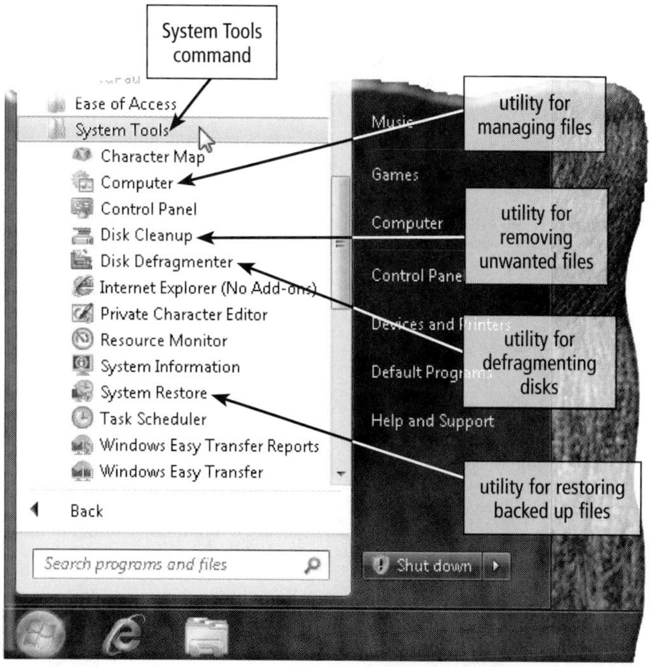

Figure 8-27 To display the utilities available in the Windows System Tools list, click the Start button, click All Programs, click Accessories, and then click System Tools.

File Manager

A **file manager** is a utility that performs functions related to file management. Some of the file management functions that a file manager performs are displaying a list of files on a storage medium (Figure 8-28); organizing files in folders; copying, renaming, deleting, moving, and sorting files and folders; and creating shortcuts. A **folder** is a specific named location on a storage medium that contains related documents. A **shortcut** is an icon on the desktop or in a folder that provides a user with immediate access to a program or file.

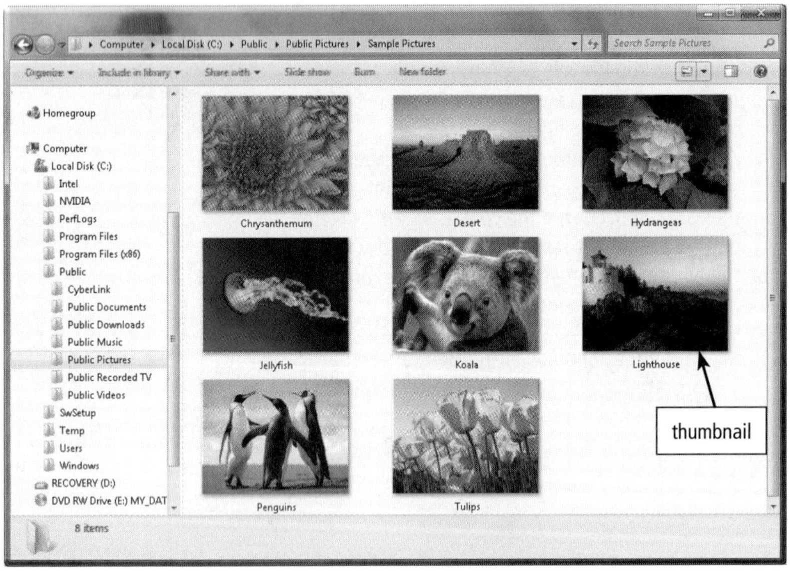

Figure 8-28 Windows includes file managers that allow you to view documents, photos, and music. In this case, thumbnails of photos are displayed.

Operating systems typically include a file manager. Windows, for example, includes Windows Explorer, which displays links to files and folders, as well as previews of folder contents and certain types of files.

Search Utility

A **search utility** is a program that attempts to locate a file on your computer based on criteria you specify (Figure 8-29). The criteria could be a word or words contained in a file, date the file was created or modified, size of the file, location of the file, file name, author/artist, and other similar properties. Search utilities can look through documents, photos, music, and other files on your computer and/or on the Internet, combining search results in a single location.

Search utilities typically use an index to assist with locating files quickly. An *index* stores a variety of information about a file, including its name, date created, date modified, author name, and so on. When you enter search criteria, instead of looking through every file and folder on the storage medium, the search utility looks through the index first to find a match. Each entry in the index contains a link to the actual file on the disk for easy retrieval. Operating systems typically include a built-in search utility. In Windows, all the Explorer windows, as well as the Start menu, contain a Search box where you enter the search criteria.

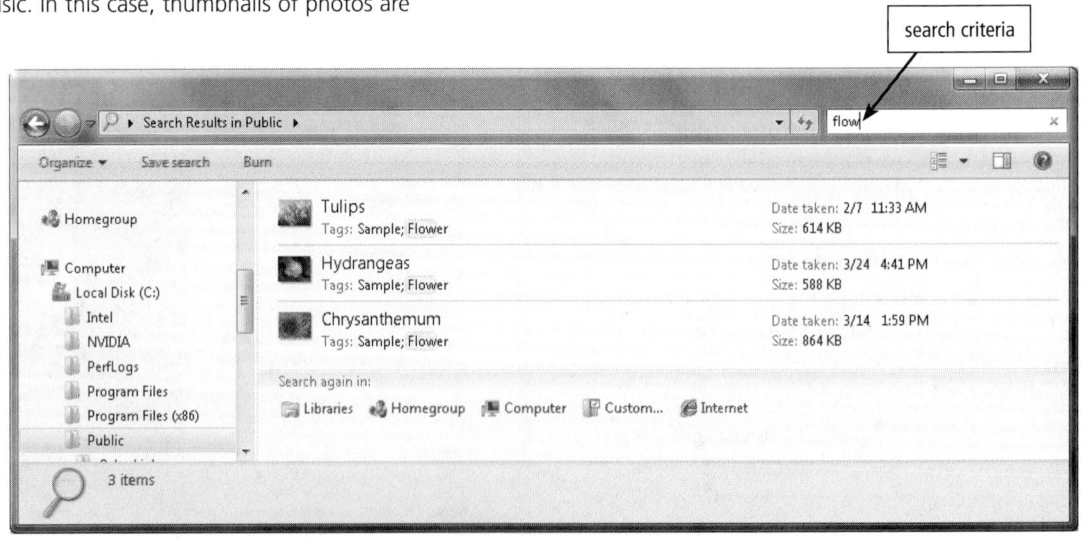

Figure 8-29 This search displays files whose name or contents contain the text, flow.

Image Viewer

An **image viewer** is a utility that allows users to display, copy, and print the contents of a graphics file, such as a photo. With an image viewer, users can see images without having to open them in a paint or image editing program. Most operating systems include an image viewer. Windows image viewer is called *Windows Photo Viewer*, which also allows you to print and e-mail photos (Figure 8-30).

Figure 8-30 Windows Photo Viewer allows users to see the contents of a photo file.

Uninstaller

An **uninstaller** is a utility that removes a program, as well as any associated entries in the system files. When you install a program, the operating system records the information it uses to run the software in the system files. The uninstaller deletes files and folders from the hard disk, as well as removes program entries from the system files. Operating systems usually provide an uninstaller.

In Windows, you are able to access the uninstaller for many installed programs through the 'Uninstall a program' command in the Control Panel. You also can access the uninstaller for some program's through that programs folder on the Start menu, or on the program's installation media.

? FAQ 8-6

Should I use Windows Explorer to delete a program?

No! If you remove software from a computer by deleting the files and folders associated with the program without running the uninstaller, the system file entries are not updated. This may cause the operating system to display error messages when you start the computer. If a program has an uninstaller, always use it to remove software.

For more information, visit the Computer Concepts CourseMate Web site at www.cengagebrain.com, navigate to the Chapter 8 FAQ resource for this book, and then click Uninstalling Programs.

Disk Cleanup

A *disk cleanup* utility searches for and removes unnecessary files. Unnecessary files may include downloaded program files, temporary Internet files, deleted files, and unused program files. Operating systems, such as Windows, include a disk cleanup utility (Figure 8-31).

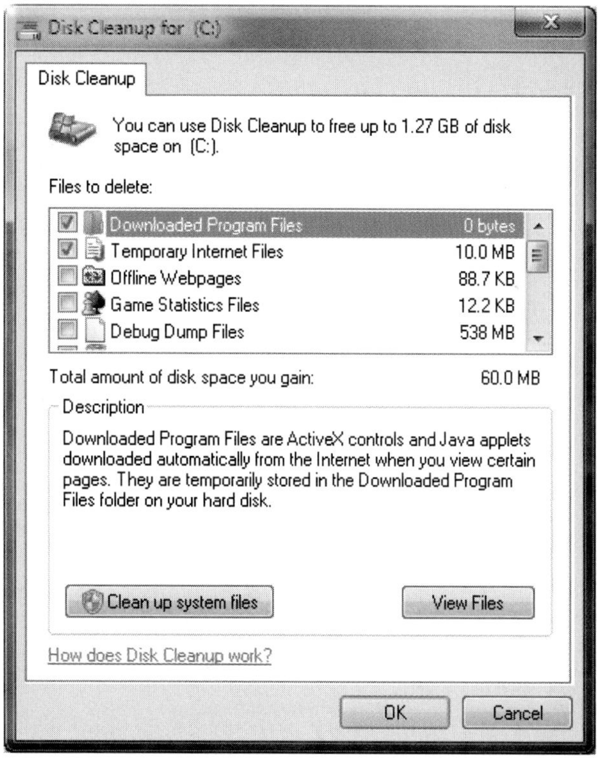

Figure 8-31 Disk Cleanup searches for and removes unnecessary files.

Disk Defragmenter

A **disk defragmenter** is a utility that reorganizes the files and unused space on a computer's hard disk so that the operating system accesses data more quickly and programs run faster. When an operating system stores data on a disk, it places the data in the first available sector on the disk. It attempts to place data in sectors that are contiguous (next to each other), but this is not always possible. When the contents of a file are scattered across two or more noncontiguous sectors, the file is *fragmented*.

Fragmentation slows down disk access and thus the performance of the entire computer. **Defragmenting** the disk, or reorganizing it so that the files are stored in contiguous sectors, solves this problem (Figure 8-32). Operating systems usually include a disk defragmenter. Windows Disk Defragmenter is available in the System Tools list.

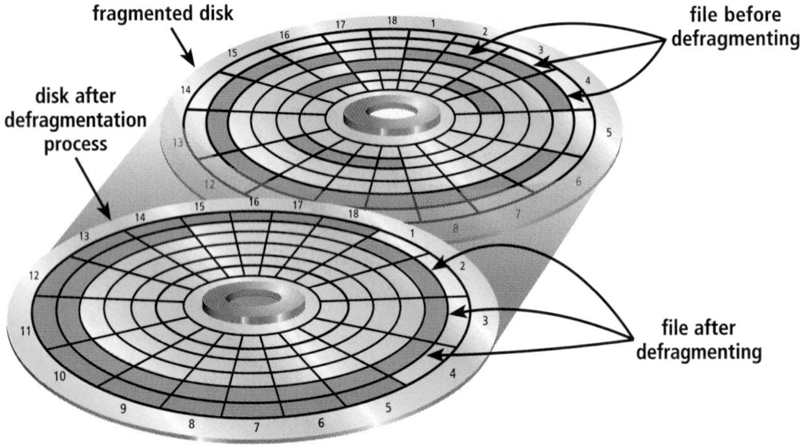

Figure 8-32 A fragmented disk has many files stored in noncontiguous sectors. Defragmenting reorganizes the files so that they are located in contiguous sectors, which speeds access time.

Backup and Restore Utilities

A **backup utility** allows users to copy, or *back up*, selected files or an entire hard disk to another storage medium such as another hard disk, optical disc, USB flash drive, or tape. During the backup process, the utility monitors progress and alerts you if it needs additional media, such as another disc. Many backup programs *compress*, or shrink the size of, files during the backup process. By compressing the files, the backup program requires less storage space for the backup files than for the original files.

Because they are compressed, you usually cannot use backup files in their backed up form. In the event you need to use a backup file, a **restore utility** reverses the process and returns backed up files to their original form. Backup utilities work with a restore utility.

You should back up files and disks regularly in the event your originals are lost, damaged, or destroyed. Most backup and restore utilities include a scheduler, which instructs the computer to perform a backup automatically on a regularly scheduled basis. Operating systems, such as Windows, include a backup and restore utility (Figure 8-33). When you purchase an external hard disk, it also usually includes a backup and restore utility. Instead of backing up to a local disk storage device, some users opt to use cloud storage to back up their files. As described in Chapter 7, cloud storage is a service on the Web that provides storage to computer users, usually for free or for a minimal monthly fee.

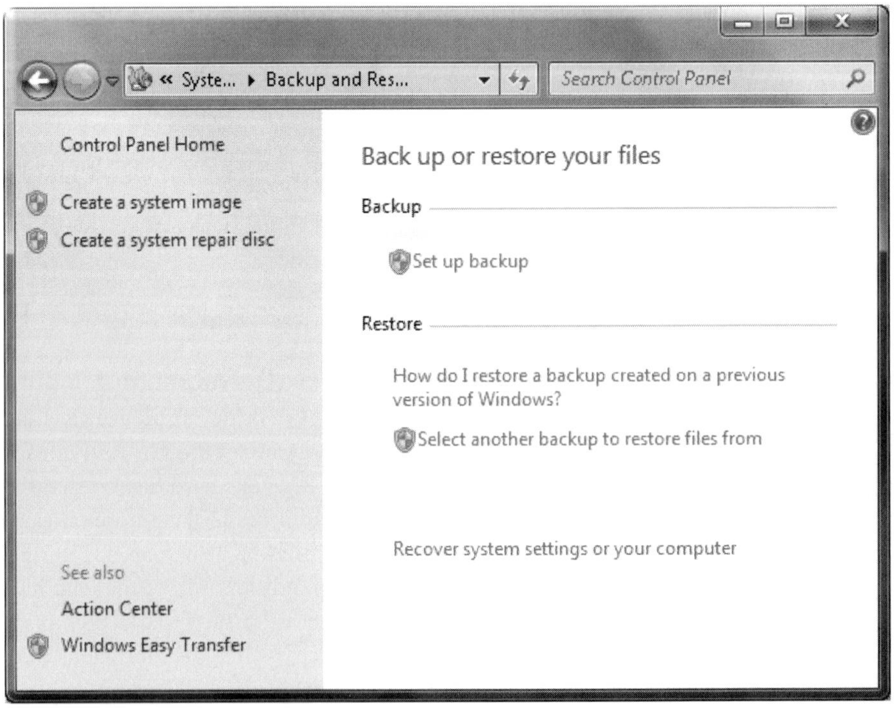

Figure 8-33 A backup utility allows users to copy files or an entire hard disk to another storage medium.

Screen Saver

A **screen saver** is a utility that causes a display device's screen to show a moving image or blank screen if no keyboard or mouse activity occurs for a specified time. When you press a key on the keyboard or move the mouse, the screen saver disappears and the screen returns to the previous state.

Screen savers originally were developed to prevent a problem called *ghosting*, in which images could be etched permanently on a monitor's screen. Although ghosting is not as severe of a problem with today's displays, manufacturers continue to recommend that users install screen savers for this reason. Screen savers also are popular for security, business, and entertainment purposes. To secure a computer, users configure their screen saver to require a password to deactivate. In addition to those included with the operating system, many screen savers are available in stores (Figure 8-34) and on the Web for free or a minimal fee.

Figure 8-34 With this screen saver software, you can create your own screen savers.

Personal Firewall

A **personal firewall** is a utility that detects and protects a personal computer from unauthorized intrusions. Personal firewalls constantly monitor all transmissions to and from a computer.

When connected to the Internet, your computer is vulnerable to attacks from a hacker. A *hacker* is someone who tries to access a computer or network illegally. Users with broadband Internet connections, such as through DSL and cable Internet service, are even more susceptible than those with dial-up access because the Internet connection always is on.

Operating systems often include a personal firewall. Windows automatically enables its built-in personal firewall, called Windows Firewall, upon installation of the operating system. If your operating system does not include a personal firewall or you want additional protection, you can purchase a stand-alone personal firewall utility (Figure 8-35) or a hardware firewall, which is a device such as a router that has a built-in firewall.

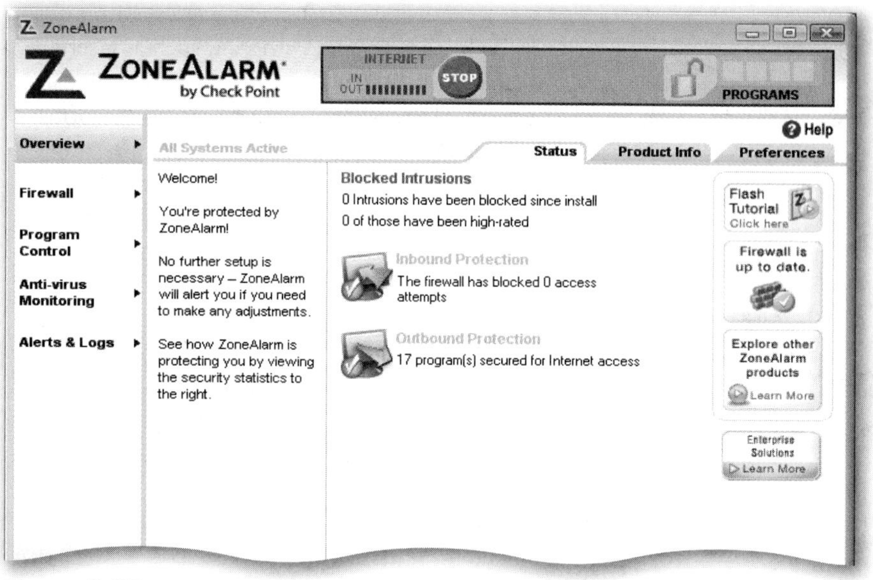

Figure 8-35 A stand-alone personal firewall utility.

Antivirus Programs

The term, computer **virus**, describes a potentially damaging computer program that affects, or infects, a computer negatively by altering the way the computer works without the user's knowledge or permission. Once the virus is in a computer, it can spread throughout and may damage your files and operating system.

Computer viruses do not generate by chance. The programmer of a virus, known as a *virus author*, intentionally writes a virus program. Some virus authors find writing viruses a challenge. Others write virus programs to cause destruction. Writing a virus program usually requires significant programming skills.

Some viruses are harmless pranks that simply freeze a computer temporarily or display sounds or messages. The Music Bug virus, for example, instructs the computer to play a few chords of music. Other viruses destroy or corrupt data stored on the hard disk of the infected computer. If you notice any unusual changes in your computer's performance, it may be infected with a virus (Figure 8-36).

Signs of Virus Infection

- An unusual message or image is displayed on the computer screen
- An unusual sound or music plays randomly
- The available memory is less than what should be available
- A program or file suddenly is missing
- An unknown program or file mysteriously appears
- The size of a file changes without explanation
- A file becomes corrupted
- A program or file does not work properly
- System properties change
- The computer operates much slower than usual

Figure 8-36 Viruses attack computers in a variety of ways. This list indicates some of the more common signs of virus infection.

Viruses are just one type of malicious software. *Malware* (short for malicious software) is software that acts without a user's knowledge and deliberately alters the computer's operations. In addition to viruses, worms and Trojan horses are malware.

A **worm**, such as Sasser or Klez, copies itself repeatedly, for example, in memory or over a network, using up system resources and possibly shutting down the system. A **Trojan horse** (named after the Greek myth) hides within or looks like a legitimate program such as a screen saver. A certain condition or action usually triggers the Trojan horse. Unlike a virus or worm, a Trojan horse does not replicate itself to other computers. Currently, more than one million known threats to your computer exist. For a more technical discussion about computer viruses, read the High-Tech Talk article in Chapter 3 on page 178.

To protect a computer from virus attacks, users should install an antivirus program and update it frequently. An **antivirus program** protects a computer against viruses by identifying and removing any computer viruses found in memory, on storage media, or on incoming files. Most antivirus programs also protect against worms and Trojan horses. When you purchase a new computer, it often includes antivirus software.

Three more popular antivirus programs are McAfee VirusScan, Norton AntiVirus (Figure 8-37), and Windows Live OneCare, most of which also contains spyware removers, Internet filters, and other utilities. As an alternative to purchasing these products on disc, both McAfee and Norton offer Web-based antivirus programs.

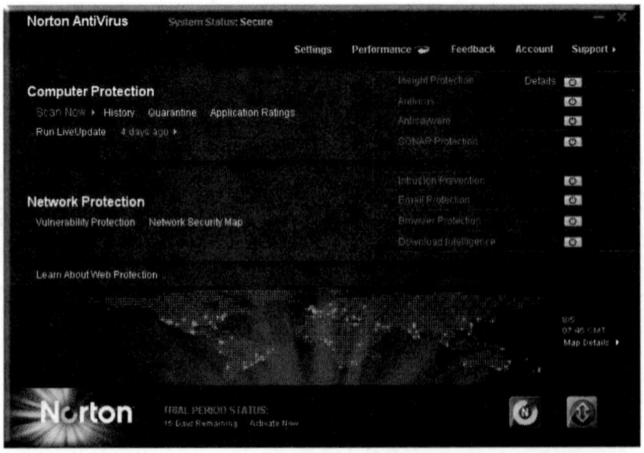

Figure 8-37 An antivirus program scans memory, disks, and incoming e-mail messages and attachments for viruses and attempts to remove any viruses it finds.

FAQ 8-7

What steps should I take to prevent virus infections on my computer?

Set up the antivirus program to scan on a regular basis. Update your virus definitions regularly. Never open an e-mail attachment unless you are expecting the attachment and it is from a trusted source. If you use Windows, install the latest Microsoft updates. Set macro security in programs such as word processing and spreadsheet so that you can enable or disable macros. Back up files regularly.

For more information, visit the Computer Concepts CourseMate Web site at www.cengagebrain.com, navigate to the Chapter 8 FAQ resource for this book, and then click Preventing Virus Infections.

Spyware and Adware Removers

Spyware is a program placed on a computer without the user's knowledge that secretly collects information about the user, often related to Web browsing habits. Spyware can enter a computer as a virus or as a result of a user installing a new program. The spyware program communicates information it collects to an outside source while you are online.

Adware is a program that displays an online advertisement in a banner or pop-up window on Web pages, e-mail, or other Internet services. Sometimes, spyware is hidden in adware.

A **spyware remover** is a program that detects and deletes spyware and other similar programs. An *adware remover* is a program that detects and deletes adware. Most spyware and adware removers cost less than $50; some are available on the Web at no cost. Some operating systems and antivirus programs include spyware and adware removers. Popular stand-alone spyware and adware removers include Ad-Aware, Spy Sweeper, Spybot - Search and Destroy, and Windows Defender.

Internet Filters

Filters are programs that remove or block certain items from being displayed. Four widely used Internet filters are Web filters, anti-spam programs, phishing filters, and pop-up blockers.

Web Filters **Web filtering software** is a program that restricts access to certain material on the Web. Some restrict access to specific Web sites; others filter sites that use certain words or phrases. Many businesses use Web filtering software to limit employee's Web access. Some schools, libraries, and parents use this software to restrict access to minors. Windows 7 contains parental controls, which allow parents to record and control the types of content their children can access on the Internet.

Anti-Spam Programs *Spam* is an unsolicited e-mail message or newsgroup posting sent to many recipients or newsgroups at once. Spam is Internet junk mail. The content of spam ranges from selling a product or service, to promoting a business opportunity, to advertising offensive material. An **anti-spam program** is a filtering program that attempts to remove spam before it reaches your inbox. If your e-mail program does not filter spam, many anti-spam programs are available at no cost on the Web. Internet access providers often filter spam as a service for their subscribers.

? FAQ 8-8

Where does spam originate?

Research indicates that spam originates from various countries throughout the world. Symantec Corporation found that in a 30-day period, the United States was responsible for more spam than any other country. The following chart illustrates the countries responsible for the most spam worldwide.

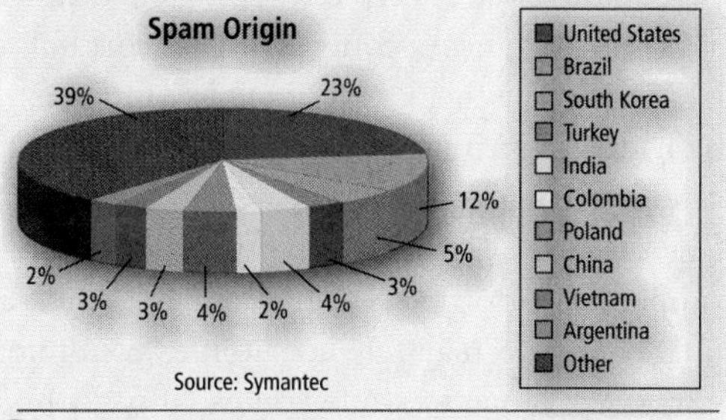

For more information, visit the Computer Concepts CourseMate Web site at www.cengagebrain.com, navigate to the Chapter 8 FAQ resource for this book, and then click Spam.

Phishing Filters *Phishing* is a scam in which a perpetrator attempts to obtain your personal and/or financial information. A **phishing filter** is a program that warns or blocks you from potentially fraudulent or suspicious Web sites. Some Web browsers include phishing filters.

Pop-Up Blockers A *pop-up ad* is an Internet advertisement that suddenly appears in a new window in the foreground of a Web page displayed in your browser. A **pop-up blocker** is a filtering program that stops pop-up ads from displaying on Web pages. Many Web browsers include a pop-up blocker. You also can download pop-up blockers from the Web at no cost.

File Compression

A **file compression utility** shrinks the size of a file(s). A compressed file takes up less storage space than the original file. Compressing files frees up room on the storage media and improves system performance. Attaching a compressed file to an e-mail message, for example, reduces the time needed for file transmission. Uploading and downloading compressed files to and from the Internet reduces the file transmission time.

Two types of compression are lossy and lossless. With *lossy* compression, because the quality of a file decreases slightly each time the file is compressed, you will be unable to restore the file to its exact original state. With audio and video files, small degradations in quality usually are not recognizable; thus, lossy compression often is used on these types of files. With *lossless* compression, by contrast, a compressed file can be returned to its exact original state. Text files typically use lossless compression.

Compressed files, sometimes called **zipped files**, usually have a .zip extension. When you receive or download a compressed file, you must uncompress it. To **uncompress**, or *unzip*, a file, you restore it to its original form. Some operating systems such as Windows include file compression and uncompression capabilities. Two popular stand-alone file compression utilities are PKZIP and WinZip.

WinZip
For more information, visit the Computer Concepts CourseMate Web site at www.cengagebrain.com, navigate to the Chapter 8 Web Link resource for this book, and then click WinZip.

Media Player

A **media player** is a program that allows you to view images and animation, listen to audio, and watch video files on your computer (Figure 8-38). Media players may also include

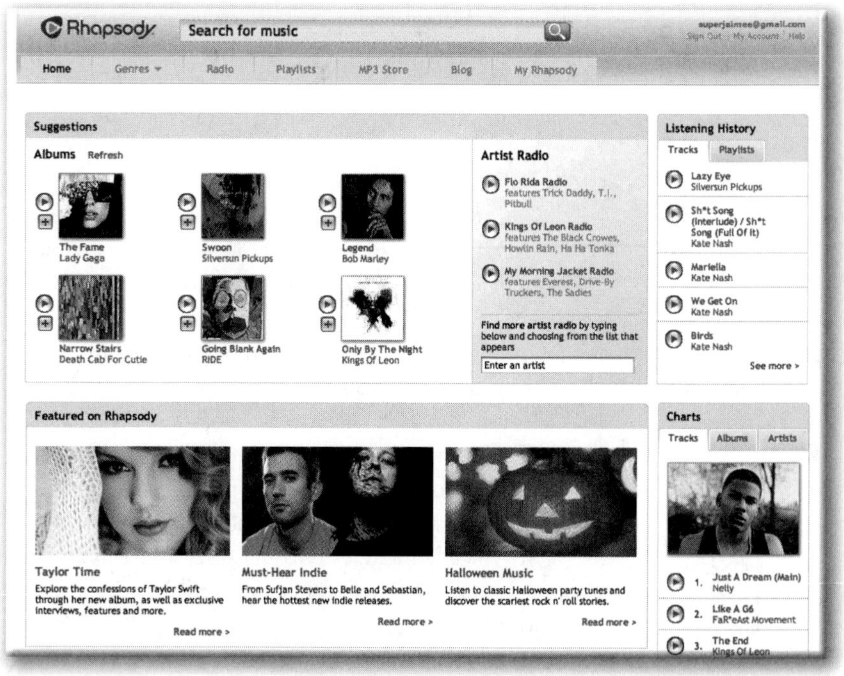

Figure 8-38 A popular media player.

the capability to organize media files, convert them to different formats, connect to and purchase media from an online media store, download podcasts and vodcasts, burn audio CDs, and transfer media to portable media players. Windows includes Windows Media Player. Three other popular media players are iTunes, RealPlayer, and Rhapsody. Read Ethics & Issues 8-4 for a related discussion.

ETHICS & ISSUES 8-4

Should the Government Tax Media Downloads?

When you purchase a DVD or Blu-ray Disc that contains a season or two of your favorite television show, chances are that you also pay a state and/or local sales tax. If you purchase and download the same material online in a digital format, however, chances are that you do not pay a sales tax. Some government taxing bodies seek to change that discrepancy. Two main reasons for the pressure to tax include: state and local governments feeling the pinch of lost revenue to legally downloaded digital content because consumers purchase less taxable, physical media; and pressure from the media industry to recoup lost sales due to illegally downloaded digital content. Some governments go as far as funneling collected taxes directly to the multimedia industry as compensation for illegally downloaded content that occurs in a region. Critics of the new taxes claim that government should not tax the greenest form of media purchases. Digitally downloaded content eliminates packaging, optical discs, trips to the store, and use of delivery vehicles. Critics also claim that governments single out multimedia content due to pressure from the multimedia industry. For example, some governments tax the purchase of newspapers, magazines and books, but often the same content is sold online and is not taxed. Typically, government taxing bodies tax goods, but not food and services.

Should the government tax media downloads, such as music, video, e-books, newspaper articles, and magazine articles? Why or why not? Should digital content delivery be considered a service rather than a good by taxing bodies? Why?

Disc Burning

Disc burning software writes text, graphics, audio, and video files on a recordable or rewritable CD, DVD, or Blu-ray Disc. This software enables the home user easily to back up contents of their hard disk on an optical disc and make duplicates of uncopyrighted music or movies. Disc burning software usually also includes photo editing, audio editing, and video editing capabilities (Figure 8-39). To learn about burning files to a disc, complete the Learn How To 2 exercise on page 440.

When you buy a recordable or rewritable disc, it typically includes burning software. You also can buy stand-alone disc burning software for a cost of less than $100.

Burning Discs

For more information, visit the Computer Concepts CourseMate Web site at www.cengagebrain.com, navigate to the Chapter 8 Web Link resource for this book, and then click Burning Discs.

Figure 8-39 You can copy text, graphics, audio, and video files to discs using the digital media suite shown here, provided you have the correct type of drive and media.

Personal Computer Maintenance

Operating systems typically include a diagnostic utility that diagnoses computer problems but does not repair them. A **personal computer maintenance utility** identifies and fixes operating system problems, detects and repairs disk problems, and includes the capability of improving a computer's performance. Additionally, some personal computer maintenance utilities continuously monitor a computer while you use it to identify and repair problems before they occur. Norton SystemWorks is a popular personal computer maintenance utility designed for Windows operating systems (Figure 8-40).

Figure 8-40 A popular maintenance program for Windows users.

QUIZ YOURSELF 8-3

Instructions: Find the true statement below. Then, rewrite the remaining false statements so that they are true.

1. A pop-up blocker shrinks the size of a file(s).
2. An anti-spam program protects a computer against viruses by identifying and removing any computer viruses found in memory, on storage media, or on incoming files.
3. A personal firewall is a utility that detects and protects a personal computer from unauthorized intrusions.
4. You should uninstall files and disks regularly in the event your originals are lost, damaged, or destroyed.
5. Web filtering software writes text, graphics, audio, and video files to a recordable or rewritable disc.
6. Fragmenting a disk is the process of reorganizing it so that the files are stored in contiguous sectors.

Quiz Yourself Online: To further check your knowledge of pages 421 through 428, visit the Computer Concepts CourseMate Web site at www.cengagebrain.com, navigate to the Chapter 8 Quiz Yourself resource for this book, and then click Objective 7.

Chapter Summary

This chapter defined an operating system and then discussed the functions common to most operating systems. The chapter introduced a variety of stand-alone operating systems, server operating systems, and embedded operating systems. Finally, the chapter described several utility programs.

Computer Usage @ Work

Education

Teachers and students have been using computers in education for many years. Teachers have been taking advantage of advances in computer technology to help provide a better educational experience for their students.

Many grade schools throughout the United States, as well as other countries, enable parents to track their child's performance online. In the past, parents would rely solely on their child bringing home graded assignments and tests to know how he or she was doing. In some cases, parents would be surprised when they saw their child's grades on report cards every two to three months. Teachers now have the opportunity to engage parents in their child's education not only by giving them an up-to-the-minute snapshot of grades, but also by posting lesson plans online so that parents know what their child is learning.

Computers and technology also benefit students in the classroom. Schools now have one or more computers in almost every classroom, enabling students to access the Internet to do research that they otherwise would have had to visit the library to perform. Schools also are able to offer additional technology courses such as Web page design, digital media, and computer programming.

At the college level, many instructors today rely heavily on e-learning systems to provide students with Web-based access to course materials and assessments, discussion forums, chat rooms, and e-mail. Once used mainly in online classes, e-learning systems provide instructors with an easy way to allow students access to the class at any time of the day.

Most instructors go beyond e-learning systems and use additional technologies to enhance their classes. For example, digital media instructors might require students to upload their assignments to a photo sharing community, and an English instructor might save paper by requiring students to upload research papers to Google Docs and share them with the instructor.

Computer use in education not only enhances the teaching experience for instructors and learning experience for students, it also provides students with technological knowledge that will benefit them for the rest of their lives.

For more information, visit the Computer Concepts CourseMate Web site at www.cengagebrain.com, navigate to the Chapter 8 Computer Usage @ Work resource for this book, and then click Education.

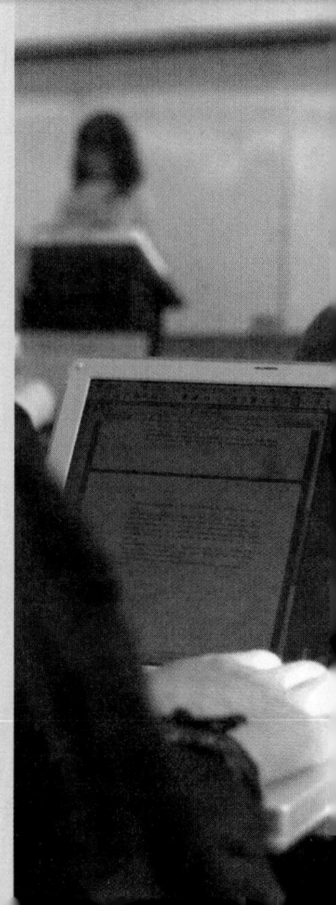

High-Tech Talk

Touch Screen Technology: How the Screen Is So Smart

Touch screen technology is becoming a larger part of everyday life for many individuals. As presented in Chapter 5, a touch screen is a touch-sensitive display device that users can interact with by touching areas of the screen. People have been using touch screens for more than 30 years, and this technology now is being used in more places, such as in smart phones, point-of-sale terminals, automated teller machines, remote controls, GPS receivers, home security systems, and Tablet PCs.

Touch screen technology has evolved since its creation in the late 1960s. The first touch screens developed allowed users to press only one area at a time with the tip of their finger, and they were much less accurate than today's touch screens. As the technology is advancing, users are able to perform additional tasks, such as dragging their finger across the screen and touching more than one area of the screen at a time. For example, the iPhone and iPod touch allow you to zoom in pictures or other objects on the screen by placing two fingers close together on the screen, and then slowly moving them apart. Three types of touch screens most in use today are capacitive, resistive, and surface wave touch screens.

A *capacitive touch screen* has a layer of material that stores electrical charges coating the surface. When a finger touches the screen, it conducts a small amount of the electrical charge, reducing the charge on the capacitive layer. Circuits located at each corner of the capacitive touch screen measure the change in electrical charge. The circuits then send this data to the touch screen controller, or software that is running on the computer. The controller then uses the data to calculate the location where the finger is touching the screen. Capacitive touch screens typically are high-quality and unaffected by items that do not conduct electrical charges. An example of the components of a capacitive touch screen is shown in Figure 8-41.

The second type of touch screen is a resistive touch screen. A metallic conductive and resistive layer held apart by spacers cover a *resistive touch screen*. When a user touches a resistive touch screen, the conductive and resistive layers connect in the location of the touch. An electronic current runs between the two layers, and the interruption in the current enables the touch screen controller to calculate the exact location of the touch. Although resistive touch screens usually are more affordable than capacitive touch screens, they are not as clear and can be damaged more easily.

The third type of touch screen uses surface wave technology. *Surface wave technology* passes ultrasonic waves over the touch screen. Touching the screen absorbs portions of the waves, which then allows the touch screen controller to calculate the position at which the object touched the screen. Because ultrasonic waves pass over the touch screen, it is easy for outside elements to damage the device. Touch screens using surface wave technology are the most advanced and often the most expensive of the three types.

Additional types of touch screen technologies exist, but they are not used as widely as the capacitive, resistive, and surface wave touch screens. *Optical touch screens* use cameras mounted at two corners of the screen to detect objects close to the surface. *Infrared touch screens* use light emitting diodes and light detectors at the edges of the touch screen to detect objects that break the beams of light traveling across the screen.

As touch screen prices continue to decrease, they most likely will be incorporated in an increasing number of computers and devices. Touch screens have increased productivity by allowing people to interact with devices more quickly than they can with a mouse or keyboard.

For more information, visit the Computer Concepts CourseMate Web site at www.cengagebrain.com, navigate to the Chapter 8 High-Tech Talk resource for this book, and then click Touch Screen Technology.

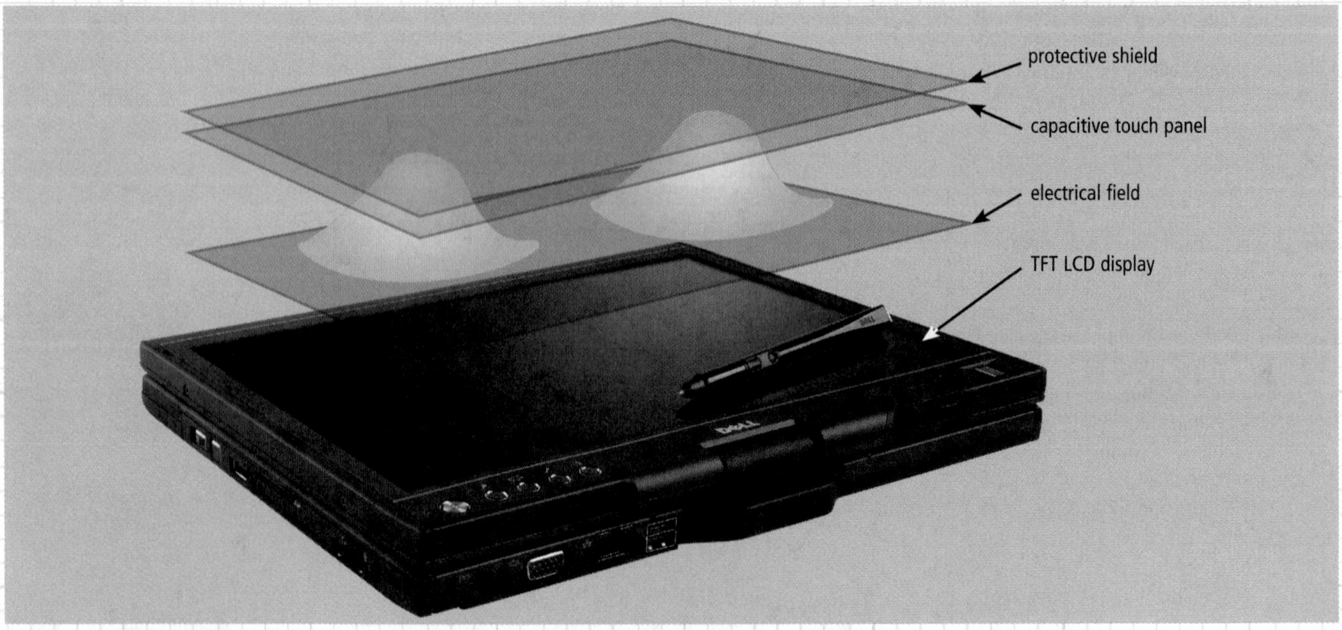

Figure 8-41 A capacitive touch screen identifies where someone touches the screen by measuring differences in electrical charges.

Companies on the Cutting Edge

VERISIGN Internet Infrastructure Services

Technology users desire immediate access to information and services. Their ability to communicate and conduct commerce securely is aided in large part by *VeriSign*. More than 30 billion times a day, people interact on the Internet, and their purchases, text messages, downloads, and other transactions are enabled and protected by VeriSign's infrastructure services.

Computer security company Semantic acquired VeriSign's Authentication division business in 2010 to strengthen encryption and identity services and help protect businesses and consumers by protecting information and detecting online fraud. Its domain name services department registers all .com, .net, .cc, and .tv domain names. The VeriSign Secured Seal, which has been issued to more than 100,000 domains in 145 countries, ensures companies and consumers that the Web site is secure.

The California-based company was founded in 1995 and has more than 2,200 employees worldwide.

RESEARCH IN MOTION (RIM) Wireless Mobile Communications Devices Manufacturer

By 2012, 800 million people worldwide are expected to access social networking Web sites on smart phones, up from 82 million in 2007. *Research in Motion (RIM)* helped fuel this networking frenzy by partnering with MySpace in 2008 to help connect networkers on the go. They can access MySpace Mobile on a BlackBerry smart phone, which is RIM's key product.

The Canadian company was founded in 1984 by Mike Lazaridis, who serves as its president and co-CEO. Lazaridis's vision for wireless technology developed in high school when he was a member of the local amateur radio and television club. He developed RIM's first major product, the Inter@active Pager, which was integrated in the first BlackBerry product in 1998. The BlackBerry gained attention for having the capability to combine a wireless mailbox with a corporate mailbox so that users could assess e-mail continuously.

Recently, Research in Motion launched BlackBerry App World, an application store that allows BlackBerry users to download personal and business programs.

For more information, visit the Computer Concepts CourseMate Web site at www.cengagebrain.com and then navigate to the Chapter 8 Companies on the Cutting Edge resource for this book.

Technology Trailblazers

STEVE WOZNIAK Apple Cofounder

Mixing fun with work comes naturally for *Steve Wozniak*. As Apple's cofounder, he says his computer designing career began and still continues to be a hobby filled with creativity, humor, games, and education. In his opinion, Apple's success evolved because he designed computers that had minimal parts and maximum performance.

Wozniak designed the original Apple computer in 1975 with Apple's current CEO, Steve Jobs, and wrote most of the software. Ten years later he cofounded Pixar, the award winning animation studio. He left Apple in 1985 to spend time with his family, work on community projects, and teach, but he still serves as an advisor to the corporation.

Wozinak was inducted into the Consumer Electronics Hall of Fame and the National Inventors Hall of Fame. One of his current passions is applying artificial intelligence to the area of robotics. He also is a member of the Silicon Valley Aftershocks, a polo team that plays using Segway electric transportation devices.

LINUS TORVALDS Linux Creator

Inductees to the Computer History Museum in Mountain View, CA, are noted for their contribution to computer technology. *Linus Torvalds* joined the Museum's Hall of Fellows in 2008 for his creation of the open source operating system, Linux.

When he developed an operating system in 1991, he announced his project in an Internet newsgroup. He made the source code available and asked readers for suggestions to enhance the product. Computer users responded by reviewing the system and offering enhancements. Three years later he released a greatly enhanced version he called Linux.

Torvalds developed this innovative operating system when he was a 21-year-old computer science student in Finland. Today, he leads the development of Linux as a fellow at OSDL (Open Source Development Labs), a not-for-profit consortium of companies dedicated to developing and promoting the operating system. Torvalds says his daily involvement with Linux involves coordinating and merging the lines of code submitted by users so that the software runs smoothly.

For more information, visit the Computer Concepts CourseMate Web site at www.cengagebrain.com and then navigate to the Chapter 8 Technology Trailblazers resource for this book.

Chapter Review

The Chapter Review reinforces the main concepts presented in this chapter.

To listen to an audio version of this Chapter Review, visit the Computer Concepts CourseMate Web site at www.cengagebrain.com and then navigate to the Chapter 8 Chapter Review resource for this book.

1. **What Is System Software, and What Are the Two Types of System Software?** **System software** consists of the programs that control or maintain the operations of a computer and its devices. Two types of system software are operating systems and utility programs. An **operating system (OS)** is a set of programs containing instructions that work together to coordinate all the activities among computer hardware resources. A **utility program**, also called a **utility**, performs maintenance-type tasks, usually related to managing a computer, its devices, or its programs.

2. **What Are the Functions of an Operating System?** The operating system starts and shuts down a computer, provides a user interface, manages programs, manages memory, coordinates tasks, configures devices, establishes an Internet connection, monitors performance, provides utilities, updates automatically, controls a network, and administers security. The **user interface** controls how data and instructions are entered and how information is displayed on the screen. Two types of user interfaces are a *graphical user interface* (*GUI*) and a *command-line interface*. Managing programs refers to how many users, and how many programs, an operating system can support at one time. An operating system can be *single user/single tasking*, *single user/multitasking*, *multiuser*, or *multiprocessing*. **Memory management** optimizes the use of random access memory (RAM). If memory is insufficient, the operating system may use **virtual memory**, which allocates a portion of a storage medium to function as additional RAM. Coordinating tasks determines the order in which tasks are processed. Tasks include receiving data from an input device, processing instructions, sending information to an output device, and transferring items between storage and memory. Configuring devices involves loading each device's driver when a user boots the computer. A **driver**, short for *device driver*, is a small program that tells the operating system how to communicate with a specific device. Establishing an Internet connection sets up a connection between a computer and an Internet access provider. A **performance monitor** is an operating system program that assesses and reports information about computer resources and devices. Operating systems often provide the capability of managing and searching for files, viewing images, securing a computer from unauthorized access, uninstalling programs, and other tasks. Most operating systems also include an **automatic update** feature that provides updates to the program. A **server operating system** is an operating system that organizes and coordinates how multiple users access and share network resources. Network administrators typically have an *administrator account* that enables them to access files, install programs, and specify network settings, including creating user accounts and establishing *permissions*.

3. **What Is the Startup Process on a Personal Computer?** **Booting** is the process of starting or restarting a computer. When a user turns on a computer, the power supply sends a signal to the system unit. The processor chip finds the ROM chip(s) that contains the **BIOS** (*basic input/output system*), which is firmware with the computer's startup instructions. The BIOS performs the *power-on self test* (*POST*) to check system components and compares the results with data in a CMOS chip. If the POST completes successfully, the BIOS searches for the *system files* and the *kernel* of the operating system, which manages memory and devices, and loads them into memory from storage. Finally, the operating system loads configuration information, requests any necessary user information, and displays the desktop on the screen. The operating system executes programs in the *Startup folder*, which contains a list of programs that open automatically when you boot the computer.

Visit the Computer Concepts CourseMate Web site at www.cengagebrain.com, navigate to the Chapter 8 Quiz Yourself resource for this book, and then click Objectives 1 – 3.

4. **What Are Features of Windows 7, Mac OS X, UNIX, and Linux Operating Systems?** A **stand-alone operating system** is a complete operating system that works on a desktop computer, notebook computer, or mobile computing device. **Windows 7** is Microsoft's fastest, most efficient operating system to date, offering quicker program start up, built-in diagnostics, automatic recovery, improved security, enhanced searching and

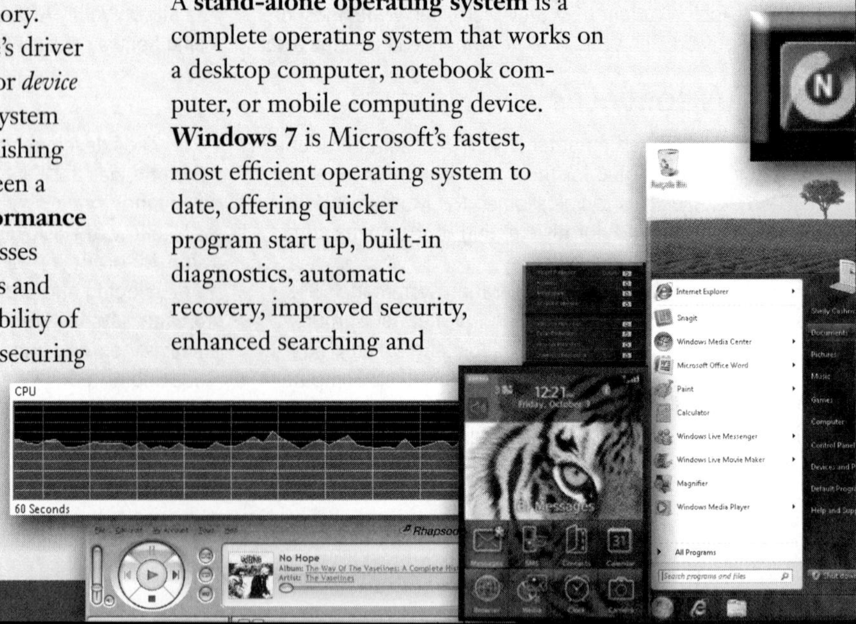

Chapter Review

organizing capabilities, and an easy-to-use interface. Most users choose from *Windows 7 Starter*, *Windows 7 Home Premium*, *Windows 7 Ultimate*, or *Windows 7 Professional* editions. **Mac OS X** is a multitasking operating system available only for Apple computers. **UNIX** is a multitasking operating system developed at Bell Laboratories. **Linux** is a popular, multitasking UNIX-type operating system that is *open source software*, which means its code is available to the public for use, modification, and redistribution.

5. What Are Various Server Operating Systems? Server operating systems include Windows Server 2008, UNIX, Linux, Solaris, and NetWare. **Windows Server 2008** is an upgrade to Windows Server 2003 and includes features of previous Windows Server versions. UNIX, like Linux, is a *multipurpose operating system* because it is both a stand-alone and server operating system. *Solaris*, a version of UNIX developed by Sun Microsystems, is a server operating system designed specifically for e-commerce applications. Novell's *NetWare* is a server operating system designed for client/server networks.

6. What Are the Features of Several Embedded Operating Systems? Mobile devices and many consumer electronics have an **embedded operating system** that resides on a ROM chip. Popular embedded operating systems include Windows Embedded CE, Windows Phone 7, Palm OS, iPhone OS, BlackBerry, Google Android, embedded Linux, and Symbian OS. **Windows Embedded CE** is a scaled-down Windows operating system designed for use on communications, entertainment, and computing devices with limited functionality. **Windows Phone 7**, which is a successor to Windows Mobile, provides a user interface designed for specific types of smart phones. *Palm OS* is an operating system used on smart phones and PDAs. **iPhone OS**, developed by Apple, is an operating system for the iPhone and iPod touch. The *BlackBerry* operating system runs on handheld devices supplied by RIM. *Google Android* is an operating system developed by Google for mobile devices. *Embedded Linux* is a scaled-down Linux operating system for smart phones, PDAs, portable media players, and other devices requiring an embedded operating system. *Symbian OS* is an open source multitasking operating system designed for smart phones.

Visit the Computer Concepts CourseMate Web site at www.cengagebrain.com, navigate to the Chapter 8 Quiz Yourself resource for this book, and then click Objectives 4 – 6.

7. What Is the Purpose of Several Utility Programs? Most operating systems include several built-in utility programs. A **file manager** performs functions related to file management. A **search utility** attempts to locate a file on your computer based on criteria you specify. An **image viewer** displays, copies, and prints the contents of a graphics file, such as photos. An **uninstaller** removes a program and any associated entries in the system files. A *disk cleanup utility* searches for and removes unnecessary files. A **disk defragmenter** reorganizes the files and unused space on a computer's hard disk. A **backup utility** is used to copy, or *back up*, selected files or an entire hard disk to another storage medium. A **restore utility** reverses the backup process and returns backed up files to their original form. A **screen saver** displays a moving image or blank screen if no keyboard or mouse activity occurs for a specified time. A **personal firewall** detects and protects a personal computer from unauthorized intrusions. An **antivirus program** protects computers against a **virus**, or potentially damaging computer program, by identifying and removing any computer viruses. A **spyware remover** detects and deletes *spyware* and other similar programs. An *adware remover* detects and deletes *adware*. Internet filter programs can include **Web filtering software**, an **anti-spam** program, a **phishing filter**, and a **pop-up blocker**. A **file compression utility** shrinks the size of a file so that it takes up less storage space. A **media player** allows you to view images and animation, listen to audio, and watch video files on a computer. **Disc burning software** writes text, graphics, audio, and video files on a recordable or rewritable CD, DVD, or Blu-ray Disc. A **personal computer maintenance utility** identifies and fixes operating system problems and improves a computer's performance.

Visit the Computer Concepts CourseMate Web site at www.cengagebrain.com, navigate to the Chapter 8 Quiz Yourself resource for this book, and then click Objective 7.

Key Terms

You should know the Primary Terms and be familiar with the Secondary Terms. The list below helps focus your study.

To see an example of and a definition for each term, and to access current and additional information from the Web, visit the Computer Concepts CourseMate Web site at www.cengagebrain.com and then navigate to the Chapter 8 Key Terms resource for this book.

Primary Terms

(shown in bold-black characters in the chapter)

anti-spam program (427)
antivirus program (426)
automatic update (409)
backup utility (424)
BIOS (400)
boot disk (402)
boot drive (402)
booting (400)
buffer (407)
cold boot (400)
defragmenting (424)
disc burning software (428)
disk defragmenter (423)
driver (408)
embedded operating system (418)
file compression utility (427)
file manager (422)
folder (422)
image viewer (423)
iPhone OS (420)
Linux (416)
log on (410)
Mac OS X (415)
Macintosh operating system (415)
media player (427)
memory management (406)
operating system (OS) (398)
password (410)
performance monitor (408)
personal computer maintenance utility (428)
personal firewall (425)
phishing filter (427)
Plug and Play (408)
pop-up blocker (427)
queue (407)
recovery disk (402)
restore utility (424)
screen saver (425)
search utility (422)
server operating system (410)
shortcut (422)
spooling (407)
spyware remover (426)
stand-alone operating system (412)
system software (398)
Trojan horse (426)
uncompress (427)
uninstaller (423)
UNIX (416)
user ID (410)
user interface (402)
user name (410)
utility (421)
utility program (421)
virtual memory (406)
virus (425)
warm boot (400)
Web filtering software (426)
Windows 7 (413)
Windows Embedded CE (419)
Windows Phone 7 (419)
Windows Server 2008 (417)
Windows Server 2008 family (417)
worm (426)
zipped files (427)

Aero Flip 3D (414)

Secondary Terms

(shown in italic characters in the chapter)

administrator account (410)
adware (426)
adware remover (426)
Aero Flip 3D (414)
back up (424)
background (404)
basic input/output system (400)
BlackBerry (420)
bugs (409)
client operating systems (412)
command language (403)
command-line interface (403)
compress (424)
cross-platform (399)
Desktop Gadget Gallery (414)
device driver (408)
device-dependent (411)
device-independent (411)
disk cleanup (423)
embedded Linux (420)
encryption (411)
fault-tolerant computer (405)
foreground (404)
fragmented (423)
gadget (414)
ghosting (425)
Google Android (420)
graphical user interface (GUI) (402)
hacker (425)
hibernate (402)
index (422)
Internet Explorer (413)
kernel (400)
lossless (427)
lossy (427)
malware (426)
memory resident (400)
multiprocessing (405)
multipurpose operating system (418)
multiuser (405)
NetWare (418)
network administrator (410)
nonresident (400)
open source software (416)
page (406)
paging (406)
Palm OS (419)
permissions (410)
phishing (427)
platform (399)
pop-up ad (427)
power-on self test (POST) (400)
preemptive multitasking (405)
print spooler (407)
proprietary software (411)
registry (401)
service pack (409)
single user/multitasking (404)
single user/single tasking (404)
sleep mode (402)
Snipping Tool (415)
Solaris (418)
spam (427)
spyware (426)
Startup folder (401)
swap file (406)
Symbian OS (420)
system files (401)
thrashing (406)
unzip (427)
virtualization (418)
virus author (425)
widget (414)
Windows 7 Home Premium (414)
Windows 7 Professional (414)
Windows 7 Starter (414)
Windows 7 Ultimate (414)
Windows Aero (402)
Windows Calendar (415)
Windows Defender (415)
Windows DVD Maker (414)
Windows Firewall (414)
Windows Live Essentials (415)
Windows Live Mail (415)
Windows Live Messenger (415)
Windows Live Movie Maker (415)
Windows Live Photo Gallery (415)
Windows Live Writer (415)
Windows Media Player (414)
Windows Photo Viewer (423)
Windows ReadyBoost (406)
Windows Server 2008 Datacenter (417)
Windows Server 2008 Enterprise (417)
Windows Server 2008 for Itanium-Based Systems (418)
Windows Server 2008 Standard (417)
Windows Touch (415)
Windows Web Server 2008 (418)

Checkpoint

The Checkpoint exercises test your knowledge of the chapter concepts. The page number containing the answer appears in parentheses after each exercise. The Beyond the Book exercises will help broaden your understanding of the concepts presented in this chapter.

To complete the Checkpoint exercises interactively, visit the Computer Concepts CourseMate Web site at www.cengagebrain.com and then navigate to the Chapter 8 Checkpoint resource for this book.

True/False Mark T for True and F for False.

_____ 1. All sizes of computers typically use the same operating system because operating systems generally are written to run on any type of computer. (399)

_____ 2. Booting is the process of permanently removing a computer from operation. (400)

_____ 3. Permissions define who can access certain resources and when they can access those resources. (410)

_____ 4. A device-independent program is one that runs only on a specific type or make of computer. (411)

_____ 5. Users can control and customize a variety of gadgets on the Windows desktop. (414)

_____ 6. Linux is open source software, which means its code can be modified and redistributed. (416)

_____ 7. BlackBerry devices provide PIM capabilities such as managing schedules, contacts, and appointments, as well as phone capabilities. (420)

_____ 8. Windows allows you to manage your documents, pictures, music, and other files using Windows Explorer. (422)

_____ 9. An adware remover is a program that detects and deletes spam. (426)

_____ 10. Phishing is a scam in which a perpetrator attempts to obtain your personal and/or financial information. (427)

Multiple Choice Select the best answer.

1. The _____ chip, which uses battery power, stores configuration information about the computer. (400)
   a. BIOS
   b. CMOS
   c. POST
   d. RAM

2. Windows users can increase the size of memory through _____, which can allocate available storage space on removable flash memory devices as additional memory cache. (406)
   a. Windows Aero
   b. Windows ReadyBoost
   c. Plug and Play
   d. a disk defragmenter

3. A _____ is a mini-program with minimal functionality that connects to another program or provides information. (414)
   a. service pack
   b. search utility
   c. gadget
   d. swap file

4. When you enter search criteria, instead of looking through every file and folder on the storage medium, the search utility looks through the _____ first to find a match. (422)
   a. index
   b. buffer
   c. file manager
   d. driver

5. Defragmenting reorganizes the files on a disk so that they are located in _____ access time. (424)
   a. noncontiguous sectors, which slows
   b. contiguous sectors, which slows
   c. contiguous sectors, which speeds
   d. noncontiguous sectors, which speeds

6. _____ is a utility that detects and protects a personal computer from unauthorized intrusions. (425)
   a. Automatic updates
   b. Sleep mode
   c. Windows Explorer
   d. Windows Firewall

7. _____ is a program that displays an online advertisement in a banner or pop-up window on Web pages, e-mail, or other Internet services. (426)
   a. Spyware
   b. A Trojan horse
   c. Adware
   d. Spam

8. A(n) _____ is a program that warns or blocks you from potentially fraudulent or suspicious Web sites. (427)
   a. phishing filter
   b. Web filter
   c. adware remover
   d. Trojan horse

STUDENT ASSIGNMENTS

Checkpoint

Matching
Match the terms with their definitions.

_____ 1. sleep mode (402)	a. the practice of sharing or pooling computing resources, such as servers
_____ 2. hibernate (402)	b. server operating system designed for client/server networks
_____ 3. page (406)	c. saves any open documents and programs to a hard disk before removing power from the computer
_____ 4. user name (410)	d. unique combination of characters that identifies one specific user
_____ 5. Aero Flip 3D (414)	e. works with the mouse to flip through windows by rolling the wheel on the mouse
_____ 6. UNIX (416)	f. saves any open documents and programs to RAM, turns off all unneeded functions, and then places the computer in a low-power state
_____ 7. virtualization (418)	g. with virtual memory, the amount of data and program instructions that can be swapped at a given time
_____ 8. NetWare (418)	h. multitasking operating system developed in the early 1970s by scientists at Bell Laboratories
_____ 9. Google Andriod (420)	i. operating system for mobile devices
_____ 10. shortcut (422)	j. an icon on the desktop or in a folder that provides a user with immediate access to a program or file

Short Answer
Write a brief answer to each of the following questions.

1. How is a cold boot different from a warm boot? __________ How is a memory-resident part of an operating system different from a nonresident part of an operating system? __________
2. What is a user interface? __________ How are graphical and command-line user interfaces different? __________
3. What is the purpose of an automatic update feature? __________ Why and when might a user receive a service pack? __________
4. What happens during a backup? __________ What is the purpose of a restore utility? __________
5. Describe four embedded operating systems. __________ What are the uses for each of the four types? __________

Beyond the Book
Follow the book element instructions below; present your findings (brief report, presentation, discussion, or other means).

1. Ethics & Issues — Select an Ethics & Issues in this chapter (410, 416, 418, 428), find a recent newspaper/magazine article that supports one point of view presented, and then evaluate the article.
2. Computer Usage @ Work — Use the Web or a recent newspaper/magazine to locate three additional unique usages of computer technology in the education field (429). What makes the use of these technologies unique to the education field?
3. Companies on the Cutting Edge and Technology Trailblazers — Use the Web or a recent business newspaper/magazine to locate an interesting fact about VeriSign, Research in Motion (RIM), Steve Wozniak, or Linus Torvalds that was not presented in the chapter (431).
4. High-Tech Talk — Locate a recent newspaper/magazine article that discusses topics related to Touch Screen Technology (430). Would you recommend the article you found? Why or why not?
5. FAQs and Web Links — Use the Web or a recent newspaper/magazine to locate three additional facts about an FAQ (402, 407, 408, 411, 412, 423, 426, 427) and Web Link (401, 402, 407, 408, 414, 415, 417, 418, 420, 427, 428) that were not presented in the chapter.
6. Looking Ahead — Use the Web or a recent newspaper/magazine to discover additional uses of the technology presented in Contact Lenses Monitor Glaucoma (409).
7. Innovative Computing — Use the Web or a recent newspaper/magazine to locate two additional interesting facts about Utility Programs Locate Deleted Files (421).
8. Making Use of the Web — Visit three of the Government sites (132) and outline the information on each Web site and the possible uses for each Web site.
9. Buyers Guide: How to Purchase Computers and Mobile Devices — Use the Buyers Guide feature (444) to determine the configuration for a desktop computer, notebook computer, smart phone, portable media player, or digital camera that you would like to purchase, then create a presentation about the reasons you made your choices using the suggested Web sites or advertisements in magazines.

Learn It Online

The Learn It Online exercises are interactive Web exercises designed to reinforce and expand your understanding of the chapter concepts. The descriptions below briefly summarize each exercise.

To complete the Learn It Online exercises, visit the Computer Concepts CourseMate Web site at www.cengagebrain.com, navigate to the Chapter 8 resources for this book, click the link for the exercise you want to complete, and then read the instructions.

1 At the Movies — Free Online Antivirus

Watch a movie to learn why it is important to run antivirus software on your computer and how to scan your computer for malware online for no cost and then answer questions about the movie.

2 Video and Audio: You Review It — Spyware

Search for, choose, and write a review of a video, podcast, or vodcast that discusses spyware.

3 Student Edition Labs — Installing and Uninstalling Software and Keeping Your Computer Virus Free

Enhance your understanding and knowledge about installing and uninstalling software and keeping your computer virus free by completing the Installing and Uninstalling Software and Keeping Your Computer Virus Free Labs.

4 Practice Test

Take a multiple choice test that checks your knowledge of the chapter concepts and review the resulting study guide.

5 Who Wants To Be a Computer Genius^2?

Play the Shelly Cashman Series version of this popular game by answering questions to find out if you are a computer genius. Panic buttons are available to provide assistance during game play.

6 Wheel of Terms

Identify important key terms presented in this chapter by playing the Shelly Cashman Series version of this popular game.

7 You're Hired!

Embark on the path to a career in computers by answering questions and solving puzzles related to concepts discussed in this chapter.

8 Crossword Puzzle Challenge

Complete an interactive crossword puzzle to reinforce concepts presented in this chapter.

9 Windows Exercises

Step through the Windows 7 exercises to learn about Windows, using a screen saver, changing desktop colors, customizing the desktop for multiple users, and backing up a computer.

10 Exploring Computer Careers

Read about a career as a systems programmer, search for related employment advertisements, and then answer related questions.

11 Web Apps — PhotoshopExpress

Learn how to use PhotoshopExpress to upload new photos as well as photos stored on other photo sharing communities, edit photos, create new pictures, and share them with others.

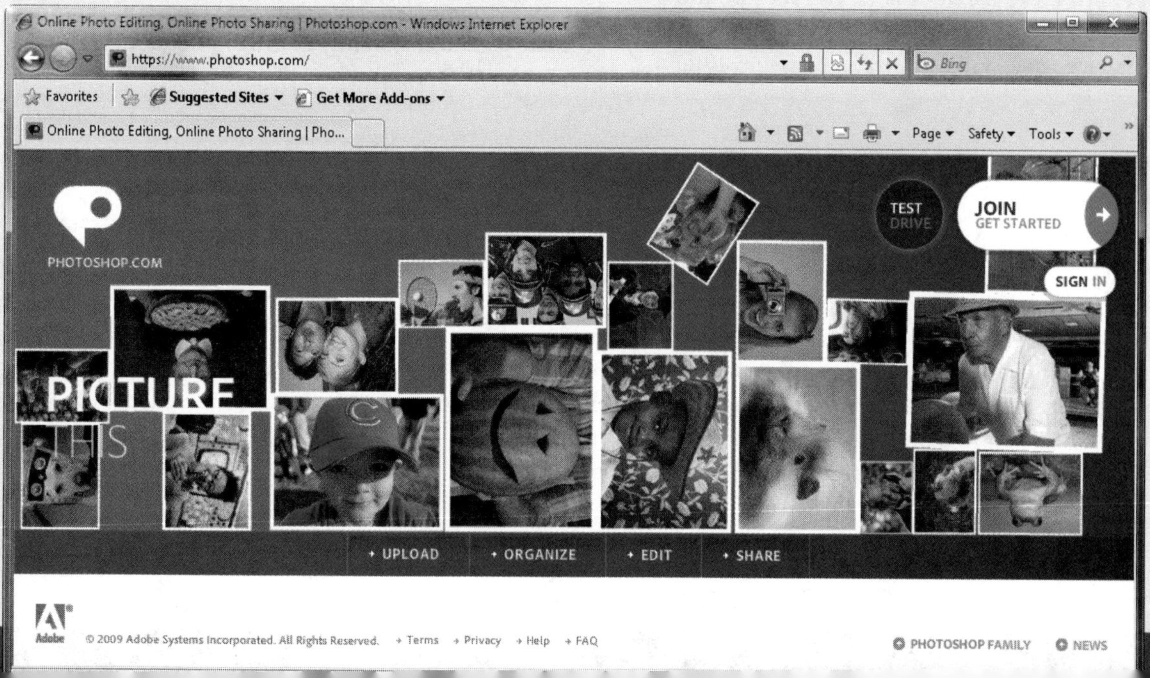

Problem Solving @ Home

The Problem Solving @ Home exercises extend your knowledge of the chapter concepts by seeking solutions to practical computer problems that you may encounter at home or school. The Collaboration exercise should be completed with a team.

In the real world, practical problems often can be solved in multiple ways. Provide one solution to each of the following problems using available resources, such as articles on the Web or in print, blogs, podcasts, videos, television, user guides, other individuals, and electronics and computer stores. You may need to use multiple resources to obtain an answer. Present your solutions in the form requested by your instructor (brief report, presentation, discussion, or other means).

1. **Computer Cannot Boot** You recently purchased a computer from a friend. When you turn on the computer, a message displays that says, "Operating system not found." What steps will you take before calling technical support?
2. **Improper Shut Down** During the startup process, your computer displays a message indicating that the computer did not shut down properly. You are certain that you shut down the computer properly when you last used it. The message also lists options to start Windows normally or start Windows in safe mode. How will you respond? Why?
3. **Incorrect Display Settings** You recently turned on your computer and noticed that the screen resolution, desktop background, and color scheme had changed, even though you have not changed the display settings since purchasing the computer several months ago. What might have caused Windows to change the display settings? What are your next steps?

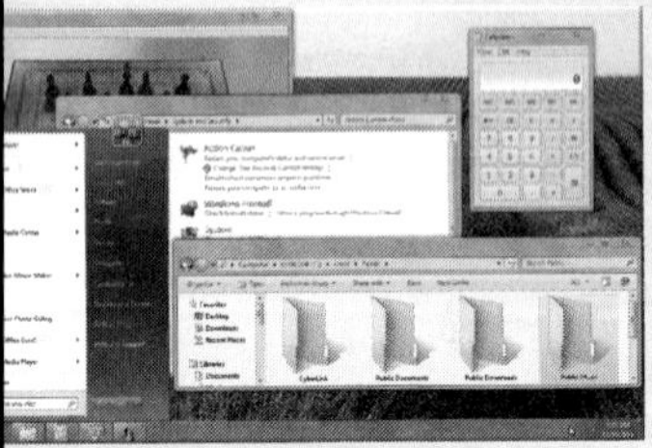

4. **Unreadable Taskbar Buttons** While using your computer for a research project, you start multiple programs. With so many programs running, you are unable to determine which buttons correspond to each program. How can you determine which button to click to access the desired program?
5. **Poor Computer Performance** Your friend sends you an e-mail message stating that her computer is running slowly. She asks if you know of any programs that are included with Windows that will help increase her computer's performance. How will you respond?
6. **Maximum CPU Usage** Because your computer is performing slowly, you start the Windows Task Manager to investigate. You see that the CPU usage is near 100%. You are not aware of any other programs currently running. What might be causing this?
7. **Command Not Displaying** While using a computer in your school's computer lab, you decide to use the Control Panel to change the desktop background. When you click the Start button, the Control Panel command does not display on the Start menu. What could be the reason for this?
8. **Unwanted Programs** The new computer that you ordered online arrived today. You anxiously unpack it, connect all components, and then turn it on. After answering a series of questions to set up the computer, you notice it includes programs that you do not want. How will you remove these unwanted programs?

Collaboration

9. **Slow Computer** A fellow classmate has been complaining that his computer does not seem to be working properly. He complains that Windows takes too long to start and that it runs very slowly. You would like more practice troubleshooting computer problems, so you offer to look at his computer. When you start Windows, you notice that the hard disk has less than 100 MB of free space, many icons appear in the notification area, no antivirus software is installed, and more than 50 Windows updates are available for the computer. Form a team of three people and determine how to use the software that is included with Windows, in addition to any third-party software that may be needed, to resolve these computer problems. Compile your findings and submit them to your instructor.

Problem Solving @ Work

The Problem Solving @ Work exercises extend your knowledge of the chapter concepts by seeking solutions to practical computer problems that you may encounter at work. The Collaboration exercise should be completed with a team.

In the real world, practical problems often can be solved in multiple ways. Provide one solution to each of the following problems using available resources, such as articles on the Web or in print, blogs, podcasts, videos, television, user guides, other individuals, and electronics and computer stores. You may need to use multiple resources to obtain an answer. Present your solutions in the form requested by your instructor (brief report, presentation, discussion, or other means).

1. **Long Defragmentation Process** You started the Disk Defragmenter in Windows and clicked the Defragment now button. Several hours have elapsed, and Disk Defragmenter reports that it still is defragmenting the hard disk, despite its initial message that the defragmenting process may take from a few minutes to a few hours. With your computer tied up in the defragmenting process, you are unable to use it to complete a report that is due to your supervisor tomorrow. How should you proceed?

2. **Password Required** After turning on your computer, it prompts you to type a password to continue the boot process; however, you forgot the password. What are your next steps to allow the computer to continue the boot process, start Windows, and access the files on the hard disk?

3. **Frozen Manufacturer Logo** After turning on your computer, the computer manufacturer's logo displays on the monitor for several minutes. Suspecting that your computer might be frozen, you turn it off. Three minutes later, you turn the computer on and the same problem arises. What might be wrong?

4. **Automatic Updates** Two or three times per month, your coworker receives a notification on his computer that the computer recently has been updated. You ask your coworker about these messages, and he says that Microsoft periodically installs updates automatically to protect the computer from various threats, as well as to improve performance. You never have seen this message appear on your computer. Does this mean that your computer does not update automatically? How can you configure your computer to update automatically?

5. **Configuring Updates** After an employee from your company's technical support department configures your computer to download and install updates automatically, you want to change the schedule so that your computer checks for and installs new updates every day instead of once per week. Your computer, however, does not allow you to change the settings for Windows Update. What could be causing this?

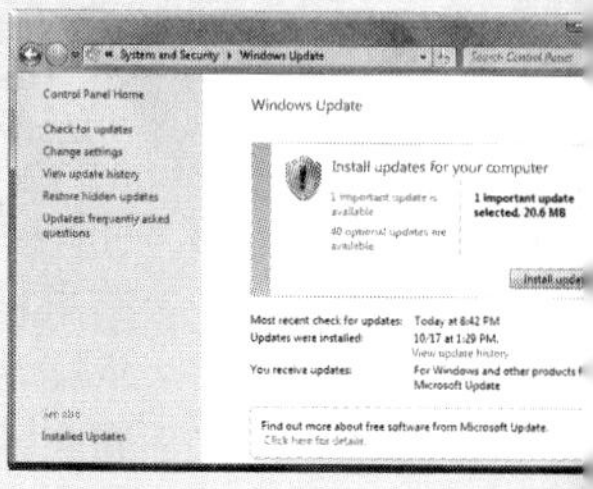

6. **Antivirus Schedule** You recently changed your work schedule so that you work until 6:00 p.m. instead of 5:00 p.m. At 5:00 p.m. each day, you notice that the antivirus program on your computer automatically begins scanning all files on your hard disk. This process slows your computer, and the program usually still is scanning when you leave the office. How can you change the configuration so that the antivirus program does not start until after you leave?

7. **Minimum Battery Power** When you use your notebook computer and it is not plugged in, the battery lasts for only one hour, but the documentation states that the computer can last for two hours on battery power. What are some ways that you can increase the battery life?

Collaboration

8. **Computers in Education** A private elementary school in your neighborhood has received a grant to create a computer lab with Internet access so that students can learn about computers and related technologies. Your neighbor, who also is a teacher at the school, asks for advice regarding how they should spend the grant money. Form a team of three people to determine the best configuration for the lab. One team member should research whether a PC or Mac is more beneficial. Another team member should research the application software that should be installed on these computers, and the other team member should determine what, if any, peripheral devices should be attached to the computers in the lab. Compile your findings and submit them to your instructor.

Learn How To

The Learn How To activities step you through fundamental technology skills when using a computer. The Learn How To exercises enable you to become more proficient with these skills.

Premium Activity: To relate this Learn How To activity to your everyday life, see a visual demonstration of the activity, and complete a short assessment, visit the Computer Concepts CourseMate Web site at www.cengagebrain.com and then navigate to the Chapter 8 Learn How To resource for this book.

Learn How To 1: Install and Maintain a Computer

Once you have purchased a computer, you must install it for use, and then maintain it. Based on years of experience, a set of guidelines for installing and maintaining your computer has been developed. To examine these guidelines, complete the following steps:

1. Start the browser on your computer.
2. Type the Web address `www.cengagebrain.com` in the Address bar and then press the ENTER key.
3. Navigate to the Chapter 8 Learn How To Install and Maintain a Computer resource for this book.
4. Read the material presented about how to install and maintain a computer.

Exercises

1. Using your Web search skills, research the latest recommendations with respect to proper ergonomics for using a computer. What information did you find that you did not know before? What changes would you make to your current computer setup that might make you more productive? Submit your answers to your instructor.
2. Many people report illnesses or injuries from using computers. Perform research in a library or on the Web to discover the five most common ailments associated with using a computer. Determine the actions people can take to minimize or eliminate these ailments. Submit a report to your instructor describing your findings.
3. On either your computer or the computer on which you are working, perform a hardware and software inventory of at least five hardware devices and five application programs. List the vendor, product, vendor Web address, vendor e-mail address, and vendor support telephone number. Submit the inventory to your instructor.

Learn How To 2: Burn Files to an Optical Disc

Many people use USB flash drives to transport files from one location to another. If they wish to share files with someone else, however, they might choose to distribute these files on an optical disc. To learn how to burn files to an optical disc using Windows 7, complete the following steps:

1. Insert a blank optical disc into the optical disc drive.
2. When the AutoPlay dialog box is displayed, click the Burn files to disc using Windows Explorer link.
3. If necessary, change the Disc title, click the 'Like a USB flash drive' option button, and then click the Next button in the Burn a Disc dialog box to prepare the blank disc.
4. Drag the files you wish to burn to the empty window that opens.
5. Click the 'Burn to disk' button.
6. Click the Next button to burn the files to the disc. When the disc has finished burning, remove the disc from the optical disc drive.

Exercise

1. Locate photos on your computer that you are willing to share with others. If you are unable to locate any photos or are using someone else's computer, download at least three photos from the Internet. Insert a blank optical disc into your optical disc drive and then burn the photos to the disc. Once you have finished burning the disc, eject it, write your name on it, and then submit it to your instructor.

Learn How To 3: Keep Windows Up-to-Date

Keeping Windows up-to-date is a critical part of keeping your computer in working order. The updates made available by Microsoft for no charge over the Internet can help to keep errors from occurring on your computer and attempt to ensure that all security safeguards are in place. To update Windows, complete the next steps:

Learn How To

1. Click the Start button on the Windows taskbar, click All Programs, and then click Windows Update in the All Programs list (Figure 8-42) to display the Windows Update window.
2. Click the link indicating that updates are available.
3. If necessary, select those updates you wish to install and then click the OK button. Be aware that some updates might take 20 minutes or more to download and install, based primarily on your Internet access speed.
4. Often, after installation of updates, you must restart your computer to allow those updates to take effect. Be sure to save any open files before restarting your computer.

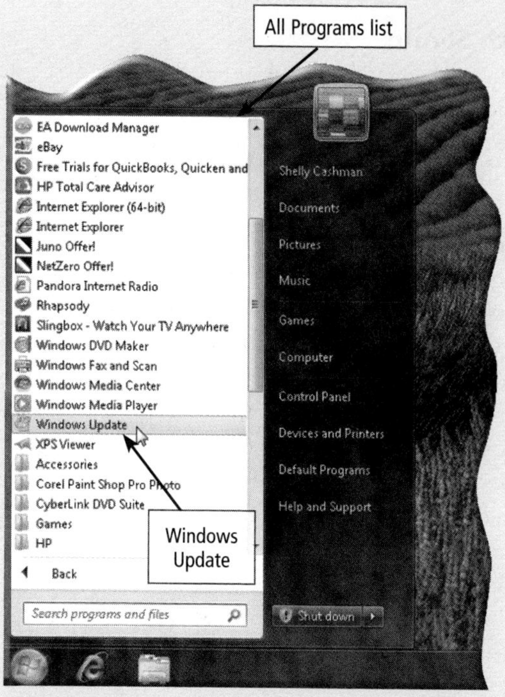

Figure 8-42

You also can schedule automatic updates for your computer. To do so, complete the following steps:

1. Click the Start button on the Windows taskbar and then click Control Panel on the Start menu.
2. In the Control Panel window, click System and Security to open the System and Security window.
3. In the System and Security window, click 'Turn automatic updating on or off' to open the Change settings window (Figure 8-43).
4. Select the option you want to use for Windows updates. Microsoft, together with all security and operating system experts, strongly recommends you select 'Install updates automatically' so that updates will be installed on your computer automatically. Notice that if you select 'Install updates automatically', you also should select a time when your computer will be on and be connected to the Internet. A secondary choice is to download the suggested updates and then choose when you want to install them, and a third choice allows you to check for updates and then choose when you want to download and install them.
5. When you have made your selection, click the OK button in the Change settings window.

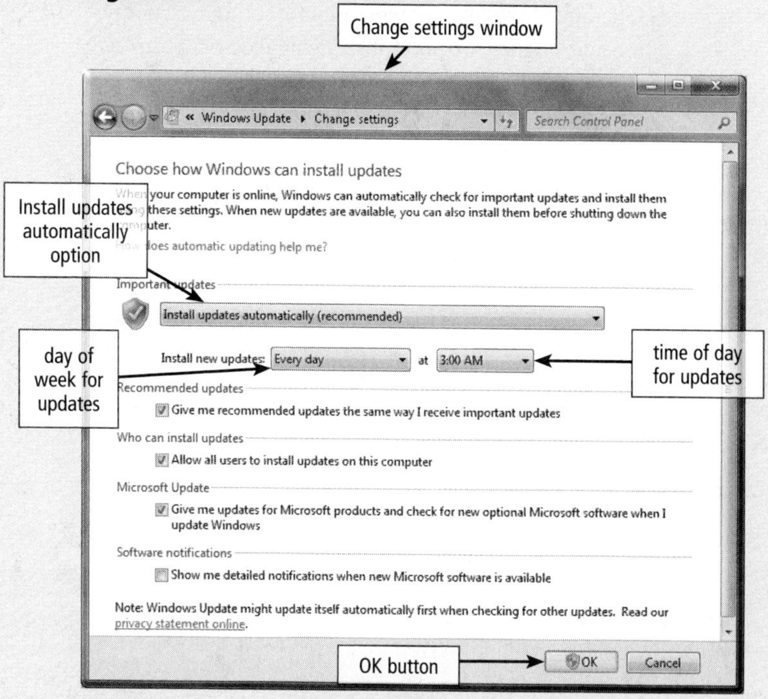

Figure 8-43

Updating Windows on your computer is vital to maintain security and operational integrity.

Exercises

1. Open the Windows Update window. Make a list of the important updates to Windows on the computer you are using. Add to the list the optional updates that are available. If you are using your own computer, install the updates of your choice on your computer. Submit the list of updates to your instructor.
2. **Optional: If you are not using your own computer, do not complete this exercise.** Open the Control Panel, click System and Security, and then click 'Turn automatic updating on or off'. Select the level of automatic updates you want to use. Write a report justifying your choice of automatic updates and then submit the report to your instructor.

Web Research

The Web Research exercises broaden your understanding of the chapter concepts by presenting questions that require you to search the Web for answers.

1 Search Sleuth

Use one of the search engines listed in Figure 2-10 in Chapter 2 on page 85 or your own favorite search engine to find the answers to the following questions. Copy and paste the Web address from the Web page where you found the answer. Some questions may have more than one answer. If required, submit your answers to your instructor. (1) Who are the "goons" who attend DEFCON? What color shirts do they wear? (2) Which product does IBM propose in its "Reincarnating PCs with Portable SoulPads" paper? (3) Which bird is the mascot for Linux? What is the mascot's name? (4) Why do some computer experts consider the term, spool, a backronym? (5) Who invented the Control-Alt-Delete (CTRL+ALT+DEL) key combination used to reboot a computer? (6) Which virus did the Farooq Alvi brothers invent? (7) Why are UNIX programmers concerned about the "Year 2038 problem"?

2 Green Computing

Operating systems can help monitor computer energy use and suggest methods of reducing electricity through efficient power management. Experts claim monitoring systems can save each computer user at least $60 per year in electricity costs. Suggestions include not using a screen saver, turning down a monitor's brightness level, and using a high performance power setting that balances processing power with notebook computer battery life. View online Web sites that provide information about power management. Which methods are effective in reducing power consumption, especially for notebook computers? Which sleep state setting gives significant power savings? Which power management settings are recommended for balanced, power saver, and high performance? Write a report summarizing your findings, and include a table of links to Web sites that provide additional details.

3 Social Networking

Social networking Web site advertisers in the United States spent $108 million in 2009, an increase of 119 percent in one year. Millions of registered online social networking users have posted demographic information about themselves, including age, gender, and geographical location. This data helps marketing managers deliver specific advertisements to each user in an attempt to raise revenue. Adknowledge (adknowledge.com) is one of the primary companies that gathers and studies data regarding online users and then sells targeted ads on social networking, e-mail, and gaming Web sites. Visit the Adknowledge Web site, view the information about targeting social network consumers, and then read articles in the About Us and Press Room sections. How are advertisers using virtual currency? How do traffic networks help advertisers create marketing campaigns? View the posts in the Adverblog Web site (adverblog.com) to read about interactive marketing trends. Summarize the information you read and viewed.

4 Blogs

A number of the search engine Web sites feature blogs describing popular search topics. Ask.com's blog (blog.ask.com), for example, lists its Blogroll, which gives recommended research and search engine Web sites. The Yahoo! Search blog (ysearchblog .com) includes news about consumer search trends (Yahoo! Buzz) and innovations in Web search technology. Google Blog Search (blogsearch.google.com) has search engines to help users find blogs about particular topics, including technology and business. Visit these sites and read the posts. What topics are discussed? Compose search queries about issues and products discussed in this chapter, such as personal firewalls or antivirus programs, and read a few of the blogs describing these topics. Summarize the information you read.

5 Ethics in Action

Several automobile insurers, including Progressive Casualty Insurance Company, are promising drivers insurance premium discounts up to 25 percent if they install a data recorder in their cars voluntarily to track their driving and then exercise good driving behavior. Privacy experts predict more insurance companies will offer this monitoring system and that it eventually will become mandatory. These critics fear that negative data will be used against poor drivers. View online sites that provide information about vehicle monitoring devices. Write a report summarizing your findings, and include a table of links to Web sites that provide additional details.

Critical Thinking

The Critical Thinking exercises challenge your assessment and decision-making skills by presenting real-world situations associated with the chapter concepts. The Collaboration exercise should be completed with a team.

To evaluate the situations below, use personal experiences and available resources such as articles on the Web or in print, blogs, podcasts, videos, television, user guides, other individuals, and electronics and computer stores. You may need to use multiple resources to form conclusions and make recommendations.

1. Class Discussion — Downloading Music
Many students at the local college have been using the college's computers to download music from the Internet. You have been asked to serve on a student committee to analyze and discuss this questionable use of the college's computers based on the following questions. Is it the college's responsibility to block music downloads? Why or why not? How would the college prevent students from downloading music? What is the difference between recording a song from the radio and downloading music from the Internet? Should violators be expelled, fined, required to attend a seminar on the ethical use of computers, or given a verbal warning? What recommendations would you give to the committee regarding the downloading of music?

2. Class Presentation — Windows 7 Editions
Your cousin is buying a new computer both for personal use and for operating his consulting business, which he runs out of his home. He is undecided about which edition of the Windows 7 operating system to purchase with his new computer. Windows 7 Professional is intended for business users. Windows 7 Home Premium is designed for home computing. Windows 7 Ultimate contains features both for home and business users. He has asked you to review the differences between each edition and help him decide which he should buy. Prepare a presentation comparing the similarities and contrasting the differences among the three editions. Be sure to include items such as features that are included with one edition that are not available in another and cost differences. At the end of your presentation, provide a recommendation and the reasons why the edition you chose would be best.

3. Research — Complete Security Solutions
Your neighbor started a new construction business and opened an office several blocks from your house. He is impressed by your computer knowledge and would like to hire you to set up his new computers. He mentions that because of the increasing security concerns on the Internet, he first would like you to install a program or programs designed to protect his computers from various security threats. What types of security threats exist on the Internet? Write a brief report describing two programs that provide a comprehensive security solution. What are the programs' functions? What computer requirements, if any, exist? Do the programs appear to be easy to install? What is their cost? Are subscription fees charged in order to receive automatic updates? In your opinion, are the programs worth the price? Why or why not?

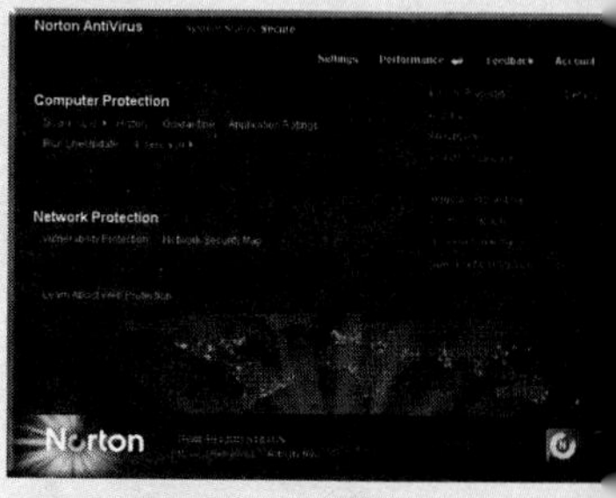

Collaboration

4. Operating Systems Your team members are employed as analysts at Soap-n-Suds, an international manufacturer of laundry soaps. The company currently uses an early version of the Windows operating system on its 5,000 desktop computers. This year, the company plans to upgrade the operating system and, if necessary, its desktop computers. The vice president of information technology has asked your team to compare the latest desktop versions of the Windows operating system, Mac OS, and the Linux operating system. Assign each member of your team an operating system. Each member should use the Web and/or print media to develop a feature/benefit analysis along with the answers to the following questions. What is the initial cost of the operating system per computer? What are the memory and storage requirements? Will the operating system require the company to purchase new computers? Are training costs involved? Which operating system is best at avoiding viruses, spam, and spyware? Which operating system is easier to use? Why? Can the latest version of Microsoft Office run with the operating system? As a team, merge your findings into a team presentation and share your findings and recommendation with the class.

Buyer's Guide: How to Purchase Computers and Mobile Devices

AT SOME POINT, perhaps while you are taking this course, you may decide to buy a computer or mobile device (Figure 1). The decision is an important one and will require an investment of both time and money. Like many buyers, you may have little experience with technology and find yourself unsure of how to proceed. You can start by talking to your friends, coworkers, and instructors about their computers and mobile devices. What type of computers and mobile devices did they buy? Why? For what purposes do they use their computers and mobile devices?

Figure 1 Computers and mobile devices.

How to Purchase a Desktop Computer

A **desktop computer** sits on or below a desk or table in a stationary location such as a home, office, or dormitory room. Desktop computers are a good option if you work mostly in one place and have plenty of space in a work area. Desktop computers generally provide more performance for your money. Today, manufacturers are placing more emphasis on style by offering bright colors, stylish displays, and theme-based displays so that the computer looks attractive if it is in an area of high visibility. Once you have decided that a desktop computer is most suited to your computing needs, the next step is to determine specific software, hardware, peripheral devices, and services to purchase, as well as where to buy the computer.

❶ Determine the specific software to use on your computer.

Before deciding to purchase software, be sure it contains the features necessary for the tasks you want to perform. Rely on the computer users in whom you have confidence to help you decide on the software to use. In addition, consider purchasing software that might help you perform tasks at home that you otherwise would perform at another location, such as at school or at work. The minimum requirements of the software you select may determine the operating system (Microsoft Windows, Mac OS, Linux) you need. If you decide to use a particular operating system that does not support software you want to use, you may be able to purchase similar software from other manufacturers.

Many Web sites and trade magazines provide reviews of software products. These Web sites frequently have articles that rate computers and software on cost, performance, and support.

Your hardware requirements depend on the minimum requirements of the software you will run on your computer. Some software requires more memory and disk space than others, as well as additional input, output, and storage devices. For example, suppose you want to run software that can copy one optical disc's contents directly to another optical disc, without first copying the data to the hard disk. To support that, you should consider a desktop computer or a high-end notebook computer, because the computer will need two optical disc drives: one that reads from an optical disc, and one that writes on an optical disc. If you plan to run software that allows your computer to function as an entertainment system, then you will need an optical disc drive, quality speakers, and an upgraded sound card.

❷ Know the system requirements of the operating system.

After determining the software you want to run on your new computer, the next step is to determine the operating system to use. If, however, you purchase a new computer, chances are it will have the latest version of your preferred operating system (Windows, Mac OS, Linux).

❸ Look for bundled software.

When you purchase a computer, it may include bundled software. Some sellers even let you choose which software you want. Remember, however, that bundled software has value only if you would have purchased the software even if it had not been included with the computer. At the very least, you probably will want word processing software and an antivirus program. If you need additional programs, such as a spreadsheet, a database, or presentation software, consider purchasing or downloading Microsoft Office, Microsoft Works, OpenOffice.org, or Sun StarOffice, which include several programs at a reduced price or at no cost.

❹ Avoid buying the least powerful computer available.

Once you know the application software you want to use, then consider the following important criteria about the computer's components: (1) processor speed, (2) size and types of memory (RAM) and storage, (3) types of input/output devices, (4) types of ports and adapter cards, and (5) types of communications devices. You also should consider if the computer is upgradeable and to what extent you are able to upgrade. For example, all manufacturers limit the amount of memory you can add. The information in Figure 2 on pages 446 and 447 can help you determine which computer components are best for you and outlines considerations for specific hardware components. For a sample Base Components worksheet that lists PC recommendations for each category of user discussed in this

Considerations for Hardware Components

Card Reader/Writer: A card reader/writer is useful for transferring data directly to and from a memory card, such as the type used in a digital camera, smart phone, or portable media player. Make sure the card reader/writer can read from and write on the memory cards that you use.

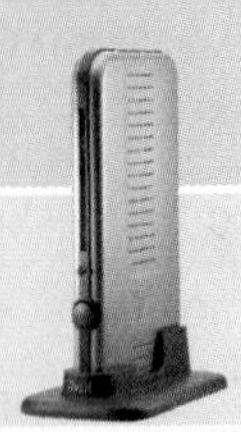

Digital Video Capture Device: A digital video capture device allows you to connect a computer to a video camera or VCR and record, edit, manage, and then write video back on an optical disc or VCR tape. To create quality video (true 30 frames per second, full-sized TV), the digital video capture device should have a USB or FireWire port.

External Hard Disk: An external hard disk can serve many purposes: it can serve as extra storage for your computer, provide a way to store and transport large files or large quantities of files, and provide a convenient way to back up data on other internal and external hard disks. External hard disks can be purchased with the same capacity as any internal disk.

Fingerprint Reader: For added security, you may want to consider purchasing a fingerprint reader. It helps prevent unauthorized access to your computer and also allows you to log onto Web sites quickly via your fingerprint, rather than entering a user name and password each time you access the site. Most use a USB connection and require software installation.

Hard Disk: It is recommended that you buy a computer with at least a 320 GB hard disk if your primary interests are browsing the Web and using e-mail and Office suite-type programs; 1 TB if you also want to edit digital photos or if you plan to edit digital video or manipulate large audio files even occasionally; and 2 TB if you will edit digital video, movies, or photos often; store audio files and music; or consider yourself to be a power user. Internal hard disk controllers are available with the RAID option for added data protection.

Joystick/Wheel: If you use the computer to play games, then you will want to purchase a joystick or a wheel. These devices, especially the more expensive ones, provide for realistic game play with force feedback, programmable buttons, and specialized levers and wheels.

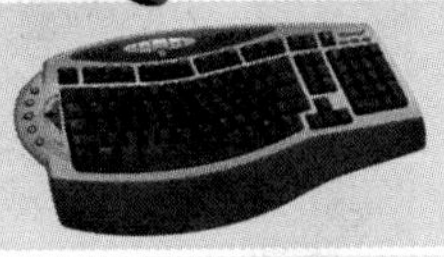

Keyboard: The keyboard is one of the more important devices used to communicate with the computer. For this reason, make sure the keyboard you purchase has 101 to 105 keys, is comfortable and easy to use, and has a USB connection. A wireless keyboard should be considered, especially if you have a small desk area.

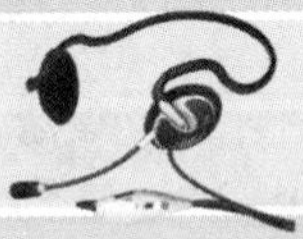

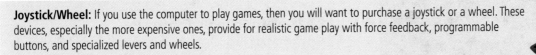

Microphone: If you plan to record audio or use speech recognition to enter text and commands, then purchase a close-talk headset with gain adjustment support.

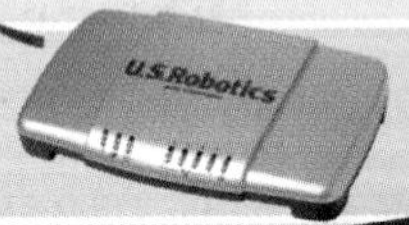

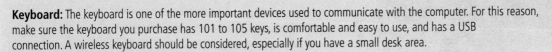

Modem: Most computers include a modem so that you can use a telephone line to access the Internet. Some modems also have fax capabilities. Your modem should be rated at 56 Kbps.

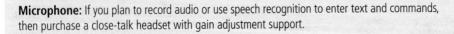

Monitor: The monitor is where you will view documents, read e-mail messages, and view pictures. A minimum of a 19″ LCD flat-panel monitor is recommended, but if you plan to use the computer for graphic design or game playing, then you may want to purchase a 22″ or 27″ monitor. Instead of a single large, widescreen monitor, you may want to consider a side-by-side monitor setup.

Mouse: While working with a desktop computer, you use the mouse constantly. Make sure the mouse has a wheel, which acts as a third button in addition to the top two buttons on the left and right. An ergonomic design also is important because your hand is on the mouse most of the time when you are using the computer. A wireless mouse should be considered to eliminate the cord and allow you to work at short distances from the computer.

Optical Disc Drives: Most computers include a DVD±RW combination drive and/or DVD/Blu-ray Disc drive. A DVD±RW or a Blu-ray Disc drive allows you to read optical discs and to write data on (burn) an optical disc. It also will allow you to store and share video files, digital photos, and other large files with other people who have access to a DVD/Blu-ray Disc drive. A Blu-ray Disc has a capacity of at least 25 GB, and a DVD has a capacity of at least 4.7 GB, versus the 650 MB capacity of a CD.

Figure 2 Hardware guidelines.

Considerations for Hardware Components

Ports: Depending on how you are using the computer, you may need anywhere from 4 to 10 USB ports. USB ports have become the connection of choice in the computer industry. They offer an easy way to connect peripheral devices such as printers, digital cameras, and portable media players. Many computers intended for home or professional audio/video use have built-in FireWire ports. Most personal computers include a minimum of six USB ports, two FireWire ports, and an Ethernet port.

Printer: Your two basic printer choices are ink-jet and laser. Color ink-jet printers cost on average between $50 and $300. Laser printers cost from $200 to $2,000. In general, the less expensive the printer, the lower the resolution and speed, and the more often you are required to change the ink cartridges or toner. Laser printers print faster and with a higher quality than an ink-jet, and their toner on average costs less.

Processor: For a personal computer, an Intel Core i7 processor at 2.93 GHz is more than enough processor power for most home and small office/home office users. Game home, enterprise, and power users should upgrade to faster, more powerful processors.

RAM: RAM plays a vital role in the speed of a computer. Make sure the computer you purchase has at least 2 GB of RAM. If you have extra money to invest in a computer, consider increasing the RAM. The extra money for RAM will be well spent because more RAM typically translates into more speed.

Scanner: The most popular scanner purchased with a computer today is the flatbed scanner. When evaluating a flatbed scanner, check the color depth and resolution. Do not buy anything less than a color depth of 48 bits and a resolution of 1200 x 2400 dpi. The higher the color depth, the more accurate the color. A higher resolution picks up the more subtle gradations of color.

Sound Card: Many computers include a standard sound card that supports Dolby 5.1 surround and are capable of recording and playing digital audio. Make sure they are suitable in the event you decide to use the computer as an entertainment or gaming system.

Speakers: Once you have a good sound card, quality speakers and a separate subwoofer that amplifies the bass frequencies of the speakers can turn the computer into a premium stereo system.

USB Flash Drive: If you work on different computers and need access to the same data and information, then this portable flash memory device is ideal. USB flash drive capacity varies from 1 GB to 16 GB.

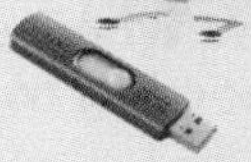

USB Hub: If you plan to connect several peripheral devices to the computer at the same time, then you need to be concerned with the number of ports available on the computer. If the computer does not have enough ports, then you should purchase a USB hub. A USB hub plugs into a single USB port and provides several additional ports.

Video Card: Most standard video cards satisfy the monitor display needs of most home and small office users. If you are a game home user or a graphic designer, you will want to upgrade to a higher quality video card. The higher refresh rates will further enhance the display of games, graphics, and movies.

Web Cam: A Web cam is a small digital video camera that can capture and display live video on a Web page. You also can capture, edit, and share video and still photos. Recommended minimum specifications include 640 x 480 resolution, a video with a rate of 30 frames per second, and a USB or FireWire port. Some Web cams are built into computer monitors.

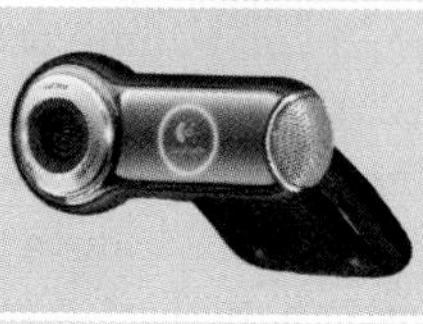

Wireless LAN Access Point: A wireless LAN access point allows you to network several computers, so that multiple users can share files and access the Internet through a single broadband connection. Each device that you connect requires a wireless card. A wireless LAN access point can offer a range of operations up to several hundred feet, so be sure the device has a high-powered antenna.

Figure 2 Hardware guidelines. *(continued)*

book, visit the Computer Concepts CourseMate Web site at www.cengagebrain.com and then navigate to the Buyer's Guide Feature resource for this book. In the worksheet, the Home User category is divided into two groups: Application Home User and Game Home User.

Computer technology changes rapidly, meaning a computer that seems powerful enough today may not serve your computing needs in several years. In fact, studies show that many users regret not buying a more powerful computer. To avoid this, plan to buy a computer that will last for at least two to three years. You can help delay obsolescence by purchasing the fastest processor, the most memory, and the largest hard disk you can afford. If you must buy a less powerful computer, be sure you can upgrade it with additional memory, components, and peripheral devices as your computer requirements grow.

5 Consider upgrades to the mouse, keyboard, monitor, printer, microphone, and speakers.

You use these peripheral devices to interact with the computer, so make sure they are up to your standards. Review the peripheral devices listed in Figure 2 and then visit both local computer dealers and large retail stores to test the computers and devices on display. Ask the salesperson which input and output devices would be best for you and whether you should upgrade beyond the standard product. Consider purchasing a wireless keyboard and wireless mouse to eliminate wires on your desktop. A few extra dollars spent on these components when you initially purchase a computer can extend its usefulness by years.

6 Determine whether to use a broadband or dial-up connection to access the Internet.

If your computer has a modem, you can access the Internet using a standard telephone line. Ordinarily, you call a local or toll-free 800 number to connect to an Internet access provider. Using a dial-up Internet connection usually is relatively inexpensive but slow.

Broadband connections provide much faster Internet connections, which are ideal if you want faster file download speeds for software, digital photos, digital video, and music. As you would expect, they can be more expensive than a dial-up connection. If you want to use a broadband connection, your computer should have an Ethernet card installed, unless you are using a wireless broadband connection such as WiMax or 3G. If you will be using a dial-up connection, your computer should have a modem installed.

7 Use a worksheet to compare computers, services, and other considerations.

You can use a separate sheet of paper to take notes about each vendor's computer and then summarize the information on a worksheet. For a sample worksheet that compares prices for a PC or a Mac, visit the Computer Concepts CourseMate Web site at www.cengagebrain.com and then navigate to the Buyer's Guide Feature resource for this book. Most companies advertise a price for a base computer that includes components housed in the system unit (processor, RAM, sound card, video card, network card), hard disks, optical disc drives, a keyboard, mouse, monitor, printer, speakers, and modem. Be aware, however, that some advertisements list prices for computers with only some of these components. Monitors and printers, for example, often are not included in a base computer's price. Depending on how you plan to use the computer, you may want to invest in additional or more powerful components. When comparing the prices of computers, make sure you are comparing identical or similar configurations.

8 If you are buying a new computer, you have several purchasing options: buying from a school bookstore, a local computer dealer, a local large retail store, or ordering by mail via telephone or the Web.

Each purchasing option has certain advantages. Many college bookstores, for example, sign exclusive pricing agreements with computer manufacturers and, thus, can offer student discounts. Local dealers and local large retail stores, however, more easily can provide hands-on support. Mail-order companies that sell computers by telephone or online via the Web (Figure 3) often provide the lowest prices, but extend less personal service. Some major mail-order companies, however, have started to provide next-business-day, on-site services. A credit card usually is required to buy from a mail-order company.

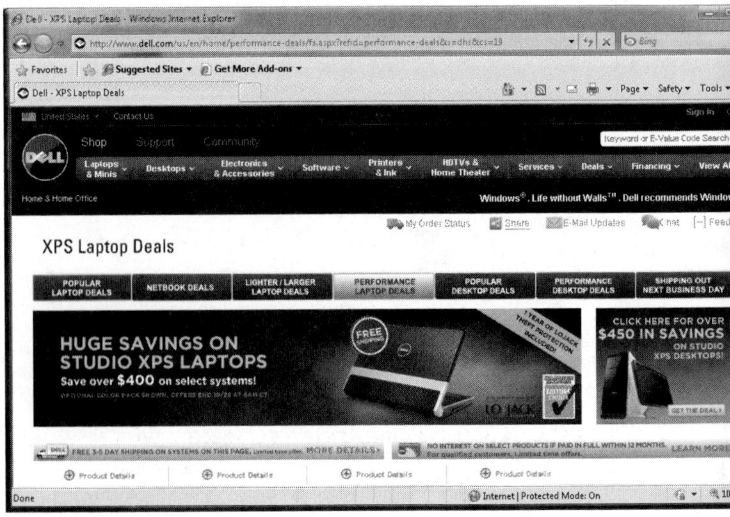

Figure 3 Mail-order companies, such as Dell, sell computers online.

9 If you are buying a used computer, stay with name brands such as Dell, Apple, HP, and Gateway.

Although brand-name equipment can cost more, most brand-name computers have longer, more comprehensive warranties, are better supported, and have more authorized centers for repair services. As with new computers, you can purchase a used computer from local computer dealers, local large retail stores, or mail order via the telephone or the Web. Classified ads and used computer sellers offer additional outlets for purchasing used computers.

10 If you have a computer and are upgrading to a new one, then consider selling or trading in the old one.

If you are a replacement buyer, your older computer still may have value. If you cannot sell the computer through the classified ads, via a Web site, or to a friend, then ask if the computer dealer will buy your old computer.

An increasing number of companies are taking trade-ins, but do not expect too much money for your old computer. Other companies offer to recycle your old computer free or for a fee.

11 Be aware of hidden costs.

Before purchasing, be sure to consider any additional costs associated with buying a computer, such as an additional telephone line, a broadband modem, an uninterruptible power supply (UPS), computer furniture, a USB flash drive, paper, and computer training classes you may want to take. Depending on where you buy the computer, the seller may be willing to include some or all of these in the computer purchase price.

12 Consider more than just price.

The lowest-cost computer may not be the best long-term buy. Consider such intangibles as the vendor's time in business, regard for quality, and reputation for support. If you need to upgrade a computer often, you may want to consider a leasing arrangement, in which you pay monthly lease fees, but can upgrade or add on to your computer as your equipment needs change. No matter what type of buyer you are, insist on a 30-day, no-questions-asked return policy on the computer.

13 Avoid restocking fees.

Some companies charge a restocking fee of 10 to 20 percent as part of their money-back return policy. In some cases, no restocking fee for hardware is applied, but it is applied for software. Ask about the existence and terms of any restocking policies before you buy.

14 Use a credit card to purchase a new computer.

Many credit cards offer purchase protection and extended warranty benefits that cover you in case of loss of or damage to purchased goods. Paying by credit card also gives you time to install and use the computer before you have to pay for it. Finally, if you are dissatisfied with the computer and are unable to reach an agreement with the seller, paying by credit card gives you certain rights regarding withholding payment until the dispute is resolved. Check your credit card terms for specific details.

15 Consider purchasing an extended warranty or service plan.

If you use your computer for business or require fast resolution to major computer problems, consider purchasing an extended warranty or a service plan through a local dealer or third-party company. Most extended warranties cover the repair and replacement of computer components beyond the standard warranty. Most service plans ensure that your technical support calls receive priority response from technicians. You also can purchase an on-site service plan that states that a technician will arrive at your home, work, or school within 24 hours. If your computer includes a warranty and service agreement for a year or less, consider extending the service for two or three years when you buy the computer.

CENTURY COMPUTERS
Performance Guarantee
(See reverse for terms & conditions of this contract)

Invoice #: 1984409
Invoice Date: 10/12/11
Effective Date: 10/12/11
Expiration Date: 10/12/14

Customer Name: Leon, Richard
Date: 10/12/11
Address: 1123 Roxbury
Sycamore, IL 60178
Day phone: (815) 555-0303
Evening Phone: (728) 555-0203

System & Serial Numbers
IMB computer
S/N: US759290C

John Smith
Print Name of Century's Authorized Signature
10/12/11
Date

How to Purchase a Notebook Computer

If you need computing capability when you travel or to use in lectures or meetings, you may find a notebook computer to be an appropriate choice. The guidelines mentioned in the previous section also apply to the purchase of a notebook computer. The following are additional considerations unique to notebook computers, including netbooks and Tablet PCs.

1 Determine which computer fits your mobile computing needs.

Before purchasing a notebook computer, you need to determine whether a traditional notebook computer, netbook, or Tablet PC will meet your needs. If you spend most of your time working on spreadsheets, writing and/or editing documents, e-mail, or using the Internet, then a traditional notebook computer will suffice. If your primary use will be to access the Internet while traveling and you are not concerned as much with processing power or hard disk capacity, consider a netbook. If you find yourself in need of a computer in class or that you spend more time in meetings than in your office, then the Tablet PC may be the answer. Before you invest money in a Tablet PC, however, determine which programs you plan to use on it. You should not buy a Tablet PC simply because it is an interesting type of computer.

2 Purchase a notebook computer with a sufficiently large screen.

Active-matrix screens display high-quality color that is viewable from all angles. Less expensive, passive-matrix screens sometimes are difficult to see in low-light conditions and cannot be viewed from an angle.

Notebook computers typically include a 12.1-inch, 13.3-inch, 14.1-inch, 15.4-inch, or 17-inch display. Netbooks have screens as small as 7 inches. For most users, a 14.1-inch display is satisfactory. If you intend to use the notebook computer as a desktop computer replacement, however, you may opt for a 15.4-inch or 17-inch display. The WSXGA+ standard (1680 × 1050) is popular with 17-inch displays, so if you intend to watch HD movies on the computer, take this into consideration. Dell offers a notebook computer with a 20.1-inch display that looks like a briefcase when closed. Some notebook computers with these larger displays weigh more than 10 pounds, however, so if you travel a lot and portability is essential, you might want a lighter computer with a smaller display. The lightest notebook computers, which weigh less than 3 pounds, are equipped with a 12.1-inch display.

Regardless of size, the resolution of the display should be at least 1024 × 768 pixels. To compare the screen size on various notebook computers, including netbooks and Tablet PCs, visit the company Web sites. Tablet PCs use a digitizer below a standard 10.4-inch motion-sensitive LCD display to make the writing experience on the screen feel like writing on paper. To ensure you experience the maximum benefits from the ClearType technology, make sure the LCD display has a resolution of 800 × 600 in landscape mode and a 600 × 800 in portrait mode.

3 Experiment with different keyboards, pointing devices, and digital pens.

Notebook computer keyboards, especially netbook keyboards, are far less standardized than those for desktop computers. Some notebook computers, for example, have wide wrist rests, while others have none, and keyboard layouts on notebook computers often vary. Notebook computers also use a range of pointing devices, including touchpads, pointing sticks, trackballs, and, in the case of Tablet PCs, digital pens.

Before purchasing a notebook computer, try various types of keyboards and pointing devices to determine which is easiest for you to use. Regardless of the device you select, you also may want to purchase a standard mouse to use when you are working at a desk or other large surface. Figure 4 compares the standard point-and-click of a mouse with the gestures made with a digital pen. Other gestures with the digital pen replicate some of the commonly used keys on a keyboard.

Mouse and Digital Pen Operations

Mouse	Digital Pen
Point	Point
Click	Tap
Double-click	Double-tap
Right-click	Tap and hold
Click and drag	Drag

Figure 4 Standard point-and-click of a mouse compared with the gestures made with a digital pen.

❹ Make sure the notebook computer you purchase has an optical disc drive.

Most mobile computers include an optical disc drive. Although DVD/Blu-ray Disc drives are slightly more expensive, they allow you to play CDs, DVDs, and Blu-ray Discs using your notebook computer and hear the sound through earbuds. If you decide to purchase a netbook, it might not include an optical disc drive. Instead, you might need to purchase an external optical disc drive.

❺ If necessary, upgrade the processor, memory, and disk storage at the time of purchase.

As with a desktop computer, upgrading a notebook computer's memory and disk storage usually is less expensive at the time of initial purchase. Some disk storage is custom designed for notebook computer manufacturers, meaning an upgrade might not be available in the future. If you are purchasing a lightweight notebook computer or Tablet PC, then it should include at least an Intel Core 2 Quad processor, 2 GB RAM, and 250 GB of storage. If you are purchasing a netbook, it should have an Intel Atom processor, at least 1 GB RAM, and 120 GB of storage.

❻ The availability of built-in ports and slots and a USB hub on a notebook computer is important.

A notebook computer does not have much room to add adapter cards. If you know the purpose for which you plan to use the notebook computer, then you can determine the ports you will need. Netbooks typically have fewer ports than traditional notebook computers and Tablet PCs. Most notebook computers include common ports, such as a video port, audio port, network port, FireWire port, and multiple USB ports. If you plan to connect the notebook computer to a television, however, then you will need a PC to TV port. To optimize television viewing, you may want to consider DisplayPort, DVI, or HDMI ports. If you want to connect to networks at school or in various offices via a network cable, make sure the notebook computer you purchase has a network port. If the notebook computer does not contain a network port, you will have to purchase an external network card that slides into an expansion slot in your computer, as well as a network cable. You also may want to consider adding a card reader.

❼ If you plan to use your notebook computer for note-taking at school or in meetings, consider a convertible Tablet PC.

Some computer manufacturers have developed convertible Tablet PCs that allow the screen to rotate 180 degrees on a central hinge and then fold down to cover the keyboard (Figure 5). You then can use a digital pen to enter text or drawings into the computer by writing on the screen. Some notebook computers have wide screens for better viewing and editing, and some even have a screen on top of the unit in addition to the regular screen. If you spend much of your time attending lectures or meetings, then the slate Tablet PC is ideal. With a slate Tablet PC, users can attach a removable keyboard.

Figure 5
A convertible Tablet PC.

❽ If you purchase a Tablet PC, determine whether you require multi-touch technology.

Newer operating systems now support hardware with multi-touch technology. If you choose an operating system that supports this technology, the Tablet PC also must support this technology.

❾ Purchase a notebook computer with an integrated Web cam.

If you will be using a notebook computer to connect to the Internet and chat with friends online, consider purchasing one with an integrated Web cam.

❿ Check with your wireless carrier to see if it offers netbooks for sale.

Most wireless carriers now offer wireless data plans allowing you to connect to the Internet from almost anywhere with a cell phone signal. Some wireless carriers now are selling netbooks with built-in capability to connect wirelessly to the Internet using a wireless data plan.

⓫ Purchase a notebook computer with a built-in wireless network connection.

A wireless network connection (Bluetooth, Wi-Fi a/b/g/n, WiMAX, etc.) can be useful when you travel or as part of a home network. Increasingly more airports, hotels, schools, and cafés have wireless networks that allow you to connect to the Internet. Many users today are setting up wireless home networks. With a wireless home network, your notebook computer can access the Internet, as well as other computers in the house, from any location to share files and hardware, such as a printer, and browse the Web. Most home wireless networks allow connections from distances of 150 to 800 feet.

⓬ If you plan to use your notebook computer for long periods without access to an electrical outlet, purchase a second battery.

The trend among notebook computer users today is power and size over battery life. Many notebook computer users today are willing to give up longer battery life for a larger screen, faster processor, and more storage. In addition, some manufacturers typically sell the notebook computer with the lowest capacity battery. For this reason, be careful in choosing a notebook computer if you plan to use it without access to electrical outlets for long periods, such as an airplane flight. You also might want to purchase a second battery as a backup. If you anticipate running the notebook computer on batteries frequently, choose a computer that uses lithium-ion batteries, which last longer than nickel cadmium or nickel hydride batteries.

⓭ Purchase a well-padded and well-designed carrying case.

An amply padded carrying case will protect your notebook computer from the bumps it will receive while traveling. A well-designed carrying case will have room for accessories such as spare optical discs, pens, and paperwork (Figure 6). Although a netbook may be small enough to fit in a handbag, make sure that the bag has sufficient padding to protect the computer.

Figure 6 A well-designed notebook computer carrying case.

⓮ If you plan to connect your notebook computer to a video projector, make sure the notebook computer is compatible with the video projector.

You should check, for example, to be sure that your notebook computer will allow you to display an image on the computer screen and projection device at the same time. Also, ensure that the notebook computer has the ports required to connect to the video projector. You also may consider purchasing a notebook computer with a built-in Web cam for video conferencing purposes.

⓯ For improved security and convenience, consider a fingerprint reader.

More than half a million notebook computers are stolen or lost each year. If you have critical information stored on your notebook computer, consider purchasing one with a fingerprint reader (Figure 7) to protect the data if your computer is stolen or lost. Fingerprint security offers a level of protection that extends well beyond the standard password protection. If your notebook computer is stolen, the odds of recovering it improve dramatically with anti-theft tracking software. Manufacturers claim recovery rates of 90 percent or more for notebook computers using their product. For convenience, fingerprint readers also allow you to log onto several Web sites in lieu of entering user name and password information.

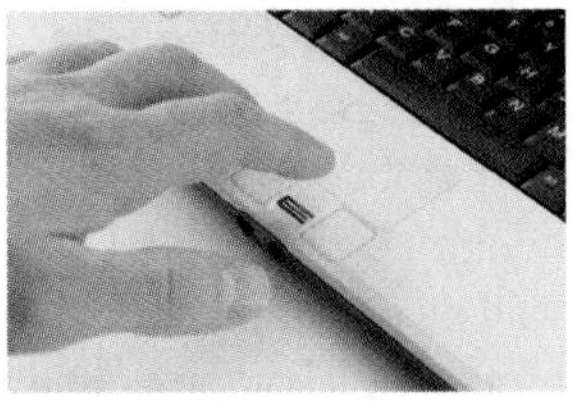

Figure 7 Fingerprint reader technology offers greater security than passwords.

⓰ Review the docking capabilities of the Tablet PC.

The Tablet Technology in the Windows operating system supports a grab-and-go form of docking, so that you can pick up and take a docked Tablet PC with you, just as you would pick up a notepad on your way to a meeting (Figure 8).

Figure 8 A Tablet PC docked to create a desktop computer with the Tablet PC as the monitor.

How to Purchase a Smart Phone

You probably will use a smart phone more often than other mobile devices. For this reason, it is important to choose a phone that is available through your preferred wireless carrier, available in your price range, and offers access to the features you will use most frequently. This section lists guidelines you should consider when purchasing a smart phone.

❶ Choose a wireless carrier and plan that satisfies your needs and budget.

Multiple wireless carriers exist today, and each one offers a different line of smart phones. For example, the Samsung Alias is available only through Verizon Wireless. Alternatively, some smart phones, such as the BlackBerry line of smart phones, are available from multiple wireless carriers. Before deciding on a smart phone, you first should research the wireless carriers in your area, and be sure to ascertain whether the coverage is acceptable. Additionally, compare the calling plans for the various carriers and determine which one best meets your needs. Once you have determined the wireless carrier to use, you then can choose from one of their available smart phones. Once you purchase a smart phone, most carriers allow you to perform a risk-free evaluation for 30 days. If you are not satisfied with the phone or its performance, you can return the phone and pay only for the service you have used.

2 Decide on the size, style, and weight of the smart phone that will work best for you.

Smart phones are available in various sizes, weights, shapes, and colors. Some people prefer larger, heavier phones because they feel that they are more durable, while others prefer smaller, lightweight phones for easy portability. Some smart phones are flip phones, meaning that you have to open the phone (like a clamshell) to display the screen and keypad, some open by sliding the phone, and others do not need to be opened to use them. Figure 9 shows the various smart phone styles.

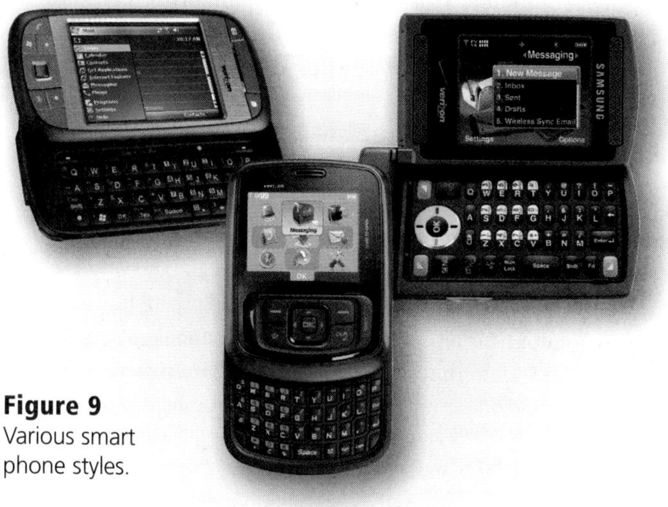

Figure 9
Various smart phone styles.

3 Determine whether you prefer a touch screen, keypad, or mini-keyboard.

Modern smart phones provide various ways to enter text. During the past several years, smart phones with touch screens as their primary input device have been penetrating the market. Some smart phone users prefer touch screens because the phone does not require additional space for a keypad or mini-keyboard, but others find it more difficult to type on a touch screen. Most newer smart phones with touch screens also include handwriting recognition. Smart phones with keypads might make it easier to type for some users, but others do not like the unfamiliar feeling of keys arranged in alphabetical order. In addition, you often have to press the keys multiple times before reaching the letter you want to type. Mini-keyboards are available on some smart phones, such as the BlackBerry and Samsung Alias. Mini-keyboards provide a key for each letter, but the keys are significantly smaller than those on a standard keyboard. Most smart phone users type on mini-keyboards using their thumbs.

4 If you will be synchronizing your smart phone with a program on your computer, select a smart phone that is compatible with the program you wish to use.

Programs such as Microsoft Outlook allow you to synchronize your e-mail messages, contacts, and calendar with your smart phone. If you would like this functionality, purchase a smart phone that can synchronize with Microsoft Outlook. Similarly, if your company uses a BlackBerry Enterprise server or Microsoft Exchange server, you should consider purchasing a smart phone that can synchronize, either using wires or wirelessly, with those servers.

5 Compare battery life.

Any smart phone is useful only if it has the power required to run. Talking and using the Internet on your smart phone will shorten battery life more quickly than when the phone is powered on but not in use. If you have a choice, be sure to purchase a battery that will allow the phone to function all day. Pay particular attention to the talk time and standby time. If you plan to talk on the phone more than the advertised talk time, you might consider purchasing a second battery or an extended battery if your phone supports it.

6 Make sure your smart phone has enough memory and storage.

If you are using the smart phone to send and receive picture, video, and e-mail messages, and to store music, purchase a memory card that not only is compatible with your computer and smart phone, but also has adequate storage space for your messages and files. If you purchase a memory card and eventually fill it, you easily can transfer the data to a larger memory card.

7 Check out the accessories.

Determine which accessories you want for the smart phone. Accessories include carrying cases, screen protectors, synchronization cradles and cables, and car chargers.

How to Purchase a Portable Media Player

Portable media players are becoming the preferred device for listening to music and watching videos on the go. When choosing a portable media player, it is important to consider features and characteristics other than the physical size and amount of storage space. This section lists guidelines you should consider when purchasing a portable media player.

1 Choose a device with sufficient storage capacity.

Audio and video files can consume a great deal of storage space, so be sure to purchase a portable media player that has enough capacity to store your audio and video files. You also should consider approximately how many media files you acquire each year, and make sure that your device has enough storage space to accommodate these files for years to come.

2 Determine which file formats your new portable media player should support and how you will add files to your library.

Some portable media players are designed to accept new audio and video files only through a program installed on a computer. For example, it is easiest to add media files to an iPod using the iTunes program. Other portable media players connect to a computer using a cable and are displayed in Windows as a removable disk. You then can add files to the media player by dragging the files to the removable disk icon in Windows. The portable media player must support the file formats you are using. You can determine the file format by looking at the file extension on the media files you wish to transfer to your portable media player. Before purchasing a portable media player, make sure that it can support the file formats you are using.

3 Consider a portable media player that can play video.

Some users prefer to watch videos on their portable media player in addition to playing music. You typically can download videos for portable media players less expensively than purchasing the movie on a DVD/Blu-ray Disc. Although the display on a portable media player is small, many still find entertainment value because they are able to watch videos and stay occupied while waiting for a bus, on an airplane, or at other locations where they otherwise might not have anything to occupy them.

4 Read reviews about the sound quality on the portable media players you are considering.

Sound quality may vary greatly among portable media players. If you are unable to try the portable media player before buying it, read reviews and make sure that those reviewing the devices find the sound quality to be acceptable. You also may consider purchasing higher-quality earbuds or headphones to enhance the sound quality.

5 Select a size and style that works best for you.

Portable media players are available in various shapes and styles. For example, Apple offers the iPod shuffle, iPod nano, iPod classic, and iPod touch (Figure 10). Each type of iPod varies in size and style, and some have capabilities (such as video) that others do not. Choose a size and style that meets your needs and fits your personality.

Figure 10 Portable media players are available in different shapes, styles, and colors.

6 Check out additional memory cards.

Most portable media players have internal storage for your media files. If you wish to increase the available storage, consider purchasing a portable media player that allows you to increase storage capacity by inserting memory cards. Similar to most computers, it is less expensive initially to purchase the largest amount of storage that you can afford, but it is helpful to be able to increase your storage at a later date.

7 Consider rechargeable batteries.

Although most portable media players include rechargeable batteries, some still use traditional alkaline batteries. Portable media players sometimes can last for only a few hours on alkaline batteries, and battery replacement can be costly. Rechargeable batteries often last longer and create less waste. If you are not near a power source, you are unable to recharge the batteries when they die. With alkaline batteries, you simply can insert new ones and continue enjoying your player.

8 Stay within your budget.

As previously mentioned, portable media players are available in a variety of shapes and sizes, and they also are available with various storage capacities. When shopping for a portable media player, be realistic when you consider how you will use the device, as well as how much storage you require. Purchasing the latest and greatest device is not always the best option, and the cost can exceed what you care to spend.

How to Purchase a Digital Camera

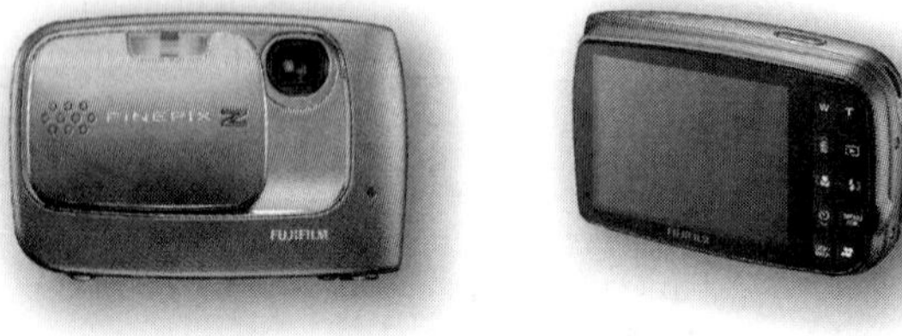

Both amateur and professional photographers now are mostly purchasing digital cameras to meet their photography needs. Because digital cameras with new and improved features regularly are introduced to the marketplace, consumers should know how to compare the differences among the multiple cameras that are available. This section lists guidelines you should consider when purchasing a digital camera.

1 Determine the type of digital camera that meets your needs.

Various types of digital cameras exist, including point-and-shoot cameras, field cameras, and studio cameras. Point-and-shoot cameras typically fit in your pocket and meet the needs of most general consumers. Field cameras, which often are used by photojournalists, are portable but flexible. Field cameras allow photographers to change lenses and use other attachments, and also are more customizable than point-and-shoot cameras. Studio cameras are used in photo studios and are stationary. These cameras give you the widest range of lenses and settings.

2 The digital camera with the highest resolution is not always the best.

Many consumers mistakenly believe that the digital camera with the highest resolution is the best camera for their needs. A higher resolution increases quality and clarity of your photos, as well as the size at which you can print the photos before noticing degradation in quality. If you never plan to print photos larger than 8" × 10", for example, you do not need a camera with a resolution greater than 5-megapixels. Many cameras available today advertise higher resolutions, but taking pictures at these high resolutions can use valuable storage space. Just because your camera can take a 10-megapixel photo does not mean that you always should set the resolution to 10 megapixels.

3 Consider size and weight.

Digital cameras are available in various sizes and weights. Some people prefer smaller, lighter cameras because they are easier to transport and take up less space. Others prefer bulkier, heavier cameras because the weight helps steady them to take a clearer picture. Many digital cameras also include an image stabilization feature that reduces the possibility of a blurry picture if you move your hands slightly while taking the picture. Some also believe that heavier cameras are of better quality, although that seldom is true. When choosing a digital camera, practice taking pictures with it and select one that feels comfortable and natural.

4 Different cameras require different memory cards.

When purchasing a digital camera, pay careful attention to the type of memory card the camera uses. Many use SD cards, some use xD Picture cards, and some use CompactFlash memory cards. Some memory cards are more expensive to replace than others, and some have a higher capacity than other cards. If you take a lot of pictures, purchase a camera that supports a memory card with a higher storage capacity so that you can avoid carrying multiple memory cards. You also might consider purchasing a camera that uses a memory card that is compatible with your other mobile devices.

5 Photo editing features can save you time.

Some digital cameras have integrated tools that allow you to edit photos directly from the camera. For instance, you may be able to crop photos, change the brightness, or remove red eye effects. Editing photos directly on the camera after taking them can save you from editing multiple photos at once when you transfer them to a computer. The photo editing capabilities available on digital cameras are limited when compared to photo editing programs, but in many cases they can edit a photo to your satisfaction.

6 Make sure that you can see the LCD screen easily.

LCD screens on digital cameras allow you to configure the settings, frame a shot before taking it, and preview photos after taking them. LCD screens vary by inches, so select a camera with a screen that does not require you to strain your eyes to view. This is especially important if the camera you are considering does not have a viewfinder, because you then will be required to use the display to frame your shots.

7 Determine whether your pictures will require you to zoom.

If you plan to take pictures of people or objects that require you to zoom in, select a digital camera that has a high optical zoom. An optical zoom enlarges the subject by adjusting the camera lens, whereas a digital zoom uses algorithms built into the camera to magnify images. Optical zooms, as opposed to digital zooms, often result in a higher quality photo. While a digital zoom might be capable of magnifying objects that are 100 feet away, the photo will suffer a loss of quality.

8 Price is important.

As with all other devices, locate a digital camera that does not exceed your budget. If you find a great camera that is available for more than you are willing to spend, consider locating a camera with a slightly lower resolution, an alternate brand, or a smaller screen. Digital cameras can last well beyond five years if properly maintained, so consider this a longer-term investment that will create memories lasting you a lifetime.

9 Know your batteries.

Some digital cameras require replaceable alkaline or rechargeable batteries (often AA or AAA), and others have a rechargeable battery. Similar to batteries in portable media players, using disposable batteries in digital cameras can get expensive, and they may not last as long as rechargeable battery packs. Digital camera battery life is not measured in hours (as is the case with smart phones and portable media players); instead, it is measured in how many pictures can be taken on a single charge or set of batteries. Turning off the LCD screen and flash when you take pictures can help to extend battery life.

10 Purchase accessories.

Accessories that are available for digital cameras include carrying cases, extra batteries and battery chargers, and extra memory cards (Figure 11). Carrying cases can help protect your digital camera, especially while traveling, and the extra batteries and chargers can stay inside your carrying case so that they are readily available should you need them. Screen protectors can help protect the LCD screen on your digital camera.

Figure 11 Digital camera accessories include memory cards, cases, batteries, and battery chargers.

Multiple Web sites on the Internet allow you to purchase computers and mobile devices (Figure 12). Some Web sites even post reviews for you to read before you commit to making a purchase.

Web Site	Web Address	Desktop Computers	Notebook Computers	Smart Phones	Portable Media Players	Digital Cameras
Acer	acer.com	X	X			
Amazon.com	amazon.com	X	X	X	X	X
Apple	apple.com	X	X	X	X	
Best Buy	bestbuy.com	X	X	X	X	X
BlackBerry	blackberry.com			X		
Canon	canon.com					X
CNET Shopper	shopper.cnet.com	X	X	X	X	X
Dell	dell.com	X	X		X	X
Fry's Electronics	frys.com	X	X	X	X	X
Gateway	gateway.com	X	X			
hhgregg	hhgregg.com	X	X	X	X	X
HP	hp.com	X	X	X		
Lenovo	lenovo.com	X	X		X	X
LG	lge.com			X		
MSN Shopping	shopping.msn.com	X	X	X	X	X
Nokia	nokia.com			X		
Panasonic	panasonic.com		X			X
RadioShack	radioshack.com	X	X	X	X	X
SAMSUNG	samsung.com			X	X	X
Sony	sony.com	X	X	X	X	X
Target	target.com	X	X	X	X	X
Walmart	walmart.com	X	X	X	X	X
Yahoo! Computers	shopping.yahoo.com	X	X	X	X	X

For an updated list of companies and their Web addresses, visit the Computer Concepts CourseMate Web site at www.cengagebrain.com and then navigate to the Buyer's Guide Feature resource for this book.

Figure 12 Web sites that sell computers and mobile devices.

Quiz Yourself Answers

Following are possible answers to the Quiz Yourself boxes throughout the book.

Quiz Yourself 1-1

1. A computer is ~~a motorized~~an electronic device that processes ~~output~~input into ~~input~~output.
2. A storage device records (~~reads~~writes) and/or retrieves (~~writes~~reads) items to and from storage media.
3. An ~~output~~input device is any hardware component that allows you to enter data and instructions into a computer.
4. True Statement
5. Computers have the ~~dis~~advantages of fast speeds, ~~high~~low failure rates, producing consistent results, storing ~~small~~ enormous amounts of data, and communicating with others.
6. Three commonly used ~~input~~output devices are a printer, a monitor, and speakers.

Quiz Yourself 1-2

1. A ~~resource~~network is a collection of computers and devices connected together via communications devices and transmission media.
2. True Statement
3. Popular ~~system~~application software includes Web browsers, word processing software, spreadsheet software, database software, and presentation software.
4. The ~~Internet~~Web is one of the more popular services on the ~~Web~~Internet.
5. Two types of ~~application~~system software are the operating system and utility programs.

Quiz Yourself 1-3

1. A ~~desktop computer~~notebook computer (or laptop computer) is a portable, personal computer designed to fit on your lap.
2. True Statement
3. Each ~~enterprise~~home user spends time on the computer for different reasons that include personal financial management, Web access, communications, and entertainment.
4. A ~~home~~power user requires the capabilities of a workstation or other powerful computer.
5. ~~Mainframes~~Supercomputers are the fastest, most powerful computers — and the most expensive.
6. The elements of an information system are hardware, ~~e-mail~~software, data, people, and ~~the Internet~~procedures.
7. With ~~embedded computers~~online banking, users access account balances, pay bills, and copy monthly transactions from the bank's computer right into their personal computers.

Quiz Yourself 2-1

1. True Statement
2. ~~A wireless Internet service provider~~An IP address (or Internet Protocol address) is a number that uniquely identifies each computer or device connected to the Internet.
3. ~~An IP address~~A domain name, such as www.google.com, is the text version of ~~a domain name~~an IP address.
4. ~~Satellite~~Cable Internet service provides high-speed Internet access through the cable television network via a cable modem.
5. The World Wide Web Consortium (W3C) oversees research and ~~owns~~sets standards and guidelines for many areas of the Internet.

Quiz Yourself 2-2

1. True Statement
2. You cannot assume that information on the Web is correct and accurate.
3. Audio and video files are ~~downloaded~~compressed to reduce their file sizes.
4. Popular ~~portals~~players include iTunes, RealPlayer, and Windows Media Player.
5. The more widely used ~~search engines~~Web browsers for personal computers are Internet Explorer, Firefox, Opera, Safari, and Google Chrome.
6. To develop a Web page, you do not have to be a computer programmer.
7. To improve your Web searches, use ~~general~~specific nouns and put the ~~least~~most important terms first in the search text.

Quiz Yourself 2-3

1. True Statement
2. An e-mail address is a combination of a user name and ~~an e-mail program~~a domain name that identifies a user so that he or she can receive Internet e-mail.
3. ~~Business~~Consumer-to-consumer e-commerce occurs when one consumer sells directly to another, such as in an online auction.
4. FTP is an Internet standard that permits file ~~reading~~ uploading and ~~writing~~downloading with other computers on the Internet.
5. ~~Spam~~Internet telephony uses the Internet (instead of the public switched telephone network) to connect a calling party to one or more called parties.
6. Netiquette is the code of ~~un~~acceptable behaviors while on the Internet.
7. VoIP enables users to ~~subscribe~~speak to other users over the Internet.

Quiz Yourself 3-1
1. True Statement
2. ~~Public-domain~~Packaged software is mass produced, copyrighted retail software that meets the needs of a wide variety of users, not just a single user or company.
3. To use ~~system~~application software, your computer must be running ~~application~~system software.
4. When a program is started, its instructions load from ~~memory~~a storage medium into ~~a storage medium~~memory.

Quiz Yourself 3-2
1. ~~Audio~~Video editing software typically includes ~~video~~audio editing capabilities.
2. ~~Enterprise computing~~Image editing software provides the capabilities of paint software and also includes the capability to modify existing images.
3. Millions of people use ~~spreadsheet~~word processing software every day to develop documents such as letters, memos, reports, mailing labels, newsletters, and Web pages.
4. Professional ~~accounting~~DTP (or desktop publishing) software is ideal for the production of high-quality color documents such as textbooks, corporate newsletters, marketing literature, product catalogs, and annual reports.
5. ~~Database~~Presentation software is application software that allows users to create visual aids for presentations to communicate ideas, messages, and other information to a group.
6. Popular ~~CAD programs~~software suites include Microsoft Office, Apple iWork, Corel WordPerfect Office, and Google Docs.
7. True Statement

Quiz Yourself 3-3
1. ~~All~~Some Web application hosts provide free access to their software.
2. ~~Computer~~Web-based training is a type of ~~Web~~computer-based training that uses Internet technology and consists of application software on the Web.
3. True Statement
4. ~~Legal~~Personal finance software is a simplified accounting program that helps home users and small office/home office users balance their checkbooks, pay bills, track investments, and evaluate financial plans.
5. ~~Personal DTP~~Photo editing software is a popular type of image editing software that allows users to edit digital photos.

Quiz Yourself 4-1
1. True Statement
2. Four basic operations in a machine cycle are: (1) ~~comparing~~ fetching, (2) decoding, (3) executing, and, if necessary, (4) ~~pipelining~~storing.
3. Processors contain a ~~motherboard~~control unit and an arithmetic logic unit (ALU).
4. The ~~central processing unit~~motherboard, sometimes called a system board, is the main circuit board of the system unit.
5. The leading processor chip manufacturers for personal computers are ~~Microsoft~~Intel and AMD.
6. The pace of the system clock, called the clock speed, is measured by the number of ticks per ~~minute~~second.
7. The system unit is a case that contains ~~mechanical~~ electronic components of the computer used to process data.

Quiz Yourself 4-2
1. True Statement
2. A gigabyte (GB) equals approximately 1 ~~trillion~~billion bytes.
3. Memory cache helps speed the processes of the computer because it stores ~~seldom~~frequently used instructions and data.
4. Most computers are ~~analog~~digital, which means they recognize only two discrete states: on and off.
5. Most RAM ~~retains~~loses its contents when the power is removed from the computer.
6. Read-only memory (ROM) refers to memory chips storing ~~temporary~~permanent data and instructions.

Quiz Yourself 4-3
1. A ~~bus~~port is the point at which a peripheral attaches to or communicates with a system unit so that the peripheral can send data to or receive information from the computer.
2. An ~~AC adapter~~expansion slot is a socket on the motherboard that can hold an adapter card.
3. Built into the power supply is a ~~heater~~fan that keeps components of the system unit ~~warm~~cool.
4. ~~eSATA~~USB ports can connect up to 127 different peripherals together with a single connector.
5. The higher the bus clock speed, the ~~slower~~faster the transmission of data.
6. True Statement

Quiz Yourself 5-1
1. A keyboard is an ~~output~~input device that contains keys users press to enter data in a computer.
2. A ~~stylus~~graphics tablet is a flat, rectangular, electronic plastic board.
3. A ~~trackball~~touchpad is a small, flat, rectangular pointing device commonly found on notebook computers, including netbooks and many Tablet PCs.
4. True Statement
5. Operations you can perform with a ~~wheel~~mouse include point, click, right-click, double-click, triple-click, drag, right-drag, rotate wheel, free-spin wheel, press wheel button, tilt wheel, and press thumb button.

Quiz Yourself 5-2
1. True Statement
2. DV cameras record video as ~~analog~~digital signals.
3. Video games and computer games use a ~~Web cam~~game controller as the input device that directs movements and actions of on-screen objects.
4. Many smart phones today have a built-in camera so that users easily can ~~type text~~take pictures.

5. The ~~lower~~higher the resolution of a digital camera, the better the photo quality, but the more expensive the camera.

Quiz Yourself 5-3

1. A fingerprint reader captures curves and indentations of a ~~signature~~fingerprint.
2. After swiping a credit card through ~~an MICR~~a magstripe (or magnetic stripe card) reader, a POS terminal connects to a system that authenticates the purchase.
3. ATMs ask you to enter a password, called a ~~biometric identifier~~PIN (or personal identification number), which verifies that you are the holder of the bankcard.
4. Four types of ~~source documents~~scanners are flatbed, pen, sheet-fed, and drum.
5. Retail and grocery stores use the ~~POSTNET~~UPC (Universal Product Code) bar code.
6. RFID is a technology that uses ~~laser~~radio signals to communicate with a tag placed in an object, an animal, or a person.
7. True Statement

Quiz Yourself 6-1

1. A ~~lower~~higher resolution uses a greater number of pixels and thus provides a smoother image.
2. An output device is any type of ~~software~~hardware component that conveys information to one or more people.
3. Documents often include ~~text~~graphics to enhance their visual appeal and convey information.
4. Types of ~~pixels~~flat-panel displays include LCD monitors, LCD screens, and plasma monitors.
5. True Statement

Quiz Yourself 6-2

1. A ~~laser~~thermal printer generates images by pushing electrically heated pins against heat-sensitive paper.
2. A ~~photo~~laser printer creates images using a laser beam and powdered ink, called toner.
3. An ink-jet printer is a type of nonimpact printer that forms characters and graphics by spraying tiny drops of liquid ~~nitrogen~~ink onto a piece of paper.
4. Printed information is called ~~soft~~hard copy.
5. True Statement

Quiz Yourself 6-3

1. A digital light processing (DLP) projector uses tiny ~~lightbulbs~~mirrors to reflect light.
2. Many personal computer users attach surround sound ~~printer~~speaker systems to their computers to generate a higher-quality sound.
3. True Statement
4. Some game controllers include ~~real-time action~~force feedback, which is a technology that sends resistance to the device in response to actions of the user.

Quiz Yourself 7-1

1. Disk ~~recording~~caching consists of a memory chip(s) on a hard disk that stores frequently accessed items.
2. True Statement
3. SATA is a hard disk interface that uses ~~parallel~~serial signals to transfer data, instructions, and information.
4. ~~Storage media~~A storage device is the computer hardware that records and/or retrieves items to and from ~~a~~ storage ~~device~~media.
5. Users can move an ~~internal~~external hard disk from computer to computer as needed by connecting the disk to a USB port or FireWire port on the system unit.

Quiz Yourself 7-2

1. ~~Cloud storage~~A solid state drive (SSD) is a storage device that typically uses flash memory to store data, instructions, and information.
2. A USB flash drive is a flash memory storage device that plugs in a ~~parallel~~USB port on a computer or mobile device.
3. Flash memory cards are a type of ~~magnetic~~solid state media, which means they consist entirely of electronic components and contain no moving parts.
4. True Statement

Quiz Yourself 7-3

1. A ~~CD-RW~~CD-ROM is a type of optical disc on which users can read but not write (record) or erase.
2. A ~~DVD-RAM~~Picture CD is a single-session disc that stores digital versions of film using a jpg file format.
3. DVDs have ~~the same~~much greater storage capacities ~~as~~than CDs.
4. Optical discs are written and read by ~~mirrors~~a laser.
5. ~~Single session~~Multisession means you can write on part of the disc at one time and another part at a later time.
6. True Statement

Quiz Yourself 8-1

1. A ~~buffer~~driver is a small program that tells the operating system how to communicate with a specific device.
2. A ~~cold~~warm boot is the process of using the operating system to restart a computer.
3. A password is a ~~public~~private combination of characters associated with the user name that allows access to certain computer resources.
4. Firmware that contains the computer's startup instructions is called the ~~kernel~~BIOS.
5. The program you currently are using is in the ~~background~~ foreground, and the other programs running but not in use are in the ~~foreground~~background.
6. Two types of system software are operating systems and ~~application~~utility programs.
7. True Statement

Quiz Yourself 8-2

1. ~~BlackBerry~~Palm OS devices use Palm OS as their operating system.
2. Examples of ~~embedded~~server operating systems include Windows Server 2008, UNIX, Linux, Solaris, and NetWare.
3. Windows 7 Starter uses Windows ~~Aero~~Vista Basic.
4. True Statement
5. ~~Aero Flip 3D~~Linux is a UNIX-type operating system that is open source software.

Quiz Yourself 8-3

1. A ~~pop-up blocker~~file compression utility shrinks the size of a file(s).
2. An ~~anti-spam~~antivirus program protects a computer against viruses by identifying and removing any computer viruses found in memory, on storage media, or on incoming files.
3. True Statement
4. You should ~~uninstall~~back up files and disks regularly in the event your originals are lost, damaged, or destroyed.
5. ~~Web filtering~~Disc burning software writes text, graphics, audio, and video files to a recordable or rewritable disc.
6. ~~Fragmenting~~Defragmenting a disk is the process of reorganizing it so that the files are stored in contiguous sectors.

Computer Acronyms

Acronym	Description	Page
AAC	Advanced Audio Coding	95
AC	alternating current	239
ADA	Americans with Disabilities Act	286
AGP	Accelerated Graphics Port	238
AIFF	Audio Interchange File Format	95
ALU	arithmetic logic unit	213
AMD	Advanced Micro Devices	216, 217
AOL	America Online	78, 89, 111
ARPA	Advanced Research Projects Agency	75
ARPANET	Advanced Research Projects Agency network	75
ASCII	American Standard Code for Information Interchange	221
ASF	Advanced Streaming (or Systems) Format	95
ATC	advanced transfer cache	227
ATM	automated teller machine	284
B2B	business-to-business	100
B2C	business-to-consumer	98
BD-R	Blu-ray Disc recordable	376
BD-RE	Blu-ray Disc rewritable	376
BD-ROM	Blu-ray Disc read-only memory	375
BIOS	basic input/output system	400
Bit	binary digit	221
BMP	bit map	93
btw	by the way	108
BSB	backside bus	237
C2C	consumer-to-consumer	100
CAD	computer-aided design	160
CAI	computer-aided instruction	171
CAM	computer-aided manufacturing	38
CBT	computer-based training	171
CCD	charge-coupled device	272

Acronym	Description	Page
ccTLD	country code top-level domain	80
CD	compact disc	8, 94, 97, 375
CD-R	compact disc-recordable	373
CD-ROM	compact disc read-only memory	372
CD-RW	compact disc-rewritable	373
CF	CompactFlash	364
CMOS	complementary metal-oxide semiconductor	229
COBOL	COmmon Business-Oriented Language	55
CPU	central processing unit	7, 213
CRT	cathode-ray tube	313
DDR SDRAM	double data rate synchronous dynamic random access memory	225
DHCP	Dynamic Host Configuration Protocol	110
DIMM	dual inline memory module	225
DL	distance learning	176
DLP projector	digital light processing projector	326
DNS	domain name system	80
dpi	dots per inch	273, 316
DRAM	dynamic random access memory	225
DSL	Digital Subscriber Line	76
DTP	desktop publishing	160
DTV	digital television	312
DV camera	digital video camera	275
DVD	digital versatile disc or digital video disc	8, 26, 64, 68, 97, 375
DVD+R	digital versatile disc or digital video disc recordable	376
DVD-R	digital versatile disc or digital video disc recordable	376
DVD+RAM	digital versatile disc or digital video disc + random access memory	376

Acronym	Description	Page
DVD-ROM	digital versatile disc or digital video disc read-only memory	375
DVD+RW	digital versatile disc or digital video disc + rewritable	376
DVD-RW	digital versatile disc or digital video disc + rewritable	376
DVI	Digital Video Interface	310
EB	exabyte	354
E-commerce	electronic commerce	30, 32, 62, 63, 98, 100, 109
EEPROM	electrically erasable programmable read-only memory	228
E-filing	electronic filing	167
EIDE	Enhanced Integrated Drive Electronics	361
E-mail	electronic mail	12, 31, 74, 75, 77, 78, 81, 88, 89, 91, 98, 100, 101, 102, 103, 105, 108, 109, 142, 144, 150, 156, 157, 159, 173, 174, 176
ENIAC	Electronic Numerical Integrator and Computer	54
eSATA	external Serial Advanced Technology Attachment	361
E-retail	electronic retail	99
FAQ	frequently asked questions	14, 108
Fax	facsimile	320, 321
FORTRAN	FORmula TRANslator	55
FSB	front side bus	237
FTP	File Transfer Protocol	107
FTTP	Fiber to the Premises	76
fwiw	for what it's worth	108
fyi	for your information	108
GB	gigabyte	223, 354
GBps	gigabytes per second	355
GHz	gigahertz	216
GIF	Graphics Interchange Format	93
GPU	graphics processing unit	310
gTLD	generic top-level domain	80
GUI	graphical user interface	15, 402
HD	high density	375
HDMI	High-Definition Media Interface	310
HDTV	high-definition television	312
HD VMD	high-density Versatile Multilayer Disc	375

Acronym	Description	Page
HIPAA	Health Insurance Portability and Accountability Act	380
HMD	head-mounted display	308
HP	Hewlett-Packard	319, 331
HTPC	home theater PC	20
http	Hypertext Transfer Protocol	82
IBM	International Business Machines	55, 56, 57, 58, 67, 76, 146
ICANN	Internet Corporation for Assigned Names and Numbers	80
IM	instant messaging	104
imho	in my humble opinion	108
IP address	Internet Protocol address	79, 110
IPng	Internet Protocol Next Generation	110
IPv6	Internet Protocol version 6	80, 110
IrDA	Infrared Data Association	235
IS	information system	27
ISP	Internet service provider	78
IT	information technology	27
JPEG	Joint Photographic Experts Group	93
K	kilobyte	223
KB	kilobyte	223, 354
KBps	kilobytes per second	355
L1 cache	Level 1 cache	227
L2 cache	Level 2 cache	227
L3 cache	Level 3 cache	227
LAN	local area network	57
LCD	liquid crystal display	308
M2	Memory Stick Micro	364
Mac OS	Macintosh Operating System	415
Mac OS X	Macintosh Operating System X	415
MB	megabyte	223, 354
MBps	megabytes per second	355
MBps	megabits per second	375
M-commerce	mobile commerce	98
MFP	multifunction peripheral	320, 329, 331
MHz	megahertz	229
MIB	Medical Information Bureau	380
MICR	magnetic-ink character recognition	281

Acronym	Description	Page
Modem	modulate/demodulate	8
MP	million pixels	269
MP3	Moving Pictures Experts Group Audio Layer 3 (MPEG-3)	94, 95
MPEG	Moving Pictures Experts Group	96
MRAM	magnetoresistive random access memory	225
μs	microsecond	229
ms	millisecond	229
MSN	Microsoft Network, The	78, 81, 85, 89
MX	mail exchange	382
NAS	network attached storage	360
Netiquette	Internet etiquette	108
NLQ	near letter quality	322
ns	nanosecond	229
NSF	National Science Foundation	75
OCR	optical character recognition	279
OLE	object linking and embedding	59
OLED	organic light emitting diode	308
OMR	optical mark recognition	279
OS	operating system	398
OSP	Open Specification Provider	78
PB	petabyte	354
PC	personal computer	19, 20
PCI bus	Peripheral Component Interconnect bus	238
PCIe	PCI Express	238
PCL	Printer Control Language	319
PDA	personal digital assistant	22
PDF	Portable Document Format	158
PDL	page description language	319
PIM	personal information manager	156
PIN	personal identification number	284
Pixel	picture element	273, 278, 308
PNG format	Portable Network Graphics format	93
POP	Post Office Protocol	103
POP3	Post Office Protocol 3	103
POS	point of sale	284
POST	power-on self test	400
ppi	pixels (picture elements) per inch	273
PROM chip	programmable read-only memory chip	228

Acronym	Description	Page
ps	picosecond	229
QT	QuickTime	95
RA	RealAudio	95
RAID	redundant array of independent disks	360
RAM	random access memory	224
RDRAM	Rambus dynamic random access memory	225
RFID	radio frequency identification	280
RIAA	Recording Industry Association of America	64
RIMM	Rambus inline memory module	225
ROM	read-only memory	228
rpm	revolutions per minute	358
RSS 2.0	Really Simple Syndication	92
SAS	serial-attached SCSI	235, 362
SATA	Serial Advanced Technology Attachment	361
SCSI	small computer system interface	235, 362
SD	Secure Digital	364
SDHC	Secure Digital High Capacity	364
SDRAM	synchronous dynamic random access memory	225
SIMM	single inline memory module	225
SMTP	simple mail transfer protocol	103
SOHO	small office/home office	30
SRAM	static random access memory	225
SSD	solid state drive	363
SVGA	super video graphics array	311
SXGA	Super Extended Graphics Array	311
TB	terabyte	223, 354
TFT display	thin-film transistor display	308
TIFF	Tagged Image File Format	93
TLD	top-level domain	80
ttfn	ta ta for now	108
TTL	Time To Live	382
tyvm	thank you very much	108
UMD	Universal Media Disc	375
UMPC	Ultra-Mobile PC	22
UNIVAC I	UNIVersal Automatic Computer	54
UPC	Universal Product Code	280
URL	Uniform Resource Locator	82
USB	universal serial bus	234, 367
User ID	user identification	410
UXGA	Ultra Extended Graphics Array	311
VoIP	Voice over Internet Protocol	100, 325

Acronym	Description	Page
VR	virtual reality	96
W3C	World Wide Web Consortium	76
WAV	Windows waveform	95
WBT	Web-based training	181
Wi-Fi	wireless fidelity	76
WMA	Windows Media Audio	95, 98
WQXGA	Wide Quad Extended Graphics Array	311

Acronym	Description	Page
WSXGA	Wide Super Extended Graphics Array	311
WUXGA	Wide Ultra Extended Graphics Array	311
WWW	World Wide Web	80
WXGA	Wide Super Extended Graphics Array	311
XGA	Extended Graphics Array	311
YB	yottabyte	354
ZB	zettabyte	354

Coding Schemes and Number Systems

Coding Schemes

As discussed in Chapter 4, a computer uses a coding scheme to represent characters. This section of the appendix presents the ASCII, EBCDIC, and Unicode coding schemes and discusses parity.

ASCII and EBCDIC

Two coding schemes that represent characters in a computer are ASCII and EBCDIC. The **American Standard Code for Information Interchange**, or ASCII (pronounced ASK-ee), coding scheme is the most widely used coding scheme to represent data. The **Extended Binary Coded Decimal Interchange Code**, or EBCDIC (pronounced EB-see-dik), coding scheme sometimes is used on mainframe computers and high-end servers. As shown in Figure C-1, the combination of bits (0s and 1s) is unique for each character in the ASCII and EBCDIC coding schemes.

When a computer uses the ASCII or EBCDIC coding scheme, it stores each represented character in one byte of memory. Other binary formats exist, however, that the computer sometimes uses to represent numeric data. For example, a computer may store, or pack, two numeric characters in one byte of memory. The computer uses these binary formats to increase storage and processing efficiency.

Unicode

The 256 characters and symbols that are represented by ASCII and EBCDIC codes are sufficient for English and western European languages but are not large enough for Asian and other languages that use different alphabets. Further compounding the problem is that many of these languages use symbols, called **ideograms**, to represent multiple words and ideas. One solution to this situation is Unicode. **Unicode** is a 16-bit coding scheme that has the capacity of representing all the world's current languages, as well as classic and historical languages, in more than 65,000 characters and symbols.

Unicode is implemented in several operating systems, including Windows, Mac OS, and Linux. Unicode-enabled programming languages and software include Java, XML, Microsoft Office, and Oracle. Some experts believe that Unicode eventually will replace all other coding schemes.

ASCII	SYMBOL	EBCDIC
00110000	0	11110000
00110001	1	11110001
00110010	2	11110010
00110011	3	11110011
00110100	4	11110100
00110101	5	11110101
00110110	6	11110110
00110111	7	11110111
00111000	8	11111000
00111001	9	11111001
01000001	A	11000001
01000010	B	11000010
01000011	C	11000011
01000100	D	11000100
01000101	E	11000101
01000110	F	11000110
01000111	G	11000111
01001000	H	11001000
01001001	I	11001001
01001010	J	11010001
01001011	K	11010010
01001100	L	11010011
01001101	M	11010100
01001110	N	11010101
01001111	O	11010110
01010000	P	11010111
01010001	Q	11011000
01010010	R	11011001
01010011	S	11100010
01010100	T	11100011
01010101	U	11100100
01010110	V	11100101
01010111	W	11100110
01011000	X	11100111
01011001	Y	11101000
01011010	Z	11101001
00100001	!	01011010
00100010	"	01111111
00100011	#	01111011
00100100	$	01011011
00100101	%	01101100
00100110	&	01010000
00101000	(	01001101
00101001	)	01011101
00101010	*	01011100
00101011	+	01001110

Figure C-1

A Unicode code for a symbol (Figure C-2) is obtained by appending the symbol's corresponding digit in the left-most column to the end of the symbol's corresponding three-digit code in the column heading. For example, the Unicode for the capital letter C is 0043. In Unicode, 30,000 codes are reserved for future use, such as ancient languages, and 6,000 codes are reserved for private use. Existing ASCII coded data is fully compatible with Unicode because the first 256 codes are the same.

Parity

Regardless of the coding scheme used to represent characters in memory, it is important that the computer store characters accurately. For each byte of memory, most computers have at least one extra bit, called a **parity bit**, that the computer uses for error checking. A parity bit can detect if one of the bits in a byte has been changed inadvertently. While such errors are extremely rare (most computers never have a parity error during their lifetime), they can occur because of voltage fluctuations, static electricity, or a memory failure.

Computers are either odd- or even-parity machines. In computers with odd parity, the total number of on bits in the byte (including the parity bit) must be an odd number (Figure C-3). In computers with even parity, the total number of on bits must be an even number. The computer checks parity each time it uses a memory location. When the computer moves data from one location to another in memory, it compares the parity bits of both the sending and receiving locations to see if they are the same. If the computer detects a difference or if the wrong number of bits is on (e.g., an odd number in a computer with even parity), an error message is displayed. Many computers use multiple parity bits that enable them to detect and correct a single-bit error and detect multiple-bit errors.

	003	004	005	006	007
0	0 0030	@ 0040	P 0050	` 0060	p 0070
1	1 0031	A 0041	Q 0051	a 0061	q 0071
2	2 0032	B 0042	R 0052	b 0062	r 0072
3	3 0033	C 0043	S 0053	c 0063	s 0073
4	4 0034	D 0044	T 0054	d 0064	t 0074
5	5 0035	E 0045	U 0055	e 0065	u 0075
6	6 0036	F 0046	V 0056	f 0066	v 0076
7	7 0037	G 0047	W 0057	g 0067	w 0077
8	8 0038	H 0048	X 0058	h 0068	x 0078
9	9 0039	I 0049	Y 0059	i 0069	y 0079
A	: 003A	J 004A	Z 005A	j 006A	z 007A
B	; 003B	K 004B	[005B	k 006B	{ 007B
C	< 003C	L 004C	\ 005C	l 006C	| 007C
D	= 003D	M 004D	] 005D	m 006D	} 007D
E	> 003E	N 004E	^ 005E	n 006E	~ 007E
F	? 003F	O 004F	_ 005F	o 006F	DEL 007F

Figure C-2

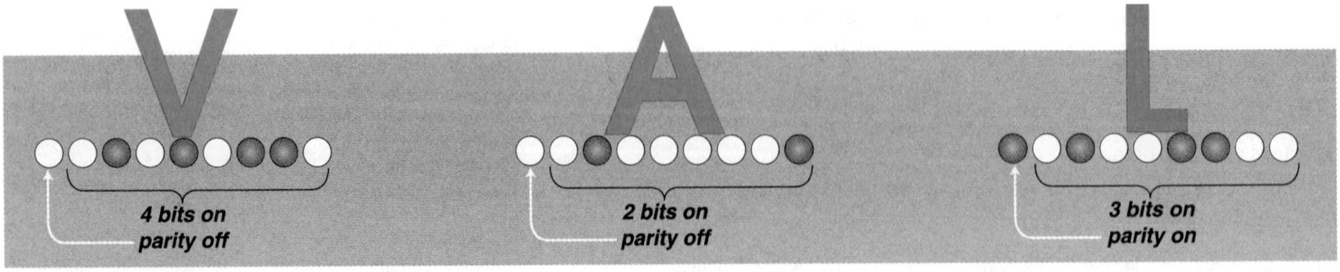

Figure C-3

Number Systems

This section of the appendix describes the number systems used with computers. Technical computer personnel require a thorough knowledge of this subject, but most users need only a general understanding of number systems and how they relate to computers.

The binary (base 2) number system is used to represent the electronic status of the bits in memory. It also is used for other purposes such as addressing the memory locations. Another number system commonly used with computers is **hexadecimal** (base 16). The computer uses the hexadecimal number system to communicate with a programmer when a problem with a program exists, because it would be difficult for the programmer to understand the 0s and 1s of binary code. Figure C-4 shows how the decimal values 0 through 15 are represented in binary and hexadecimal number systems.

DECIMAL	BINARY	HEXADECIMAL
0	0000	0
1	0001	1
2	0010	2
3	0011	3
4	0100	4
5	0101	5
6	0110	6
7	0111	7
8	1000	8
9	1001	9
10	1010	A
11	1011	B
12	1100	C
13	1101	D
14	1110	E
15	1111	F

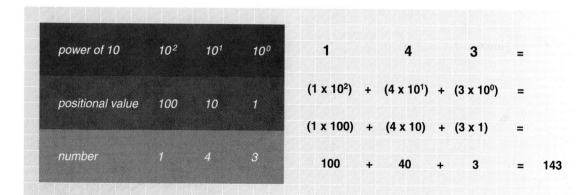

Figure C-4

The mathematical principles that apply to the binary and hexadecimal number systems are the same as those that apply to the decimal number system. To help you better understand these principles, this section starts with the familiar decimal system, then progresses to the binary and hexadecimal number systems.

The Decimal Number System

The decimal number system is a base 10 number system (deci means ten). The base of a number system indicates how many symbols it uses. The decimal number system uses 10 symbols: 0 through 9. Each of the symbols in the number system has a value associated with it. For example, 3 represents a quantity of three and 5 represents a quantity of five.

The decimal number system also is a positional number system. This means that in a number such as 143, each position in the number has a value associated with it. When you look at the decimal number 143, the 3 is in the ones, or units, position and represents three ones (3 × 1); the 4 is in the tens position and represents four tens (4 × 10); and the 1 is in the hundreds position and represents one hundred (1 × 100). The number 143 is the sum of the values in each position of the number (100 + 40 + 3 = 143). The chart in Figure C-5 shows how you can calculate the positional values (hundreds, tens, and ones) for a number system. Starting on the right and working to the left, the base of the number system, in this case 10, is raised to consecutive powers (10^0, 10^1, 10^2). These calculations are a mathematical way of determining the place values in a number system.

When you use number systems other than decimal, the same principles apply. The base of the number system indicates the number of symbols that it uses, and each position in a number system has a value associated with it. By raising the base of the number system to consecutive powers beginning with zero, you can calculate the positional value.

power of 10	10^2	10^1	10^0
positional value	100	10	1
number	1	4	3

1 4 3 =

$(1 \times 10^2) + (4 \times 10^1) + (3 \times 10^0) =$

$(1 \times 100) + (4 \times 10) + (3 \times 1) =$

$100 + 40 + 3 = 143$

Figure C-5

The Binary Number System

As previously discussed, binary is a base 2 number system (bi means two), and the symbols it uses are 0 and 1. Just as each position in a decimal number has a place value associated with it, so does each position in a binary number. In binary, the place values, moving from right to left, are successive powers of two (2^0, 2^1, 2^2, 2^3 or 1, 2, 4, 8). To construct a binary number, place ones in the positions where the corresponding values add up to the quantity you want to represent and place zeros in the other positions. For example, in a four-digit binary number, the binary place values are (from right to left) 1, 2, 4, and 8. The binary number 1001 has ones in the positions for the values 1 and 8 and zeros in the positions for 2 and 4. Therefore, as shown in Figure C-6, the quantity represented by binary 1001 is 9 (8 + 0 + 0 + 1).

power of 2	2^3	2^2	2^1	2^0
positional value	8	4	2	1
binary	1	0	0	1

$$1 \quad 0 \quad 0 \quad 1 =$$
$$(1 \times 2^3) + (0 \times 2^2) + (0 \times 2^1) + (1 \times 2^0) =$$
$$(1 \times 8) + (0 \times 4) + (0 \times 2) + (1 \times 1) =$$
$$8 + 0 + 0 + 1 = 9$$

Figure C-6

The Hexadecimal Number System

The hexadecimal number system uses 16 symbols to represent values (hex means six). These include the symbols 0 through 9 and A through F (Figure C-4 on the previous page). The mathematical principles previously discussed also apply to hexadecimal (Figure C-7).

The primary reasons the hexadecimal number system is used with computers are (1) it can represent binary values in a more compact and readable form, and (2) the conversion between the binary and the hexadecimal number systems is very efficient.

An eight-digit binary number (a byte) can be represented by a two-digit hexadecimal number. For example, in the ASCII code, the character M is represented as 01001101. This value can be represented in the hexadecimal number system as 4D. One way to convert this binary number (4D) to a hexadecimal number is to divide the binary number (from right to left) into groups of four digits, calculate the value of each group, and then change any two-digit values (10 through 15) to the symbols A through F that are used in the hexadecimal number system (Figure C-8).

power of 16	16^1	16^0
positional value	16	1
hexadecimal	A	5

$$A \quad 5 =$$
$$(10 \times 16^1) + (5 \times 16^0) =$$
$$(10 \times 16) + (5 \times 1) =$$
$$160 + 5 = 165$$

Figure C-7

positional value	8421	8421
binary	0100	1101
decimal	4	13
hexadecimal	4	D

Figure C-8

Index

A

AC adapter: External power supply, used by some external peripherals, that converts AC power into DC power that the peripheral requires. **239**
Accelerated Graphics Port (AGP): Expansion bus designed by Intel to improve the speed with which 3-D graphics and video transmit. **238**
Access provider: Business that provides individuals and organizations access to the Internet free or for a fee. 12, **77**, 112
Access time: Measures the amount of time it takes a processor or storage device to read or locate an item in memory or storage. **229**, **355**, 384
accessibility
 features, 87
 W3C guidelines, 328
Accounting software: Software that helps companies record and report their financial transactions. **158**, 159, 180
 popular (fig.), 146
Acrobat Reader, 158
Active-matrix display: LCD monitor or screen technology that uses a separate transistor to apply charges to each liquid crystal cell and thus displays high-quality color that is viewable from all angles. **308**. *See also* **TFT (thin-film transistor) display**
Adapter card: Circuit board that enhances functions of a component of a system unit and/or provides connections to peripherals. 212, **230**, 245
 types of, 230–231
Add-on: Program that extends the capability of a browser; often used to enhance multimedia. **97**, 113. *See also* **Plug-in**
Address: Unique number that identifies the location of a byte in memory. **223**, 242
 Internet, 79–80
 IP, 79, 110
 of memory cells, 242
 Web, 82–83
Address book: List of names and e-mail addresses, created and stored by a user. Also called contacts folder. **102**
Address bus: The part of a bus that transfer information about where data should reside in memory. **237**, 245
Administrator account: Computer account held by computer and network administrators that enables them to access all files and programs on the computer or network, install programs, and specify settings that affect all users on a computer or network. **410**, 432
Adobe Systems, 71, 179
Advanced Search features, 87
Advanced transfer cache: L2 cache built directly on the processor chip. **227**
advocacy Web sites, 91
Adware: Program that displays an online advertisement in a banner or pop-up window on Web pages, e-mail, or other Internet services. **426**, 433
Adware remover: Program that detects and deletes adware from a user's computer. **426**, 433
Aero Flip 3D: Windows 7 feature that works with the mouse to flip through open windows arranged in a stack. **414**
Air mouse: Motion-sensing mouse that, in addition to the typical buttons, allows you to control objects, media players, and slide shows by moving the mouse in predetermined directions through the air. **263**–264, 290
airport security, and damage to mobile media, 367
Allen, Paul, 41
All-in-one device: Output device that looks like a printer or copy machine but provides the functionality of a printer, scanner, copy machine, and perhaps a fax machine. **320**, 333. *See also* **Multifunction peripheral**
Allocation unit: Smallest unit of disk space that stores data and information. **357**. *See also* **Cluster**
ALU: Acronym for arithmetic logic unit; component of a processor that performs arithmetic, comparison, and other operations. **214**, 244
Amazon. com, 41, 60
AMD processors, 71, 216–217
Americans with Disabilities Act (ADA): Federal law that requires any company with 15 or more employees to make reasonable attempts to accommodate the needs of physically challenged workers. **286**
Analog: Continuous (wave form) signals. **221**
Anderson, Tom, 41
Andreessen, Marc, 60
Animated GIF: Animation technique that combines several GIF images in a single GIF file. **94**
Animation: Appearance of motion created by displaying a series of still images in sequence. **94**, 113
anonymous comments, and cyberbullying, 108

Anonymous FTP: Feature of many FTP sites whereby anyone can transfer some, if not all, available files. **107**
anti-aliasing, 330
Anti-spam program: Program that attempts to remove spam before it reaches a user's inbox. **427**, 433
Antivirus program: Program that protects a computer against viruses by identifying and removing any computer viruses found in memory, on storage media, or on incoming files. 144, **426**, 433
AOL (America Online), 78
Apple computers, 19–20, 41, 331
historic milestones, 57, 60, 62, 65, 66, 67, 68, 70
iPhone OS, 420
Macintosh operating system, 415
Application software: Program designed to make users more productive and/or assist them with personal tasks. **16**, 42, **142**, 180
for communications, 174–176
for home, personal, and educational use, 165–172
installing, uninstalling, 188–189
overview of, 142–145
saving files in, **188**.
See also **Specific type,** or **Program**
Archive disc: CD that stores photos from an online photo center in jpg file format, usually at a maximum resolution of 7200 pixels per photo. **374**
Arithmetic logic unit: Component of a processor that performs arithmetic, comparison, and other operations. 213, **214**–215, 244
Arithmetic operations: Basic calculations such as addition, subtraction, multiplication, and division. **214**–215
ARPA: Advanced Research Projects Agency; agency of the U.S. Department of Defense that built an early computer network called ARPANET. **75**
ARPANET: Network developed by the Pentagon's Advanced Research Projects Agency (ARPA) that linked scientific and academic researchers across the United States. 56, 75, 112
array, 242
art Web sites, 139
ASCII: American Standard Code for Information Interchange; the most widely used coding system to represent data. **221**, 222, 244
Aspect ratio: Defines a display's width relative to its height. **310**
asterisk (*), search engine operator, 87
AT&T, 78
Atanasoff, Dr. John V., 54
ATM cards, 377
Atom: Specification sometimes used by content aggregators to distribute content. **92**
attachments, e-mail, 102, 120
auctions Web sites, 133
Audio: Music, speech, or any other sound. **94**, 113
output, 305
speakers, headphones, earbuds, 323–325
Audio editing software: Application software that allows a user to modify audio clips, produce studio-quality soundtracks, and add audio to video clips. **162**, 163, 165, 170, 181
Audio input: Process of entering any sound, such as speech, music, and sound effects, into the computer. **274**
Audio output device: Component of a computer that produces music, speech, or other sounds, such as beeps. **323**–325, 333
Automated teller machine (ATM): Special-purpose terminal, connected to a host computer through a network that functions as a self-service banking machine. **284**, 291
ATM cards, 377
Automatic update: Operating system feature that automatically provides updates to a program. **409**, 432
automobiles
embedded computers in, 26
online mapping services, 173
robots in manufacturing, 38
travel and mapping software, 170–171
Autosave feature, word processing software, 150

B

Back up: To make a copy of selected files or an entire hard disk to another storage medium. **424**, 433
Background: Programs that are running, but not in use. **404**
Backside bus (BSB): Bus that connects the processor to cache. **237**, 245
Backup: Duplicate of a file, program, or disk placed on a separate storage medium that can be used if the original is lost, damaged, or destroyed. **358**
Backup utility: Utility program that allows users to copy, or back up, selected files or an entire hard disk to another storage medium such as another hard disk, optical disc, USB flash drive, or tape. 415, **424**, 433
Backward compatible: Term used to refer to a device's capability of supporting older devices, as well as newer devices. **234**
Bar chart: Chart that displays bars of various lengths to show the relationship of data. **152**. *See also* **Column chart**
Bar code: Identification code consisting of either vertical lines and spaces of different widths or a two-dimensional pattern of dots, squares, and

E

Pentium: Family of Intel processors used by less expensive, basic PCs. **216**, 244
performance
improving hard disk, 362
monitoring, 408–409
Performance monitor: Operating system program that assesses and reports information about various computer resources and devices. **408**, 432
Peripheral: Device that connects to a system unit and is controlled by the processor in the computer. **230**, 245
Permissions: Define who can access certain resources and when they can access those resources. **410**
Perpendicular recording: Storage technique in which magnetic particles are aligned vertically, or perpendicular to the disk's surface, making much greater storage capacities possible. **356**, 384
Personal computer: Computer that can perform all of its input, processing, output, and storage activities by itself and contains a processor, memory, and one or more input and output devices, and storage devices. **19**, 43, 211
PCs vs. Apple, 20
purchasing, 218–219
Personal computer maintenance utility: Utility program that identifies and fixes operating system problems, detects and repairs disk problems, and includes the capability of improving a computer's performance. **428**, 433
Personal digital assistant: Lightweight mobile device that provides personal information management functions such as a calendar, appointment book, address book, calculator, and notepad. **22**. *See also* **PDA**
Personal DTP software: Application software that helps home and small office/home office users create newsletters, brochures, advertisements, postcards, greeting cards, letterhead, business cards, banners, calendars, logos, and Web pages. **167**–168, 181
Personal finance software: Simplified accounting program that helps home users or small office/home office users manage finances. **166**, 181
Personal firewall: Utility program that detects and protects a personal computer from unauthorized intrusions. **425**, 433
Personal identification number (PIN): Numeric password, either assigned by a company or selected by a user. **284**
Personal information manager (PIM): Application software that includes features to help users organize personal information. **156**, 180
Personal paint/image editing software: Application software that provides an easy-to-use interface, usually with more simplified capabilities that allows users to draw pictures, shapes, and other images. **168**, 181
Personal photo editing software: Application software that allows users to edit digital photos by removing red-eye, erasing blemishes, restoring aged photos, adding special effects, enhancing image quality, or creating electronic photo albums. **168**–169, 181
personal Web sites, 92
perspective, 330
pet identification chips, 213
petabyte (PB), 354
Phanfare Web site, 128
Phishing: Scam in which a perpetrator attempts to obtain your personal and/or financial information. **13**, 66, **427**
Phishing filter: Program that warns or blocks you from potentially fraudulent or suspicious Web sites. **427**, 433
phones
business software for, 156
text messaging, 174
photo editing software, 159, 165
Photo management software: Application software that allows users to view, organize, sort, catalog, print, and share digital photos. **169**, 181
Photo printer: Type of nonimpact color printer that produces photo-lab-quality pictures. **317**, 332
memory card slot, 364
Photo scanner: Sheet-fed scanner model designed specifically for photos. **277**
Photo sharing community: Specific type of social networking Web site that allows users to create an online photo album and store and share their digital photos. **14**
photographs
altering digital, 162
digital camera quality, 273
digital frames for, 308
photolithography, 243
physically challenged users
input devices for, 286
output devices for, 328–329
W3C accessibility guidelines, 328
PictBridge: Standard technology used with photo printers that allows you to print photos directly from a digital camera by connecting a cable from the digital camera to a USB port on the printer. **317**
Picture CD: Single-session CD-ROM that stores digital versions of film using a jpg file format at a lower

suggested storage devices, by user (fig.), 380
Smart card: Card, similar in size to a credit card or ATM card, that stores data on a thin microprocessor embedded in the card. 352, **377**, 385
Smart phone: Internet-enabled telephone that usually also provides personal information management functions. **21**, 65, 69, 186
display, 307
input for, 268–269
memory card slot, 364
purchasing, 452–453
standard for, 418
types of, 21–22
Smart tags: Word processing screen element that appears when you perform a certain action. **148**
SMTP: Acronym for simple mail transfer protocol; communications protocol used by some outgoing mail servers. **103**
Snipping tool: Windows 7 feature that allows you to copy screen elements to a file on your computer. **415**
Social networking Web site: Online community that encourages its members to share their interests, ideas, stories, photos, music, and videos with other registered users. **14**, 52, 70, 71, **90**–91, 113, 122, 193. *See also* **Online social network**
Google's, 300
privacy on, 394
safety of, 29
Soft copy: Temporary output presented on a display device. **306**
Softbank, 179
Software: Series of instructions that tells a computer what tasks to perform and how to perform them. **15**, 42. *See also* **Program**
automatic update, safety of, 410
closed source vs. open source, 416
for home, personal, and educational use, 165–172. *see also* **Specific type,** or **Program**
types of, 15–18
Software suite: Collection of individual programs available together as a unit. **156**, 180
SOHO: Describes any company with fewer than 50 employees, as well as the self-employed who work from home. **30**, 43. *See also* **Small office/home office**
Solaris: A version of UNIX developed by Sun Microsystems that is a server operating system designed specifically for e-commerce applications. **418**, 433
Solid state drive: Storage device that typically uses flash memory to store data, instructions, and information. 69, 353, **363**, 384
Solid state media: Term used to refer to components that consist entirely of electronic components, such as integrated circuits, and contain no moving parts. **362**, 384
Sound card: Adapter card that enhances the sound generating capabilities of a personal computer by allowing sound to be input through a microphone and output through external speakers or headset. 211, **230**, 245
purchasing considerations, 447
Source document: Document that contains the original form of data to be processed. **277**
Spam: Unsolicited e-mail message or newsgroups posting sent to many recipients or newsgroups at once. 66, **108**, 113, **427**
Speakers: Audio output devices that generate sound. **323**, 333
purchasing considerations, 447
Speech recognition: Computer's capability of distinguishing spoken words. **274**, 291. *See also* **Voice recognition**
Spelling checker: Feature in some application software that reviews the spelling of individual words, sections of a document, or the entire document. **148**
Spider: Program used to build and maintain lists of words found on Web sites. **88**
Spoiler: Message that reveals a solution to a game or ending to a movie or program. **108**, 113
Spooling: Operating system process that sends documents to be printed to a buffer instead of sending them immediately to the printer. **407**
Spreadsheet software: Application software that allows a user to organize data in rows and columns and to perform calculations on the data. 57, **150**–153, 180
Spyware: Program placed on a computer without the user's knowledge that secretly collects information about the user. 66, **426**, 433
Spyware remover: Program that detects and deletes spyware and other similar programs on a user's computer. **426**, 433
Stand-alone operating system: Complete operating system that works on a desktop computer, notebook computer, or mobile computing device. **412**, 432
starting computers, 400–401
Startup folder: Contains a list of programs that open automatically when you boot a computer. **401**, 432
Static RAM: Type of RAM that is faster and more reliable than any variation of DRAM. **225**
Static Web page: A fixed Web page where visitors all see the same content. **81**
stealth virus, 178
stock market Web sites, 131
Storage: Location in which data, instructions, and information are held for future use. **352**

T

Credits

Chapter 1: Opener © Gazimal/Getty Images; Collage: Courtesy of SanDisk Corporation ; PRNewsFoto/Apple; Courtesy of Logitech; Courtesy of Apple; Courtesy of Hewlett-Packard Company; PRNewsFoto/Polaroid Corporation; © Oleksiy Maksymenko Photography/Alamy; Courtesy of Nokia; © Hugh Threlfall/Alamy; PRNewsFoto/Nintendo; 1-1© Noel Hendrickson/Getty Images; PRNewsFoto/Apple; © David L. Moore - Lifestyle/Alamy; © Jupiterimages/Comstock Images/Alamy; © curved-light/Alamy; © Brad Wilson/Getty Images; © Jupiterimages/Thinkstock/Alamy; Courtesy of Adobe Systems, Inc; Adobe product screenshot(s) reprinted with permission from Adobe Systems Incorporated; 1-3 Courtesy of Hewlett-Packard Company; Courtesy of Logitech; Courtesy of Logitech; Courtesy of Kingston Technology Corporation; Courtesy of NETGEAR; Courtesy of SanDisk Corporation; Courtesy of SanDisk Corporation; Courtesy of LaCie; Courtesy of Hewlett-Packard Company; Courtesy of Hewlett-Packard Company; Figure 1-4 Courtesy of Seagate Technology; 1-5 © Wm. Baker/GhostWorx Images/Alamy; © Jupiterimages/Thinkstock/Alamy; 1-6 © LdF/iStockphoto; Courtesy of Acer America, Inc; Courtesy of Hewlett-Packard Company; Courtesy of Hewlett-Packard Company; 1-7 PRNewsFoto/Verizon Wireless, Achille Bigliardi; Courtesy of Dell, Inc; PRNewsFoto/VerizonWireless; Courtesy of Hewlett-Packard Company; Courtesy of Nokia; © Oleksiy Maksymenko Photography/Alamy; Courtesy of Hewlett-Packard Company; Courtesy of Microsoft Corporation; Courtesy of Hewlett-Packard Company; 1-11 © Tony Freeman/PhotoEdit; 1-12 Courtesy of Hewlett-Packard Company; Courtesy of Hewlett-Packard Company; Courtesy of Kingston Technology Corporation; Courtesy of Corel Corporation; Courtesy of Hewlett-Packard Company; 1-15 Courtesy of Dell, Inc; 1-16 Courtesy of Apple; 1-17© Dmitry Bomshtein/iStockphoto; 1-18© PSL Images/Alamy; 1-19 (top) © Oleksiy Maksymenko Photography; (bottom) Courtesy of Nokia; 1-20 © Yunus Arakon/iStockphoto; 1-21 Courtesy of Intermec Technologies Corporation; 1-22 Courtesy of Apple; 1-23 Courtesy of Sony Electronics Inc; © eva serrabassa/iStockphoto; 1-24 © Ian Leonard/Alamy; © ST-Images/Alamy; © Graham Hebditch/Alamy; 1-25 Courtesy of Hewlett-Packard Company; 1-26 Courtesy of IBM Corporation; 1-27 Courtesy of IBM Corporation; 1-28 Courtesy of Toyota; Courtesy of Daimler Mercedes-Benz; © Jupiterimages; 1-29 © Stockbyte/Getty Images; © Heather Gail Delaney/Alamy; Courtesy of Xerox Corporation; Jose Luis Pelaez, Inc./Getty Images; Courtesy of Fujitsu Technology Solutions; 1-30 Courtesy of Intuit; © Kin Images/Getty Images; Courtesy of Apple; © Editorial Image, LLC/Alamy; 1-31 © Dwayne Newton/PhotoEdit; 1-32 © Lester Lefkowitz/Getty Images; © iStockphoto; © Myrleen Ferguson Cate/PhotoEdit; © blue jean images/Getty Images; 1-33 © Darryl Bush/San Francisco Chronicle/Corbis; 1-34 © Justin Pumfrey/Getty Images; 1-35 © Kin Images/Getty Images; © Dwayne Newton/PhotoEdit; © Myrleen Ferguson Cate/PhotoEdit; © Darryl Bush/San Francisco Chronicle/Corbis; © Justin Pumfrey/Getty Images; 1-36 © Thomas Barwick/Getty Images; 1-38 AP Photo/The Post-Tribune, Leslie Adkins; 1-39 © Pigeon Productions SA/Getty Images; 1-40a AP Photo; 1-40 Reza Estakhrian/Getty Images; 1-42 Courtesy of Garmin Ltd; Looking Ahead 1-1 iStockphoto; Innovative Computing 1-1 Courtesy of Banner Health; Innovative Computing 1-2 © Stockbyte/Getty Images; Computer Usage @ Work © Digital Vision; HTT1-1 1-44 © Henryk Sadura/Alamy; Looking Ahead 1-1 iStockphoto; Trailblazer 1 © Justin Sullivan/Getty Images; Trailblazer 2 © Rob Kim/Landov.

Special Feature 1: 1937 Courtesy of Iowa State University; 1937 Courtesy of Iowa State University; 1937 Courtesy of Iowa State University; 1943 Photo courtesy of The Computer History Museum; 1943 Photo courtesy of The Computer History Museum; 1945 From The Shelby White and Leon Levy Archives Center, Institute for Advanced Study, Princeton, NJ, USA/ Photo: Alan Richards; 1946 From the Collections of the University of Pennsylvania Archives; 1947 © IBM Corporate Archives; 1947 © IBM Corporate Archives; 1951 Courtesy Unisys Corporation; 1952 Courtesy of Hagley Museum and Library; 1953 © IBM Corporate Archives; 1957 © IBM Corporate Archives; 1957 © IBM Corporate Archives; 1957 Courtesy of the Department of the Navy; 1958 Courtesy of Texas Instruments; 1958 Courtesy of Texas Instruments; 1958 Courtesy of Texas Instruments; 1959 © IBM Corporate Archives; 1960 Courtesy of Hagley Museum and Library; 1964 © IBM Corporate Archives; 1964 © IBM Corporate Archives; 1964 © IBM Corporate Archives; 1965 Courtesy of Dartmouth College; 1965 Courtesy of Hewlett-Packard Company; 1969 © IBM Corporate Archives; 1970 © IBM Corporate Archives; 1971 Courtesy of Intel Corporation; 1971 Courtesy of Intel Corporation; 1975 Photo courtesy of Computer History Museum; 1975 Courtesy of Palo Alto Research Center; 1976 © Bettmann/CORBIS; 1979 Photo courtesy of Computer History Museum; 1980 © IBM Corporate Archives; 1980 © Doug Wilson/CORBIS; 1981 © IBM Corporate Archives; 1982 Courtesy of Zoom Telephonics, Inc; 1983 © PARS International; 1983 © IBM Corporate Archives; 1984 ©SSPL/The Image Works; 1984 Courtesy of Hewlett-Packard Company; 1986 © Lane V. Erickson/ Shutterstock.com; 1989 ©Photo: Fabian Bachrach. Courtesy of W3C; 1989 Courtesy of Intel Corporation; 1989 ©Wolfgang Kaehler/Corbis; 1991 ©NMPFT/SSPL/The Image Works; 1992 Courtesy of Microsoft Corporation; 1993 Courtesy of Intel Corporation; 1993 Courtesy of Microsoft Corporation; 1993 © Costa Cruise Lines/Getty

Images; 1993 Courtesy of Garmin International; 1994 AP Photo/Paul Sakuma; 1994 Courtesy of Mark D. Martin; 1994 Courtesy of Netscape Communications Corporation; 1994 Courtesy of Larry Ewing and The Gimp; 1995 PRNewsFoto/eBay, Inc; 1995 Courtesy of Oracle; 1995 © Reuters/Landov; 1996 Courtesy of Microsoft Corporation; 1996 Courtesy of Palm, Inc; 1997 iStockphoto; 1997 Associated Press; 1998 Newscom; 1998 Courtesy of Google; 1998 Courtesy of Microsoft Corporation; 1998 © Brad Cherson/Alamy; 1999 Courtesy of Intel Corporation; 1999 Courtesy of Microsoft Corporation; 1999 © CLM/Shutterstock.com; 1999 © Tan Kian Khoon/Shutterstock.com; 2000 AP Photo/PR Newswire; 2000 Courtesy of Microsoft Corporation; 2000 Courtesy of Microsoft Corporation; 2000 © B Busco/Getty Images; 2000 Courtesy of Intel Corporation; 2001 Wikimedia Foundation; 2001 Courtesy of Microsoft Corporation; 2001 Courtesy of Microsoft Corporation; 2002 © Yoshikazu Tsuno/AFP/Getty Images; 2002 Courtesy of Intel Corporation; 2003 Courtesy of ViewSonic Corporation; 2002 Courtesy of Intel Corporation; 2002 © Scott Goodwin Photography; 2002 Courtesy of Palm, Inc; 2003 © LWA- JDC/CORBIS; 2003 © Royalty-Free/CORBIS; 2003 © Jim Cummins/CORBIS; 2003 © Ed Bock/CORBIS; 2003 © Koichi Kamoshida/Getty Images; 2003 Courtesy of Microsoft Corporation; 2003 © Getty Images; 2003 © REUTERS/Mannie Garcia; 2003 Courtesy of MySpace; 2004 ISSEI KATO/Reuters/Landov; 2004 Courtesy of Facebook; 2004 Associated Press; 2004 Courtesy of Facebook; 2004 Courtesy of Sony Electronics Inc; 2004 Courtesy of SanDisk Corporation; 2004 Courtesy of Larry Ewing and The Gimp; 2004 ©Apple Computer/Handout/Reuters/Corbis; 2004 Courtesy of Palm, Inc; 2005 HANDOUT/KRT/Newscom; 2005 Courtesy of Microsoft Corporation; 2005 © PRNewsFoto/Microsoft Corp; 2006 © Courtney Weittenbiller/iStockphoto; 2006 AP Images/Nintendo; 2006 AP Images/Kevork Djansezian; 2006 © Reinhold Tscherwitschke; 2006 Courtesy of Intel Corporation; 2006 Courtesy of Intel Corporation;2006 PRNewsFoto/Nintendo; 2007 © Neville Elder/Corbis; 2007 Courtesy of Intel Corporation; 2007 © Oliver Leedham/Alamy; 2007 © Suzy Bennett/Alamy; 2007 Courtesy of Apple; 2007 iStockphoto; 2007 Courtesy of Microsoft Corporation; 2007 PRNewsFoto/Sony Electronics, Inc; 2007 Courtesy of Microsoft; 2008 AP Photo/Paul Sakuma; 2008 Justin Sullivan/Getty Images; 2008 Courtesy of Dell Inc; 2008 Courtesy of Apple; 2008 AP Photo/Mark Lennihan; 2008 Courtesy of Microsoft Corporation; 2008 Courtesy of Mozilla; 2008 AP Photo/Paul Sakuma; 2008 Courtesy of Microsoft Corporation; 2008 iStockphoto; 2009 Courtesy of Coby Electronics Corporation; 2009 © Alex Segre/Alamy; 2009 Courtesy of Microsoft Corporation; 2009 Courtesy of Intel Corporation; 2009 © Arthur Turner/Alamy; 2010 Courtesy of Microsoft Corporation; 2010 Courtesy of AMD; 2010 Courtesy of Toshiba America Electronic Components, Inc; AP Photo/Paul Sakuma; 2011© iStockphoto; 2011 © PSL Images/Alamy; 2011 PRNewsFoto/Verizon Wireless; 2011 © Joshua Kristal/Alamy; 2011 Courtesy of HTC Corporation.

Chapter 2: Opener © Jose Luis Pelaez Inc./Getty Images; Opening Collage © ST-Images/Alamy; Courtesy of Cisco; 2-1 Courtesy of Microsoft Corporation; 2-2 PRNewsFoto/AT&T Inc; © Blend Images/Alamy; © image100/Alamy; © UpperCut Images/Alamy; © Stockbyte/Alamy; © Dann Tardif/Corbis; 2-3 Step 1 © ngirish/iStockphoto; 2-3 Step 2 © blue_Iq/iStockphoto; 2-3 Step 3 ARRIS C4® CMTS Courtesy of Arris Systems, Inc; 2-3 Step 4 © Stephen Chernin/Getty Images; 2-3 Step 6 Courtesy of Fujitsu Technology Solutions; 2-7 © ST-images/Alamy; 2-21 Courtesy of Hewlett-Packard Company; © titi matei/iStockphoto; © Glowimages/Getty Images; Courtesy of Hewlett-Packard Company; 2-25 Step 1, © Colin Young-Wolff/PhotoEdit; 2-25 Step 2, © Mark Evans/iStockphoto; 2-25 Step 3, © Andrew Lewis/iStockphoto; 2-25 Step 4, © Alexander Hafemann/iStockphoto; 2-25 Step 5, Courtesy of Fujitsu Technology Solutions; 2-25 Step 6, © Ed Hidden/iStockphoto; 2-25 Step 7, © Oksana Perkins/iStockphoto; 2-25 Step 8, © Bill Aron/PhotoEdit; 2-27 Step 1 Courtesy of Hewlett-Packard Company; 2-27 Step 2 Courtesy of Hewlett-Packard Company; 2-27 Step 3, Courtesy of Juniper Networks, Inc; 2-27 Step 4 Courtesy of Hewlett-Packard Company; 2-29 Step 2 Courtesy of Fujitsu Technology Solutions; 2-29 Step 3 Courtesy of Microsoft Corporation; 2-29 Step 4 Courtesy of Acer America, Inc; 2-29 Courtesy of Hewlett-Packard Company; 2-29 Step 5 Courtesy of Hewlett-Packard Company; 2-30 Courtesy of Sony Electronics Inc; Courtesy of Hewlett-Packard Company; (center) © Blend Images/Alamy; 2-31 Courtesy of Cisco; Courtesy of Siemens; © Argunova/Shutterstock.com; Courtesy of Logitech; Courtesy of Hewlett-Packard Company; Computer Usage @ Work © Picture Contact/Alamy; Trailblazer 1 © EPA/Landov; Trailblazer 2 AP Photo/Craig Ruttle; Looking Ahead 2-1 Courtesy of W3C; Innovative Computing 2-1 Courtesy of Microsoft Corporation; Innovative Computing 2-2 PRNewsFoto/Brookstone, Inc.

Special Feature 2: © Photodisc/Alamy; © iStockphoto; © Digital Vision/Alamy; © Digital Vision/Alamy; © Alex Segre/Alamy.

Chapter 3: Opener © Janis Christie/Getty Images; Collage © Getty Images; Courtesy of Corel Corporation; Courtesy of Microsoft Corporation; Courtesy of Microsoft Corporation; Courtesy of Microsoft Corporation; Courtesy of Nokia; Pinnacle Systems, Inc., a part of Avid Technology, Inc; Courtesy of Cakewalk Inc; Courtesy of Intuit Inc; 3-1 Courtesy of Microsoft Corporation; Courtesy of Adobe Systems Incorporated; Courtesy of Corel Corporation; 3-2 © Brooke Slezak/Getty Images; Courtesy of Hewlett-Packard Company; Courtesy of Hewlett-Packard Company; 3-14 Courtesy of Microsoft Corporation; 3-15 Courtesy of Research In Motion; PRNewsFoto/Verizon Wireless; Courtesy of Research In Motion; Courtesy of DataViz Inc; 3-16 Courtesy of Computer Systems Odessa Corporation; 3-17 Courtesy of Microsoft

Corporation; 3-20 © Artiga Photo/Corbis; 3-21 Courtesy of Quark Inc; 3-22 © Picture Contact/Alamy; 3-23 Courtesy of Adobe Systems Incorporated; 3-24 Courtesy of Cakewalk Inc; 3-25 Courtesy of SumTotal Systems Inc; 3-26 Courtesy of Microsoft Corporation; 3-28 Courtesy of Intuit Inc; 3-28b © Digital Vision/Getty Images; 3-29 Courtesy of Nolo; 3-30 Courtesy of 2nd Story Software, Inc; 3-32 Courtesy of Corel Corporation; 3-33 Courtesy of Corel Corporation; 3-35 Courtesy of Encore, Inc., a Navarre Corporation Company; 3-36 Pinnacle Systems, Inc., a part of Avid Technology, Inc; 3-37 Courtesy of IMSI/Design; 3-38 Courtesy of Microsoft Corporation; 3-39 Courtesy of Encore Software, Inc. a Navarre Corporation Company; 3-40 AP Photo/Tony Giberson; 3-41a © Bernhard Classen/Alamy; 3-41b © Lon C. Dhiel/PhotoEdit; 3-41c © Fred Prouser/Reuters/Corbis; 3-46 Courtesy of Moodle; Computer Usage @ Work © iStockphoto; Trailblazer 1 AP Photo/Steven Senne; Trailblazer 2 © Tom Wagner/Corbis; Looking Ahead 3-1 Courtesy of Microsoft Corporation; Innovative Computing 3-1 © Tetra Images/Getty Images; Innovative Computing 3-2 © Wave Royalty Free/Alamy; Web Research © Brian Stablyk/Getty Images.

Special Feature 3: Figure 1 Courtesy of Microsoft Corporation; Courtesy of Verizon Wireless; © Alex Slobodkin/iStockphoto; © Image Source Black/Alamy; © iStockphoto; © David Hancock/Alamy; Courtesy of Skype; © CostinT/iStockphoto; Figure 3 Courtesy of Microsoft Corporation; © Stephen Wilkes/Getty Images; Figure 5 © CAP/Getty Images; Figure 7 © Picturenet/Getty Images; Courtesy of Research In Motion; © Gary Corbett/Alamy; Courtesy of Microsoft Corporation; Figure 9 Courtesy of Jive Software; © Jeff Greenberg/Alamy; Figure 11 © David R. Fraizer/PhotoEdit; © Jochen Tack/Alamy; Courtesy of Parliant Corporation; Figure 13 Courtesy of Cisco Systems, Inc; © Alex Slobodkin/iStockphoto; Courtesy of Zoom Technologies; Figure 15 © Reggie Casagrande/Getty Images; Figure 17 Courtesy of NASA; © PhotoAlto/Alamy; Figure 18 AP Photo/Screenshot, Peter Zschunke; Figure 21 Courtesy of Microsoft Corporation; p206a © John Lund/Drew Kelly/Sam Diephuis/Getty Images; p206b © Photodisc/Alamy; p206c © MIXA/Alamy; p206 © MIXA/Getty Images; p207 © Corbis RF/Alamy; p207 © Tetra Images/Getty Images.

Chapter 4: Opener © E Dygas/Getty Images; Collage Courtesy of Advanced Micro Devices; © imagebroker/Alamy; © Lenscap/Alamy; Courtesy of Intel Corporation; Courtesy of Kingston Technology Corporation; Courtesy of Hewlett-Packard Company; Courtesy of Hewlett-Packard Company; © Dino Ablakovic/iStockphoto; Courtesy of Intel Corporation; Courtesy of Creative Technology Ltd; 4-1 Courtesy of Dell, Inc; Courtesy of Apple; PRNewsFoto/Apple; © Mark Ralston/AFP/Getty Images; Courtesy of Palm, Inc; Courtesy of SanDisk Corporation; Courtesy of Microsoft Corporation; 4-1 Courtesy of FUJIFILM U.S.A; Courtesy of Hewlett-Packard Company; © iStockphoto; Courtesy of Dell, Inc; 4-2 Courtesy of Creative Technology Ltd; Courtesy of Sapphire Technology; Courtesy of Intel Corporation; Courtesy of Kingston Technology Corporation; Courtesy of Hewlett-Packard Company; Courtesy of Hewlett-Packard Company; 4-3 Courtesy of Intel Corporation; 4-5 © Paul Paladin/Shutterstock.com; 4-8 Courtesy of Intel Corporation; Courtesy of Advanced Micro Devices; 4-9 © KirstyPargeter/iStockphoto; 4-10 Courtesy of Puget Custom Computers; 4-12 © iStockphoto; 4-15 Courtesy of Logitech; Courtesy of Hewlett-Packard Company; 4-16 © Wayne Eastep/Getty Images; 4-18 Courtesy of Seagate Technology LLC; Courtesy of Kingston Technology Corporation; Courtesy of ViewSonic Corporation; Courtesy of Seagate Technology LLC; Courtesy of Kingston Technology Corporation; 4-20 © Andrew Howe/iStockphoto; © Jaroslaw Wojcik/iStockphoto; 4-23 © Kim Jae-Hwan/Getty Images; Courtesy of Creative Technologies Ltd; 4-25 © WireImageStock/Masterfile; © WireImageStock/Masterfile; 4-27 © Andrew Howe/iStockphoto; 4-28 © David Kilpatrick/Alamy; © Sandeep Subba/iStockphoto; Courtesy of USB Implementers Forum; 4-29 Courtesy of Hewlett-Packard Company; 4-30 Courtesy of Hewlett-Packard Company; 4-32 © Alina Solovyova-Vincent/iStockphoto; © Ruslan Kerimov/iStockphoto; © Sascha Burkard/iStockphoto; Courtesy of Hewlett-Packard Company; © Potapova Valeriya/iStockphoto; © iStockphoto; 4-33 Courtesy of Belkin International; 4-34 Courtesy of Nokia; Courtesy of Acer Inc; 4-35 Courtesy of Motion Computing, Inc; 4-36 Courtesy of Intel Corporation; Courtesy of Kingston Technology Corporation; 4-37 Courtesy of Hewlett-Packard Company; 4-38 © Kin Images/Getty Images; © Dwayne Newton/PhotoEdit; © Myrleen Ferguson Cate/PhotoEdit; © Darryl Bush/San Francisco Chronicle/Corbis; © Justin Pumfrey/Getty Images; 4-39 © Paul Maguire/Alamy; Courtesy of Merridrew Enterprises; © Lon C. Diehl/PhotoEdit Inc; © Gary Herrington Photography; Courtesy of Belkin International, Inc; © Felicia Martinez/PhotoEdit; Computer Usage @ Work © Gary Dineen/NBAE/Getty Images; Trailblazer 1 © Yoshikazu Tsuno/AFP/Getty Images; Trailblazer 2 © Andy Rain/Bloomberg via Getty Images; Innovative Computing 4-1 © China Photos/Getty Images; Innovative Computing 4-2 AP Photo/iRobot Corp; Looking Ahead 4-1 Felix Schmidberger; Web Research © Mikael Karlsson/Alamy

Chapter 5: Opener © D. Hurst/Alamy; Collage Courtesy of Hewlett-Packard Company; Courtesy of Logic3 plc; Courtesy of Logic3 plc; © Hugh Threlfall/Alamy; PRNewsFoto/Metrologic Instruments, Inc; Courtesy of Wacom Technology Corporation; Courtesy of APC by Schneider Electric; Courtesy of Hewlett-Packard Company; Courtesy of Logitech; Courtesy of Logitech; Courtesy of Logitech; Courtesy of Plantronics, Inc; 5-1 © Medioimages/Getty Images; © Carmen Martínez Banús/iStockphoto; © Getty Images; © Beaconstox/Alamy; © Tetra Images/Alamy; © Keith Morris/Alamy; © Christopher Dodge/Shutterstock.com; © Denkou Images/Alamy; © BlueSoul/Shutterstock.com; © Daniel

Acker/Bloomberg via Getty Images; © iStockphoto; © iStockphoto; © KAKIMAGE/Alamy; © Bonnie Kamin/PhotoEdit; © Stefan Klein/iStockphoto; © Anatoly Vartanov/iStockphoto; © Phil Degginger/Alamy; © Sandeep Subba/iStockphoto; © Natalie Jezzard/Alamy; © iStockphoto; 5-2 Courtesy of Microsoft Corporation; 5-4 © InstinctDesign/Shutterstock.com; 5-5 © Alex Segre/Alamy; PRNewsFoto/Verizon Wireless; © Alex Segre/Alamy; 5-6 Courtesy of Microsoft Corporation; 5-7 Courtesy of Gyration; 5-9 © Jupiterimages; 5-10 Adam Balatoni/iStockphoto; 5-11 © Photodisc/Getty Images; 5-12 Courtesy of Dell, Inc; AP Photo/Paul Sakuma; 5-13 © Henry George Beeker/Alamy; 5-14 Courtesy of Microsoft Corporation; 5-15 © Chris Rout/Alamy; 5-16 © 2licht/Alamy; © vario images GmbH & Co.KG/Alamy; © Ronald Karpilo/Alamy; 5-17 Courtesy of Nokia; Courtesy of BoxWave Corporation; Courtesy of Nokia; 5-18 Courtesy of Verizon Wireless and plawa feinwerktechnik GmbH & Co; 5-19 Courtesy of Logitech; © Arthur Turner/Alamy; Courtesy of Logic3 plc; © ST-images/Alamy; Handout/MCT/Newscom; PRNewsFoto/SplitFish GameWare Inc; 5-20 Courtesy of Sony Electronics Inc; 5-21 © Andersen RossGetty Images; 5-22 Courtesy of Nuance; 5-23 © ICP/Alamy; 5-24 Courtesy of Corel Corporation; Courtesy of Sony Electronics Inc; 5-25 © Corbis Premium RF/Alamy; 5-26 © Steve Chenn/CORBIS; 5-27 Courtesy of Hewlett-Packard Company; Courtesy of C-Technologies/Anoto Group AB; Courtesy of Visioneer, Inc; Courtesy of AZTEK, Inc.; 5-28 Courtesy of Hewlett-Packard Company; Courtesy of Acer Inc; 5-31 © Andy Sacks/Getty Images; 5-32 © Colin Young-Wolff/Photo Edit; © Phil Degginger/Getty Images; 5-33 Courtesy of Intermec Technologies; 5-34 © Spencer Grant/Photo Edit; 5-36 Courtesy of Intermec Technologies; 5-37 Courtesy of UPEK Inc; 5-38 Courtesy of Recognition Systems, Inc; 5-39 AP Photo/Canadian Press, Adrian Wyld; © Robert F. Balazik/Shutterstock.com; 5-40 © Robin Nelson/PhotoEdit; 5-41 © Bill Aron/PhotoEdit; 5-42 AP Photo/Al Behrman; 5-43 © Kin Images/Getty Images; © Dwayne Newton/PhotoEdit; © Myrleen Ferguson Cate/PhotoEdit; © Darryl Bush/San Francisco Chronicle/Corbis; © Justin Pumfrey/Getty Images; 5-44 © STUART WALKER/Alamy; 5-46 Courtesy of NaturalPoint, Inc; Computer Usage @ Work © Chloe Johnson/Alamy; Trailblazer 1 Toshiyuki Aizawa/Bloomberg via Getty Images; Trailblazer 2 AP Photo/Michael Schmelling; Innovative Computing 5-1 Courtesy of Microsoft Corporation and Avid Technology; Innovative Computing 5-2 Courtesy of Intel Corporation; Looking Ahead 5-1 AP Photo/Georgia Tech, Gary W. Meek; Web Research © iStockphoto.

Chapter 6: Opener © David R. Frazier Photolibrary, Inc./Alamy; Collage Courtesy of Nokia; Courtesy of Nokia; Courtesy of Logitech; PRNewsFoto/SANYO; Courtesy of Hewlett-Packard Company; Courtesy of Hewlett-Packard Company; © image100/Corbis; Courtesy of Palm, Inc; YONHAPNEWS AGENCY/Newscom; Courtesy of FUJIFILM USA; Courtesy of Palm Inc; 6-1 Image(s) reprinted with permission from ViewSonic Corporation; Courtesy of Hewlett-Packard Company; PRNewsFoto/Verizon Wireless; Courtesy of HTC and Microsoft Corporation; Courtesy of Nokia; Courtesy of Apple; Courtesy of Logitech; Courtesy of Sony Electronics Inc; Courtesy of Corel Corporation; © Getty Images; Courtesy of Corel Corporation; © Oleksiy Maksymenko/Alamy; 6-2 PRNewsFoto/Envision Peripherals Inc; 6-3 Courtesy of Hewlett-Packard Company; 6-4 Courtesy of Hewlett-Packard Company; © iStockphoto; © AFP/Getty Images; Courtesy of Nokia; Courtesy of Apple; 6-6 Courtesy of Advanced Micro Devices; 6-8 PRNewsFoto/LG Electronics, Inc; 6-9 AP Photo/Tina Fineberg; 6-10 Image(s) reprinted with permission from ViewSonic Corporation; 6-13 Courtesy of Hewlett-Packard Company; © Gari Wyn Williams/Alamy; Courtesy of Nokia; © Michael Newman/PhotoEdit; Courtesy of Canon; 6-14 Courtesy of Hewlett-Packard Company; Courtesy of Xerox Corporation; PRNewsFoto/Americas Best Value Inn; © JurgaR/iStockphoto; PRNewsFoto/Tabblo Inc; 6-16 Courtesy of Hewlett-Packard Company; 6-17 Courtesy of Hewlett-Packard Company; 6-18 Courtesy of Hewlett-Packard Company; 6-20 Courtesy of Hewlett-Packard Company; 6-21 Courtesy of Mitsubishi Digital Electronics America, Inc; Courtesy of Epson America, Inc; 6-22 Courtesy of Canon; 6-23 Courtesy of Intermec Technologies; 6-24 Courtesy of Hewlett-Packard Company; 6-25 Courtesy of Oki Data Amercas, Inc; 6-26 Courtesy of Creative Technology Ltd; 6-27 © Royalty-Free/Corbis; 6-28 © Hugh Threlfall/Alamy; Courtesy of Apple; 6-29 © Purestock/Getty Images; PRNewsFoto/SANYO; 6-30 Copyright 2001–2007 SMART Technologies Inc. All rights reserved; 6-31 Courtesy of Logic3 plc; Courtesy of Logitech; © picturesbyrob/Alamy; 6-32 © Kin Images/Getty Images; © Dwayne Newton/PhotoEdit; © Myrleen Ferguson Cate/PhotoEdit; © Darryl Bush/San Francisco Chronicle/Corbis; © Justin Pumfrey/Getty Images; 6-34 Courtesy of Enabling Technologies; © Don Farrall/Getty Images; Computer Usage @ Work Courtesy of NASA; 6-35 © Mark Evans/iStockphoto; Trailblazer 1 © Fujifotos/The Image Works; Trailblazer 2 Norm Betts/Bloomberg via Getty Images; Innovative Computing 6-1 Courtesy of EDGE Tech Corp; Looking Ahead 6-1 Photo: Greg Reekie, Courtesy of Xerox Corporation; PS@Home Courtesy of Hewlett-Packard Company.

Special Feature 6: Opener top © SuperStock/Alamy; Opener middle © Design Pics Inc./Alamy; Opener bottom © Somos Images LLC/Alamy; Figure 1 © Balázs Öcsi/iStockphoto; Courtesy of JVC U.S.A; PRNewsFoto/VIZIO; © Blend Images/Alamy; Courtesy of Sony Electronics Inc; © Alex Slobodkin/iStockphoto; Courtesy of Microsoft Corporation; © Silvrshootr/iStockphoto; Figure 2 Courtesy of Sony Electronics Inc; © Royalty-Free/CORBIS; Courtesy of JVC U.S.A; Figure 3 Courtesy of Hewlett-Packard Company; © mbirdy/iStockphoto; Courtesy of JVC U.S.A; screenshot photo © Ben Blankenburg/iStockphoto; Figure 4 © zoomstudio/iStockphoto; Courtesy of Hewlett-Packard